Microsoft

Microsoft® Office 2000®

Expert Companion

Tips, Tricks, and Utilities for the Power User

Reed Jacobson

PUBLISHED BY
Microsoft Press
A Division of Microsoft Corporation
One Microsoft Way
Redmond, Washington 98052-6399

Library of Congress Cataloging-in-Publication Data
Jacobson, Reed
Microsoft Office 2000 Expert Companion / Reed Jacobson.
p. cm.
Includes index.
ISBN 0-7356-0527-0
1. Microsoft Office. 2. Business--Computer programs. I. Title.
HF5548.4.M525J33 1999
005.369--dc21 99-27215
CIP

Printed and bound in the United States of America.

1 2 3 4 5 6 7 8 9 QMQM 4 3 2 1 0 9

Distributed in Canada by Penguin Books Canada Limited.

A CIP catalogue record for this book is available from the British Library.

Microsoft Press books are available through booksellers and distributors worldwide. For further information about international editions, contact your local Microsoft Corporation office or contact Microsoft Press International directly at fax (425) 936-7329. Visit our Web site at mspress.microsoft.com.

Acquisitions Editor: Christey Bahn
Project Editor: Sandra Haynes
Editorial Assistant: Kristen Weatherby
Editing and Production: Black Hole Publishing Services
Technical Editor: Sally D. Neuman

Contents at a Glance

Part 6 **Other Office Tools**

Table of Contents

Part 2 **Automation Tools**

Chapter 4 Power Up Visual Basic 123

Chapter 5 Explore Office Object Models 189

Chapter 6 Drive Office from Visual Basic 217

Part 3 Word Tools

Chapter 7 Create a Professional Appearance 259

Chapter 8 Integrate Additional Elements 301

Part 4 **Excel Tools**

Part 5 **Access Tools**

Part 6 **Other Office Tools**

Acknowledgments

This book was a major undertaking, involving the efforts of many players, often under intense pressure. Thanks, first, to Casey Doyle at Microsoft Press for asking me to write the book. Thank you to Sally Neuman for converting the manuscript into readable, accurate prose; to Jo-Anne Rosen for converting the manuscript into beautiful pages; to Jan Benes for managing the production; and to Sandra Haynes at Microsoft Press for keeping us all working together. Thanks to John Foster for arranging the bonus materials for the CD, and thank you, particularly, to Jim Buyens and Alan Neibauer for your well-written and informative chapters.

Introduction

My goal in this book is to help you, the Microsoft Office power user, take full advantage of the advanced features available in Office 2000. But what, exactly, is an advanced feature? I think of an advanced feature as one that is useful, but difficult to understand and implement. Or as one which, while technically documented, is infrequently discovered. In many cases, I've tried to show creative ways to use common tools. I have also tried to explain behavior that seems quirky or unpredictable. Sometimes, there is a valid explanation for strange behavior, and understanding the rationale makes the feature easier to use. I have attempted to cover selected topics deeply, rather than all topics shallowly. In particular, I have tried to avoid topics that are adequately covered in the Help topics, or that are well explain in other popular books about Microsoft Office, such as the Microsoft Press book *Running Microsoft Office*.

Of course, different users have different backgrounds and different expectations. An exciting new revelation for one person may be old hat to another. One person's indispensable tool is another person's example of software bloat. As an experienced Office user, you'll undoubtedly find material in the book that seems self-evident on the one hand, or that seems irrelevant and esoteric on the other. Whatever your background, I hope that you will find many explanations and instructions that will open new doors of productivity in your use of Microsoft Office.

This book does not focus merely on what's new in Office 2000, but explores how to use Office creatively to solve practical problems. You may find many new ways to use old features. One of the goals of the book is to help stimulate your creativity as you use Microsoft Office products. For example, after seeing how to create a shortcut key to toggle picture placeholders in Word, you may choose to extend the concept by creating a shortcut key to toggle revision marks, even though that topic is not explicitly covered.

You do not need to read the book from front to back; you can dip in and out almost anywhere. Some sections, however, do form an extended sequence. For example, Chapters 17 and 18 in the section on Access, work together to show you how to transition from a realistic Excel worksheet into an Access database.

Even though this book is not a tutorial, sample files are included on the CD for your convenience. They are in the Expert folder on the CD. Most of the Word and Excel macros are collected into the Expert.dot document and the Expert.xls workbook respectively. The sample files range from simple (an unformatted copy of a simple list in Chapter 9) to profound (the fully functional sophisticated product planning model in Chapter 14). In chapters that include more than one sample file, notes indicate which sample file applies to a specific section. The CD also contains a number of tools, add-ins, and other products to allow you to take full advantage of the advanced features in Microsoft Office 2000.

This book covers the six main applications of Office 2000 Premium: Word, Excel, Access, Outlook, FrontPage, and PowerPoint. These are the applications included in the main Office 2000 Premium installation program. There is not a separate chapter for PowerPoint, but the general VBA chapters in Part II do cover using VBA to manipulate PowerPoint.

From time to time, I will make additional related information available on the Web. Check my Web site at *www.expertcompanion.com*for more details. If you would like to make suggestions for additional information please send a message to reed@expertcompanion.com. If you would like to contact Jim Buyens, the author of the FrontPage and Web chapters, send a message to buyensj@primenet.com. If you would like to contact Alan Neibauer, the author of the Outlook chapters, send a message to alann@att.net.

Part 1

Office Tools

Chapter 1

Use Office Super Shortcuts

In This Chapter

The use of shortcuts can be intensely idiosyncratic. Some users prefer using keyboard shortcuts, while others prefer using the mouse. It can be frightening to see the interaction between two erstwhile friends as they debate the relative merits of different shortcut techniques. This chapter leaps squarely into that minefield. You will surely find some shortcuts in this chapter that you will consider ridiculous, while other, more common shortcuts will not appear at all. Microsoft Office 2000 obviously has far too many shortcut possibilities to cover in a single chapter. A comprehensive listing of shortcuts would be of very little value, violating the fundamental principle that you shouldn't have to learn a shortcut until you are desperate for it.

Whatever your shortcut preferences are, this chapter will help you use shortcuts to work more efficiently with the core Microsoft Office 2000 Premium applications: Word, Excel, Access, Outlook, PowerPoint, and FrontPage.

Working with Windows

Not surprisingly, Microsoft Windows applications such as those in Microsoft Office make extensive use of windows. Windows come in a variety of styles—from simple message boxes to elaborate applications. The primary purpose for using windows is to make an application intuitively easy to use. Microsoft and others have researched what features help or hurt ease of use, and the role of multiple windows has changed. The good news is that innovations have contributed to making applications increasingly easy to use. The bad news is that innovations inevitably bring inconsistencies—inconsistencies between previous versions and new versions, and inconsistencies between applications.

Before launching into specific shortcuts, you might want to review different ways in which applications can use windows—particularly as they apply in Office 2000.

Understanding the Different Types of Windows

The original Office applications—Excel and Word—both began with what is called a multiple-document interface (MDI). More recently, Office has been making a shift toward a single-document interface (SDI). In its current state, Office presents a combination of window styles that might be confusing to deal with. If you clearly understand the pure forms of MDI and SDI, you might see the pattern in the current hybrids.

Excel is an archetypal MDI application, meaning the application has a single top-level window. The top-level window will appear on the Windows taskbar, where you can easily switch between it and other top-level windows by pressing Alt+Tab, You would close the window by pressing Alt+F4. The top-level window serves as the parent window for the application. Any additional windows are created as child windows of that parent and cannot move outside the boundaries of the parent. In Excel, for example, each workbook you open creates its own child window. To create additional child windows for the active workbook, select New on the Window menu. You can create each child window as minimized, maximized, or sizeable (restored). A child window is not a top-level window; it does not appear in the taskbar, and you close it by pressing Ctrl+F4.

When a child window is sizeable, you can move it anywhere within the parent window. In fact, you can move it outside the boundary of the parent window if you want, but the parent window will then crop it. This can be quite unnerving when key portions of the window, such as the scroll bars, become invisible. In contrast, an MDI application always has a Window menu to manage its child windows. The Window menu includes commands to select a child window, arrange child windows, and perhaps create a new child window.

In a pure MDI application, only the parent window is a top-level window appearing on the Windows taskbar. To create a second top-level window, run the application a second time from Programs on the Start menu. If you run Excel twice from the Programs menu, you will have two open instances of the Excel application, each with its own MDI parent window. You will easily be able to tell that there are two instances of Excel running. Press Ctrl+Alt+Delete to display the Windows Close Program dialog box and you will see that both copies of the program are listed in the Close Program dialog box, as shown in Figure 1-1.

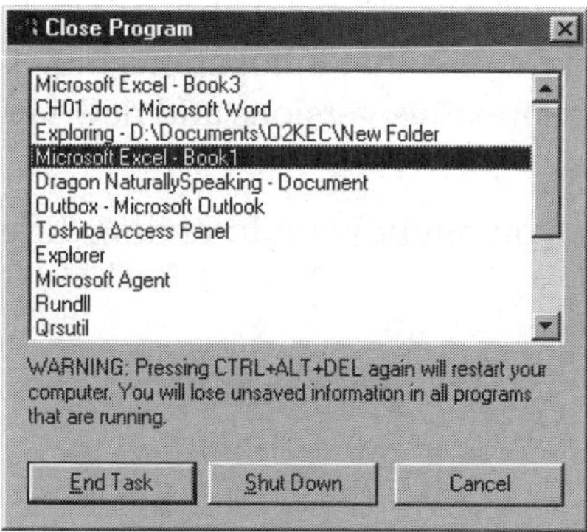

Figure 1-1
Running Excel from the Programs menu opens two copies of the program.

The Windows Notepad application is also an archetypal SDI application, meaning that there is only a single application window. To open a new file, you must first close the open file. An SDI window is similar to an MDI parent window; it appears on the taskbar—and you can create additional windows by running additional copies of the application—but the application cannot contain child windows. A pure SDI application has no need for a Window menu.

In many ways, MDI applications can be convenient, particularly when you need to see child windows side by side. MDI windows can become confusing and inconvenient, however. In Microsoft Windows, for example, most users will quickly become frustrated with the multiple windows generated as they open the My Computer icon to drill down through many subfolders. Most users will prefer the SDI Explorer interface, where the folder tree in the left pane allows you to easily select a folder to display in the right pane.

Collapsing multiple windows into a single window, with some mechanism for switching between those collapsed windows, is usually much easier to grasp. As an example, tabbed dialog boxes also create something similar to an SDI-like interface. The dialog box consists of multiple windows, but only one window at a time will fill the dialog box. The tabs at the top of the window allow you to select which window you see. Excel's workbook metaphor is another example of a move toward SDI. A single window is used for all the worksheets, and the tabs at the bottom of the workbook allow you to select which sheet will fill the window.

How Office 2000 Moves Toward SDI

Outlook 2000 is essentially an SDI application—for example, switching from the Calendar to the Inbox simply replaces the contents of the main window. But Outlook often creates additional windows—such as when you create a new mail message—that become a top-level window. The window will appear in the taskbar, and you need to press Alt+F4 to close it. The main Outlook window is obviously still the parent, because if you close it, all the auxiliary windows will also close down. If you want simultaneous windows for both the Calendar and the Inbox, Outlook allows you to open a new top-level window by running a second instance of the program.

Microsoft Word 2000 is almost completely an SDI application. Each new document you open gets a new top-level window, even though only one copy of Word is running. Each Word window is equal to each of the other windows; there is no parent window. Each window appears in the taskbar, and you can use Alt+Tab to switch from one window to another. Pressing Alt+F4 closes any of the windows, the same as if it were an individual application.

The windows in Word still maintain some vestiges of the old MDI interface, however. As mentioned earlier, all Word windows use the same instance of the Word executable program Winword.exe. In fact, even if you use the Programs menu to launch a new instance of Word, that new window is still owned by the original executable. You can still use Ctrl+F4 to close a Word document window. (When there is only one Word window open, pressing Alt+F4 will close the application, while pressing Ctrl+F4 will leaves Word running with no open documents.) Word still has a Window menu, and you can switch to any open Word document from Word's Window menu.

Aside from multiplying the number of buttons on the taskbar, the new SDI interface brings with it a few additional and surprising behaviors. If you open a dialog box that allows you to activate the document while the dialog box is open—that is, a nonmodal dialog box such as the Find And Replace dialog box—you can switch from one document to another, continuing to use the dialog box in the new window. If you open a dialog box that does not allow you to activate the modal dialog box such as the File Open dialog box, you cannot activate another Word window until you close the dialog box.

Word documents are usually independent of one another, and the SDI interface reflects that. The Windows taskbar buttons are designed to prevent novices from losing track of more than one open document because there is no option for disabling Word's new SDI interface.

Excel, Access, and PowerPoint are all still MDI applications. There is a single parent window, and multiple child windows can exist only within the parent window. In an attempt to create a consistency between Office applications, each of these applications adds a window button to the taskbar for each child window. Inexplicably, as soon as you create a second window in Excel, you get three icons on the taskbar, as shown in Figure 1-2. New windows in these applications are still child windows. Pressing Alt+F4 shuts down the entire application, not just the single window. You can turn off this feature for the three applications by clicking Options on the Tools menu and selecting View, and then clearing the Windows In Taskbar check box.

Figure 1-2
Two Excel windows will create three icons on the taskbar.

Navigating Between Child Windows

Most Office applications allow you to create multiple windows. The original specification for shortcut keys in Windows used the Ctrl+F6 key combination to switch between child windows.

Microsoft FrontPage does not recognize Ctrl+F6 for switching between child windows, (even though you might assume it would, since it is a part of Office). Outlook does not use child windows at all, and has no need to switch between windows. The remaining major Office applications—Word, Excel, PowerPoint, Access, and the Visual Basic Editor—all recognize Ctrl+F6 as the shortcut key to switch between child windows. But Ctrl+F6 really is a horrible key combination: it's hard to remember and it's hard to reach.

The introduction of Microsoft Windows brought with it the Alt+Tab key combination as a mechanism for switching between applications. In Excel, Ctrl+Tab was introduced as its replacement key combination for switching between windows. Ctrl+Tab is an excellent shortcut; it is easy to remember and easy to reach. In addition to Excel, the Visual Basic Editor uses Ctrl+Tab to switch between child windows, as do many Windows applications.

Unfortunately, you can't use Ctrl+Tab to switch between child windows in any of the other Office applications. If you press Ctrl+Tab, a Tab character is inserted inside a table. This is because pressing the Tab key either switches from one cell to the next, or it adds a row to the current table, and Pressing Ctrl+Tab indents a paragraph in Word Outline view, since pressing Tab increases the outline level. (In Excel, Ctrl+Tab never needs to substitute for Tab because you can never enter a Tab character inside a cell.) In Access, the Ctrl+Tab shortcut has the obscure function of jumping from a sub form to a main form—a horrible waste of a good shortcut.

If you choose to leave the Windows In Taskbar option selected for Excel, PowerPoint, and Access, each new child window will then have an entry on the taskbar and you can use Alt+Tab to switch between the respective windows. In Word, new Windows will always open a new instance of the application, and you can use Alt+Tab to switch between windows.

Using Panes in Windows

All Office applications except Access—whether they are SDI or MDI—use window panes. A pane is a subdivision of a window. You move from one pane to another by pressing F6.

PowerPoint, Outlook, and Word all use predefined window panes. In PowerPoint, the slide area, the outline area, and the notes area are each separate panes, as shown in Figure 1-3.

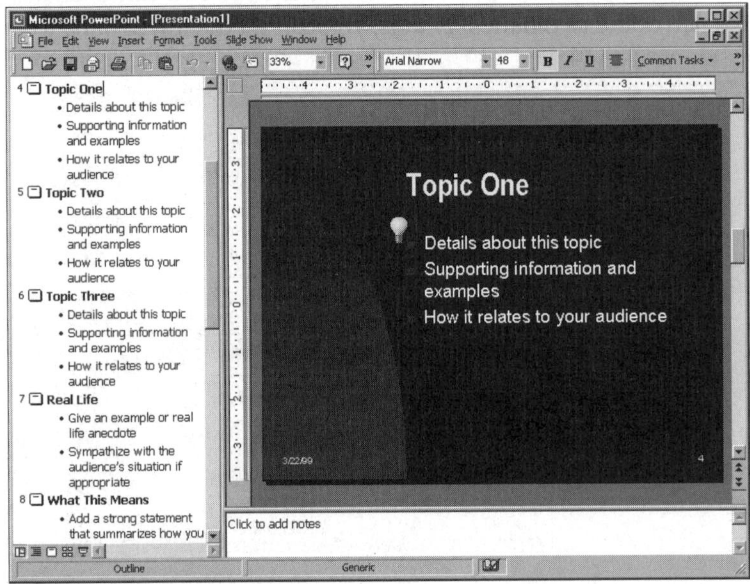

Figure 1-3
The PowerPoint window displays three panes.

In Outlook, the Inbox preview pane—which can display the contents of an e-mail message without opening it—is a pane, as is the folders list. In FrontPage, you can display a folder list which, like the folder list in Outlook, is a separate pane.

A number of Word views can display preset panes. For example, the Document Map, comments, and footnotes all appear in separate, predefined panes. In a Word window, you can have, at most, two panes—one of which is the main document pane. For example, if the Document Map is visible and you open the Comments view, the Document Map disappears while the Comments pane is visible. As soon as you close the Comments view, the Document Map pane re-appears.

In Word, you can also create a second pane in the current document window, but only if no built-in panes are visible. One way to create a pane is to drag the split bar to the desired position: At the top of the vertical scroll bar, there is a small horizontal bar right on the horizontal scroll bar above the Up arrow icon. Dragging this bar downward splits the screen and creates a new pane in the document window. Another way to create a pane is to select Split on the Window menu and set the bar that appears to the desired position. To remove the pane, double-click the divider between the panes, or select Remove Split on the Window menu.

You can scroll through a document independently in each of the two panes: Creating a second pane is useful in a long document when you want to cut and paste paragraphs from one pane to the other. You can have the beginning paragraphs of the document in the top pane and the ending paragraphs in the bottom pane, and you can then quickly cut and paste between the two. You can even assign a different view to each of the two panes. That is, you can set the lower pane to Outline view, and the upper pane to Normal view, as shown in Figure 1-4. This gives an effect similar to Word's Document Map, except that you can edit the document in the Outline view and you cannot edit it in the Document Map.

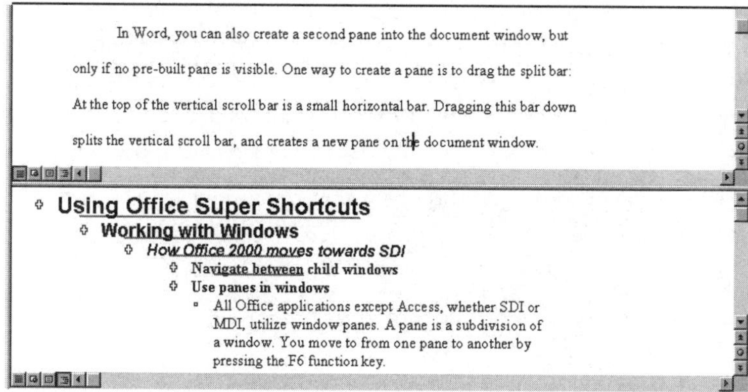

Figure 1-4
Split panes to display different views simultaneously.

Using Panes in Excel

Excel does not have pre-built panes for its windows, but you can divide the window into panes manually—both vertically and horizontally. You can also create either scrolling panes or frozen panes, although you can't mix both in the same window.

In Excel, frozen panes are typically more convenient than scrolling panes. Frozen panes add nonscrolling title rows or columns to the worksheet, making it easy to see what your row and column headings are. To create frozen panes, select the upper left cell in the non-frozen region of the worksheet, and then click Freeze Panes on the Window menu. Frozen panes affect only the worksheet window; they do not create titles for printing. To create title rows and columns for printing, select Page Setup on the File menu and click the Sheet tab. Then specify the rows and columns to be used for printing titles in the Print Titles section, as shown in Figure 1-5.

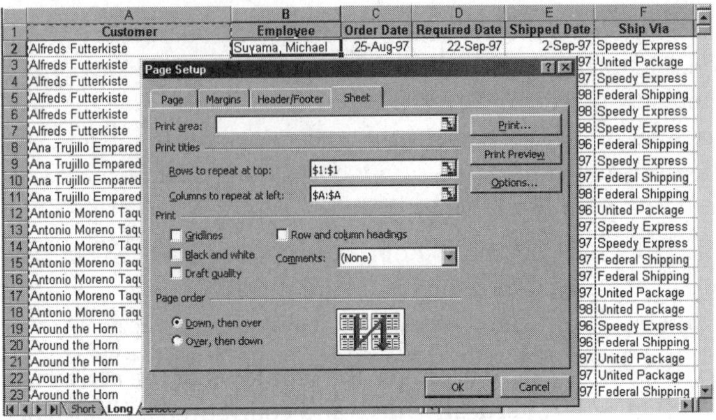

Figure 1-5
You must create print titles separately from frozen panes in Excel.

In Excel, as in Word, there are two ways to create scrolling panes. Select a cell and select Split on the Window menu, or drag the split bars in the scroll bars areas. The bar used to create a vertical split is located at the right edge of the horizontal scroll bar. Scrolling panes in an Excel window can often be confusing, because each pane can scroll anywhere on the worksheet, creating a kaleidoscope effect similar to the view shown in Figure 1-6, where you have four scrolling panes.

	J	K	L	I	J
50	Mannheim		68306	Forsterstr. 57	Mannheim
51	Mannheim		68306	Forsterstr. 57	Mannheim
52	Mannheim		68306	Forsterstr. 57	Mannheim
53	Mannheim		68306	Forsterstr. 57	Mannheim
54	Mannheim		68306	Forsterstr. 57	Mannheim
55	Mannheim		68306	Forsterstr. 57	Mannheim
56	Mannheim		68306	Forsterstr. 57	Mannheim
57	Strasbourg		67000	24, place Kléber	Strasbourg
58	Strasbourg		67000	24, place Kléber	Strasbourg
59	Strasbourg		67000	24, place Kléber	Strasbourg
60	Strasbourg		67000	24, place Kléber	Strasbourg
45	Luleå		S-958 22	Berguvsvägen 8	Luleå
46	Luleå		S-958 22	Berguvsvägen 8	Luleå
47	Luleå		S-958 22	Berguvsvägen 8	Luleå
48	Luleå		S-958 22	Berguvsvägen 8	Luleå
49	Luleå		S-958 22	Berguvsvägen 8	Luleå
50	Mannheim		68306	Forsterstr. 57	Mannheim
51	Mannheim		68306	Forsterstr. 57	Mannheim
52	Mannheim		68306	Forsterstr. 57	Mannheim
53	Mannheim		68306	Forsterstr. 57	Mannheim
54	Mannheim		68306	Forsterstr. 57	Mannheim
55	Mannheim		68306	Forsterstr. 57	Mannheim

Figure 1-6
Four scrolling panes can create a kaleidoscope effect.

You will probably find scrolling panes more useful if you split either horizontally or vertically, but not both. Scrolling panes can be very useful on a large list, because you can monitor different parts of the list.

If you have frozen panes in a window, you can't add scrolling panes. Excel does have a way to create synchronized windows to provide nearly the same effect as scrolling panes, even with frozen panes in effect. Select New on the Window menu to create a second window for the workbook. Next, add frozen panes to the new window to match those of the original. Finally, run the *SynchronizeWindows* macro shown in the following example:

```
Sub SynchronizeWindows()
    Windows.Arrange _
        ArrangeStyle:=xlArrangeStyleVertical, _
        ActiveWorkbook:=True, _
        SyncHorizontal:=False, _
        SyncVertical:=True
End Sub
```

The *SynchronizeWindows* macro arranges the windows of the active workbook like those shown in Figure 1-7: vertically tiled, and configured so that when you scroll vertically in one window, the other window will also scroll—the same as with scrolling panes. The macro leaves the horizontal scrolling independent so you can display different columns in each window. You can modify the macro to arrange or synchronize the windows any way you want.

Figure 1-7
Use an Excel macro to create scrolling windows using frozen panes.

Using the System Information Application

Microsoft Windows 98 comes with a new version of Microsoft's System Information application. Office 2000 makes that new tool available, even in Windows 95, and it also adds some additional functionality to it. To access the System Information application from any Office application, click Help, click About, and then click System Information. The System Information application displays detailed information about your computer's hardware and operating system configurations. Be sure to check out the Tools menu for interesting tools—particularly the System Configuration Utility, which allows you to modify system files such as autoexec.bat and win.ini.

(continued)

Using the System Information Application *(continued)*
Microsoft Office 2000 adds a new Applications section to the main information tree. This section displays detailed information about all currently loaded Office applications, including information about the active document.

Using Keyboard Shortcuts

My first contact with Microsoft Office came when Microsoft Excel was first introduced for the PC in 1982. At that time, an early version of Microsoft Windows was included with Excel. I was a programmer working for Hewlett-Packard, and the PC I was using did not have a mouse. (In those days, no one could think of a reason why a programmer should need a mouse.) Everything I did in Excel and Windows, I did with the keyboard. Out of necessity, I learned a lot of keyboard shortcuts. Learning the shortcuts was initially very painful, but the investment has more than made up for itself in many years of intense use of Office applications.

No one is recommending that you abandon your mouse, and the following section includes many shortcuts that use the mouse. But spending a little bit of time each week learning some keyboard shortcuts that are truly useful can make a significant difference in your productivity with Microsoft Office.

Using Shortcuts in Office Applications

Some common shortcuts are used in all Office applications, and you should be very familiar with them. For example:

- Ctrl+P to print
- Ctrl+C to copy
- Ctrl+X to cut (think of X as a proofreader's delete mark)
- Ctrl+V to paste (think of V as a proofreader's insert mark)
- Ctrl+A to select All the contents of the current window.
- Ctrl+F to open the Find dialog box
- Ctrl+H to open the Replace dialog box (try to think of a logical mnemonic for that one!)

Remembering Keyboard Shortcuts

The problem with keyboard shortcuts is that they are often hard to remember. Unlike menu commands and toolbar buttons, there are normally no visual clues to remind you of keyboard shortcuts. If you're going to learn a keyboard shortcut, you must be sure that you'll use it often enough to be able to retain it in your memory. It also helps to try to find as many tricks as possible to help you remember a keyboard shortcut.

Many keyboard shortcuts are associated with a specific letter intended to be used as a mnemonic device. For example, the original shortcut key for copy was Ctrl+Insert (which still works, by the way). Microsoft later changed the shortcut to Ctrl+C, which is much easier to remember. It is often easier to remember a shortcut key by its position on the keyboard. For example, you might remember Ctrl+Z—undo—as the bottom left key on the keyboard. As another example, Excel uses the shortcut key Ctrl+~ (Tilde) to switch between displaying values and displaying formulas on the worksheet. It's hard to come up with a good mnemonic for a Tilde, but it is easy to remember by its location on the keyboard. On a standard keyboard, the Tilde key is the top left key, to the left of the numerals. On a notebook keyboard, it can be found in a variety of locations: immediately to the right of the Spacebar, in the upper left corner, to the left of the Spacebar, and so forth.

It also helps to think of the function keys by their position. In Word, the F4 function key repeats the previous action. On many keyboards, the F4 function key is at the end of the first group of function keys, so you can think of that position as Repeat.

One technique that helps you to learn new shortcut keys is to learn patterns of similarities. Typically, the Ctrl key intensifies the behavior of an action, while the Shift key twists the behavior. For example, when using the arrow keys to move a selection, adding the Shift key extends the selection, so that the original active selection point stays as part of the selection, while the arrow keys move to the opposite end of the selection. Adding the Ctrl key intensifies the move. In Word, using the Ctrl key with the Left or Right arrow key moves the insertion point to the next or previous word, while using Ctrl with the Up or Down arrow key moves to the next or previous paragraph. In Excel, using the Ctrl key with any one of the arrow keys moves the insertion point to the beginning or end of a group of contiguously filled cells.

Using the Shift Key with Menu Commands and Toolbar Buttons

In Word and Excel, a few menus show different commands if you hold the Shift key down as you select the menu. In Word, if you hold down the Shift key as you select the File menu, the Close command changes to Close All and the Save command changes to Save All, as shown in Figure 1-8. Excel does the same with the Close command—changing it to Close All if you hold down the Shift key as you select the menu—but it does not convert the Save command to Save All.

In Excel, holding down the Shift key as you select also changes some items on the Edit menu. For example, the Copy command changes to Copy Picture, and the Paste command changes to Paste Picture, as shown in Figure 1-9. The Picture versions of these commands let you create a bitmapped image of the selected range, so that you can paste it as a graphic, rather than as cells. "Formatting Cell Backgrounds" in Chapter 16 shows some interesting uses for copying pictures. No other Office application appears to use menus modified by pressing the Shift key.

In Excel, you can also use the Shift key to reflect variations in toolbar buttons. If you hold down the Shift key as you click the Open button, it changes to a Save button,

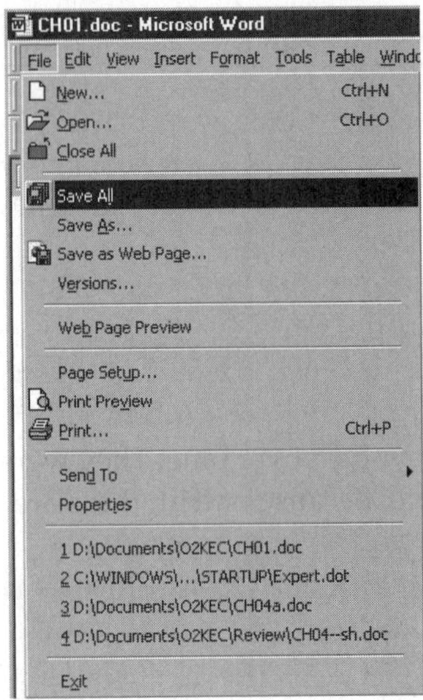

Figure 1-8
Holding down the Shift key as you click a menu will change some menu commands.

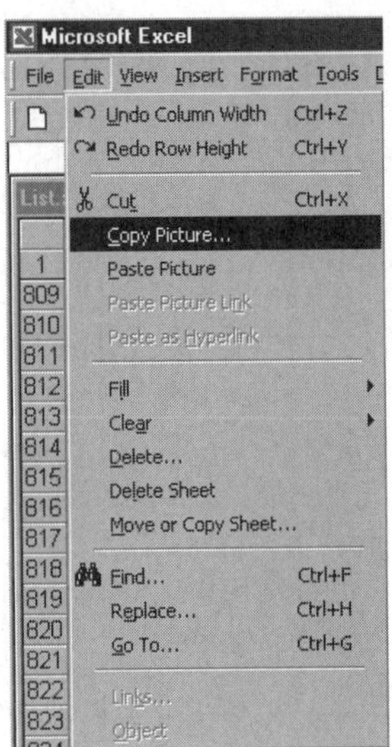

Figure 1-9
Press the Shift key to modify Excel Edit menu commands.

and vice versa. Also, the Print and Print Preview buttons trade places when you use the Shift key, as do the Sort Ascending and Sort Descending buttons, the Increase Decimal and Decrease Decimal buttons, and the Increase Indent and Decrease Indent buttons. None of the other Office applications make toolbar buttons toggle as you hold down the Shift key.

Shifted toolbar buttons are modified by pressing the Shift key; they are less cryptic than shortcut keys, and it would be nice if they were offered more extensively—and more consistently. A toolbar button modified using the Shift key does not hide a command, because the parallel button is always available. It simply allows you to extract more benefit from limited screen space, while sacrificing little in ease of remembering as the modified buttons are always logical opposites.

Using the Ctrl+G Shortcut

Shortcut keys show certain signs of having evolved over time. They were not originally designed for the Office suite as a whole. Because of that, there are some confusing anomalies in the way shortcut keys work, particularly between different Office applications. The Ctrl+G shortcut is a good example. Word, Excel, PowerPoint, Access, and the Visual Basic Editor all use Ctrl+G as a shortcut where, in each case, it is a very useful shortcut. Sometimes, there are even similarities between applications. The differences reflect the separate histories of each application.

Excel and Word both use Ctrl+G to display the Go To dialog box. In Excel's Go To dialog box, you can select a named range or you can type a cell address in the edit box. The same can be done for the Name text box at the left of the Formula bar. The advantage in using the Go To dialog box is that it remembers where you came from. After using the Go To dialog box to move to a new location—even a location in a different workbook—display the dialog box again and it will display the previous location in the Reference text box, as shown in Figure 1-10. Just click OK to jump to the previous selection. In Excel, you also access the Go To Special dialog box—which provides many more options—through the standard Go To dialog box. See "Using Go To Special to Select Cells by Attribute" in Chapter 13 for more information about the Go To Special dialog box.

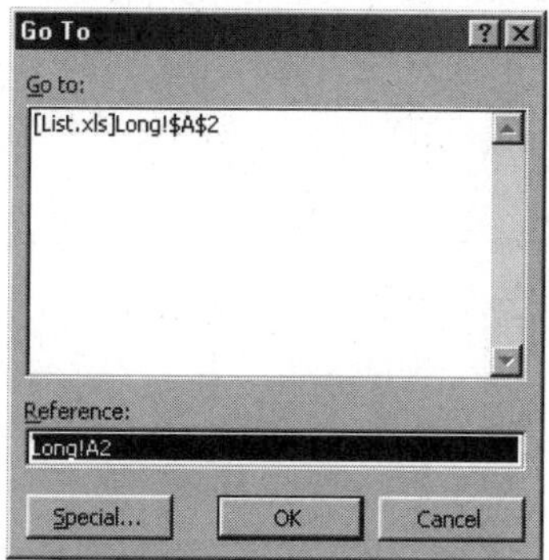

Figure 1-10
The Excel Go To dialog box will return to a previous location.

In Word, pressing Ctrl+G also displays the Go To dialog box. This is the third tabbed page in the same dialog box, which can also be accessed by pressing Ctrl+F (for Find) or Ctrl+H (for Replace). Word's Go To dialog box does not return you to a previous location, however. Instead, you must use Shift+F5 to cycle between the last four document locations it stores in memory for you. Press Shift+F5 once to jump to the previous location; press it again to jump to the location before that, and so forth.

In PowerPoint, Ctrl+G toggles the vertical and horizontal display guides. That's logical enough, but unfortunately, it is inconsistent with other Office applications.

In the Visual Basic Editor, pressing Ctrl+G displays the Immediate window. (The Immediate window was originally called the Debug window, which does contain the letter G.) In Access, even if you have never used Visual Basic, pressing Ctrl+G also launches the Visual Basic Editor and displays the Immediate window.

Using the Keyboard in a Tabbed Dialog Box

Excel was the first Office application to use tabbed dialog boxes. The Excel designers wanted to make it easy to switch from one tab to another, but they also didn't want to use up all the available accelerator letters on the tab. In Excel, when you first open a tabbed dialog box such as the Options dialog box on the Tools menu, a light gray outline appears around the active tab's caption, as shown in Figure 1-11.

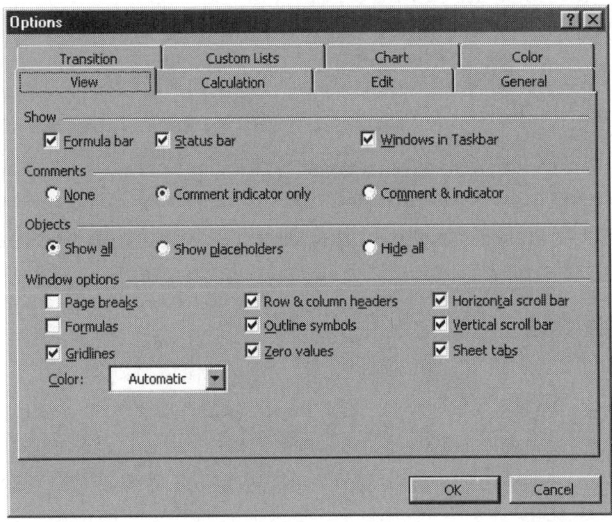

Figure 1-11
In Excel, the caption group on the tabbed page is automatically selected.

The light gray outline indicates which tab is the active control in the dialog box. The group of tabs behaves very much like a group of option buttons. If one of the tabs is the active control, you can navigate to any other tab in the group. None of the captions on any of the tabs has an underlined character for an accelerator key. But because the tabbed page is active, you can select any of the other available tabs by pressing the first letter of the caption. You can also switch between tabs by using an arrow key. Once you press the Tab key to move the active control down into the currently displayed page's options, pressing letters on the keyboard then activates the accelerator keys on that page. To switch from one page to another using the keyboard, you must press Tab or Shift+Tab to again select the tabbed page. This feature is also common to both Windows 95 and Windows 98 tabbed dialog boxes.

When tabbed dialog boxes were first introduced in Word, Word's designers chose to use a different strategy for moving between tabbed pages. When you open the Font dialog box on the Format menu, as shown in Figure 1-12, the tabbed page is not initially selected, but each of the captions has an underlined accelerator key.

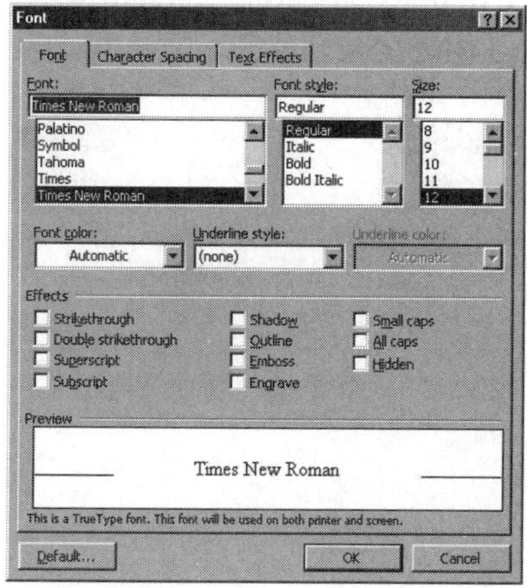

Figure 1-12
In most Word dialog boxes, tabbed page captions have accelerator keys indicated.

Pressing Alt+R key switches to the Character tab. You can also press Shift+Tab to select the tabbed page, and then use the arrow keys to switch to a new tabbed page. Word is not particularly consistent from one tabbed dialog box to another. In the Index And Tables dialog box on the Table menu, for example, the tabbed page is initially selected. In contrast, activating a new tab in the Find And Replace dialog box on the Edit menu selects a control on the page, making it impossible to continue using the arrow keys. The Options dialog box on the Tools menu does not have any accelerator letters on the tabbed page captions, probably because there are so many controls in the dialog box that it was impossible to find unused keys to use for accelerator keys.

Dialog boxes that are managed globally by Office are also generally inconsistent. For example, the New dialog box on the File menu, which is used to open a new document, does not have the tabbed page caption selected, but it also does not use accelerator keys. In all tabbed dialog boxes, regardless of which program they are in, you can use the Tab key or the Shift+Tab keys to activate the tabbed page and then use the Left, Right, Up, or Down arrow keys to move from one tabbed page to another.

In the Open dialog box on the File menu—which does not have tabs, but rather, has groups off to the side—you can still press the Tab key to select the page and then use arrow keys to change the selected item on the page. Unlike tabbed pages, once you get to the page you want, you must press Enter to activate that page.

Navigating Quickly in the File Open Dialog Box

New! Office 2000 adds a new feature to the Open dialog boxes for each application's File menu that is refreshingly friendly for keyboard-oriented users. When you enter part of the name of a file or folder in the File Name text box, the dialog box automatically fills in the rest of a matching filename or folder name, as shown in Figure 1-13. If you enter the name of a folder, the dialog box changes to that folder. This is a remarkably efficient mechanism for navigating through the endless folder trees that are inevitable on corporate network file servers.

Figure 1-13
Begin typing a file or folder name and the whole name will appear.

To use the Backspace key to move up one folder in the folder hierarchy, you must first open Windows Explorer window within the dialog box. There is a shortcut, however, that allows you to move up the folder tree very quickly while working in the File Name text box. Type a single period for the current folder and an additional period for each folder level you want to move up the tree, and then press Enter. For example, to move up four levels in the folder hierarchy, type five periods and press Enter.

Most of the Office file dialog boxes have new drop-down list box buttons that add more options to the Open button. Figure 1-14 shows the Open button displaying the options for opening a file in Excel. This new button is extremely unfriendly to keyboard users. Before you can enable the drop-down list, you must first select the button. You can't press the accelerator key to select the button; doing so executes the default command. You must press the Tab key until the button has been selected. The normal keyboard command for opening a drop-down list is Alt+Down arrow, which does not work on the drop-down button. You must press the Down arrow key once to open the list, and then again to select the desired command. The commands do have accelerator keys, but they don't work until the list has been displayed. By that time, it would have been easier just to click the arrow key to select the command.

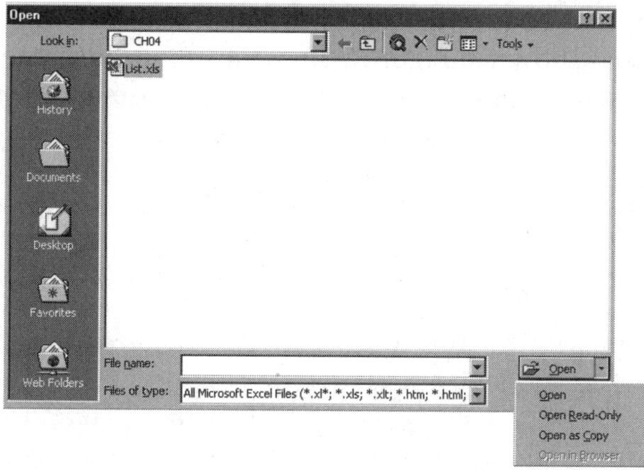

Figure 1-14
To open the drop down list box beside the Open button, you must press Tab and then press the Down arrow key.

Outlook uses a button next to the drop-down list box in instances where the accelerator key does not execute the command, but the accelerator key merely selects the button, in case you want to select a different option once you've activated the drop-down list box. When you create a message and you also have more than one e-mail service available, the Send button is a drop-down button. Pressing the Alt+S accelerator keys does not send the message; it merely selects the button. You then need to press the Down arrow key to display the list of mail options, as shown in Figure 1-15.

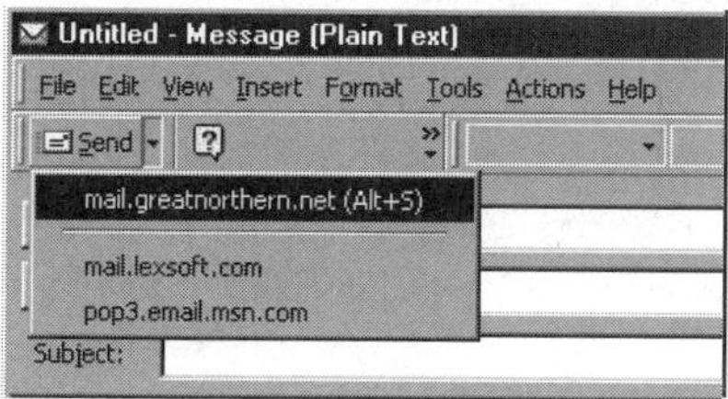

Figure 1-15
In an Outlook message, press the accelerator key to select the button next to the drop-down list.

In most Office dialog boxes, pressing the Tab key to move from control to control proceeds in logical order. Sometimes, you can tell that a new control was added to an existing dialog box, because it activates out of sequence. For example, on the View tab of the Excel Options dialog box on the Tools menu, the Windows In Taskbar check box comes at the end of the Tab sequence, rather than in its correct position. Not surprisingly, this check box is new to Office 2000. On the Transition tab of the same dialog box, the Save As Excel Files list box is also not in the proper sequence. Not surprisingly, this control was new in Excel 97.

Using Keyboard Shortcuts in Applications

In Excel, some shortcuts come in clusters, where you can access several related shortcuts for not much more work than memorizing one shortcut. This substantially improves your return-on-investment for the time you take to learn the shortcuts.

One such cluster of shortcuts is used for hiding and unhiding rows and columns. These shortcuts use the open and close parentheses keys (which are the number 9 and 0 keys on the keyboard, respectively). Use the unshifted key to hide the selected row or column, and use the shifted key to unhide the selected row or column. To remember which key goes with the row and which key goes with the column, remember that in Excel, you always speak of rows and columns, never of columns and rows. That is, the word row should always precede the word column in polite conversation, so it's only natural that the first key—the open parenthesis—should refer to rows. Thus, Ctrl+9 (without the shift key) hides the selected rows, and Ctrl+0 (again, without the shift key) hides the selected columns. By extension, Ctrl+Shift+9 (also known as open parenthesis) unhides the selected rows, and Ctrl+Shift+0 (also known as close parenthesis) unhides the selected columns.

Another related cluster of shortcuts inserts and deletes cells. Ctrl+Plus (+) inserts cells, and Ctrl+Minus (-) deletes cells. Of course, in order to insert the Plus character from the alphabetic keyboard, you must press the Shift key. On the numeric keypad, you simply press Ctrl+Plus (+) or Ctrl+Minus (-). Excel determines what to insert or delete based on the current selection. If you have one or more rows selected, Excel will insert or delete those rows. If you have one or more columns selected, Excel will insert or delete columns. If you have selected only partial rows or columns, Excel will display a dialog box asking for further guidance, as shown in Figure 1-16.

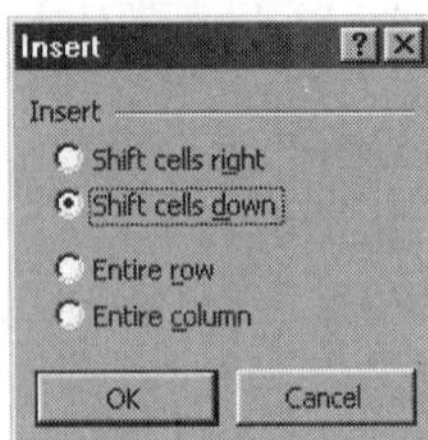

Figure 1-16
Excel prompts if you don't select an entire row or column

You can use the Ctrl+Plus sign shortcut very effectively in conjunction with Ctrl+X to rearrange cells on the spreadsheet. Suppose you want to have the range B5:D5 trade places with the range B4:D4. Select the range B5:D5 and press Ctrl+ X to cut it to the clipboard. Then select cell B4 and press Ctrl+Plus to insert the values, sliding the old values down to row 5. (For a mouse equivalent to rearrange cells, see "Using the Drag Border in Excel" later in this chapter.)

Selecting Cells In and Around an Excel List

In Excel, you will often have a block of cells similar to the cells shown in Figure 1-17, except perhaps many times larger.

	A	B	C	D	E	F	G
1	Employee	Order Date	Required Date	Shipped Date	Ship Via	Freight	
2	Suyama, Michael	25-Aug-1997	22-Sep-1997	02-Sep-1997	Speedy Express	$29.46	
3	Peacock, Margaret	03-Oct-1997	31-Oct-1997	13-Oct-1997	United Package	$61.02	
4	Peacock, Margaret	13-Oct-1997	24-Nov-1997	21-Oct-1997	Speedy Express	$23.94	
5	Davolio, Nancy	15-Jan-1998	12-Feb-1998	21-Jan-1998	Federal Shipping	$69.53	
6	Davolio, Nancy	16-Mar-1998	27-Apr-1998	24-Mar-1998	Speedy Express	$40.42	
7	Leverling, Janet	09-Apr-1998	07-May-1998	13-Apr-1998	Speedy Express	$1.21	
8							

Figure 1-17
In Excel, the currently selected range is bounded by white space.

One common task you might want to perform with a block of cells is to select the entire cell block. A block of cells—specifically, a rectangular range of cells which includes the active cell and which is surrounded by blank cells—is called the current region. The shortcut for selecting the *current region* is Ctrl+asterisk (*). Think of the asterisk key as being similar to a wildcard character in the file system. With files, the wildcard *.* refers to all files located in the current directory. In Excel, the shortcut Ctrl+asterisk (*) selects all the cells within the current region. (If you use the numeric keypad, you simply press Ctrl plus the multiplication (*) sign. If you use the standard keyboard, you press Ctrl+Shift+8 to use the Ctrl+Asterisk (*) shortcut.)

Suppose you want to select the last three columns of the range of cells shown earlier in Figure 1-18. Select the top cell in the first column you want to select, hold down the Ctrl key and the Shift key, and then press the Down arrow key. Then, without releasing the Ctrl or the Shift key, press the Right arrow key. The addition of the Ctrl key makes the arrow key jump to the end of the current block of cells, while the Shift key retains the active cell as part of the selection.

Now suppose you want to select the same range, but you want to exclude the titles in the first row. After following the instructions in the preceding paragraph to select the last three columns, you're stuck. The active cell is on the row that you want to deselect. To exclude that row from the selection, you must change the active cell without changing the selection. Technically, you can press the Enter key to move the active cell down without changing the selection. But to deselect the top row, the active cell must be in the bottom row. It would take a long time pressing the Enter key to get the active cell from the top row to the bottom row of a 10,000-row list.

The Ctrl+Period (.) shortcut shifts the active cell clockwise from corner to corner around the selection. To move the active cell from the upper left corner down to the lower right corner of the selection, press Ctrl+Period twice. With the active cell at the bottom of the selection, you can then press the Shift+Down arrow keys to deselect the top row, as shown in Figure 1-18.

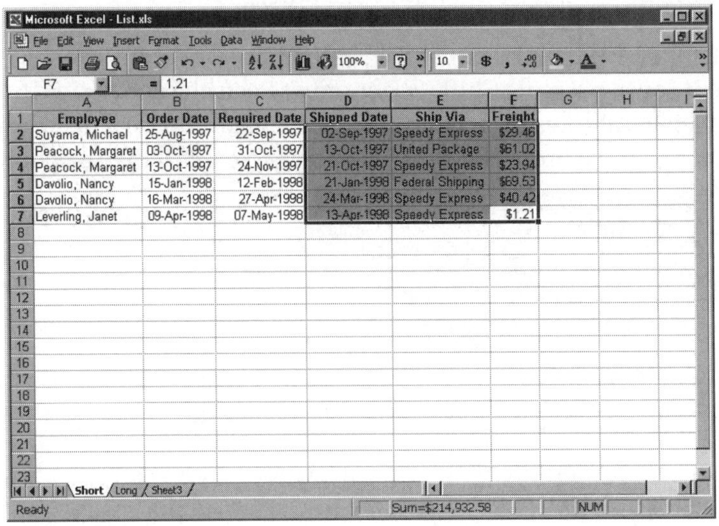

Figure 1-18
To deselect the top row, you must move the active cell to the bottom.

Extending a Selection in Word

Word also uses the Shift key to extend the selection from the starting location. The starting location is called the active end of the selection. Unfortunately, Word does not have a provision for switching the active end from one end of the selection to the other. You can, however, use a simple VBA macro to switch the end of the selection in Word, as shown in the following *SwapActive* macro:

```
Sub SwapActive()
    Selection.StartIsActive = Not Selection.StartIsActive
End Sub
```

If you assign the Ctrl+Period shortcut to the *SwapActive* macro, you can then use the same keyboard techniques to extend and contract selections in Word as you do in Excel.

Selecting Rows and Columns in Excel and Access

Excel and Access share the same shortcut keys for selecting entire rows or entire columns. To select the entire row, press Shift+Spacebar. To select the entire column, press Ctrl+Spacebar. The hardest part about these two shortcuts is remembering which one selects rows and which one selects columns. One way to remember is to think of the word Ctrl as looking similar to the word Column. Or, if you prefer, you can think of the word Shift as being similar to the word Sheet, and a bed sheet is always horizontal, like a row.

Once you've selected the entire row or column in Excel or Access, you can use Shift plus the arrow keys to extend a selection. In Excel, however, you can preselect a block of, say, four rows and four columns, and then press Shift+Space to extend the four-row selection to the entire width of the worksheet. In Access, even if you preselect cells in several rows, pressing Shift+Space only selects the entire current row. If you want to select several rows in Access, always use Shift+Space first to select the current row, and then use Shift and an arrow keys to extend the selection to include additional rows.

Expanding the Current Selection

Word and Access share the same shortcut key for expanding the current selection. Each time you press F8, the selection expands to the next largest unit. In other words, when you press F8 the first time, the selection expands to include the entire current word. When you press F8 again, the selection expands to include the current sentence (in Word) or the current cell (in Access), and so forth.

Excel also uses the F8 function key to modify the current selection, but in a slightly different way. After you press the F8 function key, Excel changes to an extended selection mode called Extend mode. In Extend mode, the arrow keys behave as if you were continuously pressing the Shift key. That is, the arrow keys extend the selection. Press F8 again to exit Extend mode.

Excel uses another variation of the F8 function key, as well. Pressing Shift+F8 in Excel places you into Add mode, which allows you to move the active cell outside of the selection without destroying the current selection, thereby creating a multiple-area selection (analogous to holding down the Ctrl key as you select multiple ranges with the mouse). Excel remains in Add mode until you enter Extend mode (either press F8, or hold down the Shift key as you move the arrow keys). Pragmatically, here's the best way to use Shift+F8 to create a multiple-area selection: Hold down the Shift key as you use arrow keys to select the first area. Then press Shift+F8 to enter Add mode and use the arrow keys to move to a new starting location. Again, hold down the Shift key as you use the arrow keys to select the second area. Repeat these steps to add as many areas as you like to the current selection.

Showing a Selected Style in Word

In Word, the Style list on the Formatting toolbar displays all the styles currently in use in a document. If you have a document with many styles, getting to the correct style in the list can be extremely frustrating. When you start typing a style name from the list, it does not automatically select a style name matching those first few letters you type. Instead, the Style box assumes you will are typing a new style name—unless you exactly match the spelling of an existing style.

The secret to forcing the list to display style names beginning with a certain letter is to select the Style box (click in it or press Ctrl+Shift+S), and then display the list of style names in the drop-down list box (click the drop-down button or press the Alt+Down arrow keys) before typing the first letter of a style name. With the list displayed, the style names scroll to display a style with the first letter you type, as shown in Figure 1-19. Scrolling the list brings you close to the desired style; it is quicker to press the Down arrow key to move to the actual style name.

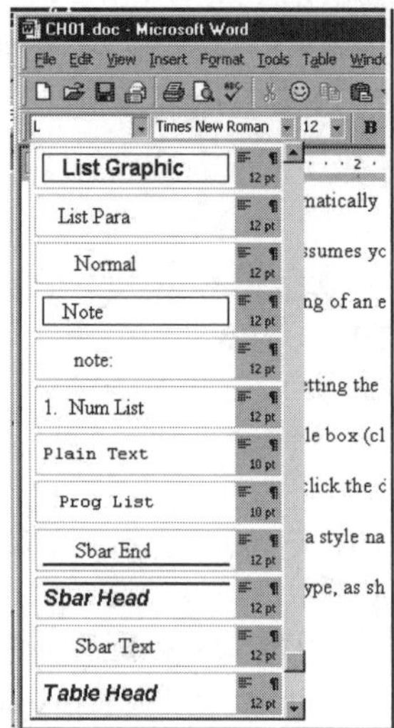

Figure 1-19
Access the Style drop-down list box before typing a letter.

Customizing Keyboard Shortcuts in Word

Both Excel and Word allow you to assign shortcut keys to macros. This is explained more fully in Chapter 5, "Make Sense of Office Object Models." Only Word allows you to customize the shortcut key for any of its built-in commands. To customize a shortcut key in Word, click Tools, Customize, and click the Keyboard button. In the Customize Keyboard dialog box, you can select a category and a command to see the current key assignment in the Current Keys list. To assign a new shortcut to the command, click in the Press New Shortcut Key text box and press the shortcut combination you want to use. If the combination you type into the box is already in use, as shown in Figure 1-20, the dialog box will show you. You can then decide whether you want to override the current assignment.

Word has an amazing shortcut that lets you determine the command associated with any shortcut key. Press Ctrl+Alt+Plus (+); you must use the plus sign on the numeric keypad. The mouse pointer will change to a cloverleaf interchange symbol. Then, simply press any key combination and Word will show you what command that key combination is currently assigned to. It will even let you change it to a different

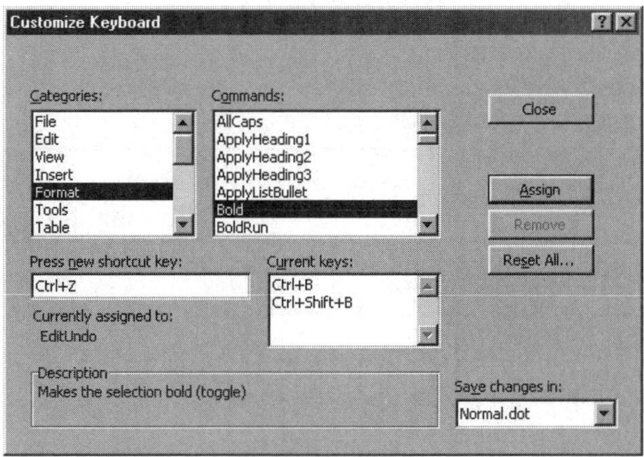

Figure 1-20
Customize the shortcut key for any command in Word.

shortcut at that time. You can use the Ctrl+Alt+Plus command for many mouse actions—such as clicking the status bar—but not for all. You can try clicking various items to see if Word will display the command.

Using the Keyboard with Graphical Objects

One reason for manipulating graphical objects with the keyboard is to work more efficiently. A more important reason is that when you are recording a macro in Word, certain activities that you normally perform with the mouse won't work while the macro recorder is running. For example, while recording a macro in Word, you cannot use the mouse to select text. And although in general you can select graphical objects with the mouse even while the recorder is running, it is often difficult to do. Keyboard techniques always work, however, even when recording a macro in Word.

Selecting Graphical Objects Using the Keyboard

Most Office applications use Office AutoShape objects—the objects that appear on the Drawing toolbar for graphical objects. Access creates objects on forms and reports using controls, which behave somewhat differently from AutoShape objects. With all graphical objects, you can select the next graphical object by pressing the Tab key. The tricky part is getting at least one graphical object selected in the first place.

One technique for selecting graphical objects with the keyboard is by working through the Drawing toolbar. You can use this technique in any application that can display the Drawing toolbar. On the Drawing toolbar, the Draw menu uses the letter R as a keyboard accelerator. So, pressing Alt+R activates the Draw menu. You can then press the Right arrow key to highlight the Select Objects toolbar button. Once the Select Objects button is highlighted, press Ctrl+Enter to select all the AutoShape objects in the document. (Pressing Enter merely turns on the button so that the mouse will select objects rather than text, which is not helpful when you're trying to use the keyboard.) Once all the objects are selected, press the Tab key to start selecting individual objects.

Note You can click any command bar button using only the keyboard. Pressing the Alt key activates the menu bar, which is the first command bar. Once a command bar is activated, you can press Tab to access the next button, or press Ctrl+Tab to get to the next command bar.

In Excel, you can select all the graphical objects on a worksheet by pressing Ctrl+G to display the Go To dialog box, clicking Special to display the Go To Special dialog box, selecting the Objects option, and clicking OK.

In PowerPoint, you don't need to do anything special to start selecting graphical objects, because everything on a PowerPoint slide is a graphical object. Simply press the Tab key to select the first object.

Using the Keyboard to Manipulate a Graphical Object

Once you have selected an AutoShape object, you can use the arrow keys to move the object on the document. By themselves, the arrow keys move the object in approximately one-eighth inch increments in the direction of the arrow key you pressed. Hold down the Ctrl key as you press an arrow key to move the object in single point increments.

To add text to an AutoShape object in Excel and PowerPoint, you simply start typing the text. The easiest way to edit text in an existing object is, again, to simply start typing new characters. Once you start typing characters, you are editing the text, which is a different mode for the object. To get back to point where the object itself is selected, press the Esc key.

Word deals with text in AutoShape objects somewhat differently. To add text to an object in Word, you must use the context menu. Right-click the object or, on the keyboard, press the context menu button. Then select Add Text from the menu. If the object already contains text, the context menu command changes to Edit Text. You cannot use the Esc key in Word to stop editing the text and reselect the object. You must again use the context menu, selecting the command Edit Text from the menu. In all Office applications, press the Esc key to deselect a selected AutoShape object.

Using the Keyboard with Access Objects

In design mode on an Access form or report, you add controls, not AutoShape objects. In Access, press Ctrl+A to select all the objects. In Access, you must always hold down the Ctrl key as you press the arrow keys to move a selected object. Access, however, allows you to hold down the Shift key as you resize the object by moving the arrow keys—an option that is available in no other Office application.

Using Mouse Shortcuts

Using the mouse effectively can enhance productivity, just as much as using shortcut keys effectively. Working with the mouse is not slow, but repeatedly switching back and forth between the keyboard and the mouse is. You will be more productive when you can perform more actions with the mouse without having to go back to the keyboard. Right-clicking context menus will substantially contribute to making the mouse an extremely useful tool. You should click the right mouse button in various locations within your application periodically just to determine whether there are any commands available to you that you might not have noticed before. Don't forget to try out the right mouse button when dragging a selection, too.

Managing Adaptive Command Bars

Office 2000 implements a new technology called adaptive menus. The Office applications initially show only the most frequently used menu commands. Other, less frequently-used menu commands appear only if you hold the mouse pointer over the menu in apparent indecision for a few seconds, or if you click the more commands button on the bottom of the menu. When you use a menu command, it moves to the visible portion of the menu. If you don't use a command for an extended period, it hides itself.

adaptive menus are intended to make the user interface less confusing for new users, and they are probably good for current users, as well. But most power users will probably find them very frustrating. Power users like to explore infrequently used—and typically powerful—menu commands. Fortunately, turning off adaptive menus is easy. Select Customize on the Tools menu. Then, on the Options tab, clear the Menus Show Recently Used Commands First check box.

Office 2000 also implements a similar feature—adaptive toolbars. Unlike adaptive menus, adaptive toolbars are convenient even for power users who typically customize their toolbars extensively. The fact that adaptive toolbars are useful is fortunate, because you can't disable this feature. To see all the commands on a toolbar, simply move the toolbar to its own row, just like the formatting toolbar is on its own row. This feature allows you to show more toolbars simultaneously without having to manually remove the buttons you don't want to see. For example, suppose that you typically use only the Run Macro and Record Macro commands on the Visual Basic toolbar. Rather than create a custom toolbar, simply drag the Visual Basic toolbar to the same row as an existing toolbar, and drag its starting position to show only those two buttons. The toolbar will always show only the two most frequently used buttons. In two or three seconds, you have achieved the same benefit as creating a custom toolbar.

Modifying Command Bars

In Word, PowerPoint, and Access—but not in Excel or Outlook—you can easily modify the shortcut menus that appear when you right-click somewhere on the display. Click View, Toolbars, Customize, and select the Toolbars tab. Turn on the Shortcut Menus toolbar. What you see are three menus which exist purely for the purpose of grouping the dozens of available shortcut menus together. Each submenu describes the context for displaying the shortcut menu. You can't change the shortcut menu itself—or certain fixed items on some of the menus—but, for the most part, you can customize them to your heart's content. Chapter 6, "Adding Commands to a Shortcut Menu in Excel," and Chapter 5, "Drive Office from Visual Basic," explain how to use macros to customize shortcut menus in Excel.

Some built-in toolbar commands have small downward-pointing triangles. These are drop-down commands. Some of the drop-down commands are really menus which you can customize. All the commands that include text, such as the Draw menu on the Drawing toolbar, are customizable drop-down menus. Most of the drop-down commands that display an icon—such as the Font Color button—are not menus, but are simply non-customizable palettes. Some of the icon commands with an icon, however, are actually customizable drop-down menus. For example, on the Drawing toolbar, the Fill Color and Line Color options are drop-down menus. The only way to tell whether a drop-down command is a menu or a palette is by trying to click the command while the Customize dialog box is open. If the drop-down opens, it is a customizable menu. Don't assume that just because a command has a graphic, you can't modify it.

Using the Drag Border in Excel

When a selection in Excel consists of a single range, it is surrounded by a thick border called the drag border, as shown in Figure 1-21. When the mouse pointer is positioned over a drag border, it changes from a normal large white plus sign into the standard Windows selection pointer. To move a range to a new location in the worksheet, select the range and then drag the drag border. Excel uses a gray outline to show you the new location for the range.

	A	B	C	D	E	F
1	Chapter 1	1st Period	Qtr1	Nov-01	11/1/01	
2	Chapter 2	2nd Period	Qtr2	Dec-01	11/2/01	
3	Chapter 3	3rd Period	Qtr3	Jan-02	11/3/01	
4	Chapter 4	4th Period	Qtr4	Feb-02	11/4/01	
5	Chapter 5	5th Period	Qtr1	Mar-02	11/5/01	
6	Chapter 6	6th Period	Qtr2	Apr-02	11/6/01	
7						

Figure 1-21
When you drag in Excel, a box shows the target location.

You can even drag the range to a new sheet within the same workbook by pressing the Alt key as you drag the range down toward the sheet tabs. Excel will switch between worksheets as you move the mouse pointer over the sheet tabs. If you have trouble remembering which key to press to drag the range to a different sheet, a message will appear in the status bar reminding you that you can use the Alt key to drag to a new sheet as soon as you start dragging the range.

Holding down the Ctrl key as you drag a range causes Excel to copy the range. (Using the Ctrl key while you drag a range to make a copy is a standard Windows behavior; it works not only in Excel, but also in Word, when dragging files in Windows Explorer, and so forth.)

In Windows Explorer, you can force Windows to move rather than copy a file, even if you are dragging the file to a different drive, by holding down the Shift key. Excel follows the same convention. If you hold down the Shift key as you drag a range, the target location appears as an I-beam rather than as a box, as shown in Figure 1-22.

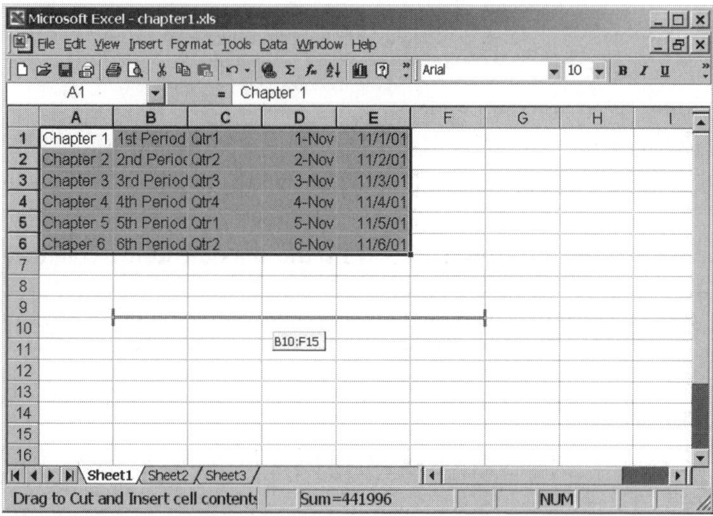

Figure 1-22
Press Shift+Drag to move a range to a new location.

If you move the range to different rows in the same column, or to different columns in the same row, Excel inserts the cells—sliding cells back in a very intuitive way. If you drag to a new range that is not part of the same column or the same row, Excel cuts the source cell—leaving blank cells—pushing cells out of the way to make room in the target area.

Note When you press the Ctrl or Shift key as you drag with the mouse, the state of the key is important only when you release the mouse button. If you drag a range without pressing any key, and then press the Ctrl key just as you release the mouse button, the range will be copied. A common error many users make is to release the Control or Shift key too early, before releasing the mouse button.

Don't forget to try dragging using the right mouse button. As you do, a menu of options will appear asking how you want to drag the cells. You can even use the mouse to convert formulas to values without changing the location of the cells. Select a range of cells containing formulas, and then use the right mouse button to drag the range slightly to the side and then back to the original location. When you release the button, the shortcut menu will give you the option to Paste Values. Selecting that option converts the range to values using nothing but the mouse.

Using the AutoFill Handle in Excel

At the bottom right corner of the drag border is a small black box called the AutoFill handle. The AutoFill handle is a powerful tool for automatically extending values in a selection. Table 1-1 illustrates some ways that AutoFill can extend a value.

If the selection consists of:	Dragging the AutoFill handle will:
Text ending in a numeral	Increment the numeral
An ordinal number such as 1st (even if it is followed by other text)	Create incremental ordinal numbers
A meaningful quarter unit such as Qtr1	Automatically restart numbering after four quarters
A date formatted to show the month and year	Extend the date in increments of a month
A date formatted to display the day	Extend the date in increments of a day

Table 1-1
Excel AutoFill Values.

If the selection consists of a single row with different types of values in each cell, dragging the AutoFill handle will increment each column independently for most types of values, as displayed in the first three columns shown in Figure 1-23. To increment dates, as displayed in the last two columns of the figure, you must AutoFill each column separately.

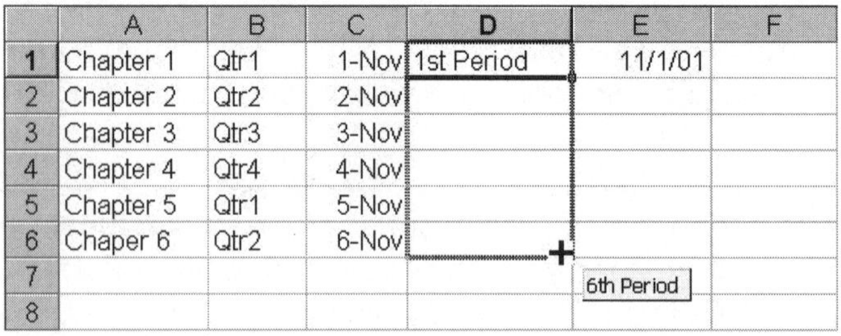

	A	B	C	D	E	F
1	Chapter 1	Qtr1	1-Nov	1st Period	11/1/01	
2	Chapter 2	Qtr2	2-Nov			
3	Chapter 3	Qtr3	3-Nov			
4	Chapter 4	Qtr4	4-Nov			
5	Chapter 5	Qtr1	5-Nov			
6	Chaper 6	Qtr2	6-Nov			
7					6th Period	
8						

Figure 1-23
Double-click the AutoFill handle to match an adjacent list.

If you want to AutoFill using a specific increment level, enter the first two values of the series into two adjacent cells, select the two cells, and then drag the AutoFill handle. (With multiple cells, the AutoFill handle uses a linear regression to extend the series! See "Using Regression to Find and Extend Patterns" in Chapter 14 for more details about linear regression.)

If the selected cell is adjacent to a column of values, you can double-click the AutoFill handle to achieve the same effect as dragging the AutoFill handle to match the number of rows in the adjacent column. Double-clicking the AutoFill handle is extremely useful when you are adding a new column of formulas to a long list.

Modifying Scroll Bars in Excel

When you drag the scroll bars in Excel, they typically move only within the range of cells that actually contain something. In other words, if you have data only in rows 1 through 200, you can't use the vertical scroll bar to scroll to row 2000. If you hold down the Shift key as you scroll, however, the scroll bars will scroll anywhere within the 65,536 rows of the worksheet.

In an Excel workbook, the sheet tabs appear on the left side, at the bottom of the workbook window, and the scroll bar uses the remainder of the width of the window. Between the two scroll bars is a small vertical bar that you can drag to change the allocation of space between the sheet tabs and the horizontal scroll bar. You can drag the bar to either extreme edge, effectively eliminating either the sheet tabs or the scroll bar. This can be an effective alternative to deselecting either the Horizontal Scroll Bar or the Sheet Tabs check boxes on the View tab on the Tools, Options dialog box.

Using Mouse Shortcuts in Tables

In Word and PowerPoint, you can use in the mouse pointer to select a column in a table. Place the mouse pointer slightly above a column in the table and it will change to a black arrow. While it is a black arrow, click to select the column directly beneath the pointer. As you click, you can drag to select additional columns. In Word (but not in PowerPoint), you can select an entire row by clicking in the margin to the left of the row—even though no black arrow appears. To select a single cell, move the mouse over the left edge of a cell until an upward pointing black arrow appears, and then click.

Word also allows you to use the mouse pointer to select, move, or resize an entire table, but you must be in either Print Layout or Web Layout view to do so. When you move the mouse over a table, a box with a four-way arrow appears slightly above the top left corner of the table, as shown in Figure 1-24. Click the box to select the table, and then drag the box to move the table. A smaller box without an arrow appears next to the bottom right corner of the table. Click and drag that box to change the height or width of the table. These boxes are a little bit quirky. They do not appear unless the mouse is over the table, but the boxes themselves are not inside the table; if you move the mouse even slightly off the box, it disappears.

If the selection consists of	*Dragging the AutoFill handle*
Text ending in a numeral	Increments the numeral
An ordinal number such as 1st (whether or not it is followed by other text)	Creates incremental ordinal numbers

Figure 1-24
In layout view, move and resize boxes appear at the corners of a table.

Note Even if you select the entire table, you cannot press Delete to delete it. Pressing Delete will only delete the contents. You can press Delete to get rid of the table if you also select at least one character—which might be the paragraph mark of an empty paragraph—outside the table.

Using Mouse Shortcuts in Word

Word has many mouse shortcuts. The margin to the left of a paragraph is a clickable area. Click once in the left margin to select an entire line of text. Double-click in the left margin to select a paragraph. Triple-click in the left margin to select the entire document.

Word's status area at the bottom of the document window also contains clickable areas. If you double-click anywhere in the first two sections of the status bar—that is, in the page number or page location section—Word will display the Find And Replace dialog box with the Go To tab highlighted.

Three browsing controls are located below the vertical scroll bar in Word. The middle control—the one with a circle icon—is the Select Browse Object button, which allows you to select an item type to browse. Once you have selected a browse object, the double arrows above and below the Select Browse Object button select the previous and next instances of the selected object type. After clicking the Select Browse Object button, you can select any of a dozen different types of objects to browse, as shown in Figure 1-25.

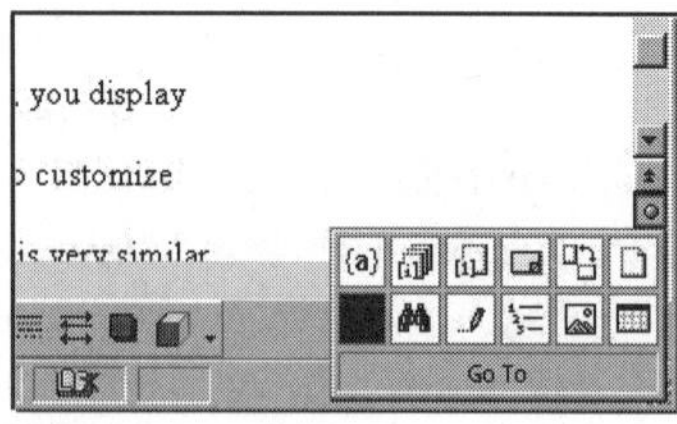

Figure 1-25
The Select Browse Object button lets you choose an object type to search for.

If you select the first item on the second row—the Go To option—you will display the Go To tab on the Find And Replace dialog box, which will then allow you to customize the browse options even further. The list of objects in the Go To What list is very similar to that in the Select Browse Object list. The Select Browse Object list contains one object type not found in the Go To What list: the object for Edits to the document. The Go To What list contains four object types not found in the Browse Object Type list: Bookmark, Equation, generic Object, and Line.

In the Go To dialog box, you can also specify a relative counter for several of the object types, which allows you to create truly customizable browsing options. Suppose, for example, that you want scroll the page on the screen by two-thirds of a page to allow a few lines' overlap between the lines of one screen and another. That is, if Word displays 30 lines at time, you want to scroll by 20 lines. In the Go To What box, select Line, and in the Enter Line Number box, type *+20*, as shown in Figure 1-26.

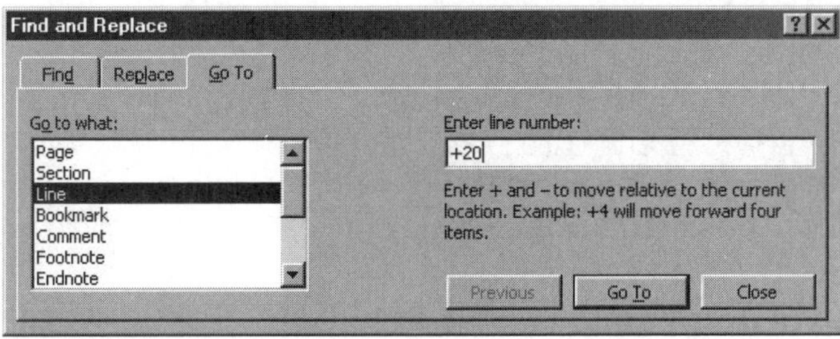

Figure 1-26
Enter a relative line number to scroll a fraction of a page.

After you click Close, you can click the Browse Previous and Browse Next buttons to scroll up or down by two-thirds of the screen. You can also use Ctrl+Page Up and Ctrl+Page Down to browse up and down.

Using Mouse Shortcuts with Graphical Objects

While it is possible to use the keyboard to manipulate graphical objects, as explained in the section "Using The Keyboard With Graphical Objects" shown earlier, it is much more natural to manipulate them with the mouse. The techniques for working with graphical objects varies somewhat from application to application.

Controlling the Alignment of Graphical Objects

All the Office applications that use AutoShape graphical objects allow you to snap the object to a grid. In Excel, the grid consists of the cell grid itself. To change the resolution of the grid, simply change the width of the columns and the height of the rows. Excel's default option keeps the object aligned with the grid, even if you resize the grid. If you want to use the cell grid to position an object and then change the grid back to its size without moving the object, here's how to change the Positioning property of the selected object: Select the object—be careful not to select the text if the object contains text—and select AutoShape on the Format menu. On the Properties tab, select the Don't Move Or Size With Cells option, as shown in Figure 1-27, and click OK.

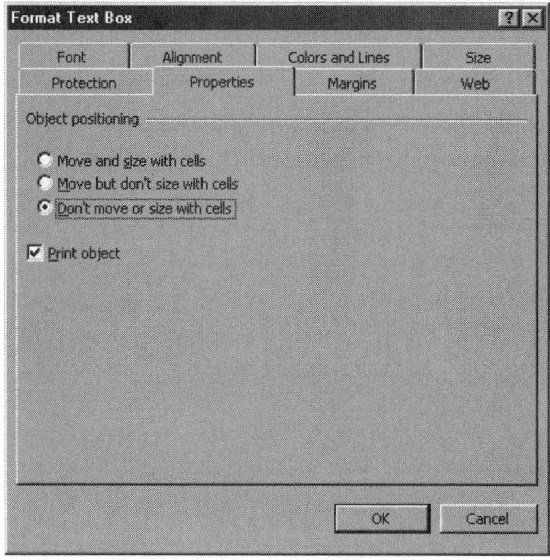

Figure 1-27
Object positioning will control what happens when you move cells.

In Word, you use a menu command to specify the size of the invisible grid. On the Drawing toolbar, select Grid on the Draw menu, enter the desired values in the Grid Settings group, and click OK.

PowerPoint does not allow you to change the size of the invisible grid. Instead, PowerPoint allows you to position guidelines for aligning the objects in addition to the built-in grid. To display guidelines, right-click the background of the slide and click Guides. Drag the guides to move them to the desired position. To make a copy, press Ctrl as you drag a guideline. To remove a guide, drag it off the edge of the slide.

In Word, Excel, and PowerPoint, you can turn Snap To Grid on or off. In Excel and PowerPoint, select Snap from the Draw menu, and then select or clear the To Grid option or the To Shape option. In Word, you must use the Draw dialog box. Select Grid from the Draw menu, and select the options in the Snap To group. The Alt key temporarily reverses the value of the Snap To Grid setting.

Aligning Controls on an Access Form or Report

In Access forms or reports, you can also use a grid to align controls. Select Align To Grid on the Format menu to turn the alignment on or off. Select Grid on the View menu to show or hide the grid dots. To change the size of the grid, double-click the form or report selector box (the square box between the rulers at the top left corner of the window) to display the Form Properties window, as shown in Figure 1-28. Change the Grid X and Grid Y properties on the Format tab.

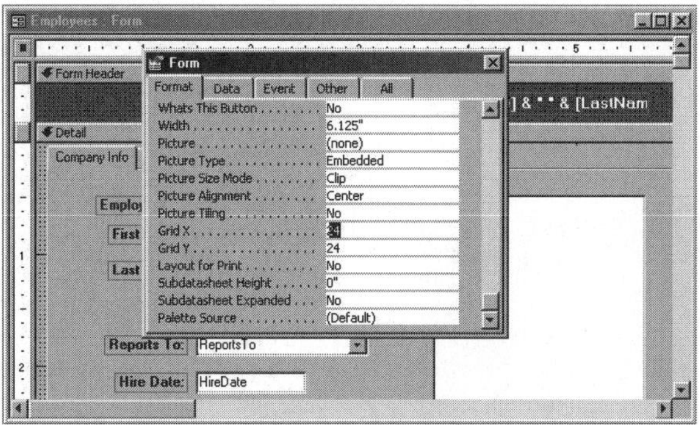

Figure 1-28
When the form selector contains a black box, you can change its grid.

To temporarily disable the Align To Grid option, hold down the Ctrl key. Unlike the Alt key used for AutoShape objects, the Ctrl key is not a toggle; it will not temporarily enable the Grid.

In Access, you cannot hold down the Ctrl key and drag a control to make a copy (Ctrl+drag temporarily disables the Align To Grid option). To make a copy of a control, select it and then select Duplicate on the Edit menu. The Duplicate command has powerful functionality, allowing you to create a uniform series of controls. When you first use the Duplicate option with a control, it creates the duplicate control just below the original you copied from. If you move the new control and then again execute Duplicate, subsequent copies will occur in the same position relative to the second control as the second is in relation to the first. Figure 1-29 shows a series of text boxes created using Duplicate on the Edit menu.

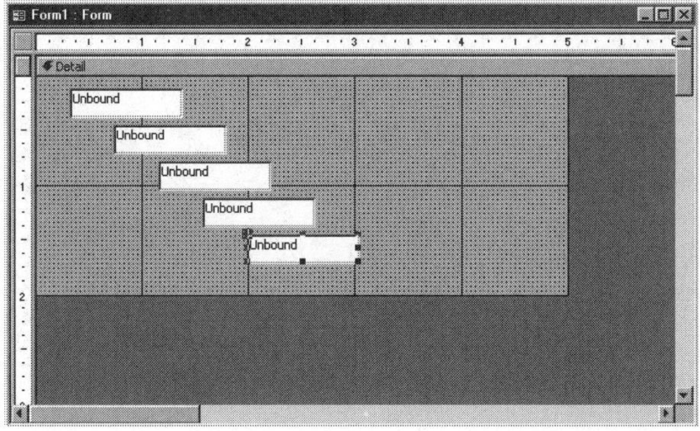

Figure 1-29
Move a control before duplicating it to create a series.

Chapter 2

Design an Office Solution

In This Chapter

Microsoft Office can be used to solve many different types of common problems. For example, a simple problem might be writing a letter to your mother, or it might be a more complex problem, such as calculating order projections for the next five years. Many resources are available in the Office applications that you can apply to problem-solving. As you build an Office solution, you need to decide which of those tools to apply to the task, and you also need to ensure that the solution you create remains intact.

As you use the many available Office tools, you need to be aware of how the applications differ from another, particularly while deciding which tool to apply to a given problem. You also need to know how the applications are similar, particularly in the ways they implement features that pertain to protecting your work.

This chapter will help you understand how to use Office applications optimally by focusing on ways in which you can use Office applications together, and on the tasks that are common among all Office applications.

Integrating Office Applications

Each Office application has its own strengths and weaknesses. For some projects—particularly large or complex projects—no single Office application will be ideal to accomplish the entire task alone. Fortunately, Office applications are designed to work well together. You can create a project planning document in Microsoft Excel, and you can include a major section of text written and formatted using Microsoft Word on each page. You can then create a list of associates involved in the project with Microsoft Outlook, and finally extract a list so you can send customized letters to associates using Word.

While many of these integration techniques will be covered in detail in later chapters of this book, this chapter will provide you with an overview of the many important ways you can integrate Office applications, and it will also give you pointers to specific sections throughout the book dealing with those tips.

Choosing an Office Tool

Each of the six major Microsoft Office applications—Word, Excel, Access, PowerPoint, Outlook, and FrontPage—has its own fundamental area of specialization. There is, however, a large degree of overlap in the many ways you can use these applications.

Following General Guidelines

For some solutions—particularly those that are small, simple, or short-lived—it really doesn't matter which tool you choose. This section will give you some general principles to help you choose between the Office applications, and then it will look, in greater detail, into the selection process used to accomplish a few important tasks.

- The single biggest reason to create a document in Microsoft Word is to manage the flow of text within and between pages. You can create a multiple-page document in Excel or Access, and you can even create blocks of text in each of these applications. But the only Office application that allows you to flow text between columns and between agents—and to applicable headers and footers to focus on the flow of those pages—is Word.
- The single biggest reason to create a database in Microsoft Access is to rigorously manage large amounts and varied types of data. Certainly, you can store or input data in Excel, and you can even input data into Word. But when you manage information in an Excel worksheet, you usually end up creating multiple copies of that data, and when the same number appears in multiple workbooks, it has a way of becoming a different number in some of them, making it difficult to know which number is right. Storing information in an Access database allows you to create a single master copy, making the data much easier to manage. You can then use that data in Access, and you can also export it to other Office applications such as Word and Excel.

- The single biggest reason you should choose to store data in Microsoft Outlook—aside from using it for e-mail—is to manage information relating to people (names, addresses, and telephone numbers, for example) or to manage activities (task lists, appointments, anniversaries, and so forth). You can easily create lists of associates or lists of things to do in any Office application, but Outlook comes ready to help, with numerous tools to simplify the management of people, activities, and information.
- PowerPoint and FrontPage exist primarily as a means for presenting information, not as repositories for the information itself. Choose PowerPoint when your presentation of information is linear. Choose FrontPage when the presentation of your information is networked—that is, when you want the person viewing the information to be able to jump from one location to another within the overall presentation and gain a better grasp of the information you're trying to present.

Choosing Between Word and Excel to Create a Table

You can use either a Word table or an Excel worksheet to organize information or perform calculations. The advantages to using an Excel worksheet over a Word table are reasonably obvious. Here are some of the most important reasons:

- You don't need to create a grid; it already exists.
- It allows you to create formulas that use relative references, or to mix relative absolute references. A Microsoft Word table allows only absolute cell addresses. See Chapter 12 for more information on creating references.
- It allows incredibly complex formulas, and it has a vast array of functions available. See Chapter 13, "Controlling Calculations," for more information on creating complex formulas.
- Formulas in an Excel worksheet can refer not only to cells on other sheets in the current workbook, but also to other workbooks and to data in other applications.
- You can create a chart graphing the data in an Excel worksheet range. See "Creating Complex Charts" in Chapter 16, for information about creating charts in Excel.

Less obviously, a Word table does have some advantages over an Excel worksheet. Here are some of the most important advantages:

- You can superimpose a Word table over a graphical image (Excel always displays a graphical image above the cells). See "Aligning a Table to a Scanned Form" in Chapter 9 for a Word project that shows how to align a table with a scanned bitmap image. See section "Formatting Cell Backgrounds" in Chapter 9 for a technique in Excel that creates the illusion of a graphical image behind the worksheet grid.

- Formulas in a Word table allow you to use relational keywords—such as Above—that are not available in Excel. See "Creating Formulas in a Table" in Chapter 9 for more information about Word formulas.
- Each cell in a Word table can contain formatted text using the full range of Word's formatting capabilities.
- You can nest tables in cells. That is, you can create a new table inside a single cell of another existing table. This makes it possible for you to use one table to organize the structure of a document, while still using other tables inside the body of the text. See "Using a Table to Add a Second Column" in Chapter 8 for information about using a Word table to structure a document.

Choosing an Application to Create a List

A list is, in simplistic terms, a block of values that can be sorted. Lists typically have a heading for each column. You can create a list in Excel, Word, Outlook, or Access. How do you choose one application over another?

- If the list deals specifically with people or activities, create it in Outlook. For most other lists, Outlook will probably be too cumbersome.
- If the list is small and you want to include it as part of a larger Word document—or if you want to use Word to merge entries from the list into fields in a document—create the list directly in a Word table. It is possible to perform simple list operations, such as sorting, on a Word table. For a list with more than a few dozen entries, however, you should create the master copy of the list in Excel or Access, even if you later plan to import the list into Word.

Excel and Access are the strongest applications to use for list management. Both applications can easily sort or filter a list. You might think that Access is appropriate only for large lists—and Access is definitely a better alternative for managing a list of more than a few thousand rows—but it is remarkably efficient at handling even a small list. Surprisingly, it can often take less time to open an Access database than to open an Excel workbook.

Access and Excel both allow you to create data validation rules for lists. Excel allows you to create data validation rules for values in a worksheet, but you are responsible for making sure that the appropriate rule is copied to all the rows in a list. (see "Validating Dates" in Chapter 14 for information about creating data validation rules in Excel.) When you define a table in Access, you can also specify data validation rules that automatically apply to all rows of the table. For certain rules—such as whether a column should contain text or numbers—it is difficult to create a list in Access that does not validate the data values. One reason for choosing Excel over Access as the best application for creating a list is if the list will contain exceptions. In Excel validation rules are nonexistent, while in Access validation rules are rigorous and unforgiving.

A list often contains values that link to other lists. For example, in a list containing order quantities by product, you might want to retrieve the price for each product from separate lists. You can create lookup formulas in Excel to link two lists. Creating lookup formulas is not difficult, but it is also not a trivial task. Conversely, one of the most powerful features of Access is the ability to link—or join—tables. "Looking Up Values in Lists and Tables" in Chapter 14 explains how to create lookup formulas in Excel. "Creating a Query that Joins Two Tables" in Chapter 18 explains how to join tables in Access.

Integrating Word and Excel

Word and Excel were the first major productivity applications offered by Microsoft, and they still form the core of Microsoft Office today. Word and Excel have more in common than most of the other Office applications. Whether you are integrating Word and Excel, or both Word and Excel with other Office applications, many activities will be similar.

Formatting Text in Excel

Suppose you want to include a large block of heavily formatted text in an Excel workbook. One possibility is to create and format the text in Excel. Figure 2-1 illustrates text which has been created and formatted purely in Excel. You can create formatted text with Excel's built-in formatting abilities.

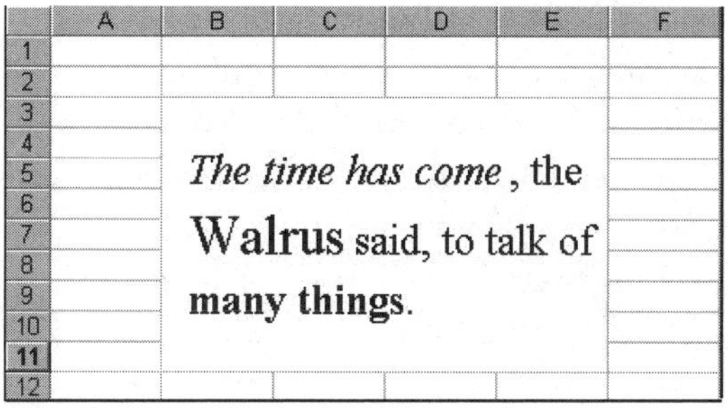

The time has come, the **Walrus** said, to talk of **many things**.

Figure 2-1
Formatting text in Excel.

As Figure 2-2 shows, using the Alignment tab of the Format Cells dialog box, you can merge cells to create one large cell, indent the text, position the text within the cell, and then wrap the text to fit across multiple lines. You can also format individual words or letters within the text in the cell using italic or bold.

Embedding and Linking Text From Word to Excel

You might want to include text in an Excel worksheet that has been formatted with all the formatting capabilities available in Microsoft Word. You do not, however, want to create a separate document and manage both of them. You want the Word document to be part of the Excel document. In Excel, click Insert, Objects, select

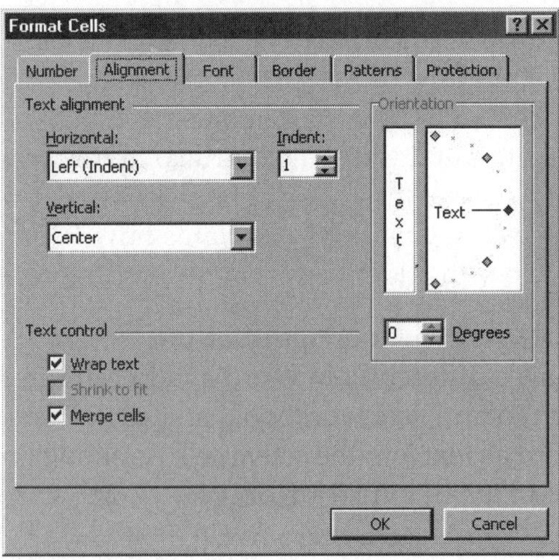

Figure 2-2
The Alignment tab provides great control over text positioning within a cell.

Microsoft Word Object, and click OK. With these commands, you have just embedded a Word object. You can type any text you want in the Word document and format it using all of Word's formatting tools. While the Word object is active, Word's menus take over the menu bar and you are, in effect, using Word formatting tools, even though you're still inside the Excel application.

Just as easily as you can embed text from a Word document into Excel, you can also embed an entire Word document into an Excel workbook. To do that, select the text and copy it. Then activate Excel, click Edit, and click Paste Special. Select Microsoft Word Document Object from the dialog box and click OK.

Suppose that rather than creating the text yourself, you retrieve it from a document created by a product manager. The product manager may change the text while you're developing the report, and you want always to be sure you are using the most recent version. In cases like this, you link to the file instead of embedding it. Click Insert, click Object, click the Insert From File tab, navigate to the file, and then click OK to insert a link to the document. When you link to a document, the other document must always be available to update or refresh the link.

As you can see, in an Office application, you can choose to either embed another object or link to another object. Collectively, this process is called Object Linking and Embedding, or OLE. You may see the OLE prefix in a number of places. The newer, more preferred term that incorporates Object Linking and Embedding is ActiveX Automation. You may see the term ActiveX Object or Automation used in place of the term OLE Object.

Note

You can paste an object from Excel or Word into PowerPoint, but when you copy from PowerPoint, you can only paste the copy as text or as a picture, not as an embedded PowerPoint object. If you do paste text from PowerPoint as a picture, the pasted text can no longer be edited; it is simply a graphical representation of the image you pasted from the PowerPoint presentation.

Dragging and Dropping Between Office Applications

The drag and drop feature behaves differently in Word and Excel. Select a block of text in Word, click Copy, switch to an Excel workbook, and click Paste. Excel then pastes the block of text from Word as text into the active cell. As shown in Figure 2-3, the process is the same if you select the text in Word, drag it to Excel, and drop it onto the active worksheet. The text is pasted as text into a cell, not as an embedded object.

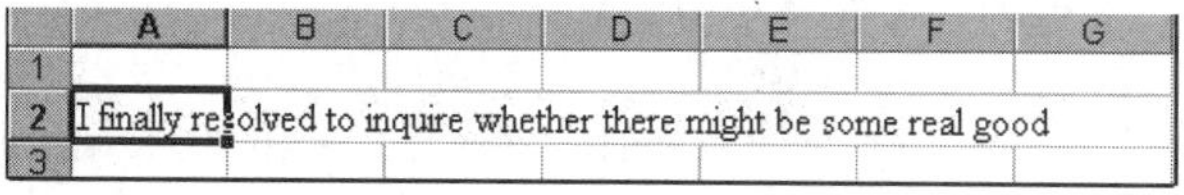

	A	B	C	D	E	F	G
1							
2	I finally resolved to inquire whether there might be some real good						
3							

Figure 2-3
Using Drag and Drop Between Office Applications.

Note

If you don't want to resize a window to drag-and-drop, you can switch between applications using the Windows taskbar. Select the item and then drag it over the application button on the taskbar. As you hold the mouse pointer over the application's taskbar button for a couple of seconds, the new application's window becomes active, and you can complete the drag-and-drop operation.

Copying a range of cells from Excel into Word is similar to copying from Word to Excel: select a block of text in Excel and click Edit, Copy. Activate Word and click Edit, Paste. Word pastes the block of cells from Excel into Word in the form of a table, as shown in Figure 2-4.

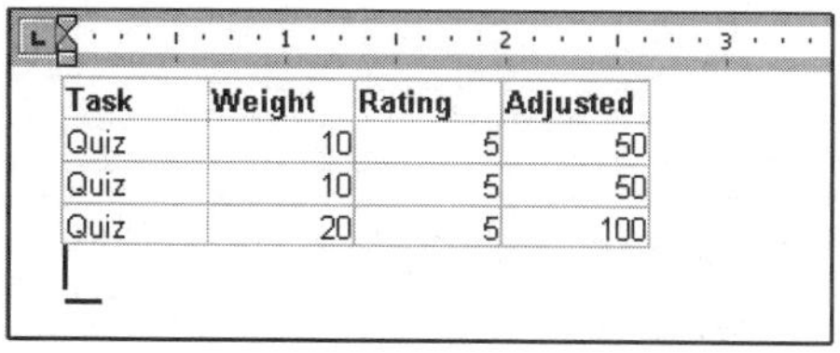

Task	Weight	Rating	Adjusted
Quiz	10	5	50
Quiz	10	5	50
Quiz	20	5	100

Figure 2-4
Copying from Excel to Word produces a table.

When you drag a range of cells from Excel to Word, however, you will see an entirely different behavior. Select a range of cells, and drag the border onto a Word document. (If you want to make a copy, hold down the Ctrl key; otherwise the range will move to the Word document.) When you release the mouse button, the Excel range becomes an embedded object, with the originally selected range visible.

If you use the Copy and Paste Special features in Word or Excel, you can select any option for copying data from one Office application to another. However, when you use the simple Copy and Paste features in either application—or when you use drag and drop—the behavior will vary.

Modifying an Embedded Object

When you drag a range of data from Excel into Word, the range of cells you see is not the only data that is being transferred. In fact, the entire workbook has been transferred. Double-click the object to activate it. In Excel, a small window opens inside the Word document, showing the cells you selected. But, as shown in Figure 2-5, you can scroll to different cells and switch to different worksheets within the workbook, showing that the entire workbook was embedded into the Word document. This makes it possible to embed a complex model in a Word document with only a few critical result cells visible. Conversely, when you embed a Word document into Excel, only the text you copy is included in the new embedded object.

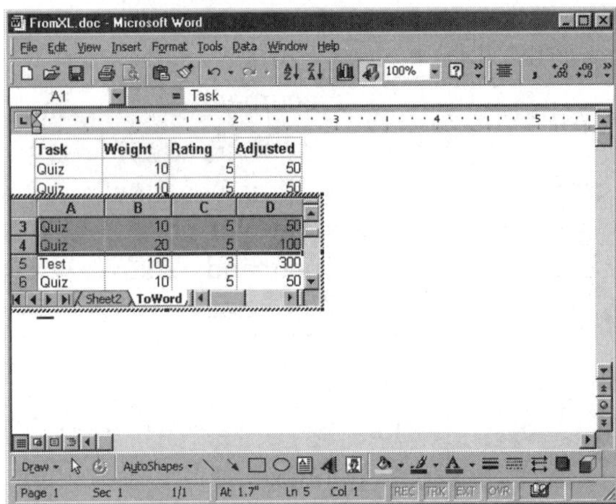

Figure 2-5
Dragging an Excel range embeds the entire workbook.

If you want to change which cells you see in the embedded Excel document—or if you want to resize the window—first activate the Excel object. If you resize an embedded object without activating it, you scale it—enlarging or reducing the contents of the window. If you activate the object and then resize the window, you change the size or the amount of the object you see. To deactivate the embedded object, click outside the object in the container.

You can open the embedded workbook in a new Excel window if using the small activation window is inconvenient. Right-click the Excel object, select Worksheet

Object from the context menu, and then click Open (using the Edit command on the Worksheet Object submenu is equivalent to double-clicking the object). The window caption in Excel will display Worksheet In Document1 or, alternatively, the name of your Word document.

To return to Word, select Close & Return To Document1 from the File menu. Any changes you made to the window size or to the selection while the object was open are not reflected once you reactivate Word.

Naturally, if you have an embedded Word document, you can double-click to activate it, or you can right-click it, click Document Object, and select Open from the context menu to display the document in a new Word window.

Note In addition to dragging a passage of text from Word or from an Excel workbook directly from one application into another, you can also drag an Office file from Windows Explorer into an open Office document. Alternatively, you can copy the file in Windows Explorer, and then use the Paste or Paste Special commands to paste the file into the application.

Fixing Broken Links

When you link from one document to another, there is always the danger of breaking a link. One way to break a link is to save the source document to a floppy disk or to another backup location while the target document is open. The target document is smart enough to know that you renamed the source document to a different location, and it changes the link for you.

Suppose, for example, that you have a source Excel worksheet linked into a Word document. If you now have both the Word document and the Excel workbook open, save the Excel workbook to a floppy disk. The Word document will then think that the source workbook is on the floppy disk.

Another way to break a link is to use the file system to move a source document, or to use Save As on the File menu to store the source document to a new location when the target document is not open. Sometimes a link may point to an old copy. Perhaps you used Save As to save the source file to a new location, and then continued to make changes to that document, while the target document continued to retrieve its information from the old location.

To fix an incorrect link in either Word or Excel, use the Links dialog box on the Edit menu. (The Links dialog box is available only if you have created links in a document.) In the dialog box, you will see a list of all the available links, similar to the one shown in Figure 2-6. Select the link you want to change and click Change Source. Navigate to the new source location, and then click OK.

Rather than link to an entire object, you can also link to a selected value from inside the source document. "Exchanging Values with Excel" in Chapter 9 explains how to link to values in source documents.

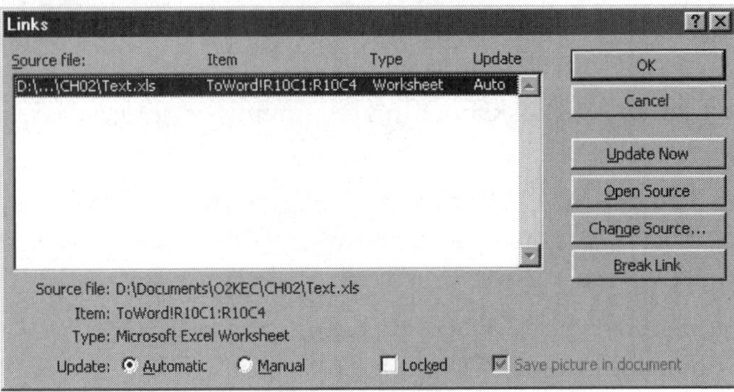

Figure 2-6
Use the Links dialog box to fix broken links.

Integrating Applications with Access

Many Office users are not as familiar with Access as they are with Word or Excel. Access is not only a powerful and useful tool, it also integrates well with other Office applications. Access is important, naturally, as the repository for a master copy of data values which can then be exported to other Office applications. Less obvious, perhaps, is its ability to integrate information from the other direction—to incorporate components from Excel and Word into Access.

Embedding and Linking into Access

You can embed objects into Access from both Excel and Word. Two different methods can be used to include Word and Excel objects in Access. One method is to create a static image on a form or a report. To do this, open the form or report in design mode and then simply drag the object to the report, or use the Copy and Paste commands from the Edit menu as you did in Excel or Word. When you drag text from Word onto an Access form or report, you paste an object and not text. You can paste text from Word onto the background of a form—it becomes a label on the form—but you must use Paste Special on the Edit menu to do so.

Another method you can use to embed or link an Office object into Access is to embed the object directly into a table. With this method, you can embed a different object for each record in a table. In the table, create a new field, giving the field an OLE Object data type. Then drag and drop objects from Word and Excel into the object field while you are in datasheet view. When you create a form or report based on a table having an OLE Object field, you can add a bound control to the form for the OLE Object. If you use the AutoForm Wizard to create a form based on the table, it will create a bound control to hold the OLE Object. As you display the form and scroll from one record to the next, any object contained in that record will appear in the frame.

You can embed different types of objects into different records. For example, you can place an Excel worksheet into the first record and a Word document into the second. The objects can be either linked—if you want to link to an official copy somewhere else—or embedded, if the official copy belongs in the Access database.

Anther possible use for embedding Office documents in a database is to store all the letters you have written in an Access table. Each time you create a document in Word, you can create an embedded object as a new record in the Access table. You can add other fields to the table to allow you to search for or sort a document. In this way, you can maintain all the Word documents in a database, rather than maintaining all your documents as separate files. (You could also store all your letters and memos as attachments to appointments in Outlook.)

Transferring a List from Excel to Access

If you create a list in Excel, you might later decide that you want to move the list to Access. The easiest way to transfer the data is to use the Import Spreadsheet Wizard. In Access, select Get External Data from the File Menu, and then click Import. Select Microsoft Excel from the Files Of Type drop-down list, select the Excel workbook you want to import from, and click Import to import the data. The first step of the wizard allows you specify either a worksheet or a named range.

The second step of the Import Spreadsheet Wizard allows you to specify if the first row contains column headings, and the third step allows you to import the data into a new table or append the data to an existing table. As Figure 2-7 shows, the fourth step allows you to link each column from the Excel range to a field in the Access table. You can change the name and specify the type of each field at this stage in the import process.

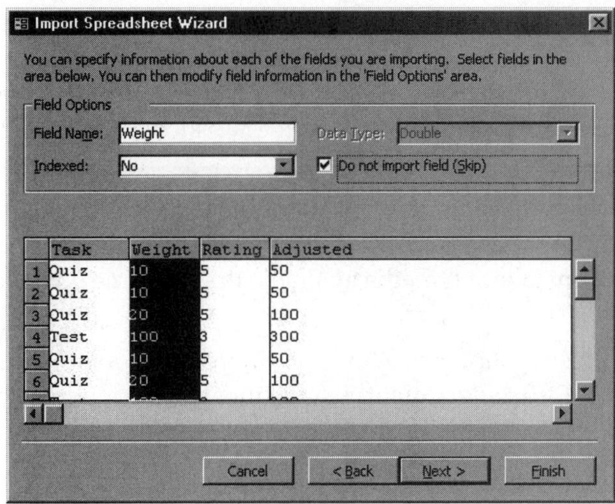

Figure 2-7
You can rename a column, or even skip it entirely.

After working your way through the rest of the Spreadsheet Wizard's steps, Access will complete the import process. If Access finds unacceptable information in the

Excel worksheet—for example, if a column that is supposed to contain numbers has a cell containing text instead—it writes that error information into a table with the file suffix Import Errors.

You can use an identical wizard to attach an Excel range to a table. Attaching is much like linking in that the master copy of the data stays in the Excel workbook. To attach an Excel file, click File, click Get External Data, and then click Attach. Everything else about the process is identical to importing data as discussed earlier in this chapter. It is usually better to store the master copy of data in Access rather than simply linking to it. Access has better tools for managing data than Excel.

Note Excel has an Access Links add-in that allows you to use Access forms and reports from within Excel. Rather than use the add-in, however, simply transfer the data into Access and create the forms and reports within Access. The Access Links add-in creates an unnecessary layer of complexity and frustration.

Data in a worksheet is often entered in a two-dimensional grid (with numbers in both rows and columns), rather than in a one-dimensional list (with numbers in, at most, a few columns). An Access table is more flexible if it is based on a list. Chapter 17, "Organize Data with Tables," and Chapter 18, "Manipulate Data with Queries" explain how to use a macro to convert a two-dimensional Excel grid into a one-dimensional Access list.

Embedding an Access Report into a Word Document

You cannot directly embed an Access report into a Word document. However, you can export a report as a snapshot using the Snapshot viewer, and you can then embed the snapshot file into a document. To create a snapshot, select the report and then click File, Export. In the Save As Type box, select Snapshot Format (*.snp).

A snapshot is a graphical representation of the report that can be viewed by anyone having a copy of the freely-distributable Snapshot viewer. The snapshot viewer is included in the Office 2000 installation, but it is not installed by default. You will need to have your Office 2000 installation media available the first time you use the Snapshot viewer.

Once you have created a snapshot, use Windows Explorer to open the file, or drag the snapshot file onto an Office document. Unlike most embedded objects, you do not need to activate the object to change how much of the snapshot you are able to see; simply change the size of the container.

Note You can easily extract data from Access into Word, Excel, or Outlook. "Extracting a List from a Database" in Chapter 15 explains how to extract a list from Access into Excel, "Using Access as a Data Source" in Chapter 10 explains how to extract a list from Access into Word.

Protecting Office Documents

An Office solution is of little value if it does not remain intact. As more and more documents are made accessible on corporate file servers, you want to retain control over the documents you create. While few of your associates would intentionally damage documents you have created, you certainly want to ensure that no one inadvertently compromises the integrity of those documents.

Protecting Documents in Word and Excel

In Word and Excel, you can protect documents on several different levels. You can prevent others from opening confidential documents. You can also prevent others from replacing your documents with changed versions. To prevent changes to the contents of documents, however, you must use a totally different mechanism.

Preventing Unauthorized Access to Documents

Both Word and Excel allow you to protect a document so that others are prevented from opening it. Select Save As from the File menu, click the Tools drop-down list, and select General Options. Figure 2-8 shows the Save dialog box for Word. As you can see, you can create one password for opening the file and another for modifying the file. Entering the Modify password does not eliminate the need to enter the Open password. In Word, you can access the same dialog box by clicking Tools, clicking Options, and clicking the Save tab. The Save dialog box on Excel's File menu has fewer controls than Word, and it can be accessed only from the Save As dialog box.

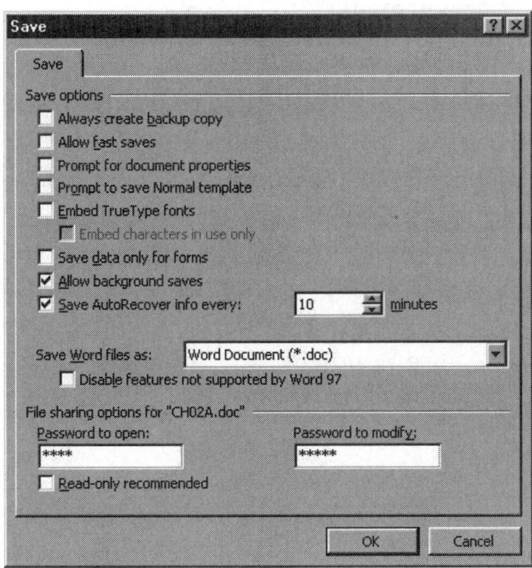

Figure 2-8
Word and Excel allow you to add two types of passwords to protect documents.

Note **Protection in PowerPoint, Outlook, and FrontPage.** If you store your Outlook information in a personal folder (.pst) file on your hard drive, you can require that a password be used to open the file. To set or change the password, right-click the Outlook Today button on the Outlook Shortcuts bar and select Properties. Click Advanced and choose Change Password. You can save the password in your password list so that you don't need to enter it once you've used your password to open the Windows desktop. You can add a password to any personal folder file, including an archive file. For more information about creating and using multiple personal folder files, see Chapter 20, "Organizing Your Life with Outlook."

Security in FrontPage deals more with users accessing Web pages over the Internet than with dealing with files on your hard drive. For information about security in FrontPage, search Help using the search words *about security*. PowerPoint does not have any option for protecting a document.

When you have finished creating a document, you might want to make it available to others, but you might not want them to be able to change the document itself. At a minimum, you may want to know what changes have been made. Word and Excel allow you to give others limited access over what they can and cannot do with documents. One way to limit access to a document is to change the attributes of the file to read-only. Using the Save dialog box to change a file's attributes does not prevent changes to the document; it merely precludes using Save on the File menu to save the file with the same name. To save changes to the document, a person reading it must save it using a new filename.

Protecting Information Within Documents

You can actually protect the contents of a document. In Word, click Tools, and then click Protect Document. The dialog box shown in Figure 2-9 appears. You can choose whether to protect a document for changes, to require tracking, to allow only comments, or to allow only entering values into forms.

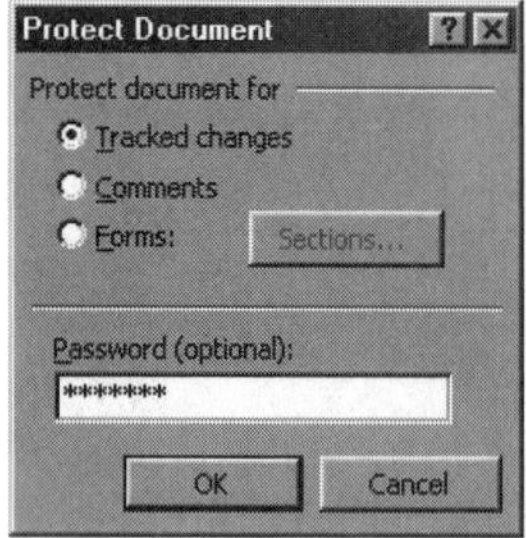

Figure 2-9
Protecting a document prevents changes to the contents.

In Excel, you can protect a document using one of two levels: one level of protection protects the workbook, and the other level protects the worksheet. To protect the workbook, select Protection from the Tools menu, and choose Protect Workbook. As you can see in Figure 2-10, you can choose to protect the contents, the windows, or both. Protecting the structure of the workbook prevents anyone from adding or deleting worksheets within the workbook. Protecting the window prevents anyone from adding, moving, or resizing windows, or from changing the panes of any worksheet.

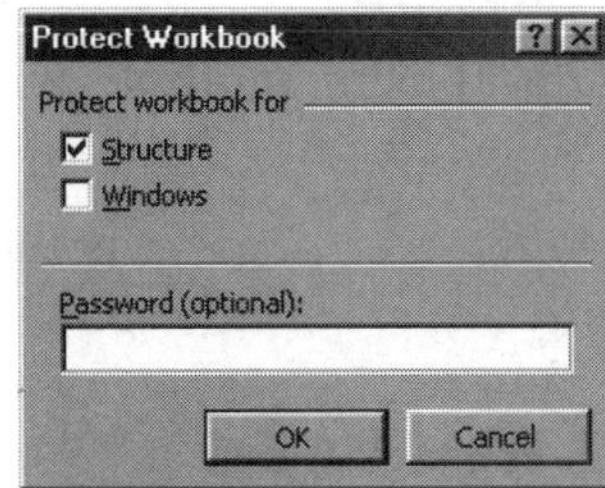

Figure 2-10
At the workbook level, you can protect worksheets and windows.

At another level, you can protect the contents of individual worksheets or chart worksheets. To choose that level of protection, click Tools, click Protection, and choose Protect Sheet. As you can see in Figure 2-11, you can choose to protect Contents, Objects, or Scenarios. Most often, you will simply choose all three.

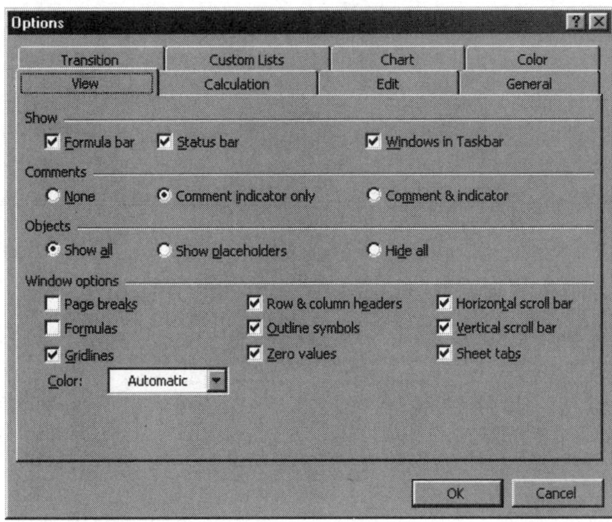

Figure 2-11
At the worksheet level, you can choose what items to protect.

After choosing to protect the contents of a worksheet, you can't modify the values in any locked cells. By default, all cells are locked. You can, however, designate a specific cell as unlocked, which means that it can be changed even if the worksheet is protected. You can only change a cell between locked and unlocked modes while the worksheet is unprotected. To unlock a range, select the range, click Format, click Cells, and then select the Protection tab as shown in Figure 2-12. Clear the Locked check box to allow users to change the values. If you don't want others to see a formula, select the Hidden check box. As with the Locked property, the Hidden property takes effect only while the worksheet is protected.

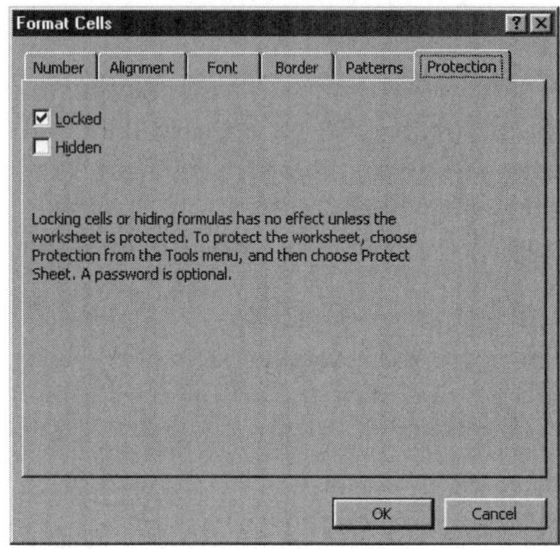

Figure 2-12
Locking a cell prevents changes while the worksheet is protected.

A password simply controls who can or cannot turn off password protection. You might want to protect a workbook or document to remind yourself not to make changes, in which case there would be no need to set a password. Even when you are distributing documents to coworkers who presumably have no desire to damage your document, you might still not need to set a password.

Using Macros to Protect All Worksheets in a Workbook

Sheet-level protection applies to each sheet separately. If you have dozens of worksheets in a workbook, you must individually protect and unprotect each worksheet. The following *LockSheets* and *UnlockSheets* macros will lock and unlock all the sheets of the active workbook:

```
Sub LockSheets
    Dim w as Worksheet
    For Each w in Worksheets
        w.Protect, "abc", True, True, True
    Next w
End Sub

Sub UnlockSheets
```

```
    Dim w as Worksheet
    For Each w in Worksheets
        w.Unprotect, "abc"
    Next w
End Sub
```

"Looping Through a Collection" in Chapter 5 contains a more detailed explanation of the *For Each* loop structure.

Protecting Access Databases

As you use Access to store important information, you will soon find that others are interested in the data you have accumulated. Access is an excellent tool for sharing data, but to the degree that you store important information in an Access database, you must also be sure to keep that information safe. Access provides powerful tools for controlling who can view or modify information stored in an Access database.

Assigning a Password to an Access Database

The easiest way to protect a database in Access is to assign a password to the entire database. First, you must open the database in exclusive mode. There are two ways to open the database in exclusive mode. Click File, click Open, select the database, and click the drop-down list box arrow beside the Open button. From the drop-down list, click Open Exclusive.

You can also change the default mode for opening a database. If you're the only one using the databases you create, you will probably want the default to be exclusive. Click Tools, click Options, and select the Advanced button. On the Default Open Mode page, choose Shared or Exclusive. Changing the default open mode does not prevent you from opening a database using the other mode.

Once you have a database open in exclusive mode, you can assign a password to it. Click Tools, click Security, and choose Set Database Password. Type the password and the confirmation in the appropriate text boxes. To remove a password, click Tools, click Security, and choose Unset Database Password.

Using a Shortcut to Open an Access Database

You can create a shortcut that opens a database in read only mode. Create a shortcut to the Access executable file, not to the database .mdb file itself. (Search for Msaccess.exe, copy it, and then paste it as a Windows shortcut.) Right-click the shortcut, click Properties, and click the Shortcut tab. Following the name of the executable file, type the name of the database .mdb file, including the full path, as shown in Figure 2-13. Put quotation marks around the database name if there are spaces in the name. Following the database name, type */ro*, which is the command-line switch used to tell Access to open the file in read only mode. (To find all the startup command-line options for Microsoft Access, ask the Answer Wizard for help using the search words *Startup command-line options)*.

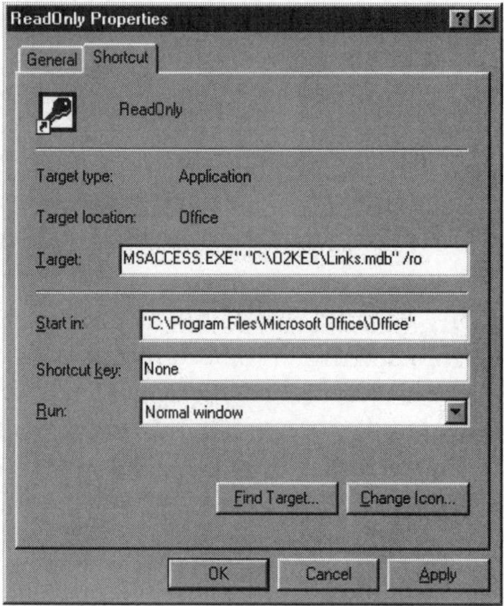

Figure 2-13
Add a command line option to open a database in read-only mode.

Note Unlike most of the Office 2000 applications which use the same file format versions as in Office 97, Access 2000 uses a new database file structure that is different from that of Access 97. You can open an Access 97 database using Access 2000, but if you do not convert it to the new file format, you will not be able to make any structural changes to the database. That means you can't add tables, queries, forms, or reports. You can only modify existing data in tables. Once you have converted an Access 97 table to Access 2000, you can convert it back to Access 97 if necessary. For detailed information about converting Access databases between the Access 97 and Access 2000 file structures, ask the Answer Wizard for help using the search words *convert a database*.

Creating User-Level Security

The problem with simply adding a password to your Access database is that it treats all people who open the database equally. A not uncommon scenario is that you create a database for your own use and it works very well for you. Others in your workgroup request permission to browse the data you have accumulated in the database. With a simple password, you can prevent unauthorized users from getting into the database, but anyone who opens the database can do anything to the database that you could—create, modify, or delete data, tables, queries, forms, reports, and so forth.

When you allow your coworkers to access your Access database, you probably want to restrict the capabilities they will have in the database. Access includes a Security Wizard that simplifies the process of adding user-level security.

Note Once you add user-level security to a database file in Access, you will need to log on each time you open any database, not just the file you originally secured.

To run the Security Wizard, click Tools, click Security, and choose the User-Level Security Wizard. The first time you use the Security Wizard, you will need your Office 2000 installation media to install the feature because it is not installed by default. Also, the first time you use the Security Wizard, it will create a new workgroup information file, which stores the rules for each user. (For details about workgroup information files, search Help using the search words *workgroup information file*.) Each user who will connect to your database will need to use this workgroup information file, so you should make note of the name and put that information in a place that is available to all users. Once you have recorded the name, accept the default options and click Next to create the information file.

The Security Wizard allows you to exclude portions of the active database from security protection. That is usually unnecessary and undesirable. Leave all objects in the database selected and click Next to go to the next step. As shown in Figure 2-14, the wizard displays several groups with predefined sets of permissions.

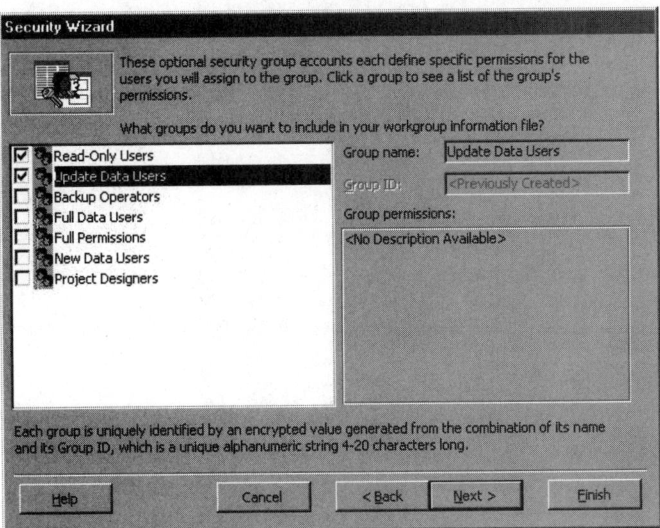

Figure 2-14
All users who belong to a group share a common permissions file for a database.

Think of a group as a security clearance level. As you create specific users for the database, you will assign each user to a group. All members of a group share the same security rules. The most likely groups you'll want to create are the Read-Only Users group and the Update Data Users group. The other groups are typically used in advanced database applications. (One other group that might be of interest is the New Data Users group, which allows a user to append data to existing tables, but does not allow the user to modify or delete data that's already there.) Once you've selected the groups you want to include, click Next.

The next screen of the Security Wizard allows you to assign permissions to a group called the Users group. This is one of the two default groups already contained within Access if you don't use the Security Wizard. Because the Security Wizard creates well-defined, specific-purpose groups, it's best to leave the Users group with no permissions at all.

Click Next to move to the next screen, where you create new users. The Security Wizard offers to create a user with your Windows log-on name. You can add as many new users as you want at this time. Figure 2-15 shows the Security Wizard dialog box during the process of adding a new user. One advantage to adding users at this stage of the Security Wizard is that you can assign an initial password for each user. When you add users later, you need to log on as that user to define a password. Be especially sure to add a password for your own user name, because you will have all power. If you don't require a password for your user name, you defeat the purpose of adding security to the database at all.

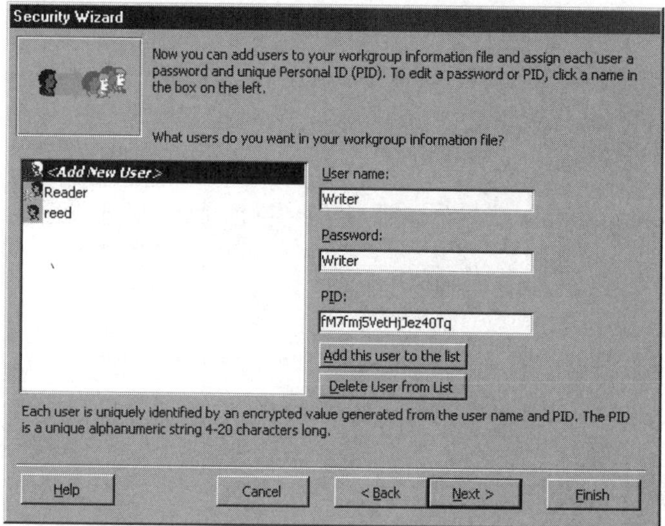

Figure 2-15
When adding a new user, assign an initial password to the user.

For now, add only one user for each group—Reader for an associate who can read the data, and Writer for one who can modify the data. Assign an initial password for both users. In most workgroups, you should create a user account for each person, as well. The purpose of having groups is to make it easy to give each user in a group a specific name. After creating user names, click Next.

The final dialog box, shown in Figure 2-16, allows you to assign each user to a group. While you can technically add a user to more than one group, a simpler security scheme would be to add each user to a single group. Add yourself to the Admins group, add Reader to the Read-Only Users group, and add Writer to the Update Data Users group. Finally, click Finish.

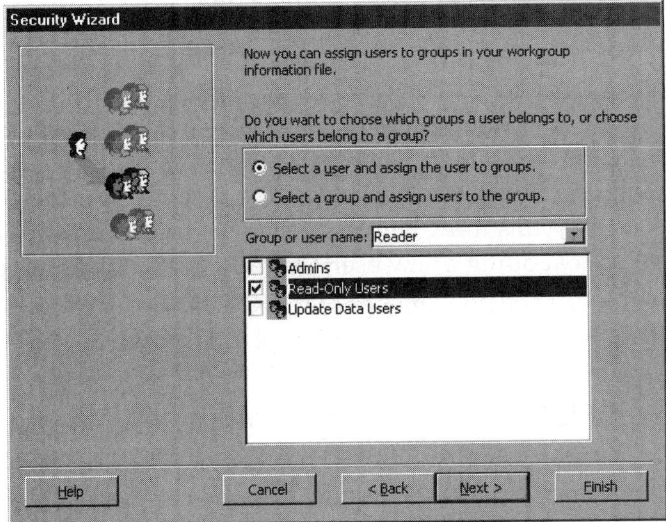

Figure 2-16
Assign each user to one or more groups.

The Security Wizard completes the creation of the new workgroup information file and secures the current database, after making a backup copy. The wizard also produces a report, if you want, that should be stored in a safe location. The report contains all the information necessary to re-create the workgroup information file should it be destroyed. You can either print the report or save it as a snapshot.

Connecting to the Access Workgroup Information File

When you create user-level security using an Access workgroup information file, each user who will connect to your database must be a member of the workgroup. If you use the default name the Security Wizard provided for the workgroup information file, the file is named Secured.mdw and is located in the same folder as the database file you originally protected. Remember, the workgroup information file must be available to any user who needs to log on to the database.

Before a user can log on to the database, that user must run the Workgroup Administrator application. If the Workgroup Administrator application does not appear in the Start menu, look in the folder where Office is installed for a shortcut named MS Access Workgroup Administrator. (The application file itself is in a language-specific folder, but the shortcut appears along with the other Office applications.) Running the Workgroup Administrator allows you to join a workgroup, which then enables you to log on to a database protected by that workgroup information file.

Connecting to a Secured Database

To make the new workgroup information file take effect, quit and restart Access. When you open the database, it will prompt you for the username and password. The workgroup information file applies to multiple databases. If you have multiple Access databases, you can log on once and open more than one database file without having to log on again. One implication of this convenience is that if you want to test different user settings, you must quit Access and log on with a different user name to test the settings.

Modifying an Existing Security File

Using the Security Wizard is the best method for creating new security levels for a database. For adding or modifying users, it is best to use the standard menu commands. Click Tools, click Security, and choose User And Group Accounts to open the User And Group Accounts dialog box shown in Figure 2-17. You can add or delete a user account, assign a user account to a group, change the group assignment for a user, or clear the password for any user.

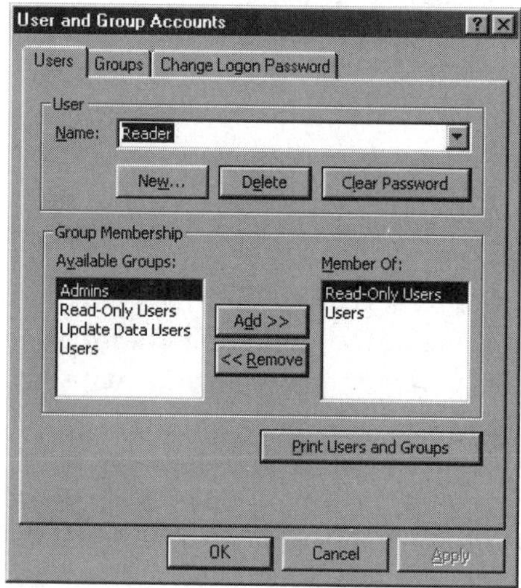

Figure 2-17
Add and delete users and change group assignments using the Security Wizard.

To add a new user, select the Users tab and click the New button. Type a name and a personal identifier. The personal identifier is not a password; Access simply uses the personal identifier value to make it impossible for a deceptive person to replicate the user name. Create a random string of bizarre characters. If you forget the user's personal identifier and have to recreate the workgroup information file, you will need to delete and recreate the user. Click OK to create the user. (You can't change the password for a user without first logging on as that user.)

Saving Office Documents

You could spend hours perfecting an Excel worksheet, only to lose everything if a power failure prevents you from saving the workbook. Just as disheartening is the knowledge that the information required by your manager today precisely matches a document you prepared a month ago—a document you can no longer find. Saving and finding files on your hard drive is critical to getting optimal use out of an Office solution.

Saving your Work

An Office project is vulnerable from many directions. You could be in the middle of an important calculation in a spreadsheet when a power failure causes your machine to shut down. You could make massive changes to a Word document, only to realize that the important new information you included came from the April Fools' Day edition of a newsletter.

In order to be safe, you must make sure that new changes are adequately saved to a file, and also that undesirable changes do not get saved to a permanent document.

Making Backup Copies in Word and Excel

Even if you conscientiously backup all your files each night—you do conscientiously backup all your files each night, right?—there is always the possibility you will accomplish some work during the course of a long day that you would prefer not to lose.

Word and Excel each allow you to make a backup copy of each document you save. If the backup option has been turned on, each time you save a document, the current file is renamed with an extension (which varies from application to application), and the new file is saved with its current filename. To enable the backup option, choose Options from the Tools menu. In the Save Options dialog box, select the Always Create Backup Copy check box.

The advantage to saving a backup copy is that you have one extra layer of protection in case you seriously damage a document and—flustered by the prospect of losing all your work—save changes as you quit the application. The disadvantage is that you get a second copy of every file you create, which not only consumes resources, but also significantly clutters up your folders.

Saving Multiple Versions of a Word Document

Word has the ability to store multiple versions of a document inside the same file. The primary purpose for this option is to create an audit trail of changes made to a document. To save the current state of the document as a new version, click File, click Versions, and choose Save Now. The dialog box shown in Figure 2-18 appears, giving you the opportunity to create a comment for each version. A comment helps you later identify a specific version for retrieval. Even if you don't add a comment, Word tags the version with the date and time.

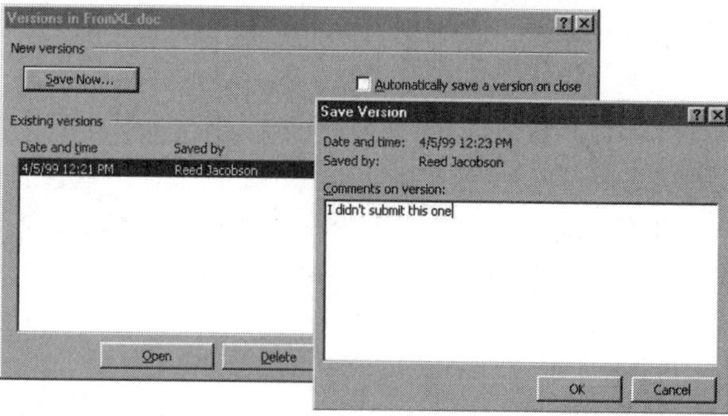

Figure 2-18
Even without a comment, Word stores the date and time of each version you save.

In the Versions dialog box, you can also select the Automatically Save A Version On Close check box. This option is particularly useful if you're using versions to create an audit trail. As an alternative to using the Versions command on the File menu, you can also create a new version using the Save As dialog box on the File menu. In the Save As dialog box, click Save Version. Saving a version using this option bypasses the Versions dialog box discussed earlier.

From one version to another, Word stores only the changes in the document. This means that you can save multiple versions using much less storage space than if you were to save each version as a separate Word document. To view an earlier version, click File, click Versions, select the version you want, and click the Open button. Word displays the new version as a document in a new window, and arranges the windows so that you can view the old version and the current version at the same time, as shown in Figure 2-19.

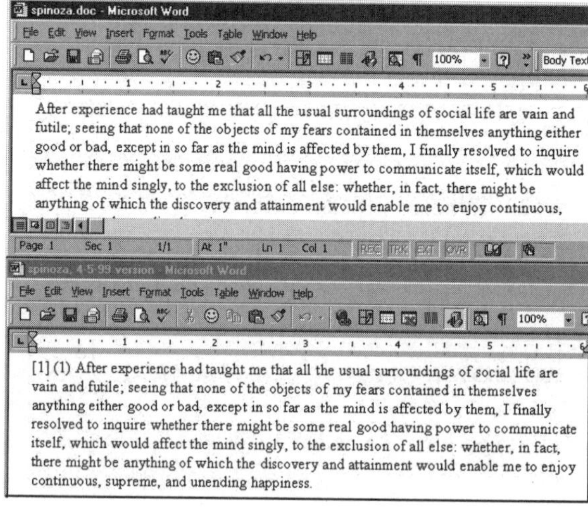

Figure 2-19
When you open a version, Word rearranges the document windows to display the old and current version.

One disadvantage to using versions—as compared to saving multiple copies of a file—is that you can't use the Merge Documents command on the Tools menu to mark detailed changes between versions. To use the Merge Documents command, you must open the version and then save it as a separate file.

Automatically Saving Documents in Word and Excel

Word provides an AutoRecover feature that allows you to recover most of the edits you have made to a document if Word should unexpectedly shut down, perhaps due to a power failure. It's hard to imagine a scenario where you would not want to take advantage of this feature. If you should want to make tentative edits in a document, reserving the ability to revert to the previous version, use either the Versions feature, or save the file using the Always Create Backup Copy option, to retain the previous generation of the document.

You might, however, want to adjust the frequency at which Word saves AutoRecover information. Click Tools, click Options, and select Save. Next to the check box labeled Save AutoRecover Info Every, you will find a control that allows you to specify the save frequency, as shown in Figure 2-20. Because saving the AutoRecover information happens very quickly and does not disrupt your work, there is little reason to increase the interval between saves. (If you're not sure, you might want to increase the frequency.)

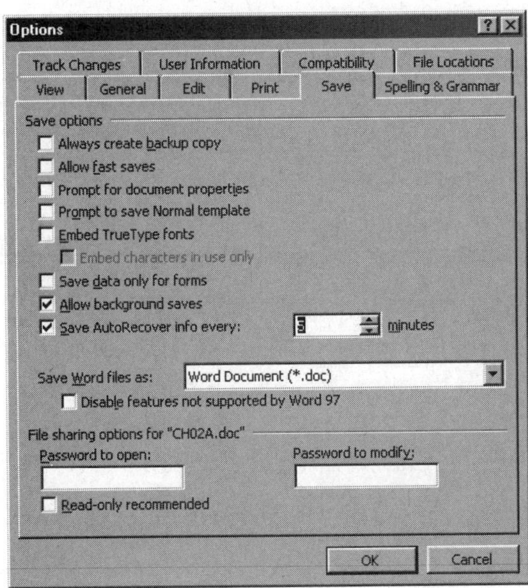

Figure 2-20
You can change how frequently Word saves recovery information.

Microsoft Excel also has an AutoSave feature you can use to automatically save your changes to a workbook. This feature is an add-in, not an integral part of the application. It was a conscious and intentional decision by Microsoft not to make Excel automatically save documents as Word does, because they found that Excel users often made extensive What-If calculations in a workbook, never intending to save the document.

Excel's AutoSave Add-in is not installed as part of the default Office installation. So the first time you use it, be sure to have your Office 2000 installation media available. To load the AutoSave Add-in, click Tools, click Add-ins, select AutoSave Add-in from the list, and click OK. The Add-in initially enables Auto-saving your document, and it also adds a menu command. Click Tools, and then AutoSave to change the configuration. The AutoSave dialog box shown in Figure 2-21 allows you to specify how frequently you want to save, what you want to save, and whether you want to be prompted.

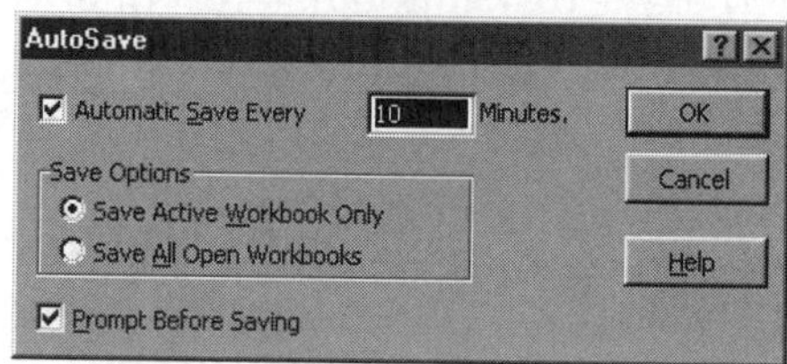

Figure 2-21
The AutoSave Add-In configuration options dialog box.

Unlike Word's AutoRecover feature, Excel's AutoSave tool does not work in the background, which means that it will interrupt your work. To temporarily disable AutoSave, deselect the Automatically Save Every check box. To permanently remove the Add-in, click Tools, click Add-ins, and clear the check box next to the Add-in's name.

Note If you find AutoSave to be overly invasive, you might want to simply discipline yourself to save your work frequently. One possibility would be to create an Outlook Task to remind you. Add a reminder to the Task for the time that you arrive at work in the morning. Each time the reminder appears, put it to sleep for 15 or 30 minutes. Within a few days, your subconscious mind will have developed the habit of frequently saving your workbook—just to get you to turn the reminder off.

Saving Your Work in Access

In Word, Excel, and PowerPoint, when you open a document, the document is loaded into memory and any changes you make affect only the copy that is currently in memory. If you close the document without saving changes, the file on your disk remains unchanged. In an Access database table, all the information is maintained on the disk. When you modify, add information to, or remove information from an

Access table, the values are, for all practical purposes, immediately written back to the database as soon as you leave the record.

The fact that an Access database is disk-based rather than memory-based makes it possible for Access tables to store vast quantities of data that would otherwise never fit in a Word or Excel document. It also makes it possible for multiple users to browse and even edit the same Access table—or the same Access record—simultaneously.

While using Word and Excel, you will have become used to the idea that all changes to a document are tentative—that you can always exit the application without saving the changes. When you work in an Access table, however, all changes you make are saved immediately to the database.

In Access, only data in tables is stored to the disk immediately. For any task requiring that you switch to Design mode—such as when you create queries, forms, or reports—you must explicitly save changes.

Finding Files

Sometimes, you need to find files that you have created, or that an Office application created for you on your behalf. Whether it is to modify a file or to back up the files properly, you need to be able to find those Office files.

Finding Application-Related Files

One of the goals for Office 2000 was to simplify the administration of Office applications, particularly for multiple users in a corporate environment. Because of this, Office has organized all application-related data into a standard set of folders in the Application Data folder. If your computer is set up for a single user in Windows 95 or later, the Application Data folder is a subfolder of the Windows folder. In Windows NT or Windows 2000—or if your computer is set up for more than one user—the Application Data folder exists under the Windows/Profiles/UserName folder.

As you can see in Figure 2-22, the Application Data folder contains a Microsoft subfolder that, in turn, contains a subfolder for each Office 2000 application, as well as subfolders for shared resources such as templates. "Storing Templates in Various Locations" in Chapter 7 discusses how Word stores template files in the Application Data folders.

Be certain you select the Application Data folder and all its subfolders in the list of files you regularly back up.

Assigning Properties to a Document

The document-centric Office applications—Word, Excel, and PowerPoint—each allow you to assign externally-visible properties to each document. To assign a property, click File, and then click Properties. The Properties dialog box contains several tabs. Most of the tabs display built-in properties. Some of the built-in properties contain calculated values, while others are properties that you can enter yourself.

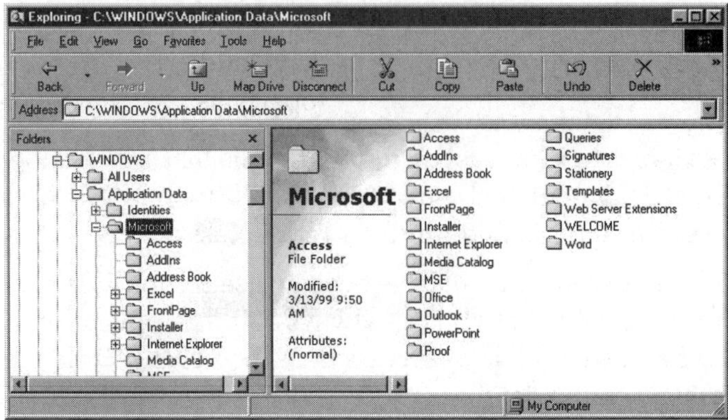

Figure 2-22
All customized Office files are stored in the Application Data folder.

On the Custom tab of the Properties dialog box, you can create your own properties. Select a name from the list (or type one of your own), select the data type of the property, and then enter a value, as shown in Figure 2-23. You can even link a custom property to a value inside a document. For more details, right-click the Link To Content check box and click What's This?

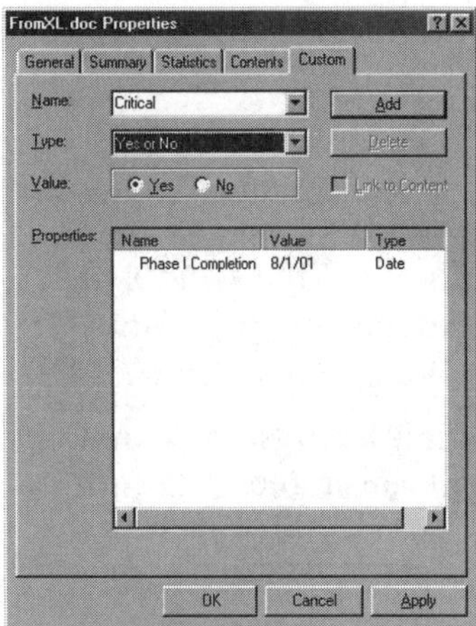

Figure 2-23
Enter any name you want for a custom property.

One of the greatest benefits of document properties is that you can view the properties from Windows Explorer without ever having to open the file. Right-click the file in Windows Explorer and select Properties. In Windows 98 or later, you can even view and edit the custom properties.

The Windows Explorer Find utility cannot search for files based on the file's properties, but the Find tool in the Office File Open dialog box can. In the File Open dialog box, click the Tools menu and select Find. Select a property in the Property list, specify a Condition, and enter a value. If you have added a custom property, the custom property name will not appear in the Property list, but you can type it yourself, as shown in Figure 2-24. To match a Yes/No property, select Is Yes or Is No from the Condition list.

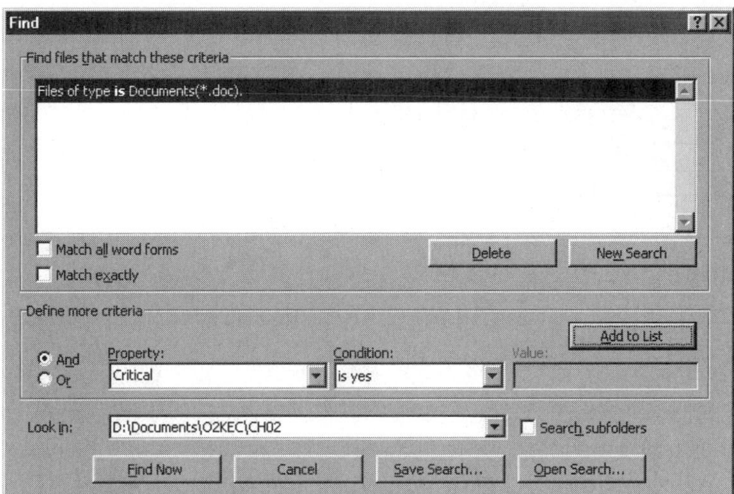

Figure 2-24
You can search for built-in or custom property values.

Using a property to find a file allows you to perform more creative searches than simply looking for names, creation dates, and text contained in files. For example, you can search for all Word documents where the Number Of Words property is at least 1000.

Note In Outlook, you can create Journal entries that track all the Office documents you work with. "Creating Journal Logs for Appointments and Tasks" in Chapter 20 contains information about using Journal entries to keep track of Office documents.

Chapter 3

Office on the Internet

by Jim Buyens

In This Chapter

The Internet is definitely the place to be for anyone in or anything involved with computing. The Internet features incorporated into Microsoft Office 2000 are among its most extensive and powerful additions. Office applications are better than ever at saving documents as Web pages, loading Web pages as documents, and creating documents uniquely suited to the Web. Office 2000 applications can open Web pages by reading them over the Internet, just as a browser would, and it can save them to a Web server using nothing more than ordinary Save commands.

In this chapter, you'll find a detailed explanation of how Office 2000 applications open and save Web pages, along with a brief overview of any features within the

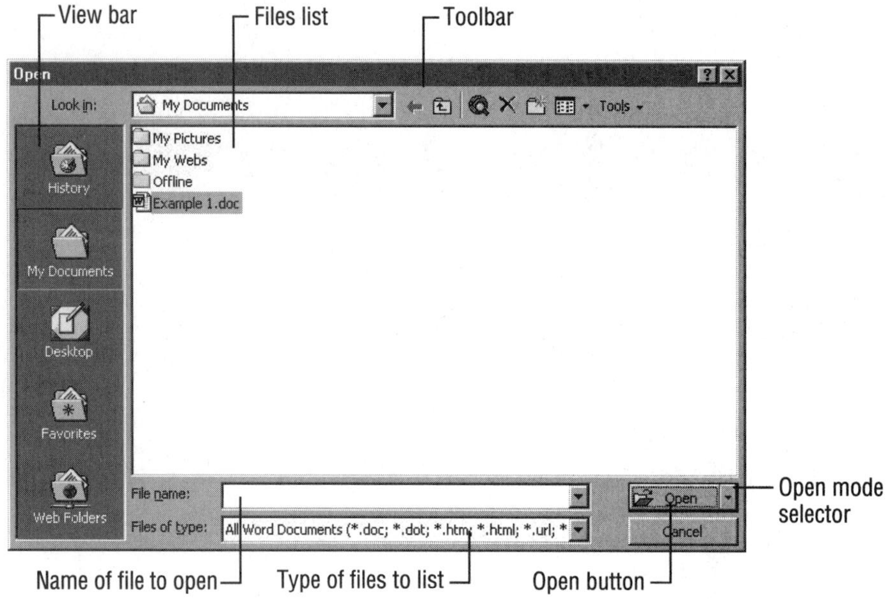

Figure 3-1
The new Open dialog box is used throughout most Office 2000 applications.

applications that are especially suited to the Web. After a brief discussion of HTML as a universal data interchange format, we'll also cover how the stand-alone Web Folders icon in Office 2000 eases the uploading of files to a Web server.

The chapter concludes with an overview of the Office Server Extensions, a group of programs your Web server administrator can install. The extensions transform Office 2000 from a collection of stand-alone programs into a company-wide or world-wide collaboration environment. These topics can be heady stuff, so let's get started.

Opening and Importing Web Documents

The new Open dialog box in Office 2000 shown in Figure 3-1 offers unprecedented flexibility in the types and locations of files you can open. Such a vast array of options can be daunting, so we'll review them one by one, highlighting the new Internet features along the way.

Using the Views Bar

The large shaded area to the left of the new Office 2000 Open dialog box contains the Views Bar. Each of the five icons (arranged vertically) specifies a different starting point for locating files. Here are the choices and their uses, in order of appearance:

- **History** displays a list of files and folders that Office applications have recently opened.

- **My Documents** displays a list of files and folders in your My Documents folder. This icon is titled Personal on Windows/NT systems.
- **Desktop** displays the same list of file locations as the My Computer icon on your Windows desktop.
- **Favorites** displays the same list of Web pages as the Favorites menu in Internet Explorer.
- **Web Folders** displays a list of Web servers that Office 2000 has recently used for opening or saving files.

The first three views—History, My Documents, and Desktop—are simply different entry points to the file system on your local computer or file server. It is entirely possible, for example, to navigate from Desktop view to the My Documents folder simply by opening the correct sequence of folders. (Double-clicking any folder in the files list will open that folder.)

The History view displays a special folder nested within the local computer's Windows folder. Each time an application opens or saves a document, the file's shortcut is updated in the folder.

Office 2000 applications can read and write files not only on your local disk or file server, but also on Web and FTP servers. This explains the presence of the Favorites and Web Folders views, where you can locate and open Web pages without having to type URLs.

Using the Favorites view is relatively straightforward because, like the History view, you are actually seeing a special folder within your Windows directory. The difference is that the shortcuts in the Favorites folder point to Internet locations—URLs. When you open one of these shortcuts, Office 2000 reads the URL the same way a browser would. However, instead of displaying the document in a browser window, Office 2000 loads the document into the current application.

The Web Folders view is especially designed for accessing Web servers that have FrontPage or Office Server Extensions installed. The Web Folders view uses information provided by the server extensions to display clickable folder lists of the Web server's content.

Understanding the FrontPage Server Extensions

Standard Web server software supports all the necessary functions for delivering Web pages to visitors, but few functions specifically for Web page development. The FrontPage Server Extensions help close this gap. The server extensions are programs that run on the Web server and supply the functions in the following list, subject to any security settings.

(continued)

Understanding the FrontPage Server Extensions *(continued)*

- They provide client software with directory lists and other information about files on the Web server.
- They provide a way for client software to upload files without leaving the application.
- They maintain various indexes and cross-references among Web files.
- They provide a variety of browse-time services such as hit counters, text search, and processing data received from HTML forms.
- They provide a standardized interface that client software can use to update the Web server's configuration.

The Office Server Extensions also include the FrontPage Server Extensions, as well as a collection of functions to support Web discussions, enhanced searching, and e-mail notification of Web changes.

For Microsoft Web servers, FrontPage Extensions are a part of the Server Extensions Resource Kit, which is optionally installed with the FrontPage or Office 2000 Premier setup. Versions for other Web servers—including non-Windows Web servers—are available from Microsoft's Web site. (Installing either version of the extensions is a job for your Web server administrator.)

The Office Server Extensions are available only for the Internet Information Server, Microsoft's Web server for the Microsoft Windows NT server and Windows 2000 server platform, and are located in the \OSE folder on the Office 2000 distribution media.

When you first click the Web Folders icon, it displays a list of the most recently visited Web servers. If the Web server containing the file you want to open isn't listed, type its URL in the Filename drop-down list box on the Open dialog box and press Enter or click Open. The URL should resemble *http://www.yoursite.com/*.

Figure 3-2 shows a Web Folders view displaying the root directory of a Web server located at *http://earring.interlacken.com*. The normal folder icons indicate normal folders on the Web server, while the folder icons with tiny globes indicate *FrontPage Webs*.

A FrontPage Web is a folder tree containing Web files that either the FrontPage desktop software or the FrontPage Server Extensions manage as a unit. Dividing the content of a large server into FrontPage Webs segregates content that requires different security or different authoring groups. It also reduces the overhead required to maintain large FrontPage indexes and cross-references. With regard to the Open dialog box, you can generally treat ordinary folders and FrontPage Webs alike. However, you should be aware that FrontPage Webs will often indicate security boundaries.

Figure 3-3 illustrates another option for opening remote files—namely, files that reside on an FTP server. Office 2000 applications can read and save files located on

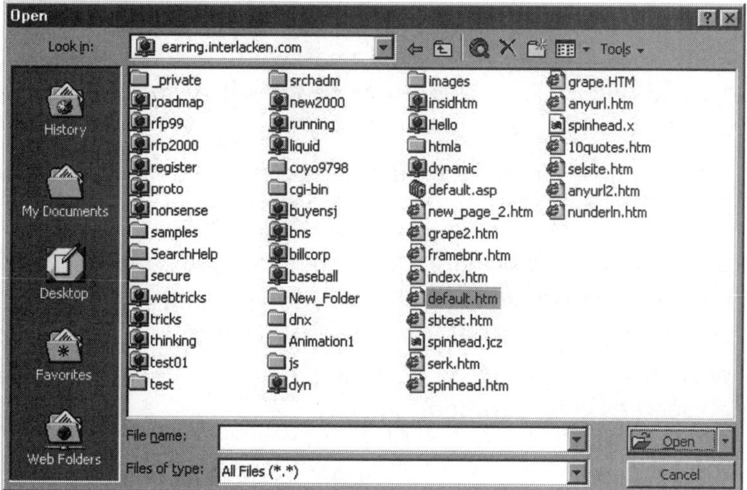

Figure 3-2

The Open dialog box displays the contents of a Web server while Web Folders view is in effect.

any FTP server in the world, provided you have a network connection and the right log-on privileges.

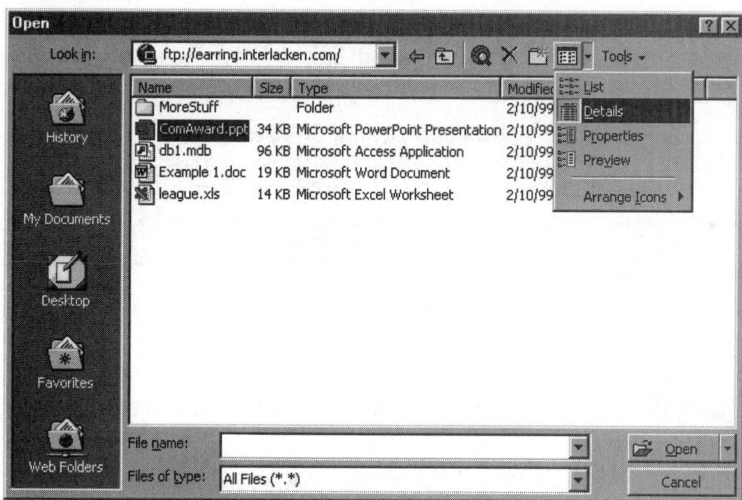

Figure 3-3

Office 2000 applications can directly open files residing on an FTP server.

There are two ways to open an FTP site from the File Open dialog box:

- Enter an FTP URL beginning with *ftp://* in the Filename drop-down list.
- Select an FTP location from the Look In drop-down list.

The first time you connect to an FTP site, you will be prompted for the site's name, the logon mode (anonymous or user), and a password. You can revisit these settings at any time by selecting FTP Locations from the Look In drop-down list box and then opening Add/Modify FTP Locations.

Regardless which view is currently in effect, you can type or paste any URL or filename into the Filename drop-down list box and the application will open the file.

- If the URL you type looks like a local or network filename, the application will open the file appropriately.
- If the URL begins with *http://*, the application will read the file using standard Web protocols.
- If the URL begins with *ftp://*, the application will obtain a copy of the file by FTP and open it.

Of course, just because a file server, Web server, or FTP server lets you read a file doesn't mean it will also let you save it. As we'll learn later in this chapter, saving files to a server requires suitable permissions and, in the case of Web servers, the presence of either the FrontPage or Office Server Extensions.

Using the File Dialog Toolbar

Most file-oriented Office 2000 dialog boxes provide the toolbar shown in Figure 3-4. There are eight controls available on the toolbar.

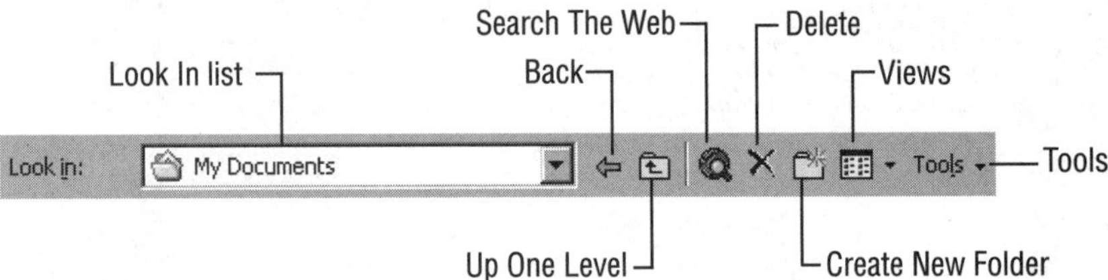

Figure 3-4
Most file-oriented Office 2000 dialog boxes provide the toolbar shown here.

- **Look In** selects and displays the folder whose contents appear in the files list.
- **Back** returns the files list to its next previous position. It works in this respect somewhat like the Back button in your browser.
- **Up One Level** sets the location in the Look In drop-down list box—and thus, the files list—to the parent of the current folder.
- **Search The Web** starts your browser and directs it to a Microsoft site that searches the World Wide Web for content.

- **Delete** deletes the currently selected object. If the object is a file or folder, the button physically deletes that object. If the object is a shortcut, the button only deletes the shortcut.
- **Create New Folder** produces a new folder in the current Look In location.
- **Views** selects any of four file listing styles—List, Details, Properties, and Preview. You can choose a specific display style after clicking the drop-down arrow on the Views control.
  - **List** displays file and folder names only, as shown earlier in Figure 3-1.
  - **Details** displays file sizes, types, and modification dates. If you've configured Microsoft Windows to display file attributes, attributes will appear here, as well. (See Figure 3-3, earlier in this chapter, for an example.)
  - **Properties** divides the files list area into two panes. The left pane displays the normal file listing and the right pane displays any values an Office 2000 document creator entered after choosing Properties from the File menu.
  - **Preview** also divides the files list area into two panes, but in the right pane, it displays a thumbnail view of the document. (This display mode is not available for all document types.)

  In addition, the Views button provides an Arrange Icons choice that controls the order in which listed files appear. In Details view, clicking the column headings accomplishes the same result.
- **Tools** provides seven useful commands: Find, Delete, Rename, Print, Add to Favorites, Map Network Drive, and Properties.
  - **Find** searches the Look In location for files matching certain criteria. The dialog box shown in Figure 3-5 controls this search.

    The large list box titled Find Files That Match These Criteria contains a list of conditions (criteria) a document must satisfy to qualify as a hit. To add a criterion, go to the Define More Criteria section of the dialog box, specify a property, a condition, and if necessary a value, then click the Add To List button. The And option means that the current criterion, as well as all other conditions, must be True for a match to occur. The Or option means that if the current property test is True, the document is a match, regardless of any other criteria. The Delete button removes a currently selected criterion, and the New Search button removes them all.

    The Save Search button saves the current search criteria with a name you provide. To repeat the same search at a later date, click the Open Search button.
  - **Delete** removes any currently selected files or folders from your file system. Choosing this command is equivalent to pressing the Delete key.
  - **Rename** edits the names of any currently selected files or folders. Pressing the F2 key is equivalent.

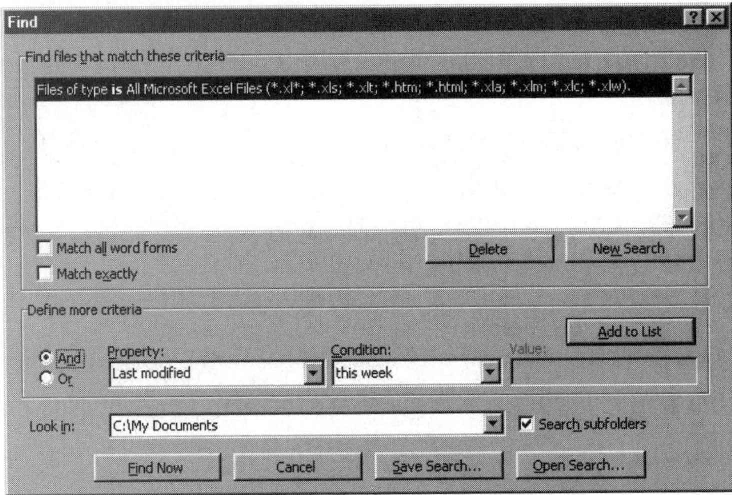

Figure 3-5
The Find tool on an Office 2000 Open dialog box can perform more complex searches than the Find Files or Folders function in Windows.

- **Print** submits any currently selected documents for printing. Windows uses the file extension to select a program capable of printing the file.
- **Add To Favorites** adds any currently selected files or folders to the Favorites folder. This option appears when you click the Favorites icon at the left of any Office 2000 Open or Save dialog box, or when you open the Favorites menu in Microsoft Internet Explorer.
- **Map Network Drive** displays a dialog box that associates a drive letter on your computer to a location on a network file server.
- **Properties** displays summary information about any currently selected folders or files.

Right-clicking any file or folder listed in the main window displays a pop-up (context) menu of operations appropriate to the object type you've selected. An example appears here.

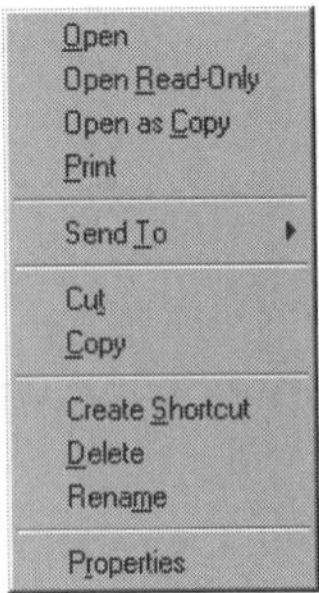

Using the Open Mode Menu

The menu shown below appears when you click the Open drop-down button in the Open dialog box (shown earlier in Figure 3-3). Some options might appear dimmed—or absent—depending on the menu's context.

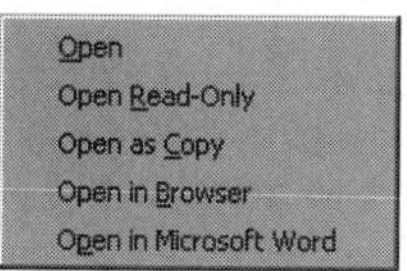

- **Open** opens any currently selected file in the normal fashion.
- **Open Read-Only** opens the selected file and prevents anyone else from making changes until you close it. However, even you cannot save the file.
- **Open As Copy** creates a temporary copy of the selected file, and then opens it. When you save the file, the application treats it as new.
- **Open In Browser** displays the selected file in your browser.
- **Open In <Application>** opens the selected file in the current application. This choice appears when the current application can open the file but another application would open it by default.

Saving Office Documents as Web Pages

Office 2000 offers two major innovations in the way it saves HTML versions of documents. First, the use of Cascading Style Sheets (CSS) provides much better rendering of documents saved as Web pages than HTML alone can provide. Second, Office 2000 uses XML to save—within the HTML file—every property and setting it saves in an application's native binary file format. For example, saving a Microsoft Excel worksheet as a Web page and then, days later, opening the HTML file in Excel produces no loss of function. All your formulas, PivotTables, and other internal details will still be there . In fact, you can set HTML as your default file format and never use native binary formats at all!

Note To always save Word documents as Web pages, choose Options from the Tools menu, click the Save tab, and set Save Word Files As to Web Page.

Using the Web-Enabled Save Dialog Boxes

Figure 3-6 shows Office 2000's Save As dialog box. The Views bar and toolbar work much as described for the Open dialog box discussed earlier, except that the application will write—rather than read—the specified file.

The following Save As controls are different from those in the Open dialog box.

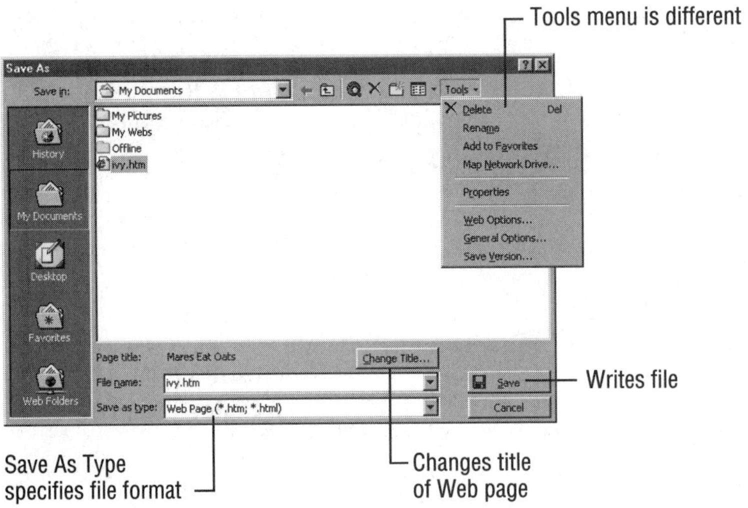

Figure 3-6
The Save As dialog box works much like the Open dialog box, except for the indicated controls.

- **Save** writes the current file to disk. Double-clicking any listed filename, or typing a filename and pressing Enter, accomplishes the same result.
- **Save As Type** specifies the file format you want the Office 2000 application to write. The choices available will depend on which application you're using and which options you've installed.
- **Change Title** appears only if the Save As Type is set to Web page. In this case, it displays a Set Page Title dialog box that controls the title text for the Web page. When a Web visitor browses the page, this text appears in the browser's title bar.

Note Some Office 2000 applications display additional Save As controls just above the Change Title button.

- **Tools Menu** contains a Web Options choice in all Office 2000 applications. Additional choices might appear, depending on the application. The choices (Delete, Rename, Add To Favorites, Map Network Drive, and Properties) work as described earlier in this chapter.

The File menu in each Office 2000 application provides a choice titled Save As Web Page, in addition to the usual Save As choice. The Save As Web Page choice defaults to Save As Type Of Web Page. The Save As choice defaults to the document's current format or, if the document has never been saved, to the Office application's native format.

Clicking the Web Pages icon in the Views bar selects file locations on Web servers running either FrontPage or Office Server Extensions. Software on your PC will compress the file you want to save and then submit it to the Web server using the same transmission protocols as an HTML form. On the Web server, the server extensions receive the transmission, decode the file, and write it to the server's file system (subject, of course, to security settings).

As with the Open dialog box, you can access an FTP site by choosing FTP Locations from the Look In drop-down list box.

Saving Word Documents as Web Pages

Figure 3-6 shows the Save As dialog box from Microsoft Word. The first four choices on the Tools menu work the same as in the Open dialog box discussed earlier, but the last three options are new.

- **Web Options** displays the four-tabbed dialog box shown in Figure 3-7, which we'll discuss in a moment. For now, suffice it to say that it controls what technologies Word can use to create the saved Web page.

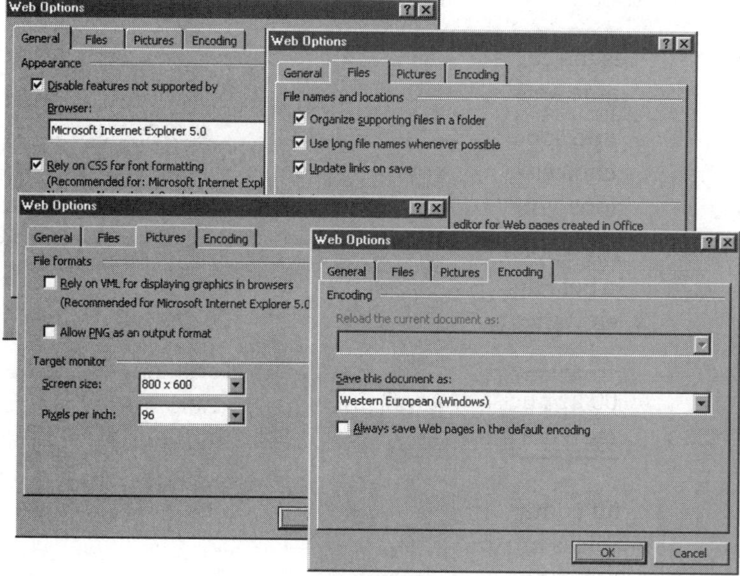

Figure 3-7
Word 2000 provides a wide array of options when saving documents as Web pages.

- **General Options** displays the same options that appear if you choose Options from the regular Tools menu and then click the Save tab. This is here simply for your convenience when the Save As dialog box is open.
- **Save Version** displays the Save Version dialog box where you can save comments related to a version of the document. The versioning of documents saves

multiple versions of the same document inside the same native binary file; this feature isn't supported when you save a file as a Web page. Web pages take long enough for visitors to download as it is, without further increasing file sizes with multiple versions embedded inside.

You can display the Web Options dialog box in either of two ways.

- Choose Web Options from the Tools menu of the Save As dialog box.
- Choose Options from the Tools menu, and then click the General tab. Finally, click the Web Options button at the bottom of the General tab.

The General tab of the resulting Web Options dialog box provides the options listed below. To follow along visually, refer again to Figure 3-7.

- **Appearance** controls the way Word formats your document for Web browsers.
  - **Disable Features Not Supported By** prevents Word from using features of the browser you specify. In effect, this lets you tell Word, "If the browser specified here doesn't support a feature, don't use it." In general, the fewer restrictions you put into place, the better the pages will look in newer browsers, and the worse they'll look in older browsers.
  - **Rely On CSS For Font Formatting** tells Word to use a technology called Cascading Style Sheets for controlling fonts in the saved Web page. CSS is much more capable than HTML in handling fonts and other aspects of typography, but again, older browsers don't support it.

The following options appear on the Files tab of Word's Web Options dialog box:

- **Filenames And Locations** controls how Word arranges and names the files that comprise a Web page.
  - **Organize Supporting Files In A Folder** tells Word where to store ancillary files the Web page must use to display the document. Although Word's normal file format can accommodate pictures and other objects in a single .DOC file, HTML can not. As a result, saving a Word document as a Web Page often creates not only a main HTML file, but also a collection of supporting files.

    If this option is selected, Word will place all these supporting files in a folder with the same name as the document, less the file extension, plus the suffix FILES. For example, if you save a document as training.html, Word will create a folder named Training Files and place all the required supporting files in that folder. If the option is turned off, Word will save the supporting files in the same folder as the main HTML file.
  - **Use Long Filenames Wherever Possible** tells Word to use long, descriptive filenames when it creates supporting files for a Web page.

- **Update Links On Save** controls whether Word should refresh any linked source document content before saving that document as a Web page.

  Suppose, for example, that you pasted part of an Excel spreadsheet into the original Word document as a link. When you save the Word document as a Web page and the Updates Links On Save option is on, Word will update the linked area (that is, copy in the current values from the spreadsheet file) before converting that area to HTML. If the option is turned off, it won't update the linked area.

- **Default Editor** monitors the assignment of HTML editors to Web files on your computer.
  - **Check If Office Is The Default Editor For Web Pages Created In Office** tells Word that whenever it starts, it should verify that your computer's default Web page editor is a program named msohtmed.exe. With this option turned off, Word won't perform this check.

Note In fact, msohtmed.exe isn't a Web page editor at all. It simply looks inside the Web page and determines whether an Office application created it. If so, it launches that application and tells it to open the Web page. If not, it opens the Web page in the current application or in the default HTML editor.

  - **Check If Word Is The Default Editor For All Other Web Pages** tells Word that whenever it starts, it should verify that Word is your computer's default editor for Web pages. With this option turned off, Word won't perform this check.

The following options appear on the Pictures tab of Word's Web Options dialog box:

- **File Formats** controls whether Word can use advanced graphic file formats within the Web page.
  - **Rely On VML For Displaying Graphics In Browsers** tells Word to use Vector Markup Language (VML) for displaying line art in your Web page. VML describes graphics as a collection of lines and shapes, rather than as individual pixels. Therefore, certain types of graphics will take less time to download than a comparable GIF or JPEG file. (Microsoft Internet Explorer 5 is the first browser to support VML.)
  - **Allow PNG As An Output Format** tells Word it can use the Portable Network Graphics (PNG) format for picture files. The GIF and JPEG formats normally used for Web images both involve compromises. For GIF files, only 256 colors can appear in any given file; for JPEG, images will lose quality because of the strong compression. PNG supports 16 million colors

per picture with no loss of quality, but at the cost of slightly larger file sizes. (Microsoft Internet Explorer 4 was the first browser to support PNG.)

- **Target Monitor** Word uses this information to make the HTML page resemble the printed document as closely as possible. Obviously, not all your Web visitors will use the same settings, and even if they did, discovering them could be impossible. However, giving your best estimate lets Word optimize its results to your primary audience.
  - **Screen Size** specifies the display resolution most prevalent among your Web visitors' browsers.
  - **Pixels Per Inch** specifies how many pixels (picture elements) usually appear in a square inch of monitor space. This will vary from user to user, depending on the resolution of their video card and the physical dimensions of their monitor.

The following options appear on the Encoding tab of Word's Web Options dialog box:

- **Encoding** refers to the character set the browser should use when displaying the Web page. Different natural languages require different character sets because of different alphabets.
  - **Reload The Current Document As** loads the current Web page into Microsoft Word using the language encoding you select. This is useful if—after opening a Web page—it appears with the wrong alphabet.
  - **Save This Document As** specifies the language encoding (that is, the character set) Word will use to save the Web page.
  - **Always Save Documents In The Default Encoding** dims the Save This Document As encoding option and specifies that Word should save each Web page using the encoding scheme already in use for that document.

The Fonts tab shown in Figure 3-8 appears only when you display Web Options by choosing Options from the Tools menu, choosing the General tab, and then clicking the Web Options button. It doesn't appear when you display the same dialog box by choosing Web Options from the Tools menu of the Save As dialog box.

- **Default Fonts** controls what fonts Word will use when displaying Web pages encoded to use a given character set. These settings only affect the Web page's appearance in Word, not its appearance on the Web visitor's browser.
  - **Character Set** selects the encoding scheme whose fonts you want to control.
  - **Proportional Font** specifies the proportional font Word will use for displaying Web pages that use the selected character set.
  - **Fixed Width Font** specifies the fixed pitch font Word will use for displaying Web pages that use the selected character set.

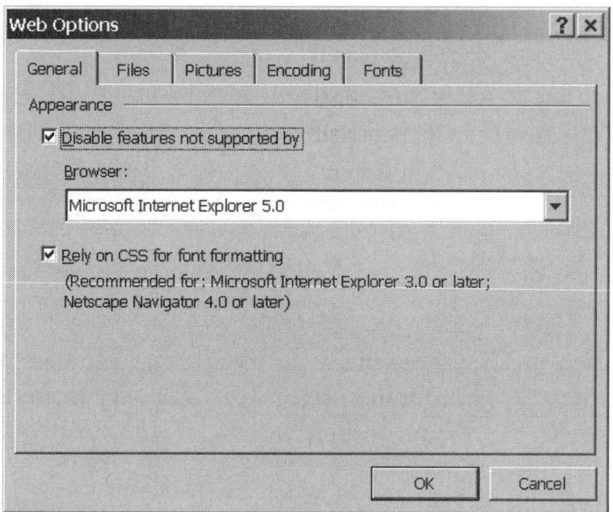

Figure 3-8
This dialog box tab controls the font used for displaying various natural language character sets.

Note A proportional font allocates different amounts of space for characters on a line. For example, the character *W* takes up more space than the character *l*. A fixed font allots the same amount of space for every character, like a typewriter. By convention, most text styles on Web pages use proportional fonts.

Viewing Word Documents as Web Pages Word 2000 has two features that display your document as Web visitors will see it.

To view your document as a Web page while you're editing it, choose Web Layout from the View menu. In this mode, Word displays your document much as a browser would—without page breaks, without a fixed page width, and so forth. Of course, you can still edit the document in all the usual ways.

The second feature uses the Save As Web Page feature to create a temporary copy of your document, and then displays the temporary copy in your browser. Of course, the browser display isn't editable, but it does provide a very accurate preview of your document's Web appearance. To use this feature, choose Web Page Preview from the File menu.

Saving Excel Documents as Web Pages

As with Word, saving an Excel spreadsheet as a Web page begins with choosing Save As Web Page from the File menu. This displays the dialog box shown in Figure 3-9. Note the additional controls below the file and folder listing, and above the Page Title field.

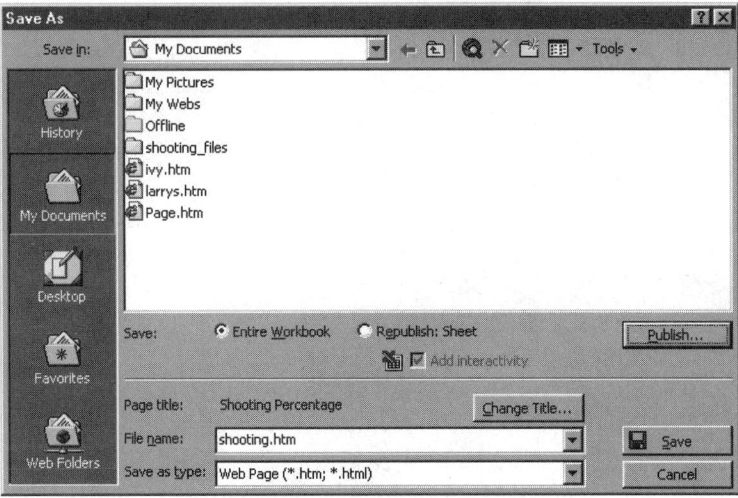

Figure 3-9
Excel 2000 provides unique Save As Web Page options.

- **Save** selects what portions of the spreadsheet will appear on the Web page.
  - **Entire Worksheet** saves everything in the current worksheet.
  - **Selection** saves only the current selection in the current worksheet.

    Note that the options above and below will never occur at the same time; one or the other will appear, depending on the circumstances. Worksheets that have never been published as Web pages will show the Save: Selection option, and previously published worksheets will show the Save: Republish option.
  - **Republish** saves the same portion of the worksheet you saved previously as a Web page.
- **Add Interactivity** controls whether the Web page is static or interactive. If the check box is not selected, Excel creates a static Web page. If it is selected, Excel creates Web pages that let Web visitors interact with a copy of the data.

At this point, you can create the Web page by clicking either the Save button or clicking the Publish button, as shown in Figure 3-9. The Save button saves using current Excel or document defaults, while the Publish button provides additional Save options. The dialog box displayed in Figure 3-10 controls these additional options.

- **Item To Publish** determines which portions of the worksheet will appear in the Web page.
  - **Choose** displays a list of the items you can choose to publish. This includes such choices as previously published items, a range of cells, the items on

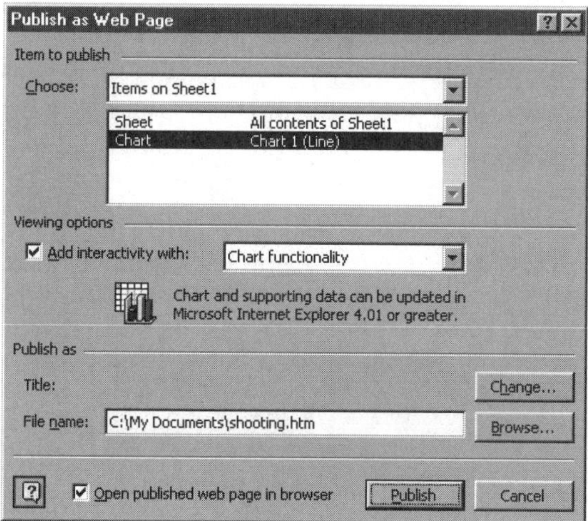

Figure 3-10
Clicking the Publish button exposes these additional settings.

one worksheet, and so forth. As you select each choice, its subcomponents appear in the list box directly below the Choose drop-down list box.

- **Remove** cancels the publishing of any currently selected subcomponents listed in the box to its left.

- **Viewing Options** predicts what capabilities your Web visitors will have when they view the Web page.
  - **Add Interactivity With** specifies that Web visitors can manipulate a copy of any worksheet data while viewing the Web page. The list box selects from among three kinds of interactivity: Spreadsheet, Chart, and PivotTable. For this option to work, any visitors must be using Microsoft Internet Explorer 4 or later, and they must have certain Office 2000 ActiveX controls installed on their system.

    If this option is turned off, Excel saves the worksheet data as ordinary Web content. Users can no longer manipulate a copy of the data, but they can display the page with any browser.
- **Publish As** controls overall aspects of writing the Web page.
  - **Title** specifies the text that will appear in the title bar of the Web visitor's browser. This defaults to the title you specify after choosing Properties from the File menu in Excel.
  - **File name** specifies the physical location where Excel will store the Web page. This can be a file and folder on your local disk or on a file server, an HTTP address on a Web server running the FrontPage Server

Extensions, or a location on an FTP server. In the case of an HTTP or FTP address, use the same URL format a browser would use to retrieve the file.

- **Open Published Web Page In Browser** tells Excel to display the page in your browser after saving it.

Figure 3-11 shows a simple worksheet opened in Excel. The data in the first three rows represent a hockey player's shots and goals during each game. The player's season-to-date shooting percentage appears in the fourth row. The chart reflects both sets of values.

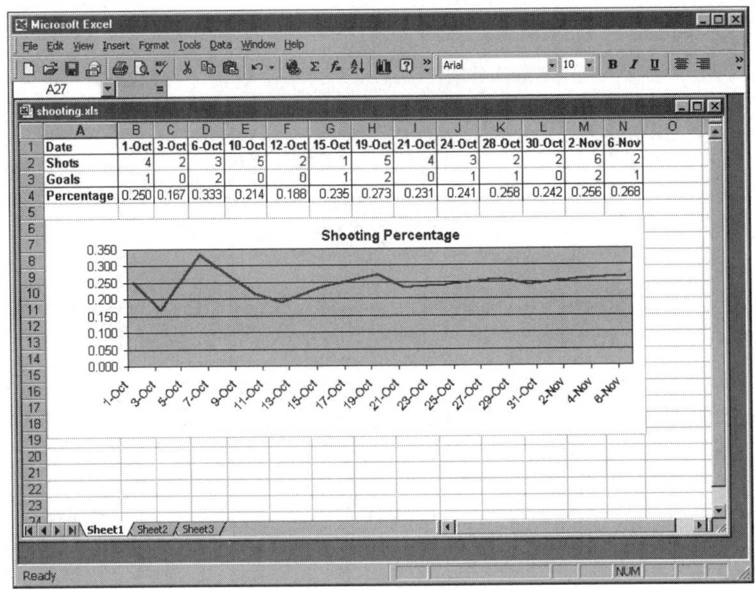

Figure 3-11
Excel 2000 displays this typical datasheet and chart combination.

Figure 3-12 shows the effect of saving this spreadsheet without interactivity added. Excel renders the datasheet as an HTML table and the chart as a GIF file. Excel has done a fairly good job of preserving fonts, cell borders, and other formatting options.

Saving the same Web page with Chart interactivity produces the results shown in Figure 3-13. A Web visitor can highlight cells, change values, sort, cut, copy, and generally manipulate the data at will. The chart will change automatically in response to changes in the data.

A Web visitor can't change the worksheet's original values, of course. Your original values appear unchanged for each visitor, when the same visitor loads the page, changes the data, and then loads the page again. Manipulating the data in the browser is essentially a What If exercise. Note the Export to Excel toolbar button,

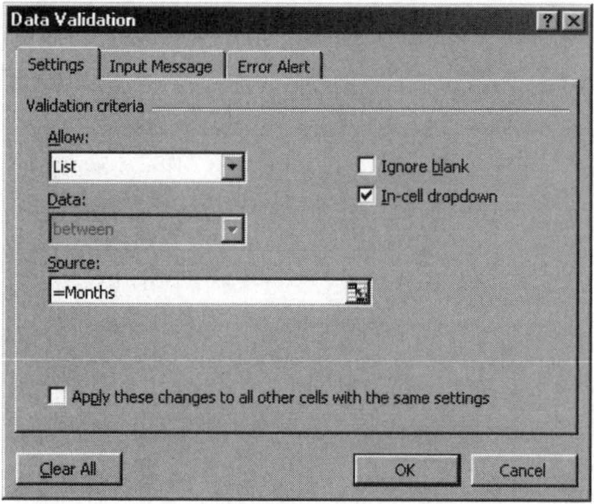

Figure 3-12
Internet Explorer displays the same worksheet saved as a Web page without interactivity.

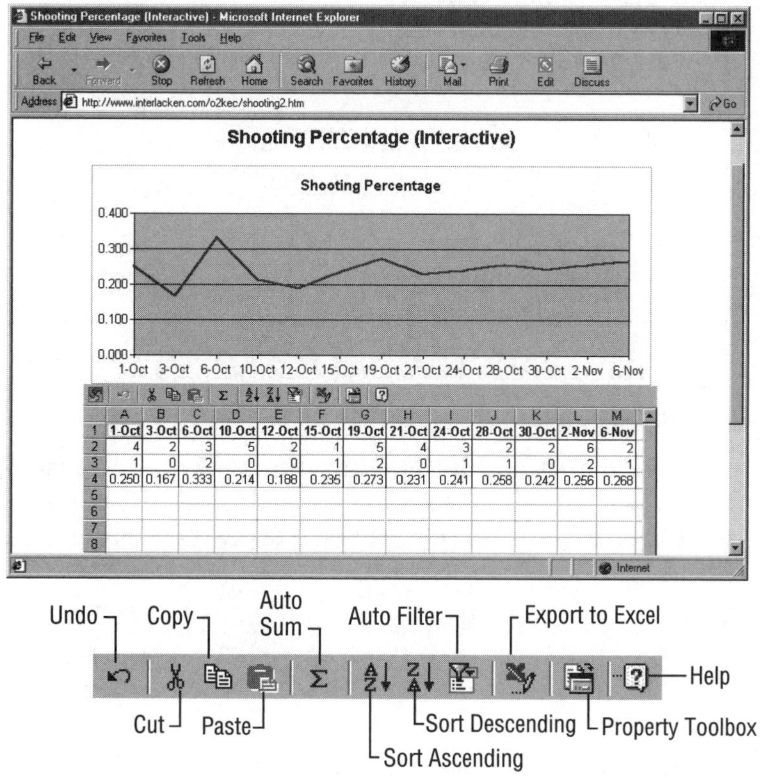

Figure 3-13
This version of the Web page lets the Web visitor try different numbers and then see their changes reflected in the Chart.

however. If a Web visitor has Excel installed on his or her computer, clicking this button will start the program and load the Web page data and chart directly into it.

Note Chart interactivity includes Spreadsheet interactivity, because the chart and the spreadsheet are linked. The same is true of PivotTables.

The Web Settings dialog box in Excel contains most of the same settings as Word, but with four additions, as shown in Figure 3-14.

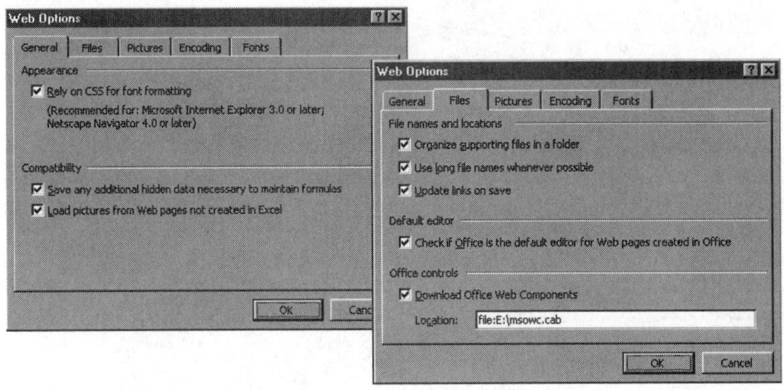

Figure 3-14
The Compatibility and Office Controls sections in these dialog boxes are unique to Excel.

- **Compatibility** controls the handling of elements that are important to Excel but not to other programs (and vice versa).
    - **Save Any Additional Hidden Data Necessary To Maintain Formulas** tells Excel to store everything in the Web page that it would normally save in its native format. Excel saves non-displayed data—such as formulas—as XML statements.

      This is an amazing feature. It means you can save a spreadsheet in HTML format, quit and restart Excel, open the HTML file, and lose nothing in comparison to saving the file in Excel's native file format. However, it does increase the size of the HTML file.
    - **Load Pictures From Web Pages Not Created In Excel** controls the handling of GIF and JPEG files when Excel opens a Web page saved by another program. If this box is selected, Excel loads the pictures. If not, Excel ignores them.
- **Office Controls** manages distribution of the ActiveX controls that Excel uses to provide interactivity at the browser level.
    - **Download Office Web Components** controls what happens when Web visitors using Internet Explorer open a page containing Excel interactivity

and they don't have the required ActiveX controls installed. If the box was selected when you saved the page, those visitors can download and install the required ActiveX controls automatically. If the box was not selected when you saved the page, those same visitors would receive an error message stating that the ActiveX control is missing.

- **Location** specifies a download location for the Office Web Components. The default location is a folder location on your computer, but this is useless to Web visitors. In practice, you should place a copy of the file msowc.cab on your Web server and enter its URL as shown in this example:

  http://www.interlacken.com/o2kec/msowc.cab

Saving PowerPoint Documents as Web Pages

Figure 3-15 shows a hypothetical presentation open in Microsoft PowerPoint 2000. The presentation concerns the inauguration of a waste disposal company named Precision Waste, Inc. PowerPoint can save such presentations as a series of Web pages, thus vastly increasing their potential audience. (For a sneak preview of the results, skip ahead to Figure 3-19.)

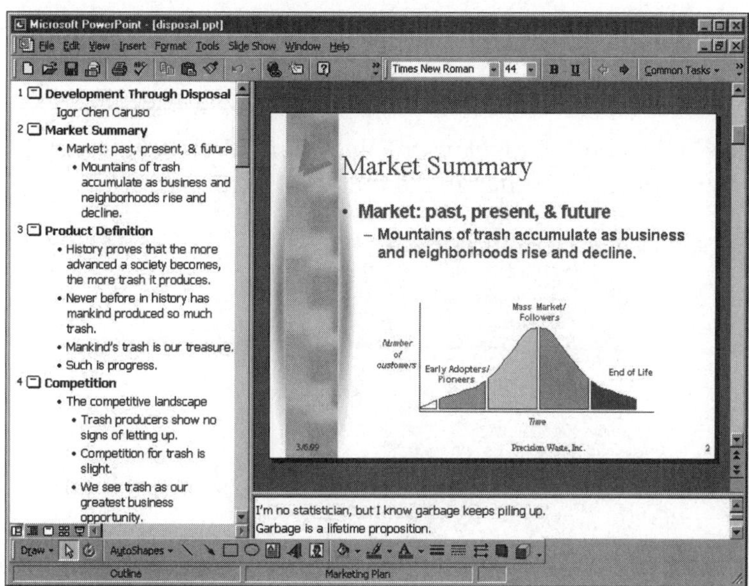

Figure 3-15
PowerPoint 2000 can save presentations as a series of Web pages.

To save a presentation as a Web page, choose Save As Web Page from the File menu in PowerPoint. Taking this action displays the Save As dialog box shown in Figure 3-16 which, by now, should be very familiar. Clicking the Save button with the Save As Type set to Web Page saves the presentation with all defaults.

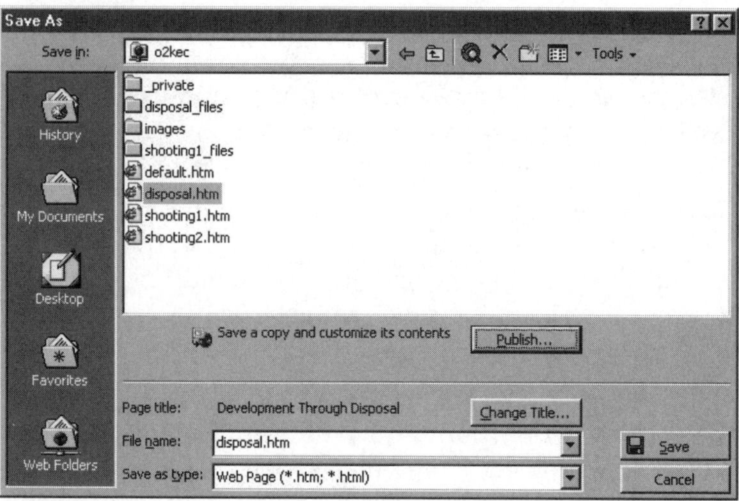

Figure 3-16
Use the Publish button to override default options when saving a PowerPoint presentation as a Web page.

Note If clicking the Publish button has no effect, try clicking Publish and then clicking Save.

Clicking the Publish button displays the Publish As Web Page dialog box shown in Figure 3-17, where you can change the following settings.

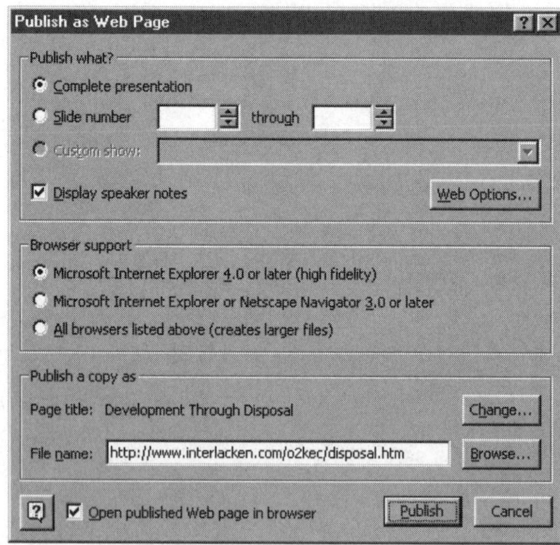

Figure 3-17
This dialog box overrides the default Save As Web Page options in PowerPoint.

- **Publish What?** controls the content of your Web-based presentation.
  - **Complete Presentation** specifies that all pages in the current presentation should appear in the Web version of your presentation.
  - **Slide Number** means that only a selected range of pages should appear. Enter the starting and ending page numbers in the spin boxes provided.
  - **Custom Show** specifies that one or more non-contiguous page ranges will appear in the Web-based presentation. Separate each page number or range of page numbers with a comma. The following is an example of this format: 2-5, 7, 9, 14-18.
  - **Display Speaker Notes** specifies that Web visitors will see the speaker notes that accompany each slide in the presentation.
  - **Web Options** displays the usual Web Options dialog box, modified slightly for PowerPoint. We'll discuss this in a moment.
- **Browser Support** specifies the least-capable browser you believe your Web visitors will have. PowerPoint can either use features of the more advanced browsers to create better-looking and faster-downloading results, or sacrifice these benefits and provide maximum compatibility with older browsers.
- **Publish A Copy As** controls the overall aspects of writing the Web page.
  - **Page Title** specifies the text that will appear in the title bar of the Web visitor's browser. This defaults to the title you specify after choosing Properties from the File menu in PowerPoint.
  - **File name** specifies the physical location where PowerPoint will store the Web page. This can be a file and folder on your local disk or file server, an HTTP address on a Web server running the FrontPage Server Extensions, or a location on an FTP server. In the case of an HTTP or FTP address, use the same URL format a browser would use to retrieve the file.
- **Open Published Web Page In Browser** tells PowerPoint to display the page in your browser after saving it.

PowerPoint provides three ways to access its Web Options dialog box. Each method produces identical results.

- Choose Options from the Tools menu, click the General tab, and then click the Web Options button.
- Choose Web Options from the Tools button on the Save As dialog box's toolbar.
- Click the Web Options button on the Publish As Web Page dialog box shown earlier in Figure 3-17.

Of the five tabs on the Web Options dialog box, only one differs from the Web Options dialog box in Word. The oddball tab is the General tab shown in Figure 3-18.

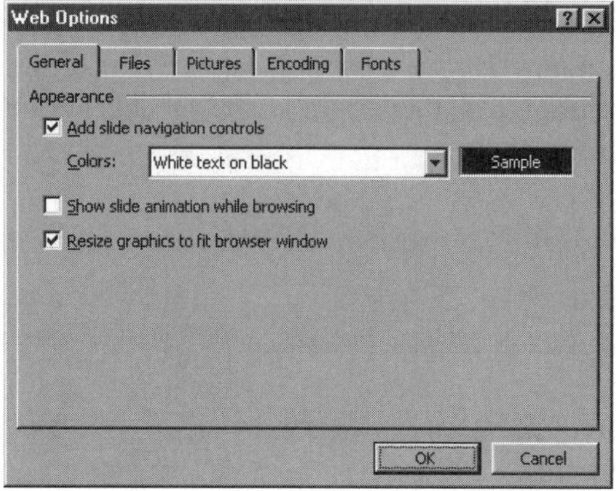

Figure 3-18
The Web Options dialog box in PowerPoint provides special options to control a presentation's appearance on the Web.

The General tab provides these options:

- **Appearance** controls the way PowerPoint formats your presentation for Web visitors.
    - **Add Slide Navigation Controls** specifies that PowerPoint should display a clickable Table of Contents, a forward button, and a back button within the Web page that displays your presentation.

      If you turn this button off, presentations saved as Web pages will have no navigational controls. This is generally suitable for single page slide presentations.
    - **Colors** controls the color scheme PowerPoint will use for the navigation controls.
    - **Show Slide Show Animation While Browsing** specifies that PowerPoint should use Dynamic HTML (DHTML) to emulate any animation effects in your presentation. This only works, by the way, for Web visitors who use Internet Explorer 4 or later.
    - **Resize Graphics To Fit Browser Window** specifies that PowerPoint will generate DHTML that resizes the presentation graphics to fit the Web visitor's browser window. Again, this only works if the Web visitors have Internet Explorer 4 or later installed. Netscape browsers have no facility to change the size of graphics in a Web page that's already displayed.

Figure 3-19 shows how Internet Explorer displays the PowerPoint presentation discussed earlier in the section "Saving PowerPoint Documents as Web Pages." In this version of the presentation, the Web page is actually a frameset—that is, a collection of rectangular areas called frames—each of which displays a different HTML file. Two frames appear along the left margin, and they contain the Table of Contents and the outline controls. The three frames along the right margin contain, from top to bottom, the current slide, its associated speaker notes, and the navigation buttons.

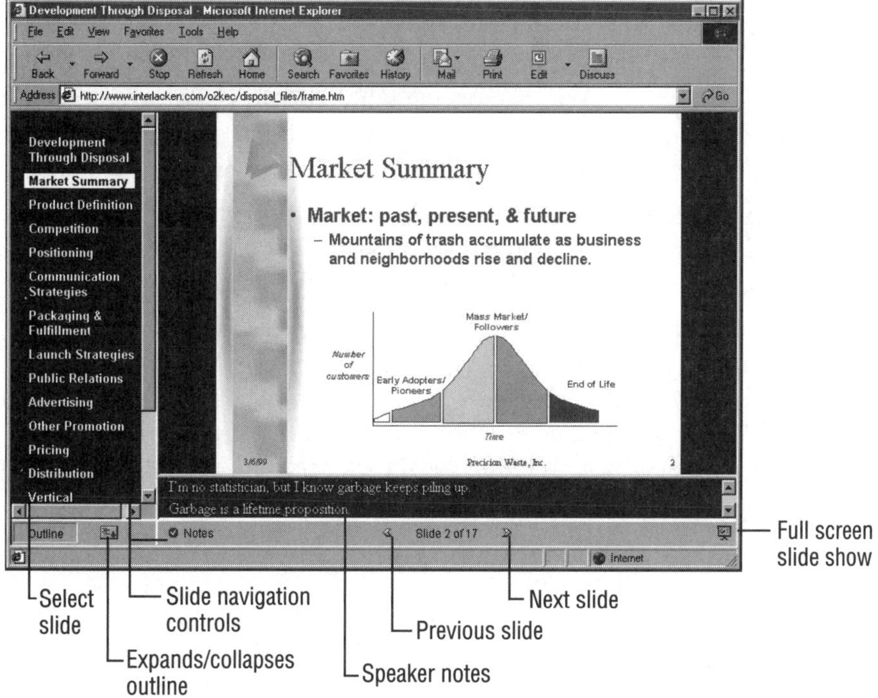

Figure 3-19
Saving the presentation of our hypothetical company as a Web page produces these results.

Saving Access Documents as Web Pages

Saving Access documents for presentation on the Web presents unique problems because the term document is really a misnomer in Microsoft Access. Instead, the basic object types are Tables, Queries, Forms, Reports, Data Access Pages, Macros, and Modules. Access can save these objects for the Web, but not in the manner you might expect. Here's how Access saves each of its basic object types for use on the Web. Subheadings later in this section will provide greater detail about each type.

- **Tables** and **Queries**. Access can save data from a table or query in a Web page format that resembles an Access datasheet view. Such Web pages can be either static or dynamic.

- A static Web page gets updated only when you export the table from Access to a new static Web page.
- An Active Server Page (ASP) queries the database and dynamically—rather than statically—displays current data each time a Web browser requests the page.

- **Forms** and **Reports**. Strictly speaking, Access can't save Forms and Reports as Web pages. For example, you can't save an Access form as an HTML form that works the same as the original Access form. Neither can you save an Access report so that it looks the same on the Web page as it does in Access. What you get in either case is a datasheet view of the table, query, or data set that underlies the form or report you're working with. This will be exactly the same datasheet view—either static or dynamic—you would create by saving the same table, query, or data set as described in the previous bullet.
- **Data Access Pages**. Because Access 2000 can't save Web-capable versions of its standard forms, it provides a second type of form designed specifically for the Web. Access 2000 calls this second form type a Data Access Page.

  Web-based database applications usually involve HTML forms that submit data to programs on the Web server. These programs, in turn, access the data in the database. Data access pages, however, take a completely different approach: the Web page serves as a carrier that invokes special ActiveX controls that access the database, through either local disk access or Windows file sharing.

  In addition, data access pages work only with Internet Explorer 5. Because of the need for Windows file sharing and Internet Explorer 5, most data access page usage will be on intranets.
- **Macros** and **Modules**. These objects are nothing more than lines of code. Because they have no visual appearance, they can't be saved for use on the Web.

The Web Options dialog box in Access 2000 consists of the single tab shown in Figure 3-20. To display this dialog box, choose Options from the Tools menu, choose the General tab, and then click Web Options.

Appearance controls the way Access formats pages for Web browsers.

- **Hyperlink Color** specifies the text or border color of hyperlinks to other Web pages.
- **Followed Hyperlink Color** specifies the text or border color of hyperlinks the Web visitor has recently visited (that is, those hyperlinks that exist either in the visitor's RAM buffer or Temporary Internet Files folder).
- **Underline Hyperlinks** specifies whether the Web visitor's browser should underline hyperlinked text. If the option is turned off, Access will create HTML pages that suppress the underlining for browsers that support this option.

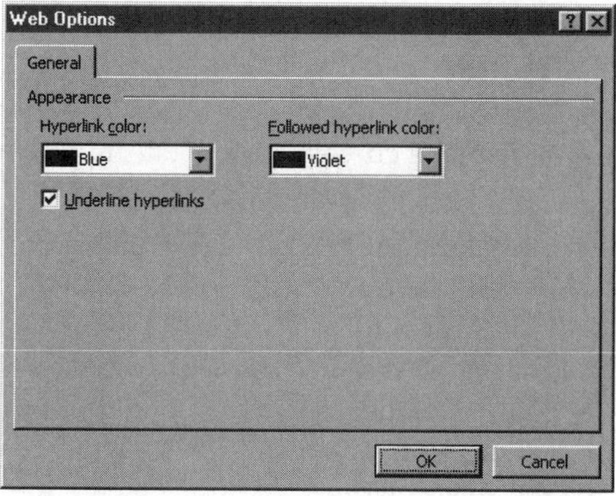

Figure 3-20
The Web Options dialog box in Access 2000 controls hyperlink formatting

Chapter 3

Exporting Access Tables, Queries, Forms, and Reports Here is the procedure for creating both static and dynamic Web-based datasheet views from any Access 2000 table, query, form, or report:

1. Start Access 2000 and open the database.
2. In the Database window, select the desired table, query, form, or report.
3. Choose Export from the File menu.
4. Choose a temporary location for saving the Web page on your local computer or on a file server. (As shown later in Figure 3-27, the Access 2000 Export dialog box provides no Web Folders choice.)
5. Choose one of the following Save As Type options:
   - **HTML Documents** if you want to create a static Web page.
   - **Microsoft Active Server Pages** if you want dynamic Web queries.
6. If you chose HTML Documents and you also want to format the Web page using an HTML template, select the Save Formatted box.
7. Click the Save button.

If you chose HTML Documents in step 5 and Save Formatted in step 6, clicking the Save button in step 7 will display the HTML Output Options dialog box shown in Figure 3-21. You can either specify the name of a template file, or you can leave the HTML Template field blank. See the sidebar "Using HTML Output Templates" on page 94 for additional explanation about this feature.

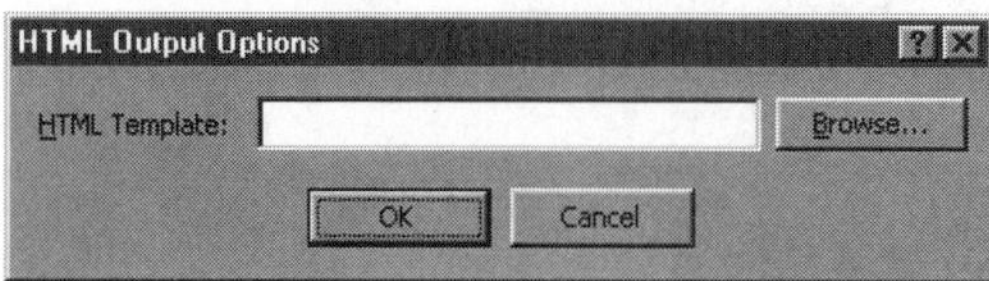

Figure 3-21
Specifying an HTML template adds formatting and other content to a datasheet view saved as a Web page.

Using HTML Output Templates

When Access 2000 exports data as an HTML page or an ASP query, the results are simple, at best, and to many people, downright unattractive. You can correct this by manually editing the output, but if you repeat the export, you'll have to repeat the manual editing, as well.

HTML output templates provide at least a partial solution. You can design a Web page as artful and complex as you like, add two special HTML comments, and then export as often as you like without the loss of other content. The two comments to use are:

HTML TAG	Use this tag for:
<!--ACCESSTEMPLATE_TITLE-->	The title of the Web page
<!--ACCESSTEMPLATE_BODY-->	The table that displays the data

A simple example appears below:

```
<HTML>
<TITLE><!--ACCESSTEMPLATE_TITLE--></TITLE>
<BODY leftmargin=200 background=grayst.jpg>
<!--ACCESSTEMPLATE_BODY-->
</BODY>
<BR><BR>
<IMG SRC = "msaccess.jpg">
</HTML>
```

If the template you specify does not contain the special comment string <!--ACCESSTEMPLATE_BODY-->, Access will export its data as the first content on the Web page.

Access 2000 Web templates normally reside on your computer in the folder C:\Program Files\Microsoft Office\Office\Samples. These templates have nothing to do with the templates used by FrontPage, Word, PowerPoint, or any other program.

You can use HTML output templates in Access 2000 two ways. First, you can create a very simple template consisting only of formatting instructions and use the same template for all related queries. This would give them all a common appearance. Second, if the exported data is only one portion of a complex page, you can place all the non-Access data into the template and then merge the Access data into the template as often as you like.

If you chose Microsoft Active Server Pages in step 5, Access 2000 will display the Output Options dialog box shown in Figure 3-22.

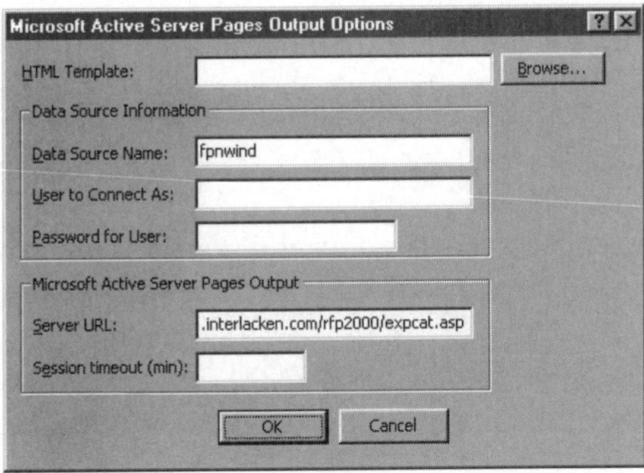

Figure 3-22
With the Output Options dialog box, Access 2000 will prompt for the ODBC Data Source that an Active Server Page will use.

- **HTML Template** provides the name of a sample Web page that provides formatting specifics. For more details on this feature, see "Using HTML Output Templates" on page 94.
- **Data Source Name** specifies the name of an ODBC system data source defined on the Web server. This is a required field, and will be discussed later in this section.
- **User To Connect As** provides a user name that is required to access the database. If accessing the database doesn't require a user name, leave this field blank.
- **Password For User** provides the authentication code for the specified user name. If accessing the database doesn't require a password, leave this field blank.
- **Server URL** specifies the page's intended URL. This field is optional.
- **Session Timeout** specifies how long the server will wait before abandoning a database query.

Because Access 2000 doesn't have a Web Folders option on its Export dialog box, the job of moving exported Web pages to the Web server must be performed manually.

Publishing Web Pages Manually

There are three ways to post Web pages on a server when you can't use the Web Folders icon in an application's Save As dialog box:

- If your Web server is also a file server—and if the Web and file sharing areas overlap—export the Web page directly to the file sharing location.

(continued)

Publishing Web Pages Manually *(continued)*

- Export the Web page to your local computer, and then upload the file to the Web server using a file transfer program such as FTP.
- If the Web server has FrontPage Server Extensions installed, first open Web Folders icon under My Computer, open the Web server, and then navigate to the desired folder where you want to post the files. Finally, drag the exported file from your local computer to the Web folder.

If you exported an Active Server Page, you have four additional requirements to satisfy:

- The Web server must be one of the following types:
    - Internet Information Server for Windows NT Server.
    - Microsoft Personal Web Server for Windows NT Workstation.
    - Microsoft Personal Web Server for Windows 95 or 98.
- The folder where the Active Server Page resides must be flagged as executable for scripts. This is something only your Web administrator can configure.
- A copy of the database must reside on the server.
- An ODBC System Data Source Name (DSN) pointing to the Access database must exist on the Web server. Again, this is a configuration option your Web administrator must configure.

Figure 3-23 provides a brief view of what is required to set up an ODBC System DSN. To display the ODBC Data Source Administrator dialog box shown in the background of Figure 3-23:

1. Open the ODBC icon in Windows Control Panel.
2. Choose the System DSN tab.
3. Click Add to display a list of available drivers.
4. Double-click the Microsoft Access driver displayed the window.

The Data Source Name field supplies the name that the exported ASP file will use for referencing the database. Clicking the Select button locates the actual database file.

Getting an ODBC System DSN set up on a Web server can be a nuisance, because it's something only an administrator working at the server's keyboard can do.

Figure 3-24 shows how a simple table looks after being saved as an HTML document. Had it been exported as an ASP page, it would look the same. But getting it to work would have required uploading it to a Web server, configuring its directory location as executable, uploading the database to the same server, and then setting up an ODBC System DSN.

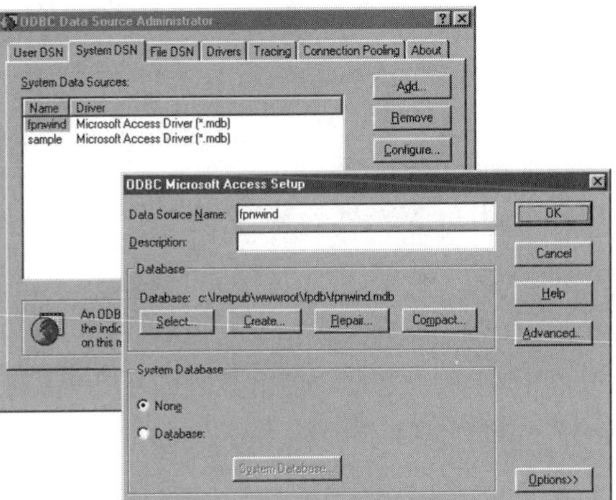

Figure 3-23
The Access database fpnwind.mdb is configured using the System DSN fpnwind.

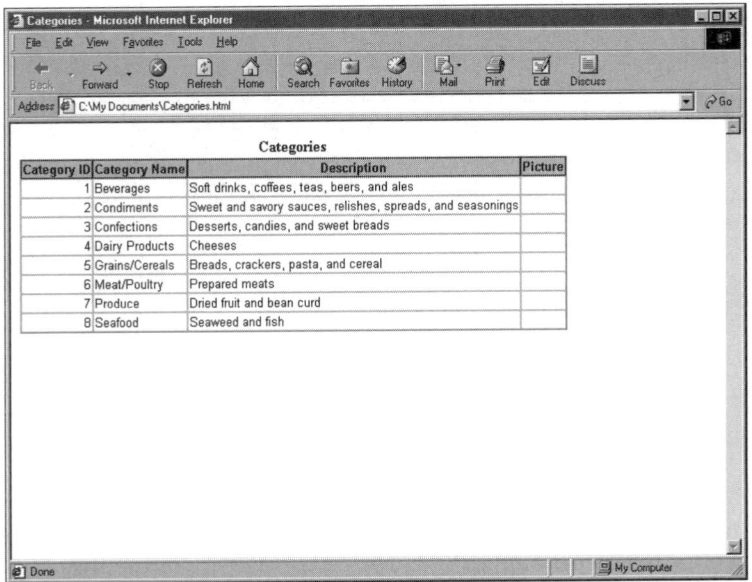

Categories

Category ID	Category Name	Description	Picture
1	Beverages	Soft drinks, coffees, teas, beers, and ales	
2	Condiments	Sweet and savory sauces, relishes, spreads, and seasonings	
3	Confections	Desserts, candies, and sweet breads	
4	Dairy Products	Cheeses	
5	Grains/Cereals	Breads, crackers, pasta, and cereal	
6	Meat/Poultry	Prepared meats	
7	Produce	Dried fruit and bean curd	
8	Seafood	Seaweed and fish	

Figure 3-24
Access 2000 displays exported tables, queries, forms, and reports as simple HTML tables.

Exporting Data Access Pages To begin working with data access pages, open a database in Access 2000 and then click the Pages icon on the Objects bar. This will list any existing Data Access Pages, and it will also display options to create a new data access page using a wizard, or edit an exiting data access page.

Figure 3-25 shows a sample data access page open in Access 2000. The Toolbox toolbar (shown detached in the figure) contains a selection of objects you can add to the data access page. The Alignment toolbar (also shown detached) aligns the form elements relative to other elements on the page. The Field List window displays the objects in the current database.

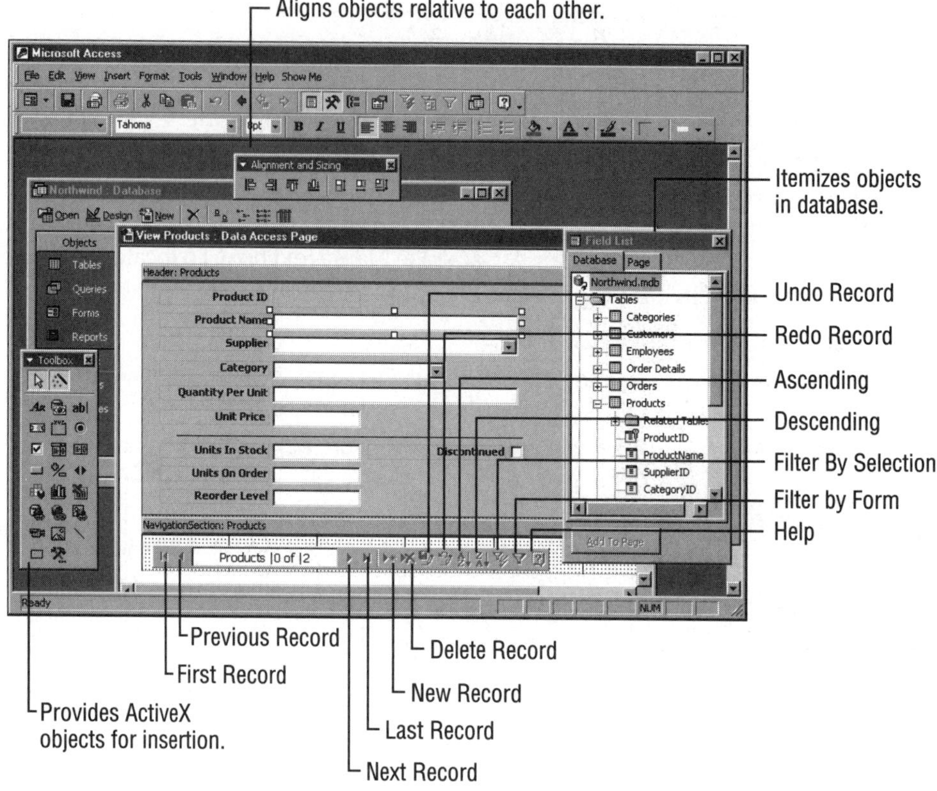

Figure 3-25
Access 2000 provides a rich development environment for Data Access Pages.

When a Web browser receives a data access page, the form and each control will be ActiveX controls. They won't be conventional HTML form fields. The ActiveX controls, plus features built into Internet Explorer 5, will function not so much as a Web page, but more like a stand-alone Access 2000 application. Putting this functionality into a Web page avoids the problems of distributing stand-alone applications to large groups of users.

Unlike the Save Results and Database Results components in FrontPage, data access pages do not submit changes or commands to a Web server for processing. For Access 2000 databases, the data access page opens the database as a file on the Web visitor's computer or on a file server. Of these two options, most real-world applications will usually involve databases on a file server, making local drive letter access to the Access database unreliable. The best approach is to place a copy of the database on a file server, open the database using universal file naming conventions—a UNC filename such as *\\server1\myapp\mydatab1.mdb*—and then create the data access page. Opening a database using a UNC filename in Access 2000 ensures that the data access page—and therefore eventual Web visitor—accesses the database using the same UNC filename. A UNC filename is independent of any drive mappings that a Web visitor might have in effect on his or her computer.

Figure 3-26 shows how to configure the location of the database that a Data Access Page will use. To display this dialog box, use the View menu in Access 2000 to display the Field List, click the database tab in the Field List, right-click the database name (the entry at the top of the list), and then choose Connection from the context menu. When the Data Link Properties dialog box appears, type the full path and database filename in the Select Or Enter A Database Name text box. To locate the database using the point-and-click method, click the ellipsis button to the right of the text box.

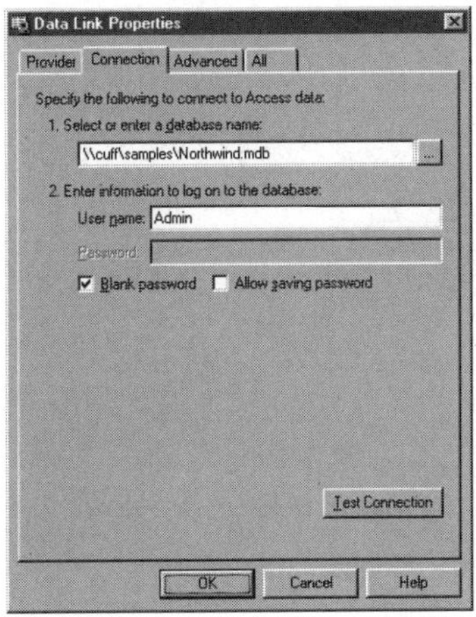

Figure 3-26
Configuring the location of a database for a data access page.

Note UNC filenames provide a way for Windows computers to access files on a file server without mapping any drive letters. To open an Access database using a UNC filename, first locate and double-click a file server in Network Neighborhood, locate and double-click its share name, and then locate and double-click the database file.

The following step-by-step procedure will show you how to transfer a data access page into a FrontPage Web. For this procedure, assume you've already tested and debugged the data access page.

1. With the data access page displayed in the active window, choose Export from the File menu.

2.. When the Export Data Access Page dialog box shown in Figure 3-27 appears, take the following steps:

- Choose a temporary location on your computer.
- Assign a filename.
- Select Microsoft Access Data Access Page as the Save As Type.
- Click the Save button to save the file.

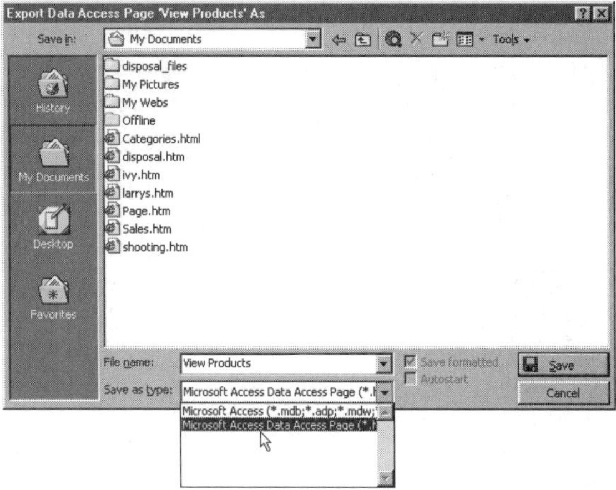

Figure 3-27
To export a data access page from Access 2000, choose Export from the File menu and then select Microsoft Access Data Access Page.

3.. To copy the data access page to a Web server, choose one of the methods listed in "Publishing Web Pages Manually" discussed earlier in this chapter.

Figure 3-28 shows the data access page in Internet Explorer developed using the steps outlined above, and shown earlier in Figure 3-26.

You can change the location of the Access database after exporting the data access page, but only with a great deal of difficulty. The database file location is stored as part of a long Extended Markup Language (XML) string that is a parameter to an ActiveX control in the <HEAD> section of the Web page. The only way to modify this information is to edit the raw HTML file, searching for the database filename or for an .MDB file extension, and to then carefully change the fully qualified filename.

Saving Publisher Documents as Web Pages

Microsoft Publisher 2000 isn't quite as powerful in its use of HTML as Word, Excel, and PowerPoint are, but it does have the ability to create Web publications from scratch, to convert existing publications to Web format, and to save publications in HTML format.

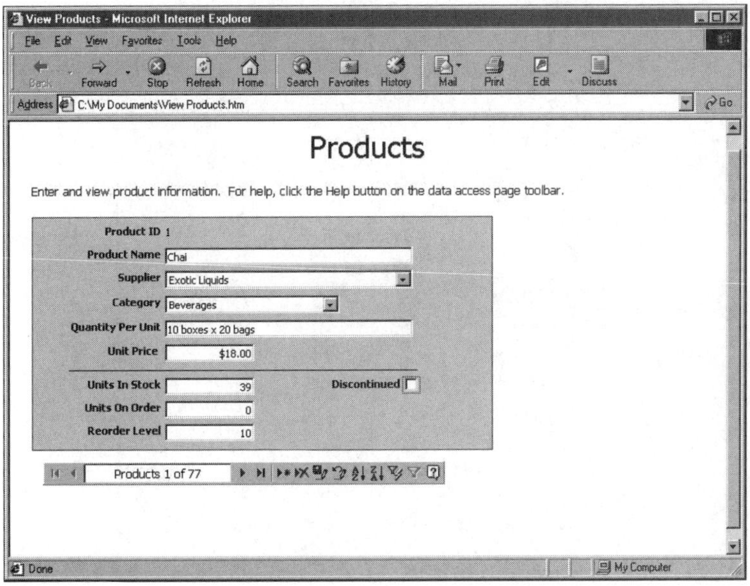

Figure 3-28
Internet Explorer displays the data access page previously shown in Figure 3-26.

To create a Web publication from scratch, first choose New from the File menu. When the Catalog window appears, choose Publications By Wizard, select Web Sites, and then click the Start Wizard button. Publisher will offer a selection of typical Web sites, and it will then run the Web Site Wizard to let you select the exact pages, colors, and other settings you want to use.

A Publisher Web site, by the way, isn't necessarily the same as a FrontPage Web. Publisher normally saves a Web site as a Publisher file rather than as Web page files. Publisher does, however, alter the publication's page layouts to make them suitable for display in a Web browser, and it also provides a Save As Web Page command on the File menu that creates true Web pages.

To convert an existing publication to a Web site, first open the publication and then choose Create Web Site From Current Publication from the File menu. Figure 3-29 shows this operation in progress.

Because the command Create Web Site From Current Publication actually creates a new publication, Publisher might display the Publisher message box shown in Figure 3-30 to ask about saving the original publication. Click the Yes button if you've made changes you want to save in the original Publisher format, as well as in the Web version. Clicking the No button will leave the original publication in its original state. Clicking the Cancel button abandons the entire process.

Unless you click Cancel, Publisher will run a style check on the publication before it performs the conversion to Web format. The style check will detect features in the

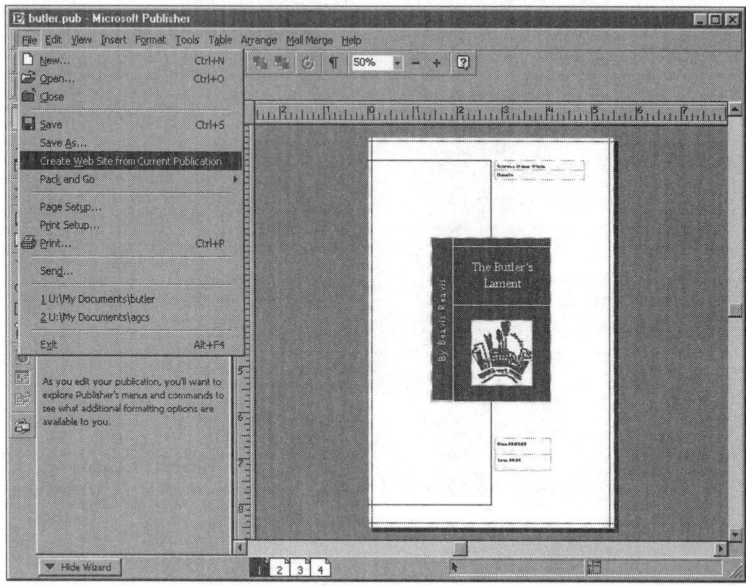

Figure 3-29
Saving a Microsoft Publisher document for the Web begins with converting the publication to a series of Web pages.

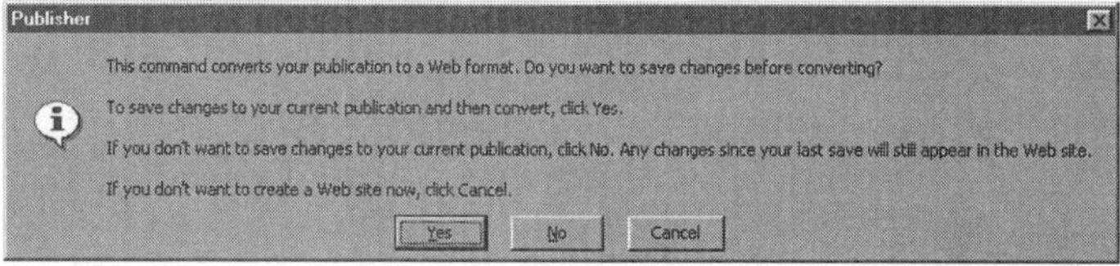

Figure 3-30
Publisher asks whether to save your changes in the original publication before converting it to Web pages.

presentation that most Web browsers can't support—such as overlapping objects—and will also provide you with alternatives for handling them.

Once you've converted the publication to a Web site, right-clicking any page and choosing Properties from the context menu will display the Web Properties dialog box shown in Figure 3-31. Here are the effects of the various settings.

- The **Site** tab controls settings that apply to the entire publication.
    - **Keywords** specifies any search terms that Web visitors might search for using Internet search engines such as Yahoo, Lycos, and HotBot. Publisher 2000 will invisibly add these keywords to your Web pages so that search engines will pick them up.

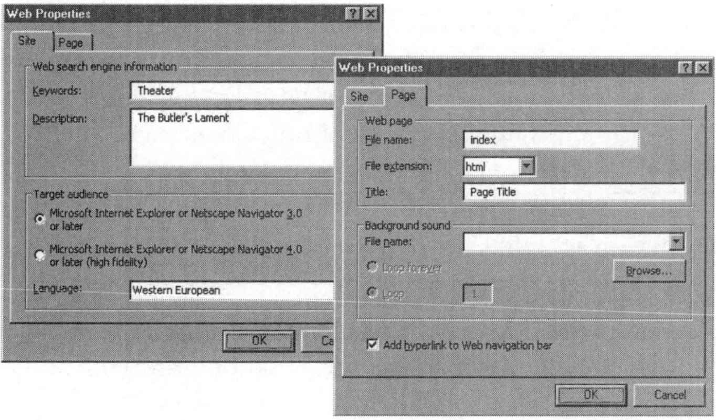

Figure 3-31
Once converted to Web format, each page in a publication acquires the properties controlled by the Web Properties dialog box.

- **Description** provides some text that search engines can use to describe your site.
- **Target Audience** specifies the type of browser you expect most of your Web visitors to use. If you specify Internet Explorer or Netscape Navigator 4 or later, Publisher will create Web pages that will look better in these browsers, but with the side effect of making them look worse in older browsers.
- **Language** specifies the character set that browsers should use when displaying the page on the visitor's system. This usually corresponds to the natural language of any text on the page.

- The **Page** tab controls settings that pertain to the page that was current before you opened the Web Options dialog box.
  - **Filename** specifies the base portion of the filename for the current Web page—that is, the portion that precedes the last period. This can be any string of characters that's valid as a filename on the Web server that will deliver the page to your Web visitors.

    The opening page of your publication should have the same filename and file extensions as the Web server's default filename setting. If the Web server's default filename is default.htm or default.html, give the opening page of your publication a filename base of default. If the Web server's default filename is index.htm or index.html, give the opening page of your publication a filename base of index.

    To specify the remainder of the filename—the extension—use the File Extension field described next.

Note A Web server's *default filename* is the value it searches for when it receives a URL that doesn't specify a filename. If the server's default filename is default.htm and you submit a URL like *http://www.example.com/stuff/*, the Web server will look for and will deliver, if found, a Web page at *http://www.example.com/stuff/default.htm*.

- **File Extension** specifies the filename extension for the current page. This will usually be HTM or HTML.
- **Title** provides the title text for the current page. This title appears in the title bar of the Web visitor's browser, and not within the body of the Web page. Search engines also make use of this value.
- **Background Sound** specifies the name of a sound file the browser should play while Web visitors view your site. The Loop Forever choice tells the browser to replay the sound file without limit until the Web visitor moves on to another page. The Loop choice tells the browser to play the file a certain number of times and then stop. If you decide to use background sound files, keep them small and remember that many Web visitors find them annoying.
- **Add Hyperlink to Web Navigation Bar** includes the current Web page in the menu page for the site. However, this option might have no effect on Web sites which have been converted from other publication types and which might still be controlled by the original Wizard.

When you're ready to actually place your publication on the Web, choose Save As Web Page from the File menu. This displays the familiar dialog box shown in Figure 3-32. However, note the following changes compared to the dialog boxes found in the other Office 2000 applications.

- The Publisher Save As Web Page dialog box specifies a folder and not a filename. The filenames come from the properties of each page in the publication, as shown earlier in Figure 3-31. Publisher saves the entire set of Web pages in the folder location you specify.
- There is no Title box and no Change Title button because, again, a single publication has a different title for each Web page it contains.
- There is no Web Options choice on the Tools menu.

If you're saving the publication to a Web server with FrontPage or Office Server Extensions, you can use the Web Folders option to save the publication directly to the server. Otherwise, save it to an intermediate location on your hard disk and then upload the entire folder as you would any other Web site content.

Figure 3-33 shows the publication saved earlier in Figure 3-32 as it now appears in FrontPage. Publisher has created a number of picture files with arbitrary names, plus

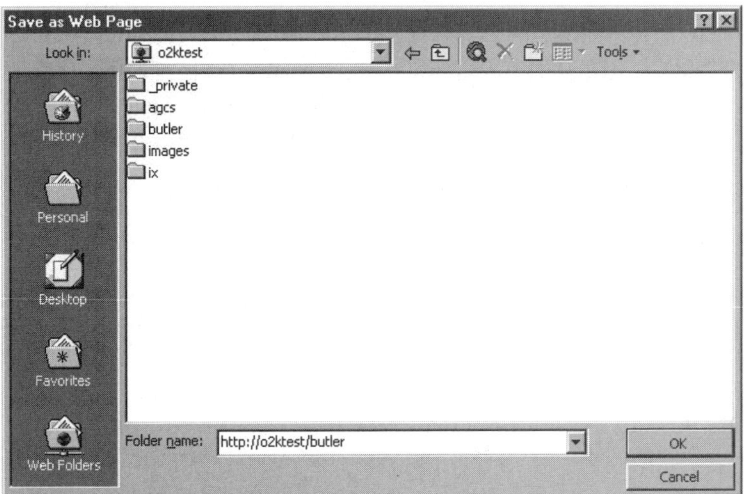

Figure 3-32
Microsoft Publisher's Save As Web Page dialog box specifies a folder location rather than a filename.

one Web page for each page in the publication. From this point, you could further modify or rename the Web pages, build hyperlinks to and from other pages in the same Web, and so forth.

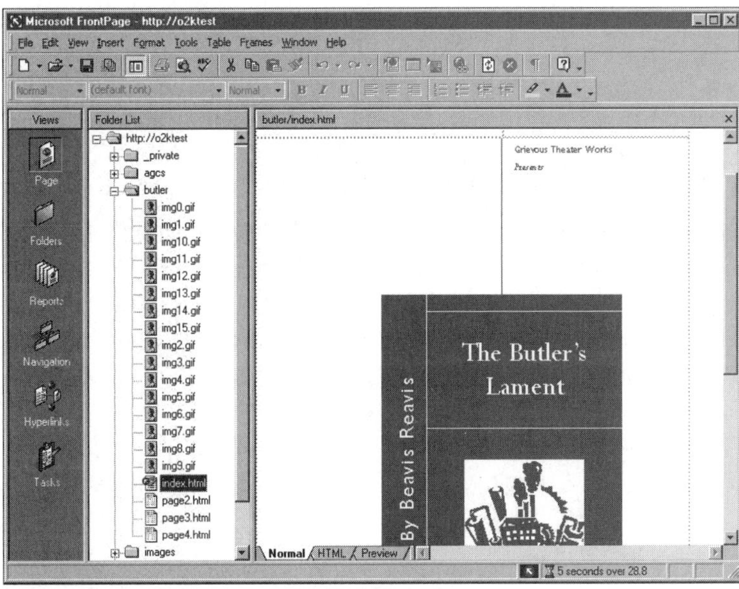

Figure 3-33
This is how a typical publication looks in FrontPage after Publisher has saved it as a Web page.

Saving Web Pages with FrontPage

Web pages are FrontPage's native file format. As such, saving them requires no special precautions or procedures. Figure 3-34 shows the FrontPage Save As dialog box, which is very similar to Save As dialog boxes in other Office 2000 applications.

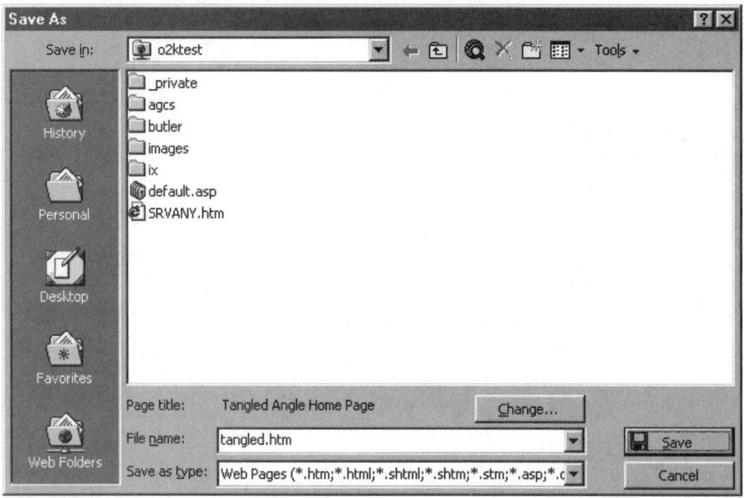

Figure 3-34
FrontPage uses the same Web-enabled Save As dialog box as the rest of the Office 2000 applications.

FrontPage is so closely tied to the Web that any distinction between Web-related settings and its general program settings tend to blur. Choosing Options from the Tools menu, for example, reveals no Web Options button. Figure 3-35 shows how options which other applications segregate as unique to the Web are simply first nature in FrontPage. Note the options Check If Office Is The Default Editor For Pages Created In Office and Check If FrontPage Is The Default Editor For Pages, for example.

FrontPage provides much more control than other Office 2000 applications over the HTML it writes. The HTML source tab at the left in Figure 3-36, for example, first specifies whether to preserve or correct the HTML formatting style of every page FrontPage saves, and then goes on to specify the exact capitalization, spacing, and indentation desired for each possible type of HTML tag. The Compatibility tab at the right specifies not only what browsers to support, but also which browser-specific technologies and which Web server features to use.

FrontPage also provides a rich assortment of formatting commands, page layout commands, and picture handling features. Through FrontPage Components, it provides easy access to a variety of useful features that would otherwise require writing complex HTML or script code. It manages all the files in your Web site as a unit, and can even generate hyperlinks among them automatically. If your Web site uses framesets, FrontPage can edit them in full WYSIWYG mode.

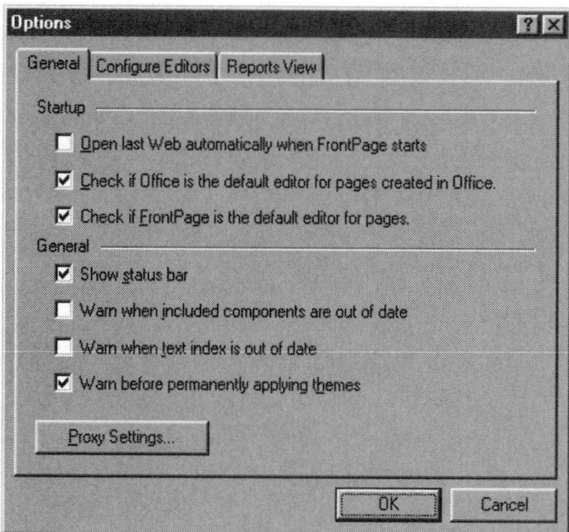

Figure 3-35
Unlike other Office 2000 applications, FrontPage doesn't segregate Web-related options from general program options.

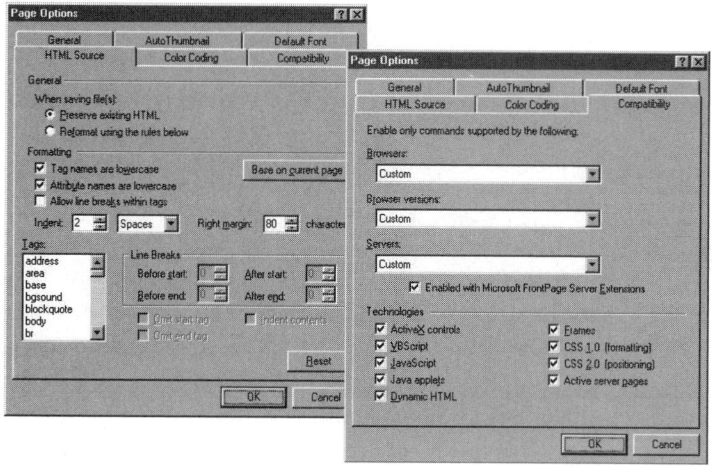

Figure 3-36
FrontPage provides detailed control over the formatting of HTML and the use of browser and Web server features.

Because of its powerful features and native orientation to the Web, FrontPage should be your application of choice for creating general-purpose Web pages and for refining Web pages created in any Office 2000 application.

Using the Web Folders Icon

Office 2000 comes with a feature that is very handy for transferring files between your computer and a Web server using either the FrontPage or Office Server

Extensions. This is the Web Folders feature shown in Figure 3-37. The Web Folders feature uses the familiar Windows Explorer interface to display the content of a Web server and, of course, you can move, copy, rename, and open files in all the usual ways—both within the Web server and between the Web server and your computer.

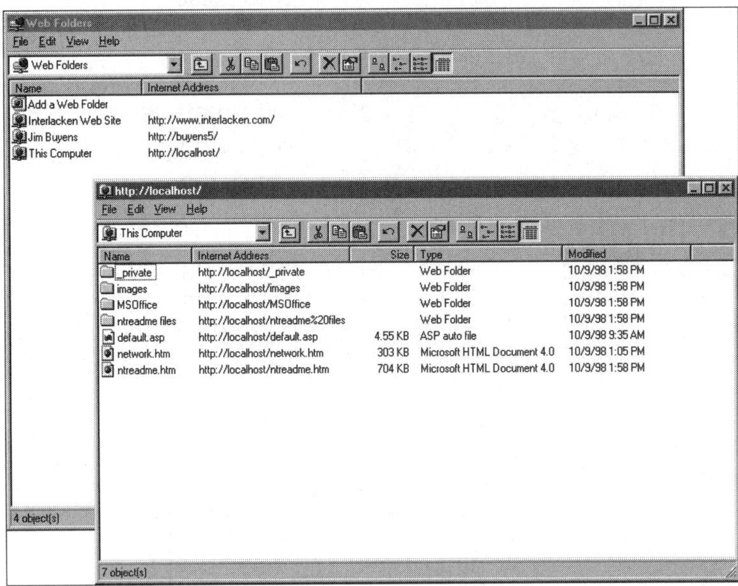

Figure 3-37
Office 2000's Web Folders feature provides drag-and-drop desktop access to server-based FrontPage Webs.

After you install Office 2000, Web Folders will appear as an icon under My Computer. Double-clicking Web Folders displays an Add Web Folder icon which, if double-clicked, prompts you for the names of Web servers to display in the future. Once the server's root folder has been displayed, you can open folders at will by double-clicking them (provided, of course, you have all the user names and passwords that might be required).

Note If you're a frequent user of Web Folders, you might find it convenient to have a Web Folders icon on your desktop. To set this up, first open My Computer, and then right-click and drag the Web Folders icon onto your desktop. When you release the mouse button, choose Create Shortcut(s) Here from the pop-up menu.

Note that just to make life a little more complicated, the Web Folders feature in Office 2000 doesn't require Office Server Extensions. Because the Web Folders feature is only a file transfer mechanism, it requires only the FrontPage Server Extensions.

Exchanging Documents via HTML

With all the Office applications capable of saving files and opening files in the same file format—HTML—you might wonder if HTML files saved from Word can be opened in, say, Excel or PowerPoint, or if presentations saved by PowerPoint can be opened in, say, Word or Publisher. The answer to these questions is yes, but with reservations.

Recall that HTML is only a markup language—that is, a notational scheme for flagging like elements in the same document for like formatting and viewing. Any intelligence in the document—the formulas in Excel, field values, footnotes, running heads, and other special elements in Word, and the structure and styles of PowerPoint applications—are saved as XML.

In theory, each application is supposed to accurately *round-trip* any XML it doesn't understand. This means if you open an Office HTML file in the wrong application, whatever XML is present is then supposed to be present on output, without modification. Consider, however, the following sequence of actions:

- You create a table of data values in Excel, with a row of totals at the bottom.
- You save the spreadsheet as HTML.
- You open the saved HTML file in Word.
- You add a row inside the table of data values.
- You save the HTML file in Word.

In Excel, inserting rows inside the range of a SUM() formula expands the range of the formula. But Word isn't a spreadsheet program—it doesn't understand the formulas Excel saved as XML, and it won't be able to enlarge the SUM() ranges. In fact, when you try to save the Web page in Word, you'll get the following warning message:

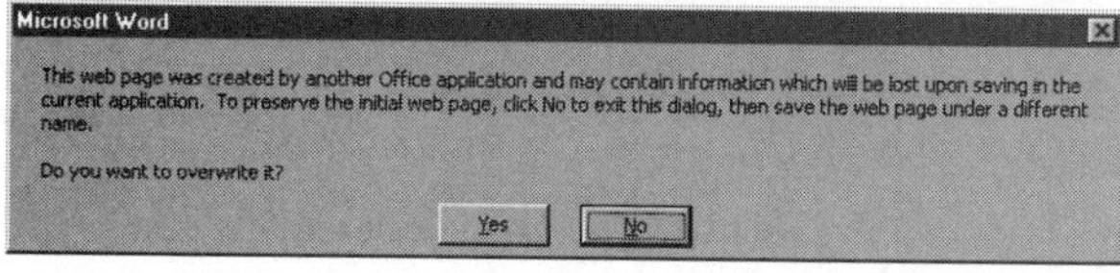

This is why Office usually opens HTML files with the applications that created or saved them, and is an excellent reason you should follow this practice whenever possible.

There is one exception to this rule, provided you're willing to be careful. It's relatively common to save documents from other Office applications, open them in FrontPage, and then use FrontPage to apply Themes, insert hyperlinks, add page banners and navigation bars, and generally enhance the page visually. Just take care to keep your changes cosmetic, and avoid areas where you know other programs will have complex logic at work.

Using Office Server Extensions

Office 2000 includes its own set of Web server extensions that provide seven applications unique to Office. Two of these applications involve both traditional Office applications and the Web, four involve only the Web, and one is a background process on the Web server. The two applications that involve traditional Office applications are:

- **Web Discussions** After an Office 2000 user has saved a document to a Web server as HTML (and recall that this is an integrated, one-step process), Web visitors browsing that document can make comments using a discussion toolbar. The Office Server Extensions store these comments as separate files on the Web server and then, when the Office 2000 user opens the document, all the comments appear seamlessly merged.
- **Web Subscriptions** With this feature, both Office 2000 users and Web visitors can ask to be notified any time a specific document or folder changes. The Office Server Extensions detect such changes and send the notifications by e-mail as requested.

The following applications involve only the Web server and a browser:

- **Start Page** This feature provides a home page for accessing the other applications.
- **Enhanced Directory Page** This enhances the normal display Web visitors receive when browsing a directory with no default document.
- **Search Page** This is a special search tool tailored for Microsoft Office documents.
- **Administration Tool** This Web-based tool provides control over the preceding applications.

The background application is a database server that keeps track of all the activity described above.

- **Workgroup Database** Providing Office Server Extensions functionality requires a database to keep track of activity data, indexes, and settings. This can be either a Workgroup database supplied as part of the extensions, or a database residing on a Microsoft SQL Server.

The clients for these features are either a browser (for the Web-based tasks) or standard Office 2000 applications (for document creation and retrieval). The server-based software comes in a package called Microsoft Office Server Extensions. The Office Server Extensions consist of the FrontPage Server Extensions, a collection of Active Server Pages and ActiveX controls, and the workgroup database server. In effect, the Office Server Extensions are an extension to—and require the presence of—the FrontPage Server Extensions.

The Office Server Extensions require Windows NT Server 4 or later and Internet Information Server 4 or later. As such, the installation is a job for your server administrator. The setup files might be present in an \OSE folder on the Office 2000 CD, or they might be downloaded from Microsoft's Web site.

Using Office Server Extensions in Word 2000

As shown in Figure 3-38, Microsoft Word 2000 can save documents directly to a server-based FrontPage Web. This might be old stuff, but it's the starting point for using the Office Server Extensions. In case you've forgotten, here is the procedure for saving a Word document into a FrontPage Web: choose Save As Web Page from the File menu, then click Web Folders in the Save As dialog box.

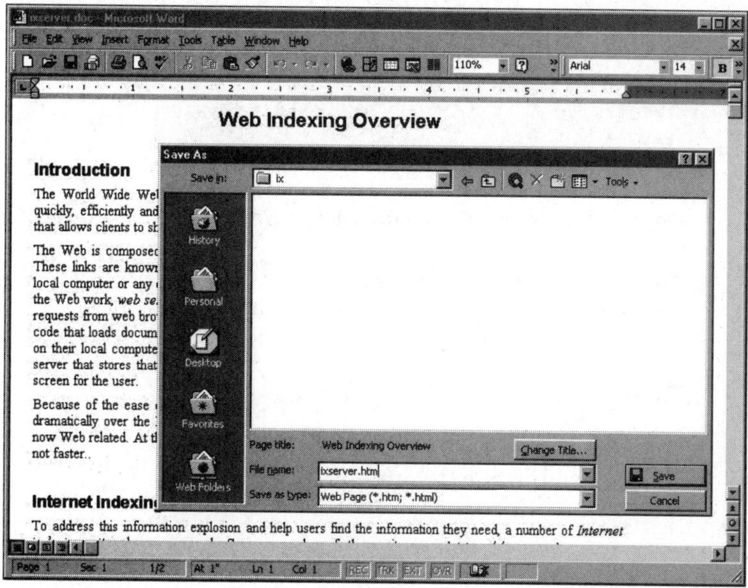

Figure 3-38
Word 2000 can save documents directly into a FrontPage Web.

Conducting Web Discussions

Once your document is on the Web server, choose Online Collaboration from the Tools menu and then select Web Discussions. This initiates discussions on the document and displays the Discussions toolbar shown at the bottom of Figure 3-39.

Note Within the Web Discussion feature, Microsoft calls each comment a *discussion.*

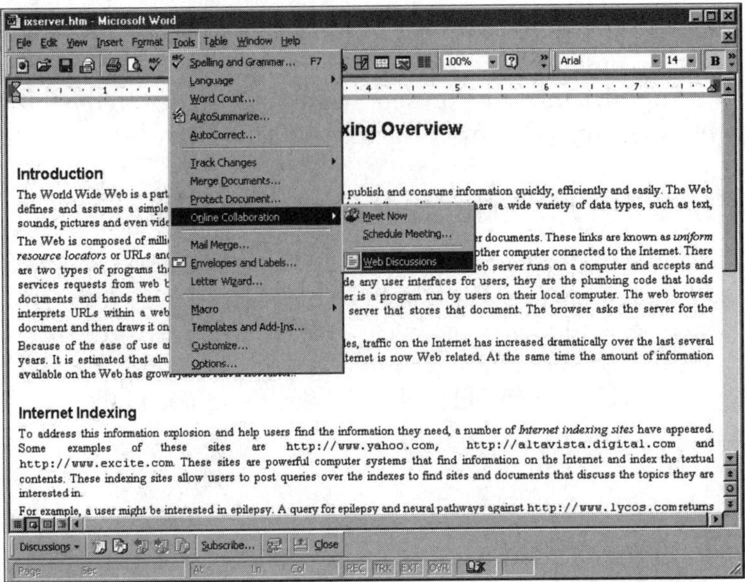

Figure 3-39
The Discussion toolbar at the bottom of this window controls Web Discussions and Web Subscriptions.

With the Discussions drop-down menu, at the left of the toolbar, you can insert a discussion, refresh the display of existing discussions, filter discussions, print discussions, and set discussion options. The five buttons left of the drop-down menu implement these five commands, respectively.

- Insert discussions in the document.
- Insert discussions about the document.
- Jump to the previous discussion.
- Jump to the next discussion.
- Toggle display of general discussions.

Collaborating With Others Online

Word, Excel, PowerPoint, and Access can all initiate online collaboration sessions using Microsoft NetMeeting. Here's how to do this:

1. If you've never used NetMeeting before, launch it from the Start menu and follow the prompts. The information you need to provide consists mostly of your name, e-mail address, and the address of an available NetMeeting server.

Note You can install NetMeeting as part of an Internet Explorer setup or by downloading it from *http://www.microsoft.com/netmeeting/*. After installation is complete, look for a NetMeeting icon under Programs on the Start menu.

2. Start the Office 2000 application corresponding to the document you want to discuss, and then open the document.
3.. If the document isn't already stored on a Web server, use the Save As Web page option to store it on a Web server now.
4. Choose Online Collaboration from the Tools menu, and then choose one of the following options:
    - **Meet Now** to collaborate immediately.
    - **Schedule Meeting** to schedule the collaboration in advance with others.
5. If you skipped step 1 above, NetMeeting will prompt you for basic identification and server information at this time.
6.. If you choose the second option, Schedule Meeting, you will next see the dialog box shown in Figure 3-40. This is an Outlook form that schedules a meeting through Microsoft Exchange. Exchange will notify the attendees you've designated and also keep track of who can participate.

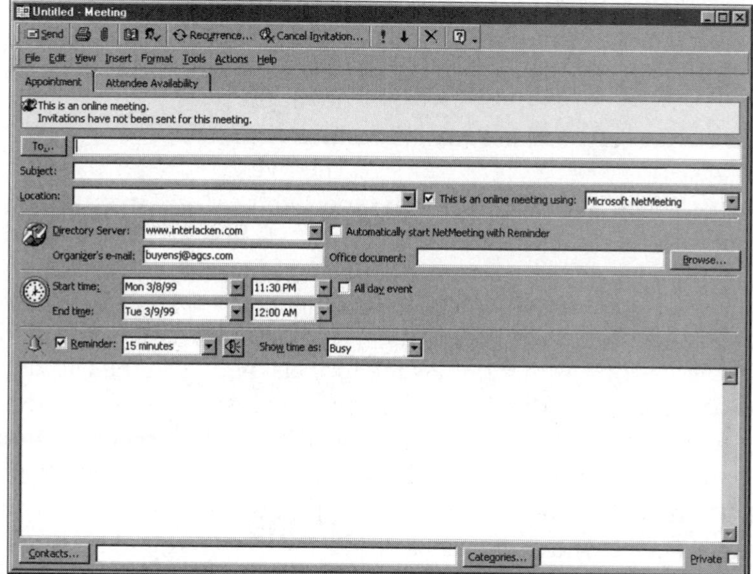

Figure 3-40
This window prompts for the details and participants of a scheduled online collaboration meeting.

7. When the NetMeeting discussion starts, participants can browse the NetMeeting server to find it, and then communicate with one another. Screen sharing is the most common form of collaboration, but if two participants both have sound cards and microphones, they can also communicate verbally while they're connected to the collaboration meeting.

Subscribing to Web Notifications

Clicking the Subscribe button, shown earlier in Figure 3-39, displays the Document Subscription dialog box shown in Figure 3-41. Here, you can subscribe to change notices for the current document or for any other document in a specified folder (subject to filters), set notification criteria, specify your e-mail address, and indicate how long the Office Server Extensions will accumulate changes before sending them on.

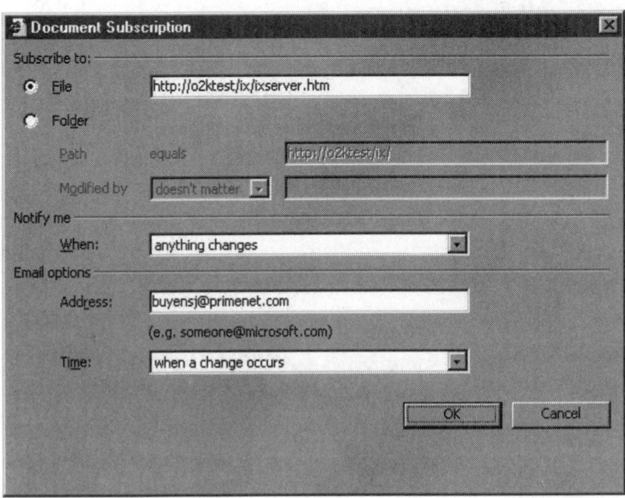

Figure 3-41
The Document Subscription dialog box subscribes an e-mail user to change notifications for a given document or folder.

Figure 3-42 illustrates the same document being discussed in Internet Explorer. The Web visitor first opened the document location shown earlier in Figure 3-38, and then chose Discussions from the View menu. This displayed the Discussions toolbar visible at the bottom of the figure. Clicking the Insert Discussion icon on the Discussions toolbar displayed a sticky note icon each place where a discussion could be inserted. The Web visitor double-clicked one of these icons to display the Enter Discussion Text dialog box, and then typed the text shown in the figure.

Note Browser users can also subscribe to change notices for discussion documents. Clicking the Subscribe button shown in Figure 3-42 displays the same dialog box as clicking the Subscribe button in Word 2000 (shown in Figure 3-41).

Clicking the OK button on the Enter Discussion Text dialog box shown in Figure 3-42 submits the discussion text and displays it as shown in Figure 3-43.

Discussion text also appears in an almost identical format when the original user opens the HTML file in Word. In fact, all discussion text from all users will appear

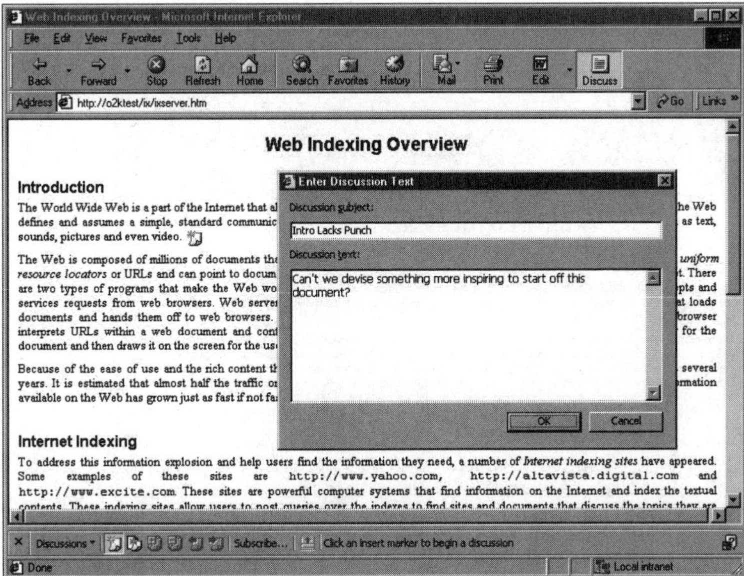

Figure 3-42
After displaying the Discussions toolbar, Internet Explorer can accept discussion text and subscribe Web visitors to change notification.

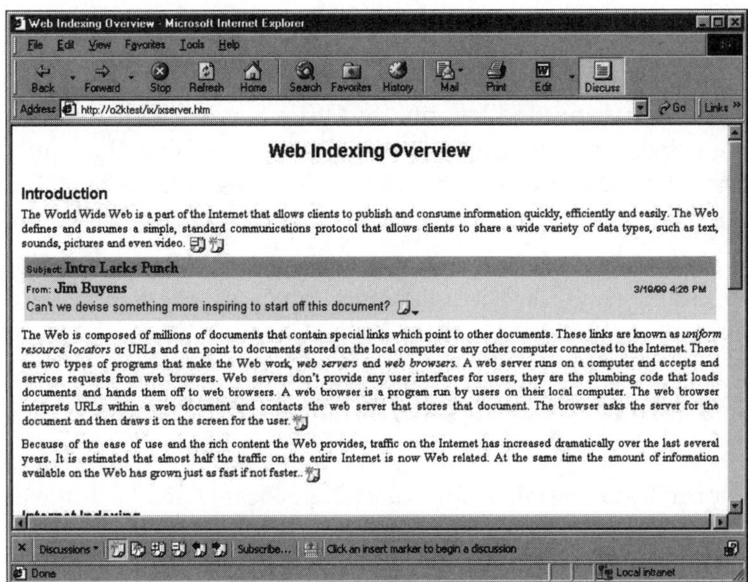

Figure 3-43
Internet Explorer displays discussions in-line with document text.

merged seamlessly into place. Figure 3-44 shows how this merging will appear in the document.

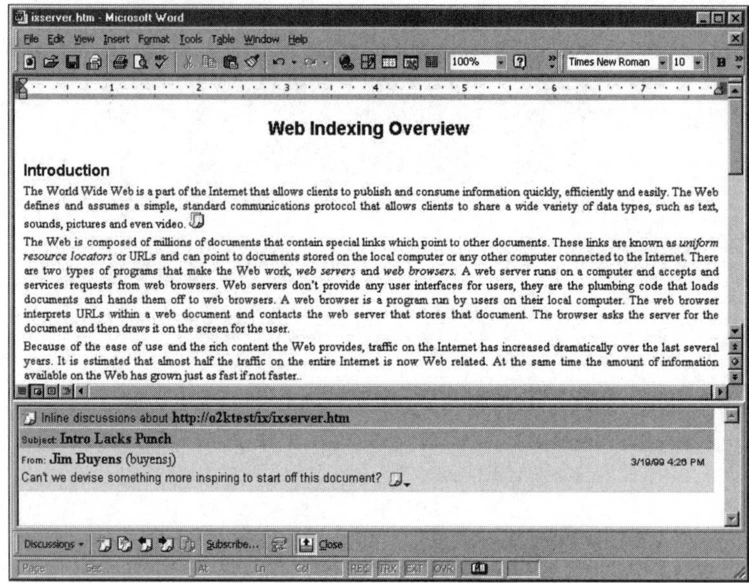

Figure 3-44
Word 2000 merges all of the Web Discussion text and then displays it in-line with document text.

Given that Internet Explorer uses a special toolbar for handling Web Discussions and Web Subscriptions, you might wonder about Netscape Navigator support. Navigator doesn't have a Discussions toolbar, but the Office Server Extensions do their best to emulate one using a frameset as shown in Figure 3-45. Note the emulated toolbar at the bottom of the window and the Document Subscription dialog box displayed as an HTML form.

Figure 3-46 shows a typical change notification message. Note that a single message can report multiple changes. The notification process periodically scans a database and combines all notifications to the same recipient.

Using Web-Based Office Server Extension Features

The Office Server Extensions also support a number of purely Web-based features which are normally accessible from a Start Page located at a Web site address such as *http://<servername>/msoffice/*. Figure 3-47 illustrates this page.

Clicking Browse Web Folders displays a listing similar to the one illustrated in Figure 3-48, provided that directory browsing for the given directory is turned on. Notice the Search option, the Filter On Name option, the customized file icons, the Last Accessed dates, and the Date Created values, none of which appear in normal directory browsing lists. Also note the contents of the browser's Address box. You

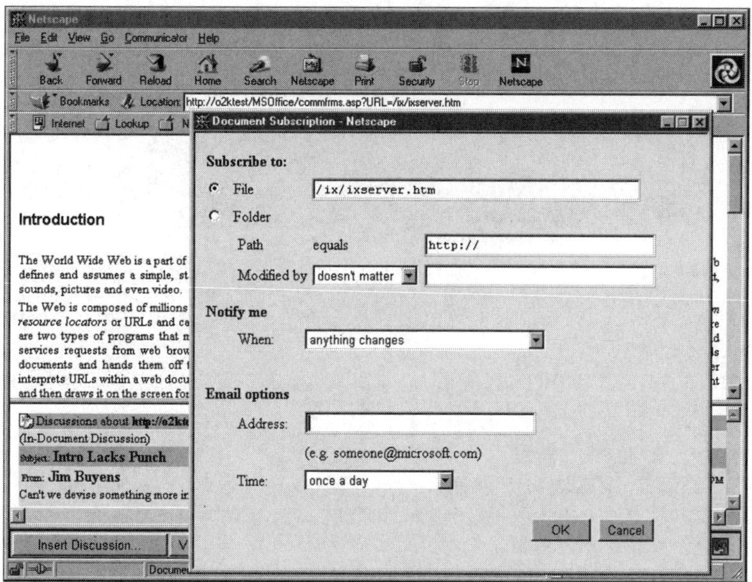

Figure 3-45
The Office Server Extensions use standard HTML to communicate with Netscape Navigator visitors.

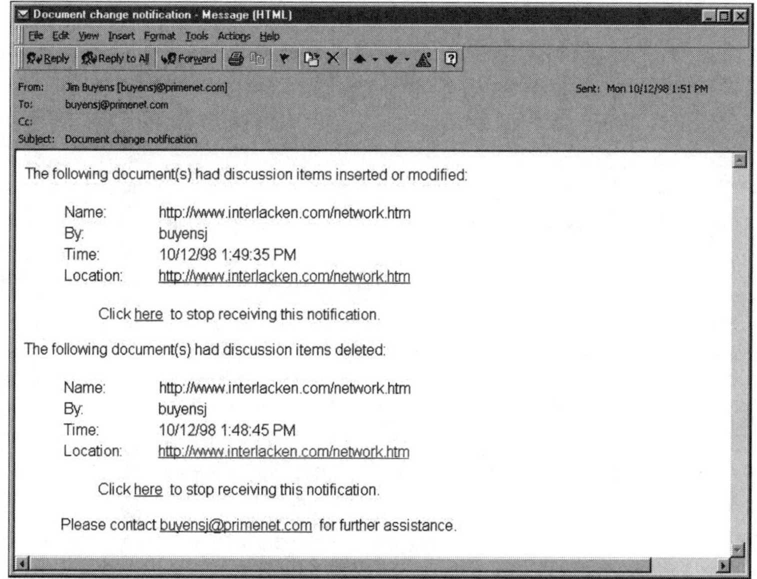

Figure 3-46
This is a notification message generated by Server Extensions.

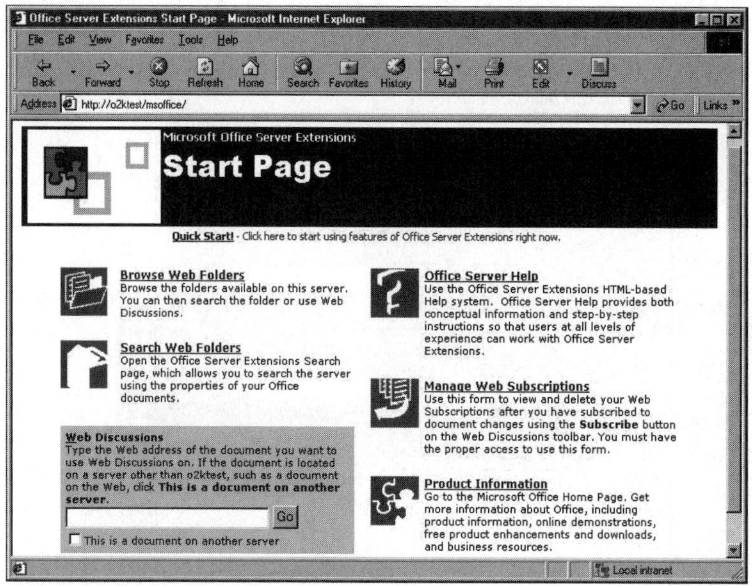

Figure 3-47
The Office Server Extensions Start Page provides the starting point for purely Web-based functions.

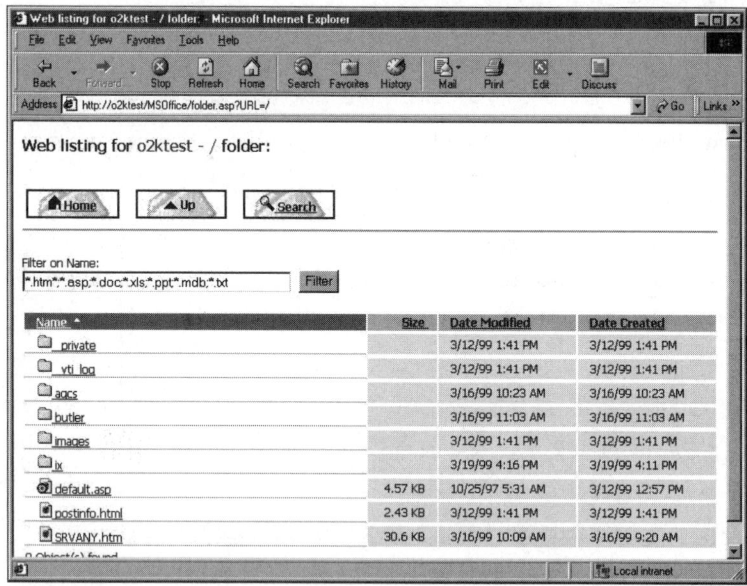

Figure 3-48
An Office Server Extension directory listing provides a Search button, filename filters, and column sorting.

can display this type of listing for any permitted folder on your server simply by modifying the *URL=* value.

Searching for Office Documents

Clicking the Search Web Folders hyperlink shown earlier in Figure 3-47 will display the Search Web Folders page shown in Figure 3-49. (Clicking the Search button shown earlier in Figure 3-48 performs the same function.)

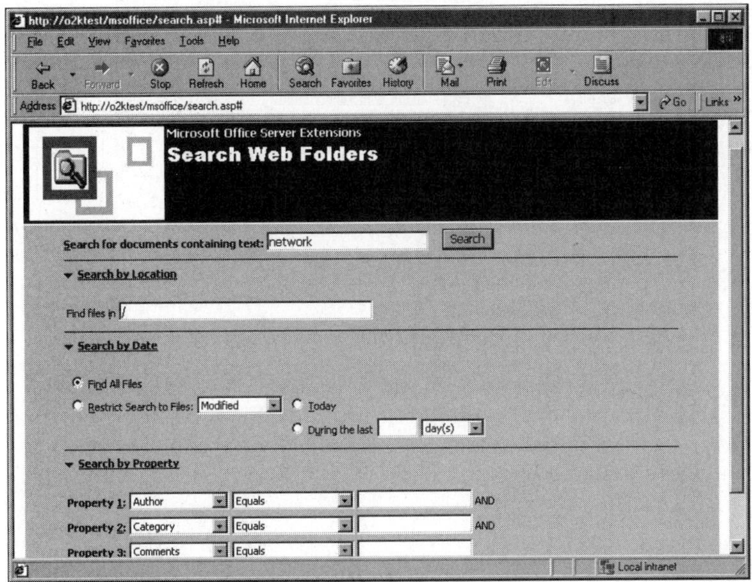

Figure 3-49
A Search Web Folders page locates documents on an Office-extended Web server.

The Search Web Folders page is just a front-end for Microsoft Index Server, a text-search engine, which is installed by default as part of Internet Information Server 4.0. This version, however, provides more options than the default Search page supplied with IIS, and it also provides more options than the default FrontPage Search form. In particular, note the Search By Property section, which searches for properties you set in Office 2000 applications (usually by choosing Properties from the File menu).

To display this Search page from any hyperlink, enter the URL *http://<servername>/msoffice/search.asp?scope=/*. To search less than the entire server, specify a directory path as the *scope =* value.

Part 2

Automation Tools

Chapter 4

Power Up Visual Basic

In This Chapter

Microsoft Visual Basic for Applications (VBA) is a special version of Visual Basic that—when added to programs—enables users to create macros and related tools that automate or customize applications. In Chapter 5, you will learn how to use VBA to control Office applications. (This chapter covers the actual Visual Basic side of Visual Basic for Applications.)

Performing Common Programming Tasks

In every application supporting Visual Basic, the same command is used to open the Visual Basic Editor. Select Macro on the Tools menu, and select Visual Basic Editor from the menu. (You can also press Alt+F11 to display the Visual Basic Editor window.) In all Office applications except Access, you can access the Visual Basic Editor simply by editing an existing macro: Select Macro on the Tools menu, click Macros on the submenu, select a macro name, and then click Edit. (In Access, the term macro has a specialized meaning. Refer to "VBA vs. Access Macros" in Chapter 6 for more information about Access macros.)

Get Help with Visual Basic

The Visual Basic Help file contains the topic *Visual Basic Conceptual Topics*, which is very useful in learning to work with VBA. In particular, the sections relating to creating *If* statements and loops are very clear. The Help topic *Looping Through Code* is an overview that links to all the relevant topics covering conditional and looping structures. From within the Visual Basic Editor, launch Visual Basic Help and ask the Answer Wizard for help using the search phrase *Looping Through Code*. (You will need to have your Office 2000 installation media handy the first time you use Visual Basic Help.)

Managing the Visual Basic Editor Windows

You use the Visual Basic Editor when you work with VBA. All editions of Visual Basic—including the Visual Studio editions—use the same editor. The first time you open the Visual Basic Editor, it fills the entire screen. If you have created any macros, the bulk of the editor window will be filled by the Code window that displays macros. Along the left side of the window are two other panes, as shown in Figure 4-1: a Project Explorer window and a Properties window.

Full-screen layout is useful when you are working in the stand-alone edition of Visual Basic. When you are using VBA in Microsoft Office, however, you will nearly always be using VBA to manipulate a document, and it will help you to see that document as you work.

Docking and Resizing Windows

The Visual Basic Editor comes with several windows that provide you with useful information. In addition to the Code window, the Visual Basic Editor also provides you with the following windows:

- A Locals window
- An Immediate window
- A Watch window

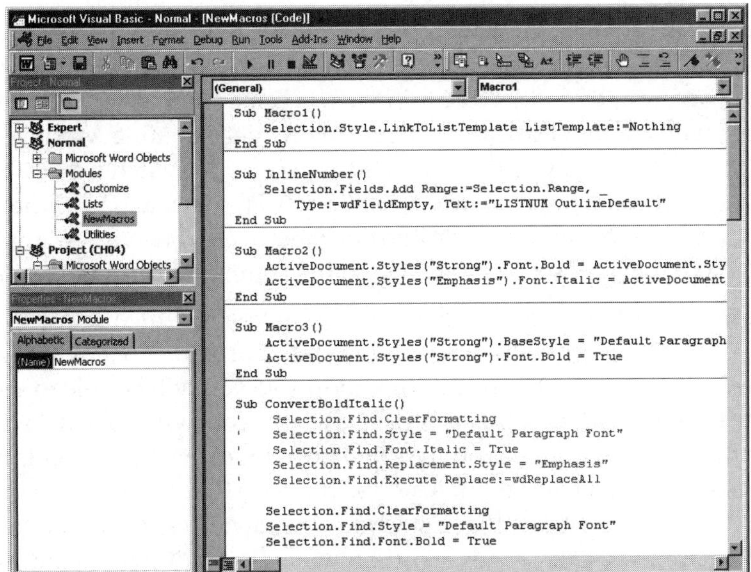

Figure 4-1
The default Visual Basic Editor window fills the screen.

- A Project Explorer window
- A Properties window
- An Object Browser window

Each window can be positioned and resized like the MDI windows in Microsoft Excel. (See "Working with Windows" in Chapter 1 for details about MDI windows.) For example, each workbook you open in Excel has its own window. Maximizing a workbook window will fill Excel's entire work area, and restoring the window will allow you to see more than one window at a time. A workbook window can never move outside the boundary of the application, however; the window is completely owned by the main application window. This type of window is called a child window.

Contrast the behavior of an MDI child window with that of a toolbar. A toolbar can either be docked or floating. You can dock a toolbar on the top, left, bottom, or right side of the application window. If you drag a toolbar away from a docked position, it will become a floating toolbar that can be placed anywhere. If the application does not use the entire screen, a floating toolbar can be moved outside the application window. A toolbar is, in essence, a dockable window.

The Visual Basic Editor uses both dockable and child windows. The Code window is a child window that can be maximized, minimized, or restored, but it can never be moved outside the boundary of the Visual Basic Editor window.

Other windows that are located around the edge of the Visual Basic Editor—the Project Explorer window, for example—are initially set to be dockable windows, just like toolbars. You can dock these windows to the top, left, bottom, or right sides of the Visual Basic Editor window, or you can transform them into floating windows by dragging them away from their docked position. You can even make a dockable window, in turn, dock with another floating window. To prevent a floating window from docking, hold down the Ctrl key as you move the window. To switch a dockable window from floating to docked, double-click its caption. All the Visual Basic Editor windows except the Code window can be made into dockable or child windows simply by right-clicking the window and selecting the Dockable command from the context menu.

When you work with macros that manipulate Microsoft Office documents, be sure to close all windows except the Code window, maximize the Code window, and then reduce the size of the Visual Basic Editor window so you will be able to see the document in the background. (In other words, make the Code window just wide enough so that the menu fits on a single row.) As you need to review the contents of the other windows, you can cause the second Code window to become a child window, sharing the same display space as the first Code window. Press Ctrl+Tab to switch between child windows. Conversely, you can make the additional window dockable but floating, as shown in Figure 4-2. The small, floating window is unobtrusive, and you can close it when you no longer need it.

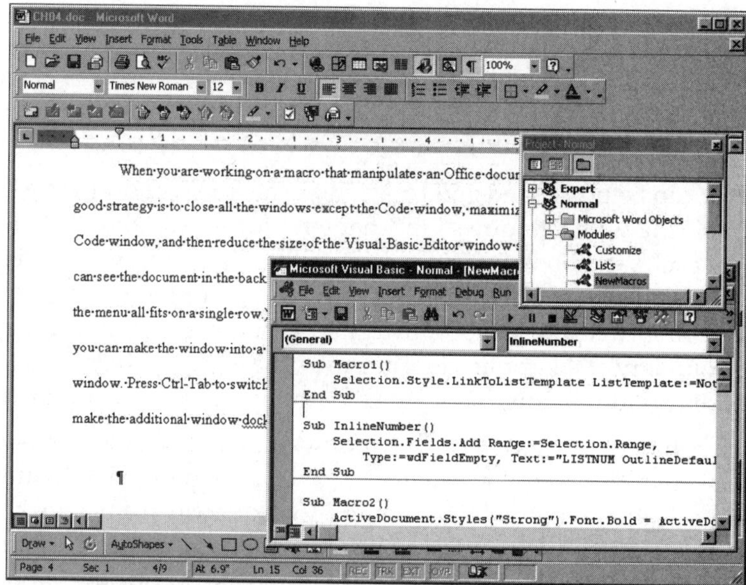

Figure 4-2
Shrink the Visual Basic Editor window so you can see the document behind it.

Changing the Default Font

Some Office applications allow you to zoom in on the text using the built-in zoom feature. You cannot zoom in on text in the Visual Basic Editor, but you can increase the font size being displayed by clicking Tools, Options, and selecting the Editor Format tab.

VBA can use any Windows font. Installing Office adds a wide selection of fonts you might want to consider. The Haettenschweilier font, which is installed with Office, is a splendid font with a splendid name. It is a very narrow font that can be increased in size up to 18 points, as shown in Figure 4-3, while still fitting just about as much on a single line as you can with the microscopic 10-point Courier New font used by default. You will see fewer lines, but that is usually not a significant problem.

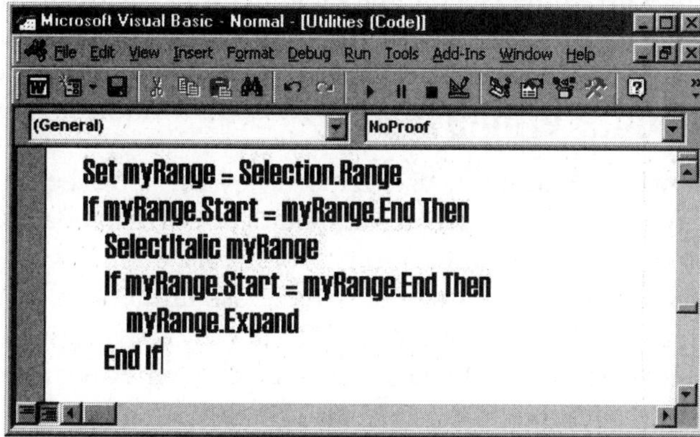

Figure 4-3
A large font is often easier to read.

Converting Code Lines to Commented Lines

When you work with macros, you will often need to indent or outdent multiple lines of code. The Visual Basic Editor makes this task very easy. As soon as you select more than a single line of code in the Code window, pressing the Tab and Shift+Tab keys will indent or outdent the lines you have selected, respectively.

A similar task consists of turning blocks of lines into commented code lines. A commented line of code does nothing in Visual Basic; Visual Basic treats the text following an apostrophe character as a comment and ignores the remaining text on the line. As you debug macros, you will occasionally need to comment out several lines of code. The easiest way to temporarily remove lines of code is to convert the lines into commented lines. This applies even if you want to convert only a portion of a macro into commented lines so you can use the macro in different programming scenarios.

The Visual Basic Editor does have commands to add and remove comment blocks in code, but they are difficult to find. You can use one of two techniques to make them easier to find and use. The Comment and Uncomment Block commands appear as toolbar buttons on the Edit toolbar, and they are the most useful (if not the only useful) buttons on that toolbar. Even though the Visual Basic Editor does not use adaptive menus commonly found in other Office applications, it does make use of adaptive toolbars. If you simply turn on the Edit toolbar and then drag it onto the same row as the Standard toolbar, it will display only the most frequently used buttons. Simply select the Comment Block and Uncomment Block buttons once to activate them as frequently used commands on the Edit toolbar. Of course, you can also copy or move the buttons to the Standard toolbar if you prefer.

If you prefer using keyboard commands, copy the two command buttons onto the Edit menu—perhaps just below the Indent and Outdent commands. For access keys, you could remove the ampersand character (&) from the Copy command and add it to the Comment command. Then, remove the ampersand character (&) from the Undo command and add it to the Uncomment command. You can then use either the mouse or the keyboard to comment and uncomment blocks of text.

Using the Immediate Window

The Immediate window is an extremely useful tool. The ability to execute statements one at a time has been one of the key features that made the original BASIC language a big hit back in the 1960s, and this same ability works for you in Visual Basic's Immediate window. To see the Immediate window, choose Immediate Window from the View menu, or press Ctrl+G. If your Visual Basic Editor window is small, you can enlarge the Immediate window by right-clicking the window and deselecting the Dockable command from the context menu.

Executing Commands in the Immediate Window

You can execute any Visual Basic statement in the Immediate window. This gives you an opportunity to test a code statement before you place it into a macro. For example, you can use the Immediate window to change the date and time on your computer. First, display the Date/Time Properties window (double-click the clock in the system tray, or right-click the time and choose Adjust Date/Time from the context menu). In the Immediate window, type *date = "12/31/1999"* and press Enter. The date in the calendar immediately changes. This is an *immediate action.* Next, type *time = "11:59:55 PM"* and press Enter again. Watch the numbers reflect the immediate action you just created, as shown in Figure 4-4.

Displaying Values in the Immediate Window

You can also use the Immediate window to display the value of an expression. An *expression* is anything that can be simplified to a single value. To display the value of an expression, type a question mark (?) and the expression, and then press Enter. For example, you can use the Immediate window to display the current date and time. Type *?Now* and press Enter. Typing *?Date* will show the current day, and typing *?Time* will show the current time. Typing *?Now* will show both values at the same time. (You cannot use *Now* to change the system clock.)

You can use a question mark to display the value of more than one expression, which is useful if you want to determine whether an expression has a trailing space, for example. If you use a space or a semicolon to separate the expressions, the values

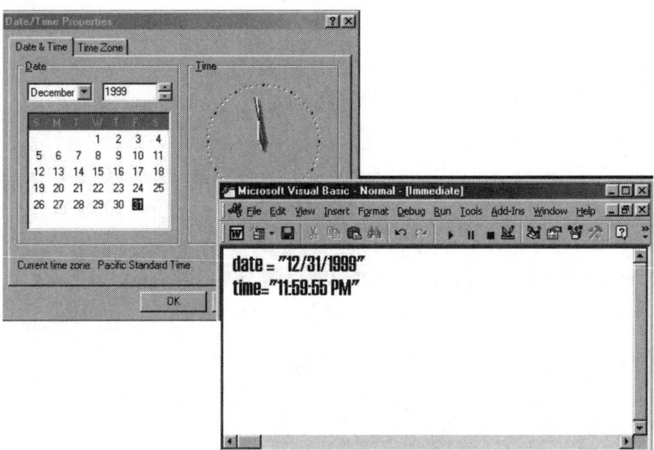

Figure 4-4
Use the Immediate window to change the system clock and calendar.

will appear with no space between them. The example shown in Figure 4-5 shows how to use semicolons to detect whether the variable *myVariable* contains a string with a trailing space. Displaying only the variable will not let you see the trailing space, but placing a bracket around the variable using short string constants will clearly reveal the space.

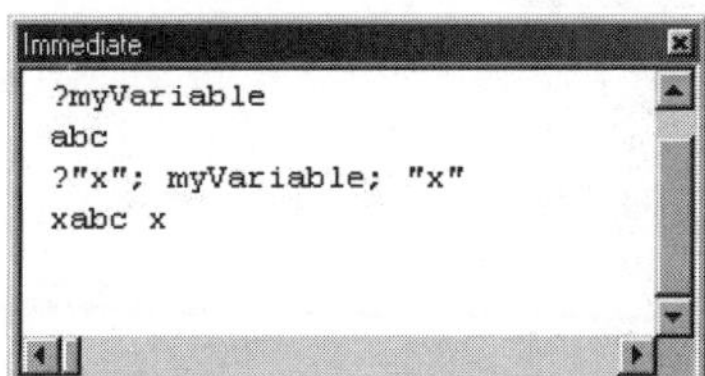

Figure 4-5
Use a semicolon to help detect trailing spaces in values.

If you use a comma to separate the expressions, the value will appear as though it has been separated by tab stops 14 characters apart.

Writing Values to the Immediate Window from a Macro

You can also use the Immediate window as a place to display information while a macro is running. The running macro can write messages to the Immediate window, and you can then view the messages as you step through the macro or after the macro has completed execution.

To write the value of an expression to the Immediate window from a macro, type *Debug.Print* and then type the expression. (Debug.Print is equivalent to adding the question mark to the statements in the Immediate window.) You can type *Debug.Print Now* into the Immediate window and it will display the date and time. You cannot, however, use the question mark in a macro.

Suppose your macro called *ChangeDirectory* is designed to change the current folder to D:\Temp, but you cannot determine why it is not working, even though you used the ChDir command to change the current directory. By adding Debug.Print statements to the macro, as shown in Figure 4-6, you will be able to see that the ChDir command really does change the directory on the D drive, but that D:\Temp does not become the current directory until you use the ChDrive command to change the current drive.

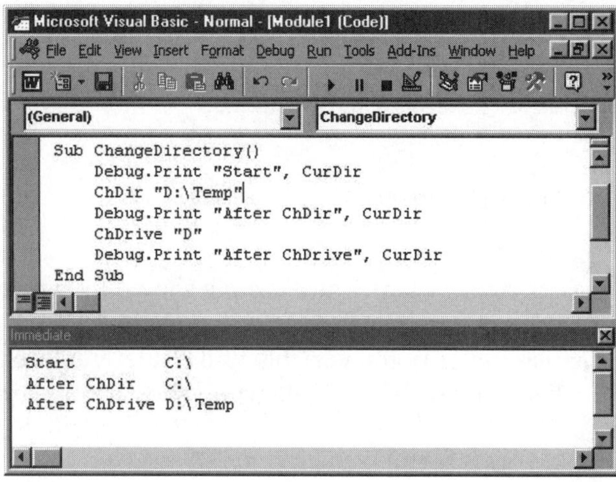

Figure 4-6
Use Debug.Print to show messages from a macro in the Immediate window.

When you print to the Immediate window from a macro, you can place a semicolon after the last expression in the statement to leave the insertion point in the Immediate window at its present location on the same line. The next time you print to the Immediate window, any value printed to the window will follow at the location of the insertion point, which is very useful when you are displaying values in a loop. You can even use a comma before the semicolon to separate the values with a tab stop. The *ShowLoop* macro shown in Figure 4-7 prints the loop counter each time it iterates through the loop, but each number from the loop execution appears on the same line. The Immediate window shows the result of running the macro three times. If you were to omit the *Debug.Print* statement from the end of the macro code, then the second time you run the macro, it would continue to print on the same line.

Executing a Loop in the Immediate Window

In the Immediate window, you can execute a single line of code. Typically, a single line of code consists of a single statement, but you can place multiple statements on a single line by separating each statement except the last with a semicolon. You can

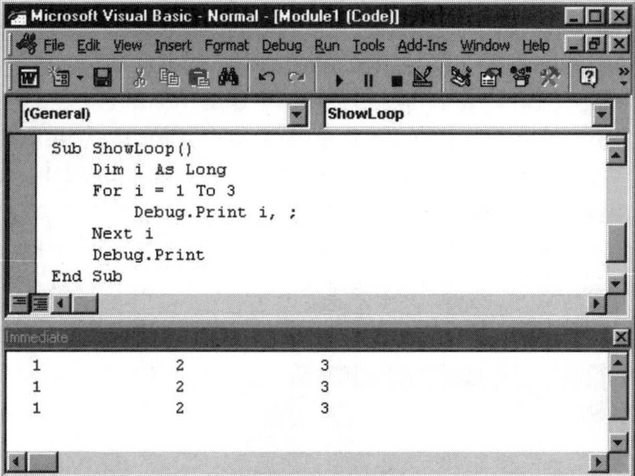

Figure 4-7
Use a semicolon to keep output on the same line.

combine statements on a single line even in a macro—which some macro writers do—but statements in a macro are easier to read if each statement is on a separate line.

In the Immediate window, however, combining statements on a single line provides significantly more flexibility. One particularly useful technique is to execute a loop entirely within the Immediate window. Figure 4-8 shows a simple loop executed multiple times in the Immediate window.

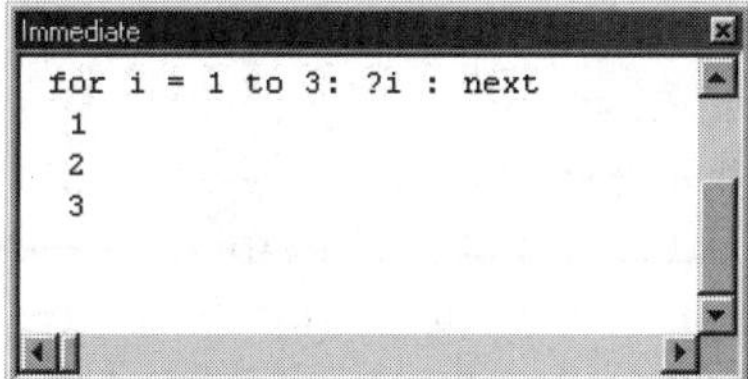

Figure 4-8
Execute a loop on a single line in the Immediate window.

Figure 4-9 illustrates a single line of code in the Immediate window, which is the equivalent of the entire *ShowLoop* macro shown earlier in Figure 4-7.

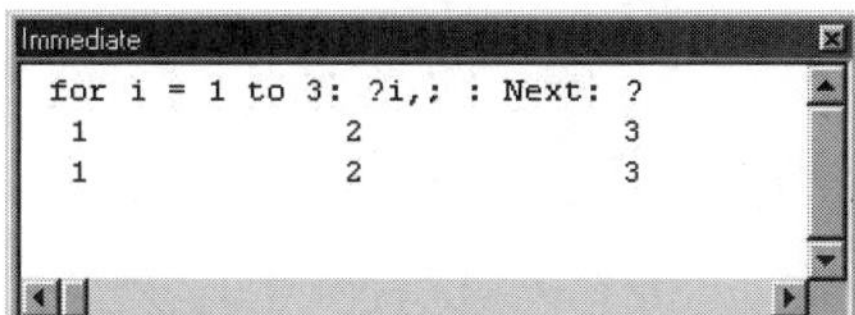

Figure 4-9
A loop in the Immediate window can be compact but cryptic.

Displaying the result of loop statements in the Immediate window is particularly useful when you are exploring a collection and are uncertain what items it may contain. For example, Word has a Tasks property that returns a Tasks collection representing all applications that are running. You use a loop structure statement to determine what applications are running so that you can display all the items from the collection in a single statement, as shown in Figure 4-10. See "Looping Through a Collection" in Chapter 5 for more information about using For Each loop statements.

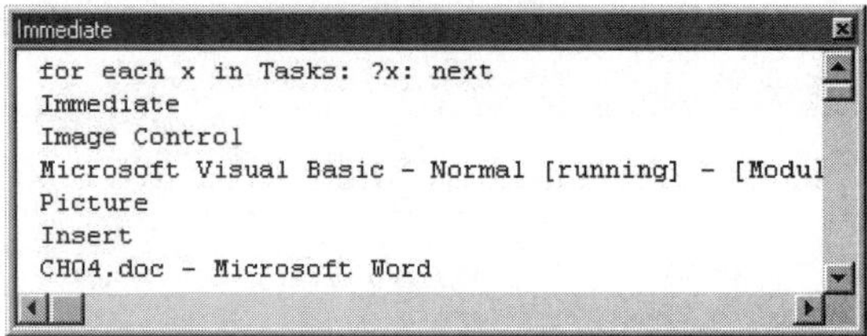

Figure 4-10
Use a loop in the Immediate window to explore a collection of objects.

Understanding the Limitations of Multiple Statements

Combining multiple program statements on a single line does have some limitations. For example, the colon cannot be used to combine statements in an If structure on a single line. The first line of code shown in Figure 4-11 produces an *End If* without Block If error message.

There are two ways to display the result of an *If* test in the Immediate window. The first method is to use a single-line *If* statement rather than the more common block If structure. The second executable statement shown in Figure 4-11 illustrates how you can enter the *If...Then...Else* statement on a single line. The second method is to use an *IIf* (Immediate If) function. The third executable statement shown in Figure 4-11 illustrates how to achieve the same result using an *IIf* function. The *IIf* function is an expression and not a statement, so the question mark is placed at the beginning of the line.

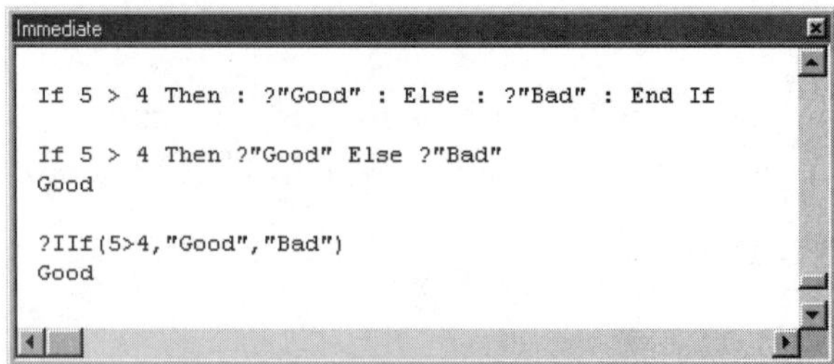

Figure 4-11
Placing an If structure routine on a single line might generate an error.

You can't use a colon to combine the parts of a With structure in the Immediate window. (For a more thorough explanation of using a With structure, see "Understanding the With Structure" in Chapter 5, "Explore Office Object Models.") For example, each Office application has Top and Height properties that describe the application window. If you want to display the value of those properties, you could use the Top statement shown in Figure 4-12. If you are displaying the values of many properties of an object, however, you may not want to type the complete object reference. You cannot use a With structure in the Immediate window. The second code statement shown in Figure 4-12 produces an error message. One way to resolve this problem is to assign the object reference to a short variable name and then use that variable name, as shown in the third statement in Figure 4-12.

```
Immediate
?Application.Top Application.Height
 125   450

With Application : ?.Top .Height : End With

Set x = Application
?x.Top x.Height
 125   450
```

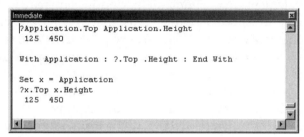

Figure 4-12
You can't combine a With structure onto a single line in the Immediate window.

If you are stepping through a macro, and the macro is in the middle of executing a With structure, the Immediate window allows you to use expressions that use the With structure. In Figure 4-13, for example, because the macro is in the middle of the With structure, the statement in the Immediate window can use the properties of the Application object.

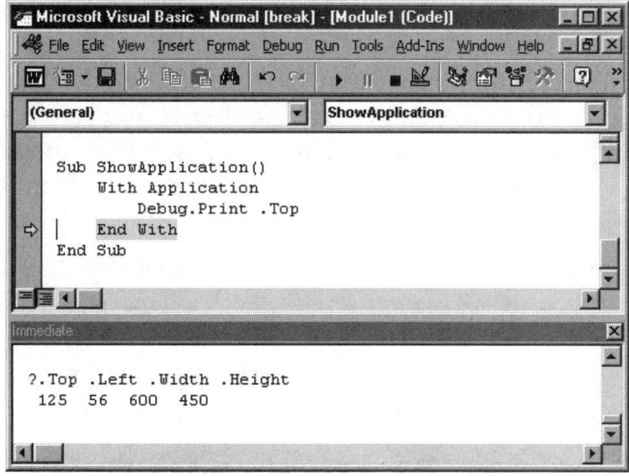

Figure 4-13
The Immediate window recognizes a With structure while you step through a macro.

Working with Existing Statements in the Immediate Window

You can execute a statement in the Immediate window by pressing Enter anywhere in the line, not just at the end. This makes it easy to execute an existing statement a second time: just press the Up arrow key as needed, and then press Enter. It also makes adding a question mark to the beginning of an expression very easy: just press the Home key, type the question mark, and then press Enter.

You might want to insert a new line into the middle of a group of existing statements in the Immediate window. The normal method for adding a new line—pressing the Enter key—doesn't work, because it simply executes the statement on the current line. To enter a new line, press Ctrl+Enter instead.

After creating several statements in the Immediate window, you may want to copy the statements into a macro. The normal rules for selecting, copying, and pasting text all apply within the Immediate window. You can even press Ctrl+A to select all the contents of the window. Remember any values that are not complete statements require a question mark to display the value. When you paste statements from the Immediate window into a macro, Visual Basic converts each question mark into the Print keyword. If you want the statement to continue printing to the Immediate window, you must add Debug and a period before the Print, as in *Debug.Print*.

Using Visual Basic Terminology

Visual Basic sometimes uses confusing terminology. You will be able to understand documentation and dialog box messages if you learn the difference between similar—but related—terms.

Working with Procedures and Macros

When you write a macro, you are really writing a Visual Basic procedure. A *procedure* (sometimes called a routine) is a chunk of program code with a name. The term macro refers to those procedures you can run from the Macros dialog box. Specifically, a macro is a procedure that begins with the word Sub and that has empty parentheses following the procedure name, as in *MyMacro()*. A macro is a procedure that you can launch directly—usually by assigning a shortcut key to the macro, by adding the macro to a toolbar button, or by selecting the macro from the Macros dialog box and clicking the Run button.

You can write procedures that are not macros. These non-macro procedures are run (or called) from other procedures or macros. Think about the hard drive on your computer for a moment. It has a root folder. That root folder can contain subfolders, which may or may not contain subfolders of their own. A macro is like a root procedure. It can call other procedures which, in turn, might call other procedures of their own.

Working with Statements and Expressions

The word *statement* refers to any command Visual Basic can execute. Most of the time, one statement occupies a single line in a Visual Basic procedure. You can break a single statement up into multiple lines by adding a space and a continuation character—the underscore character—to the end of each line except the last. The underscore must follow the space; otherwise, the underscore could be part of a variable name. A line continuation character must occur between words in a statement.

A statement is different from an expression. An expression is a series of words that are ultimately equivalent to a simple value, such as a text string, a number, or a date. For example, *5 * 3* is an expression, because it is equivalent to the simple value of *15*. For that matter, the number *15* is also an expression, because it is also equivalent to the simple value of *15*. An expression can either be simple or complex. As long as a series of words can be evaluated to a single value, it is an expression.

An expression is not a statement; Visual Basic can't do anything with an expression by itself. If you assign the value of an expression to a variable, it becomes a statement. Likewise, if you display the value of the expression, it then becomes a statement.

Working with Projects and Modules

When you first open the Visual Basic Editor window, you see one large window used for storing code, and you also see two other, smaller windows. One of the smaller windows is the Project Explorer. If you don't see the Project Explorer window, click the Project Window button or press Ctrl+R. Figure 4-14 illustrates a sample Project Explorer window. A project is a way of grouping everything relating to Visual Basic for Applications for a single Office document. Each Office document can contain a single project.

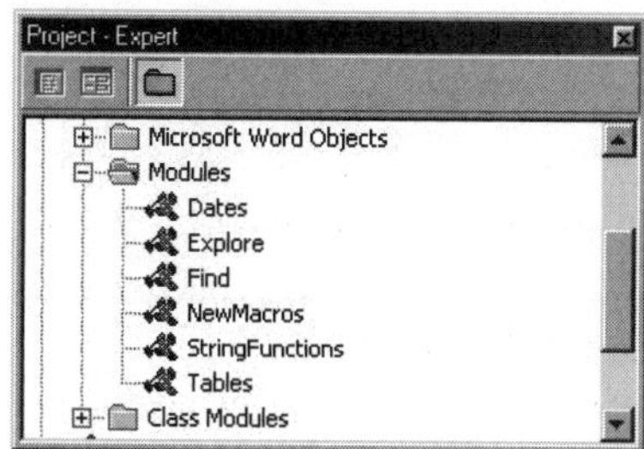

Figure 4-14
The Project Explorer window groups modules into folders.

When you create a new macro, either by creating it manually or by using the macro recorder, the macro is automatically placed into a *module*. In Word, the recorder always places new macros into the module *NewMacros*. In Excel, the recorder adds new macros into a module sheet named *Module1*, *Module2*, and so forth. Each time you close Excel and reopen it, the recorder creates a new module.

One folder that always exists is the folder for Office documents. In Word, the folder is named Microsoft Word Objects. In Excel, it is named Microsoft Excel Objects, and so on. Within the folder is a module for each component of an Office document. In a Word document, the document itself is the only component. In Excel, each worksheet is a component, plus another component for the workbook itself. These modules are used for attaching code to Office documents. "Creating Event Handlers" in Chapter 6 explains how to link code to Office documents.

Each entry within a folder in the Project Explorer window is called a module. Generic, general-purpose modules are listed in the Modules folder, while other, more specialized modules are usually placed in their own folder. To move from one module to another, double-click the module name in the Project Explorer window, or select the module and press Enter. The Project Explorer window can also contain folders named References, Class Modules, and Forms. Refer to the following sections later in this chapter for more information on the following windows:

- **References** See "Running a Procedure from an Automation Project."
- **Class Modules** See "Creating A Custom Object."
- **Forms** See "Creating A Custom Form."

Macros can move from one module to another using standard cut-and-paste techniques, and you can copy a macro from one module to another, provided the copy has a unique name within the module. To rename a macro, simply change the name in the Sub statement. To rename a module, select the module name in the Project Explorer window and click the Properties Window button or press F4, which will also display the Properties window. A module has only a single property: its name. Simply type a new name to replace the name of the module, as shown in Figure 4-15. You can then close the Properties window.

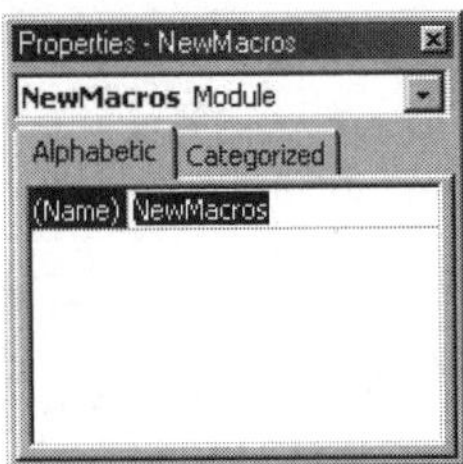

Figure 4-15
Use the Properties window to rename a module.

One effective strategy for dealing with module names—particularly when you use the macro recorder—is to let the macro recorder create a macro in its default module. You can then review and edit the macro to make sure it does what you want. Finally, rename the module, giving the module a name that reflects the type of macro it contains, or cut the macro and then paste it into an existing module. Using this approach, you can tell that any macro in a module with the default macro name is one that you have recorded but have not yet edited.

Making Macros Interactive

As you develop macros, you will want to see what is going on in the macro. You also might want to temporarily modify the behavior of a macro. Visual Basic has functions that allow you to interact with the macro.

When you create simple macros, you often want to be able to use a different value each time you run the macro. For example, in the section "Create A Dynamic Array" later in this chapter, the *ShowBigFile* macro searches the current folder for all files larger than 100-KB. What if you want to change the macro so that it checks for 5000-KB or 1-MB files?

One technique is to run the macro from Visual Basic so that you can change the value of the constant before you launch the macro. Another technique is to create a simple dialog box to prompt you for a value limit to check for. The InputBox function allows you to prompt yourself for a simple value. For example, to prompt yourself for a maximum file size and store that value in the variable *myLimit*, use the statement *myLimit = InputBox("Maximum file size")*.

The InputBox function always returns a string, even if you type a number into the box. You should always assign the value of the InputBox function to a variable that is either a string or a variant. If you assign the value to a numeric variable—such as Long—and then type a string into the input box, Visual Basic will display an error message and halt the macro. Once you've retrieved the value from the input box into a variable, you can use the IsNumeric function to test whether the variable contains a value that can be converted into a number.

Chapter 4

To check whether you clicked Cancel in the input box, check for an empty string. The statement *If myLimit = "" Then Exit Sub* will stop the macro if you click Cancel.

Displaying a Message and Asking a Question

If you want a macro to display a simple message, use the MsgBox function. Use the string that you want to display as the first argument of the function. For example, the statement *MsgBox "Today is " & Format (Date, "dddd")* displays the message Today is Wednesday, assuming you run the macro on Wednesday.

You can also use the MsgBox function to ask a simple question. The second argument for the MsgBox function is the Buttons argument. This argument allows you to specify which buttons to display on the message box. As soon as you type a comma after the first argument, Visual Basic displays a list of the possible buttons you can display. Some of the more common options are vbYesNoCancel and vbOKCancel.

You can even specify which button will be the default by adding a second component to the Buttons argument. After choosing which button configuration you want, type a plus sign (+). Visual Basic will display the same list of possible values from which you can choose. This time, select one of the options beginning with vbDefaultButton. For example, to display Yes and No buttons, with the No button as the default, use *vbYesNo + vbDefaultButton2* as the value of the Buttons argument.

You can add a third component to the Buttons argument to display an icon in the message box. At the end of the Buttons argument, type a plus sign (+), and then select one of these icon options from the list: vbCritical, vbExclamation, vbInformation, or vbQuestion.

When you use the MsgBox function to ask a question, you need to use the result—either by assigning the result to a variable or by using it in a conditional expression. Because you're using the result, you need to put parentheses around the argument. Also, when testing the value of the MsgBox function, never check for *True* or *False*. You must test for the appropriate named constant. After typing the closing parenthesis, type an equal sign (=) and Visual Basic will display the list of available constants for you to choose from.

One convenient way to use the MsgBox function is to warn yourself before you run a macro that takes a long time to execute by adding the following statement:

```
If MsgBox("This macro will take a long time. Do you want to continue?", _
    vbYesNo + vbDefaultButton2 + vbQuestion) = vbNo Then Exit Sub
```

Creating Variables

A *variable* is a place in memory where the value of an expression can be stored. You can create a perfectly usable macro without ever creating a variable; the built-in macro recorder does it all the time. For example, when you use VBA with Excel, you can always store any information you need in a worksheet cell and let the program do all the work of figuring out how to put that information into variables. So why would you ever need to create a variable?

- **You can see what you're doing.** When you write a macro, you're in a Visual Basic module. The document you're working with is in its own application. If you store a temporary value in a variable, you don't have to keep switching back to the application to see what the value of the variable is.
- **You can hide the value of the variable from the user running the macro**. If you store a value in a worksheet, for example, you or your user might inadvertently change a value that is important to a macro you are running.
- **Macros will run faster.**
- **You will do less typing.** Some Visual Basic expressions are very long, particularly expressions dealing with objects. If you store the value of the expression in a variable, you can use it repeatedly without retyping.
- **You can get Help from Visual Basic.** When you use certain types of variables, Visual Basic displays helpful tips as you type your code.

When you create a variable, Visual Basic needs some way of knowing what kind of information is to be stored in the variable. The computer stores everything as a series of ones and zeros—the exact same series of ones and zeros can be used for the number 0169 or for the symbol character ©, depending on the way the computer interprets it.

Using Simple Value Data Types

Variables come in two flavors—simple values and objects. Simple values are things like numbers, text, and dates. Visual Basic has 10 data types, in approximately the order of how likely you are to find them useful. These data types are shown in Table 4-1.

Name	Use
String	Used for text.
Long	Used for numbers having up to 9 digits that do not include a fraction.
Double	Used for large numbers, or for numbers that include fractions. Double data types use scientific (exponential) notation to store very large or very small numbers; after about 15 significant digits, they starting rounding the number.
Date	Used for date or time values.
Boolean	Used for values that can be only true or false.
Currency	Used for counting billions of dollars without loosing track of pennies.
Decimal	Used for counting galaxies without losing track of electrons.
Byte	Used for manipulating complex binary data such as pictures or sound recordings.
Integer	Used as a small version of Long (essentially obsolete).
Single	Used as a small version of Double (essentially obsolete).

Table 4-1
Simple value data types.

The *Dim* statement is used to declare (or dimension) a variable, which includes the name you want to assign to the variable, the word *As*, and the data type of the variable. The variable name can contain uppercase or lowercase letters, plus underscore characters anywhere after the first letter. A variable name cannot contain a space or any other punctuation, and it cannot match a built-in Visual Basic keyword. For details about naming rules, search Visual Basic Help using the words *Visual Basic Naming Rules.*

Some variable names are more descriptive when they contain multiple words in the name. One way to separate the words in a variable name is to use an underscore character. You might use *first_name* as a variable. Another common way to separate the words is to make the first letter of each word uppercase. For example, you might use *FirstName* as a variable name. Some programmers use the first letter of the data type name as the first letter of the variable name, followed by a descriptive term for the variable. Using that approach, you can tell that *sFirstName* is a string variable.

Another simple approach for naming variables is to prefix each variable with *my*. Using this prefix guarantees that your chosen variable name will not match any built-in keywords. In other words, you could use *myName* as a variable, even though *Name* is also a Visual Basic keyword.

Requiring Variable Declarations

Variables do not have to be declared. However, if you don't declare a variable, Visual Basic will implicitly declare the variable for you whenever you use a term it doesn't recognize. For example, the *ShowTime* macro is the shell of a macro for timing other macros. The first statement stores the current time in a variable. The last statement subtracts that time from the new current time, multiplying that value by the number of seconds in a day, to display the answer in seconds.

```
Sub ShowTime()
    myTime = Now
    ''' do something slow
    MsgBox (Now - myTine) * 86400
End Sub
```

As you can see in the code listing above, the variable *myTime* is not declared in the macro using the *Dim* statement. The first time it appears, Visual Basic implicitly declares a variable and stores the current time in it. Theoretically, the second time the variable appears, Visual Basic would retrieve the stored value. However, the macro listing contains a typographical error. The second occurrence of the variable is misspelled, but Visual Basic is unconcerned. It simply declares a new variable implicitly with an initial value of zero. Because of the typographical error, no matter how fast this macro runs, it will always appear to take a very long time (unless, perhaps, you run the macro just after midnight).

The solution to this problem is to configure Visual Basic so that variable declaration is required for each variable you use. If you take that step, Visual Basic will display an error message if you ever use an undeclared variable, which can be very annoying. On the other hand, it will also display an error message if you ever mistype a variable name, which makes the annoyance worth enduring. To require that all variables be declared, type *Option Explicit* at the top of the module. Option Explicit applies only to the module that contains it. If you create a new module, you must add Option Explicit to the top of that module, as well. The best approach is to configure Visual Basic to always place Option Explicit at the top of every module. To do that, activate the Visual Basic Editor and click Tools, then Options. On the Editor tab, select the Require Variable Declaration check box, as shown in Figure 4-16. This step does not add Option Explicit to existing modules; you'll have to do that yourself.

Using Object Data Types

Objects are a way of organizing the hundreds or thousands of values that constitute features like documents, workbooks, and databases. Visual Basic can deal with an arbitrary number of object types. Office exposes hundreds, if not thousands, of dif-

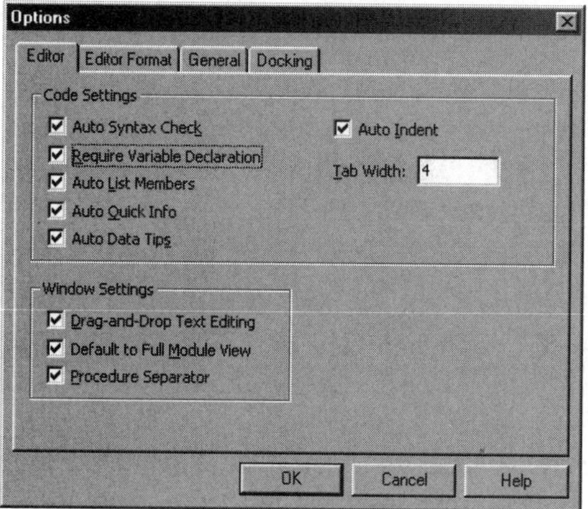

Figure 4-16
Option Explicit in each new module will force variable declaration.

ferent object types. The section "Creating A Custom Object" later in this chapter explains more about what objects are, and "Explore Office Object Models" in Chapter 5 deals with how Office applications use objects.

Using Variant Variable Types

You don't have to specify a data type at the time you declare a variable. Visual Basic will actually tag the variable with the appropriate data type at the time you assign a value to it. For example, if you have a variable named *myValue* and assign the number 52,422 to it, Visual Basic will tag its data type as Long. If you then assign *What time is it?* to the variable, Visual Basic switches the data type to String. A variable that allows Visual Basic to dynamically tag it with the correct data type is called a Variant.

Variants are, technically speaking, slightly larger and slightly slower than single-purpose variables, but not enough that you are likely to never notice any difference. In a test macro that looped 100 million times, it took 26 seconds to run when the counter was a Variant data type. When the counter was a Long data type, it took 20 seconds. The next time you need to create a loop that runs 100 million times, you might want to be concerned about whether you use a Long or a Variant data type. You also might want to empty the ashtray in your car to improve your gas mileage.

The best argument in favor of explicitly specifying a data type is that Visual Basic can help you avoid errors. Consider the *CheckTime* macro in the following code listing. This macro is the same as the *ShowTime* macro shown earlier, except that it explictly declares the *myTime* variable and there are no spelling errors. There is an error, however. In the middle of the code being timed, there is an inadvertent statement that accidentally assigns a text string to the variable *myTime*.

```
Sub CheckTime()
    Dim myTime
    myTime = Time
    ''' lots of code goes here
    ''' this statement is buried in the middle
    myTime = "Leonardo"
    ''' lots more code goes here
    MsgBox (Time - myTime) * 86400
End Sub
```

When you run the *CheckTime* macro, Visual Basic will display a Type Mismatch error. If you click Debug, it will highlight the error in the final statement where the code is attempting to subtract *myTime* from *Time*. As far as Visual Basic is concerned, this statement contains an error because you can't subtract a text string from a time value. As far as you are concerned, however, this statement is not the one that contains the real error.

If you change the variable declaration to *Dim myTime As Date* and then run the macro again, you will receive the exact same Type Mismatch error. But this time, when you click Debug, Visual Basic will highlight the statement buried in the middle of the macro at the point where you assigned the text string to the variable. The highlighted statement is the one that you need to fix. By declaring the data type of the variable, you were able to get more meaningful help in finding the error.

On the other hand, there are valid reasons why you should use a Variant data type. In some cases, you might legitimately want a variable to switch from one data type to another. This is particularly true when you assign a value from an unknown origin to a variable. For example, in Excel the value stored in a cell can be of any data type. If you are going to assign the value from a cell into a variable, you might want to declare the variable as a Variant. Once you have copied the value, you can use the Typename function to determine its actual data type.

Using Special Values For Variants

In addition, using the Variant data type allows you to take advantage of some special values that might be useful to you in some unique situations. Suppose you declare the variable *myBalance* as a Double data type. Visual Basic will automatically initialize it to contain a zero. There is no way for you to tell whether *myBalance* is zero because your expenses have exactly matched your income, or because you have never assigned a value to it. Conversely, if you declare *myBalance* as a Variant data type, it is intialized with the special value *Empty*. In the statement *myBalance = myBalance + 100*, the *Empty* value is treated like a zero and the statement works fine.

However, you could also check to see whether you had ever initialized the balance. The statement *If IsEmpty(myBalance) Then MsgBox "New Checkbook"* will display the message only if you have never assigned a value to the variable. When you are ready to begin a new accounting cycle, you can use the statement *myBalance = Empty* to restore the variable to its pristine state. A variable that contains the *Empty* value behaves the same as an empty cell in Excel.

The *Empty* value allows you to check whether a variable has been initialized, but it behaves like a zero or a Null string based on the context. Sometimes, you want to indicate that a value is not available. The special Null value means that the variable explicitly contains nothing. The statement *myBalance = Null* assigns the Null value to the variable. Visual Basic never automatically initalizes a variable to *Null.* A variable containing Null is very similar—but not the same as—a cell containing the value *#N/A* in Excel. If you use a variable containing Null in a numeric expression, the result will be *Null.* For example, if *myBalance* contains Null, then after the statement *myBalance = myBalance + 5000, myBalance* will still contain a Null. Think of it as a closed checking account.

You can't display a Null value in a message box. If *myBalance* contains *Null,* the statement *MsgBox myBalance* generates the error message Invalid Use of Null. You can, however, combine a Null with a string, where it will be treated as an empty string. The statement *MsgBox "My balance is " & myBalance* simply displays My Balance Is if the variable *myBalance* is *Null.* This is different from the value *#N/A* in Excel, which results in *#N/A* even when combined with a string.

Be careful when dealing with Null values in a comparison. If *myBalance* is *Null,* then the statement *If myBalance < 5000 Then MsgBox "Warning"* will not display a warning, because the result of the comparison is not *True,* but rather *Null.* In fact, adding *Else MsgBox "Good"* to the statement would still not display anything, because *Null* is neither *True* nor *False.*

When a variable might contain a Null value, you must explicitly test for a Null value by using the IsNull function. The statement *If IsNull(myBalance) Then MsgBox "Not available"* will display the appropriate message if the variable contains a Null. You can be tricked by a Null value: The statement *If myBalance = Null Then MsgBox "Not available"* will never display a message. This is because the Null constant will never cause the test condition to result in either *True* or *False.* Always use *IsNull* to test for a Null value.

Sometimes—particularly in the Immediate window—you might want to find out the data type of a value stored in a Variant. See "Using the Immediate Window" earlier in this chapter for more information about working in the Immediate window. The Visual Basic IsDate and IsNumeric functions return *True* if a value in the Variant can be converted to a date or a numeric value, but these don't necessarily tell you the data type in the variable. The best way to determine the data type stored in a variable is to use the TypeName function, as mentioned earlier. For example, after the statement *myValue = #1/1/2000#* assigns a date to the variable *myValue,* entering the statement *?TypeName(myValue)* in the Immediate window will display the word *Date.*

You can use the TypeName function to test the data type of any expression. With a date still stored in the variable *myValue,* typing the statement *?TypeName("Today is " & myValue)* into the Immediate window will display the word *String.* The

Chapter 4

TypeName function is particularly useful when you are exploring unfamiliar methods and properties of objects, as explained later in "Exploring With the Immediate Window" in Chapter 5.

Making a Variable Retain its Value

When you declare a variable inside a procedure using *Dim*, the variable is only valid within that procedure. As far as any other procedures are concerned, the variable does not exist. As soon as the procedure ends, the variable ceases to exist. If you run the procedure a second time, Visual Basic will create the variable anew.

You can cause a procedure-level variable to retain its value—even after the procedure has finished running—by substituting the word *Static* for the word *Dim* when you declare it. A static variable can count how many times a procedure has been run, which is illustrated in the following *AddOne* macro that will display a higher number each time you run it:

```
Sub AddOne ()
    Static i As Long
    i = i + 1
    MsgBox i
End Sub
```

Most of the time, you can make changes to macros without losing the value in a static variable. Some changes—notably adding or deleting a procedure, changing the declaration of a static variable, or changing a With structure—will reset your project, causing all static variables to lose their values. If you want Visual Basic to warn you when a change will reset your project, click Tools, Options, General, and select the Notify Before State Loss check box.

You can also force a variable to retain its value by making it a module-level variable. Module-level variables are discussed in the section "Create A Team Of Cooperating Functions" later in this chapter.

Creating Arrays of Variables

Sometimes you want to create multiple copies of a variable. For example, suppose you want to create a macro that reads through all the files in the current directory, accumulating the name of each file with a length greater than 100-KB. In principle, you could create a number of separate variables named *File1*, *File2*, *File3*, and so forth. However, it would be impossible to manipulate those filenames within a loop. Also, you probably won't know how many files there will be, so it will be difficult to create the right number of variables.

Creating and Using a Fixed-Sized Array

To create multiple copies of a variable, you create an array. To create an array, declare a variable in the usual manner, and then add parentheses after the name of the variable. Within those parentheses, place the number of elements that you want in the array. The statement *Dim myFile(5) As String* declares a string variable with six copies.

To refer to a single element from the array, place the number of the element in parentheses after the element name. The statement *myFile(3) = "Normal.dot"* assigns a filename to the fourth element of the array. Visual Basic counts array elements starting from zero; when you declare an array, the number you use specifies the highest element number, not the total number of elements. This means that the statement *Dim myFile(5) As String* creates an array with six elements, with *myFile(0)* as the lowest element and *myFile(5)* as the highest element.

When specifying the elements for an array, you can specify both the bottom and the top values. For example, the statement *Dim myFile(3 To 6) As String* creates an array with four elements numbered from three to six.

You can force Visual Basic to use *1* as the default base element within a module by adding the statement *Option Base 1* to the top of the module. You cannot, however, force Visual Basic to automatically add the statement to the top of new modules. Because you might often encounter arrays that use zero as the bottom element, you should probably get used to checking for the base value.

The LBound and UBound functions return the numbers for the bottom and top elements of a given array. For example, if you used the statement *Dim myFile(3 to 6) As String* to declare an array, the expression *LBound(myFile)* returns *3* and the expression *UBound(myFile)* returns *6*. When looping through an array, you should always use both the LBound and UBound functions, as illustrated in the following code fragment:

```
For i = LBound(myFile) to UBound(myFile)
    Debug.Print myFile(i)
Next i
```

Creating a Dynamic Array

When using arrays, you often will not know how many elements are needed until the procedure is running. The *Dim* statement that declares the array is not an executable statement, so you can't place a variable inside its parentheses. What you can do, however, is place nothing within the parentheses, creating a *dynamic array*. Once you have created a dynamic array, the *ReDim* statement can be used to change the size of the array. A *ReDim* statement looks just like a *Dim* statement (without the type declaration, since you can't change the data type), but it is an executable statement, so you can place a variable inside its parentheses.

When you use the *ReDim* statement, Visual Basic clears the existing contents of the array. When you are changing the size of an array—for example, when you want to add a new element to an existing array—add the word *Preserve* after the word *ReDim* in the statement. The following *ListBigFiles* macro shown below builds an array containing the name of each file in the current folder that is longer than 100-KB.

```
Sub ListBigFiles()
    Const myLimit = 100000
    Dim myFile() As String
```

```
    Dim myTest As String
    Dim myCount As Long

    myTest = Dir("*.*")
    Do Until myTest = ""
        If FileLen(myTest) > myLimit Then
            ReDim Preserve myFile(myCount)
            myFile(myCount) = myTest
            myCount = myCount + 1
        End If
        myTest = Dir
    Loop

    For myCount = LBound(myFile) To UBound(myFile)
        Debug.Print myFile(myCount)
    Next myCount
End Sub
```

When it is followed by a string argument, the Dir function finds all the files that match the specified string using standard Windows wildcard characters. However, it returns only the first file from the list. When you call the Dir function with no argument, it returns the next file from a previously initialized list. When there is no file remaining in the list, the Dir function returns an empty string.

The FileLen function returns the length of the file whose name you pass as an argument. In the macro, if the file length exceeds the limit defined by the *myLimit* constant, the filename is added to the array.

The sequence of the three statements inside the If structure is very important. The *myFile* array initially has no elements. Before assigning a value to the first element of the array, it must be resized to contain a single element; the number of the first element is zero. The *myCount* variable has an initial value of zero. The *ReDim Preserve myFile(myCount)* statement uses that zero value to set the top element of the array. The statement *myFile(myCount) = myTest* also uses that zero value to put the name of the file into the first element. The *myCount = myCount + 1* statement increments the value of *myCount* in anticipation of the next loop.

Note You can't add or delete elements from the middle of an array. Neither can you use a descriptive key to refer to an element; you must use the element number. Office 2000 has a new Dictionary object that enhances arrays to remove both of these limitations.

Rather than use an array at all, you can store multiple values in a Collection object. The section "Creating A Collection Object," later in this chapter, explains how to create and use a Collection object.

Storing an Array in a Variant

When you declare an array as a variable, you create multiple copies of that variable, storing the copies into an array. You can also store an entire array in a single variable, as long as the variable is declared as a Variant. This is called a Variant Array, and it is used to store the values of an existing array. Each element in a Variant Array is a Variant. That means you don't need to worry about whether all the data values for the array are the same data type.

A common use for a Variant Array is when you are working with cell values in Microsoft Excel. You can retrieve the values from entire range of cells and put those values into a single variable as a Variant Array.

Visual Basic also has an Array function that creates an array which you can store in a Variant. To use the Array function, you specify the values for the array as arguments to the function. The expression *myList=Array("January", 500, #1/1/2000#)* assigns three different values—each with its own data type—to a single Variant Array variable. Once the values have been stored in a Variant, they are retrieved the same as if you had explicitly declared the array. For example, the statement *Debug.Print myList(1)* writes the number *500* in the Immediate window, provided that there is not an *Option Base 1* statement at the top of the module.

You cannot, however, use a *ReDim* statement to change the size of a Variant Array. The only way to control the size of a Variant Array is to assign an existing array to the variable. Once a Variant Array exists, you can change the value of any element. So you can create an empty three-element Variant Array in a variable by using the statement *myList=Array(0,0,0)*. The statement *myList(2)="Dog"* could then change the value of the third element.

Because each element in a Variant Array is itself a Variant, you can assign an entirely new Variant Array to any one element. For example, given the *myList* array shown earlier, you could execute the statement *myList(0)=Array(5,4,3)*, which would assign a new Variant Array to the first element of the original Variant Array. The statement *Debug.Print myList(0)(1)* extracts the second element of the nested array and displays it in the Immediate window. (The ability to nest Variant Arrays is intriguing—and watching it work clarifies the behavior of both the Variant data type and of a Variant Array—but no practical application has been found for it yet.)

Working with Text Strings

One of the most useful skills you can develop in working with Visual Basic in Office is that of manipulating text. In Word, PowerPoint, and FrontPage, you rarely deal with anything except text. In Word, even numbers in a table are text that Visual Basic must reinterpret before using it in calculations. Even Excel and Access contain tremendous amounts of text. Visual Basic uses the term string to refer to text, because text consists of a series of characters strung together.

Using an Operator to Concatenate Strings

There is only one operator used with strings—the ampersand character (&)—which you use to join two strings together. If one of the input strings is actually a number, the ampersand operator will convert it to a string for you. If the variable *myPage* contains a number, the statement *"Page " & myPage* will prefix an introductory word to it. If you want a space between strings, you have to add it yourself.

Note Originally, Visual Basic used the plus sign (+) both to add numbers and to concatenate strings. Technically, you can still use the plus sign (+) to add strings, but if one of the values is a number, it will try to add the string to the number, which will produce an error. It is much better to leave the plus sign (+) to addition and use only the ampersand character for concatenating strings.

Using String Functions

VBA provides several string processing functions. Each function has a very good description in Visual Basic Help. You can view a list of all the string functions in the Object Browser. Click View, and then click Object Browser, or press F2. In the upper left corner of the Project/Library drop-down list, select VBA. The Members Of <Globals> list on the right side shows all the VBA functions. The Classes list on the left side shows the categories each of the functions are grouped into. In the Classes list, select Strings to see the functions relating to text strings. Figure 4-17 illustrates a few of the string functions.

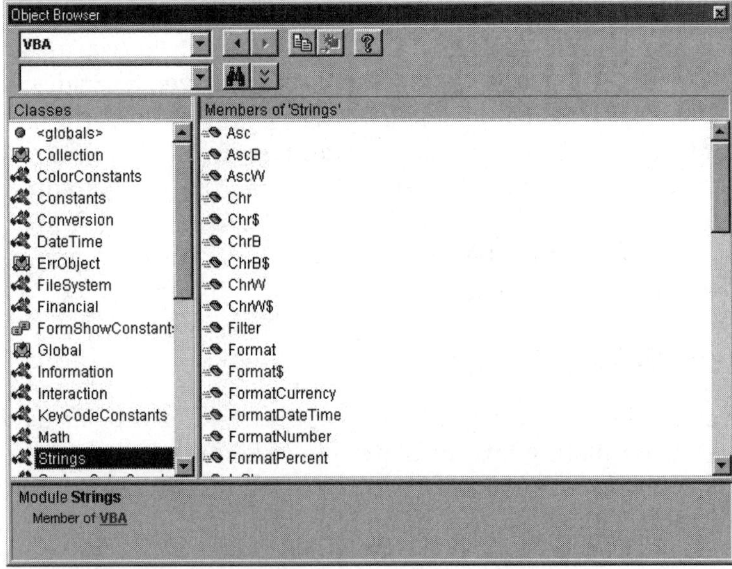

Figure 4-17
The Object Browser shows VBA functions grouped into categories.

If you see an interesting function in the right-hand list, select it and click the Help button (the question mark at the top of the Object Browser) to view the Help topic for that function.

Understanding String Function Suffixes

Many string functions come in two versions: one that ends with a dollar sign ($) and one that does not. In the early versions of BASIC, variables could not be declared and assigned a data type. To specify the type of a variable, a special character was added to the end of the variable name. The dollar sign was the secret code indicating that the variable was a string. A vestige of that old system is still in effect today. Technically, a function name ending with a dollar sign suffix returns a String, while a function name which does not end with a dollar sign will return a Variant. You will be hard-pressed to find any difference between the two versions, however. Ignore the version ending with a dollar sign and be grateful you no longer need to use special suffix characters.

Some string functions end with the letter W (for *Wide*). In an effort to deal with non-European languages, Visual Basic supports Unicode strings, which take up twice as much space (they are twice as *Wide* in variable parlance) as non-Unicode strings. The wide function versions are used to work with Unicode strings. As long as you are working only with European languages, you can ignore the wide functions. (If you want to see Unicode characters in action, activate Word and click Insert, Symbol. Then select Times New Roman as the font face and scroll through the list of available characters.)

The Trim function removes unnecessary spaces from the beginning or end of a string, which can be useful when you are working with Word documents, where the definition of a word often includes any spaces following the word. It is also useful in Excel so that you don't accidentally type an extra space at the end of a cell value. The *Trim* function is typically used in a statement such as *sInput = Trim(sInput)*, which removes extra spaces from a variable. Visual Basic also provides a Trim function for removing spaces from the beginning of a string (LTrim) or from the end of a string (RTrim). In most cases, you will want to remove all leading and trailing spaces.

The Len function tells you how many characters are in a string, and the Left and Right functions extract the first or last letters of a string. You simply provide the number of characters you want returned. The Mid function extracts letters from the middle of a string; you tell it the starting position and the number of characters you want and it does the rest. Suppose the string *sYYMMDD* contains the text string *990503*. Use the following statements to extract the year, month, and day portions from the string:

```
iYear = Left(sYYMMDD, 2)
iMonth = Mid(sYYMMDD, 3, 2)
iDay = Right(sYYMMDD, 2)
```

The *UCase* function converts all characters in a string to uppercase letters. In addition to its more obvious use, UCase is very good for making case-insensitive comparisons. Rather than work through several program options, as in *If sInput = "HTML" or sInput = "html" or sInput = "Html"* (which risks missing a meaningful combination), simply convert both strings to uppercase before comparing them, as in *If UCase(sInput) = "HTML"*. You can also use the LCase function to convert a string to lowercase letters.

Converting a Number to a Formatted String

One of the most useful tools for handling numbers and dates in Visual Basic is the Format function, which is used to convert numbers into a string using the format you specify. The Format function requires two arguments. The first argument is the number you want to convert, and the second argument is a description of how you want to format the number, which can be a text string using codes to indicate how the number is to be formatted. For example, using the expression *Format(Date, "mmm yyyy")* formats the current date to show both the month and the year. This version of the Format function is very similar to the TEXT worksheet function in Excel.

In addition to a custom formatting code, the second argument of the *Format* function can also be a predefined, named format. One advantage to using a named format is that you can use standard formats that have been defined in the Windows environment. For example, to format the current date using the long form of the date, use the expression *Format(Date, "Long Date")*. For complete information about all the formatting options, display the Help topic for *Format Function* and click See Also.

Visual Basic provides other functions for converting numbers into strings, but none are as flexible as the Format function. In particular, you will very rarely need to use the Str function, which simply transforms a number into a string, because Visual Basic will automatically convert a number into a string if the context requires it.

Note Dates in Visual Basic are very similar to dates in Microsoft Excel. See "Manipulating Dates" in Chapter 14 for additional information about working with dates.

Structuring Macros

When you create short, simple macros, you usually don't need to worry about breaking the macro into smaller pieces. But as you start to create more complex macros, you will find yourself using the same lines of code in many of your programs. You might also find that a macro becomes so long and unwieldy that it is hard to understand how it is executing. The solution in both of these situations is to break the macro into smaller pieces. Small pieces are easier to reuse, and they are also easier to understand.

Creating Procedures

When you break a macro into smaller pieces, you create new, subordinate procedures, sometimes referred to as *sub procedures*. Sub procedures are more interesting than simple macros, because you can create a more flexible procedure by passing it information as it runs, and you can also choose to have the procedure pass information back to the macro that calls it.

Note When creating general purpose macros without using the macro recorder, always create a new module by clicking Module on the Insert menu in the Visual Basic Editor. You should add procedures to the document modules only when creating event handlers, as explained in "Creating Event Handlers" in Chapter 6.

Creating Custom Procedures

When you create a procedure, it begins with either the word Sub or the word Function. In the Object Browser, you can see that the Visual Basic built-in procedures all begin with either Sub or Function. A procedure beginning with the word Sub is often called a subroutine.

Press F2 to display the Object Browser. In the Classes list on the left, select the FileSystem Class. The list on the right will show the Visual Basic procedures relating to working with files. When you select a procedure on the right, you can see the definition and syntax of the procedure at the bottom. For example, as Figure 4-18 illustrates, the *CurDir* procedure is highlighted and the text at the bottom of the window informs you that it is a function.

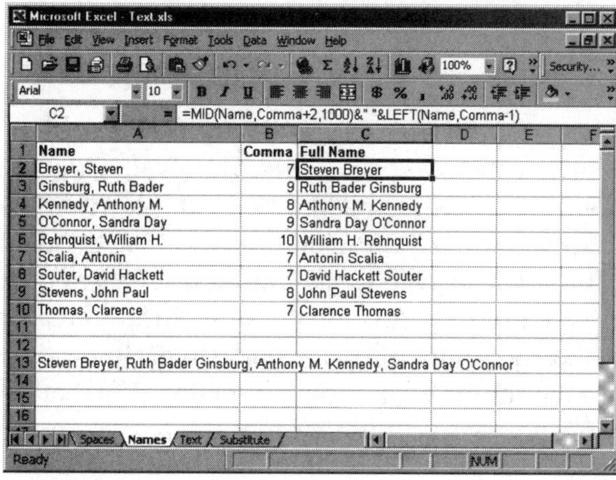

Figure 4-18
A function returns a value.

If you select the *ChDrive* procedure discussed earlier, the text at the bottom of the window shows that it is a subroutine. A function carries out an action and then returns a value; a subroutine carries out an action without returning a value. You could create a *ChangeToWindowsFolder* subroutine that changes the current drive and directory to C:\Windows, as shown in the following example:

```
Sub ChangeToWindowsFolder()
    ChDrive "C"
    ChDir "C:\Windows"
End Sub
```

This subroutine carries out an action—it changes which folder is current—but it does not return a value. It also qualifies as a macro because it begins with Sub and uses empty parentheses after the name—you could run it from the Macros dialog box. To call this subroutine from another macro, simply use the subroutine name, as the *TestProcedure* macro in the following example shows:

```
Sub TestProcedure()
    ChangeToWindowsFolder
    MsgBox CurDir
End Sub
```

Suppose you want the *ChangeToWindowsFolder* procedure to return the name of the folder it changed to. Before the procedure can return a value, you must change it to a function by replacing the word Sub with the word Function. Once you have changed it to a function, you assign the value you want to return to the name of the function—the name acts like a variable from inside the function. Here is the *ChangeToWindowsFolder* macro converted into a function:

```
Function ChangeToWindowsFolder()
    ChDrive "C"
    ChDir "C:\Windows"
    ChangeToWindowsFolder = CurDir
End Function
```

This function still carries out an action, but it now returns a value. (Incidentally, it is no longer a macro, so it does not appear in the Macros list.) What do you need to do to the *TestProcedure* macro so that it will keep working with *ChangeToWindowsFolder* converted to a function? The short answer is that you don't have to do anything. If you don't need the return value from a function, you can simply treat the function as if it were a subroutine and ignore the return value. (In early versions of Visual Basic, you could not ignore the return value from a function. You had to assign the value to a dummy variable before you could ignore it.)

New! In addition to the standard Visual Basic functions in the File System category, Office 2000 includes new tools that allow you to use objects to manipulate the file system.

Some programmers write every procedure as a function, never as a subroutine. If the function does not have a meaningful value to return, they design it to return *True*, indicating that the function completed successfully. Ultimately, the only reason you have to use Sub to define a procedure is to make it appear in the Macros dialog box.

Adding an Argument to a Function

One of the most important reasons for creating a procedure is so that you can use the same code in more than one macro. Rather than type the same five statements over and over again, you can place them into a subroutine or a function and reuse them. The *ChangeToWindowsFolder* function discussed earlier is a good example of this concept. This macro presumably does a useful task, but it does only one task without any possibility for variation. By passing an argument to the function, you can make it perform variations on a task, making it more usable.

Rather than continue with changing folders, let's explore arguments by creating functions that separate a text string into its component parts. This is called *parsing* a string, and it is a remarkably common task. The *GetFirstWord* function illustrated below does not take any arguments. The function searches for a space in the string. If it finds one, it returns everything before (but not including) the space. If it doesn't find one, it returns the entire string.


```
Function GetFirstWord() As String
    Const CheckString As String = "Beware the Ides of March"
    Dim i As Long
    i = InStr(CheckString, " ")
    If i > 0 Then
        GetFirstWord = Left(CheckString, i - 1)
    Else
        GetFirstWord = CheckString
    End If
End Function
```

As used in the previous example, the string *CheckString* is defined as a constant. A *constant* is like a variable, except that it can't be changed. *CheckString* appears three times in the body of the function. Converting it to a constant means you won't have to worry whether you typed it correctly all three times. Because it's a constant that appears at the top of the procedure, it is also easy to find and change to a new constant.

To test the function, open the Immediate window, type *?GetFirstWord; "x"*, and then press Enter. This brackets the result of the function with X characters so that you will be able to determine whether the return value includes a trailing space, as shown in Figure 4-19. Refer to the section "Using the Immediate Window," earlier in this chapter, for more details about using the Immediate window.

Changing the *CheckString* constant into an argument provides additional functionality to the function. To convert *CheckString* into an argument, place the statement *ByVal CheckString As String* between the parentheses after the function name and delete the *Const* statement, as shown in the following example:

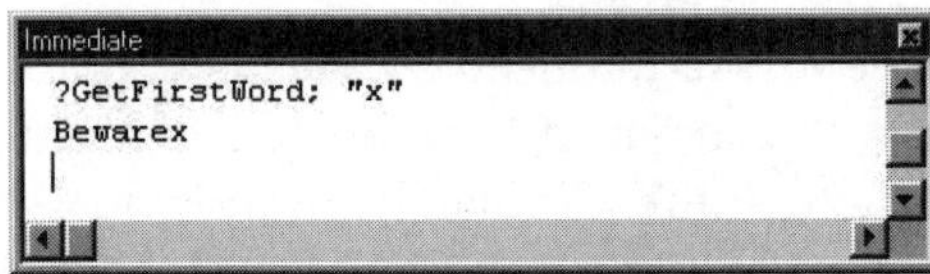

Figure 4-19
Display an extra character to check for trailing spaces.

```
Function GetFirstWord(ByVal CheckString As String) As String
    Dim i As Long
    i = InStr(CheckString, " ")
    If i > 0 Then
        GetFirstWord = Left(CheckString, i - 1)
    Else
        GetFirstWord = CheckString
    End If
End Function
```

Adding *ByVal* in front of an argument prevents the function from changing the variable's original value. In essence, it creates a local variable inside the procedure and copies the argument to it. While not required, it is a good idea to always add ByVal before any argument name unless you explicitly intend to change the argument value. This addition to the argument name prevents accidental errors, where the value of some variable suddenly changes and you can't determine what has changed it.

To test the revised function, type *?GetFirstWord("Good morrow to you"); "x"*, in the Immediate window and press Enter. The string *Goodx* should appear. You can now use the function in many more contexts than when it did not take an argument.

Adding an Optional Argument

The *GetFirstWord* function is usable in many contexts, but what if you have a text string where the component words are separated by commas instead of spaces? You could write a new function, but almost all the code inside it would be identical to the code in the *GetFirstWord* function. By passing a second argument that supplies the delimiter, you can make the function return the first string, regardless of how they are separated. The *GetFirstString* function illustrated below returns the first part of a string, delimited by the character you specify:

```
Function GetFirstString(ByVal CheckString As String, _
        ByVal Delimiter As String) As String
    Dim i As Long
    i = InStr(CheckString, Delimiter)
    If i > 0 Then
        GetFirstString = Trim(Left(CheckString, i - 1))
    Else
        GetFirstString = Trim(CheckString)
```

```
    End If
End Function
```

This function is identical to *GetFirstWord*, except that you now must explicitly provide the delimiter. It also trims the string before returning it, just in case the delimiter is not a string. You can test the new function in the Immediate window. Type *? "x"; GetFirstString("Caeser, Brutus, Cassius", ","); "x"* and press Enter. The display should show *xCaeserx*.

To use a space as a delimiter, however, you must now explicitly specify the space character. What if you use this function 90 percent of the time using a space as the delimiter? What if you added the second argument to an existing function—one you already used from several other macros? Adding the second argument would not be convenient. The solution is to make the second argument optional, using a space as the default value, as shown in this revised version of the *GetFirstString* function:

```
Function GetFirstString(ByVal CheckString As String, _
        Optional ByVal Delimiter As String = " ") As String
    Dim i As Long
    i = InStr(CheckString, Delimiter)
    If i > 0 Then
        GetFirstString = Trim(Left(CheckString, i - 1))
    Else
        GetFirstString = Trim(CheckString)
    End If
End Function
```

This function is almost identical to the preceding version—and you could use it precisely as before, always passing both arguments. The only difference is that if you omit the second argument, the function will behave as if you had passed a space. Adding an optional argument is an excellent way to increase the reusability of a function without increasing its apparent complexity—and without breaking up macros using the original version.

Changing the Value of an Argument

Often, when extracting the first word from a source string, what you really need to do is incrementally extract additional words: get the first word, and then the second word, and then the third word, and so on. One way to do this would be to add an argument telling the function which word to extract. A simpler approach, given that you want to extract the words in the order in which they come, is to delete a word from the source string as you extract it.

Because the source string is passed as an argument, deleting a word from it means that your function will change the value of the argument. This is called a *side effect*, which can be dangerous. If you call a function, oblivious of the fact that it has a side effect, inexplicable bugs can appear in your macros. Placing ByVal in front of arguments helps prevent side effects.

In this case, you are making a reasoned decision that you do want to have a side effect. The *ExtractFirstString* function shown below returns the first word from a source string, simultaneously deleting that word from the string:

```
Function ExtractFirstString(ByRef CheckString As Variant, _
        Optional ByVal Delimiter As String = " ") As String
    Dim i As Long
    i = InStr(CheckString, Delimiter)
    If i > 0 Then
        ExtractFirstString = Trim(Left(CheckString, i - 1))
        CheckString = Trim(Mid(CheckString, i + 1))
    Else
        ExtractFirstString = Trim(CheckString)
        CheckString = ""
    End If
End Function
```

Aside from changing the function name each time it appears, this new function is almost identical to the previous version of the *GetFirstString* function. One change is that the word in front of the *CheckString* argument is now ByRef instead of ByVal. The ByRef keyword means By Reference, which means that the argument does not make a copy of the original variable; rather, it points or refers to the original variable. If you make a change to the *CheckString* argument, you will also change the original variable in the macro that calls it.

The second change in this new function is that it now trims the first word from the string using the Mid function. If the function can't find the delimiter, the first word is the entire source string, and the function changes it to an empty string.

To call this function, you must use a variable to pass the source string. Naturally, if you pass the function a string constant, it can't change the constant. Figure 4-20 illustrates the two statements used to test the function.

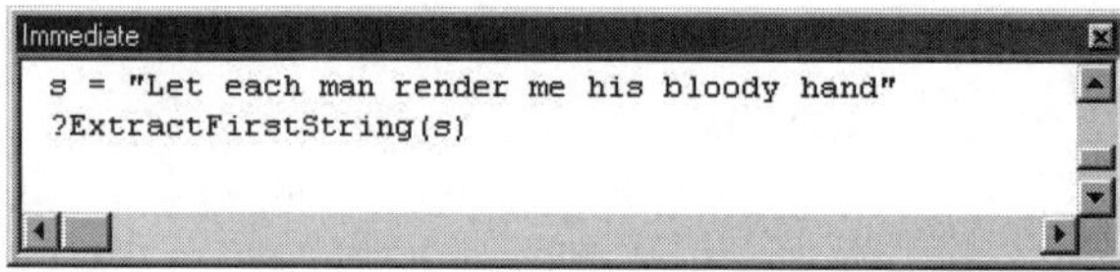

Figure 4-20
A function can modify an argument that has been passed as a variable.

If you try executing the two statements shown in Figure 4-20, Visual Basic will display a ByRef Argument Type Mismatch error message. Because a ByRef argument points to an existing variable, the variable must be of the same data type as the argument. In the macro, the *CheckString* argument is declared as a String. When you create a new variable in the Immediate window, Visual Basic implicitly declares it as a Variant. A Variant can contain a string, but a String variable can't point to a

Variant. The solution—and a good practice when you are creating a function that will modify an argument—is to define the argument in the function as a Variant.

After you change the definition of the *CheckString* argument to *ByRef CheckString As Variant*, you can execute the statements shown earlier in Figure 4-20. The first time you execute the *?ExtractFirstString(s)* statement, it displays the word *Let*. Executing the same statement a second time displays the word *each*. The third time, it displays *man*, and so forth.

Creating a Team of Cooperating Functions

The *ExtractFirstString* function behaves differently each time it is called, but that's only because the value of the argument also changes each time. The function depends on the main macro to keep track of the source string variable. Likewise, the main macro has to remember to use the same delimiter each time it calls the function.

You can create a pair of procedures—a *SetString* subroutine that initializes the source string and delimiter, and a *GetNextString* function that extracts (and removes) the first word from the previously defined string. Then, the main macro does not have to keep track of any variables. The *SetString* subroutine somehow needs to be able to communicate the values of the source string and delimiter to the *GetNextString* function. The way to do that is to create variables that come before any procedures in the module. At the top of the module, just below the *Option Explicit* statement that is surely there (see "Requiring Variable Declarations" discussed earlier), enter the following two statements:

```
Private myParseString As String
Private myDelimiter As String
```

These variables are called *module-level variables.* They are visible to any procedure in the entire module. If you replace the word Private with the word Public, the variables would be public variables—variables that are visible to any procedure in any module contained in the project. Public variables are generally dangerous to use, because it is too easy to absentmindedly change the value of a public variable without realizing the effect of that change on other procedures in your project.

Note Early versions of Visual Basic used the word *Dim* to declare a private module-level variable, and the word *Global* to declare a public variable. The keywords *Private* and *Public* were introduced to make the meaning of the module-level variables more obvious. Even though you can still use *Dim* and *Global* to declare module-level variables, you should always use the newer Public and Private terminology. You do need to use the word *Dim* to declare a variable inside a procedure.

With module-level variables in place, you can now create the two procedures that work together, as shown in the following example.

```
Sub SetString(ByVal NewParseString As String, _
        Optional ByVal Delimeter As String = " ")
    myParseString = NewParseString
    myDelimiter = Delimeter
End Sub

Function GetNextString() As String
    GetNextString = ExtractFirstString(myParseString, myDelimiter)
End Function
```

The *SetString* subroutine takes the two arguments; both use *ByVal*, but the delimiter is optional. The subroutine does nothing more than assign these values to the module-level variables. The *GetNextString* function—which takes no arguments, but which must be run after the *SetString* function has initialized the variables—simply calls the *ExtractFirstString* function using the module-level variables as arguments. If the *ExtractFirstString* function doesn't already exist, or if you don't want to keep it around, you can easily put its functionality into the *GetNextString* function.

Figure 4-21 shows how you can use the Immediate window to test these two procedures. The first statement assigns a value to the first internal variable and the second one—repeated three times—extracts successive words (which appear inverted because each new value pushes down the old values).

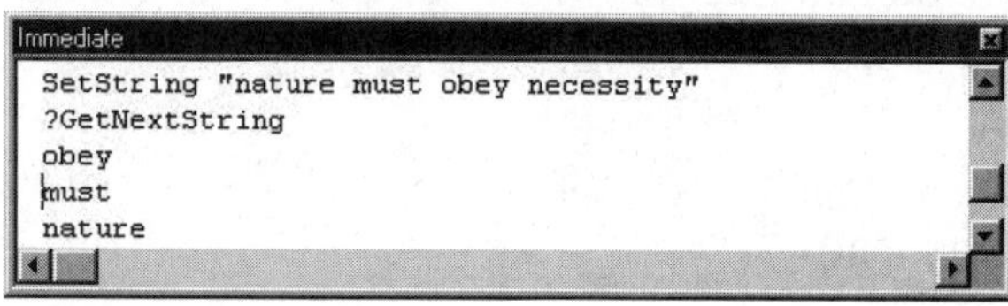

Figure 4-21
A module allows multiple, related procedures to share variables.

There are two reasons for grouping related procedures into modules. One is to make it easy to find related procedures. The other, more important reason is so that you can create private module-level variables that enable procedures to work closely together, while keeping the variables inaccessible to unrelated procedures.

Debugging Procedures

A bug is anything that keeps a procedure from running the way it's designed to run. According to legend, early computers exhibited strange behavior that was sometimes literally caused by insects crawling around inside the machine. In practice, bugs are caused by humans. It is you who will put the inevitable bugs into your macros, and it is you who must eliminate them. Fortunately, Visual Basic provides very good tools to help you track down and eliminate bugs.

Debugging a Procedure

The first step in eliminating a bug is finding it. Create a *TestString* procedure suitable for testing the *SetString* and *GetNextString* procedures, as shown in the following example:

```
Sub TestString()
    SetString "Farewell to you; and you; and you", ";"
    MsgBox GetNextString
End Sub
```

You will be able to work through this macro—and the procedures it calls, both directly and indirectly—as you learn about the Visual Basic debugging tools. In the Visual Basic Editor, the Debug toolbar contains buttons for the most important debugging tools. Figure 4-22 shows a slightly modified version of the Debug toolbar.

Figure 4-22
The Debug toolbar contains helpful buttons.

The four controls on the left side of the Debug toolbar repeat the controls found on the Standard toolbar; you can delete them without any loss. The Step To Cursor button, a very useful toolbar button, is not included on the default Debug toolbar.

Chapter 4

The Toggle Breakpoint button adds a breakpoint to the statement at the location of the insertion point. A *breakpoint* is most useful when you need to get through some introductory statements before you start stepping through the actual macro code. It causes the macro to stop execution so you can start debugging the procedure's execution one statement at a time (stepping through the procedure). Rather than use the Toggle Breakpoint button, it's easier to click in the gray margin to the left of a statement to insert a breakpoint. You can also add a more permanent breakpoint by inserting the *Stop* statement into a procedure. To start testing the *TestString* macro, click the gray margin to the left of the *SetString* statement in the Code window. A dark red circle will appear; this is a breakpoint.

Click in the *TestString* macro, and click the Run Sub/UserForm button to start running the macro. (If you want to start stepping through the macro from the beginning, click the Step Into button instead of the Run Sub/UserForm button.) The macro stops when it reaches the breakpoint, turning the statement yellow and adding a yellow arrow in the left margin, as shown in Figure 4-23.

Click the Step Into button to begin executing the *SetString* subroutine. You can watch each statement execute in turn. If you don't really want to step through this subroutine, click the Step Out button to execute the remainder of the statements and continue stepping through the macro only after returning to the calling procedure.

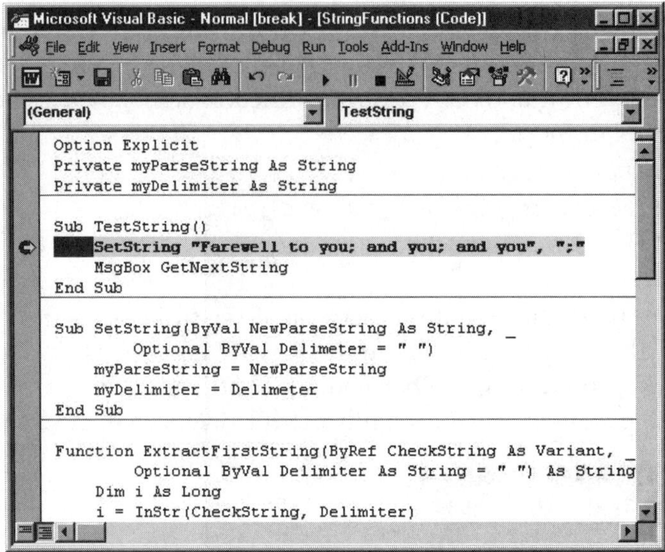

Figure 4-23
Setting a breakpoint allows you to step through a procedure.

Click the Step Into button to step into the *GetNextString* function. At this point, you can determine the value of the function name by holding the mouse pointer over the word *GetNextString* that appears in the middle of the macro. As shown in Figure 4-24, Visual Basic displays the value which, at this time, is an empty string.

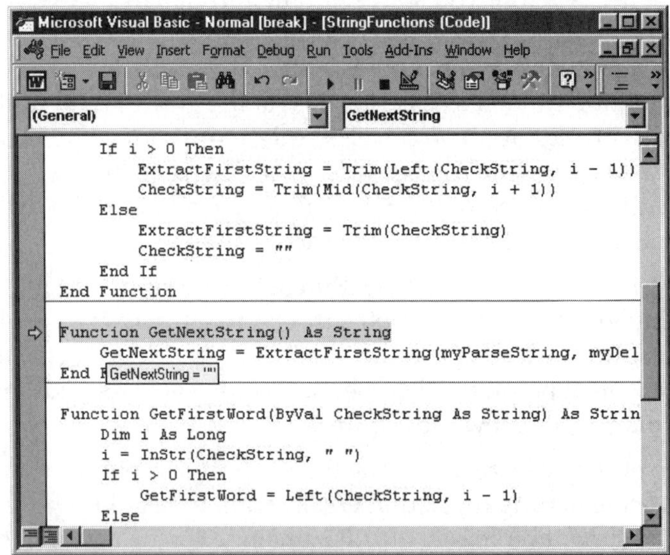

Figure 4-24
Hover the mouse pointer over a variable name to see its value.

You want to see the value assigned to the *GetNextString* function name without having to step through the entire *ExtractFirstString* function, so click the Step Over button twice. Hold the mouse pointer over the function name again to see the new value, as shown in Figure 4-25.

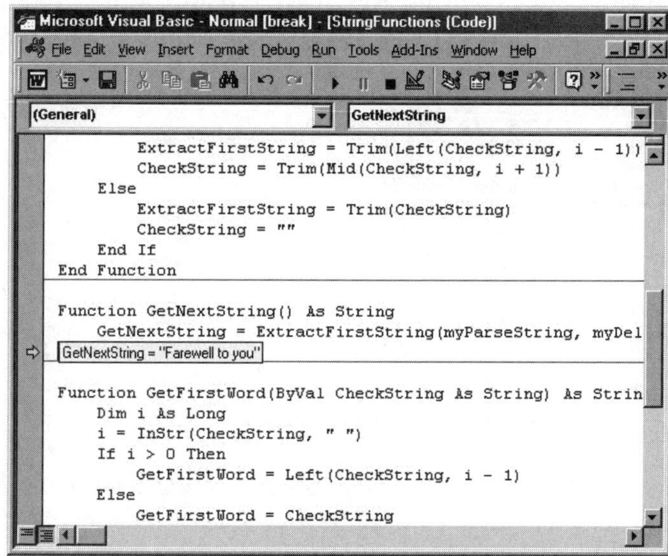

Figure 4-25
After running the function, the variable contains a value.

Suppose that you change your mind, and decide that you do want to watch the *ExtractFirstString* function at work after all. Drag the yellow arrow in the left margin back up to the statement that calls the function, and then click the Step Into button. You are now into a procedure that is nested three levels deep. It can be confusing to remember where you are. Click the Call Stack button, because the term for nested procedures is called a *stack*. This displays the Call Stack dialog box. Figure 4-26 displays the current procedure (*ExtractFirstString*), which is followed by the procedure that called it (*GetNextString*), which is then followed by the procedure that called it (*TestString*). Click the Close button to exit the dialog box. (Unlike most debugging tool windows, you cannot leave the Call Stack window open.)

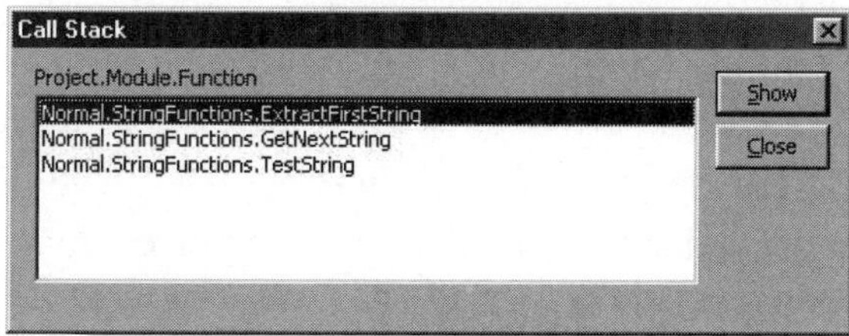

Figure 4-26
The Call Stack shows which procedure called the procedure currently executing.

The *ExtractFirstString* procedure contains a lot of variables—the module-level variables, the arguments passed, and the local variable—and you might not want to keep moving the mouse around to see each of the values. You can display a single window that shows the current value of all the variables. Click the Locals Window button. The Locals Window shows not only local variables, but also module-level variables. Just click the plus sign (+) next to the module name to see the module-level variables, as shown in Figure 4-27.

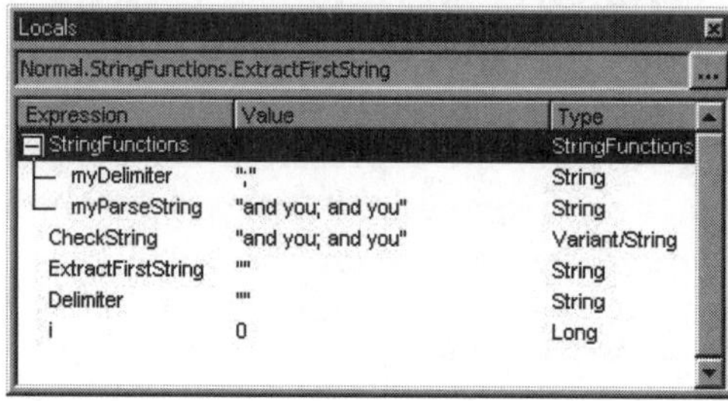

Figure 4-27
The Locals Window shows the value of each available variable.

If you want to slip back to an earlier point in the macro without changing the current statement—say, to check the values of the variables at that level—use the Call Stack dialog box to switch to a different part of the stack. The Locals Window changes to show the variables visible to the new procedure. As you step through the procedure, the values in the Locals Window change as the variable values change.

Looking at the Value of an Expression

You might want to see the value of an expression that is not a variable or an argument name. For example, suppose you want to see the value of the expression *InStr(CheckString,Delimiter)* before the statement containing it executes. You can use the mouse pointer to show you the value of most expressions. Select the expression and then hold the mouse pointer over it. Visual Basic will usually show you the expression's value.

There are some conditions where Visual Basic will not be able to show you the value of an expression. For example, Visual Basic will not show the value of an expression containing certain functions, such as Left. If you select the expression *Left(CheckString, i - 1)* and hold the mouse over it, you will see nothing. You can, however, still see the value of an expression even if the mouse pointer can't display it for you. Select the expression and click the Quick Watch button on the Debug toolbar. The Quick Watch dialog box will show you the value of the expression, as shown in Figure 4-28.

You should be careful using the Quick Watch window when you evaluate an expression that has a side effect. For example, hovering the mouse pointer will not show the value of the expression *ExtractFirstString(myParseString, myDelimiter)* in the *GetNextString* function because it would have to run the function to calculate the value. However, if you select the expression and then click the Quick Watch button,

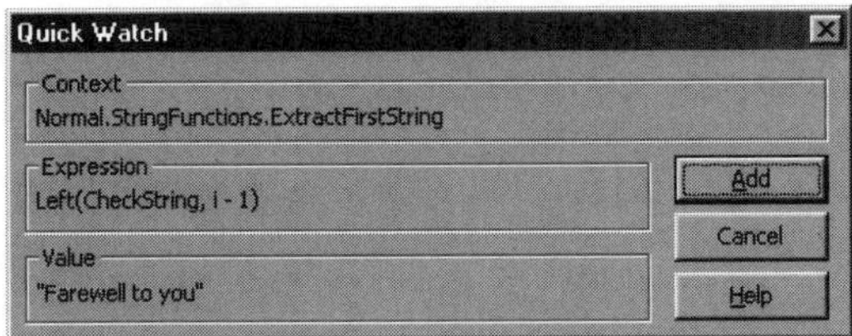

Figure 4-28
The Quick Watch window displays the value of any expression.

the dialog box will show you the value of the expression. The act of running the function to find out the value, however, removed the first word from the string, so you will receive a different answer when you execute the statement.

The Quick Watch dialog box shown earlier in Figure 4-28 contains a button labeled Add, which adds the expression displayed in the Quick Watch window as a permanent watch expression and then opens the Watches window so that you can see the new watch expression. Figure 4-29 shows an expression in the Watches window.

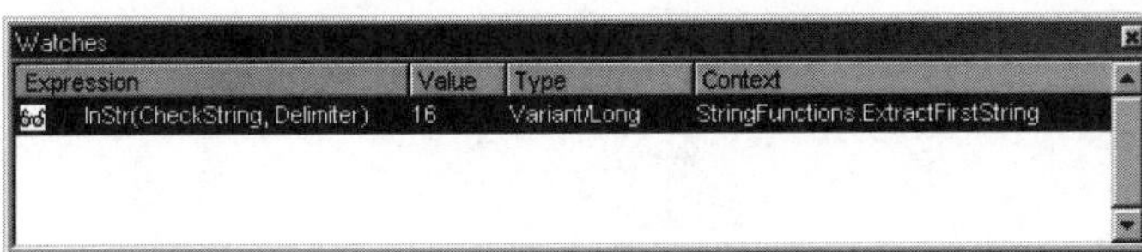

Figure 4-29
The Watch window continually displays an expression and its value.

You can also display the Watches window by clicking the Watch Window button on the Debug toolbar. You can add an expression to the Watches window by dragging the expression onto the Watches window or by selecting an expression, right-clicking in the Watches window, and choosing Add Watch from the context menu. When you add a watch expression, it doesn't have to be an expression appearing in the code itself. You can add any legitimate expression that returns a value—for example, anything that you could type after an equal sign (=) in the Immediate window.

Once you add an expression to the Watches window, it stays there until you delete it by right-clicking the expression in the Watches window and choosing Delete Watch from the context menu. If the expression is part of a function that is not currently in the Call Stack, the Value column shows the message Out Of Context. An expression in the Watches window executes once for each statement that gets executed, so the same cautions about watching an expression that has side effects also apply to the Quick Watch window—only more so.

Adding an expression to the Watches window is often more trouble than it is worth. You have to open the Window, add the expression, ignore it when the expression is out of context, and then delete the expression to remove it from the Watches window. It is often easier just to use the Quick Watch window, or to type the expression after a question mark (?) in the Immediate window.

The Watches window becomes extremely useful when you allow an expression to trigger the procedure to stop executing and start stepping through the code—in other words, to create a *dynamic breakpoint*. For example, suppose you believe there is a problem when the *ExtractFirstString* function encounters a substring longer than 10 characters, but you're not sure when you will encounter such a substring. Click in the *ExtractFirstString* procedure and then click Debug, Add Watch, and type the expression *Len(ExtractFirstString)>10*. Then select the option Break When Value Is True, as shown in Figure 4-30, and click OK to enable the watch expression.

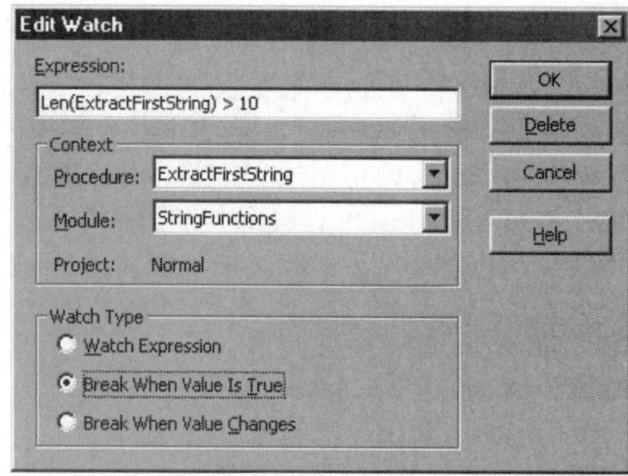

Figure 4-30
A watch expression can serve as a dynamic breakpoint.

As soon as the function encounters a sub-string longer than 10 characters, the code will shift to break mode and you can use all of Visual Basic's debugging tools to track down the error.

A dynamic breakpoint is particularly useful in a large loop, where you might want to switch to break mode when the loop counter gets to be greater than, say, 1000. A dynamic breakpoint can also be useful when the value of a variable is being changed and you're not sure what is causing the change. By setting Watch Type to Break When Value Changes, the Watch setting can help find the devious code for you.

Controlling Error Messages

Visual Basic's tools for helping you avoid errors can become intrusive. For example, the Visual Basic Editor checks for many kinds of errors, even while you create a new statement. As soon as you move the cursor away from a line, the Visual Basic Editor scans the statement for errors. If the statement contains errors, the Visual Basic Editor will turn the statement red and display a message explaining the error.

When you first start writing Visual Basic statements, you might like to see the descriptive messages, but as you become more proficient you might find that seeing the statement turn red is often enough to help you to identify and correct the error.

When you get to the point that you find the descriptive error message annoying, you can simply turn it off by clicking Options on the Tools menu, and then clicking on the Editor tab to clear the Auto Syntax Check check box. The check box label is misleading: Even with the check box turned off, Visual Basic will still automatically check for syntax errors. It simply won't show you the message that describes the error.

If a program statement turns red but you can't identify the error, turn the Auto Syntax Check option back on. You will need to make some change to the statement to display the message. It is sufficient to type a space at the end of the line, and then press the Down arrow key to trigger the message.

Handling Run-Time Errors

An error—often called a run-time error—is different from a bug. A run-time error can't be detected until the time that you actually run the statement. For example, if you assign the result of an InputBox function to a variable that is declared as a Long data type, then the statement will work fine as long as you type a numeric value into the input box. But if you type a string into the box, Visual Basic will recognize an error when it tries to assign the value to the variable.

Visual Basic has default behaviors for dealing with, or handling, errors. When Visual Basic attempts to execute a statement containing an error, it displays a dialog box that gives you the option to end the macro or to switch to debug mode. If you switch to debug mode, Visual Basic will highlight the offending statement so that you can determine what the problem is.

Visual Basic has specialized features that allow professional developers—those who develop applications that can be used by thousands of users—to create sophisticated error-handling mechanisms. As long as you are writing macros for your own use, Visual Basic's default error-handling mechanism is usually sufficient. Even if you're not trying to create a bulletproof application, however, you can add simple error-handling features to some of your macros to make them more convenient to use, even for yourself.

Ignoring Errors

Some of what Visual Basic thinks of as errors are really not errors and can simply be ignored. For example, if you use the *Kill* statement to delete a file and the file does not exist, Visual Basic considers that action an error. If you are deleting the file, however, you probably don't care that the file doesn't exist. In cases like these, you can simply ignore the error. To ignore errors, add the statement *On Error Resume Next* to your macro. After encountering this statement, Visual Basic will simply ignore errors in any subsequent statements, always continuing to the next statement.

As you can imagine, the *On Error Resume Next* statement is something you should use with discretion. You might want to ignore errors for one or two statements, and then return to the default error-handling mechanism. To restore normal error handling, enter the statement *On Error GoTo 0*. You can also add a conditional statement to check whether an error occurred. The keyword Err returns a zero if no error has occurred. If an error has occurred, Err returns the error number—the number Visual Basic displays in the standard error dialog box. For example, the error number for attempting to delete a nonexistent file is 53. If you want to be informed that the file did not exist, you could use the following statement in your code:

```
If Err = 53 Then MsgBox "The file did not exist".
```

Trapping Errors

In some macros, you might simply want to jump to the end of a macro if an error is encountered. For example, you might write a macro to modify the currently selected field in Microsoft Word. If the selection does not contain a field, you don't want the macro to run at all. Often, the simplest way to write this kind of macro is to attempt to manipulate the field, which will trigger an error if no field exists. You then force Visual Basic to jump to the end of the macro when it encounters the error.

Forcing Visual Basic to jump to a specific location whenever it encounters an error is called *trapping* the error. The target location is called an *error handler*. To create an error handler, place a label at the beginning of a line. A label is simply a word (using the same rules as creating variable names), followed by a colon, followed by nothing else on the line. Technically, you can place a label anywhere within a procedure, but you should place it very close to the bottom of the procedure to make it easy to spot.

You might want to use a standard label—such as ErrorHandler—so that you can easily copy the error handler code from one procedure to another. To set the error trap, enter the statement *On Error Go To ErrorHandler*, where ErrorHandler is the name of your error handler label. From the time the macro encounters the error trap statement, any error that would normally display the error dialog box will cause Visual Basic to jump to the specified label.

When trapping for an error, you need to consider what will happen if the error does not occur. Visual Basic does not stop executing when it reaches a label; it simply ignores the label and continues. If you put an error handler label immediately before the end of the macro, and there are no statements in the handler, then you can let the macro continue to run through the error handler to the end of the procedure.

Many times, however, the error handler will contain statements—such as displaying a message box—that should run only when an error does occur. In this case, you need to make the procedure end before it gets to the error label. To do that, enter the statement *Exit Sub* (or *Exit Function*) before the error handler label.

Creating an Error Trap in a Sub Procedure

One of the nice things about trapping errors with Visual Basic is the way error handling works when calling subroutines and functions. When you set an error handler in a main procedure, that same error handler is in effect for any sub procedures. If you add a different error handler in a subroutine, that error handler takes effect only until the sub procedure ends or until an *On Error GoTo 0* statement restores the previous error handler. For example, the *KillFile* macro shown in the following example deletes a file, adding an *On Error Resume Next* statement for the possibility that the file might not exist:

```
Sub KillFile(ByVal FileName As String)
    On Error Resume Next
    Kill FileName
End Sub
```

Even though this subroutine disables error handling altogether—a dangerous operation as previously noted—the error handler returns to its previous state at the end of the subroutine.

One effective technique for using an error handler is to create an easy way to cancel an entire macro, even from a subroutine. To do this, create an error handler in the main procedure that jumps to the end of the macro. Then, in a subroutine that displays a dialog box, enter the statement *Err.Raise 0* to trigger an error if you click the Cancel button. The error handler in the main procedure traps the error, and the macro jumps to the label at the end. You can type any number after the *Err.Raise* statement; the number becomes the error number that Err will return. For more information about error handling, see the Visual Basic Help topic for the *On Error* statement.

When you are writing macros for yourself, you don't need to create perfect error-handling procedures. Occasionally, however, adding simple error-handling features to your macros can make them run much more smoothly.

Using Procedures From Outside Your Project

In a VBA project, you can run procedures from other projects. There are two ways to do this, depending on how the external procedure was written.

Running a Procedure From an Automation Project

You might want to run a procedure contained in a project that was created using Automation. This includes any projects created using Visual Basic for Applications—whether in the same Office application or in a different Office application. To access a procedure from a different Automation project, you create a reference to that project. For example, in Word, you can create a reference to a document (or template) that contains procedures. In the Visual Basic Editor, click Tools, References, and then click Browse. Navigate to the folder containing the document, select it, and then click OK. The new document appears in the list of references with a check box next to the name. After you close to References dialog box, the new project appears in the References section of the Project Explorer window. (Word automatically creates a reference to an attached template.)

In "Using Objects From Other Office Applications" in Chapter 5, you will learn how to create a reference to a different Office application so you can use code from Excel, for example, even while you are writing a macro in Word.

Running a Procedure From a Dynamic Link Library

You might want to run a procedure from a project that stores its procedures in a *Dynamic Link Library*, or DLL. The Windows operating system includes several DLLs that contain procedures you can use. A DLL does not support Automation, and you can't simply add a reference to the DLL. You must create a specific link to each procedure in the DLL that you want to use.

Caution If you use a procedure from a DLL incorrectly, you can cause an error that will shut down your application, or even the operating system. Before trying to use a procedure from a DLL, be sure that you have saved your work in all Windows applications.

Before you can access a procedure from a DLL, you must know the definition of the procedure. The most widely used reference for using Windows DLL procedures from Visual Basic is the book *Visual Basic Programmer's Guide to the Windows API* by Daniel Appleman. With a very few exceptions, anything that you can do with a DLL in one of the standalone editions of Visual Basic, you can also do using Visual Basic for Applications.

Once you know the definition of a Windows DLL procedure, you add that definition using a *Declare* statement at the top of a module. Once you have added the declaration, you can then use the procedure as if it were part of your own project.

Using a procedure from an Automation Library is much easier than using procedures from a DLL. For one, you don't need to worry about declaring individual procedures; you simply make a reference to the entire library and all the procedures in the library then become available to you. For another, procedures in an Automation Library are designed to be used safely by Automation clients, so you are much less likely to crash your system.

Creating a Custom Object

You will, in writing macros for Office applications, use objects incessantly. One of the best ways to understand how an object works is to create one of your own. Creating a custom object is a relatively advanced technique, used primarily by application developers. As a power user creating macros for your own use, you probably will not have many occasions to create custom objects. On the other hand, custom objects are not as difficult to create as they are often made out to be.

Understanding an Object

Even if you do not commonly create objects for your own use, creating a custom object can help you understand what lies behind the terminology as you use objects from Office applications.

Creating a Custom Property

Suppose you want to use yesterday's date in a macro. The expression *Date – 1* calculates yesterday's date. If you will be using that date multiple times, you probably don't want to enter the expression each time you need the date, so you can store the value of the expression in a variable. After executing the *Yesterday = Date – 1* statement, the variable *Yesterday* contains the calculated date, and you can use the variable name in place of the expression. For example, the *MsgBox Yesterday* statement will display yesterday's date.

Rather than place the statement that calculates the date into the macro, you can make the variable calculate itself by turning it into a function as illustrated below:

```
Function Yesterday() As Date
    Yesterday = Date - 1
End Function
```

Once you have defined this function, you can use the word *Yesterday* the same as you did when it was a variable, except that you don't have to assign a value to it. The statement *MsgBox Yesterday* will still display yesterday's date, even if it is the first statement in a macro.

A function is a *read-only variable*; that is, you can't assign a new value to the function. What if you wanted to be able to use the word *Yesterday* to change the system clock? In other words, what if executing the statement *Yesterday = #12/31/1999#* would change the system clock to January 1, 2000? What if you could increment the system clock one day using the statement *Yesterday = Yesterday + 1*? You can't write a value to a function name. Instead, you have to pass a new value to the function as an argument. You could write a procedure like the following *SetYesterday* subroutine:

```
Sub SetYesterday(NewDate As Date)
Date = NewDate + 1
End Sub
```

The *SetYesterday* subroutine is a Sub, not a Function, because it doesn't return a value.

Once you have defined this new subroutine, the statement *SetYesterday #12/31/1999#* will change the system date to January 1, 2000. But this new subroutine doesn't look like a variable. You assign a value to a variable by using an equal sign. Also, you had to give this subroutine a different name from the function since you can't normally assign the same name to two different procedures. The *SetYesterday Yesterday + 1* statement does increment the system date by one day, but it is not as easy to read and understand as *Yesterday = Yesterday + 1*.

This is where Property procedures come in. A *Property* is just a clever way to allow you to take two different functions—one that retrieves a value and one that sets a value—and make them appear as though they are a single variable. To change *Yesterday* into a Property, you create a pair of Property procedures, as shown in the following example:

```
Property Get Yesterday() As Date
    Yesterday = Date - 1
End Property

Property Let Yesterday(NewDate As Date)
    Date = NewDate + 1
End Property
```

Both procedures have the same name. The only way to assign the same name to two different procedures is by creating Property procedures. The *Property Get Yesterday* procedure is identical to the *Yesterday* function shown earlier. A Property Get procedure is a function; the only difference is that a Property Get procedure can be paired with a Property Let procedure of the same name.

The *Property Let Yesterday* procedure is also identical to its counterpart, the *SetYesterday* subroutine, shown earlier. A Property Let procedure is also a subroutine with an argument for a new value. The only difference is that a Property Let procedure can be paired with a Property Get procedure of the same name.

Once you have defined the *Yesterday* Property procedures, you can use the elegant statement *Yesterday = Yesterday + 1* to increment the system date. Visual Basic determines from the context that the second occurrence of the word *Yesterday* is supplying a value, so it uses the *Property Get Yesterday* procedure. Visual Basic again determines from the context that the first occurrence of the word *Yesterday* is getting a new value assigned to it, so it uses the *Property Let Yesterday* procedure.

A property, then, is a smart variable. It looks like a variable—and you can use it in a statement as if it were a variable—but it is smart enough, thanks to the code in the *Property Get* procedure, to determine its own value. And it is also smart enough, thanks to the code in the *Property Let* procedure, to perform an action when you assign a new value to it.

Creating a Custom Data Type

Suppose you are creating a macro that manipulates an annual event, such your parents' wedding anniversary. In the first version of the macro, *AnnualDates1*, you declare three variables: one for the current year, one for the previous year, and one for next year, as shown in the following example:

```
Sub AnnualDates1()
    Dim myCurrent As Date
    Dim myPrevious As Date
    Dim myNext As Date
```

```
    myCurrent = #7/4/2000#
End Sub
```

As you continue to work with the macro, you might decide to extend it so that it will work not only with the anniversary date, but it will also work with your birthday. In the *AnnualDates2* version of the macro, you add additional variables, making sure that all the variable names are appropriately descriptive, as shown in the following example:

```
Sub AnnualDates2()
    Dim myBirthdayCurrent As Date
    Dim myBirthdayPrevious As Date
    Dim myBirthdayNext As Date
    Dim myAnniversaryCurrent As Date
    Dim myAnniversaryPrevious As Date
    Dim myAnniversaryNext As Date

    myBirthdayCurrent = #10/31/2000#
    myAnniversaryCurrent = #7/4/2001#
End Sub
```

Now you start to wonder what will happen to your macro if you decide to incorporate Groundhog Day, as well as the day you start working on your income taxes. You also wonder about the headaches you will have if you want to add a *DayOfTheWeek* variable for each of the dates. Each of the dates has a common set of variables—Current, Previous, and Next. In Visual Basic, you can define a *Type*—essentially a custom data type composed of sub-elements—that specifies a combination of variables you might want to reuse. You create a new version of your macro, *AnnualDates3*, to take advantage of this capability, as shown in the following example:

```
Type myDate
    CurrentDate As Date
    PreviousYear As Date
    NextYear As Date
End Type

Sub AnnualDates3()
    Dim myBirthday As myDate
    Dim myAnniversary As myDate

    myBirthday.CurrentDate = #10/31/2000#
    myAnniversary.NextYear = #7/4/2001#
End Sub
```

A new Type must be defined at the top of a module, not inside a procedure. A Type structure looks roughly like a procedure, with Type at the beginning and End Type at the end. You give the new Type a name, which you then use to declare actual variables. Within the Type structure, you declare any variables you want to use, except that you don't use *Dim* before the variable name. The variables inside a type are called *members*. To refer to a member of a variable, you separate the variable name from the member name with a period.

Even with only two variables and three members, the code in the *AnnualDates3* macro is much clearer than it is in its predecessor. The benefits of a Type will increase when you are ready to track another event. To declare all the variables you need to incorporate Groundhog Day, you need to add only a single new statement, *Dim myGroundhog As myDate*. If you want to add a Day Of The Week member, simply add *DayOfTheWeek As String* inside the type declaration and the new member will then be available to all the variables declared with that type.

For each variable that you declare with the *myDate* data type, Visual Basic sets aside enough memory for all the members of the Type. Each variable is called an *instance* of the data type, and each variable has its own copy of each member in the Type.

Creating a Custom Object Class

Your custom data type contains three members, and each member is a variable. You can assign values to, and retrieve values from, each of those member variables. To retrieve a value from the *NextYear* member for a variable, you must explicitly assign a value to that member. But somehow it seems that if you assign a value to the *CurrentDate* member, the *NextYear* member should be able to determine its own value since it is always just one year later. A simple, ordinary, variable isn't smart enough to determine its own value; you need to convert the *NextYear* member into a Property. Unfortunately, the Type declaration that you placed at the top of a module cannot include procedures. A *Class* is an enhanced version of a Type; it is a Type that can include procedures.

To create a Class, click Class Module on the Insert menu, and a new module will appear in the Visual Basic Editor. It looks just like an ordinary module, except that it appears in a new group named Class Modules in the Project Explorer window. To give the Class a name, click View, Properties Window, and replace the name Class1 with *AnnualDate*. (It seems somehow fitting to give a Class an official-sounding name.) You can then close the Properties window.

To declare the members of the Class, copy the three members from the *myDate* type, paste them into the Class, and then insert the word Public in front of each one. When you're through, the Class module will look like the following example:

```
Option Explicit

Public CurrentDate As Date
Public PreviousYear As Date
Public NextYear As Date
```

You now have an AnnualDate Class that replicates the functionality of the *myDate* type. You need to make a couple of minor modifications to the macro to convert it from using a Type to using a Class. The *AnnualDates4* macro shown below includes the appropriate changes:

```
Sub AnnualDates4()
    Dim myBirthday As New AnnualDate
    Dim myAnniversary As New AnnualDate

    myBirthday.CurrentDate = #10/31/2000#
    myAnniversary.CurrentDate = #7/4/2000#

End Sub
```

The first change simply replaces the *myDate* name with the *AnnualDate* name. The second, more significant change adds the word *New* after the word *As* when declaring the variables, which is required. When you declare a variable as a Type, it always sets aside new memory for the variable because there's nothing else you can do with a Type. But with a variable declared as a Class, you might want to use the variable to point to an existing instance of the Class. Adding the New keyword tells Visual Basic to go ahead and create a new copy of the variable that replicates the functionality of using Type.

When you declare a variable using New and a Class name, you create a new instance of the Class. An instance of a Class is called an Object. Sometimes, in casual conversation, people use the word Object to refer either to the Class or to the instance of the Class. The difference is whether there is actual memory reserved for the members of the Class. If you create a Class module, but you never declare a variable using the Class name, the Class does not take up any data storage space. Likewise, even if you do declare the variable, if you don't use the New keyword, the members of the Class will not take up any storage space.

Enhancing a Custom Object

Creating a Class containing only variables does not give you any significant benefit over simply creating a Type. It is in adding procedures that the Class comes into its own.

Adding a Property to a Custom Class

You can convert the *NextYear* variable in the AnnualDate Class into a Property that automatically calculates its own value—once you have assigned a date to the *CurrentDate* variable. To convert the variable to a Property, insert Property Get after the word Public. Technically, you don't need the word Public, because procedures are public by default, but adding the keyword is a good reminder. Then, insert a statement to calculate the value for the new year. Here is the finished Property as shown in the following example:

```
Public Property Get NextYear() As Date
    NextYear = DateAdd("yyyy", 1, CurrentDate)
End Property
```

The *NextYear* member is now smart and can determine its own value. You can now add statements to the *AnnualDates4* macro to use the *NextYear* value, even though the macro never assigns anything to it. In fact, because there is no Property Let procedure, you can't assign anything to the *NextYear* property. The following example shows the revised *AnnualDates4* macro:

```
Sub AnnualDates4()
    Dim myBirthday As New AnnualDate
    Dim myAnniversary As New AnnualDate

    myBirthday.CurrentDate = #10/31/2000#
    myAnniversary.CurrentDate = #7/4/2000#

    MsgBox myBirthday.NextYear
    MsgBox myAnniversary.NextYear
End Sub
```

As you type *myBirthday* and a period, Visual Basic displays an AutoList menu showing the names of the three members of the object. Each of the three members has the standard property icon beside it, as shown in Figure 4-31.

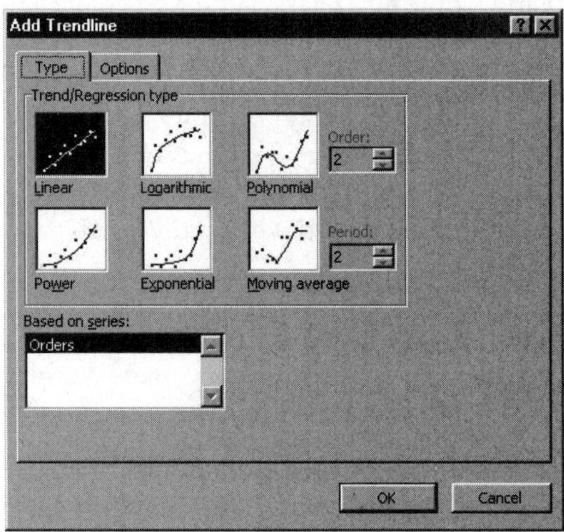

Figure 4-31
Public variables and Property procedures appear as properties.

Visual Basic treats your custom object—with its custom properties—exactly the same as it treats objects from Excel or Word. Public variables in a Class count as Properties. Technically, when you create a public variable in a Class, Visual Basic secretly creates Property Get and Property Let procedures for you, but those hidden procedures do nothing more than assign and retrieve values. That's pretty obscure, but at least you know that converting a public variable in a Class into Property procedures does not incur any additional overhead.

What is important about procedures in a Class is that the code is automatically used by any instance of the object. You do not have to do any additional work to calculate the *NextYear* value for *myAnniversary* than you did for *myBirthday*. When you create multiple instances of an object, each instance gets its own memory space for variables (such as *CurrentDate*), but they all share the same code. When the code runs, it uses the value of any variables for the currently running instance of the object.

Adding a Method to a Custom Class

Let's suppose that in your macro, you want to be able to change the system date to the current year for the object *myBirthday*. You can add a *MakeItNow* procedure to the Class, as shown in the following example:

```
Public Sub MakeItNow()
    Date = CurrentDate
End Sub
```

In the *AnnualDates4* macro shown earlier, add the statement *myBirthday.MakeItNow* just prior to the statement that displays the *NextYear* value of *myBirthday*. After you type the period, Visual Basic will display the list of Methods and Properties. The Sub procedure you added to the Class has a method icon beside it, as shown in Figure 4-32.

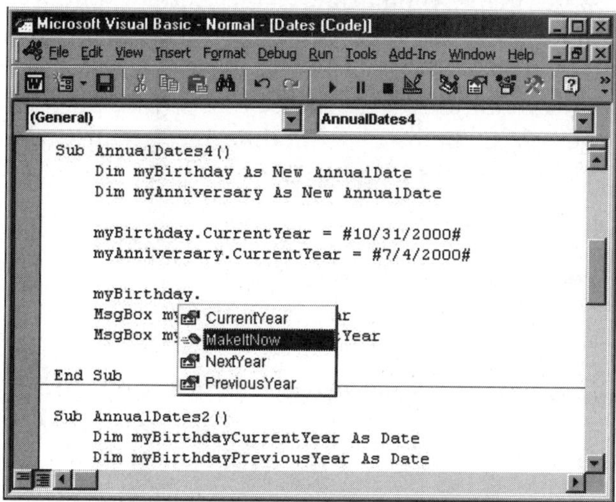

Figure 4-32
Sub and function procedures appear as methods.

The term Method applies either to a Sub procedure or to a Function procedure in a Class. In the Object Browser, you can see at the bottom of the window whether the method is a Sub or a Function when you view a method for an Office object. As shown in Figure 4-33, the *PointsToPixels* method of Word's Application object is a Function.

In the *AnnualDates4* macro, add the statement *myAnniversary.MakeItNow* before the statement that displays the *NextYear* value of *myAnniversary*. When you run the macro, each time it displays a message box, you can hold the mouse over the clock on the taskbar to see the changed system date. The same code runs, once for each

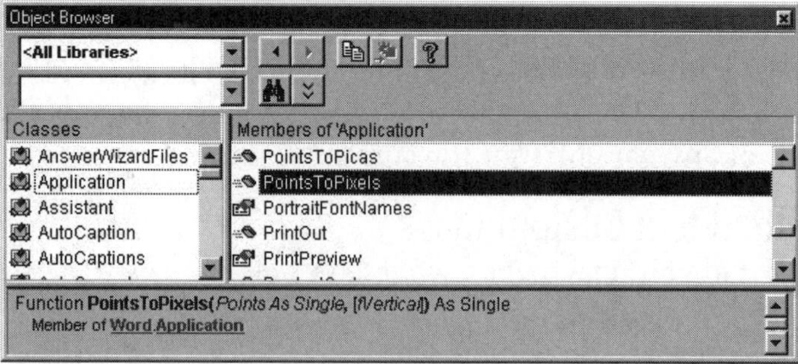

Figure 4-33
The Object Browser shows whether a method is a Sub or a Function.

object. The code simply uses the value of *CurrentDate* for the current instance of the object.

Creating a Custom Property That Returns an Object

Each of the three properties in the AnnualDate Class returns a simple value—a date value. You can also create a Oroperty that returns an object. The *PreviousYear* property is still a public variable. Turn the *PreviousYear* property into a Property procedure that returns a new AnnualDate object, whose *CurrentDate* property is one year before that of the original object. In the Class module, replace the current definition of the *PreviousYear* variable with the following:

```
Private myPreviousYear As AnnualDate

Public Property Get PreviousYear() As AnnualDate
    If myPreviousYear Is Nothing Then
        Set myPreviousYear = New AnnualDate
        myPreviousYear.CurrentDate = _
            DateAdd("yyyy", -1, CurrentDate)
    End If
    Set PreviousYear = myPreviousYear
End Property
```

The first statement declares a variable for storing the new object. The procedure checks to see whether an object has already been created and stored in the variable. Nothing is a special keyword that applies to those occasions when an object variable does not contain a reference to an object. The Nothing keyword is similar to the Empty keyword used with a Variant, except that Empty can be used only with a Variant and not with a variable declared as an object. Assigning the value *Nothing* to an object variable (as in *Set myPreviousYear = Nothing)* would destroy the object reference. An object keeps track internally of how many variables have a reference to the object. When the last object reference is destroyed, the object annihilates itself (the technical term is that the object terminates).

If the object variable does not contain a reference to an object, the New keyword creates a new instance of an object, and the Set keyword assigns a reference to the private variable. The *CurrentDate* property of the new object is then initialized to the appropriate date. Regardless of whether the object already existed or whether it was newly created, the final statement in the macro assigns the object to the Property name.

Visual Basic requires you to use the Set keyword when assigning an object to a variable. Technically, what you are assigning to the variable is a reference, or a pointer, to where the object is stored in memory. If you are just assigning a value to the variable (as when assigning a date to the CurrentDate property), the Set keyword is not used. To see the new object in action, create a new *AnnualDates5* macro that displays a value from the linked object, as shown in the following example:

```
Sub AnnualDates5()
    Dim myBirthday As New AnnualDate
    Dim myAnniversary As New AnnualDate

    myBirthday.CurrentDate = #10/31/2000#
    myAnniversary.CurrentDate = #7/4/2000#

    MsgBox myAnniversary.PreviousYear.CurrentDate
    MsgBox myBirthday.PreviousYear.PreviousYear.PreviousYear.CurrentDate
End Sub
```

The first part of the macro declares and initializes the AnnualDate objects as it did in the *AnnualDates4* macro. The macro then displays the *CurrentDate* property of the PreviousYear property for the *myAnniversary* object. In the final statement, each object gives you a reference to the next object in the chain, creating the object as necessary. You could extend the chain of *PreviousYear* objects indefinitely—or until you run out of memory or get bored, whichever comes first. It is very informative to step through this macro as it runs. (And it is even more informative to step through the macro as you run it again, when each of the *PreviousYear* objects already exists.)

The *PreviousYear* procedure is a property. In terms of the functionality of the procedure, you could just as easily have created it as a function. (Remember from the "Adding a Method to a Custom Class" section earlier in this chapter that in object terminology, a function is called a method.) There is no functional difference between a read-only property and a function (that is, a method). As you work with Office objects, you will find many methods and properties that can return a reference to an object. If you ever wonder why one is a method and one is a property, you can assume that part of the decision resulted from a whim of the designer.

Note For those of you who are historically minded, there is a little more to the story. In the first version of VBA, a *Property Get* procedure could not take any arguments. What that meant was that, in the original object models, if a procedure that returned an object had arguments, it was created as a function. If the procedure did not have any arguments, it was created as a property. Once VBA was enhanced to allow arguments for *Property Get* procedures, most procedures that returned objects were converted to properties. You will still, however, occasionally see a method—usually one with arguments—that returns an object.

Creating a Collection Object

In Office applications, you will find many objects that come in collections. To see how collections work, create your own.

Creating a Custom Collection of Values

Before creating a collection of objects, create a collection of simple values. The *MakeCollection* macro shown below creates a new collection object and adds three elements to it:

```
Sub MakeCollection()
    Dim c As New Collection
    Dim x As Variant

    c.Add "Dog", "First"
    c.Add 5000, "Second"
    c.Add #5/1/2005#, "Third"
    Debug.Print c.Count

    For Each x In c
        Debug.Print x
    Next x

    Debug.Print c("First")
    Debug.Print c(2)
    c.Remove "Second"
    Debug.Print c(2)
End Sub
```

The macro creates the first element as a string, the second element as an integer, and the third element as a date. The second argument for the Add method gives a name to the element of the collection. The final statement of the first group displays the number of elements in the collection—three in this example—in the Immediate window. All collections have a Count property that tells you the number of elements it contains.

The next group of statements in the macro consists of a *For Each* loop, which is a special looping construction designed specifically for use with collections. In a For Each loop, the inner statements of the loop are executed for each element of the collection. The For Each loop in the example shown earlier prints the value of each element in the collection to the Immediate window.

The final group of statements shows different ways to retrieve an individual item from the collection. You can retrieve an element by its position number in the collection (which can change as elements are added or deleted, as you can see by the final statement). You can also retrieve an element by its name, as a text string.

Creating a Custom Collection of Objects

You can also store objects in a collection. The *AnnualDates6* macro shown below creates and stores two AnnualDate objects in a custom collection:

```
Sub AnnualDates6()
    Dim myDates As New Collection
    Dim myDate As AnnualDate

    myDates.Add New AnnualDate, "Birthday"
    myDates("Birthday").CurrentDate = #7/4/2000#

    Set myDate = New AnnualDate
    myDate.CurrentDate = #10/31/2000#
    myDates.Add myDate, "Anniversary"
    Set myDate = Nothing

    MsgBox myDates("Birthday").NextYear
    MsgBox myDates(2).CurrentDate
End Sub
```

Chapter 4

In the statement *myDates.Add New AnnualDate, "Birthday"*, the expression *New AnnualDate* takes the place of a simple value in the *MakeCollection* macro. The *New* command creates a new *AnnualDate* object, and a reference to that object gets placed into the collection.

In the second group of statements, the *Set myDate = New AnnualDate* statement creates a new object and assigns a reference to the object to the variable *myDate.* The statement *myDate.CurrentDate = #10/31/2000#* assigns a date to the CurrentDate property of that object. (So far, this object has nothing to do with the collection.) The statement *myDates.Add myDate, "Anniversary"* copies the object reference into the collection. Even though the statement *Set myDate = Nothing* destroys the reference to the object in the *myDate* variable, the reference in the collection still remains.

The final group of statements shows that both object references are intact in the collection, and that the object whose references are stored in the collection can be accessed either by name or by number.

The Visual Basic Collection object is a generalized collection tool. It can store Variants, which means it can store any ordinary simple value, or a reference to any type of object. The collections you will find in Office applications are more specialized and can always hold only one specific type of object.

Creating a Custom Form Using VBA

In most Office applications, you can display one of the built-in dialog boxes. For an example of how to display a built-in dialog box in Word, see "Copying Styles to and from a Template" in Chapter 7. For an example in Excel, see the sidebar "Using Shortcut Keys for Names" in Chapter 12. You can also create a dialog box of your own. A VBA dialog box is called a User Form.

Programmers create User Forms when using Office to build a custom application. When you are creating macros for your own use, you might think that creating a custom User Form is more trouble than it is worth. Once you have created a user form or two, however, you might decide that it's not as hard as it originally seemed—much as the drive home from a new location often seems shorter than the outbound stretch, simply because the landmarks appear familiar.

Creating a Custom Login Form

Start by creating a simple Login form—one that asks for a user name and a password. You don't need a sophisticated security apparatus; you just want a macro to behave slightly differently if it's you who is running it.

To create a new User Form, start by displaying the Project Explorer window in the Visual Basic Editor. Right-click in the Project Explorer window, and click Insert, UserForm from the context menu. You can also click Insert, UserForm on the menu bar, or you can click the Insert UserForm button on the Standard toolbar (it shares a drop-down list with Insert Module, Insert Class, and Insert Procedure). The button for the item you most recently inserted appears in the toolbar.

As soon as you create a new User Form, the Project Explorer window acquires a new Forms folder containing your User Form. Open the folder to see your new User Form. The default name for a User Form is UserForm1. Double-click the form name to see the form; it should appear similar to the one shown in Figure 4-34. The Toolbox window will probably also appear with the User Form.

As mentioned earlier, the name of the form is UserForm1, and you will need to use this name to refer to the form later on, so you should rename it to frmLogin. You might expect that you could rename the User Form by right-clicking in the Project Explorer window and selecting a Rename command, but you can't. To rename a user form, you must use the Properties window. Click the Properties Window toolbar button or press F4, and then change the Name property to frmLogin to rename the User Form. The name of the Name property has parentheses around it in the Properties window, most likely to keep it at the top of the list.

When you change the Name property, the name changes in the Project Explorer window, but it does not change on the form itself. This is because the contents of the title bar at the top of the user form is not the name of the form. Rather, it is the name

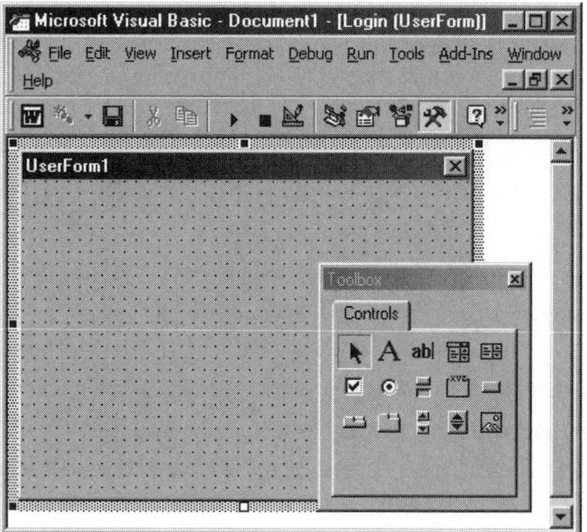

Figure 4-34
A new User Form begins as a blank dialog box.

of the form's Caption. You need to change the Caption property to Login to change the label that appears on the Form.

Adding Text Boxes to a Form

Once you have created a form, you can start adding controls to it. First select the form and then click the Toolbox button on the toolbar to display the Toolbox window. In the Toolbox, click the TextBox button and drag a box onto the form as shown in Figure 4-35.

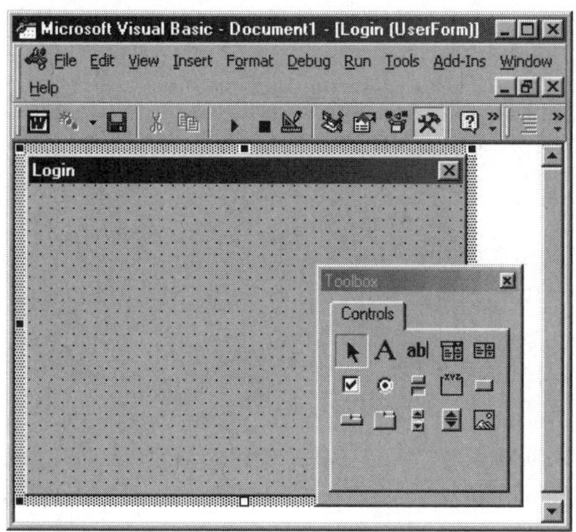

Figure 4-35
Drag a control from the Toolbox onto the form.

To create a second identical copy of the text box, select the text box and hold down the Ctrl key as you drag the box to a new location. The default name for the first text box on a form is TextBox1. Likewise, the default name for the second text box is TextBox2. You can give them more meaningful names in the Properties window. You'll use the first text box to enter your name, and the second text box to enter a password. Many people use the three-letter prefix *.txt* for a text box. Select the first text box, click the Name property in the Properties window, and type *txtName*. Give the name *txtPassword* to the second text box. Typically, when you type a password on a form, you don't want other people to be able to see the password that you type. With the second text box selected, in the Properties window, choose the PasswordChar property and replace the value with an asterisk.

Testing the Form

Before proceeding further, you should save the form. The form is stored as part of the project, and the project is stored in the Office document. Saving the form saves the project and the document as well. Click the Save Form button to save the form.

To display the form, first select the form window and then click the Run Sub/User Form button. When the form appears, type your name in the first box and type a password in the second box. You won't see the password as you type; it will be replaced by asterisk characters, as shown in Figure 4-36. To close the form, click the Close button on the top right corner of form.

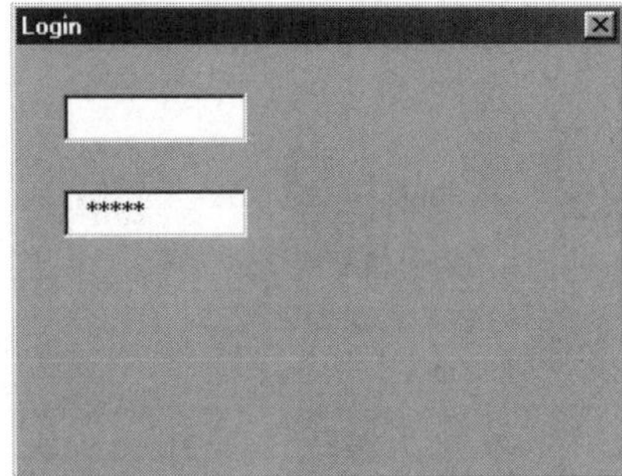

Figure 4-36
A password character keeps the text from appearing.

Adding Command Buttons to the Form

Rather than using the Close button to close the form, you can add a button for OK and another for Cancel. In the toolbox, click the CommandButton tool and drag a button onto the form, just to the right of the boxes. Hold down the Ctrl key and drag the command button to create a second button.

Assign *btnOK* as the name of the first button, with OK as the caption for that button. An OK button is the default button, which means that it gets clicked if you press the Enter key while a form is open. Change the Default property of the OK button to *True*. Assign *btnCancel* to the second command button, and change its caption to Cancel. A Cancel button typically gets clicked when you press the Escape key while the form is open. To set that feature, assign *True* as the value of the Cancel property.

Using the Keyboard with the Properties Window

You can use the keyboard with the Properties window, but it doesn't always behave the way it should. For example, if you select a control on the form, you can select a property in the Properties window by pressing Ctrl+Shift+ plus the first letter of the property name. That is, you can select the text box and press Ctrl+Shift+P to select the PasswordChar property in the Properties window. You cannot, however, type a new password character until you activate the Properties window. A few anomalies like these can discourage you from using the keyboard with the Properties window.

But if you understand how the keyboard works in the Properties window, you can use it very effectively. There are four sections in the Properties window. The column of property names is one section. The column of property values is a second section. The drop-down list of control names at the top of the window is a third section. And finally, the tabs that read Alphabetical and Categorized are the fourth section. Pressing the Tab key moves forward one section. Pressing Shift+Tab moves back one section. However, there is an error in the sequencing. When the property name list is selected, pressing Shift+Tab should select the Tab labels. Instead, it selects the list of control names, making it impossible to use Shift+Tab to cycle through all the sections. Because there are only four sections, resign yourself to using the Tab key to move from section to section.

Once you're within a section, pressing the Right arrow key or the Left arrow key will move you to a new item within the section. In all the sections except the Tab labels, you can also press the Up arrow and Down arrow keys. When you're within the property names or the property values sections, you can also press Ctrl+Shift plus the first letter of the property name to select a new property.

Unless you're fond of menu accelerator keys or function keys, it's probably easier to switch between the Properties window and the form window by simply clicking them with the mouse. If you do want to use the keyboard, press F4 to activate the Properties window, and press Shift+F4 to activate the form window. On the View menu, the Properties Window command activates the Properties window and the Object command activates the form.

Arranging Controls on a Form

Once you have added controls to the form, you can use menu commands to arrange and resize the controls. To select multiple controls, drag a rectangle that touches any of the controls you want to select. You do not need to enclose the controls. To remove the vertical spacing between the two text box controls, drag a rectangle to touch the respective controls, and then click the Format menu. On the Vertical Spacing submenu, click Decrease. Don't try to change the vertical spacing on two groups of controls at the same time. For example, don't select both the text boxes and the command buttons together before changing the vertical spacing.

If you want to make the top of the OK button align with top of the name text box, select the two controls and then click Format, Align, Tops. When you align controls, the first control you select becomes the master; all the other controls align to it. When you select controls by touching them with a rectangle, the first control the mouse touches becomes the master control.

Adding Procedures to a UserForm

Assigning the Default or Caption property of a button doesn't make the button actually do anything. You must add code to any control to make it actually do something.

Using a Command Button to Close the Form

To add code to the Cancel button, double-click the button. A code window appears with a macro already started called *btnCancel_Click*. This macro will run whenever you click the Cancel button. Add the statement *Unload frmLogin* in the body of the macro. The *Unload* command unloads a form; if *frmLogin* is the name of your form, this statement will close the form without doing anything else.

Reactivate the form window and double-click the OK button. A macro called *btnOK_Click* will appear in the code window. Add the following two statements to the body of the macro:

```
MsgBox txtName & " is running the macro"
Unload frmLogin
```

The first statement extracts the text from the *txtName* box, concatenates it with a message, and then displays the result in a message box. This is where you would place the code to run with your macro. The second statement simply closes the form.

Click the Run Sub/UserForm button to run the form. Type your name, press the Tab key, type anything as a password, and then press Enter to click the OK button. Click OK in the message box and the form will disappear. Run the form again, but this time, press the Escape key.

Creating a Procedure to Test for Valid Entries

Your form should test whether a valid password has been entered. One way to test the password is to add code to the *btnOK_Click* procedure discussed earlier. A better approach—which is no more work—is to prevent anyone from clicking the OK button unless the password is valid. On the form, double-click the OK button to display the code window and type the following new procedure in the code window:

```
Private Sub CheckOK()
    Const myPassword = "abc"
    If UCase(txtName) = "SAM" _
    And txtPassword = myPassword Then
        btnOK.Enabled = True
    Else
btnOK.Enabled = False
    End If
End Sub
```

The constant statement at the beginning of the procedure allows you to easily change the password. The procedure tests for a specific, case-sensitive user name, and whether the password entered matches the case-sensitive password constant. If both the password and the name are correct, the procedure sets the Enabled property of the OK button to *True.* Otherwise, it sets the property to *False.*

Now you need to run the *CheckOK* procedure whenever either the password or the name values might change. In the form window, double-click the name text box. In the *txtName_Change* procedure that appears, enter the single statement *CheckOK.* This will run the test procedure each time you make a change in the name text box. From the form, double-click the password text box to create a *txtPassword_Change* procedure. Enter the statement *CheckOK* into that procedure, as well.

Save the form and then run it. Type *Sam* in the name box, and type *abc* in the password box. As soon as you type the first character, the OK button becomes disabled. As soon as you finish typing the password, the OK button becomes enabled. Except for when the form first appears, you can't click the OK button without a valid user name and password. You need to run the *CheckOK* procedure one more time.

Double-click the background of the form. A new procedure called *UserForm_Click* will appear. This procedure runs whenever you click the form. But you want to run the test procedure before the form first displays, not when you click it. At the top of the code window, you will find two drop-down list boxes. In the list box on the right—the Procedure list—select Initialize. A new procedure called *UserForm_Initialize,* will appear. (You can delete the *UserForm_Click* procedure.) For the body of the *UserForm_Initialize* procedure, enter *CheckOK.* Save and test the form.

Replacing a Text Box With a List Box

Rather than type your name into the text box, you decide that you want to be able to select it from a list. Select the name text box and delete it. Click the ComboBox button in the Toolbox and drag a new rectangle for the combo box. A combo box control can function either as a drop-down list box, which only allows you to select values from the list, or it can function as a true combo box, which only allows you to select existing values or to add new ones. The Style property determines which type of list the combo box control functions as. Leave your new control as a drop-down combo box, and change the name of the new control to *lstName*.

Now that the name of the control has changed from *txtName* to *lstName*, you will need to change the name of the control in the code window. With the code window open, click Edit, Replace. Then type *txtName* in the Find What box, type *lstName* in the Replace box, and then click Replace All. You need to add values to the list. In the *UserForm_Initialize* procedure, enter the following two statements just prior to the existing *CheckOK* statement:

```
lstName.AddItem "Sam"
lstName.AddItem "Yoshiko"
```

These two statements add the names Sam and Yoshiko to the list.

The procedure that checks for the user name checks for a specific name. Now that the list can contain more than one name, the test should simply check to see if a name from the list has been selected. Replace the conditional expression *UCase(txtName) = "SAM"* with the new expression *lstName.ListIndex > -1*. The ListIndex property of a list box indicates which item in the list has been selected. The first item in the list has an index of zero. If no item is selected, the ListIndex property equals -1. As long as the ListIndex property is greater than -1, a value in the list has been selected. Save and test the form.

Note If you used the Tab key to move between the controls on the form, you probably noticed that replacing the text box with a list box placed the controls into an unnatural sequence. You should make sure that the controls on your form flow in a natural order when you press the Tab key. To correct the order of the controls, click View, Tab Order. In the Tab Order dialog box, select a control and click the Move Up or Move Down buttons as necessary.

Adding New Entries to a List Box

Because the name drop-down list box is a combo box and not a simple list drop-down list box, you can type a new value into the box. You can add code to the form which will add the new item to the list. The *lstName* control already has one procedure—*lstName_Change*—which runs whenever you select a new item from the list. It does not run, however, when you type a new value into the combo box. For that, you need to use an *AfterUpdate* procedure. In the Code window, click in the *lstName_Change* procedure. In the Procedure box at the top right corner of the Code window, select *AfterUpdate.* As the body of the new procedure, enter the following statements:

```
If lstName.ListIndex = -1 Then
    lstName.AddItem lstName
End If
CheckOK
```

The *If* statement checks to see if the value in the combo box is new. If so, it adds the value to the list. The procedure also runs the *CheckOK* test, because the *lstName_Change* procedure runs only when you select an existing value from the list. Save and test the form.

Integrating a UserForm in Office 2000

So far, the only way you have been displaying the form is by clicking the Run Sub/UserForm button. Eventually, you will want to run the form from a macro that you can execute from Office applications.

Running the Form From a Macro

Create an ordinary macro—that is, a macro which is not part of the UserForm. In the macro, enter *frmLogin* and type a period. Visual Basic for Applications recognizes the name of the form and displays a list of members when you type a period. From the list of members, select Show. The statement *frmLogin.Show* will display the form. Any statements that follow the one that will show the form will not execute until after you close the form.

Sharing a Form Between Office Applications

You can use a form you create in one Office application in any other Office application. To do so, right-click the form name in the Project Explorer window. On the shortcut menu, click Export File and save the form to an external file.

In the new Office application, open the Visual Basic Editor and right-click the project name in the Project Explorer window. On the context menu, click Import File, navigate to where you saved the file, and then click Open.

Note When you export a UserForm from Visual Basic for Applications, you can import the form only into another Visual Basic for Applications project. You cannot import the form into the Standard, Professional, or Enterprise editions of Visual Basic. Likewise, you cannot import a form from one of the stand-alone editions of Visual Basic into a Visual Basic for Applications project.

Chapter 5

Explore Office Object Models

Microsoft uses the term Automation to refer to the way Visual Basic for Applications (VBA) interacts with a program. An application program can be an Automation server, meaning that it can respond to automation instructions from VBA or elsewhere—or it can be an Automation client—meaning that it can host VBA as you create, edit, run, and store macros. All of the major Office applications—Word, Excel, Access, Outlook, PowerPoint, and FrontPage—now function either as an Automation server or as an automation client.

A program that responds to VBA instructions does so by providing an application-specific object model. Even if you are very familiar with VBA, you will still need to learn how the application's object model works as you begin automating a new application.

Understanding Object Models

An object model is also stored as an object library (sometimes referred to as a type library). An Automation Client such as VBA retrieves the object model information from the object library. It presents a way for an application to expose its objects to Automation. An object model presents an application as objects, each of which has its own attributes. Chapter 4 explains how to create a simple object. Understanding how to build a simple object can help you understand the Office object models.

Understanding Object Properties and Methods

Automation is composed of simple and complex object items. Numbers, dates, and strings of text are all examples of simple items. Objects can be very complex, but essentially, it represents the grouping together of a large number of simple object items.

Understanding Properties

Excel's object model defines a Border object, for example, which controls how a cell border is formatted. Three values are required to describe a cell border:

- **ColorIndex** identifies one of Excel's 56 available colors.
- **LineStyle** identifies one of several predefined dashed patterns.
- **Weight** identifies how thick the line is.

Each value is a number—a simple object item. The Border object is just one way of pulling these three values into a group so that you will be able to see how they relate to one other. All three values are a part of the object's properties. (The Border object's Color property gives you an additional way with which to change the ColorIndex value.)

A single Excel worksheet can contain thousands of Border objects, because each cell can have as many as six different borders (counting diagonal borders). The property values might vary from object to object, but the list of properties will be identical for any Border object. The word *Class* is used as a generic description for all objects sharing a single list of properties. For example, a line on the right edge of cell B14 is a Border object, and a line on the top edge of cell C15 is a different Border object, but they both belong to the same Border Class.

With objects, a relationship exists between the general Class and the specific instance of an object. A similar relationship exists between the general data type and the specific instance of a simple value, as well. For example, the value *512* is a number, as is the value *6,227*. These are two different values, but they are both numbers. The word number implies certain things about how these values can be used; they can all be used in arithmetic expressions, for example. The relationship of the specific value *512* to the general concept of Number is analogous to the relationship of a single Border object to the general concept of the Border Class.

Understanding Methods

In addition to defining properties, a Class can also define actions for its objects, which are called methods of that object. For example, the Word object model describes a PageNumber object that refers to a page number at the top or bottom of a page. In addition to a few properties, the PageNumber Class has four actions or methods: Select, Delete, Copy, and Cut. Each method does exactly what the name describes. Collectively, the properties and methods of a Class are called the *members* of the Class.

Understanding Object References

In addition to properties (which define attributes) and methods (which define actions), a Class can use properties and methods to create links—or references—to other objects. For example, a Border object has two additional properties linking to two related properties: the Parent property, which is the cell that the border surrounds, and the Application property, which is the Excel application itself. All Classes have both Parent and Application properties.

A Range object in Excel—which refers to one or more cells on a worksheet—has a Next property that returns a reference to the next cell, or to the cell that would be selected when you pressed the Tab key. With cell A1 selected, the expression *ActiveCell* returns a reference to cell A1, and the statement *ActiveCell.Value=100* places the value *100* into that cell. The expression *ActiveCell.Next.Next.Next* returns a reference to cell D1, and the statement *ActiveCell.Next.Next.Next.Value = 500* places the value *500* into that cell.

The Value property returns (or assigns) a simple value. The Next property returns an object reference. Both the Value and the Next properties need to be preceded by an object reference; for example, *ActiveCell.Value*, and *ActiveCell.Next*. Only the Next property can be followed by a period and an additional property.

Assigning an Object Reference to a Variable

You can use the TypeName function to determine whether an expression returns a simple value or a reference to an object. Typing the statement *?TypeName(ActiveCell.Value)* into the Immediate window will display a simple value data type of String, Double, Date, or even Empty, depending on the contents of the cell. Typing the statement *?TypeName(ActiveCell.Next)* into the Immediate window will display *Range*, the name of a Class. The TypeName function's return value shows that the expression *ActiveCell.Value* returns a simple value, and that the expression *ActiveCell.Next* returns an object reference.

You can create a new variable in the Immediate window simply by assigning a value to it. If you want to assign a simple value to a variable, you use an equal sign (=). The statement *x = ActiveCell.Value* assigns the value of the active cell to a variable, which is really a shorthand version of the full Visual Basic *Let* statement. The complete statement is *Let x = ActiveCell.Value,* but because assigning a value is such a common action to perform, you can omit the word *Let*. If you want to assign an object reference to a variable, you must use the word *Set* in place of *Let*. For example, the statement *Set x = ActiveCell.Next* assigns a Range object reference to the variable.

Many Classes provide default properties for those times when you use the object as if it were a simple value. The default property of a Range object is the Value property. For example, the statement *Set x = ActiveCell.Next* assigns an object reference to a variable, but the statement *Let x = ActiveCell.Next* must assign a simple value. To find the appropriate simple value, Visual Basic looks for the default property of the Range object, *Value,* which does return a simple value. The *Let x = ActiveCell.Next* statement is equivalent to *Let x = ActiveCell.Next.Value* statement.

Storing Objects in a Variant

Omitting the Set keyword is the same as using Let. It is easy to accidentally omit Set, which can be particularly dangerous when you are working with a Variant variable (see "Using Variant Variable Types" in Chapter 4 for details about Variants). Suppose that the variable *x* is a Variant, that you intend to assign an object reference to the variable, and that you inadvertently type the statement *x = ActiveCell,* omitting the Set keyword. Visual Basic will not detect your error, nor will it use the Devalue property to assign the value of the active cell to the variable. Later in the macro, when you try to execute the statement *x.Value = 100,* Visual Basic will detect an error because the simple value that *x* contains has no properties. Errors of this type can be difficult to track down, because the location where Visual Basic detects the error is different from the error's actual location.

If you declare the variable *x* as a Range object (*Dim x As Range*) and then try to execute the statement *x = ActiveCell,* Visual Basic will display an immediate error and you can quickly correct the statement.

Another common pitfall exists when you use a Variant to store an object reference. Suppose that *x* is a Variant and you correctly use the statement *Set x = ActiveCell* to assign a Range object reference to it. Suppose that later in the macro you want to assign the value *255* to the cell referenced by *x*. You might use the statement *Let x = 255* because you assume that Visual Basic will use the default Value property of the Range object stored in *x*. That isn't what happens. Because *x* is a Variant, Visual Basic simply assigns the new value to the variable, replacing the object reference. You must explicitly use *x.Value = 255* (or *Let x.Value = 255*) to avoid overwriting the object.

Once again, declaring the variable as a Range object avoids this problem. If you declare *x* as a Range object and assign an object reference to it, then the statement *x = 255* does use the default Value property, because *255* is not a Range object that can be assigned to the variable.

Understanding the With Structure

When you use the macro recorder, you will often see the With keyword in the resulting macro. For example, if you turn on the macro recorder in Word and then check the Picture Placeholder option on the View tab of the Options dialog box, you will end up with a macro similar to the following:

```
Sub Macro2()
    Application.DisplayStatusBar = True
    With ActiveWindow
        .DisplayHorizontalScrollBar = True
        .DisplayVerticalScrollBar = True
        .DisplayLeftScrollBar = False
        .StyleAreaWidth = InchesToPoints(0)
        .DisplayRightRuler = False
        .DisplayScreenTips = True
         With .View
            .ShowAnimation = True
            .Draft = False
            .WrapToWindow = False
            .ShowPicturePlaceHolders = True
            .ShowFieldCodes = False
            .ShowBookmarks = True
            .FieldShading = wdFieldShadingAlways
            .ShowTabs = False
            .ShowSpaces = False
            .ShowParagraphs = False
            .ShowHyphens = False
            .ShowHiddenText = True
            .ShowAll = False
            .ShowDrawings = True
            .ShowObjectAnchors = False
            .ShowTextBoundaries = False
            .ShowHighlight = True
        End With
    End With
End Sub
```

You don't need all those statements; the only thing you changed was the ShowPicturePlaceHolders property. The recorder, however, didn't know whether you changed one option or all the options, so it recorded everything. If you delete all the extraneous statements, the macro will look like this:

```
Sub Macro2()
    With ActiveWindow
        With .View
            .ShowPicturePlaceHolders = True
        End With
    End With
End Sub
```

The With keyword must be followed by an expression that returns a reference to an object. When Visual Basic sees the *With ActiveWindow* statement, it creates an invisible object variable and assigns the object reference to the variable. Each time the macro contains a period that is not preceded by an object, Visual Basic places the invisible object variable before the period. When Visual Basic arrives at the *End With* statement, it destroys the secret variable. In other words, if you replace the hidden variables with explicit variables, the macro will look something like this:

```
Sub Macro2()
    Dim w As Window
    Dim v As View
    Set w = ActiveWindow
    Set v = w.View
    v.ShowPicturePlaceHolders = True
End Sub
```

The macro recorder uses With structures to achieve the benefit of using object variables without having to generate variable names and declarations.

Whether you use a With structure or use explicit object variables is largely a matter of personal preference. When a With structure gets long, or when you start nesting With structures inside other With structures, explicit variables will make the macro more readable.

Of course, there is no need either for a With structure or for an object variable when you're going to use the object reference only once. If all you want to do is enable picture placeholders, you can convert the macro as follows:

```
Sub Macro2()
   ActiveWindow.View.ShowPicturePlaceHolders = True
End Sub
```

Understanding Collections

A *collection* is a grouping of objects. "Creating a Custom Object" in Chapter 4 explains how to create a custom collection. When you create a collection using the Visual Basic Collection object, you can store any kind of value or object in the collection. Collections in Office object models always store a single type of object (or at least very closely related objects).

A collection can contain any quantity of objects—from zero to millions of objects. For example, if the active Excel sheet does not contain any text boxes, the expression *ActiveSheet.TextBoxes.Count* returns zero. Even though there are no text boxes in the worksheet, the collection still exists; it just contains zero items. On the other hand, the expression *ActiveSheet.Cells.Count* will always return the value *16,777,216*, because that is how many cells are in the worksheet.

Selecting a Single Item from a Collection

To retrieve a single item from a collection, you use the Item property in parentheses, followed by either the item's name or number. For example, in a new Excel workbook, the expressions *Worksheets.Item(1)* and *Worksheets.Item("Sheet1")* both refer to the same Worksheet object.

The Item method is the default member for most collections. This means you can leave out the word *Item* and the expression will still work. The expressions in the preceding paragraph are equivalent to these two expressions: *Worksheets(1)* and *Worksheets("Sheet1")*.

Understanding Collections and Ranges

Most collections can be referred to as a whole, or you can retrieve a single item from the collection. For example, the Columns collection in Excel returns the cells of a worksheet as a collection of columns. The statement *Columns.Select* selects all the columns—and hence all the cells—of the worksheet. The *Columns(5).Select* statement selects column E—the fifth column of the worksheet. You cannot, however, use the Columns collection to select columns E, G, and I. With a collection, you get all or one. Interactively, you can select columns E, G, and I by selecting column E and then holding down the Ctrl key as you select columns G and I. It is reasonable to expect that you could do the same from a macro.

In most cases, when you need to refer to some, but not all, items, the Office object models use a method or property that includes the word Range. In Office terminology, a Range is like a collection, except that it does not restrict you to the single item that is typical of most collections.

Both Word and Excel have Range objects. In both cases, the Range refers to something—characters or cells—where you often refer to some, but not all, of the available items in a range. When you want to work with some, but not all, drawing objects in an Office application, you use a ShapeRange object. When you refer to some, but not all, slides in a PowerPoint presentation, you use a SlideRange object.

When you see the word Range in a Class name, a method, or a property name, you will find that dealing with multiple objects does not always fit the normal one-or-all options of a collection.

Watching for Collection Conventions

Many Classes have a corresponding collection Class. For example, the Excel Workbook Class has a corresponding Workbooks Class. The Workbooks Class consists of a collection of Workbook objects. In the vast majority of cases, the collection Class name consists of the plural form of the singular Class name, just as the word *Workbooks* is the plural form of *Workbook*. Whenever you're looking at a new object library, carefully look at the Class names to watch for pairs between singular and plural Classes.

A few collections do not have a plural name. Most often, this is because the plural form of the name is unusable. For example, one of the components of an Excel chart is a Series object. A Series object refers to a single series—a line or a series of bars—on a chart. Because the word Series already appears to be plural, a collection with the name Serieses would be silly. Excel's design team decided to give the name SeriesCollection to the collection of Series objects in the Excel object model, even though it doesn't end in an "s."

As another example, the Shape object—which is part of Microsoft Office and is available to all Office applications—has two different collection Classes associated with it. One form is the Shapes collection, which is a simple collection that allows you to create a shape or to refer to an individual Shape object. The other collection is the ShapeRange collection, which allows you to simultaneously manipulate multiple Shape objects. The ShapeRange object is a collection, even though it does not end in the letter "s." The Shapes object has already taken the plural form of the word.

Recognizing Different Types of Collections

The Shapes and ShapeRange collections illustrate another difference you will find between collections. Some collections are used purely for storing and retrieving individual objects. This type of collection object has only a bare minimum of methods available to it. Other collections serve as mega-versions of the individual object, allowing you to operate on multiple items at the same time. If the collection Class contains more than the standard list of members, it is almost certainly replicating methods of the items in the collection.

For example, even though the Shapes Class has the minimal half-dozen members, all the additional methods are simply variations of the Add method, allowing you to add different types of shapes to the collection. Conversely, the ShapeRange Class has dozens of members, most of which duplicate those of a Shape object. For example, both the Shape and ShapeRange Classes have a Left property for changing the location of one or more shapes.

Looping Through a Collection

Sometimes you want to execute a method on or refer to a property of each element of a collection. If the collection object mirrors the capabilities of the individual item, you can use the collection object directly. For example, the Excel Worksheets collection object provides a PrintOut method that mirrors the PrintOut method for the Worksheet object. The statement *Worksheets.PrintOut* will print all the worksheets in the current workbook.

When a collection does not have the method or property you need, you can use a *For Each* loop to iterate through each item in the collection. For example, the Excel Worksheets object does not have Replace method; you must execute the Replace command on each worksheet individually. The following *ReplaceAll* macro will replace a *For Each* loop through a workbook, replacing one string with another on each sheet:

```
Sub ReplaceAll()
    Const myStart = "abc"
    Const myEnd = "def"
    Dim w as Worksheet
    For Each w in Worksheets
        w.Replace myStart, myEnd
    Next w
End Sub
```

Watching for Typical Members

You will have an easier time learning about new Classes if you can recognize the methods and properties that are common to all Classes.

Members Common to All Classes Each Class has an Application property and a Parent property. The Application property returns a reference to the Office application that the object belongs to. For example, the Application property of an Excel Worksheet object returns a reference to the Excel application, while the Application property of a Word Document object returns a reference to the Word application. Even an Application object has an Application property that returns a reference to itself.

The Parent property returns a reference to the object that is next higher in the object model's hierarchy. It doesn't matter how you retrieve the reference to the initial object; it will always have the same Parent property. For example, the parent of an Excel Worksheet object is always a Workbook. It doesn't matter whether you got the reference to the worksheet by using *ActiveSheet* or *Worksheets(1)*, or by using *ActiveCell.Parent;* the Parent of a worksheet is always its Workbook. The ultimate Parent in any application is the Application object.

In most applications, each Class also has a Creator property that is used primarily on Macintosh computers. If you're not using a Macintosh, you can ignore the Creator property.

Members Common to All Collections In addition to the three common properties to all Classes, a collection Class will always have two add additional members: a Count property and an Item method. The Count property indicates how many items are contained in the collection, and the Item method allows you to access an individual item within the collection. Almost all collection Classes also have an Add method that allows you to add a new item to the collection. Some collections do not allow new items to be added and will not have an Add method.

Using Objects from Other Office Applications

Visual Basic for Application uses Automation to talk to an Office application. The Office application exposes its capabilities through an object library. An object library is sometimes called a Type Library. Visual Basic for Applications must have a reference to the application's object library to talk to the application.

References are created from within the Visual Basic Editor. Click Tools, References. The References dialog box shown in Figure 5-1 illustrates a list of available object libraries.

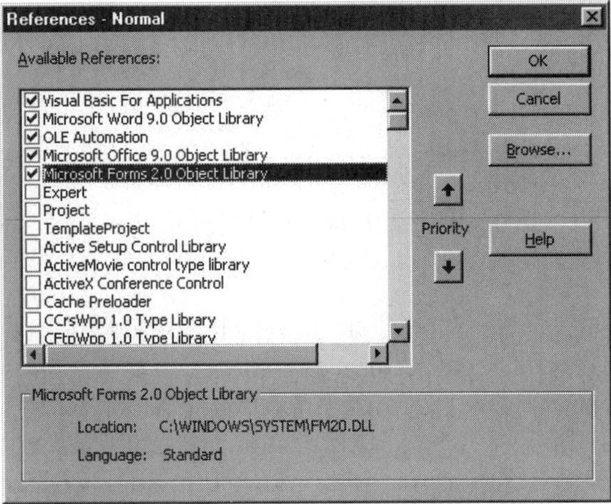

Figure 5-1
Visual Basic always requires a reference to an Object Library.

Libraries that already have a reference will appear at the top of the list with a check in the box next to the name. You will always see references to Visual Basic for Applications, OLE Automation (the original name for what is now called Automation), and the Microsoft Office object library. You will also always see a reference to the host application's object library. As shown in Figure 5-1, the References dialog box contains a reference to the Microsoft Word 9.0 Object Library. Once you have inserted a UserForm in your application, for example, the Microsoft Forms 2.0 Object Library will also appear in the list.

Creating a Reference to a Different Office Application

The References dialog box also shows the name of every Object Library that is registered on your system. To add a reference to a new library, select the check box next to the library name. For example, to add a reference to the Microsoft Excel object library, scroll down to Microsoft Excel 9.0 Object Library and select the check box next to it, as shown in Figure 5-2.

After you click OK, Visual Basic for Applications can communicate with Excel objects the same way it communicates with Word objects, even though Word is still the application hosting VBA.

To display the Visual Basic AutoList members for an Excel object, you must declare a variable with an Excel object type. If you declare a variable as simply Application, Visual Basic will assume that you are referring to the Word Application object, because the Word object library appears higher in the list of references than does the

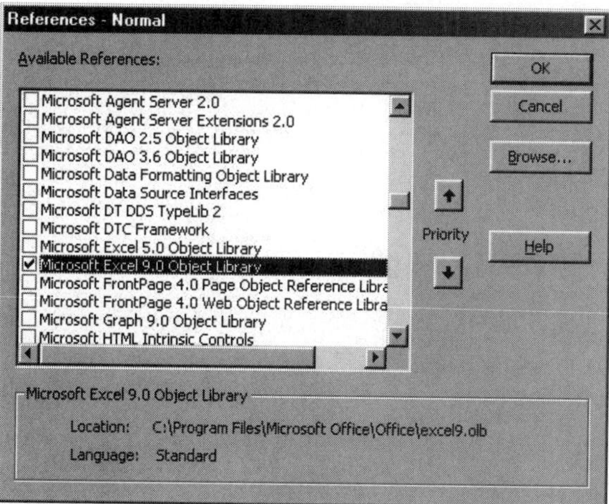

Figure 5-2
Select additional Object Models to control.

Excel object library. To declare a variable as an Excel application, you must place the library name in front of the object type as follows:

```
Dim x as Excel.Application
```

Creating a New Object

Simply declaring a variable is not enough to place an object reference into the variable. One way to add an object reference to the variable is to create a new object. In most Office applications, the only object you can create is the Application object. To create a new object, use the New keyword. Even if Excel is already running, the statement *Set x = New Excel.Application* launches a new copy—or instance—of Excel, and assigns a reference to the variable x.

The instance of the Excel Application object assigned to the variable is invisible. In the Immediate window, type *?x.Visible* and press Enter to see the value *False*, showing that the Excel application is not visible. The statement *x.Visible = True* makes the new copy of Excel appear. (Press Ctrl+Tab to get back to Visual Basic, where you can make the application invisible again.)

You can use the new invisible instance of Excel to access any of Excel's capabilities, including all the worksheet functions. For example, you can use Excel's FLOOR function to round a number down to the nearest multiple of a specified number. Type*?x.WorksheetFunction.Round(257, 50)* in the Immediate window. When you press Enter, the value *250* will appear. With this instance of the Excel application, you can also create workbooks, manipulate worksheets, or modify the values of cells—anything that you could do running VBA from within Excel.

Because the only reference to the Excel Application object is stored in the variable, when the variable ceases to exist, Excel will shut down. If you used *Dim* within a procedure to declare the object variable, as soon as the procedure ends, Excel quits. If the object variable is static, you can shut down Excel by using the *Set x = Nothing* or *x.Quit* statements.

Referencing an Existing Object

When you use New to create a new application, you will get a new copy of the application, regardless of whether the application was already running. Visual Basic's GetObject function allows you to access an existing copy of the application. The *Set x = GetObject(,"Excel.Application")* statement retrieves a reference to a currently running instance of Excel, if one exists. To use the GetObject function to obtain a reference to a running application, the first argument must simply be missing. If you use an empty string as the first argument, the GetObject function creates a new copy of the application, just as if you used the New keyword. If the application is not already running, then calling GetObject with *Nothing* as the first argument raises an error. The following code creates a reference to Excel, using the running copy if it exists, or creating a new one if it doesn't:

```
Dim x as Excel.Application
On Error Resume Next
Set x = GetObject(,"Excel.Application")
If Err Then Set x = GetObject("","Excel.Application")
On Error Goto 0
```

Exploring an Object Model

Regardless how much you know about object models in general, when you start working with a new application, you need to learn the specifics of that new application's object model.

Using the Object Model Diagram in Help

The Help file for each Office application provides a diagram of that application's object model. The object model diagram is probably the best place to start exploring a new object model.

Getting to the Correct Help File

Each Office application provides two different types of Help: Help for the application and Help for VBA. The VBA Help files are not installed on your hard drive as part of the default installation. Instead, they are set to install the first time you use them. You will need to have your Office installation media available when you first try to access Help from VBA.

Even within the Visual Basic Editor, Help is divided into Help about Visual Basic topics (the topics discussed in Chapter 4), and Help about using VBA with Office Application objects (the concepts discussed in this chapter). If you click Help, Microsoft Visual Basic Help, the Help files will not include Help about the Office application itself.

The easiest way to find topics related to using VBA with the current Office Application object—including finding the object model diagram—is to activate either the Code window or the Immediate window in the Visual Basic Editor and type the word *Application*. Then, click on the word you typed and press F1. This will take you directly to the Application object topic in the Help file, and it also ensures that the correct Help file is opened.

Finding the Object Model Diagram

Once you have the correct Help file open, click the Show button in the Help window to see the Contents, Answer Wizard, and Index tabs. Select the Contents tab and look for a section beginning with *Visual Basic Reference for,* followed by the name of the application. Then, select the topic ending with the word Objects. For example, Figure 5-3 shows the location in the Contents hierarchy for the FrontPage object model diagram.

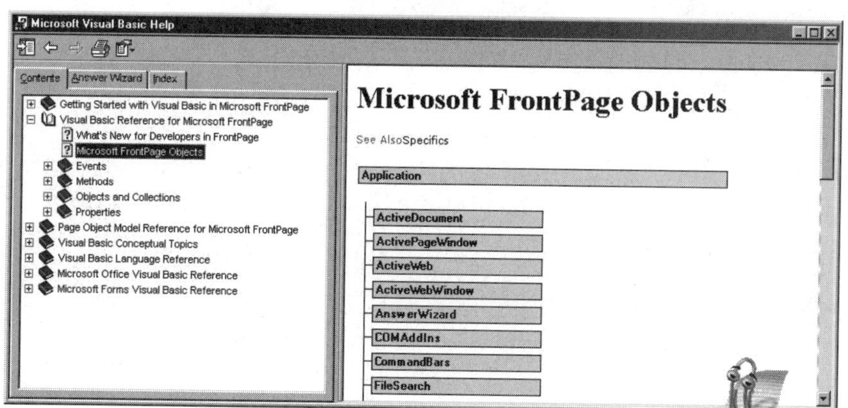

Figure 5-3
The application's Visual Basic Reference contains the FrontPage object model diagram.

In most of the Office applications, once you are in the correct Help file, you can also find the current application's object model diagram by using the Answer Wizard. In the What Would You Like To Do text box, type *Microsoft*, type the application name, and then type *Objects*. For example, for Microsoft Word, type *Microsoft Word Objects*.

In some of the Office applications—particularly Excel, Outlook, and PowerPoint—you can jump directly to the object model diagram from the Visual Basic Editor. In the Immediate window, type the name of the application. (Click Edit, List Properties/

Methods if you want to select the application name from a pop-up list.) Then select the application name and press F1. This direct link to the object model diagram is very useful. Hopefully, Word, Access, and FrontPage will implement this link in the future, as well.

Exploring an Object Model Diagram

Figure 5-4 shows the Excel object model diagram, which is similar to all the Office applications.

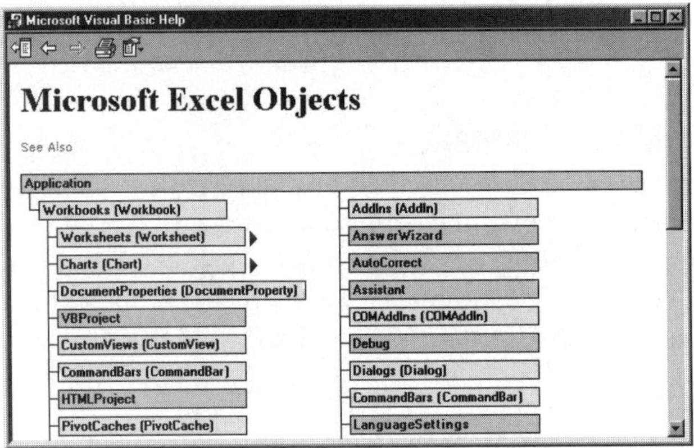

Figure 5-4
The Excel Object Model diagram is typical.

An object model diagram appears in the form of an inverted tree structure, with the Application object at the root of the tree. Each box in the diagram represents a Class. Since many Classes have corresponding collection Classes that simply add an "s" to the Class name, the diagram combines a Class and a corresponding object collection into a single box. The combination box is yellow and shows the names of both the singular and plural Classes. For example, the box labeled *Workbooks (Workbook)* refers to both the Workbook Class and the Workbooks collection Class.

An object without a corresponding collection object is blue and contains only a single Class name. For example, the AutoCorrect Class does not have a corresponding collection Class.

The object model diagram is a good overview for all the objects in an object model. Because an object model can be large, most object model diagrams extend over more than one Help topic. A small red triangle—such as the one to the right of the Worksheets (Worksheet) box—indicates an extension of the object model diagram onto a separate page. If you click the block for an object, Help jumps to the topic for that object. When you click the box for a combined object and collection, you go to the topic for the collection object, which always has a link to the singular object.

Object Model Diagrams Are Not Perfect

You should always retain a certain amount of distrust in an object model diagram in Help. The object model diagram is not generated directly from the object library, but is created by human beings and, hence is vulnerable to errors.

According to the diagram, *ActiveDocument*, *ActivePageWindow*, *ActiveWeb*, and *ActiveWebWindow* are all Classes. In reality, these are the names of properties, not Classes. The ActivePageWindow property returns a reference to a PageWindow object—which properly appears later in the diagram.

COMAddIns—which appears as a blue box with a single name, really should be a yellow box containing the label *COMAddIns (COMAddIn)*. Later in the diagram, Folder and Folders appear once as separate blue boxes, and another time (correctly) as a single yellow box.

These are not serious errors; you can still use the object model diagram to find all the Help topics you need. Once you gain some experience working with object models, you will be able to readily identify superficial errors such as these. When you are first trying to understand how an object model works, however, inconsistencies in the documentation can be confusing. Fortunately, the object models you are most likely to begin exploring are those for Word, Excel, or Access, which are more mature object models and have fewer errors in the documentation.

Browsing an Object Model

One of the most convenient tools for browsing an object model is called, not surprisingly, the Object Browser. To display the Object Browser, click the Object Browser button on the Standard toolbar in the Visual Basic Editor, or press F2. By default, the Object Browser is displayed as a child window. If your Visual Basic Editor window is small, it might be hard to see the Object Browser in the window. Enlarge the Object Browser window by right-clicking it and choosing Dockable from the context menu. Then, undock the Object Browser and make it as large as you want. When you close and re-open the Object Browser, it will remember your previous size and location settings.

Browsing Object Classes

The Object Browser displays all the objects and modules for all currently active projects. The Project/Library drop-down list box at the top of the Object Browser window allows you to specify which library you want to look at. In most cases, you can leave the Project/Library drop-down list box set to All Libraries.

Within the Object Browser, there are two lists. The list on the left side contains all the available Class names. As shown in Figure 5-5, once you select a Class name from the list on the left, the list on the right side will display all the members—the methods and properties—for that Class.

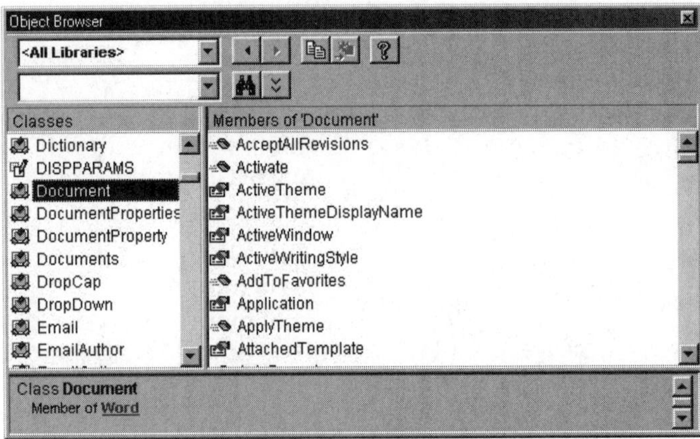

Figure 5-5
Selecting a Class name on the left displays all the members on the right.

As shown in Figure 5-6, once you select a member name from the list on the right side, the display at the bottom of the Object Browser window will provide more information about that member—for example, whether it returns a simple value or an object reference.

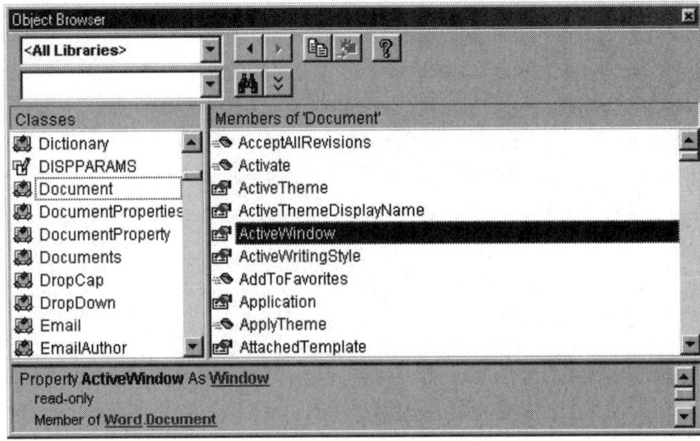

Figure 5-6
Selecting a member name on the right to display information about the member.

Note The Class marked <globals> is a particularly interesting group. Some of the methods and properties of an Application object are flagged as Global, which means that Visual Basic can understand them even when they are not preceded by an object reference. If there were no Global methods and properties, you could never get the first reference to an object. The first object method or property in any object expression must be one of the methods or properties that are flagged as Global. The <globals> section in the Object Browser simply pulls out the Global methods and properties to make them easy for you to find.

If you select the name of a Class from the list on the left and click the Help button, you will jump directly to the Help topic for that Class. If you select the name of a method or property from the list on the right and click Help, you will jump directly to the Help for that method or property. For example, if you select Application from the list of Classes on the left and click Help, you will jump to the Application object Help topic. If you select Application from the list of members on the right, you will jump to the Application Property Help topic.

Searching Within the Object Browser

You can also search for a word or a portion of a word, which can be very useful when you only vaguely remember part of a name. The Object Browser will find all the Class or member names containing the string of letters you type. For example, if you open the Object Browser from Word, type *derline* in the Search text box and then click the Find button or press Enter, a new Search Results section will appear, as shown in Figure 5-7, showing every Class and member containing the text string. When you select an item in the Search Results window, the item appears in the Classes or members list below. To hide the Search Results section, click the arrows next to the Find button.

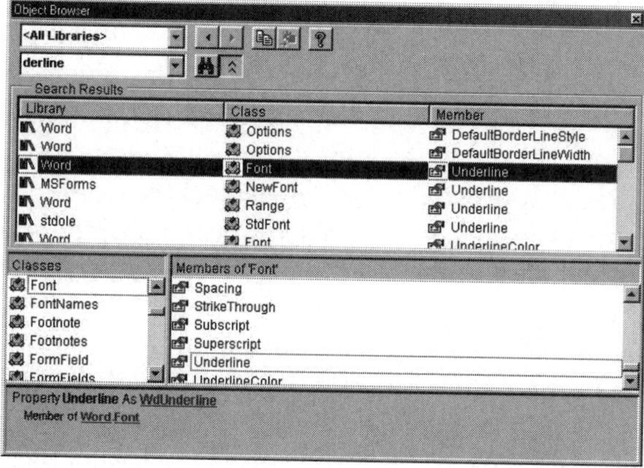

Figure 5-7
Search all Class and member names for a string.

Naming Confusions

The use of the same term for both a Property name and an Object Class name is designed as a convenient memory aid, but it turns out to be the source of a great deal of confusion.

(continued)

Naming Confusions *(continued)*

Look at the Object Browser shown in Figures 5-5 and 5-6. Essentially everything in the right-hand column is either a property name or a method name. These words go into your code. And essentially everything in the left-hand column is an Object Class name. You never place a Class name into your code.

Often, a property name will match the name of a Class. For example, Range appears as a property in the right-hand list when you select <globals>, Application, Worksheet, and several other Class names in the list. The Range property returns a reference to a Range object. You find Range in the left-hand list to find all the methods and properties you can use with a Range object in the right-hand list.

There are dozens of other properties and methods you can use to return a Range object: ActiveCell, Columns, Rows, Cells, Selection (when a range is selected), and so forth. The ActiveCell property is listed on the right, but there is no ActiveCell Class listed on the left. The ActiveCell property returns a Range object.

It might help to imagine that every name in the left-hand list was prefixed with the letter "c" (for Class). If that were the case, the Range property would return cRange object, and the Application property would return cApplication object. You would never place a word prefixed with a "c" in your code.

Exploring With the Immediate Window

You can use the Immediate window to explore an unfamiliar object model. By judiciously using the TypeName function and the AutoList members that Visual Basic provides, you can learn a lot about a new object. Try out the process of exploring a new, unfamiliar, object model. Launch PowerPoint, select the Content Wizard, and create a default presentation. A PowerPoint presentation document has many objects that you can explore.

Looking for Active Properties

You will primarily use the Immediate window to explore the object model, but it is useful to have a procedure open so that you can declare variables. On the Tools menu, click Tools, Macro, and select Visual Basic Editor to open the Visual Basic Editor. On the Insert menu, click Module to create a new module. Then, on the Insert menu, click Procedure. Type *Test* as the name and click OK.

On the View menu, click Immediate window and make the window large enough to see everything easily. The first step is to identify one of the most common objects in the application. Type *Set x =* and then hold down the Ctrl key as you press Enter. Figure 5-8 shows the AutoList that appears. Look for words that begin with the prefix *Active*.

Office applications typically have global properties for accessing important objects. In PowerPoint, there are two properties beginning with the word Active:

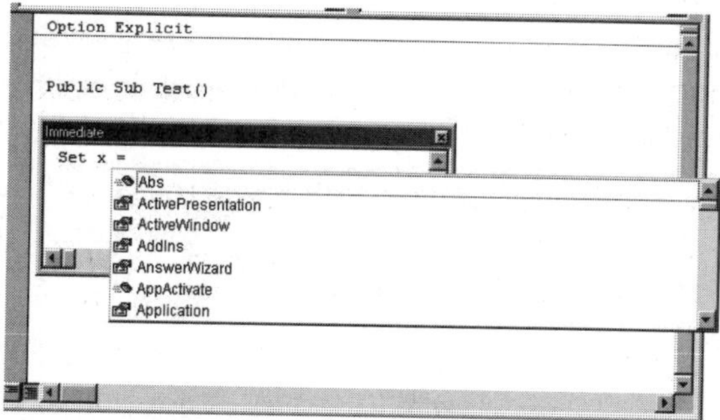

Figure 5-8
Properties for accessing key objects often begin with the word Active.

ActivePresentation and ActiveWindow. The ActivePresentation property relates to the presentation document itself. Select it and press Enter.

Declaring an Object Variable

The *Set x = ActivePresentation* statement you just executed assigned *X* to the variable as a reference to whatever the ActivePresentation property refers to. The variable is a Variant, however, so Visual Basic will not display an AutoList of its methods and properties. In order to see an AutoList, you must declare the variable as an object. To determine the name of the Class, type *?TypeName(x)* in the Immediate window and press Enter. The word Presentation will appear. This is the Class name of the object reference returned by the ActivePresentation property.

Copy the statement *Set x = ActivePresentation* from the Immediate window into the *Test* macro in the Code window. Then, above it, enter the declaration *Dim x As Presentation*. Add a breakpoint above the *End Sub* statement and then run the macro. Your screen should look similar to the one shown in Figure 5-9.

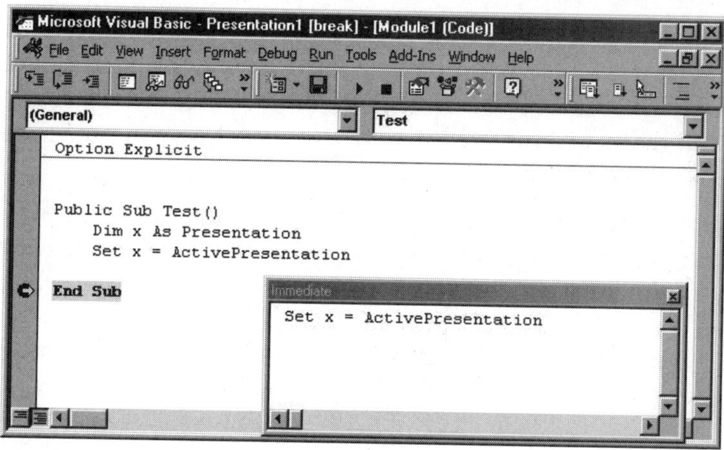

Figure 5-9
Declare object variables and step into the macro to enable AutoLists.

Once again, the variable contains a reference to the active Presentation object, but this time, you are in the middle of a macro where the variable is declared with a specific object type, so Visual Basic will display an AutoList of the object members.

Back on a blank link in the Immediate window, type X and then a period. After you type the period, Visual Basic displays the AutoList of the Presentation object members, as shown in Figure 5-10. Scroll through the list, looking for a collection that contains elements from the presentation.

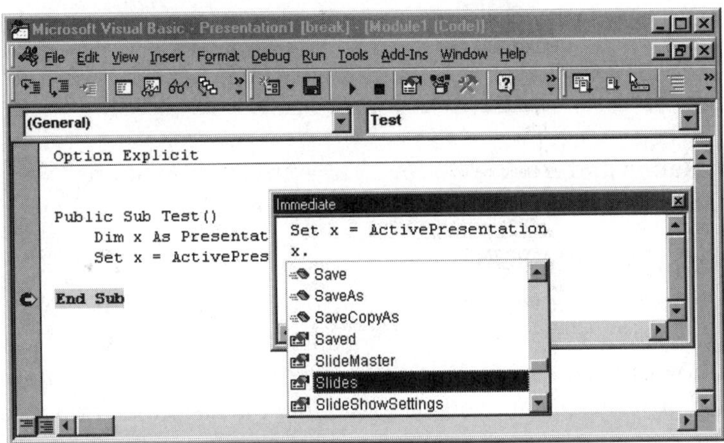

Figure 5-10
Important objects often come in collections.

You could form the hypothesis that the Slides property refers to the slides in a presentation. Select Slides and press Enter. Visual Basic displays the error message *Invalid Use Of Property*. That's because *x.Slides* is an expression that returns a reference to the Slides collection; it is not an executable statement.

Insert a question mark (?) before the *x.Slides* expression and type a period after the expression. Select the Count property from the list. When you press Enter, the number of slides in the presentation will appear. You now know that Slides really is a collection, and that it contains at least one element. You can now explore a single element from that collection.

In the Immediate window, type *y = x.Slides(1)* and press Enter. You can probably guess that the Class name for the object stored in the variable *y* is Slides, but to be sure, type *?TypeName(y)* and press Enter. You can now declare *y* as a variable. Copy the statement *y = x.Slides(1)* to the Code window, just before the *Exit Sub* statement. Then, under the first declaration, type *Dim y As Slide*. If Visual Basic resets your project, press F5 to restart the macro.

Exploring Properties and Methods

Back in the Immediate window, type a question mark *(?)* and a *y,* and then type a period. Scroll through the list of members to find an interesting property for a slide. One of the properties is the Name property, as shown in Figure 5-11.

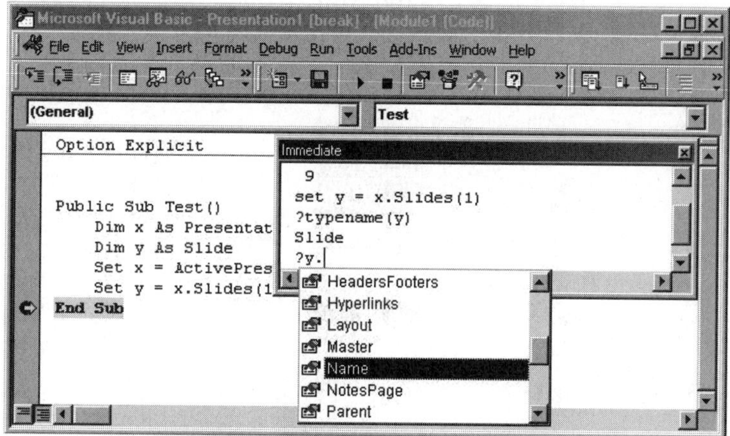

Figure 5-11
Determine unfamiliar properties.

Select the Name property and press Enter. The name of the slide—probably Slide1—will appear. Now try to change the slide's name. Type *y.name = "Opening"*. If you look at the presentation itself, nothing will appear to have changed. The name of a slide does not appear in the presentation itself. The Name property is most useful for referring to a slide from a macro. In the Immediate window, type *Set y = x.Slides("Opening")* and press Enter. Visual Basic accepts the statement, which means that you can use the name of a slide to select an item from the Slides collection.

Try executing a method of a slide. Type *y* and a period and look for an interesting method—perhaps the Duplicate method—as shown in Figure 5-12.

Select the Duplicate method and press Enter. In the PowerPoint presentation, you will see that there is now a second copy of the first slide.

Since the Slides object is a collection, you can use a *For Each* loop to look at each item in the collection. In the Immediate window, type *For Each y in x.Slides: ?y.Name: Next* and press Enter. The name of each slide appears, as shown in Figure 5-13.

The first slide is named Opening, and the second slide's name comes out of sequence—because that's the slide you just created.

After executing a *For Each* loop, the loop variable—*y*, in this case—does not contain anything. Execute the statement *Set y = x.Slides(x.Slides.Count)* to assign a reference to the last slide in the collection.

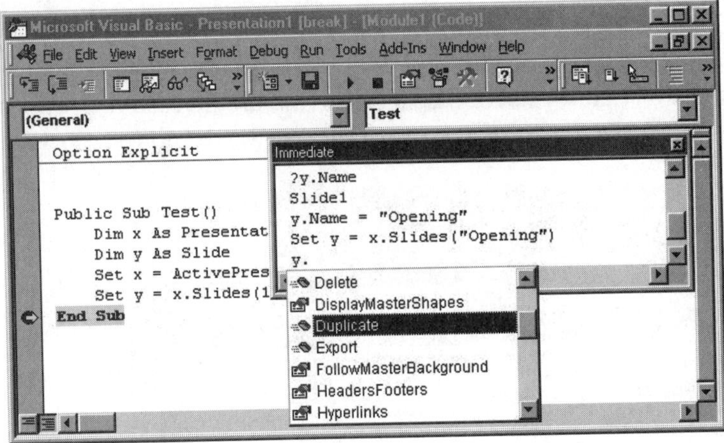

Figure 5-12
Determine unfamiliar methods.

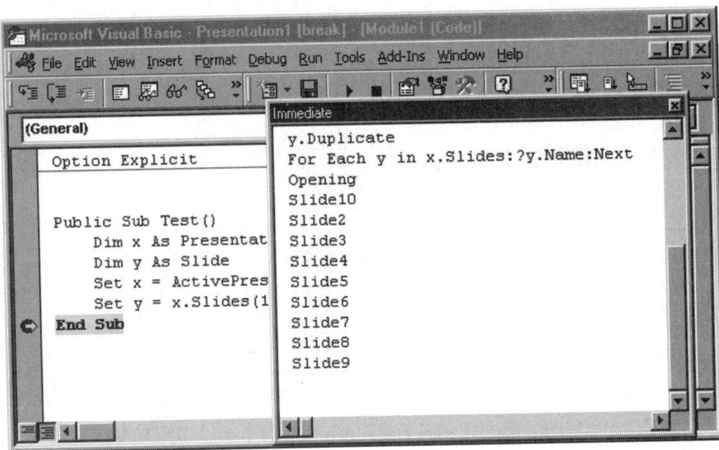

Figure 5-13
Use a For Each loop to explore a collection.

Exploring Other Levels

Next, look for an interesting collection inside the Slide object. In the Immediate window, type a question mark *(?)* and *Y*, and then a period, and observe the AutoList shown in Figure 5-14. A Slide object has very few members, and the Shapes property appears to be the most likely to contain elements of the slide.

Select the Shapes property from the list, type a period, select Count from the list, and then press Enter. The number of shapes on the current slide appears. Type *?y.Shapes(1)*, followed by a period. In the AutoList, look for property that deals with text. The TextEffect and TextFrame properties both begin with the word *Text*, as shown in Figure 5-15.

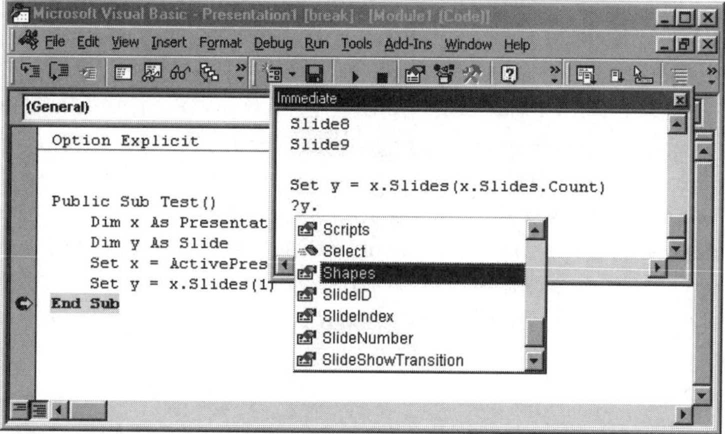

Figure 5-14
You can navigate down additional layers.

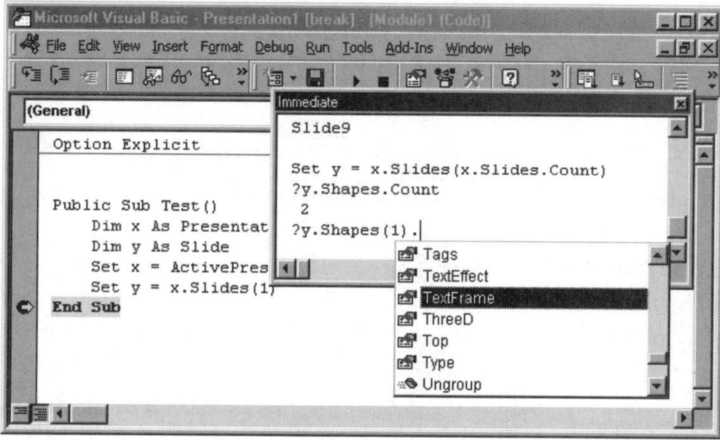

Figure 5-15
Sometimes you have to guess at a property name.

Select TextFrame and type a period. The only property that appears to have something to do with actual text is TextRange. Select that property and press Enter. The text contained in the shape should appear in the Immediate window. Try changing the text using VBA. Type *y.Shapes(1).TextFrame.TextRange = "Something new"* and press Enter. The text on the slide in PowerPoint should change.

The Immediate window is an incredible tool for poking around to determine how an Object Model works for a new application, particularly when you declare variables as a specific Class so that you can see the AutoList members.

Understanding Key Objects

Each Office application provides substantial information in the respective Help files about how to work with Objects in that particular application. The easiest way to access these introduction topics is to open the Visual Basic Editor, display the Immediate window, type Application and then select it, and then press F1. This will open the Visual Basic Help file for the application. Once Help is available, display the Contents sheet. At the top of the contents sheet is a topic labeled Getting Started with Microsoft <Application Name> Visual Basic. For example, in Excel, the topic name is Getting Started with Microsoft Excel Visual Basic. Within that topic is a description of the key objects in that application.

The layout of the Help topics is somewhat different for Microsoft Access, because in Access, the Visual Basic Help topics are not isolated from the application topics. To find a description of Access objects in the contents window, look for the section *Introduction to Programming*. This section contains the best information in the Help file regarding Access objects.

Selections and ranges, particularly in Word and Excel, can be particularly confusing. The next two sections will help clarify some of the points that might otherwise be confusing.

Comparing Selection Properties and Selection Objects

Excel, Word, and PowerPoint all have a Selection property that refers to the portion of the document that is currently selected. Word and PowerPoint, however, both have a Selection object, while Excel does not. In Excel, the Selection property returns a reference to whatever object happens to be currently selected. If, for example, a range of cells on the worksheet is currently selected, the Selection property returns a Range object. If an embedded chart is active, the Selection property returns a reference to the currently selected component of the chart, which might be a ChartArea object, a PlotArea object, or any of several other objects. These are all different types of objects, but the Selection property returns a reference to whichever one is currently selected. Likewise, if a shape—such as a TextBox—is currently selected, the Selection property returns a reference to the TextBox object.

In both Word and PowerPoint, the Selection property always returns a reference to a Selection object. However, the way you access the Selection property differs between the two applications. In PowerPoint, Selection is a property of a DocumentWindow object, so you will most likely use it in the expression *ActiveWindow.Selection*. In Word, Selection is a global property, which means that you can simply use the expression Selection without an object in front of it.

The Selection object in PowerPoint is much simpler than the Word Selection object. In PowerPoint, it is simply a redirector to take you to the actual selected object. The selected object could be one or more shapes (a ShapeRange object), text (a TextRange object), or one or more slides (a SlideRange object). In PowerPoint, it is also possible for nothing at all to be selected. The Type property tells you what kind of object is currently selected. Depending on the value of the Type property, you would then use the ShapeRange, TextRange, or SlideRange property of the selection to access the selected object. Other than methods for Cut, Copy, Delete, and Unselect, the Selection object in PowerPoint has no other significant properties or methods.

In some ways, the Selection object in Word is somewhat similar to that in PowerPoint. It also has a Type property that identifies the type of object that is selected. The *wdSelectionIP* type refers to when the selection is an insertion point, which is as close to nothing as Word seems to be able to get. Word's Selection object also has properties to redirect you to the actual selected object. That is, the Selection object has a Range property that gives you a reference to the selected Range. Likewise, the ShapeRange property gives you a reference to any shapes that might be within the selected area.

In other ways, the Word Selection object is very different from that of PowerPoint. The Selection object itself has a large number of additional methods and properties. In fact, the methods and properties of Word's Selection object are almost identical to those of Word's Range object. For example, to refer to the collection of characters within the current selection, you can either use the expression *Selection.Characters* or the expression *Selection.Range.Characters*. The lists of methods and properties for a Selection object and a Range object are almost identical.

Several methods and properties of a Range object are not available to a Selection object. For example, a Range object has 13 methods that begin with the prefix *Insert*. Of those 13 methods, 11 methods are also available to the Selection object. Only InsertAutoText and InsertDatabase are exclusive to a Range object. Meanwhile, a Selection object has 18 methods that begin with the prefix *Insert*. Of those 18 methods, 11 methods are common to the Range object. An additional seven methods—all dealing with tables—are exclusive to a selection.

This asymmetrical overlap between a Range object and a Selection object is typical. Most of the methods and properties are common between the two, but certain methods and properties—with no apparent rule for the distinction—are unique to one or the other.

To move from the Selection object to a Range object, use the expression *Selection.Range*. To get from a Range object to the Selection object, simply select the object. For example, if *myRange* is a variable that contains a Range object, the statement *myRange.Select* makes the Selection object match the Range object.

Comparing Range Properties and Range Objects

Both Word and Excel have Range objects. In both cases, the object allows you to refer to a portion of the document without having to change the selection. In Excel, a Range object always contains at least one cell. But it can also contain any number of cells, and the cells don't have to be contiguous. In Word, a Range object can consist of just the insertion point, and it can also refer to a contiguous stretch of characters. Oddly, even if a Word Range object consists of only the insertion point, its Characters collection still returns a single character—the character to the right of the insertion point.

Word's Range property does not have any arguments, which serves only to retrieve the Range from some other object. For example, the expression *Selection.Range* returns the Range that corresponds to the selection, and the expression *ActiveDocument.Sections(1).Footers(1).Range* returns the Range contained in the first footer of the first section in the active document. In the Object Browser, search for the word *Range* to see all the objects having a Range property.

Word also has a Range method. The Range method applies only to the Document object. It can take two arguments, one specifying the starting point of the range and one specifying the ending point of the range. If you omit the starting point, the resulting range starts at the beginning of the document; if you omit the ending point, the range ends at the end of the document. Thus, omitting both the starting and ending points gives you the range of the entire document.

The counting scheme for specifying a range counts the spaces between the characters. Think of a picket fence. The fence consists of two parts: the pickets, and the rails that separate the pickets. Because a fence always has a picket on each end, it will always have one fewer rail than it has pickets. For example, if you have a fence with four pickets, it will have three rails. In Word, characters are like rails, and pickets are imaginary lines between the characters. Each picket is numbered, with the number zero for the first picket in the document. Even though you think of a range as consisting of characters, you always specify it by using picket numbers. So, the expression *ActiveDocument.Range(0,5)* returns the first five characters in the document.

Excel has three different versions of a Range property. One of the versions uses no arguments and is very similar to Word's Range property. It is used to retrieve the cell range corresponding to a HyperLink object or an AutoFilter object.

The second version of a Range property corresponds to Word's Range method: it has two arguments, one for the starting cell and one for the ending cell. Word calls this a Range method because it takes arguments. Excel calls it a Range property because properties can now take arguments. (In the first version of Excel's object model, it was called a Range method.) There is no objective difference between a read-only property and a method.

When you use Excel's second Range property to specify a range, you can't use only cell numbers—because cells don't have numbers.

- You can use cell addresses as quoted text strings, as in *Range("A1", "D5")*.
- You can also use range objects, as in *Range(ActiveCell,ActiveCell.Next.Next)*.
- You can also use a mix of the two, as in *Range("A1",ActiveCell)*.

The third version of a Range property in Excel takes a single text argument and is really a free-for-all. You can enter anything as an argument that Excel could interpret as a reference in the Edit, Go To dialog box. For more details about creating exotic references in Excel, see Chapter 12, "Use Excel References to Build Better Relationships." Word has no equivalent to this third version of a Range property.

Chapter 6

Drive Office from Visual Basic

In This Chapter

Macros come in two flavors—specialized macros you create for a specific project, and general-purpose macros you create to enhance your overall productivity. For example, you might record a specialized macro to automate importing new data into a Microsoft Excel workbook each month. Conversely, you might create a general-purpose macro to toggle pictures displayed as placeholders in Microsoft Word. You can think of general-purpose macros as an extension to a Microsoft Office application—they add features you wish were built-in.

Whenever you create a macro—whether it is specialized or for general purpose—you need to think about where you will store the macro and how you will run it. All Office applications provide a default location for storing a macro, as well as a default mechanism for running it; the defaults might be sufficient for most situations. Some Office applications allow you to create an add-in, which is a way of storing a macro so that it becomes a part of the application. This chapter will help you understand the similarities—and the differences—you'll find when using Visual Basic for Applications (VBA) projects in Office applications.

Using VBA Projects in Office

A program that hosts VBA is responsible for giving the user a way to create and run macros, and for providing a place to store macros. One of the advantages of VBA is that once you learn how to use this tool, you can use those skills to automate many different programs. In fact, now that Microsoft has licensed VBA to other companies, you might even use programs that are not a part of Office but that use the same VBA used in Office applications.

Comparing VBA in Different Office Applications

Even though all Office applications host VBA, they all do so in different ways. For example, Excel, Word, and PowerPoint all utilize the VBA macro recorder, while Access, Outlook, and FrontPage do not. This chapter will help you not only learn how to use VBA in each individual application, but it will also help you understand how VBA is different in the various applications.

Comparing Macro Recorder Functionality between Office Applications

Only Word, Excel, and PowerPoint include support for the macro recorder. In those applications, automating a simple task is easy. Just click Tools, Macro, Record, type a name for the macro, and click OK. Execute the simple task, and click Tools, Macro, and choose Stop Recorder. To make the process even easier, display the Visual Basic toolbar and simply click the Record button.

Each of the three applications, however, provide individual variations to add to the macro recorder's functionality. While recording a macro in Word, some mouse actions are temporarily disabled. For example, you can't use the mouse to draw a table while the macro recorder is running, although you can still use menu commands to create the table. In addition, you can't use the mouse to select text in a text box. The Word macro recorder has the unique ability to pause while recording a macro, which can be considered a workaround to the recorder's limitations. This is an improvement over early versions of Word, when all mouse actions were disabled while you recorded a macro.

If you are recording a macro in Word and need to select text inside a text box, pause the recorder, select the text, and then continue recording. That's not as terrible an option as it sounds, particularly if you know enough about Word objects to be able to insert the missing step later. Another option is to review "Selecting Graphical Objects Using the Keyboard" in Chapter 2 to see how you can use the keyboard to select graphic objects. Even if you normally do not use keyboard shortcuts, you might want to use them while recording macros in Word.

Even if you do not need to record mouse movements, you might find the ability to pause a macro convenient. In Word, you can record part of a macro, pause the macro, switch to a different Word document to write some notes, switch back, resume the recorder, and continue right where you left off. This is not possible in either Excel or PowerPoint, because neither of these applications supports pausing while recording macros. In each of these applications, you must turn off the recorder and then start recording a new macro when you're ready to resume if you want to carry out steps that are not included in the first recorded macro. This difference is nothing more than a trifling inconvenience, however, because it is so easy to merge two macros—simply delete the closing statement of the first and the opening statement of the second.

In Word, the macro recorder always stores new macros in a module named *NewMacros*, even if it has to create the module first. You can control whether the macro will be recorded into the active document, the Normal template, or into a custom template attached to the document, but it will always be in a module named *NewMacros*. You can move the macros to a different module or rename the module, if you want.

In Excel and PowerPoint, new macros are recorded into a new module named *Module* with a number suffix sufficient to make it unique, as in *Module9*. If you record a macro, close the document, re-open it, and then record another macro, the new macro will be stored in a new module. You cannot force the recorder to store a macro into an existing module.

In Excel, you can record a macro into the active workbook, into a new workbook, or into your Personal workbook (which exists in the XLStart folder). Excel will create a Personal workbook file for you if it is needed).

- If you are creating a macro for a specific project, store it in the current workbook.
- If you are creating a general-purpose macro, store it in your Personal workbook.
- If you are creating a temporary macro but a portion of the macro task is to close the active workbook, store it in a new workbook.

In PowerPoint, you can record a macro in any open presentation. You might want to create a special presentation used only for common macros—keeping it open but minimized—to record macros into.

Undoing Macro Actions

When you run a macro in Word, PowerPoint, or FrontPage, each command is stored in the application's Undo list, just as if you had executed the command interactively. For many macros, this makes it possible to completely undo all the actions of the macro, which can be very useful when you are testing new macros.

In Excel, no macro actions will be stored in the Undo list, specifically so that Excel can warn you if an action is too massive to be undone. For example, deleting 10 cells can be undone, but deleting 4000 rows cannot. In earlier versions of Excel, statements in macros that had worked fine for months would suddenly stop, and a pop-up prompt would ask for permission to continue, simply because a range had grown larger over time. Programmers who use Excel macros extensively begged Microsoft to remove the Undo capability from Excel macros to eliminate this problem.

Storing General Purpose Macros

Office applications generally store a Visual Basic project in documents:

- In Word, a project is stored in the document.
- In Excel, a project is stored in a workbook.
- In PowerPoint, a project is stored in a presentation.
- In Access, a project is stored in a database.

FrontPage and Outlook don't have documents, per se. Each of these applications creates a special file for storing VBA projects. In FrontPage, the project is stored in a file named Microsoft FrontPage.fpm, which—for most Windows 95 and 98 users—is stored in the folder C:\Windows\Application Data\Microsoft\FrontPage\ Macros. In Outlook, the project is stored in the file VBAProject.otm located in C:\Windows\Application Data\Microsoft\Outlook.

The location of a VBA project can have implications later on when macros are constantly available. In Excel, Word, and PowerPoint, you can have more than one document open at a time, and macros can be run from any open document, regardless whether that document is the current active document. In Outlook and PowerPoint, however, because there is only one project file, all macros are always available. In Access, only one database is open within a single running instance of Access, so it is difficult to create macros that can be available all the time. The only way you can create general-purpose macros for use by all Access databases is to create an add-in. To create an Access add-in, you must directly manipulate the Windows registry. If you intend to create Access add-ins, you should obtain a copy of Microsoft Office 2000 Developer. In Access, once you develop a module with useful macros, you can export the module and copy it into any database. This creates a copy of the macros; changing one copy does not affect the others.

Storing General Purpose Macros in Excel

When you record a macro in Excel, you can choose to store the macro in what is called the Personal Macro Workbook, which is simply a workbook named Personal.xls stored in the folder C:\Program Files\Microsoft Office\Office\XLStart. (If you record a macro in the Personal Macros Workbook and the Personal.xls workbook doesn't already exist, Excel will create it for you.) The only difference between the Personal.xls workbook and a standard workbook is that Excel records macros into Personal.xls. Excel will automatically open any workbook it finds in the XLStart folder.

The Personal.xls workbook typically has a hidden window which you can unhide by selecting Unhide from the Windows menu, choosing the Personal workbook, and then clicking OK. You should unhide the Personal workbook only if you want to make any changes to the worksheets contained in the workbook—for example, to store tables of information that can be used by macros. ("Launching Macros from Office Applications," later in this chapter, shows how to create tables in the Personal.xls workbook for shortcut keys or shortcut menu commands.)

If you save the Personal.xls workbook while it is visible, it will still be visible the next time you start Excel. It can be tricky to get the workbook saved in such a way that it will open hidden. There are three ways to save your Personal.xls in a hidden state. One method is to make a change to the workbook and then hide it without saving changes, forcing Excel to prompt you to save the workbook when you exit Excel. A second way to save the workbook in a hidden state is to create the *SaveHidden* macro shown below, which hides the active workbook and then saves it for you:

```
Sub SaveHidden()
    Dim w As Workbook
    Set w = ActiveWorkbook
    ActiveWindow.Visible = False
    w.Save
End Sub
```

The macro stores a reference to the workbook in a variable, because once you hide the workbook, it is no longer active.

The third method you can use to save the personal workbook as a hidden workbook is to unhide, edit, and then rehide the workbook. Then, in the Visual Basic Editor, activate a module from the workbook and save it.

You don't need to unhide the Personal workbook to view, add, or modify macros. Simply open the Visual Basic Editor and use the Project Explorer to view the modules contained in the Personal workbook. If a module in the workbook is active in the Visual Basic Editor and you choose Save from the File menu, you will save the workbook containing the active module, even if it is not the active workbook in Excel.

You can also save a workbook as an add-in. In its simplest form, an add-in is simply a workbook where the window is super hidden so that it will not appear in the Unhide dialog box.

Comparing Add-Ins in Excel and PowerPoint

Once you create a PowerPoint add-in, you can no longer view the add-in project at all. You must be sure to save the original presentation beforehand. In Excel, even after saving the project as an add-in, you will still be able to see the project in the Visual Basic Editor. If you don't want others to be able to see the project in Excel, you must explicitly lock it. To lock a project in any Office application, click Tools, choose the <Project Name> Properties command, select the Protection tab, and then select the Lock Project For Viewing check box, as shown in Figure 6-1.

(continued)

Comparing Add-Ins in Excel and PowerPoint *(continued)*

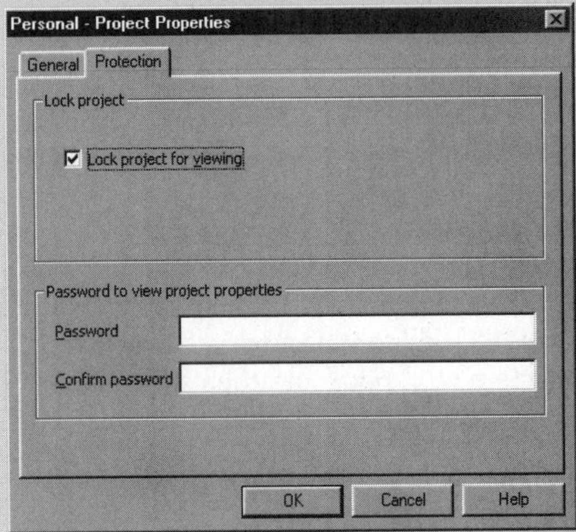

Figure 6-1
Lock a project to keep others from viewing it.

Once you save an Excel workbook as an add-in, any macros that would normally appear in the macros dialog box will no longer appear. If you know the name of the macro, you can still type its name into the Macros dialog box to run it. In PowerPoint, once you have saved a presentation as an add-in, you cannot run a macro by typing its name in the Macros dialog box.

PowerPoint add-ins are superficially similar to those in Excel. In both cases, you create an add-in by choosing File, Save As, and selecting Add-In from the Save As Type list box. In both cases, the default location for storing an add-in is C:\Windows\Application Data\Microsoft\AddIns.

Some intriguing differences do exist, however. The list of installed add-ins in Excel automatically includes any add-in files stored in the AddIns folder. Since Excel stores add-ins in that folder by default, simply saving a workbook as an add-in adds it to the list of installed files. (You will still need to select the add-in from the list to load it.) PowerPoint does not automatically install add-ins in the AddIns folder. You must explicitly choose Browse and select the file to install the add-in. This gives PowerPoint the opportunity to ask whether you want to trust the macros in the add-in, even if you had selected the Trust All Installed AddIns And Templates option in the Security dialog box.

The add-in dialog boxes have other subtle differences: In Excel, to load or unload an installed add-in, you select the check box next to the add-in name. In PowerPoint, to load or unload an installed add-in, you select the add-in name and click the load or

(continued)

Comparing Add-Ins in Excel and PowerPoint *(continued)*
unload button. PowerPoint also allows you to both install and uninstall add-ins, whereas Excel only allows you to install them. To uninstall an Excel add-in, you remove the add-in file from the add-ins folder. The next time you try to load the add-in, Excel will offer to remove the add-in name from the list of installed add-ins.

Because you can assign any macro to a command bar button in Excel, you can use the Customize dialog box to assign a macro from an add-in to a command bar button. Simply create the command or button as usual, and when you assign the macro, type the macro name, even though it doesn't appear in the macros dialog box. As long as the add-in is loaded, the macro will run whenever you click the command bar button. In PowerPoint, on the other hand, you can create command bar buttons only by dragging existing macros from the list onto a command bar. Since macros from an add-in don't appear in the list, you can't use the Customize dialog box to create a toolbar button for a macro in an add-in. The only way to run a macro from a PowerPoint add-in is by letting the add-in create a custom command bar button and attaching the macro to the button.

PowerPoint add-ins can be difficult to deal with, and if you are creating macros primarily for your own use you probably don't want to bother with them. You can get most of the benefits of PowerPoint add-ins without having to create one by simply using command bar buttons. When you assign a macro to a command bar button—that is, to a menu command or to a toolbar button—PowerPoint stores the complete name of the file that contains the macro. When you click the button, PowerPoint will open the presentation and run the macro. The fascinating part is that the presentation's window does not appear in the Windows menu, so you can't see the presentation. In other words, you create a presentation file that contains nothing but general-purpose macros, and then you add the macros to command bar buttons. To run one of those macros, simply click the command bar button.

Storing General Purpose Macros in Word

In Excel and PowerPoint, templates are different from add-ins. Add-ins contain macros, and perhaps some document data that can be used by the macros. Templates are documents that contain boilerplate text and formatting that are copied to create new documents. If a template contains macros, those macros are copied into a new document created from the template.

In Word, the roles of templates and add-ins are combined into a single file called a template. A Word template does function as a template—that is, as boilerplate text or styles for a new document. But in Word, a template also functions as an add-in—that is, in providing macros to multiple documents. A Word document remains attached to the template from which it was created, so any macros in the template are usable from any documents created from that template.

You might want to use the macros from a particular Word template in any document, not just in documents attached to that template. You can do so by making the template into a global template, which corresponds closely to the role of a PowerPoint or Excel add-in. To convert a template into a global template, simply move it to the C:\Windows\Application Data\Microsoft\Word\Startup folder. (Your Application Data folder may be under a folder for your user profile.) Word automatically opens any documents stored in the Startup folder, and any templates stored in that folder are opened as global templates. In Word, you can change the location of the Startup folder by clicking Tools, Options, File Locations, selecting Startup, and clicking Modify.

You can run any macros from a global template, but you can't open the VBA project for the template in the Visual Basic Editor to modify or edit the project. To edit the Visual Basic project, you must open the original template. (This does not apply to the Normal template. You can always edit macros in the Normal template, even if no active documents are attached to it.)

Note

Because the Normal template is used for so many things, you might want to store your general-purpose macros in a separate global template. Opening the template (so that you can edit the VBA project) is a tedious operation, because you have to navigate to the Templates folder before you can open the file. A simple solution is to add the following *OpenThisTemplate* macro into the project. The *OpenThisTemplate* macro would simply open the template containing the macro, which makes the project available for editing.

```
Sub OpenThisTemplate()
    Dim d As Document
    Set d = Documents.Open(ThisDocument.FullName)
End Sub
```

The macro will open any template it is inserted into because it uses the ThisDocument property, which refers to the document containing the macro.

Considering Alternatives to VBA

While VBA is the most important automation tool in Office, it is not the only tool. Access also has a feature that uses the name Macro, and Web-enabled applications and Outlook e-mail can use VBScript. You can also create add-ins using one of the stand-alone editions of Visual Basic. In fact, Excel even supports old-style XLM macros, but you should use those only if you are already extremely familiar with how to create and use them.

Comparing VBA and Access Macros

Access uses the term *macro* to refer to something completely different from a VBA macro. In Access terminology, a macro is a structured grid that helps you build an automated sequence to accomplish specific tasks. In Access macros, you select an action from a list, and then supply additional arguments appropriate to the selected action.

If you have never used VBA—and if you never intend to use VBA—you might want to use Access macros to automate simple actions. If you know how to use VBA, you should use VBA procedures whenever possible. The topic *Should I Use A Macro Or Visual Basic* in the Microsoft Access Help file lists several advantages of Visual Basic functions over macros. In addition, if you start creating sophisticated Access macros, you will need to learn an entirely new language and syntax that is usable only in Access. Sticking with Visual Basic reinforces skills that you can use anywhere in Office applications.

There are two reasons why you would choose to use an Access macro. One reason is to create custom shortcut keys, as explained in the section "Assigning Shortcut Keys In Access" later in this chapter. The other reason is that it is easy to create the general structure of a macro, much like using the macro recorder in applications that support it. You can create a new Access macro, enter several actions by selecting them from the list, and then let Access convert the macro to Visual Basic for you, adding error-handling code in the process. (See "Handling Run-time Errors" in Chapter 4 for details about error handling.). Save the Access macro. Then, with the Access macro selected in the database window, click Macro on the Tools menu, and choose Convert Macro To Visual Basic. Be sure that both the Add Error Handling To Generated Functions and Include Macro Comments options are selected, and click Convert. You can then use the generated VBA procedure much as you would a recorded macro—as a starting place. The feature that converts a macro to a VBA procedure is not installed as part of the default Office 2000 installation; you will need your installation media available when you use it for the first time.

Comparing VBScript to VBA

A VBA macro cannot run without the VBA engine that is hosted by the Office application. That is, in order to run a VBA macro, the Office application must be installed on your computer. If you export a document as HTML, or if you e-mail a message to someone, the person looking at the document might not have VBA available.

Visual Basic Scripting Edition (VBScript) is a lean version of Visual Basic that can be interpreted by most Web browsers without requiring Office to be installed. If you add VBScript code to a FrontPage Web document or to an Outlook e-mail message, the recipient can run the code using any modern browser. If you know Visual Basic, VBScript will be easy for you to work with. Most often, you only need to remember not to do things that are required in Visual Basic.

Comparing COM Add-Ins to VBA

The Automation mechanism used to communicate between VBA and Office applications is part of an industry standard called the Component Object Model (COM). This means that you can control Office applications from any programming language that can function as an Automation client—not just from VBA. For example, programs written in Microsoft Visual C++ or in a stand-alone version of Visual Basic can control Office applications.

Office 2000 now allows you to create add-ins using a stand-alone version of Microsoft Visual Basic that can be integrated seamlessly into the Office application. Creating a COM Add-in is better suited for programmers creating an application for widespread distribution, rather than for power users creating tools for personal use, but you will see COM Add-ins mentioned in the various Office Help files. You might also obtain commercial COM Add-ins that you want to integrate into your Office environment.

A COM Add-in is different from an Excel add-in. In Excel, you can save a workbook as an add-in, which makes it behave in a special way. The section "Storing General Purpose Macros in Excel," earlier in this chapter, gives more information about creating an Excel add-in. Help topics in Word often use the term add-in to refer to a global template. See "Storing General Purpose Macros in Word" earlier in this chapter for more information about creating a global template in Word.

Using Security in Office Applications

If you have ever had to clean up the mess caused by having your computer infected by an innocuous virus, you know how important it is to avoid new infection. Word, Excel, and PowerPoint are vulnerable to macro viruses because macros can be embedded in any of these document types.

Note Access, Outlook, and FrontPage do not include security features for VBA projects. In Outlook and FrontPage, you can create VBA projects, but only for your own use—not for distribution. An Access database is typically shared, not distributed, so different security measures are appropriate. E-mail messages with Word, Excel, or PowerPoint attachments are subject to the security provisions of those applications. Security for other types of e-mail messages is covered in Chapter 21, "Communicate Smoothly with E-Mail."

Signing a VBA Project

To protect yourself from macro viruses, Word, Excel, and PowerPoint include a security check that allows you to determine which documents that include macros you will allow to open. The default security settings prompt you with a dialog box similar to the one shown in Figure 6-2. The large buttons allow you to enable or disable macros when you open the document. To cancel opening the document altogether, click the Close button in the upper rightmost corner of the dialog box.

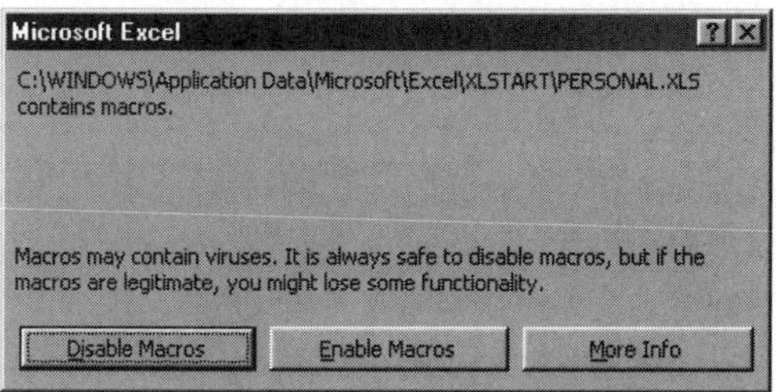

Figure 6-2
Office applications warn you if a document contains a macro.

This security feature is shared between Office applications. Changing a security option in one application changes it for all. To change whether you want to see the Macro Warning dialog box, click Tools, Macro, and choose Security. You will see the dialog box shown in Figure 6-3. The Medium security level is the only one that displays the warning dialog box. Setting the security level to High is equivalent to always clicking the Disable Macros option in the warning dialog box, and setting it to Low is the equivalent of always clicking the Enable Macros option.

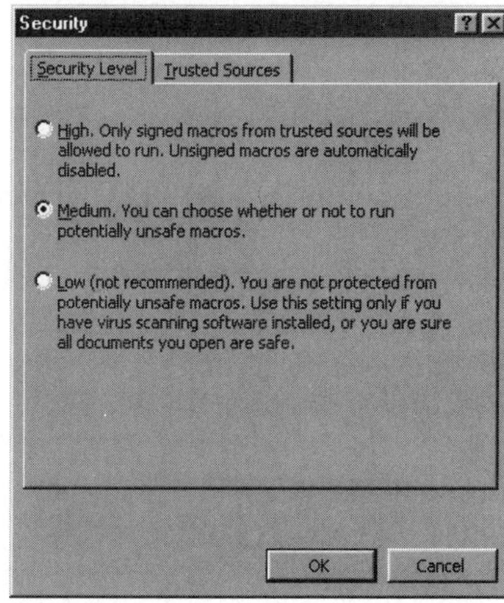

Figure 6-3
You control whether you want to see the macro warning dialog box.

The option descriptions in the Security dialog box state that some macros are "potentially unsafe." A potentially unsafe macro is one that has not been signed with a trusted *Digital Certificate*. Even if you create a macro yourself, the Office application cannot be sure that someone else did not make changes to the macro; that is, unless

Chapter 6

you signed your macro project with a digital certificate. When you use a digital certificate to sign a VBA project, you prevent anyone else from changing that project without destroying the certificate. The person who changes your project can sign the changed project with a different certificate, but not with yours.

Obtaining a Digital Certificate

To digitally sign a project, you must first obtain a digital certificate. You can obtain a certificate in one of three ways: from a commercial certifying agency, from a security administrator in your company, or by creating one for your personal use.

Typically, if you were creating applications for sale or distribution over the Internet, you would obtain a certificate from an agency. If you work for a large corporation, check with your system administrator to see if your company supplies digital certificates to employees. A personal digital certificate is good if you create macros only for yourself, but you still want maximum protection from external viruses.

For detailed instructions on how to obtain or create a digital signature, type the search words *Digital Certificate* into the Answer Wizard for Word, Excel, or PowerPoint. Be sure to access the Help file from inside the application, not from the Visual Basic Editor.

In brief, to create a personal digital certificate, search for the file SelfCert.exe on your Office installation media and run it. Type your name when prompted and click OK. You now have a personal cigital certificate you can use to sign macros you create.

Your certificate is stored in a special system area called the Certificate Store. You can export the certificate to a file that you can back up or move to a new computer, and you can also remove your digital certificate from the computer. To manage digital certificates, open the Control Panel Internet application and select the Content tab. Click the Certificates button, and then select the Personal tab. Using the dialog box shown in Figure 6-4, you can now export, import, and remove digital signatures.

Using a Digital Certificate to Sign a Project

Once you have a digital certificate, you can use it to sign a VBA project. In the Visual Basic Editor, activate a module in the project you intend to sign. Then, click Tools, Digital Signature, and click Choose to display the Select Certificate dialog box. Select the certificate and click OK. If you want to give your certificate a friendly name and description, click View Certificate, select the Details tab, and click Edit Properties. Change the friendly name, as shown in Figure 6-5, and click OK to work your way out of all the dialog boxes.

Your certificate is now attached to the project. Each time you change the project and then save the document, the certificate will be used to sign the project. If someone else changes the project and tries to save the document, a warning will appear that the Digital Certificate is not available to sign the changed project. The person making the

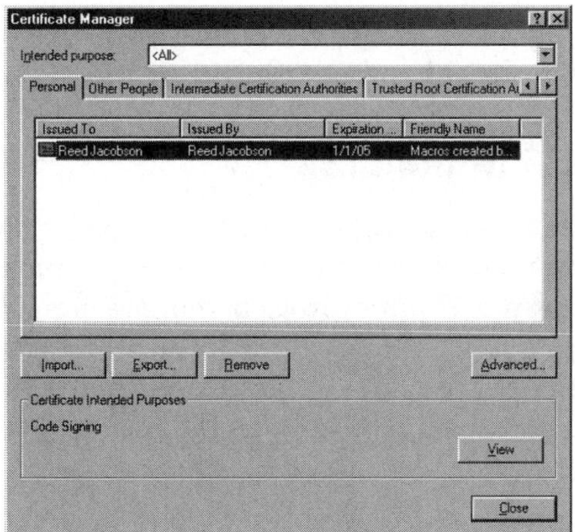

Figure 6-4
Use the Internet Options Control Panel application to manage digital certificates.

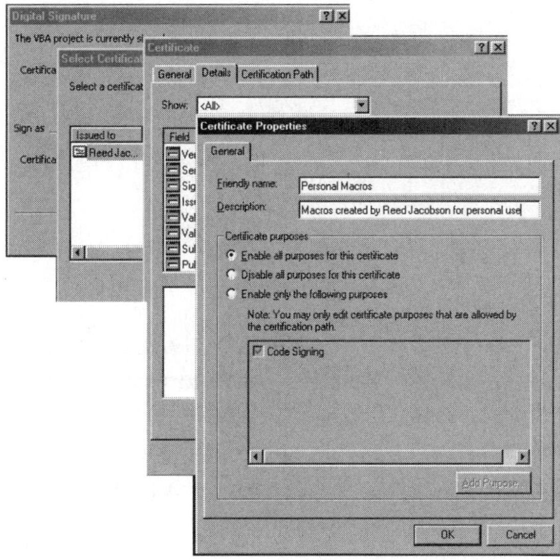

Figure 6-5
You can give your digital certificate a friendly name.

change can then add a new signature, transferring responsibility for the project away from you, or they can discard the changes.

Once you have used a certificate to sign a VBA project, that project will retain the link to the certificate until someone else changes the project, or until you explicitly remove the certificate. If you add a VBA project to a different document, you will have to attach the certificate to that project separately, but the Digital Signature dialog box will suggest the certificate you have already used.

Controlling How You Trust Signatures

When you open a document that contains a digitally signed project, you get a different security warning, as illustrated in Figure 6-6. This version of the dialog box lets you control trusted sources for macros and projects that are signed with this digital certificate. Once you trust a source, you can open documents containing macros signed by that source's digital certificate without any warnings at all. The Security Warning dialog box provides information about the certificate so that you can decide whether to trust the source.

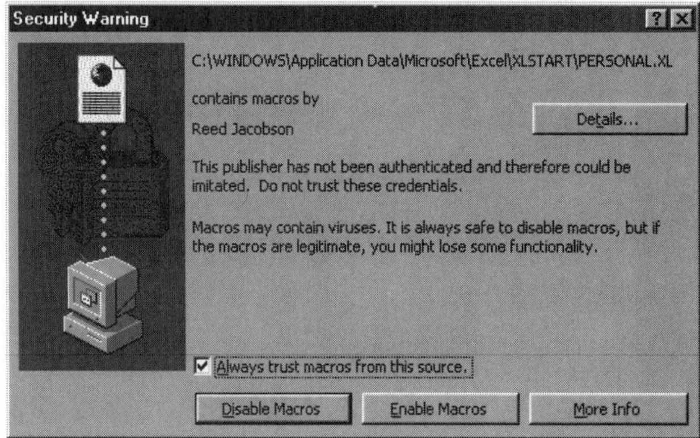

Figure 6-6
You can allow trusted projects signed with a digital certificate.

If the certificate you used to sign the project is a personal digital certificate, the dialog box will display ominous warnings about how the source has not been authenticated, but it's really nothing you didn't already know. By signing all your own projects and trusting your own certificate, you can set the security option to Medium or High (in the dialog box shown earlier in Figure 6-3), and still write macros for yourself without being plagued by constant security warnings.

You can remove any certificate from the list of trusted sources. Click Tools, Macros, Digital Signatures, and select the Trusted Sources tab. Select a signature and click Remove, as shown in Figure 6-7.

Trusting Projects Based on Location

Located at the bottom of the Trusted Sources tab is a check box labeled Trust All Installed Add-ins And Templates. This option means that all a document has to do for its VBA project to get past your security screen is reside in one of the standard Office template folders, in Word's Startup folder, or in Excel's XLStart folder. An add-

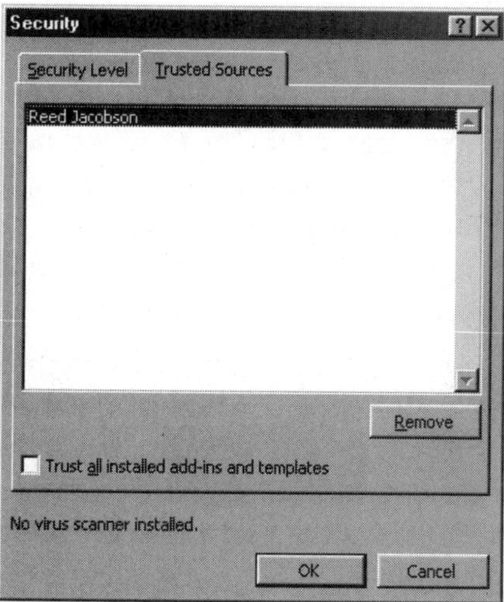

Figure 6-7
You can stop trusting projects from a source.

in that is properly registered in the Windows Registry is also excluded from screening. By default, this check box is selected.

Note Even with the Trust All Installed Add-ins And Templates check box selected, PowerPoint does not trust an add-in simply because it is located in the AddIns folder. You must explicitly install it first. See "Storing General Purpose Macros" in this chapter for more information about creating add-ins.

Trusting projects solely by their location in the file system seems to provide a loophole for virus penetration. In theory, an untrustworthy macro will never have the opportunity to place itself into one of your template folders, so you will be safe. Pragmatically, digital certificates are relatively new enough that you will have templates and add-ins that are not yet digitally signed. Without this escape hatch, you will be flooded with unnecessary security warnings.

Try clearing the check box. If you do have a lot of old templates and add-ins that generate warnings, you can once again trust all installed templates and add-ins. Some day, all legitimate macros will be signed, and this option will no longer be necessary.

Launching Macros from Office Applications

All macros are launched by some kind of an action. The most mundane way to launch a macro is by displaying the Macros dialog box, selecting a macro, and clicking Run. Here are some other ways you can launch a macro.

Linking Macros to Toolbars

In all six core Office applications—Word, Excel, Access, Outlook, PowerPoint and FrontPage—you can assign a macro to a command bar. The term command bar refers to both toolbars and menu bars. "Modifying CommandBars" in Chapter 1 discusses how to customize command bars. The information here assumes that you are familiar with that section, and also deals with how the function of adding macros to command bars differs between Office applications.

In Excel, FrontPage, and Access, you add a generic button to a command bar and then assign a macro to that button. The section "Adding a Macro to a Command Bar in Access," later in this chapter, covers how to assign a macro to a command bar in Access. To add the generic button in Excel and FrontPage, click Tools, Customize, and select Macros from the Categories list on the Command tab. Drag either the Custom Menu Item or the Custom Button to a toolbar, as shown in Figure 6-8. The only difference between a Custom Menu Item and a Custom Button is whether the button displays an icon. You can choose to add or remove an icon later.

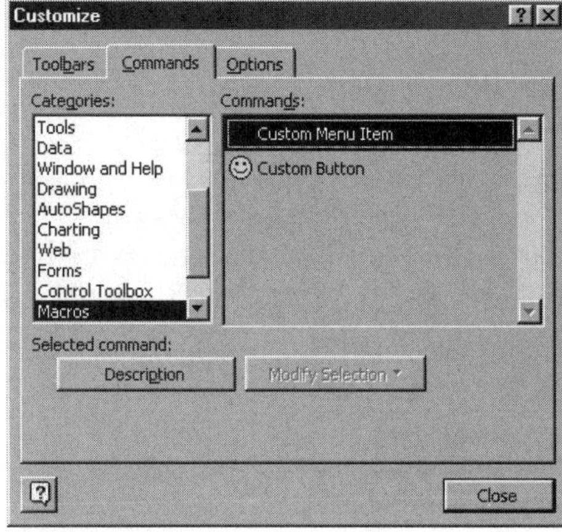

Figure 6-8
In Excel and FrontPage, you first add a generic toolbar button and then link the button to a macro.

Once you have added a generic button, you assign a macro to it. Right-click the button and click the Assign Macro command from the pop-up context menu. Select a macro and click OK. In fact, in both Excel and FrontPage, you can assign a custom macro to any command bar button—even built-in command bars.

In Word, PowerPoint, and Outlook, you assign specific macros to a command bar. In the Macros category of the Customize dialog box, each available macro appears as a separate item. After dragging the item to a toolbar, right-click the item to change its name or icon. You can't change what macro is assigned to what button; if you want to change the macro, you must delete the button and add a new one for the new macro, as shown in Figure 6-9.

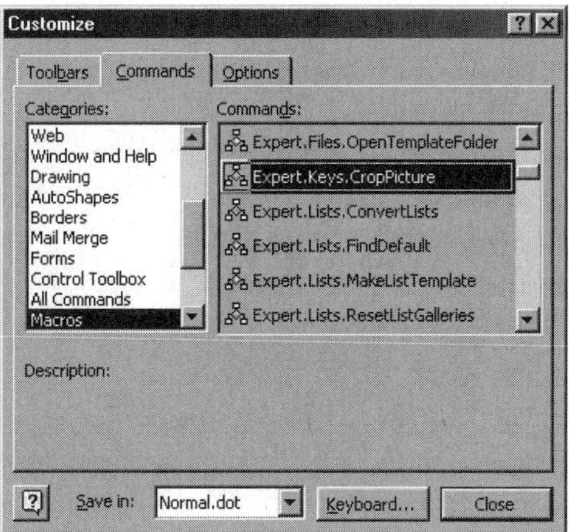

Figure 6-9
In Word, PowerPoint, and Outlook, you create a toolbar button from an existing macro.

Word, PowerPoint, and Access allow you to easily add a macro to a shortcut menu. On the Toolbars tab of the Customize dialog box, one of the toolbars is named Shortcut Menus. The toolbar contains artificial menus, each of which contains a number of submenus, as shown in Figure 6-10. Each submenu corresponds to a specific shortcut menu. When you drag a macro command onto one of these submenus, you can run the macro by right-clicking the mouse in the appropriate context.

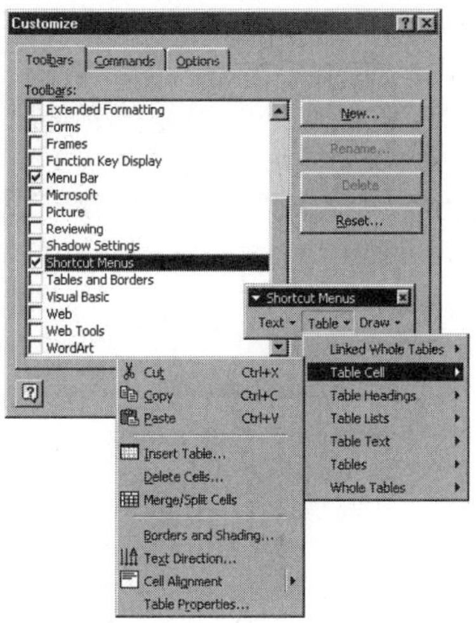

Figure 6-10
The Shortcut Menus toolbar contains all the pop-up context menus.

Adding Commands to Shortcut Menus in Excel

The ability to add commands to a shortcut menu is extremely convenient. Unfortunately, it is unavailable in Excel or FrontPage. Excel is probably the application where custom macros on shortcut menus would be the most useful. Fortunately, because command bars are programmable, you can create a macro that adds commands to shortcut menus in Excel. (You could probably adapt this macro later so that it would work in FrontPage or Outlook, but you would need a place to specify the list of menu commands.)

First, you need to create a table that specifies the shortcut menu name, the command name that you want, and the macro command to assign. Figure 6-11 shows a sample table that will add the *AddXYLabels* macro (which is described in "Creating and Labeling an XY Chart" in Chapter 16) to the Series shortcut menu, using the caption Add Labels (with L underlined as an accelerator key). Begin the table in cell A1 of a worksheet named Shortcut Menus.

	A	B	C	D
1	**Menu**	**Caption**	**Command**	
2	Series	Add &Labels	AddSeriesLabels	
3				
4				
5				

Figure 6-11
Create a table with commands for shortcut menus.

Once you have created the table, add the following *SetShortcutMenus* macro to a module within the same workbook. Run the macro to add the commands to the shortcut menus. The commands remain on the menu until you exit Excel. So that the commands will always be available, add the *SetShortcutMenus* macro to a macro that runs each time Excel is launched (as described in "Creating Workbook-Level Events in Excel," later in this chapter).

```
Sub SetShortcutMenus()
    Dim r As Range
    Dim i As Long
    Dim x As CommandBar
    Dim y As CommandBarControl
    Set r = ThisWorkbook.Worksheets _
    ("Shortcut Menus").Cells(1).CurrentRegion
    For i = 2 To r.Rows.Count
        Set x = CommandBars(r.Cells(i, 1).Value)
        Set y = x.Controls.Add _
        (Type:=msoControlButton, Temporary:=True)
        y.Caption = r.Cells(i, 2)
        y.OnAction = r.Cells(i, 3)
    Next i
End Sub
```

The macro looks for a worksheet named Shortcut Menus in the same workbook as the macro. On that sheet, it looks for the current region—that is, a rectangle of cells surrounded by blank cells—starting in the upper left cell of the worksheet. The macro skips the first row of the table and then loops through each remaining row. For each row, the macro takes the menu name from the first column of the table, finds the command bar with that name, and assigns a reference to a variable. It then adds a button to that menu, retaining a reference to the new button in a variable. Finally, the macro assigns the values from the second and third columns to the Caption and OnAction properties of the button.

The macro makes the button temporary by using *True* as the value of the *Temporary* argument when adding the button. You can make buttons permanent, but if you make it temporary, all you have to do is change the table to change the shortcut assignments. The next time you start Excel, the change will take effect.

To get a complete list of all the command bar names, type the following multiple line statement into the Immediate window and press Enter:

```
For Each x in CommandBars:?x.Name:Next
```

The list of command bar names includes both regular command bars and shortcut menus. You might need to experiment to find the correct shortcut menu name.

Adding a Macro to a Command Bar in Access

Access uses the term macro to refer to a special structured grid that contains commands. Access uses the term *Visual Basic Command* for the type of procedure that all the other Office applications call a macro.

In general, you are better off using Visual Basic commands in Access rather than macros. For a good description of the tradeoffs between the two programming approaches, see the topic *Should I Use A Macro Or Visual Basic?* in the Access Help file.

Suppose that you have the following Visual Basic command in an Access database:

```
Function ShowThisMessage()
    MsgBox "This is my custom procedure"
End Function
```

This is a function procedure, not a subroutine. In all other Office applications, making a procedure into a function is enough to remove it from the list of macros you can attach to a button. In Access, making a procedure into a function makes it easier to attach it to a button.

Now, suppose that you want to add the procedure to a custom command bar button. Like Excel and PowerPoint, you can assign a macro to any button. The method you use, however, is slightly different. You start by clicking Customize on the Tools menu to display the Customize dialog box. There isn't any Macros category in the Customize dialog box, however. There is an All Macros category, but it contains only Access-style macros. To add a Visual Basic procedure, select the File category, and then drag the Custom control to a command bar. (You can also hold down the Ctrl key as you drag an existing button from another command bar.) With the new button selected, click Modify Selection and choose Properties.

Figure 6-12 shows the Control Properties dialog box that appears. Some of the items in the dialog box—notably, the Caption and the Style items—are duplicates of commands on the Modify Selection menu. You cannot use the Properties dialog box to change the icon; to do that, you must use the Modify Selection menu. If you copied a built-in button, be sure to delete the values from the Help File field and the Help ContextID fields. For information about any of the properties, select the property box and press F1.

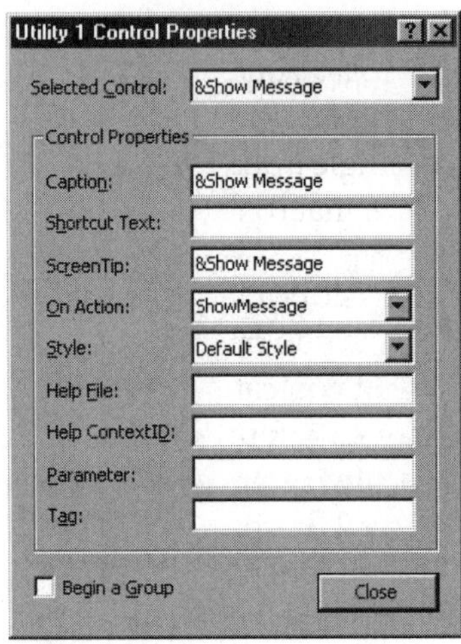

Figure 6-12
Type a Visual Basic subroutine name in the OnAction drop-down list.

The important property for assigning a Visual Basic command is the OnAction property. The drop-down list box shows only Access-style macros, not Visual Basic procedures. The F1 message says that you can enter either a macro name or the name of a Visual Basic function, in the form *=FunctionName()*. So, in the OnAction drop-down list box, type *=ShowThisMessage()*, and close both dialog boxes. You can now click the new button to run the function.

Actually, you don't need to use the full syntax as described in the dialog box. You could enter *ShowThisMessage* (without the equal sign (=) or parentheses) in the OnAction property box and it would still work. In fact, using the unembellished name of the procedure works even if you define it as a sub procedure rather than as a function.

There is a benefit, however, to creating the procedure as a function and using the full syntax—complete with equal sign (=) and parentheses: using the full syntax, you can pass an argument to the function. For example, create the following *ShowAnyMessage* function, which takes an argument.

```
Function ShowAnyMessage(MessageText)
    MsgBox(MessageText)
End Function
```

You can now add two different buttons—one with the procedure *=ShowAnyMessage("Start")* as the OnAction property value, and another with the procedure *=ShowAnyMessage("End")* as the OnAction property. The two buttons will run the same Visual Basic procedure, but with differing results.

Note In Word, Outlook, and PowerPoint, where you select a macro from the list, you can't pass an argument to the macro. In Word and FrontPage—where you assign a macro to the button—you can pass an argument, but the syntax is a little trickier than in Outlook. To run the *ShowAnyMessage* macro from a button in Word or FrontPage, type *'ShowAnyMessage("Start")'* as the macro name in the Assign Macro text box. The single apostrophes allow you to add parentheses with arguments after the macro name.

In Access, any new command bars you create are stored in the database itself. This means that custom command bars will appear when you open the database, and they will disappear when you close it. It also means that you can't create a new command bar that will be available to all databases. Changes to built-in command bars persist, regardless which database is open. Access has two empty built-in command bars available for your use named Utility 1 and Utility 2. If you want to create a custom toolbar that is always available, show one of those toolbars and add controls to it. Remember, however, that custom procedures and macros are available only when a database is open.

Attaching Macros to Shortcut Keys

In most Office applications, you can assign a shortcut key to a macro. Shortcut keys are one of the most efficient mechanisms for launching a macro. For example, you hardly have to move your fingers on the keyboard to press a sequence such as Ctrl+J. Shortcut keys also don't take up space on menus or toolbars.

Shortcut keys have two disadvantages. First, Office applications already assign shortcut keys to many common tasks. If you don't want to replace an existing shortcut such as Ctrl+C, your choices for new shortcut keys are seriously restricted. Second, you have to remember the shortcut key assignments. If you have a macro that you run frequently—and if you can come up with a shortcut key combination that is both easy to remember and also available for use—then adding a shortcut key can substantially increase your productivity.

Assigning Shortcut Keys to a Macro in Microsoft Word

Microsoft Word has a feature for assigning shortcut keys to macros that is not available in any of the other Office applications. In Word, click Tools, Customize, and then click the Keyboard button at the bottom of the dialog box. In the Categories list on the left, select Macros. In the Commands list on the right, select the specific macro name. In the Press New Shortcut Key text box, press the shortcut key combination you want to assign to the macro. If the shortcut key combination you press is already in use by a built-in command or by another macro, the dialog box will show you what is already using that shortcut key, as shown in Figure 6-13. You can then try a different key combination, or simply let the new assignment override the old one. Once you have a key combination you like, click Assign to assign the key combination to that macro.

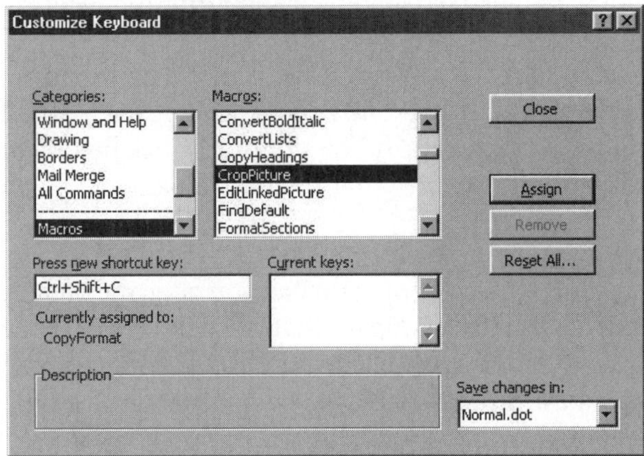

Figure 6-13
Word shows you if you try to assign an existing shortcut to a new macro.

Multiplying Available Mnemonic Shortcuts in Word

One of the problems with creating useful shortcuts is that most of the mnemonic key combinations are already used for standard Windows operations. For example, in all standard Windows applications, Ctrl+P is Print. You probably don't want to change that shortcut key combination. But if you have a macro for importing a picture, you might want to use P as the shortcut

Word has a powerful—and unique—feature for multiplying the number of shortcut combinations you have available. A shortcut key can consist of a normal shortcut combination—a key combined with Ctrl, Alt, or Shift—followed by a separate, additional key. For example, you can assign the shortcut Ctrl+DF to a macro. With this shortcut assigned, run the macro by holding down the Ctrl key and pressing D. Then, either continuing to hold the Ctrl key down or releasing it—whichever is easier for you—press the F key.

This feature was designed as a way to implement shortcut keys for accented characters in European languages. For example, to create the accented é character, you

(continued)

Multiplying Available Mnemonic Shortcuts in Word *(continued)*
press Ctrl+apostrophe (') and then press the letter e on the keyboard. You can appropriate this feature, however, as a way to give yourself a whole new alphabet of mnemonic shortcuts. Start by choosing an easily reached, but little-used shortcut key combination—something like Ctrl+D, which displays the Font dialog box. Then add the appropriate mnemonic letter for your macro. For example, for an ImportPicture macro, you could assign Ctrl+DP. For a *SaveAndMinimize* macro, you could assign Ctrl+DS. You have an entire alphabet of mnemonic combinations available to you, and you only have to remember one launcher shortcut key.

Note In Word, a keyboard shortcut is lost if you do anything to the macro itself. For example, if you so much as move the macro to a new location within a module, the shortcut key assignment is lost. The section "Using a Macro to Preserve Shortcut Keys in Microsoft Word," later in this chapter, explains a technique for maintaining Word shortcut keys.

Assigning a Shortcut Key to a Macro In Excel

Microsoft Excel offers a convenient way to assign selected shortcut keys to a macro. You can assign the control key plus any of the uppercase or lowercase alphabetic characters. In other words, you can use Ctrl or Ctrl+Shift plus a letter as shortcut keys in Excel. Unlike Word, you can't assign other keys as part of a shortcut key combination in Excel. For example, you can't assign Ctrl+Alt+F1 as a shortcut key for a macro. In Excel, you enter a shortcut key in the Record Macro dialog box at the time you record a macro.

You can also add a shortcut key to an existing macro. If you want to add the shortcut key to an existing macro, click Macro on the Tools menu, and then click Macros. Then, select the macro from the list and click the Options button. In both the Record Macro dialog box and the Macro Options dialog box, there is a box for shortcut keys. The dialog box assumes use of the Ctrl key, so you press only the second key in the combination—with or without the Shift key.

The limitations on shortcut keys in Excel apply only to shortcut keys you assign using one of the standard macro dialog boxes. You can use a VBA statement to assign virtually any key combination to a macro—which gives you roughly the same flexibility as in Word.

To use VBA to assign a shortcut key to a macro in Excel, use the Application.OnKey method. The first argument to the OnKey method is the name of the macro, as a string. The second argument is the shortcut key code. In the shortcut key code, you use special characters to refer to the Ctrl, Shift, and Alt keys. Use a caret (^) for the Ctrl key, a plus sign (+) for the Shift key, and a percent sign (%) for the Alt key. For other special keys, enter the key name in braces. For example, {F1} refers to the F1 function key and {Insert} refers to the Insert key. So the code "^%{F3}" refers to the shortcut key combination Ctrl+Alt+F3. For a complete list of the codes available in the *OnKey* function, search for *OnKey* in Excel Help.

When you use the OnKey method to assign a shortcut to a macro, that shortcut key is in effect until you close Excel. You can also use the OnKey method to explicitly turn off the shortcut key by omitting the second argument.

With very little inconvenience, you can create permanent, flexible shortcut key combinations. Create a table similar to the one shown in Figure 6-14 containing macro names, along with shortcut key codes. Then, create the following *SetKeys* macro that will run each time you launch Excel, assigning each shortcut key in the table.

	A	B	C
1	**Key**	**Macro**	
2	%+=	IncrementValue	
3	%+-	'IncrementValue -1'	
4	%+A	ToggleR1C1	
5	%m	ToggleMoveAfterEnter	
6	%c	ToggleManualCalc	
7	%s	SaveHidden	
8	%+{F3}	CreateNamesQuietly	
9			

Figure 6-14
Create a table of shortcut keys.

```
Sub SetKeys()
    Dim r As Range
    Dim i As Long
    ResetKeys
    On Error Resume Next
    Set r = ThisWorkbook.Worksheets _
    ("Shortcuts").Cells(1).CurrentRegion
    For i = 2 To r.Rows.Count
        Application.OnKey r.Cells(i, 1), r.Cells(i, 2)
    Next i
End Sub
```

The table of shortcut keys is on a worksheet named Shortcuts in the same workbook as the one containing the macro. The macro looks at the top left cell on the worksheet—Cells(1)—and then expands the range to look for the region surrounded by blank spaces—CurrentRegion. Searching for the current region makes it easy to add new items to the table. The macro loops through each row of the table after the first and calls the OnKey method using the values from the first and second cells in the row.

Before assigning new shortcut keys, the macro removes any old shortcut key combinations that might have been assigned to the macros in the list. It does that by running the following *ResetKeys* macro:

```
Sub ResetKeys()
    Dim r As Range
    Dim i As Long
```

```
    On Error Resume Next
    Set r = ThisWorkbook.Worksheets _
    ("Shortcuts").Cells(1).CurrentRegion
    For i = 2 To r.Rows.Count
        Application.OnKey r.Cells(i, 1)
    Next i
End Sub
```

This macro loops through the same table as the *SetKeys* macro, except that it omits the second argument to the OnKey method, which removes the shortcut key assignment from the macro.

You need to run the *SetKeys* macro each time Excel starts. To avoid any chance of displaying an error message, you can also run the *ResetKeys* macro each time the workbook containing the macro closes. The section "Creating Workbook-Level Events in Excel," later in this chapter, describes how to run a macro when a workbook opens or closes.

Using a Macro to Preserve Shortcut Keys in Microsoft Word Word easily forgets shortcut key assignments. Simply moving a macro around within the module is enough to make Word forget its shortcut keys. You can take advantage of Word's tools for assigning shortcut keys—and at the same time, avoid the problem of painstakingly recreating shortcut key assignments—by creating a pair of macros. One macro builds a table of shortcut key assignments, and the other assigns all the shortcut keys from the table.

Note You can print a list of all of your shortcut key assignments in Word. Click Print on the File menu. In the Print What drop-down list box, select Key Assignments and press Enter.

Word does not use an OnKey method for assigning shortcut keys. Instead, Word has an entire KeyBindings object that maintains the shortcut key assignments. One thing you need to be aware of when assigning shortcut keys in Word is where the shortcut keys KeyBindings are stored. You can store shortcut keys in the active document, in an attached template, or in the Normal template. The location for storing shortcut keys is referred to as the *customization context*. In dialog boxes, you specify the customization context by selecting a location from the Save Changes In drop-down list box.

In a macro, the Application.CustomizationContext property determines the location for changes to the keyboard shortcuts. For general-purpose macros, the most convenient place to store customizations is in the Normal template.

The following *SaveKeyBindings* macro stores the current key assignments in a table, as shown in Figure 6-15. The entire table is defined as a bookmark named KeyBindings. In the figure, you can see the brackets at the beginning and end of the table, showing the extent of the bookmark. You must create the first row of the table before running the *SaveKeyBindings* macro.

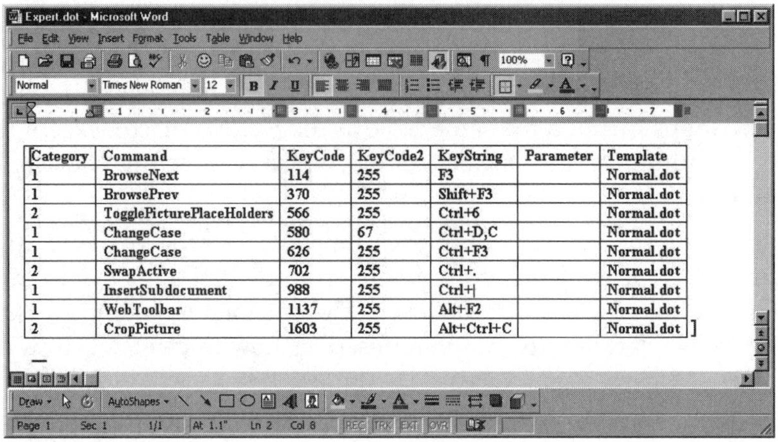

Category	Command	KeyCode	KeyCode2	KeyString	Parameter	Template
1	BrowseNext	114	255	F3		Normal.dot
1	BrowsePrev	370	255	Shift+F3		Normal.dot
2	TogglePicturePlaceHolders	566	255	Ctrl+6		Normal.dot
1	ChangeCase	580	67	Ctrl+D,C		Normal.dot
1	ChangeCase	626	255	Ctrl+F3		Normal.dot
2	SwapActive	702	255	Ctrl+.		Normal.dot
1	InsertSubdocument	988	255	Ctrl+|		Normal.dot
1	WebToolbar	1137	255	Alt+F2		Normal.dot
2	CropPicture	1603	255	Alt+Ctrl+C		Normal.dot

Figure 6-15
Store Word shortcut keys in a table to preserve them.

The *SaveKeyBindings* macro assigns a reference to the table contained in the KeyBindings bookmark range. It then deletes all but the first row of the table, so that the table will be an accurate reflection of the current shortcut key assignments. The macro then cycles through each open template—because shortcut keys can be stored in any template. Within each template, it loops through each customization in the KeyBindings collection, extracting the critical information and storing it in the table.

```
Sub SaveKeyBindings()
    Dim oTemplate As Template
    Dim oTable As Table
    Dim oRow As Row
    Dim oBinding As KeyBinding

    Set oTable = ThisDocument.Bookmarks _
    ("KeyBindings").Range.Tables(1)
    Do Until oTable.Rows.Count = 1
        oTable.Rows(2).Delete
    Loop

    For Each oTemplate In Templates
        CustomizationContext = oTemplate
        For Each oBinding In KeyBindings
            If oBinding.Command = "" Then
                oBinding.Clear
            Else
                Set oRow = oTable.Rows.Add
                oRow.Cells(1).Range = oBinding.KeyCategory
                oRow.Cells(2).Range = oBinding.Command
```

```
                oRow.Cells(3).Range = oBinding.KeyCode
                oRow.Cells(4).Range = oBinding.KeyCode2
                oRow.Cells(5).Range = oBinding.KeyString
                oRow.Cells(6).Range = oBinding.CommandParameter
                oRow.Cells(7).Range = oBinding.Context
            End If
        Next oBinding
    Next oTemplate
End Sub
```

The macro uses the ThisDocument property to refer to the Word document containing the table, rather than referring to the ActiveDocument property. The ThisDocument property refers to the document containing the macro, even if the document is not currently active.

Sometimes a KeyBinding object can remain in the KeyBindings collection without having any command associated with it. The *oBinding.Clear* statement removes any such abandoned KeyBindings. For all macros that are stored in a template other than Normal, the macro includes the template and module names. That information is not necessary, and you can delete all but the macro name. That way, if you move a macro to a different module—or even to a different template—you can still restore the shortcut key.

Once you have your shortcut keys stored in the table, you can restore all the shortcuts by running the following *SetKeyBindings* macro if Word loses any of your shortcut key assignments. The macro first clears all the shortcut keys from all the open templates, and then it reads each row of the table, assigning shortcut keys based on the information it contains. The *SetKeyBindings* macro uses an auxiliary function—*CellValue*—to extract the contents of a cell in a table, stripping off the paragraph and table cell marks that are included as part of the cell contents:

```
Sub SetKeyBindings()
    Dim oTemplate As Template
    Dim oTable As Table
    Dim oRow As Row
    Dim lCat As Long
    Dim sCmd As String
    Dim lKey1 As Long
    Dim lKey2 As Long
    Dim sParm As String

    For Each oTemplate In Templates
        CustomizationContext = oTemplate
        KeyBindings.ClearAll
    Next oTemplate

    Set oTable = ThisDocument.Bookmarks _
    ("KeyBindings").Range.Tables(1)
    For Each oRow In oTable.Rows
        If IsNumeric(CellValue(oRow.Cells(1))) Then
            lCat = CellValue(oRow.Cells(1))
```

Chapter 6

```
            sCmd = CellValue(oRow.Cells(2))
            lKey1 = CellValue(oRow.Cells(3))
            lKey2 = CellValue(oRow.Cells(4))
            If lKey2 = 0 Then lKey2 = 255
            sParm = CellValue(oRow.Cells(6))
            CustomizationContext = GetTemplate _
            (CellValue(oRow.Cells(7)))
            KeyBindings.Add lCat, sCmd, lKey1, lKey2, sParm
        End If
    Next oRow
End Sub

Private Function CellValue(InputCell As Cell) As Variant
    CellValue = InputCell.Range.Text
    CellValue = Left(CellValue, Len(CellValue) - 2)
    If CellValue = "" Then CellValue = Empty
End Function
```

The *SetKeyBindings* macro uses the seventh column of the table to determine the customization context. It switches to the correct context inside the loop, because the customization context could change for each row in the table. The *SetKeyBindings* macro never uses the KeyString column of the table (column 5). That column is purely for your convenience so you won't have to decipher the KeyCode numbers.

Assigning Shortcut Keys In Access

To assign a Visual Basic procedure to shortcut keys in Access, you need to create an *AutoKeys* macro. An *AutoKeys* macro is an Access-style macro, not a Visual Basic procedure. For detailed steps about creating an *AutoKeys* macro, search the Access Help file for the topic *Assign An Action To A Key*, which explains how to assign Access macros to a key (it does not explain clearly how to assign a Visual Basic procedure to a key). To assign a Visual Basic procedure to a key, create it as a function, not as a sub procedure. To run the procedure, select RunCode in the Action column. Then, for the command arguments, enter the name of the function, followed by any arguments enclosed in parentheses. If the function does not require arguments, use empty parentheses. Do not type an equal sign (=) in front of the function name. Save the macro with the name *AutoKeys* as described in the Help topic.

Creating Event Handlers

You always have to carry out some kind of action to get a macro to start. For example, you might click Tools, Macros, Macro, select a macro, and click Run. You might click a toolbar button, or you might press a shortcut key combination. But somehow, you must initiate some action to get the macro started.

Creating an Event Handler

Some objects have the ability to launch a macro when some other activity takes place. For example, you might want to have a macro run whenever a document opens.

Actions that can trigger a macro are called events. Macros that run automatically when an event occurs are called *event handlers*. (Not all objects have events associated with them; in fact, most objects do not. Word documents acquired several new events for the first time in Office 2000.)

When an object has events, the object appears in the Visual Basic Project Explorer in the Objects section. For example, Figure 6-16 shows the Project window for a new Excel workbook.

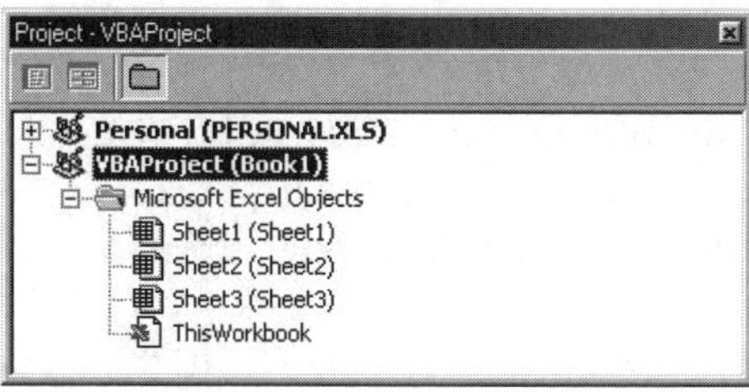

Figure 6-16
In Excel, each worksheet can have events.

In the Microsoft Excel Objects section, there are four entries: one for each of the three worksheets, and one for the workbook (labeled ThisWorkbook). In Excel, both worksheets and workbooks have associated events.

Figure 6-17 shows the Project window for new Word documents. Unlike Excel, there is only one entry in the Microsoft Word Objects section: ThisDocument. That is, only the document has any events in Word. In any application, a new module sheet appears in the Code window when you double-click an object in the Project window. This module is directly associated with the object. Deleting an object deletes the module, as well. For example, where each worksheet has its own module in Excel, if you add code to the module for Sheet1 and then delete Sheet1, the code you added is also irretrievably lost.

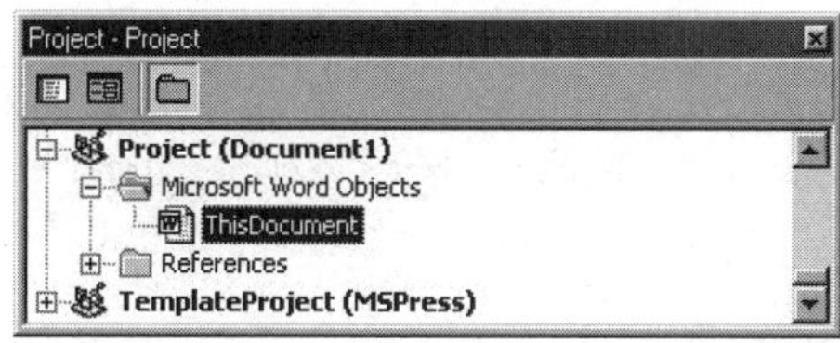

Figure 6-17
In Word, only documents have events.

You can enter any macro or procedure you like in an object's module—even ordinary macros. To create an event handler, you create a sub procedure with a special name. The first part of the name must be the name of the object. For a worksheet, the name of the object is Worksheet. The object name must be followed by an underscore, and then it must be followed by the name of the event. One of the events available for a Worksheet object is the Activate event. So, the following procedure added to the module of a worksheet object constitutes a valid event handler:

```
Sub Worksheet_Activate()
    MsgBox "The sheet is now active"
End Sub
```

After creating this procedure for Sheet1, if you activate Excel, switch to Sheet2, and then switch back to Sheet1, the message box in the procedure will appear.

It is important to get the object name and the event name just right. Visual Basic has tools to help you. At the top of the module are two drop-down list boxes: the list box at the top left is the Object list, and the list box at the top right is the Procedure list. If you create a valid event handler, the name of the event handler's object (Worksheet) appears in the Object list, and the name of the event (Activate) appears in the Procedure list.

If you drop down the Procedure list when an object is selected in the Object list, you will see all the object's possible event names. Selecting an event name creates the shell of an event handler for that event. For example, selecting Calculate from the procedure list creates a macro beginning with the words *Private Sub Worksheet_Calculate()*. This event handler will run every time Excel recalculates the worksheet.

A Private keyword means that you can't run the event handler from any other module, including the Immediate window. If you want to test the event handler from the Immediate window, remove the word Private. (Generally speaking, it's a good idea for event handlers to be private.)

Automatic Macros

In addition to attaching event handlers to events, Word and Excel also allow you to automatically run macros simply by giving the macro a special name. If for no other reason, using event handlers is better than using specially named macros because the documentation is more extensive for event handlers. Word uses one of six special names for macros: *AutoExec, AutoNew, AutoOpen, AutoClose,* and *AutoExit.* These special names are explained in the Word Help files; search for the phrase *Auto Macros.* A macro named *AutoExec* in the Normal template runs a macro when Word first starts up; the AutoExec macro is one case where there is no simple event handler that is easier to use than the macro with a special name.

Excel has four special macro names: *Auto_Open, Auto_Close, Auto_Activate,* and *Auto_Deactivate.* Excel has events that adequately replace all four of these. The only documentation available about these special macro names is in the Help topic covering the *RunAutoMacros method.*

Using Arguments in an Event Handler

Some events pass arguments to the event handler to provide it with extra information. When you select an event name from the Procedure list, Visual Basic adds all the correct arguments to the procedure.

As an example of an argument, the BeforeRightClick event occurs when you right-click a cell on the worksheet. The *Before* prefix indicates that this happens before the normal Excel action for a right-click, which is to display a shortcut menu. (In the event handler, you might want to know which cell was selected.)

One of the arguments of the BeforeRightClick event handler is Target, representing the currently selected range. You might think that the Target argument would return the cell that was clicked, but it doesn't; it returns the entire selected range. You can use Target within your code to refer to the selected range.

Another argument of the BeforeRightClick event handler is Cancel. All events that begin with the *Before* prefix have a Cancel argument. Setting the Cancel argument to *True* prevents normal processing from occurring. For example, the following event handler prevents the shortcut menu from appearing when you right-click a cell on the worksheet:

```
Private Sub Worksheet_BeforeRightClick _
    (ByVal Target As Range, Cancel As Boolean)
    Cancel = True
End Sub
```

Creating Workbook-Level Events in Excel

In Excel, worksheet events occur only for the worksheet containing the event handler. Creating a BeforeRightClick event handler on Sheet1 has no effect on Sheet2. Each of the worksheet events, however, appear in the new guise of workbook events, which do apply to the entire workbook. If you open a module for the ThisWorkbook object and select Workbook from the Object list, Visual Basic creates an event handler for the default Open event. But you can then drop down the Procedure list box and see a large number of events for the workbook. Figure 6-18 shows a portion of the list of events.

All the events that begin with the *Sheet* prefix are duplicates of the worksheet events. This time, however, they apply to all the sheets in the workbook. For example, the following event handler eliminates the shortcut menu from every sheet in the workbook:

```
Private Sub Workbook_SheetBeforeRightClick _
    (ByVal Sh As Object, ByVal Target As Range, _
    Cancel As Boolean)
    Cancel = True
End Sub
```

The SheetBeforeRightClick event has an additional argument, Sh, which returns the sheet on which the event is firing. The event handler must be in a ThisWorkbook

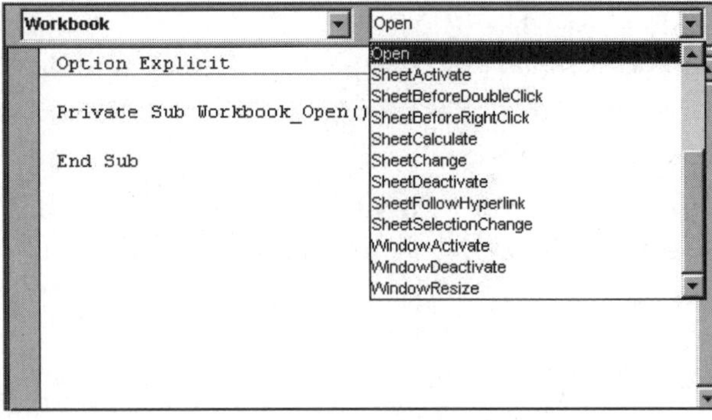

Figure 6-18
A workbook contains events for all worksheets.

module. It runs for every sheet in the workbook—even for sheets that are added after the event handler is created.

Some of Excel's workbook-level event handlers do not simply shadow worksheet level events, but apply to the workbook itself. The most important of these are the Open event and the BeforeClose event. The Open event handler runs any time you open the workbook. The BeforeClose event handler runs just before the workbook closes. As with all events that begin with the *Before* prefix, the event handler can keep the workbook from closing by assigning *True* to the Cancel argument.

Temporarily Disabling Event Handlers

Event procedures run even if the event is triggered by a macro. In other words, you can create a Worksheet_Change event handler in an Excel workbook that will fire each time you change the value of a cell. If you then run a macro that changes the value of a cell, the Worksheet_Change event will still run when the cell value changes. Because Excel has so many different events, this can be a problem. For this kind of situation, the Excel Application object has a special property: EnableEvents. Normally, the EnableEvents property is *True.* If you assign *False* to the property, no event handlers will run. Add the statement *Application.EnableEvents = False* to the beginning of a macro that might cause event handlers to run inappropriately. This will prevent other event handlers from running. At the end of the macro, be sure to add the statement *Application.EnableEvents = True.*

Handling Application Events

Excel is the only application that has workbook-level events, but all the Office applications that handle events have application-level events. (Outlook has application-level events, but you don't need to use them since Outlook has only a single project.)

What if you want an event to run for any worksheet in any workbook, anywhere in Excel? In other words, what if you want an event to occur at the application level? The good news is that application-level events do exist. The bad news is that none of the Office applications include an application object sheet—mostly because there would be no place to store it (remember that VBA projects are stored in specific documents). You must create an application object sheet yourself.

A module sheet for an object in a document is actually a Class module. You need to create a new Class module and designate it as a module for the Application Class. In the Visual Basic Editor, click Insert and choose Class Module from the menu. You might want to give the Class module the name Handlers to help identify its purpose. At the top of the module, declare a variable. Since the variable will be used to handle application events, the name *ApplicationHandler* might be appropriate. You must declare the variable as Public (so that you can refer to it from other modules). You must declare it as an application object (so that it will handle application events). Finally, you must include the word WithEvents before the variable name (to add it to the Objects drop-down list box). Here is what the final declaration will look like:

```
Public WithEvents ApplicationHandler As Application
```

As soon as you enter this statement, *ApplicationHandler* appears in the Objects drop-down list box, as shown in Figure 6-19.

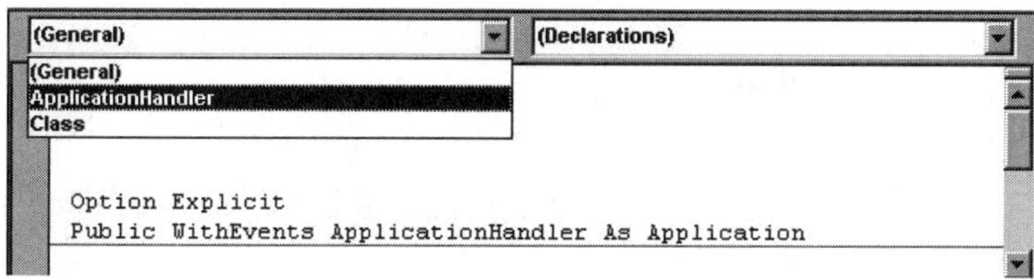

Figure 6-19
Using WithEvents adds the variable to the list of Objects.

When you select it, the Procedure list becomes populated with all the application events. One of the application events is SheetBeforeRightClick. As you can imagine, this event fires whenever you right-click on any worksheet in any workbook. The application version of the handler shown below looks suspiciously similar to the workbook version:

```
Private Sub ApplicationHandler_SheetBeforeRightClick _
    (ByVal Sh As Object, ByVal Target As Range, _
    Cancel As Boolean)
    Cancel = True
End Sub
```

The only difference between the two procedures is the name of the object. In addition to event handlers with a *Sheet* prefix, the application object also has event handlers with a *Workbook* prefix that replicate the workbook-level events for any open workbook.

In addition to creating a variable using WithEvents in a Class module, you must take one additional step to get application event handlers to work. You must assign a reference for the actual application object to the variable, and you can't do that in a Class module. In Excel, open the module for the ThisWorkbook object and create a Workbook_Open event handler that will run each time you open the workbook. In that event handler, add the statement *Set Handlers.ApplicationHandler = Application* (assuming that you used the suggested names for the module and the variable). Now, when the workbook opens, the Workbook_Open event handler assigns the Excel application to the handler variable, and any application handlers you created are now available. To test the events, select the Workbook_Open event procedure and press F5 to run it. Then try out the events that should be captured by the event handler.

Sometimes you will use an application event handler to capture events across all objects within the application, rather than creating event handlers on an object-by-object basis. Often, the application event handler has events that are not available anywhere else. For example, the Excel application object has one additional event that is not available anywhere else—the NewWorkbook event—which fires whenever you create a new workbook.

You can create application handlers for any Office application except Access, and you don't need to create them in Outlook since the ThisOutlookSession object in Outlook's Project window is Outlook's Application object.

The application object in PowerPoint is similar to that in Excel: it replicates the events of the Presentation object, adding only a NewPresentation event. The Word application object has a Quit event which fires each time you exit Word, plus a NewDocument event. All FrontPage events are associated with the application, so you must create an application event handler to capture any events in FrontPage.

Monitoring the Keyboard in a Macro

None of the Office applications includes any events that will monitor what you do with the keyboard. You can make a macro behave differently depending on which keys you press. To monitor the keyboard, you must use a function from a Windows Dynamic Link Library (DLL). Using a Windows function is an advanced technique and should be done with great caution. "Running a Procedure from a Dynamic Link Library" in Chapter 4 explains the basics of using DLL functions.

This section explains the *CropPicture* macro, which allows you to use the keyboard to interactively crop a picture in a Word document. The standard method for cropping a picture in Word is to click the Crop button on the Picture toolbar and then drag the handles on the edge of the picture. It is sometimes difficult to get the precise cropping location with a mouse.

To run the *CropPicture* macro, assign it to a shortcut key combination that includes the Ctrl key—for example, to Ctrl+Alt+C. You then keep pressing the Ctrl key until you have finished cropping the picture. The macro runs until you release the Ctrl key.

As the macro runs, it repeatedly watches for you to press the arrow keys. Initially, the macro allows you to adjust the cropping of the top and right sides of the picture, and places a thick red line on the top and right borders of the picture. In Figure 6-20 you can see the thick border. If you press the Left or Right arrow keys, the macro moves the right edge of the picture to the left or right. If you press the Up or Down arrow keys, the macro moves the top of the picture up or down.

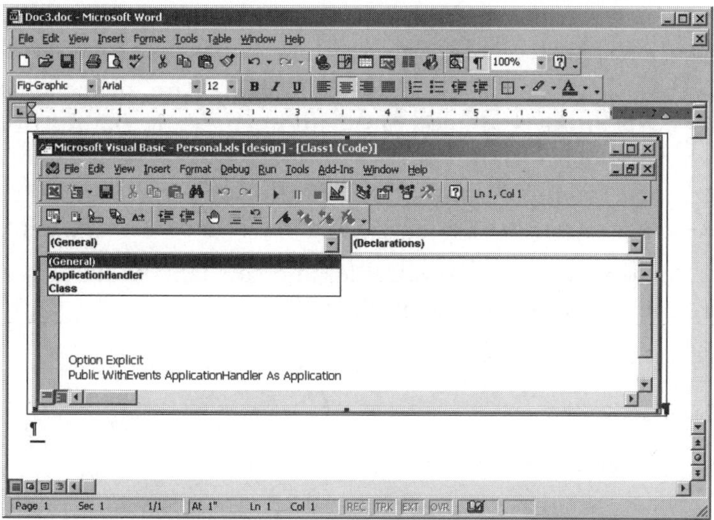

Figure 6-20
The border shows which side is active for cropping

The macro adjusts the border by about one-quarter inch each time you press an arrow key. If you hold down the Alt key as you press an arrow key, the macro adjusts the border by only a single pixel. Tapping the Shift key switches the active sides of the picture from top and right to bottom and left. Tapping the Shift key again switches the active sides back.

Even if you don't need to crop pictures, you might be interested in seeing how the macro monitors keyboard activity. The macro uses three subroutines for frequently-repeated tasks. Refer to "Structuring Macros" in Chapter 4 for information about using subroutines, arguments, and module-level variables. The first part of the macro consists of variables and constants that are stored at the module level. When you declare a Windows DLL function, you must declare it at the module level, not within a procedure.

```
Option Explicit

''' Windows function for monitoring keys pressed
Declare Function GetAsyncKeyState Lib "User32" _
    (ByVal nVirtKey As Long) As Long
''' Constant codes for Keys
```

```
Const myKeyCtrl = &H11
Const myKeyShift = &H10
Const myKeyAlt = &H12
Const myKeyLeft = &H25
Const myKeyUp = &H26
Const myKeyRight = &H27
Const myKeyDown = &H28
```

The *GetAsyncKeyState* function looks at the keyboard buffer to see if a particular key has been pressed since the last time you called the function. You pass it the code for the key you want to look at. The seven constant values are for the keys the macro watches for. The &H at the beginning of the number means that the number is entered in hexadecimal (base 16) notation. You don't need to worry about the value for a key; the number is simply a code for the particular key. A macro statement that looks for *myKeyUp* is easier to understand than one that looks for &H26.

At the module level, you also place variables and constants that need to be used in more than one procedure within the module.

```
''' Module variables for switching sides
Private CropShape As InlineShape
Private BorderSide As Long

''' Constants for border size
Const myTopRight = 1
Const myBottomLeft = -1
```

The *CropShape* variable stores the Shape object that contains the picture. The *BorderSide* variable keeps track of whether you are currently modifying the top and right sides or the bottom and left sides. The two constants show the two values that the *BorderSide* variable can contain.

The main macro handles the entire cropping operation. At the top of the macro are variables and constants used only within this one procedure.

```
''' Main macro: Runs while Ctrl key is down, arrow keys crop
Sub CropPicture()
    ''' Constants that control how much crop moves each loop
    Const BigCrop As Long = 12    ' = 1/6 inch (12 points)
    Const SmallCrop As Long = 1   ' = 1/72 inch (1 point)

    Dim iOldViewType As Long      ' for restoring view at end
    Dim p As PictureFormat
    Dim i As Long
```

The *BigCrop* and *SmallCrop* constants determine how much the cropping will change when you press an arrow key. These are listed in points, which is the unit of measure used by Word's cropping methods. The first executable statements in the macro set the object variables for the Picture and Shape objects.

```
    ''' If no picture selected, just quit quietly
    On Error GoTo ErrorCancel
```

```
''' Assign module level for shape so all proc's can use it
Set CropShape = Selection.InlineShapes(1)
''' We'll be using this subobject a lot
Set p = CropShape.PictureFormat
```

At the bottom of the module, there are two different labels to use for error handling. The ErrorCancel label is just before the *Exit Sub* statement; it does no cleanup. The ErrorHandler label comes before statements that restore the Word environment. Rather than check whether the selection includes a shape, the macro simply tries to assign the shape to an object variable. If there is no shape to assign, an error occurs and the macro quietly jumps to the end.

The next group of statements changes Word's view type to Print Layout view. This is not completely necessary, but Word does a better job of repainting the screen in PrintLayout view. The *iOldViewType* variable simply stores the original view setting so the macro can restore the original view type. Once the view type changes, the error handler switches to the label that will restore the view type.

```
''' After changing view type, quit must reset it
iOldViewType = ActiveWindow.View.Type
On Error GoTo ErrorHandler
ActiveWindow.View.Type = wdPrintView
```

The *GetAsyncKeyState* function returns *True* if the key has been pressed since the last time the function was called. It is very likely for the function to return *True* for some of the keys. By querying the state of each key, the macro clears the key buffer, assuring that a *True* return value indicates that the key was recently pressed.

```
''' Retrieve the key state of each key once
''' This clears the state of residual values
GetAsyncKeyState myKeyCtrl
GetAsyncKeyState myKeyShift
GetAsyncKeyState myKeyAlt
GetAsyncKeyState myKeyLeft
GetAsyncKeyState myKeyUp
GetAsyncKeyState myKeyRight
GetAsyncKeyState myKeyDown
```

The next statement calls the *ToggleBorder* subroutine to set the border side to top right. Among other things, the *ToggleBorder* subroutine draws a red border on the sides that will change. This subroutine is explained later in the chapter.

```
''' Initialize the thick border to top right
ToggleBorder Init:=True
```

The core of the macro exists in a loop. The loop executes repeatedly as long as you hold down the Ctrl key. A *Do While* loop keeps running as long as the condition is *True*. Each time the loop completes, it comes back to this top statement and asks Windows whether you are still holding down the Ctrl key. If you are, it executes the loop again.

Within the loop, the macro checks to see if you have pressed the Shift key (in which case, the *ToggleBorder* subroutine will switch the sides), or if you have pressed the Alt key (which determines the size of the crop movement). The Shift key toggles the border, which means that you need to merely tap the Shift key to switch sides. The Alt key sets the value of *I*, which will determine how much the cropping changes. It sets the value of *I* each time through the loop, so you must hold down the Alt key to use the small value.

```
''' Keep looping as long as the Ctrl key is down
Do While GetAsyncKeyState(myKeyCtrl)

    ''' Press (and release) Shift = Switch sides
    If GetAsyncKeyState(myKeyShift) Then
        ToggleBorder
    End If

    ''' Press (and hold) Alt = Small size move
    i = IIf(GetAsyncKeyState _
        (myKeyAlt), SmallCrop, BigCrop)
```

The next section is long, but consists merely of several variations of the same statement. This is where the actual cropping takes place. Once you have found a key that has been pressed, the *ElseIf* statement keeps the macro from checking any of the other keys (this time, through the loop).

```
    If BorderSide = myTopRight Then
        If GetAsyncKeyState(myKeyLeft) Then
            p.CropRight = p.CropRight + i
        ElseIf GetAsyncKeyState(myKeyRight) Then
            p.CropRight = p.CropRight - i
        ElseIf GetAsyncKeyState(myKeyUp) Then
            p.CropTop = p.CropTop - i
        ElseIf GetAsyncKeyState(myKeyDown) Then
            p.CropTop = p.CropTop + i
        End If
    Else
        If GetAsyncKeyState(myKeyLeft) Then
            p.CropLeft = p.CropLeft - i
        ElseIf GetAsyncKeyState(myKeyRight) Then
            p.CropLeft = p.CropLeft + i
        ElseIf GetAsyncKeyState(myKeyUp) Then
            p.CropBottom = p.CropBottom + i
        ElseIf GetAsyncKeyState(myKeyDown) Then
            p.CropBottom = p.CropBottom - i
        End If
    End If
```

While a macro is running, it takes over the computer, keeping Windows from repainting the screen. The *DoEvents* statement gives Windows permission to handle any other necessary events, such as repainting the screen. (When you execute a loop that needs to interact with Windows, you should always include DoEvents within the loop.)

Pressing an arrow key in Word moves the selection. In each iteration through the loop, the macro reselects the original shape. Theoretically, you should only need to reselect the shape when the macro ends, but selecting the shape each time throughout the loop prevents obscure errors.

```
            ''' Give the screen a chance to repaint
        DoEvents
        ''' Arrow keys deselect picture - this reselects it
        CropShape.Range.Select
    Loop
```

The macro needs to carry out several cleanup tasks before it ends. It needs to remove the red border added by the *ToggleBorder* subroutine. It needs to put the view back to its original state before the macro was run, as well. The macro also calls the *TagPictureCrops* subroutine to store the size of the cropping inside the field code. For a description of the *TagPictureCrops* subroutine, see "Creating a Macro to Store Crop Values" in Chapter 8.

```
''' Do this stuff no matter how macro ends
ErrorHandler:
    On Error Resume Next
    ''' Remove the border from all sides
    ResetBorders
    ''' Restore the original view type
    ActiveWindow.View.Type = iOldViewType
    ''' Make sure picture is still selected
    CropShape.Range.Select
    ''' Puts crop amounts into field code
    TagPictureCrops
    ''' Redraw the screen - fixes selection handles
    Application.ScreenRefresh

''' This is for quiet quit from the beginning
ErrorCancel:
End Sub
```

Chapter 6

The *ToggleBorder* subroutine primarily calls the two other subroutines, *ResetBorders* and *SetBorder*. It behaves differently depending on what the current border side is. The *Init* argument forces the subroutine to start with the editing border on the top right side.

```
Private Sub ToggleBorder _
   (Optional ByVal Init As Boolean = False)
    ''' Start with border on top right
    If Init Or (BorderSide = myBottomLeft) Then
        ''' Set module level variable
        BorderSide = myTopRight
        ''' clear any old border
```

```
        ResetBorders
        ''' Draw the borders
        SetBorder wdBorderTop
        SetBorder wdBorderRight
    Else
        ''' Ditto, except reversed
        BorderSide = myBottomLeft
        ResetBorders
        SetBorder wdBorderBottom
        SetBorder wdBorderLeft
    End If
End Sub
```

The *SetBorder* subroutine changes a single border to a solid, moderately thick, red line. This subroutine simply avoids the need to repeat these three statements four times in the *ToggleBorder* subroutine.

```
Private Sub SetBorder(wdBorder As WdBorderType)
    ''' Subroutine saves typing these three lines over and over
    CropShape.Borders(wdBorder).LineStyle = wdLineStyleSingle
    CropShape.Borders(wdBorder).LineWidth = wdLineWidth225pt
    CropShape.Borders(wdBorder).Color = wdColorRed
End Sub
```

The *ResetBorders* subroutine sets the LineStyle value for each side of the shape to *None*. If the line style is none, the color or width of the border doesn't matter. This subroutine could have used a *For Each* loop to cycle through the borders, but it would not have been much shorter or clearer.

```
Private Sub ResetBorders()
    ''' Clear them all
    CropShape.Borders(wdBorderLeft).LineStyle = wdLineStyleNone
    CropShape.Borders(wdBorderRight).LineStyle = wdLineStyleNone
    CropShape.Borders(wdBorderTop).LineStyle = wdLineStyleNone
    CropShape.Borders(wdBorderBottom).LineStyle = wdLineStyleNone
End Sub
```

Part 3

Word Tools

Chapter 7

Create a Professional Appearance

In This Chapter

Probably the single biggest reason Microsoft Word has become one of the world's most successful word processing programs is its visual appeal. As you type, words take the form of a published work. You can use Word to create reports, brochures, and even publishable books, while seeing a very a reasonable facsimile of the final result on your display.

Word has a dual task. It needs to provide precise control over minute details of a document for those users who have complex requirements. It also needs to be easy to use, particularly for creating simple memos and letters. Often, the demand for control makes Word seem harder to use than it really is. The demand for simplicity can make finding the right way to tweak a particular item very difficult.

The more you understand how Word manages formatting, the better you will be able to entice it into doing precisely what you want. This chapter will help you learn how to take control of Word's formatting to create professional documents.

Formatting Characters and Paragraphs

A Word document contains many different elements that can be formatted: characters, words, lines, paragraphs, margins, passages, columns, pages, pairs of facing pages, chapters, documents, and so forth. The Word designers have given you maximum flexibility to format any element you want, while still keeping the program's design simple enough to manage. Word tags the formatting to one of three levels of formatting within the document: characters, paragraphs, and sections. (A section, in this case, designates formatting of any unit larger than a paragraph.) At each level, Word assigns formatting attributes that cannot be applied at a lower level.

For example, a single character can have a unique font size. Font size is a character attribute, even if all the characters in a paragraph have the same font size. However, a single character cannot have a margin indentation that differs from the rest of the characters in the paragraph. Margin indentation is a paragraph attribute, and all the paragraphs in the document will adhere to the same margin. Likewise, a single paragraph cannot have a unique footer at the bottom of the page. The page footer is a section attribute.

Word has neither word-level nor sentence-level formatting. Words and sentences are simply groups of characters that are isolated from other characters by spaces or punctuation. To effectively control Word formatting—and fix surprising behaviors as they occur—always keep the three formatting levels in mind.

Word provides no easy way to identify the three formatting levels. The formatting commands are spread over various toolbar buttons and menu commands. Word uses a pattern of defaults and overrides to minimize the amount of formatting information it must store. The list at the bottom of the Modify Style dialog box shown in Figure 7-1 can help you conceptualize the formatting that applies to characters and paragraphs. (The options shown in the dialog box allow you to define character styles, which will be covered in more detail in "Using Character Styles," later in the chapter.)

The Modify Style dialog box lists seven format attribute groups. The three enabled groups—Font, Border, and Language—apply to characters. A paragraph mark stores eight groups of attributes: all three groups of character attributes, plus the five groups of its own attributes—Paragraph, Tabs, Border, Frame, and Numbering. (The character and paragraph levels have separate Border attributes which will be discussed more fully in "Defining Character and Paragraph Borders," later in this chapter.)

Every character in a document is part of a paragraph. The paragraph mark maintains default values for all the character attributes; every paragraph has a style. If you don't explicitly assign a style to a paragraph, it uses the Normal style. In a new document, the Normal style defines the default paragraph formatting, which in turn

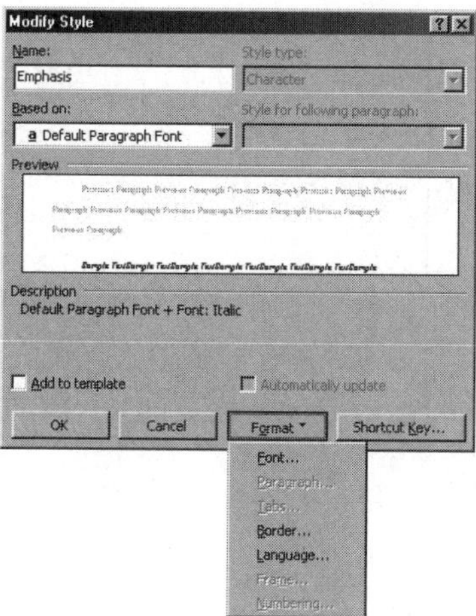

Figure 7-1
A character has three types of formatting attributes.

defines the default character formatting. Every character also has a style. If you don't explicitly assign a style to a character, it uses the default paragraph font style. Styles are associated only with paragraph and character formatting; there are no section styles. "Formatting Sections," later in this chapter, covers section-level formatting.

Revealing Character and Paragraph Formatting

Word provides a keyboard shortcut to display the Reveal Format window, which displays the character and paragraph formatting for a specific character. Press Shift+F1 and click anywhere in your document to see a description of both the paragraph and character formatting. (In the Reveal Format window, the character formatting section is called Font Formatting.) Figure 7-2 shows the formatting for new text in a new document based on the default template. As shown in figure, both the Paragraph Formatting and the Character Formatting use the default Paragraph Style.

When you change something about a paragraph, Word adds the change as direct formatting. Likewise, changes you make to the format of characters are also made using direct formatting, but these changes appear in the Font Formatting section. For example, Figure 7-3 shows the formatting after centering a paragraph and changing the font size to 24 points.

Clearing Direct Formatting

You can quickly remove all direct paragraph-level formatting from a paragraph by pressing Ctrl+Q. Why the Q key? Perhaps it stands for the Q in Quick Clean. Or perhaps it's because—like Ctrl+Z—it is on the left edge of a standard keyboard, and—like Ctrl+Z—the shortcut works like an undo command.

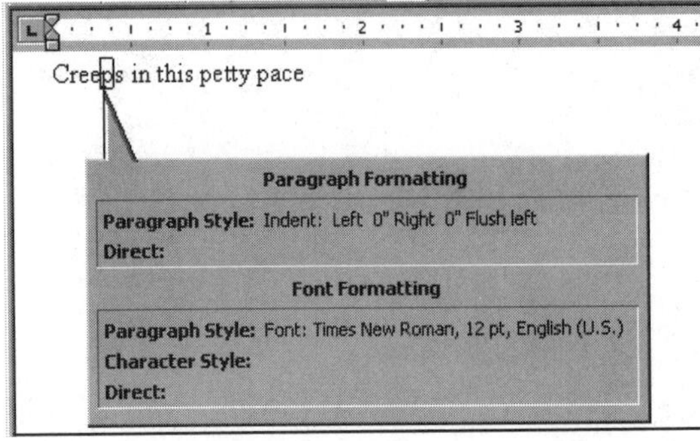

Figure 7-2
Press Shift+F1 and point to reveal formatting.

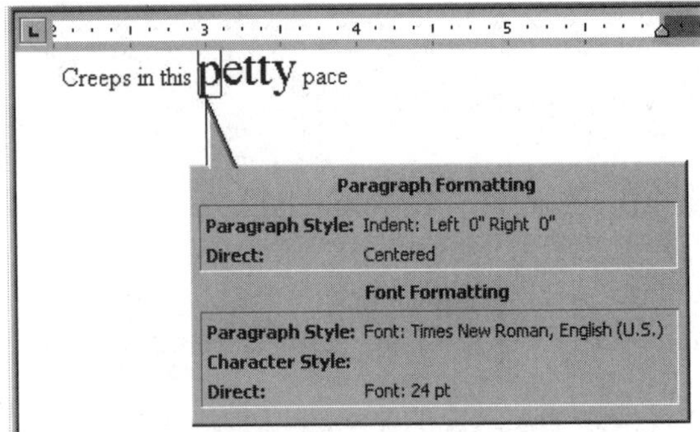

Figure 7-3
Formatting changes are applied as direct formatting.

You can remove direct character formatting from selected characters (or from the current insertion point) by pressing Ctrl+Space. Alternatively, you can press Ctrl+Shift+Z—which is a modified undo—to remove character formatting.

Technically speaking, pressing Ctrl+Space (or Ctrl+Shift+Z) does not actually clear any direct character formatting. Instead, it simply applies the default paragraph font style to the selected text. Even if you use character styles to format characters, that formatting will also be cleared when you press Ctrl+Space.

Character Formatting and Selecting Words

On the Edit tab of the Options dialog box, you will notice a check box labeled When Selecting, Automatically Select Entire Word. Despite its label, the option doesn't make much difference when you select text. You can double-click to select a word or triple-click to select a paragraph, even if this option is checked. If you then drag a selection, Word will automatically extend the selection to subsequent words or paragraphs, depending on the unit of text you originally selected.

If the option is disabled, you can select from the middle of one word into the middle of the next word, as shown in Figure 7-4. If the option is enabled, Word will select the entire first word as soon as you move the mouse into a second word—as if you had double-clicked it—and begins incrementing the selection by full-word units. However, even with the Select Word option enabled, you can still select from the middle of one word to the middle of another. Just drag the selection back into the first word and then drag into the middle of the second word. In other words, when you are selecting with the mouse, the net effect of the setting is to eliminate the need for the initial double-click.

Figure 7-4
You can select parts of two words.

The Select Word option has a more significant effect on how character formatting applies to words. If the option is disabled and the selection is at an insertion point in the middle of a word, clicking the Italic button on the Formatting toolbar (or pressing Ctrl+I) toggles the insertion point so that any new characters you type will be in Italic, while leaving the original word alone. If the option is enabled, Word will apply character formatting to the entire word when the selection is at a single insertion point in the middle of a word. Decide how you want to configure the Select Word option based on how you want entire words formatted, not on how you select with the mouse.

Assuming that the Select Word option is turned on and the insertion point is between any two letters of a word, Word extends character formatting to the entire word regardless of how you apply that formatting. Using shortcut keys, dialog box options, or toolbar buttons all extend the selection to contain the whole word. Even pressing Ctrl+Space to clear character formatting extends the selection to the entire word.

You cannot apply border or shading formatting to a word, however, if the selection is at an insertion point. Borders and shading can be applied either at the character level or at the paragraph level. If nothing is selected, Word assumes you want borders and shading applied to the entire paragraph. To apply character-level borders or shading, you must select at least a single character.

How the shortcut Ctrl+Shift+C works depends on what the selection is at the time you use the shortcut. To copy only the paragraph formatting, click within the paragraph but don't select anything. To copy only character formatting, select the character whose format you want to copy, plus—optionally—any additional characters within the same paragraph, even including the paragraph mark. To copy both the paragraph and the character formatting, select anything else: an entire paragraph, just a paragraph mark, everything in a paragraph except the paragraph mark, or a portion of one paragraph and a portion of the following paragraph.

If the selection is at an insertion point in the middle of a word, pressing Ctrl+Shift+V to paste formatting will paste any copied character formatting onto the entire word, as well as pasting any copied paragraph formatting onto the paragraph.

Paragraph Formatting: Watch the Paragraph Mark

The Help file documentation about paragraph formatting states that the paragraph mark contains all the formatting for a paragraph. In early versions of Word, that statement was quite literally true: you could manipulate paragraph formatting by manipulating the paragraph mark.

Showing Paragraph Marks

A paragraph mark is a symbol that looks like ¶ at the end of each paragraph. Normally, paragraph marks are invisible, but you can display them by clicking the Show/Hide (¶) toolbar button, or by selecting the Paragraph Marks option on the View tab of the Options dialog box.

In one advanced book covering Microsoft Word, the author argues that you should never be allowed to hide paragraph marks because they are so crucial to understanding how Word formatting works. A second author argues that you should never show paragraph marks because they clutter up the document and that it's enough just to know they are there.

I agree with both authors. On the one hand, paragraph marks—and tab and space indicators, for that matter—are indispensable in understanding what is going on with the formatting of a document. On the other hand, they do get in my way while I am reading or typing text.

The solution, of course, is to take advantage of the Show/Hide (¶) toolbar button to toggle the display status as needed. If you are trying to understand the formatting of a document, show the marks. If you are trying to understand the content of the document, hide them. Even better than the toolbar button is the shortcut key Ctrl+Shift+Asterisk (*). This shortcut—which shows all formatting marks—is easy to remember because it is similar to the file system wildcard *.*, which shows all files.

Deleting Paragraph Marks

Note The sample document shown in this section is Borders.doc.

Three paragraphs with very distinctive paragraph formatting are shown in Figure 7-5. If the formatting for each paragraph were simply stored in the paragraph mark, then deleting the paragraph mark from the end of the Right-Justified Original paragraph shown in the figure would destroy that paragraph's formatting, making it part of the Bordered Original paragraph.

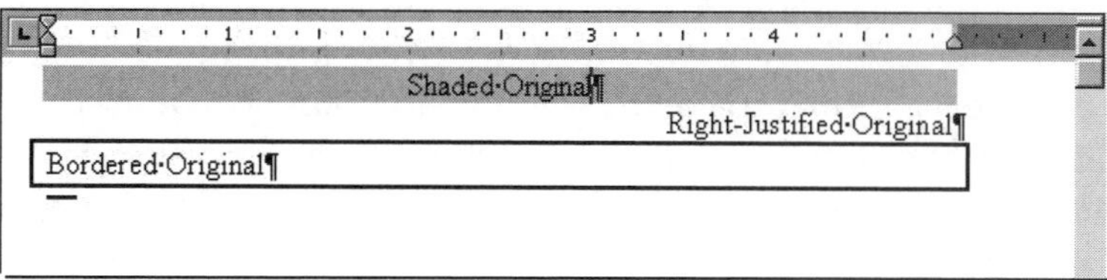

Figure 7-5
Three distinctively formatted paragraphs.

In reality, however, if you delete the paragraph mark, Word applies the formatting from the first paragraph to the newly combined total paragraph, as shown in Figure 7-6. The reason for this is simple: it more closely matches the user's natural expectations. Beginning with Word 7, the format of adjacent paragraphs is swapped when you delete a paragraph mark.

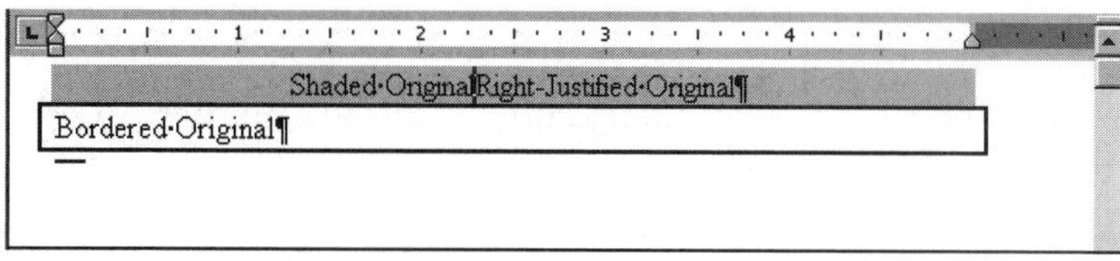

Figure 7-6
Deleting a paragraph marker keeps the format from the first paragraph.

Watch what happens, however, if you add an empty new paragraph before the Right-Justified Original, as shown in Figure 7-7, and then delete the paragraph mark of that empty paragraph. Word retains the formatting from the second paragraph, which makes the document look as it did earlier in Figure 7-5. In other words, Word does not swap the format of adjacent paragraphs if the first paragraph is empty.

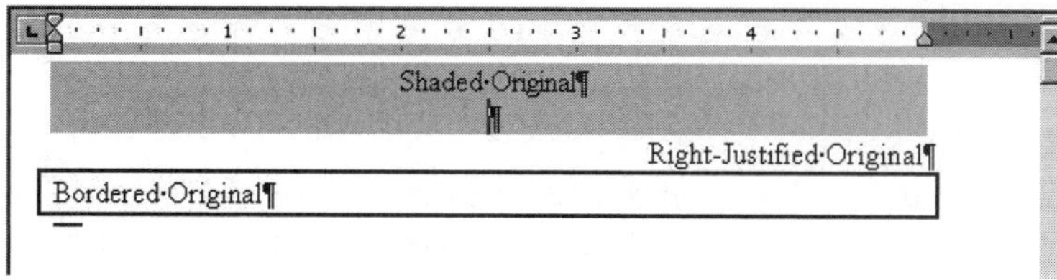

Figure 7-7
Deleting an empty paragraph marker keeps the format from the second paragraph.

The net effect is that you simply cannot merge two paragraphs and make them take on the formatting of the second. As long as the first paragraph contains any text, its format takes over in the merged paragraphs.

Note If you do want to merge two paragraphs, and you want the resulting paragraph to have the formatting of the second paragraph, you must copy the format before merging the paragraphs. One option is to use the Format Painter toolbar button to copy the format from the second paragraph to the first. Another option is to copy the format by using the shortcut Ctrl+Shift+C. This places a copy of the format on an internal clipboard so that you can copy the format, merge the paragraphs, and then use Ctrl+Shift+V to paste the format.

Copying and Pasting Paragraph Marks

Using paragraph marks to manipulate formatting becomes slightly more bizarre when you try to copy and paste a paragraph mark. Once again, consider the document shown earlier in Figure 7-5. Suppose you want to copy the format from the shaded original paragraph to the right-justified original paragraph. You could try to copy the mark of the source paragraph and paste it over the mark of the target paragraph. The target paragraph then acquires the source format, precisely as expected, as shown in Figure 7-8.

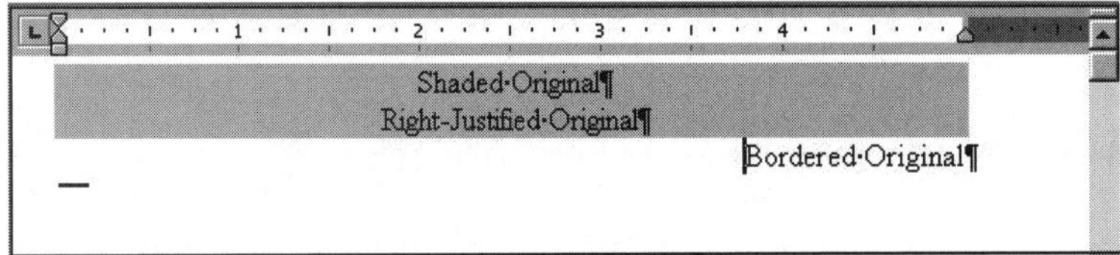

Figure 7-8
Pasting a paragraph mark pushes the replaced format down.

But, assuming that the Typing Replaces Selection option is enabled on the Edit tab of the Options dialog box, some unexpected behavior also occurs. The formatting of the Bordered Original paragraph—which you might have thought was a disinterested bystander—disappears; its formatting is replaced by the displaced formatting from the right-justified original paragraph. Thanks to the Undo command.

The behavior is entirely different if the target paragraph is empty. If you create a second right-justified paragraph and leave it empty, you can copy the mark from the shaded original paragraph, paste it over the mark of the empty paragraph, and then let Word paste the format without affecting the subsequent paragraph, as shown in Figure 7-9.

These two actions—deleting a paragraph mark and copying and pasting a paragraph mark—are suspiciously similar in the way they behave. In fact, they really are exhibiting the same behavior. When you paste one paragraph mark over another, Word first deletes the originally selected text—the paragraph mark. If the deleted mark's paragraph was not empty, Word applies its format to the (temporarily) merged paragraph. Microseconds later, when Word finally pastes the new paragraph mark, the first paragraph takes on the new formatting, but third paragraph has already received its new format.

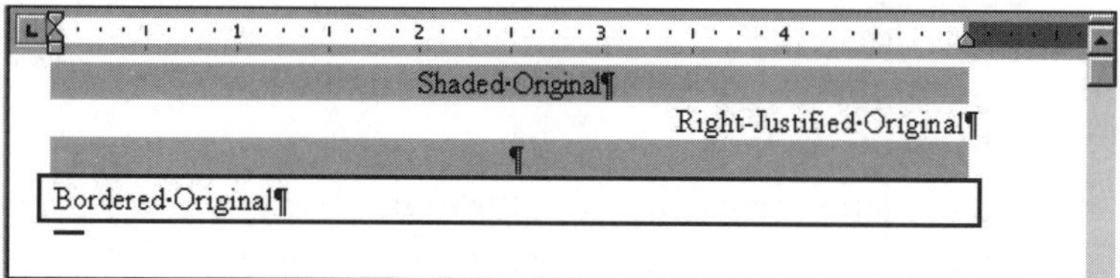

Figure 7-9
An empty paragraph behaves differently from a filled one.

Note If you do want to copy the paragraph formatting from one paragraph to another, use the Format Painter toolbar button or the Ctrl+Shift+C and Ctrl+Shift+V shortcut keys.

Paragraph marks are definitely important, and they do affect paragraphs in critically important ways. But due to Word's efforts to behave more naturally in most situations, you cannot simply manipulate paragraph marks to achieve the formatting you want.

Note The sample document shown in this section is Empty Paragraph.doc.

Formatting Pasted Text

When you apply a format to an insertion point that is not in the middle of a word, Word does not change the format of anything. Rather, it temporarily applies the format to the insertion point; and this temporary formatting evaporates as soon as you change the selection. You can see this temporary formatting when you prepare to type a word in Italic style. When you click the Italic button on the toolbar, the insertion point becomes slanted, indicating Italic style is being applied. If you then press the Left and Right arrow keys—returning to the same place—the insertion point reverts to Normal style. The opportunity for typing Italic style is gone.

Aside from the fact that Word has no way to store your clicked button action—since character formatting is stored with characters—it is perhaps good that Word does not remember the formatting placed at insertion points. Otherwise, you could edit an old document and have inserted text sporadically change to Italic style, purely due to abandoned formatting from a previous round of formatting.

Word also forgets temporary formatting the moment you paste text. So, what do you do if you want to insert some italicized text into a document? For example, what if you have an e-mail message that you want to copy some text from, and you want to change the copied text to an italic font? It would be easier to add the text in an italic font as you paste it than it would be to select and format the text after it's been pasted. You copy the text, switch to Word, find the insertion point, click the Italic button, and then click the Paste button; however, the new text is not italic.

Word can paste the text with the formatting, but only if you first think through how Word manages the formatting. Each new character takes on the formatting of the preceding character. Presumably, a space precedes the inserted text. If you click the Italic button before typing that space, Word will continue to propagate the Italic style when you paste the new text.

In short, to apply character formatting to unformatted text as you paste the text into a document, format the space that precedes the insertion point.

Defining Character and Paragraph Borders

A paragraph mark stores Font and Language information, but it does so only for characters belonging to that paragraph. Border formatting information—which includess shading—is different. Borders exist at both the character and the paragraph level, and a paragraph mark stores both types of information. Figure 7-10 shows text formatted with both character and paragraph borders.

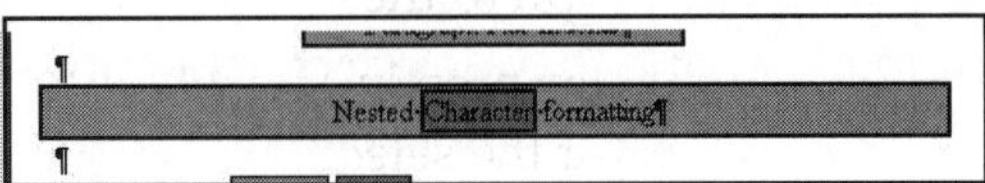

Figure 7-10
Character borders are different from paragraph borders.

The Borders And Shading dialog box offers an Apply drop-down list from which you can select whether to apply borders at the paragraph or the character level. (In the drop-down list, the character level is referred to as Text.) The Text option is available only if at least one character is selected.

The main difference between character and paragraph formatting is that character formatting applies only to the actual characters, not to any spaces around the characters, while paragraph formatting applies to the entire paragraph. Paragraph formatting extends to the paragraph margins, but it does not include the space before or after that might be assigned to a paragraph, unless the adjacent paragraph has the same format. Figure 7-11 shows the difference between a paragraph whose characters are formatted and one where the paragraph itself is formatted.

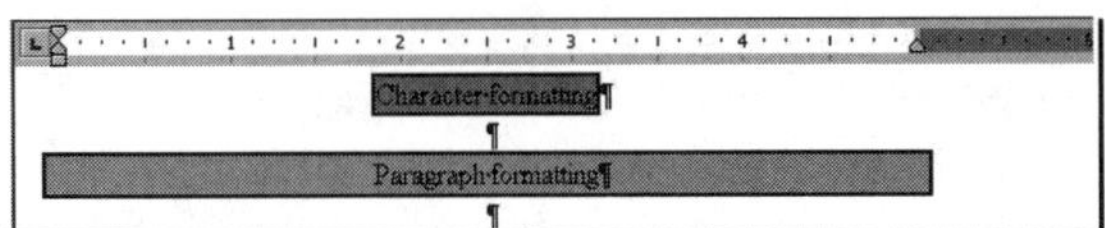

Figure 7-11
Paragraph borders and shading extend to the margins.

Character formatting will not extend to trailing spaces in a paragraph. Suppose you have a centered title and want shading to extend slightly past the words. The top paragraph of Figure 7-12 shows what happens if you use character formatting and add spaces before and after the text. Word formats the spaces at the beginning of the paragraph but ignores the trailing spaces. (Word ignores those spaces completely—even when centering a paragraph.) The ignored spaces retain their formatting information. If you type an *x* or a period at the end of the spaces, Word will suddenly format all the spaces.

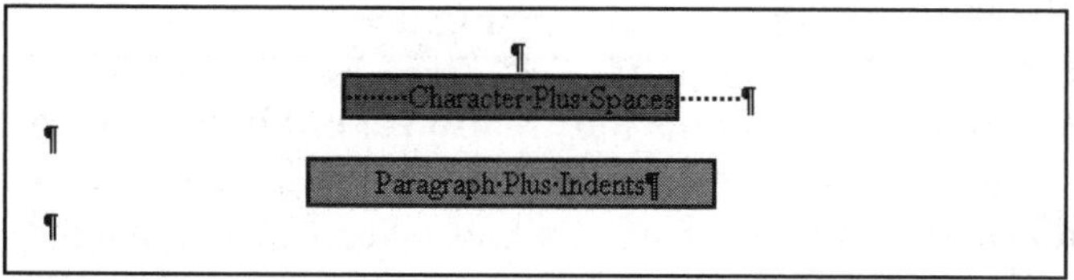

Figure 7-12
Paragraph borders and shading extend to the margins.

To add shading or borders to the edges of a title, use paragraph formatting and add left and right indentation to reduce the paragraph to the desired width.

When you select a word by double-clicking it or by pressing F8 twice, Word includes trailing spaces—but not punctuation—as part of the selected word. When you apply character formatting to the word, however, Word formats only the characters, not the trailing spaces. This is true for all character formatting, not just borders and shading. This is by design; Word does not format the space so it will be easy for you to insert a new word without accidentally picking up character formatting. There are a few cases, however, when you might want the space to be formatted.

For example, suppose you want to shade adjacent words using different colors. The first paragraph shown in Figure 7-13 shows what happens to the text when you format a single word and then format the second. With each word—including the trailing space, if you selected it—Word excludes the space from the formatting. The result is an unformatted gap between the words. If you want the space formatted, one option is to carefully select the space and format it. If you select only the space, Word will indeed format it.

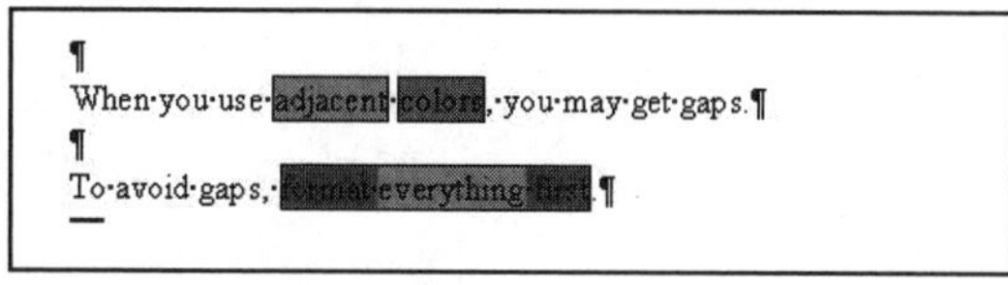

Figure 7-13
Word does not format spaces at the end of a word.

A second option is to select all the words and format them with the shading you want the spaces to have—Word does format spaces in the middle of a selected block of text. Then select and format the other word.

Improving Character Spacing

Note The sample document for this section is Kerning.doc.

Each letter in most font faces contains information about how much room to leave before and after the letter. This sizing box is the amount of space you see highlighted when you select a single character, and it allows Word to fit most letters together nicely. Some letters have portions that extend past their sizing boxes. For example, the top of the letter f extends to the right. If a small letter such as an o follows the letter f, Word can make the two letters overlap, as shown in Figure 7-14.

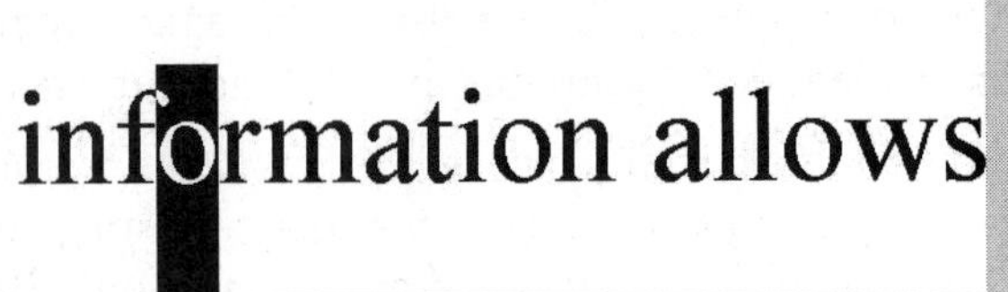

Figure 7-14
Letter spaces can overlap.

Normally, Word appropriately handles letter spacing. However, some combinations are notoriously poor at fitting together. For example, the letters W and A, when placed next to each other, allow too much room. In the first line of Figure 7-15, the first three letters appear as if they are separated by spaces, which is particularly true for capital letters. Letters that are too far apart are particularly noticeable in headings, where the font is usually large. The font size in Figure 7-15 is 36 points, large enough for the extra space to be significant.

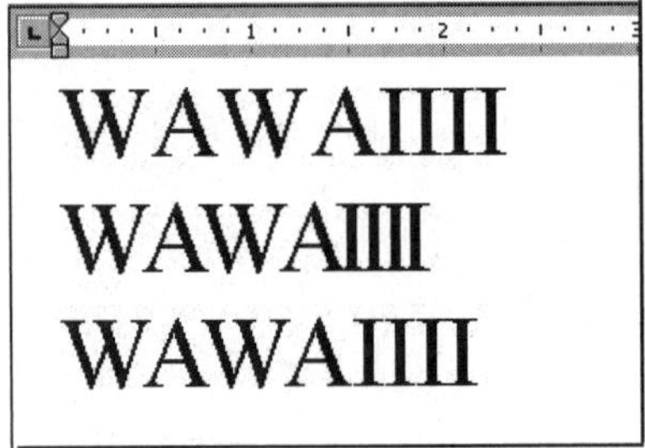

Figure 7-15
Kerning condenses the space between letters that need it.

Some fonts contain additional information that allows Word to automatically move certain character combinations closer together. Adjusting pairs of letters is called kerning. The Character Spacing tab in the Font dialog box allows you to enable kerning for the characters if the font is larger than a specified size. Most fonts that contain kerning information do limit the size of font that can be kerned, so this limit is somewhat redundant. If you have any concern about the spacing of the fonts in your document headings, kerning is efficient and automatic.

Kerning is a character format, but it has no effect unless you apply it to two adjacent characters. Kerning is usually set at the paragraph level.

You can achieve kerning manually by applying character spacing. Kerning looks at the relationship between two adjacent characters and is built into a font. Character spacing changes the right side of a single character's sizing box, and you must set it manually. Kerning has no effect when applied to a single character, but character spacing does.

Character spacing is typically used to apply either a "squished" or an "airy" feeling to an entire heading, but you can also use it to perform manual kerning. The third example shown in Figure 7-15 has the spacing on all the letters condensed by 4 points. The effect of the character spacing adjustment on the A and W characters is identical to that of kerning. The effect on the I characters, however, is excessive. If you apply the character spacing to the first three characters only, the effect is identical to the effect obtained by kerning.

Why would you want to kern letters manually? If you are fanatical about character spacing, you know that automatic kerning is not always sufficient. Automatic kerning almost exclusively involves capital letters. However, lowercase letters like y and x often have too much space around them. Figure 7-16 illustrates three versions of the names of the men from a famous Russian family (the Brothers Karamozov). The first line shows the names with no kerning. The second line includes automatic kerning. The primary effect of the automatic kerning was to remove space before two of the commas. Automatic kerning did not remove the extra space between the F and the y, after the d, or around the x. The third line is kerned manually.

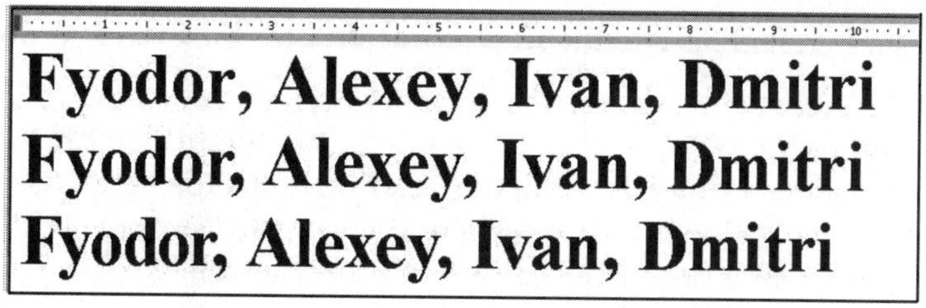

Fyodor, Alexey, Ivan, Dmitri
Fyodor, Alexey, Ivan, Dmitri
Fyodor, Alexey, Ivan, Dmitri

Figure 7-16
Use character spacing to fine-tune kerning.

For casual documents, automatic kerning is more than sufficient. But if you are using Word to prepare documents for publication or to present to upper management, you might want to fine-tune the character spacing in major headings.

Creating Hidden Macros to Adjust Character Spacing

Adjusting character spacing is largely a matter of trial and error. You decrease the spacing by 1 point and see how it looks. Then you decrease it by another point and review it again. And you quickly learn that opening and closing the Font dialog box makes the process very frustrating.

Unless you have the unlikely job of full-time Character Adjuster, you would not want to set up shortcut keys for character spacing. You probably don't even want infrequently used macros cluttering up the macros list in the Macros dialog box, either. An effective solution is to create macros in a private Module. You can run the macros from a small Visual Basic Editor window as you watch the effect in Word, but the macros will not appear in the Macros list.

In the Visual Basic Editor, create a new module and add the statement *Option Private Module* at the top. This makes the module invisible outside the current Visual Basic project, which means that it will not appear in the list in the Macros dialog box.

The following *ExpandOne* and *ContractOne* macros increase the spacing for the first selected character (or the first character after the insertion point):

```
Sub ExpandOne()
    Selection.Characters(1).Font.Spacing = _
        Selection.Characters(1).Font.Spacing + 1
End Sub

Sub ContractOne()
    Selection.Characters(1).Font.Spacing = _
        Selection.Characters(1).Font.Spacing - 1
End Sub
```

The standard expression *Selection.Font* refers to the font for the entire current word if the selection is an insertion point within a word. Adding *.Characters(1)* after *Selection* specifically refers only to the first character after the insertion point, even if the insertion point is not in the middle of a word.

As you are fine-tuning the spacing of a heading, you might like the relative spacing between the letters, but you think the heading looks too condensed or too expanded overall. The following *ExpandAll* and *ContractAll* macros add or subtract 1 point from the spacing of each character in the paragraph:

```
Sub ExpandAll()
    Dim c As Range
    For Each c In Selection.Paragraphs(1).Range.Characters
        c.Font.Spacing = c.Font.Spacing + 1
    Next
End Sub

Sub ContractAll()
    Dim c As Range
    For Each c In Selection.Paragraphs(1).Range.Characters
```

```
        c.Font.Spacing = c.Font.Spacing - 1
    Next
End Sub
```

These macros loop through each character in the first paragraph of the selection. A Paragraph object does not have a Characters collection, so the macro must first go to its Range object.

Finally, you might want to see the result of your character spacing adjustments. The following *ListSpacing* macro simply writes the spacing for each character to the Immediate window:

```
Sub ListSpacing()
    Dim c As Range
    For Each c In Selection.Paragraphs(1).Range.Characters
        Debug.Print c.Font.Spacing
    Next
End Sub
```

Because these macros are in a private module, you can't run them from the Macros dialog box, nor can you assign them to shortcut keys or toolbar buttons. To run them, resize the Visual Basic Editor window so that you can see Word in the background, click inside one of the macros, and then click the Run Sub button or press F5.

Rather than creating macros—which are permanent—you could set up any of these commands to run directly in the Immediate window instead. In the Immediate window, you simple move the cursor onto a line and press Enter to run the line. To run a loop in the Immediate window, place colons between each line. For example, to display the spacing for each character in the current selection, type the following line—all on one line—and press Enter:

```
For each c in Selection.Characters:?c.Font.Spacing:Next
```

In the Immediate window, a question mark (?) is shorthand for *Debug.Print*.

Incidentally, for the third paragraph shown earlier in Figure 7-16—which already had kerning enabled—the character spacing values are:

-5, -3, 0, -3, -3, 0, 0, 0, -2, 0, -1, -2, 0, -2, 0, 0, 0, -2, -1, 0, 0, 0, 0, -1, 1, -1, -1, 0, and 0

Dealing with Toggle Formats

Some character formats—most notably Bold and Italic—toggle the underlying format. This can have strange effects as the character formatting interacts with the paragraph formatting.

If you select a word and click the Bold and Italic buttons, Word adds Bold and Italic as direct character attributes, as shown in Figure 7-17.

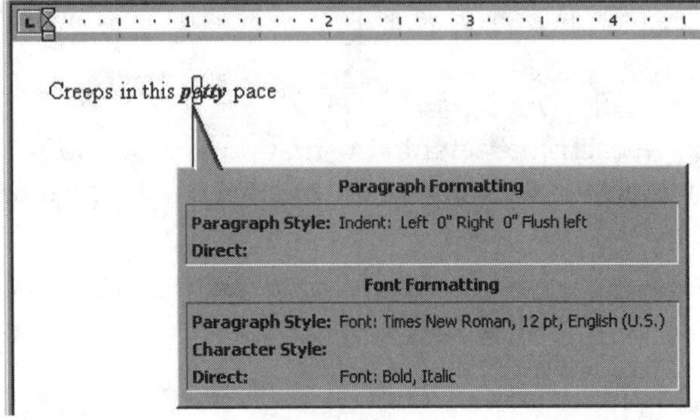

Figure 7-17
Changing a font style applies Direct character formatting.

A strange thing happens if you now assign the paragraph a style that also includes Bold and Italic formatting—the built-in style Heading 2, for example—as shown in Figure 7-18. (Before assigning the Heading 2 style, change the selection to an insertion point or Word will use the character portion of the paragraph style to format only the selected characters.)

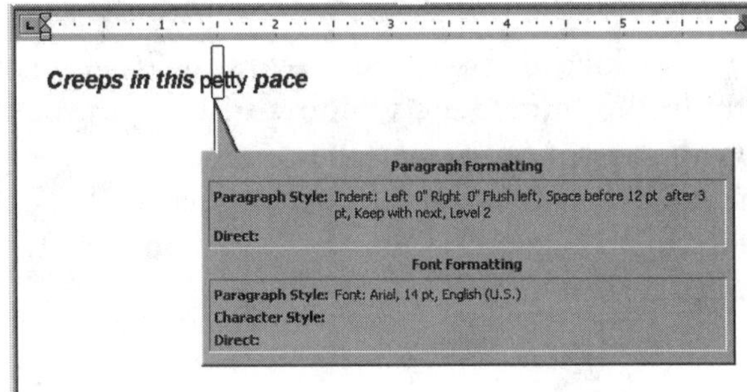

Figure 7-18
Reveal Formats does not show character formatting that undoes paragraph formatting.

It is not surprising that the emphasized word is now neither bold nor italic. Bold and Italic are toggle settings, so applying a Bold character format to a Bold paragraph format should result in non-bold characters. It is strange that the Bold and Italic character attributes no longer appear in the Direct formatting section, however. Logically, these attributes should appear both in the Paragraph Style section and in the Direct formatting section, thus canceling each other out. Instead, the Bold and Italic attributes simply disappear from the Paragraph Style section.

The fault, unfortunately, does not appear to be in the Reveal Formats window, where the problem would be merely superficial. The formatting actually becomes confused: if you change the paragraph style back to Normal, the Bold and Italic formats are lost. In reality, the confusion is slightly more complicated than that. If you apply the Heading 2 style directly—that is, using the Style box on the formatting toolbar, the

Format Style dialog box, or the Ctrl+Alt+2 shortcut key—Bold and Italic character formats are simply lost when you change the paragraph style back to Normal. If you apply the Heading 2 style by increasing the outline level, however—that is, pressing Ctrl+Shift+Right arrow—Bold and Italic formats are retained when you change the paragraph style back to Normal, except that from then on, the character formats do not toggle properly against the paragraph style.

None of this is a problem as long as you never apply Direct character formatting to a heading, or you never change heading levels or heading formats. (That was supposed to be sarcastic.) As it is, you can have a document with two apparently identical headings—where even the Reveal Format window shows identical information for each character in the two headings—as shown in Figure 7-19.

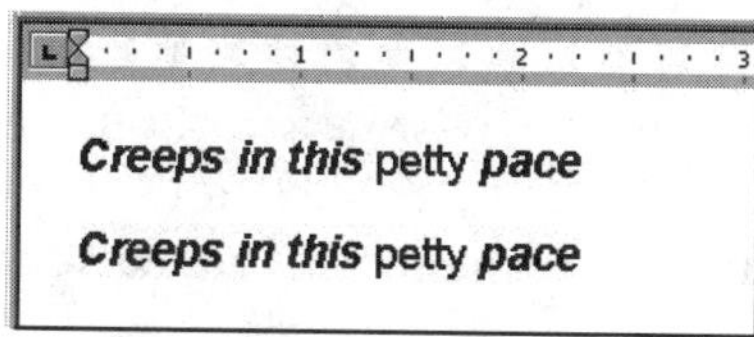

Figure 7-19
Two headings appear to be identically formatted.

Simply by removing Bold and Italic from the definition of the style for that heading level, the headings will behave differently, as shown in Figure 7-20, depending solely on which method you used to apply the original heading style.

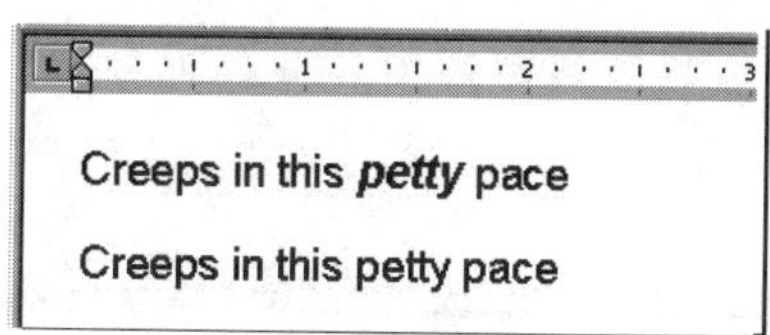

Figure 7-20
Changing the definition of a paragraph style can have inconsistent results.

Chapter 7

The bottom line is that if you apply direct character formats such as Bold and Italic to headings, you might lose important emphasis when you change the heading style. One way to protect yourself against this problem is to use styles for character formatting using the tips you'll find in the next section.

Formatting Sections

A section in Word handles the formatting of attributes larger than a paragraph. Section formatting falls into two categories: attributes that apply to a whole page, and attributes that can change within a page. For example, page margins can change within a page, as can the number of columns on a page. But page borders, headers, footers, and orientation can apply only to an entire page.

In general, you use a continuous section break when you want to modify one of the changeable attributes, and you use one of the page section breaks when you want to modify a page-level attribute. Continuous sections can contain page-level formatting, however. If a single page has more than one section, then the section in effect at the top of the page controls the formatting for that page.

If you delete a section mark, the formatting for the subsequent section takes over both sections. This is the opposite of a paragraph mark, where deleting a paragraph mark applies the formatting from the previous paragraph to both paragraphs.

Using Multiple Sections

Sections serve several different purposes. When you change a portion of a document to display multiple columns, for example, Word adds a continuous section break at the beginning and end of the multi-column region. The section breaks identify where the formatting starts and where it stops.

You can use sections to give one part of a document portrait orientation and another part landscape, to change paper sizes, or to place borders around some pages but not others. Each time one aspect of the overall page layout changes, you need to insert a new section break. Even if you have only one section in your document, you will use sections extensively if you add multiple headers or footers to the pages. The next section discusses headers and footers in some detail. In "Enhancing the Background of a Document" in Chapter 8, you will also learn how to use headers and footers to add a background picture to your documents.

Using Headers and Footers

Every page in a Word document has a header and a footer. Headers and footers are portions of the document that repeat on additional pages. Because headers and footers are entirely analogous, everything I describe in this section about headers applies equally to footers.

In a new document, click Headers And Footers on the View menu to switch to Print Layout view and display the headers and footers. Any text you enter in the header area will appear on all pages of the new document. If you want the header to change in a predictable way throughout the document—for example, if you want to include page numbers or chapter numbers—find an appropriate field to include in the header. (See "Adding Page Numbers," below, for more information about using fields in headers.) If you want the header to change radically—for example, if you don't want chapter headings to appear once you get to the index—insert a new section break.

Each section implicitly contains the definitions for three headers: one for the first page, one for even pages, and one for odd pages. Unless you use a template with the headers created, all three headers are empty in a new document. When you add a header to a document, you are adding an odd—or primary—page header. In much the same way that some stereo earphones play the left channel through both ears when you play from a monaural source, a Word document displays the odd headers on both pages if you don't explicitly request headers for even pages. Because of this, the header for an odd page is called a primary header.

To see the even headers, click File, Page Setup, Layout, and select the Different Odd And Even check box. This option applies to the entire document, regardless of whether you select This Section or Whole Document from the Apply To drop-down list. An even page header starts out blank. If you define an even header and then clear the Different Odd And Even check box, the section quietly retains the invisible heading, waiting for the time that you might choose to display it again.

Likewise, the first page of a section has its own header. To see the header for the first page, click File, Page Setup, Layout, and select the Different First Page check box. Unlike even and odd header display, this option does respect the Apply To value. In other words, if you select Different First Page only for the current section, you will obtain exactly that: a different first page only for the current section.

Note If you select This Point On from the Apply To list, you might not get the result you want. This option does not apply the setting to all the remaining sections in the document. Rather, it inserts a new section break at the current insertion point, and then applies the setting to that one new section.

Managing Headers and Footers with Section Breaks

To change the layout of a header in the middle of a document, you must first create a new section and then break the link between that section's header and the previous section's header. Each newly inserted section links headers to those of the previous section. To remove a link, click the indented Same As Previous button on the Header And Footer toolbar. When the button is not indented, there is no link. You can link or break links independently for each of the three headers in a section. In other words, the even page header can change from the previous section while you keep the same first page header.

Even a continuous section—the kind that is inserted when you create a section with multiple columns—has its own header. The section that is in effect at the start of a page is the one that governs the header (and the footer) for that page. If you assign different headers to different continuous sections, you might find that the header of a page changes simply because you have inserted text earlier in the document (thus changing which section happens to be at the top of a page).

In practical terms, you should only unlink headers when the current section begins on a new page. That way, you're guaranteed that the section will always be in effect at the beginning of the page. The fact that a continuous section quietly links to the previous section simply makes it safe to add continuous sections freely without disrupting the headers.

Adding Page Numbers

A header does not change from page to page. That is, the structure of a header does not change. You probably do have information in a header that you want to have change—such as the page number.

Page numbers are used by almost almost everyone who creates documents. Because page numbers are so pervasive, Word provides a special Page Numbers command on the Insert menu to simplify creating them. In case you ever want more (or less) than the Page Numbers command gives you, you might want to know more about how it does what it does.

You might expect that the Page Numbers command would use a field to add the page number and, in fact, it does. The {PAGE} field—with or without the Page Numbers command—displays the current page number anywhere you put it. The Page Numbers command adds the {PAGE} field into a header (or a footer) so that it will appear on all pages.

When you clear the Show Number On First Page check box, the Page Numbers command simply turns on the Different First Page option for the first section of the document. Even if you do not have Different Odd And Even pages enabled for the section, the Page Numbers command adds the page number to the even page, as well as the odd page.

The Page Numbers command always inserts the page number in a frame. (See "Using Text Boxes and Frames" in Chapter 8 for more details about frames.) The frame allows Word to align the number wherever you specify—left, right, center, inside, outside—without disrupting any text that might already be in the header. A frame also has options for inside and outside that does not require separate headers for even and odd pages.

If you request a left-justified page number and already have left-justified text in the header, Word will adjust the first-line indent to make room for the page number. If you request a centered or right-justified page number, however, and there is already text in that position, the page number will simply appear over the top of the text. To reposition the text, select the frame (click when the mouse pointer becomes a four-headed arrow) and drag the border (not the sizing handles) to reposition the frame.

Frames can extend outside the bounds of the normal page footer. In other words, if you select the frame and change the font size of the number to 48 points, it will extend into the body of the page, effectively increasing the size of the footer.

You can remove the frame so that you can integrate the page number with the rest of your heading by double-clicking the frame and clicking Remove Frame. The field will remain intact, but it will be left-aligned, regardless of where the frame was aligned.

If you already have a page number in a frame—even if you created it yourself—and use the Page Numbers command to change the alignment, Word will move the frame to the new position, retaining any character formatting you might have added to the number. If you have a {PAGE} field that is not inside a frame—even if the Page Numbers command created it originally—and you use the Page Numbers command to change the alignment, Word will remove the existing {PAGE} field and add a new one in a frame, losing any formatting you might have added.

If you are viewing headers and footers, the Page Numbers command will add a number in the header or footer only, whichever is currently active. If you are in the main body of the document, you can specify whether to add the number in the header or the footer. If you already have a page number in a header and you use the Page Numbers command to add a page number to the footer (or vice versa), Word will simply create a new page number field and frame.

Formatting Page Numbers

The Page Numbers command can format the page number as Arabic or Roman numerals, or it can format it as uppercase or lowercase letters. A {PAGE} field has formatting switches for these same options. However, the Page Numbers command does not use the formatting switches for the field. Let me repeat that: The Page Numbers command does insert a {PAGE} field, but it does not add any formatting switches to the field.

Instead, the Page Numbers command uses the format option you select to set the default format for any {PAGE} field appearing in the current section. If you manually insert a {PAGE} field and then select a formatting switch other than Use Default Numbering in the Field Options dialog box (which merely clears any formatting switch you might have previously selected), Word warns you that you are not changing the default number format for the section and instructs you to use the Page Numbers command to change that default.

So, if you already have a {PAGE} field without an explicit formatting switch and you want to change its format, use the Page Numbers command. Don't select any options in the main Page Number dialog box. Just click the Format button and change the format in the Page Number Format dialog box.

Word stores the default page number format independently for each section, and it provides no linking between the sections. This means that you can have different styles of page numbers within the same document. For example, you can use lowercase Roman numerals in a table of contents section, while the remainder of the document uses Arabic numerals. It also means that if you decide to change the default format for a portion of the document that includes more than one section (for example, if your introductory pages include a preface in a separate section from the table of contents), you will need to select a range of text that includes both sections before changing the number format default.

If, for some reason, you want to show the page number in lowercase Roman numerals in the header and in Arabic numerals in the footer, add a formatting switch to one of the {PAGE} fields.

Customizing Page Numbers

Each section in a document stores either the starting page number for that section or a flag indicating that the page numbering should be continued from the previous section. If the first page numbering definition for the first section of the document continues from the previous section, the page numbering starts with page 1. There is a substantial difference, however, between starting the first section at page 1 and carrying forward the preceding section's numbering.

Suppose you create a document that has a single section. You set the page numbers to begin at page 1. Now, at the beginning of page 4, you insert a section break that launches a new page—page 4 will change to page 1. This is because inserting a new section copies the section formatting—including the numbering options—from the original section. The original section started numbering on page 1, so the new section will start numbering on page 1.

This is true even if you insert a continuous section break—which you might do without even knowing you did. For example, suppose that in a single-section document explicitly starting its numbering with page 1, you select from the middle of page 3 to the end of the document and then format the range as two columns. What used to be page 4 becomes page 2, because Word inserts a new continuous section break at the beginning of the two-column region. The page where the new section starts is now page 1 (even though you don't see the page number, because the section was not in effect at the top of the page), and the subsequent page is page 2.

Note Never explicitly number a document from page 1. If the first section continues numbering from the preceding section, any new sections you insert will do the same.

If you do need to specify the starting page number of a section—perhaps because you are printing separate chapters from individual documents or because you start numbering each chapter with page 1—you have two choices. The easiest option is to wait until the very last minute to specify the starting page number of the first section. By that time, any new sections will have already been created with numbering set to continue appropriately. The other option is always to remember to reset the renumbering option whenever you insert a new section break in the middle of the first section.

Note The sample document used in this section is Levels.doc

Heading Styles vs. Outline Levels

Word uses nine levels of numbering in at least four features: outline levels, numbered heading style, the document map, and the table of contents (TOC). The way these nine number levels interact can be somewhat confusing.

Each Word paragraph is assigned one of ten outline levels. Outline level 10 is called body text; it is the default if no other outline level is assigned. The Document Map and Outline view both use outline levels one to nine to provide a hierarchical view of your document. The table of contents field does not use outline levels.

Each of the nine built-in styles—Heading 1 to Heading 9—is assigned to the corresponding outline level. You cannot change the outline level of these nine built-in styles. All other built-in styles are assigned the body-text level. If you use one of the nine built-in heading styles, you automatically obtain the outline level that goes with it. Keep in mind it's the outline levels that matter to the Document Map and Outline view, not the heading style.

When you display the Document Map in a document that does not use built-in heading styles and that uses the body text outline level for all its paragraphs, Word will identify and assign outline levels to paragraphs. Try this: with the Document Map turned off, create a new document and enter short headings, each followed by an empty paragraph. Now switch to Outline view. All the paragraphs are displayed as body text, as shown in Figure 7-21.

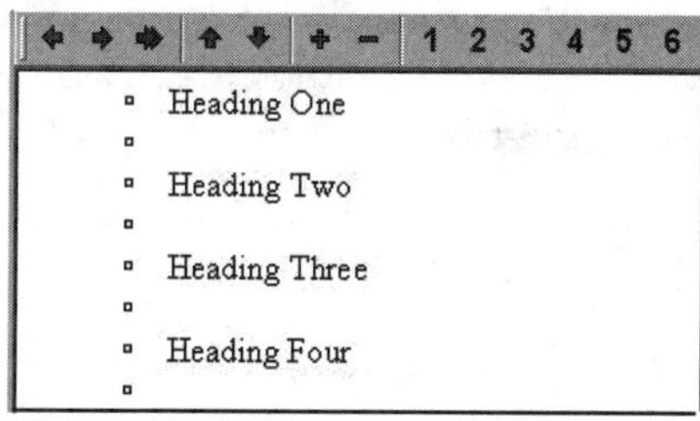

Figure 7-21
Ordinary text is displayed at the body-text level.

Now turn the Document Map on. The paragraphs will suddenly be promoted to Outline level 1, but the paragraphs still have the Normal style. The Document Map merely added the outline level to the paragraph as direct formatting, as shown in the Reveal Format window in Figure 7-22.

The Document Map assigns outline levels completely without permission. This is not an AutoCorrect action, and even if you disable all the AutoCorrect options, the Document Map will still try to create outline levels. As with AutoCorrect actions, you can press Ctrl+Z to restore text to body text if you don't want the levels assigned (that is, if you even notice that the Document Map assigned them). Once you restore them, Document Map will never again assign outline levels within that document. If you discover at a later time that some body text paragraphs have an outline level

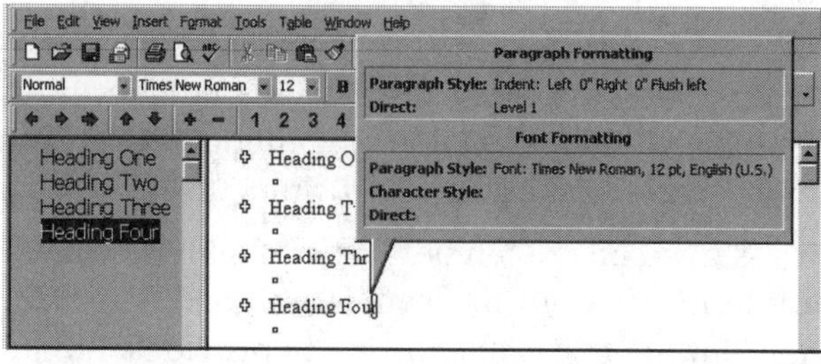

Figure 7-22
The Document Map tries to assign outline levels.

applied, you can press Ctrl+Q to remove direct formatting from the paragraph, or you can set the outline level on the Indents And Spacing tab of the Format Paragraph dialog box.

A table of contents field can display—by some remarkable coincidence—up to nine levels. The nine levels for the table of contents can be tied to any styles used in the document. In fact, a single table of contents level can be associated with as many styles as you want. The default table of contents associates the style Heading 1 with table of contents level 1, and so forth, but that is merely a convenience for you if you happen to use the built-in heading styles in that way. The table of contents function never looks at the outline level of any paragraphs or styles. It looks only at styles, and not at outline levels, because the table of contents is really a generalized tool that can create all kinds of lists—tables of figures, lists of tables, detailed chapter contents—in addition to an ordinary table of contents.

Chapter numbers used in page numbering require the use of built-in heading styles, not outline levels, which is covered in the next section.

Adding Chapter Numbers

The Page Numbers command also allows you to add chapter numbers to the page number. This feature works only if you assign one of the heading styles (Heading 1 to Heading 9) to the paragraph containing the chapter number and you use outline numbering to automatically number the heading style. ("Creating and Managing Numbered Lists" in Chapter 9 contains more information about creating numbered lists.) You cannot add chapter numbers using the Page Numbers command unless you use the specific built-in styles. It is not enough to assign an outline level to a style, even if you link that style to an outline numbering level.

Once you assign a numbered heading style to the chapter heading, you simply designate which heading level corresponds to the chapter numbers you want to use. (You can have the prefix be a subchapter or a part number, if that's the heading level you assign.) The compound page number will become the result of any {PAGE} field in the section, regardless of who or what added the {PAGE} field.

The format of the chapter number will be the format you assigned in the Customize Outline Numbered List dialog box. That is, you cannot use Roman numerals for the chapter number in the heading paragraph and Arabic numerals for the chapter number in the page number. The page number does, however, remove any text prefix from the chapter number, so the heading paragraph can be defined as Chapter 1, while the page number is defined as 1–15. If you want the text prefix to appear in the page number, simply add the text next to the {PAGE} field in the header or footer.

For example, if you assign the chapter number heading as, say, Heading 3, and format the numbering to include higher levels, the page number will also display the higher levels.

Creating a Macro to Add Section Breaks

Suppose you have multiple chapters in a document and you want to include chapter numbers and to restart page numbers with each chapter. You have assigned Heading 1 style to each new chapter title and have established numbering in the heading style. To force the pages to start renumbering with each new chapter, you must also make sure that each new chapter begins with a section break.

You can add a Page Break Before option to the Heading 1 paragraph style, but a page break is not sufficient. You need a section break and, unfortunately, you can't add a Section Break Before option to a paragraph style. Each section break must be created manually. The following *AddSections* macro will scan through the document searching for a paragraph with the Heading 1 style that is not preceded by a section break, inserting a section break if needed. The macro then scans each section, making sure that the only time a section is set to restart numbering is when it begins with a Heading 1 style.

```
Sub AddSections()
    Const ChHead = "Heading 1"
    Dim p As Paragraph
    Dim r As Range
    Dim s As Section

    ''' Insert section mark before each chapter heading
    For Each p In ActiveDocument.Paragraphs
        ''' must have the right style and not be section
        Set r = p.Range
        If p.Style = ChHead _
        And r <> vbFormFeed Then ''' vbFormFeed is a section break
            ''' don't add if there's already a section before
            r.Move wdCharacter, -1
            If r <> vbFormFeed Then
                ActiveDocument.Sections.Add p.Range
            End If
        End If
    Next p
```

```
    ''' Restart numbering only if chapter heading
    For Each s In ActiveDocument.Sections
        With s.Headers(1).PageNumbers
            ''' always have same chapter/page format
            .NumberStyle = wdPageNumberStyleArabic
            .IncludeChapterNumber = True
            .HeadingLevelForChapter = CLng(Right(ChHead, 1)) - 1
            .ChapterPageSeparator = wdSeparatorHyphen
            ''' Renumber if and only if right heading style
            If s.Range.Paragraphs(1).Style = ChHead Then
                .RestartNumberingAtSection = True
                .StartingNumber = 1
            Else
                .RestartNumberingAtSection = False
            End If
        End With
    Next s
End Sub
```

At the top of the macro, *Heading 1* is defined as a constant. This way, if you change the chapter heading to Heading 2, you will need to change it only in this one place.

The first loop scans each paragraph in the document, searching for the Heading 1 style. When you insert a section, it takes on the style of the paragraph it precedes. As a result, some of the section breaks will have a Heading 1 style, which the macro needs to ignore. A section break paragraph consists of a single character that corresponds to the Visual Basic vbFormFeed constant. Comparing the contents (the Range) of the paragraph to vbFormFeed identifies a section break.

Once the loop finds a Heading 1 paragraph that is not a section break, it must check to see if the paragraph is already preceded by a section break. Setting the range of the paragraph to a Range variable and then moving that range back by a single character allows the macro to check for a preceding section. If the macro doesn't find one, it adds one.

The second loop scans each section in the document. In each section, the macro sets the page number formatting. You could delete this portion of the macro if you were to select the entire document and assign the number formatting you want to all the sections. The *.HeadingLevelForChapter = CLng(Right(ChHead, 1)) – 1* statement is there to make sure the heading level is set to the same one used in the constant at the top of the macro. It extracts the last character from the heading level (which will be a digit from 1 to 9) and subtracts 1 from it, because the HeadingLevelForChapter property counts from 0, not from 1.

The most useful portion of the second loop is the If structure, which turns on or off the Restart Numbering property of the section, depending on if it begins with Heading 1. This prevents the problem discussed earlier in the "Customizing Page Numbers" section.

You probably wouldn't run a macro like this often enough to need a shortcut key. Just switch to the Visual Basic Editor, skim the macro to make sure the heading is set to the proper level, and press F5 to run the macro.

Adding Other Fields to a Header

The Header And Footer toolbar that appears when you are viewing a header contains an Insert AutoText menu. This menu contains several common entries you might want to use in a header.

Four of the AutoText entries include a page number. When the AutoText entry inserts a page number, it simply includes a {PAGE} field in the text of the header. It does not add the {PAGE} field into a frame. The {PAGE} field is affected, however, by changes you make using the Page Number Format dialog box, so you can change the format of the numbers, add a chapter number, or start with an arbitrary page number (even if you use the AutoText entry to add a page number).

Other AutoText entries add other useful fields, often with a descriptive label. For example, you can automatically add your name, the full path where the document is saved, the date the document was printed, and so forth. If you want to include any of these AutoText field combinations when the Header And Footer toolbar is not visible, click Insert, AutoText, Header/Footer.

Word has other fields that might be useful in a header. To find them, click Insert, Field, and look in the categories listed under Document Information, User Information, Date And Time, and Numbering.

- The **Document Information** category includes such options as Title, Subject, Keywords, and Category—values you enter using the File, Properties command.
- The **User Information** category contains UserName, UserInitials, and UserAddress, all of which you can update by clicking Tools, Options, User Information.
- The **Date And Time** category includes fields for printing the date the document was created, saved, or printed, and also includes a field to show how much total time the document has been open for editing.
- The **Numbering** category includes many fields. Those that are most useful for a header might be the section number, the number of pages in the section, and the number of times the document has been saved.

One additional field worth pointing out is the DocProperty field. This field is in the Document Information category, but it is like a super field: it displays any information available on any of the tabs in the Document Properties dialog box. Many of the fields overlap those of custom fields—such as Title and Subject—but some additional fields are available only through DocProperty. Click Options after selecting DocProperty in the Fields dialog box to see a list of all the available properties. If you add custom properties in the Properties dialog box, those properties also appear in the Property list for this field.

Managing Styles

Styles allow you to manage paragraph and character formatting. One benefit of using styles—particularly paragraph styles—is to ensure that your document looks professional. If you define and use paragraph styles in a document, you can be confident that the look and feel of your document will be consistent.

Another benefit of using styles—and this applies equally to both character styles and paragraph styles—is that they allow you to quickly and consistently change the look of a document. If your document is built on styles, you can quickly change the look from formal to casual by switching the font of one or two styles from Times New Roman to Comic Sans MS or Lucida Handwriting. (Installing the Microsoft PhotoDraw 2000 component of Office 2000 Premium adds dozens of creative fonts you can also use in Word.)

Word applies character styles to several automatically entered elements, such as line numbers, page numbers, footnote references, and comment references. You can change the look of any of these elements simply by changing the character style. Even though Word does not automatically use the Strong and Emphasis character styles, they are available as built-in styles for your use. If you consistently use these styles to add bold or italic formatting, you can instantly and easily change the look of those attributes.

Word includes a large number of built-in styles—both character and paragraph—that you might want to use. These styles are actually part of the Word program; the first time you use one of them, it is copied into your document so that you can modify it if you want. To see the complete list of built in styles, click Format, Style, and select All Styles in the List drop-down list.

Printing a List of Styles

For documentation or for improved understanding, you might want a printed list of the styles in a document. Click File, Print. In the Print What drop-down list, select Styles and click OK. This option prints all the styles that are currently defined in the active document. It does not print the definition of the built-in styles that have not been used.

Basing One Style on Another

Any style except Normal can be based on another style. When you base a style on another style, Word looks at all the attributes you define for the new style, compares them to the attributes of the base style, and only stores those that are different. Normal is the root paragraph style. You can change the attributes of the Normal style, but you can't base it on any other style.

Of the approximately 85 built-in paragraph fonts, all but three are based on the Normal paragraph font. Some of those—such as Normal (Web), Note Heading, and Salutation—are based on the Normal font, but have not changed; they are Normal plus nothing. These styles illustrate an important concept in defining styles. Whenever possible, you should define (and use) styles according to the intent of the paragraph, not according to its current formatting. If you apply the style Note Heading to the heading of notes—even though the format is no different from the Normal style—you can change the look of all your note headings simply by changing that one style definition.

The three built-in styles that are not based on Normal illustrate additional principles of creating styles. One of the three, Macro Text, is used to include macro text in your document. It is similar to the style used in this book to display macros. It is radically different from the normal font, and you would not want to change even if you change the font for all the remaining paragraphs. There are two purposes for basing a style on another style: First, it can help you understand the relationship between the styles if all you have to look at are the differences between them. Second, basing one style on another allows you to change both of them simply by changing the base style. Basing the Macro Text style on Normal would serve neither of those purposes, so it is simply based on nothing.

The other two non-Normal styles are Body Text First Indent (which is based on the Body Text style, with the addition of an indented first line), and Body Text First Indent 2 (which is the same except that it is based on a version of Body Text that already has all lines indented). These styles show how you can build a hierarchy of styles. The Body Text style is defined as Normal + Space after 6 pt. The Body Text First Indent style is defined as Body Text + Indent: First 0.15". If you change the font of Normal, it will change all three styles (plus many others). If you change the font of Body Text, it will change only two styles. If you change the first indent of Normal, it will change the Normal style and the Body Text style, but it will not change the Body Text First Indent style, because that one style has an explicit setting for first indent.

You can also learn principles of defining styles by looking at built-in styles that are based on Normal. For example, the styles List, List 2, List 3, List 4, and List 5 all form a related group. Each level is indented a quarter-inch further than the previous level. These are not defined in terms of each other, however; each style is based independently on Normal. Each of the styles has an explicit setting for the same attribute: Left Indent. Basing the List 5 style on the List 4 style (rather than on the Normal style) would give you no additional information and would not make it easier to change all the List styles in tandem. If you do want to change all the lists at the same time without changing the Normal style, base the styles List 2 through List 5 on the List style.

Heading styles Heading 1 through Heading 9 are also all based independently on Normal. Even though each of these styles customizes a new attribute—for example, indentation, font size, italic, or bold—do not base Heading 2 on Heading 1, Heading 3 on Heading 2, and so forth. The headings with the lowest numbers actually have the most formatting, and each new level would have to remove formatting, which would be backward. When forming a hierarchy, always base the style that is most like Normal on Normal. Then base the one that is next most like Normal on that one, and so forth. So, if you want to build a hierarchy with headings, start by basing Heading 9 on Body Text. Then base Heading 8 on Heading 9, and so on. That way, if you want to change the font of all the headings above, say, Heading 4, you can change just that one style.

When you switch an existing style from one base style to another, watch out for the notorious toggling attributes: bold, italic, and no proofing. If you apply bold character formatting to a paragraph that is already bold, the characters become Not Bold. (See "Character Formatting and Selecting Words," earlier in this chapter.) In the same way, if you base Style 1 (with bold formatting) on Style 2 (also with bold formatting), Style 1 changes to be Not Bold, which is probably not what you want.

If you want to hierarchically nest styles, you might want a macro to help you do it. The following *NestStyles* macro creates a hierarchy of styles Heading 4 to Heading 1, basing Heading 4 on the Body Text style.

```
Private Sub NestStyles()
    Dim ss As Styles
    Dim sList As Variant
    Dim i As Long
    Dim s1 As Style
    Dim s2 As Style

    ''' Put styles collection into variable
    Set ss = ActiveDocument.Styles
    ''' Make custom list of styles to nest
    sList = Array( _
        "Body Text", _
        "Heading 4", _
        "Heading 3", _
        "Heading 2", _
        "Heading 1")

    ''' loop through all but the first style (base 0)
    For i = 1 To UBound(sList)
        ''' The style to be changed
        Set s1 = ss(sList(i))
        ''' The target base style
        Set s2 = ss(sList(i - 1))

        ''' Turn off toggle attributes that match
        s1.Font.Bold = s1.Font.Bold <> s2.Font.Bold
        s1.Font.Italic = s1.Font.Italic <> s2.Font.Italic
        s1.NoProofing = s1.NoProofing <> s2.NoProofing

        ''' assign the new base style
        s1.BaseStyle = s2
        ''' set first in list as the Next Paragraph
```

```
        s1.NextParagraphStyle = sList(1)
    Next i
End Sub
```

In the macro, *sList* is an array of style names to nest, so you can easily change the macro by simply adding or deleting style names from the list. For example, you could add the remaining styles Heading 9 to Heading 5 to create a complete hierarchy. Each style name in the array must either already exist in the document or must be a built-in style.

The *Array* function creates an array where the first element is numbered 0. To loop from the second element, the macro begins the loop with item 1. The macro then assigns the current and base styles to variables.

The trickiest part of the macro consists of the statements that allow toggling attributes to remain intact. Each of these three statements turns the value of the attribute to *True* only if the values for the current and base style differ. If you discover an additional toggling attribute that is important to you, simply add another statement following the same pattern.

Finally, the macro assigns the new base style. It also assigns the first style in the list as the style for the next paragraph. If you don't want to change the style for the next paragraph, add an apostrophe to the beginning of the statement to comment out the line. (You could also create a macro with two lists of style names and let the macro assign the style from list 2 as the next paragraph style for the corresponding style in list 1.)

Modifying Style Definitions

When you apply a style to a paragraph and then make changes to that paragraph, Word adds those changes as direct formatting; they don't affect any other paragraphs formatted with the style. To have the changes apply to other paragraphs, you must change the style.

You can update a style in three ways: manually, automatically, and semi-automatically. To manually update a style, click Format, Style, select the style you want to change, and click Modify. In the Modify Style dialog box, click Format, and then select one of the formatting options, as shown in Figure 7-23.

To modify a style semi-automatically, first make changes to the paragraph. Then select the same style name in the Style box on the Formatting toolbar and press Enter. Word will ask whether you want to change the style to match the paragraph, or if you want to change the paragraph to match the style, as shown in Figure 7-24. This semi-automatic method does not work for the Normal style. If you try this with the Normal style, the paragraph is changed to match the existing definition of the style.

To automatically modify a style, select the Automatically Update check box either in the Modify Style dialog box shown earlier in Figure 7-23, or in the Modify Style message box shown earlier in Figure 7-24. You must set this option for each style you want to modify.

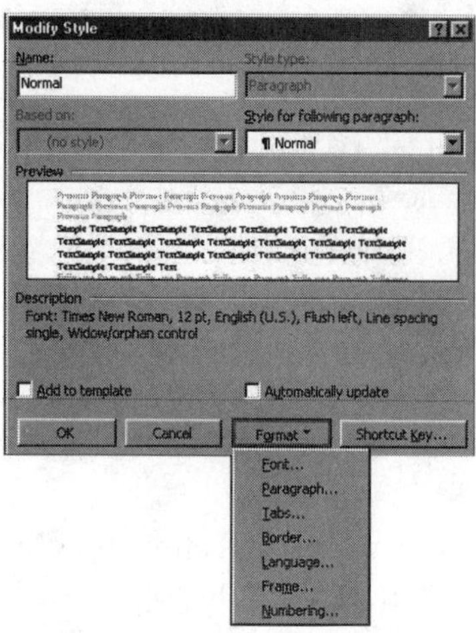

Figure 7-23
Use the Modify Style dialog box to manually change a style.

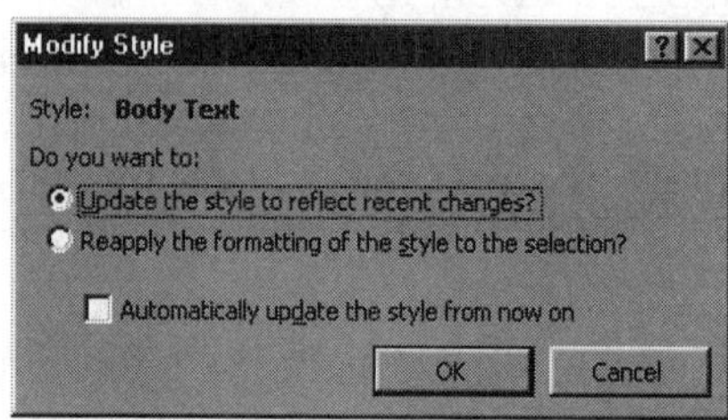

Figure 7-24
Reapply the same style name to semi-automatically change the style.

Automatically updating styles seems convenient, but it has certain quirks you should be aware of. First, not all style attributes will update automatically. Of the seven types of formatting you can define in a paragraph style (see the list at the bottom of Figure 7-23 shown earlier), only three—Font, Paragraph, and Numbering—actually modify the style automatically when you change them in a paragraph. If you change Tabs, Borders and Shading, Language, or Frame, the changes do not automatically apply to the style. To propagate changes in those attributes to the style, you need to use a variation of the semi-automatic method: select the style name from the list and press Enter. If you have set the style update to automatic, Word changes the style without asking you to confirm the update.

Another surprising thing about automatically updating a style is that you can automatically update the Normal style (or at least the Font, Paragraph, and Numbering attributes of the style). It seems backward that the Normal style should be left vulnerable to automatic updating when it is protected from semi-automatic updating because so many styles are based on it. More confusing still is that with the Normal style, you can't use semi-automatic updating even to complete the automatic updating of the four less-automatic attributes. To change those attributes of the Normal style, you must use the manual method.

I don't like using automatic updating for styles. The behavior is too hard to remember (which attributes make it back to the style?), and the effects can be more than expected. On the other hand, manual updating is too tedious, and it makes trying out possibilities too hard. A good compromise is to use semi-automatic formatting for most styles and use manual formatting for the Normal style, which does deserve extra consideration.

Using Character Styles

Paragraph styles—at least the common built-in styles such as Normal and Heading 1—are easy to understand and use. Word also has styles specifically for character formatting. The built-in Strong style adds Bold character formatting, while the built-in Emphasis style adds Italic formatting. You can, of course, create your own custom character styles.

In theory, if you always use the Strong and Emphasis styles, rather than directly applying Bold and Italic character formats, you can easily change the look of the document. For example, if the document will be viewed on a computer, you could quickly change all the bold text in the document to have a blinking background (which might make everyone who reads it hate you, but that's a different matter).

Unfortunately, the Strong and Emphasis styles—at least in their unmodified forms—have a slight problem. They do not properly toggle the underlying paragraph style. For example, if you format a heading with the default Heading 1 style—which has a bold character format—and then apply the Strong style to one of the words, you will see no difference. The boldness of the Strong character style is imperceptible against the boldness of the Heading 1 paragraph style. If you switch the paragraph to Normal style, the boldness readily appears, but that is not helpful for headings. Perhaps this unexpected behavior has discouraged people from taking advantage of character styles.

Fortunately, you can easily fix the Strong style so that it does work properly by merely pretending to modify it. And if you save the pseudo-modified style back to the Normal template, you never have to worry about it again. To do this, click Format, Style, and select the Strong style (you might first need to specify All Styles in the List drop-down list). Then click Modify, Format, Font, and, without making any changes, click OK, Save To Template, OK, and Close. Once you make this non-change, the Strong style will work perfectly in all contexts. Make the same pseudo-change to the Emphasis style.

In "Finding and Replacing Formatting" in Chapter 10, you will learn how to convert direct formatting in a document to character styles.

Copying Styles to and from a Template

When you create a new document, it is always based on a template. If you create a new, blank document, it is based on the Normal template. At the time you create the document, any styles that exist in the template are copied into the new document. After that, when you use or modify a style in the document, it is the document's style you are using, not that of the template.

If someone changes the styles in the template, you might want to use the new versions of the styles in your document. The template never forces changes to the styles in previously created documents based on that template, but the document can retrieve style changes from the template. There are several ways to retrieve updated styles from the template.

The easiest—but also the most dangerous—way to update styles is to always retrieve updated style definitions from the template whenever you open the document. To do this, click Tools, Templates And Add-Ins, and select the Automatically Update Document Styles check box, as shown in Figure 7-25.

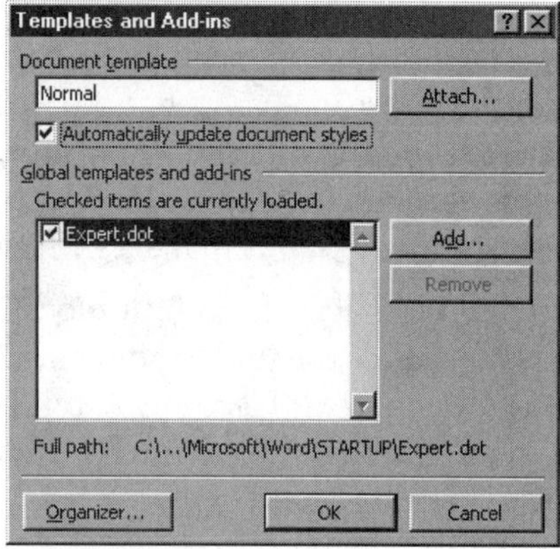

Figure 7-25
This check box will ensure that updated styles are copied from the template each time you open the document.

You could use this option if your workgroup has very strict—but constantly changing—conventions for how a document should look. If the workgroup style manager maintains the styles in a master template, everyone in the workgroup bases documents on that template. If everyone selects the Automatically Update Document Styles check box and no one uses direct formatting, then all the documents currently used in the workgroup will always have the current standard formatting.

You can also use the Automatically Update Document Styles check box to semi-automatically update the styles. Just select the check box and click OK. Then, disable the option you just enabled so you can regain control of the document. For a quicker version of this semi-automatic update, use the following simple *RefreshStyles* macro. It updates the styles from the attached template, but only when you run the macro, not each time you open the document.

```
Sub RefreshStyles()
    ActiveDocument.UpdateStyles
End Sub
```

When you update the styles from the template, you get all the styles in the template—you can't be selective. If you want to update only certain styles, use the Style Organizer. The button to open the Organizer appears in several dialog boxes—among them the Template And Add-Ins dialog box, the Style dialog box, and the Macros dialog box. Surprisingly, the Organizer button does not appear in the AutoCorrect or the Toolbars Customize dialog boxes, although the Organizer can organize those features, along with macros and styles.

To use the Organizer to update styles from the template, open the Organizer and click the Styles tab. On the left is a list of all the styles in the active document. On the right is a list of all the styles in the attached template, as shown in Figure 7-26. Select any or all of the styles in the template list. (Hold down the Shift key to select a range of styles; hold down the Ctrl key to select multiple individual styles.) Then click the Copy button to copy the styles to the active document. Word will ask your permission to replace existing styles.

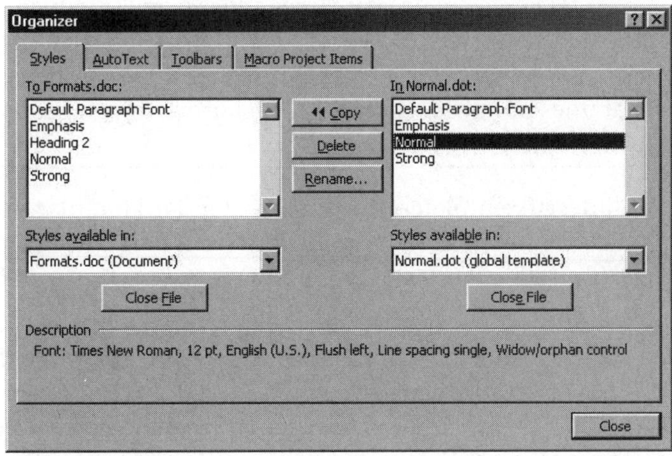

Figure 7-26
Use the Organizer to copy styles between documents or templates.

You can use the Organizer to do more than merely update styles from the template to the active document. You can copy styles from the active document back into the template—in case you have made some nice enhancements to some styles and want to propagate them into other documents. You can also copy styles from one document to another, or from one template to another. Just click the Close File button below one of the lists of styles, and then click the Open File button that takes its place and locate the template or document you want to open.

Opening a file in the Organizer does not affect any documents or templates—at least, not until you click the Copy, Delete, or Rename buttons. Opening a file does not change the template your document is attached to; it simply allows you to organize styles in two documents or templates.

If you like the Organizer, but you want to be able to access it more directly, use the following *ShowOrganizer* macro, perhaps adding it to a command on the Tools menu bar:

```
Sub ShowOrganizer()
    Dialogs(wdDialogOrganizer).Show
End Sub
```

One other tool for bringing the styles from a template into the active document is the Style Gallery. The Style Gallery copies all the styles from a template into your document. Each template in the Style Gallery is designed to provide a coherent set of styles that look good together. To access the Style Gallery, click Format, Theme, and then click Style Gallery at the bottom of the Theme dialog box. The Style Gallery includes all the templates available to Word—including some you might not have installed yet.

Note Like the Style Gallery, the Theme dialog box copies styles from a template into your document. The Theme tool, however, is primarily intended to provide beautiful background graphics for HTML pages. If you are creating a document that does not need a graphical background, you probably don't need the Theme tool.

The Style Gallery includes all templates in any of the standard template folders. (See "Managing Templates" in the next section for more information about template folders.) You can use the Style Gallery as a brute-force organizer to copy all the styles from a template into the active document.

If you like the Style Gallery, you might not like having to go through the Theme dialog box to get to it. There is a Style Gallery command in the Format category of the on the Commands tabbed page of the Toolbars Customize dialog box (accessed from the View menu) (it is about twentieth from the bottom in the category). Drag the command onto the Format menu and you can go directly to the Style Gallery.

The Style Gallery can display any of three preview options: the active document with the new styles applied, an example document (as shown in Figure 7-27), or samples of each style. If you select the Example or Style Sample option for a template you have created, you will probably see the fearsome statement "There is no example for this template." If you are so inclined, it is easy to add an example or style sample to your template. Create an AutoText entry named Gallery Example for the example and create an AutoText entry named Gallery Style Samples for the style samples.

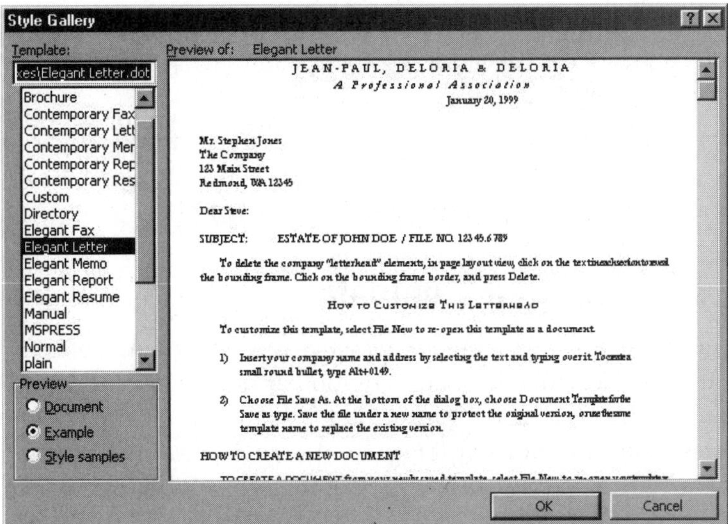

Figure 7-27
The Style Gallery can display an example document from a template.

Of course, creating the sample itself might not be easy, but adding it to the template certainly is. You can add AutoText only to a template, so if you are converting a document into a template, save it as a template first. To create an AutoText entry, select the portion of the text you want to include, click Insert, AutoText, and choose AutoText. In the Look In drop-down list, select the template in to which you want to store the AutoText, type a name in the Insert AutoText Entries Here box, and click Add.

Remember, the Style Gallery is an all-or-nothing proposition. It copies all the styles from the template into your document. If you want to copy selected styles from one of the templates, you can use the Organizer to do that.

Managing Templates

Word uses templates much more extensively than do other Office applications. For example, an Excel template is simply a workbook that creates a copy of itself when you open it. In Word, templates continue to play a role, even after you have created a new document. You can use a Word template in any of four different ways:

- As a **custom template**, which serves as the source of text and styles for a new document. See "Creating a Customized Template" for details about creating a custom template.
- As an **attached template** for updating styles and storing macros. It is easy to transfer styles to or from, or create new macros in, an attached template. See "Switching to a New Template" for details about attaching a template.

- As a **global template**, which contains macros, AutoText entries, and toolbars that you can use. See "Creating a Global Template" for details about creating and using a global template.
- As a **library template**, which serves as a repository for styles, macros, AutoText entries, or toolbars without being opened. See "Creating a Library Template" for details about creating and using a library template.

Creating a Customized Template

Each time you create a new document, it copies text and styles from some template. When you click the New Blank Document toolbar button, or select the Blank Document template in the New dialog box on the File menu, the new document copies text and styles from the Normal template. Word comes with a large number of predesigned templates, grouped into eight categories in the New dialog box.

You can create a template of your own. Create a document and include in it the text and styles you want included in new documents based on the template. Click File, Save As, select Document Template (*.dot) in the Save As Type drop-down list, type a name for the template, and click the Save button. (As soon as you select Document Template, Word switches to the default template folder.) Once you've saved the template, you can close it.

If you want to simplify the process of saving a document as a template, select Template in the File, New dialog box when you create a new document, as shown in Figure 7-28. If you create the file as a new template, Word automatically selects the Document Template option for you when you save the document, preventing you from changing it to anything else. Selecting the Template option when you create the document has no other effect. You can just as easily save an ordinary document as a template; Word simply switches the default folder when you change the file type to Document Template.

Once the template safely exists in the default Template folder, it will appear on the General tab whenever you use the New command to create a new document (assuming you saved the templates in the default Templates folder).

To make changes to the template, simply open the template file. Click the Open toolbar button, navigate to the folder containing templates, and double-click the template file you want to open. The only difficulty is finding the location of the template folder.

To see the default storage location for templates, click Tools, Options, File Locations, and look at the User Templates entry. If you can't read the folder name, double-click the entry to see the Modify Location dialog box. (Be careful that you don't accidentally change the file location.) The default location for document templates is the Application Data\Microsoft\Templates folder. If you are on a computer that has

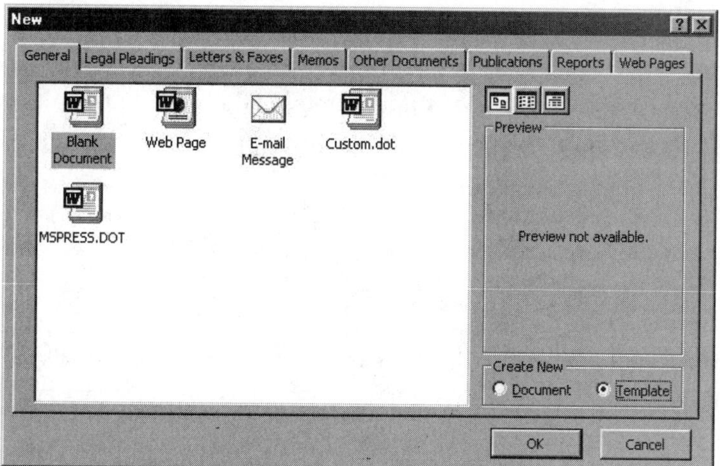

Figure 7-28
Select Template when creating a document to simplify saving the template.

user profiles, the Application Data folder will be under the folder for your profile. Otherwise, it will be under the Windows folder.

It seems inconsistent that Word switches to the template folder for you when you are saving a template but doesn't do the same when you attempt to open a template. Navigating to the template folder can be frustrating. If you do it often, you might want to use this *OpenTemplateFolder* macro:

```
Sub OpenTemplateFolder()
    ChangeFileOpenDirectory Application.Templates("Normal.dot").Path
    Dialogs(wdDialogFileOpen).Show
End Sub
```

This macro first changes to the folder containing the Normal template (which is always open), and then displays Word's built-in, Open dialog box.

Customizing a Built-In Template

Word comes with many beautifully designed templates. Almost all the templates have placeholders labeled Company Name Here or Click Here And Type Return Address. That's fine if you intend to use the template only once, but if you want to really use the template, you should update it to include at least your company name.

Even though the built-in templates are grouped into eight sections, all the built-in templates are stored in the same folder. The folder for built-in templates is not actually in the Application Data hierarchy; it is in the Program Files hierarchy, where the Word application files are stored. (This storage notation actually represents a pseudo-folder. The true physical folder where your templates are actually stored is C:\Program Files\Microsoft Office\Templates\1033.) The folder where the Word executable file (Winword.exe) is stored is called Office. It has a sibling folder named Templates. Under that Templates folder are one or more language-specific folders. The folder for English (US) is 1033. That folder contains the built-in templates.

The following *OpenBuiltInTemplateFolder* macro will open the folder for you.

```
Sub OpenBuiltInTemplateFolder()
    ChangeFileOpenDirectory Application.Path
    ChangeFileOpenDirectory "..\Templates\1033"
    Dialogs(wdDialogFileOpen).Show
End Sub
```

The macro changes the file open directory to the location of the Word executable file, moves up one level (using the double-dot notation for a parent folder), and then moves back down to the Templates folder and the 1033 subfolder for English, respectively.

While you can customize the original built-in template, that's probably not a good idea, for the following reasons:

- Reinstalling Office might erase your modifications.
- You might not be as likely to back up files stored in the Program Files hierarchy as you would files stored in the Application Data hierarchy.
- You might want to refer to the original template.

To create a customized copy of a built-in Memos template, use the File New command to open a new document based on the template (and specify that you will create a new template). Make the changes and then save the customized template.

Assigning Categories to a Template

If you save the template in the default folder, it will appear on the General tab, not on the Memos tab. To store your template under the Memos tab, create a new subfolder under the default Templates folder and name it Memos. (The name of the new subfolder must exactly match the name of a standard built-in tab.) Then save your template in the Memos subfolder.

Let's go over the rules again: the built-in templates are all stored in a single folder. Word has internal mechanisms to know which built-in tab to assign them to. If you create a custom template and want to assign it to a tab other than General, you must store it in a subfolder with the same name as the built-in tab.

In addition to the eight tabs that appear in Word's File, New dialog box, Office has four other built-in tabs intended for PowerPoint, Excel, and Access. If you still have the New Office Document command on your Start menu, you can see all 12 of the built-in tabs. Word will display any tab that matches the name of a subfolder under the Templates folder, provided the subfolder contains a file that can be opened by Word. For example, even though Presentations is a tab used by PowerPoint, if you create a subfolder named Presentations and store a Word template in it, the Presentations tab will appear in the File, New dialog box in Word.

Storing Templates in Various Locations

In addition to the User Templates folder, Word also defines a Workgroup Templates folder. You can find—and define—this folder on the File Locations tab of the Tools Options dialog box. When you open the File, New dialog box, Word includes templates stored in this folder (and its appropriately named subfolders). If you want to save a template into the Workgroup Templates folder, you will need to navigate to that folder, or create the template in the User Templates folder, and then move it using Windows Explorer.

Word can open templates from three different locations: the built-in folder in the Program Files hierarchy, the User Templates folder in the Application Data hierarchy, and the Workgroup Templates folder, which could be anywhere. A template in the User Templates folder takes precedence over an identically named file in the Workgroup Templates folder, and a template in the Workgroup Templates folder takes precedence over an identically named file in the built-in templates folder.

You can store a template anywhere, but unless it is in one of those three standard template locations, it will not appear in the File, New dialog box and you will not be able to base a new template on it. Conversely, any Word file—an ordinary document, for example—that exists in one of the template folders will appear in the File, New dialog box as if it were a template.

Switching to a New Template

Every document is attached to one template, initially—the template used to create the document. The attached template is the one where a style is stored if you choose the Add To Template option in the Modify Style dialog box. The attached template is also where a style comes from if you choose the Automatically Update Document Styles option in the Templates And Add-Ins dialog box.

You can use the Templates And Add-Ins dialog box to change the template that is attached to a document. Changing the attached template does not copy text from the template into the document, and it also does not copy the styles from the template into the document unless you explicitly request to. Unless you explicitly update or modify styles, switching the attached template for a document has no effect on the document whatsoever.

Changing an attached template can, however, change your Word environment. Word always opens an attached template, so an attached template acts just like an open global template.

Creating a Global Template

Any template that is open supplies the Word environment with macros, toolbars, and AutoText entries. A template that is neither the Normal template nor the one attached to a document is called a global template.

A global template can be open in one of two ways. If you use the Open command, the template is completely open. A completely open template has a document window, and you can edit anything about it, including macros, toolbars, and AutoText entries.

If you use the Templates And Add-Ins command to add the template, the template is then loaded. A loaded template does not have a document window and you can't edit it. You can use the macros, toolbars, and AutoText entries, but you cannot change them. In fact, if a template is loaded, you can't even use the Organizer to modify it. If you want to modify a loaded template, you must explicitly open it.

When you load a template using the Templates And Add-Ins command, the template quietly unloads when you exit Word. It does not automatically reload the next time you start Word, but it does remain in the list of global templates so that all you have to do is select the check box to load it.

If you want a global template to load automatically each time you start Word, store the template in the Startup folder. The default location of the Startup folder is Application Data\Word\Startup folder (where Application Data is either in the Windows folder or in your user profile folder). You can click Tools, Options, File Locations to change the location of the Startup folder.

You might want to store a template with commonly used macros in the Startup folder—which makes it an automatically loading global template. The only problem with this is that you can't add new macros to the template. To edit a template, you only need to open it, but navigating to the template folder can be tedious. If you add the following *OpenTemplate* macro into a global template, you can run it whenever you want to make changes to the macros in that template.

```
Sub OpenTemplate()
    Documents.Open FileName:=ThisDocument.FullName
End Sub
```

The ThisDocument property refers to the document that contains the currently running macro. This is different from the ActiveDocument property, which always refers to the currently active document, regardless of whether that document contains the macro or not. The FullName property includes everything needed to open the document, so you don't need to worry about what the current directory is.

Creating a Library Template

A library template is one that you open only with the Style Gallery or the Organizer. To use a template in the Style Gallery, it must be in one of the three template locations described in "Storing Templates in Various Locations" earlier in the chapter. If you will use the template only from the Organizer, you can store it anywhere you like—although storing it into a folder that is easy to navigate to is a good idea.

Chapter 8

Integrate Additional Elements

In This Chapter

Word maintains 11 different types of text—called stories—within a document, with the main text of a document being the main story. The various types of headers and footers account for six story types, and comments, footnotes, and endnotes account for an additional three story types. The last story type is for text encased in text boxes.

A document's Normal view presents only the main story. Headers, footers, footnotes, comments, and text boxes do not appear in Normal view. Secondary story elements can be added only to the main story; that is, you can't add a comment to a comment—or to a header, footer, endnote, footnote, or text box. In addition, only main story elements are included in a Table of Contents or an Index.

Simple documents might contain nothing more than a main story. As you develop more complex documents, however, you will add other elements—such as graphics—to the main story, and additional stories—such as text boxes—to the document.

This chapter will help you understand how to integrate these extra components into your document.

Adding Graphics

Documents have two layers: the text layer and the drawing layer. The main story of a document occupies the text layer; graphics can be added either to the text layer or to the drawing layer. If you add a graphic to the text layer, it is called an Inline Graphic. If you want to explicitly position a graphic on the page, you must place it on the drawing layer, which you will not be able to see in Normal view.

The drawing layer is not above or below the text layer. Objects on the drawing layer can appear behind text, in front of text, or wrapped by text.

Note The sample document for thid section is Graphics.doc

Wrapping Text Around Graphics

When you add a graphic to the drawing layer of a document, the text from the main story wraps around the graphic. Microsoft Word provides many options for wrapping text. For example, the text can follow closely along the edge of the object, as shown in Figure 8-1. (The graphic in Figure 8-1 is an AutoShape object. To add an AutoShape object, display the Drawing toolbar, and choose a shape from the AutoShapes menu. ("Creating a Forceful Presentation with PowerPoint," in Chapter 22 covers Office Clip Art objects in more detail.)

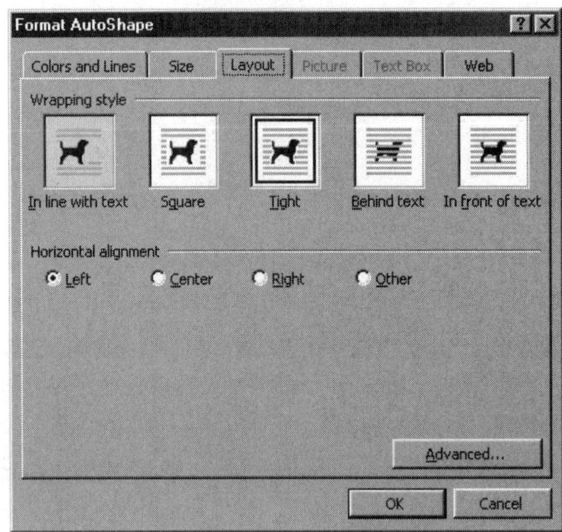

Figure 8-1
Text can wrap closely around a graphical object.

To change how text wraps around an object, double-click the edge of the object and select the Layout tab. The star graphic shown earlier in Figure 8-1 is set to use a tight wrapping style, left-aligned on the page, as shown in the dialog box in Figure 8-2. An object must be on the drawing layer—that is, not inline with text—for text to wrap around it. You can only display the drawing layer when you view the document in Print Layout or Web Layout views.

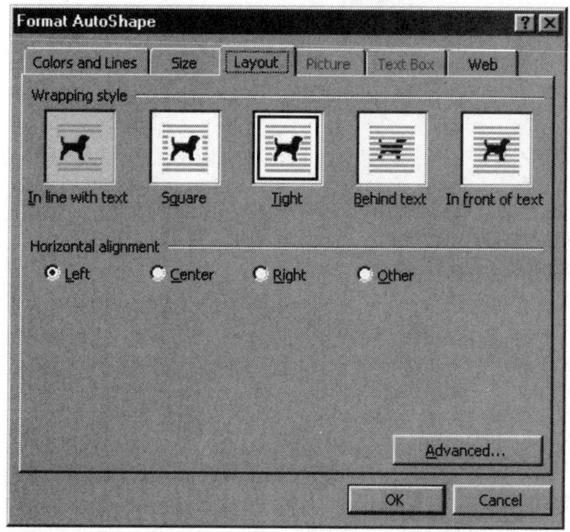

Figure 8-2
Format the layout of the object to choose the wrapping type.

Refining How Text Wraps

Even though the graphic shown earlier in Figure 8-1 is left-aligned to the page, some of the text wraps on the left side of the image and looks out of place. One of the options for wrapping text is to keep all the text on only one side. On the Layout tab of the Format AutoShape dialog box, click the Advanced button to see the Advanced Layout dialog box, as shown in Figure 8-3. This dialog box adds two more wrapping styles:

- **Top And Bottom** makes the graphic appear to be in line.
- **Through** lets text wrap into open spaces in the middle of object, such as between the dog's legs or between the bottom points of the star.

The Advanced Layout dialog box also lets you control precisely how close text can be placed to an object.

It is often very useful to be able to wrap text only on the largest side of an object, because it eliminates the choppy look of having text break for an object, while still giving you the flexibility to move the object wherever you want. Figure 8-4 shows the embedded star with text wrapping on only one side of the image, even after the star has been moved away from the left edge.

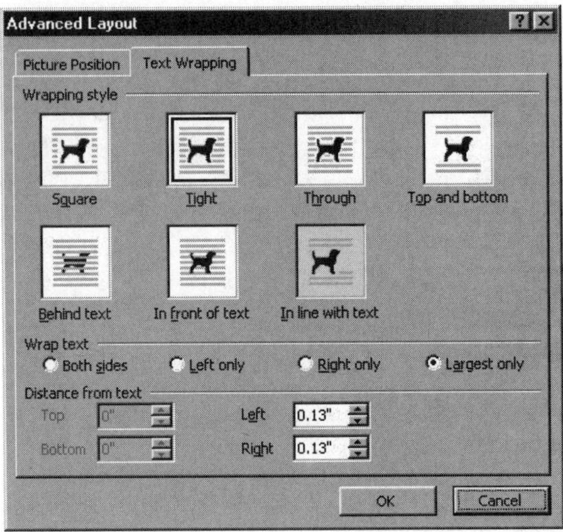

Figure 8-3
Advanced layout options let you wrap on only one side.

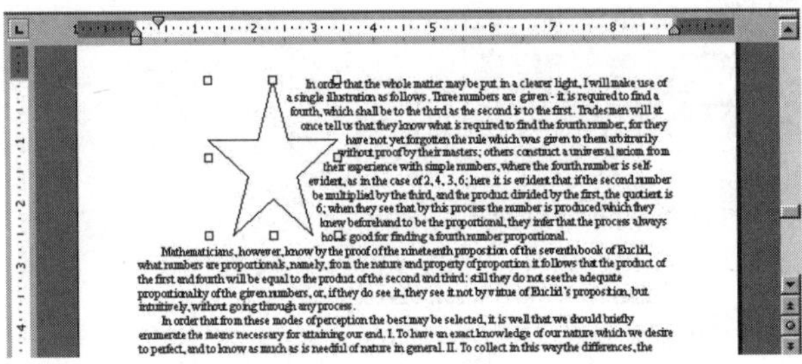

Figure 8-4
Text is less choppy when it wraps on only one side.

Note If you prefer to always have text wrap on the larger side of an image, you can change the default behavior of all AutoShape objects. Simply change an object to the desired format, and then right-click the object and choose Set AutoShape Defaults from the shortcut menu.

Changing the Wrapping Outline

Suppose you don't like how closely the text aligns between the arms of the star. You could change the Distance From Text option, but that would also move the text farther from the points of the star. An option on the Drawing toolbar allows you to change what the wrapping mechanism perceives as the shape of the object. On the Drawing toolbar, click Draw, Text Wrapping, and then select Edit Wrap Points. The object gains several small sizing dots separated by a red dashed line, as shown in

Figure 8-5. You can drag the dots to any shape you like and the text will track to the shape of the dots, regardless of the shape of the object.

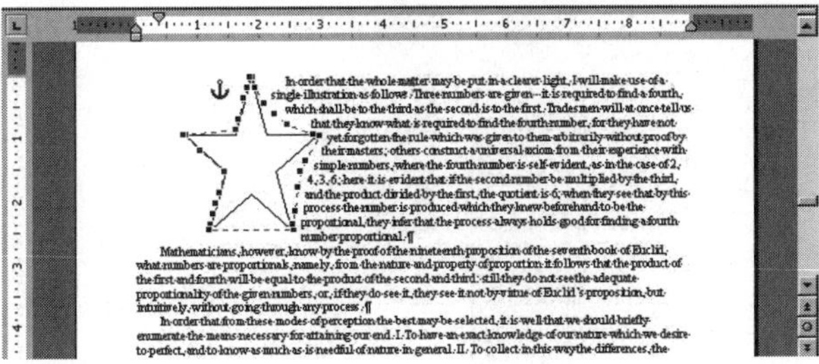

Figure 8-5
Edit wrapping points to change how text flows.

You can't add or delete wrapping points. You can, however, borrow the outline from one shape to use with another. The Change AutoShape option on the Draw menu allows you to change an Office Clip Art object to a new AutoShape. Normally, when you change one shape into another, the wrapping points change to the new shape as well. If you have made even the slightest edits to one of the wrapping points, however, the object will retain the customized wrapping points, even if you switch object types. Figure 8-6 shows text wrapping around the modified outline of the star, even after the shape has been changed to a diamond.

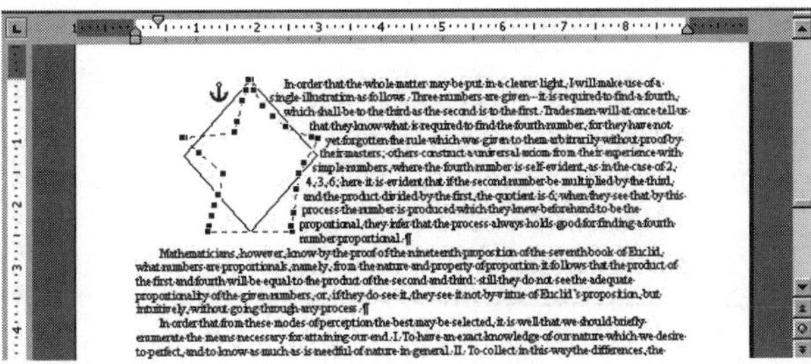

Figure 8-6
You can apply the outline from one shape to a different shape.

Most of the time, you will want the wrapping shape of an object to at least approximate the object's actual shape. Sometimes, however, you might find yourself wanting you could add wrapping points. You can—by borrowing the wrapping points from a similar, but more complex, object.

Using Columns to Control Wrapping

If you want to place a graphic in the middle of the page, you might want text on both sides of the image, as shown in Figure 8-7. But lines of text that have been split in the middle are sometimes hard to read, because you need to match the lines across the gap.

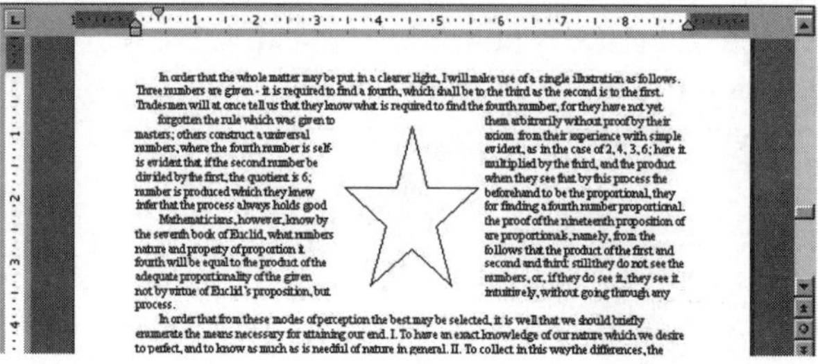

Figure 8-7
Text that is split in the middle can be hard to follow.

In situations like these, you might prefer to have the text flow down the left side of the graphic, and then continue to flow down the right side. You can do this by adding columns for the range of text that includes the graphic. (This kind of fine-tuning is best saved for last, after you have made most of the necessary changes to the content and layout of the document.)

First, make sure to orient the graphic as centered relative to the page rather than relative to the column. The Picture Position tab on the Advanced Layout dialog box allows you to fine-tune the position, as you can see in Figure 8-8.

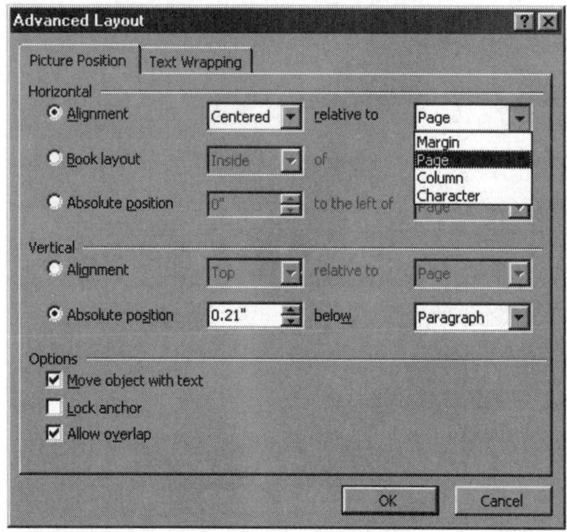

Figure 8-8
Advanced layout options allow you to precisely control the position of the graphic.

Select the text surrounding the graphic, click the Columns button on the toolbar, and create two columns. Word inserts continuous section breaks at the beginning and end of the region you selected. Because a section break acts like a paragraph mark, if you have indented paragraphs or extra spacing after a paragraph, you will need to manually change the formatting of one or two paragraphs to make them appear as a single paragraph. Figure 8-9 shows the document with revised wrapping. The text flows down the left side of the star before moving on to the right side.

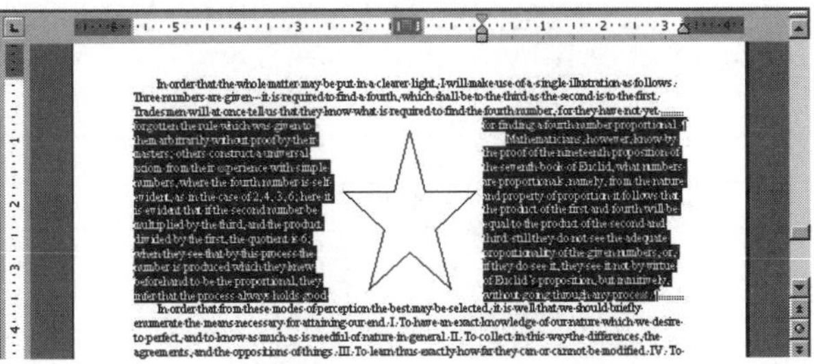

Figure 8-9
Text that flows vertically within a column is easier to read.

Enhancing the Background of a Document

In addition to wrapping text around a graphic, you might want to use a graphic to enhance the background of a document.

Adding a Background Fill

Use the Background option on the Format menu to add any background available for an Office Clip Art object to the background of your document (but only when the document is displayed in Web Layout view). Figure 8-10 shows a gradient background for a document viewed in Web Layout view.

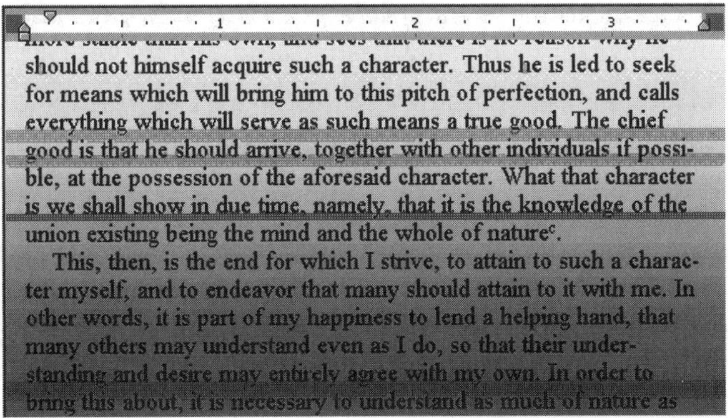
should not himself acquire such a character. Thus he is led to seek for means which will bring him to this pitch of perfection, and calls everything which will serve as such means a true good. The chief good is that he should arrive, together with other individuals if possible, at the possession of the aforesaid character. What that character is we shall show in due time, namely, that it is the knowledge of the union existing being the mind and the whole of nature[c].

This, then, is the end for which I strive, to attain to such a character myself, and to endeavor that many should attain to it with me. In other words, it is part of my happiness to lend a helping hand, that many others may understand even as I do, so that their understanding and desire may entirely agree with my own. In order to bring this about, it is necessary to understand as much of nature as

Figure 8-10
The Background command creates a background for Web Layout.

To create this background, select Format, Background, Fill Effects, and then select the first variation of the horizontal shading style. When you apply a background, Word automatically switches the view to Web Layout. If you switch to any of the other views, the background disappears.

Note In Office 2000, you can now create the same kind of background for a printed page using the new capability to position Office Clip Art objects behind text. Figure 8-11 shows a document with a shaded fill in Print Layout view, very similar to the kind of fill you can create using the Format Background option.

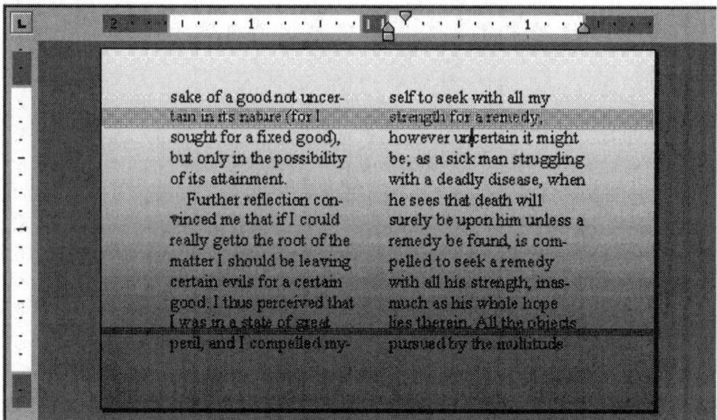

Figure 8-11
Use Office Clip Art to create a background for a printed document.

Creating a background fill for a printed page is only slightly more complicated than creating one for a web page. If you want the shaded background for a single page, add the Office Clip Art object while viewing the document page. If you want the shaded background to appear on all pages, add the object while viewing Headers And Footers for the appropriate section. Refer to "Using Headers and Footers" in Chapter 7 for more information on using headers and footers with sections.

To add a background fill, click the Rectangle button on the Drawing toolbar and draw a small rectangle on the screen. You don't want to make the rectangle fit the page until after you move it under the text. Click Draw on the Draw menu, click Text Wrapping, and then select Text Wrapping Behind Text, which corresponds to the option in the Format AutoShape dialog box. Again on the Drawing toolbar, select Fill Effects from the Fill Color list box and choose the effect you want, such as the first variation of the horizontal shading style used earlier. Once the rectangle has been formatted, resize it to cover the portion of the page you want to cover.

Note The sample document for this section is Background.doc.

Adding a Watermark

A watermark is a pale image that appears behind the text of a page. Adding a watermark is very similar to adding a shaded background. You can use any graphic you like as a watermark—an image from the Office Clip Gallery, a scanned picture, your company's logo, or a block of text displayed at an angle. Figure 8-12 shows a simple clip art image used as a watermark.

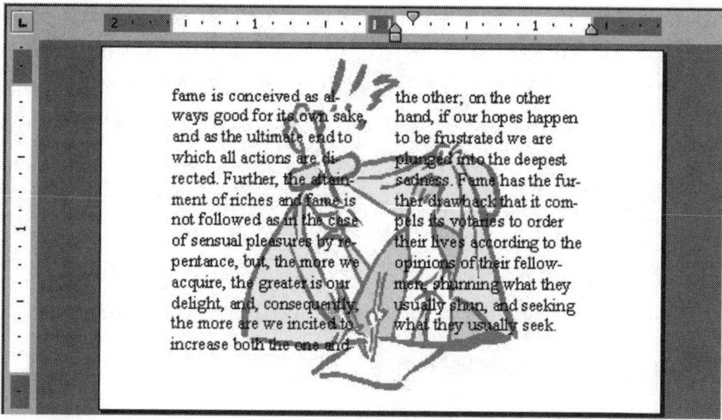

Figure 8-12
A watermark is a pale image behind the text of a page.

To convert an image to a watermark, click Insert, Picture, and choose the source of the graphic. When you insert a graphic from the Office Clip Gallery or from a file, Word initially positions it in-line with the text. An inline graphic behaves like a single character. If you reduce the size of an inline graphic, as shown in Figure 8-13, you can see how the text moves around it. You can do anything with an inline graphic that you can do with a single (oversized) character. An inline graphic is visible in Normal, Outline, Print Layout, and Web Layout views.

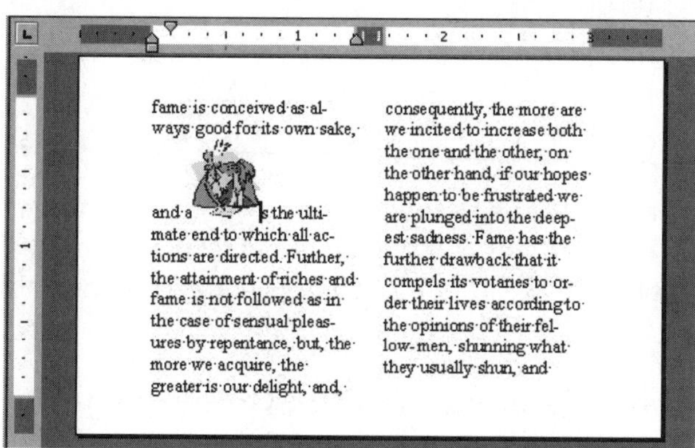

Figure 8-13
An inline graphic behaves like a single character.

You cannot, however, specify wrapping options for an inline graphic. As soon as you set a wrapping option, the graphic ceases to be in-line. To place the graphic behind the text, select it and click Draw, Text Wrapping, and then choose Text Wrapping Behind Text. Finally, resize the picture.

Most graphic images are too strong to be placed behind text; they tend to make the text illegible. You can create a better watermark by reducing the contrast (to make it more subtle) and increasing the brightness (to make the background lighter). Double-click the picture to open the Format Picture dialog box. On the Picture tab, select Watermark from the Color list. The Watermark option is simply a shortcut to setting the Brightness to 85% and the Contrast to 15%. You can fine-tune the brightness and contrast values if they are not optimal for your graphic. Unlike the Watermark option—which merely adjusts the values of other controls—the Grayscale and Black & White options in the Color list actually change the apparent color of the picture. None of these settings changes the actual picture, and you can always return the picture to its original state by choosing Automatic from the Color list.

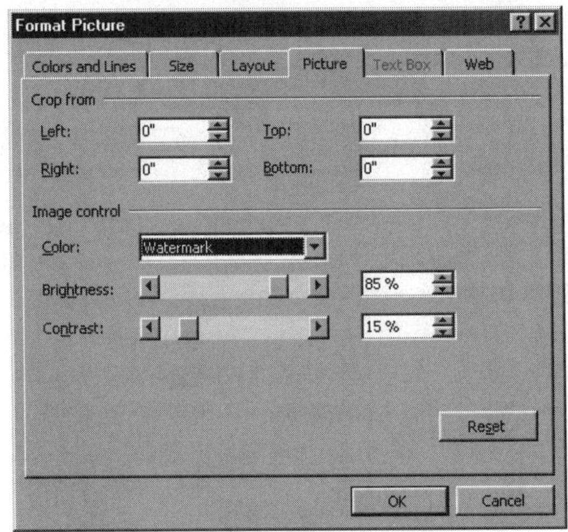

Figure 8-14
A watermark shows the low contrast and high brightness settings.

As with all background images, place the image directly on the document page if you want it to be on a single page only. If you want the image to appear on all the pages in the section, view the section's headers and footers before you insert the graphic.

Creating Rotated Text

The text contained in a text box—or any Office Clip Gallery object—can be rotated, but only in 90-degree increments. You can't rotate a text box to create the kind of watermark that appears in Figure 8-15. You can, however, use the WordArt tool to add text as a graphic that can be freely rotated.

On the Drawing toolbar, click WordArt, select the upper-left style, and then click OK. Type the text you want in the watermark and click OK. Use the Draw menu to move the graphic behind the text. To rotate the text, select the object and then click the Free Rotate button on the Drawing toolbar. Drag one of the rotation handles in the direction you want to rotate your text. (You can resize the text later, even after you have

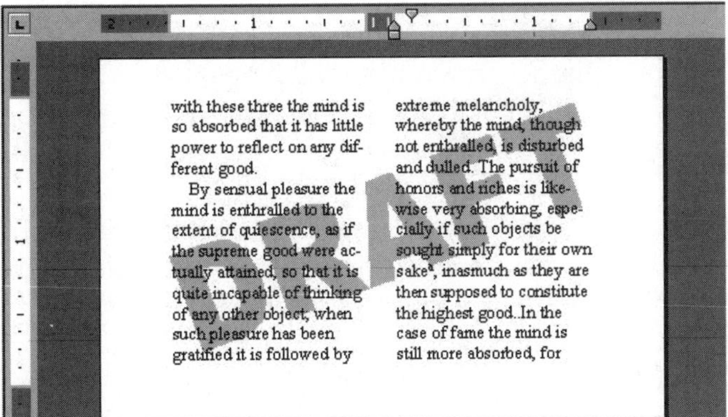

Figure 8-15
Use WordArt to add a text watermark that can be rotated.

rotated it.) WordArt will not let you use the Contrast and Brightness settings from the Picture toolbar, so select a subtle fill color that won't make your document unreadable. To turn off the outline around the letters, click the arrow next to the Line Color button on the Drawing toolbar and select No Line from the pop-up menu.

Including Inline Bitmaps

Many documents require figures, such as screen captures—like the figures you see in this book. You can purchase special programs designed specifically to capture screens, but you can also capture screens easily using built-in Windows tools and Word.

To capture an entire screen, press the PrintScreen key on your keyboard. To capture only the active window—the window with the active title bar (which is good for capturing dialog boxes, screen options, and so forth)—press Alt+PrintScreen. Using either of these options places the image onto the Windows Clipboard. Once an image is on the Clipboard, you can simply paste it into Word. (You can only capture one image at a time. Each time you press PrintScreen or Alt+PrintScreen, the existing image is replaced with the new image you just captured.)

Estimating the Size of a Bitmap

Pasting a captured image into your Word document can increase the size of your document.

When you capture the screen, you create what is called a bitmap image. A bitmap stores the value of each pixel on the screen. If your computer displays 256 Colors, each pixel requires one byte—the same as a single character of text. To calculate the size of a bitmap, you multiply the storage for a single pixel by the size of the screen.

A standard VGA screen has 640 by 480 pixels, for a total screen area of 307,200 pixels. That means that a bitmap of the entire screen set at 256 colors would require

(continued)

Estimating the Size of a Bitmap (continued)
roughly .33-MB of storage. Larger screen sizes and higher color settings increase the size of the bitmap geometrically. For example, a 1024 by 768-pixel screen set to True Color (24-bit) requires roughly 2.5-MB of storage for a single screen capture.

You can keep your document small and still display the graphic image by saving the graphic to a file on your hard disk and then simply creating a link to it in your document. To save the graphic image to a file, paste the file into Windows Paint and then save it as a bitmap file (Paint's default format). Refer to "Create a Forceful Presentation with PowerPoint," in Chapter 22 for more information about working with bitmap files.

To link to the image file from Word, click Insert, Picture, From File, and then select the file, but don't click the Insert button at this point. Clicking the Insert button will insert the image directly into your document—just as if you pasted the image from the Clipboard. Instead, click the drop-down arrow on the right side of the Insert button, and then choose Link To File from the list. (The other option, Insert And Link, stores the entire image in the document and also maintains a link to the image so that if the external file changes, you can update the document to match the external file.)

Note If you prefer using the keyboard, the Insert button's drop-down arrow is somewhat frustrating. Pressing Alt+S clicks the button; it doesn't just select it. To choose the Link To File option using the keyboard, press Alt+T to select the Files Of Type text box and then press the Tab key to select the Insert button. Press the Down arrow key to open the drop-down list box, and then continue to press the Down arrow key as many times as necessary to select the option you want.

When you print a document containing linked pictures, be sure to set the Update Links print option, which is available on the Print tab of the Tools, Options dialog box, or by clicking Options from the Print dialog box. If this option is turned off, some of the pictures might appear as empty boxes or as substitute images on the printed page.

Creating a Macro to Link to a File

If you will be creating multiple screen captures in a document, you will need a new filename for each captured file. The actual filename might not matter, but each filename must be unique. You can write a macro to simplify the task of giving each file a unique name and then linking the file to your document.

When you use Paint to save a new bitmap, it defaults to the filename Untitled.bmp—probably in the My Documents folder. The following *InsertPictureFromFile* macro looks for that filename; if it does not exist, the macro stops. If the file exists, the macro searches for the highest numbered file in a subfolder of the folder containing the active document, and then renames the bitmap file to a name with the next available number. It then inserts a link to the newly renamed file and changes the style of the new paragraph to a custom style named Figure.

Before running the macro, you must capture the screen, paste it into Paint, and save the file. You must also have added a style named Figure to the active document, saved the document, and created a subfolder named Screens. (The definition of the Figure style is not important, but the macro assumes that the type name exists.)

```
Sub InsertPictureFromFile()
    ''' Put default folder\file that Paint uses
    Const sBase As String = "C:\My Documents\untitled.bmp"
    Dim iNumber As Long
    Dim iMatch As Long
    Dim iMax As Long
    Dim sFile As String
    Dim sNew As String

    ''' Check for new bitmap file
    sFile = Dir(sBase)
    If sFile = "" Then
        MsgBox "No picture available as " & sBase
        Exit Sub
    End If

    ''' Change to active document's child folder
    ChDir ActiveDocument.Path & "/Screens"
    ChDrive ActiveDocument.Path

    ''' Find highest existing file number
    sNew = Dir("*.bmp")
    Do Until sNew = ""
        iNumber = Mid(sNew, 4, 2)
        If iNumber > iMax Then iMax = iNumber
        sNew = Dir
    Loop
    iMax = iMax + 1

    ''' Change to parent folder and rename the file
    ChDir ".."
    sNew = "SCREENS\FIG" & Format(iMax, "00") & ".bmp"
    Name sBase & sFile As sNew

    ''' Add graphic to new paragraph with set style
    Selection.InsertParagraph
    Selection.InlineShapes.AddPicture FileName:=sNew, _
        LinkToFile:=True, SaveWithDocument:=False
    Selection.Style = "Figure"    ''' Style must already exist
End Sub
```

After declaring variables, the macro checks for the existence of the bitmap file. (See "Creating a Dynamic Array" in chapter 4 for more information about using the *Dir* function to find files.)

In the second block of code, the macro changes to the path of the active document. In the statement *ChDir ActiveDocument.Path & "/Screens"*, the Path property contains the complete path for the active document, and the subfolder name is appended to it. The ChDir function changes to the specified directory but leaves the current drive unchanged. The statement *ChDrive ActiveDocument.Path* changes to the desired drive. The ChDrive function looks only at the first letter of the argument you give it, so you can give it the full path of the active document.

In the third block of code, the macro looks for all files with the extension .BMP in the current directory (the Screens subfolder under the active document). Because the filenames will all have the form FIGnn.bmp (where nn is a sequential number), the number portion of the filename is always in the fourth and fifth character positions. The statement *iNumber = Mid(sNew, 4, 2)* extracts those characters, converting them into a number by assigning them to a variable that has been declared as *Long*. The Dir function retrieves the files in an unpredictable order, and you might have deleted an unwanted file, so the loop searches through all the files, keeping track of the highest number.

In the next section, the *ChDir ..* statement changes back to the directory containing the active document (the .. notation moves up one folder), the *sNew = "SCREENS\FIG" & Format(iMax, "00") & ".bmp"* statement constructs a new filename, and the statement *Name sBase & sFile As sNew* renames the bitmap to the new filename.

The final section adds a paragraph mark, inserts the file as a link, and changes the style of the paragraph. When you run this macro, you don't even need to know what the filename is for the bitmap. If you do want to see the filename, select the picture and press Shift+F9 to convert the field codes. Press Shift+F9 again to restore the picture.

Editing a Linked File

What if you need to replace a captured bitmap with a new one? The Edit Picture command on the shortcut menu does not work for linked pictures. Even for an embedded picture, it displays the Word picture editor, which cannot be used for working with a bitmap. It would really be nice if there were an Edit Linked Picture command that could open the linked file in Paint so that you could replace it with a new picture.

The following *EditLinkedPicture* macro extracts the filename from an IncludePicture field. If no field is selected, or if the first field in the selection is not an IncludePicture field, the macro will simply do nothing.

```
Sub EditLinkedPicture()
    Const LinkCode As String = "INCLUDEPICTURE "
    Dim sCode As String
    Dim sFile As String
```

```
    Dim iStart As Long
    Dim iLen As Long

    ''' Fail quietly if no field selected
    If Selection.Fields.Count < 1 Then Exit Sub

    ''' Fail quietly if wrong field code
    sCode = UCase(Trim(Selection.Fields(1).Code))
    If Left(sCode, Len(LinkCode)) <> LinkCode Then Exit Sub

    ''' Extract filename from field
    iStart = Len(LinkCode) + 2
    iLen = InStr(iStart, sCode, " ") - iStart - 1
    sFile = Mid(sCode, iStart, iLen)

    ''' Run Paint with extracted file
    Shell "C:\Program Files\Accessories\MSPAINT.EXE " & _
        ActiveDocument.Path & "\" & sFile, vbMaximizedFocus
End Sub
```

In the statement *If Selection.Fields.Count < 1 Then Exit Sub,* the Fields collection returns all the fields contained within the current selection. If the Count property of the collection is zero, then there are no fields within the selection and the macro quits. In the statement *sCode = UCase(Trim(Selection.Fields(1).Code)),* the macro looks at the first field within the selection. The Code property of a Field returns a range that corresponds to the instructions for the field. The *Trim* function removes leading and trailing spaces to make sure that the field code is at the beginning, and the UCase function converts the code to all capital letters to avoid being deceived by irrelevant variations.

To extract the filename, the statement *iStart = Len(LinkCode) + 2* calculates the location two spaces after the name of the field, thereby skipping the space and the quotation mark. The *iLen = InStr(iStart, sCode, " ") - iStart – 1* statement then searches for the next space and calculates the length of the entire filename, excluding the closing quotation mark.

The statement *Shell "C:\Program Files\Accessories\MSPAINT.EXE " & ActiveDocument.Path & "\" & sFile, vbMaximizedFocus* launches Microsoft Paint. If your MSPAINT program is in a different folder, you will need to change the path. The *Shell* statement is approximately equivalent to executing the command from the Run command on the Start menu.

To add this command to the shortcut menu, customize the toolbars and activate the ShortcutKeys toolbar. Place the macro onto the first Inline Picture submenu on the Draw menu, and change the name to Edit Linked Picture. (See "Modifying Command Bars" in Chapter 1 for more details about adding macros to shortcut menus.)

After you use the command to edit the picture, make any changes in Paint (including replacing the picture by pasting a new picture). Then save the file and close Paint. In Word, refresh the link by selecting the picture and pressing F9.

Cropping a Bitmap Image

When you place an image in your document, it might not be the size you want. There are two ways to change the size of an image. You can scale the image, which reduces (or enlarges) the image to fit the desired space, or you can crop the image, which trims (or adds a margin to) the edges.

When you scale a bitmap image, you can't change the number of pixels in the original bitmap. If you increase the size of a bitmap, you also increase the chances for jagged edges to appear on diagonal or curved lines. (Chapter 22, "Create a Forceful Presentation with PowerPoint," contains more details about working with graphics.)

When you crop a bitmap image, you don't change the number of pixels; you simply don't include pixels from the edges of the bitmap. Cropping a bitmap image in Word does not change the original image, even if you pasted it directly into the document. Cropping simply tells Word how much of the image to display. If you crop by a negative amount, Word adds a border around the bitmap.

To crop an image with the mouse, show the Picture toolbar. Select the bitmap and click the Crop button on the toolbar. Clicking the Crop button displays the document in Print Layout view if your document was in any other view mode. You can display an inline picture in Normal view, and you can see the cropped image in Normal view, but you can't use the Crop tool to change the image unless you are in one of the layout views. When the Crop button is selected, the mouse pointer changes to reflect the crop tool image on the button. Drag the image handles to crop the image.

Creating a Macro to Store Crop Values In the beta versions of Office 2000, Word would sometimes lose the cropping information for a bitmap, scaling the bitmap instead. The following macro goes through the document, storing the cropping values for each bitmap. The *TagCrop* macro stores the crop values as a custom switch in the IncludePicture field. Even if Word never loses your cropping information, you might find this macro useful. It shows how you can store your own information in a field code by creating a custom switch. It also shows how to manipulate field codes. If you want to use the same crop values for more than one bitmap, you can simply copy the custom switch from one field code to another.

```
Sub TagCrop()
    Const LinkCode As String = "INCLUDEPICTURE "
    Dim myFields As Fields
    Dim myField As Field
    Dim myFormat As PictureFormat
    Dim myStart As Long
    Dim myCode As String

    On Error GoTo ErrorHandler

    ''' If no selection, process entire document
    If Selection.Start = Selection.End Then
```

```
        Set myFields = ActiveDocument.Fields
    Else
        Set myFields = Selection.Fields
    End If

    ''' Store crop values in custom field switch
    For Each myField In myFields
        myCode = Trim(myField.Code.Text)
        If Left(myCode, Len(LinkCode)) = LinkCode Then

            ''' Discard custom switch if already there
            myStart = InStr(myCode, "\x")
            If myStart Then myCode = Left(myCode, myStart - 1)

            ''' append new switch and crop amounts
            Set myFormat = myField.InlineShape.PictureFormat
            myCode = myCode & " \x "
            myCode = myCode & Format(myFormat.CropTop, "0.00 ")
            myCode = myCode & Format(myFormat.CropRight, "0.00 ")
            myCode = myCode & Format(myFormat.CropBottom, "0.00 ")
            myCode = myCode & Format(myFormat.CropLeft, "0.00 ")

            ''' put revised code back into the field
            myField.Code.Text = myCode
        End If
    Next myField
ErrorHandler:
End Sub
```

The *On Error GoTo ErrorHandler* statement causes the macro to quit if something goes wrong.

Many of Word's functions—find and replace, for example—operate on only the current selection unless nothing is selected, in which case the function processes the entire document. The *If* block at the top of this macro emulates that behavior. By the end of the block, the *myFields* variable contains a collection of either all the fields in the document or all the fields in the selection.

The macro then loops through all the fields in the *myFields* collection. If the trimmed field code does not begin with the appropriate keyword, the macro skips that field. Of the three groups of statements that do the actual work in the macro, the first checks for the existence of the custom switch. If the *myStart = InStr(myCode, "\x")* statement finds the custom switch, then the *If myStart Then myCode = Left(myCode, myStart - 1)* statement truncates the field code to discard the switch and all its values. The second group of statements appends the custom switch code, along with a crop value, for each of the four sides of the image. The statement *myField.Code.Text = myCode* in the third group places the updated field code back into the field.

To test the macro, select a cropped picture and then run the macro. Then, press Shift+F9 to see the full field code with its newly acquired custom switch. Press

Shift+F9 again to redisplay the picture. Even with the custom switches in the field code, you can still press F9 to refresh the picture if the bitmap file changes. Word simply ignores the custom switch values.

Creating a Macro to Reapply Crop Values To reapply the crop values, you need a second macro. (You would also run this macro if you copy the crop switch values from one field to another.) The *ReCrop* macro is the inverse of the *TagCrop* macro. It also searches either the selected range or the entire document looking for IncludePicture fields. If the field has a custom switch, the macro applies the crop settings to the picture.

```
Sub ReCrop()
    Const LinkCode As String = "INCLUDEPICTURE "
    Dim myFields As Fields
    Dim myField As Field
    Dim myFormat As PictureFormat
    Dim myStart As Long
    Dim myCode As String

    On Error GoTo ErrorHandler

    ''' If no selection, process entire document
    If Selection.Start = Selection.End Then
        Set myFields = ActiveDocument.Fields
    Else
        Set myFields = Selection.Fields
    End If

    ''' Extract crop values from custom field switch
    For Each myField In myFields
        myCode = Trim(myField.Code.Text)
        If Left(myCode, Len(LinkCode)) = LinkCode Then

            ''' Select new field range to watch macro work
            myField.Code.Select

            ''' Find custom switch
            myStart = InStr(myCode, "\x")
            If myStart Then

                ''' Extract values and apply
                myCode = Mid(myCode, myStart + 3)
                myField.InlineShape.Reset
                Set myFormat = myField.InlineShape.PictureFormat
                myFormat.CropTop = FirstNumber(myCode, " ")
                myFormat.CropRight = FirstNumber(myCode, " ")
                myFormat.CropBottom = FirstNumber(myCode, " ")
                myFormat.CropLeft = FirstNumber(myCode, " ")
            End If
        End If
    Next myField
```

```
ErrorHandler:
End Sub
```

This macro differs from the *TagCrops* macro only after the *If myStart Then* statement. The statement *myCode = Mid(myCode, myStart + 3)* extracts the values from the custom switch. The *myField.InlineShape.Reset* statement removes any scaling or cropping from the picture. The macro applies each number from the custom switch, in turn, to the sides of the picture. Extracting the first number from a string is not a trivial task and needs to be done four times for this macro. Any time you need to perform the same task more than once in a macro, you should create a custom function, which is what the *FirstNumber* function is.

Creating a Function to Extract Numbers from a String The *FirstNumber* function searches a string for a delimiter. (In this case, the delimiter is a space, but why not write the function so that it could use anything as a delimiter?) If the portion before the string is a valid number, it returns that number. Otherwise, it returns a zero. The function also strips the extracted number from the *InputString* argument.

```
Private Function FirstNumber(InputString, Delimiter) As Double
    Dim i As Long
    Dim s As String

    ''' If not a valid number, return a zero
    On Error GoTo ErrorHandler

    ''' Return everything to the left of the first delimiter
    InputString = Trim(InputString)
    i = InStr(InputString, Delimiter)
    s = Left(InputString, i)

    ''' Remove the first number from the string
    InputString = Trim(Mid(InputString, i + 1))

    ''' Attempt to convert the first part to a number
    FirstNumber = s
    Exit Function

ErrorHandler:
    FirstNumber = 0
End Function
```

The *InputString = Trim(InputString)* statement trims the input string, in case there is a leading space that would erroneously match the delimiter character. The statement *i = InStr(InputString, Delimiter)* searches for the delimiter and the statement *s = Left(InputString, i)* extracts the left part of the input string, up to the delimiter. If there is no delimiter in the string (for example, if it is at the end of the string), trying to extract the left portion will raise an error. The error-handler then simply returns zero.

The *InputString = Trim(Mid(InputString, i + 1))* statement then removes everything before the delimiter from the *InputString* argument. It can do this because the argument was passed By Reference. (See "Changing the Value of an Argument" in Chapter 4 for more details about passing an argument By Reference.) Trimming the first number makes it easy to use the function repeatedly to get the next number each time.

Finally, the *FirstNumber = s* statement tries to assign the extracted left portion of the input string to the function name. Since the function is declared as a Double, this converts the string into a number. If the extracted portion does not contain a valid number, this raises an error and the macro returns zero.

The *FirstNumber* function isolates the complexity of extracting a number from a string, thus making the *ReCrop* macro easier to read.

Note "Monitoring the Keyboard in a Macro" in Chapter 6 describes a macro that will crop the edges of a picture as you hold down the arrow key. That macro illustrates an interesting way to make a macro keep working as long as you hold down a particular key.

Using Drop Caps to Learn About Frames

The Drop Cap option appears on the Format menu. A drop cap, such as the one in Figure 8-16, is normally an extra-large first character of a word, with the paragraph text wrapping around it. The Drop Cap command creates a frame to cause a paragraph to wrap around the drop cap character, but it can also add other formatting options.

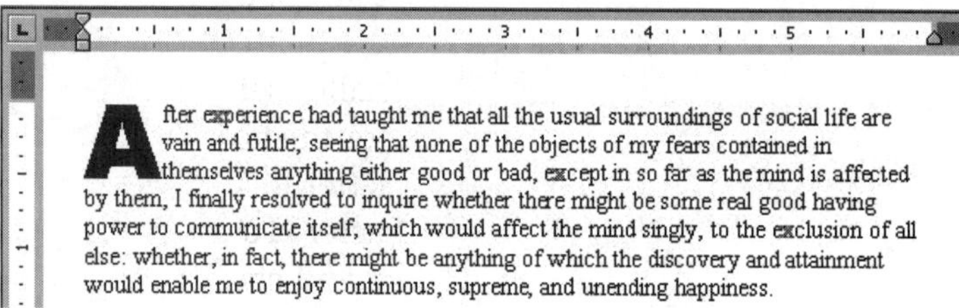

Figure 8-16
A drop cap highlights the beginning of a section.

While you would almost never create a drop cap without using the Drop Cap command, replicating the character, paragraph, and frame formatting that the Drop Cap command achieves can be a useful way to learn how these formats interact. You can also see what the command adds, in addition to simply doing the dirty work of applying the formatting. In the process, you can learn ways to use the Drop Cap command to create more than simply drop caps.

Replicating a Drop Cap

To replicate a drop cap, add a frame around the first letter of the paragraph, remove any border from the frame, and then set the frame's distance from the text to zero. Then format the first letter with the desired font at the appropriate size, which can be defined as the size of the paragraph font times the desired number of lines, allowing for the amount of spacing between the lines. Trial and error is always necessary. Because adding a frame inserts a paragraph mark (a frame is a paragraph attribute), remove any initial formatting from the remaining paragraph (such as a first line indent or the space before the paragraph) that would give away the secret that it is now a separate paragraph.

So far, the process of adding a drop cap is reasonably straightforward. As shown in Figure 8-17, the drop cap, however, still has substantial space both above and below it, even though the frame's vertical distance from the text is set to zero.

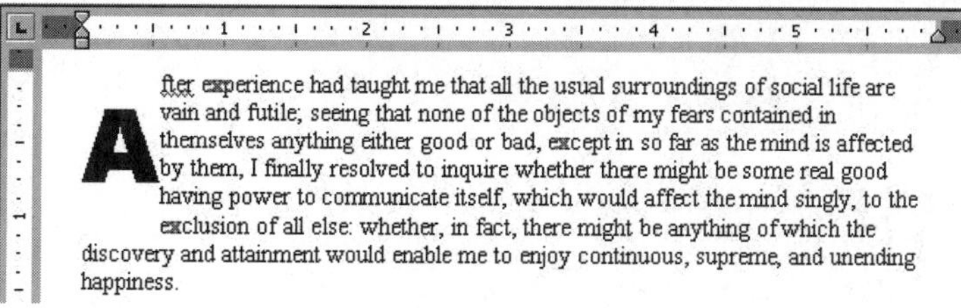

Figure 8-17
Creating a frame leaves spaces above and below a character.

The vertical spacing does not come from the frame; it comes from the paragraph itself. Format the drop cap paragraph to remove any space above or below it. Then set the paragraph's line spacing to Exact, but a few points smaller than the font size for the letter. Adjusting the line spacing to a smaller setting than the point size of the document will clip the top of a capital letter or the bottom of a lower case letter that descends below the base-line, such as the letter g. The final step is to raise or lower the character position to center the character. To do that, click Font on the Format menu, choose the Character Spacing tab, and choose an option in the Position drop-down list box to raise or lower the character's position relative to the paragraph text.

At this point, your drop cap would appear the same as the one generated by the Drop Cap command, but there are some additional capabilities that you simply cannot replicate using standard formatting tools. First, when generating a drop cap with the Drop Cap command, you can resize the character by dragging one of the sizing handles on the frame. If you try to do the same thing with your hand-created drop cap, you will get a frame that no longer fits the character. Second, text continues to wrap around a drop cap created by using the Drop Cap command, even if the column with the text becomes narrow enough to hold only three or four characters. If the column containing your hand-made drop cap becomes narrower than a few words, the text will no longer wrap.

Note The sample document for this section is SpinCap.doc.

Using a Drop Cap for More Than an Initial Letter

Now that you know more about what the Drop Cap does, you can extend its applicability far beyond its original intent. Suppose, for example, that you want to create an initial bold word, such as the one shown in Figure 8-18. Use the Drop Cap command to drop the first letter, and then add the rest of the word (or words) inside the frame. (If you want to cut and paste a word into the frame, use Paste Special to paste unformatted letters. Otherwise, they will keep their original small size.)

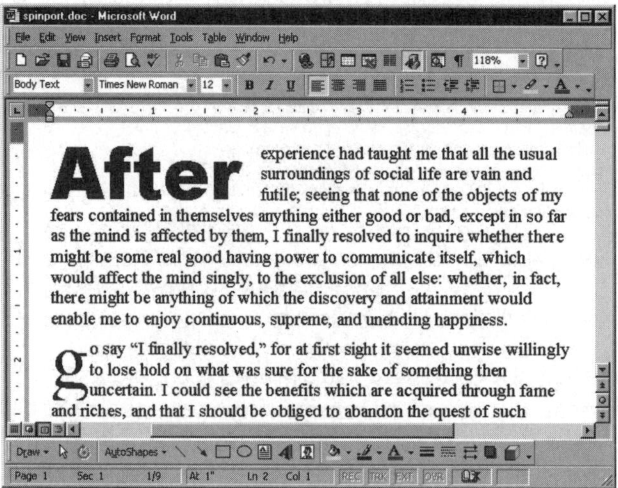

Figure 8-18
A drop cap can be more than a single letter.

If you place a word in the frame, you will need to increase the frame's horizontal Distance From Text option to insert a space after the word. If you add letters that descend below the line, such as the letter g, those letters might be clipped. If this happens, simply click Format, Drop Cap, and then click OK without changing any options. The command will shrink the font to make the new characters fit. You can also use the Drop Cap command to quickly change the number of lines the drop character or word uses. Re-executing the Drop Cap command does not extract a single letter from the word or change the horizontal spacing you added to the frame.

You can also exploit the font resizing capability of a drop cap by simply resizing the frame. You might want to insert a bold word in the middle of a page, like the one shown in Figure 8-19. If you're not sure what size you want the word to be, you can make it easy to resize by making the word into a Drop Cap at the beginning of the paragraph, and then moving it to the center of the page. Because of the automatic sizing, a drop cap is not useful for more than one or two short words. Also, if you use the Drop Cap command again, it will then move the frame back to the top left corner of the paragraph.

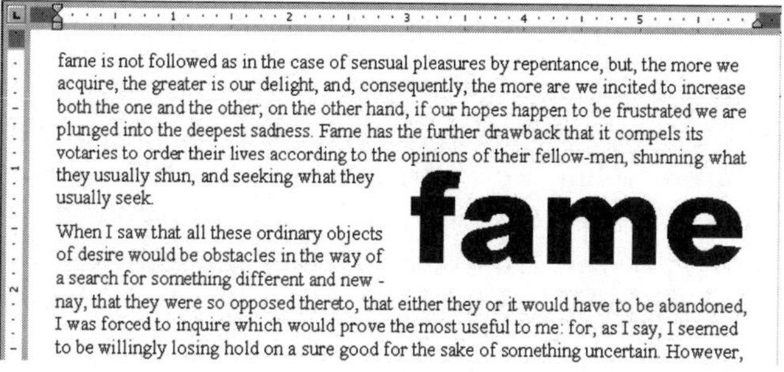
fame is not followed as in the case of sensual pleasures by repentance, but, the more we acquire, the greater is our delight, and, consequently, the more are we incited to increase both the one and the other; on the other hand, if our hopes happen to be frustrated we are plunged into the deepest sadness. Fame has the further drawback that it compels its votaries to order their lives according to the opinions of their fellow-men, shunning what they usually shun, and seeking what they usually seek.

fame

When I saw that all these ordinary objects of desire would be obstacles in the way of a search for something different and new - nay, that they were so opposed thereto, that either they or it would have to be abandoned, I was forced to inquire which would prove the most useful to me: for, as I say, I seemed to be willingly losing hold on a sure good for the sake of something uncertain. However,

Figure 8-19
A drop cap can be placed anywhere on the page.

Now that you know which attributes the Drop Cap command directly modifies—paragraph spacing, character font and vertical position, and frame location—you can change any other attributes of the paragraph, font, or frame and still gain the benefits of a drop cap. For example, you can condense or expand the spacing between characters. Or you can add space above and below by changing the Vertical Distance From Text option for the frame. You can also make some—or all—the letters italic, or you can change the color of the font. Just because you used the built-in tool doesn't mean you must limit yourself to built-in results.

Note The sample document for this section is Quote.doc.

Creating Pull Quotes

A pull quote is a quotation that is pulled from a document in a large font to capture the reader's attention. Pull quotes provide an interesting example of the trade-off between text boxes and frames in Word.

There are two parts to creating a pull quote:

- First, you need to extract a quote from the document to place into the box.
- Second, you need to create a formatted box to place the quote into.

There are two basic ways to extract text from a document. You can use a bookmark, or you can use a StyleRef field.

Using a Bookmark to Extract a Quotation

When you use the Cross-reference command on the Insert menu to add a cross-reference to a heading or a figure caption, Word creates a hidden bookmark to complete the link. If you are creating several pull quotes, you want to make sure that each bookmark is unique. It's easy to create unique bookmarks by simply using a prefix with a trailing number. Give the first bookmark a name like PQ001, the second PQ002, and so forth.

To reference the text from a bookmark, you simply add a field that contains the name of the bookmark. (If you are feeling lazy, you can use the Insert Cross-Reference command and select the Bookmark Reference type. The Cross-Reference command will do all the work of adding the field. Just create the bookmark before you create the cross-reference.) To add the field directly, press Ctrl+F9, type the bookmark name, and then press F9.

Using a bookmark to extract a quotation is effective if you are selective about what you quote, or if the pull quote does not appear on the same page as the quotation in the text. With a bookmark, you have complete control over what text is quoted where.

Using a Style to Extract a Quotation

The second way to extract text from a document is to use a StyleRef field, which was designed so that you could create a header showing the current chapter name. If you always format the chapter name heading with the Header 1 style (or the My Chapter Heading style), then you can add the StyleRef Header 1 (or StyleRef My Chapter Heading) field to the header and it will always show the current chapter name. When you insert the StyleRef field into a header, it starts searching for the specified style from the top down to the bottom of the current page. If it doesn't find the style on the current page, it searches toward the beginning of the document. This is precisely the behavior you would want to show the chapter heading at the top of the page: if a new chapter begins on this page, use its name, otherwise use the name of the chapter that began most recently.

With the advent of character styles, it became possible to use a StyleRef field to create a header for a dictionary. With a dictionary style header, you want to place the first and last words on the page into the header. A telephone directory uses the same type of header. To create this kind of header, you assign a character style (such as KeyWord) to each defined word in the dictionary (or to each last name in the directory). You then create a StyleRef field in the header that references the KeyWord style. This field gives the first occurrence of the style on the page. For the last occurrence, you add the /l switch (for "last"). Using /l with StyleRef causes it to search the current page for the style starting from the bottom and working toward the top of the page. If the StyleRef field can't find the style by the beginning of the page, it continues toward the front of the document, the same as without the switch.

You can appropriate the dictionary header's use of a StyleRef field to extract any text you might want from the page. Create a Character Style named PullQuoteText, for example—which is defined as default paragraph font, with nothing added—and apply it to any likely quotation candidates. You can apply the style as many times as you like on a page, but you should always define at least one on any page that will have a pull quote displayed. If you want to extract two different quotations from the same page, use two StyleRef fields, one with the /l switch, and one without. That way, one of the fields will extract the first possible quote and the other will extract the last possible quote.

Creating a Pull Quote Using a Text Box

When it comes to displaying a pull quote on a page, you have two options: you can place the quote into a text box or into a frame.

A text box has more formatting options. You can add a gradient background or a fancy border to a text box. You can also create a realistic shadow on the box, as shown in Figure 8-20, or you can make the shadow three-dimensional. (If you do make the text box three-dimensional or add a shadow, be sure to move the box behind the text, since the text will not wrap around the Office Clip Art embellishments.) A text box, however, can have only a single border, the same on all four sides. If you want a border only on the top—or only on the top and the bottom—do not place a border on the text box. Instead, add borders to the paragraph inside.

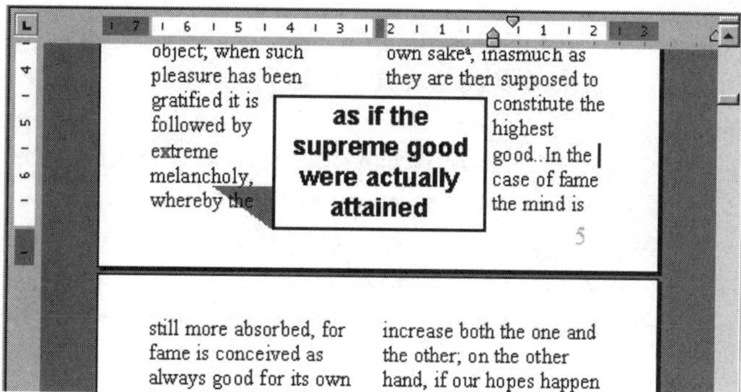

Figure 8-20
A text box can have realistic shadows.

The functionality of a StyleRef field, however, is limited when it is within a text box. Inside a text box, the /l switch has no effect. A StyleRef field within a text box always starts searching from the location of the text box's anchor, and always searches toward the top of the document. Trying to manage the location of the text box anchor is probably more trouble than maintaining bookmarks.

A text box cannot be made to automatically resize based on the text it contains. This means that if you change from a long quotation to a short one, you must manually adjust the size of the text box to fit the text. In addition, the fields within a text box do not update if the text box is in a header or footer, so you can't simply add a text box to the design of the page and have it automatically appear on each page.

Copying a Text Box While Maintaining Alignment Let's suppose that you do want to use text boxes (for formatting purposes), and you want the pull quote for each page to be centered at the bottom of the page. To set up the first text box with those attributes, double-click the border, select the Layout tab, and click Advanced. In the Horizontal group, select Centered Relative To Page; in the Vertical group, select Bottom Relative To Margin.

The first text box is now appropriately positioned. If you carefully select the border—the text box, not its contents—copy it, and then switch to the new page and paste it, the text box will not be in the appropriate location. It will have absolute horizontal and vertical coordinates that are not quite centered at the bottom of the page.

To create a copy of the text box that you can paste onto any page—while keeping the alignment settings intact—create an AutoText entry. That is, select the original text box and click Insert, AutoText, and then click New. Give the AutoText entry an appropriate name (perhaps Quote, Bottom Center). Now, go to the new page and insert the AutoText entry. The copied text box will appear with the alignment intact.

You could also use a formatted AutoCorrect entry to store the text box. To enter the AutoCorrect entry, you must type the replacement characters into the document and press the Spacebar, and it is hard to control which page Word will use to actually insert the text box.

An AutoText entry is stored in a template, so you can't create a template style for your Quote, Bottom Center AutoText entry for a single document based on a shared template. (You could always delete and recreate the AutoText entry each time you need to use it. You could also keep a template just for formatted text boxes, attach the active document to that template just long enough to add text boxes, and then switch it back to the original template.) Formatted AutoCorrect entries are all stored together and are all available for use, regardless of which template a document is attached to.

Creating a Pull Quote Using a Frame

You can also create the box for a pull quote in a frame. A frame is ideal if you want to place a pull quote in the same place on each page, because you can place a frame in a header or footer, and the StyleRef field still works from within a frame.

Create a paragraph style with the desired font format and name it PullQuote. Then, in the Modify Style dialog box, add frame attributes to position the frame on the page—perhaps centered on the bottom margin. Set the width to a constant amount and set the height to Auto. Next, create a character style for PullQuoteText, and apply it to all the phrases that could be potential quotations in the document. In the section header, add a paragraph with the StyleRef field searching for either the first or the last matching style on the field. Then, apply the PullQuote style to the paragraph to center it on the page. The pull quote automatically displays the first (or the last) quotation on a page, changing height to fit the text.

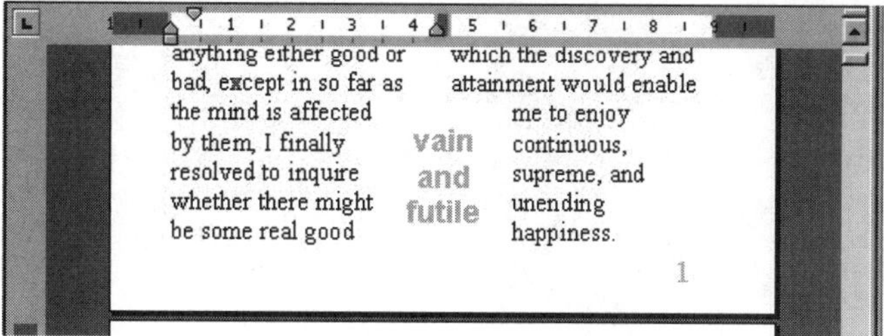

Figure 8-21
A field in a header frame appears as a gray box.

Unlike most fields, a StyleRef field in a header updates itself whenever you apply or remove the designated style. This makes it easy for you to test different quotes on a page simply by applying the character style or by pressing Ctrl+Space to remove it.

In summary, a frame is better than a text box if you want to include a field that needs to be updated on each page. A text box is better than a frame if you want more formatting options.

Creating Multiple Columns

The default layout for a Word page is to place everything into a single column. A single column is good for many purposes, but there are a variety of reasons for placing text into more than one column on the page. Word has at least four different mechanisms you can use to place text into multiple columns, and each one is best for certain purposes.

Using a Section to Add a Second Column

A single, wide column across a page of text is often difficult to read. As the reader's eye completes a line and scans back to the left, it must find the appropriate new line. The wider the column of text is, the harder it is to find the next line.

Adjusting Line Spacing to Enhance Readability

One way to make it easier to read a wide column is to increase the amount of space between lines. The amount of space between lines is called leading, because typesetters used to add strips of lead between rows of text. In Word, you specify the amount of leading by selecting Exactly in the Line Spacing value on the Format Paragraph dialog box, as shown in Figure 8-22. The amount of leading is the difference between the line spacing value and the point size.

When you select single spacing, Word adds an amount of leading that is appropriate for the default six-inch column width. The leading amount varies depending on the point size. For a 12-point font, Word adds approximately 2 points of leading. If you have a wide column of text, you can make the text easier to read by increasing the line spacing value.

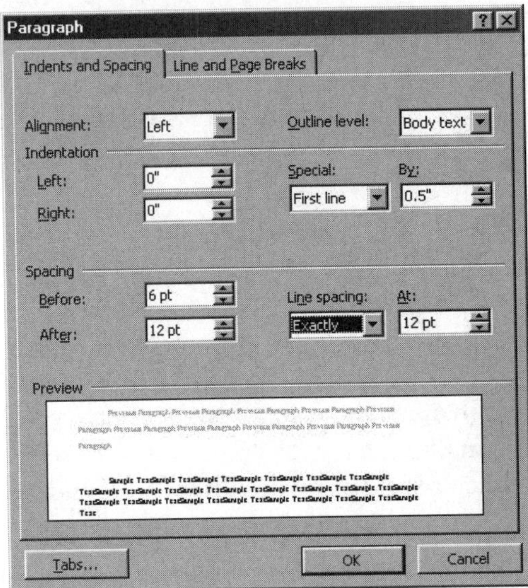

Figure 8-22
Use Exact Line Spacing to specify leading between lines.

Adding Columns To Improve Readability

If you have a wide page, an alternative to increasing the spacing between the lines is to decrease the column width. Newspapers and magazines use multiple columns because the narrow columns are easy to read, even with little or no leading between the lines. The reduced leading more than compensates for the space between the columns, and they can fit more text on the same page by using columns.

The Format Columns command in Word creates columns that are appropriate for making text easy to read on a wide page. To create a section with multiple columns, simply select the range you want to convert to columns and click the Columns button on the Standard toolbar. The Columns button initially shows one to four columns, but you can use it to create as many as six columns. If you change your mind about creating columns, you must drag the mouse to the left—where no columns would be. Dragging below or to the right of the button creates columns.

When you convert a portion of a document to columnar format, Word adds continuous section breaks to the beginning and the end of the section. You can use the Columns button to remove columns—by selecting 1 Column, but that won't remove the section breaks. In fact, selecting a range that is already one column and assigning the 1 Column setting to it is a simple way to add continuous section breaks before and after a range of text. If you want to remove the section breaks, you need to delete them manually. (Be sure to show all formatting marks so you can see the section break marks.) If you use the Columns button when nothing is selected, Word will apply the columns to the current section, which might comprise the entire document or a single space.

In addition to using the Columns button, you can create or refine multiple columns by using the Format Columns command. This command displays the dialog box shown in Figure 8-23.

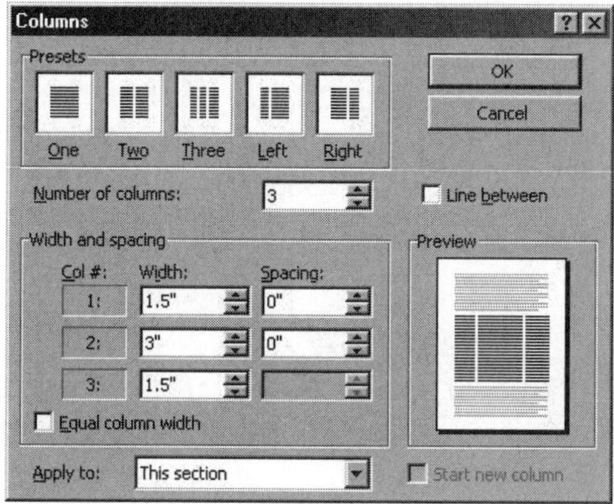

Figure 8-23
The Columns dialog box gives you complete control over column settings.

The Columns dialog box lets you create as many columns as will fit on the page, with a minimum width of 0.5 inches per column. So, in principle, on a 22-inch wide piece of paper with narrow margins, you could have as many as 43 columns on the page, which could be mighty difficult to follow.

You can choose whether to have the columns equal in width or not. In Figure 8-23, the columns are set to one wide central column, with narrower columns down each side. The preset boxes at the top of the dialog box give you some common combinations.

If your selection includes a range of text, the Apply To drop-down list box defaults to Selected Sections if there are multiple sections in the document (even if the selection is completely contained in one of the sections), or to Selected Text if the document has only one section. When you apply the columns to the Selected Text, Word adds new continuous section breaks both before and after the selection.

If the selection is an insertion point, the Apply To drop-down list box defaults to This Section if there are multiple sections in the document, or to Whole Document if there are none. It also offers a This Point Forward option, which adds a new continuous section break at the insertion point.

Note The sample document for this section is SpinCol.doc.

Creating a Section That Starts with a New Column

Choosing the option This Point Forward enables the Start New Column check box. If you have a document with, say, three columns, and you add a new continuous section break in the middle of the document, Word will start the new section at the left margin, wrapping the columns from the preceding section, as shown in Figure 8-24. You can achieve the same result by choosing the option This Point Forward in the Columns dialog box, but without changing the number of columns.

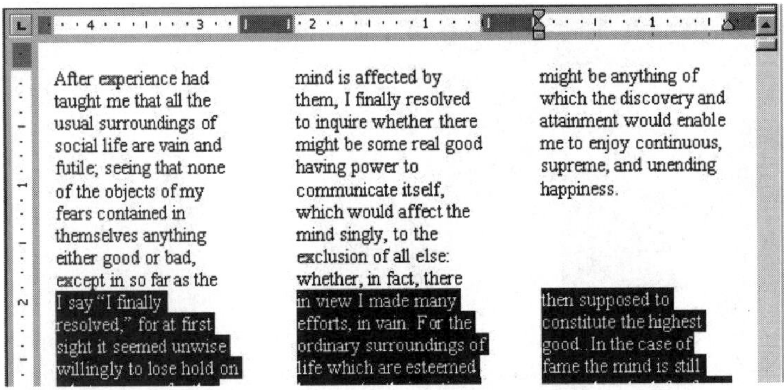

Figure 8-24
A new, continuous section restarts columns at the left margin.

If you use the Columns check box to add a new section—selecting both This Point Forward and Start New Column—the preceding section will continue in its own column, and the new section will begin at the top of the next column, as shown in Figure 8-25.

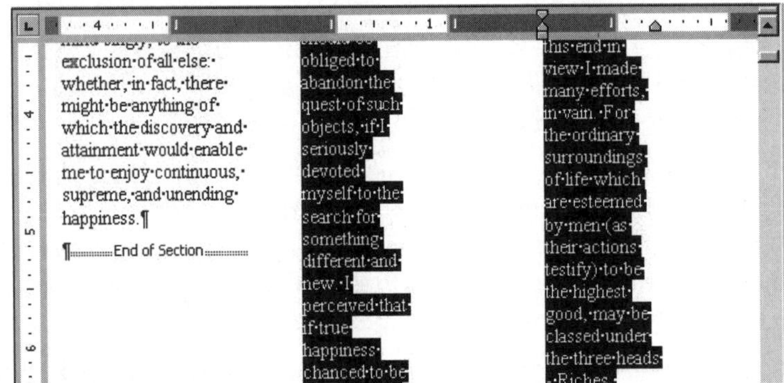

Figure 8-25
Choose Start New Column to start a new section at the top of the page.

This effect is very similar to inserting a new column break. The difference is subtle, but real. A new column section break is an actual section break. That means there are certain section attributes that you can change for the new columns that you could not change if you had inserted a standard Column Break. For example, notice that the selected columns shown earlier in Figure 8-25 are narrower than the first column. When you insert a new column section, you can change the column width and spacing for the new section. You can also change the page margins.

Some section formatting, such as headers and footers, take effect only on a new page after the section begins. Other section formatting, such as changing the number of columns or changing the paper size, force the new section to change to a new page.

The Insert Break dialog box shown in Figure 8-26 displays only four section break styles, while there are really five styles. The fifth section break is a new column break which can be created only from the Format Columns dialog box.

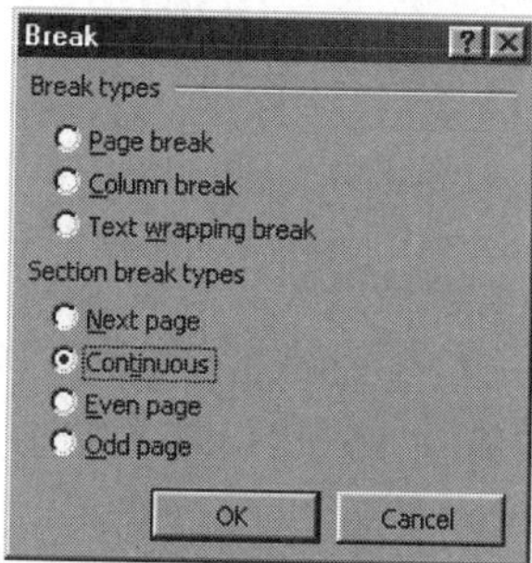

Figure 8-26
The Insert Break dialog box shows only four section break styles.

You can, however, change an existing section break into a new column break using the Layout tab on the Page Setup dialog box, as shown in Figure 8-27.

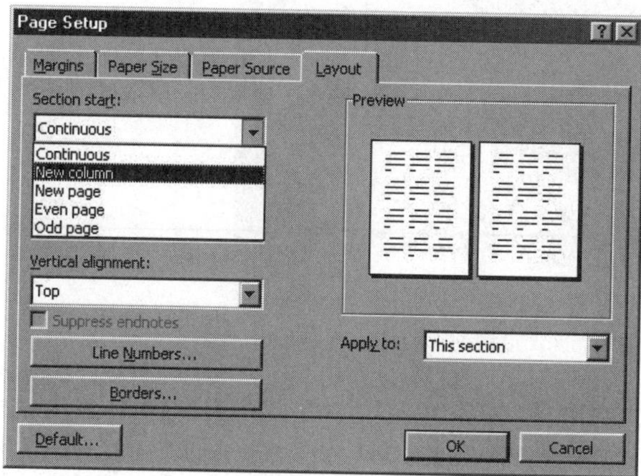

Figure 8-27
The Page Setup dialog box shows all five section break styles.

In summary, the new page, even page, odd page, and continuous section break types are all available from the Insert Break dialog box. The new column section break can only be added by choosing the option This Point Forward, together with the option start new column, from the Format Columns dialog box. Any section break type can be changed to any other type using the Page Setup dialog box. If a new column section changes the number of columns, or if either of the two flavors of continuous section breaks changes the paper size or orientation, they behave in the same manner as a new page section.

Note The sample file for this section is SpinTube.doc

Using Linked Text Boxes to Add a Second Column

A second way to create multiple columns is to place the text into text boxes and then link them so the text flows from one text box to the next. A linked text box is a good choice if you want the text to fit into unusual spaces on the page, or if you want to use unusual backgrounds for the columns. Figure 8-28 shows columns of text formatted as if they were printed in physical columns like a booklet. The text boxes were shaded using a vertical gradient fill effect. The left and right internal margins (which can be found on the Text Box tab of the Format Text Box dialog box) were increased to avoid overlapping the text onto the dark portion of the columns.

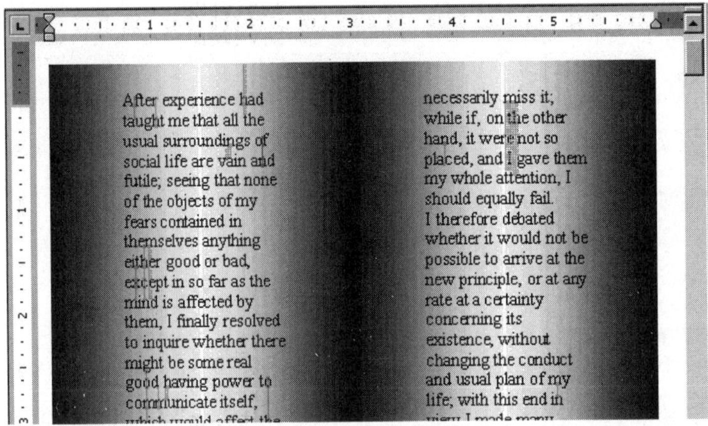

Figure 8-28
Linked text boxes allow unusual background effects.

The contents of a text box are not part of a document's main story, so you can't use any of the normal extras such as footnotes or comments. You can use character and paragraph styles within a text box—including heading styles—but none of the contents appears in Outline or Normal view, and the headings will not be included in a Table of Contents.

Creating a Macro to Link Text Boxes

One of the most frustrating aspects in dealing with linked text boxes is that you must create a new, empty text box each time you want to flow text into a new box. You must then resize, format, and position the new text box.

A macro can create and link as many copies of a text box as necessary in order to use all the text in the box. The following *MakeBoxes* macro shown below adds as many linked boxes as necessary to use up all the text in a chain. Each linked box is anchored to a separate paragraph, and each anchoring paragraph is on a new page. This makes it easy to switch the text boxes between pages. Each new text box also copies the formatting of the first text box in the chain.

The *MakeBoxes* macro is not trivial. Using a macro to work with text boxes means dealing with a lot of little quirks along the way. An explanation follows the macro to describe in detail how the macro works. If you want to create other macros that deal with shapes or text boxes, you should find the analysis of this macro very helpful.

```
Sub MakeBoxes()
    Dim oFirst As Shape
    Dim oLast As Shape
    Dim oNew As Shape
    Dim oRange As Range

    GetEndBoxes oFirst, oLast
    oFirst.RelativeHorizontalPosition = wdRelativeHorizontalPositionPage
    oFirst.RelativeVerticalPosition = wdRelativeVerticalPositionPage

    Do While oLast.TextFrame.Overflowing

        Set oRange = oLast.Anchor
        oRange.InsertParagraphAfter
        oRange.Move wdParagraph, 1
        oRange.InsertBefore vbFormFeed
        oRange.Collapse wdCollapseEnd
        oRange.Select

        Set oNew = ActiveDocument.Shapes.AddTextbox( _
            msoTextOrientationHorizontal, _
            oFirst.Left, oFirst.Top, oFirst.Width, oFirst.Height, _
            oRange)
        oNew.LockAnchor = True

        oFirst.PickUp
        oNew.Apply
        oNew.RelativeHorizontalPosition = oFirst.RelativeHorizontalPosition
        oNew.RelativeVerticalPosition = oFirst.RelativeVerticalPosition
        oNew.Top = oFirst.Top
        oNew.Left = oFirst.Left
        oNew.WrapFormat.Type = wdWrapNone
        oNew.ZOrder msoSendBehindText

        oLast.TextFrame.Next = oNew.TextFrame
        Set oLast = oNew
    Loop
End Sub
```

Chapter 8

A text box is really a Shape object that happens to contain text. A Shape object is any Office Clip Art object, including AutoShape objects. When you deal with a text box, you work with three levels of objects:

- The container Shape object determines the general formatting and position on the page.
- The TextFrame object inside the Shape object controls the links between text boxes and also controls the internal margins of the text box.
- A TextRange is inside the TextFrame object, which is the actual text inside the text box. (In this macro, you don't need to manipulate the TextRange object.)

The first action the macro performs is to run the *GetEndBoxes* subroutine that finds the first and last shapes already existing in the chain. This subroutine is described later in the chapter. The macro then makes sure that the first text box in the chain is positioned relative to the page. This will make it easier for other text boxes to be positioned at the same place on the page.

If the Overflowing property of a TextFrame object is *True,* the box contains too much text to display. The *Do While oLast.TextFrame.Overflowing* statement starts a loop that runs as long as there is more text to display. A chain of linked text boxes can include up to 32 text boxes—that is, 31 links. If the macro tries to add a 33rd text box, the macro will stop with an error.

The next few statements in the macro create a new paragraph to serve as the anchor for a new text box. Each text box—each shape on the drawing layer, actually—is linked to an anchor in the document's main story. An anchor is an invisible character that resides at the very beginning of a paragraph. You can't see or select an anchor character, but it is added each time you create an object that is not in-line. The Anchor property of a Shape object returns a Range object that refers to that hidden character.

The *Set oRange = oLast.Anchor* statement assigns the anchor range of the last text box in the chain to a variable. The invisible anchor character is the first character in a paragraph. Interactively, if an anchor is attached to an empty paragraph, it is difficult to add a new paragraph without shifting the anchor to the new paragraph. You must add a real character to the paragraph containing the anchor and then select just after that character before pressing Enter. In a macro, you can insert a paragraph after the anchor range, which is what the *oRange.InsertParagraphAfter* statement does.

The next statement, *oRange.Move wdParagraph, 1,* moves the Range variable down to the new paragraph, and the *oRange.InsertBefore vbFormFeed* statement adds a page break to the beginning of the new paragraph. The Range object in the variable now includes both the page break character and the paragraph mark. The statement *oRange.Collapse wdCollapseEnd* collapses the range to a single insertion point at the end of the new paragraph, which is now on the new page. The *oRange.Select* statement is there only to make it easier to watch what the macro is doing.

The *oRange* variable is now positioned, ready to be an anchor to a new text box. The very long statement *Set oNew = ActiveDocument.Shapes.AddTextbox (msoTextOrientationHorizontal, oFirst.Left, oFirst.Top, oFirst.Width, oFirst.Height, oRange)* adds a new text box, using *oRange* as the anchor range. The statement *oNew.LockAnchor = True* then locks the anchor to the paragraph so that the anchor won't move around if you move the text box.

The *Pickup* method of a Shape object is the equivalent of the CopyFormat method of a Range object: it is what happens when you press Ctrl+Shift+C. Analogously, the Apply method of a Shape is equivalent to the PasteFormat method of a Range object: it is what happens when you press Ctrl+Shift+V. The statement *oFirst.PickUp* and the statement *oNew.Apply* copy the formatting from the first shape in the chain and apply it to the new shape.

The *Pickup* and *Apply* methods don't copy all the formatting from an object; they don't copy the relative position type—changing that can affect the object's Top and Left properties. They also don't copy the object's wrapping type, or its Z-Order, which determines whether the object is in front of or behind the text. The next six statements explicitly copy each of these attributes from the first shape to the new shape.

```
oNew.RelativeHorizontalPosition = oFirst.RelativeHorizontalPosition
oNew.RelativeVerticalPosition = oFirst.RelativeVerticalPosition
oNew.Top = oFirst.Top
oNew.Left = oFirst.Left
oNew.WrapFormat.Type = oFirst.WrapFormat.Type
oNew.ZOrderPosition = oFirst.ZorderPosition
```

Finally, the macro is ready to link the new text box to the existing chain, pouring the excess text into it. The *oLast.TextFrame.Next = oNew.TextFrame* statement links the text boxes. (It is hard to understand why this statement works.) The Next property is a property of a TextFrame object. The Help topic for the Next property indicates that it is a read-only property. Obviously, the Next property of the TextFrame object is not read-only. The Next property does, however, return a TextFrame object. Logically, you should use the Set keyword to assign a new object to the property. But, not only is the Set keyword not required, it is also not allowed. Despite all logic and documentation to the contrary, the statement in the macro does link the two text boxes.)

As the final statement in the loop, the macro uses the *Set oLast = oNew* statement to make the old-new shape into the new-last shape in preparation for repeating the loop, checking whether the new-last shape still overflows.

Finding the First and Last Text Boxes in a Chain

The *MakeBoxes* macro also uses the *GetEndBoxes* subroutine to find the first and last text boxes in a chain. This macro illustrates the convoluted path you need to use to navigate from one container shape to the next in a text box chain. It also shows you how to get around a bug in that path.

```
Private Sub GetEndBoxes(First As Shape, Last As Shape)
    Dim oText As TextFrame
    If Selection.ShapeRange.Count = 0 Then
        Set oText = ActiveDocument.Shapes(1).TextFrame
    Else
        Set oText = Selection.ShapeRange(1).TextFrame
    End If

    Do Until oText.Previous Is Nothing
        Set oText = oText.Previous
    Loop
    Set First = oText.Parent

    Do Until oText.Next Is Nothing
        Set oText = oText.Next
    Loop
    Set Last = oText.Parent
End Sub
```

The subroutine takes two arguments, both declared as Shape objects, and both passed By Reference so that the macro can use them to pass back the desired Shape objects. (See "Changing the Value of an Argument" in Chapter 4 for more information about passing arguments by reference.) If the subroutine needed to pass back one Shape object, you could make it into a function that returns a Shape object, but the only way to return two or more objects is to use arguments.

The first section of the macro simply checks to see whether a Shape object is already selected. If so, the macro assigns the text box contained in it to the *oText* variable. If not, the macro assigns the text box contained in the first object in the document's Shapes collection, which might or might not be the first shape in the document. (The name TextFrame is somewhat ironic, since a TextFrame is what enables a text box to compete with a frame for positioning text on a page.) It's the TextFrame object that has links to other TextFrame objects.

The second section searches for previous text boxes until it finds the first. The statement that begins the first loop is *Do Until oText.Previous Is Nothing*. The variable *oText* contains a TextFrame object. The Previous property returns the preceding TextFrame object in the chain. The keyword Nothing means that no object exists in a property that could refer to an object.

The single statement inside the loop, *Set oText = oText.Previous*, replaces the *oText* object with the Previous TextFrame object. The loop can now test to see whether that object is linked to a previous text frame. If it is not, then it is the first text box in the chain and its Parent—the Shape object that contains it—can be returned as the value of the *oFirst* argument.

The third section is a mirror image of the second; it searches for the next text box until it finds the last one.

Adding Continued Tags to Linked Text Boxes

Word can link text boxes so that text from the first page can flow smoothly onto a fourth page. Word does not have a convenient tool, however, for adding a notice to the bottom of the text on the first page to inform the reader where to find the continuation. (Microsoft Publisher, included in the editions of Office 2000, does have a convenient tool for adding a notice to linked text boxes.) Figure 8-29 shows a notice for a continued text box.

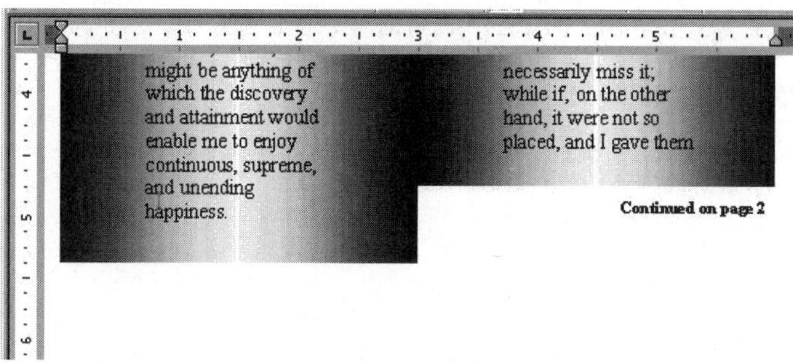

might be anything of
which the discovery
and attainment would
enable me to enjoy
continuous, supreme,
and unending
happiness.
necessarily miss it;
while if, on the other
hand, it were not so
placed, and I gave them
Continued on page 2

Figure 8-29
Text boxes that link to a different page should provide a notice.

It would be hard to imagine anyone creating a text box that flows to a different page—especially if it flows to something other than the immediately following page—without having a notice at the bottom of the text box. Unfortunately, it can be difficult to set up such a link. Ideally, you want the page number to automatically recalculate if you shift pages around. Unfortunately, if you insert a bookmark inside a text box, any cross-reference you make to that bookmark will always indicate "1" as the page number, because the text box is not part of the main story.

The best way to create a cross-reference between text boxes (at least without using a macro) is to select the target text box and find its anchored paragraph. Lock the anchor so it won't change paragraphs, and assign a unique bookmark name to the anchor paragraph. Then, select the source text box and insert any caption. Provided the text box was positioned relative to a paragraph, Word adds the caption directly to the bottom of the text box. Replace the contents of the caption box with a cross-reference to the bookmark, preceded by whatever text you would like.

If you like using linked text boxes, you might want a way to automate adding cross-reference captions as needed. The *ContinueAllBoxes* macro is a Shell macro that looks at each shape in the document. If it finds a shape containing text in the first box in a chain, it launches a second macro to add a continuation caption.

```
Sub ContinueAllBoxes()
    Dim oStartRange As Range
    Dim oShape As Shape

    On Error GoTo ErrorHandler
```

```
    Set oStartRange = Selection.Range
    For Each oShape In ActiveDocument.Shapes
        If oShape.TextFrame.HasText Then
            If oShape.TextFrame.Previous Is Nothing Then
                If Not oShape.TextFrame.Next Is Nothing Then
                    oShape.Select
                    ContinueBox
                End If
            End If
        End If
    Next oShape
    oStartRange.Select
    Application.ScreenRefresh
    Exit Sub
ErrorHandler:
    MsgBox "Problem adding link tags"
End Sub
```

The *ContinueAllBoxes* macro is relatively straightforward. It sets an error-handler at the beginning, to provide feedback if something does not work. You might want to remove the error-handler so that Visual Basic will show you where the problem occurs.

The *oStartRange* variable exists purely for the purpose of restoring the original selection when the macro is finished. It has no real effect on the macro. When a macro switches selections—particularly when shapes are involved—the screen can end up with strange blotches. The *Application.ScreenRefresh* statement repaints the screen to remove any remnants.

The real work of linking text boxes takes place in the *ContinueBox* subroutine. In general, the subroutine checks for an existing cross-reference box, deleting it if one exists. Then it checks to see if the next text box in the chain is on a different page. If so, the macro adds a caption and some formatting. At the end, if the target text box has another link, the macro simply restarts itself.

```
Private Sub ContinueBox()
    Dim oSource As Shape
    Dim sName As String
    Dim iSourcePage As Long
    Dim iTargetPage As Long
    Dim bNeedsTag As Boolean
    Dim oTag As Shape

    Set oSource = Selection.ShapeRange(1)

    On Error Resume Next
    sName = SubSpaces(oSource.Name & "_Z")
    ActiveDocument.Shapes(sName).Delete
    On Error GoTo 0
```

```
    iSourcePage = oSource.Anchor.Information(wdActiveEndPageNumber)
    iTargetPage = oSource.TextFrame.Next _
        .Parent.Anchor.Information(wdActiveEndPageNumber)

    If iTargetPage <> iSourcePage Then
        Selection.InsertTag Label:="Figure", _
            TitleAutoText:="InsertTag3", _
            Title:="", Position:=wdTagPositionBelow
        Set oTag = Selection.ShapeRange(1)
        oTag.Name = sName
        oTag.Line.Visible = msoFalse
        oTag.RelativeHorizontalPosition = wdRelativeHorizontalPositionPage
        oTag.RelativeVerticalPosition = wdRelativeVerticalPositionPage
        oTag.Left = oSource.Left
        oTag.Top = oSource.Top + oSource.Height
        oTag.TextFrame.MarginTop = 0#
        oTag.TextFrame.TextRange.ParagraphFormat.Alignment = _
            wdAlignParagraphRight
        oTag.ZOrder msoSendToBack
        oTag.TextFrame.TextRange.Text = "Continued on page " & iTargetPage
    End If

    oSource.TextFrame.Next.TextRange.Select
    If Not Selection.ShapeRange(1).TextFrame.Next Is Nothing Then
        ContinueBox
    End If
End Sub
```

The macro needs a way to know whether a text box already has a caption, which it does by giving the caption text box a name consisting of the name of the main text box with a _Z appended to the name. One would think that if Word can create a text box named Text Box 1, with spaces, it would be possible for a macro to give the name Text Box 1_Z to a different text box. It's not. You can't give a name that contains a space to a Shape object. The macro gets around this ridiculous rule by sending the name to the *SubSpaces* function, covered later in this chapter, which converts any space characters to underscores.

The macro deletes any text box that already happens to have the invented name. The reason for the *On Error Resume Next* statement is to intentionally ignore the error that is raised if the text box does not already exist. The macro is going to delete it anyway, so it doesn't matter if it doesn't exist. The *On Error GoTo 0* statement resets the macro back to the original error-handler. (For more information about error-handers, see "Handling run-time Errors" in Chapter 4.)

Next, the macro retrieves page numbers from the pages containing the source and target text boxes. In the *oSource.Anchor.Information(wdActiveEndPageNumber) expression, oSource* contains a reference to the source text box and Anchor returns the range with the secret anchor character (which must be on the same page as the anchored shape). To determine the page number of a range, use the Information method, which has about 35 possible pieces of information it can provide to you. Many of them are very useful, and some are surprising. For example, through the Information method, any character in the document can tell you not only how many pages are in the document, but also whether the Overtype key is turned on.

Finding the page number of the next linked text box is much the same. In the *oSource.TextFrame.Next.Parent.Anchor.Information(wdActiveEndPageNumber)* expression, *oSource* is once again a reference to the source shape. TextFrame navigates to the text box within it, Next navigates to the next linked text box, and Parent navigates back up to the Shape object that contains it. From here, the expression copies the one that calculates the source page number.

The major block of the macro—the one that creates a new continuation caption—only occurs if the two page numbers are not the same. This section of the macro inserts an arbitrary new caption and assigns a reference to that shape to the *oTag* object variable, giving the shape the secret name that will allow the macro to delete it later, if necessary. The rest of the statements simply format the caption, adding a suitable message using the calculated page number.

After the *If* block—even if no caption was created—the macro selects the next shape and, if there is still a linked box, runs the macro again. Running a macro from within itself is called *recursion*, which is very similar to looping. If you do recursively run a macro, be sure you provide a way for the macro to end. In this case, the macro ends when there is no Next text frame.

Creating a Macro to Replace Spaces

Word adds spaces to object names, but will not allow a macro to do the same. To get around this hypocritical behavior, use the *SubSpaces* function below, which replaces all spaces in a text string with underscore characters.

```
Private Function SubSpaces(sText As String) As String
    Dim i
    For i = 1 To Len(sText)
        If Mid(sText, i, 1) = " " Then
            SubSpaces = SubSpaces & "_"
        Else
            SubSpaces = SubSpaces & Mid(sText, i, 1)
        End If
    Next i
End Function
```

The *SubSpaces* function uses the Visual Basic Mid function to extract each character from the input string. If the character is not a space, the character is appended to *SubString*—the name of the function—which is the value the function returns. (See "Creating Custom Procedures" in Chapter 4 for details about returning a value from a function.) If the character is a space, the macro appends an underscore in its place. (From within a function, you can use the name of the function as if it were a variable.)

Note The sample document for this section is Table.doc.

Using a Table to Add a Second Column

A third way to add a second column to a document is to use a table. You can create the entire document in a table using parallel columns. A table is particularly useful when you want to present parallel sentences or paragraphs. Figure 8-30 shows a document with the column on the right displaying a French translation of the column on the left.

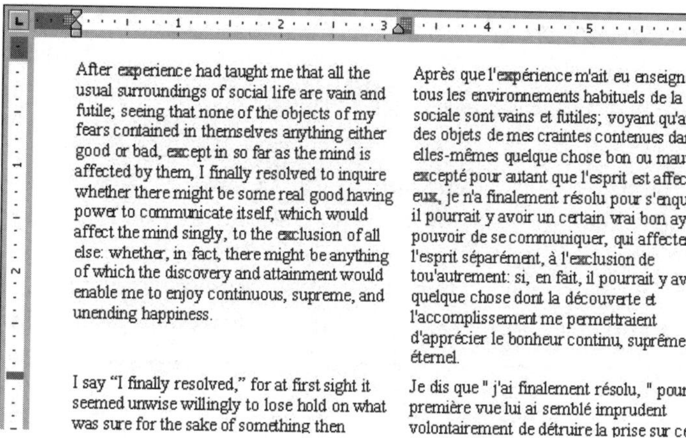

Figure 8-30
Use a table to create balanced parallel columns.

In a translated text situation, one column will sometimes get ahead of the other, or vice versa. By placing each paragraph into a new row in a table, a table keeps the columns synchronized. If the text in one column is always wider than the text in the other column, click Table, AutoFit, and choose AutoFit To Contents to allow Word to decide how wide each column should be, and to minimize the gaps at the end of the paragraphs.

Because a table is part of the document's main story, you can include comments, footnotes, and even text boxes and drawing objects within the table. You cannot, however, place a frame within a table. If you have a heading that transcends both columns, simply merge the cells for that row.

Combining Table Columns from Different Documents

Normally, when you create a table, either you create an empty table—adding text later—or you convert existing text in the document into a table. If you want to print translated text in two columns, you probably already have the text in two separate documents. First, convert each of the documents to a table. Select the text of the document and Click Table, Convert, and click Text To Table. Then, select Paragraphs as the Separate Text At option. The result is shown in Figure 8-31.

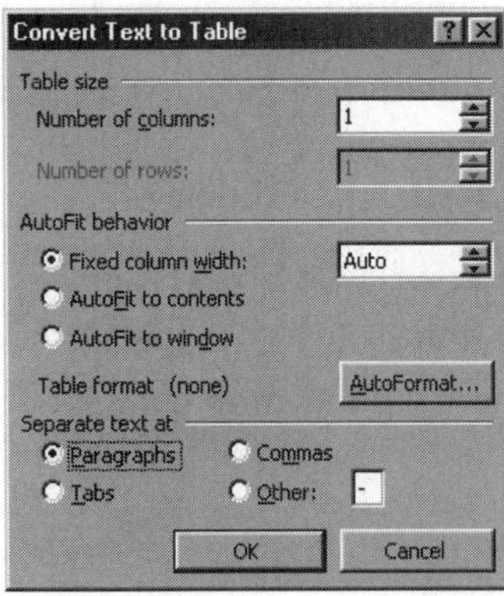

Figure 8-31
Separate text at paragraphs to convert a document into a table.

Once both documents are converted, activate the document with the text for the left column. Click above the table, selecting the entire column, and copy the column. Select the document containing the right column, select the entire column, and paste. Be careful when copying and pasting to select only the one column, not the entire table. If you select the entire table, you will replace the existing table, rather than add to it.

Note The sample document for this section is SpinNote.doc.

Using a Margin Frame to Add a Second Column

A fourth and (possibly) final way to create two text boxes is to create margin notes using frames. Margin notes create the effect of parallel columns. They allow you to achieve an effect similar to that of a table, but without the worry of managing a table. You would, however, need to interleave the paragraphs. Margin notes are best when suited to text where the note is shorter than the paragraph it is adjacent to. A long margin note will extend past the end of the paragraph, pushing down any margin note below it.

Figure 8-32 shows a column of margin notes added to a main document. The margin notes are simply paragraphs that have been formatted with a frame.

To use frames to create a column in the margin, create a style named Margin Note to apply to all the margin paragraphs. Give the style the paragraph and character formatting that you want, and specify frame attributes for a style similar to those shown in Figure 8-33. That is, specify an exact width (perhaps 2 inches), and a negative horizontal position relative to the column—slightly greater than the width of the column (perhaps -2.25 inches). Set the horizontal distance from the text to the difference between the width and the inverse of the horizontal position (perhaps .25 inches). Specify a vertical position of 0 inches, relative to the paragraph. It doesn't matter what text wrapping option you use.

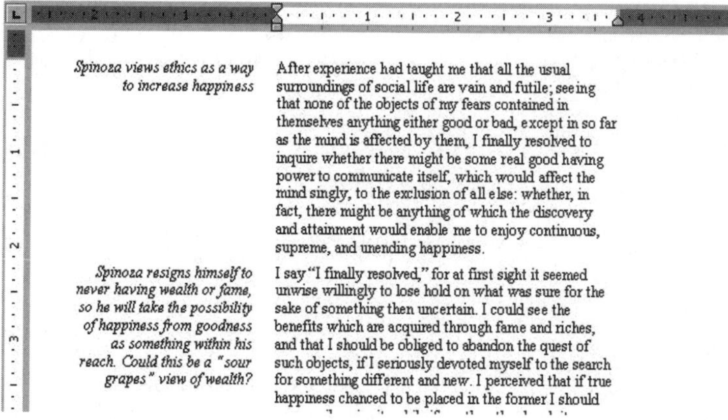

Figure 8-32
Use frames to create a column of margin notes.

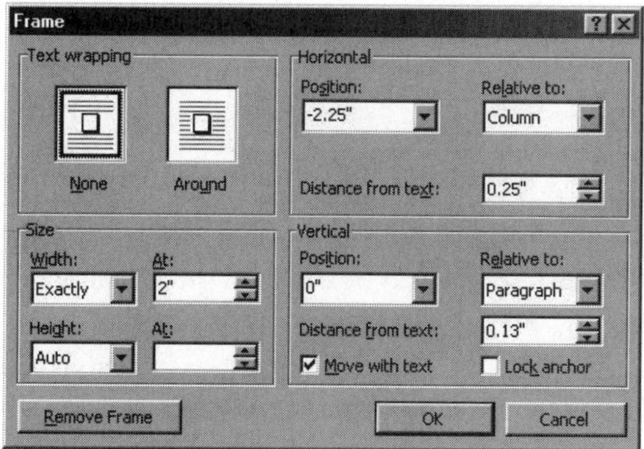

Figure 8-33
Use a negative horizontal position for a margin note.

Once the style is defined, simply assign that style to the paragraphs that you want to appear in the margin. Unlike text boxes, text in framed paragraphs, as shown in Figure 8-34, appears as part of the document flow in Normal view, making the text easy to edit.

Using Text Boxes and Frames

The functionality of text boxes and frames overlaps quite a bit. They can both contain text, and they can both position text anywhere on a page. Either one can attach to a paragraph, to move with text as the document layout changes. The Help file descriptions—and the way menu commands are set up—imply that text boxes are superior to frames; text boxes are certainly newer than frames. Text boxes were introduced in Word 97, while frames have been around from time immemorial. But

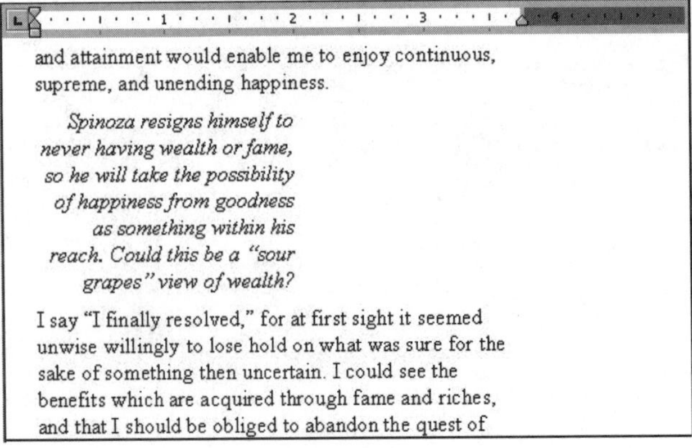
and attainment would enable me to enjoy continuous, supreme, and unending happiness.

Spinoza resigns himself to never having wealth or fame, so he will take the possibility of happiness from goodness as something within his reach. Could this be a "sour grapes" view of wealth?

I say "I finally resolved," for at first sight it seemed unwise willingly to lose hold on what was sure for the sake of something then uncertain. I could see the benefits which are acquired through fame and riches, and that I should be obliged to abandon the quest of

Figure 8-34
Framed paragraphs appear as part of the flow in Normal view.

each has its own strengths. The essential differences between the two are illustrated in Table 8-1.

Frames All the benefits of a frame lie in its ability to integrate with the story of your main document:	Text Boxes All the benefits of a text box lie in its ability to manage the appearance of a portion of the page:
A frame takes a portion of the main story and sets it apart visually.	A text box takes a graphical portion of a page and adds text to it.
The text in a frame can have comments, footnotes, and endnotes.	The text in a text box can have fancy borders or fill patterns.
The text in a frame can be included in either side of a cross-reference or in a reference table.	The text in a text box can flow from one box to another, thus creating its own independent story.
A frame can be added as part of a paragraph style.	A text box provides many options to determine how to position it on the page.
A frame can automatically resize to fit the text.	A text box can go over or under the text of the main story.
The text in a frame appears even when shown in Normal view.	The text in a text box appears even when shown in Normal view.

Table 8-1
Differences between Frames and Text Boxes.

Word has a variety of methods for breaking up the flow of text in a document, because documents have a variety of flow needs.

Chapter 9

Create Dynamic Documents

In This Chapter

As I watched my daughter finish up her high school Senior English paper in the middle of the night, it brought back memories of my using a typewriter to crank out my own high school English paper in the middle of the night. For better or worse, my first draft with a typewriter was my final draft. My, how things have changed.

Word processing programs are powerful tools for creating beautiful and functional documents. One of the most important uses of a word processing program like Microsoft Word, however, is to allow you to make changes to documents. It is inevitable that as you develop documents, you will surely make changes to them. You might need to rearrange items in a numbered list, make changes to numbers in an expense report, or you might need to send customized letters to different people. Whenever you change your documents, there is always the inevitable ripple effect. The more you know about Word's powerful document processing tools, the more you can do to keep your documents correctly structured, even when you make changes.

Creating and Managing Numbered Lists

Note The sample document for this section is ListNull.doc.

Suppose you and your associates are getting ready to submit a proposal to manage a special task force. You want to create a document that highlights the process—along with major headings and numbered steps—similar to the one illustrated in Figure 9-1.

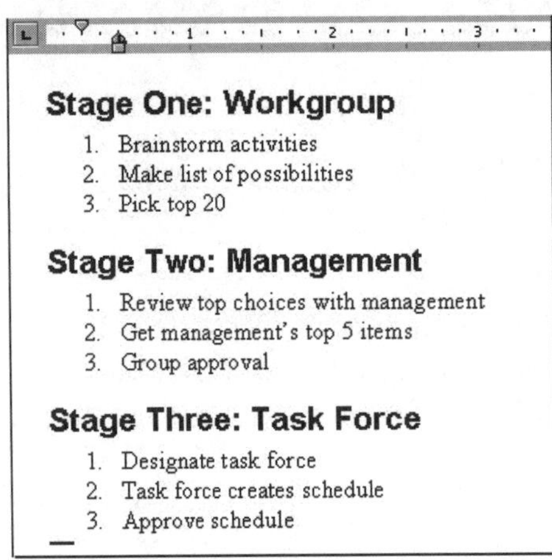

Figure 9-1
Your goal is to create a simple numbered list.

Word manages numbered lists very effectively, making it easy to create and modify those lists. But how you create the numbered list can affect what happens when you change the document. There are at least three different approaches for creating list styles:

- Automatic numbering
- Built-in numbering styles
- Outline numbering

Each of these numbering styles has its strengths and weaknesses. As you will see, the approach that is the best for simple lists is not necessarily the best for a document you will make changes to later.

Creating a Numbered List Using AutoFormat

Word can automatically create numbered lists for you based on what you type. To enable (or disable) automatic list creation, click AutoCorrect on the Tools menu, and select AutoFormat as As You Type, and select (or clear) the Automatic Numbered Lists check box. Using the automatical numbering method is enticingly easy. The numbers are convenient for simple lists, but they have some interesting quirks. If you understand the strengths and limitations of automatic numbered lists, you will know when to use them and when to create lists a different way.

Beginning an Automatic List

Start by typing the heading for the first group, and then press Ctrl+Shift+Left arrow to promote the paragraph to Heading 1. Then, type the number *1*, a period, two spaces, and the first item. As soon as you press Enter, Word indents the list, converts your number into a number format for the paragraph, and automatically adds a second number for you.

What Starts an Automatic List?

Word watches as you type at the beginning of a paragraph to see if you are starting a list. It looks for three indicators:

- A counter—a number or letter at the beginning
- A separator—a period or closing parentheses
- A spacer—either a Tab character, or two or more Space characters

If the counter is an Arabic numeral, a list will begin as long as you provide either a separator or a spacer. For example, the number 1 will start a list if it is followed by two spaces and no period, or if it is followed by a closing parenthesis and only one space.

A Roman numeral or a letter must be followed by a separator, but the spacer is optional. For example, Roman numeral IV, followed by a period and only one space (a separator but no spacer) will work, but the letter B followed by a tab (a spacer but no separator) will not work.

You can use double letters as a counter, but only if the letters are identical and are followed by both a separator and a spacer. For example, typing *cc* followed by a close parenthesis and a tab will work, but typing *cd* or *aaa* will never begin a list, regardless of what follows the letters.

When you use a Tab character as the spacer, Word always creates a .50 inch hanging indent. If you use space characters, Word creates a hanging indent that approximates the width of the spaces you typed.

In the list you're creating, Word obligingly creates a fourth list entry for you after you add the second and third list entries. But what if you don't want a fourth list item—what if you want a new heading instead? Pressing the Alt+Shift+Left arrow keys to promote the paragraph to Heading 1 style does nothing. The behavior of the Alt+Shift+Arrow keys in a numbered list is explained in more detail in "Exploring Issues With Automatic Lists" later in the chapter. For now, simply press the Backspace key to turn off list numbering (this removes the number but leaves the paragraph indented), or press Ctrl+Q (this removes all the direct formatting from the paragraph). You can then press Ctrl+Shift+Left arrow to convert the paragraph to Heading 1 style and type the second heading.

Continuing a Previous List

You are now ready to start typing the second list. This time, type *1*, forget to type the period, type the two spaces, type the text for the item, and then press Enter. The result, as shown in Figure 9-2, might surprise you: Word indents the list to a new level.

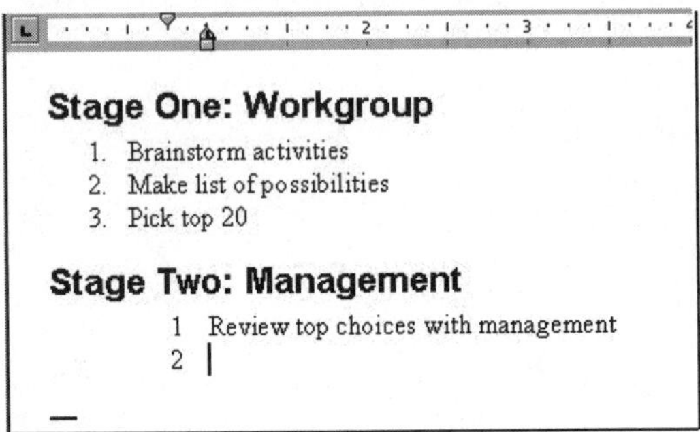

Figure 9-2
A new separator creates a new list level.

As always, Word watches at the beginning of the paragraph to see if you are typing a list. In this case, Word recognizes it as being a list because of the Arabic numeral counter and the two-space spacer. Word then checks to see whether you are continuing a previous list or starting a new one. If either the counter or the separator is different from the previous list—for example, if you change the counter from a number to a letter, or if you change the separator from a period to a parenthesis or to nothing—Word assumes you are continuing the previous list using a new outline level. Changing only the spacer—for example, changing it from two spaces to a tab—is not enough to make Word change your outline levels.

After you press Ctrl+Z to undo the change to the list and then insert a period after the number, however, you think you might want to insert a couple of new items into the list at this stage. So you change the item number from 1 to 3. Then, moving the cursor to the end of the line, you press Enter.

This time, Word changes the number from 3 to 4. Why? Word is trying to determine whether you are starting a new list or continuing the previous one. Here's how it makes the guess: If you are continuing a list, you probably use the next sequential number—that is, a 4—but it's human nature to make minor mistakes; you might accidentally type a number that is either too high or too low. If the first number in a new list is within one number—up or down—of the next sequential number, Word assumes that you are continuing the previous list. Once Word combines the lists, it renumbers the paragraph for you.

Chapter 9

Press Ctrl+Q to remove direct paragraph formatting, which removes the number. Type *1*, a period, two spaces, move to the end of the line, and press Enter. Word now interprets the list as a new list formatted the same as the first one. You continue creating the outline shown earlier in Figure 9-1.

Working with Multiple Lists

When you work with lists in a document, it is helpful to use Visual Basic for Applications (VBA) to see what is going on. In the Immediate window of the Visual Basic Editor, type *?ActiveDocument.Lists.Count*. The number 3 appears, showing that there are three lists in the document. The Lists property of a document refers to a collection of all the unique lists in the document.

You can create the following macro to color each list so that you can see them easily. The *ShowLists* macro changes the formatting of each paragraph that is part of a list. Before using this macro, always be sure to save your document.

```
Private Sub ShowLists()
    Dim oList As List
    Dim oPara As Paragraph
    Dim i As Long

    ActiveDocument.Content.Shading.ForegroundPatternColorIndex = wdWhite
    For Each oList In ActiveDocument.Lists
        For Each oPara In oList.ListParagraphs
            oPara.Range.Select
            oPara.Shading.ForegroundPatternColor = QBColor(i Mod 14 + 1)
        Next oPara
        i = i + 1
    Next oList
End Sub
```

First, the macro changes the shading color of the entire document to white so that any residual colors will not mask the formatting that the macro adds. The Content property returns a Range object that refers to the entire main story. It is precisely equivalent to using the Range method of a document with no arguments. If your document contains lists other than in the main story—for example, in text boxes—the looping portion of the macro will format those lists, but the first statement in the macro will not clear the format.

The loop works through each entry in the Lists collection. Within a single list, it loops through each of the paragraphs managed by that list, shading the paragraph. The QBColor function, a function left over from the old Quick Basic days (hence the QB), returns any of 16 basic colors numbered from 0 to 15. Color 0 is black and color 15 is white. The QBColor function is useful when you need a small number of clear, strong colors. The Mod operator gives the remainder of a division. There are only 14 usable colors, excluding black and white. If the active document contains more than 14 lists, the macro simply cycles back through the same colors. The expression *i Mod 14 + 1* converts any number stored in the variable *i* into a number between 1 and 14.

After you run the *ShowLists* macro, you will be able to see each list with its own color. If you want to remove the colors, step into the *ShowLists* macro and then stop after the statement that sets the shading for the entire document to white.

Exploring Issues with Automatic Lists

Automatic numbered lists are ideal for simple lists, particularly where you don't need to make many changes to the document. If you do start making changes to a document, you will see the strengths and limitations of automatically generated lists.

First, look at a one of the strengths of a list: You can switch the order of items within a list and the numbering will automatically adjust. For example, suppose you want to change Group Approval, shown earlier in Figure 9-1, from third place to first place within its section. Click in paragraph 3 and press Ctrl+Alt+Up arrow a couple of times, and the paragraph becomes number 1. The paragraphs renumber, regardless how you move them around; using a shortcut key, cut and paste, or drag and drop makes no difference.

But what happens if you decide that Group Approval should be the last step of stage one? If you click in paragraph 1 and press Ctrl+Alt+Up arrow, the paragraph moves up, and the number is now—still—paragraph 1. If you run the *ShowLists* macro, you will see the three lists, still intact. When you have multiple lists in a document, moving a paragraph within the document does not change which list it belongs to. In fact, if you ever have the need, you can interleave paragraphs from two lists, as shown in Figure 9-3, and they will retain their separate list numbering.

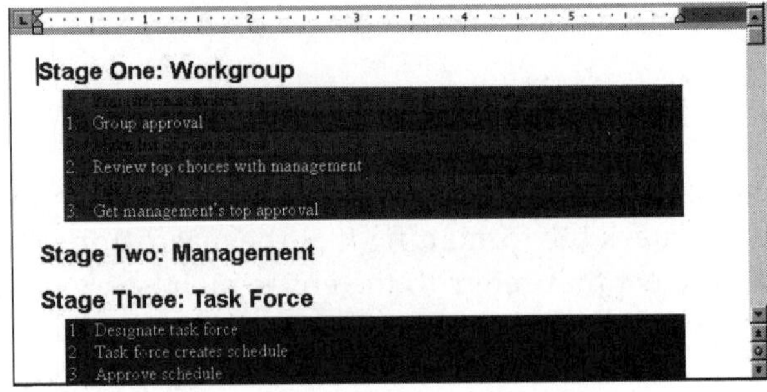

Figure 9-3
A paragraph does not change lists, even when you move it.

To move a paragraph from one list to another, press Ctrl+Shift+C to copy the paragraph. In most situations, where automatic numbering creates multiple lists, you really have a single list that simply starts renumbering after a heading. This is covered in "Creating a Numbered List Using Outline Formatting" later in this chapter.

Manipulating paragraph formatting can also be a problem if you're using automatic list . When Word creates an automatic list, it applies the numbering as direct paragraph formatting. So if you press Ctrl+Q to reset the paragraph formatting (say, to remove a shaded background), the number format will disappear, as well. When you need control over the format of your document, you don't want numbers capriciously disappearing when you remove a completely unrelated bit of formatting.

Because automatic numbering is applied as direct paragraph formatting, you can convert a paragraph from one list type to another by copying and pasting the paragraph format. Use the Format Painter, or use the Ctrl+Shift+C and Ctrl+Shift+V key combinations.

Creating a Numbered List Using Built-In Paragraph Styles

Automatic numbering applies the formatting as direct paragraph formatting. Word also has built-in styles that are already linked to number formats. For example, the number format of the List Number 2 style is virtually identical to the format produced using automatic numbering if you type the text according to the instructions in the "Begin An Automatic List" section, earlier in this chapter. The other List Number styles behave identically, but with varying amounts of indentation. Using built-in paragraph styles is the second approach to creating numbered lists. To see the built-in numbered styles in the Style dialog box, select Style from the Format menu, and then select All Styles in the List drop-down list.

Each built-in list style has a corresponding List Continue style that has the same amount of indentation but no number. The pairs of styles are valuable if you have a document with unnumbered comments sprinkled between numbered items. If you will be using the List Number 2 style interleaved with the List Continue 2 style, you might want to modify the style and set Style For Following Paragraph for each style to the opposite style.

The built-in numbered styles are good if you have only a single list in the document. They have some strange behaviors, particularly if you need the list numbers to restart, as in the case of the document being prepared for your task force.

Applying Built-In Numbered Styles

To practice using numbered styles, add numbering to the task force list you are creating using the following steps:

1. First, select the entire document and press Ctrl+Q to remove direct paragraph formatting, thus removing any existing numbers.
2. Save the unformatted list with a new name, perhaps List Test.
3. Apply List Number 2 style to all the previously numbered paragraphs. The result appears in Figure 9-4. The numbers do not restart after each heading; they form a single list.
4. To force the numbers to restart, select the first item in step 2 and click Bullets And Numbering on the Format menu. Select the Restart Numbering option at the bottom of the dialog box. The number changes to 1. Then, repeat step 3.

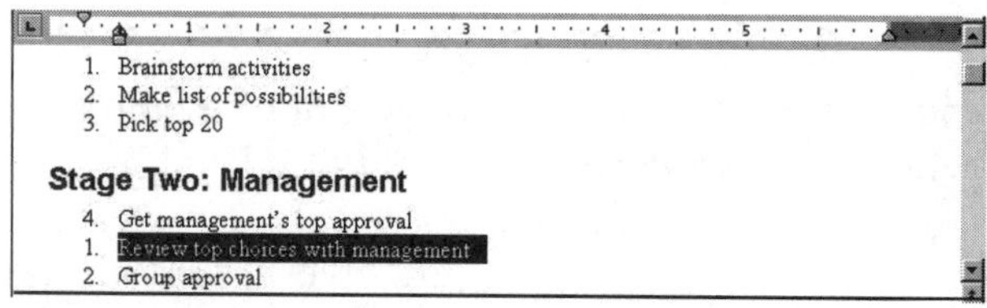

Figure 9-4
Using built-in numbered styles creates a single list.

The document should now look very much like the goal outline shown earlier in Figure 9-1.

Rearranging Paragraphs with a Numbered Style

The fun starts, however, when you try making changes. Choosing Restart Numbering simply breaks the list, starting a new one; now you have three lists. That brings with it all the problems of the three lists created by automatic numbering. As you should expect, if you move the first item from the second group up into the first group, it retains the number 1. However—and perhaps unexpectedly—if you move the first item of the second group down to the second position, as shown in Figure 9-5, it still retains the number 1, while the old number 2 suddenly becomes item 4 from the first list.

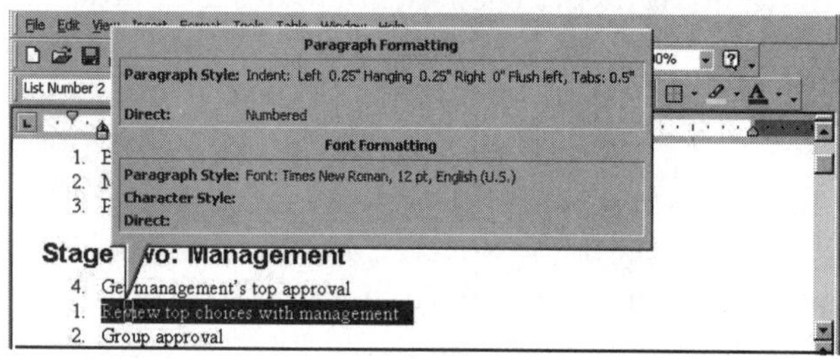

Figure 9-5
A paragraph tagged with Restart Numbering keeps its number.

Once you understand how list formatting works, this behavior actually makes sense. The List Number 2 style is linked to this particular number formatting scheme. All the paragraphs formatted with the style possess the number formats with no direct formatting; you can see the formatting by pressing Shift+F1. When you click in one of the unmodified paragraphs, all the formatting, including numbering, is part of the paragraph style. When you click in the paragraph you tagged with Restart Numbering, the numbering portion of the format changes to direct paragraph formatting, as shown earlier in Figure 9-5.

The format that became part of direct formatting is called the Restart Numbering attribute. Because it is an attribute of the paragraph, it naturally moves with the paragraph.

The paragraph that changed to number 4 in Figure 9-5 does not have any direct formatting telling it to start a new list, so it simply became part of the preceding list.

Modifying the Number Format of a Style

One more aspect of formats linked to styles is worth investigating. Suppose you are using the List Number 2 style, but you want to change the numbering format to display Roman numerals. To do that, you use the Bullets And Numbering dialog box.

1. Select the final paragraph in the third group.
2. Click Bullets And Numbering on the Format menu, and select the last style in the dialog box—the one with lowercase Roman numerals (if a different numbering scheme is in the final position, select the position and click Reset).
3. Click OK.

You would like all the paragraphs formatted with the same number format to change, but that seems too much to hope for. What you really expect is that the one selected paragraph would change formats, and you would need to retype the style name in the Style box to apply the new format to all the paragraphs. In reality, what you do get is the completely unexpected result shown in Figure 9-6. All the previously numbered paragraphs change, but only a seemingly random sample changes to the new numbering format, while all the others lose their numbers completely!

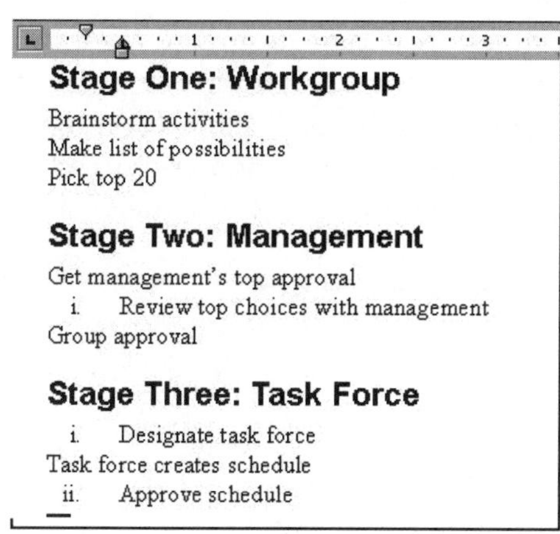

Figure 9-6
In a numbered style, the numbering is part of the Style formatting.

At first, this outcome seems nothing short of erratic. But in fact, it is almost understandable. All the paragraphs have the List Number 2 style. The three paragraphs that display numbers have Numbered as part of their direct paragraph formatting, not as part of the style. (The first two were previously set to Restart Numbering; the third is the one you just changed.)

Before you used the Bullets And Numbering dialog box to redefine the number format, the List Number 2 style was linked to the numbering template. The process of redefining one of the paragraphs erased the link between the style and the numbering template. The paragraphs with no direct formatting were left with no numbering. The paragraphs with direct formatting are still linked to the (updated) numbering template.

This behavior might not seem very clear, but it is at least predictable. You already expected that you would need to redefine the style based on the updated paragraph. In fact, that really is all you still have to do. Click in the Style box, press Enter, and accept Word's offer to update the style.

If you want to avoid having the style lose its link to a numbering template, use the Style dialog box to modify the format of the style: Click Style on the Format menu, and then click, Modify, Format, Numbering, select a numbering template from the Bullets And Numbering dialog box that appears. Click OK as needed to exit all the dialog boxes.

Creating a Numbered List Using Outline Formatting

Both automatic numbering and the built-in numbered styles create single-level lists. With a single-level list, the only way to restart numbering is to break the list into multiple lists. Once you break a list into separate lists—even if all the lists are based on the same list template—the list becomes difficult to manage because you can't freely move items from one list to another.

When you create a document with numbering that continually restarts, you probably have an outline list. An outline is a list whose template contains nine outline levels. Even if you use only two or three of the levels, the template contains all nine levels. For any level lower than the first one, you can choose to restart the numbering after any higher level. This gives you a tremendous amount of control over how numbering works within a list.

Creating an Outlined List

As you work on your task force outline, you decide to apply outline formatting to the list you have already created. Here are the steps:

1. Start by selecting the entire list and applying the Normal style. This resets all the paragraph formatting, including numbering.
2. Then, with the entire list still selected, click Format and choose Bullets And Numbering. Then select the Outline Numbered tab, and select the box with the first list format, as shown in Figure 9-7. (Click the Reset button if the first list template does not match the one in the template.)
3. Click OK. The entire list—including the headings—will be numbered with a simple series of numbers.

All the items are now set to List level 1. If you select the first item in the list and increase the indent (press Alt+Shift+Right arrow, or click the Increase Indent button on the

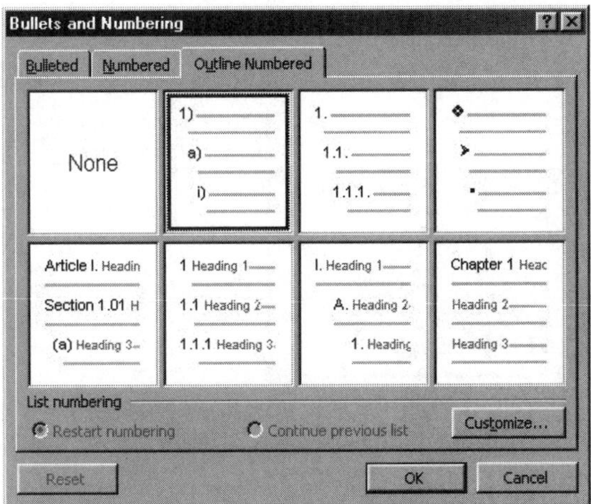

Figure 9-7
Restart Numbering becomes part of a paragraph's direct formatting.

toolbar), Word increases the indentation of the entire list, but leaves everything at List level 1. (Press Ctrl+Z to put the list back.) If you select the second item in the list (any item other than the first one) and increase the indent, however, the level for that item increases by one and the numbering restarts for that level, as shown in Figure 9-8. You can now increase the level for each task item, leaving the stage headings at List level 1.

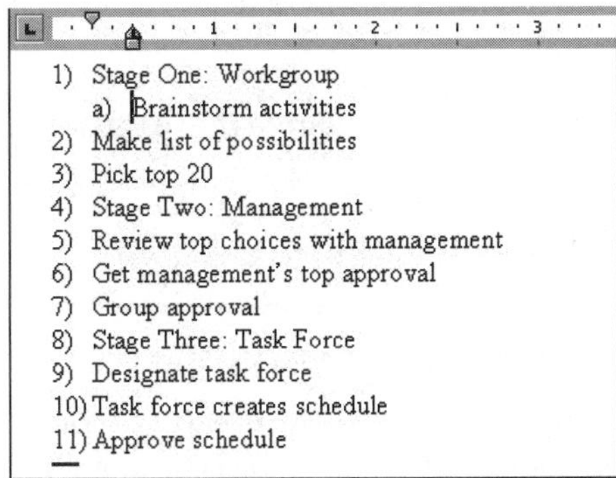

Figure 9-8
Changing one paragraph changes everything.

Now you have a single list, but the numbering of the lower level items resets each time you have a paragraph with a higher level number. Because this is a single list, you can change the format of the entire list at once by following the steps below:

1. Click anywhere within the list.
2. Click Bullets And Numbering on the Format menu, and select the second list format (resetting it if necessary).
3. Click OK.

The entire list changes to legal style formatting as shown in Figure 9-9, even though the selection consists of only a single insertion point. You simply changed the template the list is linked to.

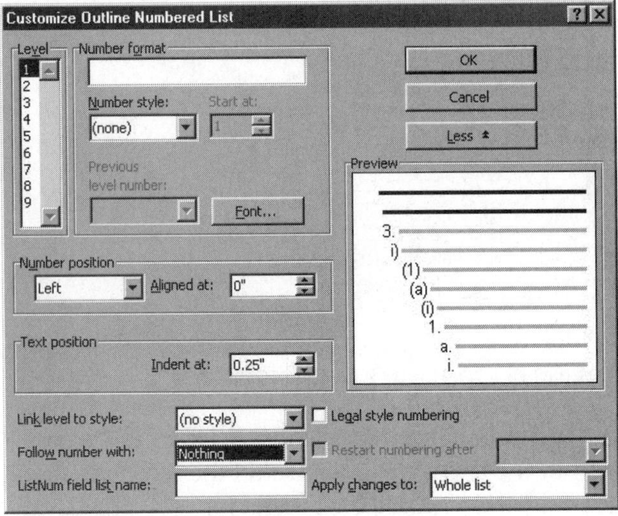

Figure 9-9
An outline numbered list has multiple levels.

Customizing an Outlined List

Once you have the outline list created, you can customize it to a remarkable degree. Here's how:

1. With the insertion point anywhere within the list, display the Bullets And Numbering dialog box.
2. Select the first list template (resetting it if necessary), and click Customize.
3. You don't want numbers on the top level of the list, so select 1 from the Level list box, and then select and delete the entire contents of the Number Format text box. This changes the value in the Number Style drop-down list box to None.
4. You want the second-level numbers to be Arabic, followed by a period. Select 2 from the Level list box, select the Arabic numerals from the Number Style drop-down list box, and change the parenthesis in the Number Format text box to a period.
5. Click OK. Word changes the number formatting for the entire list, as shown in Figure 9-10. The headings are still indented.

If you click the Show/Hide (¶) button on the Standard toolbar to show formatting marks, you will see that Tab characters precede the headings. The number formatting provides the Tab characters. You cannot select them, but you can press the

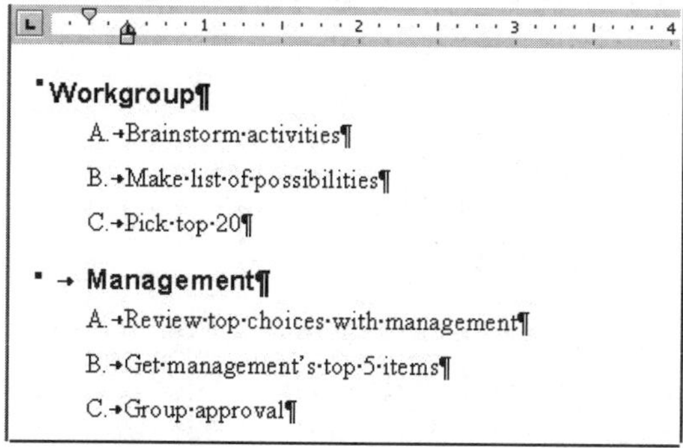

Figure 9-10
Increasing the indent of any item other than the first changes the level.

Backspace Key to delete them (doing so removes number formatting from the paragraphs, and the second level paragraphs no longer restart numbering).

To remove the Tab characters from the number formatting, you must display the extended version of the Customize Outline Numbered List dialog box, which is shown in Figure 9-11, using the following steps:

1. Click Bullets And Numbering on the Format menu, select 1 from the Level list box, and click the More button.
2. In the Follow Number With drop-down list, select Nothing.
3. Click OK.

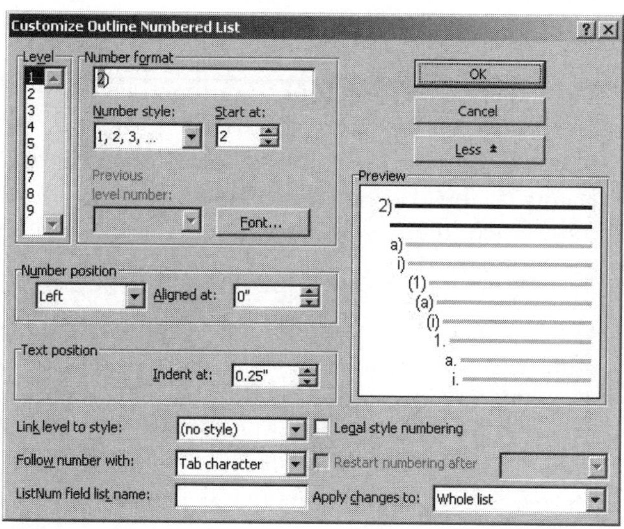

Figure 9-11
Extend the Customize dialog box to see additional options.

Note If you close the dialog box while it is extended, it will open in the extended position the next time you use it.

You can also make List level 1 of the list add the stage numbers, so that you could swap the Management part with the Workgroup part in your task force list without renumbering using the following steps.

1. First, remove the introductory numbers from each of the paragraphs.
2. In the Customize Outline Numbered List dialog box, select 1 from the Level list box and select One, Two, Three from the Number Style drop-down list.
3. Insert the word Stage at the beginning of the Number Format text box, and add a period at the end.
4. In the Follow Number With text box, select Space.
5. Click OK. The results are shown in Figure 9-12.

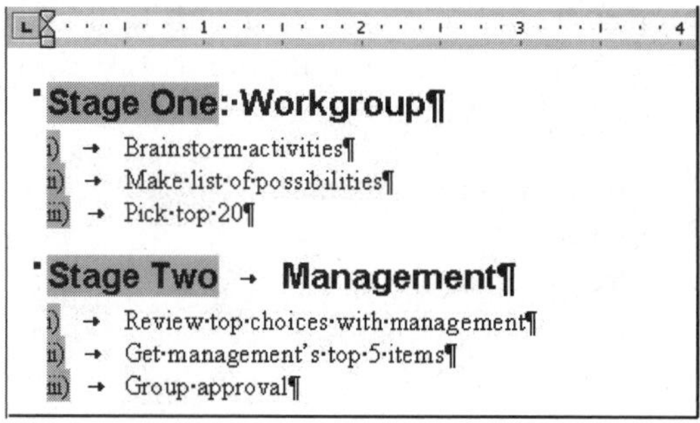

Figure 9-12
Add text to outline level numbering.

You can add numbers at any or all levels of an outlined list. At any level other than the first level, you can decide whether to restart the numbering and at which level to restart it. For all levels, you decide the style for the number and the text, if any, will precede and follow it. You also decide how much indentation you want for both the number and for the text in any subsequent items in the outline.

Linking Styles to a Numbered Outline

You might notice that some of the templates show faint style names for the different levels in the Outline Numbered tab of the Bullets And Numbering dialog box shown earlier in Figure 9-7. With an outline numbered list, you can assign a style to any or all levels of the list. Four of the built-in templates already have the nine heading styles assigned to the nine list levels. You do not, however, need to assign heading styles to the list levels, and you do not need to assign styles to all the levels.

A list template forms an interesting relationship with a style. You can use either the Customize Outline Numbered List dialog box to create the link, or you can use the Modify Style dialog box. Either way, you achieve the same link.

The list you are creating for the task force is currently an outline list, but it is not linked to any styles. If you select one of the numbered items and press Ctrl+Q, the numbers will disappear. You can now link styles to the list using the following steps:

1. After clicking anywhere in the list, click Bullets And Numbering on the Format menu, leave the current template selected, and click Customize.
2. Click More if the dialog box is not already extended.
3. Select List level 1. In the Link Level To Style drop-down list, select the Heading 3 style. The Heading level of the style does not need to match the list level of the template.
4. Select level2. In the Link Level to Style drop-down list, select Body Text. You can link to any style, not just to heading styles.
5. When you click OK, the list changes to use the Heading 3 style for each List level 1 entry, and the Body Text style for each level two entry.

The list template and level has been added to each of the two styles. Pressing Ctrl+Q will no longer remove the numbers from the numbered items, and assigning the Body Text style to any new paragraph will automatically number it as part of this list.

Placing Automatic Numbers in the Middle of a Paragraph

Word's automatic numbering features relate to numbers that appear at the beginning of a paragraph. When you have sequential numbers in the middle of a paragraph, you can still integrate these numbers into a normal Word outline. The ListNum field creates a sequential number anywhere in a document. It also contains an option switch—\l—that controls the level of the number within an outline. To link the ListNum field to an outline number, add a name to the field code. Then type that name in the ListNum Field List Name in the Customize Outline Numbered List dialog box.

Changing List Levels While Linked to Styles

Word provides two pairs of commands that behave very differently under normal circumstances, but behave similarly when used with numbered lists. They are Increase Indent and Decrease Indent, and Outline Promote and Outline Demote.

The Increase Indent and Decrease Indent buttons appear on the Formatting toolbar. (They'll be referred to collectively as change indent commands in this chapter.) These buttons change the amount of space a paragraph is indented. With a normal unformatted, unindented, unnumbered paragraph, clicking the Increase Indent button increases the left indent by 0.50 inch.

Use the Alt+Shift+Right arrow and Alt+Shift+Left arrow keys as the equivalent of the Outline Promote and Outline Demote commands, respectively. (They'll be referred to in this chapter, collectively, as change outline commands.) With an unformatted paragraph selected, pressing Alt+Shift+Right arrow changes the style to Heading 2, and pressing Alt+Shift+Left arrow changes the style to Heading 1. With a normal, unnumbered paragraph, the change indent and change outline commands each behave differently.

When you are working with a numbered paragraph, however, these two sets of commands behave similarly. If you select a numbered paragraph that is not associated with a style, the change outline commands suddenly behave just like change indent commands. For example, if the numbered paragraph is at the beginning of a numbered list, both the change indent and the change outline commands then change the indentation of the paragraph—the same as if the paragraph were not numbered. Likewise, if the numbered paragraph is part of a single-level list—that is, a list that is not part of an outline numbered list—the change indent and change outline commands then change all the indentation.

If the numbered paragraph is part of an outline numbered list, however, and if it is not the first paragraph in the list, both the change indent commands and the change outline commands will then change the level of the list paragraph.

Understanding How Word 2000 Formats Lists

An enhancement in Word 2000 complicates the rule. When you create what seems to be a single-level list in Word—either by using automatic list numbering or by using the Numbered tab (not the Outline Numbered tab) of the Bullets And Numbering dialog box—you might think that the list is not an outline numbered list. In fact, it is. Word 2000 now formats all lists as outline numbered. This is actually a good thing, because outline numbered lists are much more powerful than single-level lists.

The only problem with using a simple list as an outlined list—aside from the fact that list might behave differently than you expect—is that you cannot use the Bullets And Numbering dialog box to modify the various levels of the list. The Bullets And Numbering dialog box always activates the template you used when you created the numbered list. On the Numbered tab of the dialog box, you can customize the template, and the template really is an outline numbered list, but you can customize only the top level of the outline.

The behaviors of the change indent and change outline commands diverge again when any level of the outline is associated with a style. If the selected numbered paragraph is part of an outline numbered list, but the current level is not associated with the style, the change outline commands change the outline level (as do the change indent commands). If the level of the selected paragraph is linked to one of the heading styles, however, the change outline commands revert to their natural behavior of changing outline levels.

If you link each level of a numbered outline with the corresponding Heading level, the change indent and change outline commands will always behave the same within a numbered list. They will always behave differently outside of a numbered list.

Managing Links within Styles and Templates

A document can contain more than one list. Separate lists can share a single template, and each list can have its own template. Each outline numbered template has nine levels. Any level of any template can be linked to a style. You cannot, however, link the same style to more than one level, or to more than one template. As soon as you link a style to a new level or template, any old links are broken.

It is perfectly acceptable to link the Heading 1 style to List level 1 of one list, and the Heading 2 style to List level 5 of a different list. If you do, promoting or demoting the Heading style of a paragraph will switch the paragraph between the two lists.

Removing Links from Styles

Suppose you apply one of the built-in templates that links styles to list levels—such as the first template on the bottom row of the Outline Numbered tab (reset to the default value, if necessary). What if you then want to remove the links to the heading styles?

If you use the Customize Bullets And Numbering dialog box and clear the style from the Link Level To Style drop-down list, Word does remove the link between the numbering format and the style definition. When you close the dialog box, however, you will still see the same number format applied to the paragraph, with the same style name in the Style box. Word simply converted the number format of the paragraphs that were formatted with that style to use direct paragraph formatting rather than style paragraph formatting. You can see this by pressing Shift+F1 and clicking in the paragraph.) To remove the number formatting from the paragraph, press Ctrl+Q to remove direct paragraph formatting.

If you create a new style name linked to a numbering level, you might think that you could remove the link by deleting the style. Deleting the style does remove the style from the list of styles, and it does remove the formatting from any paragraphs formatted with that style, but it does not really remove the relationship. The definition of the style is still stored within the Style Gallery template. If you open the Bullets And Numbering dialog box, the style name still appears in the definition of the style. If you assign that numbering template to a paragraph, Word re-creates the style in the active document. To remove the definition of the style, you must reset the template in the Bullets And Numbering dialog box. Resetting the template does not delete the style, but it removes the numbering portion of the style definition, and it removes the style definition from the numbering template gallery.

Adding Numbers Formatted as Words

You might have noticed that the stage headings of your outline document each contain a number, even though the numbers are written out as words. What if you wanted to rearrange the order of the stages? Wouldn't it be nice if Word could automatically renumber the stage for you? It can, using the following steps:

1. First delete the numbered prefixes from each of the top-level paragraphs so you won't have duplicate numbers later.
2. Select the first paragraph. Click Bullets And Numbering on the Format menu, and click Customize to display the Customize Outline Numbered List dialog box. Select List level 1 if it is not already selected.
3. In the Number Style drop-down list, select One, Two, Three. This formats the numbers as words.
4. In the Number Format text box, type *Stage* and a space before the word One.
5. In the Follow Number With drop-down list, select Space.
6. Click OK to format the paragraph.
7. Copy the format to the other two headings. (Use Ctrl+Shift+C and Ctrl+Shift+V, or use the Format Painter.)

Each of the List level 1 paragraphs now has an automatically numbered heading, and you can freely rearrange the stages and the individual tasks of your project.

Formatting Automatic Numbers

Suppose you want to format the words "Stage One:" as bold italic, without changing the formatting of the rest of the heading. You have two options. One option is to format the paragraph mark. The numbering takes most of its format from the paragraph mark. Simply select the heading's paragraph mark and apply the bold and italic formats to it. Formatting the paragraph mark works for font name, style, size, and color, but not for underlining. It also works for all the standard effects (strikethrough, superscript, embossed, all caps) except small caps and hidden text.

Actually, using the paragraph mark to format the number is best when you do want the number format to match that of the paragraph, because the number format will follow if you change the format of the paragraph. In most cases, if you want the format of the number to differ from that of the paragraph, you are probably better off using the second option, which is to use the Font button on the Customize Outline Number Format dialog box. This button brings up the Font dialog box, which lets you change any character formatting you want. Character formats you apply to the number using the Font dialog box take precedence over character formatting applied to the number from the paragraph mark.

The formatting of the paragraph mark is important if you want to format the text of a paragraph without affecting the format of the number. For example, suppose you want to format the word "Management" as bold italic, without changing the formatting of the number. If you simply select the word Management—remembering to carefully avoid the paragraph mark—and apply the format, the number will change to match the format, anyway. This is not because the rule about paragraph marks is wrong; it is because how Word works.

When you select all the text in a paragraph—even if you don't select the paragraph mark or any trailing spaces that might exist—Word assumes that omitting the paragraph mark was accidental and formats the paragraph mark, as well. If you do want to apply character formatting to everything except the paragraph mark, type an X or some other letter at the end of the paragraph, format everything before the X, and then delete the letter.

Using Template Galleries

The Bullets And Numbering dialog box provides three formatting tabs: Bulleted, Numbered, and Outline Numbered. Each tab on the dialog box displays eight boxes: None, which turns off the numbering, and seven pre-defined numbering templates. These three groups of seven templates are called template galleries. When the selected paragraph already has numbering applied—for example, a paragraph formatted with the List Number 2 style—the dialog box replaces one of the default gallery templates with the template used by the current paragraph.

When you customize a template in the gallery, you do not change the original gallery template. Rather, you create a new template that takes the place of the built-in gallery template. Word uses the Windows registry to store the detailed definitions of customized templates that are in the gallery. After you customize a template in one document—thus adding the customized template to the gallery—you can then apply the same template to a list in an entirely new document.

When you select a gallery position that contains a customized template in the Bullets And Numbering dialog box, the Reset button becomes enabled. Resetting the template removes your custom template from the gallery, restoring the built-in gallery template to its normal position. The template you created is still intact, however; it just doesn't appear in the gallery. To add your custom template back into the gallery, select a paragraph that uses the customized template and display the Bullets And Numbering dialog box. (You have no control over which position Word will use for the customized template.)

Calculating in Tables

Note The sample documents for this section are Expense.doc and Expense.bmp.

In Word, a table provides the opportunity to structure the contents of a document. "Using a Table to Add a Second Column" in Chapter 8 explains how to use a table to organize the text of a document into columns. You can also use a table to organize numbers in rows and columns, similar to a spreadsheet. In fact, you can even perform some spreadsheet-like calculations on the cells within a table.

You might wonder why you would ever want to use a Word table as a spreadsheet when you can simply embed an Excel worksheet directly in the document. For small tables, it might simply be easier to create the spreadsheet grid using a Word table than to embed an Excel object in the document. Even for a large grid, there will be times when you might prefer to create the grid directly in Word.

Suppose you have a printed form that you want to fill in by printing from a document. You can scan the printed form into the computer and use it to help align a grid for printing to the form. Even though you can import the scanned document into Excel, you cannot place it behind the cell grid. In Word, however, you can place a scanned document behind the text layer, which is where a table grid exists.

This section will show you how to build a grid—complete with calculations—on top of an expense report. Figure 9-13 shows the scanned expense report form. Both the grid layout and the calculations on this expense report are quite complex, and you can learn much about refining the layout of a table and about using calculations within a table in this example.

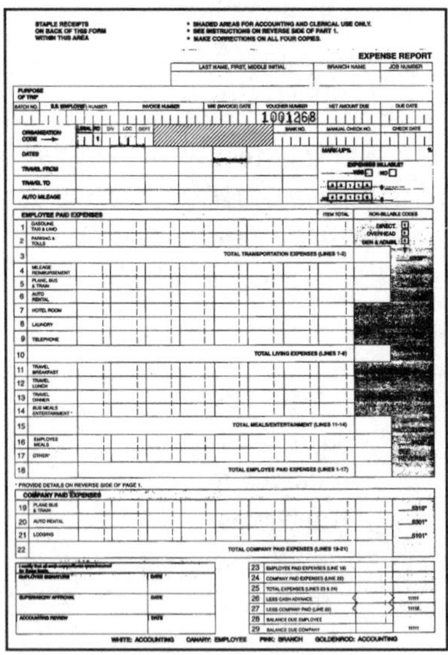

STAPLE RECEIPTS
ON BACK OF THIS FORM
WITHIN THIS AREA

- SHADED AREAS FOR ACCOUNTING AND CLERICAL USE ONLY.
- SEE INSTRUCTIONS ON REVERSE SIDE OF PART 1.
- MAKE CORRECTIONS ON ALL FOUR COPIES.

EXPENSE REPORT

LAST NAME, FIRST, MIDDLE INITIAL	BRANCH NAME	JOB NUMBER

PURPOSE OF TRIP

BATCH NO.	S.S. (EMPLOYEE) NUMBER	INVOICE NUMBER	W/E (INVOICE) DATE	VOUCHER NUMBER	NET AMOUNT DUE	DUE DATE
				1001268		

ORGANIZATION CODE → | DIV | LOC | DEPT | BANK NO. | MANUAL CHECK NO. | CHECK DATE

DATES | MARK-UP% %

TRAVEL FROM | EXPENSES BILLABLE? YES ☐ NO ☐

TRAVEL TO

AUTO MILEAGE

	EMPLOYEE PAID EXPENSES	ITEM TOTAL	NON-BILLABLE CODES
1	GASOLINE TAXI & LIMO		DIRECT
2	PARKING & TOLLS		OVERHEAD / GEN & ADMIN.
3	TOTAL TRANSPORTATION EXPENSES (LINES 1-2)		
4	MILEAGE REIMBURSEMENT		
5	PLANE, BUS & TRAIN		
6	AUTO RENTAL		
7	HOTEL ROOM		
8	LAUNDRY		
9	TELEPHONE		
10	TOTAL LIVING EXPENSES (LINES 7-9)		
11	TRAVEL BREAKFAST		
12	TRAVEL LUNCH		
13	TRAVEL DINNER		
14	BUS MEALS ENTERTAINMENT *		
15	TOTAL MEALS/ENTERTAINMENT (LINES 11-14)		
16	EMPLOYEE MEALS		
17	OTHER*		
18	TOTAL EMPLOYEE PAID EXPENSES (LINES 1-17)		

* PROVIDE DETAILS ON REVERSE SIDE OF PAGE 1.

	COMPANY PAID EXPENSES		
19	PLANE BUS & TRAIN		5310*
20	AUTO RENTAL		5301*
21	LODGING		5101*
22	TOTAL COMPANY PAID EXPENSES (LINES 19-21)		

EMPLOYEE SIGNATURE	DATE
SUPERVISORY APPROVAL	DATE
ACCOUNTING REVIEW	DATE

23	EMPLOYEE PAID EXPENSES (LINE 18)		
24	COMPANY PAID EXPENSES (LINE 22)		
25	TOTAL EXPENSES (LINES 23 & 24)		
26	LESS CASH ADVANCE		
27	LESS COMPANY PAID (LINE 22)		
28	BALANCE DUE EMPLOYEE		
29	BALANCE DUE COMPANY		

WHITE: ACCOUNTING CANARY: EMPLOYEE PINK: BRANCH GOLDENROD: ACCOUNTING

Figure 9-13
You want to print values onto this form.

Aligning a Table to a Scanned Form

The first part of the process consists of adding the embedded bitmap into the document so that you can begin to construct a table over the top of it.

Because you will be printing the document directly onto the printed form, you won't want the scanned bitmap to print. You'll be using it only to help you align the cells on the form's grid.

Importing and Placing Bitmaps

Even though you do not need a scanned form to repeat on more than one page, it will stay out of the way better if you add it to the page header. Before inserting the scanned image, click View and then click Header And Footer to display the page header. To insert a scanned image into your document, follow these steps:

1. Click Picture on the Insert menu, and choose From File.
2. Navigate to the folder that contains the picture, select the image file, and click Insert. To position the image, you need to prevent Word from wrapping text around it.
3. Click Picture on the Format menu, and select the Layout tab. Select Behind Text as the Wrapping Style, but don't click OK yet. If the image is close to the size of the page, Word will probably reduce it to fit within the page margins.
4. In the Format Picture dialog box, click the Size tab and adjust the size to match the original size of the document.
5. After you click OK, adjust the position of the document to match its position on the actual printed form.
6. Print a copy of the page and compare the scanned image with the original form.

Adding the scanned form to the header also has the desirable effect of making the form's shading faint while you're creating the table. If the form in the background still appears too dark, select the picture, activate the Picture toolbar, and use the More Brightness button to lighten it.

Aligning Text Outside a Table

On the expense form shown earlier in Figure 9-13, your social security number needs to be typed into the appropriate block at the top of the form. Rather than create a table with one cell for each character, it is much easier to adjust the character and paragraph spacing to force the characters to fit the boxes. This job is much easier if you create a couple of macros to help you. First, type the sample social security number *999-99-9999* in the first paragraph of the document. To align the row vertically, use the following *IncreaseParagraphSpace* macro:

```
Sub IncreaseParagraphSpace()
    Selection.ParagraphFormat.SpaceBefore = _
        Selection.ParagraphFormat.SpaceBefore + 1
End Sub
```

The *IncreaseParagraphSpace* macro simply increases the amount of space before the selected paragraph by one point (one-twelfth of an inch) each time it is run. Reduce the size of the Visual Basic Editor window so that you can see the Word document in the background, and press F5 repeatedly until the numbers in the paragraph are vertically aligned with the row on the form.

Drag the left indent indicator on the ruler to align the first digit of the social security number with the first box on the form. Normally, dragging the left indent mark on the ruler adjusts the indent in one-eighth-inch increments. To get more precise control over the amount of the indent, hold down the Alt key as you drag the indicator. Once the first character of the social security number aligns with the box, you can select all the characters and use the following *IncreaseCharacterSpace* macro to increase the spacing between characters:

```
Sub IncreaseCharacterSpace()
    Selection.Font.Spacing = Selection.Font.Spacing + 0.25
End Sub
```

The *IncreaseCharacterSpace* macro simply increases the amount of space between all selected characters by one-quarter point each time it is run. Run the *IncreaseCharacterSpace* macro repeatedly until the characters align with the social security number boxes. If the characters are spaced too far apart, you can press Ctrl+Z to undo the action of the macro. After formatting the first paragraph, press Enter to create a new paragraph. The new paragraph will default to the same paragraph and character spacing as that of the social security number box. Press Ctrl+Q and Ctrl+Spacebar to remove both the direct paragraph and direct character formatting.

Creating the First Row of the Table

Performing calculations in a table is easiest when all the calculations take place in the same table, and it is best to simply create the entire table at one time. Before you create the table, add sufficient paragraphs so that the insertion point is located at approximately the first row of the grid. To control the left edge of the table, change the left indent of the paragraph; adjust the left indent for the paragraph slightly to the right of the left edge of the first style. When Word creates a table, it places the left edge of the table to the left of the indent so that the contents of the paragraph will begin at the current indent location.

To control the right edge of the table, don't set the right indent of the paragraph because the table will ignore it. Rather, change the right margin of the document; set the margin slightly inside the right edge of the rightmost cell on the form.

Here are the steps to create the table itself:

1. Click Insert Table on the Table menu.
2. Specify the maximum number of columns in the Number Of Columns box. The expense form has a maximum of nine columns.
3. Add the approximate total number of rows for the grid in the Number Of Rows box, counting any gaps between sections as a row. The expense form has approximately 26 rows.

4. Click OK to create the table.

To align the top of the table with the top of the form grid, select a paragraph that precedes the table, and run the *IncreaseParagraphSpace* macro as needed. The columns in the new table should match the columns on your form.

- If the left edge of the table is not sufficiently close to the left gridline on the form, hold the Alt key as you drag the left edge of the table to the proper location.
- If the right edge of the table is not sufficiently close to the right edge of the form's grid, move the mouse pointer over the lower right corner of the table; a small box will appear. Move the mouse pointer over that box until it changes into a double-headed arrow pointing up to the left and down to the right. Then drag the small box—holding down the Alt key as necessary for increased control—until the right edge of the table matches the right grid mark on the form.

By default, Word adjusts the width of table columns to fit the contents. When you're matching a printed form, you don't want the column widths adjusting automatically. Follow these steps to adjust the column width settings:

1. Select Table Properties on the Table menu.
2. On the Table tab, click Options.
3. In the Table Options dialog box, clear the Automatically Resize To Its Contents check box.

If you ever need to create a table where the cell contents completely fill each cell—with no space on either side—set the values of the left and right boxes to zero.

Formatting Cell Rows

Type a number into one of the cells of the table. You can use this sample number to check the format of the contents. Decrease the font size to a small enough size so that the values you need to type can fit into the cells. Select the entire table and change the font size to 10 points.

The rows in the table will probably be shorter than the rows in the grid on the form. If the rows of the table are taller than the rows in the form grid, you need to reduce the height of the paragraphs in the table. A macro can make the task of adjusting the row heights easy. The following *IncreaseRowHeight* macro increases the row height of all selected rows in a table:

```
Sub IncreaseRowHeight()
    With Selection.Rows
        .HeightRule = wdRowHeightExactly
        .Height = .Height + 1
    End With
End Sub
```

This macro increases the height of the selected rows of the table by one point each time it is run. By default, Word increases the row height as necessary to fit the contents of the row. Setting the HeightRule property to *wdRowHeightExactly* turns off automatic row height adjustment. Run the *IncreaseRowHeight* macro until the row height is correct for a single block of cells in the grid. Gaps between sections of the form will need a different row height.

Once you set the row height for the table as a whole, select individual rows that might need to be refined. For example, the gaps between the sections need to be taller, and some rows might need to be shorter. Run the *IncreaseRowHeight* macro as needed, changing between a plus sign (+) and a minus sign (-) as appropriate. Remember, too, that you can undo the macro actions by pressing Ctrl+Z.

After increasing the row height, the sample cell value might appear too high in the cell. To move the text down, change the paragraph format by adjusting the Space Before value on the Format Paragraph dialog box to 4 points.

When you're through, you should have a Word table whose grid matches the grid of the scanned form. You will eventually turn off the gridlines. For now, however, the visible gridlines make it easier to tell the difference between the table cell borders and the grid of the scanned form.

Creating Formulas in a Table

Now that you have imported and positioned the bitmap form, and you have created a table that aligns with the bitmap form, you're ready to add some sample values and formulas into the grid

Entering Formulas using Bookmarks and Cell Addresses

In the Auto Mileage row, type *100* in the first column, type *150* in the second column, and type *300* in the third column.

The fourth line of the expense report includes a mileage reimbursement dollar amount for the miles listed in the Auto Mileage line. The mileage rate does not appear anywhere on the form. You can add it in a bookmark above the table. (A bookmark is simply a named location in the document.) Somewhere above the table, type the rate per mile—perhaps 0.34. Select the mileage rate. On the Insert menu, click Bookmark, type *MileageRate* for the name of the bookmark, and click the Add button.

The formula that calculates the mileage reimbursement in each column multiplies the mileage rate—which is now in a bookmark—by the number of miles in the Auto Mileage cell for the column. You can refer to a cell in the Auto Mileage row by using its cell address. (Cell addresses in a table are named using A1 notation, much like an Excel spreadsheet.)

1. Click in the first column of the Mileage Reimbursement row, and then click, Formula on the Table menu.

2. In the Formula text box, type *=A4*MileageRate*. You can also select the correct bookmark to use from the Paste Bookmark drop-down list.)
3. When you click OK, the reimbursement amount appears in the cell.

A Word table does not use relative references. If you copy the formula to the right, each cell will still retrieve the mileage from cell A4. You must type a new formula in each cell of the Mileage Reimbursement row, substituting the appropriate column letter each time. (For more information about relative and absolute addresses, see "Managing References in a Grid" in Chapter 12.)

Even though Word does not use relative references to summarize formulas, it has a feature that gives you all the benefits of relative references—plus a few extra features.

Entering Formulas using the SUM Function

You can create formulas in Word that use functions similar to those found in Excel. Word has only 18 functions, as opposed to the hundreds of functions available in Excel. Those 18 functions are useful for the most common tasks in a table. Many of the functions summarize values. Those summarizing functions (such as the SUM function) are very similar to the corresponding functions in an Excel worksheet except that, in place of a relative address, you use a relative directional word: Left, Right, Above, and Below. Once you understand how to use directional words, you'll find they are extremely powerful.

Before creating a summarizing function, type sample values into the Gasoline, Taxis, and Limos row of the expense report.

1. Type *$200.00* in the first column, *$300.00* in the second column, and *$450.00* in the third column.
2. The eighth column on the expense form contains the row totals. Click in the total cell of the first row, and then click Formula on the Tables menu. Because you typed sample numbers in the row, the dialog box now contains the default formula *=SUM(LEFT)*. (If there are no numbers entered in the vicinity of a cell, the Formula box will display only an equal sign, as it did in the previous exercise.)
3. When you click OK, the value *$950.00* appears in this cell. The SUM function summarizes the values to the left of the cell containing the formula.

The SUM function attempts to copy the formatting of the source cells. Because the source cells were formatted as dollars, the result of the SUM function is also formatted as dollars. If you don't want the dollar sign in the total cell—or if you want to control the format of the result— select a format in the Number Format text box drop-down list on the Formula dialog box. The Formula dialog box will not replace an existing formula; it only creates a new one. If you want to replace an existing formula, be sure to delete the original formula first.

Once you've created a formula you like, you can copy it to all the other cells requiring an equivalent formula. When you copy a cell, you can copy either the contents of the cell or the entire cell, including the cell mark at the end. If you're only pasting this cell into a single new cell, it doesn't matter which method you select. However, if you're pasting this cell into multiple new cells, Word's behavior becomes quirky. If you select only the contents of the source cell, when you paste those contents into multiple cells, the cells will then lose any paragraph formatting they already had, even if the source cell and the target cells have the same paragraph formatting. If you select the entire cell and then paste it into multiple cells, the target cells will acquire the formatting of the source cell.

To select an entire cell, select the cell mark at the end of the cell. (If you are displaying paragraph marks, the cell mark looks like a miniature sun.) If you're not displaying paragraph marks, select the blank space at the end of the cell to select the entire cell. Then select all the cells that require an equivalent total and paste the cell into them. The new cells will display the old value until you select the document and press F9 to recalculate the field totals.

Type sample values into the first three columns of several rows and then recalculate the document fields to make sure that the new formulas are working correctly.

Creating Subtotal Formulas

The Total Transportation Expenses field is the third row of the table, and it contains a subtotal. The subtotal appears in the ninth column, however, not in the eighth column, as do the line-item totals. Word does not have a directional word indicator for "above and to the left". To use directional words, you must use one formula to calculate a subtotal in the same column as the totals, and then use a second formula to copy that subtotal over to column nine.

- Make sure there are sample values in the first three columns of the first two rows. Recalculate the formulas in column eight so that each total cell in the first two rows contains a number.
- Select the cell in column eight of the third row, just below the total formulas, and click Formula on the Table menu. The Formula dialog box appears showing the default Formula *=SUM(ABOVE)*. Word correctly guessed that the numbers are above the formula.
- Click OK to accept the formula.
- In the ninth column of the third row, insert a formula to sum the cells to the left. (You can copy the formula from one of the total cells in column eight.) After recalculating the formulas, both the eighth and the ninth columns contain the subtotal from the first section.

Typing the formula *=SUM(LEFT)* in the subtotal column of the third row makes sense. Column eight is the only cell that will ever contain a value. In the fourth, fifth, and sixth rows of the expense report, the value in the subtotal column copies the value from the total column. If you type the formula = *SUM(LEFT)* in column nine of one of these rows, you might expect that it would sum all the cells in the first eight columns, double-counting the totals. In fact, the formula in column nine sums only the value in column eight.

The directional word references in a Word table are designed to allow you to create subtotals. The formula =*SUM(LEFT)* starts scanning with the cell immediately to the left of the one containing the formula. It proceeds to the left until it finds a non-blank cell. It then sums all the contiguous non-blank cell values. As soon as the formula reaches a blank cell that follows one or more non-blank cells, it quits. In other words, all you need to create subtotals is a blank cell.

This is a brilliant design. It allows you to use relative directional words to create subtotals in a table. Unfortunately, the only description of how this feature works that is listed in the Help file treats it as if it were a defect. In the Help topic *Total The Numbers In A Row Or Column,* one of the notes says, "If your column or row contains blank cells, Word will not total the entire column or row. To total the entire row or column, type a zero in each blank cell." There is no hint that this is a conscious design intended to multiply the power of formulas in a table.

You can control subtotals in a different context when you create the formula for the Living Expenses subtotal in line 10. As with the subtotal in the third row, to create a subtotal in column nine, you must first create the subtotal in column eight. But when you insert the formula =*SUM(ABOVE)* into line 10 in the eighth column (and recalculate it), the result is the total of all the cells from row one through row nine. That's because none of the cells is blank; they all contain formulas, which calculate either a total or a zero.

You want the formula in line 10 to get the subtotal of only lines 7 through 9. To stop subtotaling at the seventh row, you need a blank cell in the row immediately above it. To do that, insert a new row in the table, leaving the cells blank. The subtotal formula now calculates correctly, but the rows no longer line up with the grid on the form. The trick is to make the new blank row too small to see. The following *MakeRowSmall* macro changes the height of a row in a table to 1 point:

```
Sub MakeRowSmall()
    With Selection.Rows
        .HeightRule = wdRowHeightExactly
        .Height = 1
    End With
End Sub
```

As with the *IncreaseRowHeight* macro, the *MakeRowSmall* macro must first set the HeightRule property to *wdRowHeightExactly,* or Word will take the new Height property value as merely a suggestion (that is, a minimum value). Select the new row and run the *MakeRowSmall* macro. Even though the row is only a single point high, you might need to use the *IncreaseRowHeight* macro—changing the plus sign (+) to a minus sign (+)—to adjust the height of the rows immediately following the new row.

In the ninth column of row 10, create a formula that copies the subtotal from column 8. In this expense report, you'll also need a small blank row after row 10 to allow the subtotal from the Meals and Entertainment section to summarize only the one section. You don't need a blank row after the Meals and Entertainment section, because the following rows don't have subtotals. You will need formulas in column 9 of rows 16 and 17 to copy the row totals into the subtotal column.

Creating Grand Totals

Column nine of row 18 contains the grand total of all rows from row 1 through row 17. You can enter the formula=*SUM(ABOVE)* into the cell, but there are too many blank cells interspersed between the rows for it to properly calculate the entire column. Simply enter a zero in all the blank cells. Be sure to also include zeros in column nine of the small rows that separate the sections.

The summary section at the bottom of the expense report refers to specific subtotals in the report. You could use cell addresses to refer to those cells, but the farther down the table you get, the more chance there is that you might insert or delete a row above the source cell. Assigning bookmarks to the source cells is a safer option.

You have several choices for creating the summary section. You can extend the existing table, you can create a new separate table, or you can simply position the text using paragraph formatting. None of these options is vastly superior to any other.

Hiding Values in a Table

The document contains a number of values that you don't want to print. Specifically, you don't want to print the subtotals that appear in column eight, you don't want to print the extras zeros in column nine, and you don't want to print the mileage rate at the top of the document. For most of the values that you don't want to print, you can select the text or value, and then click Font on the Format menu, and select the Hidden check box on the Font tab.

Hidden values have interesting effects in Word formulas. Formulas still calculate values that are formatted as hidden, as long as they are currently displayed on the screen—which happens if you display the paragraph and other marks. If you hide hidden text, the formulas treat the values as zero. This is not a problem, because you can leave the hidden values visible on the screen (so that they are included in calculations) and still exclude them from printing. To do so, in the Print dialog box, click the Options button and make sure that the Hidden Text check box in the Include With Document section is not selected.

Hidden values behave differently when determining which values are included in a subtotal. The algorithm calculates which values to include in formulas such as =*SUM(ABOVE)*. These directional formulas watch for blank cells. Unfortunately, they consider hidden text to be blank, even if the text is currently displayed. If you hide the zero value row in the ninth column of the report, the subtotal values become bizarre and unpredictable. The best available alternative is to set the Font Color of the unwanted cells to White. The white text won't print, but it will allow the entire column to be included in the total.

Before printing the document, select the entire table and change the gridlines to nothing. Then, only the numbers will print onto the form. (If you need to use a laser printer to print onto both a heavier top sheet and a thinner back sheet, try layering the thinner sheet on top of the heavier sheet in the printer's auxiliary tray. Of course, some papers are too thin to work in any printer.)

Calculating Outside a Table

You can also perform calculations outside a table. Even though the Formula command is on the Table Menu, that doesn't mean that you can't use it to create formulas anywhere in your document. Outside a table you need to use bookmarks as a source for the values; you can use cell notation or the relative directional indicators only within a table. You can even use the SUM function to add up all the numbers that appear within a bookmarked range.

For example, suppose you bookmark Contributions to the entire sentence, "George contributed $50, Anique contributed $75, and Tony contributed $37.83." You can then add the sentence "That results in *XREF* as the total department contribution," with the intention of replacing the *XREF* with a SUM formula that calculates the $162.83 as the total contribution. The SUM function requires a minimum of two arguments. To add the values from a single bookmark, add zero as a second argument. To create the formula, select *XREF* and click on the Table menu Formula. Type *=SUM(Contributions,0)* in the Formula box and click OK.

Of course, when you sum all the numbers within a bookmark, you must be careful that the bookmark does not inadvertently include numerals that should not be added to the total. You also must not include an exclamation mark (!) within the bookmark or the result of the SUM function will be zero!

Exchanging Values with Excel

"Integrating Office Applications" in Chapter 12 explains how to link or embed one Office document inside another. For example, you can link a Word document to an Excel spreadsheet, or you can embed an Excel spreadsheet in a Word document. But what if you need to retrieve a single value from the linked document? What if you want to send a date value from a Word document to an Excel spreadsheet, perform calculations on that date value, and then return the result to Word? Linking values is different from linking entire worksheets or charts, but it does allow you to reap the benefits of an Office application's power while working in another application.

Extracting a Value from a Linked Workbook

Note The sample documents for this section are Orders.doc and Orders.xls.

Suppose someone in your department maintains an Excel workbook that includes the total order quantity for the previous month. You create a Word report that discusses the previous month's orders. To ensure that your document has the most current information, you want to retrieve the current value from the workbook into your document. You want to refer to the quantity in descriptive text, not as an Excel table. In other words, you need to extract a value from a linked Excel workbook.

Creating a Link

Your coworker's Excel worksheet looks like the one in Figure 9-14. It includes the date in cell A3 and the order total in cell B3.

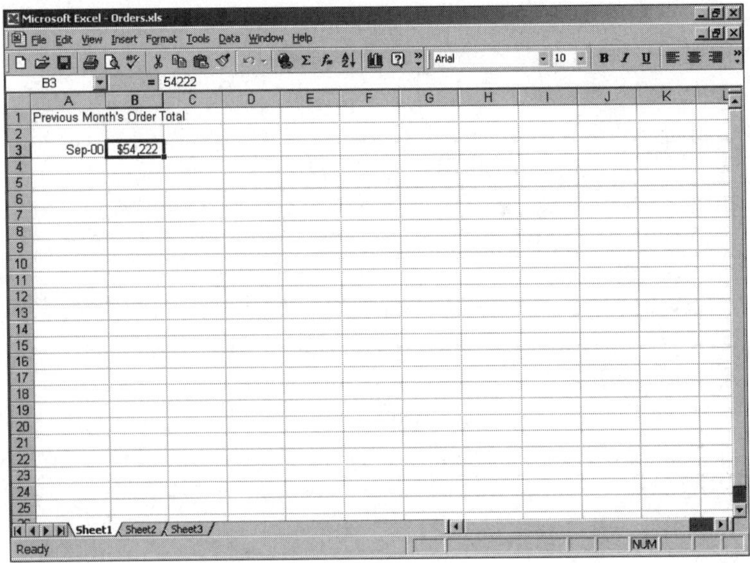

Figure 9-14
Your coworker created an Excel workbook with values you want.

In your document, you include a summary sentence that looks like this:

> "In August 2000, the order total was $53,152."

You want to retrieve both the date value and the dollar amount from the Excel workbook. Open the Excel workbook and select the cell containing the date—cell A3. Copy the cell and switch to your Word document. Select the date constant in your original sentence and click Paste Special on the Edit menu. One option in the Paste Special dialog box allows you to specify how you want the value pasted. If you select Formatted Text (RTF) from the list, the values will retain the font formatting of the

Excel worksheet. Select Unformatted Text to use the default character formatting of your Word paragraph.

The Paste Special dialog box also provides the option to paste a link. If you select the Paste option, the value appears in your document with no indication of its origin. Select the Paste Link option to create a link to the source document. As in Figure 9-15, click OK to paste the new value into the document.

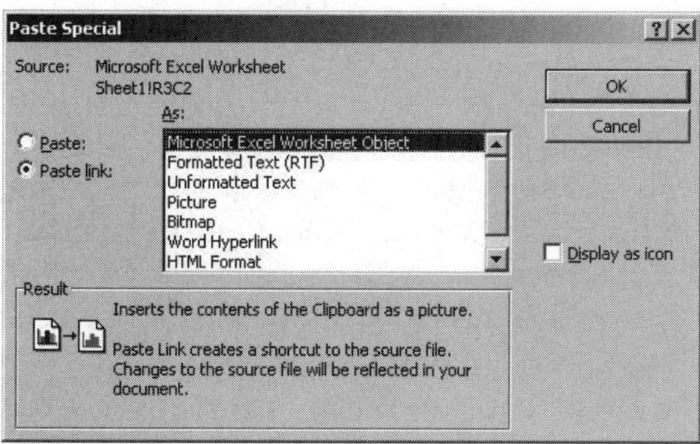

Figure 9-15
Paste unformatted text as a link.

How Word Interprets a Link

When you paste a link, Word inserts a Link field. The Link field contains several arguments that control the link. To display the field codes, click in the new Link field and press Shift+F9. Here is an example field code for linking to a cell in Excel:

{ LINK Excel.Sheet.8 C:\\ExpertCompanion\\Orders.xls Sheet1!R3C1 \a \t }

The first argument, Excel.Sheet.8, indicates the type of object you're linking to. The version number for Excel 2000 is actually 9, but the link still works, because the file format for Excel 2000 is the same as that for Excel 97, which was version 8. You could change Excel.Sheet.8 to Excel.Sheet.9 and the link would still work. In fact, for a simple link where the version is completely irrelevant, you could leave the version number off altogether and simply use Excel.Sheet as the object type.

The second argument lists the fully qualified path of the source document. Any backslash characters in the path are doubled. That's because field switches—which appear at the end of the field code—use a backslash character to identify the switch. Because the link stores the entire path of the workbook, you can move your Word document to a different folder without breaking the link. If you intend to move both the source workbook and the target Word document to a new folder, however, the link will continue to look at the old location.

(continued)

How Word Interprets a Link *(continued)*

You can create the link as a relative link so that Word will always look for the workbook in the same folder as the Word document. To make the relative link, delete everything except the actual filename. Before pressing F9 to recalculate the field, be sure that the current folder is the one containing the Word document. To do that, click Open on the file menu, navigate to the folder containing the Word document, and then click Cancel. Once you're in the correct folder, Word recalculates the field when you press F9, retrieving the value from the workbook in the current folder.

Somewhat strangely, if you press Shift+F9 to display the actual field code, you will again see the full current path in the field code, even though the filename is now relative. When displaying the field code, the relative path looks the same as the absolute path. The only way you can really tell them apart is to move the document to a different folder and open it. After moving the file, an absolute path will still refer to the original path, while a relative path will show the folder of the document.

The third argument in the Link field is the location in the file. For an Excel worksheet, this location shows both the sheet name and the cell address on that sheet. The link uses R1C1 notation for the address. (See "Picking the Right Reference Style" in Chapter 12 for details about R1C1 notation.) If the person who manages the Orders workbook renames the sheet or moves the location of the cell, the link will break. The section "Creating A Robust Link to A Named Range," later in this chapter, explains how to make the link more robust.

Switches appear at the end of the field code. The \a switch tells Word to automatically refresh the field each time you open the document. If you remove this switch, Word will leave the old value in the field, updating only when you press F9. The \t switch tells Word to import the value as unformatted text. If you had selected the formatted text option when you created the link, this switch would be \r, Rich Text Format. (If you created a link as Rich Text Format and want to convert it to unformatted text, change the \r switch to \t.)

As you can see, you don't have to use the Paste Special command to create a link. Once you understand the arguments in the Link field code, you can create a link by inserting a field. It is probably easier, however, to simply take advantage of the Paste Special command.

Adding Custom Formatting to a Field

When you extract a value from an Excel spreadsheet, it maintains the same numeric format it had in the original worksheet. You might want to convert a date or number value to your own format. For example, suppose you don't like the format of the date in the Orders workbook. Word fields provide general formatting switches that you can use to create nearly any date format you want. You can add a general formatting switch to a Link field, even though general formatting switches aren't mentioned under Options for the Link field.

To add a general date formatting switch, type \@ followed by a date code just before the closing brace of the field code. The date code to format the date with a full month name and four-digit year is *MMMM D, YYYY*. This formatting code causes the date from the Orders workbook to appear as *November 2000*. For details about general formatting switches, ask the Word Answer Wizard about *general switches.*

Creating a Robust Link to a Named Range

In the Orders.xls workbook, your coworker gave the name Orders to cell B3—the cell that contains the order total. After copying that cell, using Paste Special to paste an unformatted link, and then pressing Shift+F9, the field code will appear like the one shown in Figure 9-16. A link to a named range includes the range name instead of a cell address.

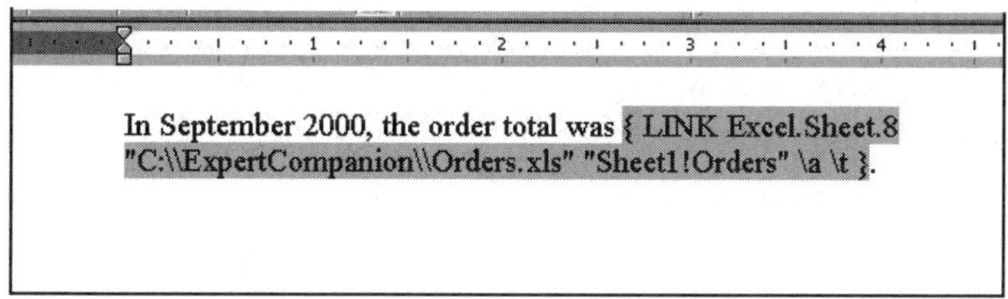

In September 2000, the order total was { LINK Excel.Sheet.8
"C:\\ExpertCompanion\\Orders.xls" "Sheet1!Orders" \a \t }.

Figure 9-16
A link to a named range includes the range name instead of a cell address.

Because the cell you copied was named, the argument that shows the location in the file displays the range name—rather than the cell address—after the sheet name. Once you link to a named range, the person who manages the workbook can change the location of the cell without disrupting your document. You are still vulnerable if the name of the worksheet changes, though. To make the link truly robust, remove the worksheet name and the exclamation point (!) from the field code. Because the range name is global to the entire Excel workbook, you don't need the worksheet name.

Making a Round-Trip Link to an Excel Worksheet

Excel has many functions that are not available in Word. For example, Excel is adept at manipulating dates. Suppose you have a generic overdue notice form letter. You type the date that a book was due in the department library into the letter. At another location in the document, a sentence explains that library privileges will be revoked on the Saturday following the two-month anniversary of the due date. Word does not have a function that will calculate the revocation date. In Excel, the formula *=CEILING(A1+60,7)* will calculate the first Saturday two months after the date stored in cell A1. (For more details about using dates in Excel, see "Manipulating Dates" in Chapter 14.)

To calculate the revocation date from the due date using Excel, first you type the due date in Word, and then you pass the value to Excel to calculate the revocation date.

Finally, you retrieve that date from Excel into the Word document. This requires a round-trip link.

Creating Links between Word and Excel

Your overdue notice form letter looks like the example shown in Figure 9-17. The filename for the letter is Overdue.doc.

Figure 9-17
Excel can calculate a value, even in Word.

You want to use Excel to calculate the revocation date. To create an embedded Excel worksheet, follow these steps:

1. Click Object on the Insert menu, select Microsoft Excel Worksheet, and click Insert. This creates an embedded worksheet.
2. Double-click the object to activate it. To change the number of cells in the grid, resize the window while the Excel object is active.
3. Click outside the object to reactivate Word.
4. Select the due date in the Word document and give it the bookmark DueDate. (If you don't give a bookmark name to the range that you will link to in Excel, Word will give it the bookmark name OLE_Link1. You're better off giving it a meaningful bookmark name of your choice.)

Note When you change the contents of a bookmark range in Word, you must be careful that the changes stay within the bookmark. Any characters that you type immediately before the first character of the bookmark range will be included within the bookmark. Any characters that you type at the end of the bookmark range will not.

If you want to change the year, at the end of the bookmark range from 2001 to 2002, type the number 2 before the number *1,* and then delete the final digit. You'll save yourself a lot of grief if you display bookmark brackets. To display bookmark brackets, click Options on the Tools menu, select the View tab, and in the Show section, select the Bookmarks check box. The Show/Hide ¶ toolbar button does not affect the bookmark brackets.

5. Select the due date and copy it.
6. Activate the embedded Excel worksheet, select cell A1, click Edit, and then click Paste Special.
7. In the Paste Special dialog box, select the Paste Link option and select Text from the As list.
8. Click OK to paste a link to the value. The linked value probably looks like a five-digit number, not like a date.

9. To change the value so it looks more like a date, you must format it. Click Cells on the Format menu, and select the Number tab.
10. In the Category list, click Custom. In the Type box, type *mmmm d, yyyy*.
11. Click OK to format the cell. Make sure column A is wide enough to allow for long month names, such as September.

Creating a Macro to Update Links

Linking a calculation through an Excel worksheet is an exciting tool—particularly if you get the worksheet to perform multiple calculations. There is only one small problem: when you close and reopen the document, the links stop automatically updating. Having the links update manually is actually not a bad thing, particularly if you create a document with multiple links going each way. You can wait until you change all the values before updating the link. If you have a macro to help you, manually updating even becomes painless.

The following *RefreshLinks* macro updates all the links both in the embedded Excel workbook and in the Word document:

```
Sub RefreshLinks()
    Dim myField As Field
    Dim myCode As String
    ActiveDocument.Shapes(1).OLEFormat.Object.updatelink Type:=2
    For Each myField In ActiveDocument.Fields
        If myField.Type = wdFieldLink Then
            myField.Update
        End If
    Next myField
End Sub
```

The first executable statement in the macro updates all the links in the Excel workbook. Here's how it works. As far as the Word document is concerned, the embedded Excel object is a Shape object. (It is possible to embed a worksheet as an InlineShape object; in that case, you would need to change Shapes to InlineShapes in the macro.) A Shape object has an OLEFormat property (which returns an OLEFormat object). One use of the OLEFormat object is to allow you to use a macro to activate an embedded object. The object also has an Object property that provides a reference to the object embedded inside the shape. In the case of an embedded Excel worksheet, the Object property returns a reference to the Workbook object.

The Workbook object has an UpdateLink method that allows you to update one or more links in the workbook. You can specify either the name of the link or its type. If you specify the name of the link, you can update only one link at a time. If you specify the type of the link, you can update all the links of that type. The type number for an OLE link is 2.

The loop in the macro updates each Link field in the document. It loops through all the fields, but it only updates if the type of the field is *wdFieldLink*.

To run the macro, create a custom toolbar—just for this document—that allows you to refresh the links. To create the toolbar, follow these steps:

1. Click Customize on the Tools menu, and select the Toolbar tab.
2. Click New to create a new toolbar. Choose the current document name as the location for the toolbar.
3. Give the toolbar the name *Overdue*, and click OK to create the toolbar and return to the Customize dialog box.
4. On the Controls tab, select the Macros category, select the RefreshLinks macro from the list of items, and drag the macro to the toolbar.
5. Right-click the new button and change the name to *Refresh*. Close the Customize dialog box.

The toolbar will appear when you open the document, and disappear when you close it. Each time you change the due date, click the Refresh button to update the links.

Chapter 10

Fine-Tune a Document

In This Chapter

After you finish creating a document, you often want to fine-tune it. For example, you might want to globally replace items within the document, you might want to proofread the document, or you might want to make customized copies of the document. Microsoft Word's Find and Replace tools help you make those global modifications; its proofing tools help you check spelling and grammar; and its mail merge tools help you customize document copies. For the most part, these tools are straightforward, easy to use, and well documented. Each of these tools has features, capabilities, and quirks, however, that might not be so obvious. This chapter will help you make the most of Word's fine-tuning tools.

Finding and Replacing Text

Finding and replacing is a familiar activity in Word. Word has additional find and replace capabilities, however, that are often under-utilized. The most interesting of these under-utilized capabilities appear when you click the More button on the Find And Replace dialog box.

Finding and Replacing Formatting

One advanced replace option allows you to replace formatting throughout a document. Suppose, for example, that you want to convert any text that is formatted using the Italic font style to the Emphasis style. Use the following steps to convert all italicized text to use the Emphasis character style:

1. Click Replace on the Edit menu to display the Find And Replace dialog box.
2. Click the More button.
3. Click in the Find What drop-down list, but don't type anything.
4. Click the Format button, and then select the Font command.
5. Select Italic from the Font Style list, and then click OK.
6. Click in the Replace With drop-down list and then click the Format button.
7. Select the Style command, and then select the Emphasis style. Click OK. The dialog box will look similar to Figure 10-1.
8. Click the Replace All button. Nothing will appear to have changed, since the Emphasis style already has the italic format.

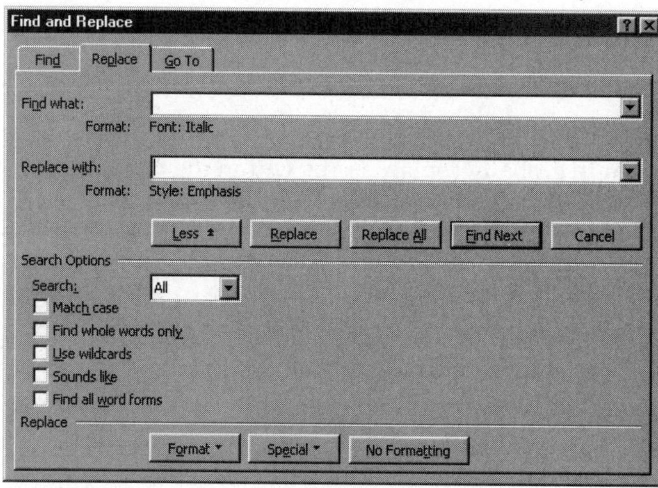

Figure 10-1
Replace character formatting with a character style.

Once you have converted the italicized text to the Emphasis style, you can change all italicized text in the document at once simply by changing the style. For example, once the formatting has been converted, if you use the Style dialog box to add the Blinking Background animation text to the Emphasis style, all the italicized text will then be both italic and blinking text. Of course, you could also replace the formatting directly—that is, replace the italic font with the italic, blinking background text effect—but converting the formatting to use a character style makes it easier to make additional changes to the style in the future. In fact, you could switch the format of the emphasis simply by copying new styles from a different template, as explained in section "Copying Styles to and from a Template" in Chapter 7.

Finding Special Characters

When the Find What box is the active control, the extended Find And Replace dialog box uses the Special button at the bottom to provide an additional 21 common elements that can be found and replaced, as shown in Figure 10-2.

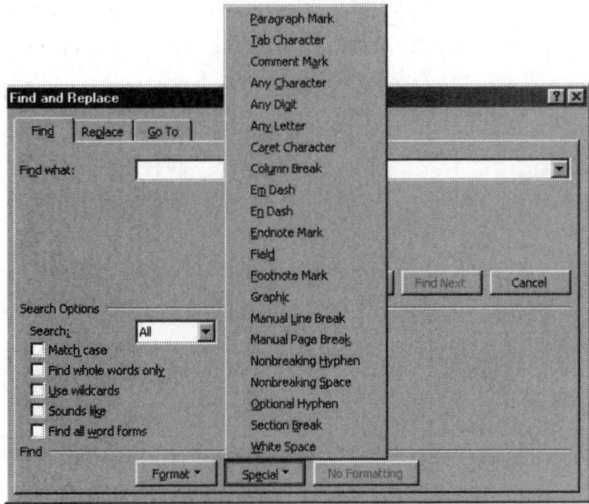

Figure 10-2
Word makes it easy to search for 21 named marks.

When you select one of the elements in the list, Word places a code prefixed by the caret character (^) into the Find What drop-down list. Most of these special elements are self-explanatory, and several elements in the list are particularly useful.

The White space code (^w) refers to any sequence of spaces, non-breaking spaces, or tab characters. Suppose you want to remove any spaces at the end of paragraphs. Insert the code for White Space (^w) and the code for Paragraph Mark (^p) in the Find What drop-down list, and then insert the code for Paragraph Mark (^p) in the Replace With drop-down list. (The White Space code does not match a paragraph mark or a manual line break.)

Even without using pattern matching (which is discussed in the following section), you can insert the codes for Any Character (^?), Any Digit (^#), or Any Letter (^$) into the Find What drop-down list. This allows you to search for simple combinations such as a product number code that begins with a letter and that is followed by two digits. The result code would be (^$^#^#), representing Any Letter, Any Digit, and Any Digit.

If the Replace With box is the active control, some of the options drop off, but two new and very useful codes are added: Clipboard (^c) and Find value (^&). Use Clipboard (^c) to insert the contents of the clipboard. This is particularly useful when you want to find or replace an item that cannot be typed directly from the keyboard into the Find What or Replace With drop-down lists, such as a graphic or a field code. By copying the item in the document to the clipboard, you can then paste the copied item into the Find What drop-down list or the Replace With drop-down list. In "Creating Sequentially Numbered Labels," later in this chapter, this feature is used to insert sequential numbers into labels.

Use the Find What Text (^&) command option to paste the string that matches the search. This is particularly useful when you are searching for wildcards or for all word forms. For example, suppose you want to enclose any verb that is a form of *to be* in parentheses. Select the Find All Word Forms check box, type *is* in the Find What drop-down list, and type *^&* in the Replace With drop-down list, as shown in Figure 10-3. (You do not need to include *^&* in the Replace With drop-down list when you are changing the formatting of the text that has been found.)

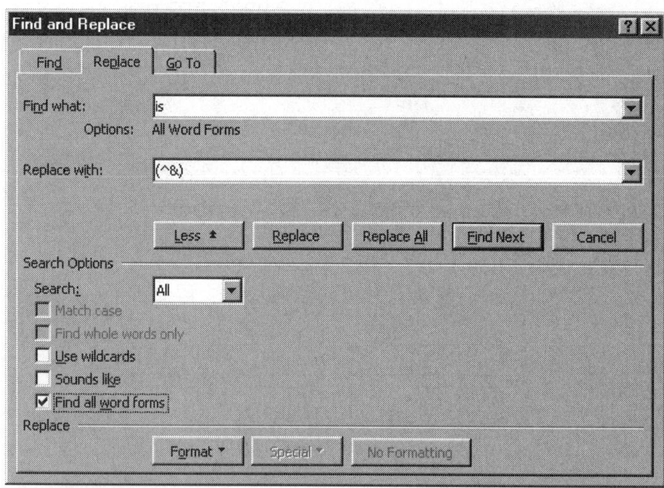

Figure 10-3
The special code ^& refers to any found item.

There is one additional search code available for either the Find What or the Replace With drop-down lists. It is used for specifying a character based on its ANSI

(American National Standards Institute) code. This code was originally designed so that you could find any character that is difficult to type into the Find What drop-down list—most notably, accented characters from other languages such as the é character. You can insert these characters using the Insert, Symbol command. Rather than use the ANSI code, it's easier to simply type an example of the character and then select it before you open the Find dialog box. If the current selection is a single word or portion of a word, the Find What drop-down list defaults to containing the character you have selected.

Chapter 10

Note The Help file does contain a topic that describes all the Find codes; it is hidden away. Search for the topic *Find and Replace Formatting* within that Help topic, click the link to the topic *Find and Replace Paragraph Marks, Page Breaks, and Other Items.* Finally, click the link to the topic *Type a Code for the Item.*

Finding Patterns

Note The sample document for this section is Spinoza.doc.

If you select the Use Wildcards check box in the Find And Replace dialog box, Word uses the Windows Explorer wildcard characters—a question mark (?) to match a single character, and an asterisk (*) to match any string of characters. You do not need to prefix the wildcard with a caret, and you cannot use the wildcard codes ^#, ^?, and ^$ while the Use Wildcard check box is selected. These simple wildcards are convenient, but they barely scratch the surface of Word's pattern matching capabilities.

Finding a Regular Expression

Suppose you have a document that contains numbered paragraphs and sentences such as the example shown in Figure 10-4. The numbers are each surrounded by parentheses or brackets.

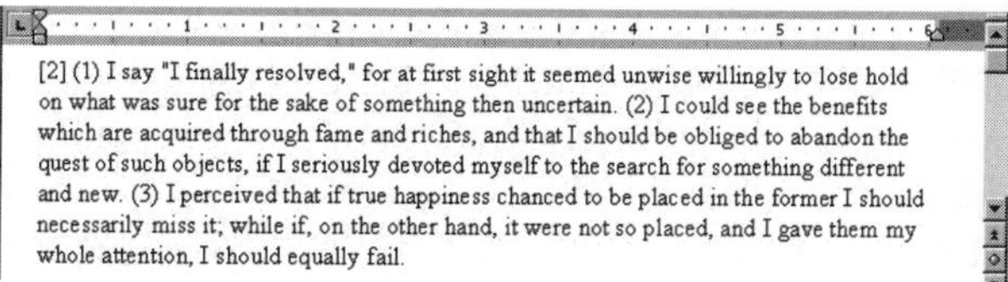

[2] (1) I say "I finally resolved," for at first sight it seemed unwise willingly to lose hold on what was sure for the sake of something then uncertain. (2) I could see the benefits which are acquired through fame and riches, and that I should be obliged to abandon the quest of such objects, if I seriously devoted myself to the search for something different and new. (3) I perceived that if true happiness chanced to be placed in the former I should necessarily miss it; while if, on the other hand, it were not so placed, and I gave them my whole attention, I should equally fail.

Figure 10-4
You might want to remove text that matches a pattern.

Now suppose that you want to remove all the numbers, along with the surrounding parentheses or brackets. You can't use an ordinary find and replace operation because each instance you want to remove will be different from the previous one.

What you need to use is a *Regular Expression* pattern. An *expression* is a string of characters, and it is a regular expression if you can use a pattern to define it. A regular expression is like a wildcard character, only much more powerful and expressive. For the numbers in the sample document, you need to find the following pattern: an opening bracket or parenthesis, one or more digits, a closing bracket or parenthesis, and a space.

When you search for files in Windows Explorer, you can use a question mark (?) to replace a single character and an asterisk (*) to replace one or more characters in a filename. With an ordinary wildcard, you use a question mark (?) to indicate a single character at a given position in the filename. With a regular expression, you identify a list of acceptable characters for the position by enclosing the characters in brackets. For example, to find win, won, or wan, you can use the expression *w[ioa]n.*

You can also use a hyphen to indicate a range of characters. For example, to find any digit, use the expression *[0-9]*. Even though there are multiple characters within the brackets, the expression matches only a single character—the brackets tell Word to match any one of the characters. To reverse the set contained in the brackets, insert an exclamation point (!) as the first character within the bracket. For example, to find any character except a digit, use the expression *[!0-9]*.

With ordinary wildcards, you use an asterisk (*) to indicate one or more characters at the given position. (It is true that Word will also help you find the existence of zero characters; you'll need to experiment with this option to fully understand its methods.) With a regular expression, you specify precisely how many occurrences of a character (or set of characters) to match by typing the minimum and maximum numbers in braces. For example, to match a three- to five-digit number, use the regular expression *[0-9]{3,5}*. If you specify only the first number, the expression matches exactly the number of characters you specify. For example, the expression *[0-9]{3}* matches a three-digit number. If you omit the second number but leave the comma, the maximum number becomes infinite. For example, the expression *[0-9]{2,}* matches two or more sequential digits. Because the pattern *{1,}*—meaning one or more—is so common, it can be replaced by a single @ character. For example, the expression *[0-9]@* matches one or more digits.

The brackets that specify a set of characters are smart enough to let you include a bracket as one of the characters. For example, to find either an opening bracket or an opening parenthesis, use the expression *[[(]*. Likewise, to find either a closing bracket or a closing parenthesis, use the expression *[])]*. If you include a bracket, brace, or parenthesis as a simple character—that is, not within brackets—you must precede it with a backslash—an escape character. The escape character tells Word to treat the subsequent character as an ordinary character and not as a regular expression code.

Replacing a Regular Expression

You now have all the pieces necessary to eliminate of the numbers from the sample document. Take the following steps to find and replace regular expression text:

1. On the Replace tab of the Find And Replace dialog box, type the regular expression *[[(][0-9]@[])]* in the Find What drop-down list. There is a space after the final bracket in the expression. Do not type anything in the Replace With drop-down list.
2. Click the More button to extend the dialog box.
3. Select the Use Wildcards check box.
4. Click the Find Next button a few times to validate the search.
5. Click the Replace All button to complete the replace operation.

You can even use regular expressions to swap the order of expressions. Enclose each of two or more regular expressions within parentheses. You can then refer to each matching expression by a number preceded by a backslash. Suppose that rather than deleting the paragraph and sentence numbers of the document shown earlier in Figure 10-1, you want to swap the order—so that the paragraph number follows the sentence number. In the Find What drop-down list, type the expression *(\[[0-9]@\])(\([0-9]@\)).* In the Replace With drop-down list, type *\2\1.*

Regular expressions are extremely powerful. They can also be intimidating. Microsoft seems reluctant for users to find out about them. There is documentation in Help about regular expressions, but it is very hard to find, and it avoids the technical term regular expression. To find the specifics on regular expression codes, search Help using the words *Find and Replace.* Then select the topic *Fine-Tune a Search by Using Wildcard Characters,* and click the *Type a Wildcard character* link.

Managing Proofing Tools

At twelve, my son was a very creative a writer. Unfortunately, the creativity applied not only to his plots and characterizations, but also to his spelling and grammar. Sometimes, as I tried to clean up a story so that others could enjoy it, I had to have him dictate the story so I could decipher the language. One day, he brought me a story he had written that was immaculate: everything was spelled correctly, and the grammar was impeccable. I asked him who helped him clean it up, and he told me he did it himself. He said that whenever he saw a red or green squiggly line, he right-clicked and chose the correct option from the shortcut menu. Then I remembered that I had just installed a new version of Word—complete with enhanced proofing tools.

As wonderful as Word's proofing tools might be, there are times when they can become frustrating, particularly when writing technical documents or when creating sophisticated subordinate clauses. Word often detects as an error something that really is not an error.

One option for dealing with the problem, of course, is to simply ignore the squiggly lines, or to turn them off by clicking Options on the Tools menu, selecting the Spelling And Grammar tab, and then selecting both the Hide Spelling Errors In This Document check box and the Hide Grammatical Errors In This Document check box, as shown in Figure 10-5.

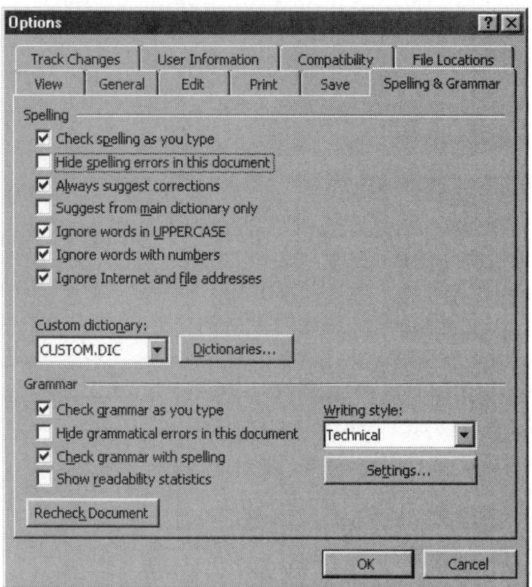

Figure 10-5
You can hide spelling and grammatical error marks.

Disabling proofing marks does hide invalid marks, but it also hides marks for legitimate errors. What if you want Word to notify you of real errors, but not to display non-errors? Word checks for two types of errors in documents: spelling errors and grammatical errors. Spelling errors are underlined in red, and grammatical errors are underlined in green. In many ways, the two types of errors behave similarly, but ignoring an invalid error requires a different strategy for dealing with each error type.

Ignoring Spelling Errors

When you right-click an ostensible spelling error, Word provides two options for removing the error mark, as shown in Figure 10-6.

You can ignore the word for the entire document, or you can add the word to a custom dictionary. Adding a word to a custom dictionary is perfect for a legitimate word that is not in Word's built-in dictionary. As a good general rule, add a word to a custom dictionary if you intentionally use the word in multiple documents. If the unique spelling occurs in only one document—for example, if it is the name of a macro or

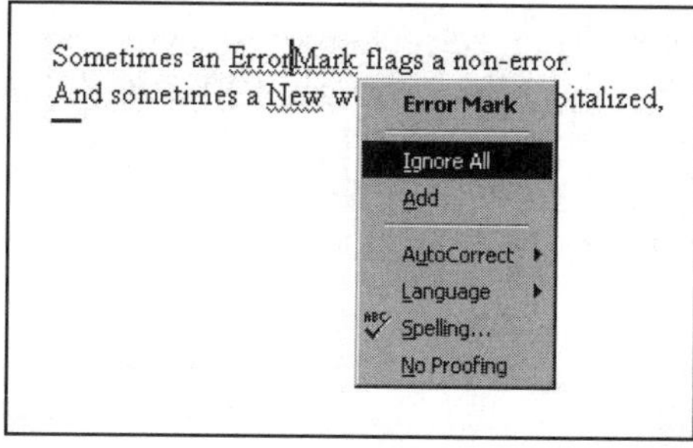

Figure 10-6
You can ignore or add a word improperly flagged as misspelled.

Chapter 10

a variable—you might not want to add it to your custom dictionary. In cases like those, choose Ignore All to ignore all instances of the word in the current document.

The problem with using Ignore All is that if you inadvertently ignore a word that truly is misspelled, the only way to reset that single word is click the Recheck Document button in the Spelling & Grammar dialog box, which will clear the ignore flag for all words in the document. In other words, there isn't any way to selectively remove the ignore status from a single word. In fact, even Undo on the Edit menu does not restore the error state of the word.

Ignoring Grammatical Errors

When you right-click a grammatical error, Word only offers the option to ignore the error mark, as shown in Figure 10-7.

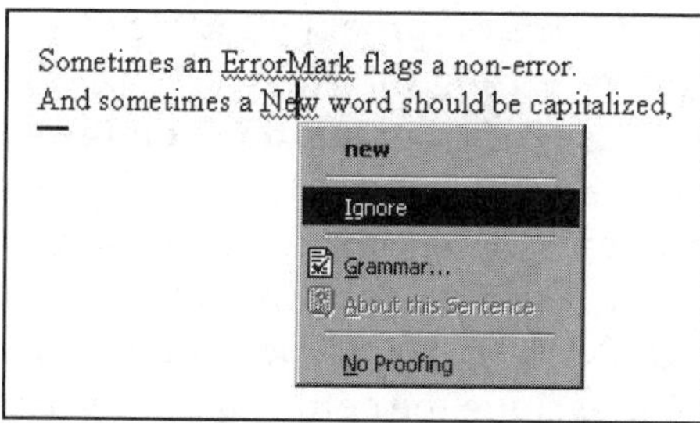

Figure 10-7
Word allows you to ignore an apparent grammatical error.

Ignoring a grammatical error does not ignore the error throughout the entire document; it ignores only that specific grammatical error. The problem with the ignore command is that it is reset each time you edit the sentence. It can be frustrating to ignore a grammatical error, only to see it reappear when you make a completely unrelated edit to a different part of the sentence. If you want to ignore a grammatical error permanently—without having the error mark reappear—change the language of the offending portion of the sentence to use No Proofing. Specifically, select the text and then click Language on the Tools menu. Then select Set Language. Select the Do Not Check Spelling Or Grammar check box as shown in Figure 10-8, and then click OK.

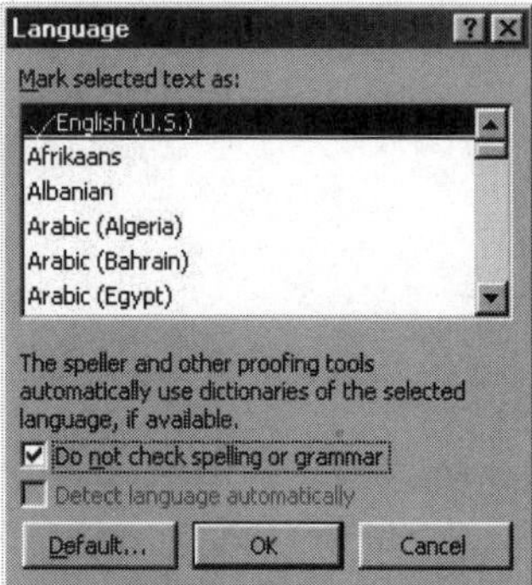

Figure 10-8
Set the Language to Do Not Check Spelling or Grammar (No Proofing) for selected passages.

The check box caption is a long-winded way of saying No Proofing, which is a Character property. It is assigned as a character attribute, and it is removed by clearing the character attributes (pressing Ctrl+Spacebar).

Turning off proofing for grammatical errors is actually very effective. You eliminate the error mark, but you retain complete control over whether the error is detected. If you want Word to redetect the error, select the range of text that includes the error and reset the character formatting using Ctrl+Spacebar.

Creating a Macro to Ignore Grammatical Errors

You might want to create a macro that turns off proofing for the selected text. The following *NoProof* macro does just that. Setting the NoProofing property for the selected range is trivial, but also frustrating. If the insertion point is in the middle of a range of text that contains an error, setting the No Proofing property for the selection does not eliminate the error mark. To eliminate the error mark, you must disable proofing for the entire range of text that includes the error. The *NoProof* macro calls two subroutines: one that extends the range to include any contiguous italicized text, and one that extends the range to include the entire current error. It then sets the NoProofing property of the resulting range to *True*.

```
Sub NoProof()
    Dim myRange As Range
    Set myRange = Selection.Range

    If myRange.Start = myRange.End Then
        ExpandItalic myRange
        ExpandError myRange
        myRange.Expand
    End If
```

```
    myRange.NoProofing = True
End Sub
```

The macro assigns the selected range to a Range object variable so that it can adjust that range without changing the selection on the screen. If the initially selected range is larger than zero characters—that is, if the End position of the range is not the same as the Start position—the macro does not expand the range, it only checks the selected text. A Selection object has a Type property that simplifies the process of checking the Start and End positions of a range. The expression *Selection.Type = wdNoSelection* returns *True* if the selection is an insertion point. A Range object does not have a Type property, however, so you must explicitly compare the Start and End positions.

ExpandItalic and *ExpandError* are subroutines which are explained in the following sections. Expand is a method of a Range object, which is similar to pressing the F8 function key to expand the range to the next larger unit. The default unit is a word, so using Expand with no argument expands to include a word. If you want to expand a range to include the entire paragraph, use the *myRange.Expand wdParagraph* statement. Once the range has been determined, you can simply set its NoProofing property to *True*.

Creating a Subroutine That Finds Contiguous Italics

Often, nominally improper grammatical expressions are in italicized statements. The following *ExpandItalic* subroutine expands a range to include all italic characters on either side of the selection. First, it expands the Start of the range, and then it expands the End of the range.

```
Private Sub ExpandItalic(r As Range)
    Dim i As Long
    Do While ActiveDocument.Range(r.Start - 1, r.Start).Font.Italic
        r.MoveStart wdCharacter, -1
    Loop
    Do While ActiveDocument.Range(r.End, r.End + 1).Font.Italic
        r.MoveEnd wdCharacter, 1
    Loop
End Sub
```

A *Do While* loop repeats as long as the condition expression returns *True*. In this subroutine, the first loop checks the font of the character just preceding the Start of the range. As long as that character is italic, the macro moves the Start of the range to include it. The second loop does the same for the character just following the End of the range. Technically, this routine will fail if you are searching at the very beginning or the very end of a document. When creating macros for your own use, it is often better to allow for the rare possibility of an error, in favor of keeping the macro easy to understand.

Creating a Subroutine That Finds a Complete Error

To turn off the green underline for a grammatical error, you must turn off proofing for the entire range that includes the error. The following *ExpandError* subroutine extends a range to include the entire error it might be a part of. If the range is not part of an error, the subroutine does not change the range.

```
Private Sub ExpandError(r As Range)
    Dim g As Range
    For Each g In r.Paragraphs(1).Range.GrammaticalErrors
        If r.InRange(g) Then
            Set r = g
            Exit Sub
        End If
    Next g
End Sub
```

The subroutine wants to find the grammatical error (if any) that contains the specified range. A Range object has a GrammaticalErrors property, but that property does not refer to grammatical errors that contain the range; rather, it refers to grammatical errors contained within the range. The subroutine needs to cast a wider net. Grammatical errors always occur at a level smaller than a paragraph, so by finding all the grammatical errors contained within the paragraph and then checking each one to see if the specified range is within it, the subroutine can find the error that contains the range. You could make the subroutine slightly faster by adding the statement *If g.Start > r.End Then Exit Sub* after the *End If* statement.

Creating a Macro That Checks Each Error in the Document

When you click Spelling And Grammar on the Tools menu, Word cycles through each spelling or grammatical error in the document, allowing you to correct or ignore each one it finds. As you inspect a grammatical error, the dialog box appears to provide the option to ignore the error or skip the sentence, presumably leaving the error marked. In fact, both the Ignore button and the Next Sentence button ignore the error—and they both do so it in such a way that editing the sentence causes the error to reappear.

Unfortunately, you cannot add a No Proofing button to the dialog box. But you can create the following *NoProofAll* macro which will cycle through each grammatical error in your document and ask if you want to set the No Proofing property for the error:

```
Sub NoProofAll()
    Dim r As Range
    For Each r In ActiveDocument.GrammaticalErrors
        r.Select
        Select Case MsgBox("Disable proofing for this selection?", _
            vbYesNoCancel)
        Case vbCancel
            Exit Sub
```

```
        Case vbYes
            Selection.NoProofing = True
        End Select
    Next r
End Sub
```

This macro loops through the collection of grammatical errors for the entire document. For each error range, it selects the range—to make it easy to see—and then prompts you whether to assign *True* to the NoProofing property.

Managing Mail Merge Documents

On the one hand, I fail to feel appropriately elated when I receive a friendly bulk mailing from the local auto plaza assuring me, "Reed Jacobson (might have) won the grand prize!" On the other hand, I fail to feel appropriately reassured when I get a letter from the local HMO clinic assuring me, "the patient(s) test(s) resulted in negative diagnosis(es) for the specified illness(es)." A merged mailing can insult, or it can personalize.

Choosing a Mail Merge Data Source

A mail merge document consists of two components: a main document—which serves as a template for the output document, and a data source—each record (or row) which typically results in a new copy of the main document. A mail merge document requires a source of records for the merge. The data source must be a simple list with a field heading for each column. Word can use almost anything as a data source, as long as it is a list with column headings. In fact, the interplay of possible data sources can be confusing. This section will elucidate the most likely—and the most confusing—data source options.

Word provides four ways to communicate with a data source:

1. Open the data source in the file directly.
2. Use Dynamic Data Exchange (DDE) to communicate with an application that has the data source file open.
3. Use an Open DataBase Connectivity (ODBC) driver to retrieve the data source.
4. Use Microsoft Query to retrieve a data source.

Regardless of the actual nature of the data source file, Word always uses one of these four mechanisms to retrieve the data. In the sections that follow, the implications of these options are explained in the context of different source document types.

Note The Microsoft Query option typically uses both DDE (for Word to communicate with Query) and ODBC (for Query to communicate with the ultimate data source). This is the most complex option, and it can usually be avoided. The primary reason for using Microsoft Query is that you can create a customized query similar to what you could create in Access. If you have Access available, much of the benefit of using Microsoft Query disappears. Simply create a query in Access using all its available tools. "Extracting a List From a Database" in Chapter 15 explains more about using Microsoft Query.

Using a Word Table as a Data Source

The simplest data source is a Word table—or something that Word can interpret as a Word table, such as a tab-delimited text file or an HTML document containing a table. To create a new Word table you can use as a data source, choose the Create Data Source option in the Mail Merge Helper. To open an existing document as a simple Word data source, choose the Open Data Source option and select either All Word Documents or Text Files from the Files Of Type drop-down list.

When you choose any of these simple data source options, Word opens the document directly. The advantage of a simple Word table is that Word does not need to negotiate with any other application to retrieve the data, and you can easily edit the values in the data source—either by using the Data Form dialog box or by opening the data source directly. The biggest reason not to use a simple Word table is that you most likely already have suitable data sources available in other applications. Excel, Access, and Outlook are the most likely alternative sources.

Using Excel as a Data Source

Note The sample document for this section is Products.xls.

If you open an Excel workbook as a data source in the Mail Merge Helper, Word uses DDE to communicate with Excel. Word has two other options available, as well. To access the other options, select the Select Method check box before opening the Excel file. With the Select Method check box selected, you are given three options, as shown in Figure 10-9.

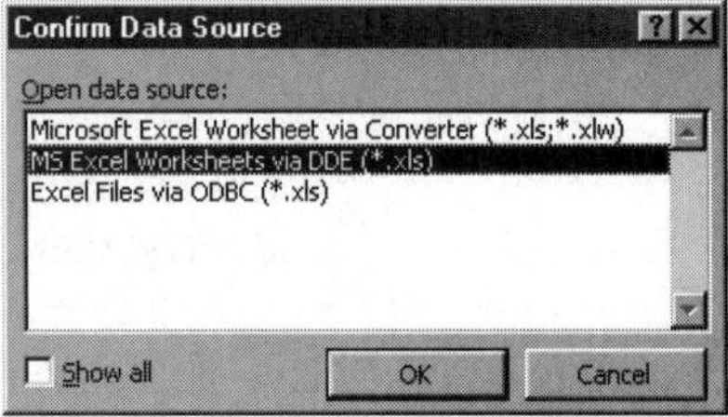

Figure 10-9
The Select Method check box gives you three additional options for retrieving data from Excel.

Converting an Excel Worksheet If you choose the Converter option, Word opens the actual Excel workbook and uses it directly as the data source. The Converter uses the same mechanism if you open an Excel file directly in Word. That is, it is the same as if you clicked Open on the File menu, and selected Microsoft Excel Workbook in the files of a type drop-down list. Word uses its converter to import all the worksheets, a selected worksheet, or a named range within the worksheet into a Word table. Word does not create a copy of the workbook in a Word document; it literally opens the Excel workbook as if it were a Word document. This is similar to what Word does if you open a WordPerfect document; Word simply translates the document as it opens it.

Unlike many of Word's import filters, however, Word does not have a corresponding export filter for Excel. This means that if you make changes to the data source—if you click the Edit button in the Mail Merge Helper dialog box—you get into a strange situation: you can make changes to the data, but if you save the file, Word saves the file as a Word document with the Excel extension. This makes the file essentially unusable to Excel. The Converter option is very good, but only if you don't need to edit the document.

Using Excel as a DDE Data Source The second option is to open the workbook or worksheet via DDE. The DDE approach launches the Excel application and requests that Excel provide the data for the mail merge. Each time you retrieve the values for the workbook, the DDE option launches Excel, if it is not already running. (Excel must be open the entire time a mail merge operation takes place. Word does not simply extract the data all at once from the worksheet; it retrieves the data dynamically as it processes the records in the mail merge.)

Using DDE, you can select the entire first worksheet in the workbook, or you can select a named range that is defined in the first worksheet. If the workbook is open, DDE looks at the open copy of the workbook—that is, any changes that you have made to the workbook since the time you last saved or opened it are reflected in the retrieved values. Even if the Excel workbook is already open, however, Word closes the workbook after it extracts the data.

Using Excel as an ODBC Data Source The third option for retrieving data from an Excel workbook is to use ODBC. Like Word's direct Excel import filter, ODBC does not require that Excel be running to work. In effect, the Excel ODBC driver disguises the Excel workbook as a database. Using the ODBC approach, you can retrieve all the data from any worksheet in the workbook, as well as from any named range in the entire workbook. When you first see the list of tables in the dialog box, you see only the list of defined range names. To see the list of worksheets, click Options and select the System Tables check box, in addition to the Tables check box (which is selected by default), as shown in Figure 10-10.

With both Tables and System Tables selected, Excel will display both range names and worksheet names. There is no logical reason why worksheets should be called

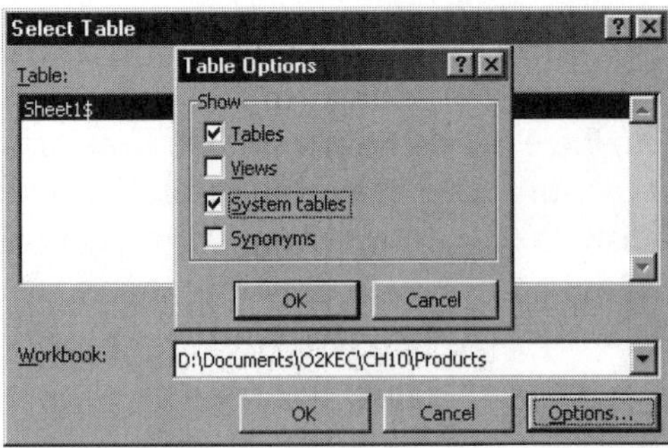

Figure 10-10
To see Excel worksheet, select the System Tables check box.

system tables; that's just the way the worksheet driver works. Each worksheet name ends in a dollar sign; you can simply ignore that suffix.

At the bottom of the dialog box is a list that allows you to select any Excel workbook within the current folder. This is an artifact of the fact that the same ODBC dialog box can be used for dBase files, as well as for Excel workbooks. Selecting a different workbook changes the list of sheet or range names, but it does not actually change the workbook that ODBC uses as a source. In other words, do not select a different workbook from the list or you might thoroughly confuse the ODBC driver.

Using Access as a Data Source

Note The sample document for this section is Toys.mdb.

When you retrieve data from an Access database, Word typically uses DDE to communicate with Access. If you select the Select Method check box, you will see two of the three previous options that were available to Excel, as shown in Figure 10-11.

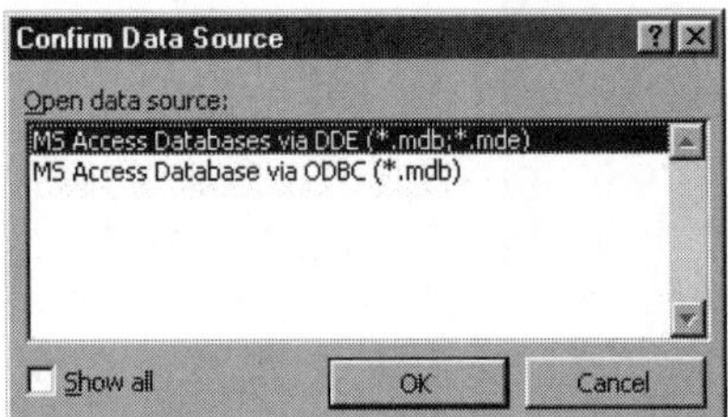

Figure 10-11
The Select Method box shows two options for communicating with Access.

As with Excel, the DDE option launches Access and communicates with the application to retrieve the data. The DDE option for Access has a couple of twists that are worth exploring. When you select DDE, Access displays the list of all the visible tables and queries in the database.

When you select a query, the dialog box includes the Link To Query option. The meaning of this check box can be a little bit confusing. (In fact, even the example in the Help topic on the subject is incorrect.) Here's how it works: An Access Query is a Structured Query Language (SQL) statement. If the check box is cleared, Word copies the SQL statement from the query into Word. After Word copies the query definition, the original Access query becomes irrelevant—you could even delete it with no effect. If the Link To Query check box is selected, Word creates a new, simple SQL statement that retrieves the contents of the query. In either case, Word always extracts the most current data values from the table.

The Link To Query check box does make a difference if you try to edit the data source. If the data source is linked to a query, clicking the Edit button opens the query in Access, where you can then switch to Design view and change the definition of the query. If you do not link to the query but subsequently edit the data source, Word breaks the link to Access, copying the current values to a Word table.

Initiating a Link From Access Another way to achieve the same effect as a DDE link to an Access query is to initiate the new link from Access. In Access, select the query or table you want to use as the data source and click the OfficeLinks drop-down button. Select Merge It With MS Word from the menu. This gives you the option of choosing an existing Word document or creating a new one (which will use the default Form Letters 1 style), as shown in Figure 10-12. In either event, the Merge To Word Wizard creates a DDE link from the document to the Access data source.

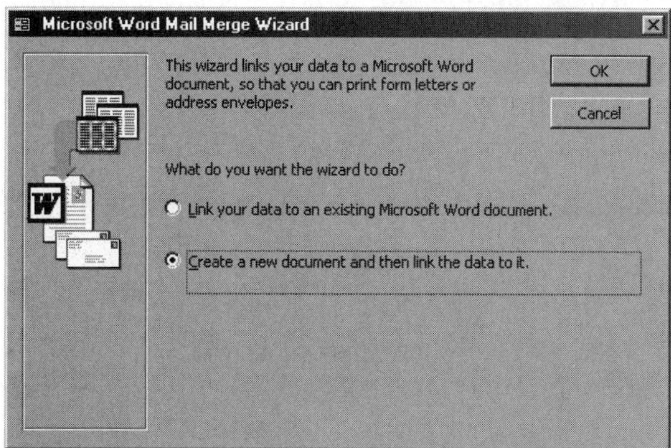

Figure 10-12
Initiating a mail merge from Access results in a DDE connection.

If you want to extract constant values from Access, first select the query or table. Then, on the OfficeLinks button, click the Publish It With MS Word option. This exports the resultant records set to a Word table in Rich Text Format, which you can then use as a Word data source for a merge operation.

Using ODBC to Link to an Access Data Source As with Excel, you can choose to link to Access via ODBC. When you use ODBC, Word does not need to launch Access; it talks directly to the database. The ODBC driver typically shows only tables, but you can also link to a query. Click Options and select Views, in addition to Tables, as shown in Figure 10-13. The word View is the ODBC-equivalent of the word Query.

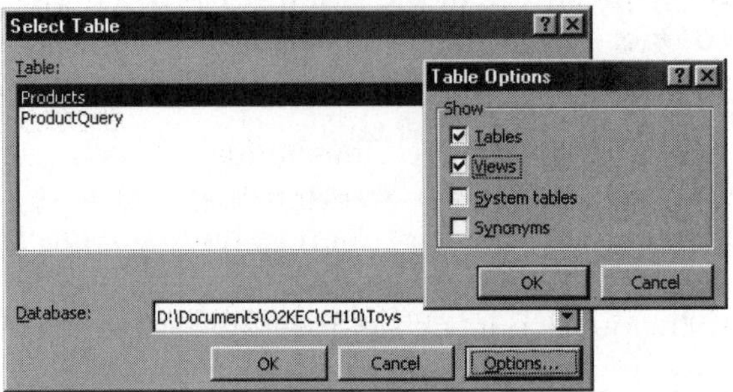

Figure 10-13
To link to an Access query via ODBC, select the Views option.

When you use ODBC to link to either a table or a query, you cannot edit the source data. If you link to a table, Word breaks the link to Access when you edit the data source, converting the table to a Word table. If you link to a query, Word offers to let you use Microsoft Query to edit the data. In Microsoft Query, however, you can change only the definition of the query—for example, you can add new criterion to the query—you cannot change the values in the source table.

Using Outlook as a Data Source

If you are creating a mailing to send to associates, you will probably store the contact information in Outlook. Outlook and Word work well together to create mail merge documents.

Initiating the Mail Merge from Word When you select Use Address Book in a Mail Merge document and then choose Outlook Address Book, Outlook exports the entire contents of the address book to a temporary document, which then serves as the data source for Word. After that, Word uses the document as if it were a Word table.

When you use the Outlook Address Book as the data source, Word creates a temporary, virtual file, which is the data extracted from your Outlook Address Book. It might take a few seconds to create the virtual file, but once the file is created, you can make several changes to the Word document without having to extract the address book data again. If you click Tools, Mail Merge, and click the Edit button under Data Source, you can edit the values in the virtual Outlook data source file. Editing the virtual file does not propogate changes back to Outlook. Conversely, changes you make to the Outlook Address Book while merging a document are not reflected in the merged file.

The virtual Outlook file disappears once you close Word. The next time you open the main document, Word will complain that it cannot find the data source and prompt you to locate the source. From the Word dialog box, click Options and then click Remove Data/Header Source to remove the data source and open the document. Once the document is open, click Tools, Mail Merge, and click the Get Data button to recreate the virtual file. You can use this method of closing and opening the file to reflect changes in Outlook.

There is a simpler way, however, to refresh the virtual file. In the merge main document, click Mail Merge on the Tools menu. In the Data Source group, click Edit, then click the View Source button to open the virtual file in Word. Immediately close the file. When you are prompted to save changes, click No. Word then recreates the virtual address book.

Initiating the Mail Merge from Outlook One problem with initiating the transfer of your Address Book data in Word is that the entire address book will be retrieved; any filtering happens solely in Word. If your address book is large, the mail merge can really bog down. If you initiate the mail merge from Outlook, you will have a lot more control over which contacts and which fields are included in the merge.

In Outlook, select the Contacts folder and select specific contacts. You can also use a View to filter the contacts. For more information on using Views in Outlook, see "Creating and Changing Views" in Chapter 20. Once you have selected the contacts in Outlook, click Tools, Mail Merge. In the Mail Merge Contacts dialog box, select the All Contacts In Current View, or select the option Only Selected Contacts, as shown in Figure 10-14.

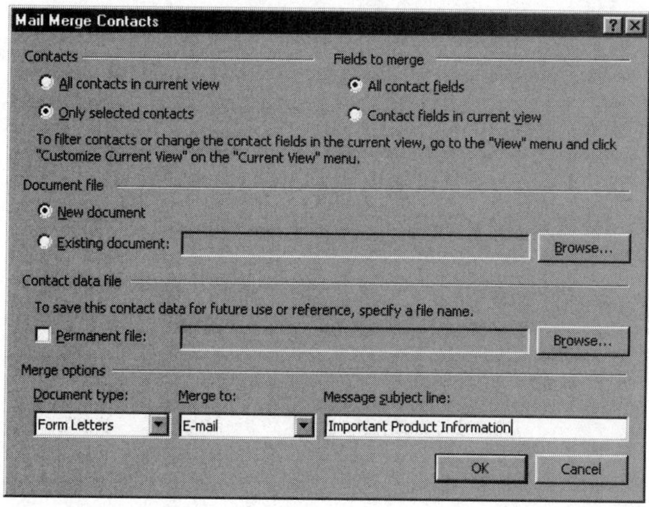

Figure 10-14
To specify only certain contacts, initiate the merge from Outlook.

The Mail Merge Contacts dialog box also allows you to specify which document type you want, and what the target for the merge operations should be. In principle, you can change these later in Word, but it is more convenient to do so while you are initiating the Mail Merge in Outlook. If you will be generating merged e-mail messages, it is particularly helpful to specify the merge information in Outlook, because you can conveniently enter the Subject of the message and Outlook will automatically flag the e-mail address field, which is required when merging to e-mail.

When you initiate a Mail Merge operation from Outlook, Outlook generates a file containing the exported records, which Word then uses as the data source. If you specify a filename when you begin the export operation, you have control over the location of the file. If you don't, Outlook will create a file in the Windows Temporary folder. That file remains, even after you close the main document, until you clear out the temporary folder.

Creating Mail Merge Output

Typically, when you think of a mail merge operation, you think of creating form letters or perhaps envelopes. Word can create other types of documents, as well. The four types of documents you can create actually overlap quite a bit. If you understand how these four document types work, you can create sophisticated merge results that go far beyond a simple form letter.

Understanding Merge Fields

When you add a merge field to a document, you implicitly add an ordinary Word field—MergeField. The argument for MergeField is the name of a merge data source field. In a merge document, Word simply displays the field in a way that makes it easier to understand. Unlike most fields, MergeField can appear in any of three forms: as the underlying field code, as the merge field name, or as the result of the merge operation. Press Alt+F9 to see the underlying field codes, as shown in Figure 10-15.

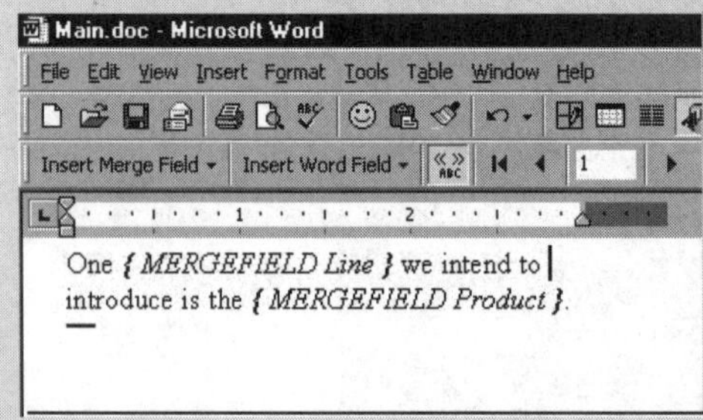

Figure 10-15
A Merge field is really a Word field in disguise.

(continued)

Understanding Merge Fields *(continued)*

Press Alt+F9 again to return to the merge field names. To display the output values from each record in the data source, click the Merge Text button and scroll through the records of the data source. This is an effective way to determine whether you've set up the fields properly. The Mail Merge toolbar also makes it easy to add other standard Word fields to the main merge document as you go.

Choosing a Document Type

Word's Mail Merge Helper allows you to create four different types of merge documents: Form Letters, Mailing Labels, Envelopes, and Catalogs. The relationship between these four different types of merge documents can be a little bit confusing. Table 10-1 shows how the four different merge document types relate to each other.

Document Type	Structured to Match a Specific Page Layout	Multiple Records on a Single Output Page
Form Letters	No	No
Envelopes	Yes	No
Mailing Labels	Yes	Yes
Catalog	No	Yes

Table 10-1
Output options fit into a simple grid relationship.

Two of the document types allow you to place multiple records on the same output page, while the other two document types create a new page for each new record. Likewise, two of the document types require you to define a specific output page format, providing a dialog box to assist you in laying out the fields for a record, while the other two are free-form formats. You can use the table to help determine which type of document to create. For example, if you want to create a document that allows multiple records on a single page, and you want to define the layout of each record, then choose Mailing Labels.

The Envelope option will prompt you for the shape of the envelope, and it provides a dialog box for laying out fields within the address area, as shown in Figure 10-16.

It then changes the page setup and positions the fields on the page. Once the main document is created, there is no significant difference between an envelope and a form letter. Each creates a new page—or a new section if you are outputting the results to a new document—for each record.

Both the Envelope and Mailing Labels options simply help you generate a document. Once you have created the envelope or label document, the document is identical to a Form Letter as far as Word is concerned. That is, you could create a form letter document and manually change the Page Setup and fields, and you would have exactly the same document as if you had used the Envelopes option. Likewise, you

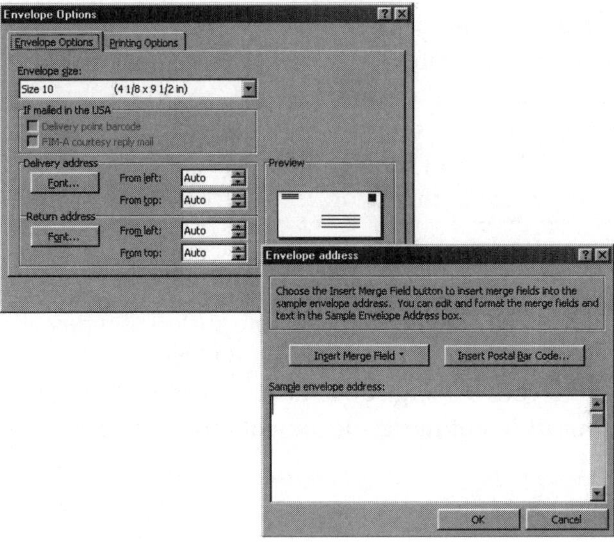

Figure 10-16
The Envelope option structures the fields to match a specific document.

could create a Form Letter document, add a table, and then enter field codes into each cell using the Next field to move from record to record, and you would have exactly the same result as if you had created a Labels document. Envelopes and mailing labels are purely convenience tools for creating a main merge document.

While both the Mailing Labels and Catalog document types allow you to place more than one record on a single page, each uses a different method. The Mailing Labels option inserts a Next Record field to retrieve the values from the next record in the data source. The Catalog option is completely different. It affects the way Word generates the output, not the way it sets up the source document. With a Catalog document, Word simply appends the next copy of the output directly to the same page, without creating a section break. In fact, if you create a standard Form Letter document, output it to a new document, and then replace all the section marks with nothing, you will have exactly the output produced with a Catalog merge document. Of all the document types, the Catalog type is the only one that affects the way Word generates the output. Catalog is the only document type that cannot generate e-mail or fax messages.

Creating a Hybrid Merge Document

Note The sample documents for this section are Catalog.doc and Catalogs.doc.

Once you understand how the different document types interact, you can create a hybrid document. For example, suppose you want to create a catalog-style report that uses indentation to create groups of three rows, as shown in Figure 10-17.

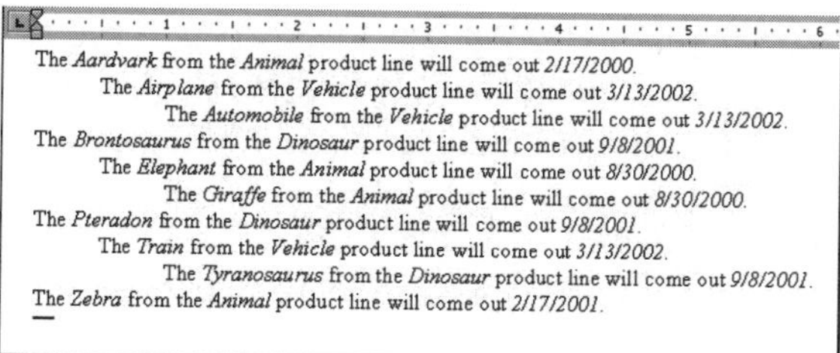

The *Aardvark* from the *Animal* product line will come out *2/17/2000*.
The *Airplane* from the *Vehicle* product line will come out *3/13/2002*.
The *Automobile* from the *Vehicle* product line will come out *3/13/2002*.
The *Brontosaurus* from the *Dinosaur* product line will come out *9/8/2001*.
The *Elephant* from the *Animal* product line will come out *8/30/2000*.
The *Giraffe* from the *Animal* product line will come out *8/30/2000*.
The *Pteradon* from the *Dinosaur* product line will come out *9/8/2001*.
The *Train* from the *Vehicle* product line will come out *3/13/2002*.
The *Tyranosaurus* from the *Dinosaur* product line will come out *9/8/2001*.
The *Zebra* from the *Animal* product line will come out *2/17/2001*.

Figure 10-17
You can create a hybrid output document.

To achieve this effect, take the following steps:

1. Create a Catalog merge document and enter the fields for the first record.
2. Copy the paragraph and paste it twice.
3. At the beginning of the first new paragraph (the second row), insert a tab and a Next Record merge field.
4. At the beginning of the second new paragraph (the third row), enter two tabs and a Next Record merge field. When you output the document, the result will be a document similar to the one shown above in Figure 10-17.

Note

If your intent is to create an actual catalog with multiple product entries on a page, you might want to produce the catalog using Access instead. The primary reason for using Word's mail merge feature is to embed variable fields within a block of text. If you simply enter each field in a separate column—in the fashion of an ordinary catalog—you might want to use an Access report. Even if you will be embedding a few text items within a longer text string, Access might work better.

In an Access report, you can create multiple heading levels, separating categories of products. You can also add subtotals for sections and subsections of the catalog, which is something that you cannot easily do in Word.

See "Creating Dynamic Reports" in Chapter 19 for information about creating groups in an Access report.

When you create a catalog style report, you can add textual material to the top or bottom of the entire document once you've output the results to a document. If you add a header, a footer, or column breaks to the original document, those headers and footers will propagate throughout the merged document.

Extending Mail Merge Operations

A mail merge operation can become very sophisticated. You can add filters to the data source, and you can create conditional expressions for filtering data. Many of the customization options are explained adequately in the Help file. Search for the topic *Mail Merge Overview* and then select the topic *How Do I Customize a Mail Merge?* The following section provides additional tips for customizing a mail merge.

Managing the Return Address for an Envelope

The Mail Merge feature interacts in an interesting way with the standard Envelopes And Labels feature.

- If you have defined the merge documents either as a Form Letter or a Catalog, the Envelopes And Labels command will function the same as if the document were a normal document.
- If you have defined the document as Mailing Labels, the Envelopes And Labels command will be completely disabled.
- If you define the merge documents as Envelopes, the Envelopes And Labels command will display only the Envelope Options dialog box, which will allow you to change the envelope size and how the envelope will print. This is the same dialog box you access when you click the Options button from the Envelopes tab of the ordinary Envelopes And Labels dialog box, or when you first set up a new Envelopes main document.

When you set up a mail merge document as Envelopes, you are not provided with a spot to enter a return address, because you usually do not include merge fields in the return address. Add the return address to the master envelope once it has been created. The Mail Merge Helper does utilize a standard return address that you might have created previously using the Envelope And Labels dialog box, as shown in Figure 10-18.

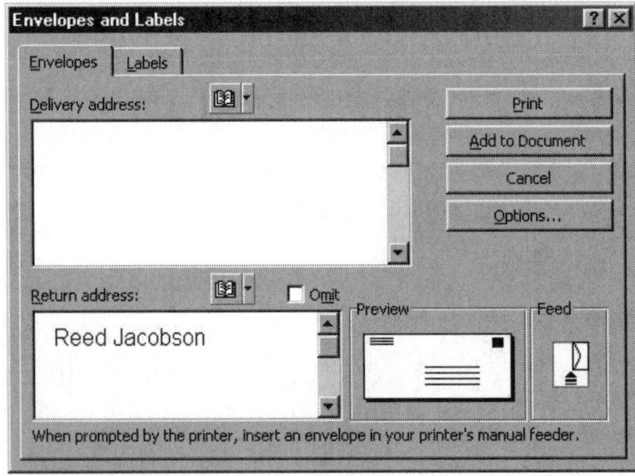

Figure 10-18
If you create a default return address, the mail merge Envelopes will use it.

You can also add a graphic to the default return address by creating the graphic as an AutoText item named either EnvelopeExtra1 or EnvelopeExtra2. (For more information about creating AutoText entries for the return address, search Help using the search words *Graphics on Envelopes*.) If you create AutoText entries with both names, the EnvelopeExtra2 item will appear before the EnvelopeExtra1 item.

Changing the Setup of a Merge Document

After you specify Mailing Labels or Envelopes as the document type, the Mail Merge Helper provides you with a Setup button only when you first create the merge document. If you want to use the Setup dialog box a second time—that is, to replace the structured contents—click the Create button and select the same document type (Envelope or Mailing Labels). Word asks if you want to change the document's type, even though you selected the same type. After changing the type, you can access the Setup button again.

If you change the Setup in a document that already contains text, Word warns you that the existing text in the document will be replaced. If you convert a document from Envelopes to Envelopes type, however—that is, restore the Setup button without changing the type—the Mail Merge Helper does not delete the existing return address, and it does not add text from the default return address. Inconsistently, however, it does add the EnvelopeExtra1 and EnvelopeExtra2 AutoText items, even if they already appear on the envelope.

Creating Sequentially Numbered Labels

Note The sample documents for this section are Ticket.doc and Tickets.doc.

Suppose you want to print a series of sequential numbers on labels. The easiest way to do this is not with Mail Merge as you might expect, but instead by using the Labels portion of the Envelopes And Labels dialog box. Take the following steps to prepare this document:

1. Click Envelopes And Labels on the Tools menu, and select the Labels tab.
2. Click the Options button to choose the type of label you want to use. For example, select Avery Standard Label Products and choose 3110 - Sticker .
3. Type some dummy characters—such as *XXX*—into the Address text box and click the New Document button to create a new document filled with the labels, as shown in Figure 10-19.
4. In a separate temporary document, type the text you want to appear on the label, along with a SEQ field code. For example, type *Ticket* and then click Insert, Field, select Numbering, and select the SEQ field.
5. Type *Ticket* as the sequence field name and click OK, as shown in Figure 10-20.

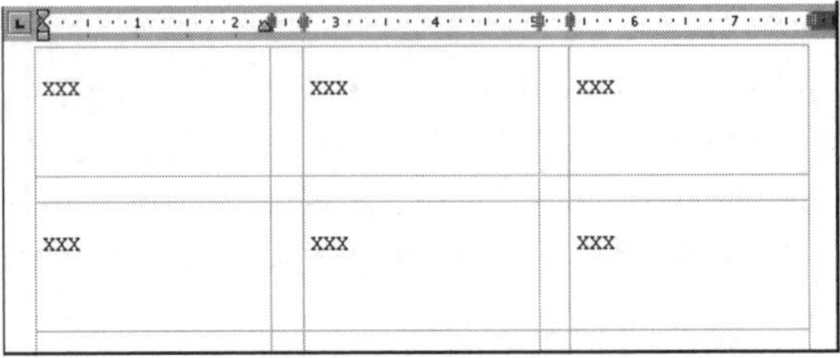

Figure 10-19
To create sequentially numbered labels, type some dummy text on the label design first.

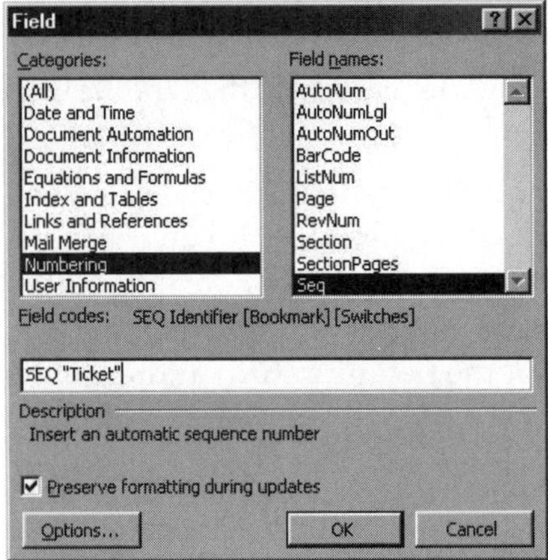

Figure 10-20
Create a SEQ field and copy the field code.

6. Copy all the text. It doesn't matter whether you display the field codes or the field results.
7. Switch back to the labels document and click Replace on the Edit menu. In the Find What drop-down list, type your dummy text. In the Replace What drop-down list, type *^c* to insert the contents of the clipboard.
8. Click the Replace All button to replace the contents of each label with the text and field code from the clipboard.
9. Press Ctrl+A to select the entire document, and press F9 to recalculate all the fields.
10. If you need more labels, simply copy the entire table and paste it onto a new page.

If you would like to add both mail merge fields and sequential numbers to labels, create a Mailing Labels main document that includes the dummy text, along with normal merge fields. Once the labels are created, click the Insert Word Field toolbar button, and select Merge Record # or Merge Sequence #. (The record number counts records in the data source; the sequence number counts records in the output document.) Copy the inserted field and then replace your dummy text with the contents of the clipboard.

Calculating Using Mail Merge Fields

Note The sample document for this section is Price.doc.

You can include mail merge fields within a formula calculation. For example, suppose you have Price and Cost fields in a data source and you want to calculate a Profit amount. You can insert Mail Merge fields inside an ordinary Word formula field. This is much easier to do, however, if you first display field codes in the document.

Press Alt+F9 to display field codes. Click Field on the Insert menu, select the Equations And Formulas category, and double-click the = (Formula) field. Click inside the field code, right after the equals sign (=), and then click the Insert Merge Field button and select the Price field. Word will insert the field code for a merge field, as shown in Figure 10-21.

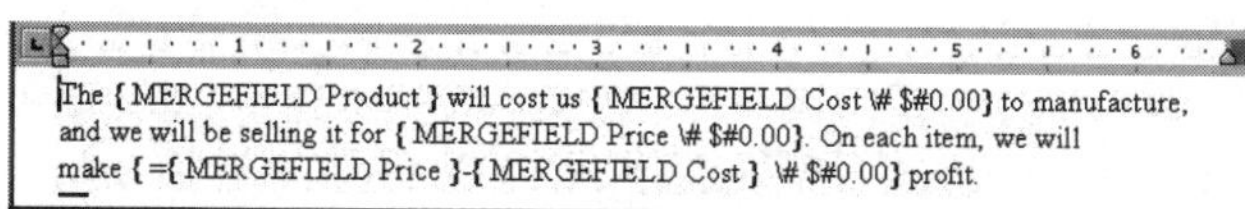

Figure 10-21
Display field codes before inserting a Mail Merge field into a formula.

After the Price merge field, type a minus sign (-), and insert a Cost merge field. Before switching the document back to field results display, add a formatting string to the field so that it will display the field value as currency.

Type \# *$#,##0*. The final field code should look like this:

```
{ = { MERGEFIELD Price } - { MERGEFIELD Cost } \# $#,###0 \* MERGEFORMAT }
```

When you press Alt+F9 to restore field values, Word displays the result of the formula using the values from the current record, even if the View Merged Data button is not indented.

Using a Macro to Control Mail Merge

Note The sample document files for this section are Intro.doc and Intros.doc.

Some calculations you might include in a merge document require a custom VBA routine to calculate. "Exchanging Values with Excel" in Chapter 9 describes some situations that require custom calculations. As one example, suppose your data source includes a product introduction date, and you want to add a notice that you will be accepting orders two weeks earlier than the actual product introduction, creating a document like the one shown in Figure 10-22.

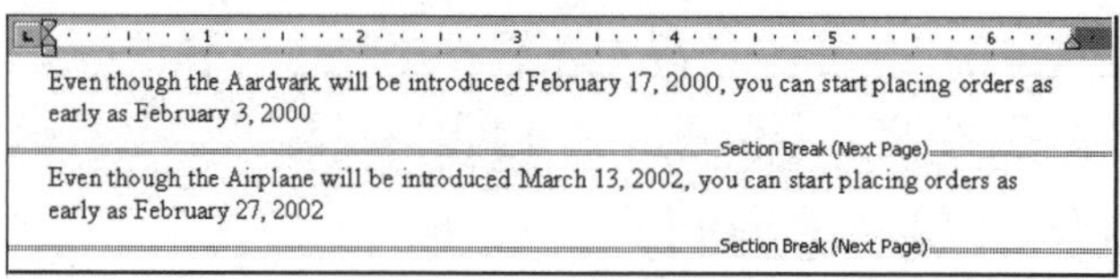

Even though the Aardvark will be introduced February 17, 2000, you can start placing orders as early as February 3, 2000
Section Break (Next Page)
Even though the Airplane will be introduced March 13, 2002, you can start placing orders as early as February 27, 2002
Section Break (Next Page)

Figure 10-22
You need to use VBA to manipulate a custom date calculation.

Word does not have the ability to calculate dates within a field. It is easy, however, to manipulate a date in a VBA routine. It would be ideal if Word allowed you to call a custom function from a Word field, or if you could fire a BeforeMergeRecord event before each output record was generated, but neither of those exists. Unfortunately, you can't hook a VBA routine into a mail merge operation.

Word does allow you to use VBA to manipulate the current record number—essentially, to click the record navigation fields in the Mail Merge toolbar. Word also allows you to choose which record (or records) to include in a merge operation. Because of this, it is possible to create a rather clumsy macro that can execute a mail merge operation one record at a time under macro control. This gives you an opportunity to make custom calculations during the mail merge.

The following *MailWithDates* macro adds an initial order date to each record as the record goes into a Catalog output document. The macro must execute a separate mail merge for each record of the data source—which produces a new, separate document for each record. After the first record, therefore, the macro must move the output for each record to the end of the original document.

```
Sub MailWithDates()
    Dim o As Range
    Dim m As MailMerge
    Dim d As MailMergeDataSource

    Application.ScreenUpdating = False

    Set m = ActiveDocument.MailMerge
    If m.State <> wdMainAndDataSource Then
        Exit Sub
    End If

    Set d = m.DataSource
    d.ActiveRecord = wdFirstRecord
    Do
        d.FirstRecord = d.ActiveRecord
        d.LastRecord = d.ActiveRecord
        m.Parent.Variables("StartDate").Value = _
            CVDate(d.DataFields("Intro").Value) - 14
        m.Execute
        If o Is Nothing Then
            Set o = ActiveDocument.Range
```

```
        Else
            ActiveDocument.Range.Copy
            o.Paste
            ActiveDocument.Close False
        End If
        o.MoveStart wdStory
        d.ActiveRecord = wdNextRecord
    Loop Until d.ActiveRecord = d.FirstRecord
End Sub
```

The purpose of the *Application.ScreenUpdating = False* statement is to minimize the amount of jumping around that you see on the screen as Word shifts from document to document. Even with screen updating turned off, however, you will see a tremendous amount of flashing, so you might choose to omit this statement and watch the action.

Each Word document has a MailMerge property, whether the document is part of a mail merge operation or not. The MailMerge object has a State property that corresponds to the state of the buttons in the Mail Merge Helper dialog box. If a document is not part of a mail merge operation, the State property equals *wdNormalDocument*. If the document does not have both a main document and a data source identified, then the macro can simply quit.

The DataSource object returned by the DataSource property of a MailMerge object allows you to manipulate the records in the data source. The DataSource ActiveRecord property behaves in an interesting manner. When you get the value of the property, it returns the current record number—the number that appears in the Go To Record box on the Mail Merge toolbar—and you can assign a record number to the property to change to that absolute record number. In addition, you can assign the relative values for *wdFirstRecord, wdLastRecord, wdNextRecord,* and *wdPreviousRecord.*

The looping body of the macro sets the first and last record of the data source to the active record. This limits the output of the merge operation to a single record. It then calculates the effective date. The statement that calculates the date is the entire reason for the macro's existence.

```
        m.Parent.Variables("StartDate").Value = _
            CVDate(d.DataFields("Intro").Value) - 14
```

This one statement does a lot. Starting from the end, it retrieves the value of the *Intro* field from the DataSource object. The DataSource object always returns a value from the active record, and it always returns values as a string. The statement uses the Visual Basic CVDate function to convert the string into a date that can be used as the basis for an arithmetic operation. The statement subtracts *14* from the date—moving the date forward two weeks, and then assigns the adjusted date to what is called a document variable. (A document variable is like a bookmark, except that it does not refer to a range. It simply stores the value somewhere in the depths of the document.) (Document variables are completely different from VBA variables, which are discussed in the section "Creating Variables" in Chapter 4.) On the Word side, you simply insert a DocVariable field to use a document variable, and you include the name that the VBA macro gave to the variable.

After the macro calculates the date, which allows the Word field that accesses *DocVariable* to calculate, it executes the mail merge. The mail merge takes place, but only within the bounds of the DataSource object's FirstRecord and LastRecord properties. In this case, it generates only a single record.

The macro behaves differently on the first execution than on subsequent executions. The first record output goes to a new document. You want to keep that initial document, appending subsequent records to it. The macro stores a reference to the range of the document in a variable. That variable is thus able to serve as an indicator of the first record: if the variable contains something other than nothing, then the first record has already been processed. For all records other than the first, the macro copies the entire contents of the new document, pastes it into the original output document, and closes the new document without saving changes.

At the end of the loop, the macro moves the output range—the location where the next record will be pasted—to the end of its document. The macro then moves to the next record in the data source, and if there really was a next record to move to—that is, if changing to the next record actually did change the active record number—the loop starts over. Otherwise, the macro is finished.

If the output of the merge operation is sent to the printer, or even to e-mail or fax, you can omit the portion of the macro that copies the output to the original document. Instead, simply execute the mail merge one record at a time. This macro solution does not work when generating mailing labels.

Chapter 11

Work with Large Projects

In This Chapter

Large document projects bring with them special considerations that are insignificant with smaller document projects. For example, you might need help keeping track of how a document is organized, you might want to print drafts of a document that minimizes the amount of paper you use, and you might want to split the document into component parts. This chapter focuses on tools related to working with large documents—Outline View, Master Documents, and Zoomed Printing. Each of these features is powerful and useful, but each feature also has aspects that are hard to understand or are frustrating to deal with.

Working in Outline View

Outline view is a tool for organizing material in a large document. With it, you can collapse a document so that you see only the headings at any desired level. You can then manipulate an entire section of the document as if it were a single line of text.

Making Selections in Outline View

Using the keyboard to move or extend a selection within your document can result in some very strange behaviors in Microsoft Word.

Extending Selections Within Outline View

When you extend a selection in Outline View, Word always applies two rules:

- **Rule 1** Selecting the paragraph mark of any paragraph selects the entire paragraph.
- **Rule 2** Once a paragraph is selected, Word extends the selection in increments of only a paragraph.

These rules are actually very logical and very beneficial. By design, they make it difficult for you to butcher a document by tearing paragraphs in half as you rearrange the document. However, in certain situations—which are most obvious when you are using the keyboard to change the selection, but which are also evident when you use the mouse—the implications of these simple rules causes behavior that is nothing short of bizarre.

For example, Figure 11-1 shows an outline paragraph with the last word in the paragraph selected. In Normal view, starting from that selection, if you press the Shift+Right arrow keys twice and then press the Shift+Left arrow keys twice, you end up with the same selection as when you started.

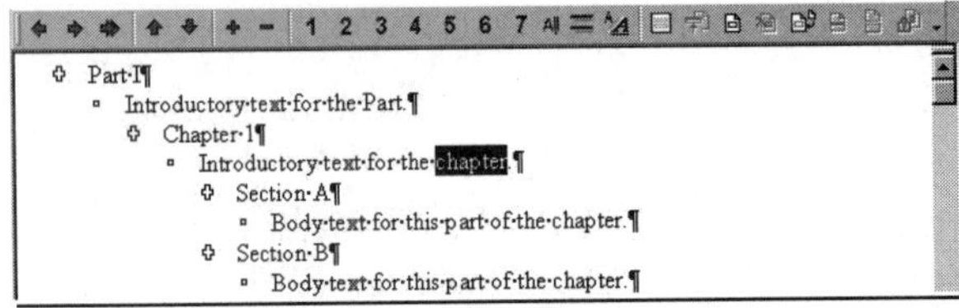

Figure 11-1
Start with a single word selected.

In Outline view, you obtain a completely different result. Starting with the selection shown earlier in Figure 11-1, pressing the Shift+Right arrow keys once extends the selection to include a single additional character—the period—the same behavior as in Normal view. Pressing the Shift+Right arrow keys a second time, however, selects the entire paragraph, as shown in Figure 11-2. This is due to Rule #1, and is a completely different behavior than Normal view.

Once the paragraph is selected, pressing the Shift+Left arrow keys collapses the selection to an insertion point at the beginning of the paragraph. Because the paragraph mark is no longer selected, pressing the Shift+Right arrow keys would again increment in units of a single character. With the insertion point at the beginning of the

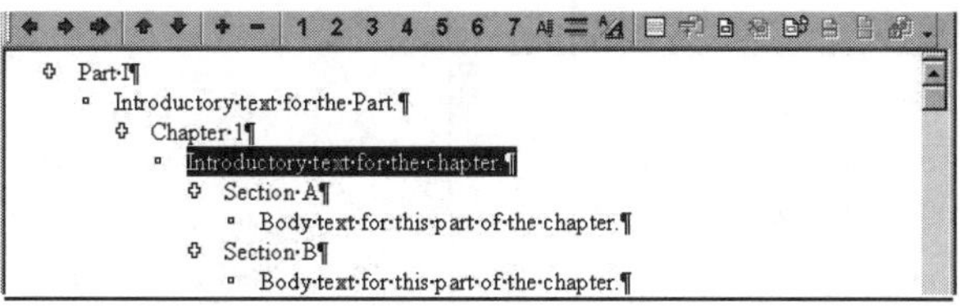

Figure 11-2
Selecting the paragraph mark selects the paragraph.

paragraph, pressing the Shift+Left arrow keys selects the preceding paragraph mark, which selects the entire preceding paragraph, as shown in Figure 11-3.

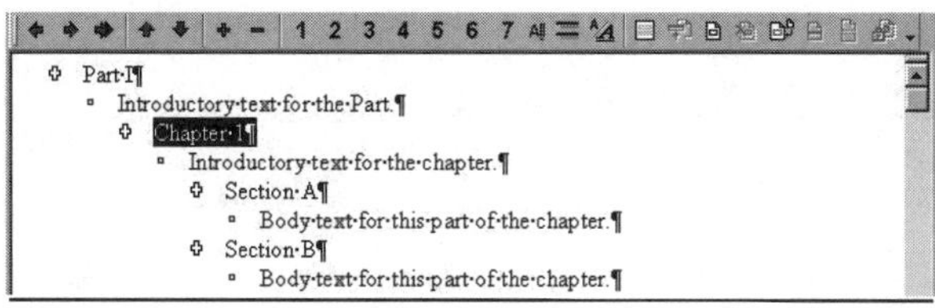

Figure 11-3
With a paragraph selected, the selection unit becomes a paragraph.

In short, the same simple four-keystroke sequence that effectively does nothing in Normal view selects a completely different paragraph in Outline view. Unless you consciously think of the Outline view selection rules, this can be a very unnerving experience.

If you do want to select the last word of a paragraph, start by selecting the end of the word and press the Shift+Left arrow keys to select toward the beginning of the paragraph. Otherwise, one too many Right arrow key presses will select the paragraph mark and land you in selection chaos.

Selecting Headings with Collapsed Text

When you select a heading with collapsed text below it, Word automatically selects all the collapsed text. You can tell the collapsed text is selected by switching to another view or by showing all levels. This makes it easy to move a large chunk of a document as if it were a single line.

The asymmetry between selecting to the right and selecting to the left becomes even more egregious when portions of the outline are collapsed. When selecting around collapsed text, Outline view adds one more rule: if a paragraph is selected, Word will not move the active end of the selection down into a heading with collapsed text. If possible, it will move to a paragraph that is not followed by collapsed text; otherwise, it will not move down. I cannot find a logical explanation for this rule, and I cannot find a concise explanation that adequately describes the behavior. Take the outline in Figure 11-4, for example.

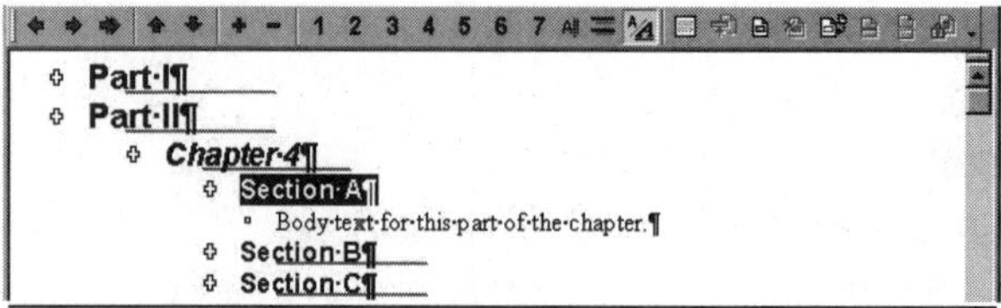

Figure 11-4
Word extends the selection to uncollapsed text.

With the Section A paragraph selected, pressing Shift+Down arrow key extends the selection to include the following body text. That is a natural and logical result. If you start with the Part I heading selected, however, pressing Shift+Down arrow key results in the selection shown in Figure 11-5.

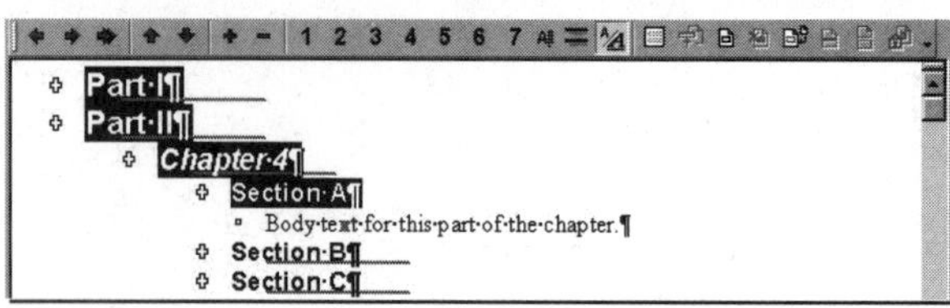

Figure 11-5
Word extends the selection to the first heading without collapsed text.

Word extends the selection to include the Section A paragraph because that is the first heading that does not have collapsed text below it. As a final and quite bizarre implication of Word's selection rule, if you start with the Section B heading selected—or even with the body text paragraph selected—Word will refuse to budge when you press the Down or Right arrow keys, with or without the Shift key. All remaining heading paragraphs have collapsed text, so Word will not move or extend the selection into any heading.

Curiously—and fortunately—Word does not apply the same rule when moving the active end of the selection up in the document. Given the outline and the selection shown in Figure 11-5, you can press the Shift+Left arrow keys to contract the selection so that it is similar to the one shown in Figure 11-6.

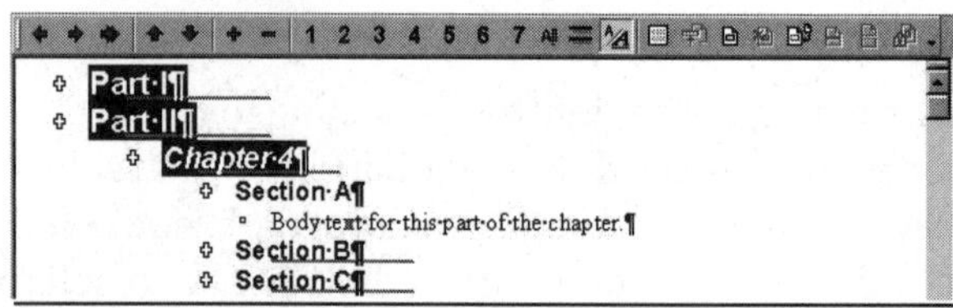

Figure 11-6
Moving the end of the selection to the left ignores collapsed text.

The net effect is that as you select downward in the document, Word might jump farther than you intended, while shrinking the selection behaves in a predictable manner. Unfortunately, if your document has no headings with uncollapsed text, you can never jump far enough to start collapsing the selection backward.

The bottom line is that when you want to select headings in a document with collapsed text, you should always work your way up from the bottom. Place the insertion point at the beginning of the first heading you do not want to select. Then press the Shift+Up arrow keys to extend the selection.

Shortcut Keys in Outline View

All the shortcut keys that relate specifically to Outline view use the prefix keys Alt +Shift. If you remember that prefix, it's very easy to remember the shortcut keys. Following the Alt+Shift prefix, the shortcut for each button on the Outline toolbar is the symbol you see on the toolbar button. Table 11-1 lists the command name, the toolbar button, and the shortcut key.

Command Name	Toolbar button	Alt+Shift+Key
Promote	⬅	Left arrow
Demote	➡	Right arrow
Move Up	⬆	Up arrow
Move Down	⬇	Down arrow
Show Heading 1 (etc.)	1	1, 2, 3, etc.
Show All Headings	All	A
Expand	+	Plus sign (+)
Collapse	−	Minus sign (-)

Table 11-1
Shortcut keys in Outline view.

The keyboard shortcut for Show First Line Only is Alt+Shift+L (for Line). For Show All Headings, the letter L is underlined on the button, indicating that Alt+L works as a keyboard shortcut, in addition to Alt+Shift+A. The Demote To Body Text button does not have a shortcut, but because it simply changes the paragraph to the Normal style, you can use the keyboard shortcut Ctrl+Shift+N. There is also no shortcut for Show Formatting; if you want one, you'll have to come up with it on your own.

Collapsed Text and VBA

The collapsed text that is included when you copy text differs depending on whether you reference the text from the user interface or from VBA—and on which method you use within VBA. This can be important when creating a macro to manipulate an outline (such as the one in "Using a Macro to Paste Part of an Outline," later in this chapter). Consider the outline illustrated in Figure 11-7. The selected paragraph is both preceded and followed by hidden text.

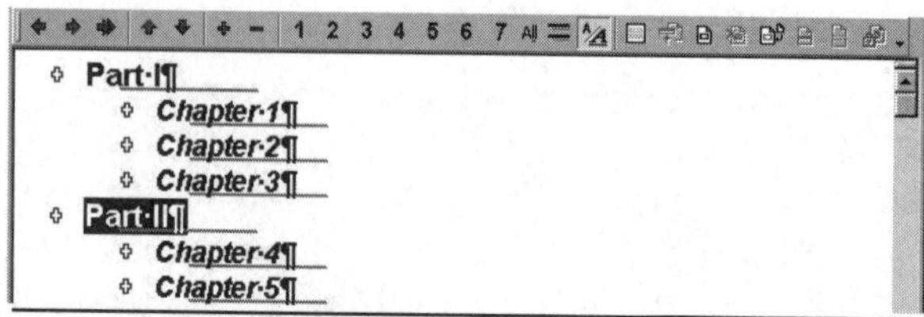

Figure 11-7
Select a single paragraph preceded and followed by collapsed text.

If you use menu commands to copy the selected paragraph and paste it into a new document, you obtain the result reflected in Figure 11-8. Word pastes the visible heading, along with the subordinate, collapsed text.

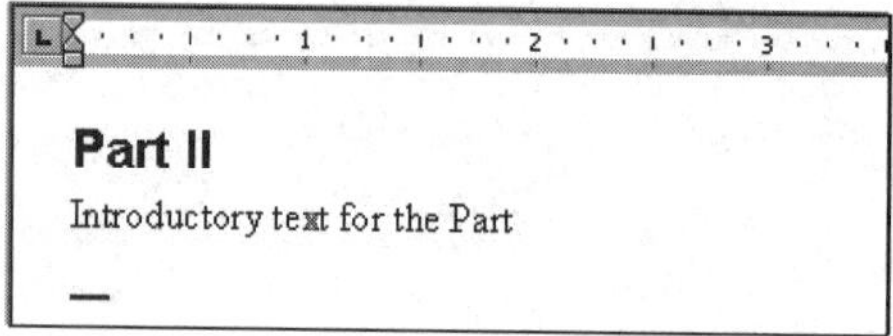

Figure 11-8
Word pastes collapsed text that follows a copied paragraph.

Executing the *Selection.Copy* statement in the Immediate window of the Visual Basic Editor before pasting the text into a new document has the same effect as copying from the user interface. Understandably, the *Selection.Range.Copy* statement has the same effect, as well. Surprisingly, however, the *Selection.Paragraphs(1).Range.Copy* statement—which, from all logical considerations, would be identical for a single-paragraph selection—produces the result shown in Figure 11-9.

The collapsed text that follows the selected heading is not pasted at all. Rather, all the collapsed text that precedes the heading is pasted! When a paragraph is preceded by collapsed text, the first character of its VBA Paragraph object refers to the entire collapsed range.

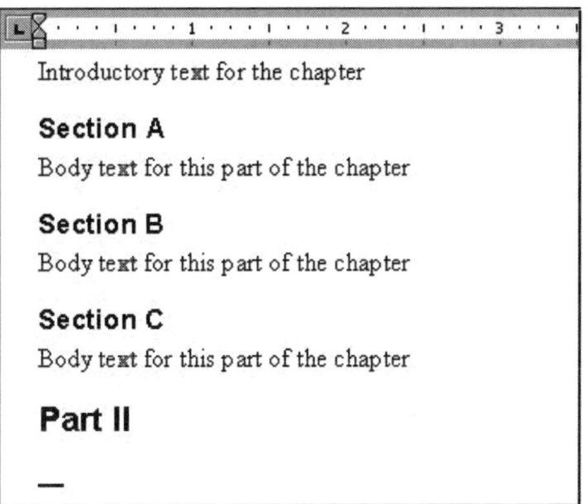

Figure 11-9
Copying the paragraph in VBA pastes the preceding collapsed text.

Switching Between Outline View and Other Views

When you switch between Outline, Normal, Print Layout, and Web Layout views, Word tries to display the same approximate location in each view. Two factors compete, however, when deciding what constitutes the same location: the currently selected text, and the text at the top of the window. In Outline view, where much of the document can be collapsed, there can be a considerable difference between the location of the selected text and the text at the top of the window. When switching from Outline view to either of the Layout views, Word keeps the selected text visible, even if the text at the top of the window changes. Because you typically focus on the selected text, this is logical and not confusing.

When you switch between Normal and Outline views, however, Word can make you think that it lost your place within the document. This is because it displays the same text at the top of the window as was at the top in Outline view. (Approximately; it actually displays about one extra line at the top of the window when you switch views, so switching repeatedly back and forth between Outline view and Normal view gradually scrolls up through the document.) Figure 11-10 shows a document in Outline view, where most of the text is hidden in the first two-thirds of the document. The first line of the document is at the top of the window.

When you switch to Normal view, Word displays the top of the document, matching the text that was at the top of the window in Outline view. This might make you think that Word has lost the selection, as you are scrolling back to the bottom of the document. In fact, Word did not lose the selection at all; it just displayed a different part of the document. If you press an arrow key, thus modifying the selection, Word instantly scrolls to where the action took place.

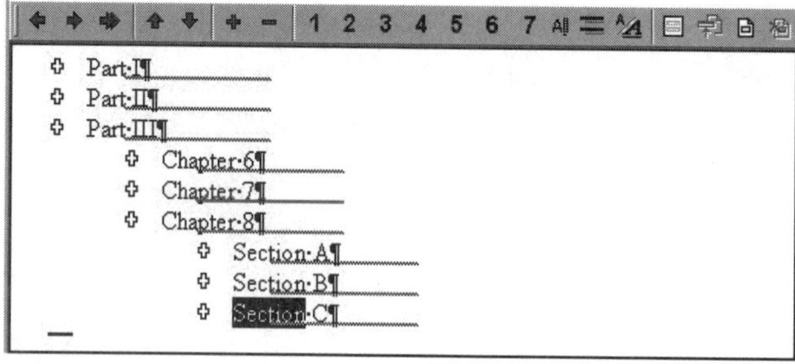

Figure 11-10
Collapsed text can separate the selection from the top of the window.

Copying and Pasting in Outline View

Outline view provides a convenient way to select large blocks in a document. One obvious reason for selecting a large block of a document is to cut, copy, or paste it. You might cut, copy, or paste within a single Outline, or you might transfer material from an outline to another document—or even to another application.

Pasting Into an Outline

If you cut and paste paragraphs to move them around in an outline, always place the insertion point at the beginning of the paragraph that follows the target, rather than at the end of the paragraph that precedes the target location. Pasting a paragraph onto the end of an existing paragraph combines the two paragraphs, gives the new paragraph the style of the pasted paragraph, and leaves a lingering, empty paragraph. (This behavior is identical to the paste behavior in Normal view, but you are more likely to take the wrong approach in Outline view.)

Using a Macro to Paste Part of an Outline

Sometimes, you want to print only the top levels of an outline. If you search Word's Help file using the search terms *Print an Outline,* the topic describes how to print only the visible portion of an outline. Unfortunately, it doesn't work. Even if you show only the top headings in an outline, Word will print all the collapsed text, as well as the visible headings.

One alternative is to create a Table of Contents that shows only the desired heading levels, and then print that Table of Contents. The Table of Contents is an excellent solution, but it does not let you print detailed headings for one part while showing high-level headings for another.

You might try selecting the visible headings and copying them into a new document. For good or for ill, when you paste headings from an outline, you get the detail as well.

A final approach is to create a macro that copies only the non-collapsed paragraphs to a new document, which is exactly what the following *CopyVisibleOutline* macro does. You can then print the new document, or copy it and paste it somewhere else.

```
Sub CopyVisibleOutline()
    Dim ps As Paragraphs
    Dim p As Paragraph
    Dim r As Range

    ''' Make sure document is in outline view
    ActiveWindow.View.Type = wdOutlineView
    ''' Set paragraphs while still active doc
    If Selection.Type = wdNoSelection Then
        Set ps = ActiveDocument.Paragraphs
    Else
        Set ps = Selection.Paragraphs
    End If

    ''' Create output doc in outline view
    Documents.Add
    ActiveWindow.View.Type = wdOutlineView

    ''' Loop through each (visible) paragraph
    For Each p In ps

        ''' Get the range that doesn't include
        ''' collapsed text from previous paragraphs
        Set r = p.Range
        If Asc(r.Characters(1)) = 13 Then
            r.Start = r.Characters(2).Start
        End If

        r.Copy
        Selection.Paste
        Selection.MoveEnd wdDocument
    Next p
End Sub
```

The macro first makes sure the document is in Outline view. It then assigns a reference to the collection of paragraphs in either the active document or the selection. It assigns this reference before creating a new document because the new document will become the active document. Next, the macro creates a new document, changing it to Outline view as well.

The main body of the macro occurs in the loop, with one iteration of the loop for each paragraph. When the Word window is in Outline view, the Paragraphs collection contains only uncollapsed headings. Ideally, you can simply copy each paragraph from the collection to a new document. Unfortunately, as explained in "Collapsed Text and VBA" earlier in this chapter, a Paragraph object that follows a section of collapsed text includes the range of collapsed text in its first character.

Therefore, the *CopyVisibleOutline* macro must check to see if the first character in the paragraph's range is a paragraph mark—that is, if the ASCII number for the character is 13. If so, the macro adjusts the starting position of the copy range to skip the paragraph's first character.

This macro illustrates the counterintuitive relationship between the Characters collection and a Range object. Intuitively, if a paragraph contains 15 characters of text, and the Start property of the first character's range is, say, 150, you would expect the End property of the final character's range to be 165—or perhaps 166, counting the paragraph mark. In actuality, when a paragraph follows collapsed text, the Start property of the paragraph's first character is the starting position of the collapsed text, and the End property of the paragraph's first character is the End position of the collapsed text—which might include hundreds, or even thousands, of characters.

At the end of each iteration through the loop, the macro copies the adjusted range and pastes it into the new document, shifting the selection to the end of the document in anticipation of the next iteration.

Note In addition to printing a portion of an outline, you might also use this macro to copy the top headings of a Word outline to Excel.

Extracting Clues From the Mouse Pointer

When you use the mouse, pay particular attention to the shape of the pointer. If the arrow is pointing northeast, dragging with the mouse extends the selection. If the arrow is pointing northwest, dragging with the mouse uses drag-and-drop to move the current selection. If you drag while the pointer is a four-way pointing arrow, you get an outline move, which moves a paragraph to a new location within the outline while still keeping both the paragraph and its style intact.

Managing Master Documents

In Word, a master document is a way for multiple documents to appear as if they are a single document. A book with chapters is a good example of a document that could be constructed beneficially as a master document. On the one hand, you probably want to create and edit each chapter independently. Perhaps you will even assign different chapters to different authors. On the other hand, you probably want to create a single Table of Contents and a single Index, or add cross-references from one chapter to another, as if all the chapters were part of a single large document.

Creating Subdocuments

Working with master and subordinate documents can be confusing, but a master document is just like any other ordinary document—that is, it can contain text of its own. A master document is one that contains pointers to other documents. Adding a subdocument is what transforms an ordinary document into a master document.

Before working on a mission-critical quarterly report, you should first practice with small subordinate document files.

Creating a Simple Master Document

You and your associates are writing an instruction manual. So far, you've created a simple introductory outline like the one illustrated in Figure 11-11, having two parts, and with two chapters in each part.

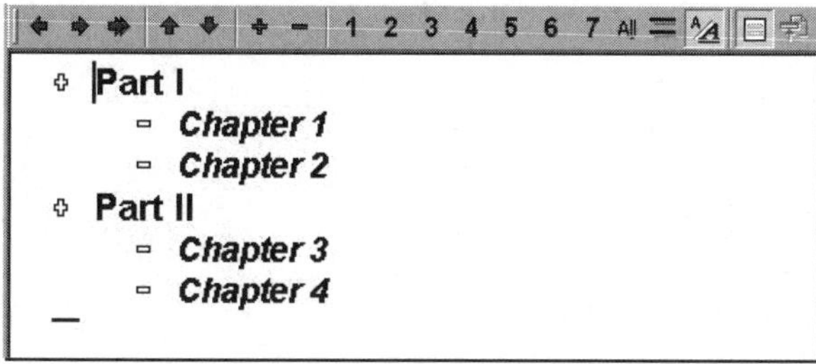

Figure 11-11
A sample outline has parts and chapters.

The parts use the Heading 1 style, and the chapters use the Heading 2 style. Before you actually begin writing a book, you want to split the documents into subdocuments so that each team member can work on specific chapters. See what happens if you select from Chapter 1 through Chapter 4, as shown in Figure 11-12, before creating the subdocuments.

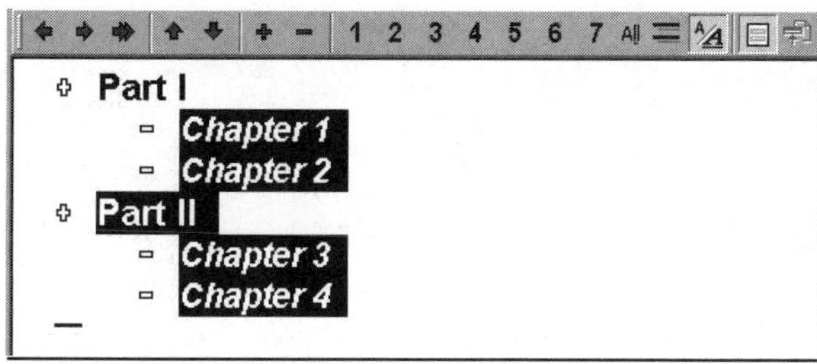

Figure 11-12
The first selected heading determines the subdocument level.

On the Outlining toolbar, make sure the Master Document view button is indented. Then, on the same toolbar, click the Create Subdocument button. The resulting master document will look like the one shown in Figure 11-13.

The first selected heading belongs to outline level 2, so Word creates a new subdocument each time there is a new outline level 2 paragraph. As you can see in the figure, the Part II heading is included as part of the Chapter 2 subdocument.

Word adds a paragraph before and after each subdocument. If you press the Ctrl+Asterisk (*) keys to show paragraph marks, you see that each added paragraph is really a continuous section break, as illustrated in Figure 11-14.

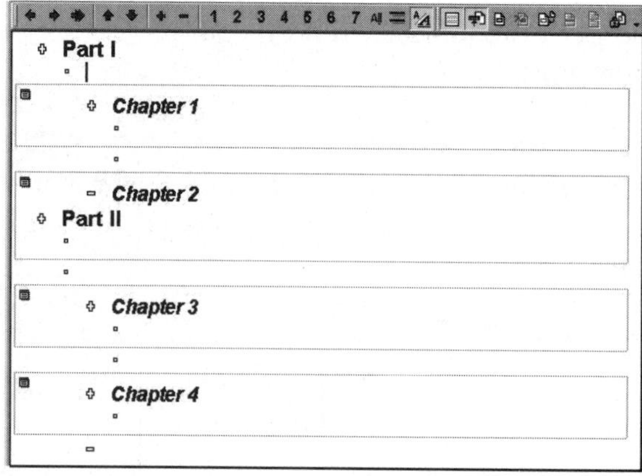

Figure 11-13
Each matching heading starts a new subdocument.

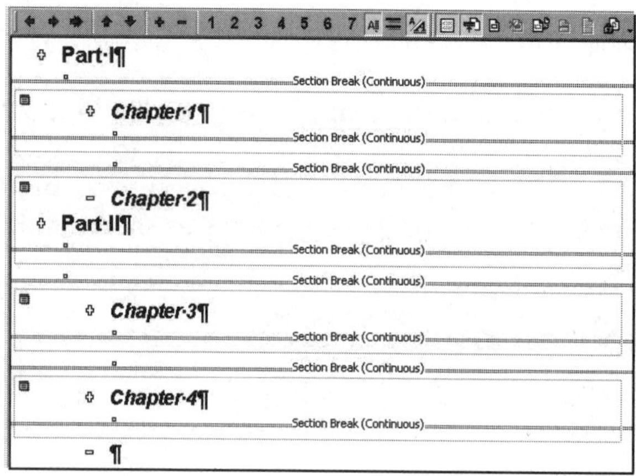

Figure 11-14
Each subdocument receives two new section breaks.

Word adds the section marks purely for your convenience, to make it easy to force a page break or a column break. You can convert the section break to the desired type by clicking Page Setup on the File menu, selecting the Layout tab, and then choosing an option from the Section Start drop-down list. For more information about working with section breaks, see "Formatting Sections" in Chapter 7. The section mark preceding each subdocument is part of the master document; the section mark at the end of each subdocument is part of the subdocument. If you do not want the section breaks, you can remove them without affecting the status of the subdocuments.

The gray box highlight around each subdocument is visible because the Master Document View button is selected. If you deselect the Master Document View button, the gray boxes disappear. The state of the Master Document View button has no effect on the status of the subdocuments themselves. If the button is selected, you see a highlight box around each subdocument and an icon in the top left corner of each box. When Master Document View is enabled, Word does not show section marks unless you display all marks. If Master Document View is not enabled, Word always shows the section breaks, even if other marks are not visible. The Master Document View button has no effect except while in Outline view.

Note Interestingly, there is no mention of the Master Document View button in the Help file. In fact, if you choose the What's This? command from the Help menu and click the Master Document View button, an error message indicates that there is no Help associated with that item.

Creating Subdocument Files

Each subdocument is a separate file that is integrated into the master document. You can open a subdocument in its own window. Double-click the subdocument icon for the Chapter 1 subdocument. Word displays the chapter—such as it is—in a new window, as shown in Figure 11-15.

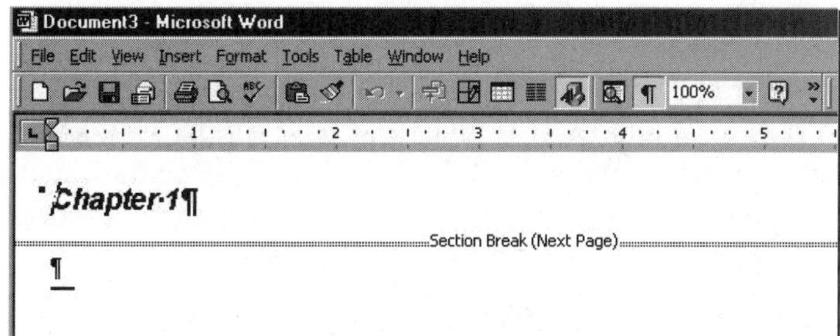

Figure 11-15
You can view a subdocument in its own window.

Close the window to return to the subdocument.

As shown in Figure 11-15, the caption for the subdocument window displays a generic document name—Document3. Even though you see subdocument boxes in the master document, and even though you can open the subdocument in its own window, Word has not actually saved the subdocument yet. Word does not save changes to the master document or create a subdocument until you save the master document.

When you save the master document, Word prompts you for a name for the file. Save the file with the name Parts.doc. Word does not prompt for the name for any of the subdocument files. It automatically generates each filename based on the text in the heading, and it then stores each subdocument file in the same folder as the master document.

You can change the name of a subdocument—even saving it in a completely different folder—but you must make the change from within Word, not from Windows Explorer. Double-click the subdocument icon to open the subdocument in its own window. Then, using the Save As command on the File menu, give the document a new name, and then close the document. (Don't forget to delete the old file.) If you do move the subdocument to a new folder, see "Understanding Subdocument Names" for possible implications you might encounter.

Understanding Subdocument Names

Word automatically generates subdocument filenames based on the text of the first heading in the file. To create the filename, Word starts with the beginning of the heading and continues until encountering either a punctuation mark or the 54th character. That becomes the tentative filename. If the tentative filename already exists, Word adds a numeric digit to the filename, incrementing the digit as necessary to create a unique filename.

If the headings for subdocument sections of your document end in numbers, you might encounter an interesting situation when Word automatically generates the subdocument filenames. Suppose that you will be converting the headings Chapters 1, 2, and 3 into subdocuments. Also suppose that you already have a file in the master document's folder named Chapter 1. When Word automatically generates the name for the Chapter 1 section, it finds that the filename Chapter 1.doc has already been used. So, it increments the number at the end of the filename, saving the Chapter 1 section with the name Chapter 2.doc. Consequently, it must also increment the next filename, saving the Chapter 2 section with the name Chapter 3.doc, and so forth.

Before you allow Word to automatically generate filenames, be sure you have removed any unnecessary files from the master document's folder. If Word does generate a nonsensical filename, use File Save As to rename the file.

Note When you create a subdocument from text that is already in the document, the text must be a heading so that Word can construct a filename for the subdocument. Once you have created a subdocument, you can demote its text to body text without harming the subdocument. You can also add an external file as a subdocument, even if the file does not contain any headings. Word uses the heading only to create the filename for the subdocument.

Moving Text Between Subdocuments

In Outline view, you can easily move paragraphs or even sections of the document from one subdocument to another, or between a subdocument and the master document. Simply move the text as if it were all a part of the same document. For example, given the subdocuments illustrated in Figure 11-14, you might not want the Part II heading to be part of the Chapter 2 subdocument. Simply drag the heading outside the subdocument box to move it into the master document. When you save the master document, Word also saves changes to any modified subdocuments.

If you move all the text out of a subdocument, the subdocument disappears. If you want to move all the text from a subdocument into the master document, you can click inside the subdocument and then click the Remove Subdocument button on the toolbar. Moving all the text of a subdocument into the master document has the same effect as clicking the Remove Subdocument button. That is, the Remove Subdocument button does not delete the subdocument file or the text from the subdocument; it simply moves the text into the master document. After removing a subdocument, don't forget to delete the file in case you might need to reuse the filename later.

If you want to switch the order of two subdocuments, do not use the standard Word outline tools. If you do, you will move the text out of a subdocument, thus removing it. Instead, drag the icon in the upper left corner of the subdocument box to the desired location.

Master documents are closely integrated with the Outline View in Word. Conceptually, a subdocument replaces any heading, along with all its subordinate text. The heading does not need to be a top-level heading; it can occur at any level. It must correspond to a heading somewhere in the outline. You can even have subordinate documents at different levels of the outline. For example, one subordinate document could replace a level 1 heading, while a different subordinate document replaces a level 3 heading. A document can serve as both a subordinate document and as a master document of its own, thus nesting master documents.

Creating Nested Subdocuments

In the Parts master document, remove all the subdocuments. To remove a single subdocument, the selection must be within that subdocument. To remove multiple subdocuments, the selection must begin within the first subdocument and end within or after the last subdocument. Save the Parts document to incorporate the change to the file.

Even after removing all the subdocuments from a master document, you cannot immediately delete the old subdocument files in Windows Explorer. Word does not release the lock on the removed file until you close the master document. Close the Parts document, delete the files for Chapters 1, 2, and 3 (but leave the file for Chapter 4 available), and then reopen the Parts document.

Select the entire outline, including Part I, Part II, and all the chapters. Click the Create Subdocument button on the toolbar to create two subdocuments. Word does not create separate subdocuments for the lower level headings. Select the Chapter 1 and Chapter 2 headings and click the Create Subdocument button. Word creates subdocuments nested within the Part I subdocument, as shown in Figure 11-16.

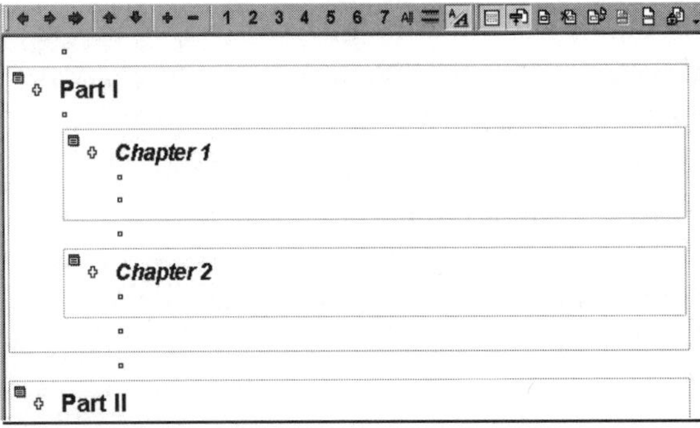

Figure 11-16
You can nest subdocuments.

If you don't want Chapter 2 to be nested within the Part I document, there are two ways to convert it to a parallel subdocument:

- Drag the icon in the subdocument box to the space between the Part I and the Part II subdocuments.
- Remove the nested subdocument: click within the Chapter 1 subdocument and click Remove Subdocument. Then click at the beginning of the Chapter 1 heading and click the Split Subdocument button on the toolbar.

There are also two ways to convert a parallel subdocument into a nested subdocument:

- Drag the icon for the Chapter 1 subdocument up into the Part I subdocument.
- Merge the subdocuments.

To merge subdocuments, select from the beginning of the Part I subdocument to the end of the Chapter 2 subdocument and click the Merge Subdocuments button on the toolbar. Once the two subdocuments are merged, click in the Chapter 2 heading and click the Create Subdocument button on the toolbar again.

You can create, remove, split, rearrange, and nest subdocuments, all without changing any actual files. Nothing happens to the files on your hard disk until you save the master document. Save the Parts document now to create four new files: one for each part, and one for each of the two nested chapters in Part I. If you double-click the subdocument icon for Part I, the file will look just like an ordinary master document, as shown in Figure 11-17. A master document is nothing more and nothing less than a document that just happens to contain a subdocument.

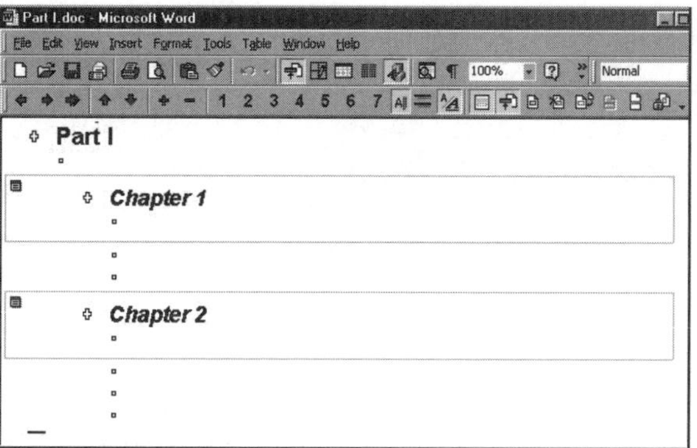

Figure 11-17
A subdocument can be a master document, too.

Understanding Toolbar Button Behavior

Word attempts to enable the toolbar buttons that relate to master documents only when they are meaningful. Unfortunately, the buttons are sometimes enabled when they can't be used and disabled when they can. Because the buttons are sometimes incorrect, it can be difficult to determine exactly how—and when—to use them.

The Create Subdocument button is always enabled (as long as subdocuments are not collapsed (see "Expanding and Collapsing Subdocuments" later in this chapter). But if the selected text is not a heading, clicking the button generates an error message. Word should just disable the button unless the selection begins with a heading, but it doesn't.

To split a subdocument, the selection must begin within a subdocument at the beginning of a paragraph, and be the first paragraph. Word is not perfect at identifying these conditions.

Word enables the Split Document button on the toolbar, even in the first paragraph in a subdocument—even though nothing happens when you click the button. It disables the Split Document button—even in a later paragraph—if you have just inserted the paragraph. (To enable the button, move off the new paragraph and then back onto it.) Ideally, you do not even have to select the beginning of a paragraph (Rule #2 mentioned earlier in this chapter), and the Split Subdocument button will simply split at the beginning of the current paragraph.

Word enables the Remove Subdocument button any time the beginning of the selection is within a subdocument. Word will remove any subdocument that is even partially included within the selection. Fortunately, the button remains enabled even if the end of the selection extends into the master document, but it should be enabled any time at least part of the selection includes any part of a subdocument.

(continued)

Understanding Toolbar Button Behavior *(continued)*

Word enables the Merge Subdocument button only if the beginning of the selection is at the exact beginning of a subdocument and the end of the selection is at the exact end of a different subdocument. (Any subdocuments in between are merged as well.) It seems reasonable that the button should work as long as the selection includes at least part of at least two subdocuments, but it doesn't.

Inserting a Subdocument

You can also insert existing files as subdocuments within a master document. This is particularly useful if you have already written all the chapters of a book and want to pull them together to create a single paginated document, with one Table of Contents and one Index.

In the Parts document, delete both chapter headings from the Part II section. Click inside the Part II subdocument box and click the Insert Subdocument button on the toolbar. Open the Chapter 3 document; it will appear as a new subdocument. The text has not been copied into the master document yet; it only appears as if it has. Click below the Part II section and insert the Chapter 4 document. Save the master document.

If you look at the relevant files in Windows Explorer, you will see that the Parts document and the Part II document were both modified at the time you saved the master document. That's because they each contain new pointers to subdocuments. The time for the Chapter 3 and Chapter 4 subdocuments, however, should be earlier. Adding the subdocuments to a master document does not change the subdocuments in any way.

When you add a subdocument to a master document that has a different template than the subdocument, Word warns you that the master document's template will take precedence. For details about how styles interact between a master document and a subdocument, see "Using Styles in Subdocuments and Master Documents" later in this chapter.

Expanding and Collapsing Subdocuments

An important principle to understand in working with master documents is that subdocuments can appear in either of two modes. In the first mode—the default mode—when you create subdocuments, each subordinate document is visually integrated into the master document so that there is no apparent distinction between the two. In the second mode, you see only the links to the subdocuments.

In the first mode, the subdocuments are expanded. In the second mode the subdocuments are collapsed. Effectively expanding and collapsing a master document can help you understand how the pieces fit together.

Collapsing Subdocuments

Click the Collapse subdocuments button on the toolbar to collapse the subdocuments. A file with collapsed subdocuments looks similar to the one shown in Figure 11-18. Word will not collapse the subdocuments without first saving the master document.

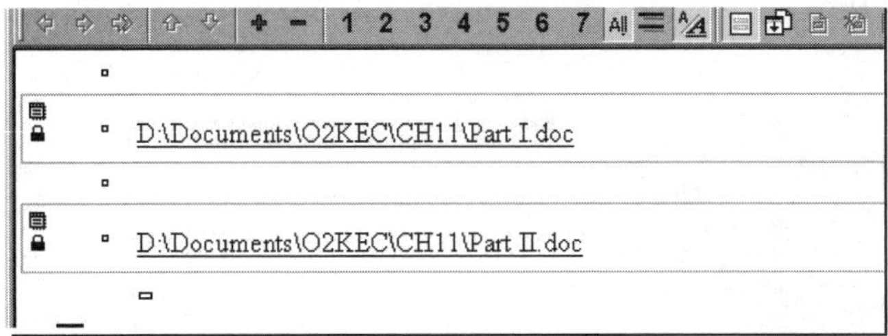

Figure 11-18
When subdocuments are collapsed, they appear as hyperlinks.

Unlike the Master Document View button, which has an effect only in Outline view, the Collapse/Expand Subdocuments button affects any view of the document. In fact, when using a master document, you might want to be able to switch between collapsed and expanded subdocument view at any time. Use the following steps to customize your Standard toolbar to include the Collapse Subdocuments button:

- Click Toolbars on the View menu, and then click Customize.
- Hold down the Ctrl key as you drag a copy of the Collapse Subdocuments button from the Outlining toolbar onto the Standard toolbar.

You can also use the Ctrl+Backslash (\) shortcut key to toggle between views of your collapsed and expanded subdocuments. This shortcut key works in any view.

Exploring Subdocument Hyperlinks

When subdocuments are collapsed, you see only the filename as a hyperlink. This is an ordinary Word hyperlink. Word's Hyperlink submenu is on its shortcut menu, as shown in Figure 11-19, but the Edit and Remove commands are disabled on the Hyperlink menu.

The only way that you can create or delete a subdocument is by using the buttons on the Outlining toolbar. The Copy Hyperlink command is available on the shortcut menu for a subdocument. That means you can copy a subdocument hyperlink. But if you paste the link, you get an ordinary hyperlink, not a new subdocument hyperlink. If you press Alt+F9, you will see the underlying hyperlink field codes, as shown in Figure 11-20.

When you create a subdocument, Word's default is to store the new subdocument in the same folder as the master document. When you collapse subdocuments, Word displays a link that shows the full path, but it does not store the full path of a subdocument file; rather, the link is actually relative. If you move the master

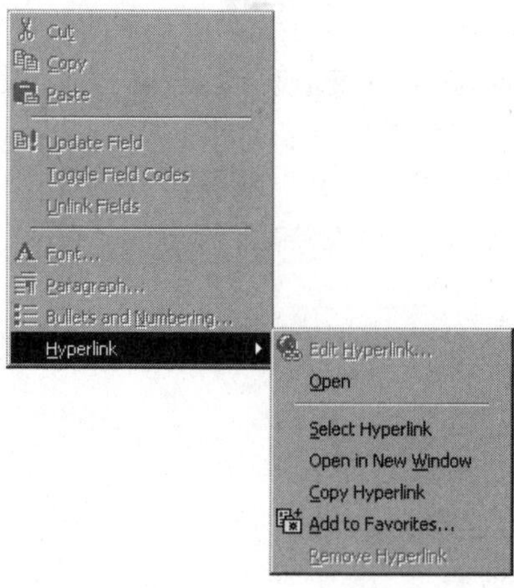

Figure 11-19
A subdocument hyperlink is not editable.

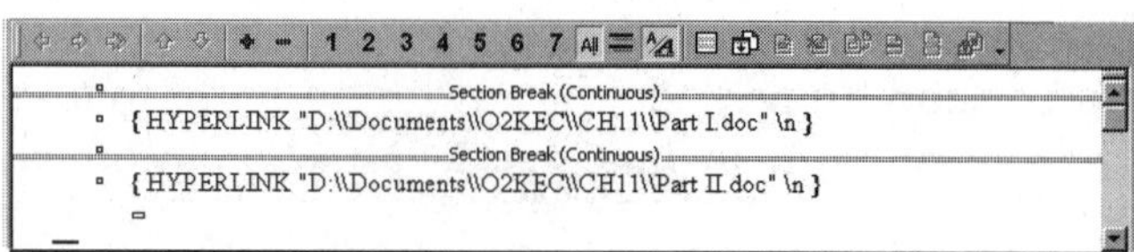

Figure 11-20
Subdocuments use Hyperlink fields.

document and all the subdocuments together to a new folder, Word automatically adjusts the document links.

If you want to move the subdocuments into new folders—for example, if you want each chapter subdocument to be in its own folder—you can move the subdocument to a new folder in the same way that you would rename it. That is, open the subdocument in its own window, and then click Save As on the File menu. Navigate to the subfolder you want to save the file in, and then save the file. You can also save subdocuments in a folder that is separate from the master document if you use the Insert Subdocument button on the toolbar to add the subdocument. As long as a subdocument's folder is a subfolder of the master document folder, Word maintains a relative reference to the subdocument. That is, as long as you move the entire folder tree to a new location, the links remain intact.

If you store a subdocument in a folder outside of the master document's folder tree, Word stores the link as an absolute reference. You could have a master document on your hard disk that links to subdocuments on a network path. You could then move the subdocument to a different location and it would still point to the same absolute location on the network.

Note If you move the subdocument to a folder on a network that was assigned a drive letter, you must always use the same drive letter to maintain the link.

Using Styles in Subdocuments and Master Documents

When you expand subdocuments, the portions of the document that belong to a subdocument act exactly as if they have been included in the master document itself. This has some interesting positive and negative side effects. For example, any styles assigned to paragraphs or characters use the style definition from the master document, not from the definition in the subdocument. In addition, if the Normal style in the subdocument is bold and centered, while the Normal style in the master document is italic and left justified, the text will switch formats, depending on whether you open the file separately or as part of the master document.

Once you get used to this behavior, this feature can be very useful. It allows you to create a stand-alone document that has one custom look, and include the same document—without modification—as part of a larger report, with the formatting automatically changing to match that of the master report.

If the subdocument contains a style that is not defined in the master document, Word copies the style to the master document as soon as you expand the subdocuments. As always, the master document style controls the formatting.

If you create subdocuments that you intend to integrate into a master document, you might want to use Heading 2 as the top-level heading in each subdocument. Then, as you combine the subdocuments into a master document, the Heading 1 level is available for headings that group documents together, such as parts. A master document can change the formatting of subdocument styles, but it cannot automatically demote heading levels.

Linking to Graphical Files from Subdocuments

The fact that subdocument text behaves precisely as if it were part of a master document has implications for other linked files if the subdocuments are not in the same folder as the master document.

For example, imagine that you have a master document in the folder C:\Report, and you create a subfolder named C:\Report\Sub1. You save a subdocument named Chapter1.doc in the subfolder. You also include a graphic image file named Picture1.bmp in the same subfolder, and you then use the field {INCLUDEPICTURE Picture1.bmp} to include the picture in the Chapter1.doc file.

If you open the Chapter1 document in its own window, it will display the picture properly. However, if you display the subdocument as part of the master document (stored in the folder C:\Report), Word looks unsuccessfully for a file named Picture1.bmp in the folder C:\Report. This behavior is probably not a feature intentionally designed into Word. Most likely, it is simply a consequence of the fact that everything in a subdocument acts as if it is part of the master document.

In theory, you could take advantage of this behavior to intentionally make a document display one set of graphics when it is opened by itself, but a different set of graphics when it is opened as part of a master document. Most likely, however, this linking behavior is something you will have to consciously avoid.

If you do have a large number of graphic image files for each subdocument, it is reasonable to want to isolate those that support files into separate folders. If you have links, however, you cannot effectively keep each subdocument in a separate folder from the master document. A reasonable alternative is to store only the graphic image files in separate folders, while storing the subdocuments in the same folder as the master document.

Create a relative link from each subdocument to the relevant graphic image files. Using the earlier example, you would store the Chapter1.doc file in the folder C:\Report, but you would change the picture field link to {INCLUDEPICTURE Sub1\Picture1.bmp}. Because both the subdocument and the master document are in the same folder, the same relative reference will work for either one, and you are still able to segregate the graphic image files for each chapter into separate subfolders.

Locking Documents

A subdocument can be accessed from more than one direction. It can be opened in its own window, or it can be opened as an expanded subdocument within a master document. It caneven be opened in multiple master documents at the same time. If you are editing a master document at the same time that an associate is editing Chapter 1, it will be unfortunate if both of you try to make changes to the same passage at the same time. Word uses a locking mechanism to allow only one person to edit the document at a time.

Locking a Subdocument

If you have Chapter 1 open independently, and you then open the Part I document—which opens Chapter 1 as a subdocument—Word automatically locks the Chapter 1 portion of the Part I document. You can look at Chapter 1, but you can't change it. You can tell whether a document is locked by looking at the subdocument box in Outline view. If there is a small padlock next to the subdocument icon, the subdocument is locked.

Word automatically locks a document that is protected on the file system. Before opening the Part I document, you can change the Read-Only property of the Chapter 1 file. (In Windows Explorer, select the file and click File, Properties. On the General tab, select the Read-Only box and click OK.) If you then open the Part I document, the Chapter 1 subdocument is locked. If the subdocument exists on a network file share that does not grant read-write permissions, you see the same effect.

You can manually lock a subdocument. In Outline view, select anywhere within the subdocument and click the Lock Document button on the toolbar. Locking the subdocument saves any changes you have made and releases the file so that another person can open it for editing. You can also click the Lock Document button to unlock a locked subdocument—but only if it is not locked by another person or by the file system.

You can manually lock or unlock only one document at a time. If the selection transcends more than a single subdocument—that is, if it includes a portion of the main document as well as a subdocument, or if it includes more than one subdocument—Word disables the Lock Document button. Word also will not change the locked status of the master document or expand or collapse subdocuments without first saving the master document.

The final method used to lock subdocuments is to collapse them. Collapsed subdocuments are locked by default. A collapsed subdocument is locked in two senses: First, because you can't see the contents of the file, you can't edit it. Second, the link itself is locked.

Negotiating Simultaneous Changes

Locking is most useful when multiple individuals are working on various subdocuments of a single master document. If you open the Part I document, you have the unlocked version of the document. If an associate then opens the Chapter 1 subdocument over the network, Word displays the message shown in Figure 11-21.

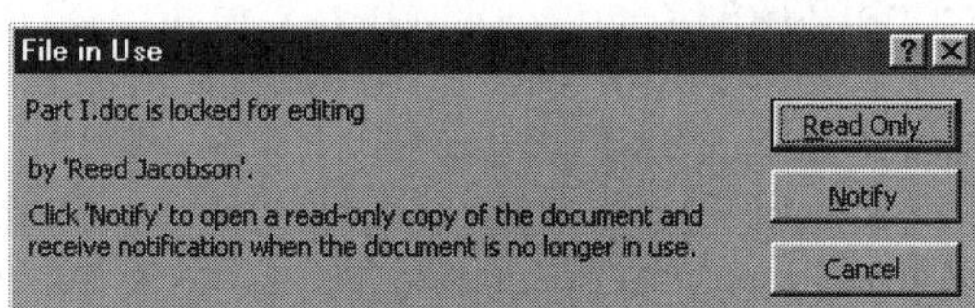

Figure 11-21
Only one user can have a document open for editing at a time.

Let's say that your associate chooses the Notify button. After you have finished making changes to the Chapter 1 portion of the document, you can lock just that portion. In Outline view, with the selection inside the Chapter 1 subdocument, click the Lock Document button. You can then make no further changes to the document. After a few seconds, your associate will see the message illustrated in Figure 11-22.

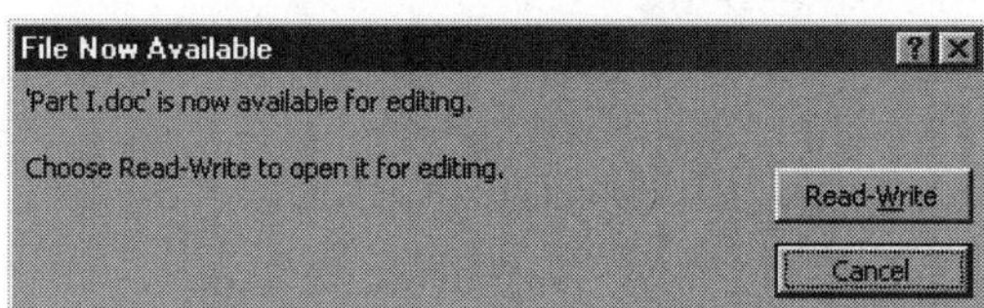

Figure 11-22
Word notifies others when a lock has been released.

If your associate clicks the Read-Write button, but you made changes to the document while it was open as Read Only, there will be a conflict between the changes you made and the new changes. Word gives your associate limited options, as shown in Figure 11-23.

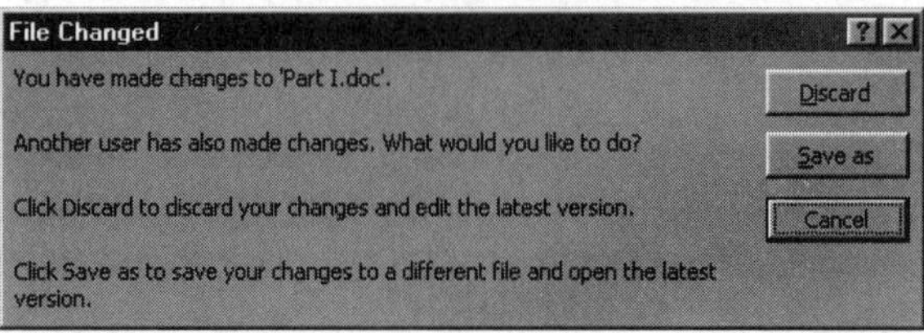

Figure 11-23
Word does not allow a user to discard unseen changes.

Your associate can select the Discard button to discard the visible changes, but there is no option to discard the invisible changes you made.

Comparing Locking with Other Protection Mechanisms

In addition to locking a subdocument, you can also use the Lock Document button to lock the master document itself. (That's why the button caption is Lock Document and not Lock Subdocument.)

When you write-protect an ordinary document—or when you add a Modify password—Word opens the file in read-only mode. Read-only mode does not prevent the person reviewing the document from making changes to the file; the reader simply cannot save the file with the same filename. When a document or subdocument is locked within the context of a master document, however, the read-only status becomes very rigorous; it does not allow any edits to the document at all.

You could use this effect as a feature for a document that you want to place on your company's network, when you want to remind users that the file cannot be modified. Create a subdocument and add a single subdocument to it—perhaps a security notification text document. Then, change the network file status to make the file read-only. When anyone opens the document—which will be in read-only mode—Word prevents any changes to the file at all. If someone tries to type anything in the file, Word will display a status bar error message that the command is not available because the document is locked for editing.

It would be very nice if Word had a way of locking a document for editing without adding a subdocument to it. Of course, locking a file does not provide absolute security. A user can always save the master document with a different name and, in the process, remove the Modify password. It does, however, serve as an effective reminder to someone reading the document that it should not be modified.

Creating References Between Subdocuments

One of the real benefits of using a master document is the ability to create references between subdocuments. With the master document open, you can create a cross-reference from one subdocument to another. In Figure 11-24, Chapter 2 contains a cross-reference to Chapter 4.

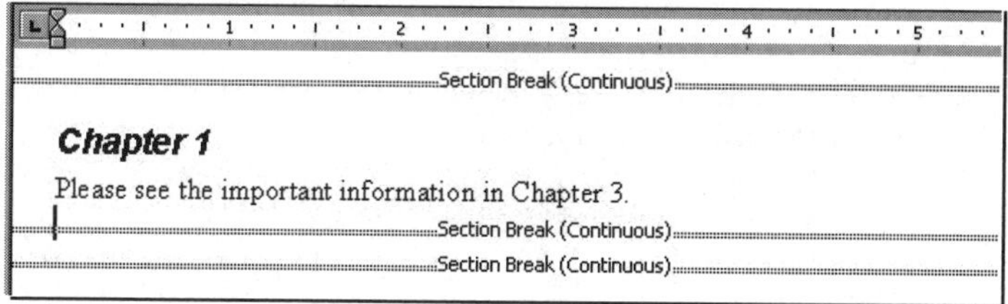

Figure 11-24
Within a Master Document, you can reference text in other subdocuments.

To create a cross-reference like the one illustrated in the previous figure, click Cross-Reference on the Insert menu, select Heading as the Reference Type, select Heading Text as the Insert Reference To option, and then select the target heading in the For Which Heading list box. When you create a cross-reference, Word creates a unique bookmark at the target location and adds a {REF} field at the location of the reference. Figure 11-25 shows a field code for a cross-reference.

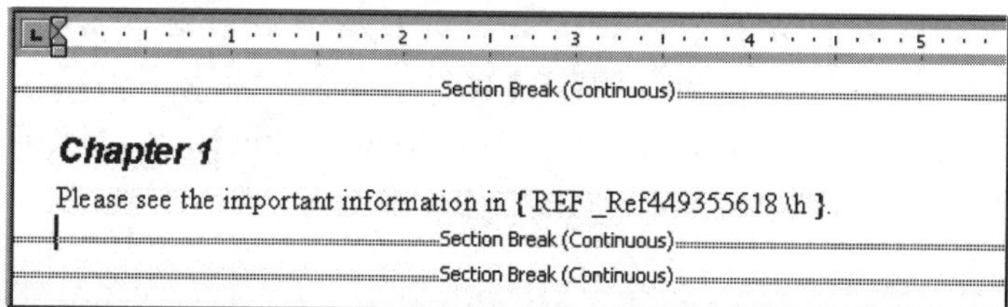

Figure 11-25
A {REF} field refers to other subdocuments within the master document.

If you calculate the {REF} field while the subdocuments are expanded, Word finds the bookmark and displays the cross-referenced text. If you open the subdocument on its own, it retains the reference until you recalculate the field. When you recalculate the {REF} field, Word is unable to find the bookmark because the bookmark target is not in the same subdocument.

Using a Macro to Convert References to External References

If you want to create cross-references between separate documents, one effective strategy is to include all documents in a master document and create the references there. Then, create the following *ConvertReferences* macro to convert {REF} fields—which look for a bookmark in the same document—into {INCLUDETEXT} fields—which can look for a bookmark in a different document.

```
Sub ConvertReferences()
    Dim myField As Field
    Dim myReference As Range
    Dim sCode As String
    Dim sBookmark As String

    For Each myField In ActiveDocument.Fields
        ''' Don't do anything unless it is a reference field code
        If myField.Type = wdFieldRef Then
            ''' get the code from the current REF field
            sCode = Trim(myField.Code)
            ''' extract (and discard) the field type name
            sBookmark = ExtractFirstString(sCode)
            ''' extract (and keep) the referenced bookmark name
            sBookmark = ExtractFirstString(sCode)

            ''' Get a reference to the bookmarked range
            Set myReference = ActiveDocument.Bookmarks(sBookmark).Range
            ''' Composite a new field code
            sCode = "Includetext """ & myReference.Subdocuments(1).Name _
                & """ " & sBookmark & " " & sCode

            ''' replace the field's code
            myField.Code.Text = sCode
        End If
    Next myField
End Sub
```

The macro loops through all the fields in the document, ignoring all fields other than the {REF} field. If you want to convert {PAGEREF} fields to cross-reference page numbers, you need to modify the macro and make sure the start page for each separate document is correct. The macro uses the *ExtractFirstString* function described in Chapter 4, "Power Up Visual Basic." The function extracts the first string—delimited by a space—and removes it from the original string. In a {REF} field, the bookmark is the second string, so calling *ExtractFirstString* the first time extracts (and discards) the {REF} field code, and calling it the second time extracts (and keeps) the field code. The *sCode* string is left with anything that followed the bookmark name in the field code (for example, a * MERGEFORMAT switch).

The macro then finds the range referred to by the bookmark, finds the subdocument that contains the range, and reconstructs a new field code—this time using the {INCLUDETEXT} field, which takes both document name and bookmark as arguments. For good measure, the macro tacks on any remaining text from the original {REF} field code, and finally replaces the {REF} field code string with the new string. Figure 11-26 shows the reference after it has been converted.

While the macro runs, the document must be open with all the subdocuments expanded. After the macro runs, the subdocuments can be opened separately—and the

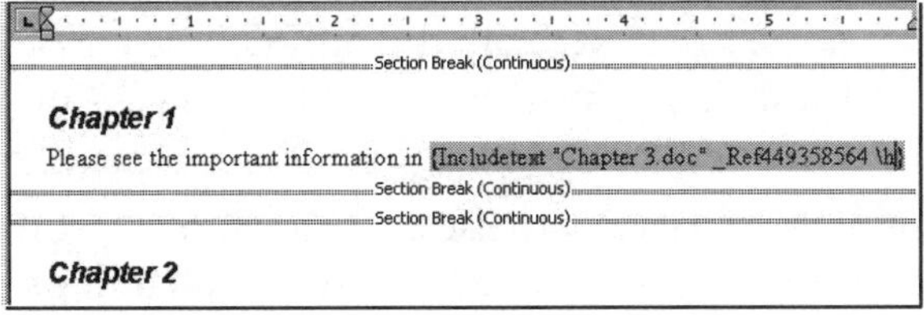

Figure 11-26
An IncludeText field can refer to another document.

fields recalculated—without losing the references. The subdocuments must all remain in the same folder.

Printing a Large Document

Printing a large document can consume a considerable amount of paper. Word offers a new feature that allows you to print two to four logical pages on a single physical sheet of paper, called 2-up and 4-up printing. In the Print dialog box, select the desired number of pages in Pages Per Sheet drop-down list, as shown in Figure 11-27.

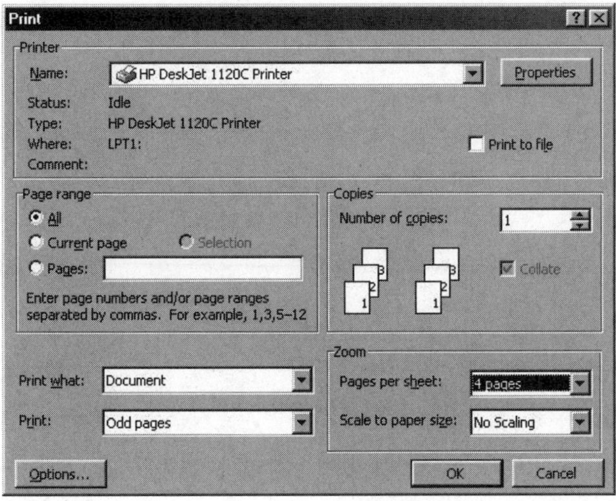

Figure 11-27
Print multiple pages per sheet to save paper.

Some printers also have the capability of printing on both sides of paper automatically—called duplex printing. Duplex printing is another way to substantially reduce the amount of paper you use. Word's Print dialog box makes it possible to do duplex printing even on an ordinary printer that can print on only one side of a page at a time. You simply specify that you want to print all the odd pages; then, you take the paper out, turn it over and place it back into the printer's paper tray facing the right direction. Finally, you print all the even pages. In Figure 11-27, the Print drop-down list shows Odd Pages selected.

Unfortunately, Word does not make it easy to use both the duplex print feature and the 4-up feature together. When you select all even pages or all odd pages, you are specifying logical pages, not physical pages.

Create a Macro to Print Multiple Pages on Each Side of a Printed Sheet

To print four logical pages on each side of a duplexed physical page, you must print pages 1-4, print pages 9-12, and so forth, skipping every other group of four pages. In other words, you must print even or odd physical pages, not logical pages. Depending on the nature of your printer, you might need to print the backside of the sheets in reverse order after reinserting the paper.

The following *Print4Duplex* macro prints 4-up duplex pages. It sends all the odd physical pages to the printer, and then waits for you to switch the paper to print the even physical pages. The macro is designed so that you can switch it to print 2-up duplex pages (which might be easier to read than 4-up duplex pages) simply by changing a constant value.

```
Sub Print4Duplex()
    Const iFit As Long = 4
    Dim x As Document
    Dim i As Long
    Dim n As Long
    Dim iStop As Long
    n = ActiveDocument.BuiltInDocumentProperties(wdPropertyPages)
    iStop = ((n + (iFit - 1)) \ (iFit * 2)) * (iFit * 2) - (iFit - 1)
    For i = 1 To iStop Step (iFit * 2)
        DoPrint i, iFit
    Next i
    If i > 1 Then MsgBox "After page " & i - iFit - 1 & _
        " has printed, invert the stack in tray and click OK."
    For i = iStop To 1 Step -(iFit * 2)
        DoPrint i, iFit
    Next i
    i = iStop + iFit
    If i <= n Then
        DoPrint i, iFit
    End If
End Sub
```

The constant *iFit* controls how many logical pages are printed on a single physical page; it must be either 4 or 2. The macro determines the number of pages in the document, and then uses that number and the *iFit* variable to determine how many pages it will take to print halfway through the document. The *iStop* variable stores the number of the first page that should be printed on the back side. One factor that complicates calculating the halfway point is having an uneven number of pages in the document. If the document is 12 pages long, the halfway point is four pages, not six pages, because the second physical piece of paper will have nothing on the back; the first page for the back side is page five. If the document has 13 pages, however, the halfway point is eight pages, since the second physical page will have a single logical page on the back; the first page for the back side is page nine.

The statement that calculates the *iStop* variable is messy, but it uses mostly simple algebraic calculations. The backslash operator (\) divides one number by another, producing an integer result and discarding the remainder.

The macro executes two loops, one for the front sides of the page and one for the back. The contents of each loop are identical, so it is moved into a separate *DoPrint* subroutine. The subroutine needs the first page to print and the number of pages to print on the sheet as arguments. The first loop starts with page 1 and continues to the halfway point, incrementing by twice the number of pages per sheet. It then displays a message box to allow time to invert the paper. The second loop starts with the first page to be printed on the back, but loops from the back to the front. If your printer doesn't require the back copies to be printed in reverse order, change the statement that begins the second loop to *For i = iFit + 1 To iStop Step (iFit * 2)*. (In other words, make it the same as the first loop, except that it starts with the first logical page on the second physical sheet.)

The following *DoPrint* subroutine is almost trivial. The only complexity is handling the variable number of pages per sheet. You can extend the macro to print other numbers of pages per sheet by adding additional case statements to the macro.

```
Private Sub DoPrint _
    (ByVal StartPage As Long, ByVal PagesPer As Long)
    Dim iCol As Long
    Dim iRow As Long
    Select Case PagesPer
    Case 2
        iCol = 2
        iRow = 1
    Case 4
        iCol = 2
        iRow = 2
    Case Else
        MsgBox "Unable to print " & PagesPer & "pages per sheet."
        Exit Sub
    End Select
    ActiveDocument.PrintOut _
        Range:=wdPrintRangeOfPages, _
        Pages:=StartPage & "-" & StartPage + (PagesPer - 1), _
        Item:=wdPrintDocumentContent, _
        Copies:=1, _
        PageType:=wdPrintAllPages, _
        Collate:=False, _
```

```
        Background:=False, _
        PrintToFile:=False, _
        PrintZoomColumn:=iCol, _
        PrintZoomRow:=iRow, _
        PrintZoomPaperWidth:=0, _
        PrintZoomPaperHeight:=0
End Sub
```

The subroutine passes the actual pages to print as a string to the *Pages* argument. The string looks like what you would type in the Pages text box on the Print dialog box: for example, "1-4". In principle, you could construct a single string for printing all the first side. It would look something like this: "1-4,9-12,17-20." It might or might not make the printing go faster. If you look at the documentation for the PrintOut method for a document, the *From* and *To* arguments should allow you to specify starting and ending page numbers without constructing a string. They don't work. Stick with the *Pages* argument.

The macro does not allow you to select a printer. It simply prints to the default printer. If you need to print to a special network printer, you will need to change the default printer in the Printers control panel.

Part 4

Excel Tools

Chapter 12

Use Excel References to Build Better Relationships

In This Chapter

References are the lifeblood of formulas. The better you learn how to use (and manage) references, the better models you will be able to build. Microsoft Excel provides several powerful tools for creating, tweaking, adjusting, and using references. This chapter briefly reviews the basics of relative and absolute references, and then continues to reveal the incredible power of Excel references.

Managing References in a Grid

The simplest cell reference is an address based on a grid. The letter prefix indicates the column and the number suffix indicates the row, much like finding an address on a map. The reference A1 refers to the upper, leftmost cell on the worksheet, and the reference IV65536 refers to the lower, rightmost cell on the worksheet. This part of cell references is easy. The fun begins when you copy a cell containing a formula.

Suppose you have a simple worksheet with price values in the cell range B1:E1 and quantity values in the cell range A2:A5, as shown in Figure 12-1. To create a formula that calculates the revenue in cell B2, take the following steps:

1. Type an *equal sign* (=) and select cell B1.
2. Type an *asterisk* (*) and select cell A2.
3. Press Enter.

B2 = =B1*A2

	A	B	C	D	E	F
1		$5	$10	$15	$20	
2	2	$10				
3	4					
4	6					
5	8					

Figure 12-1
A typical model in a grid.

The resulting formula, *=B1*A2,* is simple. However, what happens when you copy the formula you just created to the rest of the cells from the range B2:E5? None of the copied formulas will be correct, because the reference =B1 does not actually point to cell B1. What it means depends entirely on the cell containing the reference. If cell B2 contains the reference =B1, then it means "point to the cell directly above".

To anchor either the row or the column portion of the reference, you must prefix the reference with a dollar sign ($). In the price and quantity example shown in Figure 12-1, you want the price reference in column B to adjust to the values in columns C, D, and E as you copy the formula to the right. In addition, you want the quantity reference in row 2 to adjust as you copy the formula down. The correct formula for cell B2 is *=B$1*$A2.* If you want to multiply the revenue by a fixed quantity—say, a commission percentage stored in cell G1—that reference requires that the references from both the row and the column be anchored, with the resulting formula becoming *=B$1*$A2*$G$1.*

Cell references come in one of four types:

- Completely relative
- Row relative
- Column relative
- Completely absolute

To cycle between the four reference types, select the cell reference in the formula bar and repeatedly press F4 to cycle through the options. Whenever you have a formula that you will copy both horizontally and vertically, you almost certainly will need an absolute reference somewhere in the formula.

Excel's default reference type is *completely relative*. A relative reference is simple and easy to view; there are no distracting dollar signs to worry about. You need to make all or part of a reference absolute only if you intend to copy the formula. If you don't copy a formula, relative and absolute references in the formula will make no difference at all.

Of course, spreadsheets have a way of becoming more complex over time. You start by calculating a single revenue value based on a single price and quantity. Before long, you want to compare the effect of various price, quantity relationships, so you start copying formulas. You begin seeing errors in your answers, and you hope you notice them before your boss or client does.

Picking the Right Reference Style

It is important that you watch out for references which should be absolute as you create formulas, even though doing so requires as much disciplined foresight as changing your car's wiper blades before the rainy season hits. Excel provides an alternative reference notation that is nearly as good as having your wiper blades pop up red "change me" flags in August. It's called R1C1 notation. When you refer to cells by letter and number, it's called *A1 notation* because that's what the reference in the upper left cell in the worksheet displays. In R1C1 notation, Excel refers to cells using two sets of numbers, preceding each set of numbers with the letter R or C to show which is a *Row* and which is a *Column*. This is called *R1C1 notation*, again because that is the reference for the upper leftmost cell. Regular numbers indicate absolute row and column positions, and bracketed numbers indicate relative positions. A simple R or C all by itself indicates the same row or same column, respectively.

The difference between R1C1 notation and A1 notation is that in R1C1 notation, the reference describes what it literally does. You cannot say "one cell above me" using A1 notation without knowing which cell contains the formula. Consequently, the phrase "one cell above me" appears as =B1 in cell B2, while "one cell above me" appears as =AZ22 in cell AZ23. In R1C1 notation, the reference "one cell above me" will always display =R[–1]C, regardless of what cell contains the formula, making this reference type very useful in macros and named formulas.

As mentioned earlier, relative and absolute references come in four types. R1C1 notation stands out from A1 notation in that in any given context, the correct reference type almost always has the fewest characters of the four choices. Take the reference to price in cell B2 of the example from Figure 12-1 shown earlier, for example. In A1 notation, the four possible relative and absolute combinations for referring to cell B1 are B1, $B$1, B$1, and $B1. The simplest of the four—B1—is not the correct reference type in this context. In contrast, when using R1C1 notation, the four reference types for referring to the same cell are R[–1]C, R1C2, R1C, and R[–1]C2. The simplest of the four—R1C—is the correct reference type in this context.

Try the same test with the reference to quantity. In A1 notation, the four possible reference types are A2, $A$2, A$2, and $A2. The simplest, again, is the completely relative but completely incorrect reference. In R1C1 notation, the four possible reference types are RC[–1], R2C1, R2C[–1], and RC1. The simplest in this notation style is the fourth reference—RC1—which is the correct reference.

Toggling R1C1 Notation

When you are viewing cell references in a formula to determine if you have used the proper relative and absolute reference types, R1C1 notation can be extremely useful. It is also the most difficult to read. You probably don't want to live with R1C1 notation enabled, but it is very easy to switch between the two notation styles. On the Tools menu, click Options, select the General tab, and select or clear the R1C1 Reference Style check box. If you want to be able to switch frequently, make it even easier to toggle types by adding the following *ToggleR1C1* macro to your personal workbook, and then assign the macro to a toolbar button or a shortcut key:

```
Sub ToggleR1C1()
    If Application.ReferenceStyle = xlA1 Then
        Application.ReferenceStyle = xlR1C1
    Else
        Application.ReferenceStyle = xlA1
    End If
End Sub
```

Letting Excel Decide Between Relative and Absolute References

If you look closely at relative and absolute references, you will notice that most of the time, the portion of a cell reference that is in the same row or column as the formula is relative, while the portion that is in a different row or column is absolute. Look again at the revenue calculation shown earlier in Figure 12-1. When you refer to the price in cell B1 from a formula in cell B2, both the reference and the formula are in the same column, so the column portion of the reference is relative. Conversely, the reference and the formula are in different rows, so the row portion of the reference is absolute. When the formula in cell B2 refers to the commission value in cell G1, neither the row nor the column is the same between the formula and the reference, so both portions are absolute.

This "same is relative, different is absolute" nature of most formulas is what allows the R1C1 notation style to provide the simplest form for the correct reference: in R1C1 notation, the only time a relative reference is simple is when it is in the same row or column.

The Excel development team noticed this recurring pattern of relative references and built an extremely powerful feature into Excel to deal with relative and absolute references. It's called *implicit intersection*, which allows you to create formulas that are easy to read and easy to copy, simply by naming a couple of ranges.

Take the price and quantity grid shown earlier in Figure 12-1. If you name the cell range B1:E1 as *Price*, and you name the cell range A2:A5 as *Quantity*, you can then type the formula =*Price**Quantity* into cell B2 and it will return the proper value. Here's why this technique works: When Excel looks at the formula, it sees a multiplication sign (*). Multiplication is an operation that requires two single-value *operands*. The price operand in the formula, however, is not a single-cell; it is a single-row by multiple-column range. Excel then intersects the column containing the formula with the price range. The result is a single value, which it uses in the formula. Excel then goes through the same process with the quantity operand, but this time, it's the row containing the formula that successfully produces a single value when intersected with the quantity reference.

You can copy the formula =*Price*Quantity* to all the cells in the cell range B2:E5, and in each case, the implicit intersection calculation derives the correct relative reference. You are using the named range to give the formula the absolute portion of the reference (which is the part it needs to know), and letting it determine the relative portion by intersecting the current row or column.

If you try to extend the =*Price*Quantity* formula past the limits of the named range—say to cell F2—the formula will result in a #VALUE! error. When Excel tries to intersect the range *Price* with the current column, there is no overlap. Because of this need to intersect, if there is any possibility you might need to extend a block of the formula, create the name to refer to the entire row or column. Give the name *Price* to the entire first row and the name *Quantity* to the entire first column. Including the extra cells in the named range will not harm the formulas you have—they will intersect with the current row or column to produce a single cell—but this will make it easier to extend the model later.

Managing References in a List

Sometimes, you need to create formulas that are part of a list similar to the one illustrated in Figure 12-2. In your list, you often have two or more input (value) columns, and one or more output (calculated) columns, both based on the value columns. There are at least three alternatives for dealing with formulas in a list, each of which has its advantages and its disadvantages.

One option is simply to use cell addresses in the formula. Technically, the appropriate form for the reference would show the row as relative and the column as absolute, as in =*$B2-$C2*. Because you will not be copying formulas horizontally, you also could use simple relative references, as in =*B2-C2*. As you enter values and formulas into the list, you can simply copy the formula from the preceding row.

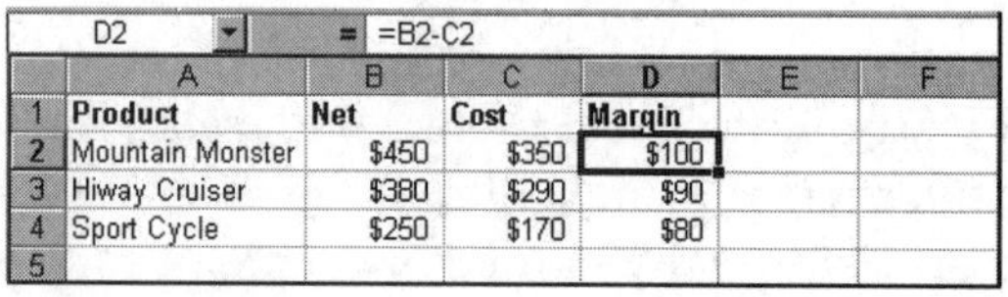

	A	B	C	D	E	F
1	**Product**	**Net**	**Cost**	**Margin**		
2	Mountain Monster	$450	$350	$100		
3	Hiway Cruiser	$380	$290	$90		
4	Sport Cycle	$250	$170	$80		
5						

D2 = =B2-C2

Figure 12-2
A typical model in a list.

Note To copy the formula from the preceding row, press Ctrl+Shift+". Think of it as Ctrl+ditto.

New! A strange thing happens after you have begun entering values and formulas into as few as four rows in your list: Excel begins entering the formulas for you. This ability to extend formulas in a list is new in Excel 2000. This feature can be disabled by clicking Options on the Tools menu, clicking Edit, and then clearing the Extend List Formats And Formulas check box.

Creating Readable Formulas Using Names

One disadvantage of using cell addresses in a formula is that the formula can become difficult to decipher. If you have complex relationships defined in a list, readable formulas are worth a lot. One way to create formulas that are more readable is to define names for ranges of cells. If you give the name *Net* to column B and the name *Cost* to column C, you can then enter the formula *=Net-Cost* into any cell on the worksheet and Excel will calculate the difference between the two columns for the row containing the formula.

One disadvantage to using names in a formula is that Excel will extend formulas to new rows in a list only if the cells contain cell addresses. If you use readable formulas, you will have to manually copy them to the new rows. One useful technique—after defining new names—is to ask Excel to convert formulas that use cell addresses into formulas that use range names. Click Names on the Insert menu, click Apply, select all the names you care about in the Apply Names list, and then click OK. The Use Row And Column Names check box tells Excel that you want it to use implicit intersection where possible. As you can see in Figure 12-3, if you click the Options button, the subordinate check boxes show you precisely how Excel will apply implicit intersection. The result of applying the names to the list shown earlier in Figure 12-2 is *=Net-Cost.*

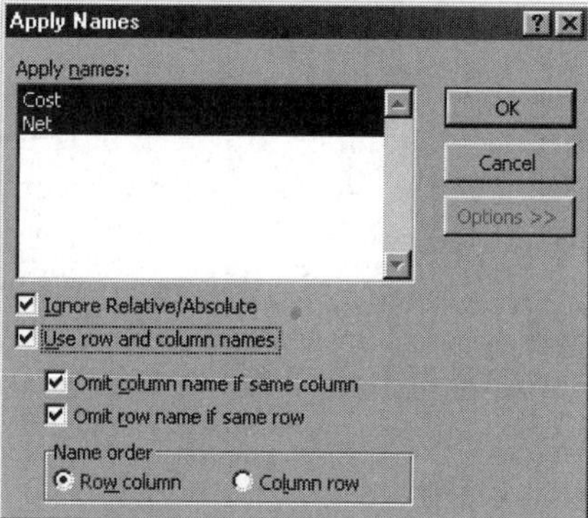

Figure 12-3
Applying names uses implicit intersection.

Creating Readable Formulas Using Labels

Another way to create readable formulas is to use the labels at the top of the columns as if they were names. Before you can use labels in formulas, you must change the workbook option so it can accept them. Click Options on the Tools menu, click Calculate, and select the Accept Labels In Formulas check box. This setting applies to the entire workbook and is saved with the workbook (the default for a new workbook is not to accept labels).

Chapter 12

In the workbook shown earlier in Figure 12-2, suppose you deleted all the names but accepted labels in the formula. If you type the formula *=Net-Cost* into cell D2 of the worksheet, Excel will look at the current region, see the labels in the top row or the left column, and behave as if the entire column or row were named with that label. Labels in formulas were new in Excel 97, and were designed to make it easy to create readable formulas in simple models. As with names, Excel will not automatically extend formulas using labels to new rows in a list.

Note If you have already created formulas using names and then delete the names, Excel does not recognize the labels until you edit and reenter each formula. To quickly re-enter all the formulas on a worksheet, search for and replace "=" with "=" throughout the entire worksheet.

Excel uses an internal algorithm to determine which labels refer to which rows or columns, so you will not have the same control over how labels are interpreted as you would with explicitly defined names. Sometimes, the way Excel interprets labels is logical and sometimes it is surprising. If you have the same label twice in a worksheet—for example, a Plan version and an Actual version—Excel will either prompt you for which label you want to use, use the first label without prompting, or use the second label without prompting. If you ever get frustrated trying to control labels, your model is getting too complex for labels and you should switch to defined names.

Understanding How Excel Interprets Labels

If you want to see how Excel interprets labels in a formula, you can disable the label option, which will convert the formulas with labels into cell addresses. (If you don't want to permanently lose the labels, save the workbook first, because you can't undo this conversion.) To disable labels, click Optionson the Tools menu, click Calculation, and clear the Accept Labels In Formulas check box. The label formula *=Net-Cost* from the list shown earlier in Figure 12-2 converts to the cell address formula *=B$2:B$65536-C$2:C$65536.* Excel has interpreted these column labels to be all cells below the label and to the bottom of the sheet. The row portion of the reference is absolute and the column portion is relative. If you copy the formula to the right, it will shift to whatever labels are in the new columns. In the list shown in Figure 12-2, copying the formula from column D to column E changes the formula from *=Net-Cost* to *=Cost-Margin.* The relative nature of labels can actually be very useful if your list contains columns comparing one month to the previous month, or for some types of running totals.

If a label contains spaces, or if it matches something that Excel could otherwise interpret as a reference, you need to precede the label with apostrophes ('). Specifically, you need apostrophes if a label matches a defined name in the workbook. (If you define a name after creating a formula that uses a label, Excel will place apostrophes into the formula for you.) You need apostrophes if you have a label that matches a potential cell address in either A1 or R1C1 notation. For example, if you have a product named B52 in a cell as a label, you would need apostrophes to prevent Excel from interpreting the label as a cell address. Seemingly innocuous labels such as R2001C—or even just C or R—are potential cell addresses in R1C1 notation and require apostrophes in formulas.

The option to allow labels in formulas is a workbook-level setting. You can disable labels for one workbook, while having labels enabled on another, even when both workbooks are open at the same time.

Making New Workbooks Accept Labels in Formulas

In Excel 97, new workbooks would accept labels in formulas as the default. In Excel 2000, the default has been changed to not accept labels. If you like to use labels, you can write a simple macro to change the default. First, you must set up an event handler for application events as described in "Handling Events with VBA" in Chapter 5. Then add the following event handler to the Handlers class:

```
Private Sub ApplicationHandler_NewWorkbook(ByVal Wb As Workbook)
    Wb.AcceptLabelsInFormulas = True
End Sub
```

Once you have the handler set up, the macro will run each time Excel creates a new workbook. It simply selects the check box for you.

Managing References Beyond the Worksheet

Note The sample documents for this section are Client.xls and Source.xls.

Worksheet models are often interrelated. You might have one model developed for product pricing plans, another model developed for unit forecasts, and a third model combining the two to create a revenue plan. In the same way that references can refer to other cells within a worksheet, they can also refer to cells in other worksheets, or even to cells in other workbooks. Links are generally easy to create. You can create links by pointing to cells, or by copying cells and then using the Paste Link button from the Paste Special dialog box.

Linking Within a Workbook

If you need to link to a single cell within the workbook, name the cell and refer to the cell by name. If you use a name, you don't need to include the sheet portion of the reference because names are, by default, global within a workbook. See "Using Names to Simplify Relationships" later in this chapter for information on using names in a workbook.

Links to another cell in a workbook always refer to an absolute worksheet. You cannot create a link using the reference "cell A1 on the worksheet before this one."

Viewing a Linked Cell

If a cell refers to a cell on a different worksheet within the workbook, you might want to see both the source and the target cells at the same time. To do that, you will need to open a second window in the workbook. Click Window and then New Window. Next, click Arrange on the Window menu, and select Tiled. Finally, select the source and target worksheets to display in each window.

Range finder boxes do not appear around source references on a different worksheet, even if the source worksheet is visible in a separate window. If you use the Auditing toolbar to display precedent arrows, the arrows point to boxes if the cell is linked. Clicking the arrow displays the Go To dialog box on the Edit menu with any precedent cells listed, as shown in Figure 12-4.

Excel provides a shortcut key for selecting precedent cells that will select a precedent on a different worksheet with no intermediate steps. The shortcut key is Ctrl+[(Left Bracket). (You can remember the left bracket as pointing to the left, in the direction of a precedent.) The corresponding key—Ctrl+] (Right Bracket)—points to the right in the direction of a dependent. If a cell has precedents on both the active sheet and on the linked sheet, Ctrl+[selects only the precedents on the active sheet. Unfortunately, Ctrl+] finds dependents on only the active sheet.

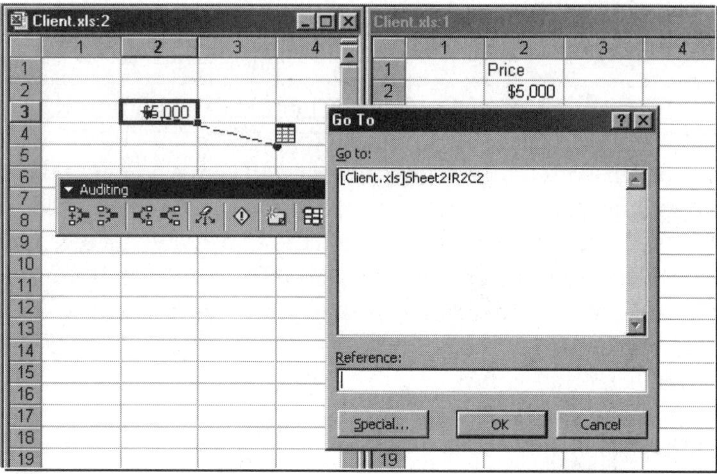

Figure 12-4
Click the precedent arrow to go to a linked cell.

Creating Three-Dimensional Formulas

Three-dimensional formulas are formulas that work across multiple worksheets within a workbook, and only function with aggregate functions such as SUM or AVERAGE. A three-dimensional formula must use the same cells on each worksheet. To create a three-dimensional formula, insert a colon between two worksheet names. The three-dimensional range refers to the two worksheets, plus all worksheets between them. For example, in a workbook with sheets named Sheet1, Sheet2, and Sheet3, the formula *=SUM(Sheet1:Sheet3!A1:B2)* summarizes a total of 12 cells (3 sheets times 4 cells on each sheet). If you move Sheet2 after Sheet3, it is immediately—and without warning—removed from the three-dimensional range. Conversely, if you insert a worksheet between the two endpoint worksheets, it becomes part of the three-dimensional range.

You can give a name to a three-dimensional reference in the same way that you can name a formula that calculates a reference. See "Naming Constants and Formulas" later in this chapter for details about naming reference formulas. You cannot use a formula, however, to manipulate a three-dimensional reference. See the section "Using Reference Functions" later in this chapter for details about how to use formulas to manipulate references.

Linking Outside a Workbook

Linking to a cell in a different workbook is very similar to linking to a cell on a different worksheet. In fact, if you move a source sheet to a new workbook, Excel automatically converts the formulas to include the new workbook name. Worksheets usually stay together since they're in the same workbook. However, workbooks can move around, and links between workbooks easily become broken. If you understand how Excel works with linked formulas, you usually can prevent links from breaking, and you can fix them if they do.

Managing Links Between Folders

When you create a link to a separate workbook. Excel needs to store the location of the source workbook to do so. If the source workbook is in the same folder as the target, Excel stores only its name, not its full path. If the source workbook is in a subfolder of the folder containing the target workbook, Excel stores only the relative path. If the source workbook is higher in the folder tree, however, or if it is in a different branch altogether, Excel stores its complete path.

Suppose you have one workbook named Conclusions in a folder named C:\Forecast, and another workbook named Assumptions in the subfolder named C:\Forecast\Draft. You create a link from the Conclusions workbook to a cell in the Assumptions workbook. You now want to share your forecast draft with a coworker, so you copy the Forecast folder to the network path \\COMPANY\Users\Shared. Everything works perfectly, because the source document is in a folder below the folder containing the target; Excel just copies the whole model intact.

Suppose you had stored the Assumptions workbook (the source for the link) in the C:\Forecasts folder, and the Conclusions workbook (the target for the link) in the C:\Forecast\Draft subfolder. In this case, the source document is in a folder above the one containing the target. When you copy the pair of folders to the network, strange things can happen.

If you open both network files, you will see a message asking if you want to update links, even if you open the Assumptions file first. If you change the Assumptions, the new values will not transfer to the Conclusions file, because the links in the Conclusions workbook are still looking at the file on your local drive.

If your coworker opens both network files (or if you moved the files rather than copying them), stranger things happen. When she answers yes to the puzzling question about updating the linked values, Excel will inform her that the file does not exist (since the source workbook is not on her C: drive) and will offer to let her look for it. Even if she finds the Assumptions file on the network, the link will work properly only until she closes the workbook. After that, it will revert to its original state before she closed the file. Finding a file when Excel detects a broken link only temporarily fixes the problem. This can be very frustrating when you think you have fixed a problem but it keeps coming back.

Whenever possible, store the source workbook either in the same folder as the target workbook or in a subfolder. If you must link to a workbook that is either higher in the tree or in a different tree entirely, plan to repair broken links if you ever move the source workbook to a new folder.

Repairing Broken Links

To repair broken links in a workbook, activate the target workbook and then click Edit, Links. Select the link you want to repair and click Change Source. Find the correct source workbook and click OK.

You also can change links from an external workbook to the active workbook (for example, if you have an Assumptions sheet in the active workbook, as well as in a separate workbook). Act as if you are repairing a broken list, but select the currently active workbook as the source. After you convert a link so that the source is the same as the target, it ceases to be an external link, and you won't be able change it back without changing each formula.

Finding All the Links in a Workbook

Sometimes you will see a phantom link in a workbook. Excel will prompt you to update links, but you won't know if you have any links to update. Links can occur either in worksheet cells or in named references. To find all the possible links in a workbook, you must search not only all the worksheets, but also all the named references. The latter can be tricky because, as explained in the "Managing Local and Global Names" later in this chapter, all the names might not be visible in the Define Name dialog box. The *FindLinks* macro shown later in this chapter will create a log of all the links in a workbook, including links to invalid cell addresses. Figure 12-5 shows a sample log generated by the macro. With the log, you can quickly determine which links are desirable and which links are forgotten leftovers.

	A	B	C
1	**Links in names**		
2	BadName	=[source.xls]Sheet1!#REF!	
3	GoodName	=[source.xls]Sheet1!$B$5	
4	**Links in Sheet1**		
5	$B$3	=source.xls!Discount	
6	$B$5	=[source.xls]Sheet1!B2	
7	$C$5	=[source.xls]Sheet1!C2	
8	$B$6	=[source.xls]Sheet1!B3	
9	$C$6	=[source.xls]Sheet1!C3	
10	**Links in Sheet2**		
11	**Links in Sheet3**		
12	$D$4	=[source.xls]Sheet1!D4	
13	$E$4	=[source.xls]Sheet1!E4	
14	$D$5	=[source.xls]Sheet1!D5	
15	$E$5	=[source.xls]Sheet1!E5	
16	$D$6	=[source.xls]Sheet1!D6	
17	$E$6	=[source.xls]Sheet1!E6	
18			
19			
20			

Figure 12-5
The FindLinks macro helps you find invalid links.

The *FindLinks* macro is complex, so you might not immediately understand it all. The comments are preceded by apostrophes at the beginning of the respective lines, and they should help you understand the section of code listed.

```
Sub FindLinks()
    Dim myStartBook As Workbook
    Dim myLogRange As Range
    Dim myName As Name
    Dim mySheet As Worksheet
    Dim myFindCell As Range
    Dim myFirstCell As Range

    ''' Initialize a log workbook
    Set myStartBook = ActiveWorkbook
    Workbooks.Add
    Set myLogRange = ActiveSheet.Cells(1)
    myStartBook.Activate

    ''' Log all names that contain a !
    myLogRange.Value = "Links in names"
    myLogRange.Font.Bold = True
    Set myLogRange = myLogRange.Offset(1)
    For Each myName In Names
        If InStr(myName.RefersTo, "!") Then
            myLogRange.Value = myName.Name
            myLogRange.Offset(0, 1).Value = "'" & myName.RefersTo
            Set myLogRange = myLogRange.Offset(1)
        End If
    Next myName
    ''' Search each worksheet in turn
    For Each mySheet In Worksheets
        myLogRange.Value = "Links in " & mySheet.Name
        myLogRange.Font.Bold = True
        Set myLogRange = myLogRange.Offset(1)
        ''' Search for a ! character
        Set myFindCell = mySheet.Cells.Find("!", , xlFormulas)

        ''' Find returns Nothing if it can't find a match
        If Not myFindCell Is Nothing Then
            Set myFirstCell = myFindCell
            Do
                ''' Log the cell only if it is a formula
                If myFindCell.PrefixCharacter = "" _
                And Left(myFindCell.Formula, 1) = "=" Then
                    myLogRange.Value = myFindCell.Address
                    myLogRange.Offset(, 1) = "'" & myFindCell.Formula
                    Set myLogRange = myLogRange.Offset(1)
                End If
                Set myFindCell = mySheet.Cells.FindNext(myFindCell)
            ''' Check against first find to know when done
            Loop Until myFindCell.Address = myFirstCell.Address
        End If
    Next mySheet

    ''' Display the log
```

Chapter 12

```
    myLogRange.Parent.Parent.Activate
    Columns.AutoFit
End Sub
```

Links are valuable tools, but you also need tools like the Change Source command and the *FindLinks* macro to help you keep them in line.

Manipulating References

Note The sample document for this section is References.xls.

You can use references in Excel for many years without ever understanding their true nature. For all appearances, a reference is a simple, static pointer to a cell. Even the relative vs. absolute distinction has significance only at the time you copy a formula to a new cell. In every spreadsheet program in the world except Excel, references really are the static links they appear to be.

Excel introduced the concept of references as objects that can be manipulated using formulas. In Excel, you can manipulate references much the same as you can manipulate numbers, dates, or text strings. References are a little more abstract than numbers, so the idea of manipulating references is a little more abstract than the idea of manipulating numbers. Numbers themselves are more abstract than teddy bears, and you made the leap a long time ago from counting toys to multiplying integers. In this section, you will learn how to manipulate references and unleash the full power of Excel.

Understanding Reference Operators

Think of numbers. Operators—the plus (+), minus (-), multiplication (*), and division (/) symbols—enable you to manipulate numbers. What if you had a spreadsheet program that allowed you to use numbers but not numeric operators?

Excel provides *Reference operators*—range, union, and intersection—that work with references in much the same way that *Numeric operators* work with numbers. Looking at ranges on a worksheet can make the abstractness of range operators a little more concrete. Figure 12-6 illustrates named ranges on a worksheet. These ranges will provide you with concrete values to look at as you manipulate references. These sample ranges aren't ones you would use in building a model, but they are very useful when you create named formulas (as explained below in the "Naming Constants And Formulas" section, and used in a practical example in "Charting an Algebraic Function" in Chapter 13).

The best way to physically manipulate references is to use the Go To dialog box on the Edit menu. Press Ctrl+G and then type a reference expression in the Reference text box. When you click OK, Excel selects the reference you specified, or it informs you of an error in the expression.

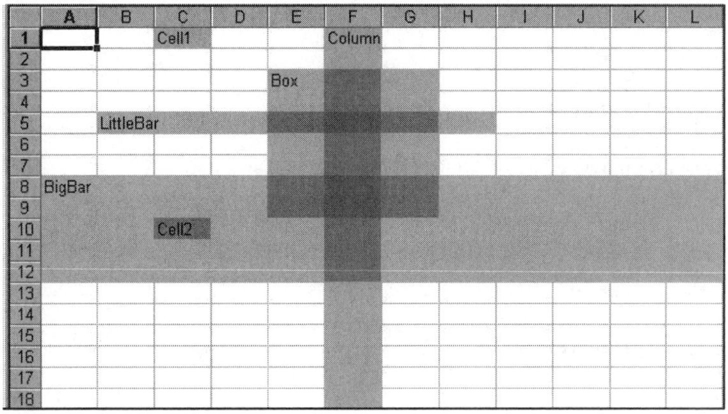

Figure 12-6
Ranges ready to manipulate.

Extending a Reference with the Range Operator

The *Range operator* is a colon. The result of a range operation is always a rectangle. Normally, you specify the rectangle for a range by using the upper left and lower right cells. The expression *Cell1:Cell2* produces the range C1:C10. The range operator can actually use any two references as its operands. The true definition of a range is the rectangle that bounds any two references. The expression *Cell1:LittleBar* produces the range B1:H5, although B1 (the upper left cell) is not in either of the original references.

You can string multiple range operators together into a single expression, much the same as adding 3+4+5 in a single expression. The expression *Cell1:LittleBar:Cell2* produces the range B1:H10, because that rectangle bounds all three ranges.

You can use a range operator to extend an entire column to include a new cell. The expression *Column:Cell1* will produce the range C:F, and the expression *Column:LittleBar* will produce the range B:H.

Reference operators that require all references be on the same worksheet. You can't use a range operator (or any of the reference operators) with cell addresses to construct a three-dimensional reference. (See the sidebar "Creating Three-Dimensional Formulas" for information about creating three-dimensional references.)

The range operator corresponds to VBA's Range method—the version with two arguments. The Range method will accept either Range objects, or strings that refer to range names or cell addresses. If you enclose a reference expression in square brackets instead of quotation marks, Excel will interpret it as a Range object. If you want to use the Range method to combine more than two references, nest the methods. The following VBA statements correspond to selecting the cell addresses described above. The comment above each statement restates the reference as you would enter it in the Go To text box on the Edit menu.

```
''' Cell1:Cell2
Range("Cell1","Cell2").Select
''' Cell1:LittleBar
Range("Cell1","LittleBar").Select
''' Cell1:LittleBar:Cell2
Range(Range("Cell1","LittleBar"),"Cell2").Select
Set myColumn = [Column]Set myCell1 = [Cell1]''' Column:Cell1
Range(myColumn,myCell1).Select
''' Column:LittleBar
Range(myColumn,[LittleBar]).Select
```

Combining References with the Union Operator

The *Union operator* is a comma. A union is a simple combination of ranges, and is achieved when you select a range and then press the Ctrl key as you select a different range. A union is sometimes called a *noncontiguous selection* or a *multiple-area selection.* If you set the print area for a worksheet to a union of ranges, each area of the union will print on a separate page.

The expression *Cell1,Cell2* produces a union of the cells C1 and C10. When you create a union for two or more ranges that overlap, the overlapped cells occur in each area of the union. The expression *LittleBar,Column,Box* produces a union of all three ranges, with cell F5 occurring three times in the final reference. For example, if you use Paste Special on the Paste menu to add values to a union with overlapping ranges (see "Using Paste Special to Adjust Values" in Chapter 13), Excel will repeatedly add the values to the overlapped ranges.

The union operator corresponds to VBAs Union method. You must pass Range objects to the Union method; you can't use strings in quotation marks. You can use references in square brackets, because Excel will interpret them as Range objects. You can also create a union of up to 30 ranges in a single Union method; you don't need to nest Union methods the way you do Range methods. The following VBA commands correspond to selecting references described above. The comment above each Select statement describes the reference you would type in the Go To text box on the Edit menu:

```
''' Cell1,Cell2
Union([Cell1],[Cell2]).Select
Set myLittleBar = [LittleBar]
Set myColumn = [Column]
''' LittleBar,Column,Box
Union(myLittleBar,myColumn,[Box]).Select
```

Restricting a Reference with the Intersection Operator

The *Intersection operator* is a space. When you intersect two ranges, the result will be all the cells that are common between them. The expression *BigBar Column* produces the range F8:F12, and the expression *BigBar Box* produces the range E8:G9.

Excel implicitly intersects ranges when necessary in a formula (see "Letting Excel Decide Between Relative and Absolute References," earlier in this chapter). You can use the intersection operator to explicitly intersect ranges. A common use for the intersection operator is to specify a single cell in a grid having named columns and rows. If you have a grid with month labels across the top and Revenue, Expenses, and Profit labels down the side, you can refer to "January expenses" from any cell on the worksheet with the expression *January Expenses*.

The intersection operator gets more interesting when you combine it in an expression with the range and union operators. By default, Excel processes the range operator first, then the union operator, and finally the intersection operator. As with arithmetic expressions, you can control the order of evaluation by using parentheses. The expression *LittleBar:BigBar Box* produces the range E5:G9, while the expression *LittleBar:(BigBar Box)* produces the range B5:H9. The expression *LittleBar,BigBar Box* produces the two ranges E5:G5 and E8:G9, while the expression *LittleBar,(BigBar Box)* produces the two ranges B5:G5 and E8:G9.

It is fun—and instructive—to define ranges on a worksheet and determine what reference expression can give you that range. With Reference operators alone, there are combinations you cannot achieve. When you add the reference functions in the next section, you become omnipotent. For example, using only the named ranges, how would you specify the range from C1:F9? Because *Column* intersecting with *Box* will give you cell F9, the expression *Cell1:(Column Box)* would work.

Chapter 12

If you intersect an overlapped union with itself, each cell will occur only once in the result. The expression *(LittleBar,Box,Column) (LittleBar,Box,Column)* appears to refer to the same range as the nonintersected union, but it includes cell F5 only once. It also changes the reference from having three (overlapping) areas to having nine (nonoverlapping) areas, since each area must be rectangular. The nine areas in the result are: B5:H5,E5:G5,F5,E5:G5,E3:G9,F3:F9,F5,F3:F9,F:F. Say that three times fast.

The intersect operator corresponds with VBAs Intersect method. As with the Union method, you can intersect up to 30 ranges in a single method, but each one must be a Range object, not text. The following VBA statement— all using the bracketed forms of Excel names for clarity—select references described above. The comment before each Select statement gives the corresponding reference you would type in the Go To text box on the Edit menu:

```
''' BigBar Column
Intersect([BigBar],[Column]).Select
''' BigBar Box
Intersect([BigBar],[Box]).Select
''' LittleBar:BigBar Box
Intersect(Range([LittleBar],[BigBar]),[Box]).Select
''' LittleBar:(BigBar Box)
Intersect([LittleBar],Range([BigBar],[Box])).Select
''' LittleBar,BigBar Box
Intersect(Union([LittleBar],[BigBar]),[Box]).Select
```

```
''' LittleBar,(BigBar Box)
Intersect([LittleBar],Union([BigBar],[Box])).Select
''' Cell1:(Column Box)
Range([Cell1],Intersect([Column],[Box])).Select
```

Unfortunately, the intersect method does not completely match the functionality of the intersection operator: it does not keep cells in overlapped unions from occurring multiple times.

Incidentally, as explained in "Comparing Range Properties and Range Objects" in Chapter 5, the single-argument form of the Range method will accept anything that works in the Go To dialog box on the Edit menu, provided you use A1 notation for cell references. That means that any of the preceding reference expressions would work as a single argument to the Range method. Here are a few examples:

```
Range("LittleBar,Column,Box").Select
Range("Cell1:LittleBar:Cell2").Select
Range("Cell1:(Column Box)").Select
```

The single-argument version of the Range method is completely different from the two-argument version. The two-argument version corresponds—along with the union and intersect methods—to the reference operator. The single-argument version is a general-purpose reference interpreter. Because the Excel object model uses the term Range object to refer to any reference, not just a rectangular range, the Range method ends up with a split personality.

Intersecting Labels and Names

The intersection operator allows you to combine the relative benefits of names and labels. One of the advantages of labels is that you can copy a formula to a new column and labels in the column automatically

Using Reference Functions

Just as Excel has functions like SUM and AVERAGE that work with numbers, it also has functions that work with references. Reference functions give you even more flexibility in manipulating references. As with reference operators, you can see the effect of reference functions by entering them in the Go To dialog box on the Edit menu.

Shifting a Reference with the OFFSET Function

The OFFSET function can do anything. It is a most amazing reference manipulation machine. You must give it any reference as a starting point, along with how much you want to shift the reference vertically and horizontally. In return, it gives you a beautiful, custom-designed reference.

Using the named references shown earlier in Figure 12-6, suppose you want to refer to the range immediately below the *Box* range, E10:G16. Perhaps the *Box* range contains units and you want a range for calculating dollars. The expression

OFFSET(Box,7,0) will return that range. The first argument gives the base range, which must be rectangular. The second argument tells how many rows down to shift the range. (Imagine yourself standing in the upper left cell of the base range, facing the bottom of the worksheet. Enter the number of steps you would take. To leave the range in the same place, you take zero steps. To move the range up, you take backward, or negative, steps.) The third argument tells how many columns to the right to shift the range. (For columns, imagine yourself facing the right side of the worksheet.) The OFFSET function does not change the base range; it creates a new reference.

You can also let Excel count the number of rows or columns in a range, which is often convenient when using the OFFSET function. The ROWS function counts the rows in a range and the COLUMNS function counts the columns. To refer to the range immediately to the right of the *Box* range, whatever size you make the *Box* range, use the expression *OFFSET(Box,0,COLUMNS(Box))*.

In VBA, the Offset method corresponds to this use of the OFFSET function. Rather than give the base range as an argument, state the range first, and use *Offset* as a method of that range. To find the number of rows or columns of a range in VBA, you must use both the Rows or Columns propert,y followed by the Count property. The following statements correspond to the reference expressions above:

```
Set myBox = Range("Box")
myBox.Offset(7,0).Select
myBox.Offset(0,myBox.Columns.Count).Select
```

Chapter 12

Resizing a Reference with the OFFSET Function

In addition to shifting a reference, the OFFSET function can also resize it, using two optional arguments. The first optional argument specifies the number of rows you want in the new reference, and the second specifies the number of columns. If you omit either argument, Excel retains the number of rows or columns from the base range. To select the first row below the *Box* range (E10:G10, where totals would likely go), use the expression *OFFSET(Box,ROWS(Box),0,1)*. To select the two rows above the *Box* range (E1:G3), use the expression *OFFSET(Box,-2,0,2)*.

If you want to resize a range while leaving the same starting location, use zero for both the second and third arguments. If you want to change the number of columns, while leaving the rows the same, use a comma to indicate the empty argument. To select the first column of the *Box* range (E3:E9, where row labels would likely go), use the expression *OFFSET(Box,0,0,,1)*.

To resize a reference in VBA, use the Resize method, which makes it easier to resize without shifting. The following are VBA equivalents to the expressions referenced above, with the comment before each *Select* statement giving the reference you would type in the Go To text box on the Edit menu:

```
''' OFFSET(Box,ROWS(Box),0,1)
myBox.Offset(myBox.Rows.Count).Resize(1).Select
```

```
''' OFFSET(Box,-2,0,2)
myBox.Offset(-2).Resize(2).Select
''' OFFSET(Box,0,0,,1)
myBox.Resize(,1).Select
```

A Range object contains a Rows collection and a Columns collection which allow you to select a single row or column from a range. The following are functionally equivalent alternatives to the above statements using the Rows and Columns collections:

```
''' OFFSET(Box,ROWS(Box),0,1)
myBox.Rows(myBox.Rows.Count+1).Select
''' OFFSET(Box,-2,0,2)
myBox.Rows(-1).Resize(2).select''' OFFSET(Box,0,0,,1)
myBox.Columns(1).Select
```

Retrieving a Cell from a Range with the INDEX Function

The INDEX function has three required arguments: a range, a row number, and a column number. Ostensibly, you give it these three pieces of information, and it gives you back the value from that row and column position in the range. For example, if you enter the formula *=INDEX(BigBar,3,3)* into a cell, that cell will display the Cell2 text label found in cell C10. However, contrary to appearances, it is not the value from cell C10 that the INDEX function returns. Rather, the INDEX function returns the reference to cell C10. Excel simply displays the result of the reference in the cell, just as if you had typed the formula *=C10* directly into the cell.

Because the INDEX function returns a reference, you can use it in the Go To dialog box on the Edit menu. You can also use it as an operand with reference operators. (The expression *INDEX(BigBar,3,3):Box* is perfectly legitimate, and refers to the range C3:G10.) Likewise, you can use the INDEX function as an argument to the OFFSET function (the expression *OFFSET(INDEX(BigBar,1,3),0,0,4,2)* refers to the range C8:D11).

With the INDEX function, you specify row and column positions starting from one, and you can't go outside the bounds of the base range. You can use zero as the row or column value, in which case the INDEX function returns all the rows or all the columns. The expression *INDEX(BigBar,0,2)* refers to the range B8:B12.

In principle, you never need the standard INDEX function, since its capabilities are a subset of those of the OFFSET function. To refer to a single cell in a grid, it is much easier to start counting from one and not to have to resize the result.

To retrieve a single cell from a range in VBA, use the Cells property of a Range object. To retrieve a single row or column, use the Rows or Columns property. The following are VBA equivalents to the above expressions:

```
Set myBigBar = Range("BigBar")
''' =INDEX(BigBar,3,3)
myBigBar.Cells(3,3).Select
''' INDEX(BigBar,3,3):Box
```

```
Range(myBigBar.Cells(3,3),[Box]).Select
''' OFFSET(INDEX(BigBar,1,3),0,0,4,2)
myBigBar.Cells(1,3).Resize(4,2).Select
''' INDEX(BigBar,0,2)
myBigBar.Columns(2).Select
```

The default collection for a range is the Cells collection, so you can actually omit *.Cells* from the VBA statements. For example, you could use this statement in place of the next to the last one above.

```
''' OFFSET(INDEX(BigBar,1,3),0,0,4,2)
myBigBar(1,3).Resize(4,2).Select
```

Retrieving an Area from a Union with the INDEX function

In addition to its regular job, the INDEX function also has extra secret powers. It has an optional fourth argument that specifies the area from a multiple-area selection. The expression *INDEX((Box,BigBar),3,3,1)* refers to cell G5, while the expression *INDEX((Box,BigBar),3,3,2)* refers to cell C10. "Searching by Column, Row, and Table" in Chapter 4 uses the INDEX function to extract values from multiple areas.

Use the Areas property of a multiple-area range to select the specific area in VBA. The following are VBA statements that select ranges equivalent to those shown in the expressions above:

```
''' INDEX((Box,BigBar),3,3,1)
Union([BigBar],[Box]).Areas(1).Cells(3,3).Select
''' INDEX((Box,BigBar),3,3,2)
Union([BigBar],[Box]).Areas(2).Cells(3,3).Select
```


Converting Text into a Reference with the INDIRECT Function

The INDIRECT function does not manipulate an existing range. Rather, it converts a text string into a reference. If you type *BigBox* in the Go To dialog box on the Edit menu, Excel will select the BigBox range. If you type *"BigBox"* with quotation marks, as a text string, you will get an error. On the other hand, if you type *INDIRECT("BigBox")*, Excel will again select the *BigBox* range.

So, why put quotation marks around a range name, just so that you can use the INDIRECT function to convert it back to a reference? There are two common uses for the INDIRECT function:

- Using a text expression to construct a reference
- Placing reference labels into worksheet cells

As an example of using a text expression, suppose that you want to refer to the third cell in the first row of the LittleBar range, and you might also want to refer to the corresponding cell in the BigBar range. Type *Little* into cell A1. The expression *INDEX(INDIRECT(A1&"Bar"),1,3)* refers to cell D5. Type *Big* into cell A1, and the same expression suddenly refers to cell D3.

As an example of putting reference labels in cells, consider the example shown in Figure 12-7. The labels in column B indicate the names of the shaded ranges to the right. The Short range name refers to cells C2:D2, while the range name Long refers to cell C4:F4. Without the INDIRECT function, it would be very difficult to create a single formula—one you can copy without modification from row to row—that would sum only the shaded cells.

	A	B	C	D	E	F	G	H
1								
2	10	Short	5	5	5	5	5	
3	15	Medium	5	5	5	5	5	
4	20	Long	5	5	5	5	5	
5								
6								

Figure 12-7
The INDIRECT function lets you use a label to refer to a named range.

In VBA, the equivalent to the INDIRECT function is the single-argument form of the Range method, which converts any valid text string into a Range object.

Note "Searching by Column, Row, and Table" in Chapter 14 contrasts the use of the INDIRECT function with a special use of the INDEX function in a Lookup Table.

Using Names to Simplify References

Note The sample document for this section is Names.xls.

Using names in a workbook is the hallmark of an experienced Excel model builder. Names make formulas easy to understand, and they make it easy for you to redefine what the formulas refer to without changing the formulas themselves.

Defining and Redefining Names

Creating a new name is easy: select the range you want to name and then type a name into the Name Box above cell A1. This simple method works if you don't mind typing the name, the name is not already defined in the workbook, and you don't need to adjust the name. Excel provides other tools that are almost as easy to use, and they provide more control over how names are defined in your workbooks.

Using Shortcut Keys for Names

Excel provides four commands on the Insert Names menu for creating and manipulating names: Define, Paste, Create, and Apply. The first three have function key equivalents. The function keys are easier to remember if you think of them as a family, because they all use the F3 key. Once you remember that F3 has to do with names, you just need to remember which flavor goes with which command.

- The plain version—F3—displays the Paste Name dialog box. This is an ordinary task, since you use names more often than you define them. Paste Name works only if you have already defined at least one name.
- The intensified function key—Ctrl+F3—displays the Define Name dialog box, which gives you more power than merely using the name.
- The extreme form of the function key—Ctrl+Shift+F3—displays the Create Names dialog box, which is the superhero command, giving you the ability to create hundreds of names in a single blow.
- The remaining standard-flavor F3 function key—Shift+F3—displays the Paste Function dialog box. Functions can be thought of as built-it Excel names.
- The F3 family can be augmented by adding the final name command—Apply Names—to the Alt+Shift+F3 function key.

You can use the following macro, *ApplyNames,* to quickly display the Insert Name dialog box:

```
Sub ApplyNames()
    Application.Dialogs(xlDialogApplyNames).Show
End Sub
```

Create a keyboard handler routine as described in "Assigning a Shortcut Key to a Macro in Excel" in Chapter 6, using %+{F3} as the Key value and *ApplyNames* as the macro value.

Chapter 12

Defining a Name Using a Label

The Name box might not be the best way to define a new name, particularly if the name you want to use appears as a label in a cell. The Define Name dialog box (click Name on the Insert menu and select Define to access the dialog box) looks at and around the active cell to find a likely label to propose as a name for the selection. If a label contains a space or other illegal character, Excel replaces it with an underscore in the proposed name. If a label begins with a number, Excel prefixes the name with an underscore. (For valid naming rules, ask the Answer Wizard for help using the search words *Name Guidelines.*)

Excel will always propose that label for the name if the active cell contains a label. If it does not contain a label, Excel looks at the shape of the selection. If the selection contains more columns than rows, it looks at the cell to the left of the upper left cell for a label to propose as a name. In the worksheet shown in Figure 12-8, if you select the range C2:E3, Excel will propose *Revenue* as the range name. If the selection contains more rows than columns, Excel looks at the cell above the top left cell for a suitable label. If you select the range C2:D5, Excel will propose *January* as the range name. If the selection contains the same number of rows and columns (this situation applies when you select a single cell), Excel looks first to the left of the upper left cell and then above it. If you select the range C2:E4, Excel will propose *Revenue*, but if you select the range D2:F4, Excel will propose *February*.

If Excel's first choice for a name is already in use, it simply leaves the name box blank. If you want to use a label to name an entire row or column, the label must be in the active cell. For example, in the worksheet shown in Figure 12-8, to give the name *Revenue* to all of row 2 (without having to type the name), you must select row 2 and then press Tab to make cell B2 the active cell.

	A	B	C	D	E	F
1		Budget	January	February	March	
2		Revenue	$1,000	$1,500	$2,000	
3		Expenses	$800	$1,000	$1,200	
4		Profit	$200	$500	$800	
5						
6						

Figure 12-8
Excel proposes an adjacent label as the name for a cell.

Redefining an Existing Name

You can use the Name text box to define a name only if the name does not already exist. That's because when you type a valid reference into the dialog box, Excel selects that reference. Likewise, the Define Name dialog box will not propose a label for a name if that name already exists.

One option you can use to redefine a name is to delete the existing name, and then use either the Name text box or the Define Name dialog box to create a new name. A second option you can use is to select the new range within the Define Name dialog box. Without worrying about the current selection, open the dialog box and select the name you want to redefine. Then click in the Refers To text box and select the new range.

Note When you first click in the Refers To text box, the status bar message changes to Point. As you select a new range using either the mouse or the keyboard, Excel replaces the currently defined reference. If you again click in the Refers To text box, the status bar message changes to Enter. Then, when you try to select a new range, Excel will append it to the existing reference joined by a plus sign (+), which can be very unnerving. To get back to where you are able to replace the reference, click the name again and then click in the Refers To text box. The name doesn't actually change until you click OK or Add (OK and Add are identical, except that Add leaves the dialog box open). If you change a reference and then click a name in the list without first clicking Add, the change is lost.

A third option you can use is to select the range before opening the Define Name dialog box. If you choose this option, you must type the name in the Names In Workbook text box. Do not select the name from the list, because doing so will replace the currently selected range in the Refers To text box with the existing definition of the name. This is a very common error in redefining a name. The result is that you redefine the name to mean the same thing it did before, which can also be very confusing.

Defining Multiple Names Based on Labels

If you have a table with labels down the side, labels across the top, or both, you can define all the rows and/or columns in the table with the Create Names command. In the worksheet shown earlier in Figure 12-8, if you select the range B1:E4 and display the Create Names dialog box (click Names on the Insert menu and choose Create), and you then accept Excel's proposal to create names using the top row and left column, Excel will define the following seven names for you:

- January will define C2:C4, with February and March defining the adjacent columns.
- Revenue will define C2:E2, with Expenses and Profit defining the adjacent rows.
- Somewhat cleverly, Excel uses Budget to define C2:E4.

The Create Names dialog box is a very powerful way to define names quickly. If you choose the Accept Labels In Formulas option, however, it might be superfluous. The labels Excel can interpret most easily are precisely the names that the Create Names dialog box creates, except that Labels In Formulas interprets a corner label such as Budget as a column label. If you do prefer to use real names, however, the Create Names dialog box can be convenient. If you are naming the columns in a list, be sure to clear the Left Column option, because the Create Names command is very likely to propose that, even when you don't want it.

One of the frustrations in using the Create Names dialog box comes when you need to redefine a block of names, usually because you have added additional rows or columns to the range. Where Create Names would redefine existing names, it first prompts for a confirmation for each name it proposes to change, but without any option to confirm all the changes at once. You can create the following simple macro, *CreateNamesQuietly,* which will run the Create Names dialog box for you without any confirmation prompt:

```
Sub CreateNamesQuietly()
    Application.DisplayAlerts = False
    Application.Dialogs(xlDialogCreateNames).Show
```

Chapter 12

```
    Application.DisplayAlerts = True
End Sub
```

If you are confident, you can modify the Create command on the Names menu so that the Ctrl+Shift+F3 shortcut will run this macro in place of Excel's built-in command.

Managing Local and Global Names

When you define or create names, those names are available throughout the workbook. Excel only interprets labels in formulas on the current worksheet. When you move or copy a worksheet to a new workbook, Excel copies the names with the sheet. What happens if you copy a worksheet that contains those names to a workbook that already has those names defined? What happens if you make a duplicate copy of a worksheet within the current workbook? What happens if you delete a worksheet that has names defined on it?

If you are not aware of how Excel manages names in a workbook, these scenarios can create some very confusing situations. If you do understand names in a workbook, you can blissfully avoid—or fix—any problems you might encounter with names.

Understanding Workbook Names

Names in an Excel workbook are governed by two pragmatic principles. First, multiple worksheets sometimes use the same name and you want them to be unambiguous. Second, a name usually occurs only once and you want it to be available throughout the workbook. Each Excel workbook maintains a single list of names. Any name within the list can be prefixed with a worksheet name, which makes that name visible only on that worksheet. A prefixed name is called a *local name*. A name without a prefix is visible on all worksheets, and is called a *global name*. Let's see what this means in practical terms.

Suppose you have a division budget similar to the one shown earlier in Figure 12-8 on a sheet named NorthWest. You use the Create Names command to create named ranges. The new names are all global names, because Excel creates global names by default. You add formulas that use the names. Next, you decide to create a second copy of the budget for a second division, so you copy the worksheet and name the new sheet NorthEast.

Think about what Excel could do with the names. If Excel replaced the global names with the names on the NorthEast worksheet, the formulas on the NorthWest worksheet would refer to NorthEast ranges. Likewise, if Excel simply left the names as they were, the NorthEast formulas would refer to NorthWest ranges. Instead, Excel creates new local copies of the names for the NorthEast worksheet, while leaving the NorthWest names as they were. The new formulas on the NorthEast worksheet properly refer to the NorthEast ranges, while the original formulas work as they always did.

Creating Local Names

If you create names on a new worksheet by copying labels and using the Create Names command, the new names will be local names. When names already exist as global names in the workbook, Excel creates local names. Any time you bulk-create names in a workbook—whether by copying a worksheet within the same workbook, by using Create Names, or by copying a worksheet from a different workbook—Excel follows the same rule when creating each name: if a matching global name does not already exist, it creates a global name; otherwise, it creates a local name. If you copy a worksheet having local names, Excel always makes the new names local.

In the Define Name dialog box, you manually create a local name by entering the worksheet name followed by an exclamation point, in turn followed by the name you are defining. In the list of defined names, however, Excel shows the worksheet name to the right of the name. If the name of the worksheet contains a space or is otherwise an invalid Excel name, you must place apostrophes around the worksheet name.

Note If you want to define the local name Revenue on the Current Forecast worksheet, you can avoid having to type the apostrophes in the name 'Current Forecast'!Revenue. To avoid the apostrophes, temporarily rename the worksheet to Temp and create the name as Temp!Revenue. When you rename the worksheet back to its original name, Excel will add the apostrophes for you.

Using Local and Global Names

In the Define Name dialog box, you see only the local names for the active sheet, plus any global names that do not have local equivalents. Local names will mask global names in the dialog box. When you use a name in a formula, you get the local name if there is one; otherwise, you get the global name.

Just because you don't see local names from other worksheets does not mean that you cannot use them. If you want to enter a formula on the NorthWest division worksheet that refers to *Revenue* for the NorthEast division, use the formula *=NorthWest!Revenue.* The rules for implicit intersection are the same whether you refer to a range on a different worksheet or on the same worksheet. (See "Managing References in a Grid" earlier in this chapter), For example, entering *=NorthWest!Revenue* in cell D6 of the NorthEast worksheet will return the February revenue number from the NorthWest sheet, because cell D6 is in the same column as February. In a workbook called Names.xls, if the NorthEast worksheet contains global names and you enter the formula *=NorthEast!Revenue* on a different worksheet, Excel will change the formula to *=Names.xls!Revenue* to reflect that the name is global to the workbook.

Creating a List of Workbook Names

In the Define Name dialog box, you can see only the names that are visible to the active sheet. Likewise, in the Paste Name dialog box, the Paste List button pastes a list of names into the worksheet. It also pastes only the names that are visible to the active sheet. The following *ListNames* macro pastes all the names—global and local—from the workbook onto the active sheet:

```
Sub ListNames()
    Dim myLog As Range
    Dim myName As Name

    Set myLog = ActiveCell
    For Each myName In Names
        myLog.Value = myName.Name
        ''' prefix an apostrophe to turn formula to text
        myLog.Offset(, 1).Value = "'" & myName.RefersTo
        Set myLog = myLog.Offset(1)
    Next myName
End Sub
```

Figure 12-9 shows a sample result from the *ListNames* macro. You can easily see both the global and local names. The macro begins the list in the active cell, so be sure there is room available on the worksheet before you run it.

	A	B	C	D	E	F
2		**Revenue**	$1,000	$1,500	$2,000	
3		**Expenses**	$800	$1,000	$1,200	
4		**Profit**	$200	$500	$800	
5						
6						
7						
8						
9	NorthEast!Budget	=NorthEast!$C$2:$E$4				
10	Budget	=NorthWest!$C$2:$E$4				
11	NorthEast!Expenses	=NorthEast!$C$3:$E$3				
12	Expenses	=NorthWest!$C$3:$E$3				
13	NorthEast!February	=NorthEast!$D$2:$D$4				
14	February	=NorthWest!$D$2:$D$4				
15	NorthEast!January	=NorthEast!$C$2:$C$4				
16	January	=NorthWest!$C$2:$C$4				
17	NorthEast!March	=NorthEast!$E$2:$E$4				
18	March	=NorthWest!$E$2:$E$4				
19	NorthEast!Profit	=NorthEast!$C$4:$E$4				
20	Profit	=NorthWest!$C$4:$E$4				
21	NorthEast!Revenue	=NorthEast!$C$2:$E$2				
22	Revenue	=NorthWest!$C$2:$E$2				
23						

Figure 12-9
Sample output from the ListNames macro.

Converting Global Names to Local Names

If you have a workbook with a mixture of global and local names similar to the one shown in Figure 12-9, you might want to convert the global names into local names.

The easiest way to convert the names is to copy the worksheet that contains the global names (hold down the Ctrl key as you drag the worksheet tab to create local names on the new copy). Then delete the original worksheet and rename the copy.

When you delete a worksheet, Excel automatically deletes all the names that are local to that worksheet. Excel does not delete global names, however, even if you delete the worksheet they reference. The sheet name portion of the reference simply shows #REF. These orphaned names just remain in the workbook. In fact, if all the worksheets that remain in the workbook have local names, you can't even see the global names in the Define Name dialog box in order to delete them!

You can make a name invalid by deleting the rows or columns in the name reference. In that case, the cell address portion of the reference becomes #REF!. Either by deleting sheets or by deleting rows or columns, you can accumulate invalid names in a workbook. Of course, an invalid global name might not be a bad thing. It will force the Create Names command to create a local name from matching labels.

If you do want to remove invalid names from your workbook, you can insert a new worksheet (which has no local names), and then use the Define Name command from that sheet to delete any names that show #REF as part of the reference. You can also use the following *CleanNames* macro, which deletes any name that contains #REF as part of its reference:

```
Sub CleanNames()
    Dim myName As Name
    Worksheets.Add
    For Each myName In Names
        If InStr(myName.RefersTo, "#REF") Then
            myName.Delete
        End If
    Next myName
    Application.DisplayAlerts = False
    ActiveSheet.Delete
End Sub
```

Caution A macro always interprets a name in the current context. If a workbook contains both the sheet local name Sheet1!Prices and the global name Prices, and if Sheet1 is the active sheet, the VBA expression *Names("Prices")* will refer to the local name, not the global name. To force a macro to refer to a global name, temporarily insert a new worksheet into the workbook. The new worksheet will be the active sheet, and it will not contain any local names. After accessing the global names, the macro can then delete the temporary worksheet.

Creating Hidden Names

If you create a large number of names in your worksheet models, you might want to allow only some of the names to appear in the Name Box or in the Define Name or Paste Name dialog boxes, while hiding the rest. Hidden names are similar to the hidden bookmarks Microsoft Word creates, which you can either show or hide in the Bookmark dialog box. In Excel, you must use VBA to hide or unhide a name. Even if a name is hidden, you can still use it in formulas, and you can still delete it from the Define Name dialog box, as long as you type the name correctly in the box before clicking Delete.

An easy way to hide names is to add a specific prefix to each name that you want to hide. Then you can run a macro that hides all the names with that prefix. The *HideNames* macro in the following example hides all the names in the workbook that have t. as a prefix:

```
Sub HideNames()
    Const Prefix As String = "t."
    Dim myName As Name

    For Each myName In ActiveSheet.Names
        ''' Instr for sheet local name
        If Left(myName.Name, Len(Prefix)) = Prefix _
        Or InStr(myName.Name, "!" & Prefix) Then
            myName.Visible = False
        End If
    Next myName
End Sub
```

The macro uses a two-part test to determine if a name contains the specific prefix. The first part of the test looks for the prefix at the beginning of the name. This retrieves the global names. With local names, however, the sheet name comes before the actual name, so the second part of the test looks for the prefix immediately after an exclamation point (!), which must always immediately precede the defined name. You might want to create an additional *ShowNames* macro that unhides all the hidden names in a workbook.

Creating Unconventional Names

Most Excel users rarely use names in their workbooks. When they do create formulas, they just point at cells and call it complete. For those who do use names, however, they use them only in their limited, conventional way: to refer to a cell. The few who have figured out what names in Excel can really do rarely do anything without using names. Many of those uses are anything but conventional.

Naming Relative References

Give the name *TaxRate* to cell A2 on Sheet1 of a new workbook and then select the name in the Define Name dialog box. In the Refers To text box, you will see the formula *=Sheet1!$A$2*. Excel makes the reference absolute so that you will always get cell A2, regardless of what cell you use the name from.

A named reference does not have to be absolute; you can give a name to a relative reference, as well. On Sheet1 of a new workbook, select cell B1 and display the Define Name dialog box. Type *LastMonth* as the name and activate the Refers To text box. The default location in the Refers To text box is =Sheet1!$B$1. Press the Left arrow key to change the Refers To location to =Sheet1!$A$1. Then press F4 three times to change the reference to =Sheet1!A1. Click OK to define the name. You now have a name with a relative reference. Select cell F5 and look at *LastMonth* in the Define Name dialog box. The reference is now =Sheet1!E5.

A relative name is relative to the location of the cell where it appears in a formula and has nothing to do with the location of the active cell. Names with relative references can be very confusing to work with in A1 notation because the reference changes whenever you change the active cell. If you intend to work with a named relative reference, switch to R1C1 notation—at least while you are working with the name. In R1C1 notation, the definition of *LastMonth* is =Sheet1!RC[–1], and that definition stays the same, regardless of which cell is currently active. See "Picking the Right Referenc Style" at the beginning of this chapter for details about R1C1 notation.

Chapter 12

As we discussed earlier, relative names are particularly useful when comparing a current value with a previous value. One effective way to use relative names is to give the name *Previous* to the reference =R[–1], which names the entire row above the cell with the formula. Excel always adds a sheet name to a reference. For example, if you enter =R[-1] as the reference for a name on the Sheet1 worksheet, Excel will convert the reference to =Sheet1!R[-1]. Unfortunately, you cannot create a sheet-relative name that works on any sheet in the workbook. If you want the name *Previous* to refer to the previous row on more than one worksheet, you must create it as a local name on each sheet.

You can combine a relative name with labels in formulas in the same formula. In Figure 12-10, the name *Previous* is defined as =R[–1]. There are no other defined names, but the Accept Labels In Formulas option is enabled for the workbook. Excel interprets the *Revenue* label as referring to all of column 2. The formula in cell R3C3 implicitly intersects with the *Revenue* column to get the current revenue, and explicitly intersects the *Previous* row with the *Revenue* column to get the previous month's revenue.

	A	B	C	D	E	F
1	Month	Revenue	Growth			
2	Jan-00	$10,000				
3	Feb-00	$10,180	180			
4	Mar-00	$10,060	-120			
5	Apr-00	$9,870	-190			
6	May-00	$9,950	80			
7	Jun-00	$10,240	290			
8						
9						
10						

Figure 12-10
Use explicit intersection to combine a relative name and a label.

When using labels in formulas, Excel usually interprets the label to refer to the entire column; that is, *Revenue* refers to B$2:B$65536. When used with explicit intersection, however, Excel interprets the label to refer only to the currently filled cells; that is, when used with explicit intersection, the *Revenue* label refers to only B$2:B$7. If you copy formulas to new rows and see the value #NULL!, re-enter the formulas (replace = with =) to force Excel to reinterpret the label range.

Naming Constants and Formulas

In casual conversation, a user might say that a name defines cells. Another user might respond that a name could also define a constant or a formula. In fact, even the Excel Help topics use this terminology. The terminology is technically incorrect, however. Names in Excel never define cells, and they never define constants. The only thing a name ever defines is a formula. Define the name *TaxRate*, type *28%* in the Refers To text box, and then click Add. Excel changes the constant you typed to *=0.28,* which is a formula. All formulas in Excel begin with an equal sign (=), and everything that begins with an equal sign is a formula. Admittedly, *=0.28* is a very simple formula—a formula that consists of a numeric constant—but it is a formula nonetheless.

Likewise, when you give the name *Revenue* to cell B7 on the NorthWest worksheet, the contents of the Refers To text box is =NorthWest!$B$7. This is a very simple formula, a formula that consists of a reference constant. Nevertheless, it is a formula. If the value of cell B7 is *4500,* the result of the *Revenue* name is not *4500*. The result is the reference to cell B7. When you use the name in a context that requires a value, Excel converts the reference into the value from the cell. Up until that final moment, the formula in the name calculates a reference, not a value. That makes it possible to use defined names with reference operators and functions as described in "Manipulating References" earlier in this chapter.

Naming a Formula to Reduce Complexity

One way to use a named formula is to move a complex formula into a name. You probably have a list somewhere with an extremely complicated formula. In Figure 12-11, the formula to calculate *Volume* is not extremely complicated, but it can illustrate the process of turning a formula into a named formula.

	A	B	C	D	E	F
1	Width	Height	Depth	Volume		
2	35	35	45	55,125		
3	50	20	25	25,000		
4	10	50	20	10,000		
5	40	20	35	28,000		
6	25	10	50	12,500		
7						
8						
9						
10						

Figure 12-11
A named formula can hide complexity.

Building a formula in the Define Name dialog box is difficult, so create the formula in the location it will be used first, using appropriate relative and absolute references. Select and copy the formula, and then exit the formula bar. Display the Define Names dialog box and enter the name *Volume!Volume,* if you want it to be a local name on the Volume worksheet. Select the entire contents of the Refers To text box and paste in the formula. If you do try to modify a formula in the Define Name text box, press F2 to change from Enter mode to Edit mode before using the arrow keys to move around in the formula. You can see the mode you are working in on the status bar. In Enter mode, arrow keys select cells on the worksheet, destroying the formula. In Edit mode, arrow keys move around within the formula, allowing you to modify the formula.

When the workbook is set to use A1 reference notation, the formula in the Define Name text box changes, depending on which cell is active. In R1C1 notation, the formula for *Volume* is always *=RC1*RC2*RC3,* regardless of which cell is active. If you need to examine a named formula, you might want to switch to R1C1 notation. To use the name, type *=Volume* in the relevant cells of the worksheet.

Named formulas can use the results of other named formulas. In this simple example, you could create the name *Width* defined (in R1C1 notation) as =RC1, the name *Height* defined as =RC2, and the name *Depth,* defined as =RC3. You could then define *Volume* as *=Width*Height*Depth.* If you want to use names within a named formula, make sure they are relative names. A named formula can't use implicit intersection. "Charting an Algebraic Function" in Chapter 13 describes how to use named formulas to calculate mathematical functions and chart the results without copying the formulas to worksheet cells.

Chapter 13

Manage Calculations to Control Excel

In This Chapter

Microsoft Excel is interactive. Excel is analytical. You can create lists using Microsoft Access, Microsoft Outlook, or even Microsoft Word, but it is only in Excel that you can experience the tactile sensation of manipulating the list, dragging columns to different positions, instantly sorting by any combination of list values, and filtering and unfiltering. You can create formulas in Access, but only in Excel can you create formulas that let you change input values and then watch the results percolate through whatever implications you might have imagined.

When you create formulas that change output values while you change input values interactively, you are creating a model. A *model* is a small-scale, simplified representation of some real-world phenomenon. In the same way that you can build an HO scale model representation of alpine villages with trains trafficking between them, you can use Excel to build a model representation of profits and losses, of order projections, or of interest payments. The essential ingredient for linking formulas together into models is the cell reference. Excel's cell references are not as simple as they first appear, but you can use them to create powerful models of your world.

Calculations drive Excel models. The better you can control how Excel calculates, the better models you can build.

Controlling Calculations

A worksheet cell has two content layers. The layer you see is the *value layer*. Excel uses the value of this layer when you reference the cell from a formula. The value layer might also be embellished, justified, colored, or indented, but that won't change the value of the cell. The other layer is the *formula layer*. The formula layer is what you see in the formula bar. If a cell contains a constant, the formula layer matches the value layer.

Typically, Excel displays formatted values in a worksheet. You can have Excel display the formulas instead. Figure 13-1 shows two windows in the same workbook, one showing the formatted values and the other showing the formulas. To toggle between values and formulas, press Ctrl+` (accent grave), which is on the same key as the tilde, located either in the upper left corner of the keyboard or next to the Spacebar on most keyboards.

Client.xls:1

	A	B
1		
2	5000	
3	$2,500.00	
4	25%	
5	1-Mar-97	
6	4:45 PM	
7	5-Sep-71	
8	35490	
9	0.697916667	
10		
11		

Client.xls:2

	A	B
1		
2	5000	
3	2500	
4	0.25	
5	35490	
6	0.697916666666667	
7	=A5*10	
8	=VALUE(A5)	
9	=VALUE(A6)	
10		
11		

Figure 13-1
Press Ctrl+` to see cell formulas.

When Excel calculates, it causes the values you see in the value layer to match the values calculated by the formulas. You can control the way Excel performs those calculations.

Using Manual Calculation

If you have very large, very slow models, you might want to change the workbook to use manual calculation. Click Options on the Tools menu, and then click the

Calculation tab, and select the Manual option. When calculation is set to manual, Excel uses the word Calculate in the status bar to indicate any open workbook changes, leaving the potential that a formula somewhere is inconsistent. Press F9 to recalculate all open workbooks.

If you want to recalculate only the active sheet, press Shift+F9. Pressing Shift+F9 will not clear the Calculate flag in the status bar, even if the active sheet is the only sheet that has changed.

If you want to recalculate a single cell, re-enter the formula. (Press F2 and then press Enter.) If you want to recalculate a range of identical formulas, select the range, press F2 to edit the active cell, and then press Ctrl+Enter to enter the formula into all the cells of the range. Entering formulas using Ctrl+Enter recalculates the formulas, just as if you re-enter them one by one. Copying and pasting—or using Edit, Fill Down (Ctrl+D) or Edit, Fill Right (Ctrl+R)—to re-enter formulas does not recalculate the formulas. Those operations merely retain the original value of the copied formula.

If you want to recalculate all the formulas within a workbook where the formulas are not identical, select the range and then search for all equal signs (=), replacing them with "=", as in "=" with "=".

Preventing Propagation of Manual Calculations

Manual calculations are stored in a workbook. Once you change a workbook to use manual calculation, it will use manual calculation each time you open it thereafter. This setting, however, is global; it affects all open workbooks. This means that a single workbook using manual calculation can contaminate workbooks that are set to use automatic calculation. If you open Big.xls, which is set to calculate manually, Excel's workspace becomes manual. If you then open Small.xls, which is supposed to calculate automatically, its calculation mode also changes to manual. If you save Small.xls while calculation is set to manual, it will store the setting in the workbook and will be manual forever after.

Manual calculation emulates a virus-like effect, then, infecting new workbooks in an ever-widening circle. It can be particularly frustrating for your coworkers who have never opened your Big.xls workbook. They still find their calculation mode set to manual, often not even knowing what manual calculation is, furious because their worksheets suddenly contain errors.

One solution is not to set calculation to manual. If you have huge models, here's a macro solution that can help. You create a macro (a handler) that runs whenever you try to save any workbook. The macro checks whether Excel's calculation mode is set to anything other than automatic. (The other two options are manual and semi-automatic, which is rarely used.) If so, it prompts and offers to switch the calculation mode back to automatic before you save the workbook. If you are saving Big.xls, simply click No. If you have already closed Big.xls and are now saving Small.xls, click Yes. If you still have Big.xls open and you are saving Small.xls, you have a couple of options: you can choose to switch calculation mode and wait; you can go ahead and save Small.xls with the wrong setting (promising yourself you will go back and fix it later); or, you can cancel the save so you can close Big.xls before you save Small.xls.

To set up the handler, activate Visual Basic. In your Personal.xls workbook create a new Class module with the name *Handlers* and add the following code to it:

```
Option Explicit

Public WithEvents ApplicationHandler As Application

Private Sub ApplicationHandler_WorkbookBeforeSave( _
    ByVal Wb As Workbook, _
    ByVal SaveAsUI As Boolean,
    Dim r As VbMsgBoxResult

    If Application.Calculation <> xlCalculationAutomatic Then
        r = MsgBox("Excel is currently set to use " & _
            "Manual calculation. Do you want Excel " & _
            "to switch to Automatic calculation before " & _
            "saving this workbook?", vbYesNoCancel)
        Select Case r
        Case vbYes
            Application.Calculation = xlCalculationAutomatic
        Case vbCancel
            Cancel = True
        End Select
    End If
End Sub
```

This handler runs before any open workbook is saved. If the application's calculation mode is not set to automatic, it offers to switch to automatic, save anyway, or cancel the save altogether. For the handler to work, you must now set it up so it loads when the Personal.xls workbook opens. In the Personal.xls workbook's ThisWorkbook module, enter the following code:

```
Private Handlers As New Handlers
Sub Workbook_Open()
    Set Handlers.ApplicationHandler = Application
End Sub
```

This creates a new variable using the *Handlers* Class module you previously created. Then, when the workbook opens, it assigns the Excel Application object to it. You can initialize the handler by clicking within the Workbook_Open procedure and pressing F5. This code is now standing guard to help you avoid propagating manual calculation mode throughout all your workbooks.

Calculating Within a Formula

Perhaps you received a worksheet from a coworker and you want to understand the formulas it contains. You might have one formula—a large and very complicated formula—that appears to be giving an incorrect answer, and you want to isolate the problem by deciphering the formula. Suppose, for example, that you acquire a worksheet that contains the following simple formula:

```
=IF(AND($B2<=S$1,$G2>S$1),$F2+$E2*S$1,
  IF(AND($B2<=S$1,Sheet2!$A2>=S$1),$K2+$J2*S$1,
  IF(AND(Sheet2!$A2<=S$1,Sheet2!$F2>S$1),
    Sheet2!$E2+Sheet2!$C2*S$1,0)))
```

The formula does not appear to produce the correct answers. In fact, the formula contains two errors. How can you ever find them? (I don't want to make you nervous, but in "Creating a Product Planning Model" in Chapter 14, you will learn how to create a slightly more readable version of this formula.)

As soon as you press F2 to edit a formula, Excel draws colored boxes around each of the precedent cells. These are called *Range Finders*, and they are certainly helpful for determining what goes into a formula. They do not, however, show you how the formula calculates. To understand a complex formula, you often need to calculate segments of the formula, much like stepping through a macro in Visual Basic.

Calculating an Expression Using F9

If you select any meaningful expression within a formula in the formula bar and then press F9, Excel will calculate that expression for you right in the formula bar. You can then either select another expression and calculate further, or press Ctrl+Z to restore only the expression you just calculated. (The formula bar does not support multiple levels of undo.) When you're finished, be sure to press Esc to avoid changing the formula. Figure 13-2 shows an expression selected in the formula bar.

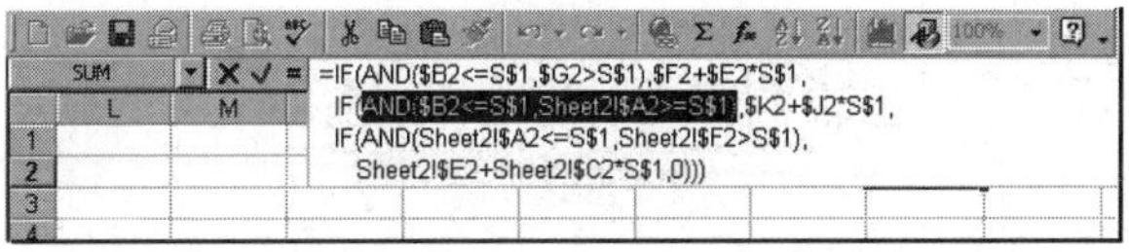

Figure 13-2
An expression selected in the formula bar.

Figure 13-3 shows the same formula after pressing F9 to calculate the expression.

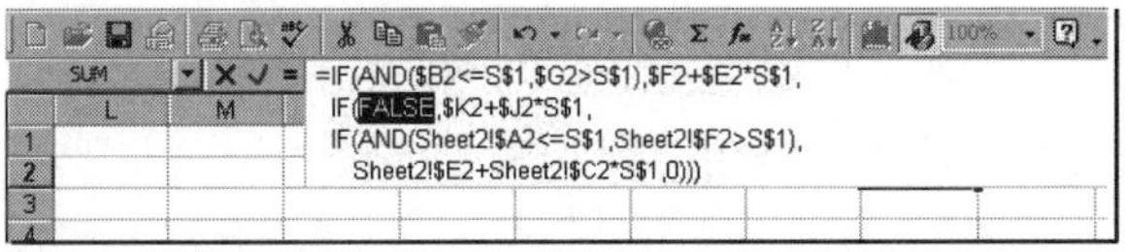

Figure 13-3
Press F9 to calculate an expression in the formula bar.

You can also use F9 to see the current value of a reference that is not immediately visible—one that is in a hidden column, or one that is on a different worksheet.

Navigating to the Reference Source with F5

You can also work within the formula bar to temporarily go to referenced ranges. This is particularly useful if you want to see references on a different worksheet, or if you want to see the cell addresses used by a name. Select any expression within a formula that calculates a range—usually a cell address—and press F5. Be sure to include the sheet name in the reference or you will get the corresponding cell on the active sheet. When the Go To dialog box appears, simply click OK to select the referenced range, as shown in Figure 13-4.

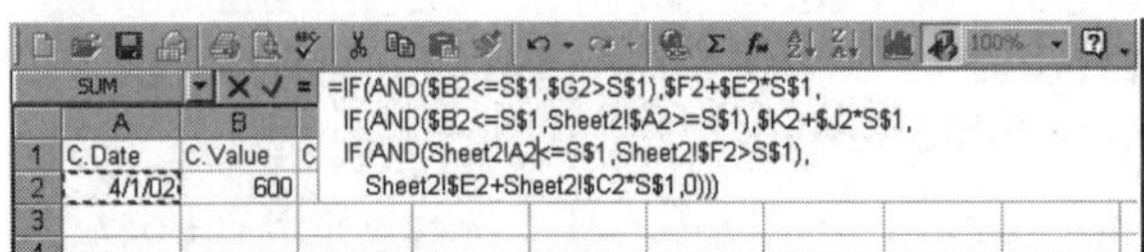

Figure 13-4
Press F5 to go to a reference from the formula bar.

To return to the worksheet containing the formula, either click the worksheet tab or press Esc.

Changing a Reference by Pointing with F2

When you edit an existing formula, Excel places the formula bar in Edit mode, which you can see on the status bar. While you're in Edit mode, you can use the arrow keys to navigate within the text of the formula. If you want to change a reference in the formula by using the arrow keys to point, first select the entire reference you want to change, and then press F2 to switch to Enter mode before pressing the arrow keys.

Incidentally, to include a line break within a long formula, press Alt+Enter. You can also insert spaces at any convenient break in the formula.

Controlling Circular References

In most circumstances, a circular reference is a bad thing. It means that you accidentally caused a formula to refer to a cell that depends on the value of the formula itself. When a circular reference is accidental, you just need to find and fix it. Excel warns you and provides a handy Circular Reference toolbar to help you browse through all the cells in the circular chain to find the problem.

Iterating to Count Calculations

Sometimes, however, you can intentionally use a circular reference. Perhaps you want cell A1 to show how many times the worksheet has calculated. If calculation is automatic, the worksheet calculates each time you change any cell. If calculation is manual, the worksheet calculates each time you press F9. You can use a circular reference to count each calculation. Click Options on the Tools menu, and then click

Calculation, select the Iteration check box, and change Maximum Iterations to *1*, as shown in Figure 13-5.

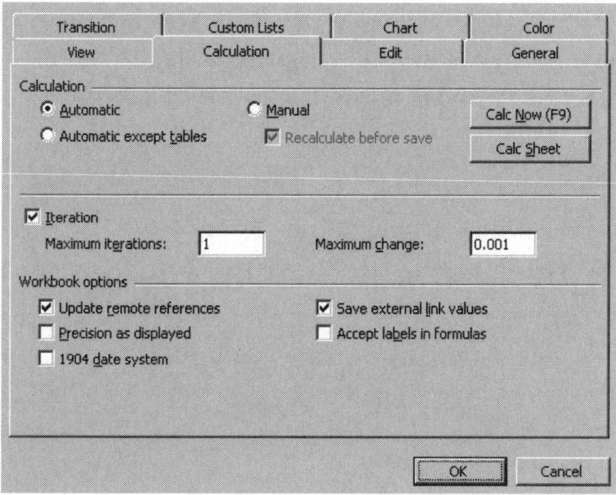

Figure 13-5
Set iteration options to control circular references.

Next, enter the formula *=A1+1* in cell A1. The number 1 will appear in the cell. The original value of the cell was 0, adding one to that value changes it to 1, which—without a restriction on the number of iterations—would cause Excel to recalculate the worksheet, changing the number to 2, which would cause Excel to recalculate the worksheet, ad infinitum. Because you limited the number of iterations to 1, the value of cell A1 stops at 1.

When you type a value in cell B1, the number in cell A1 changes to 2. When you press F9, the number in cell A1 increases by one more. Each time the worksheet calculates, the counter increases by one. To reset the counter, re-enter the formula in the cell. (Select the cell, press F2 and then press Enter.)

Iterating to Converge on an Answer

Some models do require circular calculations to resolve to an answer. Most are a variation on a taxation theme. If you must pay a 10 percent tax on your net income, and you subtract the tax from the gross income to determine the net income, then each time the net income changes, the tax changes, which changes the net income, which changes the tax, and so on. Fortunately, the amount of each change becomes smaller and smaller with each iteration in this kind of situation until you do stabilize on an answer. Next to the box where you set the number of iterations in Figure 13-5 is a Maximum Change box. If you have a feedback system that needs to recalculate until it converges on an answer, you can leave it set to a large number of iterations, and Excel will stop recalculating as soon as the amount of each change comes below the threshold.

Calculating Without Formulas

Formulas are what make Excel interactive. You change a number here, and hundreds of numbers all over the spreadsheet change as a result. Formulas also consume resources. They take time to calculate, and they also increase the size of a workbook. You can't type a value into a cell that contains a formula without destroying the formula. Sometimes, you want to modify a number of cells, but don't want to leave formulas behind when you're done. Excel has some very powerful tools for calculating without using formulas.

Modifying Your Worksheet with Special Tools

You've just spent the last three weeks working out a department budget. Everything is set to finalize when you receive word that all salaries must be cut two percent across the board.

Using Paste Special to Adjust Values

Figure 13-6 shows a portion of your budget worksheet. You need to reduce all the values in the range D4:F8 by two percent. Excel has a special feature that allows you to do precisely that: reduce all the values in a range by a constant amount—without using formulas.

	A	B	C	D	E	F	G	H
1	**Expenses**			**Jan-2000**	**Feb-2000**	**Mar-2000**		
2								
3	**Salaries**							
4		Owner		$8,000	$8,080	$8,160		
5		Bookkeeper		$2,500	$2,525	$2,550		
6		Ship/Rcv		$1,232	$1,244	$1,257		
7		Orders		$2,464	$2,489	$2,513		
8		Designer		$2,350	$2,374	$2,397		
9	**Total Salaries**			**$16,546**	**$16,711**	**$16,877**		
10		Benefits & Taxes	0.35	$5,791	$5,849	$5,907		
11	**Total Salaries and Benefits**			**$22,337**	**$22,560**	**$22,784**		
12								
13	**Supplies**							
14		Art supplies		$300	$303	$306		
15		Office Supplies		$200	$202	$204		
16		Production Supplies		$100	$101	$102		
17		Screens		$140	$141	$143		
18		Squeegies		$60	$61	$61		
19	**Total Supplies**			**$800**	**$808**	**$816**		
20								
21	**Total Expenses**			**$23,137**	**$23,368**	**$23,600**		
22								

Figure 13-6
Salaries that need to be reduced by two percent.

First, you need to come up with a number that you can add to, subtract from, multiply by, or divide into the existing values in the cells. To reduce by two percent, you need to multiply by 98 percent. Type *98 percent* into a convenient blank cell, and then copy that cell. Select the range you want to change, click Edit, and then click Paste Special. Select the Values option from the Paste group (to avoid changing the number format of the cells), and select the Multiply option from the Operation group, as shown in Figure 13-7. Clear the copied cell when you finish.

If you need to undo a Paste Special operation—once it's too late to simply press Ctrl+Z—simply apply the inverse operation using the same constant. To reverse the action of reducing all the expenses by two percent, copy a cell containing 98 percent and divide it into the block of cells.

Figure 13-7
Use Paste Special to calculate without formulas.

Using Go To Special to Select Cells by Attribute

The Paste Special command makes it easy to modify a block of values. But what if the values you need to modify are not in a convenient block? What if the constants you want to change are interspersed with formulas that you don't want to change? Another special Excel feature allows you to select just the constants. To reduce all expenses (but not total rows) by two percent, copy a cell that contains 98 percent and select the entire range that includes the constants and the formulas. Then click Go To on the Edit menu, click Special, and select the Constants option, as shown in Figure 13-8.

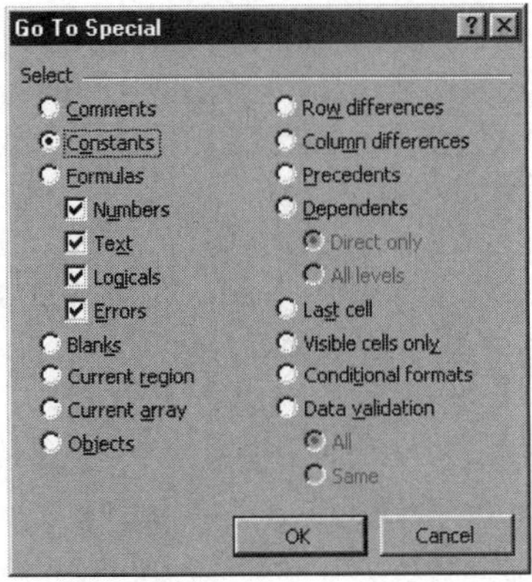

Figure 13-8
Select any type of cell you want.

When you click OK, Excel selects from your original selection only those cells with the attribute you specified, as shown in Figure 13-9. If you have only a single cell selected when you use the Go To Special dialog box, Excel will behave as if you had selected the entire worksheet.

	A / B	C	D	E	F	G
1	**Expenses**		**Jan-2000**	**Feb-2000**	**Mar-2000**	
2						98%
3	**Salaries**					
4	Owner		$8,000	$8,080	$8,160	
5	Bookkeeper		$2,500	$2,525	$2,550	
6	Ship/Rcv		$1,232	$1,244	$1,257	
7	Orders		$2,464	$2,489	$2,513	
8	Designer		$2,350	$2,374	$2,397	
9	**Total Salaries**		**$16,546**	**$16,711**	**$16,877**	
10	Benefits & Taxes	0.35	$5,791	$5,849	$5,907	
11	**Total Salaries and Benefits**		**$22,337**	**$22,560**	**$22,784**	
12						
13	**Supplies**					
14	Art supplies		$300	$303	$306	
15	Office Supplies		$200	$202	$204	
16	Production Supplies		$100	$101	$102	
17	Screens		$140	$141	$143	
18	Squeegies		$60	$61	$61	
19	**Total Supplies**		**$800**	**$808**	**$816**	
20						
21	**Total Expenses**		**$23,137**	**$23,368**	**$23,600**	
22						

Figure 13-9
With only constants selected, you are ready to use Paste Special.

Using Paste Special to Modify Text Formulas

If you use Paste Special to modify a cell that contains a formula, Excel adds parentheses around the existing formula and then adds the operator and value you pasted. You can use Paste Special only with numbers—there is no option to concatenate text. If the cells you are modifying contain formulas, however, you can use Paste Special to trick Excel into letting you append a constant to the end of the formula.

Suppose you want to append the string *& "(assumed)"* to a number of different formulas. Type a unique number into a blank cell—a number like *-9999* that doesn't occur anywhere else in the worksheet. Copy the cell and select the range of formulas you want to modify. Then use Paste Special with the Add operator to add the number. (The formula might temporarily result in an error.) Each formula will now have parentheses around it, followed by *+-9999*, which is a delightfully unique string. Once you have a unique string, you can replace it globally. Without changing the selection, use Edit Replace to replace *+-9999* with *& "(assumed)"*.

If you want to prefix a number of formulas with *& "(assumed)"*, replace "=" with the string=*"(assumed) "&*. Globally replacing equal signs (=) in formulas is a little bit dangerous because there might be an equal sign in the middle of a formula. If you do have equal signs in formulas and want to insert something at the beginning of a number of them, you can try this little four-step maneuver using Paste Special:

1. Use Paste Special to add *-9999* to all the formulas (which adds parentheses around the original formula).
2. Replace the *"=("* string—which is now at the beginning of each formula—with a *"|=("* string. (That's a vertical bar in front of the equal sign.) This changes the formulas into ordinary text so that you can temporarily create illegal formulas.
3. Replace the *")+-9999"* string at the end with nothing.
4. Replace the *"|=("* string at the beginning with *"="*, plus the desired prefix.

Globally modifying formulas might seem a bit far-fetched, but now that you know it can be done, you might be surprised at how many times you end up doing it.

Dynamically Calculating New Formatting

You have a model that you use to analyze the departmental budget. You normally focus on one month at a time, and you would like to add a column for that month. Rather than applying and removing formatting from columns, let the worksheet format itself. You can set up the worksheet so that merely typing a new month name in cell A1 changes the column that has the highlight, as shown in Figure 13-10, without using any macros or formulas—at least without any formulas in cells.

Note The sample document for this section is Condition.xls.

	A	B	C	D	E	F	G
1	February			January	February	March	
2			Revenue	$1,200	$1,400	$1,800	
3			Expenses	$800	$900	$1,100	
4			Profit	$400	$500	$700	
5							
6							

Figure 13-10
Use conditional formatting to highlight an arbitrary column.

Conditional formatting is frequently used to show whether a number is exceptional—typically unusually high or low. Simple conditional formatting is very easy to create. You also can use conditional formatting to represent any condition you can describe with a formula. In the example in Figure 13-10, you want a column to be shaded if the value in row 1 does not match the value in cell A1.

To set up the formatting, you must create a formula that returns *True* when the format should change. It is easier to create and test a formula in a worksheet cell than in the Conditional Formatting dialog box.

1. Select the range D6:E7 (enough cells to make sure that you also select the relative and absolute portions of the reference correct by), and type the formula *=D$1<>$A$1*.

2. Use Ctrl+Enter to enter the formula into all the selected cells at once. You should see the value *False* in the column that does match cell A1 and the value *True* in the other column.
3. Once the formula is correct, select it in the Formula Bar and copy it.
4. Then select the range you want to format and click Conditional Formatting on the Format menu.
5. In the Condition 1 drop-down list box, select Formula Is.
6. Paste the copied formula into the formula box, as shown in Figure 13-11. (In R1C1 notation, the formula would be *=R1C=R1C1,* which has a positively elegant ring to it.)

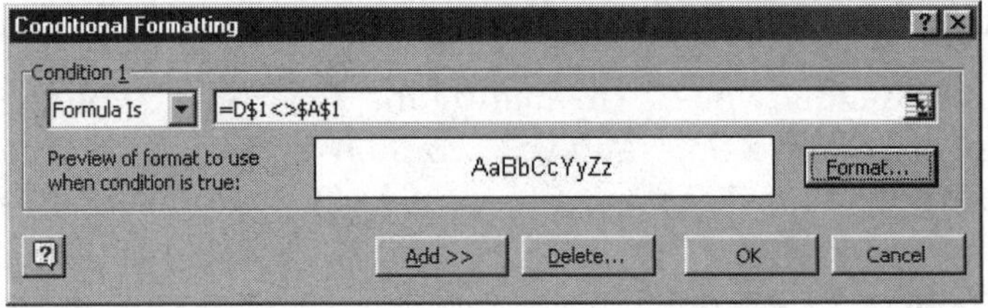

Figure 13-11
Use any formula that calculates True or False to set a format.

7. Click Format to set the Pattern to light gray.

Once you specify that the condition is a formula, you can enter any formula that evaluates to *True.* (Any nonzero number counts as *True.*) If you do try to edit the formula in the Conditional Formatting dialog box, press F2 to change from Enter mode to Edit mode before using the arrow keys to move around in the formula.

Selecting an Item from a List

In the budget worksheet shown earlier in Figure 13-10, you might decide that you don't like typing the full month name each time; you would prefer to select the name of the month from a list. You can use Data Validation to turn any cell into a list box.

First, assign the name *Months* to the range D1:F1.Then select cell A1 and click Data Validation. Select List in the Allow box, clear the Ignore Blank check box, and type *=Months* in the Source box. Be sure to include the equal sign (=) at the beginning of the range name or Excel will think you are entering a list directly into the box. (If you do want to enter a list of values directly in the box, separate values with commas.)

Now you can select the month from the list in cell A1 and watch the formatting change, without any formulas in any cells and without any macros.

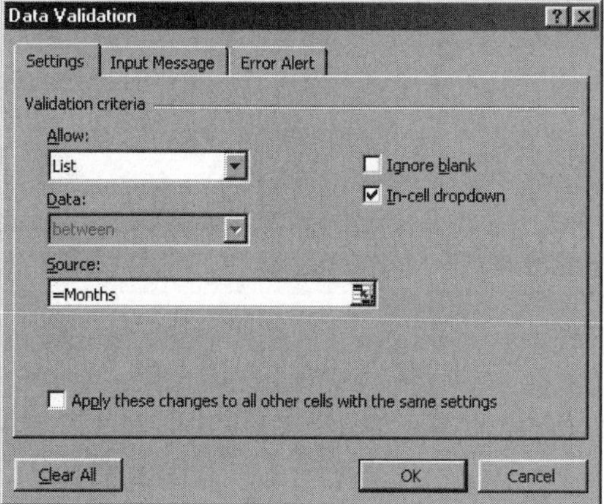

Figure 13-12
Use Data Validation to turn a cell into a list box.

Calculating Using Array Formulas

In early versions of Excel, array formulas were incredibly hard to understand. The documentation on array formulas was obscure, and the examples were not universal. Using array formulas became an almost religious experience for those who learned how to use them, however. They could make worksheet models compact, elegant, and incredibly fast—not to mention the fact that they made possible otherwise impossible formulas. Proficiency with array formulas was the true badge of the elite, as was proficiency with hieroglyphics for the ancient Egyptians.

In later versions of Excel, the development team has made great efforts to eliminate the need for array formulas. They optimized the calculation speed of large blocks of identical formulas so that ordinary formulas in current versions are now as fast—or faster—than the equivalent array formulas. They changed the mechanism for linking cells between workbooks so that array formulas are no longer needed. They added new functions to allow common conditional totals without an array formula. Array formulas are no longer the "Rosetta Stone" that unlocks the mysteries of Excel they way they once were. However, array formulas are still very useful. Here are some situations that call for the use of array formulas.

- Some functions are capable of returning multiple values. An array formula lets you share the results of a single function over many cells.
- Some formulas require intermediate calculations. An array formula lets you perform intermediate calculations in a single formula.
- Array formulas are also much easier to understand and use than they once were. The relevant help topics are much better than they once were, as well.

- You now have this book to show you how to get the benefits of array formulas without the pain.

Sharing Results Between Multiple Cells

Note The sample document for this section is Transpose.xls.

Several Excel functions return more than a single value. One common function that returns more than one value is the TRANSPOSE function. TRANSPOSE converts rows into columns and vice versa. Excel's Paste Special command provides a Transpose option you can use to copy a range and then use Paste Special to transpose it as you paste it into a new location. But the Paste Special command is an action, not a function. If you change any of the values in the original range, you would need to copy and paste it again. The TRANSPOSE function refreshes the transposed values whenever the original values change. The TRANSPOSE function will serve as a useful tool for learning the ropes in dealing with array formulas.

Note Almost all of Excel's regression functions (which look for patterns in a series of numbers) return multiple values. These functions will be covered in "Using Regression to Find and Extend Patterns" in Chapter 14. Some advanced mathematical functions—such as matrix multiplication—return multiple values. If you understand the mathematics of matrix multiplication, you will be able to apply the array formula techniques described here to use those advanced functions, as well.

You have a worksheet like the one shown in Figure 13-13, that imports a list with results for each of your company's products. The list comes with products listed down the side. You need to prepare a report that looks just like the imported list, but with the products listed across the top. You refresh the numbers weekly, and would like the transposed report to automatically reflect the new numbers.

	A	B	C	D
1	Product	Revenue	Expenses	
2	Mountain Blaster	$1,200	$800	
3	Goat Herder	$1,500	$1,200	
4	Cycle Magic	$1,100	$1,300	
5				
6				

Figure 13-13
You import a report that you need to transpose.

You can use the formula bar to watch how the TRANSPOSE function works. First, look at what the TRANSPOSE function sees as input. Give the range A1:C4 the name *Results.* Select cell A1 on a new worksheet. Type =*Results* and, before pressing Enter, press F9 to see how Excel interprets the value of the range. Figure 13-14 shows the formula bar.

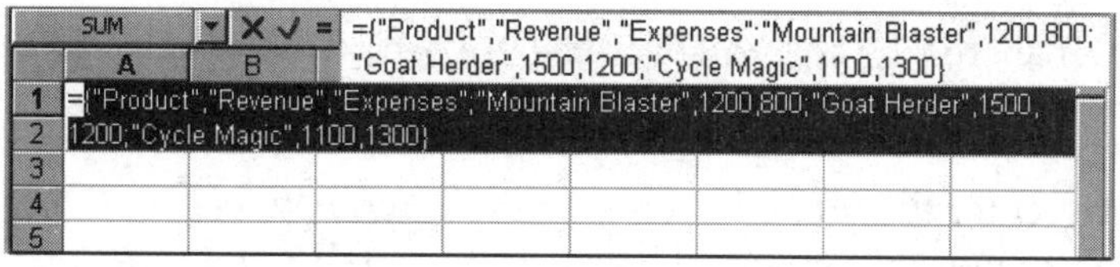

```
SUM  X ✓ = ={"Product","Revenue","Expenses";"Mountain Blaster",1200,800;
"Goat Herder",1500,1200;"Cycle Magic",1100,1300}
1 ={"Product","Revenue","Expenses";"Mountain Blaster",1200,800;"Goat Herder",1500,
2 1200;"Cycle Magic",1100,1300}
```

Figure 13-14
An array constant is enclosed in braces.

What you see is called an *array constant*, which represents multiple results from a single formula. Braces enclose the entire array constant, commas separate items in the same row, quotation marks enclose text items, and semicolons separate rows. An array constant must be equivalent to a rectangular range. That is, all rows must have the same number of columns.

You can always tell whether a formula will return an array by pressing F9 in the formula bar. (The formula bar can display approximately 1000 characters. If an array constant is larger than that, Excel will display a message that the formula is too long.) Press Esc to exit the formula bar.

Next, look at what the TRANSPOSE function generates as output. Type =*TRANSPOSE(Results)* and press F9. Figure 13-15 shows the result. The array constant appears very similar, except that the product names are now in the first row of the array. Press Esc to get out of the formula bar.

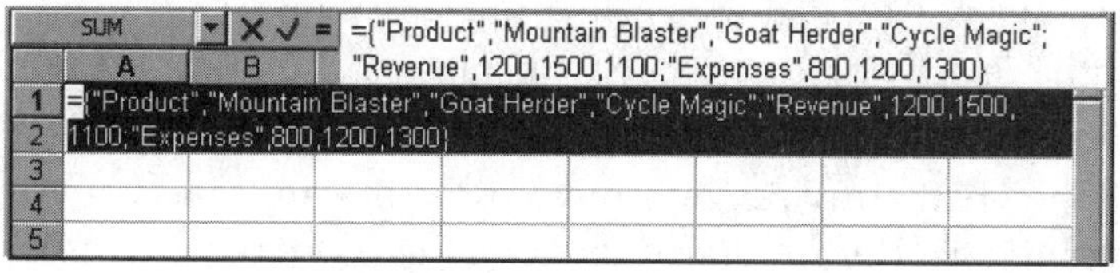

```
SUM  X ✓ = ={"Product","Mountain Blaster","Goat Herder","Cycle Magic";
"Revenue",1200,1500,1100;"Expenses",800,1200,1300}
1 ={"Product","Mountain Blaster","Goat Herder","Cycle Magic";"Revenue",1200,1500,
2 1100;"Expenses",800,1200,1300}
```

Figure 13-15
A transposed array constant reverses rows and columns.

The result of the TRANSPOSE function consists of 12 values. Excel cannot display all 12 values in a single cell. To see the result of the function, you must share the formula between 12 cells. The *Results* range has four rows and three columns. The transposed array has three rows and four columns.

Select the range A1:C4. Type =*TRANSPOSE(Results)* and press Ctrl+Shift+Enter to enter the formula as an array formula.

Note It might help you remember to use Ctrl+Shift+Enter for array formulas if you think about all the other variations of the Enter key. Enter places the formula into the active cell and selects the next available cell. Shift+Enter is the same as Enter, but it selects the previously available cell. Ctrl+Enter puts a copy of the formula into each selected cell.

Ctrl+Shift+Enter shares the current formula between all the selected cells. Ctrl+Enter and Ctrl+Shift+Enter do not change the selection.

When you array-enter the formula, it becomes shared between all the selected cells, and you can no longer edit any of the cells individually. If you try, Excel displays the message, "You cannot change part of an array." When you array-enter a formula, Excel displays braces around the formula in the formula bar.

To select all the cells that are shared by a single array formula, select any one of the cells and press Ctrl+forward slash (/) (which corresponds to the Current Array option in the Go To Special dialog box). If you need to modify an array formula, you don't need to pre-select the array. Just edit the formula from any of the cells and press Ctrl+Shift+Enter. Excel will automatically select the current array and enter the formula.

Resizing Array Formulas

Suppose you have a formula that returns an array with three rows and four columns. If you enter it into a range that has four rows and five columns, Excel will populate the extra cells with the error value #N/A. If you enter it into a range with two rows and three columns, Excel simply will not display any of the values that don't fit.

Suppose that your company adds a new product, and the range named *Results* changes to have five rows. The transposed array will now have five columns, but the fifth column will not appear. Expanding an array range is easy: simply select the new range (with the active cell on a cell that contains the formula), press F2 to edit the formula, and press Ctrl+Shift+Enter to enter the formula into the expanded range.

Reducing the size of an array range is more difficult. Suppose that your company drops a product and the *Results* named range changes to have three rows. The transposed array no longer has enough columns to fill the cells, and the extra cells display #N/A. If you try to delete the formula from those cells, Excel reminds you that you can't change part of an array. If the formula is long and complex, you might not want to clear the range and start over. The secret is to temporarily split the formula into individual cells. Here's how to reduce the size of an array formula:

1. Select any cell that is part of the array and press Ctrl+/ (forward slash) to select the current array.
2. Press F2 to edit the formula, and press Ctrl+Enter (not Ctrl+Shift+Enter) to copy the formula into all the cells. The cells might display bizarre values or errors.
3. Clear the cells that no longer need to be part of the array, and then select the remaining cells.
4. Press F2, and then array-enter the formula by pressing Ctrl+Shift+Enter.

Disabling Implicit Intersection

Note The sample document for this section is Arrays.xls

In the worksheet shown in Figure 13-16, the name *Price* refers to cells B1:E1, and the name *Quantity* refers to cells A2:A6. The formulas use implicit intersection to calculate individual revenue totals. Because the block of formulas does not align with the names, the first revenue value corresponds to the second price and quantity, and the last row and column, which don't belong to rows or columns that intersect with the named ranges, produce the #VALUE! error values.

C3 = =Price*Quantity

	A	B	C	D	E	F	G	H
1		$5	$10	$15	$20			
2	10							
3	20		$200	$300	$400	#VALUE!		
4	30		$300	$450	$600	#VALUE!		
5	40		$400	$600	$800	#VALUE!		
6	50		$500	$750	$1,000	#VALUE!		
7			#VALUE!	#VALUE!	#VALUE!	#VALUE!		
8								
9								
10								

Figure 13-16
Implicit intersection requires row and column alignment.

You might have worksheets where you want to use named ranges, but the formulas do not suitably align for implicit intersection. One of the attributes of array-entering a formula is that Excel no longer uses implicit intersection with the formula. Instead, the formula produces however many values it can, and it is your responsibility to either find them homes or discard them.

The worksheet shown in Figure 13-17 is identical to the one shown in Figure 13-16, except that the block of formulas has been array-entered. (Notice the braces in the formula bar.) The multiplication operator expects to multiply identically sized arrays, but the *Price* range has four columns, while the *Quantity* range has only one column. When an input array has only one row or column, and the corresponding array has more than one, Excel simply duplicates the one row or column. (Excel follows the same rule when you copy a single row and then paste it into a multiple row range.)

So, in effect, this one formula is multiplying the *Quantity* range (replicated to produce a 5-row by 4-column array) by the *Price* range (replicated to produce a 5-row by 4-column array). The result, then, is a 5-row by 4-column array. If you click on the formula in the Formula Bar and press F9, you see the following array constant:

```
={50,100,150,200;100,200,300,400;150,300,450,600;200,
400,600,800;250,500,750,1000}.
```

It is this result array that you're sharing between the cells of the destination range.

C3 = {=Price*Quantity}

	A	B	C	D	E	F	G	H
1		$5	$10	$15	$20			
2	10							
3	20		$50	$100	$150	$200		
4	30		$100	$200	$300	$400		
5	40		$150	$300	$450	$600		
6	50		$200	$400	$600	$800		
7			$250	$500	$750	$1,000		
8								
9								
10								

Figure 13-17
Array-entered formulas do not require alignment.

If you array-enter the formula into the cell C3, the result is 50, because array-entering the formula disables implicit intersection. If you then copy cell C3 and paste the formula into the remaining cells of the range C3:F7, each cell will display the number 50. Each cell will calculate all 20 numbers but will display only the first, discarding the rest. If you want to display the array of results, you must share the formula between many cells.

Note You might wonder if there's a way to array-enter a formula into a single cell and then somehow retrieve the other values from the cell—perhaps using a special argument with the *INDEX* function or something. You cannot. Even if an array formula is calculating hundreds of values, there is no way to get to any of the values that are not allocated to a worksheet cell, either with a formula or with VBA.

Preventing Inconsistent Formulas

Suppose you move the formulas in Figure 13-17 into the range B2:E6 to align them with the *Price* and *Quantity* ranges. In that case, it is easier to use the non-array formula, because you can delete or change formulas without worrying about which cells are included in the array formula.

On the other hand, one of the problems with many worksheet models is that formulas might become inconsistent. You have a block of formulas, and some helpful person converts one of them into a value, or adds +150 to the end of one of them.

You might want to turn one of the greatest inconveniences of an array formula into a virtue: it is impossible to make any of the formulas inconsistent.

Eliminating Intermediate Formulas

Note The sample document for this section is Grades.xls.

Even more valuable than sharing the results of a single formula among many cells is the ability to eliminate the need for formulas altogether.

Some calculations require intermediate values in order to arrive at the correct result. Suppose you are teaching a class and are using Excel to calculate the students' grades. You give a variety of quizzes and tests, and rate each task on a 5-point scale, as you can see in Figure 13-18. At the end of the term, you need to come up with an average grade for each student. Since each item is weighted differently, the simple average (shown in cell C10) gives the incorrect answer. To get the correctly weighted rating (shown in cell D10), you must first multiply each rating by its corresponding weight. To get the average, you divide the sum of the adjusted values by the sum of the weights. For the student rating illustrated in Figure 13-18, the difference between the correct and incorrect calculation is unfortunate, but striking.

D5 = =Weight*Rating

	A	B	C	D	E	F	G	H
1	**Task**	**Weight**	**Rating**	**Adjusted**				
2	Quiz	10	5	50				
3	Quiz	10	5	50				
4	Quiz	20	5	100				
5	Test	100	3	300				
6	Quiz	10	5	50				
7	Quiz	20	5	100				
8	Test	100	3	300				
9	Final	500	1	500				
10	**Average**		**4.0**	**1.9**				
11								
12								

Figure 13-18
Calculating a weighted average requires intermediate calculations.

You must create an entire column of intermediate formulas just to calculate the weighted rating. It would be easier to create grades for an entire class of students if each student's ratings and total could fit into a single column. Excel actually provides several options for dealing with this situation; an array formula is one of them. We'll look at how to solve this problem using an array formula, because it can help you see how array formulas work. Then we'll compare the array formula approach with some alternatives so that you can decide which approach would work best for you in the models you build.

Calculating a Weighted Average by Using an Array Formula

An array formula makes it possible to calculate dozens, hundreds, or even thousands of intermediate calculations in a single formula. As an example, see what an array formula does to the multiplication operator (*). You normally use the multiplication operator to multiply two single numbers. When you enter a formula that uses the multiplication operator in a cell, Excel expects it to multiply two single numbers, and it uses implicit intersection where possible to reduce ranges of numbers down to two single numbers for the operator to use. In Figure 13-18, the range B2:B9 is named *Weight*, and the range C2:C9 is named *Rating*. In cell D5, the formula =*Weight*Rating* plucks the single values from cells B5 and C5 to produce the single answer: 300.

The multiplication operator, however, is capable of multiplying two entire arrays of numbers, producing a corresponding array of values as the result. You can see the capabilities of the multiplication operator by calculating the formula in cell D5 in the formula bar. If you select cell D5, click in the formula bar, and press F9, you see the result ={50;50;100;300;50;100;300;500}. This is an array constant with one column and eight rows. The native capability of the multiplication operator is to calculate entire arrays. It is only when you enter it into a single cell that you defeat the operator's ability to calculate only two single values.

Using Ctrl+Shift+Enter to array-enter a formula reenables the array capabilities of the operators. Of course, you then have an array of answers to deal with. In this example, the only reason you need the intermediate values is so that you can sum them up and then divide that sum by the sum of the weights. The result is a single number that will easily fit into a single cell. The one formula =*SUM(Weight*Rating)/ SUM(Weight)* entered into cell C10 will produce the correct weighted average rating.

You must use Ctrl+Shift+Enter to enter the formula, or Excel defeats the multiplication operator and attempts to intersect row 10 with the *Weight* and *Rating* ranges. Since those ranges end at row 9, the result of the non-array formula is #VALUE!. (If you enter the non-array formula into cell D5, it produces the result 0.1, because row 5 intersects with the *Weight* and *Rating* ranges at cells B5 and C5.) After you array-enter the formula, you can see the braces around the formula. This is an array formula, even though it eventually produces a single value that requires only a single cell.

Copying an Array Formula to Multiple Columns

The grades for the first student now all fit in a single column, with no cells that require intermediate formulas. You are ready to expand the worksheet to handle all the students in your class. Figure 13-19 shows the worksheet with additional students. The original array formula used the range *Rating*, which referred to the ratings for one student (now identified as Martha). You can't use the same range name multiple times on a single worksheet. You could name each column of ratings with the name of the student, but that would require you to customize each formula, and would also cause serious problems with the three Sara's in your class.

A better solution is to extend the name *Ratings* to refer to the entire block of rows that contain ratings, rows 2:9, and then use explicit intersection in each formula to get just the current student's rating. In A1 notation, to specify the entire current column, you must enter the column letter twice, with a colon in between. The column letter also changes from column to column. In R1C1 notation, you specify the entire current column with the letter C, regardless of the column. In R1C1 notation, the formula is =*SUM(Weight*Rating C)/SUM(Weight)*.

An even better way to implement the explicit intersection option is to use the labels from the top of each column. If you give the name *Ratings* to rows 2:9, and the name *Weight* to the cell range B2:B9, you can use the expression *Martha Ratings* to refer to the range C2:C9, so the formula array-entered into cell D10 is:

```
=SUM(Weight*Martha Ratings)/SUM(Weight)
```

When you copy the formula to the right, Excel automatically adjusts the label to refer to the new column. Even if two students have the same name, the formula works properly as long as you don't actually edit the cell containing the duplicate label. (That's because the formula secretly uses the cell addresses—the label displayed in the formula is purely for your convenience.)

D10 = {=SUM(Weight*Rating D:D)/SUM(Weight)}

	A	B	C	D	E	F	G	H
1	Task	Weight	Martha	Albert	Jose	Jasmine		
2	Quiz	10	5	2	3	5		
3	Quiz	10	5	2	2	3		
4	Quiz	20	5	3	2	3		
5	Test	100	3	4	4	4		
6	Quiz	10	5	1	1	5		
7	Quiz	20	5	2	5	3		
8	Test	100	3	5	1	5		
9	Final	500	1	4	2	4		
10	Average		1.9	4.0	2.2	4.1		
11								
12	MMULT		1.9	4.0	2.2	4.1		
13								
14								
15								

Figure 13-19
Use explicit intersection to extract a column from a range.

If you want to push array formulas to the limit, you can also calculate all the average ratings in a single array formula that returns average ratings for all the students at once (one row with four columns in the worksheet in Figure 13-19). The mathematical procedure known as *matrix multiplication* (and implemented in Excel's MMULT function) can multiply the weights times each of the students and sum the numbers in each column—all in a single function. You just have to transpose the *Weight* range so that it has the same number of columns as the *Rating* range has rows. You'll get the same values you see in the range C10:F10 if you array-enter the following formula into the range C11:F11:

```
=MMULT(TRANSPOSE(Weight),Rating)/SUM(Weight)
```

Calculating a Weighted Average Without an Array Formula In the interest of total disclosure, there is an alternate method for creating the formula to calculate the grades—a method that does not require an array formula. The weighted average example is useful for understanding how array formulas work, but Excel does have a special function that will multiply corresponding elements of two arrays of numbers, summing the total into a single cell: the SUMPRODUCT function. The formula

=SUMPRODUCT(Weight,Martha Ratings)/SUM(Weight), entered as an ordinary formula in cell C10, will calculate Martha's average rating. This formula uses the combination of label and named ranges discussed in the preceding section, and can be copied to new columns.

Array Formulas and Names

Note The sample document for this section is Array2.xls.

When you define a formula in a name, the formula calculates the same as it does in the formula bar—that is, it calculates all the possible values, without any implicit intersection.

Suppose you have a worksheet with prices and quantities in lists, as shown in Figure 13-20, rather than arranged as row and column headings. Then suppose that you don't need the entire grid of revenues, but you want to retrieve only a single revenue value from the array of possible combinations.

You can calculate all the possible combinations in a named formula, from which you can retrieve values as needed. To get all the possible combinations, you need to transpose the prices, but you can do that as part of the same formula. A formula on the worksheet—as shown in cell E3 in the figure—can use the INDEX function to select a particular value out of the array calculated by the name.

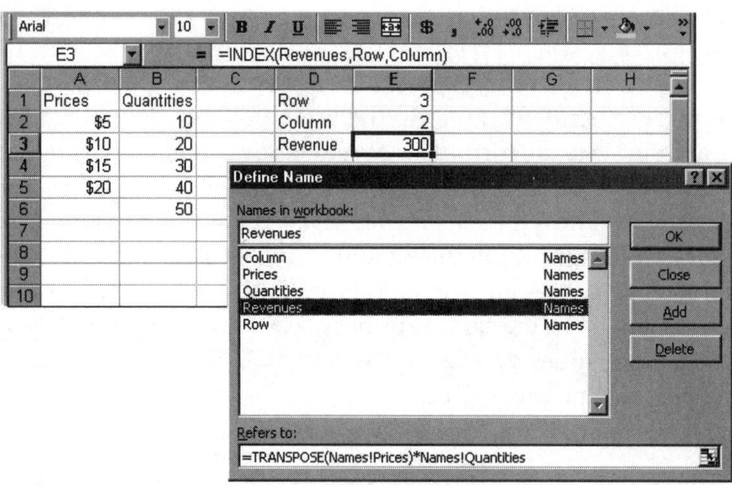

Figure 13-20
A named formula can calculate an entire array.

The *Revenues* formula calculates all the values it needs without using any worksheet cells. If you insert three more prices into the *Prices* list, the *Revenues* formula will instantly and automatically change its result array from 20 values to 35 values. This ability of named formulas to calculate a dynamically sized result array is particularly powerful if you need to chart mathematical functions. The following section shows how to create a series with anywhere from five to 5000 data points, none of which appear anywhere on a worksheet.

Charting an Algebraic Function

Note The sample document for this section is Poly.xls.

An algebraic function specifies what the value on the y (vertical) axis of a chart should be for any given value on the x (horizontal) axis. Traditionally, when creating a chart of an algebraic function, you create a range of x values in a column on a worksheet, and then add a formula in the adjacent column that calculates the y value for each of those x values.

The problem with the traditional approach is that some functions require only a few data points to chart properly, while other functions require many data points to properly display the behavior of the function. Figure 13-21 shows a chart of a polynomial function. Changing the values in column B changes the shape of the line. The chart in the Figure 13-21 displays only five data points, ranging from –10 to 10. (The number in cell E4 specifies the number of segments; there is one more point than there are segments.) There are no cells on the worksheet that contain the x values. There are also no cells on the worksheet that contain the calculated y values. The x values and the y values are calculated dynamically using a named array formula.

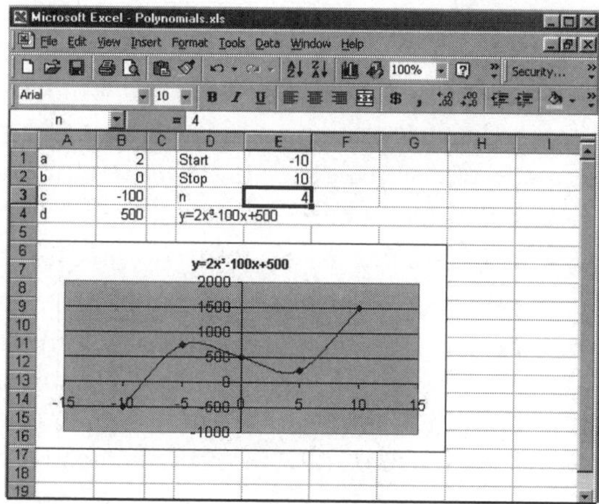

Figure 13-21
Use named array formulas to generate points for a chart.

The advantage of using named array formulas to generate the chart data is that you can instantly change from charting five data points to charting 51 data points—as shown in Figure 13-22—or even 5001 data points (which would appear as merely a thick line for this function on this small chart), simply by typing a new number into a cell.

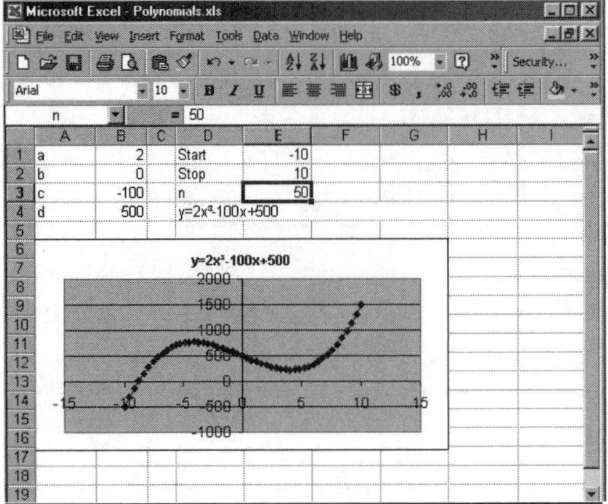

Figure 13-22
Dynamically change the number of data points.

The goal is to create a formula that will generate an array of x values. You need one more value than the number in cell *n*. The values should begin with the *Start* value and end with the *Stop* value. Since the formula to create those values might seem complicated, let's build it gradually.

The seed for creating an arbitrary array of numbers is the OFFSET function, which can specify a range of arbitrary size. The expression *OFFSET(A1,0,0,100)* returns a range that begins with cell A1 and has 100 rows. It's best not to use cell A1 as the starting cell, because it's too easy to accidentally delete that cell when reformatting or rearranging the worksheet. Instead, use the cell named *n*, because you are unlikely to accidentally delete it. The revised expression *OFFSET(n,0,0,n+1)* returns a range that begins with the cell named *n* and has as many rows as the value of cell *n* plus 1.

The ROW function returns the row number of a given cell. If you give it a range of cells that encompasses more than one row, it returns an array of row numbers. The expression *ROW(A1:A5)* returns the array {1;2;3;4;5}. If cell E3 is named *n* and contains the value 4, then the expression *ROW(OFFSET(n,0,0,n+1))* returns the array {3;4;5;6;7}. To get a series beginning with 0, subtract the row number of the original cell. The expression *ROW(OFFSET(n,0,0,n+1))-ROW(n)* returns the array {0;1;2;3;4}.

The next step is to scale the numbers. To do that, divide by *n* (to get numbers between 0 and 1), and then multiply by the difference between the *Start* and *Stop* values. The expression *(ROW(OFFSET(n,0,0,n+1))-ROW(n))/n* returns the array {0;0.25;0.5;0.75;1}, and the expression *(ROW(OFFSET(n,0,0,n+1))-ROW(n))/n*(Stop-Start)* returns the array {0;5;10;15;20}.

The final step is to shift the numbers to the correct starting value by adding *Start*. The formula =(ROW(OFFSET(n,0,0,n+1))-ROW(n))/n*(Stop-Start)+Start returns the array {-10;-5;0;5;10}, which happens to match the range of desired x values. The beauty of the formula is that by changing the value of *n* to *10*, the result of the formula instantly becomes {-10;-8;-6;-4;-2;0;2;4;6;8;10}.

When dealing with an array formula such as this—one that will eventually become a named array formula—always begin by entering the formula into a cell. You can then use the F9 key to calculate selected parts of the formula. Just be sure to press Esc to keep from converting the formula into a constant.

Once the formula is correct, copy the formula from the formula bar (don't just copy the cell), define a name, and paste the formula into the Refers To text box, as shown in Figure 13-23. When charting an algebraic function, you might want to give the formula the name *X*, or *PlotX*.

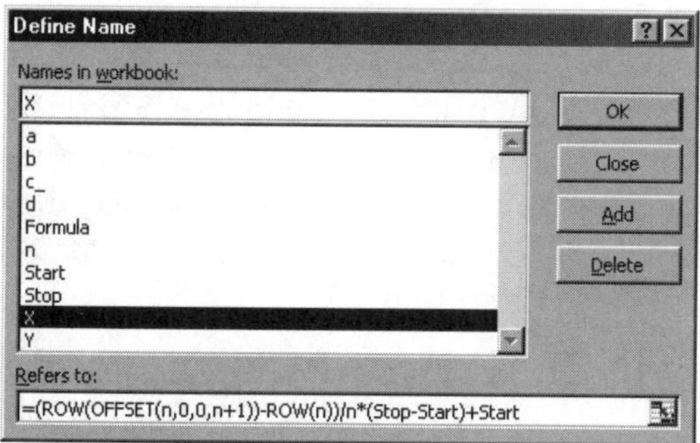

Figure 13-23
Create the formula first, and then paste it into a name.

You can then define the name *Y* to implement the function. For the polynomial equation, the formula for *Y* is =a*X^3+b*X^2+c_*X+d. (The name *c* by itself is not a legal name because in R1C1 notation, it is a cell reference. An underscore at the end of the name makes it legal.) Once again, you might want to create and test the formula in a cell before pasting it as the definition of a name.

Once the X and Y formulas are defined, you can assign them to a chart. Normally, when you create a chart, Excel assigns cell addresses as the source data. You can replace those cell addresses with names. If a name refers to a worksheet range, it can be either a global name or a local name. If the name defines a formula that returns values, however, it must be a global name.

Select any two or more arbitrary cells and begin creating an XY (Scatter) chart. In step 2, select the Series tab, and type the defined names into the X Values and Y Values boxes. You must specify each name as external references. You can prefix the name with either the workbook name or the name of the active sheet, as shown in Figure 13-24. Either way, Excel converts the reference to use the workbook name.

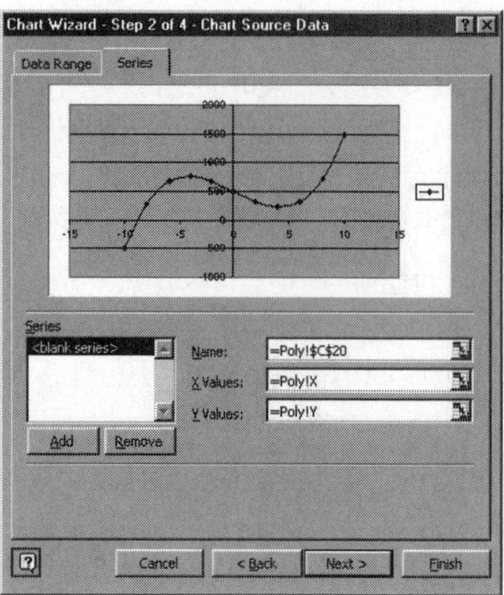

Figure 13-24
Assign named formulas as the data source.

The only remaining complexity in this workbook is the creation of the label that displays the equation in standard algebraic form. There are two steps required to create this formula. The first step is a named formula that constructs the formula for all terms that are not zero. Once again, the formula appears more complicated than it really is. The name *Formula* has this definition:

```
="y="&
 IF(a,"+"&a&"x³ ","")&
 IF(b,"+"&b&"x² ","")&
 IF(c_,"+"&c_&"x","")&
 IF(d,"+"&d,"")&
 IF(SUM(a*RAND(),b*RAND(),c_*RAND(),d*RAND()),"","0")
```

This formula starts with the y= prefix. Next, each value is checked to see if it is not zero (any non-zero number counts as *True* in the IF function). If the value is not zero, it is added to the equation, along with the appropriate power of *x*. To enter the symbol ^{2} for a square, hold down the Alt key as you type *0178* on the numeric keypad. To enter the symbol ^{3} for a cube, type *Alt 0179.* The final IF component of the formula simply displays a zero if all the other values are zero. Multiplying each value by RAND keeps –1 and 1 from canceling each other.

For the constants in Figure 13-22, the result formula is $y=+2x^3+-100x+500$. The squared term is properly eliminated, but the combinations =+ and +- are redundant. The formula in cell D4 eliminates all redundant combinations using the SUBSTITUTE function. Here's the formula in the cell:

```
=SUBSTITUTE(SUBSTITUTE(SUBSTITUTE(SUBSTITUTE(
 Formula,"+1x","+x"),"-1x","-x"),"=+","="),"+-","-")
```

For an explanation of how to use the SUBSTITUTE function, see "Replacing Portions of Text Strings" in Chapter 14.

Chapter 14

Use Functions and Let Excel Do the Work

In This Chapter

I once taught a class in advanced Microsoft Excel techniques to a group of engineers. One morning, one of the students came in very excited about an extremely complex formula he had spent half the night creating that implemented some obscure mathematical function. In my typical diplomatic fashion, I commended him on his work and then asked if he knew whether Excel had a built-in function to do that calculation.

He was startled at the thought. So we looked at the list of available functions and, sure enough, there it was. He was morbidly depressed the rest of the day.

Excel has well over 200 functions built directly into the product. The Analysis Toolpak add-in supplies roughly another 100 specialized functions, plus a dialog box containing several analytical tools. If you are using Excel for statistical or engineering work, install the Analysis Toolpak immediately. To learn more about installing the Analysis Toolpak, ask the Answer Wizard for help using the search words *Analysis Toolpak.*

The Help topics for Excel functions are generally very good, providing clear examples of function usage. There is no need to repeat any of that information here. This chapter will discuss some of the more easily overlooked functions—most likely to be useful to power users.

If you need to search for a function, try the categorized list in the Paste Function dialog box. For more assistance, click the Help button at the bottom of the dialog box (click it twice if you have turned off the Office Assistant). Accept the offer for Help with the feature and then type a brief description of the function you want to search for. A new "Recommended" category will appear in the dialog box, as shown in Figure 14-1, listing all the functions that might be relevant to your search.

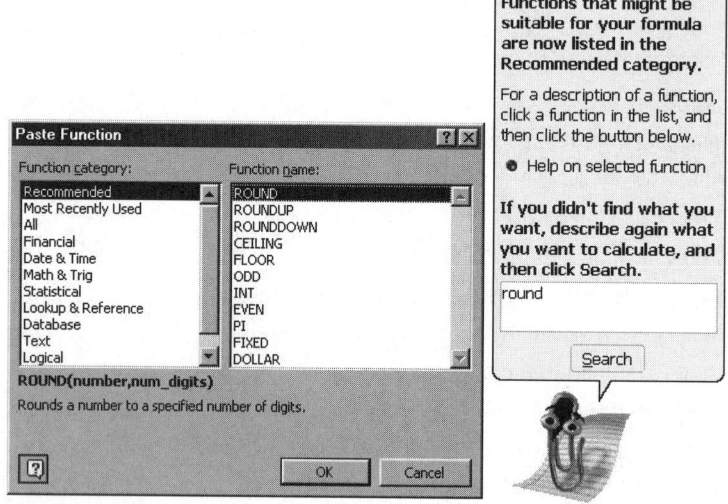

Figure 14-1
The Office Assistant can help you find Functions.

If you don't like having the Office Assistant around, you'll have to turn it off again after using this feature; the customized list of functions is worth keeping the Office Assistant around long enough to get it.

Manipulating Dates

My first job after college was as a COBOL programmer. Dealing with dates was one of the biggest headaches of the job. We gave occasional thought to what would happen to dates as the year 2000 arrived, but most of the frustration centered around handling the more routine transitions from one month to another and from one year to the next. Simply formatting a date value suitable for displaying on a report required dozens of lines of code. Leap years were particularly obnoxious coding challenges.

All that changed when I started developing applications on a personal computer, first using Lotus 1-2-3 and then using Microsoft Excel. Managing dates suddenly became trivial. Formatting dates became a delight. Once you understand how dates work in Excel, you'll find they are very powerful tools.

Understanding Excel Dates

Dates in Excel after March 1, 1900, are identical to dates in Microsoft Visual Basic and Microsoft Access. They are really floating point numbers, with the day—since the beginning of the twentieth century—stored in the integer portion and the time of day stored in the fractional portion. If you format a positive number as a date, it becomes a date. If you remove the formatting from a date, it becomes a regular number. If you see an unfamiliar number in a cell that looks vaguely like 36526, it is probably a date that has lost its date formatting. Dates in Visual Basic, Access, and Excel are valid up to December 31, 9999.

Before March 1, 1900, dates are different in Excel from those in Visual Basic and Access, for two reasons. One reason is that Excel bases dates only on positive numbers, so they stop at the first of the twentieth century; Visual Basic and Access use both positive and negative numbers and carry dates back to January 1, 100. The other reason is that Excel dates are off by one day for dates before March 1, 1900. The Lotus 1-2-3 developers erroneously thought that the year 1900 was a leap year and created a February 29 date for that year. When Excel moved from its original Macintosh base to the PC world, it was critical for a worksheet to be compatible with Lotus 1-2-3, so Excel emulated the date error. Access and Visual Basic later borrowed the concept of dates from Excel, but refused to perpetuate the Lotus date error.

If you transfer data between Excel and Access, you might encounter this date inconsistency. Suppose you use the date 1/1/1900 to indicate a starting date in the indefinite past. In Excel, the date 1/1/1900 has the value 1. If you copy that date to Access, the date does not change to 12/31/1899; it remains 1/1/1900. But in Access, the date 1/1/1900 has the value 2. The effect of this inconsistency—when transferring dates between Excel and Access—is not always apparent, so you should be aware of the underlying situation in case you see some completely inexplicable anomalies with dates early in the twentieth century.

(continued)

Understanding Excel Dates *(continued)*
Another artifact of the Lotus date error is an inconsistency between dates in Microsoft Windows and Macintosh versions of Excel. Excel was originally introduced on the Macintosh. In an effort to bypass the date error, the Excel developers chose to make the value of day 1 equal to January 1, 1904 rather than January 1, 1900. To provide compatibility with Lotus 1-2-3 on the PC, the Windows version of Excel opted to go with the January 1, 1900 date system.

Each workbook has an option under Options, Calculation on the Tools menu, that indicates whether the workbook is using the 1904 date system. On the Macintosh, the default value for that setting is checked. In Windows, the default value is unchecked. If you move a workbook between operating systems, the date style goes with the workbook and you have no apparent problems. If you attempt to copy cells containing dates from a migrated workbook to a native workbook, however, the dates will shift. For example, if you create a workbook on the Macintosh and type the date January 1, 2000, and then copy that cell into a Windows-style workbook, the date will change to December 31, 1995. There is a difference of 1462 days between the two date systems. If you need to fix a migrated date, either add or subtract 1462, as necessary.

Using Date Functions

The most useful date functions are the ones that deconstruct and reconstruct dates. The YEAR, MONTH, and DAY functions extract the appropriate components from a date. The DATE function constructs a date using year, month, and day values. (Equivalent functions deal with time.) To calculate the date exactly one month later than the date in cell B2, for example, use the formula *=DATE(YEAR(B2),MONTH(B2)+1,DAY(B2)).*

The TODAY function returns the current date. You can find the first day of the current month with the formula *=DATE(YEAR(TODAY()),MONTH(TODAY()),1).* (Even though the TODAY function does not take any arguments, you must add parentheses after it or Excel will think you are entering a defined name. This differs from functions in VBA, where you can omit parentheses if they are empty.)

One of the incredibly useful features of the DATE function is that it allows seemingly illegal values. Calculating the last day of a month could be very difficult, because months have different lengths, particularly during leap year. The DATE function, however, obligingly gives you the last day of the previous month when you use 0 as the day value. To find the last day of the month for an arbitrary date in cell B2, use the formula *=DATE(YEAR(B2),MONTH(B2)+1,0).*

Because dates simply count days, you don't need a special function to count the number of days between two dates. Just subtract the earlier date from the later date—unless, that is, you want to ignore weekends and holidays. If you want to count the net working days between two dates, install the Analysis Toolpak and use the

NETWORKDAYS function it supplies. This function skips weekends, and it allows you to create a list of dates to use as holidays that it will skip as well.

Adding a Shortcut Key to Increment Dates

Checkbook management programs such as Microsoft Money or Intuit's Quicken allow you to adjust dates by using a shortcut key. You can add your own shortcut keys to adjust dates in Excel. The *IncrementValue* macro (later in this section) adjusts a date by the number of months passed as an argument. Passing 1 (or nothing) moves the month up by one, passing –1 moves the month down by one.

Assigning a Shortcut Key to a Macro That Takes an Argument

Before looking at the macro, consider how to set it up as a shortcut key. "Assigning a Shortcut Key to a Macro" in Chapter 4 describes how to add custom shortcut keys in Excel. The *IncrementValue* macro is complicated, however, because it uses an argument. If you want to pass an argument to a macro, you must enclose the macro name and the argument between apostrophes. Using the shortcut key Ctrl+Shift+plus (+) to increment a month and the shortcut key Ctrl+Shift+minus (-) to decrement a month, you would add these entries in the shortcut table:

```
%+= IncrementValue
%+- 'IncrementValue -1'
```

Even if you think of the increment shortcut as Ctrl+Shift+plus (+), the actual unshifted key value is an equal sign (=), so that is the code you must use in the table.

Creating a Macro to Increment Dates

The following *IncrementValue* macro adds one month to or subtracts one month from the value in the active cell—but only if that value is a valid date. As an added bonus, the macro also adds 10 to or subtracts 10 from any other numeric cell. If the active cell contains text, the macro does nothing. (If the active cell contains the logical value *True,* the macro treats it like the number –1. If it contains the logical value *False,* the macro treats it like the number 0.)

When you change the month of a date, the macro retains the same day of the month, unless the day happens to be the last day of the month. If it is the last day of the month, the macro changes to the last day of the new month. Also, if the current day is 29 or 30 and the new month does not have that many days, the macro shifts the date to the last day of the new month.

Here's the macro code, which will be explained in detail.

```
Sub IncrementValue(Optional ByVal Amount As Long = 1)
    Dim d As Date
    On Error GoTo ErrorHandler
    If IsDate(ActiveCell) Then
        d = ActiveCell.Value
        If Month(d) <> Month(d + 1) Then ''' last of month
```

```
            d = DateSerial(Year(d), Month(d) + Amount + 1, 0)
        Else
            d = DateSerial(Year(d), Month(d) + Amount, Day(d))
            If Day(ActiveCell.Value) <> Day(d) Then
                d = DateSerial(Year(d), Month(d), 0)
            End If
        End If
        ActiveCell.Value = d
    ElseIf IsNumeric(ActiveCell) Then
        ActiveCell.Value = ActiveCell.Value + Amount * 10
    End If
ErrorHandler:
End Sub
```

After declaring a date variable, the macro sets the error handler to jump to the end. In other words, if the macro hits any kind of an error, it will quit—doing nothing.

If the active cell contains a value that can be interpreted as a date, the macro assigns that value to the date variable to avoid having to type *ActiveCell.Value* repeatedly.

If the month of the date is different from the month of the next day, the date must be the end of the month. In that case, the macro simply adds 1 to the new month, and takes its "zero-th" day, which is the last day of the preceding month. The *Amount* argument will either be 1 or –1. Adding that amount to the month portion correctly shifts the month.

If the date is not the end of the month, the macro tries to adjust the month, while keeping the day of the month the same. If the resulting day is in a new month, the month was too short and the date should shift back to the last day of the preceding month.

If the macro makes it through all those tests without any errors, it enters the new date back into the cell.

By contrast, the numeric portion is very easy. As long as the active cell can be interpreted as a number, the macro multiplies the argument amount (1 or –1) by 10 and adds the result to the active cell.

Watching for a Formula When Incrementing Dates

The *IncrementValue* macro works very well. Too well, perhaps. If the active cell contains a formula, it will quietly replace it with the incremented value. You can configure the *IncrementValue* macro to ask you whether you intended to replace a formula simply by adding a couple of calls to a simple subroutine.

After the statement that begins *If IsDate* and after the statement that begins *ElseIf IsNumeric*, type the statement *CheckFormula ActiveCell*. Then add the following *CheckFormula* macro code:

```
Sub CheckFormula(ByVal r As Range)
    If Left(r.Formula, 1) = "=" Then
        If MsgBox("The cell contains a formula. " _
            "Do you want to replace it with a value?", _
```

```
            vbQuestion + vbYesNo + vbDefaultButton2) = vbNo Then
            Err.Raise 0, , "Canceled"
        End If
    End If
End Sub
```

The macro checks any cell passed to it, looking for an equal sign (=) as the first character in the formula. If one exists, the macro asks whether to replace it with a value. If the answer is *No*, it raises an error, which causes the calling macro to quit.

The statement calling the *CheckFormula* subroutine must be inserted twice into the *IncrementValue* macro; you want to run the subroutine only if the macro would otherwise replace the value in the cell.

The MsgBox function uses three flags for the *Button* argument: vbQuestion, vbYesNo, and vbDefaultButton2. To use multiple flags, you simply add them together. The only portion that is necessary is the vbYesNo flag, which determines what buttons will appear. The vbQuestion flag adds a charming little question mark icon. The vbDefaultButton2 flag makes the second button—the *No* answer—the default. It's a good idea to make the safest choice the default.

Creating Expense Report Headers

Say you travel a lot and that you create a lot of expense reports. Your company requires a particular look to the expense report, and you have to match that look. Figure 14-2 shows the top portion of the expense format. You must display the departure date for the trip, and the column headings must show all the days of the week that include that date. The dates must show the day of the week, along with the month, day, and year. Just to keep everything interesting, you work for an outsourcing agency, so the first day of the week varies, depending on the client company.

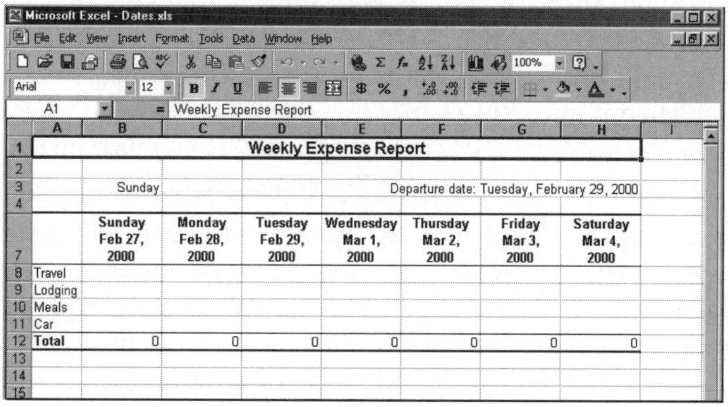

Figure 14-2
Create date headings that adjust automatically.

Note The sample document for this section is Expenses.xls.

Displaying Long, Custom-Formatted Dates

You want the departure date to appear right-justified in cell H3, including the cell label *"Departure Date: "* in the cell. Because you will want to use this date in formulas, you must enter it as a date. But because the length of the date shifts, the label prefix must be part of the date. What's more, Excel does not have a built-in date format that includes the day of the week. You can create the date style you want by using a custom number format.

Type the date *2/29/00* in cell E3. With that cell selected, display the Number tab on the Format Cells dialog box. Select the Custom category, and in the Type text box, type *"Departure date: "dddd, mmmm d, yyyy* as the custom format. In a custom format, many letters function as codes that tell Excel how to format different types of numbers. When you enclose text in quotation marks, Excel simply includes the text as part of the format. The rest of the format consists of date codes. These codes tell Excel to display the full weekday name, the full month name, a one or two-digit day, and the full four-digit year. For a list of all the possible custom date format codes, ask the Answer Wizard for Help using the search term *Format Codes for Dates*.

After you format the date, if you keep the column the standard width, the value in the cell will appear as a series of number signs (#####). When you enter a number that can't fit into a cell, Excel does not extend the value into the next cell as it does with text. You can extend a formatted date beyond the cell boundaries by merging cells. To do that, select the range E3:H3 and click the Merge And Center button on the Formatting toolbar. After you merge the cells, click the Align Right button on the same toolbar to right-align the formatted date in cell H3.

Caution The Ctrl+; (semi-colon) shortcut key enters the current date into the active cell. When you use this shortcut key in Office 2000, it adds the custom date format m/d/yyyy to the active workbook. This appears to be a change designed to minimize the chance for error associated with two-digit dates. Unlike the built-in date formats, you can delete this date format in the Format Cells dialog box, just as if you had created it yourself.

Do not delete it. If you do delete that custom date format, Excel will try to use any other custom date format you have defined the next time you use the Ctrl+; shortcut key. In some cases, deleting the custom format m/d/yyyy can cause Excel to crash. If you ever see m/d/yyyy as a custom format in the Format Cells dialog box, pretend that it is a built-in format and leave it alone.

Wrapping Long, Formatted Dates Within a Cell

You also want long, formatted dates at the top of each column, in cells B7:H7. The formatted values in these cells cannot merge into the cells to the right or the left; they must wrap into multiple lines. Creating formatted dates that can wrap within a cell is easier if you can base them on dates with simple formats. If you enter simple dates into row five, you can hide rows five and six before submitting the expense report. (Leave a blank row between the hidden row and the visible table so that AutoFormat will interpret the table correctly.)

For the time being, enter the first day of the week as a constant. Later, you can make it calculate based on the departure date. In cell B5, type *2/27/00*. In cell C5, type *=B5+1*, and then fill that formula to the right, through cell H5.

Excel can wrap only text values, not numbers or dates. The TEXT function allows you to convert a number or date into text using any formatting codes you could use as a custom number format.

In cell B7, type the formula = *TEXT(B5,"dddd mmm d, yyyy")*. Format the cell to wrap. (Use the Alignment tab on the Format Cells dialog box.) If you want to control where Excel wraps the contents of the cell, press Alt+Enter to insert returns within the text string itself (perhaps before the *mmm* and *yyyy* codes). To set the column widths, select the cell that displays Wednesday, make the column extra wide, and then click Format, Column, AutoFit to set the width for that column. Then apply that same width to the other date columns.

Rounding Dates Within a Week

For your expense report, you need to calculate the first day of the week containing the departure date. First, give the name *Departure* to the departure date cell, E3.

Excel's date with the value of 1—January 1, 1900—occurred on a Sunday. That means that the date with the value of 7—January 7, 1900—was a Saturday. In fact, every date that is a multiple of 7 occurs on a Saturday. If you round any date up or down to the next multiple of 7, you will always get a Saturday. Use the CEILING function to round any date up to the following Saturday, and use the FLOOR function to round any date down to the preceding Saturday.

In cell B5, type the formula *=FLOOR(Departure,7)*. Excel displays the date as an unformatted number (even though cell B7 still interprets it properly as a date). Format the cell with the default date format (use the shortcut Ctrl+Shift+#). The number is now the Saturday preceding the departure date. You still need to adjust this formula to start the week on any arbitrary day.

A week always has seven days, so you must always round down to a multiple of 7, which will always be a Saturday. The way to round down to a Sunday is to temporarily pretend that Sundays are multiples of 7, not Saturdays. To do that, subtract 1 from the departure date before rounding, and then add 1 back to the date when you're through. In other words, change the formula in cell B5 to *=FLOOR(Departure-1,7)+1*.

Now you can generalize the formula to start the week on any day. Give the name *StartWeek* to cell B3, and type the number 1 in it. Format the cell to display only the day of the week. (Use *dddd* as a custom number format.) The number changes to display "Sunday" (and the formula bar changes to show the number as the date 1/1/1900).

In the formula in cell B5, you always want to subtract only the day of the week—a number between 1 and 7. You can either limit yourself to allow only 1 to 7 in the StartWeek cell or you can use the WEEKDAY function to extract the day of the week from whatever date happens to be in the cell.

Change the formula in cell B5 to=*FLOOR(Departure-WEEKDAY(StartWeek),7)+ WEEKDAY(StartWeek).*

This is the final formula. It will calculate the first day of the week containing the departure date, regardless of which day of the week you choose that to be. You can now hide rows five and six in the workbook.

If you don't want to see the *StartWeek* cell, you can either move it to the hidden row five, unhiding the row when you need to change to a different first day of the week, or you can give it the custom number format ;;; (that's three semicolons in a row), which will hide the value in a cell.

Validating Dates

If you enter a value that is not a date in the StartWeek cell—that is, text, a negative number, or a very large number—the WEEKDAY function will be unable to extract the day of the week, and all the date formulas will display the #VALUE! error. You can prevent this by using the Data Validation command to restrict entry to valid dates. With the *StartWeek* cell selected, click Data and then click Validation. In the Allow drop-down list box, select Date. In the Data list, select Between.

Caution You must always use Between when validating dates. If you use an option such as Greater Than, Excel will allow you to enter a very large number into the cell, even though it is not a legitimate date.

For the *StartWeek* cell, you want to accept any possible date, so type *1/1/1900* in the Start Date box, and type *12/31/9999* in the End Date box. Click the Error Alert tab and type something like *"Please enter a date or a positive number"* for the error message.

For the Departure cell, you want to be more restrictive in the dates you allow. Your company allows expense reports for trips that occurred only within the past 90 days. You can enter formulas in the Data Validation dialog box that implement that rule. With the Departure cell selected, click Data, click Validation, select Date in the Allow drop-down list box, and select Between in the Data drop-down list box. In the Start Date box, type *=TODAY()-90.* In the End Date box, type *=TODAY().* Clear the Ignore Blank check box, because you do need a valid date. Select the Error Alert tab and type an Alert message like *"You can enter reports for trips only within the past three* *months."* In the Style drop-down list, select Warning, which allows you to enter a value, even if it does not meet the validation criteria.

Manipulating Numbers

Numbers are the lifeblood of a spreadsheet model. You change a number in cell A7, and the value pulses through all dependent formulas, giving life to the model. Numeric formulas can also make sense out of massive quantities of numbers. Even the simplest of spreadsheets use summation formulas. Sophisticated users can wring phenomenal information from a data set, or bend numbers to any desired form.

Analyzing Averages

When you have a large pool of numbers, taking an average is a good way to get a feel for the overall value of the pool. An average is somehow supposed to represent the typical value, but it can sometimes be misleading. Last year, when my daughter was in fifth grade, she had to learn the difference between three types of averages: the *mean*, the *mode*, and the *median*. She was given several examples of where one or another average seriously misrepresented the population.

Note The sample document for this section is Stats.xls.

For example, suppose that in a group of 10 people, one person has an annual income of $1 million, two people have incomes of $50,000 each, and each of the seven remaining individuals has a salary ranging from $400 to $1,000, in $100 increments. The mean annual salary (the sum of the salaries divided by the number of people, as calculated by Excel's AVERAGE function) is well over $100,000. The mode salary (the most common value, as calculated by the MODE function) is $50,000. The median salary (the halfway mark, calculated by the MEDIAN function) is only $900. You have three different averages for a community; they range from $110,490 to $900, and the least representative of the three is the mean—the one calculated by Excel's AVERAGE function.

The whole point of teaching fifth graders about mean, mode, and median is to help instill in them a healthy distrust of averages. (Now that my daughter is in sixth grade, she assures me that she can't remember anything except the need to distrust averages.) The reason for using mode and median is that they are easy for fifth graders to calculate. Otherwise, they don't give you a lot of information about the data set.

For statisticians, Excel has an incredible wealth of functions, ranging from CHITEST (the chi-squared distribution test for independence) to WEIBULL (the Weibull probability density function for mean time to failure). Unfortunately, that wealth of functions makes it difficult for nonstatisticians to find the three most useful functions for analyzing an average: STDEVP (the standard deviation), SKEW (skewed result), and KURT (kurtosis). Even though these functions might sound bizarre, they are no more complicated to use than the mode and median calculations my daughter learned. They are simply harder to calculate than the mode and the median, which is why they don't teach them to fifth graders. Fortunately, Excel will do all the hard calculations for you.

Checking for Unrepresentative Averages

In the earlier income example, the average income was $110,490. We can tell by quickly scanning the salaries that the average income does not represent the average member of the group. But what if the group were larger and the numbers were less obvious? For example, if you calculate that the average monthly revenue for a division over the past five years was $100,000, how would you know how representative that average is?

In rough terms, the *standard deviation* of a number tells you how far away from the average you would have to go to capture about two-thirds of the population. In the income example, the standard deviation is $297,140, which is more than twice as much as the average itself! The standard deviation fairly shouts that $110,000 does not typify the population at large.

If the average monthly revenue for a division is $100,000, and the standard deviation is $10,000, you know that revenues haven't fluctuated very much, with the implication that you can probably count on similar numbers in the future. If the standard deviation is $80,000, then you know that revenues have varied dramatically from month to month, so you really don't know what next month will bring.

To calculate the standard deviation, use the STDEVP function. You use it the same as you would the AVERAGE function; just give it the range of values. Like the AVERAGE function, the STDEVP function ignores any cells that are blank or that contain text or logical values.

Note The STDEVP function returns the standard deviation of an entire population (the P stands for population). This is the function you should use if you are analyzing order history values, where you do know every data point. If the numbers you are looking at are really a statistical sampling (for example, if you want to find the average height of your fellow employees by measuring the height of every twentieth person coming into the cafeteria), you should use the STDEV function, which returns a larger standard deviation to compensate for the possibility of error in a small sample. In most business analysis situations, you are not analyzing a statistical sample, so you should use STDEVP. Of course, if you are just using the standard deviation as a general indicator—which is all you should be doing unless you are a trained statistician—it doesn't really matter which flavor of the function you use.

A standard deviation is often used as a measure of risk in investments. A stock fund that claims an average annual return of 12 percent might have a standard deviation of 20 percent (which means that you need to be prepared for a year with returns as low as –8 percent, or even worse). On the other hand, a fund with an average annual return of 6 percent might have a standard deviation of 2 percent, which might make it a better choice if you are unprepared to weather a year or two of bad returns.

If you know the mean and the standard deviation of a bunch of numbers, you might want to know how unusual a particular value is. For example, looking at five years of monthly revenue, if the average is $5,000, the standard deviation is $250, and one of the months was $8,000, you might wonder just how exceptional a month that was.

The STANDARDIZE function tells you how many standard deviations away from the mean that one month was. The formula *=STANDARDIZE(8000,5000,250)* returns the value 12. In other words, the $8,000 month was incredibly unusual. You can probably guess what the STANDARDIZE function is doing—it takes the difference between the number and the average and divides the standard deviation into it.

Checking for Distorted Averages

When an average is *skewed*, it means that you have a few very big (or very small, if the skew is negative) values that are throwing off the average. The highest a skew value can get is the square root of the number of data points.

In the income example from my daughter's fifth grade class, the skew value is 3.14. In that example, there were 10 data points. The square root of 10 is 3.16. That sample was just about as skewed as you can get.

If you're looking at five years of monthly revenue in a range named Revenue, and want to check for skewed values, first calibrate your expectations by finding the square root of the number of months using the formula *=SQRT(COUNT(Revenue))*. The result for 60 months is 7.75. Then use the SKEW function with the range of values. If the result of the SKEW function is less than 1 (positive or negative), it's probably not worth worrying about. If the skew is between 1 and 6 (positive or negative), you probably have one or two months that are significantly out of line with the rest, but they might not be affecting the average that much. If the skew is greater than 7 (positive or negative), you should not trust the average until you find out more about the aberration.

A skewed result has nothing to do with whether the values have a trend or not. The series 10, 20, 30, 40, 50 has a definite trend, but it is not skewed at all. Skew results only have to do with how balanced the numbers are. With all these statistical functions, the sequence of the numbers is irrelevant. Both the series 10, 20, 30, 40, 50 and the series 50, 10, 30, 40, 20 have the same average (30), the same standard deviation (14), and the same skew (0). (The section "Using Regression to Find and Extend Patterns" later in this chapter deals with finding the trend of an ordered sequence of numbers.)

If you have skewed numbers, you might want to ignore the fringe values while calculating an average. Excel provides a TRIMMEAN function to calculate the average after trimming off a percentage of the data points. TRIMMEAN always removes the upper and lower values together. For example, in the incomes example, there are 10 data points. To remove the highest data point using TRIMMEAN, you would also need to remove the lowest data point. With 10 data points, you must trim 20 percent of the values to make a difference. There are no corresponding functions with a TRIM prefix for calculating other statistics, such as standard deviation. Rather than use the TRIMMEAN function to deal with skewed data, you might prefer to sort the data and use a range name to trim aberrant values.

Checking for Abnormal Averages

Even with the same mean, the same standard deviation, and no skew, two sets of values can represent very different pictures. The chart in Figure 14-3 shows histograms of two large sets of data. Both sets have the same mean (1000), the same standard deviation (225), and no skew. The values represented by the solid line are in what is called a *normal distribution.* A normal distribution is sometimes called a *bell curve,* because the curve looks like someone's conception of a bell. The average in an unskewed normal distribution actually does adequately represent most of the values.

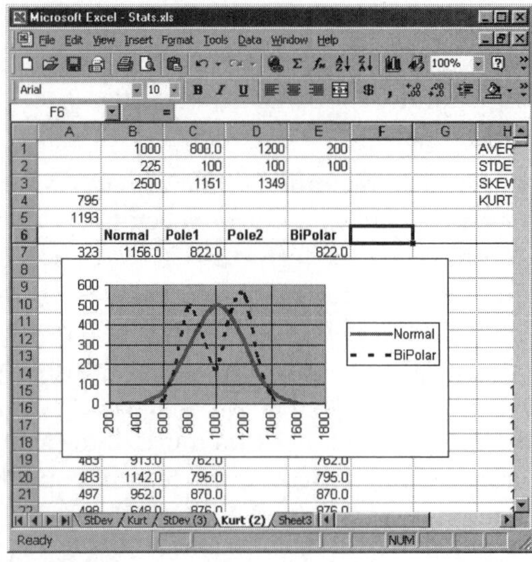

Figure 14-3
In a normal distribution, most values are near the middle.

The values represented by the dashed line are not in a normal distribution. They come in two humps. This is sometimes called a U-shaped—or *bipolar*—distribution. The average in a bipolar distribution does not represent most of the values very well. If your values fall in a bipolar distribution, your data might be summarizing two different activities that are inappropriately lumped together.

The degree to which a set of data diverges from a normal distribution is called *kurtosis* and can be calculated using the KURT function. A negative kurtosis means that the values are less peaked than the normal distribution. The most negative kurtosis you can get happens when half the data points are one value and the rest are a different value, and that is approximately –2, (as long as you're dealing with more than a dozen or so data points). The bipolar values in Figure 14-3 have a kurtosis of –1.2.

A positive kurtosis means that the values are more peaked than the normal distribution. What that usually means is aberrant outlying data points are making the numbers appear more spread out than they would be otherwise.

The data sets represented in Figure 14-4 both have the same mean (1000), the same standard deviation (about 200), and no skew. If you looked only at those three statistics (and not at the chart), you would assume that the data sets were very similar. The Extreme series, however, has two outlying data points—one low and one high, which keeps the data from being skewed. If it weren't for those two aberrant points, which don't even show up on the chart because there's only one of each, the standard deviation of the Extreme series would change from 200 to 100.

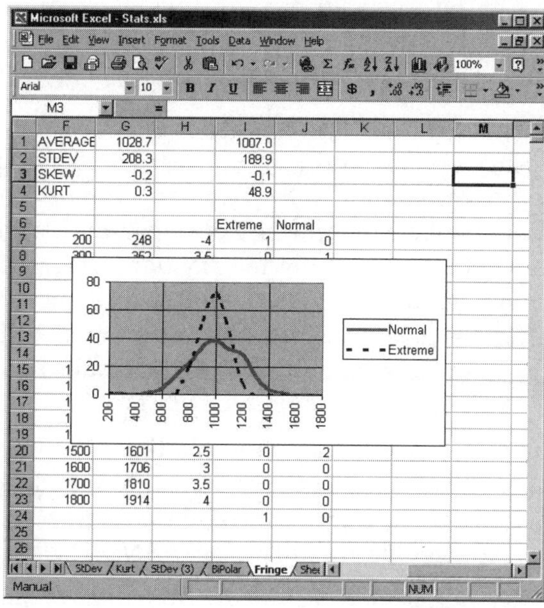

Figure 14-4
Extreme values can overstate a standard deviation.

The kurtosis for the Extreme series is about 55. The high positive value means that the series is more peaked than a normal distribution with the same standard deviation would be.

Kurtosis interplays with the standard deviation. If the standard deviation is large, you can expect a relatively large negative kurtosis. If the standard deviation is small, and the kurtosis is lower than –1, you probably have bipolar data. A large kurtosis tells you that the standard deviation would probably be smaller than it is if you could eliminate a few aberrant data points.

The internal calculations made to calculate the standard deviation, skew, and kurtosis are horrendous. If you want to see the gory details, look at the relevant Help topics. But Excel takes care of all that for you. All you have to do is use the functions. Whenever you take an average of a large data set, check these additional statistics to see how meaningful that average really is.

Creating Random Numbers

Sometimes you need to create random numbers—perhaps you have a model you want to test, or you are creating a prototype of a report. Excel's RAND function will create random numbers, but they all fall between 0 and 1. Typically, you want random numbers that fall between two larger numbers, perhaps between 1000 and 5000.

Creating Random Numbers Between Two Values

The Analysis Toolpak provides a RANDBETWEEN function that will give you random numbers between specified low and high values. That is, the formula *=RANDBETWEEN(5,10)* returns a random integer that might be as low as 5 or as high as 10. RANDBETWEEN returns only whole numbers.

If you don't want to use the Analysis Toolpak (perhaps you will be giving the workbook to someone who hasn't installed the Toolpak add-in), you can easily create random numbers between two numbers by using simple algebra. To create random numbers between 5 and 10, start by subtracting the smaller number (5) from the larger number (10) to get the spread. If you want your numbers to include both end values (as RANDBETWEEN does), you need to add 1 to the spread. Multiply the spread by RAND, and then add the lower number (5) to the result. To get random numbers between 1000 and 5000, use the formula *=RAND()*(5000-1000)+1000.*

If you want your formula to return whole numbers, add the INT function, which truncates all but the integer portion of a number. (If you were to round the numbers, rather than truncating them, some of the numbers would round up to 11.) Entering all that into a single formula, you get the formula *=INT(RAND()*(10-5+1)+5).*

Once you've created the random numbers, you probably want them to quit changing, so copy the range and use the Paste Special command to convert them to values.

You can create your personalized RANDBETWEEN function in Visual Basic for Applications (VBA). Here's what it would look like:

```
Function RandBetween(Min As Long, Max As Long) As Long
    Application.Volatile True
    Randomize
    RandBetween = Int(Rnd * (Max - Min + 1) + Min)
End Function
```

The *Application.Volatile True* statement makes the function volatile. A volatile function calculates whenever the worksheet recalculates. A nonvolatile function calculates only when its precedent cells change. You might want to create a nonvolatile random number function so that you can leave automatic calculation and have the random numbers change only when you reenter the formula (either by using Ctrl+Enter, or by replacing "=" with "=").

If you take out the *Randomize* statement, this function will return the same value the first time it is called each time you launch Excel. The *Randomize* statement initializes Visual Basic's random number generator to something very close to a truly random number. (Excel's RAND function has a built-in randomizer.For details about the Randomize statement, see the Randomize Help topic.)

The main statement in the macro is very similar to the formula for a worksheet cell. You use argument names in place of the constants, replace Excel's RAND function with the VBA Rnd function, and assign the value to the name of the function.

Creating Normally Distributed Random Numbers

If you are creating random numbers that represent normally distributed values, using the RAND function will not produce a very natural-looking simulation. Figure 14-5 displays histograms comparing a normal random curve with numbers generated by the RAND function. To create normally distributed random numbers, you specify the mean and the standard deviation.

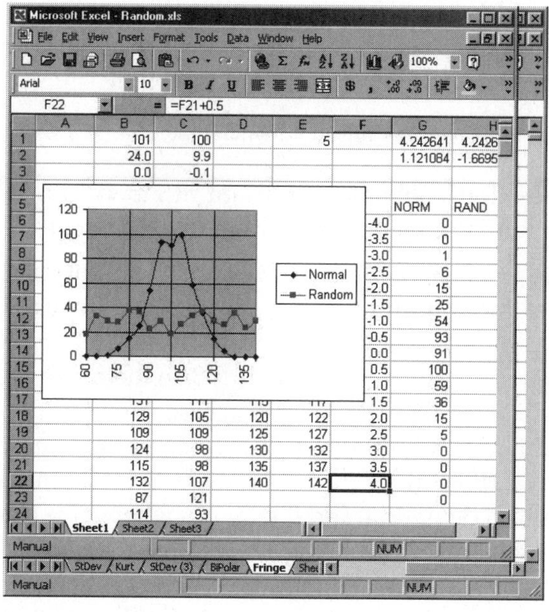

Figure 14-5
The RAND function does not create a normal distribution.

Excel does not have a function for creating normally distributed random numbers, but if the Analysis Toolpak is installed, the Data Analysis dialog box can create them for you as constant values. Click click Data Analysis on the Tools menu (after installing the Analysis Toolpak add-in), and select the Random Number Generation tool. In the Random Number Generation dialog box (see Figure 14-6), select Normal as the Distribution method and enter the Mean and Standard Deviation you want. You can specify how many random numbers you want by entering the number of columns in the Number Of Variables text box and the number of rows in the Number Of Random Numbers text box. You can also select the Output Range option and specify a range of the proper size. If you do both, it's the same as if you had entered a single cell in the Output Range text box.

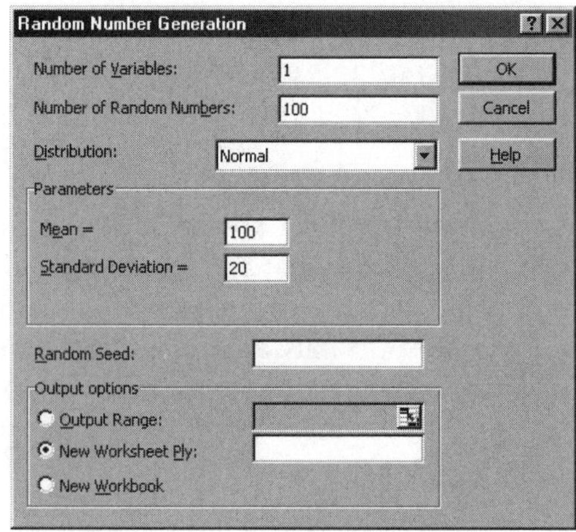

Figure 14-6
The Analysis Toolpak will generate normally distributed random numbers.

The Random Number Generation Tool enters constant numbers into cells. The results are not integers, so you might need to round them or change the formatting.

If you don't want to use the Analysis Toolpak, or if you want a formula that recalculates normally distributed random numbers, you can create your own formula. The formula is a little convoluted, but it works. For example, the formula for generating normally distributed random numbers with 100 as the mean and 20 as the standard deviation is *=NORMINV(RAND(),100,20)*. In case you're interested, here's how it works: The NORMINV function returns an inverse normal cumulative distribution. Got that? You give NORMINV a percent probability (0 to 100 percent), along with a mean and standard deviation, and it tells you what value has that probability. The RAND function generates numbers between 0 and 1 (which is the same as 0 percent and 100 percent). The formula uses the RAND function to seed the NORMINV function, converting ordinary random probabilities into normally distributed numbers. If you want integer random numbers, just enclose the whole formula in the INT function.

You can also create the following custom *RandNormal* worksheet function of your own:

```
Function RandNormal(Mean As Double, StDev As Double) As Double
    Application.Volatile
    Randomize
    RandNormal = WorksheetFunction.NormInv(Rnd, Mean, StDev)
End Function
```

The only tricky part about this VBA function is that Visual Basic does not have a NormInv function of its own, so you need to use Excel's function instead. All the Excel worksheet functions are grouped under the WorksheetFunction object. The function uses Double for the arguments and the return value to allow noninteger values.

Random numbers are useful for testing or for getting feedback on report or chart layouts. Normally distributed random numbers can add a significant amount of realism.

Rounding Numbers

Rounding numbers seems to be a simple task. In fact, you can do a lot of rounding with nothing but cell formatting, as you'll see later in "Rounding Numbers with Cell Formatting."

But rounding numbers can get complicated. What if you need to round up to the next higher multiple of 5—or to the nearest multiple of 5, which is an entirely different matter? What if you need to round to the next available pallet size for shipping? (Rounding to a pallet size is particularly interesting, because you need to accumulate units as you go.)

Excel has an interesting mixture of functions that round in one way or another. The rounding functions are grouped in the Math & Trig section of the Paste Function dialog box, so they are sometimes hard to find. Moreover, the functionality overlaps so much that some of the functions become irrelevant. The arguments are often inconsistent, and there are quirks to most of the functions. To complicate matters even further, some of Excel's rounding functions correspond to similar VBA functions, which have their own quirks. Before exploring how to put rounding functions to work, start by taking a brief tour of the rounding functions available in Excel and VBA.

- **The ROUND function** is the workhorse rounding function. It rounds to a multiple of any power of 10. The expression *ROUND(123.456,2)* rounds to 123.46, while the expression *ROUND(123.456,-2)* rounds to 100. Excel's ROUND function differs from VBAs Round function in the way it handles numbers that end in .5. Excel's ROUND function always rounds away from zero. In contrast, VBAs Round function always rounds to the nearest even integer. Therefore, the Excel expression *ROUND(4.5,0)* equals 5, while the VBA expression *Round(4.5,0)* equals 4. Also, VBA's Round function does not take a negative second argument, so it can't round to the nearest 10 or 100. If you want to use VBAs Round function from an Excel worksheet, create a custom function. If you want to use Excel's ROUND function from a VBA macro, use the WorksheetFunctions object.

- **The CEILING and FLOOR functions** are extremely useful. You use them to round (up or down) to any multiple of a number you designate. So, the expression *CEILING(123.456,3)* rounds up to the next multiple of 3 (126) and the expression *FLOOR(123.456,3)* rounds down to the next multiple of 3 (123). This is more general than the number of decimal places approach of the ROUND function. To get the equivalent of the expression *ROUND(123.456,2)*—which rounds to the second decimal place—but rounding down, use the expression *FLOOR(123.456,0.01)*, which returns 123.45. The CEILING function interprets up as away from zero, and the FLOOR function interprets down as toward zero. Unfortunately, both the CEILING and FLOOR functions require that the second argument—the one that tells what multiple you want to round to—must have the same sign as the number you want to round. The CEILING and FLOOR functions are used with dates in the "Rounding Dates Within a Week" section earlier in this chapter.
- **The ROUNDUP and ROUNDDOWN functions** are part of the Analysis Toolpak and are made unnecessary by the CEILING and FLOOR functions, which are much more general. These functions, like the ROUND function, can round only to decimal digits, not to multiples of any number.
- **The INT and TRUNC functions** don't really round; they simply remove the fractional portion of a number. You can think of them as "rounding down" to the nearest integer. The difference between them is in how they deal with negative numbers. The INT function always rounds down (to the left in the string of digits); the TRUNC function always rounds toward zero, like the FLOOR function. The VBA functions Int and Fix correspond to the Excel functions ING and TRUNC , respectively.
- **The EVEN and ODD functions** are a bit odd, really. You never need the EVEN function because you can just use the CEILING function with a multiple of 2. The ODD function does add the useful feature of shifting the EVEN function by 1, which you can't do with the CEILING function. But why should you have a special function that shifts only by 1? When working with dates, you might want to round up or down to the nearest week.

Creating a Function That Rounds Everything

The ROUND function would be better if you could round to any multiple (the way CEILING and FLOOR do). The CEILING and FLOOR functions would be better if you didn't have to worry about whether the significance has the same sign as the value. The ODD function would be better if you could round and shift by any amount, not just by two and one.

The *RoundX* function is an enhanced version of all these functions. When you use it with its two required arguments, it behaves just like the ROUND function, except that you give it a multiple rather than a decimal place. When you use a positive number as the optional third argument, it rounds up, like the CEILING function.

When you use a negative number, it rounds down, like the FLOOR function. Unlike those functions, it works with whatever signs the numbers have. The optional fourth argument shifts the number, like ODD, but by a variable amount.

So the expression *RoundX(123.456,0.01)* is equivalent to the expression *ROUND(123.456,2)*, but you can also use the expression *RoundX(123.456,4)* to return 4, which is something the ROUND function can't do. Likewise, the expression *RoundX(123.456,3,1)* returns 126, the same as the expression *CEILING(123.456,3)*, but you can also use the expression *RoundX(-123.456,3,1)* to return -126, which the CEILING function can't do unless you change the signs to match. Further, the expression *RoundX(124,2,1,1)* returns 125, the same as the expression *ODD(124)*, but you can also use the expression *RoundX(TODAY(),7,1,3)* to return the next Tuesday, which the ODD function can't do.

Of course, a function that uses a lot of optional arguments can be confusing, so you might choose to break the *RoundX* function up into enhanced replacements for the ROUND, CEILING, and FLOOR functions, and add new functions for rounding to a day of the week. The following *RoundX* function just puts all the tricks in one place:

```
Function RoundX(ByVal Number As Double, _
    ByVal Significance As Double, _
    Optional ByVal Direction As Long = 0, _
    Optional ByVal Shift As Long = 0) As Double

''' Flip sign of significance if signs are not the same
    Significance = Significance * Sgn(Number) * Sgn(Significance)
''' Shift means to pretend number is smaller - shift back at end
    Number = Number - Shift

    Select Case Direction
    Case Is > 0 ''' Ceiling
        Number = WorksheetFunction.Ceiling(Number, Significance)
    Case Is < 0 ''' Floor
        Number = WorksheetFunction.Floor(Number, Significance)
    Case Else   ''' General
    ''' Scale to significance - then scale back
        Number = Number / Significance
        Number = WorksheetFunction.Round(Number, 0)
        Number = Number * Significance
    End Select
    Number = Number + Shift
    RoundX = Number
End Function
```

The *RoundX* function just calls the Excel ROUND, CEILING, or FLOOR worksheet functions to do the real work. The function always shifts the number, because the default value for the Shift argument is zero, which doesn't do any harm. The function converts the sign of significance if it differs from that of the Number, to avoid errors from CEILING or FLOOR. The Sgn function (the VBA equivalent to Excel's

Chapter 14

SIGN function) returns –1 for a negative number and 1 for a positive number. Multiplying the two signs together produces –1 only if they differ. The function scales the number to the correct significance only before rounding to the nearest whole number, because CEILING and FLOOR already use significance as a multiple.

Rounding Numbers with Cell Formatting

If you work for a large company, you probably create reports that display values in the millions of dollars. On the report, you rarely want to display all those digits. You probably display amounts as thousands or even millions. One way to scale the numbers is to use Paste Special to divide the numbers by 1000 or 10,000, as described above. Another way is to simply format the numbers as thousands or millions. One advantage of using cell formatting to scale the numbers is that you can append a scaling suffix such as K or M to the number itself. For example, if you have a cell that contains the number 34,543,221.83, you can format it to display $34,543K or $34.5M.

Click Cells on the Format menu. On the Number tab, select the Currency category. Then click the Custom category. The Type box shows the underlying codes that create the default Currency format: $#,##0.00. The # characters indicate that you want to show a digit if there is one; the 0 characters indicate that you want to show a digit even if it is zero. To format the number as thousands with no decimal places and K as a suffix, change the code in the Type box to *$#,##0,K*. You should see the number from the active cell displayed in the Sample box, as shown in Figure 14-7. The extra comma at the end of the number divides the number by 1000. To format the number as millions with one decimal place and M as a suffix, change the Type code to *$#,##0.0,,\M*. You need the backslash in front of the M because custom number formats use M as the code for a single-digit month number.

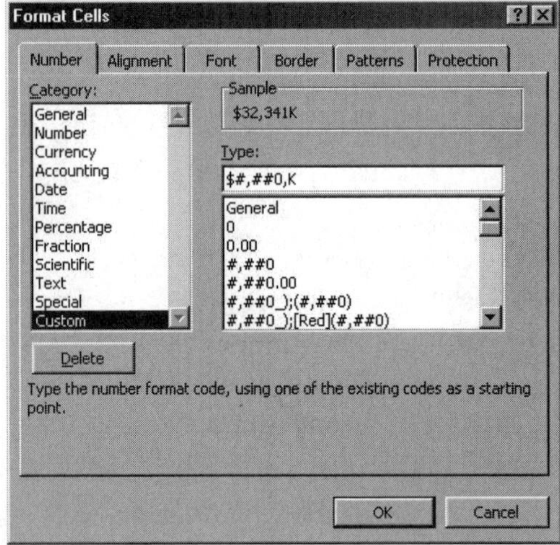

Figure 14-7
Insert a comma in a number format to divide by 1000.

Once you create a custom format, it is available (at the bottom of the Custom category) to apply to any additional cells in the workbook.

Formatting Numbers as Fractions

Several options allow you to format numbers as fractions. One of these options is As Eighths (4/8). Because this formatting option was added at the request of people dealing in investment securities, it does not reduce fractions to their simplest form. There is no simple way to format the number 4.5 as 4-½, while also formatting 4.75 as 4¾. You can't use conditional formatting to adjust the format based on the cell's value, because conditional formatting changes only the font, border, and interior of a cell, not its number format.

The *FormatEighths* macro gets around the problem by applying the appropriate As Halves, As Quarters, or As Eighths number format to each cell. The macro could have been implemented in many ways, but there are a couple of issues to deal with: how do you deal with a number such as 4.51123, which is not exactly a half, but still appears as 4-4/8 when formatted As Eighths? Also, the macro must not change the value in the cell from a number to a text string, because you still want to use the number in formulas.

```
Sub FormatEighths()
    Dim r As Range
    Dim s As String

    Selection.NumberFormat = "# ?/8"
    For Each r In Selection.Cells
        If IsNumeric(r) Then
            s = Left(Right(r.Text, 3), 1)
            Select Case s
            Case "4"
                r.NumberFormat = "# ?/2"
            Case "2", "6"
                r.NumberFormat = "# ?/4"
            End Select
        End If
    Next r
End Sub
```

The macro first gives the As Eighths number format to all the selected cells. It then loops through each individual cell looking at the numerator of the fractional portion—the third character from the last. (The Text property returns the formatted contents of the cell.) Finally, if the numerator is one that can be reduced, the macro applies the appropriate number format.

Unfortunately, the macro can only apply the formatting based on the current contents of the cell. If the cell contents change, you need to run the macro again to reapply the formats.

Eliminating Apparent Rounding Errors

The formatted value of a cell is not always the same as the value that is stored internally in the cell. Regardless of the way a number is displayed, Excel stores the number with up to 15 digits of accuracy. There are situations, however, when you might want to control how much accuracy Excel actually does retain.

Say you are a teacher and you've put together spreadsheets to track each child's progress for the term. The report for one of the students is in Figure 14-8. Halfway through what started out as an amicable parent-teacher conference, the father suddenly blurts out, "What's the matter with you? These numbers are all wrong!" While the worksheet clearly shows the total as 79—and you are certain the formula is correct—the father argues very convincingly that the total should be 81.

	A	B	C	D	E	F	G
1		**Points**					
2	First	12					
3	Second	23					
4	Third	14					
5	Fourth	32					
6	**Total**	**79**					
7							
8							
9							

Figure 14-8
Sometimes the total doesn't seem correct.

The problem, of course, is a rounding error. The actual scores for each of the projects were 11.53, 22.61, 13.58, and 31.70. Because the fractional part of the student's scores was a little more than .5 on each project, each score rounded up to the next higher number. The unrounded total is 79.42, which, while higher than 79, does not match the apparent 81. The discrepancy itself is not important. What is important is the embarrassment while appearing to be incorrect.

You can force Excel to internally round numbers to match what appears on the screen. Click Options on the Tools menu, click Calculation, and then select the Precision As Displayed check box.

When you enable the Precision As Displayed option, Excel warns you that the data in your workbook will permanently lose accuracy. You can watch how a value with several decimal places loses accuracy. Select the cell and click the Decrease Decimal toolbar button a couple of times. Then click the Increase Decimal toolbar and see zeros appear in place of the original numbers.

You can also use the Precision As Displayed option to round values temporarily. In some situations, such as when you scale constants using Paste Special, you end up with constants that have more apparent accuracy than is really necessary. If the values in the worksheet represent dollars—or units of a product—and the number stored in the cell has 10 decimal places, the worksheet does not accurately model the business situation. Rather than create formulas to round the numbers, format them with the appropriate level of precision, turn Precision As Displayed on, and then immediately turn it off again. Any future calculations, and any calculations made with formulas, will then maintain all the internal accuracy available to Excel, but the constants will be properly rounded, without the overhead of any formulas.

The Precision As Displayed option applies to the entire workbook. Before enabling it, make sure there aren't any values on other worksheets that will lose important internal accuracy.

Creating Pallet Sizes for Shipping If you ship large quantities of identical boxes, you might group units into pallets to reduce shipping costs. The size of a pallet is not often correlated with the number of units you manufactured. The pallet size might also vary from product to product and from customer to customer.

Note The sample document for this section is Pallet.xls.

Suppose you have a weekly shipping plan for a particular customer. You receive weekly production numbers, and you need to convert those to the weekly shipping numbers using the pallet size for each product. Calculating the number of items to ship for one week is easy—just round the available quantity down to the nearest pallet size. But for the next week, you must also include any units that were built but not shipped the previous week.

To keep the worksheet as simple as possible, you want to avoid any cells with intermediate calculations. That way, you can model multiple products simply by copying the formulas to the right. You also want the formulas to be the same in all the rows. Figure 14-9 shows one way that you could model the shipments.

SUM =FLOOR(SUM(B$3:B9)-SUM(F$3:F8),F$1)

	A	B	C	D	E	F	G	H	I
1	Pallet					11	44	88	
2									
3	**Week**	**Cycle**	**Scooter**	**Roadster**		**Cycle**	**Scooter**	**Roadster**	
4	1/3/00	30	45	50		22	44	0	
5	1/10/00	45	35	40		44	0	88	
6	1/17/00	5	45	30		11	44	0	
7	1/24/00	10	50	35		11	44	0	
8	1/31/00	30	50	25		22	88	88	
9	2/7/00	40	20	25		=FLOOR(SUM(B$3:B9)-SUM(F$3:F8),F$1)			
10	2/14/00	20	30	10		22	44	0	
11	2/21/00	35	10	50		33	0	88	

Figure 14-9
Include headings in a SUM formula range to keep formulas identical.

To avoid intermediate cells, the easiest way to calculate the number of units available to ship is to total the units that have been built (through the current week), and subtract the units that have already shipped (through the previous week). The ranges

Chapter 14

for the two SUM functions must expand as you copy the formula down the worksheet, so make the ending point of each range relative. When calculating the quantity already shipped, the SUM function must add everything from the first week through the previous week. That causes a problem when you want to use the same formula for the first week, because you don't want it to include itself. The solution is to anchor the ranges with the label row, because the SUM function ignores cells that contain text. In cell F4, the formula changes to *=FLOOR(SUM(B$3:B4)-SUM(F$3:F3),F$1),* which sums the value in cell F3(0) and subtracts it from the number built in the first week.

Making Formulas More Readable The formula shown earlier in Figure 14-9 is identical between all rows and columns of the model. It is also, however, somewhat hard to decipher, and in A1 notation, it appears to change from cell to cell. Switching to R1C1 notation doesn't really help. Even though the formula appears to stop changing, the relative column references make it completely unreadable: *=FLOOR(SUM(R3C[-4]:RC[-4])-SUM(R3C:R[-1]C),R1C).*

You can't use column labels in this model, because formulas that use column labels (unfortunately) can never refer to the cell that includes the label. You can't use the dates as row labels because Excel discards the $ sign (dollar) absolute marker when a label is a date (apparently a bug) and because Excel will always interpret the Week label as a column label, never as a row label. You can use *Pallet* as a row label, provided that you prefix it with a $ sign (dollar) to keep it absolute, but why not just define names for everything?

Start with the easy name: define the range name *Pallet* to refer to all of row 1. The best you can do with the other references is to name the relative reference, which at least documents the purpose of the reference.

Select a typical cell containing the relative reference formula, for example, F8. In the Formula Bar, select just the cell range that refers to the quantity built to-date (B$3:B8), copy it, and press Escape. Define a new range name, *BuiltToDate,* press Alt+R to select the current contents of the Refers To text box, type an equal sign (=) to start the formula, paste the reference from the cell, and click OK. Repeat the process with the range that refers to the quantity shipped to-date (F$3:F7), giving it the name *ShippedToDate.*

You now have three names defined in the workbook. It's time to convert the formulas to use the names. Select any single cell, click Name on the Insert menu, and then click Apply. The most recently defined name will be selected. Click the other two names so that all three are selected, and click OK. Excel should convert all the formulas to use names: *=FLOOR(SUM(BuiltToDate)-SUM(ShippedToDate),Pallet).* Making the formula use names was a little work, but the formula doesn't change from cell to cell, and it is easy to understand the intent of the summed ranges.

There is a risk, however, with using named relative references. When you have relative references in cells and then insert rows or columns, Excel automatically adjusts the reference. When the relative reference is in a name, Excel cannot adjust it if you change the worksheet. The *BuiltToDate* range refers to the column four to the left of the one with the formula. (The reference R3C[-4]:RC[-4] in R1C1 notation makes this very obvious.) If you delete column E, the formulas will still refer to the column four to the left, which will then be incorrect.

Summarizing Numbers

Excel has several functions that summarize numbers.

Note The sample document for this section is Budget.xls.

Using the SUM Function with Named Ranges

The most obvious summarizing function is SUM, and its usage is straightforward. One difference between the addition operator and the SUM function is that the SUM function does not use implicit intersection. Say you have a model similar to the one in Figure 14-10—with columns A, B, and C named January, February, and March. To create quarter totals with the addition operator, you simply use the column names =January+February+March, and implicit intersection takes care of the rest. If you try to use the column names in a SUM function, Excel merrily adds all the numbers from each column.

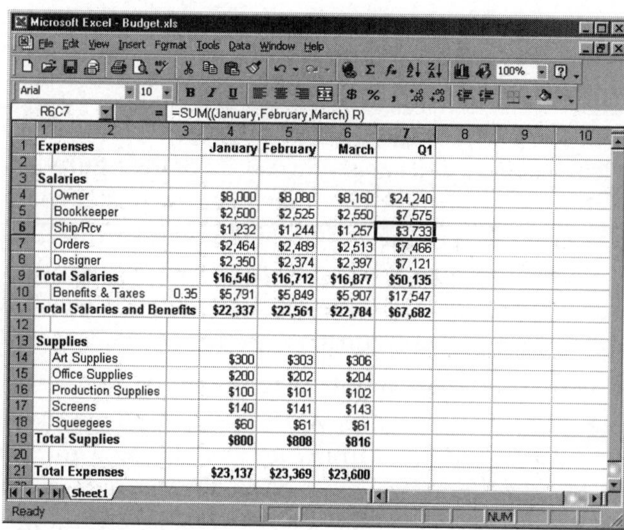

	1	2	3	4	5	6	7
1	**Expenses**			**January**	**February**	**March**	**Q1**
2							
3	**Salaries**						
4		Owner		$8,000	$8,080	$8,160	$24,240
5		Bookkeeper		$2,500	$2,525	$2,550	$7,575
6		Ship/Rcv		$1,232	$1,244	$1,257	$3,733
7		Orders		$2,464	$2,489	$2,513	$7,466
8		Designer		$2,350	$2,374	$2,397	$7,121
9	**Total Salaries**			**$16,546**	**$16,712**	**$16,877**	**$50,135**
10		Benefits & Taxes	0.35	$5,791	$5,849	$5,907	$17,547
11	**Total Salaries and Benefits**			**$22,337**	**$22,561**	**$22,784**	**$67,682**
12							
13	**Supplies**						
14		Art Supplies		$300	$303	$306	
15		Office Supplies		$200	$202	$204	
16		Production Supplies		$100	$101	$102	
17		Screens		$140	$141	$143	
18		Squeegees		$60	$61	$61	
19	**Total Supplies**			**$800**	**$808**	**$816**	
20							
21	**Total Expenses**			**$23,137**	**$23,369**	**$23,600**	

Figure 14-10
The SUM function does not use implicit intersection.

You can use the names in a SUM function, but only if you use explicit intersection to restrict the formula to the current row. Switch to R1C1 notation, if only long enough to enter the formula. The formula *=SUM(January:March R)* will calculate the quarter total for the current row. So will the formula *=SUM((January,February,March) R)*. You need the extra set of parentheses for two reasons: to keep the SUM function from interpreting the commas as new arguments and to make the union operation happen before the intersection.

One advantage of using the SUM function over using the addition operator is that the SUM function ignores text values, while the addition operator returns an error if one of the operands is text. In the budget in Figure 14-10, suppose that you enter a text value—such as none—into one of the budget cells. If you use the addition operator, you will get the #VALUE! error, but the SUM function will simply treat the cell as a zero. (See the "Creating Pallet Sizes for Shipping" project earlier in this chapter for an example of how this feature helps in creating formulas in lists.)

All Excel's basic summarizing functions have these same two important qualities: they don't use implicit intersection and they ignore cells containing text. (Some of the summarizing functions have specialized versions that do not ignore text.)

Using the PRODUCT Function

The PRODUCT function is similar to the SUM function, except that it multiplies values rather than adding them. When you deal with rates—such as interest rates or growth rates—the values in a list often compound, so the SUM function would give the wrong answer. Suppose you have an investment that has the monthly growth rates shown in column B of Figure 14-11. You want to calculate the total return on the investment so far this year. Simply using SUM to add the monthly rates gives the value 8 percent, but that is wrong, because it does not take into account the compounding that occurs with growth rates.

One way to calculate the total return is to create a sample investment of an arbitrary amount ($100 is a typical base), as you can see in cell C2 of the figure. Then enter the formula *=C2*(1+B2)* into cell C3, and copy it down one row past the last rate. These formulas calculate the period-by-period growth of the investment. To calculate the overall growth, you subtract the beginning value from the ending value and divide by the beginning value—in the example, use the formula *=(C10-C$2)/C$2*. The result of this formula is the correct total return, 7.3 percent.

If you don't want to calculate all those monthly values, you can use the PRODUCT function to get the total directly. In essence, you add 1 to each monthly rate, multiply the adjusted rates, and then subtract 1 from the result. If you want, you can create a column that adds 1 to each rate and then use the PRODUCT function on that range. But if you're willing to use an array formula, you can enter everything into a single cell. With the rates in the range B2:B9, use Ctrl+Shift+Enter to enter the formula *=PRODUCT(B2:B9+1)-1* into any convenient cell. The reason you need to array-enter the formula is so that the addition operator can add the 1 to all the rates before turning them over to the PRODUCT function to multiply. The PRODUCT function does not need to be array-entered, any more than a SUM function does.

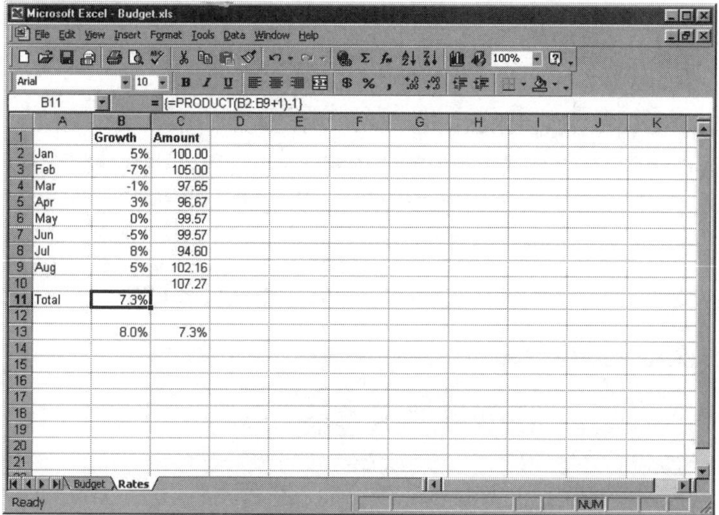

Figure 14-11
Use the PRODUCT function to summarize rates.

Like the SUM function, the PRODUCT function does not fail when the input range includes text. Instead, the PRODUCT function treats non-numeric cells as if they contained the value 1, which does not affect the final product.

Using the COUNT Function

The COUNT function, like other summarizing functions, ignores any non-numeric cells. That makes it possible to replicate the AVERAGE function by using SUM and COUNT. If you want to count all the cells that contain a value, use the COUNTA function (the A stands for All). Not even the COUNTA function counts the blank cells, though. The COUNTBLANK functions counts only the blank cells; if you want to count all cells in the *Data* range, use the formula *=COUNTA(Data)+COUNTBLANK(Data)*. The COUNT and COUNTA functions work fine with multiple-area references, but the COUNTBLANK function requires a single rectangular range.

In VBA, the expression *Range("Data").Cells.Count* returns the total number of cells in the range, regardless of their content. If you want to count only the blank cells, you can use the expression *Range("Junk").SpecialCells(xlCellTypeBlanks).Count*. (The SpecialCells property will not work if the worksheet is protected. These properties work whether the range is a simple range or a multiple-area range.)

For a rectangular range, you can use the ROWS function to count all the rows, empty or full; likewise, you can use the COLUMNS function to count all the columns. An alternative formula, *=ROWS(Data)*COLUMNS(Data)*, will count all the cells in the *Data* range. In VBA, the expression *Range("Data").Rows.Count* returns the number of rows in the first area of the *Data* range, equivalent to the *Range("Data").Areas(1).Rows.Count* statement.

All the basic summarizing functions except SUM and PRODUCT have versions with an A suffix that treat text as 0, *True* as 1, and *False* as 0.

Summarizing Data Conditionally

In an effort to make array formulas unnecessary for common tasks, Excel developers added a special summarizing function, SUMIF, that lets you summarize selected values from one range based on a value from a different range. The worksheet in Figure 14-12 shows monthly sales for three products for three months. Suppose that you want to know the total for only one product. The SUMIF function will let you do this.

Microsoft Excel - Budget.xls

C12 =SUMIF(Product Data,B12,Sales Data)

	A	B	C
1	Month	Product	Sales
2	1/1/00	Mountain Blaster	328,000
3	1/1/00	Goat Herder	154,000
4	1/1/00	Cycle Magic	37,000
5	2/1/00	Mountain Blaster	379,000
6	2/1/00	Goat Herder	469,000
7	2/1/00	Cycle Magic	311,000
8	3/1/00	Mountain Blaster	346,000
9	3/1/00	Goat Herder	174,000
10	3/1/00	Cycle Magic	77,000
11			
12		Mountain Blaster	1,053,000

Budget / Rates / Products

Figure 14-12
The SUMIF function lets you summarize part of the data.

In the example worksheet, rows 2:10 are named **Data** to make it easy to use the labels. Rather than use column labels, you could give the names *Month, Product,* and *Sales* to columns A, B, and C.

The formula *=SUMIF(Product Data,B12,Sales Data)* compares each value in the *Product* data range (B2:B10) with the value in cell B12. If the values match, the formula includes the corresponding value from the *Sales* data range (C2:C10) in the sum. To double-check the total, press and hold the Ctrl key as you click each sales amount that matches the criteria. Then look at the SUM value in the status bar.

You can also use relative comparisons with SUMIF. For example, if you wanted to sum all the products except for the one in cell B12, you could prefix the test value with a quoted string containing Excel's not equal to symbol (<>)—a greater than sign followed by a less than sign. The revised formula would be *=SUMIF(Product Data,"<>"&B12,Sales Data)*. When you don't include a relative operator, SUMIF assumes that you want an exact match.

You can also compare to dates. Just enter a date into a cell and point to it, or enclose the date in quotation marks. The formula *=SUMIF(Month Data,"<3/1/2000",Sales Data)* sums the sales for all months before March 2000.

Note The COUNTIF function is completely equivalent to SUMIF, except that you do not include a third argument. The function simply counts the matches in the first range.

In early versions of Excel, anytime you wanted to create a conditional sum, you needed to create an array formula. The SUMIF function handles the most common scenarios and can be entered as an ordinary formula. Some situations, however, require the full flexibility of the array formula version. For example, the SUMIF function cannot satisfy multiple conditions. What if you want to summarize the sales for one product, but only before March?

First, let's compare the single-condition formula with the array formula version.

The formula *=SUMIF(Product Data,B12,Sales Data)* (entered with Enter) is equivalent to *=SUM(IF(Product Data=B12,Sales Data))* (entered with Ctrl+Shift+Enter). In the array formula version, the equal sign compares all the values in the *Product* data range with the value in cell B12, resulting in an array of *True* and *False* values. For each element, if the value is *True,* the value from *Sales* data is used; *False* values stay *False.* The SUM function then adds up the result, ignoring the *False* values. You need to enter the formula as an array to release the power of the equal sign.

The array formula version is not that much more complicated than the SUMIF version, except that you have to remember to enter it as an array. In exchange, you can tinker with the internal processes all you want. Which brings us back to adding the second condition.

Type the date *3/1/2000* into cell A12, and array-enter this formula into any convenient cell: *=SUM(IF(Product Data=B12,IF(Month Data<A12,Sales Data)))*. This formula does the same thing as the preceding one, only twice. For all the array elements that are *True* as a result of the product criteria, the second IF function tests the date. Only the values that match both conditions are summed.

When creating an array condition, you can't use the AND function. For example, the formula *=SUM(IF(AND(Product Data=$B$12,Month Data<$A$12),Sales Data))* would not give the desired result—it will almost always be equal to zero. That's because AND is an aggregating function; you always give it an array of conditions, and it always returns a single value. It returns *True* only if every condition is true. To filter the sales data, you need an array of *True* and *False* values that corresponds to the values.

Taking Advantage of the Subtotal Function

Excel has one more fascinating aggregation function, SUBTOTAL, which corresponds to 11 different functions: AVERAGE, COUNT, COUNTA, MIN, MAX, PRODUCT, STDEV, STDEVP, SUM, VAR, and VARP. You give it a number from one to 11 as its first argument—the number that corresponds to the alphabetical order of the 11 function names. The most common and important use of the SUBTOTAL function is as a replacement for the SUM function, number nine.

The SUBTOTAL function was designed to facilitate the Data Subtotals command, which adds subtotals into the middle of a list. Use the Data Subtotals command and Excel will add SUBTOTAL functions for you.

One attribute of the SUBTOTAL function that makes it remarkably useful is that it doesn't double-count. In the budget worksheet in Figure 14-13, the total at the bottom of the worksheet summarizes the entire data range from the top to just above the function. In that range are three other summary functions. If cells D9, D11, D19, and D21 all had SUM functions rather than SUBTOTAL functions, the value of cell D21 would be *$80,162,* almost four times the correct value of *$23,369.*

The SUBTOTAL function simply ignores any cells that contain a SUBTOTAL with the same function number. With an ordinary SUM function, each formula must be custom crafted to reference only one level of summary. Inserting or removing rows from a budget can become a nightmare. With the SUBTOTAL function, each function can simply refer to its natural range.

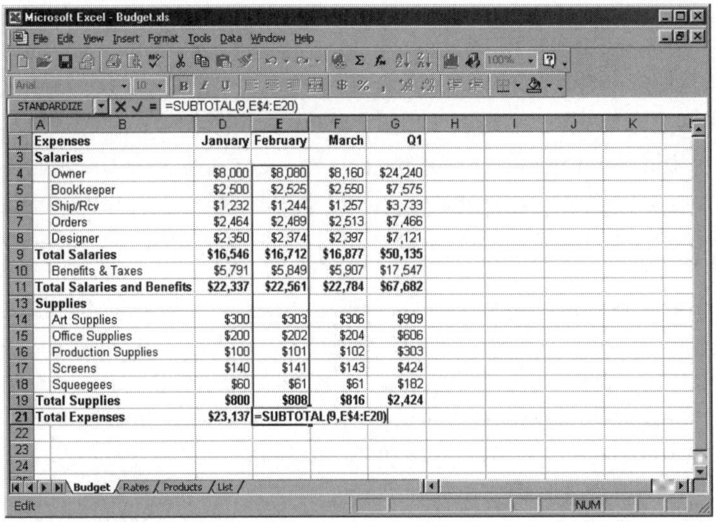

Microsoft Excel - Budget.xls

=SUBTOTAL(9,E$4:E20)

	A	B	D	E	F	G
1	Expenses		January	February	March	Q1
3	Salaries					
4		Owner	$8,000	$8,080	$8,160	$24,240
5		Bookkeeper	$2,500	$2,525	$2,550	$7,575
6		Ship/Rcv	$1,232	$1,244	$1,257	$3,733
7		Orders	$2,464	$2,489	$2,513	$7,466
8		Designer	$2,350	$2,374	$2,397	$7,121
9	Total Salaries		$16,546	$16,712	$16,877	$50,135
10		Benefits & Taxes	$5,791	$5,849	$5,907	$17,547
11	Total Salaries and Benefits		$22,337	$22,561	$22,784	$67,682
13	Supplies					
14		Art Supplies	$300	$303	$306	$909
15		Office Supplies	$200	$202	$204	$606
16		Production Supplies	$100	$101	$102	$303
17		Screens	$140	$141	$143	$424
18		Squeegees	$60	$61	$61	$182
19	Total Supplies		$800	$808	$816	$2,424
21	Total Expenses		$23,137	=SUBTOTAL(9,E$4:E20)		

Budget / Rates / Products / List

Figure 14-13
The SUBTOTAL function doesn't double-count.

If a worksheet has subtotals both vertically and horizontally (that is, if you summarize months into quarters and years in addition to summarizing accounts into groups), pick one of the directions for the SUBTOTAL function. While not impossible, it is exceptionally difficult to design two-dimensional SUBTOTAL functions that don't confuse each other. Pick the dimension that is most likely to change.

(Usually the relationship of months, quarters, and years is a very stable dimension, well-suited to using traditional formulas.)

If you already have a worksheet laden with SUM functions, you can quickly convert them into SUBTOTAL functions. Select a single column (you can copy the formulas to other columns later) and replace the *SUM(* string with the *SUBTOTAL(9,* string, as shown in Figure 14-14.

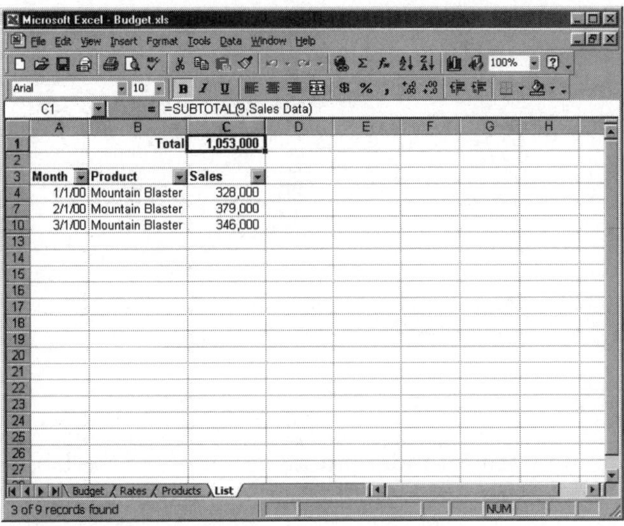

Figure 14-14
Calculating a single column subtotal.

Another remarkably useful attribute of the SUBTOTAL function is that it ignores any cells that have been filtered. (See "Summarizing Filtered Values" in Chapter 5 for more about using the SUBTOTAL function with filtered lists.)

One disadvantage of the SUBTOTAL command is that you can't use it in 3D formulas across worksheets as you can all the other summarizing functions. That is probably because you can filter rows differently from sheet to sheet within a 3D range, which would cause bedlam with the SUBTOTAL function.

Manipulating Text

You generally do not enter as much text in Excel as in, say, Word, but in Excel you are much more likely to need to manipulate the text using formulas. Excel has powerful functions that make it easy to manipulate text.

Note The sample document for this section is Text.xls.

Trimming Spaces Before Indenting Text

Many worksheets have labels that are logically indented. Figure 14-15 shows three different ways of indenting labels. In column A, the indented cells have extra spaces at the beginning. In column B, the Increase Indent toolbar button was used. In columns E and F, the indented values are in a separate column.

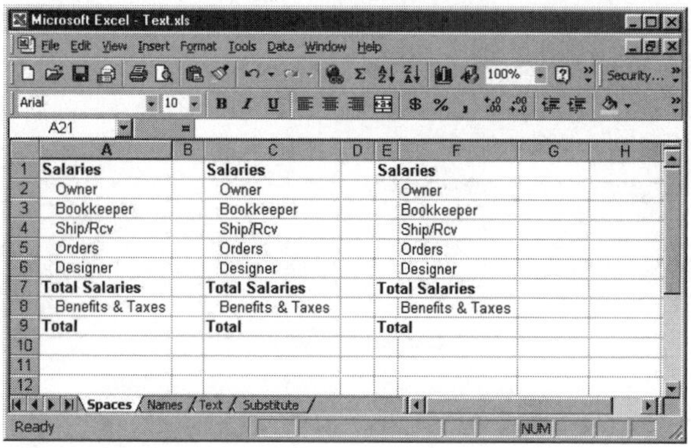

Figure 14-15
Labels can be indented using various methods.

Regardless of the method used for indentation, you can use the labels to identify adjacent ranges in formulas. However, in the version that uses spaces (column A) the labels end up looking strange. If you type the formula *=Owner+Bookkeeper*, Excel changes it to *=' Owner'+' Bookkeeper'*. It includes the apostrophes and the extra spaces. (What's really amazing is that the labels algorithm is able to determine out the indented labels at all.) The other two options leave the labels more readable.

The separate column option allows you to change the indent for all the relevant rows simply by dragging the column border. You can also use Ctrl+Up arrow and Ctrl+Down arrow keys to jump to the top and bottom of each section. You could even merge the cells to the left of the indented column and enter the rotated label into that cell, as shown in Figure 14-16.

Using the Increase Indent button and using a separate column are both useful techniques. Unfortunately, the mechanism most frequently used to indent labels is adding spaces. If you inherit a workbook from a colleague who has used spaces to indent the labels, you need to remove the spaces as part of the process of converting the labels to use either indentation or separate columns.

Using a Function to Remove Spaces

Excel's TRIM function removes spaces from the beginning and the end of a text string. If you have labels with spaces in column A, here's how to use the TRIM function to remove the spaces: Insert a new column B. Type the formula *=TRIM(A1)* in cell B1. Copy the formula down the column. Paste values over the original range. Then delete the temporary column B.

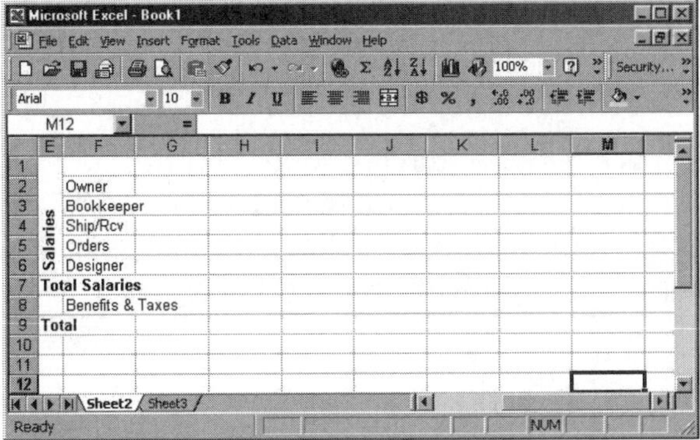

Figure 14-16
Rotate a merged label.

VBA also has a Trim function that corresponds to Excel's TRIM function, and it has functions for trimming spaces from only the left (LTrim) or the right (RTrim) of a string.

Using a Command to Remove Spaces

If you would prefer to use a command to trim the spaces from a column of text all at once, you can appropriate the Text To Column command on the Data menu. This command was designed for parsing text data files into a worksheet, but you can use it to trim spaces from a single column.

Select the column you want to trim, click Data, and click Text To Columns. In the first step of the wizard, select Fixed Width as the Original Data Type, as shown in Figure 14-17. (The Delimited option will not trim spaces.) Then click Finish. That's all there is to it; the default target range in the wizard will put the trimmed values back into the original cells.

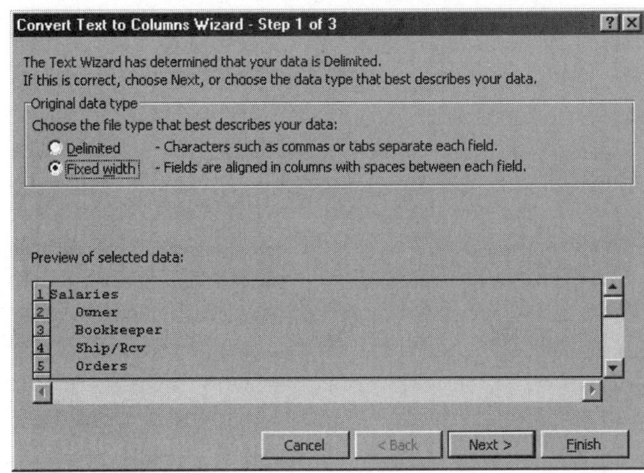

Figure 14-17
Select Fixed Width to use Text To Columns to trim spaces.

Note In addition to trimming spaces from indented labels, you might also need to trim spaces from the ends of cells. Some people inadvertently type a space at the end of labels. Those spaces are very hard to spot. (Press F2 and see whether there is space between the last letter and the cursor.) Some database programs include extra spaces at the end of labels. If data you have imported from a database doesn't behave properly—when sorting, searching, or comparing—check for trailing spaces.

Dividing and Conquering Text

Say you have a file containing the names of the current Supreme Court justices. The names are listed last name first, like a telephone book entry. You want them to appear first name first, as shown in Figure 14-18. To rearrange the names, you must find where the comma is, use that location to split the name into first and last names, and then recombine the parts into a whole.

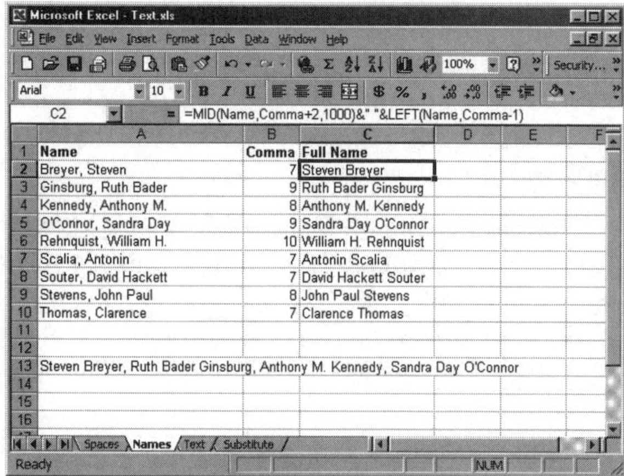

Figure 14-18
Use text functions to divide and recombine text strings.

Using Functions to Parse Text

The formula for finding a comma is *=SEARCH(",",Name).* The SEARCH function returns the number of the first matching letter. You can search for more than one letter. You can also search for the second occurrence of a match by adding 2 as a third argument. Excel has another function, FIND, that is just like SEARCH except that it is case-sensitive.

Excel's FIND and SEARCH functions are similar to VBA's InStr function, which can be case sensitive or not. The order of the arguments is different, and InStr returns 0 if it doesn't find a match, while Excel's functions return #VALUE!.

Once you find the location of the comma, you can use the LEFT function to retrieve characters from the left side of the string. The formula *=LEFT(Name,Comma)* returns the last name, including the comma. Subtract 1 to get just the last name. The correponding RIGHT function finds characters on the right side of the string.

To find characters beginning at a known location in the middle of the string, use the MID function. You give the MID function the original string, the starting position, and the number of characters to retrieve. When you want to retrieve all the remaining characters in a string, you can just use a large number as the third argument. (More precisely, you can use an argument as large as 2,147,483,647, which happens to be 1 less than 2^{31}. This is longer than most words you will encounter.) The formula *=MID(Name,Comma,1000)* returns everything from the comma on. Add 2 to get just the first name.

Using Commands to Parse Text

Rather than use the SEARCH, LEFT, and MID functions to split the names, you could use the Text To Columns command. Select the column you want to split, click Data, and click Text To Columns. In step 1, select Delimited. In step 2, select Comma as the delimiter (it is not necessary to clear Tab as a delimiter). In step 3, select a starting cell for the output and click Finish.

When used with a delimiter, the Text To Columns command doesn't trim spaces, so you will end up with spaces at the beginning of the first names. You can then use the Text To Columns command again on that one column, using the Fixed Width option, as described in the section "Using a Command to Remove Spaces" earlier in this chapter.

Using Formulas to Combine Text

You need to use a formula to combine pieces of text into a single text string. Because you need a formula to piece the judges' names together anyway, you might want to use the functions to extract the text while you're at it. To join text, use the concatenation operator (&). Don't forget to add a space between the names. The formula *=MID(Name,Comma+2,1000)&" "&LEFT(Name,Comma-1)* returns the entire, properly rearranged name.

If you find the concatenation operator distasteful, you can use the CONCATENATE function to join strings together. An equivalent substitute for the formula in cell C2 is *=CONCATENATE(MID(Name,Comma+2,1000)," ",LEFT(Name,Comma-1))*. You cannot use the CONCATENATE function with a range; its arguments must be single cells or constants. (The function will convert numbers into unformatted text.)

Creating a Custom Function to Merge Text

What if you want to create a comma-separated list with the names of the first four judges, as shown in Figure 14-19? Excel does not have a function that will do this, but you can create one of your own.

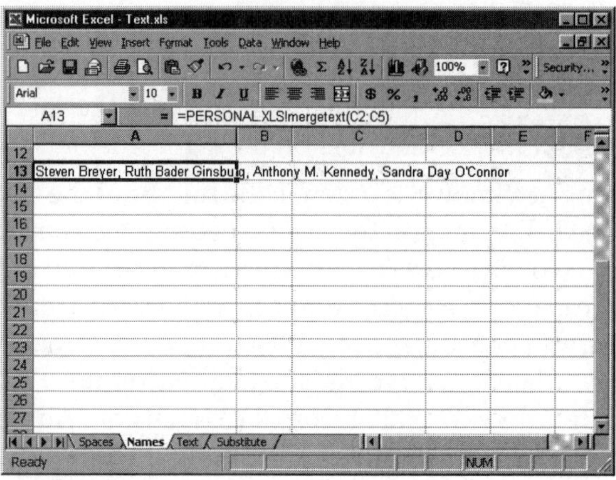

Figure 14-19
Create a custom function to merge text into a comma-separated list.

The following *MergeText* function takes one range argument. The function merges the (formatted) value from each cell into a single text string, with commas (and spaces) separating each element.

```
Function MergeText(ByVal InputRange As Range) As String
    Dim myCell As Range
    Dim myText As String
    For Each myCell In InputRange.Cells
        If myCell <> "" Then
            myText = myText & Trim(myCell.Text) & ", "
        End If
    Next
    If Len(myText) = 0 Then
        MergeText = ""
    Else
        MergeText = Left(myText, Len(myText) - 2)
    End If
End Function
```

The function loops through each cell in the input range. If the cell is blank, the function skips it. The function uses the Text property of the cell, which is the formatted value, trimming the value because some formats add an extra space to a value. Finally, if the resulting string has anything in it, the function strips the final comma and space.

Turning Numbers into Text

Numbers that don't fit into a cell appear as number signs. Cell B1 in Figure 14-20 contains the same date, with the same format as cell A1, but the column is not wide enough. When you concatenate a number with some text, you see the underlying value. Cell C1 of Figure 14-20 contains the formula = *"Start: x"&A1*. The result of the formula shows the unformatted number for the date.

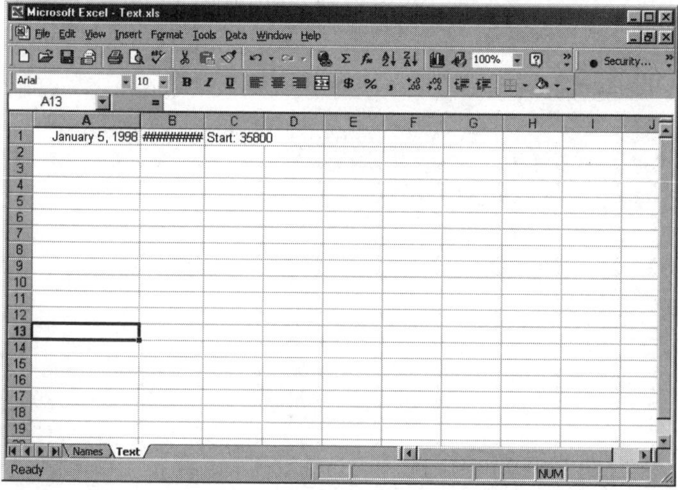

Figure 14-20
Numbers sometimes don't look right.

If you want to make a number act like text, you must change it to text. The TEXT function converts a number into a text string. You give the TEXT function two arguments: the number and a formatting string. The formatting string is anything that can appear in the Type box of a custom number format.

To convert the date in cell A1 into a text string with the same format, use the formula *=TEXT(A1,"mmmm d, yyyy")*. To make the start date in cell C1 concatenate a formatted date to the text, use the formula = *"Start: "&TEXT(A1, "mmmm d, yyyy")*.

To enclose a quoted text string within the date format argument, you must double the quotation marks.

Excel has two functions for simple formatting. The DOLLAR function formats a number as currency, and the FIXED function formats a number with commas and decimal places. You can control these functions somewhat with arguments, but if you need more than the default format, you might as well get the format string from the Number Format dialog box and use the all-purpose TEXT function.

You can also use the Text To Columns command to convert dates that are in the form 19990101 or 990101 (that is, YYYYMMDD or YYMMDD).

Managing Text That Looks Like Numbers

Excel does a very good job of interpreting a value as you type it into a cell. If you type a date, for example, Excel recognizes and interprets the date. In general, if Excel can interpret what you type as a number, it will. But sometimes you have a value—a product or part number, for example—that looks like a number but is actually text.

Figure 14-21 contains a list of product numbers. The part numbers in cells A1 and A2 have a letter suffix, and Excel automatically interprets them as text. Cell A3 shows what happens if you try to type the part number *0003* into a cell: Excel interprets it as a number. You have a number of options for convincing Excel to leave a number as text.

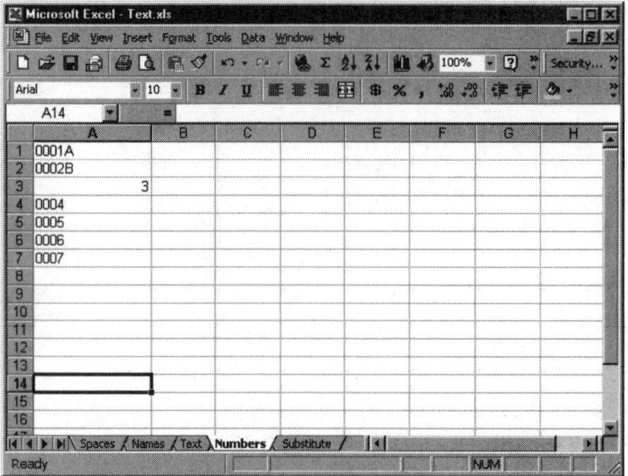

Figure 14-21
You can prevent Excel from interpreting a value as a number.

One option is to use the Format dialog box to give the cell the Text number format before entering the value into the cell. When a cell is formatted as text, Excel does not interpret anything you enter in the cell, not even a formula. If you need to enter numeric text values into a lot of cells, formatting the cells might be the best option. Be careful when you clear the cells, because the format remains unless you clear the format along with the contents.

A second option is to prefix the value with an apostrophe as you enter it in the cell. This option doesn't require any preparatory work, and it doesn't leave any residue in the cell. But you do need to remember to type the apostrophe.

You can also enter a number as a formula in quotation marks. Cell A6 contains the formula *="0006"*. Because the number is in quotation marks, it is text. Because it is a formula, the quotation marks don't appear in the cell.

The value in cell A7 is not a formula, the cell does not have the Text format, and the value does not have an apostrophe prefix. This fourth way to enter numbers as text produces a strange, unstable state. If you edit the cell and reenter the value, Excel will convert the value into a number, the same as cell A3. This final condition is less valuable as a way to get a number into a cell than as a way to get a number out of one.

To produce the strange state in cell A7, copy the formula in cell A6 and use Paste Special with the Value option to paste it into cell A7. When you use Paste Special to convert a formula to a value, Excel does not interpret the value as it does when you type it in the formula bar.

To convert a value back to a number, you need to edit and reenter the value. With a single cell, you can reconvert the text to a number by editing and reentering the cell. With multiple cells, the fastest approach is to search for and replace a digit that is common to all or most of the cells, even if you have to do it more than once with different digits to get all the cells.

Replacing Portions of Text Strings

Suppose that you want to use parameters to plot a line. The standard form of the formula for a straight line is $y = ax + b$. You want to type the coefficient *a* and *b* values into cells, but you then want to display the formula with those coefficients in the standard form. Cell B4 of Figure 14-22 shows the formula for the coefficients in cells B1 and B2. The Excel formula in that cell is *="y="&A&"x"&"+"&B*. In cell B4, the formula looks perfect. But in column C, the value of the *a* coefficient is *0*. The formula in cell C4 is a copy of the one in cell B4. Ordinarily, if a coefficient is *0*, you drop the entire term.

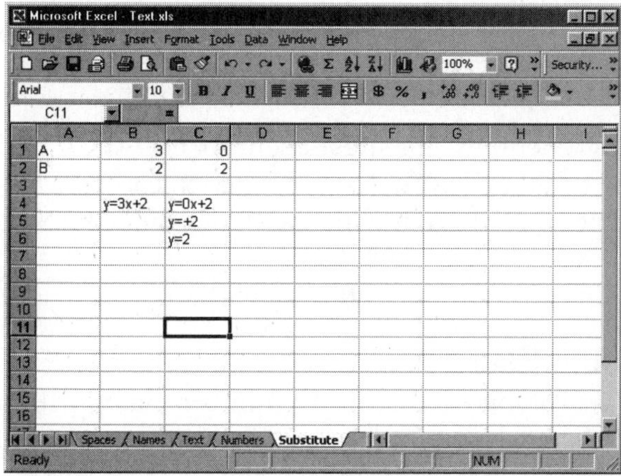

Figure 14-22
Use the SUBST function to replace portions of a text string.

Cell C5 has a revised version of the formula: *="y="&IF(A,A&"x","")&IF(B,"+"&B,"")*. This version displays a term only if the coefficient is not zero. The result in cell C5 is better, but it still looks funny to have a plus sign after the equal sign. Adding an IF condition to eliminate the plus sign is difficult because the sign could come from either term.

The formula in cell C6 uses the SUBST function to replace a portion of the text string in cell C4. You give the function the original string, the substring you want to replace, and the substring you want to replace it with. The formula is *=SUBSTITUTE(C5,"=+","=")*. If SUBST does not find a match, it doesn't change the original string. The SUBST function can solve tricky situations with text formulas that are difficult to solve in any other way. There is no VBA function equivalent to

Excel's SUBST function; in a VBA macro, use the WorksheetFunctions object to access Excel's function.

"Charting an Algebraic Function" in Chapter 13 has a more complete implementation of this formula—one that handles a third-order polynomial equation with positive and negative numbers for any term.

Looking up Values in Lists and Tables

Much of the appeal of a spreadsheet is in its ability to link data. You might enter a part number and need to find a price, or you might need to find the right discount percentage for a customer's order. You can find these values using table lookups. Excel has two basic kinds of lookups: *exact lookups*, which are good for looking up prices, and *range lookups*, which are good for looking up discount rates. (This kind of range is completely different from a range of cells.)

Note The sample document for this section is Lookups.xls.

Looking Up Values in a Table

Excel has various lookup functions. The most useful is the VLOOKUP function, which looks up a value in a table. The VLOOKUP function can search for either an exact or a range match. The VLOOKUP function searches the leftmost column of a vertically arranged table. Excel also has an HLOOKUP function that searches the top row of a horizontally arranged table, but vertical tables are much more common.

Searching for a Discount Rate

You use a range lookup when you need to find a number that is within a possible range of values. For example, you might need to give letter grades based on test scores, or find a tax rate given a certain income level.

Suppose that you give discounts based on the total value of an order. Figure 14-23 shows a worksheet that calculates the discount. The shaded range A2:B7 is named *Discounts*. Use the VLOOKUP function to look up a value in the list. For the first argument, give the value that you want to look up. For the second argument, give the list range. The VLOOKUP function always searches for the value in the leftmost column of the list. As the third argument, give the column number you want to return the value from. Cell E2 shows a formula for calculating the discount amount.

The list does not have to be a range on a worksheet. It could also be an array constant. The formula *=VLOOKUP(Order Total,{0,0;100,0.02;200,0.04;300,0.06;400,0.08;500,0.1},2)* in cell C2 would return the same discount as the current formula.

Conceptually, the range version of the VLOOKUP function begins at the top of the list and searches down to find the last value that is less than or equal to the search value. Technically, the function performs a binary search. In other words, it looks

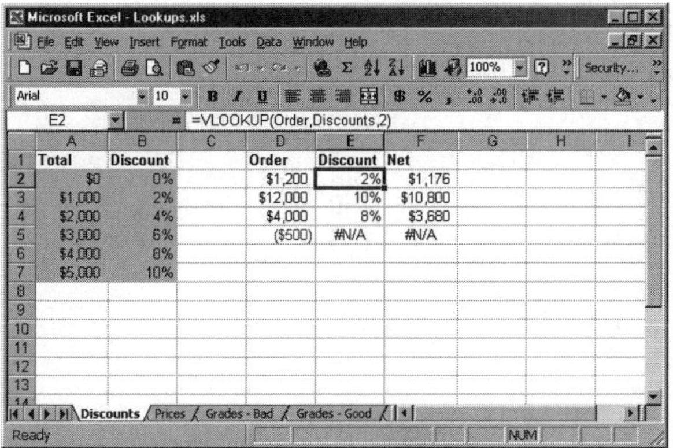

Figure 14-23
Use VLOOKUP to find a discount percent.

at the middle value of the list. If that value is greater than the search value, it looks at the middle value of the upper half of the list. If that value is greater than the search value, it looks at the middle value of the top half of that half. If the top value in the list is still greater than the search value, the function returns the #N/A error value. If the bottom value in the list is less than the search value, the function considers it a match. If the search value is a number and the list contains text, the function scans to find the next available number. When you have multiple identical values in the lookup column, the function always finds the last one.

The fact that the search is a binary search has a few implications for you. First, the list must be sorted in ascending order. An unsorted value at one of the key midpoints can cause the search to move to the wrong half of the remaining list. Second, because the search doesn't start at the top, you can include text labels at the top of a numeric list without affecting the function. In Figure 14-23 shown earlier, if the *Discounts* range were defined as A1:B7, the lookup functions would return identical results. Third, a range lookup is extremely fast, even with very large lists. Doubling the size of the list adds only a single comparison test.

Searching for a Price

A range lookup is very useful for some things, but it is terrible when you are looking up a product name in a price list. The worksheet in Figure 14-24 is completely analogous to the one shown in Figure 14-23 (through column E), except that it uses product names instead of dollar amounts. The range A2:B7 is named *Prices*, and the list is sorted in ascending order. The formulas in column E are similar to the ones in the discount example. They even appear to give correct answers. Do not be deceived.

As long as a range lookup happens to find an exact match, everything is fine. But the product name in cell D5 is accidentally mistyped. As a result, the price, which should have been $2.00 for the donuts, is the $0.89 that would be appropriate for carrots. The insidious thing about using a range lookup inappropriately is that it

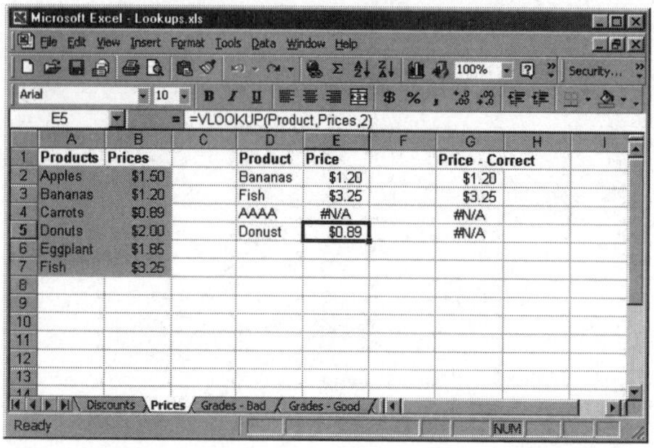

Figure 14-24
Using a range lookup with product names gives misleading answers.

gives correct answers as long as the data is perfect, which is often the case when you are first testing a model. What's worse, even when you make the inevitable, inadvertent typographical error, the function still appears to return a valid result.

You might even test an invalid answer, like the AAAA in cell D4. But the error in cell E4 occurs only because AAAA is less than any of the values in the table. If you mistype a product name, you want the worksheet to announce the fact loudly, so you can find and fix the error before anyone else sees the problem. What you need is an exact match lookup.

The VLOOKUP function has an optional fourth argument, named, appropriately enough range_lookup. If this argument is missing or *True*, the function performs a range lookup. By entering *False* as the fourth argument, you change the VLOOKUP function to perform exact match lookup. The formulas in column G, which give appropriate invalid values, simply have the fourth argument: *=VLOOKUP(Product,Prices,2,False)*. It's a simple difference in the formula, but it can make a profound difference in your model.

Change the Appearance of a Lookup Table

The range lookup version of VLOOKUP is very particular about what the first column looks like: the column must be sorted in ascending order. The first value in the list must be less than the smallest value you want to look up. And the result values must align with the value at the low end of the lookup range. Sometimes you need a list that doesn't look like that.

For example, suppose you are using an Excel worksheet to calculate grades for your class of students. The grade corresponds to the total number of points. You want to display the list equating scores and grades to look like the shaded area of Figure 14-25. Unfortunately, as you can see from the formulas in column E, that table is inappropriate for a range lookup. (However, those invalid values do show you

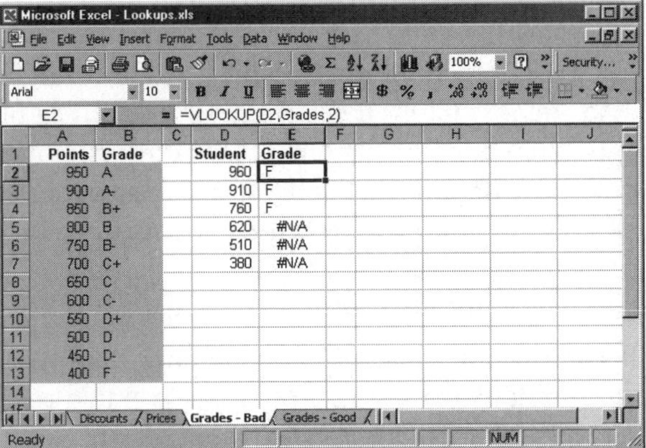

	A	B	C	D	E
1	Points	Grade		Student	Grade
2	950	A		960	F
3	900	A-		910	F
4	850	B+		760	F
5	800	B		620	#N/A
6	750	B-		510	#N/A
7	700	C+		380	#N/A
8	650	C			
9	600	C-			
10	550	D+			
11	500	D			
12	450	D-			
13	400	F			

Figure 14-25
A list sorted in descending order gives invalid results.

how the binary search works. Compare the student's points to the middle value in the list. If the mid-value is greater, move down; otherwise, move up and repeat the process. Because the list is inverted, all point totals greater than the middle value percolate to the bottom, F, while all point totals less than the middle value percolate to the top, where they become #N/A.)

The displayed list has multiple problems. Not only is it sorted in descending order, but the lowest value in the list (400) also does not truly represent the lowest possible value.

In a situation like this, the easiest solution is to make a separate, clean copy of the table, use that as the actual source of the lookup, and then hide it. Figure 14-26 shows the corrected model. Once the worksheet is correct, simply hide columns A through C before printing it.

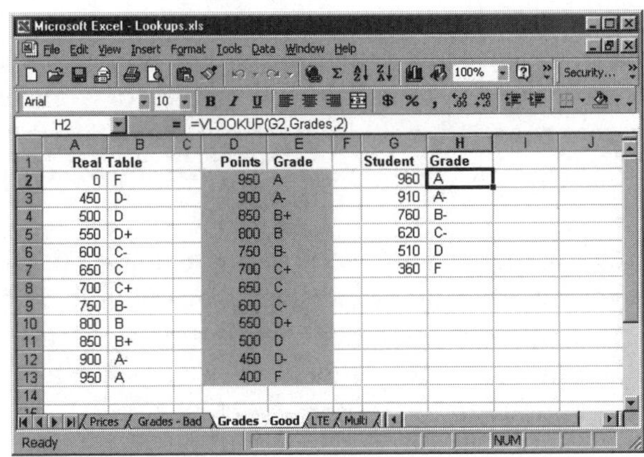

	A	B	C	D	E	F	G	H
1	Real Table			Points	Grade		Student	Grade
2	0	F		950	A		960	A
3	450	D-		900	A-		910	A-
4	500	D		850	B+		760	B-
5	550	D+		800	B		620	C-
6	600	C-		750	B-		510	D
7	650	C		700	C+		360	F
8	700	C+		650	C			
9	750	B-		600	C-			
10	800	B		550	D+			
11	850	B+		500	D			
12	900	A-		450	D-			
13	950	A		400	F			

Figure 14-26
Use a hidden table if the display table is not set up for lookups.

Chapter 14

Using Other Lookup Functions

The VLOOKUP (and HLOOKUP) functions are not the only functions Excel has for finding a value in a list. It also offers a LOOKUP function, which you might never need to use. LOOKUP comes in two flavors: two-argument and three-argument versions. The two-argument version decides for you whether a list is vertical or horizontal, based on whether there are more rows or columns. You are probably better off retaining control over that decision; the Help topic indicates that this version of the function was implemented purely for compatibility with other spreadsheet programs.

The three-argument LOOKUP function is useful in certain unusual contexts. You give the LOOKUP function a value to look up, a single-column (or single-row) list to find it in, and a separate single-column (or single-row) list to get the answer from. If your lookup table is split into two pieces—even on different worksheets—you might want to use this three-argument LOOKUP function. Unfortunately, LOOKUP can perform only range lookups, which severely limits its usefulness.

The MATCH function, on the other hand, is a powerful tool. You give it a value to look up and a single-column (or single-row) list in which to find the value. You also specify whether you want a range or exact-match lookup. The MATCH function then returns the position of the value in the list, and you are free to do with that number whatever you want. Since the INDEX function returns a value from a list, given row and column positions, the combination of MATCH and INDEX give you a generalized equivalent to the VLOOKUP and HLOOKUP functions.

Searching by Two Columns

The fact that the MATCH function can perform either a range lookup or an exact match lookup has interesting consequences when the same value occurs multiple times in a list. The exact-match lookup always finds the first value that matches. The range lookup always finds the last value that matches. This allows you to find sublists within a larger, sorted list.

For example, suppose that you have a list similar to the gray region of Figure 14-27. You can think of this list as a combination of three lists, one for each model of bicycle. Since the model names are sorted, you can use MATCH to find the beginning and end rows of each smaller list. Within the smaller list, you can then search for the appropriate assembly.

The entire process—calculating the start and end rows, calculating the range of the sub-list, and finding the value within that range—requires functions that use the result of other functions. You can implement this completely with named formulas, or you can implement the same sequence of functions in a custom function. We'll look at both approaches, starting with the custom function.

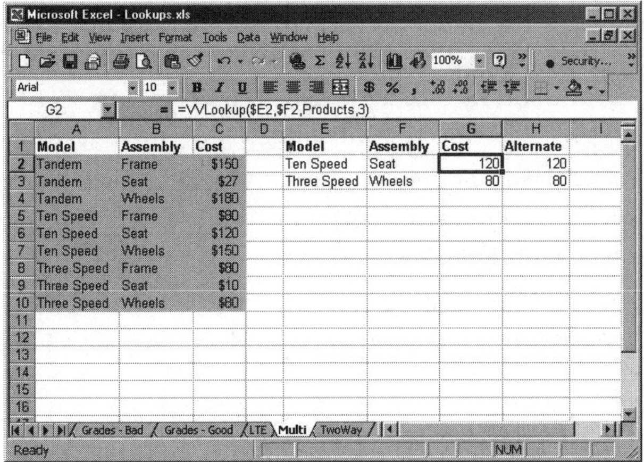

Figure 14-27
Use MATCH to create a custom function that searches by two columns.

Using Functions to Match Two Columns

The custom function acts like VLOOKUP, except that it has two vertical lookup columns: *VVLookup*. Here's what it looks like:

```
Function VVLookup(lookup_value, lookup_value2, _
    table_array As Range, col_index_num As Long) As Variant
    Dim myTop As Long
    Dim myRows As Long
    Dim myMatch As Long
    Dim myMini As Range
    On Error GoTo ErrorHandler

    myTop = WorksheetFunction.Match(lookup_value, _
        table_array.Columns(1), 0)
    myRows = WorksheetFunction.Match(lookup_value, _
        table_array.Columns(1), 1) - myTop + 1
    Set myMini = table_array.Cells(myTop, 2).Resize(myRows)
    myMatch = WorksheetFunction.Match(lookup_value2, myMini, 0) _
        + myTop - 1
    Set VVLookup = table_array.Cells(myMatch, col_index_num)
    Exit Function

ErrorHandler:
    VVLookup = CVErr(xlErrNA)
End Function
```

The argument names are modeled after those for the VLOOKUP function. The function is declared as a Variant because it will return either a range (if it does find a match) or the error value #N/A (if it doesn't). The error handler causes the function to return #N/A if anything goes wrong. Excel has names for each of the error values, but you must convert that value into an error using the Visual Basic CVErr function or it simply appears as 2042 in the cell.

The first real statement in the function finds the first matching row and assigns the position number to the variable *myTop*. It uses the worksheet's MATCH function, giving it only the first column of the table. The MATCH function uses 0 as the third argument for an exact match and 0 as the third argument for a range lookup.

The next statement finds the number of matching rows by executing MATCH again, this time as a range lookup, and then adding 1 and subtracting the starting row. It assigns this row count to the *myRows* variable.

The next statement creates a mini-lookup range named *myMini*. The range begins with the second column of the first matching row and extends for as many rows as the table has.

Now it's time to find the matching inner column. This is a simple exact match against the mini-range. Adding the starting position of the top range (and adjusting by 1) gives the matching position within the original lookup table.

Finally, the function returns the matching value from the original table, using the column number that was passed as an argument.

Using Named Formulas to Match Two Columns

If you use named formulas, you use the apparently simple formula *=INDEX(Products,Match,3)* to look up the cost based on the two values. In fact, even though you can't see it, this is the formula in cell H2 of Figure 14-27. The named formulas follow the same progression as the statements in the *VVLookup* function, although they look somewhat different because of the differences between Excel and VBA. The formulas appear in the Define Names list in alphabetical order, but they have a logical sequence that corresponds to the sequence in the macro.

The logical first name is *Top*; its formula is *=MATCH(Multi!$E12,INDEX (Multi!Products,0,1),0)*. (When you enter formulas, you don't need to include the active sheet name. If you type this formula as *=MATCH($E12,INDEX(Products,0,1),0)*, Excel will add the sheet names.) This formula uses MATCH to perform an exact-match search of the first column of the Products range.

The next name is *Rows*; its formula is *=MATCH(Multi!$E11,INDEX(Multi!Products,0,1),1)-Multi!Top+1*. This corresponds very closely to the VBA statement.

Next comes the minirange (Minirange); its formula is *=OFFSET(Multi!Products,Multi!Top-1,1,Multi!Rows,1)*. In VBA, the Resize property is separate from the Offset property, so you can use it anywhere. In Excel, the resize functionality is bundled in as part of the OFFSET function. With the OFFSET function, you just need to be sure to count from 0, rather than from 1.

The last named formula is Match; its formula is *=MATCH(Multi!$F8,Multi!MiniRange,0) +Multi!Top-1*. This is almost identical to the VBA statement.

The final VBA statement is the function itself. Once you know the row number, which is calculated by the Match defined name, retrieving the value is easy.

Searching by Column and by Row

The MATCH function is quite versatile. You can use it to search both the top row and left column of a table at the same time. For example, given the shaded table of calories in Figure 14-28, you might want to calculate the total number of calories burned by a specified individual doing a specified activity for a specified time.

D14 =INDEX(Calories,
MATCH(Activity,Activities,0),
MATCH(Weight,Weights,1))
*Minutes

	A	B	C	D	E
3	*Calories burned per minute*				
4		*90*	*130*	*170*	*210*
5	*Bicycling*	5	7	9	12
6	*Calisthenics*	4	5	6	8
7	*Handball*	7	9	12	15
8	*Running*	10	13	19	22
9	*Swimming*	6	8	12	15
10	*Walking*	3	5	7	8
11					
13	Activity	Weight	Minutes	Calories	
14	Walking	175	10	70	
15	Swimming	215	10	150	
16	Bicycling	90	10	50	

Figure 14-28
Use MATCH to calculate a two-way lookup.

If you give the name *Calories* to the range B5:E10, Activities to the range A5:A10, and *Weights* to the range B4:E4, you can use the formula in Figure 14-28. The INDEX function takes a table, a row number, and a column number. For the row number, use MATCH to find the exact match position of the current activity in the *Activities* list. For the column number, use MATCH to find the range for the current weight in the *Weights* list. (Using Alt+Enter to break lines can make a formula like this easy to read.)

If you don't want to name the individual ranges but want to give the single name *Table* to the entire shaded area, you can still use a modified version of the same formula. You simply use the INDEX function to extract the first row or column, as needed. Here's the single-name version of the same formula:

```
=INDEX(Table,
 MATCH(Activity,INDEX(Table,0,1),0),
 MATCH(Weight,INDEX(Table,1,0),1))
 *Minutes
```

The lookup ranges in this version extend to include the blank cell A4, but that doesn't hurt the formula at all.

If these simple, elegant formulas are too much work for you, and you would rather have a Wizard create a formula that calculates the two-way lookup (even though the resulting formula doesn't use any names and is hard to read), you can use the Lookup

Wizard add-in. On the Tools menu, click Add-Ins, and then select the Lookup Wizard. (You will need the Office 2000 installation media the first time you use the wizard.)

Once the Wizard is installed and enabled, a Wizard submenu appears on the Tools menu; it has a Lookup command. Follow the instructions carefully in the wizard. They can be confusing—perhaps more trouble than creating the formula using INDEX and MATCH. Once the Lookup Wizard creates a lookup formula, the formula will continue to work even if you disable or remove the add-in.

Incidentally, here is the formula the Lookup Wizard created for the lookup table in Figure 14-28: *=HLOOKUP(B16, $B$4:$E$10, MATCH(A16,$A$4:$A$10,)).* (You have to add the **Minutes* yourself.)

Searching by Column, Row, and Table

You might sometimes have a situation where you need to search in three dimensions. For example, suppose that your company uses three different carriers for shipping purposes. Each company has its own rate schedule based on weight and distance. You have a worksheet that contains the shipping tables, similar to the one shown in Figure 14-29. You need to find the correct shipping cost for a given carrier, weight, and distance. This is the same problem as selecting by row and column, with the added twist that you also need to select the correct table.

You can use either of two methods to select one of several tables. The first method is to use the often-forgotten fourth argument of the INDEX function to select a range from a multiple-area reference. (See "Combining References with the Union Operator" in Chapter 12 for more information about creating a multiple-area reference.)

In the worksheet, the range B3:D5 is named *Carrier1,* the range B7:F11 is named *Carrier2,* and the range B19:B22 is named *Carrier3.* The worksheet also has a named formula that combines the three areas into a single reference: The name *Tables* is defined as *=Carrier1, Carrier2, Carrier3.*

As you can see in Figure 14-29, the formula that calculates the Rate in cell E20 is the same one as in the preceding section, except that each occurrence of the INDEX function uses the multiple-area *Tables* reference, along with *Carrier* as the fourth argument to select one area from the reference.

The second method for dealing with multiple tables is to use the INDIRECT function, which calculates a reference based on a name. (See "Converting Text into a Reference with the INDIRECT Function" in Chapter 12 for more information about the INDIRECT function.) To use the INDIRECT method, give the same names to the three tables, but don't create the *Tables* name to combine them into a single reference. In the Carrier column, type the name of the carrier range (*Carrier1, Carrier2,* or *Carrier3*), and use this formula for the rate:

```
=INDEX(INDIRECT(Carrier),
 MATCH(Weight,INDEX(INDIRECT(Carrier),0,1)),
 MATCH(Distance,INDEX(INDIRECT(Carrier),1,0)))
```

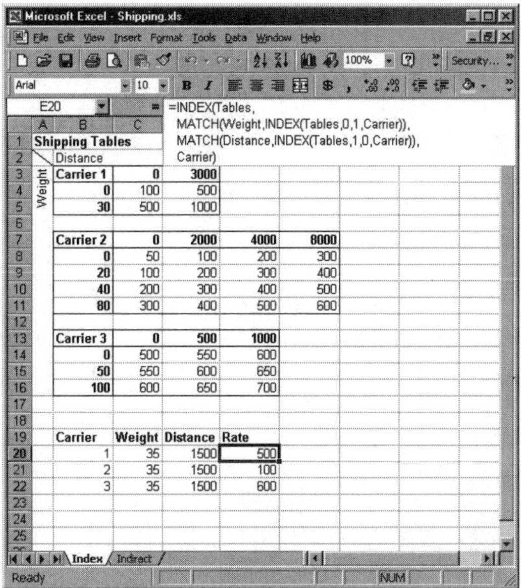

Figure 14-29
Use INDEX to select one of several tables.

Finding and Extending Patterns using Regression

Excel's ability to manipulate numbers and dates makes it an ideal tool for calculating models that project order volumes, revenue streams, population densities, and other time-series data. Extrapolating from the past is often a reasonable way to predict the future. If orders have been increasing steadily over the last few years, barring any new factors in the marketplace, orders should continue to increase next year. Of course, such predictions can be dangerous, because countless new factors continually enter the marketplace. Sometimes, however, the best way to project the future is to simply draw a straight line through the past and see where it leads.

All Excel's extrapolation tools are based on a technique called *least-squares regression.* The basic idea of a regression is to find a line such that the distance between the data points and the line is as small as possible. You don't need to know how least-squares regression works to take advantage of Excel's tools. If you are interested in the internal calculations, look at the Help topic for the LINEST worksheet function.

Excel has some extremely simple regression tools. Probably the simplest regression method is to select a range of historical values and then drag the AutoFill handle to include new cells. Excel fills the new cells with values that are calculated based on a straight-line regression of the existing values.

If you want trend values for the existing data points as well as the new ones, select the original values (or a copy, if you don't want to destroy the original values), along with any new cells you want to extrapolate into. On the Edit menu, click Fill, and then click Series and select the Trend check box.

Creating Trends with a Chart

Almost without exception, when you create a trend from historical data, you want to see the original values and the trend line on a chart. Excel can shortcut the whole process by enabling a chart to create trend lines on its own. A chart trend line can extrapolate into the future, and it can even display the formula for the line along with a statistical indicator, called the *R-squared value*, of how well the line fits the data. The chart in Figure 14-30 shows 16 months of orders along with a linear trend line extrapolating the remaining 8 months of the year.

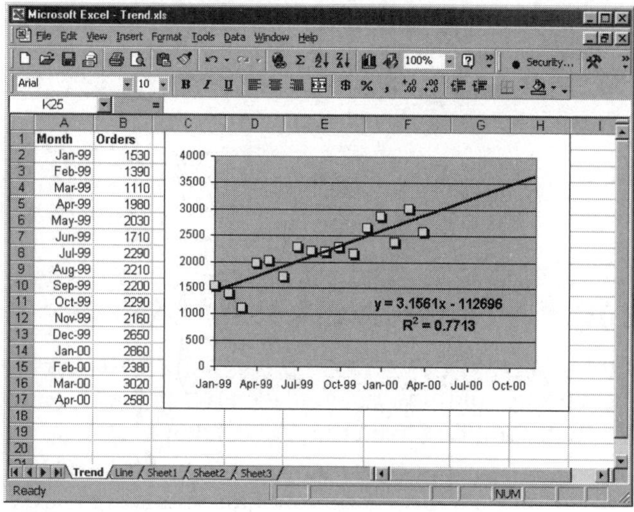

Figure 14-30
A chart can create a trend line on its own.

The chart also shows the equation for the line—which you will learn more about in the following section—and the R-squared value. If a trend line fits the data perfectly, it will have an R-squared value of 1. If a trend line is exactly the opposite of the data, it will have an R-squared value of 1. If the trend line and the data have no relationship whatsoever, it will have an R-squared value of 0. Other things being equal, the closer the R-squared value is to 1, the greater the chance that an extrapolation might be valid.

Not all data values fit in a straight line, and Excel can calculate curved trend lines in addition to straight ones. A chart can generate five different types of trend lines, as you can see in the Add Trendline dialog box in Figure 14-31. (A moving average does not use regression and is not really a trend line.)

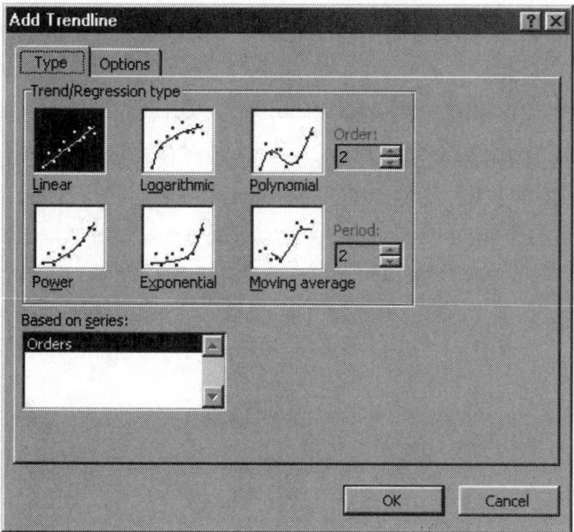

Figure 14-31
A chart can create five trend lines and a moving average.

Excel's Help file has an excellent discussion of how to choose which trend line works best with your data. To see it, type *Choosing a Trend Line* in the Answer Wizard.

Suppose, however, you have decided that the linear trend line shown earlier in Figure 14-30 does adequately represent your data. The real problem is that the extrapolated numbers—which look so good on the chart—are not in your spreadsheet where you can use them for planning. With a little work (and a little help from this chapter), you can recreate the values from any of the five types of trend lines in your worksheet.

Using the Slope-Intercept Equation for a Line

To create a trend line on your own, you need to be able to use the formula displayed on the chart. The most fundamental formula is the equation for plotting a straight line. This equation is called the *slope-intercept* form of a line, and if you haven't looked at it since high school, you might want to review it now. All the other trend line equations are variations of this formula.

Note The sample document for this section is Slope.xls.

The chart in Figure 14-32 plots a line between two data points. The first data point has a value of 0 on the horizontal (x-) axis and a value of 4 on the vertical (y-) axis. The second data point has a value of 4 on the x-axis and a value of 12 on the y-axis. Given those two data points, you can construct an equation that defines all the points on the line that connects them (and can extend past them, as well). The difference between the two y values, 12 and 4, is 8. The difference between the two x values, 4 and 0, is 4. Dividing the 8 by the 4, you get 2, which is the slope of the line. Every time the line moves one unit to the right, it moves two units up. When x is zero, the value of y is 4. This is called the intercept of the line. The intercept is where the y-axis (the vertical line where x equals zero), crosses, or intercepts, the line.

For the line in Figure 14-32, the slope is 2 and the intercept is 4. In Excel, if the value on the x-axis is in cell A2, then the formula for the value on the y-axis is *=2*A2+4*, as you can see in cell B2. If you use the letter x to refer to any arbitrary value on the x-axis, and the letter y to refer to the corresponding value on the y-axis, you can define the line with the equation $y = 2x + 4$, which is called the slope-intercept equation for the line. This equation has the same form as the one displayed by the trend line shown earlier in Figure 14-30.

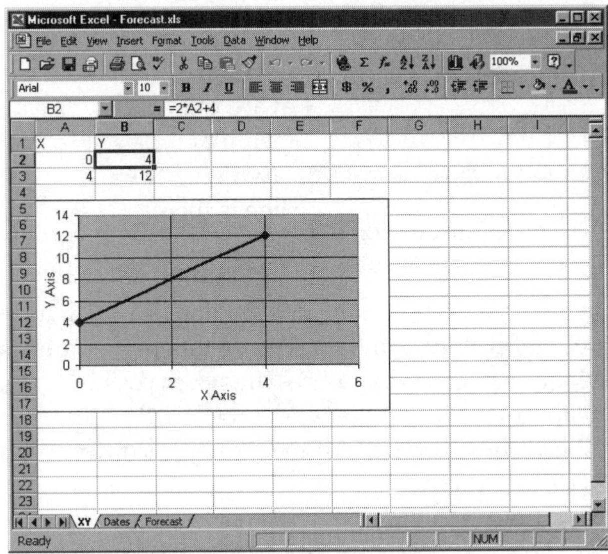

Figure 14-32
Slope and intercept define a line.

Increasing the slope makes the line steeper. Using a negative slope makes the line slope downward. Increasing the intercept makes the line shift up. Decreasing the intercept makes the line shift down. The generalized equation for a straight line is $y = ax + b$, where a is the placeholder for the slope value, and b is the placeholder for the intercept value.

If you know the x and y values for any two points on a line, you can calculate the slope and intercept by taking the difference between the y values and dividing it by the difference between the x values, as in the paragraph above. (It doesn't matter which point you subtract from, as long as you use the same order for both the x and y values.)

Given three of the four values—slope, intercept, any x, and any y—you can calculate the fourth value by using algebra to rearrange the slope-intercept equation. If your algebra is getting rusty, here are the four versions, already worked out for you. If you want the y value, use the standard form of the equation, $y = ax + b$. If you want the intercept, use the equation $b = y - ax$. If you want the x value, use the equation $x = (y - b) / a$. If you want the slope, use the equation $a = (y - b) / x$. In the forecasting project below, you will see Excel versions of all these equations except the one for the slope.

Using the Slope-Intercept Equation with Dates

Excel dates work marvelously as x values in the slope-intercept equation for a line because, as explained more fully in "Understanding Excel Dates"earlier in this chapter, dates in Excel simply count the days since January 1, 1900. How could you hope for more perfect evenly spaced values?

The only confusing part about using dates is that January 1, 1900, was a long time ago, and most date ranges you are likely to look at are pretty far to the right on the x-axis. Figure 14-33 contains a graph that looks very similar to the one in Figure 14-32, except that the x values are *37000* and *37004* (which correspond to April 19 and 21, 2001), instead of 0 and 4. The slope of the line is the same in the two figures. In each case, y increases by 2 for each increase in x. But the true y-axis does not intersect the line on April 19, 2001. It intersects when x is equal to zero, which was December 31, 1899. If you extrapolate the line back that far, it actually crosses the y-axis when the y value is *-73996*. That's *-74000* (which is twice the *37000* for April 19), plus the 4 that is the apparent intercept on April 19.

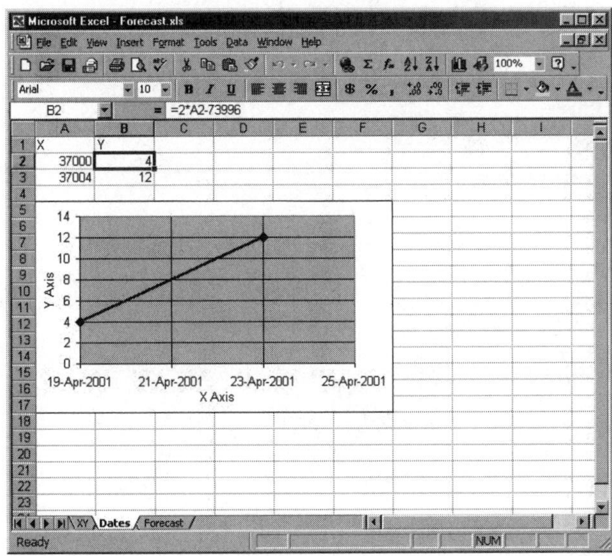

Figure 14-33
Dates require a negative intercept.

When you use dates as the x values for an upward-sloping line, the intercept is almost always a very large negative number. Conversely, for a downward-sloping line, the intercept is almost always a very large positive number.

The slope of the trend line in Figure 14-30 is 3.1561, meaning that the order rate is increasing by about three units each day. The intercept of that trend line is –112696, as expected, a very large negative number.

Note Dates work well with linear trends, but when you start using nonlinear trends, you are better off creating a column of period numbers starting with 1 or 0 to use as the x values.

Calculating a Straight-Line Trend

Excel has three functions that calculate the slope, intercept, and R-squared values of a linear regression: SLOPE, INTERCEPT, and RSQ. When you use them as arguments, you give them the known (that is, the actual) y values and the known (actual) x values. In the worksheet in Figure 14-34, if you give the name *Actual* to rows 2 through 17, you can use the labels at the top of columns A and B to specify the actual y and actual x values. The formula to calculate the slope is *=SLOPE(Actual Orders, Actual Month)*. The formula to calculate the intercept is almost the same: *=INTERCEPT(Actual Orders, Actual Month)*. The formula to calculate the R-squared value is also predictable: *=RSQ(Actual Orders, Actual Month)*.

Note The sample document for this section is Trend.xls.

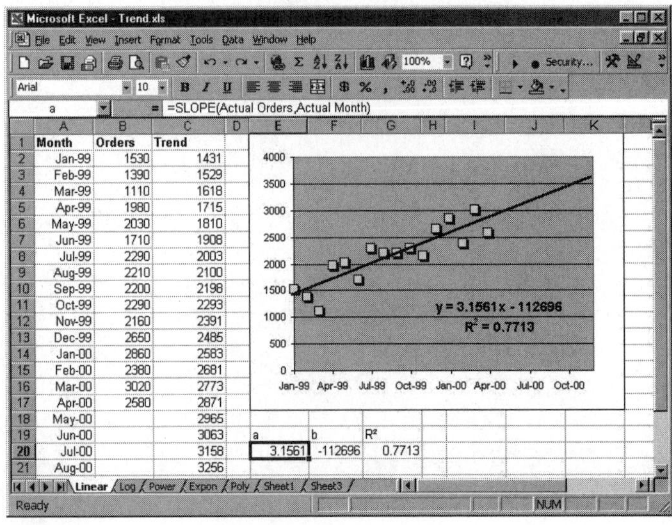

Figure 14-34
Excel has functions for calculating a straight-line regression.

These three values correspond exactly to the slope, intercept, and R-squared numbers that the trend line displayed on the chart in Figure 14-30. You can use this slope and intercept to calculate the values that make up the trend line on the chart. In cell C2, type the formula *=a*Month+b*, and copy the formula down to all 24 rows.

Excel has other functions that calculate a linear trend. The TREND function will calculate the resulting trend values—the ones in column = C of Figure 14-34—without going through the intermediate steps of calculating the slope and intercept. When you use TREND to extrapolate new y values, you need to give it the corresponding new x values. If you give the name *All* to rows 2 through 25, you can use the *Month* label from the top of the column. To get the same values as those in column C, select cells D2:D25, and array-type the formula *=TREND(Actual Orders, Actual Month, All Month)*. The TREND function is a single function that returns multiple answers, so you need to array-enter the formula to share those answers over multiple cells.

Excel also has a function that calculates the slope, intercept, and R-squared value (and several other statistics) all at once: LINEST. The LINEST function returns several values, so it, too, must be array-entered. The easiest way to know how many cells to use is to select more than you need. Excel will fill all the unused cells with #N/A. Select a range with at least six rows and three columns and array-enter the formula *=LINEST(Actual Orders, Actual Month, TRUE, TRUE)*. You will see values similar to the ones in Figure 14-35. The values in the top row are the slope and intercept. The first value in the third row is the R-squared statistic. The other values in the second to the fifth rows are various statistics about the regression. The LINEST Help topic provides a description of these statistics.

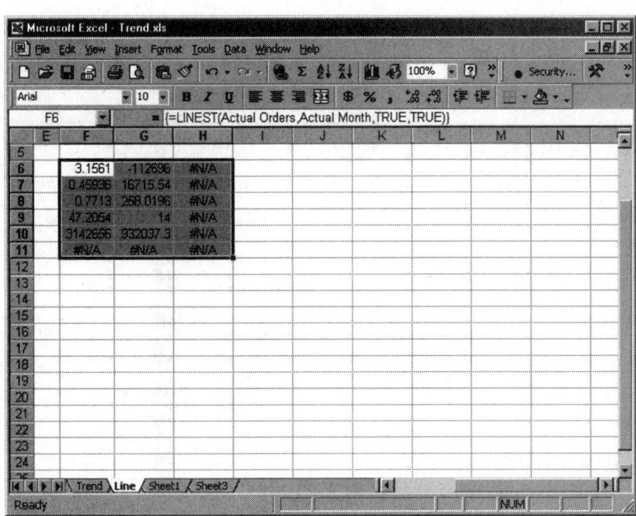

Figure 14-35
The LINEST function calculates many regression statistics.

Chapter 14

The third and fourth arguments—the ones that are both *True* in this example—are optional. If you enter *False* as the third argument, LINEST will force the intercept to equal zero. If you enter *False* as the fourth argument (or omit it), LINEST will not return the statistics in the last five rows.

You might wonder why you would use the LINEST function when you can just use SLOPE, INTERCEPT, and RSQ. In fact, those three functions were added to Excel precisely so that you would not have to deal with entering the LINEST function as an array formula. You need the LINEST function if you want any of the additional statistics it returns or if you have multiple x variables—as in the polynomial regression below.

Calculating a Logarithmic Trend

Sometimes values grow quickly at first and then taper off, similar to the values in Figure 14-36. Of an Excel chart's five data types, the logarithmic trend usually fits best with growth that gradually slows down. Suppose that in analyzing the historical order data on the worksheet, you determine that the best representation of your data is the logarithmic trend. You would once again like to get the projected values into your worksheet.

The *least-squares regression* method technically works only with straight lines. To make a curved regression line, you must somehow include an exponent in the equation. Back in 1614, a man named John Napier, frustrated with how hard it was to multiply and take roots of large numbers, invented a mechanism for converting multiplication into addition and exponentiation into multiplication. He gave the name *logarithms* to his invention. Logarithms allow Excel to use the straight-line regression calculation to calculate curved lines.

The equation for the logarithmic trend in Figure 14-36 has the same form as the standard $y = ax + b$. The only difference is that the formula uses the LN function to "curve" the x values before using them.

To calculate the slope, intercept, and R-squared values, you use the same SLOPE, INTERCEPT, and RSQ functions as if you were calculating a straight line. Just enclose the x values (Actual Month) in the LN function. The three formulas are *=SLOPE(Actual Orders, LN(Actual Month)), =INTERCEPT(Actual Orders, LN(Actual Month)),* and *=RSQ(Actual Orders, LN(Actual Month).*

To calculate the trend numbers—the ones in column C of Figure 14-36—you use the standard equation, only modifying the x values. After assigning the names *a* and *b* to the slope and intercept cells, use the formula *=a*LN(Month)+b* to calculate the trend.

Calculating an Exponential Trend

Exponential growth is simply compounded interest. When you put $100 in a savings account at 4.3 percent interest, your money is growing exponentially—not growing very fast, perhaps, but it is growing exponentially.

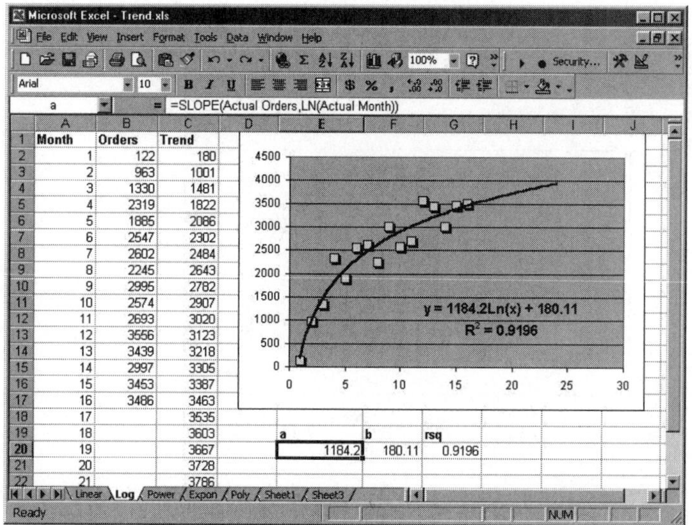

Month	Orders	Trend
1	122	180
2	963	1001
3	1330	1481
4	2319	1822
5	1885	2086
6	2547	2302
7	2602	2484
8	2245	2643
9	2995	2782
10	2574	2907
11	2693	3020
12	3556	3123
13	3439	3218
14	2997	3305
15	3453	3387
16	3486	3463
17		3535
18		3603
19		3667
20		3728
21		3786

Figure 14-36
A logarithmic regression tapers off.

In an exponential regression, the standard linear equation $y = ax + b$ gets escalated a notch: addition becomes multiplication and multiplication becomes exponentiation. The exponential equation is $y = a^x b$, or in Excel, *y=a^x*b*. In interest rate terms, the b value is simply the amount of the original deposit, and the a value is 1 plus the interest rate. (When the chart displays the equation, it uses a logarithmic manipulation that means the same thing: $y=be^{xa}$, except *a* is now the log of the growth rate. The symbol e refers to the natural logarithm constant that the brilliant blind mathematician Leonhard Euler subtly named after himself in 1720.)

Excel has many financial functions that work with interest rates. The RATE function, for example, calculates the average interest rate of an investment. However, this function only considers the original deposit, the number of periods, and the ending value. It determines what constant interest rate you would achieve from the original amount to the ending amount in the given number of periods. Calculating an exponential trend is different because it takes into consideration the growth of each period.

For example, suppose that 16 years ago, your grandmother bought you $1,000 worth of shares in a mutual fund. You have a report that shows the value of those shares at the end of each of the 16 years. The second column of Figure 14-37 shows the value of the stock at the end of each year. The chart shows the values plotted, and the dark line is an exponential trend line generated by the chart.

The cell labeled (and named) *Rate* contains the rate as calculated by Excel's RATE function. The *Start* cell contains the amount of the original $1,000 investment. Column C calculates what the fund's value would have been if it had earned 14 percent

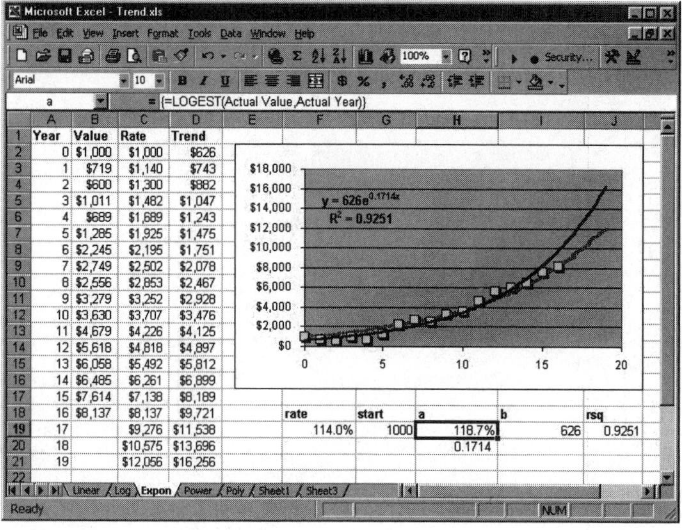

Figure 14-37
An exponential trend tracks compounding interest.

each year. The formula in column C is *=rate^Year*start*. You would get the same result by entering *=start in cell C2, =C2*rate* in cell C3, and copying the formula down. The value at the end of year 16—in cell C18—exactly matches the actual ending value in cell B18. The RATE function determines that you would need a 14 percent annual interest rate to get from $1,000 to $8,137 in 16 years, compounding annually.

But the actual growth of the fund was lower than 14 percent during the first few years (in fact, it lost value in some years), and its growth was higher than 14 percent during the more recent years. The annual growth rate calculated by the trend line is 18.7 percent. (The value displayed in the equation on the chart is 0.1714, which is the log of 18.7 percent.) In effect, the trend adjusted the original deposit down to $626 to account for the bad early years.

You can use the SLOPE, INTERCEPT, and RSQ functions to calculate the a, b, and R-squared values for an exponential trend. You just use the log of the y value and then use the EXP function to take the inverse log of the result for the *a* and *b* values. Here are the three formulas: *=EXP(SLOPE(LN(Actual Value),Actual Year))* for the *a* value, *=EXP(INTERCEPT(LN(Actual Value),Actual Year))* for the *b* value, and *=RSQ(LN(Actual Value),Actual Year)* for the R-squared value.

Excel also has a single-function equivalent, similar to LINEST, that might be easier to use. In a range at least two columns wide by three rows high, array-enter the formula *=LOGEST(Actual Value, Actual Year)*. As with LINEST, the a value is in the top left cell, the b value is in the next cell to the right, and the R-squared value is first in the third row.

Once you have the *a* and *b* values, you can calculate the exponential trend. The formula is essentially identical to the one in column C. It is *=a^Year*b.*

Incidentally, the actual formula for calculating the rate (in cell F19) is *=RATE (16,0,-start,B18)+1.* The first argument gives the number of periods. The second gives the value of any periodic payments. The third argument gives the amount of the initial deposit (payments out are negative numbers). The fourth argument gives the ending amount. The function returns an interest rate, so you need to add 1 to get a value that can be used as an exponent in the formulas in column C. The RATE function arrives at the interest rate by guessing various values until it arrives at one that works. Incidentally, you can calculate the same interest rate (without intermediate guesses) by using an algebraic variation of the formula in column C: *=(B18/start)^(1/16).* This formula divides the ending value by the starting value and solves for the 16th root.

Calculating a Power Trend

The chart's power regression is probably not extremely useful in business situations. It extrapolates very quickly to extreme values. If you do find some data values where the power trend is the best, here's how to reproduce the values from the chart as shown in Figure 14-38.

The equation for a power trend is similar to that of an exponential trend, except that *a* and x trade places. Instead of $y = a^xb$, it is $y = x^ab$ or, in Excel, *y = x^a*b.*

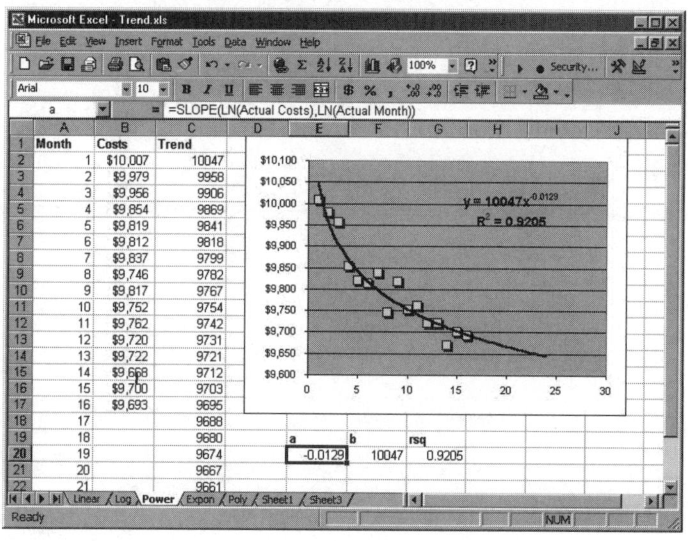

Figure 14-38
A power regression changes very quickly.

To calculate the coefficients, you simply convert both the x and y values to logarithms before using the SLOPE, INTERCEPT, and RSQ functions. With cells *a* and *b* named, the formula that calculates the trend in column C is *=Month^a*b.*

Calculating a Polynomial Trend

The fifth and final type of trend line that you can create in a chart is a polynomial trend. "Charting an Algebraic Function" in Chapter 13 uses a polynomial equation as an example of how to plot the value of a function without entering formulas in any cells. You can look at that project if you want to learn more about polynomial functions.

A polynomial trend on an Excel chart has an *order* that can range from 2 to 6. (A polynomial with an order of 1 is simply a straight line.) Each additional order allows the line to "bend" one more time. A second-order polynomial can bend once. A third-order polynomial can bend twice, and so on. Those bends might be meaningful, or they might simply be tracking the historical values, giving you a meaninglessly high R-squared value. Polynomials—particularly third-order and higher—are very dangerous for extrapolating into the future. New y values are seldom meaningful with x values that are outside the original range.

You might be able to use a polynomial, however, to *interpolate* missing values. In the worksheet in Figure 14-39, the original monthly values for a two-year period are shown in columns A and B. Approximately half the periods are missing. The remaining values appear on the chart as square boxes. You determine that the third-order polynomial accurately describes what happened. You can replicate the polynomial trend line from the chart to interpolate the missing months.

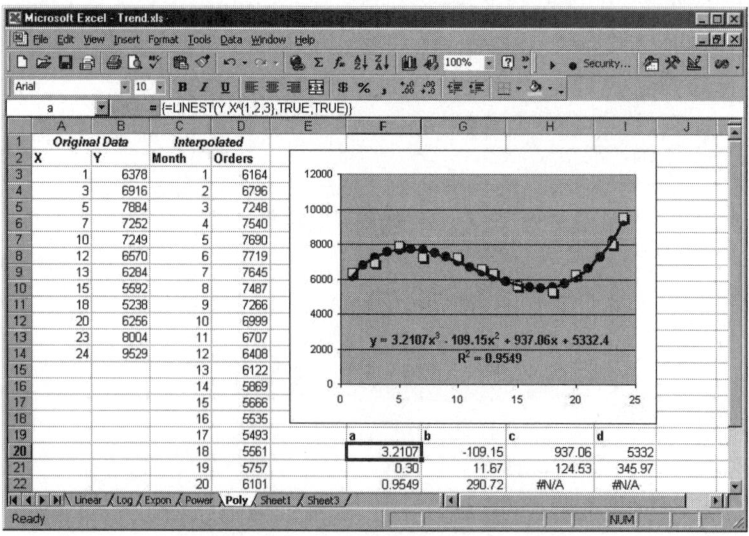

Figure 14-39

Use a polynomial to interpolate missing values.

The equation for a polynomial is the same as that for a line, except that it gets an additional term, with the x value raised to a higher power, for each new order. The equation for a third-order polynomial has the form $y = ax^3 + bx^2 + cx + d$. In fact, the equation for a straight line is simply the last two terms of a polynomial.

To calculate the *a, b, c,* and *d* values, you must use the LINEST function. Select a range that is at least four columns wide (one more than the order of the polynomial), and at least three rows high (if you want to see the R-squared statistic). With the ranges A3:A14 named X and B3:B14 named Y, array-enter the formula *=LINEST (Y,X^{1,2,3},TRUE,TRUE)*. You need to enter the formula as an array formula to share the results over multiple cells. The x range in the formula is raised to an exponent. The exponent is actually three values—1, 2, and 3—entered as an array constant. Excel applies each of these exponents to a new copy of the x values, resulting in the three columns of x values that the function needs. If the x range is horizontal, you need to put the three exponents in a vertical array by separating them with semicolons instead of commas.

The constants for the equation match those in the chart, and the R-squared value in the third row matches the one from the chart as well.

The formula for column D is simply the Excel implementation of the polynomial equation. Name the cells for the *a, b, c,* and *d* values. (The letter c is invalid as a name in Excel, because it is a meaningful reference in R1C1 notation. If you create the names using the Create Names dialog box, Excel will add an underscore to create the name c_. If you use Define Names, you will need to add the underscore yourself.) In cell D3, type the formula *=a*Month^3+b*Month^2+c_*Month+d*, and copy it down the column.

Creating a Product Planning Model

A worksheet model that projects product sales over several years is a powerful use for the slope-intercept equation. You want to create a model similar to the one in Figure 14-40. Each product's lifecycle consists of three phases, an introductory growth phase, a plateau maturity phase, and a decline phase. You want to graph the volumes for each product, stacked so that you can see the total unit volumes for all your products.

Note The sample document for this section is Forecast.xls.

For the growth phase, you will specify the starting date (the date you introduce the product) and a monthly ramp amount (the amount each month's sales will increase over those of the previous month). For the mature phase, rather than specify a start date, you will specify the mature monthly sales quantity. (The mature phase will begin when the product reaches that quantity.) Even during the mature phase, the product will have a ramp—its sales might continue to increase, but the increase is slower than during the growth phase. For the decline phase, you will specify the date the decline will start (which might coincide with the expected introduction date of a new product), and the rate at which the sales will drop off each month.

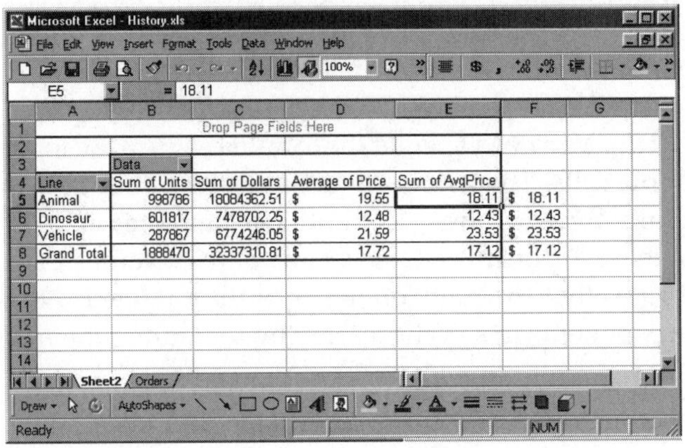

Microsoft Excel - History.xls

E5 = 18.11

Drop Page Fields Here

Data					
Line	Sum of Units	Sum of Dollars	Average of Price	Sum of AvgPrice	
Animal	998786	18084362.51	$ 19.55	18.11	$ 18.11
Dinosaur	601817	7478702.25	$ 12.48	12.43	$ 12.43
Vehicle	287867	6774246.05	$ 21.59	23.53	$ 23.53
Grand Total	1888470	32337310.81	$ 17.72	17.12	$ 17.12

Sheet2 / Orders /

Figure 14-40

Project product sales using three lifecycle phases.

As shown in Figure 14-40, each of the three products has identical parameters, except that each product begins and ends one year later than the previous product. You can see how even with almost identical parameters, the interaction between the three products can get quite complex.

Calculating Parameters for Each Phase

To project the monthly orders for the products, you need to create slope and intercept values for each phase. For consistency, you can create five columns for each phase: *Date, Value, Ramp, Slope,* and *Intercept*. The model in Figure 14-40 hides three of the five columns for each phase. Figure 14-41 shows all five columns for the Growth phase.

In the Growth phase, the *Slope* column simply converts the ramp from a monthly number to a daily number. The formula *=A.Ramp/(365/12)* divides the monthly ramp amount by the average number of days in a month. Given that the value of the Growth phase is zero on the Start date and that the growth rate is the *Slope* amount per day, the Intercept column must equal what the quantity would have been on day zero. In the slope-intercept formula $y = ax + b$, the intercept is the b variable. Solving the equation for b gives the equation $b = y - ax$. Translated to use the column labels, the equation becomes *=A.Value-A.Slope*A.Date.*

In the Mature phase (see Figure 14-42), the Slope and Intercept formulas are equivalent. In the mature phase, however, you need to calculate the start date—the date at which the growth phase would reach the mature value. In the slope-intercept formula $y = ax + b$, the *Date* is the x variable. Solving the equation for x gives the equation $x = (y - b) / a$. Translated to use the column labels, the equation becomes *=(B.Value-A.Intercept)/A.Slope.*

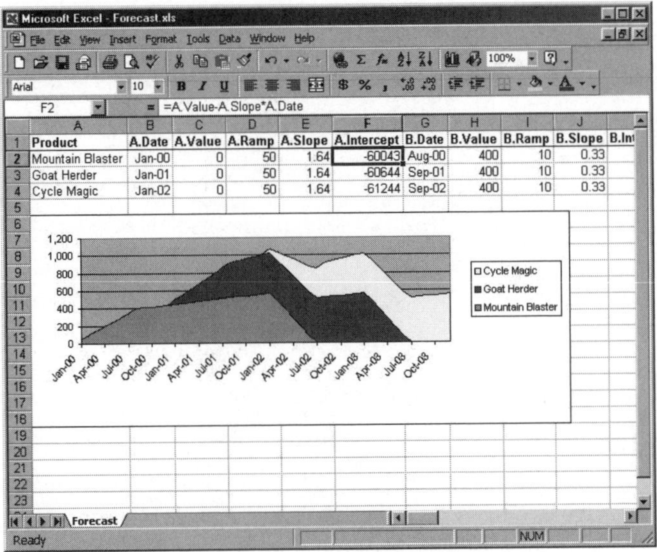

Figure 14-41

For the Growth phase, you must calculate the slope and intercept.

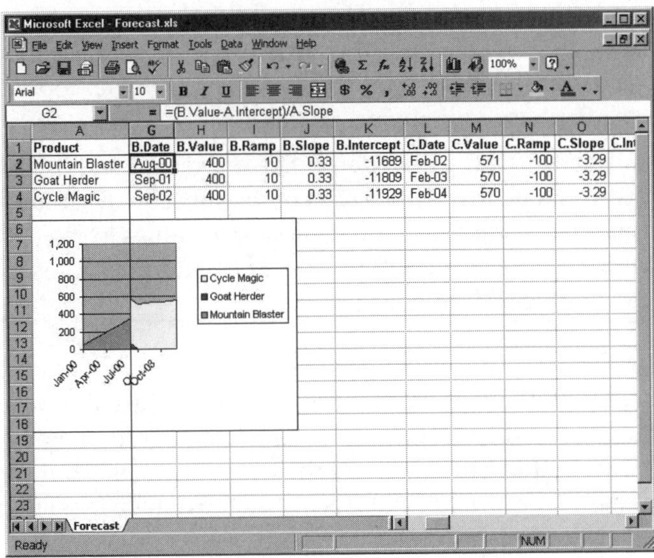

Figure 14-42

For the Mature phase, you must also calculate the start date.

In the Decline phase (Figure 14-43), the *Slope* and *Intercept* formulas are analogous to those in the other two phases. You do, however, need to calculate the initial *Value*. This formula uses the slope-intercept equation intact, $y = ax + b$. Translated to use column labels, the equation becomes *=B.Intercept+B.Slope*C.Date.*

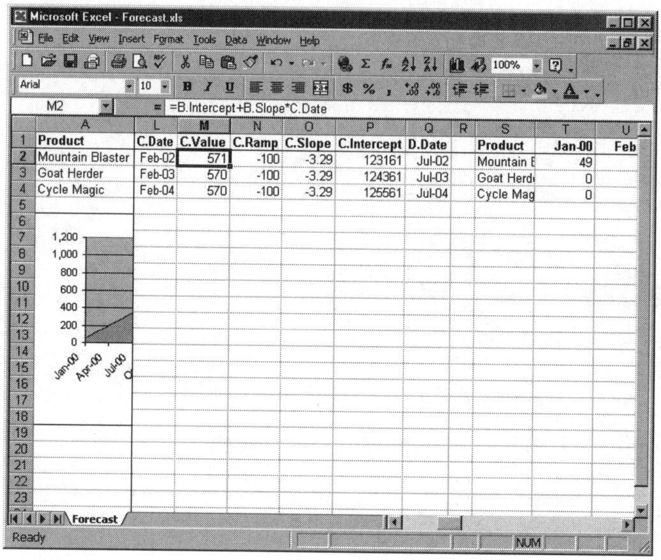

Figure 14-43
For the Decline phase, you must calculate the initial value.

To end the Decline phase properly, you also need the Start date of a post-Decline phase. The formula for the final date is *=(0-C.Intercept)/C.Slope*. This is equivalent to the formula that calculates the start date of the Mature phase, except that the ending value of the Decline phase will always be zero.

You now have three phases (plus a final date). The important values for each phase are the Start date, the End date (that is, the start of the subsequence phase), the *Slope*, and the *Intercept*. You will use the *Slope* and the *Intercept* values to calculate the value for each month within a phase. You will use the Start and End dates to determine whether to calculate a value for the phase or not.

Calculating the Forecast Formulas

Give the name *Month* to the row of dates across the top of the column. You can use column labels for the forecast formulas—as long as you prefix them with a dollar sign to keep Excel from shifting them as you copy the formulas—but you must use a real name for the row of dates, since there is no way to enter a label that Excel will not misinterpret as a column label.

The essence of the forecast formula is the standard form of the slope-intercept equation $y = ax + b$. Using names and labels, the formula is *=$A.Slope*Month+$A.Intercept*. If you were to copy that formula to all the columns in the forecast range, you would get a line corresponding to the Growth phase, but it would continue both forward and backward indefinitely.

You need to restrict this portion of the line to the dates after the start of the Growth phase. To do that, change the formula to *=IF($A.Date<=Month,$A.Slope*Month+$A.Intercept,0)*.

This tests for whether the start date is less than or equal to the date of the current month. If so, it calculates the value for the month. If not, the value for the month is zero. This formula would still extrapolate the first phase out indefinitely.

You need to further restrict this portion of the line to the dates before the start of the Mature phase. To do that, change the formula to *=IF(AND($A.Date<=Month,$B.Date>Month),$A.Slope*Month+$A.Intercept,0)*. This creates a compound test for the first phase. The date of the current month must be both greater than or equal to the start of the phase and less than the start of the next phase. This formula correctly creates all the values—and only the values—for the first phase.

Expanding the formula to include the second phase appears more complicated than it really is. You simply replace the zero value in the formula with another copy of the entire formula. Then you convert the *Dates, Slope,* and *Intercept* to refer to the new phase. Here is the two-phase formula, broken into two lines to make the two phases easy to compare:

```
=IF(AND($A.Date<=Month,$B.Date>Month),$A.Slope*Month+$A.Intercept,
 IF(AND($B.Date<=Month,$C.Date>Month),$B.Slope*Month+$B.Intercept,0))
```

In brief, this formula says, "If I'm in the first phase, return the first phase value; otherwise, if I'm in the second phase, return the second phase value; otherwise, return zero."

Expanding the formula to include the third phase simply requires repeating the same process one more time. Here's the complete formula to calculate the entire lifecycle of a product:

```
=IF(AND($A.Date<=Month,$B.Date>Month),$A.Slope*Month+$A.Intercept,
IF(AND($B.Date<=Month,$C.Date>Month),$B.Slope*Month+$B.Intercept,
IF(AND($C.Date<=Month,$D.Date>Month),$C.Slope*Month+$C.Intercept,0)))
```

This is a triple-decker nested IF function with compound conditions. If you type it into a cell without adding spacing to make the phases align, you can really impress your friends. To add the spacing that makes it easy to read, use Alt+Enter at the end of each line and add two spaces at the beginning of the second and third lines.

Replacing IF Functions with Algebra

Think back to an arithmetic concept you learned in kindergarten: adding zero to a number doesn't change the number. By applying that seemingly simple concept to the forecasting formula, you can eliminate the need to nest the IF functions. If you give each of the three phases in the formula its own self-contained IF function, you can simply add the three phases together. As long as the expression for each phase returns 0 when it's out of range, the final answer will be correct. Here's the revised formula.

```
=IF(AND($A.Date<=Month,$B.Date>Month),$A.Slope*Month+$A.Intercept,0)
+IF(AND($B.Date<=Month,$C.Date>Month),$B.Slope*Month+$B.Intercept,0)
+IF(AND($C.Date<=Month,$D.Date>Month),$C.Slope*Month+$C.Intercept,0)
```

Think back to another arithmetic concept, one you learned in second grade: multiplying a number by one doesn't change the number, but multiplying by zero turns the number into 0. By applying that simple concept to the forecasting formula, you can eliminate the need for IF functions altogether. The expression *$A.Date<=Month* returns either *True* or *False*. When used in an arithmetic context, Excel treats the value *True* as 1, and the value *False* as 0. If you multiply the formula for the value of a phase by the expression that checks for whether the date is in range, you will get 0 when the date is out of range and the unchanged value when the date is in range. Here is the forecast formula without any functions at all:

```
=($A.Date<=Month)*($B.Date>Month)*($A.Slope*Month+$A.Intercept)
+($B.Date<=Month)*($C.Date>Month)*($B.Slope*Month+$B.Intercept)
+($C.Date<=Month)*($D.Date>Month)*($C.Slope*Month+$C.Intercept)
```

You need parentheses around the logical expressions to make Excel calculate the comparison before the multiplication. You need parentheses around the value expressions to make Excel calculate the addition before the multiplication.

In early versions of Excel, using arithmetic was faster than using IF functions. Formulas have now been optimized to the point where it doesn't make much difference. The choice between the three versions of the formula boils down to which one you find the easiest to understand.

Using the Forecast Model

The Forecast workbook accompanying this book contains a usable forecasting model, with three rows. Each of the three rows uses one of the three versions of the forecast formula.

The workbook contains two *Custom Views* to make it easy to show and hide the parameter columns. To show the detail, click Custom Views on the View menu and show the Detailed view. To hide the detail, show the Compact view.

The dates in the *Months* range are all end-of-month dates, and are adjusted based on the date in cell T1. That is, if you change the date in cell T1, all the other dates will automatically adjust in increments of one month.

The workbook has a macro associated with the Ctrl+Shift-plus (+) and Ctrl+Shift+minus (-) keys. If the active cell contains a date, press the Plus shortcut key to add one month to the date. Press the Minus shortcut key to subtract one month. If the active cell contains a number, press the Plus shortcut key to increment the value by 10. Press the Minus version to decrement the value by 10.

The formulas and macros for dealing with the dates are explained in "Manipulating Dates" at the beginning of the chapter.

The only named range in the worksheet is the *Months* range. If you want to change the number of months in the forecast, you will need to adjust that named range. Everywhere else, the worksheet uses column labels, so to add a new product, simply copy one of the existing rows down to a new, blank row. The product names are duplicated in column S to make it easy to change the source data range of the graph: show the Detailed custom view, and then use the contiguous range of cells as the chart's source data range.

Chapter 15

Extract Information from Lists

In This Chapter

A few years ago, when the Microsoft Excel design group first began extensively researching actual usage patterns, they were surprised to learn how much Excel was used to manipulate lists. Partly because of that research, Excel provides extensive tools for working with lists in various forms. You can sort and filter lists, link lists to databases, and slice and dice lists with PivotTable reports. You can even share lists—and other workbooks—for multiple users to simultaneously edit. This chapter will explore some of the less familiar—but extremely powerful—Excel list capabilities.

Filtering a List

Note The sample document for this section is Lists.xls.

In addition to sorting a list (which is ridiculously easy to do), you also might want to filter a list, hiding some of the rows. You are undoubtedly familiar with adding an AutoFilter to a list but AutoFilters and Advanced Filters might provide additional capabilities you have not yet explored.

Utilizing AutoFilters, you have a list of all the previous quarter order totals by product and by customer. Figure 15-1 shows the beginning of a list, sorted by product and by reseller.

	A	B	C	D	E	F	G	H
1	**Product**	**Line**	**Reseller**	**Channel**	**Contract**	**Units**		
2	Pteradon	Dinosaur	Hiabuv Toys	Toys	C5055	7,650		
3	Elephant	Animal	West Coast Sal	Distrib	C5017	1,650		
4	Tyranosaurus	Dinosaur	Wide World Imp	Distrib	C5068	300		
5	Aardvark	Animal	Baldwin Museur	Museums	C5028	7,350		
6	Brontosaurus	Dinosaur	West Coast Sal	Distrib	C5017	4,050		
7	Elephant	Animal	Industrial Smok	Retail	C5038	-		
8	Pteradon	Dinosaur	Wide World Imp	Distrib	C5068	450		

Figure 15-1
Excel has great tools for manipulating lists.

Your job is to generate a forecast for each product and for each company. You can use the historical values as a starting point.

Using AutoFilter to Limit Changes to Rows

Suppose you need to change the channel in all the rows for Industrial Smoke and Mirrors from the value *Retail* to the value *Distrib*. You can use AutoFilter to filter and display just the reseller you need.

Click any single cell in the list. Click Filter on the Data menu, AutoFilter. Excel immediately transforms each column heading into a drop-down list with arrows in the upper row of each column. You filter the list by selecting an item from one of the drop-down list. From the Reseller list, for example, select Industrial Smoke And Mirrors. Excel hides all rows except those for the reseller you selected, changing the color of the row numbers to blue in the process. (You can tell that rows are hidden because there are gaps in the row number sequence.) Change the channel in the first visible row to *Distrib.*

Now you can fill the channel down using the AutoFill handle. Select cell D7, the first visible cell in the Channel column, and double-click the AutoFill handle. Excel selects only the visible cells before extending the value, as shown in Figure 15-2. Select (All) from the list of resellers to see that only the selected rows were changed.

D7 = Distrib

	A	B	C	D	E	F	G	H
1	**Product**	**Line**	**Reseller**	**Channe**	**Contrac**	**Units**		
12	Automobile	Vehicle	Industrial Smok	Distrib	C5038	150		
13	Zebra	Animal	Wingtip Toys	Toys	C5015	-		
14	Elephant	Animal	Wingtip Toys	Toys	C5015	-		
15	Tyranosaurus	Dinosaur	Hiabuv Toys	Toys	C5055	2,400		
16	Elephant	Animal	Baldwin Museur	Museums	C5028	1,200		
17	Tyranosaurus	Dinosaur	West Coast Sal	Distrib	C5017	2,100		
18	Elephant	Animal	Lakes & Sons	Distrib	C5004	750		
19	Giraffe	Animal	Lakes & Sons	Distrib	C5004	1,350		
20	Train	Vehicle	Lakes & Sons	Distrib	C5004	3,750		

Figure 15-2
Excel changes only the visible rows when you double-click the AutoFill handle.

You now need to delete all the rows for one of the resellers. To delete rows from a list, simply filter the list to show the rows you want to delete, and then delete them. Excel preserves all the hidden rows. To avoid the confirmation dialog box when you delete rows from a filtered list, select the row numbers on the left side of the list. This selects the entire row. If the entire row is selected when you click the Delete Row command on the Edit menu, Excel will not ask you for confirmation.

Note Most changes you make to a filtered list automatically apply only to the visible rows.

Explicitly Selecting Filtered Cells

You want to increase each unit value for the Hiabuv Toys Company to 120 percent of the current quantities. The Paste Special dialog box is an effective way to multiply a entire range of cells by a constant. Unfortunately, the Paste Special dialog box pastes a value on to both the visible and invisible rows. Rather than sacrifice this extremely useful tool, you can manually select only the visible rows before you use the Paste Special command. To do that, type *120%* into cell H1 (or any convenient empty cell) and then copy that cell. Select Hiabuv Toys from the list of resellers to filter the rows. Select the range F2:F119 (the visible cells from the Units column). Press Ctrl+G to display the Go To dialog box. Click Special, select the Visible Cells Only option (as shown in Figure 15-3), and click OK.

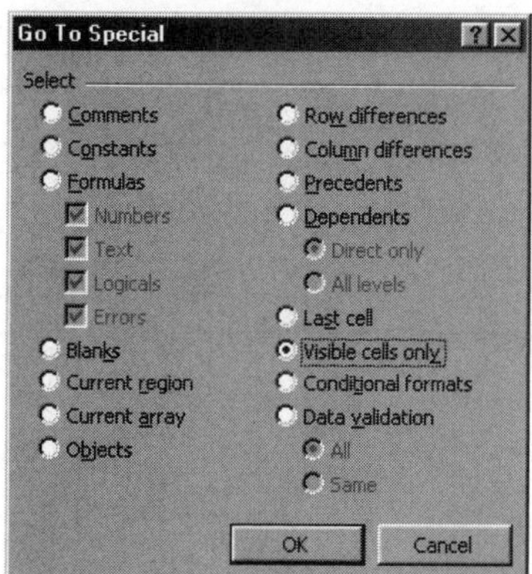

Figure 15-3
When using Paste Special in a filtered list, you must manually select the visible rows.

After confirming that you can see distinctive white lines between the rows—indicating that only the visible cells will be affected by the next command—click Paste Special on the Edit menu, enable both the Values and the Multiply options, and click OK. (Clear the cell containing the temporary 120 percent value.) Your result will be similar to the worksheet shown in Figure 15-4.

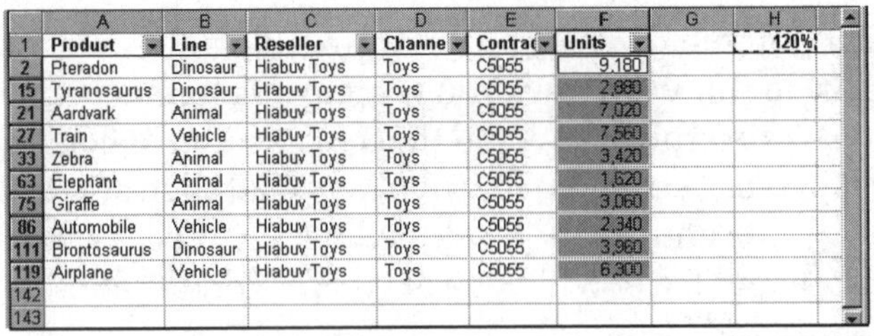

	A	B	C	D	E	F	G	H
1	Product	Line	Reseller	Channe	Contrac	Units		120%
2	Pteradon	Dinosaur	Hiabuv Toys	Toys	C5055	9,180		
15	Tyranosaurus	Dinosaur	Hiabuv Toys	Toys	C5055	2,880		
21	Aardvark	Animal	Hiabuv Toys	Toys	C5055	7,020		
27	Train	Vehicle	Hiabuv Toys	Toys	C5055	7,560		
33	Zebra	Animal	Hiabuv Toys	Toys	C5055	3,420		
63	Elephant	Animal	Hiabuv Toys	Toys	C5055	1,620		
75	Giraffe	Animal	Hiabuv Toys	Toys	C5055	3,060		
86	Automobile	Vehicle	Hiabuv Toys	Toys	C5055	2,340		
111	Brontosaurus	Dinosaur	Hiabuv Toys	Toys	C5055	3,960		
119	Airplane	Vehicle	Hiabuv Toys	Toys	C5055	6,300		
142								
143								

Figure 15-4
When you manually select visible cells, you see gaps within the selection.

Excel normally applies changes only to the visible rows in a filtered list. When you use Paste Special, however, you can manually select only the visible cells by using the Go To Special dialog box. Use this manual selection option when you don't want to take chances with values in the hidden rows in a filtered list.

Summarizing Filtered Values

Suppose you want to display the average monthly units across products for a particular reseller. You can use the AutoFilter feature to display only the rows for that one reseller, but the AVERAGE function will calculate the average of all resellers, whether they are visible or not. In addition to avoiding double counting, the SUBTOTAL function also ignores any cells that are hidden in a filtered list. (For more details about the SUBTOTAL function, see "Taking Advantage of the Subtotal Function" in Chapter 14.)

Start by creating a place to calculate the average. Insert two blank rows at the top of the worksheet. Type the formula *=SUBTOTAL(1, Units)* into cell F1 and press Enter. For the SUBTOTAL function, the value *1* calculates an average for the first argument. You can use a column label from a list to specify a range for the second argument. When all the rows in the list are visible, the formula calculates the average for the entire list, as shown in Figure 15-5.

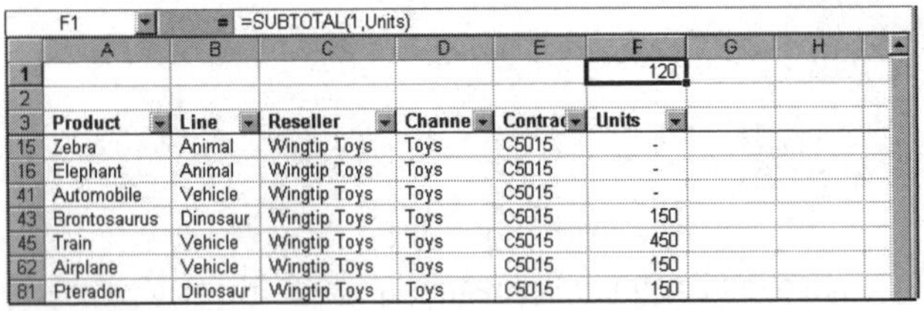

F1 = =SUBTOTAL(1,Units)

	A	B	C	D	E	F	G	H
1						120		
2								
3	Product	Line	Reseller	Channe	Contrac	Units		
15	Zebra	Animal	Wingtip Toys	Toys	C5015	-		
16	Elephant	Animal	Wingtip Toys	Toys	C5015	-		
41	Automobile	Vehicle	Wingtip Toys	Toys	C5015	-		
43	Brontosaurus	Dinosaur	Wingtip Toys	Toys	C5015	150		
45	Train	Vehicle	Wingtip Toys	Toys	C5015	450		
62	Airplane	Vehicle	Wingtip Toys	Toys	C5015	150		
81	Pteradon	Dinosaur	Wingtip Toys	Toys	C5015	150		

Figure 15-5
The SUBTOTAL function ignores rows that are hidden by filtering.

When you filter the list, the formulas will ignore everything except the visible cells. Watch the average change by selecting the reseller Wingtip Toys. You can verify that the subtotal is a correct average by replacing all the quarter totals for the reseller with a single value. In cell F1, type *460*. Then copy the cell and paste it into the visible Unit cells. The white stripes that appear between each row show you that Excel deselected all the hidden cells so that you could paste the number only into the visible rows. The average at the top of the worksheet changes to show that the new average is also 460, confirming that the AVERAGE function works correctly.

The SUBTOTAL function is an effective tool to summarize numbers from a filtered list. It ignores only those rows hidden by filtering, not rows that you hide using the Format Rows command. Once again, you can see that common operations—such as pasting values—automatically apply only to the visible rows.

Customizing a Filter

Suppose that after making changes for two resellers, you want to change all the remaining resellers. You need to hide the two resellers you already changed, while leaving all the other resellers visible. Each AutoFilter drop-down list contains a Custom option. The Custom option allows you to create complex criteria for a filter.

Select (Custom) from the Reseller drop-down list. The first drop-down list in the Custom AutoFilter dialog box gives you a selection of comparison operators, and the second drop-down list directly to the right shows a list of Resellers. To exclude a specific reseller, select Does Not Equal in the left drop-down list. In the drop-down list directly to the right, select Hiabuv Toys.

To exclude a second reseller, you need to combine two filters. The two lower drop-down list boxes serve the same purpose as the two upper list boxes. In the lower list box's group of operators, select Does Not Equal. In the drop-down list box directly to the right, select Wingtip Toys. To hide both resellers, leave the combination option under the first list box with the default And option button selected, and click OK to display all the remaining resellers, as shown in Figure 15-6.

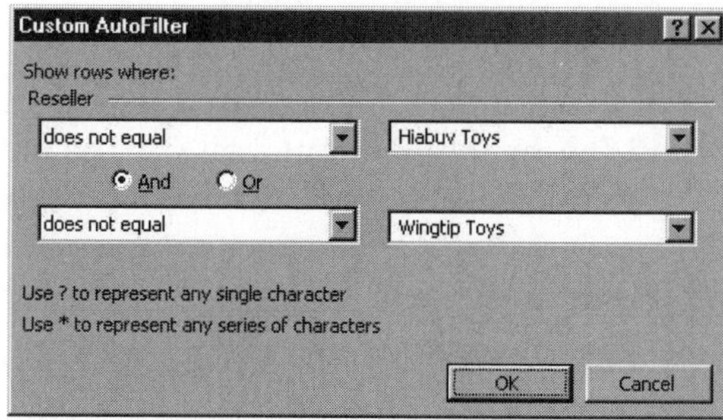

Figure 15-6
A Custom AutoFilter lets you combine conditions.

Note If you want to display only two resellers, use Equals for each of the comparison operators, and then select the Or option button to combine the two criteria.

Most of the time, you can use AutoFilter to select a simple value. Every now and then, however, you need a slightly more complex filter. The Custom dialog box gives you a few more options, while still being very easy to use.

Selecting Top Items from a List

You want to determine which resellers and which products are the most popular. First, make sure that all rows are displayed. To do that, on the Data menu, select Filter, and then click Show All. To filter the list to show 5 percent of the rows with the greatest numbers of units, select the item Top 10 from the AutoFilter drop-down list.

In the drop-down list for the Units column, select Top 10. The Top 10 AutoFilter dialog box lets you select from either the top or the bottom units, and it allows you to specify the number of items. (It doesn't have to be 10, in spite of the name displayed on the dialog box.) It allows you to choose between specifying the actual number of rows to show and specifying a percentage of the total rows to show. To show the top 5 percent of the rows, leave Top selected in the leftmost drop-down list box, click the down arrow to select 5 in the middle drop-down list, select percent in the drop-down list on the right, and click OK. The values in the Top 10 AutoFilter dialog box should look like Figure 15-7.

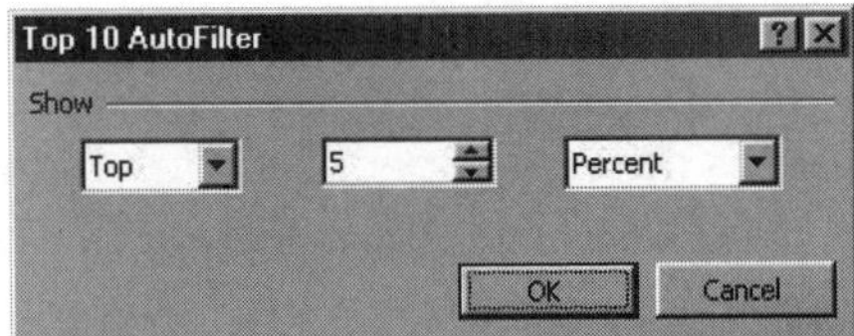

Figure 15-7
The Top 10 filter does more than AutoFilter the top 10.

Unfortunately, the Top 10 filter always looks at the entire list. You can't see, for example, the top 5 percent of the rows for the Dinosaur product line. If you select Dinosaur from the drop-down list for the Line column, you will see only one row, since there is only one Dinosaur product in the top 5 percent list. To see the top 5 percent of each product line, you can use a PivotTable report, as described in "Calculating in a PivotTable" later in this chapter.

Using Advanced Filters

AutoFilters are easy to use, but there are limits to what you can do with them. For example, you can't extract a portion of the list to a new location, you can't see the criteria you used to filter the list, and you can't create a list of unique values. Advanced Filters are slightly more complex than AutoFilters, but they give you much more control over the filtering process.

Creating a List of Unique Values

Suppose you want to extract a list of reseller names from the list. Extracting a list of unique values is a perfect task for an Advanced Filter. Start by selecting just the portion of the list you want to extract values from—the Reseller column. Excel uses the term *filter database* to refer to the range you will extract values from.

To use Advanced Filter to extract a list of unique values from this filter database, click Filter on the Data menu, and choose Advanced Filter. Select the Unique Records Only check box. In the Action group, select the Copy To Another Location option button. The List Range reference box should already contain the range $C$3:$C$143, as shown in Figure 15-8, which is the range you preselected as the filter database.

Figure 15-8
The List Range is called a filter database.

Note If you don't preselect a range before you use the Advanced Filter command, you will need to type the filter database range in the dialog box.

In the Copy To reference box, enter a blank cell off to the side of the list—perhaps cell H3. Select the Unique Records Only check box and click OK. When you scroll to see cell H3, you see the list of unique resellers Excel created. Looking at the extract, however, you realize that you really wanted not just the list of reseller names, but also their respective channels. Delete this extracted list and try again.

After you have used a subset of the list as the filter database, Excel remembers that subset and ignores the current selection the next time you use the Advanced Filter command. If you want to reset the Advanced Filter command, the easiest way is to Click Filter on the Data menu, and then click AutoFilter twice to enable and then disable AutoFilter.

Select both columns C and D within the list as your filter database. Click Filter on the Data menu and select, Advanced Filter. Select the Copy To Another Location option button. Make sure the List Range reference box contains the range $C$3:$D$133. Type *K3:L3* in the Copy To reference box. Select the Unique Records Only check box and click OK. Then scroll to cell K3. Widen column K as needed to fit the reseller names in the column.

Remember that if you ever try to use the Advanced Filter command with a portion of the list and the dialog box does not recognize the current selection, simply turn AutoFilter on and off to reset the list.

Note Excel uses the Extract range name to remember the range you specify as the Copy To range in the Advanced Filter dialog box. To remember the filter database, Excel uses the hidden name _FilterDatabase (complete with the underscore character as the first letter). Each time you turn AutoFilter on, Excel resets _FilterDatabase to the current region; Advanced Filter assigns _FilterDatabase when you click OK.

Advanced Filter uses the current definition for _FilterDatabase if either of the following are true:

1. AutoFilter is turned on.
2. AutoFilter is turned off and the _FilterDatabase range name does not match the current region—the block of cells surrounding the active cell.

To see the current definition of the _FilterDatabase range name, click Go To on the Edit menu and then type _FilterDatabase in the Reference box and press Enter.

Filtering Using a Criteria Range

The Advanced Filter dialog box contains an extra box labeled Criteria Range. A *criteria range* works like drop-down AutoFilter list boxes, except that you type the value you want to match in a cell rather than selecting it from a list. A criteria range requires a little more preparation than turning on AutoFilter lists, but it also has a couple of advantages. For example, you can easily see what you used as the criteria.

A criteria range consists of two rows on the worksheet. The top row contains column labels from the list. The second row contains the criteria you want to use. A good place to create a criteria range is at the top of a worksheet, above the list. Insert two new rows above row 1. Select cell A5, the label for the first column. Press Ctrl+Shift+Right arrow to select all the contiguous cells in the row (or hold down the Shift key and double-click the right edge of the cell). Copy the range and paste it into cell A1, as shown in Figure 15-9.

This pastes the labels for the criteria range. The criteria range also needs to include one blank row below the labels. Hold down the Shift key and press the Down arrow key to extend the selection to include one additional row.

A1 = Product

	A	B	C	D	E	F	G	H	
1	Product	Line	Reseller	Channel	Contract	Units			
2									
3						3,315			
4									
5	Product	Line	Reseller	Channel	Contract	Units		Reseller	Cl
6	Pteradon	Dinosaur	Hiabuv Toys	Toys	C5055	9,180		Hiabuv To	Tc
7	Elephant	Animal	West Coast Sal	Distrib	C5017	1,650		West Coa	Di
8	Tyranosaurus	Dinosaur	Wide World Imp	Distrib	C5068	300		Wide Wor	Di
9	Aardvark	Animal	Baldwin Museur	Museums	C5028	7,350		Baldwin M	M
10	Brontosaurus	Dinosaur	West Coast Sal	Distrib	C5017	4,050		Industrial	Di
11	Elephant	Animal	Industrial Smoke	Distrib	C5038	-		Main Stre	Re
12	Pteradon	Dinosaur	Wide World Imp	Distrib	C5068	450		Wingtip Ti	Tc
13	Giraffe	Animal	Main Street Mar	Retail	C5080	900		Lakes & S	Di

Figure 15-9
A useful criteria range copies headings from the list columns.

If you use the name Criteria for the criteria range, Excel will automatically know the range you want to use. Use a name that is local to the active worksheet, in case you add a criteria range to another worksheet in this workbook at a later time. (See "Managing Local and Global Names" in Chapter 12 for more information about using local names.)

Your criteria range is now ready. Suppose you want to see all the resellers in the retail channel who sell Elephant models. You must type the value you want to match under each of the labels, so you type *Elephant* in cell A2, and you type *Retail* in cell D2. Reset the filter list range by turning AutoFilter on and then off again. Select cell A5 (or any single cell in the list). On the Data menu, select Filter and then click Advanced Filter. Leave all the options with their default values, as shown in Figure 15-10, and click OK.

Figure 15-10
Advanced Filter automatically uses a range named Criteria.

As you can see in Figure 15-11, Excel filters away all rows except the three retail resellers who sell Elephants. You can also easily see the criteria that you used. By defining the range names, you enabled Excel to correctly fill in all the dialog box options for you.

When you type a text value into the criteria row, Excel searches for any cell that begins with the same characters you typed. If you want to search for a range of values, you can add a *comparison operator* at the beginning of a criteria field. For

A5 = Product

	A	B	C	D	E	F	G
1	**Product**	**Line**	**Reseller**	**Channel**	**Contract**	**Units**	
2	Elephant			Retail			
3						1,600	
4							
5	**Product**	**Line**	**Reseller**	**Channel**	**Contract**	**Units**	
28	Elephant	Animal	Enchantment La	Retail	C5064	1,050	
93	Elephant	Animal	Main Street Mar	Retail	C5080	450	
96	Elephant	Animal	Adventure Work	Retail	C5044	3,300	
146							
147							

Figure 15-11
An explicit criteria range is self-documenting.

example, to see all the resellers who ordered at least 2000 Elephants each quarter last year, clear cell D2 and type >=*2000* in cell F2. Then select cell A5 and click Filter on the Data menu and select, Advanced Filter. Then click OK. Excel displays only the three resellers that sold a lot of Elephants. Once again, you can easily see the criteria that gave you these three resellers in the list.

You can also use wildcard characters to specify criteria. Use a question mark (?) to match any single character, or an asterisk (*) to match one or more characters. For example, to see all the resellers whose contract numbers begins with C and ends with 1, clear cell F2 and type *C???1* in cell E2. Then select cell A5 and click Filter on the Data menu, and select Advanced Filter. Then click OK. Excel displays the two resellers that meet the criteria you specified.

Once you set up the criteria range, the Advanced Filter command is not much more difficult to use than the AutoFilter command, and it has the advantage of letting you see what the filter criteria was. If you are going to print a copy of the filtered list and distribute copies in a meeting, you might be grateful for the reminder.

Note When you type a text value in the criteria range, Excel treats it as if you typed an asterisk (*) at the end of the value. For example, if you type *C50* in the Contract column of the criteria range, Excel would interpret that as C50* and display all the rows that begin with the characters C50. To force Excel to match only cells that have exactly C50 as the contract, you must type the formula ="=*C50*" (with two equal signs) into the criteria range. The result of this formula is =*C50*.

This applies only to the Advanced Filter command. When you use the AutoFilter command's (Custom) option, you can use wildcard characters, but AutoFilter never assumes there is an asterisk at the end of the item.

Extracting a Portion of a List

You also can use Advanced Filter to extract a portion of a list. For example, suppose you want to create a list showing the reseller name, the contract number, and the units for all resellers who sell Aardvarks. You do not want all the columns from the original list, only the Reseller, Contract, and Units columns.

First, set the criteria range to select every reseller who sells Aardvarks by clearing all the cells in row 2 and then typing *Aardvark* in cell A2. If you want to extract only certain columns, you can create an extract range that includes only the column labels you want. The easiest way to make sure the labels are correct is to copy them from the original list. Holding down the Ctrl key as you select allows you to select nonadjacent cells. Copy cells C5, E5, and F5, and paste them into a range starting at cell H5. You can now use H5:J5 as the Copy To range in the Advanced Filter dialog box.

Select cell A5. Click Filter on the Data menu, select Advanced Filter, and select the Copy To Another Location option button. In the Copy To list box, type *H5:J5* and click OK. Then you can scroll to see that the extract range contains only the columns with specified labels.

The Advanced Filter command allows you to filter by both rows and columns. You use the criteria range to control the rows that will be used, and you use column labels in the extract area to control which columns are used.

Using Calculated Criteria to Select Random Rows

Suppose you want to select a random 2 percent of the rows in a list. One way to select a random 2 percent of the rows is to add an extra column to the list and type the formula *=RAND()<2 percent* (which would generate the value *True* approximately 2 percent of the time). Then, you use AutoFilter to select all the rows with the value *True.* You can accomplish the same result using the Advanced Filter command, without having to add an extra column to the list.

Normally, when you create a criteria range, you fill the top row with the column labels from the list. If you use a label that does not appear in the list, you create what is called a *calculated criterion.* A calculated criterion adds a virtual column of formulas to the list. You add the sample formula in the cell below the label. Excel then, in effect, adds an exact copy of that formula into a cell in the first row of the list and copies the formula to the rest of the list. Each row where the formula returns a *True* value meets the criterion.

One way to create a calculated criterion is to replace one of the labels in a regular criteria range with a word like Calc. Type *Calc* in cell A1. Because the word Calc does not match any of the column labels, cell A2 is now a calculated criterion. Clear all the cells in row 2 and type *=RAND()<2 percent* in cell A2. This is the formula that Excel will virtually copy to each row of the list. The Advanced Filter command will display any row where the formula returns *True.* Select cell A5, click Filter on the Data menu, select Advanced Filter, and click OK. Excel displays approximately 2 percent of the rows, as shown in Figure 15-12. If you repeat the Advanced Filter command, different rows will remain visible.

A2 = =RAND()<2%

	A	B	C	D	E	F	G	H
1	Calc	Line	Reseller	Channel	Contract	Units		
2	FALSE							
3						2,700		
4								
5	Product	Line	Reseller	Channel	Contract	Units		
23	Giraffe	Animal	Lakes & Sons	Distrib	C5004	1,350		
27	Airplane	Vehicle	West Coast Sal	Distrib	C5017	2,550		
80	Giraffe	Animal	Mightyflight Toy:	Toys	C5011	4,200		
146								
147								
148								

Figure 15-12

A criteria label that doesn't match a list column creates a calculated criteria.

Using Calculated Criteria to Compare Columns

You can also use calculated criterion to compare the value in one column with that in another. For example, suppose you want to see the rows where the first letter of the product name matches the first letter of the reseller name. Because you could add a new column with the formula *=Left(Product,1)=Left(Reseller,1)*, you also could use that formula as a calculated criterion.

In cell A2, type the formula *=Left(Product,1)=Left(Reseller,1)*. Even though the formula in the criteria range displays an error, it calculates properly when it is virtually copied to the list. Select cell A5, click Filter on the Data menu, and select Advanced Filter. Then click OK. Excel displays the matching rows, as shown in Figure 15-13.

A2 = =LEFT(Product,1)=LEFT(Reseller,1)

	A	B	C	D	E	F	G	H
1	Calc	Line	Reseller	Channel	Contract	Units		
2	#VALUE!							
3						6,475		
4								
5	Product	Line	Reseller	Channel	Contract	Units		
28	Elephant	Animal	Enchantment La	Retail	C5064	1,050		
29	Automobile	Vehicle	Adventure Work	Retail	C5044	2,250		
54	Aardvark	Animal	Adventure Work	Retail	C5044	9,750		
86	Pteradon	Dinosaur	Peck n Order To	Toys	C5001	8,850		
106	Brontosaurus	Dinosaur	Baldwin Museur	Museums	C5028	4,350		
125	Airplane	Vehicle	Adventure Work	Retail	C5044	12,600		
146								
147								

Figure 15-13

A calculated criterion can compare values from different columns.

Note If you want to use cell addresses rather than column labels, type the addresses as if you were typing them into a cell in the first row of the database. For this example, where the list begins on row 5, you could type *=G6*3>F6* as the formula.

You also can make a calculated criterion refer to a cell that is not in the list. Just use dollar signs ($) to create an absolute cell reference.

Many Excel users are unaware of calculated criteria, possibly because the feature is not mentioned anywhere in Excel's Help files. You can always avoid calculated criteria simply by adding additional columns to your list. But once you understand the secret of calculated criteria, they are not hard to use.

Integrating a List with a Database

Note The sample documents for this section are Query.xls and Forecast.mdb.

Managing order history and other information can be cumbersome in Excel worksheets. It is often more efficient to store the information in a database from which you can retrieve the information you need—when you need it. (The introduction in Chapter 17 discusses some of the reasons why you might want to move data from an Excel worksheet into a database.) The database contains master copies of critical lists, but it is often convenient to have working copies in Excel workbooks. You can link a list to a database so that you will always have a fresh copy of the master list.

Extracting a List from a Database

Suppose you have a master copy of a product list in a database. Anyone who wants the list in a spreadsheet should retrieve a copy. You can easily create a dynamic list—called a *QueryTable*—to retrieve the product list from the database.

Creating a New Data Source

To retrieve a list, you need to create a query. When you create a query, Excel launches the Microsoft Query application to communicate with the database. (The Microsoft Query component of Excel is not included as part of the default installation. You will need your installation media the first time you use Microsoft Query.)

Click Get External Data on the Data menu, and select New Database Query to launch Microsoft Query. The database from which you retrieve the information is a *data source*. The first time you retrieve information from a database, you need to create a new data source.

In the Create New Data Source dialog box, select New Data Source and click OK. You can communicate with a database from any vendor as long as the vendor provides a driver that translates between the database and Microsoft Query. When you create a new data source, you give the data source a name so that you can use it again in the future. You must also specify which database driver to use.

Type *ForecastDB* as the name of the data source and press the Tab key. In the Select A Driver drop-down list, select Microsoft Access Driver (*.mdb). Each driver has a different way of identifying the database you might choose, and some databases will require a user login and password. Once you specify the database driver, a dialog box specific to the driver appears to connect to the database, as shown in Figure 15-14.

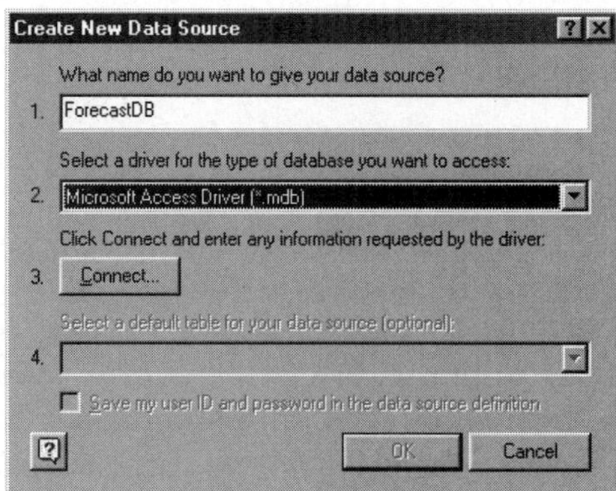

Figure 15-14
Once you specify a driver, you can connect to the database.

Click the Connect button to display the ODBC Microsoft Access Setup dialog box. In the Database group, click the Select button. Navigate to the folder containing the database. Then, click OK twice to finish defining the new data source.

Note You need to create a new data source only the first time you use it.

Retrieving a List from a Database

Once the data source exists, you can retrieve a list from the database. In the Choose Data Source dialog box, select ForecastDB. Make sure that the Use The Query Wizard check box is selected and click OK. The Query Wizard - Choose Column dialog box will display a list of tables and queries in the database. Clicking the Options button will display the Table Options dialog box shown in Figure 15-15, which allows you to choose the database objects you want to include.

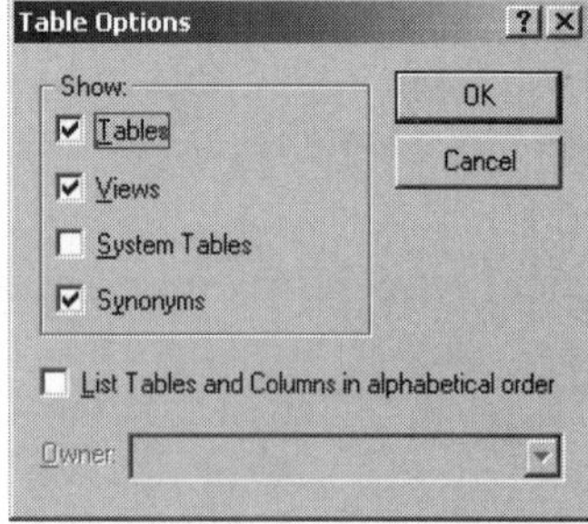

Figure 15-15
You can display queries as if they were tables.

If you double-click one of the table names in the list, you will see a list of all the columns in that table. If you want to use all the columns from a table, you can simply select the table name. Select tblProduct from the list of tables and click the right-pointing arrow (>) in the center of the dialog box to move the table's columns from the list on the left into the Columns In Your Query list on the right, as shown in Figure 15-16.

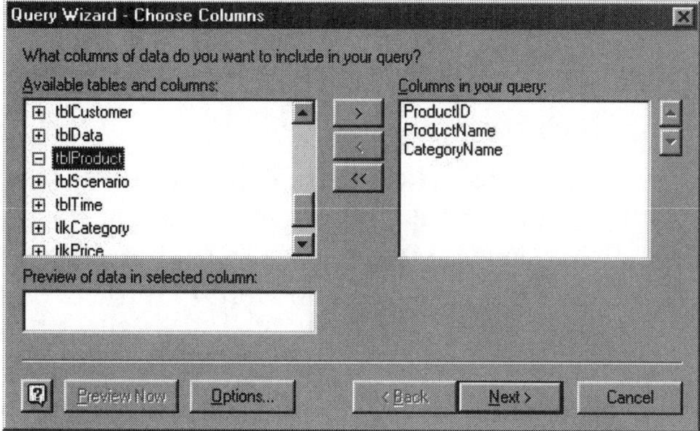

Figure 15-16
Click the table name to add all the columns from the table.

That's all you need to do if you are going to retrieve the entire table into the worksheet. Click the Next button three times and then click Finish. When you are prompted where you want to place the list, just click OK. The products list will appear in the Excel worksheet, as shown in Figure 15-17.

A1 = ProductID

	A	B	C
1	ProductID	ProductName	CategoryName
2	1	Bratwurst	Meats
3	2	Dried Apples	Produce
4	3	Gnocci	Cereals
5	4	Pasties	Meats
6	5	Pate	Meats
7	6	Sauerkraut	Produce
8	7	Tofu	Produce
9	8	Tourtiere	Meats
10	9	Tunnbrod	Cereals
11			
12			

Figure 15-17
When you retrieve a list, it retains a link to the data source.

If the values in the database change, you can update the values by refreshing the list. To refresh the table, either click the Refresh Data command on the Data menu or click the Refresh Data button on the External Data toolbar.

The Query Wizard is an effective tool for creating simple queries. As long as you can define the data source, the Query Wizard can help you select the records you want. In addition to using the Query Wizard, you can directly design or modify a query in Microsoft Query. For certain types of requests, you must directly interact with Microsoft Query.

Retrieving a Filtered List from a Database

As you add products to the database in the future, you might not want to retrieve the entire list of products. You can add a filter—or criteria—to a query, limiting the retrieved rows to those that meet the criteria. So that you can have as much control as possible over the definition of the query, you can bypass the Query Wizard and work directly with Microsoft Query.

With any cell selected in the query list, click the Edit Query button on the External Data toolbar. Click the Next button three times to get to the last step of the Query Wizard. Choose Column dialog box you used. Select the option View Data Or Edit Query In Microsoft Query and click Finish. If you want to retrieve only the products with Meats as the category name, for example, click one of the Meats cells, and then click the Criteria Equals button. A criteria grid will appear that is similar to the bottom portion of the field grid in Access. The criteria grid contains the Criteria Field and Value, as shown in Figure 15-18.

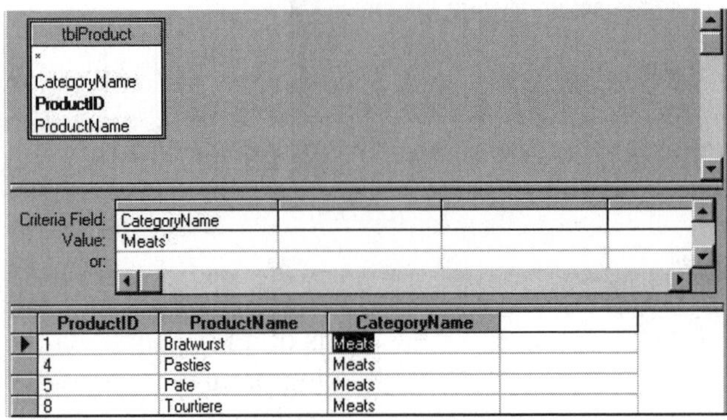

Figure 15-18
Microsoft Query is a simplified version of the Microsoft Access Query editor.

If you want to be able to switch which category you select, you can replace the criteria value with a *parameter*, which is simply a prompt that allows you to specify a value at the time the query executes. To create a parameter, replace a value in the criteria area with a prompt surrounded by square brackets. For example, replace the word *Meats* in the criteria area with the text *[Category Name]*. Then press Enter. As soon as you press Enter, Microsoft Query executes the query and prompts you for the parameter value. If you type *Produce* as the parameter value, the grid will display all the products having that category name. When you close Microsoft Query, you will be able to specify a parameter value when you execute the query from Excel.

On the File menu, click Return Data To Microsoft Excel. The table in Excel displays only the three produce products. To query again with a new parameter value, click the Refresh Data button.

A *parameter query* allows you to interactively adjust the criteria for a list you retrieve from a database. You can even use the value of a cell to determine the parameter value for criteria.

In cell E1, type *Cereals*, and then click cell A1 (or any cell in the query list). On the External Data toolbar, click the Query Parameters button. Select the option Get The Value From The Following Cell, click cell E1, and select the Refresh Automatically When Cell Value Changes check box in the Parameters dialog box, as shown in Figure 15-19. Then click OK. Click the Refresh Data button on the External Data toolbar to update the list. The list will change to display the two cereals.

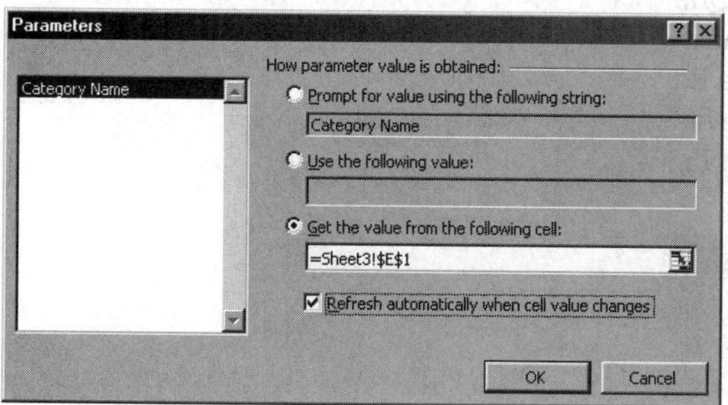

Figure 15-19
Link a parameter to a worksheet cell.

Using criteria allows you to retrieve only portions of a list. Adding parameters allows you to dynamically change the criteria. Linking parameters to cells allows you to avoid a dialog box, or to create formulas to calculate the appropriate value.

Manipulating a List with a PivotTable

Note The sample document for this section is Pivot.xls.

A PivotTable is a great way to review and analyze numerical data. Whether the numbers are in a local Excel list or a corporate database, you can use a PivotTable to analyze them.

Linking a PivotTable to a Data Source

Linking a PivotTable to a database is very similar to retrieving a list from a database. Once you specify that you want to use an external data source, you specify the source and then use the Query Wizard to define the data you will bring into the PivotTable.

Retrieving Data From a Database into a PivotTable

Click PivotTable And PivotChart Report on the Data menu. In step 1 of the PivotTable and PivotChart Wizard, double-click the External Data Source option. In step 2 of the Wizard, click the Get Data button. The Choose Data Source dialog box appears, precisely the same as when querying a list. Double-click the ForecastDB data source.

Add all the fields from the table qryDataX. The Query Wizard is defining a query that the PivotTable can use to retrieve data from the database. As you continue, you will return the definition of the query to the PivotTable Wizard; Excel uses Microsoft Query only to create the query definition. Once you have created a PivotTable, Excel refreshes the data by going directly to the data source. Figure 15-20 shows the qryDataX query.

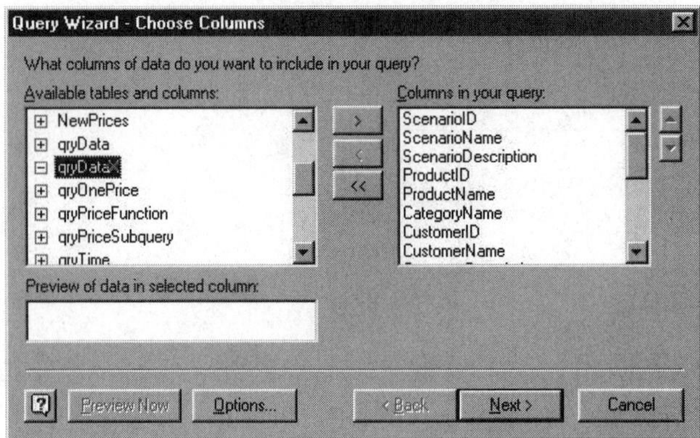

Figure 15-20
Add the table name to add all the columns from the table.

The qryDataX query contains numerical ID codes that are meaningless in Excel. Before returning the query, remove each of the three columns with ID as the column name suffix. When you remove a column from the query, select the column name and click the single left-pointing arrow (<) in the center of the dialog box. (If you click the double arrow, you will remove all the columns from the query.)

Click the Next button three times, and make sure the option Return Data To Microsoft Excel is selected. Then click Finish. You are back in step 2 of the PivotTable wizard, but now the message in the box is telling you that data fields have been retrieved. The PivotTable has not yet retrieved the data from the database, but it has retrieved the names of all the columns. You can now define the appearance of the PivotTable.

Note If you want to change the definition of the query once you have created the PivotTable, select a cell anywhere within the PivotTable, display the PivotTable Wizard, click the Back button to get back to step 2 of 3 above, and click the Get External Data button.

Click Finish to create the shell of the PivotTable on the worksheet. Then drag the ScenarioName button onto the page area. (To tell the difference between two field names that begin with similar letters—such as ScenarioName and ScenarioDescription, hold the mouse pointer over the field button.)

Drag the CustomerName button on to the page area, drag the ProductName button on to the row area, and drag the Units button on to the data area. The ScenarioName field contains different types of forecasts. If the value of the ScenarioName field drop-down list is All, you will double-count forecasts. Instead, select Corporate in the ScenarioName field drop-down list.

Excel normally retrieves all the data for the PivotTable and places it into a cache—or holding place—when you create a PivotTable. You might not want to retrieve all the information at one time if the database is large. When a PivotTable links to an external data source, you can add a page field configured to retrieve only the rows from the database that match the one field. This is particularly useful when you have a field—such as ScenarioName—where you want to select only a single value at a time; linking the page field to the database eliminates the All option.

To convert the ScenarioName field, double-click the field button in the page area, and then click the Advanced button. In the Page Field Options group, select the second option, Query External Data Source As You Select Each Page Field Item (Requires Less Memory), as shown in Figure 15-21. Then click OK twice.

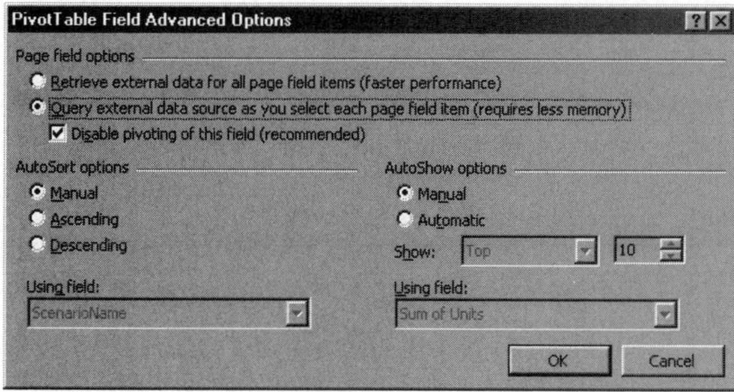

Figure 15-21
You can restrict data to a single page field item.

When you click Finish to create the PivotTable, Excel first retrieves the list of unique values for the ScenarioName field. It then arbitrarily selects the first scenario and retrieves only the data for that one scenario. (Watch the status bar as the PivotTable communicates with the data source, both as you create the PivotTable and as you change the page field item.) Setting one page field to retrieve a single item at a time does not affect any other page fields you might have.

Click Finish. Then change the ScenarioName field from *Corporate* to *Customer*. Each time you change the item in the page field, Excel reconnects to the data source and retrieves the new information; the first query takes far longer than subsequent queries. If you have a large database and a single page field accounts for relatively few of the rows, you might want to link the page field to the database. However, if the data source is relatively small, you might find the PivotTable more responsive if you retrieve all the information into the cache at one time.

Note A PivotTable that retrieves data for a single page field item cannot share its cache with other PivotTables in the workbook. If you create multiple PivotTables from a single data source, you might use less memory if you base all the PivotTables on a single cache than if you were to make each PivotTable retrieve its own data, one page field item at a time.

When you retrieve data from an external database into a PivotTable, you have several options, depending on how large the database is and what kind of analysis you will perform in the PivotTable. You can use the Query Wizard or Microsoft Query to filter the rows before they ever get to the PivotTable. You can use page fields to retrieve only a portion of the rows at a time, or you can import the entire data source into the PivotTable cache.

New!

Using an OLAP Data Source

A new feature in Office 2000 is the ability to integrate a PivotTable with an OLAP Cube. (For a description of the OLAP acronym, see the introduction of Chapter 17.) The following two sections explain how to create an OLAP Cube, and they also show how a PivotTable based on an OLAP Cube differs from a traditional PivotTable.

In the final step of the Query Wizard, you are given the option of creating an OLAP Cube from the query, as shown in Figure 15-22.

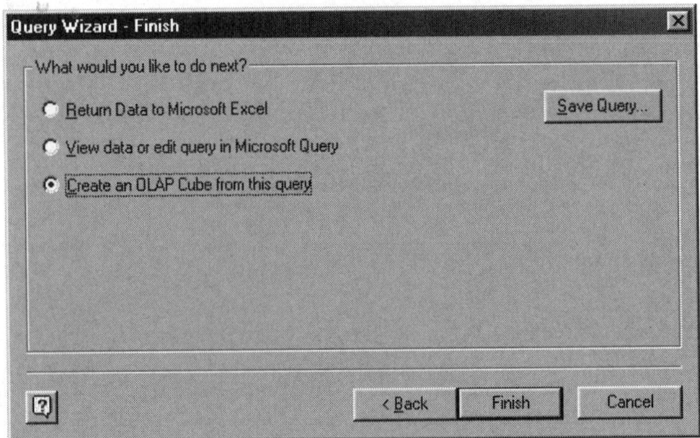

Figure 15-22
You can create an OLAP Cube from an ordinary query.

If you choose to create an OLAP Cube, the Query Wizard will launch the OLAP Cube Wizard when you click Finish. The first step of the OLAP Cube wizard allows you to select the data fields for the OLAP Cube, as shown in Figure 15-23.

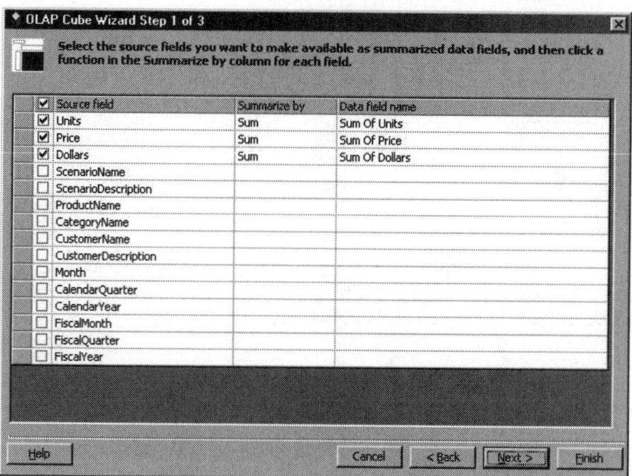

Figure 15-23
An OLAP Cube contains summarized numbers as data fields.

The OLAP Cube Wizard suggests that you sum each numeric field in the data source. In addition to Sum, you can choose Count, Min, and Max. You cannot choose Average, or any of the other calculation methods available for a PivotTable field. If you add a text field as a data field, Count is the only summarization option.

Step 2 of the OLAP Cube Wizard allows you to group related text fields from the data source into dimensions. A dimension is a hierarchically arranged grouping of fields. When you add a date/time field—such as Month—to the list of dimensions, the wizard automatically generates common summary levels—Day, Month, Quarter, and Year. If you have fields in the database that calculate these time periods, you do not need to add them to the dimension. If you have calculated fiscal date fields in the database, you can create a separate dimension for the alternate hierarchy. You should always combine logically related fields—such as Product Category and Product Name—into a single hierarchy. Figure 15-24 shows the most likely dimensions for the Forecast database.

The final step of the OLAP Cube Wizard lets you decide how to store the cube. You can store it simply as a definition—so that the values are refreshed from the database as you use them—or you can store the data values themselves on your computer. This final option, as shown in Figure 15-25, is useful if you need to extract data from a data source on a network source to a notebook computer so that you can perform analyses, even when you are disconnected from the network.

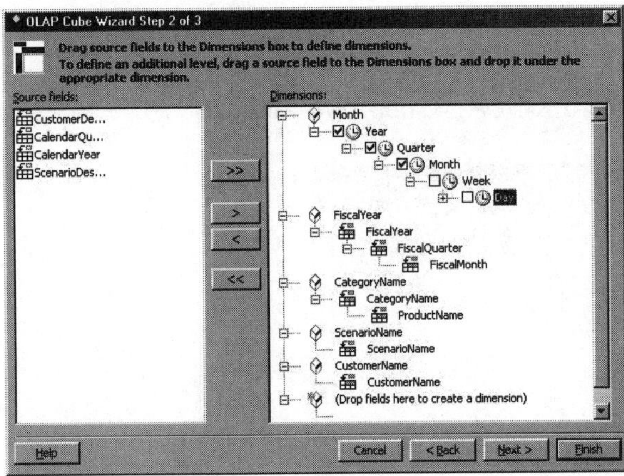

Figure 15-24
Dimensions group related fields into hierarchies.

Microsoft Excel - Lookups.xls

E2 =VLOOKUP(D2,Grades,2)

Points	Grade		Student	Grade
950	A		960	F
900	A-		910	F
850	B+		760	F
800	B		620	#N/A
750	B-		510	#N/A
700	C+		380	#N/A
650	C			
600	C-			
550	D+			
500	D			
450	D-			
400	F			

Discounts / Prices / Grades - Bad / Grades - Good

Ready NUM

Figure 15-25
You can store just the definition, or you can store the entire cube.

Once you have created an OLAP Cube as the source for a PivotTable, some of the PivotTable behaviors change. For example, in the list of fields, you see only one field for each dimension. All fields in the hierarchy are automatically included. Once you have added a dimension to the PivotTable, you can select items from any level of the hierarchy, as shown in Figure 15-26.

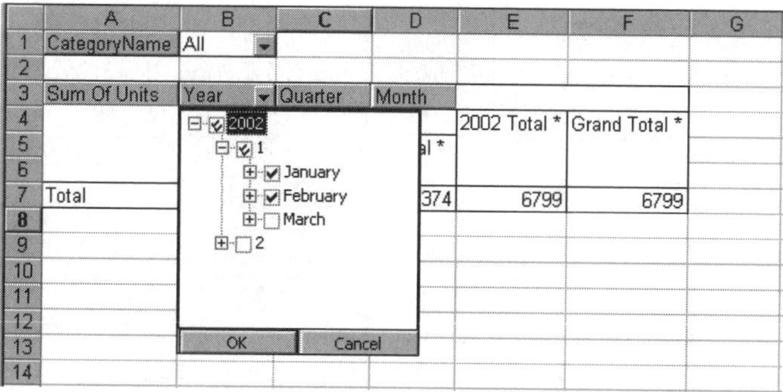

Figure 15-26
In an OLAP PivotTable, you can select from multiple levels in a hierarchy.

Understanding an OLAP PivotTable

An OLAP Cube can be based either on the server or as a cube file on your own computer. Two different tools manage these cube files:

- On the server side, a cube is created and managed by an OLAP product, such as the Microsoft SQL Server OLAP Services 7.0, which is an Enterprise Data Warehousing solution.
- On the client side, a cube is managed by the Microsoft OLE DB Provider for OLAP Services that ships with Office 2000.

The OLE DB Provider that ships with Office 2000 actually serves two roles. On the one hand, it creates and manages local cube files, either by retrieving data from a traditional data source using Microsoft Query, or by slicing a piece of a server-based cube using the Client/Server Settings command on the PivotTable toolbar. On the other hand, even if you are linking to a server-based cube, the OLE DB provider communicates with that server cube. When a server database provides a cube, an Excel PivotTable uses the OLE DB provider to link directly to the server cube. If the data source is a traditional database, you can choose whether to create an OLAP Cube for the PivotTable data.

It might be helpful to understand the differences between a traditional PivotTable and an OLAP PivotTable.

First, in a regular PivotTable, all the detail is pulled into a pivot cache in your computer's memory, and the summary values are calculated at the time they are displayed. In an OLAP PivotTable, the values are presummarized on the server (or in the cube), and only the summarized values are pulled into your computer's memory. This can make a file with an OLAP PivotTable open faster and require less memory; it doesn't need to load the PivotTable cache with detail values. If the cube

(continued)

Understanding an OLAP PivotTable *(continued)*

is on the network with a slow network connection, it can make it slower to change a PivotTable because the new data must be retrieved from the server. Also, you can no longer specify new ways to dynamically aggregate the data (for example, by switching from a Sum to an Average), because the summarization was predefined on the server.

Second—and this tremendously affects the way you interact with the PivotTable—each row and column field in a regular pivot table is independent of any other, while an OLAP PivotTable understands that some fields belong in a hierarchical relationship with one another. For example, if you have a field containing dates (let's say the field is named Month) in a regular PivotTable, you can group the dates to create new fields such as Quarter and Year. But once those new fields are created, they are all independent. You can move both the Quarter and the Month fields to the page area and then select Quarter 1 from the Quarter field and September from the Month field, even if September is not in Quarter 1. In an OLAP Cube, on the other hand, the Year, Quarter, and Month fields are sure to be defined in a hierarchical relationship. If you try dragging the Month field to the page area, it's the Year field—the top field in the hierarchy—that actually moves there. When you select an item from the list, you get a hierarchical tree view display that prevents you from selecting an illogical combination.

The same is true, of course, if you group your products into product lines. In a regular pivot table, you could select Go Carts in the Product Line page field and Climber Bike in the Product page field, even though the two choices do not intersect. In a properly structured OLAP Cube, the hierarchical relationship between the product line and the products would be predefined.

Calculating in a PivotTable

A PivotTable creates summary calculations as a matter of course. A PivotTable also can create less orthodox—but analytically interesting—calculations.

Finding the Top Values for a Dimension

Using AutoFilter, you can select the top items from a list, but not from subgroups within a list. With a PivotTable, you can sort and select based on rankings within a category.

Create a new PivotTable based on the qryDataX query in the ForecastDB data source. Once you have created the shell of the PivotTable, drag the ScenarioName field button to the page area and select the Corporate scenario. Then drag the CategoryName field and the CustomerName field buttons to the row area, and drag the Dollars field button to the data area. Since you will not be making changes to the page field or to the data, hide rows 1 through 3 to eliminate clutter. The PivotTable should look like the one shown in Figure 15-27.

A4 = CategoryName

	A	B	C	D	E
4	CategoryName	CustomerName	Total		
5	Produce	Lazy K	8037		
6		Trail's Head	10991		
7		White Clover	8187		
8	Produce Total		27215		
9	Meats	Lazy K	15171		
10		Trail's Head	19923		
11		White Clover	14980		
12	Meats Total		50074		
13	Cereals	Lazy K	13995		
14		Trail's Head	7250		
15		White Clover	15305		
16	Cereals Total		36550		
17	Grand Total		113839		
18					

Figure 15-27
Item names in a PivotTable appear in random order.

The item labels appear in an arbitrary order, which corresponds to their creation order in the database. You can sort the categories so they appear in descending order based on the total dollars for the category. To do that, double-click the CategoryName tile. In the PivotTable Field dialog box, click Advanced. In the PivotTable Field Advanced Options dialog box, select Descending as the AutoSort option, and select Sum Of Dollars in the Using Field drop-down list, as shown in Figure 15-28. Then click OK twice to change the PivotTable.

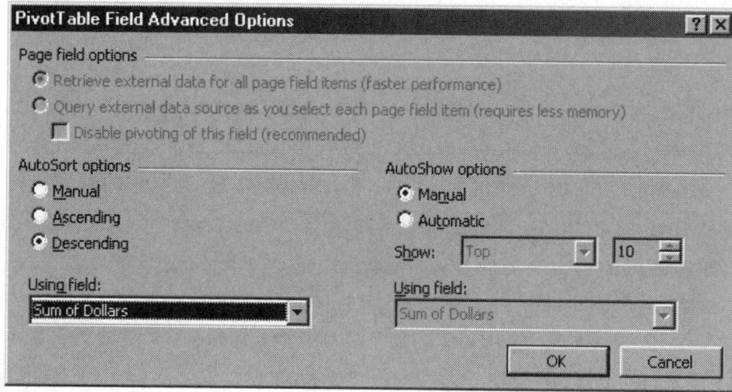

Figure 15-28
You can automatically sort items within a field.

To automatically sort the item labels in alphabetical order, select Ascending in the AutoSort Options group and CategoryName in the Using Field list.

Within each product category, you can sort the reseller names based on total dollars. You can even filter the names to show only the top two resellers for each product category. To do that, double-click the ResellerName field button and click Advanced. In the AutoShow Options group, select Automatic, and select Top and 2 from the Show drop-down list. Leave the default Sum Of Dollars in the Using Field drop-down list box. (If you also want to sort the items, you must select AutoSort options, as well. Showing only the top items does not automatically sort the item labels.) Click OK twice to show the revised PivotTable, as shown in Figure 15-29.

	A	B	C	D
4	CategoryName	CustomerName	Total	
5	Meats	Lazy K	15171	
6		Trail's Head	19923	
7	Meats Total		35094	
8	Cereals	Lazy K	13995	
9		White Clover	15305	
10	Cereals Total		29300	
11	Produce	Trail's Head	10991	
12		White Clover	8187	
13	Produce Total		19178	
14	Grand Total		83572	
15				
16				

Figure 15-29
You can select only the top items within each group.

The totals for the categories and for the entire PivotTable include only the visible customers. You cannot display the entire total without displaying all the items.

Counting Items in a PivotTable

While you are creating a PivotTable, you use columns containing text as row, column, and page fields, and columns containing numbers as data fields. You can reverse the roles and use the order size as the row label. This is particularly useful for grouping the order sizes into ranges.

For example, suppose you want to know which products have the highest unit volumes. You can create a new PivotTable that shares the data cache with an existing PivotTable. If the new PivotTable will be similar to the old one, hold down the Ctrl key as you drag the PivotTable's worksheet tab to create a clone of the sheet. If the new PivotTable will be substantially different, you might want to start with a blank structure. To create a new, blank PivotTable based on the same cache as an existing PivotTable in the workbook, select any cell that is not part of a PivotTable and click PivotTable And PivotChart Report Wizard on the Data menu. In step 1, select Another PivotTable Or PivotChart. In step 2, select the existing report. In step 3, select New Worksheet.

In the new empty structure, drag the ScenarioName field button to the page area and select Corporate as its value. Drag the Units field button to the row area, and drag the Product field button to the data area. The resulting PivotTable will appear similar to the PivotTable shown in Figure 15-30.

The data field label is Count Of ProductName. When you drag a numeric field to the data area, the PivotTable suggests summing the numbers. When you drag a text field (or a numeric field with some blank cells) to the data area, the PivotTable suggests counting the rows. That is exactly what you need for this analysis. (You could

A1 = ScenarioName

	A	B	C	D	E
1	ScenarioName	Corporate			
2					
3	Count of ProductName				
4	Units	Total			
5	3	1			
6	4	2			
7	5	4			
8	6	3			
9	7	3			
10	8	2			

Figure 15-30
You can use labels as data and numbers as row headings.

have used any text field as the data field, since each row counts as one, regardless of what text happens to be in the field.)

The PivotTable shows all the different quantity levels on the left, and the number of times that quantity occurs on the right. There are dozens of different order quantity levels. You can get the PivotTable to group the quantities into useful ranges. Select any cell within the PivotTable. Then click Group And Outline on the Data menu, and then select Group to display the Group dialog box as shown in Figure 15-31.

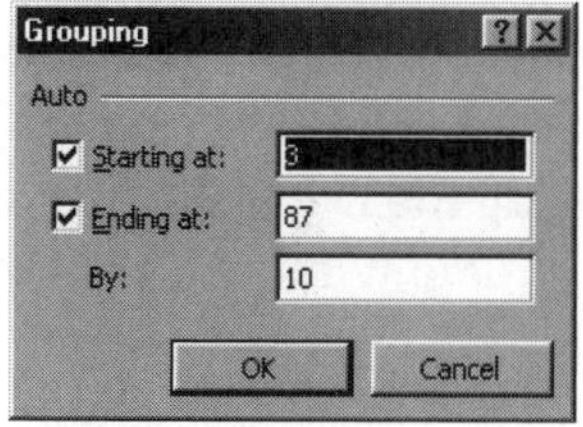

Figure 15-31
The grouping dialog box suggests minimum and maximum values.

The Grouping dialog box suggests starting with the smallest value, ending with the largest value, and grouping by 10s. To create groupings with more logical boundaries, change the Starting At value to *0* and click OK. The PivotTable changes to resemble Figure 15-32.

	A	B	C
1	ScenarioName	Corporate	
2			
3	Count of ProductName		
4	Units	Total	
5	0-9	18	
6	10-19	68	
7	20-29	47	
8	30-39	17	
9	40-49	6	
10	Grand Total	156	
11			
12			

Figure 15-32
You can group numeric labels into ranges.

It appears that most products sell between 10 and 19 units each month.

Note

In addition to grouping numeric fields, you can also group text fields and date fields. When you group text fields, the Grouping dialog box does not appear. Before you click the Group button, select the items you want to group. If the items are not adjacent, hold down the Ctrl key as you click each one. When you group date fields, a different version of the Grouping dialog box allows you to group by years, quarters, months, days, or even intervals of days.

When you group text or date fields, however, you create new virtual fields in the PivotTable. These virtual fields appear in every PivotTable that shares the same cache. Changing the grouping in one PivotTable affects—sometimes with unpleasant consequences—related fields in other PivotTables. Rather than use groups to add virtual fields to text and date fields, you might prefer to add new fields to the source list itself.

Calculating the Percent of Total

You might want to analyze orders based not only on units, but also on dollars. In fact, you might like to know not only how many dollars each order size group accounts for, but also the specific percent of total.

Drag the Dollars field button onto the data area. Drag the Data field button to cell C3 to place the data columns side by side. The PivotTable will look similar to the one shown in Figure 15-33.

	A	B	C	D
1	ScenarioName	Corporate		
2				
3		Data		
4	Units	Count of ProductName	Sum of Dollars	
5	0-9	18	4728	
6	10-19	68	36127	
7	20-29	47	42239	
8	30-39	17	20300	
9	40-49	6	10445	
10	Grand Total	156	113839	
11				
12				

Figure 15-33
Absolute numbers might be hard to compare.

Products that sell in slightly higher quantities account for the bulk of the dollars, but you can't tell how much just by looking at the dollar totals. To see the percent of the dollar total for each level of units, you can add an additional calculated data field.

Drag the Dollars field button onto the data area a second time. You now have both a Sum Of Dollars field and a Sum Of Dollars2 field. To change the way the new field calculates, right-click the Sum Of Dollars2 label, click Field Settings, and then click Options. The dialog box shown in Figure 15-34 will appear.

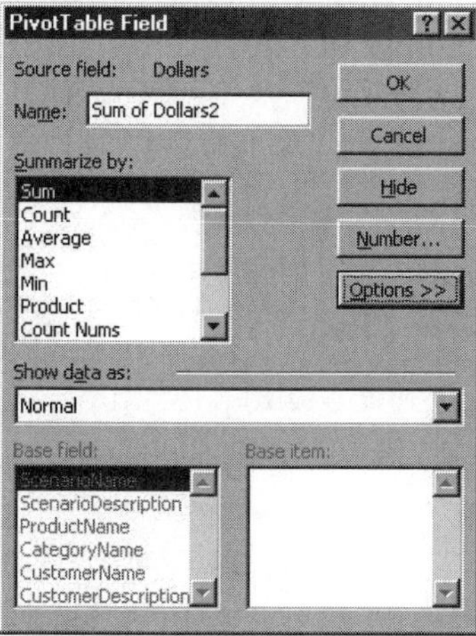

Figure 15-34
Field Options let you control how a field is calculated.

This is where you control whether the PivotTable sums or counts an item. You can also choose to average, multiply, or find the smallest or largest values, along with several other options. In this case, you still want to sum the dollars, but then you want to determine what percent of the total that sum is. Calculating a percent of total is a secondary calculation, because you first have to sum the numbers before you can determine the percent value. From the Show Data As drop-down list, select the Percent Of Column, type *Percent* as a new name for the field, and then click OK. The PivotTable now appears as shown in Figure 15-35.

D7 = 37.1041558692539%

	A	B	C	D	E
1	ScenarioName	Corporate			
2					
3		Data			
4	Units	Count of ProductName	Sum of Dollars	Percent	
5	0-9	18	4728	4.15%	
6	10-19	68	36127	31.74%	
7	20-29	47	42239	37.10%	
8	30-39	17	20300	17.83%	
9	40-49	6	10445	9.18%	
10	Grand Total	156	113839	100.00%	
11					
12					

Figure 15-35
Percent Of Totals allows for easy comparison.

You want to replace the Sum Of Dollars label with simply Dollars, but that label already exists as a field name, so you can't use it for the summary name. However, a computer is inherently stupid. You can trick the PivotTable by adding a space after the name that duplicates a field name. Click cell C4, type *Dollars*, press the spacebar, and then press Enter. As far as you are concerned, the label appears the way you want. As far as the PivotTable is concerned, the label Dollars (with a space) is completely different from the label Dollars (without a space).

Calculating New Detailed Values

Note The sample document for this section is Prices.xls.

Excel allows you to create both calculated fields and calculated items. You might wonder about the difference between adding a new column of formulas to the source list and adding a calculated field. The difference has to do with an arithmetic concept you learned in fifth grade. Consider the simple grid of numbers shown in Figure 15-36.

	A	B	C	D
1	2	4	8	
2	2	5	10	
3	4	9	???	
4				
5				

Figure 15-36
Sequence matters when combining multiplication and addition.

Column C is equal to column A times column B. Row 3 is equal to row 1 plus row 2. What value should go into cell C3? If C3 is the *product* of A3 and B3, then the result is 36. But if C3 is the *sum* of C1 and C2, then the result is 18. Whenever you combine multiplication (or division) with addition (or subtraction), you have this choice.

Do you multiply values in each detail row and then add the result? If so, add a new column of formulas to the source list. Do you add each column of values and then multiply the result? If so, use a calculated field. Consider a practical example using the dollars from the Forecast database.

Suppose you have a database containing historical order amounts. The database includes both units and dollars, and the dollar amounts reflect actual customer discounts. Figure 15-37 shows the order history list.

	A	B	C	D	E	F	G	H	I
1	Product	Line	Reseller	Month	Units	Dollars			
2	Elephant	Animal	Baldwin Museum c	9/1/99	363	$ 8,884.61			
3	Elephant	Animal	Enchantment Lake	9/1/99	352	$ 8,351.64			
4	Elephant	Animal	Kimball Museum o	9/1/99	1,204	$ 29,167.80			
5	Giraffe	Animal	Baldwin Museum c	9/1/99	1,552	$ 29,620.70			
6	Giraffe	Animal	Enchantment Lake	9/1/99	425	$ 7,863.03			
7	Giraffe	Animal	Kimball Museum o	9/1/99	1,305	$ 24,652.43			
8	Elephant	Animal	Baldwin Museum c	10/1/99	38	$ 930.07			
9	Elephant	Animal	Enchantment Lake	10/1/99	382	$ 9,063.43			
10	Elephant	Animal	Kimball Museum o	10/1/99	180	$ 4,360.64			
11	Giraffe	Animal	Baldwin Museum c	10/1/99	1,320	$ 25,192.86			
12	Giraffe	Animal	Enchantment Lake	10/1/99	513	$ 9,491.14			
13	Giraffe	Animal	Kimball Museum o	10/1/99	775	$ 14,640.33			
14	Elephant	Animal	Baldwin Museum c	11/1/99	127	$ 3,108.39			

Figure 15-37
A history database often contains actual units and dollars.

One way to calculate the prices is to add a calculated column to the list before creating a PivotTable. In cell G1, type *Price*. In cell G2, type *=Dollars/Units*. Select cell G2, click the Currency Style button, and then double-click the AutoFill handle. Press Ctrl+Shift+asterisk (*) to select the list, including the new Price column. Click Name on the Insert menu, Define, type *Database* in the Names In Workbook text box, and click OK.

Create a new PivotTable using the Database range as the source. After creating the structure, drag the Line field button to the row area. Drag the Units field, the Dollars field, and the Price field buttons onto the data area. Drag the Data field button onto cell C3 to add the data values into the columns. Convert the Sum Of Price field to calculate an average (see "Calculating the Percent of Total," earlier in this chapter, for details about changing the calculation method for a field).

You now have a report that shows the units, dollars, and average price for each product line over the past two years, as shown in Figure 15-38.

	A	B	C	D	E
1					
2					
3		Data			
4	Line	Sum of Units	Sum of Dollars	Average of Price	
5	Animal	998786	18084362.51	$ 19.55	
6	Dinosaur	601817	7478702.25	$ 12.48	
7	Vehicle	287867	6774246.05	$ 21.59	
8	Grand Total	1888470	32337310.81	$ 17.72	
9					
10					
11					

Figure 15-38
You can calculate an average of detailed values.

Calculating Values Based on Totals

As you consider the averages based on the detailed values, you think about what others might do when they receive your report. A likely scenario is that someone will divide the units into the dollars to double-check your numbers. Doing so would result in the numbers shown in column E of Figure 15-39.

F5 = =C5/B5

	A	B	C	D	E	F	G
1							
2							
3		Data					
4	Line	Sum of Units	Sum of Dollars	Average of Price			
5	Animal	998786	18084362.51	$ 19.55		$ 18.11	
6	Dinosaur	601817	7478702.25	$ 12.48		$ 12.43	
7	Vehicle	287867	6774246.05	$ 21.59		$ 23.53	
8	Grand Total	1888470	32337310.81	$ 17.72		$ 17.12	
9							
10							

Figure 15-39
Dividing the sums produces a different result than averaging the detail.

The inconsistency, of course, comes from the associative property of division. If you want an average that matches the ratio of the total values, you cannot base the calculation on row-level numbers. You must divide the sum of the Dollars by the sum of the Units. To do that, you must use a calculated field. A *calculated field* is a new data field (you can't create a new calculated row or column field) that calculates based on the results already calculated by other data fields.

Select any cell in the PivotTable. On the PivotTable toolbar, click PivotTable, Formulas, and select Calculated Field. Give the field a name and then create a formula that includes other data fields. Type *AvgPrice* in the Name text box, and *=Dollars/Units* in the Formula text box. Then click OK. The new Sum Of AvgPrice data field automatically appears in the PivotTable, and the numbers match the test numbers in the worksheet, as shown in Figure 15-40.

Line	Sum of Units	Sum of Dollars	Average of Price	Sum of AvgPrice	
Animal	998786	18084362.51	$ 19.55	18.11	$ 18.11
Dinosaur	601817	7478702.25	$ 12.48	12.43	$ 12.43
Vehicle	287867	6774246.05	$ 21.59	23.53	$ 23.53
Grand Total	1888470	32337310.81	$ 17.72	17.12	$ 17.12

Figure 15-40
A calculated field calculates based on existing totals.

Note The label Sum Of AvgPrice is slightly deceptive. The word *Sum* in the label really means that the formula is operating on the sum of each field in the formula. In other words, the formula *=Dollars/Units* really means =Sum Of Dollars/Sum Of Units. You cannot create a calculated field that uses averages or any other operation other than Sum.

Merging Data into Worksheets

Note The sample document for this section is Mapping.xls.

One of the greatest benefits of using spreadsheets is that you can have formulas right next to input numbers so that when you change a number, you immediately see the effect of the change. One of the greatest frustrations of using spreadsheets, however, is that values and formulas are intermingled, making it difficult to move data into or out of a spreadsheet. This is often an issue when you create multiple copies of a spreadsheet and need different values in each copy, while still keeping the formulas and the formatting constant.

For example, if you create a budgeting worksheet and distribute it to 20 departments, you have 20 copies of the worksheet. Each copy of the worksheet contains identical copies of the formulas, but each department worksheet has unique data values intermingled with those formulas. If you need to change a formula in the worksheet, you cannot make the correction just on one copy and redistribute the new worksheet, because each department would then lose its unique data.

Because formulas and values are intertwined on a worksheet, extracting data from a worksheet is also difficult. Suppose you need to extract the input values from the budgeting worksheets and upload them to a centralized accounting system in a database. Because the input values are all intermingled with the formulas, isolating just the data values to pass to the database can be a great deal of work.

On the one hand, you do want to separate input values from the formulas when you import or export the data values or when you change the structure of the worksheets. On the other hand, you want the input values interlaced between formulas so that users of the worksheet can get the most benefit from the spreadsheet. This is definitely a case where you want to have your cake and eat it too.

Merging Rows and Columns with Single Labels

Excel's *Data Consolidate* command can help. Data Consolidate was originally designed to combine values from different spreadsheets, and it does a great job of doing that, but its powerful and flexible design also makes it an effective tool for solving problems that require repositioning—or mapping—numbers without actually consolidating (that is, summarizing) anything. The Data Consolidate command can solve the problem of separating code and data in a worksheet. First consider a very simple example, and then explore a more realistic scenario.

Extracting Data from Formulas

Suppose you have a budgeting worksheet with input data and formulas intermingled, as shown in the worksheet in Figure 15-41.

You want to create a worksheet that contains a simple grid with no formulas. To extract the input values from the Formulas worksheet into the Table worksheet, insert a new column B and type unique labels (presumably budget account numbers) on each budget row. Then give the name *DataValues* to the range B1:E9, as shown in Figure 15-42.

To use Data Consolidate to map values, the top row and the left column of the consolidation range must contain unique labels.

	A	B	C	D	E	F
1		Jan	Feb	Mar		
2	Salaries	4000	4000	4200		
3	Benefits	1800	1800	2000		
4	**Total**	**5800**	**5800**	**6200**		
5						
6	Office Supplies	80	80	80		
7	Books	50	50	50		
8	Software	450	0	130		
9	**Total**	**580**	**130**	**260**		
10						
11						
12						

Figure 15-41
In a budget, values and formulas are intermingled.

DataValues =

	A	B	C	D	E	F	G
1			Jan	Feb	Mar		
2	Salaries	10	4000	4000	4200		
3	Benefits	20	1800	1800	2000		
4	**Total**		**5800**	**5800**	**6200**		
5							
6	Office Supplies	30	80	80	80		
7	Books	40	50	50	50		
8	Software	50	450	0	130		
9	**Total**		**580**	**130**	**260**		
10							
11							

Figure 15-42
Name a range that includes labels on both the left and the top.

On a new worksheet, select cell A1. Click Consolidate on the Data menu, and type *DataValues* in the Reference list box. Select both the Use Labels In Top Row and Left Column check boxes. Click Add to add the reference to the All References list—which will verify the range—as shown in Figure 15-43. Then click OK.

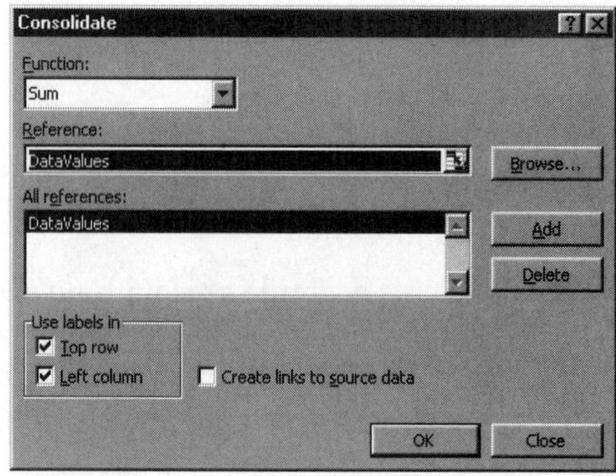

Figure 15-43
Consolidate using labels in the top row and the left column

In the first column of the output sheet, Excel creates a list of the unique row labels from the left column of the source reference. In the first row, Excel creates a list of the unique column labels from the top row of the source reference. Then, as it works through the source reference, Excel adds each value to the cell where the row and column headings match in the source and the output areas. The result is a simple grid with only values and no formulas, as shown in Figure 15-44.

	A	B	C	D	E	F
1		Jan	Feb	Mar		
2	10	4000	4000	4200		
3	20	1800	1800	2000		
4	30	80	80	80		
5	40	50	50	50		
6	50	450	0	130		
7						
8						
9						
10						

Figure 15-44
When you consolidate to a blank sheet, Excel generates unique labels.

Because you have only one source reference, and because all the row and column headings are unique, this has the effect of copying the values. While the range with unique labels at the top and left is selected, give it the name *DataSource.*

Merging Imported Data into Formulas

Now, suppose that management has dictated that all budgets should be cut by 10 percent. It is easy to reduce each number in the tabular block by 10 percent. (See the section "Explicitly Selecting Filtered Cells," earlier in this chapter for an example of how to scale numbers.) After changing the budget values, you want to merge them back into the Formulas worksheet. This process is the same as extracting the values, only in reverse.

Activate the worksheet containing the formulas and select the DataValues range. Click Consolidate on the Data menu, and type *DataSource* as the Reference. Select both of the Use Labels In check boxes and click Enter.

Excel merges the revised values into the Formulas worksheet, precisely as you requested. (If everything does not work the way you want, click the Undo button to put everything back so you can try again.)

The merged data values are constants, so you can modify them directly and the formulas will be left intact; you can immediately see the effects of any changes. After you make changes on the Formulas worksheet, switch back to the Table worksheet and use the Data Consolidate command again to extract the revised data. If you change numbers on the Tables worksheet, switch back to the Formulas worksheet and use the Data Consolidate command again to merge the new data into the formulas.

Note When consolidating into a worksheet, Excel uses the selected range as the target. However, if you have defined the range name *Consolidate_Area* on the worksheet, Excel uses the Consolidate_Area named range, regardless what the current selection is.

The Data Consolidate tool is a remarkable tool for merging and extracting input values in the midst of formulas. Data Consolidate works only if your worksheet meets certain conditions:

- The input values must be numbers; Data Consolidate does not transfer text data.
- You must create unique keys in the left column and top row of the data ranges. You can hide this row and column if you don't want it to show in the reports.
- The worksheet must not have any constants—text or numbers—within the area where the data and formulas will be merged. Excel clears all constants from the target area before it begins consolidating.

Excel always clears all the cells below and to the right of the labels in the target range, so add any additional labels to the left of or above the labels. (You can work around this restriction in some cases by adding a constant as a formula. For example, type the value *500* as *= 500.*)

Merging Rows and Columns with Multiple Labels

The most impressive part about using Data Consolidate to map data values is that you can go both directions—using Data Consolidate to integrate values with formulas, and then using Data Consolidate again to extract the values after you change them. Often, you will have the need to transfer values that require more than two keys. For example, the table of forecasting values in Figure 15-45 has a single row of labels at the top, but two columns of labels at the left.

	A	B	C	D	E	F	G	H
1	**ProductName**	**CustomerName**	**Month1**	**Month2**	**Month3**	**Month4**	**Month5**	**Month6**
2	Bratwurst	Lazy K	180	150	150	210	90	150
3	Bratwurst	Trail's Head	240	330	240	150	270	510
4	Bratwurst	White Clover	120	120	210	210	180	180
5	Dried Apples	Lazy K	390	480	420	420	450	270
6	Dried Apples	Trail's Head	690	570	420	900	750	570
7	Dried Apples	White Clover	360	570	420	330	630	330
8	Gnocci	Lazy K	930	900	870	870	840	1470
9	Gnocci	Trail's Head	450	420	990	450	360	540
10	Gnocci	White Clover	1440	1230	1080	960	810	960
11	Pasties	Lazy K	750	720	510	750	660	780
12	Pasties	Trail's Head	630	990	810	750	870	690
13	Pasties	White Clover	690	420	630	870	660	600
14	Pate	Lazy K	840	810	900	1050	840	810

Figure 15-45
Some tables contain two or more row labels.

The secret to working with multiple row labels is to create a *Key* column that concatenates the separate labels into one. Figure 15-46 shows the forecasting table with a new column added. Assuming that the data is on a worksheet named Grid, give the sheet-local name *Grid!Consolidate_Area* to the range with the exportable data (C1:I28 in the sample worksheet). See "Managing Local and Global Names" in Chapter 12 for information about creating sheet-local names.

C2 = =B2&"#"&A2

	A	B	C	D	E	F	G	H	I
1	**ProductName**	**CustomerName**	**RowKey**	**Month1**	**Month2**	**Month3**	**Month4**	**Month5**	**Month6**
2	Bratwurst	Lazy K	Lazy K#Bratwurst	180	150	150	210	90	150
3	Bratwurst	Trail's Head	Trail's Head#Bratwurst	240	330	240	150	270	510
4	Bratwurst	White Clover	White Clover#Bratwurst	120	120	210	210	180	180
5	Dried Apples	Lazy K	Lazy K#Dried Apples	390	480	420	420	450	270
6	Dried Apples	Trail's Head	Trail's Head#Dried Apples	690	570	420	900	750	570
7	Dried Apples	White Clover	White Clover#Dried Apples	360	570	420	330	630	330
8	Gnocci	Lazy K	Lazy K#Gnocci	930	900	870	870	840	1470
9	Gnocci	Trail's Head	Trail's Head#Gnocci	450	420	990	450	360	540
10	Gnocci	White Clover	White Clover#Gnocci	1440	1230	1080	960	810	960

Figure 15-46
Create a concatenated key for multiple row labels.

The formula for the concatenated key simply combines the customer name with the product name. The order of the keys does not matter as long as you are consistent. Adding an unusual character—such as the pound sign (#)—between the keys can prevent any mismatches where the beginning of the second key could be the end of the first key.

In a situation like this, you will often create multiple worksheets—perhaps one for each customer. First, create a template for a single customer, and then create a macro to copy it. Create a worksheet named Master. Type a sample customer name into cell A1 and give the cell the sheet-local name *Master!Customer*. Add product labels—grouped by categories as desired—to the rows, and create a key column that concatenates the customer name with the product name, as shown in Figure 15-47. The concatenated key should match the key on the tabular worksheet.

C3 = =Customer&"#"&B3

	A	B	C	D	E	F	G
1	***Lazy K***			**1/1/02**	**2/1/02**	**3/1/02**	**4/1/02**
2				**Month1**	**Month2**	**Month3**	**Month4**
3	Cereals	Gnocci	Lazy K#Gnocci	930	900	870	870
4		Tunnbrod	Lazy K#Tunnbrod	510	540	480	360
5	**Cereals Total**		**Lazy K#**	**1440**	**1440**	**1350**	**1230**
6	Meats	Bratwurst	Lazy K#Bratwurst	180	150	150	210
7		Pasties	Lazy K#Pasties	750	720	510	750
8		Pate	Lazy K#Pate	840	810	900	1050
9		Tourtiere	Lazy K#Tourtiere	540	450	300	570
10	**Meats Total**		**Lazy K#**	**2310**	**2130**	**1860**	**2580**

Figure 15-47
Create a concatenated key for the target worksheet.

Chapter 15

The column labels must match the column labels from the tabular worksheet. If you want different labels for cosmetic reasons, place them above the actual column labels. Select the target range (C2:I15 in the sample worksheet) and give it the name *Master!Consolidate_Area*.

Consolidate the data into the Master worksheet. This serves both to set the consolidation properties and to test the worksheet layout. To execute the consolidation, click Consolidate on the Data menu, type *Grid!Consolidate_Area* in the Reference text box, and click Add. Select the Top Row and Left Column check boxes and click OK. The numbers from the source should appear in the worksheet. If the numbers do not appear, check the order of the concatenated labels in the keys, and check the range name definitions.

Once the numbers are pulled into the worksheet, add any desired analytical formulas, hide the key row and column, and format the worksheet.

Creating a Macro that Generates Template Worksheets

The next task is to create a copy of the master template for each customer. If you have only a few customers, you can easily clone the worksheets. If you need to create multiple worksheets, or if you need to modify and recreate the worksheets multiple times, it is worth creating a simple macro to clone the worksheets.

First, create a list that contains the name for each worksheet—which is also the name that will go into the *Customer* range on the worksheet. Give the list the name Customers. The following *CreateSheets* macro will make a copy of the master sheet for each cell in the Customer range:

```
Sub CreateSheets()
    Dim r As Range
    Dim s As String
    For Each r In Range("Customers")
        s = r.Value
        DeleteSheet s
        Worksheets("Master").Copy Worksheets(1)
        ActiveSheet.Name = s
        Range("Customer").Value = s
    Next r
End Sub
```

The macro loops through the cells in the *Customer* range, assigning the text from the cell to a string variable. It then calls a subroutine to delete the sheet in case it already exists. The macro copies the master worksheet to the beginning of the active workbook, renames it, and then changes the customer name cell.

The task of deleting a sheet is delegated to a subroutine, because Visual Basic will display an error message if the sheet does not exist. The following *DeleteSheet* subroutine can easily ignore the error:

```
Sub DeleteSheet(ByVal SheetName As String)
    Application.DisplayAlerts = False
    On Error Resume Next
    Worksheets(SheetName).Delete
End Sub
```

Setting the Application.DisplayAlerts property to *False* prevents Excel from asking permission to delete the selected sheet.

Creating a Macro to Consolidate Multiple Worksheets

Once you have created each worksheet, all you need to do to populate each worksheet with the values appropriate for the sheet's reseller is to activate the sheet, click Consolidate on the Data menu, and click OK. The proper information is already retained in the Consolidate dialog box. To make the process even simpler, the macro can execute the calculation on each sheet. Create a range named *Customers* that includes the name of each worksheet you need to calculate, and then run the following *DistributeValues* macro:

```
Sub DistributeValues()
    Dim r As Range
    For Each r In Range("Customers")
        Worksheets(r.Value).Range("Consolidate_Area").Consolidate
    Next r
End Sub
```

The macro is very simple. It loops through each cell in the *Customers* range and executes the Consolidate method on the range named *Consolidate_Area* for the sheet named in the cell. The range name on the worksheet does not need to be Consolidate_Area; any name will do.

Creating a Macro to Extract Data from Multiple Worksheets

You can use the generated forecast worksheets to modify the forecast for each customer. You could even save each worksheet in its own workbook and distribute a workbook to each customer account to let the accounts revise their own forecasts. Eventually, you will want to re-assemble the forecasts into a single table, either for analyzing with a PivotTable or for exporting to a database.

Consolidating from multiple worksheets is essentially the same as consolidating from a single worksheet. You simply add an entry to the References list in the Consolidate dialog box for each worksheet you will use as a source. For two or three worksheets, adding each worksheet separately to the dialog box is not difficult. If you have dozens of worksheets to extract values from, adding each one to the dialog box can get tedious.

You can createthe following *RetrieveValues* macro that adds all the worksheet references for you. The macro consolidates the range named *Consolidate_Area* for each worksheet named in the *Customers* range. The target for the consolidation is the *Consolidate_Area* range on the active worksheet, so be sure to select the desired target worksheet before running the macro.

```
Sub RetrieveValues()
    Dim v As Variant
    v = [TRANSPOSE("[Mapping.XLS]" & Customers & "!Consolidate_Area")]
```

```
    Range("Consolidate_Area").Consolidate _
        Sources:=v, _
        Function:=xlProduct, _
        TopRow:=True, LeftColumn:=True, CreateLinks:=False
End Sub
```

If you use the Consolidate method without specifying any arguments, it uses the values typed previously in the dialog box. You can also use arguments that correspond to each control in the dialog box.

Sources is the most interesting—and most complex—argument of the Consolidate method. You pass the *Sources* argument an array containing a string entry for each reference. Each reference consists of a modification of a single value from the *Customers* range. Specifically, an exclamation mark (!) and the name of the consolidation range must be appended to the sheet name. If the consolidation sources are in the same workbook as the target, you do not need to prefix the range name with the workbook name. Adding the workbook name is always acceptable, and the macro includes a sample workbook name so you can see how to add it; it must be enclosed in brackets, immediately before the worksheet name. For example, for a range named *DataSource* on a worksheet named Master in a workbook named sample.xls, the appropriate final reference string is [sample.xls]Master!DataSource.

The formula includes a TRANSPOSE function because the Consolidate method requires a horizontal array. The list in the worksheet is a vertical array of cells. In the unlikely event that you store the names of the worksheets in a row (horizontal), you don't need the TRANSPOSE function.

In Visual Basic, you cannot create a statement that modifies an entire array of cells at once, but you can in Excel. (See "Calculating Using Array Formulas" in Chapter 13 for details about calculating with arrays.) Visual Basic can use a special syntax to ask Excel to perform a calculation that returns an array. Take any formula that you could type into Excel's formula bar, remove the equal sign, and add brackets around it. Visual Basic passes the expression to Excel, which calculates it and returns the result. If the result is an array, you can store it in a variable declared as a Variant.

Other than creating an array of reference sources, the macro is very simple. It simply calls the Consolidate function. You need to use the macro only once, because after that, the list of references is stored in the dialog box. Always using the macro means that you don't have to worry whether you changed the list of worksheets.

Sharing a Workbook

In Excel, you can dynamically share a workbook. Unlike Word, where only a single user can open a document at a time for editing, Excel makes it possible for multiple users to make simultaneous, interactive changes to a workbook. You might want to experiment with how sharing works before you start sharing workbooks with others. It might seem difficult to test sharing a workbook by yourself; the easiest way is to run two copies of Excel.

Making Simultaneous Changes to a Workbook

When multiple users share a workbook, Excel identifies which user makes which change. To make it clear which copy of Excel is which, assume that the first copy belongs to a person named Boris. You can change the user name in the Options dialog box (assuming your name is not Boris). To change the user name, click Options on the Tools menu, and then select the General tab. In the User Name text box, type *Boris* and click OK. Then save the workbook. Reduce the size of the window so you can tell which copy of Excel belongs to Boris.

To launch a second copy of Excel, click Programs on the Start menu and choose Microsoft Excel. Assume that this second copy belongs to a coworker of Boris named Natasha. Use the Options dialog box to change the user name. Arrange the copies of Excel so that you can see both of them.

Note Boris and Natasha are main characters from Leo Tolstoy's epic novel *War and Peace*. This example has nothing to do with "The Rocky and Bullwinkle Show."

Using the Boris copy of Excel, open a workbook for editing. While Boris has the workbook open, if Natasha tries to open it she will see a warning message like the one shown in Figure 15-48.

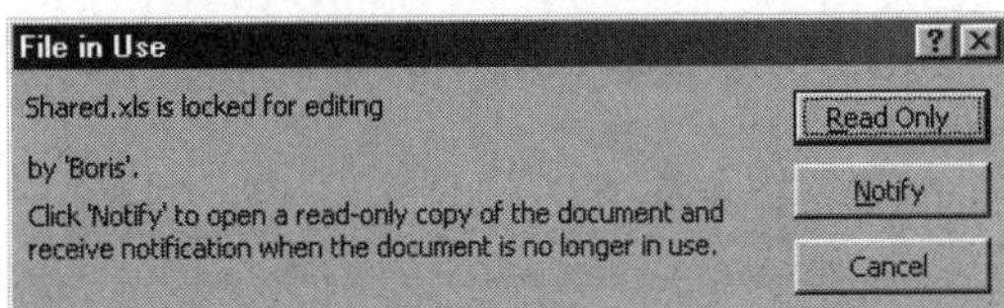

Figure 15-48
Only one person can edit an ordinary workbook at a time.

Only one person can have a workbook open for editing at a time—unless that person chooses to share the workbook. When you share a workbook, more than one person can make changes at the same time. While a workbook is shared, most normal Excel functions are available, but certain actions that are difficult to share are disabled. For example, you can insert or rename a worksheet, but you can't delete one.

To share the workbook, in Boris's copy of Excel, click Share Workbook on the Tools menu, and then select the Editing tab. Enable the check box Allow Changes By More Than One User At The Same Time, as shown in Figure 15-49. This will allow changes by more than one person at the same time. Click OK.

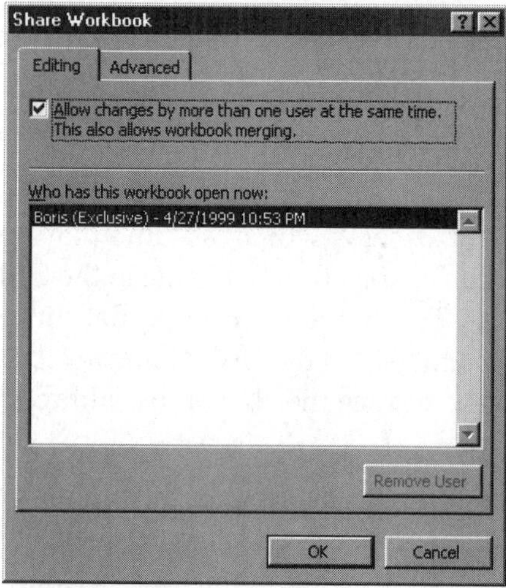

Figure 15-49
You can grant permission for others to simultaneously edit the workbook.

Click OK again when Excel informs you that this action will save the workbook. The title bar shows that the workbook is being shared. Natasha can now open and edit the workbook.

In Natasha's copy of Excel, open the same workbook. Now both Natasha and Boris can make changes to the workbook.

Excel posts Natasha's changes back to the shared copy on the network each time she saves the workbook. With a logic that might seem backward—but which is actually very convenient—Excel imports Natasha's changes from the network copy when Boris saves his copy of the workbook. To see how this works, change the value of cell A1 in Natasha's copy of the workbook. Then save the workbook. Change the value of cell A2 in Boris' copy of the workbook and save the workbook. Click OK when Excel notifies you that the workbook was updated with changes from another user.

Excel not only copies Natasha's change to cell A1, it also highlights the change with a colored border and a comment on the cell. You can see the history of the change by moving the mouse pointer over the changed cell, as shown in Figure 15-50.

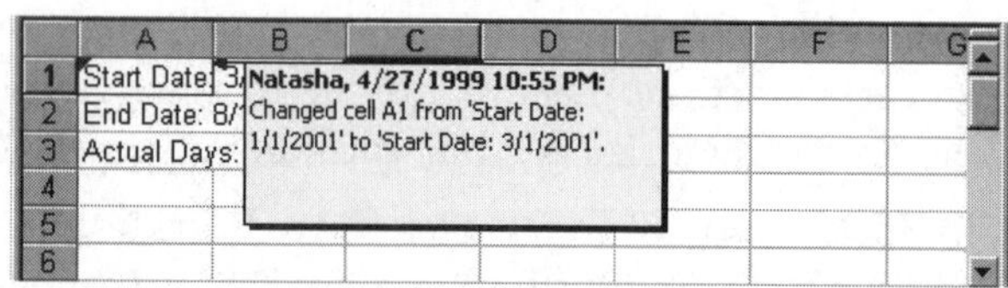

Figure 15-50
Excel uses comments to notify users of changes.

Boris's copy of the workbook now includes both his and Natasha's changes. Natasha's copy, however, shows only her own changes. That is because she hasn't saved her workbook since Boris saved his changes. As soon as she saves her workbook, the two copies will be synchronized. Save Natasha's copy the workbook to synchronize her workbook.

Managing Conflicts

As long as each person editing a shared workbook changes a different cell, Excel is able to smoothly integrate the changes. But when two or more users change the value of a single cell, someone must decide which value will "win." The first person that encounters the conflict is the one who gets to make the decision, but Excel does retain a history of all the changes, even the changes that "lost."

Change the value of cell A3 in Natasha's copy of the workbook and then save it. Change the value of cell A3 in Boris's copy of the workbook, and then save the workbook. As shown in Figure 15-51, the Resolve Conflicts dialog box shows all the conflicting changes and allows Boris (who happened to be the one saving the workbook at the time the conflict was detected) to decide whose changes win. To accept Boris's changes, click the Accept All Mine button.

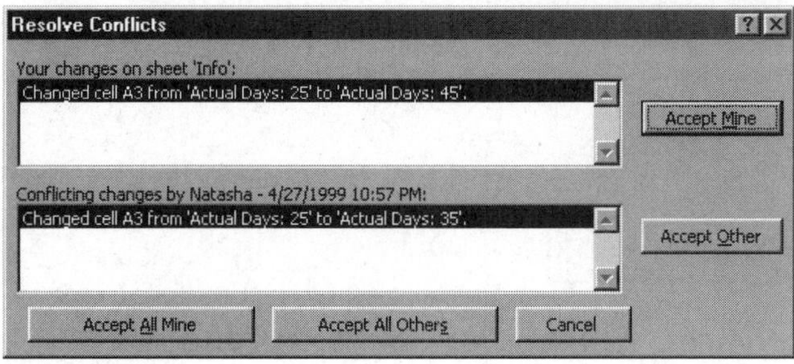

Figure 15-51
The first person to encounter a conflict gets to decide which change to accept.

When you save Natasha's copy of the workbook, there will be no conflict. Excel merely notifies you that a change occurred. Natasha's previous value for cell A3 is gone, but Natasha still has an opportunity to reject Boris's change. To exercise that option, in Natasha's copy, click Track Changes on the Tools menu and select Accept Or Reject Changes. Click OK to accept the default options. Accept any uncontested changes. The dialog box shown in Figure 15-52 now shows a history of the changes to cell A3, which both users changed.

Natasha can see her earlier change, and she can see that Boris overwrote it. She can also reaffirm her previous decision by selecting her previous change and clicking Accept. Saving the workbook posts the revised changes back to the network.

Now it is Boris's turn to find his change rejected when saving his copy of the workbook. Rather than go through the process of accepting or rejecting changes, he can

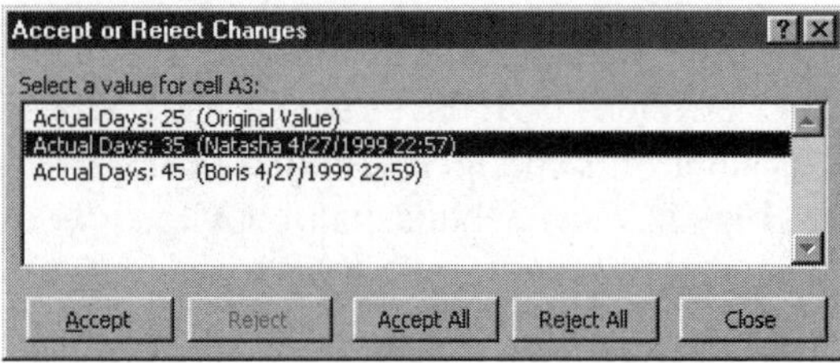

Figure 15-52
Any user can change which conflicting value is accepted.

chose to see an audit trail of all the changes that have occurred. To do that, in Boris' copy, click Track Changes on the Tools menu, and then click Highlight Changes. The Highlight Changes dialog box has the same choices as the Select Changes To Accept Or Reject dialog box, plus a few extra check boxes, as shown in Figure 15-53.

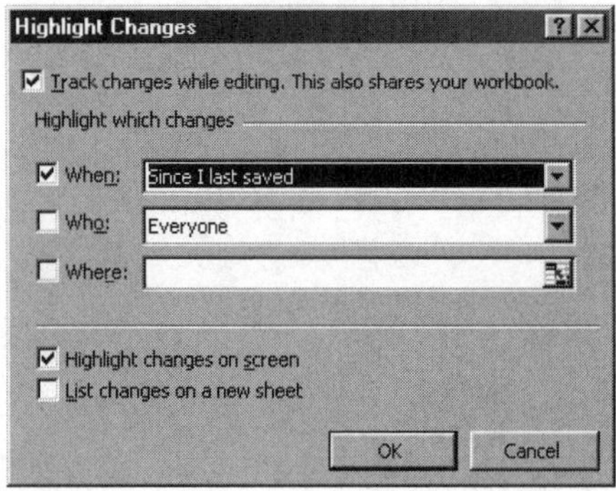

Figure 15-53
You can choose which changes you want to see.

To display a complete log of changes, clear the When check box, select the List Changes On A New Sheet check box, and click OK. Excel displays a new worksheet that lists all the changes that have been made since the worksheet was shared. You can use AutoFilters to select specific history values.

The History worksheet is a special worksheet that is owned by Excel. You cannot make any changes to it, and you cannot give the name History to a worksheet of your own. Because the History worksheet can change any time you save a workbook, it hides itself when you save the workbook.

After closing one copy of Excel, remember to reset your user name before you close the second copy. When you click Share Workbook on the Tools menu, select Editing, and clear the Allow Changes check box, Excel stops sharing the workbook and erases the history of changes from the workbook.

Sharing with Remote Users

Allowing multiple users to edit a workbook at the same time is a powerful feature for people who have access to a shared network folder. Sometimes, however, you might want to share a workbook with people who do not have access to a network file. For example, you might distribute a workbook as an e-mail attachment or on a Zip disk. The recipients make changes and send the files back to you. You need to integrate the changes and manage any conflicts, the same as if the users were simultaneously editing the file.

When you share a workbook, that workbook retains a history of all the changes that have been made to it. If you make copies of the workbook, each copy retains a history of the changes. To save a workbook as shared, click Track Changes on the Tools menu, and click Highlight Changes. In the Highlight Changes dialog box, select the Track Changes check box. This has exactly the same effect as selecting the Allow Changes check box in the Share Workbook dialog box discussed earlier.

Once you track changes, you can make a copy of the workbook either by copying the file in Windows Explorer (or File Manager), or by using the Save As command on the File menu.

After you distribute copies of the workbook and receive the changed versions back, you need to merge the changes into the original workbook. Open the original workbook and then click Merge Workbooks on the Tools menu. Select the modified copies of the workbook (hold down the Ctrl key to select multiple workbooks), and click OK to incorporate the changes.

Merging workbooks is identical to simultaneously sharing a single workbook, except that you can integrate copies of the file that have different names or that are located in different folders. Otherwise, managing conflicts, accepting or rejecting changes, and reviewing history all work the same, whether you are sharing a single file or merging copies of the file.

Chapter 16

Present Excel Information Meaningfully

In This Chapter

Data values found in database and reports are of very little value unless you can properly interpret them. Interpretation occurs at two different levels: first, you must analyze the data, looking for important information, implications, and trends. Charting is a powerful tool for finding implications in large sets of data. Next, you must present the results of the analysis in a way that is meaningful to others. When you present the results of an analysis, your charts are important tools, but properly controlling the formatting of worksheet ranges is also critical.

Formatting Worksheet Ranges

A Microsoft Excel worksheet has two layers. The bottom, fundamental layer consists of the worksheet cells. Graphical objects appear on a separate layer above the worksheet grid. AutoShapes objects—which are available in Excel and in other Microsoft Office applications—appear on the graphical layer, as do embedded charts. (“Using the Keyboard with Graphical Objects” in Chapter 2 covers keyboard techniques you can use with AutoShapes objects in Excel.)

Even within a worksheet grid, you can apply formatting either to the contents of a cell or to a cell's border and background. Excel provides a number of cell formatting options you can use to change how cells are displayed.

Formatting Labels

Note The sample document for this section is Dates.xls.

Labels typically appear in the top row or the left column of a block of cells and give meaning to the contents of that row or column. Labels are often longer than the other cells in the row or column, and they often require special treatment to highlight their meaning, while still making them look good on a report.

Converting Labels into Dates You Can Format

In Excel, a date is a numeric value. You can use dozens of formats with a date value. ("Manipulating Dates" in Chapter 14 contains details about using formulas to manipulate dates in Excel.) A text string might look like a date, but if it is not stored internally as a date, you can't change its formatting. Suppose you have a document that contains text dates, such as those shown in the top row of the worksheet in Figure 16-1.

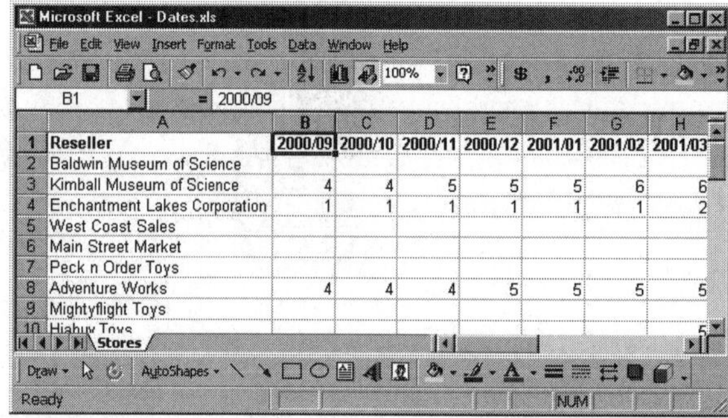

Figure 16-1
You cannot reformat text that looks like a date.

The dates appear as labels in the format YYYY/MM, which is difficult for most people to understand. Because the dates are labels and not Excel date values, you can't simply reformat them the way you want.

Excel's Text To Column feature converts labels into one or more columns of cells. This feature can interpret a variety of date formats. However, to use this feature, the labels must be in a column. You can transpose the row of dates, convert them to Excel dates, and then transpose them back to their original position using the following steps:

1. Copy the range of dates.
2. Choose a new out-of-the-way cell location—such as cell AA1—where you can paste a copy of the date range.

3. Click Paste Special on the Edit menu. Click the Transpose check box and click OK. Once the dates are in a column, you can use the Text To Columns feature to convert the text dates into Excel dates.
4. Select the vertical range of text dates and select Text To Columns from the Data menu.
5. In the Convert Text To Columns Wizard dialog box, click the Next button twice to skip steps 1 and 2. These steps are unnecessary because you are converting from a single column of labels to a single column of dates.
6. In the Column Data Format group in step 3, select the Date option, select YMD from the list of date formats in the Date drop-down list, and then click Finish. The result should look like the detail shown in Figure 16-2.

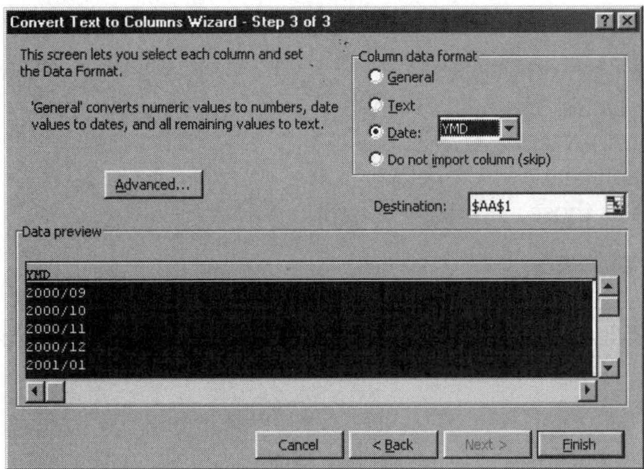

Figure 16-2
The Text To Columns Wizard can interpret various date formats.

Excel converts the labels into dates that you can format. Both the Copy and the Paste Special commands transpose the text and values, replacing the original labels.

If you want to divide a column of labels into separate columns, you can use the Text To Columns command on the Data menu. You can also use the Convert Text To Columns Wizard to translate any of several different possible date formats into dates that Excel can format. If the values you need to convert are in a row, use the Paste Special command on the Edit menu to transpose them into a column, temporarily converting the values.

Creating a Custom Date Format

The default date format for months uses a three-letter abbreviation for the month, followed by a two-digit number for the year. You can convert the format to display the full name of the month, followed by the full four-digit year. The Format Cells dialog box does not contain the precise format that you want, but it contains one that is close.

Select the range of dates, select Cells on the Format menu, and then select the Number tab. From the Type drop-down list, select the built-in March-97 format. This format is the closest format to the one you want to use. You can now customize this format to get exactly the look you want. In the Category list, select Custom. At the top of the Type drop-down list, a box appears containing the formatting code for the format you previously selected, as shown in Figure 16-3.

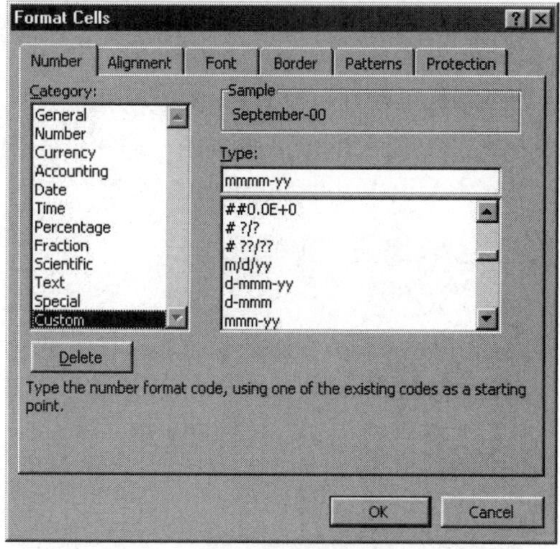

Figure 16-3
You can modify a built-in number format.

The letters MMMM tell Excel to use the full month name, and the letters YY tell Excel to use a two-digit year abbreviation. As you might guess, you can replace the hyphen with a space and add two more Y's to the year code. (Technically, three Y's are enough to display a four-digit year.) You can watch the contents change in the Sample box as you make changes in the Type drop-down list.

Formatting Oversized Labels

If a number (or a date) cannot fit in a cell, Excel does not truncate the number, because that might give you invalid information. Instead, it displays a series of number signs. Select Column on the Format menu, and then click the AutoFit Selection button to force the columns to fit the long dates. This method often makes columns wider than you would like, particularly if the remaining values in the column are narrow.

Excel provides a number of tools to make long labels fit better on a report. Some worksheets are wider than they are tall. In some situations, if cells can take up less horizontal space and more vertical space, your report will fit better on a page. You can orient long labels at an angle so they will take up very little horizontal space using the following steps:

1. Select all the wide labels and set a column width that would be appropriate if the labels were the same width as the data in the columns. Select Column from the Format menu, and then select Width. Type *3.5* and press Enter.
2. Select Cells from the Format menu, and then click the Alignment tab. Select General in the Horizontal list, and then drag the red dot in the Orientation box upward until the Degrees box displays the value 45, as shown in Figure 16-4.
3. Click OK.

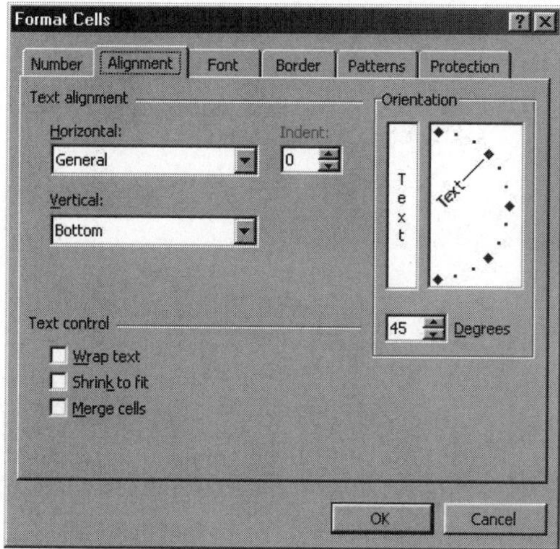

Figure 16-4
Rotate labels to consume less horizontal space.

Angled column labels take up very little horizontal space on a report. Figure 16-5 displays the result of the column label formatting.

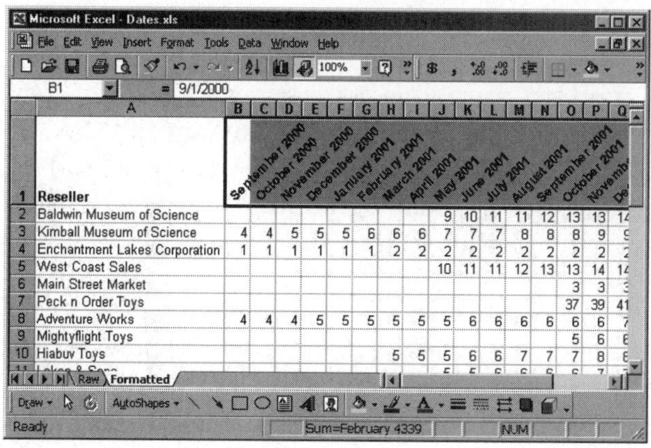

Figure 16-5
Angled text labels consume less column space.

Chapter 16

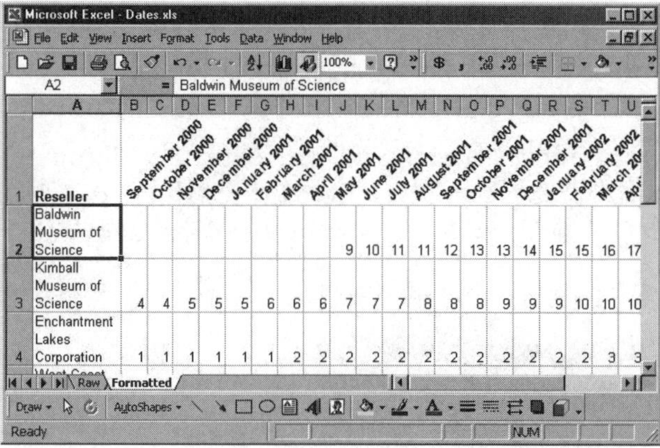

Figure 16-6
Wrapped text takes up less row space.

Sometimes—as with the reseller names on the sample worksheet—a single column takes up a lot of horizontal space. If you make the column narrower by dragging the column heading, the labels spill over into the blank cells on the right. Long labels can fit in a single column if the labels wrap within a cell. To wrap labels, select the cells (or the column) you want to change and choose Cells from the Format menu. Select the Wrap Text check box and click OK. The row height expands and the text wraps, as shown in Figure 16-6.

When you change the Wrap property for a cell, or when you edit the text in the cell, Excel automatically adjusts the row height. However, if you later change the column width, Excel does not adjust the row height, which might result in extra blank space or in truncated text. To fix the row height, select the rows you want to change and double-click the horizontal edge of any row label.

Formatting Cells

An Excel grid forms a rigid structure. One of the strengths of Excel is that rows and columns are guaranteed to line up for the entire worksheet. When you format a worksheet, however, the unwavering structure of the worksheet grid might be frustrating. Excel provides options for visually grouping cells, as well as for physically combining cells, to soften the rigidity of the grid.

Using Borders to Group Columns

An uninterrupted series of month labels can seem to go on endlessly. You can make it easier to interpret a report by grouping months by fiscal quarter. One way to group months is to add a border around each group of three months.

Start by adding a box around the first three labels. Select three label cells (if the labels are tilted, ignore the portion of a cell that overlaps the cell to the right). Click the arrow next to the Border button and select the third border option, Outside Borders. Once you have a block of cells formatted with a pattern, you can repeat the pattern with other cells in a series. Now you can copy the format of this block of columns to the rest of the columns. Click the Format Painter button. Then press Ctrl+Shift+Right arrow to select the entire row of labels. The Format Painter applies the pattern of the selected cells to the new selection, as shown in Figure 16-7. (For more control over duplicating the format, you can copy the source range, select the target range, and then use the Paste Special command on the Edit menu to paste the format.)

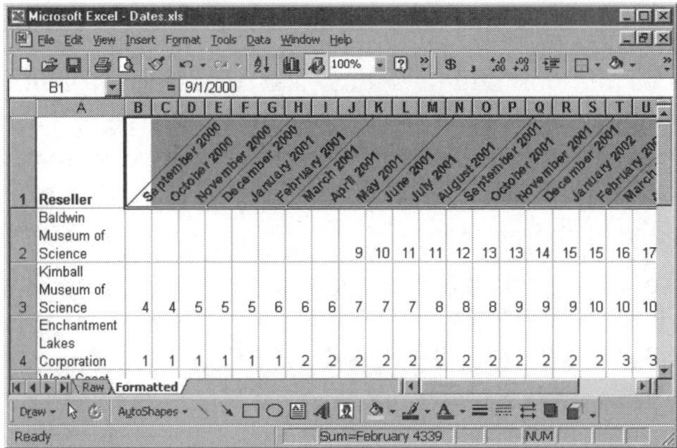

Figure 16-7
The Format Painter can copy a multiple-cell formatting pattern.

Creating Labels in Merged Cells

Perhaps you want to add a row below each month's label that shows the quarter for each group of columns. To do that, insert a new row under the month labels. The new row retains the formatting from the row above it. Select the row, select Clear from the Edit menu, and then click Formats to remove the formatting. In the new cell under the first month label (cell B2), type *2000Q1* for the quarter label.

The quarter label should apply to three columns. To merge the three cells into a single cell for the quarter label, select the three cells and click the Merge And Center button on the Formatting toolbar. (Clicking the toolbar button is equivalent to displaying the Format Cells dialog box and then selecting the Merge Cells and Center Horizontal options.) Cell B2 now takes up the space of all three cells. (Cells C2 and D2 no longer officially exist; if you refer to them in formulas, they are treated as empty cells.) Add a border around the cell before you copy the cell format to the other columns.

To use AutoFill to extend the quarter labels to the right, drag the AutoFill handle for cell B2 to the right until you reach the right edge of cell Y2, just below the August 2002 label. (If the quarter labels were in a column, you could double-click the AutoFill handle to extend the selection to match the adjacent column. To use AutoFill in a row, you must drag the handle.)

Merging cells is a useful way of dealing with labels that apply to multiple rows or columns. After you merge cells, you can format the resulting cell the same as any ordinary cell.

Note After you merge cells, you can no longer select an entire row or column that passes through the merged cell without selecting all the rows and columns that pass through that cell. If you frequently select individual rows or columns, you might want to limit your use of merged cells.

Creating and Modifying Styles

By default, Excel formats numbers snugly against the right side of a cell. The Comma Style toolbar button will add a little bit of space to the right side of a cell. Select the range of cells that you want to format and click the Comma Style button. The Comma Style button does not format only the cells; it also applies a style to the cells. A *style* is a named group of formatting attributes.

The default Comma Style displays two decimal places when formatting numbers. You can remove the decimals by clicking the Decrease Decimal button twice. You can also change the cells by adjusting the definition of the style. Before you change the style, select an unformatted cell so that you can clearly see the effect of redefining the style.

Click Style on the Format menu. In the Style Name drop-down list, select Comma. (The Style Name drop-down list defaults to show the style assigned to the active cell.) In the Style Includes group, there are six check boxes—one for each tab in the Format Cells dialog box. For the Comma style, only the Number check box is selected, because that style changes only the number format of a cell. To change the number format for the style, click the Modify button, and then click the Number tab. Change the Decimal Places option to zero.

While you're at it, why not change the Comma style to make the cell background pale yellow? Click the Patterns tab. In the second group of colors, select the pale yellow color box in the top row. Then click OK to return to the Style dialog box. Both the Number and the Patterns check boxes are now selected in the Style dialog box. You can still apply the Comma style to cells without affecting the alignment, font, border, background, or protection.

Click the Add button to change the style definition without applying the style to the active cell, and then click the Close button. All the previously formatted cells change to the new style. One of the advantages of using a style is that when you change the definition of the style, all the cells assigned to that style automatically change.

Note When you redefine a style, the style changes for the entire workbook. The Normal style applies to all unformatted cells, so modifying the Normal style changes all unformatted cells in the workbook.

You can't undo a style modification, but you can restore the styles in a workbook to the default by merging the styles from an unmodified workbook. To restore the styles in the workbook Book1, for example, create a new workbook (Book2), activate Book1, and then display the Styles dialog box. Click Merge. In the Merge Styles From list, select Book2 and click OK.

Formatting Cell Backgrounds

AutoShapes objects provide beautiful formatting options—gradients, textures, patterns, and more. Unfortunately, you can't apply Clip Gallery formatting to the cell backgrounds of cells on a worksheet. There is a way you can achieve the same effect, however. You can create a picture of a range on a worksheet and format that picture, which then gives the appearance of formatting a worksheet.

Creating a Linked Picture

The first step is to create a drawing object that is a picture of a worksheet range. Suppose you have a simple worksheet grid of facts like the one shown in Figure 16-8. You want to add a striking gradient format to the background of the range.

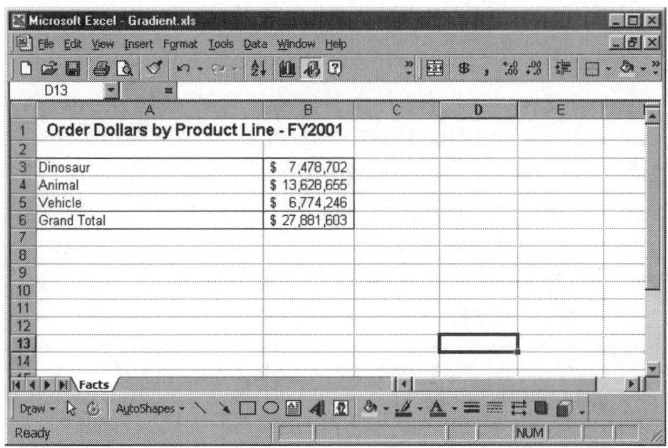

Figure 16-8
To add a gradient background, you must first create a picture.

Start by copying the range A1:B6. Then, to create a picture, you use the Paste Picture Link command, which only appears on the Edit menu if you hold down the Shift key while you open the Edit menu. Select cell A9, and hold down the Shift key as you select Paste Picture Link from the Edit menu. A visual copy of the original range appears, as shown in Figure 16-9.

This copy is a picture object, and it precisely copies the visual appearance of the original—including items such as the worksheet gridlines. (It sometimes produces an overlapping gridline effect.) To remove gridlines from the picture, you must

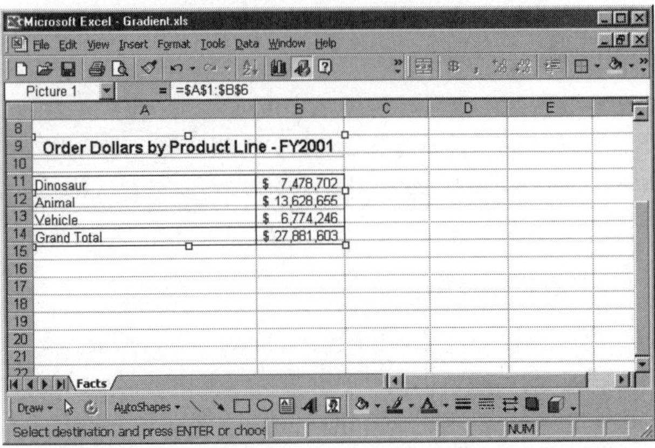

Figure 16-9
A picture of a range can create doubled gridlines.

remove them from the original sheet. Select Options on the Tools menu. Then select View, clear the Gridlines check box, and click OK.

Formatting a Linked Picture

You can format the picture using all the available AutoShapes tools. For example, to change the background of the picture to a gradient fill, select the picture, click the small arrow on the Fill Color button on the Drawing toolbar, and then click Fill Effects. On the Gradient tab, select the Preset option. From the Preset Colors list, select Nightfall. Select the bottom right variation and click OK. The result, which is terribly difficult to read, is shown in Figure 16-10.

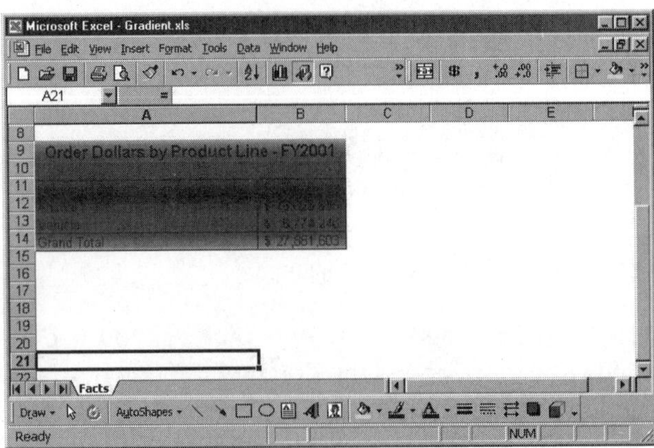

Figure 16-10
A dark background can make text hard to read.

The background is beautiful, but it is so dark, you can't see the text. You can't change the font color on the picture because the font is part of the original cell, not part of the picture. You can change the original text to white, but then you won't be able to see the text on the worksheet. If the font on the worksheet is set to Automatic, changing the foreground colors of the picture will not affect the font color.

If the font color is set to anything other than Automatic, you can control the shading with controls on the Picture toolbar. Change the font color of the original text to Gray-80%, which is barely distinguishable from black, and then select the picture. On the Picture toolbar, click the More Brightness button repeatedly until it reaches its maximum level and becomes disabled—about 16 clicks.

To add a finished look to the picture report, you can give it a multiple line border. To do that, click the Line Style button on the Drawing toolbar and select the bottom style in the list.

You now have a worksheet table that does not look anything like a worksheet table. It is still linked, however, to the original cells. If the numbers in the original cells change, the formatted table will change, as well.

Note A linked picture does not need to be located on the same worksheet—or even in the same workbook—as the original object. Simply cut the object and paste it where you want it to be. If you decide you want to break the link to the cells—leaving an unchangeable picture—select the picture object, clear the reference from the formula bar, and press Enter.

Creating Complex Charts

Most business charts consist of pie charts, line charts, and bar charts. Excel can create these basic charts, and it also can create more interesting charts.

Creating a Pie of a Pie

When you create a pie chart, you might find that some segments are significantly smaller than the rest. Figure 16-11 shows a table, along with a default pie chart.

Note The sample document for this section is Pie.xls.

Creating a Pie of Pie Chart

It's hard to see what is going on with this pie chart. To begin with, the title takes up valuable space and does not provide useful information; it can be removed. The legend takes up a lot of room, but is still not large enough to show all the resellers; you can replace the legend with labels for each segment. Delete the legend and double-click anywhere on the pie. In the Format Data Series dialog box, select the Data Labels tab, select the Show Labels option, and click OK. Double-click the new labels, select the Font tab, and change the font size to 9 points. Clear the Auto Scale check box and click OK. The result appears in Figure 16-12.

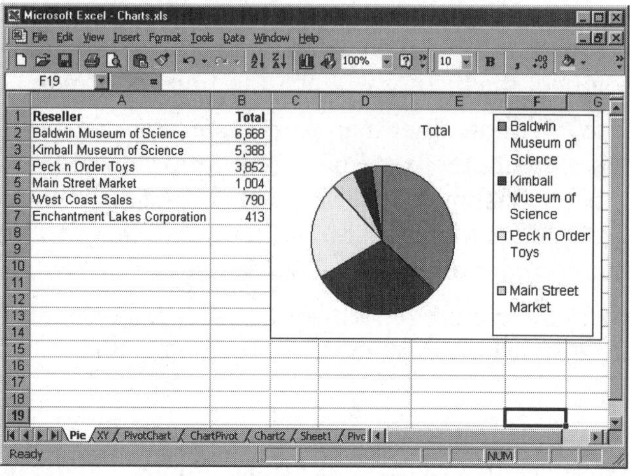

Figure 16-11
A default pie chart can be hard to interpret.

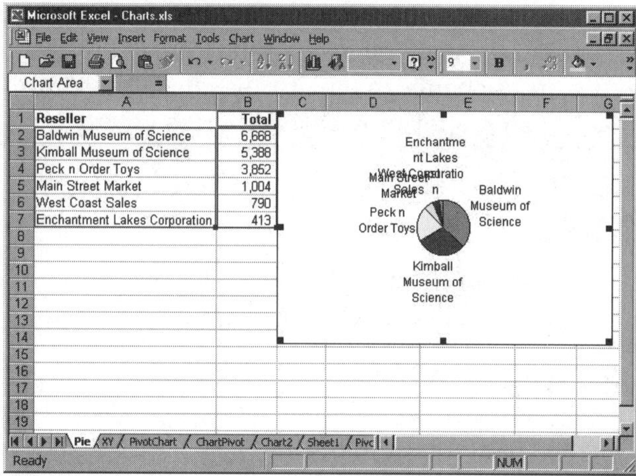

Figure 16-12
Small segments can have overlapping labels.

Because some of the segments are small, the labels overlap. Excel's Pie Of Pie chart option allows you to combine these small segments into a single segment, along with a separate pie chart that shows just the small segments. Select Chart Type on the Chart menu. Select the Pie Of Pie chart option (the third chart on the top row) and click OK.

By default, Excel adds two segments to the second pie. In this chart, there are three small segments. To change how many segments are added to the secondary pie chart, double-click either pie chart, select the Options tab, change the value of Second Plot Contains The Last to 3, and click OK.

The labels in each pie chart no longer overlap, but some of the labels between the segments still overlap. To move a single segment's label, click the label once (to select all the labels) and then click it a second time (to select the single label). Drag it to a new location; a line appears linking the label to the segment. You can't change the width of a text box, but you can edit the text within the box—abbreviating or hyphenating long words. You can also delete an individual label. For example, you might want to delete the Other label.

You can also resize the plot area to make it fill as much of the chart box as possible. To do that, click between the two pies to select the plot area, which will reveal its move border and sizing handles. When you resize the inner box of the plot area, Excel then expands the label area around the chart. Figure 16-13 shows the modified Pie of Pie chart.

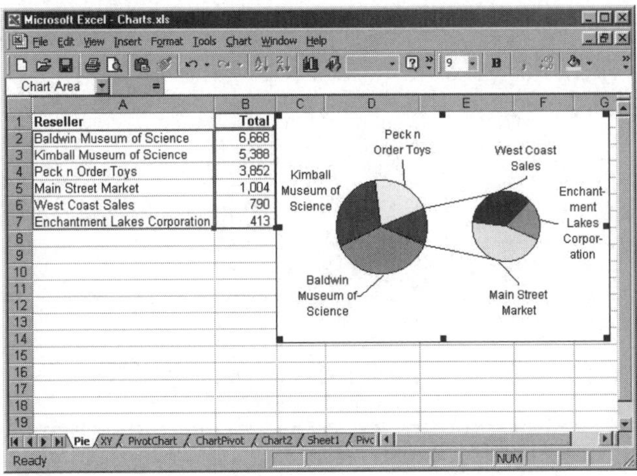

Figure 16-13
A pie of pie chart can make small segments easier to see.

The pie of pie chart allows you to clearly see the relationship between the resellers. You can see that combined, the smaller three resellers accounted for only a fraction of the orders that month—less than the other three resellers. However, you can still see the detail for the small resellers without their being lumped into the Other label.

Creating a Macro to Normalize the Size of a Pie Chart

One of the benefits of a pie chart is that the size of each segment is proportionate to the value for that segment—a segment that accounts for twice as many orders as another has twice the area. A default pie of pie chart does not maintain that equal area relationship.

On the Options tab of the Format Data Series dialog box, you can specify the radius of the secondary pie as a percentage of the radius of the primary pie. The default radius for the secondary pie is 75 percent of the main chart. The formula for the area of a circle is $a=\pi r^2$. In other words, the area is proportionate to the square of the radius. With a radius 75 percent of that of the primary pie, the secondary pie has an area that is 56 percent (75 percent x 75 percent) of that of the primary pie.

In the example, the sum of the three smaller segments is 12 percent of the total. For the smaller pie to have the same area as the Other segment of the larger pie, the radius needs to be the square root of 12 percent:35 percent. If you double-click the pie, select the Options tab, and change the Size Of Second Plot value to 35, you get the result shown in Figure 16-14.

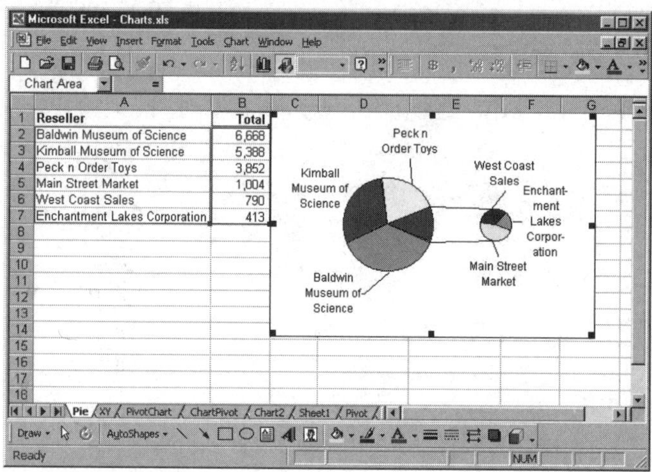

Figure 16-14
You can make the area of the second pie match the area of the Other segment.

Having to calculate a new radius percentage for the smaller pie each time you change any of the data values might discourage you from keeping the areas proportional. To relieve the tedium, you can create the following *SetSmallPieSize* macro to calculate the appropriate radius for you. The hardest part of the macro consists of summing up the values for the large and small pies to calculate what percentage the small pie is of the large pie.

```
Sub SetSmallPieSize()
    Dim myGroup As ChartGroup   ' Pie Chart portion of chart
    Dim mySeries As Series      ' Data series
    Dim myBigTotal As Double    ' Total value for main pie chart
    Dim myCutoff As Long        ' Number of segments on small pie
    Dim mySmallTotal As Double  ' Total of segments in a small pie chart
    Dim mySmallSize As Long     ' Size for small pie
    Dim n As Long               ' Number of points in series
    Dim i As Long               ' Loop counter

    Set myGroup = ActiveSheet.ChartObjects(1).Chart.PieGroups(1)
    Set mySeries = myGroup.SeriesCollection(1)
    n = mySeries.Points.Count
    myCutoff = myGroup.SplitValue
```

```
    ''' Pie of Pie has extra "virtual" segment
    ''' Loop through all "real" segments
    For i = 1 To n - 1
        myBigTotal = myBigTotal + mySeries.Values(i)
        ''' Count small values only if greater than cutoff
        If i >= n - myCutoff Then
            mySmallTotal = mySmallTotal + mySeries.Values(i)
        End If
    Next i

    ''' Calculate new radius (as sqrt of ratio)
    mySmallSize = Sqr(mySmallTotal / myBigTotal) * 100
    ''' Minimum legal size of small pie is 5
    myGroup.SecondPlotSize = IIf(mySmallSize < 5, 5, mySmallSize)
End Sub
```

To reference an embedded chart, the macro uses the ChartObjects collection on the worksheet. The ChartObject collection object is the box that contains the chart; it has a Chart property that returns a reference to the Chart object inside the box. (When a Chart sheet is active, the ActiveSheet property returns a Chart object directly.)

In the hierarchy of a Chart object, a Chart object contains a collection of ChartGroup objects. A ChartGroup contains all the series that share a single chart type and that use the same axis for labels. Using the PieGroups property returns only the ChartGroups that have Pie as the chart type. Ordinarily, a pie chart has only a single group and a single series within the group, but the property is still associated with the group.

The SplitValue property (which corresponds to the Second Plot Contains The Last on the Options tab in the Format Data Series dialog box) is a property of the ChartGroup.

The first executable statement in the macro, *Set myGroup = ActiveSheet.ChartObjects(1).Chart.PieGroups(1)*, stores the first (only) ChartGroup object in a variable, because the macro refers to it three times. The second statement, *Set mySeries = myGroup.SeriesCollection(1)*, saves a reference to the first (only) series in the group. For a chart with only one chart group, getting the series collection from the group is equivalent to getting it from the chart.

The next two statements simply store the number of points in the series and the cutoff point for the secondary pie. The loop accumulates the value from each point in the series, accumulating the values separately for those points that are on the secondary pie.

Note You might expect that the value of a data point is a property of the point, but that is not how the object model works. The values for a series are all stored in a single Values array that is affiliated with the series. Values are associated with the series because you might create a macro that replaces all the values of a series at one time—perhaps even changing the number of points in the process. See "Creating a Properly Labeled Bubble

Chart" later in this chapter for details on how to use a macro to change the values of a series.

The final two statements of the macro are the raison d'être for the macro. Dividing the small total by the big total produces the percentage of total for the small pie. Taking the square root produces the desired radius percentage, which must be multiplied by 100 to get the value for the SecondPlotSize property. The final statement simply ensures that the value of the property is not less than the minimum value of 5 (which produces a remarkably small pie).

Making a Macro Run When a Data Value Changes

You can run the *SetSmallPieSize* macro when you change the value of any data point, or when you change the number of points assigned to the second pie. It might be nice to have the macro run itself when you change a value on the worksheet. The easiest way to do this is to add an event handler to the worksheet's Calculate event.

The worksheet will recalculate only if the input cell for a formula changes. In cell B8, type the formula *=SUM(B2:B7)*, which will calculate each time any of the values on the chart change. Then right-click the worksheet tab and select View Code to open the worksheet's module. Select Worksheet from the Object drop-down list and select Calculate from the Properties drop-down list to create the following *Worksheet_Calculate* handler procedure. Add the statement *SetSmallPieSize* to the procedure. It should look like this (see "Creating Event Handles" in Chapter 6 for details about creating event handlers):

```
Private Sub Worksheet_Calculate()
    SetSmallPieSize
End Sub
```

Changing a value on the worksheet will cause the total formula to recalculate, which will cause the event handler to run, which will run the macro, which will adjust the size of the secondary pie chart (in the house that Jack built).

Creating and Labeling an XY Chart

Charts are often used to visually detect correlations. For example, if the return of a mutual fund is correlated to the risk of the fund, you can predict that if a fund's return is high, the risk also will be high.

Note The sample document for this section is XY.xls.

Adding Labels to an XY Chart

An XY (scatter) chart is very effective in showing the correlation of two variables. Unlike a line chart—which uses the X-axis (the horizontal axis) for evenly spaced labels and which scales values only on the Y-axis (the vertical axis)—an XY (scatter) chart scales values on both the X-axis and the Y-axis.

Note XY charts are often used to graphically represent mathematical functions. In Excel, you can use named array formulas to graph a mathematical function without filling the function into worksheet cells. See "Charting an Algebraic function" in Chapter 13 for details about how to use a named array formula in an XY chart.

Figure 16-15 displays an XY chart that shows the correlation of risk and return for four fictitious companies.

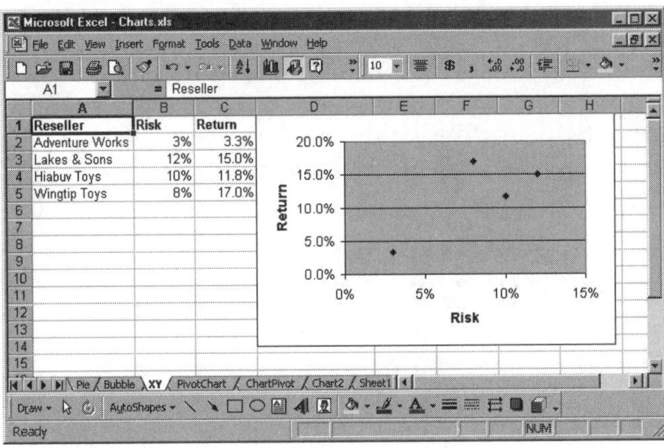

Figure 16-15
An XY chart correlates two variables.

To create the XY chart on the sample worksheet, select the range B1:C5, click the Chart Wizard button, select XY (Scatter) from the Chart Type list, and click the Next button twice. On the Titles tab, type *Risk* in the Value (X) Axis box, and type *Return* in the Value (Y) Axis box. Clear the Show Legend check box on the Legend tab and click Finish.

On this chart, you expect points to fall roughly on a line extending from the lower left corner to the upper right corner. Three of the companies fall roughly on the expected line, but one company has better returns for the risk than the others. However, it is hard to identify which point represents which company.

Unfortunately (and unbelievably!), Excel does not have an easy way to link the list of company names to the chart. To link the labels to points, first create automatic labels for the points, and then replace each automatic label with the company name. To add the X-axis value as a label for each point, double-click a point on the chart to display the Format Data Series dialog box. Click the Data Labels tab, select the Show Label option, and click OK. Now you must replace each default label with a link to the company name.

To replace one label, click the label to select all the labels. Click the label again to select the one label. Type an equal sign (=), click the cell containing the label (the reseller name next to the value on the worksheet), and press Enter. To center the label, double-click it, select the Alignment tab, select Center from the Label Position drop-down list, and click OK. You must repeat the process for each additional label, which might not be a serious problem for four data points, but it would certainly get old fast if you were labeling 200 points.

Note After you add labels to a data point, clicking a marker always selects the label. To select the series of markers, click the arrow next to the Chart Objects list on the Chart toolbar and select the series name. Once you've selected the series, you can select an individual point by pressing the Right arrow key.

Creating a Macro to Add Labels to an XY Chart

You can create the following *AddXYLabels* macro to automate the process of adding centered labels to a chart. The macro assumes that the label for each point is immediately to the left of the X value cell. Rather than enter the label as a constant, it assigns a link back to the label cell.

```
Sub AddXYLabels()
    Dim myChart As Chart
    Dim mySeries As Series
    Dim myData As Range
    Dim myPoint As Point
    Dim sFormula As String
    Dim sRange As String
    Dim i As Long

    Set myChart = ActiveSheet.ChartObjects(1).Chart
    Set mySeries = myChart.SeriesCollection(1)

    sFormula = mySeries.Formula
    ExtractFirstString sFormula, ","
    sRange = ExtractFirstString(sFormula, ",")
    Set myData = Range(sRange).Offset(0, -1)

    For i = 1 To mySeries.Points.Count
        Set myPoint = mySeries.Points(i)
        myPoint.ApplyDataLabels xlDataLabelsShowLabel
        myPoint.DataLabel.Text = "=" & myData(i).Address(1, 1, xlR1C1, 1)
        myPoint.DataLabel.Position = xlLabelPositionCenter
    Next i
End Sub
```

The first two executable statements simply assign references to the chart—assuming that the chart is the first chart on the active sheet—and to the XY series—assuming that the series is the first series on the chart.

The Chart object model does not provide any convenient method to determine the range source for a data series. The only way to retrieve the source range address is to parse the SERIES formula. You can see the SERIES formula in the formula bar when you select the series. In the SERIES formula, the X value range is the second argument. In other words, it is between the second and third commas. The macro uses the *ExtractFirstString* function described in "Creating Procedures" in Chapter 4. The macro calls the function once to discard everything through the first comma, and a second time to extract the X Value range address. Inserting the address from the SERIES formula as an argument in a Range method converts the address to a Range object. The Offset method shifts the range one cell to the left—the presumed location of the labels.

Inside the loop, the macro assigns a reference to the current point and adds a default label to the point. The macro then extracts the address from the corresponding cell in the label range. The arguments to the Address method specify that the address should be an absolute, external reference in R1C1 notation—including the worksheet name. The equal sign (=) prefixed to the address converts it into a formula. The final statement in the loop simply centers the label.

Creating a Properly Labeled Bubble Chart

Note The sample document for this section is Bubble.xls.

A bubble chart is like an XY chart. It plots one value against another in a grid. However, a bubble chart allows you to correlate a third value—usually some kind of magnitude value. Suppose, for example, that in addition to risk and return rates, you also have market capitalization values for several companies.

Creating a Bubble Chart with Series Labels

Unfortunately, the Chart Wizard does not seem to understand how to properly create a bubble chart. Figure 16-16 shows two different default bubble charts.

The chart to the right of the table is the result if you select the entire table (A1:D5) before starting the Chart Wizard. It includes two company names, but the markers are all wrong. The chart below the table is the result if you select only the data range (B2:D5) before starting the Chart Wizard. It has the correct markers, but in only one of the series, so you can't tell which company is which. With a bubble chart, you need a legend that shows the name of each company because text labels would clutter the chart. To show the company names as a legend, each company must be a separate series on the chart.

The only way to add each company to a separate series is to add the companies one at a time. To create an appropriately labeled bubble chart, select the range B2:D2 and click the Chart Wizard button. In the Bubble category, select the 3-D option and click the Next button. In step 2 of the Chart Wizard, select the Series tab, click in the Name

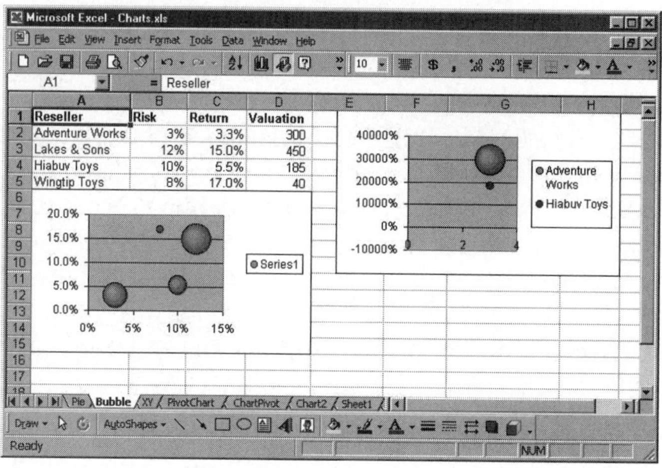

Figure 16-16
Default bubble charts don't work well.

box, and then click the cell containing the label, as shown in Figure 16-17. Click Finish to add the series to the chart.

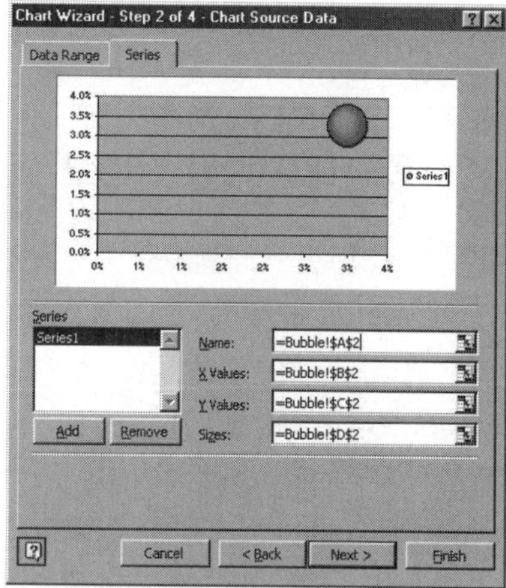

Figure 16-17
After creating the marker, add the series name.

To add additional series to the chart, select the data range (for example, B3:D3). Drag the border of the range onto the chart, and then click OK in the Paste Special dialog box. After adding all the new series, activate the chart and click Source Data on the Chart menu. On the Series tab, add the Name reference to each of the series. After you add all the series and assign names to each, the chart looks like the one shown in Figure 16-18.

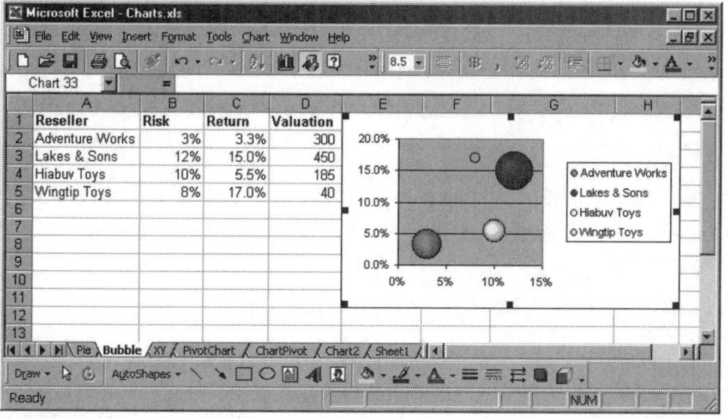

Figure 16-18
A proper bubble chart has a legend entry for each data point.

As with adding labels to an XY chart, creating a bubble chart with an appropriate legend is not too bad with just a few series, but it is not fun if you have to do it very often.

Creating a Macro to Create a Bubble Chart with a Legend

The following *MakeBubbleChart* macro creates a bubble chart from a table with legend entries in the first column. Before running the macro, make sure the active cell is somewhere in the table.

```
Sub MakeBubbleChart()
    Dim myRange As Range
    Dim myRow As Range
    Dim myChart As Chart
    Dim mySeries As Series
    Dim i As Long

    Set myRange = ActiveCell.CurrentRegion
    Set myRange = Intersect(myRange, myRange.Offset(1, 1))

    Set myChart = ActiveSheet.ChartObjects.Add(100, 50, 300, 150).Chart
    For i = 1 To myRange.Rows.Count
        Set myRow = myRange.Rows(i)
        myChart.SeriesCollection.Add Source:=myRow, Rowcol:=xlColumns, _
            SeriesLabels:=False, CategoryLabels:=True, Replace:=False
        Set mySeries = myChart.SeriesCollection(i)
        mySeries.Name = myRow.Cells(1).Offset(0, -1)
        myChart.ChartType = xlBubble3-DEffect
    Next i
End Sub
```

The macro first assigns a reference to the current region around the active cell. It then eliminates the first row and column from the range. The Intersect method finds the intersection of two Range objects. The Offset method returns a new Range object that is shifted from the original. The first argument tells how many rows to shift down; the second argument tells how many columns to shift to the right. The intersection of a range—with the same range shifted down one—and right one removes the first row and first column.

The macro then uses the Add method of the worksheet's ChartObjects collection object to create a new chart. The arguments of the Add method provide the *Left*, *Top*, *Width*, and *Height* values for the chart. Because the Add method returns a ChartObject object, the macro can retrieve the chart from that object and assign it to an object variable.

Note The Chart Wizard creates an embedded chart by first creating a chart sheet and then changing the location of the chart to a worksheet. The Add method of the ChartObjects object is a more direct route to the same end. Even though the Add method of the ChartObjects collection object is no longer documented, it is essentially identical to the Add method of a TextBoxes object.

The macro loops through each row in the (shrunken) source range. For each row, the macro adds a new Series object, passing as a source range the same three data cells you would drag onto the chart if you were manually adding a series. The arguments to the Add method correspond to the arguments that appear in the Paste Special dialog box when you drag the range onto the chart.

With very rare exceptions, all Add methods in the Excel object model return a reference to the newly added object. The Add method of the SeriesCollection object is one of those exceptions. This Add method merely returns *True* if it successfully adds a series. The statement after the one with the Add method compensates for the deficiencies of the method by retrieving a reference to the newly created series. If the Add method returned a reference to the new object, the macro could have used a *For Each* loop, rather than the more cumbersome *For* loop. (You must use a *For* loop if the macro needs to reference corresponding elements of two different collections.)

Once the macro obtains a reference to the Series object, it adds it as the name of the cell to the left of the current row.

The final statement in the loop converts the chart to a bubble chart. This might seem like a strange location for changing the type of the chart, because it executes each time through the loop while the chart type should need to be set only once. The problem lies in convoluted rules regarding a bubble chart.

Unlike any other chart series, a bubble chart series requires an additional property—the BubbleSizes property. In the SERIES formula, the *BubbleSizes* value becomes a fifth argument that appears in no other chart type. In an effort to avoid errors, a chart refuses to be converted into a bubble chart unless at least one series contains a valid BubbleSizes property. However, with a perverse turn of logic, you can't assign a BubbleSizes property to a series unless the series belongs to a bubble chart! In fact, if you record the process of creating a bubble chart, running the recorded macro fails with an error because the recorder assigns the chart type before creating the first series.

You might find it educational to step through the first loop in the *MakeBubbleChart* macro. When you use a range with three horizontal cells to create a data series, Excel actually creates two series using the first of the three cell values as the category label for each of the other two cells. When the macro converts the chart to a bubble chart, Excel collapses the two series into one, thus providing the extra value for the bubble chart.

Creating Gradient Surface Charts

A surface chart is a special chart that looks like a topographical map of the data. It is used primarily to plot complex mathematical functions, but you also can use a surface chart for simple business data, creating either a banded area chart or a banded ribbon chart. Creating a gradient sequence of colors is an effective touch for a surface chart, and the technique can be applied to coloring any chart.

Note The sample document for this section is Surface.xls.

Creating a Banded Area Chart by Using a Surface Chart

You can create a chart that looks like an area chart with colored bands using a surface chart. A surface chart requires a minimum of two series. In effect, a surface chart stretches an elastic sheet between the two data series, and then colors sections of the sheet according to which pair of gridlines the stretched sheet passes between. To create the effect of an area chart, you simply make all the values of one series equal to zero. Figure 16-19 shows an example of a simple banded area chart.

To create a surface chart, select cells A2:C5, click the Chart Wizard button, select a surface chart, and click Finish. Remove the legend; it is redundant with the Y-axis labels. Make the plot area as large as possible, and set the font size of the chart area to a reasonable, small size. To remove the 3-D effect on the chart, click 3-D View on the Chart menu, type *0* (zero) in the Elevation, Rotation, and Perspective boxes, and click OK. To remove the S1 label for Series 1, click Source Data on the Chart menu, select the Series tab, type ="" in the Series1 Name text box, and click OK.

You can also create a 3-D banded ribbon effect with a surface chart. For the ribbon effect, use the same values for the two data series for the chart. Figure 16-20 shows the effect of the chart.

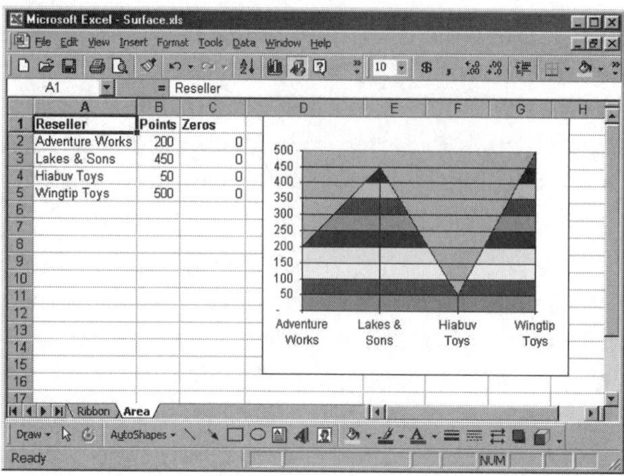

Figure 16-19
A surface chart can create a banded area chart.

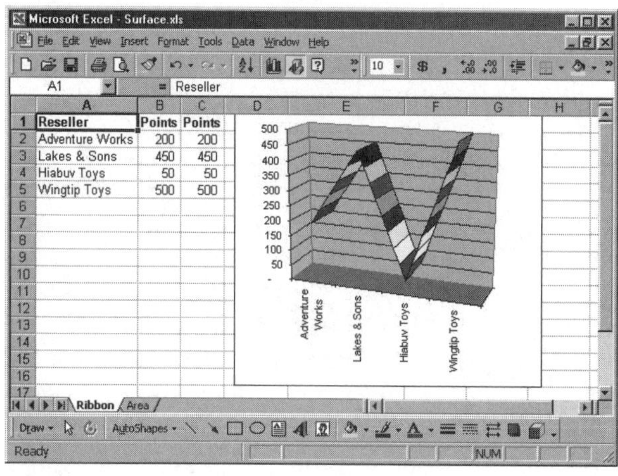

Figure 16-20
A surface chart can create a banded ribbon chart.

The steps for creating this chart are the same as for the banded area chart, except that you don't need to remove the 3-D effect.

Changing Colors for a Chart to an Even Gradient

A surface chart usually looks better if the colors in the bands are an even gradient, similar to a topographical chart. Excel does not let you select the series on a surface chart. To change the color of a band, you must modify the legend. Turn on the legend, click once to select the legend box, click a legend entry to select the entry, and then click the marker box to select only the box. Double-click the box to format the color of the band.

Editing each band by using the legend entry is not only painstaking, it is also ineffective, because you can select colors only from Excel's default palette and the palette has a limited number of colors that form smooth gradients. For example, by using the default palette, you cannot create a smooth gradient of 10 shades of green. Excel can display any of millions of different colors, but any one workbook can display only 56 colors at one time.

Before creating a macro to modify the palette, see what is involved in changing it directly. To change the colors of the workbook palette, click Options on the Tools menu, and then select the Color tab. As you can see in Figure 16-21, a certain row of colors is designated as Chart Fills.

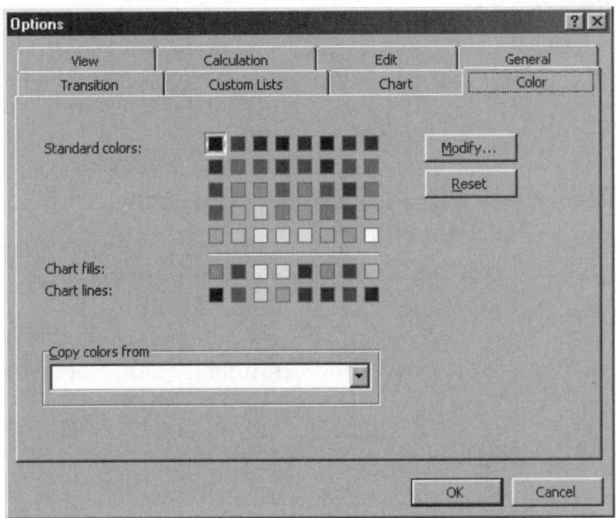

Figure 16-21
Default chart fill colors come from specific locations in the color palette.

The Chart Fill colors are those that a chart uses when the color is set to Automatic. To modify a color, select the position in the palette and click the Modify button. In the Colors dialog box, select the Custom tab to specify any of the millions of available colors, as shown in Figure 16-22.

Computers and—not surprisingly—macros think of color in terms of Red, Green, and Blue components. These correspond to the three colors of receptor cones on the retina of your eye. Most people think of colors, however, in terms of a color wheel. The grid box represents a flattened color wheel, and you can select a color by moving the white marker or by changing the numbers below the grid.

- The **Hue** number specifies a color on the color wheel that is represented across the top of the color grid.

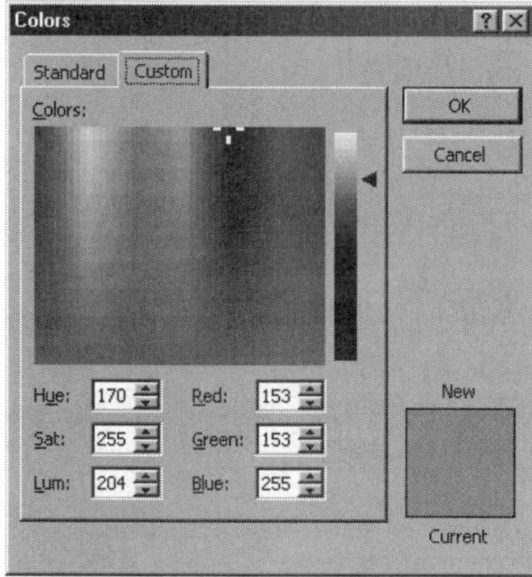

Figure 16-22
You can assign any of millions of colors to a palette position.

- The **Sat** number determines the *saturation*—or grayness—of the color, which is reflected in the vertical axis of the grid.
- The **Lum** number determines the color's *luminosity*—or brightness—as shown in the bar to the right of the grid.

You can use the "human" Hue, Saturation, and Luminosity values to find a color you want, and then make note of the Red, Green, and Blue values so that you can use them later in a macro. All the numbers in the dialog box are scaled between 0 and 255. As you will see by experimenting in the Color box for a few minutes, identical Red, Green, and Blue values that increase evenly between 0 and 255 create uniform shades of gray.

When you click OK in the Color box, the color of the selected palette position changes to that color. Changes to a color palette affect an entire workbook. If you need different color schemes for different charts, you need to keep them in separate workbooks. To restore all the colors of the palette to the default values, click the Reset button on the Color tab of the Options dialog box.

Creating a Macro to Change Palette Colors

You can create a very simple macro to change the palette colors for charts. The following *SetSimpleColors* macro changes the chart colors to shades of gray for a specified number of positions:

```
Sub SetSimpleColors()
    Const iMax = 4
    Dim i As Long
    Dim iStep As Long
    iStep = 256 / iMax
    For i = 0 To iMax
```

```
        ActiveWorkbook.Colors(17 + i) = _
            RGB(i * iStep, i * iStep, i * iStep)
    Next i
End Sub
```

The *iMax* constant determines how many colors (in addition to black) the macro will set. To create five colors ranging from black to white (with three intermediate gray values), set *iMax* to 4. The *iStep* variable stores the uniform increment for each step. The macro loops from zero to the maximum number (zero will produce black). The first chart color position in the palette is at number 17. (When the palette numbering scheme was first worked out, chart colors began on the third row of the palette—which was position number 17—because each row contained eight entries.)

You can create a fancier version of the macro specifically for a surface chart that determines how many legend entries there are to color.

```
Sub SetSurfaceColors()
    Dim myChart As Chart
    Dim iMax As Long
    Dim iColor As Long
    Dim iStep As Long
    Dim i As Long

    Set myChart = ActiveSheet.ChartObjects(1).Chart
    If Not myChart.HasLegend Then
        myChart.HasLegend = True
        iMax = myChart.Legend.LegendEntries.Count
        myChart.HasLegend = False
    Else
        iMax = myChart.Legend.LegendEntries.Count
    End If
    iMax = iMax - 1
    iStep = 255 / iMax
    For i = 0 To iMax
        If i < 40 Then
            iColor = 17 + i
        Else
            iColor = i - 39
        End If
        ActiveWorkbook.Colors(iColor) = _
            RGB(iStep * i, iStep * i, iStep * i)
    Next i
End Sub
```

The macro has only two significant differences from the simple macro. First, the macro must determine the number of legend entries for the surface chart, temporarily displaying the legend as necessary. The *iMax* value is one less than the number of legend entries. Second, the macro handles the possibility of more than 40 legend entries. The chart colors begin at palette position 17. If a chart has more than eight colors, the chart simply uses incremental palette positions until it runs out at 56 colors.

At that point, the chart starts using the palette positions starting from position one. The *If* block inside the loop mimics that behavior.

Figure 16-23 shows the banded area surface chart with 25 levels of gray. Compared to Figure 16-19 shown earlier, this figure shows the benefits of smooth, gradient colors for a surface chart—although smooth, gradient colors are useful in many other types of charts, as well.

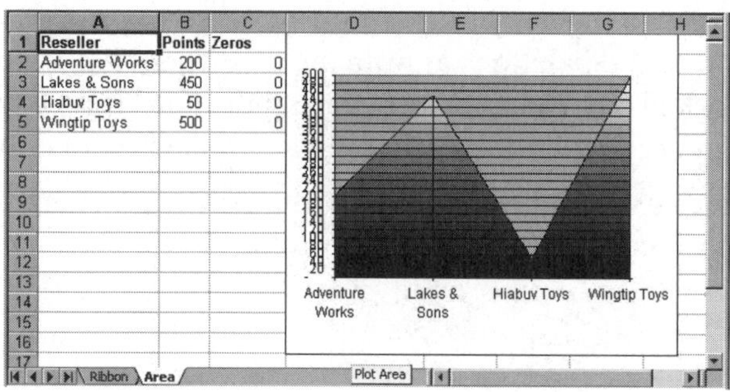

Reseller	Points	Zeros
Adventure Works	200	0
Lakes & Sons	450	0
Hiabuv Toys	50	0
Wingtip Toys	500	0

Figure 16-23
Change the palette to get smooth gradient colors.

Creating Charts Associated with PivotTables

New! PivotCharts—graphical PivotTables—are new in Office 2000. Like PivotTables, you can drag and drop, rearrange, and reselect freely. Unlike PivotTables, however, PivotCharts allow you to instantly see a visual representation of the data. PivotCharts bring with them many benefits. However, as with many program feature changes, there might be disruption to previous activities. For example, now that PivotCharts are available, it is more difficult than before to create a chart that is not a PivotChart if you use a PivotTable grid as a data source.

Note The sample document for this section is Pivot.xls.

Creating an Ordinary Chart Based on a PivotTable Range

You might find it useful to create a PivotTable combined with a chart on the same page of a report. One typical use is to display a chart—along with the tabular data from the chart—in a PivotTable below the chart. In previous versions of Excel, you could simply create the PivotTable and then select a range on the table and create a chart from it. The new PivotChart feature in Excel 2000 takes over the creation of the chart. If you select any portion of the PivotTable and then attempt to create a chart, the result is a new PivotChart.

If you just want a nonpivoting chart that displays the values in a PivotTable, a PivotChart can be problematic. Many PivotTable reports display time-series data with dates running across the top. When you create a time-series chart, you typically want the dates to appear across the category (X) axis of the chart, as shown in Figure 16-24.

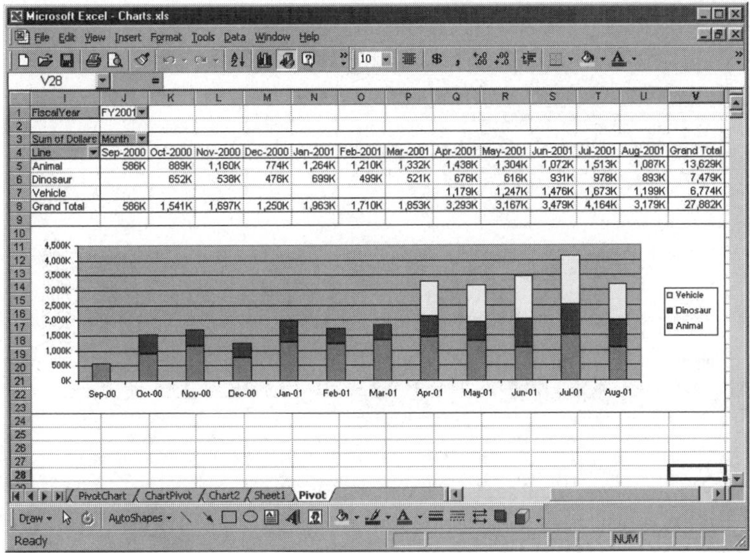

Figure 16-24
Time-series tables and charts often display dates horizontally.

Conversely, a PivotChart always displays the vertical row labels from the PivotTable as horizontal category labels. If you rearrange the chart to make the dates horizontal when you link a PivotChart to a PivotTable, you automatically rearrange the PivotTable.

One possible solution is to create two PivotTables—one PivotTable to be displayed and another hidden one based on the same data source or Pivot cache—that supports the chart. When you create reports with multiple worksheets, each containing a PivotTable report coupled with a chart, managing hidden tables makes it easy to introduce errors. Another solution is to create a traditional chart based on the range of data in a PivotTable. This second solution works well, but it requires a couple of tricks to implement.

Suppose, for example, that you want to create a regular chart based on a PivotTable range, similar to the worksheet shown earlier in Figure 16-24. If you simply select the range I4:U7—everything in the main part of the PivotTable except the grand totals—and create a chart, Excel will create a PivotChart.

The secret to creating a chart that is not a PivotChart is to first create an empty chart and then move the data into it. Select a cell that is not part of the PivotTable and click the Chart

Wizard button. In step 1 of the Chart Wizard, select a stacked column chart and click Finish. This creates an empty chart on the worksheet, as shown in Figure 16-25.

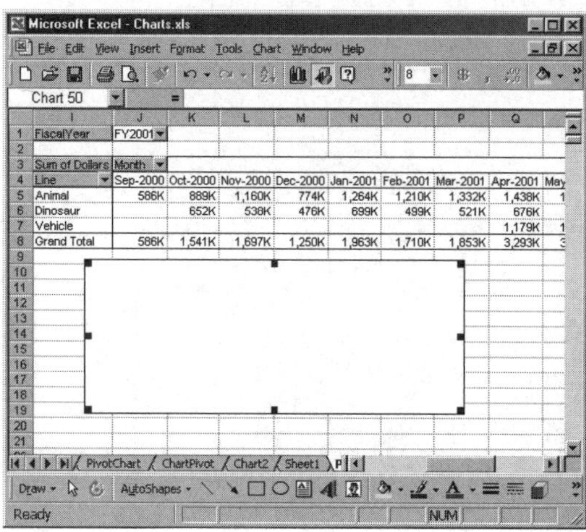

Figure 16-25
To create a regular chart, you must first create an empty one.

Position this empty chart at the location where you want the final chart to appear. Next, drag data from the PivotTable onto the chart. Don't drag any range that includes a PivotTable Field button—in other words, any selection that includes both the row headings and the column headings—or Excel will change the chart into a PivotChart. Instead, drag just the data—that is, range I5:U7—onto the chart. This creates a chart based on the cell addresses, not on the PivotTable.

However, the category axis labels on the new chart are simple numbers, not dates. As a separate action, drag the dates—range J4: U4—onto the chart. This creates an ordinary chart that links not to the PivotTable itself, but to the cells underlying the PivotTable. Naturally, if you change the PivotTable in any way, you will need to adjust the data range for the chart. If you're creating a static report, you don't need to worry about pivoting the table.

Creating a PivotChart Based on an Existing PivotTable

You might want to create a PivotChart based on an existing PivotTable. A PivotChart must always be linked to a PivotTable. When you pivot the chart, Excel actually pivots the linked PivotTable. If you want to base a PivotChart on an existing PivotTable—without having the chart modify the table—you should create a new PivotTable along with the new chart. To do that, take the following steps:

1. Select a cell that is not part of the existing PivotTable.
2. Select PivotTable on the Data menu, and click PivotChart Report.

3. In step 1 of the wizard, select the Another PivotTable Or PivotChart option, select the PivotChart (Cap with PivotTable) option, and then click the Next button.
4. In step 2 of the wizard, select the PivotTable you want to use as a base and click the Next button.
5. In step 3, specify that the new PivotTable will be created to support the chart on a new worksheet and then click Finish. Excel creates a new worksheet for the PivotTable, and it creates a new chart sheet for the PivotChart, as shown in Figure 16-26.

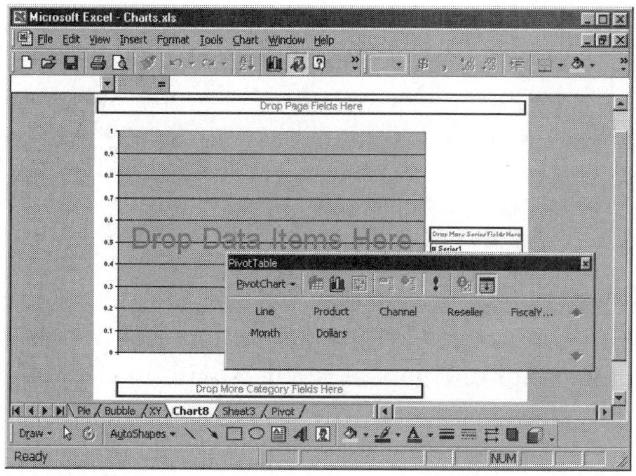

Figure 16-26
Creating a new PivotChart creates an accompanying PivotTable.

You might want to give a meaningful name to each sheet. You also might want to hide the sheet that contains the linked PivotTable.

A PivotChart has four areas: Page, Category, Series, and Data Items. These areas correspond to the four areas of a PivotTable. The Categories—that is, the X-axis labels—correspond to the Row fields of the PivotTable. The Series fields correspond to the Column field. Data Item fields and Page fields have the same name on a PivotTable as they have on a PivotChart.

In the chart, drag the Month field to the Category area, drag the Dollars field to the Data Items area, drag the Reseller field to the Series area, and drag the Product field to the Page area. As with a PivotTable, you can easily drag Field buttons from one area to another or select different Page Field values on a PivotChart. Each time you change the PivotChart, you actually change the linked PivotTable.

The Field buttons can take up quite a bit of space on a chart. Once you have finished pivoting, you can hide the buttons. To hide the buttons, click PivotChart on the PivotTable toolbar, and then select Hide PivotChart Field Buttons.

Note Although Excel creates a new PivotChart on a chart sheet, you can still embed the chart on an existing sheet. To do so, click Chart Location, select the As Object In option, and choose a worksheet location for the chart.

As with any chart, Excel defaults to display the chart as it would appear printed on a sheet of paper. If you intend to only use the chart interactively (not printed), you might want to size it to automatically fit the window. To do that, click View and choose Size With Window. A chart defaults to automatically scaling the font size as you adjust the size of the chart. This prevents Excel from rearranging the chart each time you resize it, but it can have the effect of creating a microscopic font if you shrink the size of the chart window.

To retain the font size even in a small window, first—while the font still automatically scales with the window size—adjust the size of the window until the font is an appropriate size. Then select the Chart Area—by clicking in the white area around the edges of the chart—and choose Selected Chart Area on the Format menu. On the Font tab, clear the Auto Scale check box and click OK. You can then reduce the size of the window and Excel will shrink the chart as needed to keep the font the same size.

Animating a PivotChart

Sometimes it is difficult to convey all the information you want in a static chart. For example, you might want to compare resellers with individual products as you maintain the perspective of time. One way to capture multiple dimensions in a chart is to animate the chart. This can be particularly effective if you transfer the time dimension into the page field, because you can watch your business change over time.

Before creating an animation macro, you should add a specially named text box to the chart so that the macro can use it as a title. When you animate a PivotChart, the Page Field value will continually change, but you probably want to keep the PivotChart Field Buttons hidden. A good solution is to make the animation display the value of the current page field in a text box. A text box takes up less room on the chart than a title.

To create a text box on the chart, select the Chart Area, and type some sample text. (Type a label as long as the longest page field item label.) After you press Enter, Excel creates a text box in the center of the chart. Position and format the text box. To assign a name to the text box you can use from the macro, select the text box border. In the name box (to the left of the formula bar), type *myTitle* and press Enter.

The following *AnimateChart1* macro cycles through each item of a page field, switching the chart, displaying the item name in the myTitle text box, and pausing for a half second after displaying each chart. (Expanded versions of this macro will be created later.)

```
Option Explicit
Declare Sub Sleep Lib «kernel32» (ByVal dwMilliseconds As Long)
```

```
Sub AnimateChart1()
    Dim mySleep As Long
    Dim myField As PivotField
    Dim c As Chart
    Dim s As Shape
    Dim i As Long

    Application.ScreenUpdating = False
    mySleep = 500

    Set c = ActiveChart
    Set myField = c.PivotLayout.PageFields(1)
    Set s = c.Shapes(«myTitle»)

    For i = 1 To myField.PivotItems.Count
        myField.CurrentPage = myField.PivotItems(i).Name
        s.TextFrame.Characters.Text = myField.CurrentPage

        Sleep mySleep
        Application.ScreenUpdating = True
        Application.ScreenUpdating = False
    Next i
End Sub
```

The most effective way to pause a macro during animation is to use the Sleep function from the Windows DLL. To use the Sleep function, you must place the Declare statement at the top of the module. ("Running a Procedure From a Dynamic Link Library" in Chapter 4 provides more background on using DLLs.) Once you have declared the Sleep function, you can use it in the macro as if it were part of Visual Basic for Applications (VBA). The Sleep function takes one argument that specifies how long, in thousandths of a second, to pause.

The first executable statement turns screen updating off. This keeps the chart from flashing while it is being switched to a new page. The *mySleep* variable will be used as the argument of the Sleep function. Setting it to *500* will make the macro pause for a half second.

The macro stores some useful objects in variables for later use. Because the chart is on a chart sheet, the ActiveChart property returns a direct reference to the chart. A text box on a chart is part of the generic Shapes collection.

Inside the loop, the macro assigns the Name property of the current PivotItem object to the CurrentPage property of the page field. Even though the CurrentPage property is really an object reference, you must assign the name of the item directly to the object name; you can't assign the value to the Name property or the Value property. In addition, although Name is the default property of a PivotItem object, you must explicitly specify the property when assigning the name to the CurrentPage object.

After assigning the new name to the CurrentPage property, the macro assigns the same name to the text box. Changing the text of a Shape object requires all the intermediate steps taken in the macro, although several of them seem as though they should be optional.

After preparing the new page, the macro pauses for the one-half second and then turns on screen updating (to display the page) and then off again (to prepare for the next cycle). Excel automatically turns on screen updating when the macro ends.

You can now run the *AnimateChart1* macro to cycle through the each page field in the chart. The macro displays each item for a moment before continuing the loop.

Creating an Event Handler that Starts a Macro

VBA allows you to create event handlers that respond to certain actions. Each application determines, as part of its object model, which events it will expose to VBA. ("Creating Event Handlers" in Chapter 6 explains how to create event handlers.) A Chart object in Excel—including a PivotChart—responds to many events. A Chart object has more events than all other aspects of Excel combined. When a chart is on a chart sheet, it is easy to add event handlers for the chart events. If a chart is embedded on a worksheet, you can still add event handlers using the same process as creating an event handler for application-level events, as described in "Handling Application Events" in Chapter 6.

First, create an event handler that runs the *AnimateChart1* macro when you click the chart. To do that, right-click the chart tab and select View Code from the context menu. In the Object drop-down list, select Chart. In the Procedure drop-down list, select MouseUp. This adds a *Chart_MouseUp* event handler procedure. A Chart object does not have a Click event; rather, clicking consists of pressing the mouse button down (a MouseDown event) and releasing the mouse button (a MouseUp event). You can choose to respond to either. As the body of the event handler procedure, type the name of the macro to run: *AnimateChart1*. The event handler should look like this:

```
Private Sub Chart_MouseUp(ByVal Button As Long, _
        ByVal Shift As Long, ByVal x As Long, ByVal y As Long)
    AnimateChart1
End Sub
```

Once the handler is in place, click the chart to run the macro. In effect, the *Chart_MouseUp* event handler simply turns the entire chart into a button.

Creating an Event Handler that Stops a Macro

The event handler still does not interact with the macro in any way. It simply runs the macro as a subroutine. Event handlers can also interact with a running macro. To allow this interaction, you must modify the *AnimateChart1* macro. Before making the changes, copy the macro and give the new version the name *AnimateChart2*.

You will change the macro to run in a loop that continues until you click the mouse button a second time. In other words, if the macro is not running, clicking will start it; if the macro is running, clicking will stop it. In the code listing, changed portions of the macro are bracketed with rows of asterisks.

```
Option Explicit
Declare Sub Sleep Lib «kernel32» (ByVal dwMilliseconds As Long)

'************************************
Public myRun As Boolean
'************************************

Sub AnimateChart2()
    Dim mySleep As Long
    Dim myField As PivotField
    Dim c As Chart
    Dim s As Shape
    Dim i As Long

    Application.ScreenUpdating = False
    mySleep = 500
    Set c = ActiveChart
    Set myField = c.PivotLayout.PageFields(1)
    Set s = c.Shapes(«myTitle»)

    '************************************
    s.Fill.Visible = msoTrue
    s.Fill.ForeColor.RGB = vbGreen

    Do
        i = i + 1
        If i > myField.PivotItems.Count Then i = 1
    '************************************

        myField.CurrentPage = myField.PivotItems(i).Name
        s.TextFrame.Characters.Text = myField.CurrentPage

        Sleep mySleep
    '************************************
        Application.ScreenUpdating = True
        DoEvents
        Application.ScreenUpdating = False
    Loop While myRun
    s.Fill.ForeColor.RGB = vbRed
    Application.StatusBar = False
    '************************************
End Sub
```

You need a way to communicate between the event handler and the macro, letting the macro know that it's time to stop. The public variable *myRun* at the top of the module is accessible to any procedure in the workbook, including event handlers. The first time you click the chart, the event handler will set the value of this variable to *True* before launching the macro. The second time you click the chart, the event handler will set this variable to *False.* The loop will continue as long as the variable *myRun* equals *True.*

As an extra clue that the macro is currently running, the revised macro changes the color of the title text box to green when it starts, and to red when it stops.

This macro replaces the *For* loop with a *Do* loop. A *Do* loop continues while—or until—a condition is *True*. The condition for stopping the loop is later in the macro. With the loss of the self-incrementing *For* loop, the macro needs a way to increment the *i* loop counter. You simply add 1 to the counter for each iteration through the loop, converting back to 1 when the number becomes larger than the count of items in the page field.

The next group of modified statements comes at the end of the loop. While a macro runs, it does not allow Microsoft Windows to monitor other events. To override that behavior, the macro needs a *DoEvents* statement. The *DoEvents* statement works only if ScreenUpdating is *True*. At the end of the loop, the macro now has a *DoEvents* statement between the two *Application.ScreenUpdating* statements.

In conjunction with changing the *For* loop to a *Do* loop, the macro also replaces the *Next i* statement with the statement *Loop While myRun*. This loop will run as long as the *myRun* variable is still equal to *True*. The macro itself will never change the value of the variable; the event handler will do that.

Now that the *AnimateChart2* macro has been modified, you need to enhance the *MouseUp* event handler. The handler needs to manage the *myRun* variable; it also needs to use a new mechanism for launching the macro. Here is the revised event handler:

```
Private Sub Chart_MouseUp(ByVal Button As Long, ByVal Shift As Long, _
        ByVal x As Long, ByVal y As Long)
    myRun = Not myRun
    If myRun Then
        Application.OnTime Now, «AnimateChart2»
    End If
End Sub
```

First, the procedure simply toggles the *myRun* variable. Then, if *myRun* is *True* (meaning that the handler is starting up the macro), the handler launches the *AnimateChart2* macro.

The event handler must be tricky about how to launch the macro. If it runs the macro as a subroutine, the handler will keep running until the subroutine finishes. Obviously, if the handler is processing an old event, it can't respond to a new one. The secret is to use the OnTime method, which tells Excel when to launch a macro. The handler tells Excel to launch the *AnimateChart2* macro immediately, which means to launch it as soon as the handler concludes.

Note If you use the OnTime method to launch a macro when the macro is in a regular module—that is, when its name appears in the Tools, Macro, Run dialog box—all you need is the name of the macro. If you add the macro to a class module such as the worksheet code module that contains the event handlers, you must prefix the macro name with the code name of the worksheet. The code name might be different from the name on the worksheet tab. In the Project Explorer window, the code name for a worksheet is the name that does not appear in parentheses.

Once both the macro and the event handler have been modified, you can click the chart to start the animation, which will be repeated until you click the chart a second time.

Creating an Event Handler that Modifies the Behavior of a Macro

Starting and stopping a macro are both very good events, but you also can use an event handler to modify the behavior of a macro while it continues to run. For example, while the animation macro is running, you might want to change the speed of the animation, or change the direction—scrolling backward through the months instead of forward. With only a few fairly simple modifications to the macro-end along with a new event handler-end, you can change the way the macro behaves based on the location of the mouse pointer without requiring any mouse clicks at all.

This technique makes use of the MouseMove event. The MouseMove event occurs each time you make the slightest move with the mouse. The MouseMove event tells the event handler the exact location of the mouse pointer. You can use Public variables in the chart code module to pass the mouse location to the *AnimateChart* macro, allowing it to change behavior depending on the location of the mouse.

Change the macro so that if the mouse pointer is inside the plot area, nothing changes on the chart.

- If you move the mouse pointer above the plot area, the animation will speed up.
- If you move the mouse pointer below the plot area, the animation will slow down.
- If you move the mouse pointer to the left of the plot area, the animation will be reversed.
- If the mouse pointer is anywhere on the plot area or to the right of the plot area, the animation will occur in normal forward order.

Because reverse is an atypical action, it's appropriate that you should have to move the mouse pointer to a small area to capture it.

To give visual clues as to what the macro is doing, have the status bar display a message if the macro is speeding up, slowing down, or going in reverse. While the mouse pointer is in the normal position—in the middle of the plot area—the status bar should show nothing.

The following *MouseMove* event handler is very simple. You can create it before modifying the *AnimateChart2* macro.

```
Private Sub Chart_MouseMove(ByVal Button As Long, _
        ByVal Shift As Long, ByVal x As Long, ByVal y As Long)
    myX = x / 1.33
    myY = y / 1.33
End Sub
```

To create this event handler, all you need to do is select MouseMove from the Procedure drop-down list to generate the procedure shell, and then add the two statements that communicate the mouse position to the public variables.

The purpose for dividing the mouse position by 1.33 is to convert between pixels and points. The positions on a chart are in units of points—or one seventy-second of an inch. The MouseMove event gives the x and y positions of the mouse in units of screen pixels. Depending on your screen resolution, the ratio between points and pixels varies. Excel's ActiveWindow object has methods that ostensibly convert pixels to points—*ActiveWindow.PointsToPixelsX* and *ActiveWindow.PointsToPixelsY*.

Unfortunately, these methods appear to assume that your screen has a resolution of 800 by 600. If your screen resolution differs from that, the Excel methods return incorrect values. Microsoft Word has a PointsToPixels method that returns the correct conversion value. To verify the ratio on your monitor, start the Visual Basic Editor in Word. In the Immediate window, type the expression *?PointsToPixels(100)* and press Enter. You will then see a number that is a valid conversion ratio between points and pixels. Divide the number by 100, and then divide that number in the x and y mouse pointer locations into the point measurement scale used by Chart objects. For example, if the value the Word function returns is 133, you should divide the mouse pointer's x and y positions by 1.33.

You are now ready to change the *AnimateChart2* macro. Make a copy of the macro and change the name to *AnimateChart3*. (Remember to change the name of the macro in the *MouseUp* event handler, as well.)

Here is the *AnimateChart3* macro, with new statements bracketed by asterisks.

```
Option Explicit
Declare Sub Sleep Lib «kernel32» (ByVal dwMilliseconds As Long)

Public myRun As Boolean
'***********************************
Public myX As Long
Public myY As Long
'***********************************

Sub AnimateChart3()
    Dim mySleep As Long
    Dim myField As PivotField
    Dim c As Chart
```

```
Dim s As Shape
Dim i As Long
'***********************************
Dim myTop, myBottom, myLeft As Long
'***********************************

Application.ScreenUpdating = False
mySleep = 500
Set c = ActiveChart
Set myField = c.PivotLayout.PageFields(1)
Set s = c.Shapes(«myTitle»)

'***********************************
myLeft = (c.ChartArea.Left + c.PlotArea.InsideLeft)
myTop = (c.ChartArea.Top + c.PlotArea.InsideTop)
myBottom = myTop + c.PlotArea.InsideHeight
'***********************************

s.Fill.Visible = msoTrue
s.Fill.ForeColor.RGB = vbGreen
Do
'***********************************
    Select Case myY
    Case Is <= myTop
        mySleep = mySleep * 0.8
        Application.StatusBar = «Faster»
        If mySleep < 10 Then mySleep = 10
    Case Is > myBottom
        mySleep = mySleep * 1.2
        Application.StatusBar = «Slower»
    Case Else
        Application.StatusBar = « «
    End Select

    If myX < myLeft Then
        Application.StatusBar = «Reverse  « & Application.StatusBar
        i = i - 1
        If i < 1 Then i = myField.PivotItems.Count
    Else
        i = i + 1
        If i > myField.PivotItems.Count Then i = 1
    End If
'***********************************
    myField.CurrentPage = myField.PivotItems(i).Name
    s.TextFrame.Characters.Text = myField.CurrentPage

    Sleep mySleep
    Application.ScreenUpdating = True
    DoEvents
    Application.ScreenUpdating = False
Loop While myRun
```

```
    s.Fill.ForeColor.RGB = vbRed
    Application.StatusBar = False
End Sub
```

At the top of the module, the *myX* and *myY* public variables receive the mouse position information from the event handler. Inside the macro, the macro needs new variables to store the top, bottom, and left edge locations of the plot area.

The first new executable statements calculate the edges of the plot area. To calculate the left edge of the plot area, you start with the Left property of the ChartArea object and add the value of the Left property of the PlotArea object. In Excel terminology, the PlotArea object includes the axis labels. To exclude the axis labels, use the InsideLeft or InsideTop properties of the PlotArea, rather than the Left or Top properties.

Inside the loop, the macro changes the value of the *mySleep* variable, depending on the location of the mouse pointer. The *Select Case* structure says that if the y position is less than *myTop*—the mouse is above the top of the chart—it must decrease the time the macro sleeps in each loop and add the word *Faster* to the status bar. Of course, you don't want the *mySleep* value to go as small as zero, because multiplying it by a ratio would never make it large again. Therefore, the statement *If mySleep < 10 Then mySleep = 10* adds a 10 millisecond-per-frame limit on how fast the macro runs.

Note The next portion of the *Case* structure does the inverse: if the y position is below the bottom of the chart, it increases the *mySleep* value—which increases the amount of time the macro sleeps on each iteration.

The *Case Else* portion of the structure—which occurs if the mouse is within the plot area—doesn't change the sleep increment, but it sets the status bar message to a space. (If you assign an empty string ("") to the StatusBar property, Excel behaves as if you assigned *False* to the property, restoring it to Excel's default Ready message.)

When determining the forward or reverse directions, the macro does not need a *Select Case* statement because there are only two conditions. If the x location of the mouse is to the left of the plot area, prefix the status bar message with the word Reverse and subtract 1 from the counter *i*. Then check to see if the counter needs to be moved to the last item number. Otherwise, increment and check the counter as before, leaving the status bar message alone.

Part 5

Access Tools

Chapter 17

Organize Data with Tables

In This Chapter

Databases can have many different purposes. You can use a database to create simple inventory style lists; Microsoft Access has many built-in design templates to help you create inventory style lists, so they will not be covered in this book. You might also need a database to manage business transactions such as those used in Order Processing and Accounts Receivable. A database that manages day-to-day transactions is often called an Online Transaction Processing (OLTP) database. Because of their complexity, OLTP systems should generally be created by database professionals, and will not be covered in this book

A third—and very important—type of database accumulates data for use in analyzing business activities. This third type of database is called an Online Analytical Processing (OLAP) database. An application based on an OLAP database is sometimes called a Decision Support System (DSS). While OLAP databases are often built using Back Office servers that accumulate information from various corporate databases, this chapter will show you how to use Microsoft Access 2000 to design and build a simple OLAP database based on information currently stored in Microsoft Excel workbooks.

You are probably maintaining analytical or decision support information for your activities in Excel workbooks. If so, you are probably frustrated with managing the multiple versions of the numbers that inevitably result from storing the master copy of your data in a workbook. The focus of this chapter is on helping you analyze the information you currently store in Excel worksheets, and to help you understand how you can use Access to manage that information, making it more usable for yourself and your department.

Designing a Database

Note The sample document for this Chapter is Forecast.xls. The Forecast.mdb database contains the finished, empty tables.

Most people enter numbers into a database so that the numbers can be used in multiple ways while only having to enter them once. Within the database, you can display the values you've entered in multiple forms or in various reports. But even beyond the database itself, once you've stored numbers in a database, you can then retrieve data into a PivotTable or QueryTable in Excel where you can use it as the basis for multiple analyses. Because you will be using values stored in a database in a variety of contexts, it is important to think carefully about how you will organize the information you store in the database. When you store values in a worksheet that will be used only once, it doesn't matter how you arrange the data values. But when you store values in a database that will be used in a variety of situations, it is crucial that you design the database with reusability in mind.

A personal or departmental database is often very dynamic in structure. You might need to start tracking information in ways that you have not thought of before. For example, after creating a database to store planning information, you might find that you obtain different planning numbers from the Products Planning Group than you obtain from the Field Marketing Group. Suddenly, you have the need to store two different sets of planning numbers. This volatility means that as you design your database, your design must be flexible, and that you can modify its design over time.

Understand Your Data

You will rarely create a database from thin air. Almost always, you'll have data in an Excel worksheet that you want to move into a database. Suppose you have created a forecasting document like the one illustrated in Figure 17-1, and you want to move the forecast into a database. If you understand certain terminology that describes data, you'll have an easier time translating data stored in a worksheet into a structure you can use in a database.

	A	B	C	D	E	F	G	H
1	**Product**	**Jan**	**Feb**	**Mar**	**Apr**	**May**	**Jun**	
2	Gnocci	145	115	140	125	115	133	
3	Tunnbrod	48	68	58	55	51	54	
4	Pate	103	114	79	114	73	92	
5	Pasties	69	71	65	79	73	69	
6	Bratwurst	18	20	20	19	18	28	
7	Tourtiere	52	44	53	67	61	66	
8	Dried Apples	48	54	42	55	61	39	
9	Sauerkraut	43	39	55	56	36	48	
10	Tofu	58	48	45	50	58	43	
11								

Figure 17-1
A typical worksheet has labels for rows and columns.

Understanding Measures and Dimensions

Your document has product names down the side, months across the top, and forecast quantities in each cell of the grid. In its simplest form, a typical spreadsheet has some variation of this pattern: labels down the left, labels across the top, and values in the grid.

The numerical values that populate a grid are called *facts*: it is a fact that you forecast 500 units for Gnocchi in March 2002. A fact is sometimes called a *measure*, because facts are quantitative—or measurable—values. The labels in the left column and the top row identify the fact, letting you know what that particular fact means. These labels are called keys. Keys are grouped into a dimension, and the forecasting worksheet has two dimensions.

Now, suppose you create a separate forecast for each of your five major customers. In Excel, you create a separate copy of the forecast worksheet for each customer, as shown in Figure 17-2. In a database, the customers fall into the third dimension.

	A	B	C	D	E	F	G	H
1	**Product**	**Jan**	**Feb**	**Mar**	**Apr**	**May**	**Jun**	
2	Gnocci	66	44	75	64	60	52	
3	Tunnbrod	20	23	25	25	30	22	
4	Pate	39	44	24	46	22	36	
5	Pasties	21	33	27	25	29	23	
6	Bratwurst	8	11	8	5	9	17	
7	Tourtiere	18	16	27	31	32	30	
8	Dried Apples	23	19	14	30	25	19	
9	Sauerkraut	16	16	24	21	11	20	
10	Tofu	24	24	15	25	19	16	
11								

Trail's Head / White Clover / Lazy K

Figure 17-2
Separate worksheets form a third dimension.

With three dimensions, you will need three keys to uniquely identify a fact—one key for each dimension. The forecast should resemble the information in Table 17-1.

Value	Dimension
Trail's Head Store	Customer dimension
Gnocchi	Product dimension
March 2002	Time dimension
75 units	Fact

Table 17-1
Forecast Table Structure.

With product keys as row labels, month keys as column labels, and customer keys as sheet labels, the Forecast workbook looks like a cube; the term *dimension* captures the metaphor of a cube. You can rearrange the workbook, however, without changing the nature of the dimensions. For example, suppose you entered all the customers on the same worksheet, as shown in Figure 17-3, which includes only two products per customer for clarity.

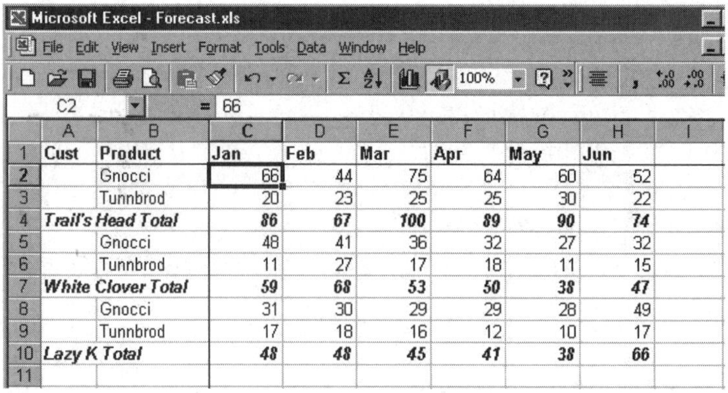

Microsoft Excel - Forecast.xls

Cust	Product	Jan	Feb	Mar	Apr	May	Jun
	Gnocci	66	44	75	64	60	52
	Tunnbrod	20	23	25	25	30	22
Trail's Head Total		***86***	***67***	***100***	***89***	***90***	***74***
	Gnocci	48	41	36	32	27	32
	Tunnbrod	11	27	17	18	11	15
White Clover Total		***59***	***68***	***53***	***50***	***38***	***47***
	Gnocci	31	30	29	29	28	49
	Tunnbrod	17	18	16	12	10	17
Lazy K Total		***48***	***48***	***45***	***41***	***38***	***66***

Figure 17-3
Dimensions can be arranged in many different ways.

The workbook now contains only a single worksheet, and the worksheet has two columns of row labels—one each for the Customer and Product dimensions. But the workbook still contains the same cube. There are still three dimensions, and you still need one key from each dimension to uniquely identify a single fact.

Designing Dimension Attributes

Adding a new label does not necessarily add a new key or a new dimension. After moving the Customer dimension back to the separate worksheets, Figure 17-4 illustrates a different way of arranging the worksheet.

Microsoft Excel - Forecast.xls

B2 = 145

	A	B	C	D	E	F	G	H
1	**Product**	**Jan**	**Feb**	**Mar**	**Q1**	**Apr**	**May**	**Jun**
2	Gnocchi	145	115	140	**400**	125	115	133
3	Tunnbrod	48	68	58	**174**	55	51	54
4	***Grains/Cereals Total***	***193***	***183***	***198***	***574***	***180***	***166***	***187***
5	Pate	103	114	79	**296**	114	73	92
6	Pasties	69	71	65	**205**	79	73	69
7	Bratwurst	18	20	20	**58**	19	18	28
8	Tourtiere	52	44	53	**149**	67	61	66
9	***Meat/Poultry Total***	***242***	***249***	***217***	***708***	***279***	***225***	***255***
10	Dried Apples	48	54	42	**144**	55	61	39

Figure 17-4
An attribute appears similar to a dimension.

The Category labels in Figure 17-4 are visually similar to the keys from a Customer dimension. There's a big difference, however. Customers are independent of products. Each customer key has a complete set of product keys. The category labels group as product keys; a product key that appears in one category does not appear in any other category. In a spreadsheet, attributes often appear as subtotal rows.

A category is not an additional key, and there is no new Category dimension. A category is an attribute of a product. An *attribute* is an additional piece of information about a key, which allows you to summarize several keys into one group, or to select related keys while excluding unrelated keys.

Attributes sometimes form a hierarchy. For example, a product might belong to a product category, which belongs to a product line, which belongs to a product group, and so forth. The levels of an attribute hierarchy do not correspond to facts that need to be stored in the database. You can always summarize the facts to recreate the summary facts. In the database, you need to store only the lowest level facts.

Attributes do not need to come in a single, clear-cut hierarchy. For example, a customer dimension might have two hierarchies: a geographical hierarchy (city, state, country) and a sales organization hierarchy (sales representative, district, region). Some attributes might not belong to a hierarchy at all. For example, a customer attribute might be the size of the company.

When you create a grid in a worksheet, there is rarely enough room to include auxiliary attributes of a dimension. But attributes give you the ability to slice and dice the data, per se. The more meaningful the attributes you include with a dimension, the more ways you can look at the data. One of the benefits of moving information into a database is that you can add many useful attributes for each dimension.

Most dimensions have the potential for attributes. Even the Time dimension might warrant additional attributes. For example, you might add the month name, the month number, the quarter number or name, and the year to the Time dimension. If your company's fiscal year does not align with the calendar year, you'll certainly want to store fiscal date attributes in the Time dimension.

Creating a Scenario Dimension

In addition to any logical dimensions your database might require—Time, Product, and Category are common—there is one additional dimension that you will probably find useful while you are trying to manage information overload.

Suppose that after you give the original forecast to customers, each customer makes changes to the forecast and a revised version returns to you. After assembling the revised forecasts, you have two identically structured workbooks—one containing the original (corporate) forecast, and the other containing the revised (customer) forecast. What do you do with the new forecast?

Your first option is to scrap the original forecast and replace it with the revised customer forecast. That is probably not an acceptable option, however, because you would like to compare the two forecasts.

Your second option is to create a second fact field in the database. You could have one fact field for Corporate Forecast Units and another for Customer Forecast Units, for example. This is also not a good idea, because it makes the database inflexible. If you add Dollars (which is a legitimate new data type), you would have to add Corporate Forecast Dollars and Customer Forecast Dollars. If—after reconciling the two forecasts—you end up with a third revised forecast you would need to create a new field in the database for Revised Forecast. Existing reports and PivotTables would not know what to do with the new fact fields.

Your third option—and the best solution—is to add another dimension. You can call the new dimension Version, Type, Iteration, or any of a number of other possible names. One useful and commonly used term is *scenario*. The Scenario dimension corresponds to the different versions of a workbook you accumulate. (You might even use separate folders to differentiate multiple versions of a workbook.) Initially, you will create the Scenario dimension with two keys: Corporate and Customer. Later, if you want to create a new Revised scenario, all you need to do is add another key and store the new forecast into the database. You might even want to store multiple versions, including the date as part of the Scenario name: "2002 Fall Customer Forecast," for example. Adding a new dimension means that you now have an additional key you must specify to uniquely identify a single fact.

The Scenario dimension is different from all the other dimensions because you never, ever summarize the keys in it. It is easy to imagine a case where you would want to know the total of all the months in a year, or of all the customers, but you never need to know the total of the Customer and Corporate forecasts. Once you add a Scenario dimension to a database, you must always be careful to display data for only one scenario at a time.

The distinction between a key, an attribute, and a dimension is important. If you add a new key to an existing dimension, you add one new fact for each key in each remaining dimension. For example, if your store starts carrying pita bread, you need to develop a pita bread forecast for each month and for each customer. If you add a new product attribute, you don't add any new facts. For example, you can add a

Domestic attribute—which has the value *True* or *False* for each product—without having to invent any new forecast numbers at all. If you add a new dimension, you redefine the entire database.

Designing Database Tables

A table is essentially a list. A row in a table is called a record. A column in a table is called a field. Think of a field as a named column that can contain only a single type of information. In Excel, a list typically stands alone, although it is possible to use lookup formulas to retrieve values from a second list. In Access, a table almost always relates to other tables, and the equivalent to creating lookup formulas is called *joining* the tables.

Designing Tables

When you create the database, you'll create one table to store the facts. This is called the primary fact table, and will include one row for each fact.

Each record of the primary fact table will include only one fact plus the key value from each dimension. All the auxiliary information for each dimension will be stored in a separate table for the dimension. When you retrieve data from the database, you will retrieve values from the primary fact table, and look up the attributes from the dimension tables. This design—with the central fact table in the middle and dimension tables sprouting around—is called a *star database*. Figure 17-5 displays a diagram showing the dimension tables around the primary fact table.

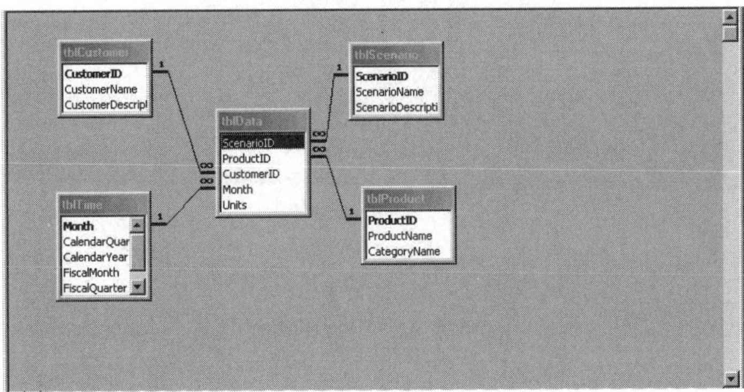

Figure 17-5
A star database design captures dimensioned data.

A star database design is simple, flexible, easy to understand, and easy to use. It's easy to add an additional attribute to a dimension at any time because you add the attribute only to the dimension table, not to the primary fact table.

The primary fact table contains one record for each unique combination of keys, which is equal to the product of the number of keys in each dimension. The (very small) Forecast database has four dimensions: two keys in the Scenario dimension, nine keys in the Product dimension, 12 keys in the Time dimension, and three keys in the Customer dimension. That means that the database will contain 2 x 9 x 12 x 3 = 648 records in the primary fact table. The size of the primary fact table increases geometrically as you add keys to each dimension.

Each dimension table contains one record for each key. That means that the Forecast database will have 2 + 9 + 12 + 3 = 26 records in all the dimension tables. The size of each dimension table increases arithmetically as you add keys. There are many records in the primary fact table, but each record is very small. A record in a dimension table might be large, but there are not very many of them. A star database design is, therefore, very efficient.

Looking at the Sample Northwind Database

As you learn to use Access, you might want to look at the sample databases that accompany Office 2000. The Northwind database is the most important of all the sample databases; it includes a wide variety of queries, forms, and reports. Figure 17-6 shows the structure of the Northwind database which, as you can see, does not have a star structure.

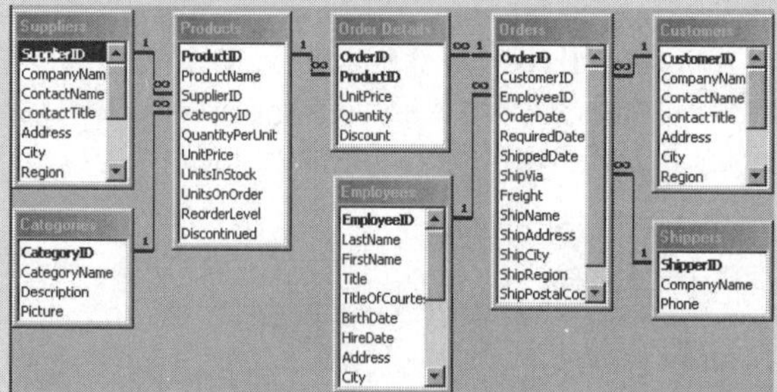

Figure 17-6
The Northwind sample database does not have a star structure.

The most important difference between the Northwind database and a star database is that Orders and Order Details appear in two levels. This is called a Header/Detail structure. Essentially, the primary fact table for the Northwind database is the Order Detail table. This is the table that contains information about products, quantities, and prices. But the fields that pertain to the entire order—for example, the date of the order and the customer name—are not stored with the Order Detail table. Rather, they are in the Orders table. Many corporate databases are designed using this Header/Detail structure.

A Header/Detail structure is useful for a transaction database, but it is more complicated than necessary for an analytical OLAP database.

Planning Table Names

When you create the database, you will give it a name. Access stores the entire database in a single file, with the extension .mdb. You don't need to worry too much about the name of the database, because you can easily move or rename it in Windows Explorer. With a simple database, renaming the database normally does not disrupt any internal database processes.

The names you use for tables and fields are much more critical. Table and field names are embedded in any queries, forms, or reports you might create.

Note Access 2000's new AutoCorrect feature fixes the names you use when you rename a table or a field, but it does not catch every instance. Try very hard to design table and field names that you will not need to change later.

You will need a name for the primary fact table and a name for each dimension table. Even though the primary fact table originally contains only forecast information, you can easily expand it to contain other types of information simply by adding new Scenario keys. Use Data for the table name so that it will reflect multiple information types. For each of the dimensions, use the name of the dimension as the table name. There is no need to add a plural suffix to the table name because database tables contain multiple records as a matter of course.

You might want to add a short prefix to the table name. Sometimes Access adds tables of its own—for example, to log errors or other changes to the database. If you add a standard prefix such as *tbl* to the names of the primary tables in the database, you can easily distinguish them from temporary tables that you or Access might create. A prefix can also help distinguish tables from queries, which are discussed in Chapter 18, "Manipulate Data with Queries." In Figure 17-7, you can see how the prefix distinguishes the core tables from temporary tables created either by you or by Access.

Planning Fields

When you create a field for a fact, give it a name that represents the type of fact the field contains. If you're forecasting dollars, use the name Dollars; if you're forecasting units, use the name Units. A fact is almost always a number. Some facts—such as units—never have a fractional component and can be created as Long Integers (refer to Chapter 12 for more information about data types). It is generally safe using a Double as the data type for a fact column in a database.

Adding a Second Fact Field

Suppose you want to add Dollars to your database, in addition to Units. One option would be to add a new Data Type dimension with two keys: Units and Dollars. But that might not be a good approach. Normally, units are whole numbers and can be stored using a Long Integer data type, while dollar values are not whole numbers and are usually stored using a Double data type. Even if you use the same type of field for both units and dollars, you would usually want to format them differently.

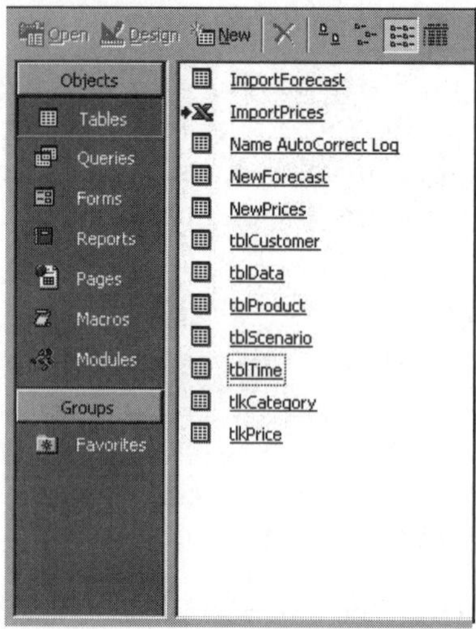

Figure 17-7
Adding a prefix to table names isolates permanent from temporary tables.

Units and dollars are fundamentally different data types and each can warrant a fact field of its own if you do store it in the database. If the Dollar forecast is simply the units times the price, however, you should not store the dollars in the database. Instead, you should calculate them at the time you extract the numbers from the database, either into a report or a PivotTable. See "Planning a Table for Prices" and "Creating an Auxiliary Price Table," later in this chapter for more information about dealing with prices.

Designing Field Names

An Access field has two similar properties. One is the name of the field. The name is the value that is used internally in queries. The other is the caption. The caption is what the wizards use when creating new forms and reports.

Although the program allows you to include spaces and most special characters in a field's name, it will be easier to use the field in queries if the field name consists of a single word. Enter the long descriptive name—complete with any spaces—as the Caption property of the field instead. Use proper case letters to differentiate the logical words within a field name. (For detailed rules about naming a field, search the online Help using the search term "Guidelines For Naming Fields.")

Most dimensions have several predictable fields; typically, one for the key name, one for a longer description, and one for the key. If you always use a consistent naming strategy for fields, it will be easier to know what each field contains. For example, if you use fields named ProductID, ProductName, and ProductDescription in the Product dimension, then you should use fields named CustomerID, CustomerName, and CustomerDescription in the Customer dimension to maintain consistency. Using consistent names also increases the amount of work Access will do in your behalf. For example, if two tables contain a field with the same name, Access will automatically create a link between the two tables if required.

Designing Keys for Linking Tables

When you link information from one list to another in Excel, you use a lookup formula; a separate lookup formula is created for each row and for each column. Access has a much more powerful mechanism for joining tables. All you need is a field that exists in both tables. (The fields do not need to have the same name, but it makes the linking easier if the name is identical in both tables.) Access links the tables together using a field that will be designated a primary key field.

Each dimension table in Excel already has a logical key, the label, which is usually a text value. The product name is an example of a logical key. When you create a dimension table, you must decide whether to use the familiar label as the primary key or to let Access create a sequential number as the key. The most important rule for a key is that it must be unique within the dimension. Also, it's better to have a key that does not change values. For example, if you are creating an attribute table for products, and each product already has a unique product identifier—perhaps an SKU or a product number—you might want to use that identifier as the product key.

If you're planning for the future, you might plan for a product that does not yet have a finalized product identifier. You might also sell products that do not have a computer-generated key. In that case, you will want to let Access create a sequential number as the key, which guarantees that the key will be unique.

Access is more efficient if the primary key is a Long Integer data type. Each dimension's primary key will be repeated in every record of the primary fact table. As described in the sidebar "Estimating the Size of a Database" below, integer keys can significantly reduce the size of a database.

Perhaps more important than size, Access can be more efficient at lookup values when you use integer keys, particularly as your database grows in size. Integer keys also eliminate the possibility of errors, because you enter the descriptive name only once. Also, if you need to change the textual logical key, you change it only once in the dimension attribute table.

Estimating the Size of a Database

The primary fact table contains one record (row) for each fact in the database. If your database has nine products, three customers, 12 months, and two data types, you have 648 facts, which means 648 records in the primary fact table. If each dimension key is text with an average length of 20 characters, and the fact field is an eight-byte Double data type, the approximate total size of the fact table is (20 + 20 + 20 + 20 + 8) * 648, or 57,024 bytes, which is not very large.

(continued)

Estimating the Size of a Database *(continued)*
If you use Long Integers, which are four bytes for keys, the size of the table will be approximately 15,552 bytes–(4 + 4 + 4 + 4 + 8) * 648—about one-quarter the size of the table with text keys. The difference is not significant.

A database with nine products and three customers is quite unrealistic, but the size ratio between the text and integer key tables is the same for larger tables. If you have 50 products, 200 customers, and six data types, then the primary fact table suddenly has 720,000 records, and the size difference changes to 60 MB for text keys vs. 20 MB for integer keys. With a typical computer hard drive being five or six gigabytes in size, a difference of 40-MB in the size of a database is not trivial, but it is also not terribly significant. In a small database, the primary fact table does not take up that much more space than the dimension tables. As the database grows larger, the primary fact table completely dwarfs the dimension tables, making their size immaterial.

Even for the Scenario dimension, you might want to specify its name as an attribute and use an integer key to link to the primary fact table. You might decide later that you want change the name in the type field. As you appreciate the usefulness of your forecast database, you might decide to add more data types to it. For example, you might later decide to compare the forecast numbers with actual numbers, which is easy to do. You simply add an Actual data type. As soon as you add Actual as a data type, however, Corporate and Customer no longer clearly identify that these keys refer to forecasts. You might want to change the names to Corporate Forecast and Customer Forecast. Those names are descriptive and accurate, but they are also long. When you display the data type in a report or in a PivotTable, you might want to use a shorter name. Now, not only do you need to change the name of data type, but you also need to add a second attribute—the short name.

For the Time dimension, you will simply use the date for the first day of the month. Any space or performance savings in using an integer key would not compensate for having to link to a dimension table just to select a range of months.

Designing Auxiliary Tables

A star database consists of a single fact table surrounded by dimension tables. Most of the information in an analytical database fits into this standard organization. Occasionally, however, you will find the need for a few auxiliary tables.

Planning a Table for Prices

Sometimes a dimension contains an attribute that changes over time. For example, consider the price attribute. A product has a price. But the price in February 2002 might be different from the price in March 2002.

Typically, you do not change prices every month. Prices could be stable for three, four, five, or six months and then change. You could call Price a slowly changing attribute of the dimension. Each product has too many prices to store in the dimension table, but prices are constant over customers and scenarios, so it doesn't make sense to store them in the central fact table. Changing the date triggers the price change, but there isn't a price change every month. You can create a separate table that keeps track of these slowly changing prices. The table requires three columns: one column for the ProductID, one column for the effective (or As Of) date, and one column for the price on that date. Each product will have at least one entry in the Prices table—that is, the price as of the date the product is first introduced. Each time there is a price change for the product, the product gets a new entry in the Prices table.

Planning Lookup Tables

Most links between tables form what is called a *one-to-many relationship*. That means that for each single record on the one side of a link, the many side of the link might have any number of records—from none to millions. Each dimension table forms a one-to-many relationship with the primary fact table. Access has the ability to easily keep one-to-many relationships synchronized.

In any one dimension, some attribute values apply to several items. For example, several products all share the Cereals category attribute. If you create a separate table that stores each category attribute once, that table will form a one-to-many relationship with the product table. If you create a Category table, you will be able to change the name of a category in the Category table and have Access automatically replicate the change to all the related products.

Keep as much of the database as possible in a clean star structure. Adding complexity makes a database hard to understand and hard to manage. Some auxiliary tables can actually help keep a database consistent.

Creating a Database

Once you have identified the facts, dimensions, and keys for your database, you are ready to create a database itself. When you're creating the database, Access offers to use its wizard to create the database for you. Dispense with the wizard for two reasons. First, it will be clearer for you to understand what's going on if you create a database from scratch. Second, the wizard creates databases that might not be practical for your intended use.

Creating an Initial Dimension Table

In the Forecast database, Scenario is the simplest dimension, so create its table first. Don't use the wizard to create this table; you need to see what goes into defining a table.

Using Design View to Create the Scenario Table

Launch Access. In the Microsoft Access window that appears, select Blank Access Database. Give the database the name Forecast.

In the Database window, select Tables as the object type and then click Create Table In Design View. A grid appears, as illustrated in Figure 17-8.

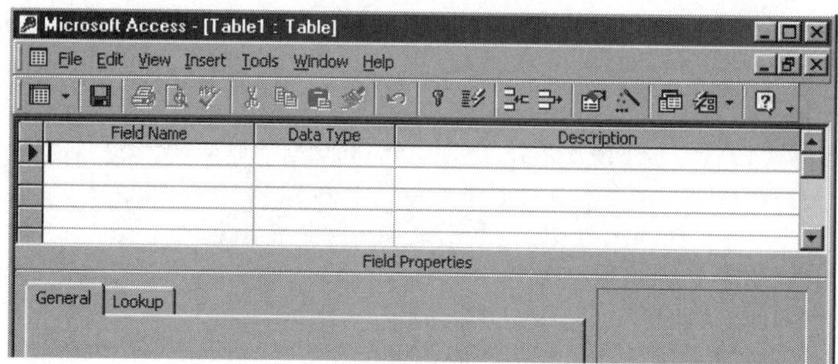

Figure 17-8
Each row of the Design view grid defines one field.

Each row in this grid corresponds to one field—or column—in the table. The first field for the table will be the index, or the automatic key that Access will generate for you. For the index name, type ScenarioID. Press the Tab key to move to the Data Type portion of the field definition. As you type the field name, Field Properties appear in the bottom half of the window. Before continuing, enter the name *Scenario ID* for the Caption property, including the space.

In the grid next to the field name, select AutoNumber from the Data Type drop-down list. After you specify a Data Type, Access will display information about that data type in the Field Properties section at the bottom of the Table Design window. For the AutoNumber field, the field size is Long Integer. The New Values property allows you to choose whether the key numbers should increment, starting from zero, or whether they should be random numbers.

The default value for the Indexed property is Yes (Duplicates OK). When you choose an AutoNumber Data Type, Access also assumes that you want to index the field. You want to set this field as the *primary key*. A primary key is a special index that does not allow duplicates. In the Standard toolbar, click the Primary Key button. The Indexed property changes to Yes (No Duplicates), as shown in Figure 17-9.

In the second row, type *ScenarioName* for the field name and press the Tab key. This will be the short name for the Scenario field, and Text is an appropriate data type. Most dimension attribute fields will use Text as the Data Type. In the Field Properties section, the default Field Size is 50. This specifies the maximum size of the field, and Access will use only as much space as necessary to store the actual characters in the field. Type *Scenario Name* as the Caption for the field.

In the third row of the table, type *ScenarioDescription* for the field name and press the Tab key. This will be a long descriptive name of the scenario. Type *Scenario Description* as the Caption for the field.

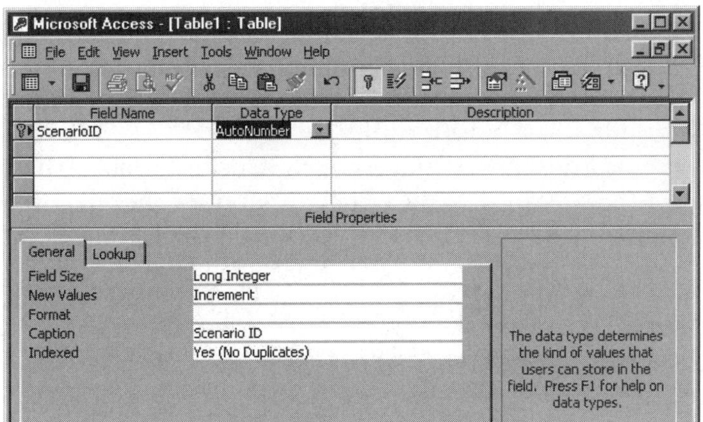

Figure 17-9
Adding a primary key prevents duplicates in an index.

These are enough fields for the Scenario table at this time. Remember that you can always add additional attribute fields to a dimension table later. Click the Save button on the toolbar. When Access prompts you to give a name to the table you have created, type *tblScenario* as the table name and click OK to save the table.

You can enter values into the table. Click the View button to open the table in Datasheet view. The first column of the table contains the value (AutoNumber). This lets you know that you should not enter value because Access will do it you. In the Scenario Name column, type *Corporate,* and press the Tab key. As soon as you start entering a value into a row of the table, Access will generate a value for the primary key field of the record, as shown in Figure 17-10. In the Scenario Description column, type *Corporate Forecast*.

	Scenario ID	Scenario Nam	Scenario Desc
✎	1	Corporate	
*	(AutoNumber)		

Figure 17-10
As soon as you start typing, Access generates a new automatic key.

In the second record, type *Customer* as the short name, and type *Customer Forecast* as the Scenario description. As you enter values into a record, Access changes the icon at the left margin of the current row to show a pencil, indicating the record is currently being modified but has not been saved. When you press Enter or press an arrow key to move to the next record, the pencil disappears and the record is saved. You also can click the pencil icon to save the record at any time.

Because the primary key value is automatically generated for you, you might not want to see it in the Datasheet grid. To hide the column, select the column by clicking the column's title, clicking Format, and then clicking Hide Columns. Even with the key field column hidden, Access will continue to generate new values for you. After you hide a column, click the Save button to save the layout of the table.

Creating Additional Dimension Tables

Close the table tblScenario. Next, you'll create the Customer table. This time, create the table using the Table Wizard. In the Database window, click the Create Table By Using Wizard button. In the Table Wizard, select the Business option and, in the list of sample tables, select Customers. The Sample Fields list will display a number of attributes that are commonly used in a Customer table, as shown in Figure 17-11.

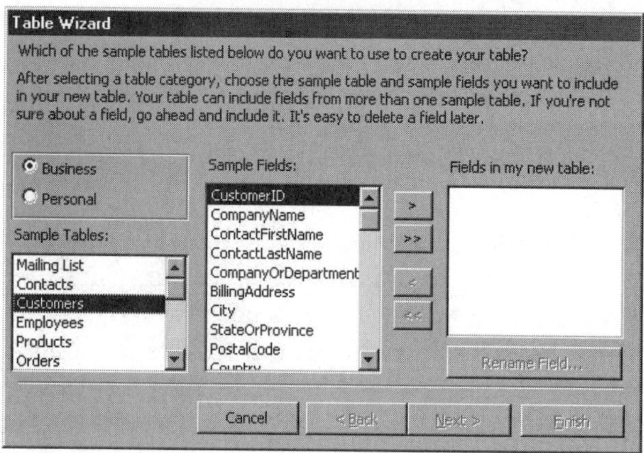

Figure 17-11
The Table Wizard lets you choose predefined fields.

Select CustomerID and click the right-arrow button to add the field to the Field In My New Table list. You also can double-click a value in the Sample Fields list to add the field. Double-click CompanyName and Notes to add two new fields. Click the Next button, and then give the table the name tblCustomer. Leave the option selected for Yes, Set A Primary Key For Me and click Finish.

Note The wizard preselects the entire table name. Oddly, you can't press arrow keys to insert a prefix in front of the name. Instead, you have to press the F2 function key and then press the Home key to move to the beginning of the table name.

After you have finished creating the table, Access will open it in Datasheet view. Click the Design button on the Standard toolbar to display the now-familiar design grid. The CustomerID field has a key in the column next to it to designate that Access automatically assigned the field as the primary key field. For each field, the wizard also created a descriptive caption, and it also specified that each field should be indexed, as shown in Figure 17-12. Adding an index speeds up retrievals, but it does make the database larger, which can make updates slow.

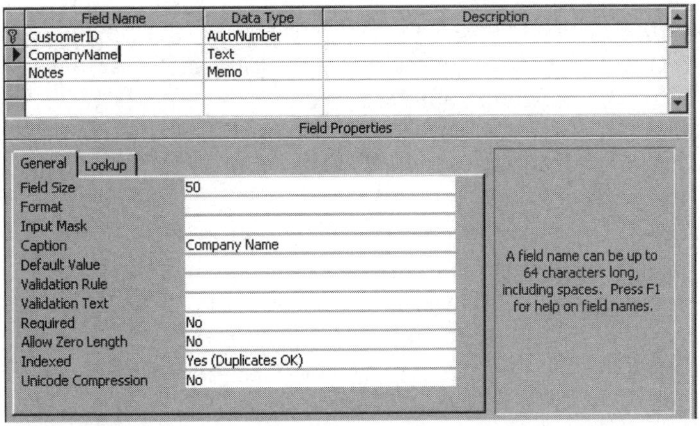

Field Name	Data Type	Description
CustomerID	AutoNumber	
CompanyName	Text	
Notes	Memo	

Field Properties

General | Lookup

Field Size	50
Format	
Input Mask	
Caption	Company Name
Default Value	
Validation Rule	
Validation Text	
Required	No
Allow Zero Length	No
Indexed	Yes (Duplicates OK)
Unicode Compression	No

A field name can be up to 64 characters long, including spaces. Press F1 for help on field names.

Figure 17-12
The Table Wizard indexes most fields.

The customer table will probably not contain more than a few hundred records, so indexes will probably not speed up retrievals significantly. On the other hand, because the table is so small, indexes will not consume much space either; because you will change attribute values only infrequently, slightly slower updates will not be a problem. If you do want to remove the indexes, change the Indexed property to No for each field other than the primary key.

The Table Wizard does not offer a good sample for creating a Time Table, so you'll need to use Design view to create it manually.

In the Database window, select Tables and then click Create Table In Design View. In the Table Design window, enter Month as the first field name, and select Date/Time as the field type. As additional field names, enter FiscalMonth, CalendarQuarter, FiscalQuarter, CalendarYear, and FiscalYear, all as Text types. Assign the primary key to the Month field and save the table as tblTime. Figure 17-13 shows the design of the Time Table.

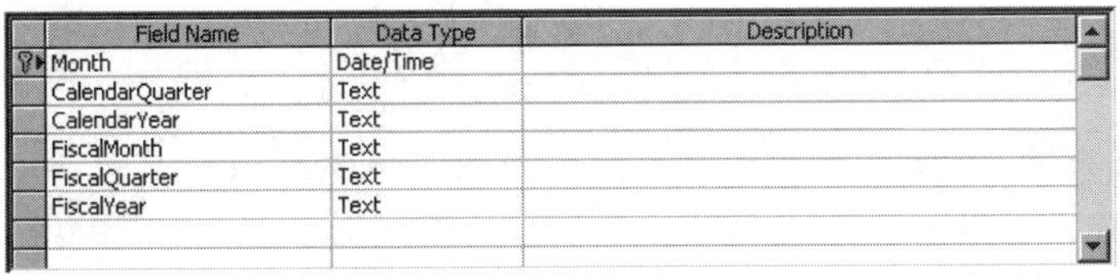

Field Name	Data Type	Description
Month	Date/Time	
CalendarQuarter	Text	
CalendarYear	Text	
FiscalMonth	Text	
FiscalQuarter	Text	
FiscalYear	Text	

Figure 17-13
You can add several attributes to the Time Table.

Also create a table for the Product dimension. Use the Table Wizard, select Products from the Sample Tables list, and add ProductID, ProductName, and ProductDescription fields. You also want to add a field for the product category name. In the Sample Tables list, select Categories. In the Sample Fields list, double-click CategoryName. Give the table the name tblProduct, let Access create the primary key, click Finish, and then switch to Design view.

Creating a Lookup Table for Categories

The values in the Product Name and Product Description fields can differ for each record in the Product table, but there are only a limited number of categories you can use for a product. Access can help prevent invalid entries in the table, and it also can generate a list of values you can use when you add products to the table. Select the CategoryName field, and click the Lookup tab in the Field Properties section. Change the Display Control property to List Box. In the Row Source Type box, select Value List. In the Row Source box, enter a list of valid categories separated by semicolons, as in Cereals; Meats; Produce, as shown in Figure 17-14.

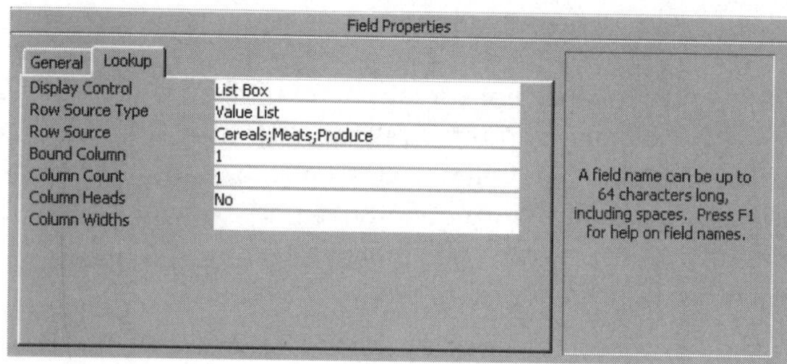

Figure 17-14
You can enter a list of values for a drop-down list.

Save the table and click the View button to switch to Datasheet view. Enter a product name and a product description. In the category name box, press the Alt+Down arrow keys and select the appropriate category from the list.

Note When you choose List Box as the Lookup control type, you can only select items from the list. If you choose Combo Box as the Lookup control type, you can select from the list or enter an item that is not in the list.

Rather than store lookup values as a list of constants in the Lookup definition, you might prefer to create a separate table that includes the category names. The purpose of this second table is simply to create a list that is easy to modify for validating and entering category names into the Product table.

In the Database window, click Create Table By Using Wizard, select Categories from the Sample Tables list, and double-click CategoryName. Then click the Next button and save the table with the name tlkCategory. The *tlk* prefix stands for lookup table, which helps keep this table separate from the main tables prefixed with *tlb*.

If you allow Access to create a primary key for you, it will add a new CategoryID field. For a lookup table like this, you don't want an additional integer key. Select the No, I'll Set The Primary Key option. In the subsequent step , the wizard proposes setting the CategoryName field as the primary key, as shown in Figure 17-15. The options in the dialog box control the data type of the primary key. Leave the option at the default, which sets the data type as Text.

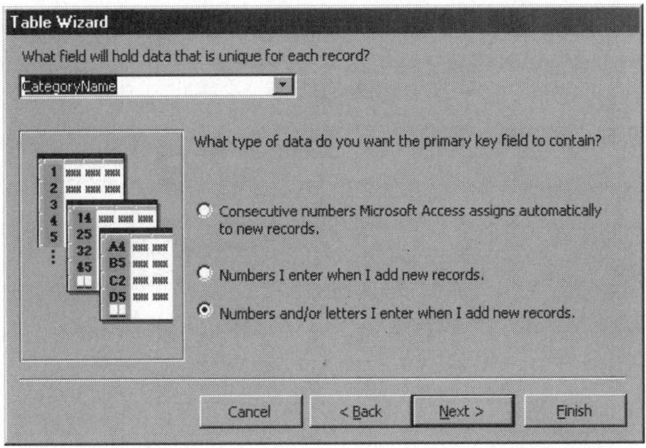

Figure 17-15
To use a text field as the primary key, chose the third option.

When you click the Next button, the wizard will confirm table relationships. Because the Category lookup table does not contain an integer key, the wizard assumes that it is not related to any of the other tables; in fact, it is related to the Product table. Select the Product table and then click the Relationships button on the Standard toolbar to specify the relationship. As shown in Figure 17-16, the second option is used when one record in the Category table will match many records in the products table—the correct option. Select it and click Finish.

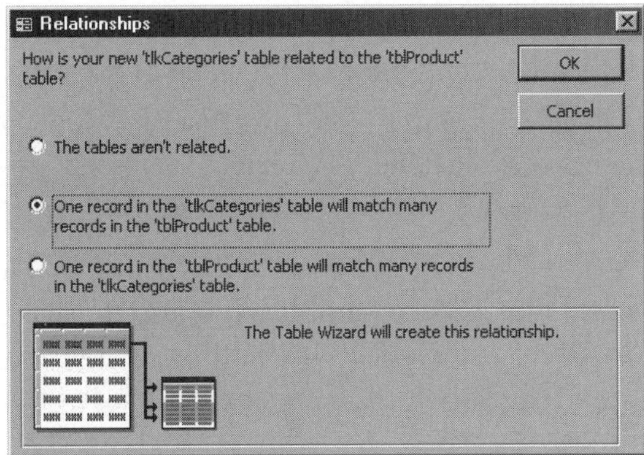

Figure 17-16
In the Relationships dialog box, select one to many.

You can now enter the category names—Cereals, Meats, and Produce—in the Category Name field of the table. Once you've created and populated the Category table, you can change the definition of the Product table to use the lookup table rather than the hard-coded list you created earlier. Open the Product table in Design view, select the CategoryName field, select the Lookup tab, and change the Row Source Type value to Table/Query. Then change the Row Source value to the tlkCategory table, as shown in Figure 17-17.

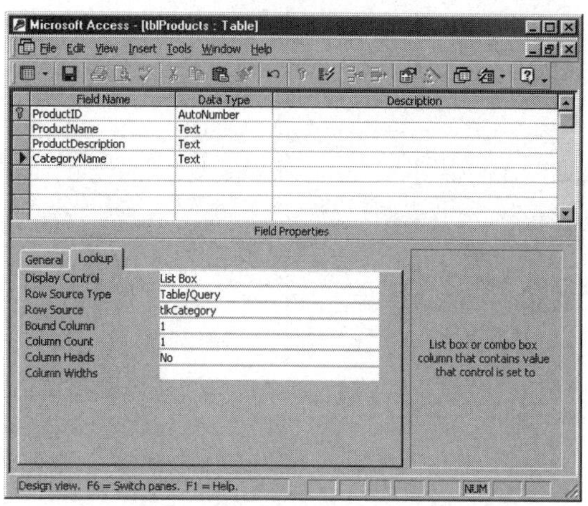

Figure 17-17
You can use a Table as the source of a lookup list.

Leave the rest of the options alone, save the table, and then switch to Datasheet view. When you click the drop-down arrow in the Category Name field, you will see the same list as the list you hard-coded, but you can now easily add additional categories to the list using the Category table.

Creating a Primary Fact Table

Once you have created all the dimension tables, you can create the primary fact table. As you create the primary fact table, you will link it to each of the other tables.

Use the Table Wizard, to select ProductID from the Product sample table and CustomerID from the Customers sample table. The wizard doesn't have predefined fields for Scenario and for date. Here's how to add an existing field that has the appropriate data type:

1. For the Scenario field, select the Contacts sample table, add the ContactID field, click the Rename Field button, and change the field name ScenarioID.
2. For the Month field, select the Orders sample table, add the OrderDate field, and rename it to Month.

3. For the Units field, select the Order Details sample table, add the Quantity sample field, and rename it to Units.

   Figure 17-18 shows the fields for the fact table.

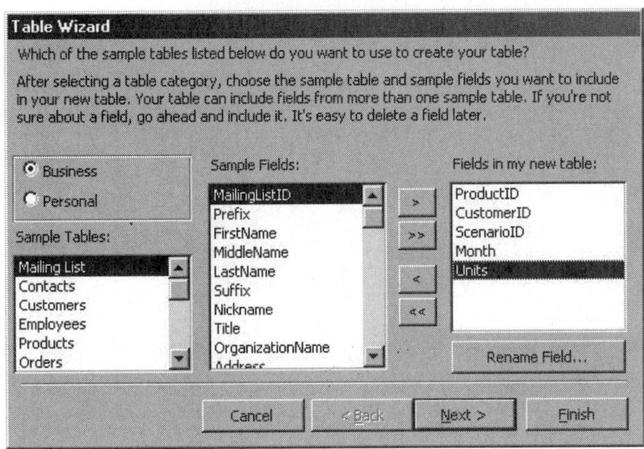

Figure 17-18
You can rename fields from the Table Wizard.

4. Click the Next button, name the table tblData, choose to set the primary key yourself, and click the Next button.

   The primary key for the Data table actually consists of a combination of four different fields: the key field for each dimension table. The Table Wizard does not allow for a multiple-field primary key, so simply select one of the fields as the primary key and click the Next button. You can fix the primary key later.

5. In the Relationships screen, the wizard suggests that the new Data table is related to each of the four dimension tables, as shown in Figure 17-19. This is correct, so click the Next button. In the final page of the wizard, select the option Modify The Table Design option and click Finish.

The only change you need to make to the design is to replace the primary key. The only way to obtain a primary key that is unique within the table is to use all four fields. Select from ProductID through Month, and then click the Primary Key button. Key icons will appear to the left of all four columns, as shown in Figure 17-20. Click the Save button to save the table and close the Design view.

Creating an Auxiliary Price Table

The Data table will contain units. If you want to convert those units to dollars, you will need to have the price of each product available. The "Planning a Table for Prices" section earlier in this chapter describes a design for an auxiliary price table.

Create the table using Design view. Create a field named ProductID as a Number data type, with the Long Integer size. The automatic key Access generates for the

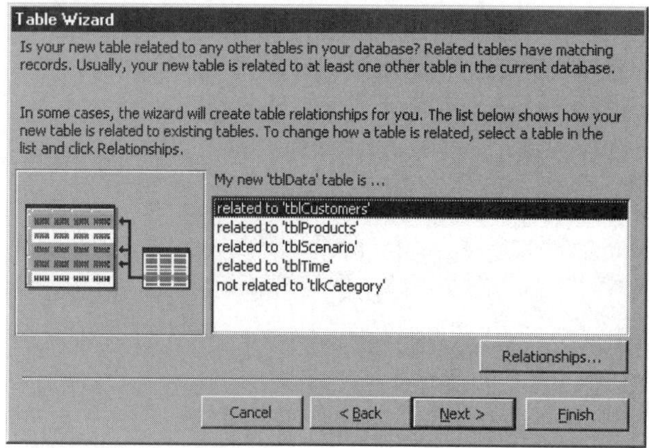

Figure 17-19
The Table Wizard detects relationships when key names are identical.

Field Name	Data Type	Description
ProductID	AutoNumber	
CustomerID	Number	
ScenarioID	Number	
Month	Date/Time	
Units	Number	

Figure 17-20
Select multiple fields to create a compound primary key.

price is a Long Integer. Add a Date/Time field named AsOfDate for the effective date of the price change. Add a Number field with a field size of Double to store the price. As the primary key, create a concatenated key with ProductID and AsOfDate. Figure 17-21 shows the Prices table with some sample entries.

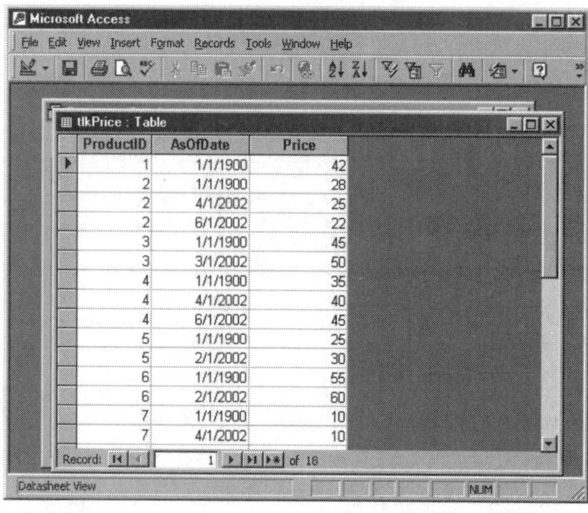

ProductID	AsOfDate	Price
1	1/1/1900	42
2	1/1/1900	28
2	4/1/2002	25
2	6/1/2002	22
3	1/1/1900	45
3	3/1/2002	50
4	1/1/1900	35
4	4/1/2002	40
4	6/1/2002	45
5	1/1/1900	25
5	2/1/2002	30
6	1/1/1900	55
6	2/1/2002	60
7	1/1/1900	10
7	4/1/2002	10

Figure 17-21
Prices are linked to Product ID and Date.

You probably don't want to have to remember the ProductID number to create a new price. Add a Lookup field to link the ProductID field to the Product table. On the Lookup tab for the ProductID, select List Box, select Table/Query as the Row Source Type, and select tblProduct as the Row Source. The Product ID is the first column of the Product table, so specify *1* as the Bound column. To show the Product Name in the lookup list, change the Column Count field to 2 and the Column Widths field to *0;1* This will make the Product ID column invisible, while still showing the Product Name column using approximately one inch of space.

Save the table and display it in Datasheet view to see the prices listed by product name. Now, if you need to add a new product or a price change, select the product name in the drop-down list, as shown in Figure 17-22, and then add the As Of date and the price. Section "Using a Macro to Transfer a Grid to a List" in Chapter 18 shows how you can enter the prices into a grid in Excel and then use a macro to import them into Access.

tlkPrice : Table

ProductID	AsOfDate	Price
Bratwurst	1/1/1900	42
Bratwurst	1/1/1900	28
Dried Apples	4/1/2002	25
Gnocci	6/1/2002	22
Pasties	1/1/1900	45
Pate	3/1/2002	50
Sauerkraut	1/1/1900	35
Tofu	4/1/2002	40
Tourtiere	6/1/2002	45
Pate	1/1/1900	25

Figure 17-22
Use the lookup list to enter price changes.

To use the prices, you will need to fill in the prices for each month. That will require a query, which you will learn how to do in "Calculating Prices" in Chapter 18.

Setting Access Environment Options

If you know how to click the New button at the top of the database window, you might not want to have the icons showing for creating a table in Design view, creating a table using the Table Wizard, and so forth. To remove those icons, click Options on the Tools menu. On the View tab, clear the New Object Shortcuts check box, as shown in Figure 17-23. One advantage to removing the shortcuts from the database window is that the New button displays additional options and wizards that are not available from the shortcuts.

(continued)

Setting Access Environment Options *(continued)*

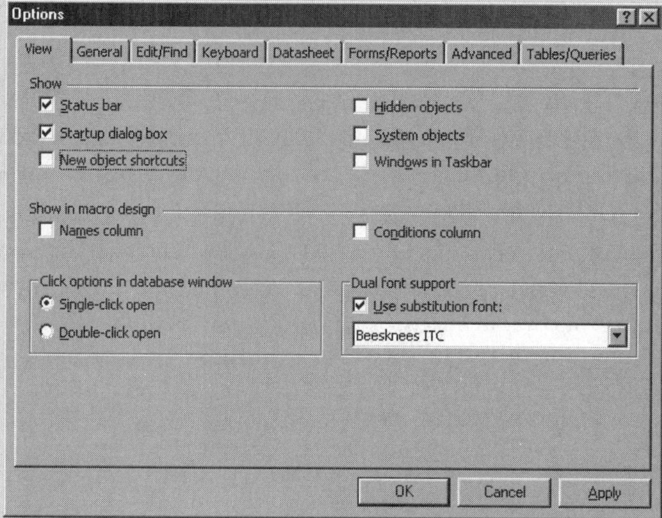

Figure 17-23
Change View options to remove New Object shortcuts.

While you're on the View tab of the Options dialog box, you might want to switch the options in the database window to allow you to open an object by simply clicking it. You might also want to remove the Windows In Taskbar check box to avoid overpopulating your taskbar.

If you don't like seeing the confirmation dialog box each time you delete a record and each time you delete a form or query, clear the appropriate check boxes in the Confirm group on the Edit/Find tab of the Options dialog box, as shown in Figure 17-24.

Modifying Table Relationships

When you created your database, the Table Wizard created a relationship between your fact table and each of the dimension tables you created. It did not, however, create optimal relationships. You can modify those relationships.

Using the Relationships Window

Click Relationships on the Tools menu. The Relationships window shows the primary fact table, along with the four dimension tables. Rearrange the tables so that they appear in a star configuration, as shown in Figure 17-25.

The lines between the fields show the relationships created by the Table Wizard. Click the Save button so as not to save the changes to any of the relationships. Those changes have already been saved.

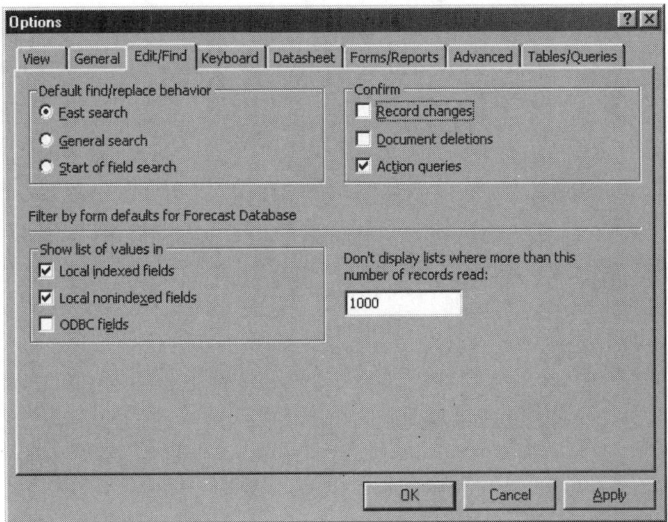

Figure 17-24
Clear confirmation check boxes that annoy you.

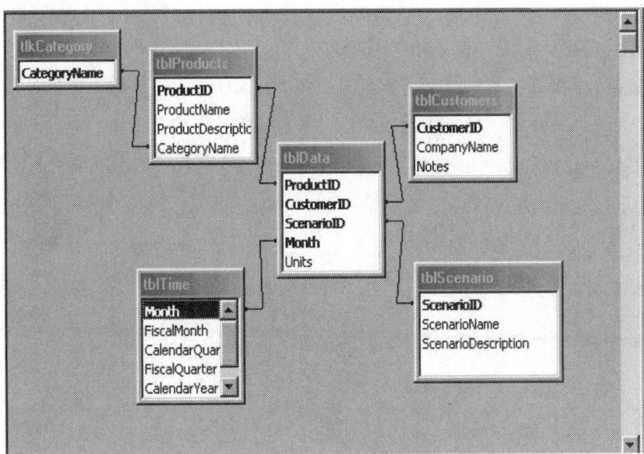

Figure 17-25
Arrange the tables in the Relationships window.

Modifying a Relationship

Each key field in the fact table corresponds to the identically named field in a dimension table. Double-click the line between the two ProductID fields. In the Edit relationships dialog box that appears, you can choose the Enforce Referential Integrity option. *Referential integrity* identifies one of the tables as having a single value that corresponds to multiple values in the other table. This is called a one-to-many relationship. It's all right to have an entry on the one side of the relationship with no corresponding values on the other side; that is, you can have a product in the Product table, but not create a forecast for it. You cannot, however, have an entry on the many side of the relationship if there is no entry on the one side; that is, you cannot create a forecast for a nonexistent product.

Referential integrity is a very good thing. Select the Enforce Referential Integrity check box. Once you have selected the option, the dialog box enables the other two check boxes, as shown in Figure 17-26.

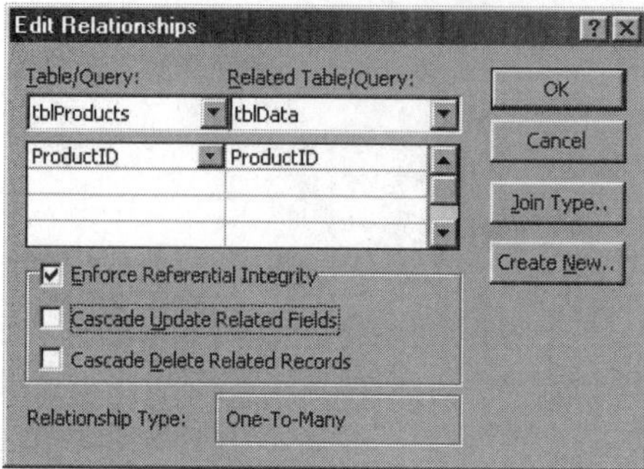

Figure 17-26
Enforcing referential integrity enables cascading changes.

Selecting the Update Related Fields check box tells Access to automatically change the key in all related records in the fact table if you change the key in the Product table. Because the product key is an artificially generated number, there's never any reason to change it. If you were to use a preexisting product number as your ProductID, it is possible that number would change—particularly if you are planning for products before they are introduced. In that case, select the Cascade Update Related fields option so that changing the ProductID in the Product table will automatically change the ProductID for all the related records in the fact table.

You might also delete a product In the Forecast database, and you would want all the related records to disappear from the table as a result. Select the Cascade Delete Related Records check box and click OK. The relationship connection line between the two tables changes slightly, showing the one-to-many relationship between the tables, as shown in Figure 17-27.

Update the relationships for the other three tables, selecting the Enforce Referential Integrity and the Cascade Delete Related Records check boxes.

Adding New Relationships

You can adjust the relationship between the Category lookup table and the Product table so that if you ever renamed a category, you could simply change the name once in the category table and have the corresponding name change for all the products in that category. Double-click the relationship connection line and select all three referential integrity check boxes. Then click Create to create the relationship.

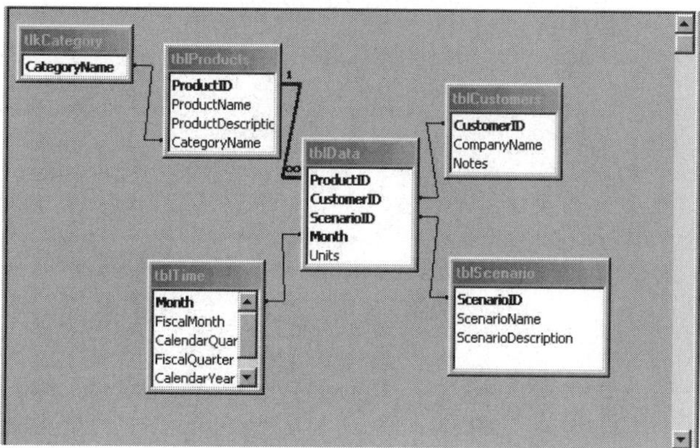

Figure 17-27
The one-to-many icons indicate referential integrity.

The Prices table is also related to the Product table. If you delete a product, you want Access to remove all the associated prices. Because you added the Prices table using Design view and not the Table Wizard, Access did not add the relationship. Click the Add Table button and double-click tblPrice. Move it to an appropriate location, and then create a relationship between the ProductID in the Price table and the Product table. Select both Enforce Referential Integrity and Cascade Deletes and click Create to create the relationship.

Entering Values in the Database

You have now completely defined the structure of the Forecast database. You can manually add entries to each dimension table, and also to the fact table. Creating new records in Access for all your products and customers is tedious, particularly if you already have those names entered as labels in an Excel spreadsheet. "Using Queries to Import Excel Data" in Chapter 18 will show how to use queries to extract the numbers and labels from Excel and populate not only the dimension tables, but also the fact table.

Chapter 18

Manipulate Data with Queries

In This Chapter

Tables are static in Microsoft Access. Essentially, all you can do with a table is add records, delete records, and browse records. A query, on the other hand, is dynamic. It makes things happen. A query allows you to filter, sort, combine, and rearrange information from a table. Think of a table as a repository for data, and think of a query as an interactive tool.

You may recall that you can sort and filter tables in Access. However, when you sort or filter a table, Access actually creates an implicit, but very limited, query to carry out the action on the table. To gain the full power of queries, create them yourself.

Using Queries to Import Excel Data

Chapter 17, "Organize Data with Tables," explains how to create the structure of an analytical database. Conceptually, the database is an extension of a Microsoft Excel grid. To fill the tables in the database, you typically want to extract data that you have already accumulated in Excel. The data in Excel does not look anything like the data in the Access table. To transfer the data from Excel to Access, you will need to create queries. You can also create macros to automate parts of the process.

Note The sample document for this chapter is Forecast.xls. To replicate the instructions, start with the Forecast.mdb database from the CH17 folder.

Introducing a Round-Trip PivotTable

In a well-designed Access table, each record contains only one fact (or one group of related facts). A single set of keys uniquely identifies each record. From the point of view of extracting data from the database, storing one fact in each record is a powerful design. It provides a great deal of flexibility in how the data can be rearranged. From the point of view of entering or updating values, however, having one fact in each record is extremely cumbersome. For each new fact you enter, you must create a new record, which entails creating a whole new set of keys. When you update existing values, you must scroll vertically through a large, unwieldy list, like the list shown in Figure 18-1.

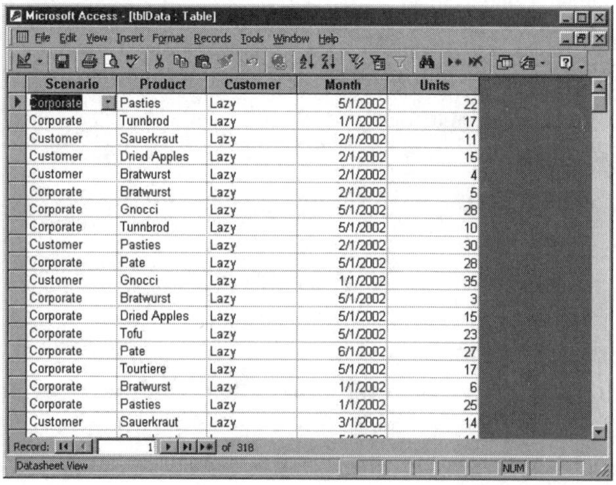

Scenario	Product	Customer	Month	Units
Corporate	Pasties	Lazy	5/1/2002	22
Corporate	Tunnbrod	Lazy	1/1/2002	17
Customer	Sauerkraut	Lazy	2/1/2002	11
Customer	Dried Apples	Lazy	2/1/2002	15
Customer	Bratwurst	Lazy	2/1/2002	4
Corporate	Bratwurst	Lazy	2/1/2002	5
Corporate	Gnocci	Lazy	5/1/2002	28
Corporate	Tunnbrod	Lazy	5/1/2002	10
Customer	Pasties	Lazy	2/1/2002	30
Corporate	Pate	Lazy	5/1/2002	28
Customer	Gnocci	Lazy	1/1/2002	35
Corporate	Bratwurst	Lazy	5/1/2002	3
Corporate	Dried Apples	Lazy	5/1/2002	15
Corporate	Tofu	Lazy	5/1/2002	23
Corporate	Pate	Lazy	6/1/2002	27
Corporate	Tourtiere	Lazy	5/1/2002	17
Corporate	Bratwurst	Lazy	1/1/2002	6
Corporate	Pasties	Lazy	1/1/2002	25
Customer	Sauerkraut	Lazy	3/1/2002	14

Microsoft Access - [tblData : Table]

Record: 1 of 318

Datasheet View

Figure 18-1
Updating one fact per row is cumbersome in Access.

A person who is experienced in working with Excel spreadsheets will usually find updating data values in an Access table to be a frustrating experience. Even if you package the database table using forms, you can't easily get around the list nature of a database. It is much easier to update values for a multidimensional analysis when one of the dimensions—most commonly, the Time dimension—appears in columns, as in a typical spreadsheet like the one shown in Figure 18-2.

Excel and Access work very well together for pulling data from a database into a spreadsheet grid using a PivotTable. The problem occurs when it is time to update values. When you are dealing with historical information, such as orders or financial data, updating values is not a problem. By definition, historical values cannot

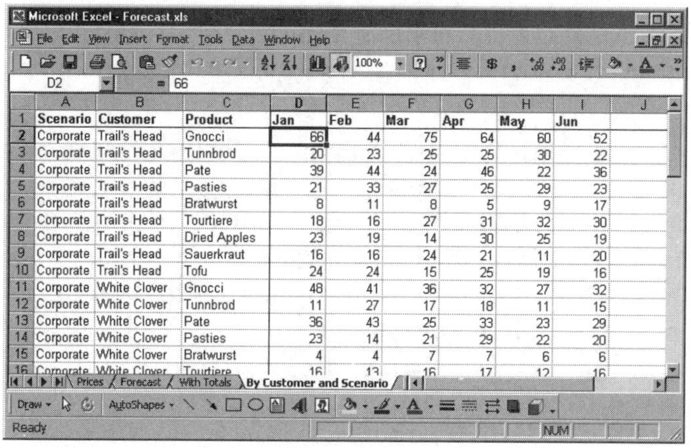

Microsoft Excel - Forecast.xls

D2 = 66

	A	B	C	D	E	F	G	H	I
1	Scenario	Customer	Product	Jan	Feb	Mar	Apr	May	Jun
2	Corporate	Trail's Head	Gnocci	66	44	75	64	60	52
3	Corporate	Trail's Head	Tunnbrod	20	23	25	25	30	22
4	Corporate	Trail's Head	Pate	39	44	24	46	22	36
5	Corporate	Trail's Head	Pasties	21	33	27	25	29	23
6	Corporate	Trail's Head	Bratwurst	8	11	8	5	9	17
7	Corporate	Trail's Head	Tourtiere	18	16	27	31	32	30
8	Corporate	Trail's Head	Dried Apples	23	19	14	30	25	19
9	Corporate	Trail's Head	Sauerkraut	16	16	24	21	11	20
10	Corporate	Trail's Head	Tofu	24	24	15	25	19	16
11	Corporate	White Clover	Gnocci	48	41	36	32	27	32
12	Corporate	White Clover	Tunnbrod	11	27	17	18	11	15
13	Corporate	White Clover	Pate	36	43	25	33	23	29
14	Corporate	White Clover	Pasties	23	14	21	29	22	20
15	Corporate	White Clover	Bratwurst	4	4	7	7	6	6
16	Corporate	White Clover	Tourtiere	16	13	16	17	12	16

Prices / Forecast / With Totals / By Customer and Scenario

Figure 18-2
Updating multiple facts per row in Excel is convenient.

and should not be updated. However, when you are dealing with planning information, or with tactical data repositories that are not populated by the IS department, updating data values is an essential part of the process. The ideal situation, essentially, would be to have an updateable PivotTable. You could use a PivotTable to extract values from a database, update values as necessary, and have the updated values reflected back to the database.

One reason that PivotTables are not updateable is that they typically display summarized values, not values at the lowest level of detail. However, PivotTables cannot transfer data back to the data source, even at the lowest level of detail. Hopefully, later versions of Excel will have that update functionality. In the meantime, the standard tools leave you with the options of entering data in a spreadsheet, which typically results in multiple, unmanaged copies of each value.

This chapter gives you tools for creating a second option: creating a round-trip process for moving values between a database and a worksheet. The outbound portion of the trip, extracting data from Access into Excel, is covered in "Linking A PivotTable to a Data source" in Chapter 15. This chapter will help you with the inbound portion of the trip: moving values from an Excel grid into a list in an Access database.

The solution suggested in this chapter is not as simple as you might like, but given the current alternatives, the chapter does provide a workable solution, particularly when new values are repeatedly transferred into the same Access table. The process consists of three overall steps. First, convert multiple dimensions into a two dimensional grid in Excel. Second, transfer the grid from Excel to Access. Finally, convert the grid into a one-dimensional list.

Assembling Data in Excel

If your Excel grid contains only two dimensions—one row dimension and one column dimension—you can simply transfer the grid to Access. If your Excel grid contains multiple dimensions, one or more dimensions probably extend over multiple worksheets or even multiple workbooks. If so, the first step is to pull the items from the multiple dimensions into a single grid.

If you have a forecast by product and by month—with multiple customers, each on a separate worksheet—you'll copy the forecast for each customer and append it to the bottom of a single list in Excel. Before appending customers into a single grid, insert a new column into which you will add a key for each new customer. Each time you paste a forecast for a customer, you insert the keys for that customer into the Customer column, as shown in Figure 18-3.

	A	B	C	D	E	F	G	H
1	Customer	Product	Jan	Feb	Mar	Apr	May	Jun
6	Trail's Head	Bratwurst	8	11	8	5	9	17
7	Trail's Head	Tourtiere	18	16	27	31	32	30
8	Trail's Head	Dried Apples	23	19	14	30	25	19
9	Trail's Head	Sauerkraut	16	16	24	21	11	20
10	Trail's Head	Tofu	24	24	15	25	19	16
11		Gnocci	48	41	36	32	27	32
12		Tunnbrod	11	27	17	18	11	15
13		Pate	36	43	25	33	23	29
14		Pasties	23	14	21	29	22	20
15		Bratwurst	4	4	7	7	6	6
16		Tourtiere	16	13	16	17	12	16
17		Dried Apples	12	19	14	11	21	11
18		Sauerkraut	13	14	16	16	14	11
19		Tofu	22	12	15	15	16	11

Figure 18-3
Paste blocks from separate worksheets into a single list.

If you have different scenarios in separate workbooks, you'll need to add yet another column to the left side of the table, and then begin assembling the components of the forecast, adding a new key for each scenario. "Merging Data into Worksheets" in Chapter 15 provides a technique for exporting values from a single grid into separate worksheets, and importing the values back into a single grid.)

When you finish assembling the components of the forecast in Excel, it should resemble the sheet shown in Figure 18-4. The combined forecast still looks like a grid. Each month is still in a separate column. The other dimensions are all combined together into rows.

Importing an Excel Worksheet into Access

Once you have combined all the forecasts into a single large grid—with one dimension for the columns and all the remaining dimensions as rows—you're ready to transfer the table to Access.

If you need to import the data into Access only one time, you can import the table. If you will continually update numbers in Excel and you will need to refresh the values in Access on a recurring basis, you should link to the table. The process is

Scenario	Customer	Product	Jan	Feb	Mar	Apr	May	Jun
Corporate	Trail's Head	Gnocci	66	44	75	64	60	52
Corporate	Trail's Head	Tunnbrod	20	23	25	25	30	22
Corporate	Trail's Head	Pate	39	44	24	46	22	36
Corporate	Trail's Head	Pasties	21	33	27	25	29	23
Corporate	Trail's Head	Bratwurst	8	11	8	5	9	17
Corporate	Trail's Head	Tourtiere	18	16	27	31	32	30
Corporate	Trail's Head	Dried Apples	23	19	14	30	25	19
Corporate	Trail's Head	Sauerkraut	16	16	24	21	11	20
Corporate	Trail's Head	Tofu	24	24	15	25	19	16
Corporate	White Clover	Gnocci	48	41	36	32	27	32
Corporate	White Clover	Tunnbrod	11	27	17	18	11	15
Corporate	White Clover	Pate	36	43	25	33	23	29
Corporate	White Clover	Pasties	23	14	21	29	22	20
Corporate	White Clover	Bratwurst	4	4	7	7	6	6
Corporate	White Clover	Tourtiere	16	13	16	17	12	16

Figure 18-4
A grid with multiple dimensions is ready to import to Access.

virtually identical whether you link or import. While you experiment, it's faster to use an imported table because Access does not need to continually reconnect to Excel. With Tables selected in the Access Database window, click the New button. In the New Table dialog box, select Import Table and click OK.

The first step is to specify the source location of the file. Change the value in the File Of Type drop-down list to Microsoft Excel (*.xls), and then navigate to the folder containing the workbook with the composite forecast. Select the workbook and click the Import button. The Import Spreadsheet Wizard lets you select a worksheet or a named range. Click Finish. You now have an Access table. Rename your new table to ImportForecast.

Figure 18-5 shows the table you imported from Excel. It is not quite ready to append to the data table in Access; there are two changes you need to make first. First, you need to convert the table from a grid into a list. Second, you need to convert key names into key numbers.

Creating Queries to Extract a Column from a Grid

The general process for converting a grid into a list is to add one column of facts at a time from the grid to the list. If you have six columns in your grid—corresponding to six months—you will append six blocks of rows into the Access table. This is a tedious job—one that would clearly benefit from macro processing. Before creating the macro, however, you should manually convert at least a portion of the grid to a list using queries. One reason for converting the grid manually is so that you will appreciate the macro. A more important reason is so that you can understand what the macro does, because the macro simply automates the actions of the query.

Microsoft Access - [ImportForecast : Table]

Scenario	Customer	Product	Jan	Feb	Mar
Corporate	Trail's Head	Tunnbrod	20	23	25
Corporate	Trail's Head	Pate	39	44	24
Corporate	Trail's Head	Pasties	21	33	27
Corporate	Trail's Head	Bratwurst	8	11	8
Corporate	Trail's Head	Tourtiere	18	16	27
Corporate	Trail's Head	Dried Apples	23	19	14
Corporate	Trail's Head	Sauerkraut	16	16	24
Corporate	Trail's Head	Tofu	24	24	15
Corporate	White Clover	Gnocci	48	41	36
Corporate	White Clover	Tunnbrod	11	27	17
Corporate	White Clover	Pate	36	43	25
Corporate	White Clover	Pasties	23	14	21
Corporate	White Clover	Bratwurst	4	4	7
Corporate	White Clover	Tourtiere	16	13	16
Corporate	White Clover	Dried Apples	12	19	14
Corporate	White Clover	Sauerkraut	13	14	16
Corporate	White Clover	Tofu	22	12	15
Corporate	Lazy K	Gnocci	31	30	29
Corporate	Lazy K	Tunnbrod	17	18	16

Record: 2 of 53

Datasheet View

Figure 18-5
An Excel grid after it has been imported into Access.

Extracting a Single Column from a Grid

The first step is to create a query that appends the first column—or month—from the grid into the data table—or rather, into a surrogate for the data table. First, you will create a temporary table that uses the descriptive names for the dimension keys. Later, you'll create a query that converts descriptive names into numeric keys.

In the Database window, with the Tables object selected, select the ImportForecast table and click the Query option on the New Object toolbar button. In the New Query dialog box, select Design View and click OK. This step creates a new query based on the selected table.

A query allows you to choose which rows and columns of a table you want to display. The upper half of the Query Design window displays any tables from which you'll be retrieving data. The lower half of the window displays a field grid that shows the fields you want to include in the query.

You want to add the three dimension keys—Scenario, Customer, and Product—and the first fact column—Jan—to the field grid. In the ImportForecast table, select the Scenario field and then hold down the Shift key as you click the Jan field. This selects all four fields. Drag the selected field names down to the field grid. (You can also double-click fields to move them to the field grid one field at a time.)

Click the View toolbar button to display the results of the query. The Datasheet view displays the dimension name fields, along with Jan, as shown in Figure 18-6.

These are the records you'll add to the temporary data table, except that the column labeled Jan needs to have the caption Units at the top, and there should be a column captioned Months that contains the date January 2002. Click the View button, which now displays the Design View icon, to get back to design mode.

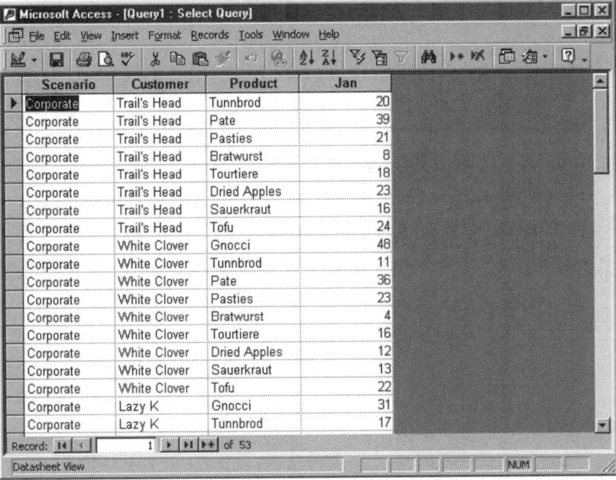

Scenario	Customer	Product	Jan
Corporate	Trail's Head	Tunnbrod	20
Corporate	Trail's Head	Pate	39
Corporate	Trail's Head	Pasties	21
Corporate	Trail's Head	Bratwurst	8
Corporate	Trail's Head	Tourtiere	18
Corporate	Trail's Head	Dried Apples	23
Corporate	Trail's Head	Sauerkraut	16
Corporate	Trail's Head	Tofu	24
Corporate	White Clover	Gnocci	48
Corporate	White Clover	Tunnbrod	11
Corporate	White Clover	Pate	36
Corporate	White Clover	Pasties	23
Corporate	White Clover	Bratwurst	4
Corporate	White Clover	Tourtiere	16
Corporate	White Clover	Dried Apples	12
Corporate	White Clover	Sauerkraut	13
Corporate	White Clover	Tofu	22
Corporate	Lazy K	Gnocci	31
Corporate	Lazy K	Tunnbrod	17

Figure 18-6
Create a query that extracts a single column from the grid.

The query is currently a *Select Query*. It selects fields and records, and allows you to look at them. Before continuing, save the current state of the query. Give it the name qryForecast.

Use Prefixes on Query Names

You can create several different kinds of queries. To keep the different types of queries separate, you may want to use a different three-letter prefix for each query type, as shown in Table 18-1.

For this Query Type	Consider Using this Prefix
Select Query	qry
Crosstab Query	qxt
Make-Table Query	qmt
Update Query	qup
Append Query	qap
Delete Query	qdl

Table 18-1
Three-letter prefixes you can use for query names.

The first row of the field grid lists the name of the source field. If you don't specify otherwise, the name of the source field serves as the caption in the query results. You can create a caption that is different from the source field name. To specify a caption, insert it before the source field name, separating the two names with a colon. In this query, insert *Units:* in front of the *Jan* field name, as shown in Figure 18-7.

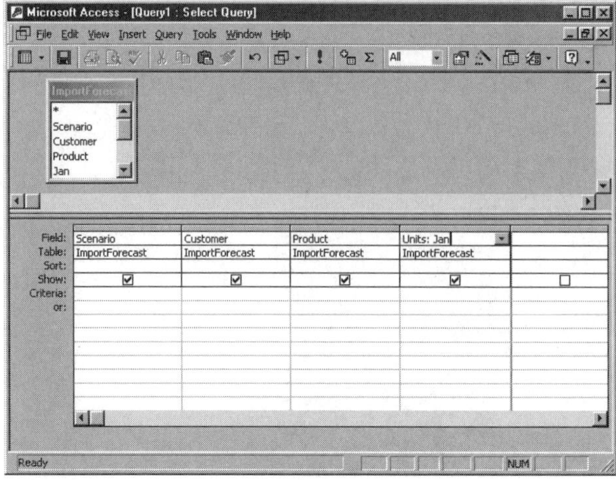

Figure 18-7
Add a label and a colon to create a custom caption.

Switch to Datasheet view to see the new caption, and then switch back to Design View.

The Months field does not retrieve data from the source table at all. You'll enter a constant for that field. First select the Units field and press the Insert key. This inserts space for the new field.

In the same way that you specified a caption for the Units field, you can enter a caption for a field where the source is a constant. Type *Months:* in the Field row of the new column. Type the source for the field after the colon. In this case, the source is a constant date expression. Type *#1/1/2002#,* as shown in Figure 18-8. Click the View button to see the results of the table. This query does match what you want to add to the new temporary table.

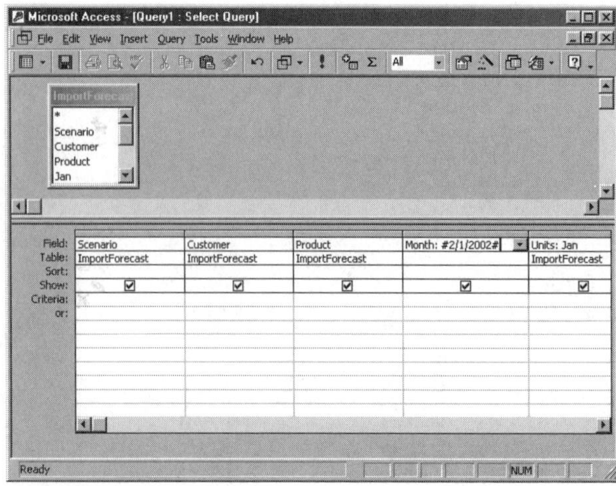

Figure 18-8
A field can contain a constant.

The query is currently designed as a Select query, by default. You want to change it to a query that adds the selected fields and records into a new table. On the Query Type button, select the Make-Table Query option. Type *NewForecast* as the name of the new table and click OK.

A Make-Table Query is an *Action Query*. It does more than simply display values; it changes the content of the tables in the database. Save the revised query with the name qmtForecast and then close the Query window. In the Database window, switch to the Queries object group to see the two queries you have created, as shown in Figure 18-9. The Select query—qryForecast—displays a double-grid icon. The Make-Table Query—qmtForecast—displays a grid with a shiny new mark accompanied by an exclamation mark. The exclamation mark identifies the query as an Action query.

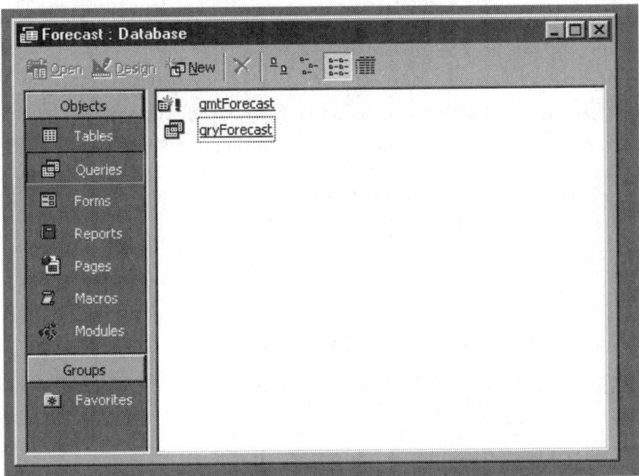

Figure 18-9
The icon for an Action query includes an exclamation mark.

When you double-click the query, Access warns you that you will be modifying the table. Click Yes to run the query. You'll see another warning confirmation box telling you that you are about to paste rows into a new table. Click Yes again. Switch to the Tables tab and open the NewForecast table that you just created. You will add these records to the data table (after converting each key to the appropriate numeric key).

Adding a Column from a Grid to an Existing Table

The qmtForecast query creates a new table and populates it with facts from the first column of the imported forecast table. You can modify it so that it appends the second column from the grid to the same table.

In the Database window, select the qmtForecast query and click Design. In Design View, change the name of the source field for the Units column from *Jan* to *Feb*, and change the date constant from *#1/1/02# to #2/1/02*. Then click the drop-down button

Microsoft Access - [NewForecast : Table]

Product	Customer	Scenario	Month	Units
Tunnbrod	Trail's Head	Corporate	1/1/2002	20
Pate	Trail's Head	Corporate	1/1/2002	39
Pasties	Trail's Head	Corporate	1/1/2002	21
Bratwurst	Trail's Head	Corporate	1/1/2002	8
Tourtiere	Trail's Head	Corporate	1/1/2002	18
Dried Apples	Trail's Head	Corporate	1/1/2002	23

Record: 1 of 318

Figure 18-10
The month column heading is now a dimension key.

next to Query Type and select Append Query. Leave the table name as NewForecast, because you will be appending to the same table you previously created. A new row, Append To, appears in the field grid. The Append To row contains field names from the target table. Since the target table has field names that match the field names in the grid, Access fills in the names for you.

Save the revised query with the name qapForecast. Before executing the query, add one more enhancement. You don't need a row in the Access table, if the fact for a particular set of keys equals zero. In the criteria row, under the Units column, type <>*0*, as shown in Figure 18-11.

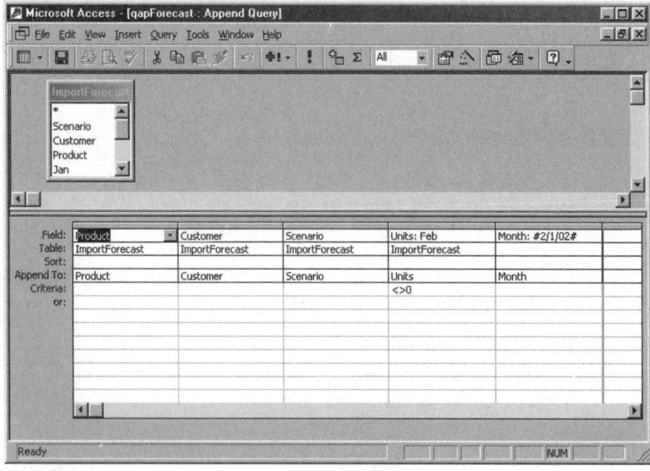

Figure 18-11
Add a condition to the Criteria row to filter records.

This criteria means that you will only include records in the result where the value does not equal zero. Save the query.

In an Action query, the View button and the Run button (which looks like an exclamation mark) behave differently. The Run button executes the Action query, while the View button displays the Datasheet as if the query were a Select query. The View button gives you a chance to preview the results of an Action query. Click the View button to preview the results. Then, switch back to Design View and click the Run button to execute the query. After the query executes, open the NewForecast table to view the results of the query. It now has rows for both January and February.

Analyzing an SQL Statement for a Query

To add the remaining months, you need to repeat the same change: that is, you need to change the source field for the Units column and the date in the Months column. Once you've created the original query, converting it to append additional columns becomes a mechanical process—a process perhaps better performed by a macro. The macro must dynamically create the Make-Table and Append queries you just created manually. However, a macro does not interact with a query in Design View. A macro must modify the Structured Query Language (SQL) statement of a query. When you interact with query in the Design View grid, Access is generating an SQL statement behind the scenes. To see the SQL statement Access generates, open the *SQL view* of the query.

Select the qmtForecast query, open it in Design View, and select the SQL View option from the View button. What you see, as shown in Figure 18-12, is the SQL statement that actually carries out the query's actions.

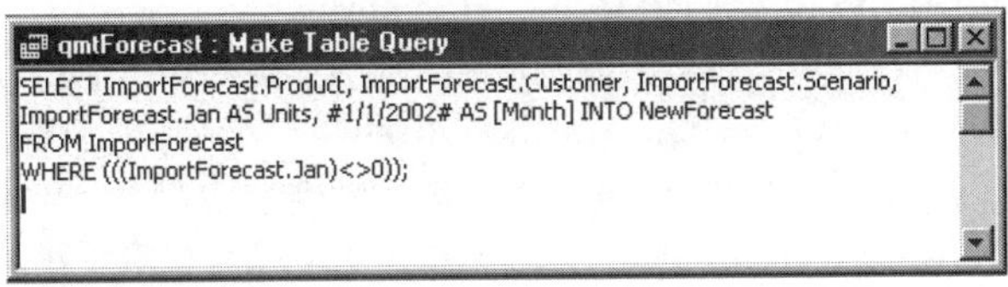

qmtForecast : Make Table Query
SELECT ImportForecast.Product, ImportForecast.Customer, ImportForecast.Scenario,
ImportForecast.Jan AS Units, #1/1/2002# AS [Month] INTO NewForecast
FROM ImportForecast
WHERE (((ImportForecast.Jan)<>0));

Figure 18-12
The Query Design grid generates an SQL statement.

The Make-Table Query consists of four clauses, each introduced by a keyword. Although case is not important, by convention, the keyword in an SQL statement is written in all uppercase letters. Line breaks are not important either, but by convention, each new clause appears on a new line.

The first—and most important—keyword is SELECT. After the SELECT keyword and a query, you list the name of each field you want to include in the query. This corresponds to the top row of the field grid in Design View. Before each field name, the SQL statement includes the name of the table the field originates from. Including the table name is important if you are selecting fields from multiple tables, as well as if the same field name appears in more than one table. In this case, you are selecting data from one table, so the macro will omit the table name prefixed to each field name.

The first three fields are Product, Customer, and Scenario. The last two fields are the fields where you specified a customized caption. The first customized field displays the date constant *#1/1/2002#*, followed by the keyword AS, followed by the name Month in square brackets. The name Month is the caption; it is enclosed in brackets because Month is a keyword in SQL syntax. The brackets tell SQL to interpret Months as a name you have defined, not as a built-in name. Brackets around field names are always safe. The AS keyword precedes a custom caption.

The syntax in an SQL statement is the inverse of that in the field grid. In the field grid, you enter the caption, followed by a colon, followed by the source of the field. In an SQL statement, you enter the source of the field, followed by the word AS, followed by the caption.

The final field gets its values from the Jan column of the ImportForecast table, with Units as the caption. If a SELECT clause contains more than one field (as this one does), names must be separated by commas. There is no comma after the final name in the clause.

The second clause begins with the keyword INTO. This gives the name of the table to create.

The third clause begins with the keyword FROM. This clause specifies one or more tables from which you extract the data. In this SQL statement, there's only one table—the ImportForecast table.

The final clause begins with the word WHERE. This clause corresponds to the Criteria row of the field grid. When Access generates an SQL statement, it tends to add excessive parentheses in a where clause. In this clause, you could remove all the parentheses without affecting the meaning of the statement.

The SQL statements end with the semicolon, which is optional. Here is the SQL statement with all the optional elements removed. Following is the string the macro needs to generate:

```
SELECT Product, Customer, Scenario, Jan AS Units, #1/1/2002# AS [Month]
INTO NewForecast FROM ImportForecast WHERE Jan<>0
```

Comparing Different Types of Queries

The only difference between a Make-Table Query and a Select query is the INTO clause. If you remove the INTO NewForecast clause from the query, it becomes an ordinary Select query.

Look at the SQL statement for the qapForecast query (the one that appends the second month) to see the slightly different syntax for an Append Query. Open the query in Design View and select SQL View from the View button. The SQL statement should look like the one shown in Figure 18-13.

In an Append Query, the SELECT, FROM, and WHERE clauses are identical to those in a Make-Table Query. The only difference is that a Make-Table Query has an INTO

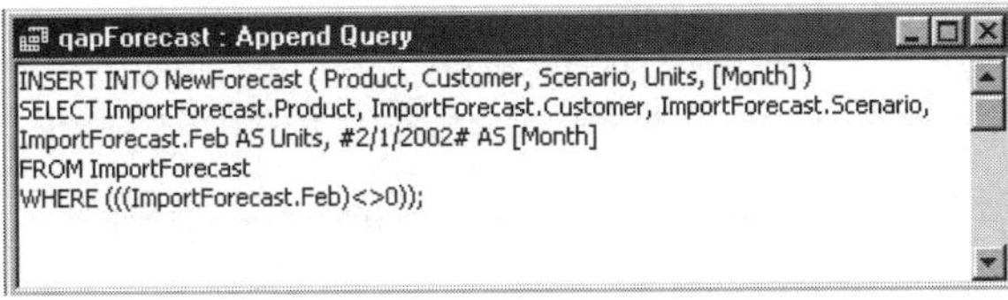

Figure 18-13
An Append Query is almost identical to a Make-Table Query.

clause that follows the SELECT clause, while an Append Query has an INSERT INTO clause that precedes the SELECT clause.

The SELECT INTO clause contains the name of the target table, followed by a list of field names enclosed in parentheses. If the captions of the columns generated by the SELECT clause match field names in the target table, you do not need the list of field names surrounded by parentheses. Here is the SQL statement with all the optional elements removed:

```
INSERT INTO NewForecast SELECT Product, Customer, Scenario, Feb AS Units,
#2/1/2002# AS [Month] FROM ImportForecast WHERE Feb<>0
```

Using a Macro to Transfer a Grid to a List

You are finally ready to create a macro that transfers the grid to a list. The task of transferring a grid to a list is one that you may need to do for more than one grid. If you construct the bulk of the macro as a subroutine, you can use it in multiple contexts. You can then create a macro that sets up the specifics for a given conversion and calls the subroutine that does the work. When you need to convert a different grid into a list, all you need to create is a new set up macro. In fact, "Importing Prices from an Excel Grid into an Access List," later in this chapter, will use the same macro to convert product prices from an Excel grid into an Access list.

Creating a Macro to Convert a Specific List

The following *ForecastToList* macro automates the process of converting the ImportForecast grid table into the NewForecast list table. The macro assigns values to module-level variables and then runs the *Convert* subroutine, which does all the work.

```
Sub ForecastToList()
    sSourceTable = "ImportForecast"
    sTargetTable = "NewForecast"
    vRowFields = Array("Product", "Customer", "Scenario")
    sFactField = "Units"
    sTargetColumnField = "Month"
    vSourceColumnLabels = Array("Jan", "Feb", "Mar", "Apr", "May", "Jun")
    vTargetColumnKeys = Array("#1/1/2002#", "#2/1/2002#", "#3/1/2002#", _
        "#4/1/2002#", "#5/1/2002#", "#6/1/2002#")
    Convert
End Sub
```

The module-level variables isolate the qualities that make the ImportForecast table unique. To convert a table, there are certain pieces of information you must provide:

- The names of the source and the target tables. These values go into the variables *sSourceTable* and *sTargetTable,* respectively.
- A list of the row dimensions—those that will be transferred directly from the source table to the target table. These dimension field names go into the *vRowFields* variable as an array. The Visual Basic Array (VBA) function lets you store multiple values in a single Variant variable. (For more information about variants, see "Creating Variables" in Chapter 4.)
- A name for the new dimension field. This name goes into the *sFactField* variable.
- Two parallel lists that correspond to the columns labels in the grid. The first list is the original list of column labels. These labels are field names in the imported grid table. You store these names as an array in the *vSourceColumnLabels* variable. In the Forecast table, these are the names of the months.
- The value you want to use as key for each new block of rows that will be appended, is provided in the corresponding parallel list. In the Forecast table, these correspond to date constants for the months. These are stored as an array in the *vTargetRowKeys* variable. You will be using these values to construct an SQL statement—which is a string—so enter dates as strings with number signs surrounding the date values.
- A name for the fact field. This will be stored in the *sFactField* variable.

All the variables are declared at the module level. (Alternatively, you could change the *Convert* subroutine to use seven arguments, but it is difficult to add comments to multiple arguments.) Here are the declarations for the module-level variables. Each variable is prefaced by a descriptive comment.

```
Option Compare Database
Option Explicit
''' Imported table with "grid" layout
    Private sSourceTable As String
''' New Table to be created with "list" layout
    Private sTargetTable As String

''' Row fields will be transferred straight across
    Private vRowFields
''' Name for new field to hold Column dimension items
    Private sTargetColumnField As String
''' Names of column labels in the "grid" table
    Private vSourceColumnLabels
''' Output key Names (must correspond to vSourceColumnLabels)
    Private vTargetColumnKeys
''' Name for Fact field in new table
    Private sFactField As String
```

Using a Subroutine to Convert the Grid

The actual work of converting the grid is done by the *Convert* subroutine, as mentioned earlier. For each column in the grid, it creates and executes an SQL statement. For the first column, the SQL statement creates a Make-Table Query. For each remaining column, the SQL statement creates an Append Query.

```
Private Sub Convert()
    Dim iField As Long
    Dim iKey As Long
    Dim sSQL As String

    On Error GoTo ErrorHandler
    DoCmd.SetWarnings False

    For iField = LBound(vTargetColumnKeys) To UBound(vTargetColumnKeys)
        ''' Initialize the SQL string
        sSQL = ""
        ''' Other than first time, make it an Append Query
        If iField <> LBound(vTargetColumnKeys) Then
            sSQL = "INSERT INTO " & sTargetTable & " "
        End If
        sSQL = sSQL & "SELECT "

        ''' Put in all the constant keys
        For iKey = LBound(vRowFields) To UBound(vRowFields)
            sSQL = sSQL & vRowFields(iKey) & ", "
        Next iKey

        ''' Insert a constant key value for the current cross-tabbed field
        sSQL = sSQL & vSourceColumnLabels(iField) _
             & " AS [" & sFactField & "], "

        ''' Insert the field name for the current cross-tabbed field
        sSQL = sSQL & vTargetColumnKeys(iField) _
             & " AS [" & sTargetColumnField & "] "

        ''' First time, make it a Make-Table Query
        If iField = LBound(vTargetColumnKeys) Then
            sSQL = sSQL & "INTO " & sTargetTable & " "
        End If
        sSQL = sSQL & "FROM " & sSourceTable & " "

        ''' Eliminate zero records
        sSQL = sSQL & "WHERE " & vSourceColumnLabels(iField) & "<>0;"

        ''' Execute the command for this field
        DoCmd.RunSQL sSQL
    Next iField

ErrorHandler:
```

```
    DoCmd.SetWarnings True
End Sub
```

This macro generates an SQL statement and then executes the statement once for each column. The macro uses a lot of string manipulation—mostly concatenating strings together. Each statement appends a little bit more to the one SQL statement. Each statement that adds to the SQL statement always includes a space at the end. One common error when constructing an SQL statement is to omit a space between clauses. An SQL statement can all be on a single line—not broken onto separate lines as in the Query SQL View—but there must be one or more spaces separating each word.

Control Warning Messages in an Access Macro

You might want to use the *DoCmd.SetWarnings False* statement at the beginning of your Access macros. This statement prevents Access from asking your permission to carry out actions such as creating new tables and appending rows—particularly when the macro includes a loop. The problem with the *SetWarnings* command is that it remains in effect even after the macro finishes, which can cause unnerving effects. For example, suppose you start creating a new query, and then decide to abandon the query. If warnings are disabled, Access will not let you close the query without saving changes. That's because the initial dialog box—the one that asks whether you want to save changes to the query—does not appear. The only dialog box that appears is the one that asks what name you want to assign the query. If you click OK, Access saves the query; if you click Cancel, Access drops you back into Design View. This is very disconcerting.

When you turn off warnings in a macro, you must to be absolutely certain to turn the warnings back on at the end of the macro. For an extra tip on how to create a keyboard shortcut to reset warnings, select the search word *SetWarnings* in the Visual Basic Editor, and press F1.

The purpose of the *On Error Go To ErrorHandler* statement is to ensure that the macro executes the final statement of the macro—the one that turns warnings back on—even if the macro encounters a run-time error. (For more information about error handling, see "Handling Run-Time Errors" in Chapter 4.)

After setting an error handler and disabling warnings, the macro enters a loop. Not surprisingly, most of the work of the macro occurs in the loop.

The loop executes once for each entry in the array of column labels. The LBound function returns the number of the lowest entry in an array, and the UBound function returns the number of the highest entry. Looping a variable from the LBound of an array to the UBound ensures that you execute the loop once for each item in the array. (For more information about working with arrays, see "Creating Arrays of Variables" in Chapter 4.)

The first statement in the loop is *sSQL = ""*. Because statements append to the *sSQL* variable, this statement ensures that nothing is left over from the previous loop. (Technically, this is not necessary in this loop, but it is good practice to get in the habit of being safe.)

For the first column, the loop creates a Make-Table Query. For every other column, the loop creates an Append Query. An Append Query has an INSERT INTO clause at the beginning. The first statement within the loop checks to see if the current column number is equal to the lowest possible column number. If so, it adds an INSERT INTO command with the target table name.

Each SQL statement will include a SELECT clause. The statement *sSQL = sSQL & "SELECT"* appends the SELECT clause to the existing statement. If this is not an Append Query, then the existing statement will be blank.

The next section of the macro loops through each of the row fields, merely copying the name of the field from the *vRowFields* array to the SQL statement, with each field name followed by a comma. This inner loop is executed each time it iterates through the main loop.

The *sSQL =sSQL & vSourceColumnLabels(iField) & " AS [" & sFactField & "], "* statement inserts the appropriate column label as the source for the field data, but it always uses the fact field name as the caption for the column. This statement appends a comma to the end, because there is one remaining field for the SELECT clause.

The *sSQL = sSQL & vTargetColumnKeys(iField) & " AS [" & sTargetColumnField & "] "* statement appends the appropriate date for the current column into the field for the new dimension. This field does not have a comma at the end, because it is the final field of the SELECT clause.

The next block of the statement executes only if the loop is processing the first column. If this is the first column, the SQL statement needs to create a Make-Table Query. In a Make-Table Query, the INTO clause comes immediately after the SELECT clause.

The *sSQL = sSQL & "FROM " & sSourceTable & " "* statement appends a FROM clause to each statement.

The statement *sSQL = sSQL & "WHERE " & vSourceColumnLabels(iField) & "<>0;"* adds a WHERE clause that skips any rows that have a zero value for the current column. After this statement, the SQL statement is complete.

The statement *DoCmd.RunSQL sSQL* executes the SQL statement. You may want to add a breakpoint on this statement and display the contents of the *sSQL* variable in the Immediate window before proceding. The first time through, it should match (aside from line breaks) the SQL statement in the qmtForecast query. The second time through, it should match the SQL statement in the qapForecast query.

With the *GridToList* module in the database, you can convert the entire ImportForecast table into the NewForecast table by simply executing the one *ForecastToList* macro. The macro replaces the NewForecast table if it already exists.

Debugging an SQL Statement Generated by a Macro

If an SQL statement generated by a macro does not work properly, it can be tricky to debug. Here's how to move the SQL statement back into the Design View grid:

- Add a breakpoint to the command that executes the SQL statement.
- Type *?sSQL* in the Immediate window to display the SQL statement when the macro stops at the breakpoint. Simply examining the statement may reveal the error. If not, select and copy the SQL statement.
- Before leaving the Visual Basic Editor, restore warnings by dragging the yellow current line in the Code window indicator down to the *DoCmd SetWarnings True* command, and press F5 to finish the macro.
- Switch to Access, create a new simple query with no tables, and switch to SQL view.
- Delete the entire default SQL statement, and paste the one generated by the macro.
- Then switch to Design View where you can use the graphical grid interface to identify any problems.

Importing Prices from an Excel Grid into an Access List

The Convert macro introduced earlier in this chapter also can be used to import prices from Excel into the Prices table created in Chapter 17. Assume that you have already created prices in an Excel worksheet, as shown in Figure 18-14.

For each product, specify the price at its introduction—which may be the price at the beginning of the planning period—and then enter only price changes in the grid.

In Access, here's a brief recap of how to link a table to the Prices worksheet (so that if you make changes to the prices, you can easily import the revised prices into Access):

1. In the Database window, select the Tables object group and click New.
2. Select Link Table and click OK.
3. Navigate to the folder that contains the workbook, change the Files Of Type drop-down list box value to Microsoft Excel (*.xls), and then click the workbook and click Open.
4. Select the worksheet that contains the prices, and click Finish.
5. Rename the links table to ImportPrices.

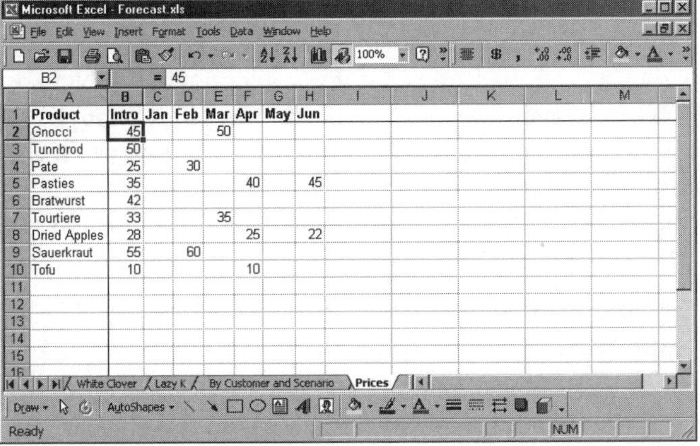

Product	Intro	Jan	Feb	Mar	Apr	May	Jun
Gnocci	45			50			
Tunnbrod	50						
Pate	25		30				
Pasties	35				40		45
Bratwurst	42						
Tourtiere	33			35			
Dried Apples	28				25		22
Sauerkraut	55		60				
Tofu	10				10		

Figure 18-14
It's easy to edit a grid that contains only price changes.

Copy the following *ForecastToList* macro and rename the copy to *PricesToList*. Change the macro to read as follows:

```
Sub PricesToList()
    sSourceTable = "ImportPrices"
    sTargetTable = "NewPrices"
    sFactField = "Price"
    sTargetColumnField = "Months"
    vRowFields = Array("Product")
    vSourceColumnLabels = Array("Intro", "Jan", "Feb", "Mar", _
        "Apr", "May", "Jun")
    vTargetColumnKeys = Array("#1/1/1900#", "#1/1/2002#", "#2/1/2002#", _
        "#3/1/2002#", "#4/1/2002#", "#5/1/2002#", "#6/1/2002#")
    Convert
End Sub
```

The values you assign in the *PricesToList* macro are very similar to those in the *ForecastToList* macro. There is only one row dimension, but you still need to assign the value as an array. The first column label is Intro, referring to the introductory price for the product. Because each product can have a different introduction date, it's safe to enter a very early date as the standard introduction date. You can enter an arbitrary value such as 1/1/1900. (You could enter a date as early as 1/1/100. Dates earlier than 1/1/100 have a two-digit year and are interpreted as belonging to the current century.) Run the *PricesToList* macro to create the NewPrices table.

Before you can use either the imported forecast or the imported prices, you will need to convert descriptive dimension names to integer dimension keys. Before you can do that, you must populate the dimension tables.

Using Queries to Populate Dimension Tables

Now that you have imported the forecast data, you can use the NewForecast table to populate the Product, Customer, and Time dimension tables. In the Database window, with the Tables object group activated, select—but don't open—the NewForecast table. On the Standard toolbar, click the drop-down arrow next to the New Object button and Select Query. In the New Query dialog box, select Design View and click OK.

In the NewForecast table, double-click the Customer field to add it to the field grid. You now have a query that will display only the customer names from the NewForecast table. Click the View toolbar button to display the results of the query. The Datasheet view displays all the customers from the imported forecast, as shown in Figure 18-15.

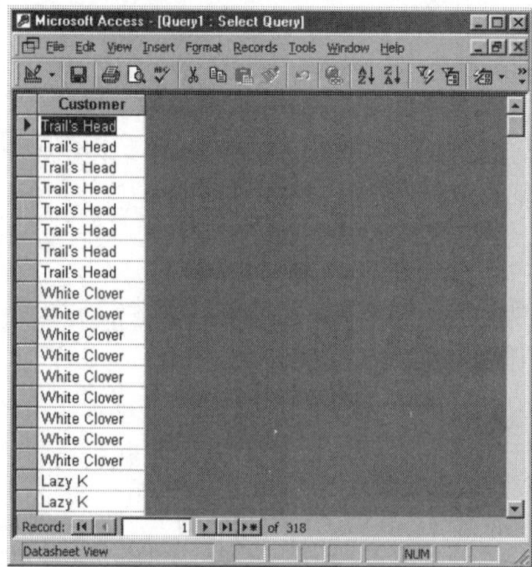

Figure 18-15
You need to extract only unique values.

If you were to append this list to the Customer table, you would have multiple copies of each customer name. In the dimension table, the key must be unique. As far as the table is concerned, the key is unique because it contains the automatic number that Access generates. Access sees the customer name as simple text and allows multiple values; you want each customer name to appear only once.

Click the View button to return to Design View. On the toolbar, click the Properties button to display the Properties window. The Properties window can display properties either for an individual field or for the entire query. If you click the Customer field in the field grid, the Properties window will display the properties of the customer field. If you double-click the background in the upper part of the window, the Properties window will display the properties of the query itself. You want to include each customer name only once in the output of the query. Change the Unique Values property to Yes, as shown in Figure 18-16.

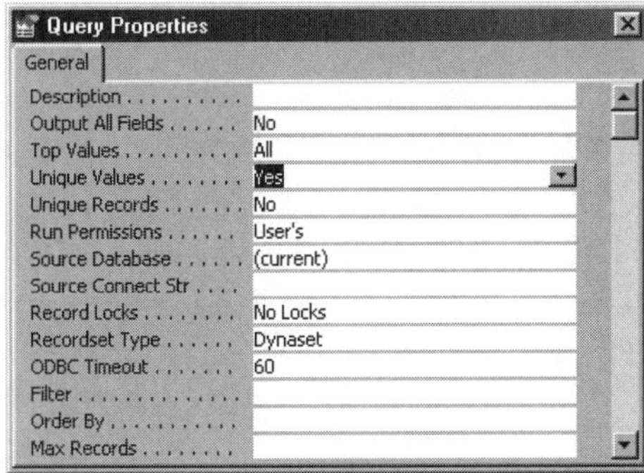

Figure 18-16
Select the Unique Values property to remove duplicates.

Click the View button to switch to Datasheet view. This time, the query displays each customer name only once. These customer names are now ready to append to the Customer table.

To convert this Select query into an Append Query, select Append Query from the Query Type toolbar button. Select tblCustomer as the append target and click OK. Access does not fill in the name of the Append To field in the field grid, because the target table does not contain a field named Customer. Select CustomerName as the Append To field, as shown in Figure 18-17.

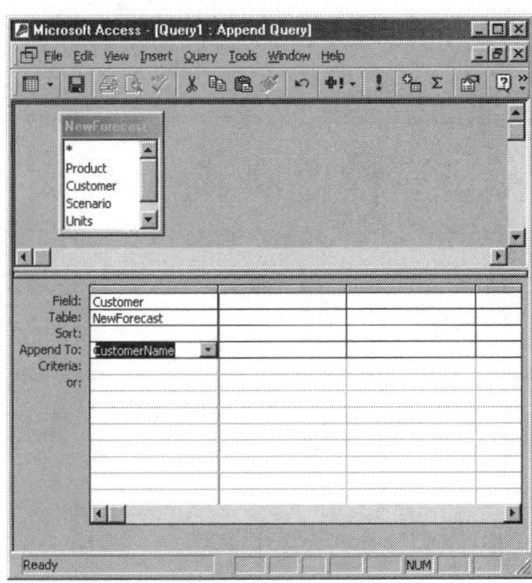

Figure 18-17
If the target field name is different from the source, you must select it.

This query can now append each unique customer name from the imported Excel worksheet into the CustomerName field of the Customer table. Save the query with the name qapCustomer and click the Run button.

You have now appended the names to the Customer table. In the Database window, switch to the Tables object group and open the Customer table. The customer names appear in the list, complete with automatically generated customer ID numbers.

Create a query for populating the Product table by modifying the Customer query. Before making changes, save the query with the name qapProduct to avoid accidentally replacing the original query. After running the query, open the Products table and assign a category to each product. Gnocci and Tunnbrod are Cereals; Bratwurst, Pate, Tourtiere, and Pasties are Meats; and Sauerkraut, Tofu, and Dried Apples are Produce.

Create and run a query to populate Months in the Time table. Save this query with the name qapTime.

Control Automatic Record Numbers

When you add entries to a table that has an automatic numbering key, Access always adds from the next available number, even if you delete records. For example, if you add 10 records to a new table, they will be numbered from 1 to 10. If you delete the records and add more records, the new records will be numbered from 11 to 20. To reset the numbering of a table back to zero, you must delete all the records in the table, and then compact the database.

To compact a database, click Database Utilities on the Tools menu, and then click Compact And Repair Database. This command temporarily closes the database, compacts it, repairs any invalid links, rebuilds the indexes, and reopens the database. (If you'll want to start automatic numbering at a specific location, search the Answer Wizard using the words *Start AutoNumber*.

Creating an Update Query to Populate the Time Table

The Time dimension table contains attribute columns that can be derived from the Month column. You can create a query that calculates the value of each derived attribute. Because the records already exist, you'll use an *Update Query* to fill the attribute columns.

In the Database window, select the existing Time table. Click the New Objects toolbar button, Select Query and choose Design View. This creates a new query with the Time table as a single source table.

Note As with all Action queries, when you are in design mode, an Update query allows you to click the View button to execute a select version of the query. Unfortunately, when you click the View button with an Update query, you see the old value in each field, not the new value. When you create an Update query, you may find it convenient to first create the query as a Select query—so you can see the values you are calculating. After the query calculates the correct values, you can convert it to an Update query.

Save the Select version of the query as qryTime. Double-click the Month field to move that field into the field grid. You won't be updating the Month field, but as you develop the query, it can be useful to see it so you can tell whether the attribute calculations are correct.

Each of the attribute columns in this table extracts a part of the date in the Month column. Access has two different formulas you can use to extract a portion of a date: DatePart and Format. Technically, DatePart returns an integer, while Format returns a string. Pragmatically, Access automatically converts a string that looks like a number into an integer as needed, so that the difference is not significant. On the other hand, the Format function can create a much wider variety of results. For example, with the Format function, you can extract either a two-digit or a four-digit year, while the DatePart function can extract only a four-digit year.

Each column must have a caption. If you enter a formula for a column without specifying a caption, Access will generate one for you. You're better off creating a short, temporary caption of your own. Type the label *CY* (short for calendar year) and then a colon. After the caption, type the expression *Format(Month, "yyyy")*. As soon as you press Tab, Enter, or an arrow key, Access interprets the formula for you, inserting brackets around the Month field name, as shown in Figure 18-18. Click the View button to see the results of the formula. You should see the original Month value, with the four-digit calendar year next to it. Click the View button to return to Design View.

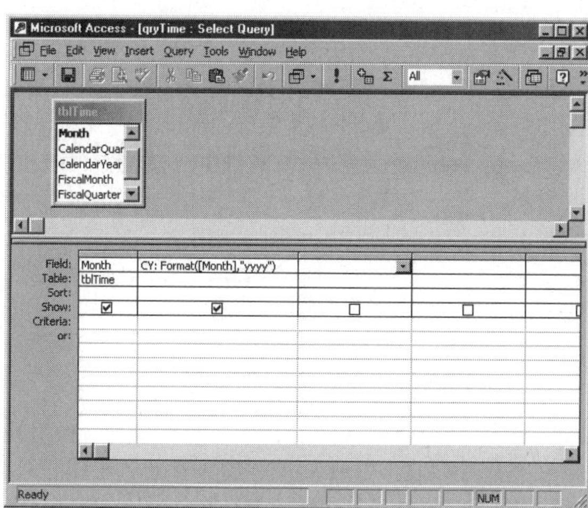

Figure 18-18
Use the Format function to extract the year from a date.

Next, calculate the calendar quarter. The *Format* function allows you to format a date as a quarter. Type the label *CQ* (for calendar quarter) followed by a colon, followed by the expression *Format(Month, "q")*. Click the View button to look at the value. It should show the numerical quarter for each month.

Suppose that your company likes to display the prefix Q before the quarter number. You can easily add a one-character prefix as part of the *Format* function. In design view, change the calendar quarter formula to *Format([Month], "\Qq")*, as shown in Figure 18-19. Use Datasheet view to check the results of the query.

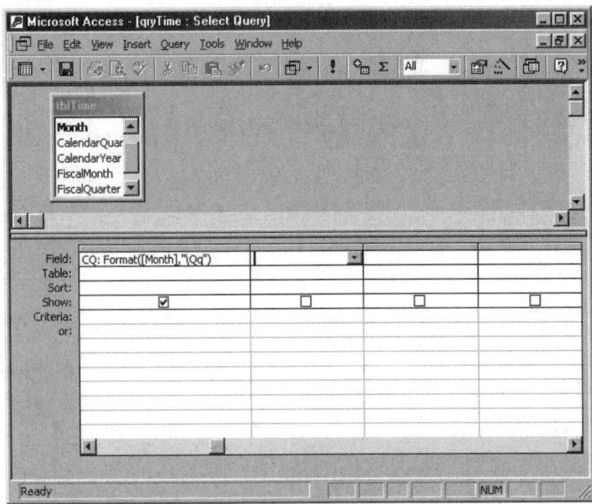

Figure 18-19
A backslash lets you include a text character in a formatting code.

Note A backslash character (\) is called an escape character. It causes the Format function to interpret the following letter as text, not as a format code. The backslash character applies only to a single letter. If you want to include more than one letter in the format string, you must enclose the text in double-quotation mark pairs (""""), which can make the formula very difficult to read. When you want a prefix with more than a single letter, you're better off adding the prefix in front of the Format function, concatenated with an ampersand (&).

Calculate Fiscal Dates

Suppose your company's fiscal year begins in February. That means that January 2002 would be the twelfth month of Fiscal 2001. You can let the Format function do all the work of shifting between years and quarters in a fiscal date. To calculate fiscal equivalents for a date with a fiscal year that begins in February, simply subtract 15 from the date inside the Format function. With a fiscal year that begins in November, add 75 to the original month. Because fiscal dates are typically displayed as months, quarters, or years—not as days—you should add or subtract enough to put the date into the middle of the month. That avoids having to deal with varying month lengths.

To create the Fiscal Year field, type the label *FY* and a colon as the field caption. Then enter the formula *"FY" & Format(Month-15, "yyyy")*. To create the Fiscal Quarter field, type the label *FQ* and a colon, and then enter the formula *"FQ" & Format(Month-15, "q")*. To create the Fiscal Month field, which you'll prefix with FM, type *FM* and a colon, and then type the formula *"FM" & Format(Month-15, "m")*, as shown in Figure 18-20.

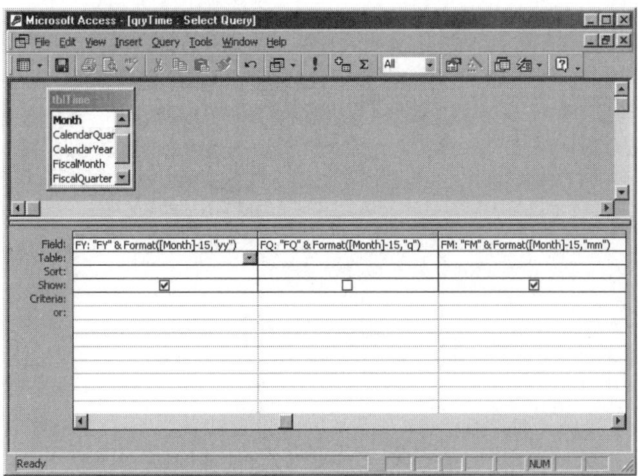

Figure 18-20
Add or subtract a constant to calculate fiscal dates.

After creating all the fields, display them in Datasheet view. The result should look like Figure 18-21.

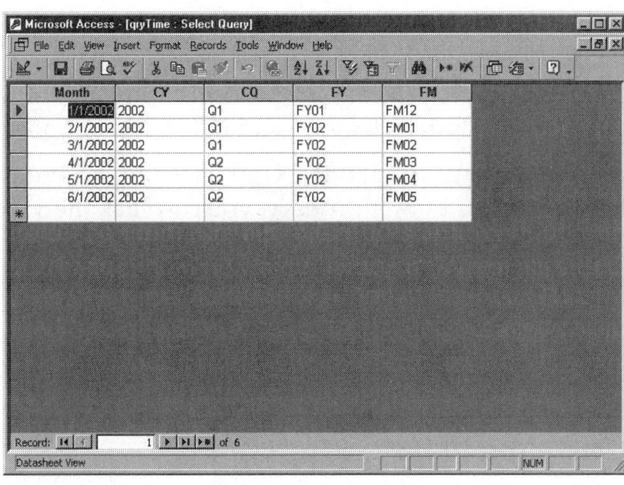

Figure 18-21
Create a Select query before converting to an Update Query.

You are now ready to convert the query to an Update query. In Design View, select Update query on the Query Type toolbar button. An Update To row appears in the field grid. Unlike a Make-Table Query or an Append Query, when you create an Update query, you do not need to enter a table name because, by definition, you will update the source table.

Select the field definition for the calendar year field. Access should select the entire definition. Copy the definition to the clipboard by pressing Ctrl+C. Then, in the Field row, click the drop-down list box and select the CalendarYear field from the source table. Move to the Update To row of the grid and paste the field definition by pressing Ctrl+V. Delete the caption and the colon from the formula. The result should look like Figure 18-22.

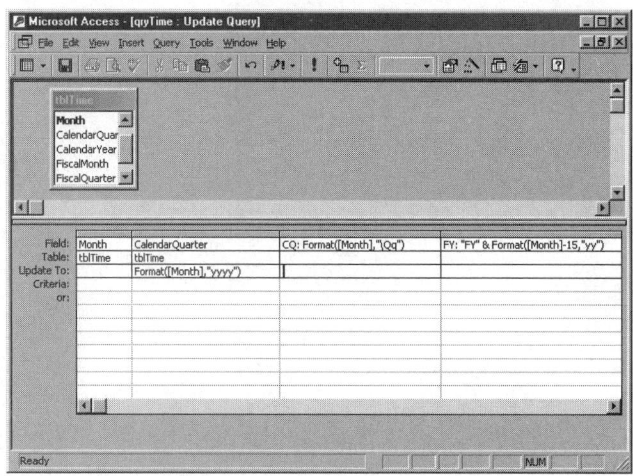

Figure 18-22
Move field definitions from the Field row to the Update To row.

For each remaining field, repeat the process: cut the definition, select the target field name, paste the formula in the Update To row, and delete the temporary caption.

After moving the formula for each field to the Update To row, save the query as qupTime and then run it. After running the query, you can click the View button to see the values that now populate the table.

Creating a Query that Joins Two Tables

You have already converted the Forecast and Price grids into temporary lists. However, the lists still contain text names for the keys. You need to convert those text names to integer keys. Start by converting the keys in the NewPrice table, as it has only one dimension table.

In the Database window, switch to the Queries object group and click the New button. In the Show Table dialog box, double-click NewPrices and tblProduct, and then close the dialog box. Access should not create a link between the tables, because the ProductID primary key name in the Product table does not match a field name in the NewPrices table.

You need to create a link between the text key field in the NewPrices table and ProductName field in the dimension table. Drag the Product field from the NewPrices table to the ProductName field in the Products table. Dragging a field from one table to another creates a *Join*—essentially a super-fast lookup field. Figure 18-23 shows the joined tables.

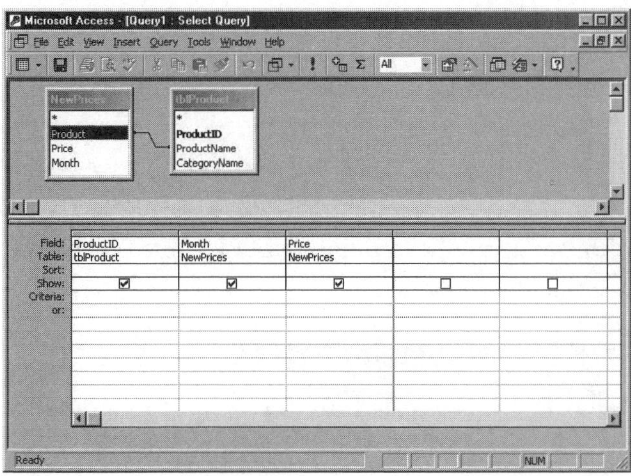

Figure 18-23
Drag a field between tables to create a join.

Double-click the ProductID, Price, and Month fields to add them to the field grid. Click View to see the converted price list, and click View again to return to Design View.

When you drag a field from one table to another, you create what is called an *inner join*. An inner join discards output from either table if it can't find a match in the other table. If you created prices for a product not appearing in the Product table, an inner join would simply exclude those prices from the output. Conversely, if you accidentally forgot to enter prices for one of the products, an inner join would simply not include that product in the output. (Try deleting one of the products from the NewPrices table—perhaps Bratwurst—to see what happens.)

Suppose there is a real possibility that you forgot to enter prices for a product, and you don't want that product to just disappear. You can modify the join so that it always includes all records from one side of the join. This is called an *outer join*. To create an outer join, double-click the join line. In the Join Properties dialog box that appears, select the option that includes all rows for the left or right table, as shown in Figure 18-24.

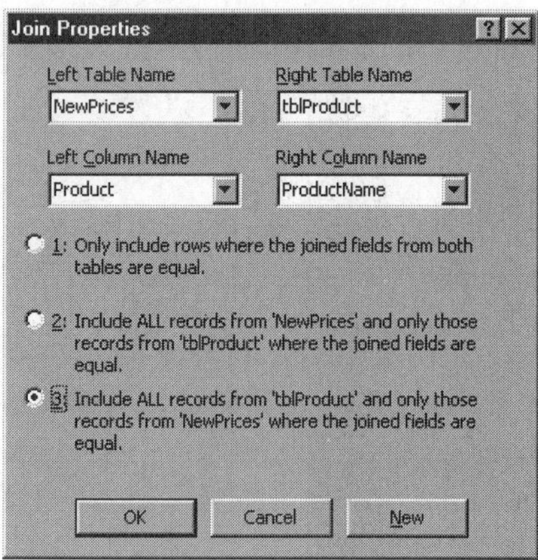

Figure 18-24
An outer join includes all records from one of the tables.

In this case, you want to be sure to retain all the products. After you click OK, the join line changes to show an arrowhead pointing at the table that can be ignored, as shown in Figure 18-25.

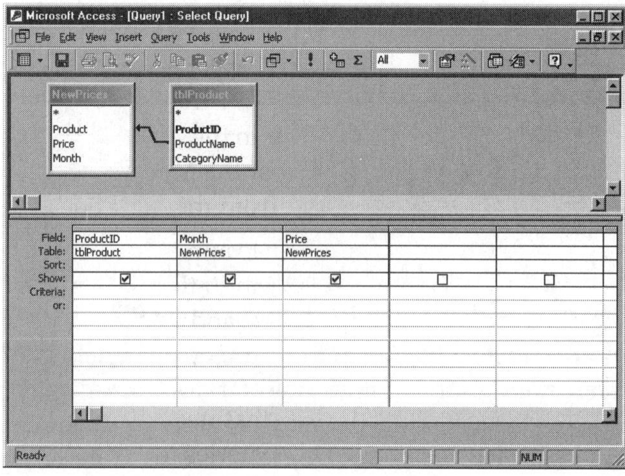

Figure 18-25
An outer join displays an arrowhead.

When you display the output for an outer join, you will see empty cells where the joined table lacked a corresponding record, as shown in Figure 18-26.

Note If you want to add criteria to search for records that don't have a match, enter *Is Null* in the criteria row for a field from the second table.

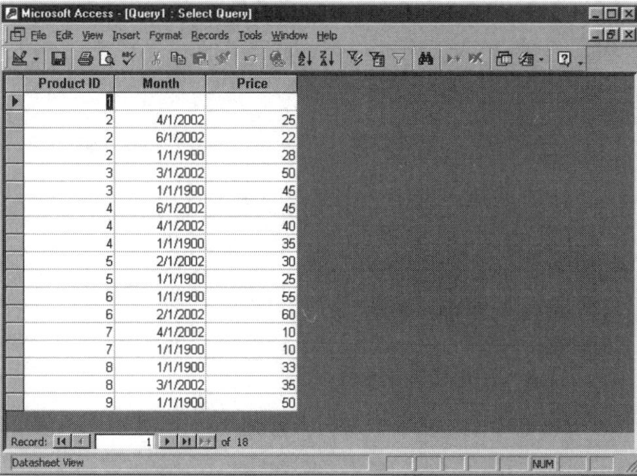

Product ID	Month	Price
1		
2	4/1/2002	25
2	6/1/2002	22
2	1/1/1900	28
3	3/1/2002	50
3	1/1/1900	45
4	6/1/2002	45
4	4/1/2002	40
4	1/1/1900	35
5	2/1/2002	30
5	1/1/1900	25
6	1/1/1900	55
6	2/1/2002	60
7	4/1/2002	10
7	1/1/1900	10
8	1/1/1900	33
8	3/1/2002	35
9	1/1/1900	50

Figure 18-26
An outer join leaves holes.

(If you deleted a row from the NewPrices table, run the *PricesToList* macro to repopulate the table.) You can now convert the prices query into an Append Query to add the records to the tlkPrice table.

In the Query Type list, select Append Query, and select tlkPrice as the target. The target field names should automatically appear in the Append To list for the ProductID and the Price. A field name will appear in the Append To row only if the spelling does not match that of the source field. For the Month, the name of the target field is AsOfDate, so you need to select that from the list, as in Figure 18-27.

Save the query as qapPrice and click the Run button to append the prices. Now all you have to do to replace the prices—if you change them in the Excel worksheet—is delete the prices from tlkPrice, run the *PriceToList* macro, and execute the qapPrice query.

Creating a Query that Joins Multiple Tables

The NewForecast list has three dimension fields that need to be converted to integer keys. In the Database window, switch to the Queries object group and click the New button. In the Show Table dialog box, double-click the NewForecast, tblProduct, tblScenario, and tblCustomer tables, and close the dialog box. Access should not create any links between the tables.

Drag the Product field in the NewForecast table to the ProductName field in the Products table. Drag the Customer field to the CustomerName field in the Customer table. Finally, drag the Scenario field to the ScenarioName field in the Scenario table. Inner joins are all right for the Product and Customer tables, since you used the NewForecast table to fill them. Convert the join for the Scenario table to an outer join that displays all records for the NewForecast table. Figure 18-28 shows the query

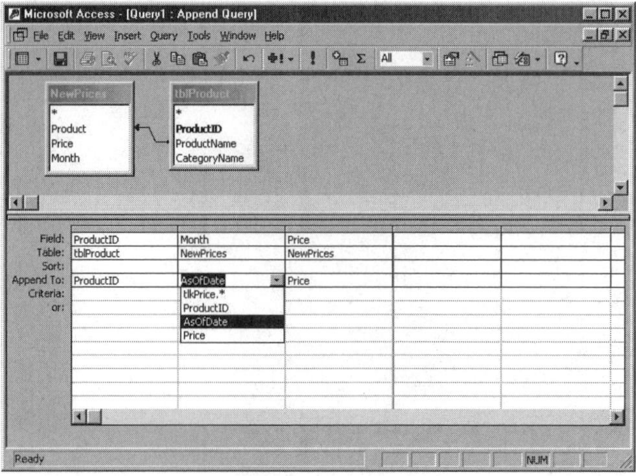

Figure 18-27
You must select an Append To field if the field names don't match.

grid, complete with the joins. (You can drag the tables around to make the join lines easier to see.)

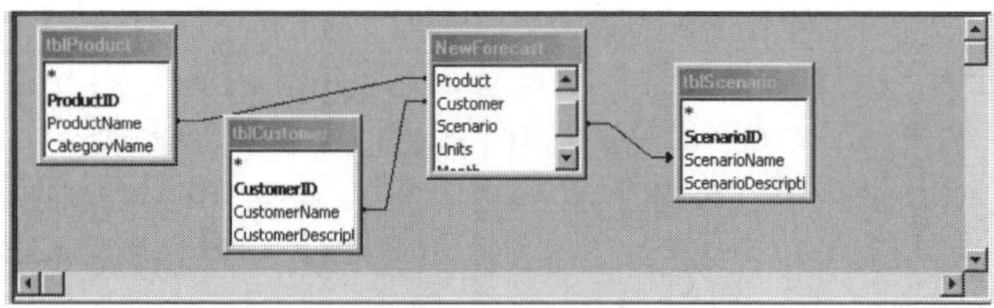

Figure 18-28
Rearrange tables to make joins easy to see.

You can now move the key numbers to the field grid. Double-click ProductID in the Product table, CustomerID in the Customer table, and ScenarioID in the Scenario table. In addition, double-click Month and Units in the NewForecast table. Click the View button to see the values, which should appear similar to Figure 18-29, with ID numbers in place of the key names.

Watch for missing Scenario keys. Click the View button to return to Design mode so you can append the records to the data table. In the Query Type list, select Append Query, and select tblData as the target. The target field names should automatically appear in the Append To list.

Save the query as qapData and run it to append the records. After appending the records, look at the data table to make sure that the values were properly added.

	Product ID	Customer ID	ScenarioID	Month	Units
▶	4	10	1	5/1/2002	22
	9	10	1	1/1/2002	17
	6	10	2	2/1/2002	11
	2	10	2	2/1/2002	15
	1	10	2	2/1/2002	4
	1	10	1	2/1/2002	5
	3	10	1	5/1/2002	28
	9	10	1	5/1/2002	10
	4	10	2	2/1/2002	30
	5	10	1	5/1/2002	28
	3	10	2	1/1/2002	35
	1	10	1	5/1/2002	3
	2	10	1	5/1/2002	15
	7	10	1	5/1/2002	23
	5	10	1	6/1/2002	27
	8	10	1	5/1/2002	17
	1	10	1	1/1/2002	6
	4	10	1	1/1/2002	25
	6	10	2	3/1/2002	14

Figure 18-29
The query converts names to numbers.

Creating Queries To Extract Data

Once the data tables are populated, you can create queries to extract data from the tables—either to analyze the information directly, or as a vehicle for transferring the data in a report into a PivotTable. The data table is the primary fact table of the database. It contains one record for each key combination that has a forecast. The primary fact table, however, does not contain attribute information from the dimension tables. A good initial query for an analytical database such as the Forecasting database is one that combines the primary fact table with the attributes from the dimension tables.

Creating a Combination Query

On the Queries page of the Database window, click the New button and select Design View. In the Show Table dialog box, double-click the data table, and then add each dimension table in the order in which the key appears in the data table. After adding all five tables, close the Show Table dialog box. The upper half of the Design window should appear similar to Figure 18-30.

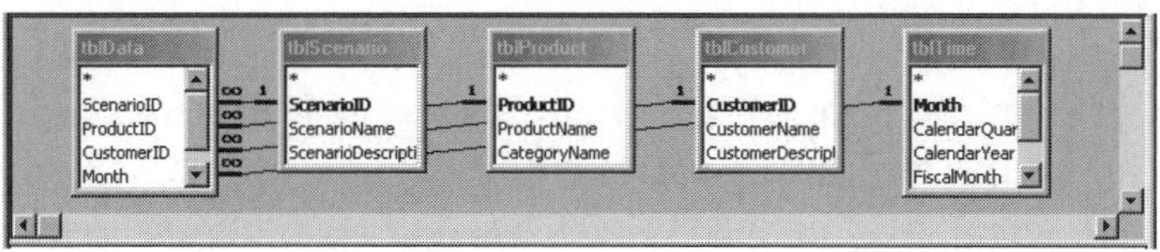

Figure 18-30
Access automatically creates joins when field names match.

The lines that connect the tables indicate how Access will join the tables. Access was able to automatically link the tables because you defined Relationships, and also because the names of the key fields match.

Adding All Fields from a Table

You want to include all the attributes from each dimension table. One way to select all the fields of a table is to double-click the caption bar of the table. After selecting all the field names, you could drag the names to the field grid. However, this is not the best way to add field names from the attribute tables, because if you add a new attribute to one of the dimension tables, you would have to modify the query.

An asterisk (*) appears above the top field of each table. The asterisk means all the fields of this table. You can add the asterisk directly to the field grid. Double-click the asterisk from each of the dimension tables.

Do not double-click the asterisk for the data table. If you add all the fields from the data table, each key field will appear twice in the query result, which you do not need. The only field from the data table that is not represented in the grid is the Units field. Double-click the Units field to add it to the field grid. When you have finished, the field grid should look like the one shown in Figure 18-31.

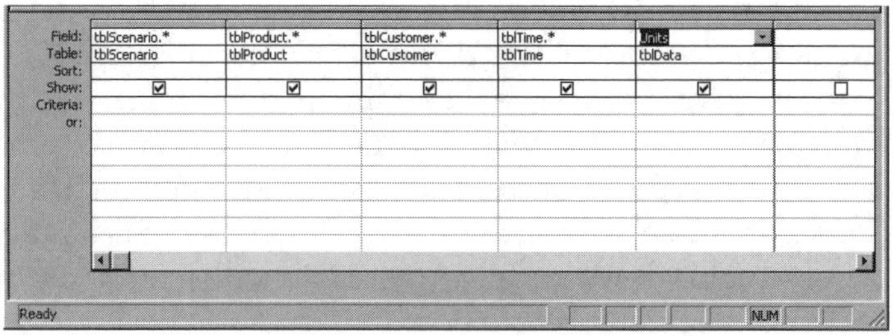

Figure 18-31
Use an asterisk to include all fields.

Save the query with the name qryData, and switch to Datasheet view to look at the results of the query. The query displays all the fields in each dimension, along with the Units from the data table. You can now use this query as the basis for other queries or reports.

Creating a Summary Query

Once you have created the data query, you can base any number of analytical queries on that query. For example, suppose you want to create a query that summarizes the Corporate version of the forecast by Product Category. On the Queries page of the Database window, select the data query, click the New Object: Query button and select Design View. Double-click the ScenarioName, CategoryName, and Units fields.

In every summary query, you must remember to include a Scenario field—that is, you must either display both scenarios or select only one. Otherwise, you will get the total of the two scenarios, which is not meaningful. To include only the Corporate forecasts in the query, type *Corporate* in the Criteria row of the ScenarioName field. If you don't want the ScenarioName field to appear in the report, clear the Show check box for the field.

To create a summary query, click the Totals toolbar button. This adds a new Total row to the field grid. The default value in the total row is Group By, which means that the field appears as a row heading. For the Units field, change the Total property to Sum. For the ScenarioName field, change the Total property to Where, which means that the value is used only in the criteria row and that the show check box is cleared. (Leaving the total as Group By will not hurt the report, but Access can create a more efficient SQL statement for the query if you choose Where for fields that will not be displayed.) The field grid should look like Figure 18-32.

Field:	ScenarioName	CategoryName	Units
Table:	qryData	qryData	qryData
Total:	Where	Group By	Sum
Sort:			
Show:	☐	☑	☑
Criteria:	"Corporate"		
or:			

Ready NUM

Figure 18-32
A Summary query includes Total options.

Click the View button to see the summarized values.

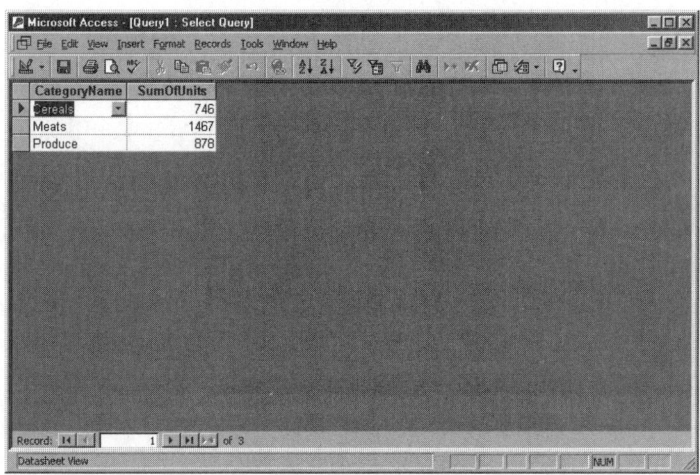

Figure 18-33
The summary report shows totals.

Although the query has a drop-down arrow on the Category button, you can't change the value because it is the composite of multiple rows. The caption for the Units column is SumOfUnits. This caption does reflect the nature of the values, but it would not look good on a printed report. Whenever there is a function in the Total row, Access creates a caption by combining the function name with the field name. One way to override that default caption is to prefix the field name with the new caption (Units: Units). Another way is to change the field property. Select the Units field and click the Properties toolbar button. In the Field Properties window, change the Caption to Units. While you're at it, you can add a comma to the units by selecting Standard as the Format property, and 0 as the Decimal Places property, as shown in Figure 18-34.

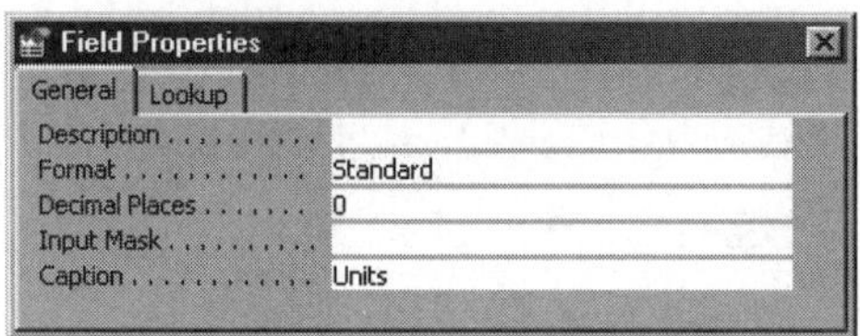

Figure 18-34
Each field in a query has its own properties.

Save the query using the name By Category. For analytical queries that you can print, you might want to include spaces and omit a prefix. If you print the query, the name will appear as a title. In addition, the lack of a prefix will keep this query distinct from utility queries that you use to build the database.

Creating a Crosstab Query

Suppose you want to compare the Corporate and Customer forecasts for each product in the database. It will be easiest to compare the two forecasts if they are side by side on a row. This requires a Crosstab query.

Create a new query based on the data query. Double-click the ScenarioName, ProductName, and Units fields. Select Crosstab Query from the Query Type list. This adds a Total row, the same as if you were creating a simple summary report. Change the Total property of the Units field to Sum. A Crosstab query also adds a new Crosstab row to the field grid. The Crosstab row indicates where to place the field. In the Crosstab row for the ScenarioName field, select Column Heading. For the ProductName field, select Row Heading. For the Units field, select Value. The field grid should look like the one shown in Figure 18-35.

Save the report as By Scenario And Product, and view the result of the query. It should look like Figure 18-36.

Field:	ScenarioName	ProductName	Units
Table:	qryData	qryData	qryData
Total:	Group By	Group By	Sum
Crosstab:	Column Heading	Row Heading	Value
Sort:			
Criteria:			
or:			

Figure 18-35
For a Crosstab query, specify the location of the fields.

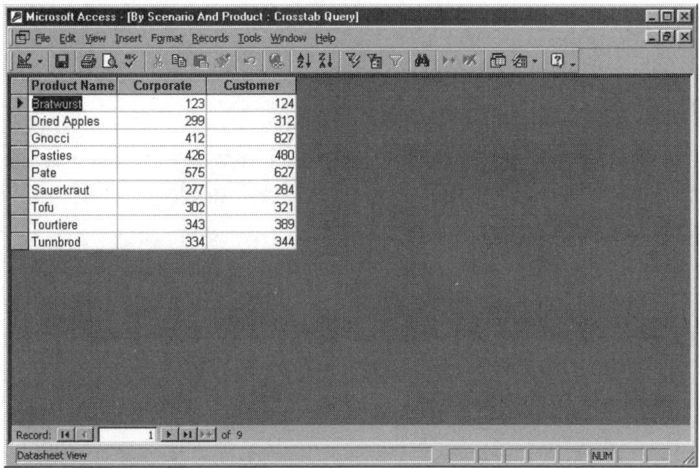

Product Name	Corporate	Customer
Bratwurst	123	124
Dried Apples	299	312
Gnocci	412	827
Pasties	426	480
Pate	575	627
Sauerkraut	277	284
Tofu	302	321
Tourtiere	343	389
Tunnbrod	334	344

Figure 18-36
A Crosstab query converts a list to a grid.

Calculating Prices

What if you want to calculate dollars for the forecasted units in the database? The Price table includes all the price changes, but it is not in a form suitable for joining to the data table. Before you can join the prices to the data table, you must have a price for each Month. In other words, you must fill in the gaps between the price changes.

Creating a Cartesian Product Query

The first part of the process consists of creating a query that has one record for each product for each month. To do this, you create what is called a *Cartesian product* of the Product and the Time tables. The Cartesian product of two tables creates a copy of all the records in one table for each record in the other table. As you can imagine, a Cartesian product can quickly become very large, and you should be very careful not to create one accidentally. In this case, there are very few records in the Time table, and a Cartesian product is precisely what you need.

Create a new query, and include the tables tblTime and tblProduct. After adding the two tables, the upper part of the Design window will look like Figure 18-37.

Figure 18-37
Two tables with no join lines form a Cartesian product.

Access did not draw a join line between the two tables, because the Time table and the Product table do not share a common key. Whenever you have two tables in a query with no joins between them, you will get the Cartesian product of the two tables.

Add the Month field from the Time table, and the ProductID and ProductName fields from the Product table to the field grid. (Include the ProductName field so that you can identify the products.) Click the View button to see the Cartesian product of the Months and Products, as shown in Figure 18-38.

Month	Product ID	Product Name
1/1/2002	1	Bratwurst
2/1/2002	1	Bratwurst
3/1/2002	1	Bratwurst
4/1/2002	1	Bratwurst
5/1/2002	1	Bratwurst
6/1/2002	1	Bratwurst
1/1/2002	2	Dried Apples
2/1/2002	2	Dried Apples
3/1/2002	2	Dried Apples
4/1/2002	2	Dried Apples
5/1/2002	2	Dried Apples
6/1/2002	2	Dried Apples

Figure 18-38
A Cartesian product includes all Months for each Product.

Now that you have the Cartesian product, you need to calculate the price for each product and month combination. Conceptually, the appropriate price for any month is the last price change before the current month. There are two different ways to calculate the most recent price for a given month. One approach uses a Domain Aggregate function, and the other approach uses a Subquery. The subquery is a more efficient way to calculate the prices, but you should also understand how a Domain Aggregate function works.

Using a Domain Aggregate Function to Calculate a Field

Access has several functions that select or aggregate values from a set of records. In database terminology, a set of records is called a Domain. The functions that operate on a set of records are called *Domain Aggregate* functions. Each Domain Aggregate function begins with the letter D. The DLast function retrieves the last value from a set of records. (For information about other Domain Aggregate functions, search Help using the search words *domain aggregate function*.)

The DLast function takes three arguments. As the first argument, you supply the name in quotes of the field that you want to retrieve values from. In this case, you want to retrieve the value of the Price field. As the second argument, you supply the name of the table or query that contains the field, again in quotes. In this case, the table is the tlkPrice table. As the final argument, you supply criteria for selecting the records, again as a quoted string. This corresponds to the WHERE clause of an SQL statement.

First create the string using sample constant values for the Month and Product. Type *#6/1/2002#* as the sample Month, and type *2* as the sample ProductID. The criteria string for these examples would be *"ProductID = 2 And AsOfDate <= #6/1/2002 #"*. In the Field row of the fourth column of the field grid, type *Price: DLast ("Price", "tlkPrice", "ProductID = 2 And AsOfDate <= #6/1/2002 #")*. After entering the formula, click the View button. You should see the result records with the same price in each row.

To get different prices for each product and month, you must insert the ProductID and Month from the current record. To do that, remove the constants from the criteria string and replace them with field name in brackets, joined to the remainder of the string using ampersands. The final condition string, with field names properly embedded, is shown in Figure 18-39.

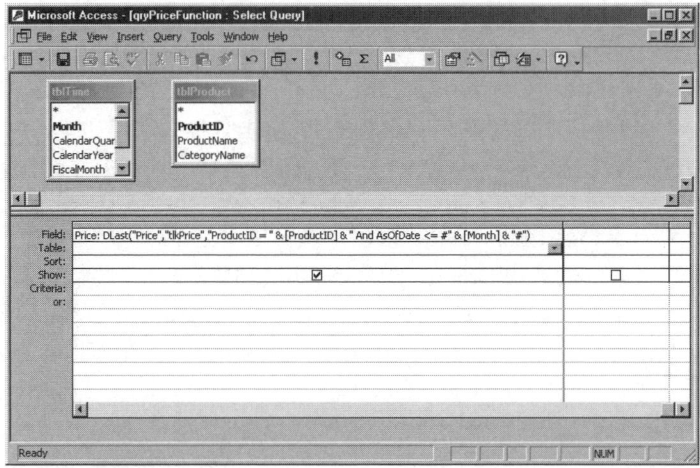

Figure 18-39
For an aggregate function, you must construct a text string.

Click the View button to check the result. You should see changing prices as shown in Figure 18-40. Save the query with the name qryPriceFunction.

Month	Product ID	Product Name	Price
6/1/2002	3	Gnocci	50
1/1/2002	4	Pasties	35
2/1/2002	4	Pasties	35
3/1/2002	4	Pasties	35
4/1/2002	4	Pasties	40
5/1/2002	4	Pasties	40
6/1/2002	4	Pasties	45
1/1/2002	5	Pate	25

Figure 18-40
The function returns a different value for each row.

Using a Subquery to Calculate a Field

The Domain Aggregate function calculates the price properly, but it does not calculate as quickly as an embedded query. Before changing the query, save a copy using the name qryPriceSubquery. By creating two separate queries, you can compare them when you're finished.

A *subquery* uses a complete SQL statement to calculate the value of the field. The only requirement for a subquery is that it results in a single value for each record of the table. The easiest way to create the appropriate SQL statement is to create a query that retrieves the price sample for a single product and a single month.

Create a new query with the Price table as the only source. Save it with the name qryOnePrice. Add the Price field, the AsOfDate field, and the ProductID field. In the criteria row for the AsOfDate, type <= *#6/1/02#*. As the criteria for the ProductID field, type 2. Click the View button to see the result of the query. Depending on the specific price changes for the product, you'll probably see more than one record, as shown in Figure 18-41.

You need to determine a way to select only the one correct price from this list. If you sort the list in descending order by date, the correct price will be in the first record. Return to Design View and in the Sort row of the AsOfDate field, select Descending.

To select the top one record in a query, set a Query Property. Click the background of the query (to deselect any field), and then click the Properties button to display the Query Properties window. Change the Top Values property to 1, as shown in Figure 18-42. (The number 1 does not appear in the list of choices, but you can type it anyway.)

Click the View button to see the result of the query. You should see one record with the most recent price (as of 6/1/2002). Switch back to Design View and clear the Show check box for the AsOfDate and ProductID columns. This is the correct query for the sample product and month. Save the query.

To see the SQL statement, click the drop-down button next to the View button and select SQL View. Simplify the query by removing the table name prefixed to the field and remove the parentheses in the WHERE clause. Add a space at the end of each

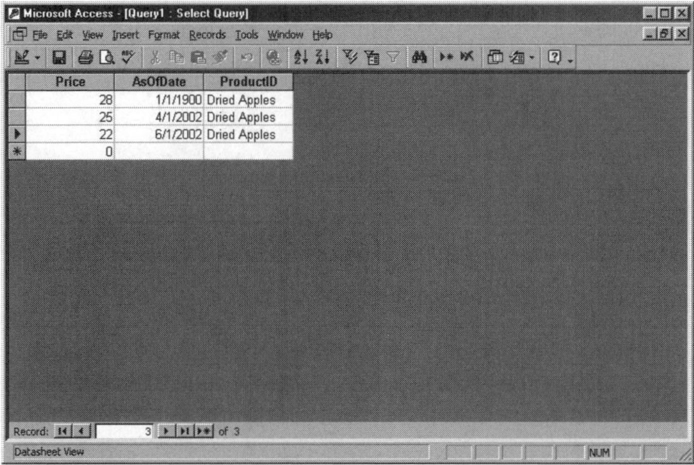

Figure 18-41
You need only the last price.

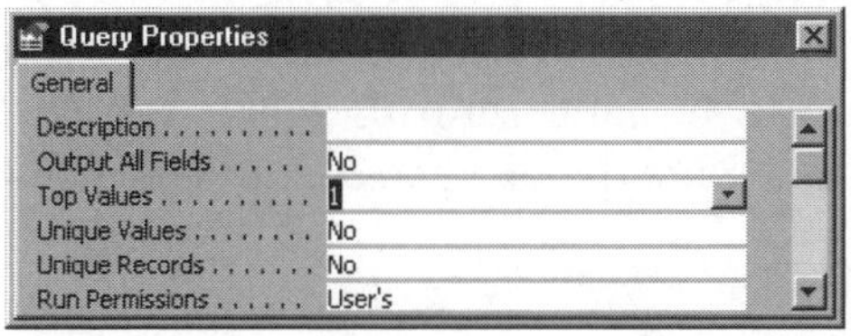

Query Properties
General
Description . . . .
Output All Fields . . . . . . No
Top Values 1
Unique Values . . . . No
Unique Records . . . . No
Run Permissions . . . . . . User's

Figure 18-42
The Top Values property lets you select only the first record.

line, remove the line break between the lines, and remove the semicolon from the end. The resulting SQL statement should look like this:

```
SELECT TOP 1 Price FROM tlkPrice WHERE AsOfDate<=#6/1/2002#
AND ProductID=2 Order by AsOfDate DESC
```

Enclose the statement in parentheses and copy it. Switch to the qryPriceSubquery window. Because the SQL statement is long, you can display it in a Zoom window. Click in the Price field definition cell and press Shift+F2. Delete everything after the colon in the Price field, and paste the SQL subquery. It should look like Figure 18-43.

Click OK, and then click the View button to make sure the query works with the constant date and product.

You now need to extend the query to refer to the ProductID and Month fields of the current record. A subquery is not a text string. It is a complete SQL statement enclosed in parentheses, which is then included within another SQL statement. (Remember that the whole purpose of the field grid is to create an SQL statement.) To substitute the month and product from the current record for the sample constants,

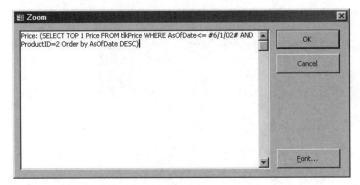

Figure 18-43
Press Shift+F2 to Zoom a field definition.

simply replace the constants with the field names. Press Shift+F2 to see the field definition in the Zoom window. Replace the date #6/1/02# with the word *Month*. Replace the ProductID 2 with *tblProduct.ProductID*. (You must specify the table name along with the ProductID field name, because the ProductID field exists in both the Product table and in the Price table. You don't need to include the table names in front of AsOfDate and Month, because the names are different in the two tables.) The enhanced field definition should look like the one shown in Figure 18-44.

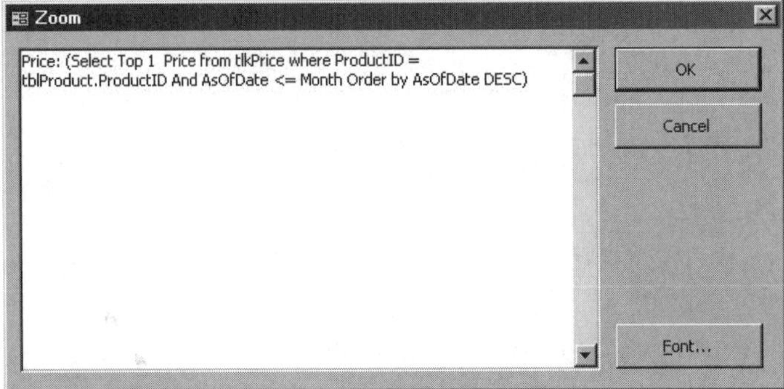

Figure 18-44
In a subquery, you do not use quotation marks and ampersands.

Save the query and click View to see the prices changing according to the price changes in the Prices table.

The subquery version of the query generates the same results as did the function version. Even for a small database such as this one, the subquery version calculates the prices substantially faster. You will have to decide for yourself which version you think is easier to understand. In many situations, either a Domain Aggregate function or a subquery can be used. Access is much more efficient using a subquery. (For more information about creating a subquery, search Help using the search word *subquery*.)

Using a Double Join to Link Two Tables

Once you have created a query that calculates the price for each product and month combination, you can join that query with the data table. This allows you to calculate Dollars for the forecasted Units. A good place to add Dollars is in the data query. The data query combines Units from the central fact table with the attributes from all the dimension tables. Once you add Dollars to that query, you'll be able to create summary queries of Units and Dollars, representing a complete picture of the forecast.

Open qryData in Design View and save a copy as qryDataX (for extended). Click the Show Table toolbar button, select the Queries tab, double-click qryPriceSubquery, and click Close. Access creates a join line between the ProductID of the Prices query and the ProductID of the Product table, as shown in Figure 18-45.

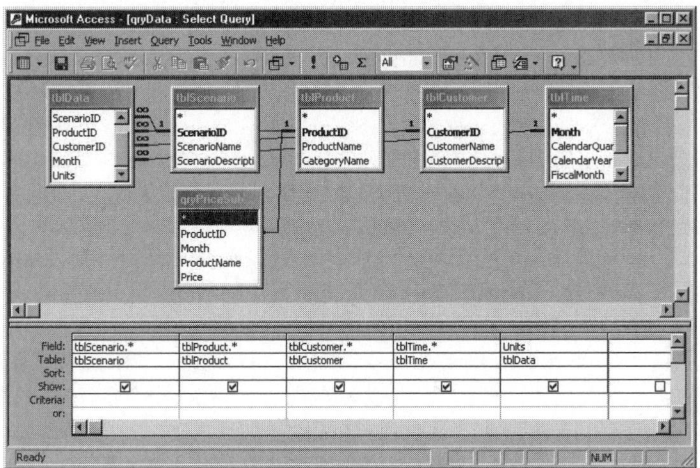

Figure 18-45
Access automatically joins the ProductID, but not the Month.

Although both the data table and the Product table have a ProductID field, the ProductID field is the primary key of the Product table, so that it is the table Access joins. You can either leave the join between the Price query and the Product table, or remove that join and join the ProductID fields of the Price query and the data table.

The ProductID is not sufficient to fully determine which record of the Prices query to use. You must also designate the Month. Drag the Month field of the data table to the Month field of the Prices query to create a join.

Double-click the Price field to add it to the field grid. To add a Dollars field, you simply multiply Units times Price. As a new field, type *Dollars* followed by colon as the caption, and then type the formula *Units * Price*. Figure 18-46 shows the resulting query.

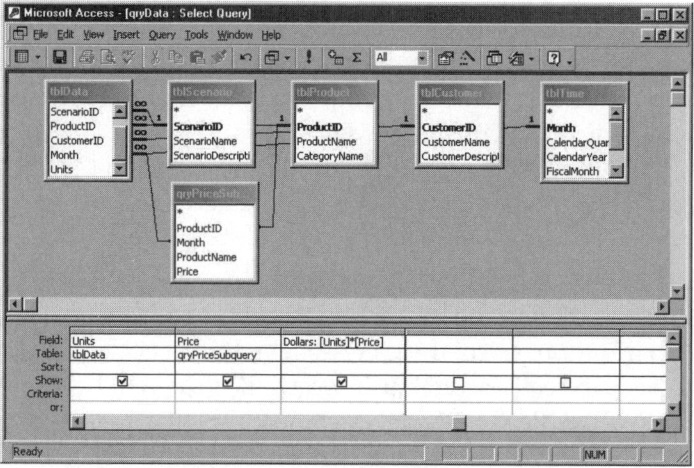

Figure 18-46
A new field can be the arithmetic result of other fields.

Save the query, click the View button, and scroll to the right to see the Price and Dollar fields. Save the data query.

You can now use the data query to summarize Dollars as well as Units. You also can use this query as the source for a PivotTable in Excel, completing the round-trip from Excel to Access and back to Excel.

Chapter 19

Present Data Using Forms and Reports

In This Chapter

A Microsoft Access database can serve both as a tool for updating information and as a mechanism for reporting the results of analysis. In many cases, you can adequately update and review information using nothing more than tables and queries. But tables and queries limit you to a datasheet grid structure. Forms and reports enhance both the updating and reviewing of tasks by opening doors of flexibility. In a form or report, you can position fields in any location. You can group related items, show summary totals, add headings, and add charts to display information graphically.

Note The Forecast database in the CH19 folder contains the completed samples from this chapter. If you want to replicate the exercises as they're described in this chapter, create a copy of the database, and then delete all the forms and reports.

Creating Dynamic Forms

A simple form displays the values for a single record. Single-record forms are easy to create, but they can be frustrating to use. Most people think more clearly when they group related items together. You can create dynamic forms that group related records into a cohesive whole.

Creating a Form You can Filter

You might want to use a form to facilitate the updating of product prices. Let's assume that you have a product table similar to the table shown in Figure 19-1.

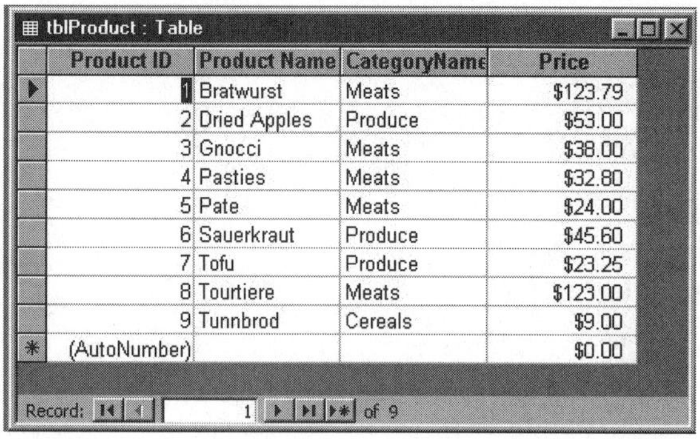

tblProduct : Table

Product ID	Product Name	CategoryName	Price
1	Bratwurst	Meats	$123.79
2	Dried Apples	Produce	$53.00
3	Gnocci	Meats	$38.00
4	Pasties	Meats	$32.80
5	Pate	Meats	$24.00
6	Sauerkraut	Produce	$45.60
7	Tofu	Produce	$23.25
8	Tourtiere	Meats	$123.00
9	Tunnbrod	Cereals	$9.00
(AutoNumber)			$0.00

Record: 1 of 9

Figure 19-1
You can create a form to update product prices.

You would like to be able to update the prices for all the products in a given category. Begin the design process for the form using the New Form Wizard.

Creating and Modifying a Simple Datasheet Form

In the Database window, activate the Forms object group and click New. Select AutoForm: Datasheet as the form type, select the Product table name (tblProduct) in the drop-down list, and click OK. The Form Wizard will create a form similar to the one shown in Figure 19-2.

A datasheet form looks very much like a simple table. In Datasheet view, you can adjust the column widths while displaying the datasheet, but to change the caption of the form, or to delete or rename columns, you first must switch to Design view.

To change the form's caption, switch to Design view and double-click the Form Selector box (the small box in the upper left corner of the form, at the intersection point of the horizontal and vertical rulers). In the Form Properties window, select the Format tab and change the Caption property to Update Prices. Save the form with the name frmPrices, and then close the Properties window.

Next, delete the ProductID column by selecting the ProductID text box in the Detail section and pressing Delete (or clicking the Cut button on the toolbar). You don't

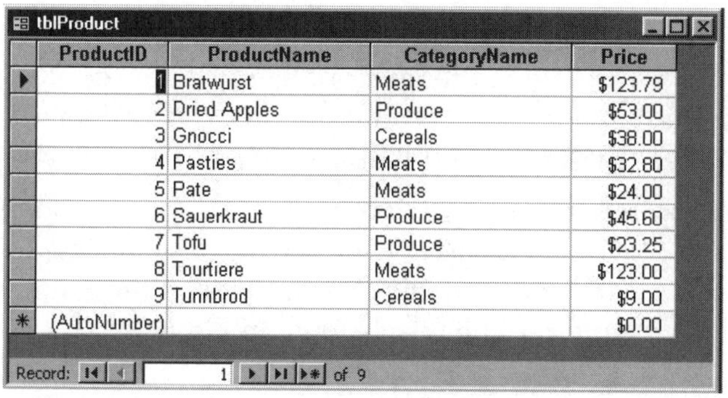

tblProduct

ProductID	ProductName	CategoryName	Price
1	Bratwurst	Meats	$123.79
2	Dried Apples	Produce	$53.00
3	Gnocci	Cereals	$38.00
4	Pasties	Meats	$32.80
5	Pate	Meats	$24.00
6	Sauerkraut	Produce	$45.60
7	Tofu	Produce	$23.25
8	Tourtiere	Meats	$123.00
9	Tunnbrod	Cereals	$9.00
(AutoNumber)			$0.00

Record: 1 of 9

Figure 19-2
A datasheet form looks just like a table.

need to rearrange the remaining controls yet; the Datasheet view will ignore the position of the controls on the form.

The form created by the Form Wizard provides a Form Header section containing a text label for each column. The header will be ignored when you display the form in Datasheet view, so it doesn't matter if you delete a form header label. The header label does not affect the Datasheet view in any way; specifically, the spelling of the header label does not determine the column header content in Datasheet view.

To change the column header in Datasheet view, you need to change the field control's name. For example, to change the datasheet column header of the ProductName field, double-click the field's text box control in the Detail section. In the Form Properties window, select the Other tab and change the Name property to the caption you want to use. Changing the Name property of the control does not affect the column that the control is linked to; that is determined by the Control Source property on the Data tab. After you delete the ProductID field and rename the ProductName field, save the form. Then click the View button to switch back to Datasheet view.

When you click in the CategoryName field, a combo box control appears. You can select Cereals from the drop-down list control, but that selection action does not restrict the grid to displaying only those products from the Cereals category; it simply changes the category for that one product. You can choose to display only the Cereal products by right-clicking any field in the datasheet containing the word Cereal and then selecting the Filter By Selection option from the shortcut menu. To remove the filter, click the Remove Filter button in the toolbar, or right-click the field and choose Remove Filter/Sort option. Even after you click the Remove Filter button, the filter still exists; it has only been temporarily disabled. To reapply the previous filter, click the Apply Filter button.

Converting a Datasheet Form to a Tabular Form

You might want a more intuitive way of filtering by category. You would like to add a drop-down list at the top of the form from which you can select a category. In fact, you might want to remove the category field from the grid altogether to prevent anyone from inadvertently changing the category name for a product. A datasheet form does not provide any space at the top of the form to add a combo box control, but you don't need to leave the form as a datasheet form.

A tabular form displays a separate box for each field, and it has a header section. To view a tabular version of the form, click the Down arrow connected to the View toolbar button and select Form view (or click Form View on the standard toolbar). The Form view will look similar to the form shown in Figure 19-3.

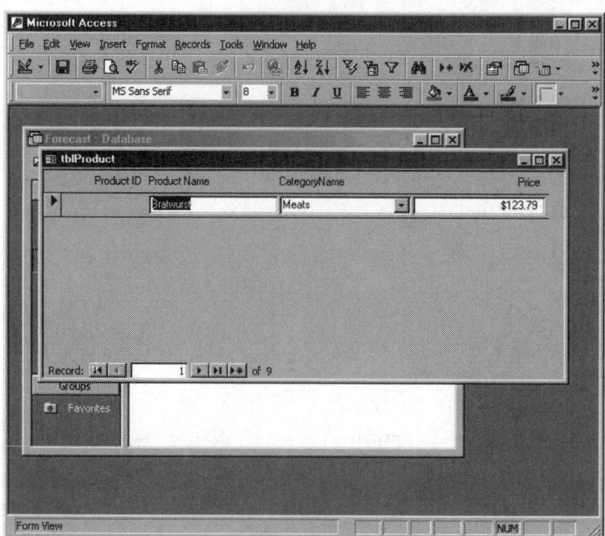

Figure 19-3
Form view has a separate control for each field.

In Form view, the column headings from the table are shown as individual label controls, and the layout and field sizes correspond to the controls in Design view. Form view is, essentially, what the wizard creates if you select a Tabular form design. The only difference is that the Tabular form created by the wizard displays multiple records. When a form displays multiple records, it simply repeats the Detail section of the form.

To convert the form so it will repeat the Detail section of the form, switch to Design view and double-click the Form Selector box. In the Form Properties window, select the Format tab and change the Default View property from Datasheet to Continuous Forms. Then close the Properties window.

Before switching back to Form view, delete the ProductID label from the form header and slide the rest of the controls over to the left side of the form. (To select the labels and text box controls together, click and drag in the ruler at the top of the form.) Click the View button to switch to Form view, which should look similar to the form shown in Figure 19-4.

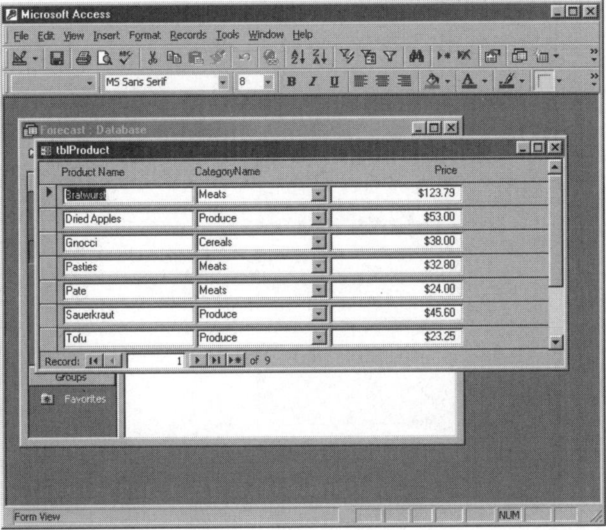

Figure 19-4
Continuous Form view displays multiple rows.

Adding a Combo Box to the Header of a Form

Unlike Datasheet view, the labels in Continuous Form view are located in a form header at the top of the form. You can increase the size of the header to provide a place to add a Category combo box control.

Switch to Design view and drag the top edge of the Detail separator down about one-half inch. Select all the column heading labels (click in the ruler area on the left side of the form and then drag to select the header controls), and then click and drag the controls down to just above the Detail separator. If the Toolbox window is not open, click the Toolbox button in the toolbar. In the Toolbox window, click the Combo Box control, and then click above the labels in the form's header to launch the Combo Box Wizard shown in Figure 19-5.

The Combo Box Wizard offers helpful options for filtering the list. The third option, Find A Record On My Form Based On The Value I Selected In My Combo Box, will help you create the combo box you want, but you will need to do a lot of customizing. Select the third option and click the Next button twice. (You will define the record source later in this section.)

In the third step of the Combo Box Wizard, double-click the CategoryName field in the Available Fields list box to add the field to the Selected Fields list. None of the remaining steps offers helpful options for this example, so click the Next button until the Finish button becomes enabled, and then click the Finish button to complete the initial combo box control design.

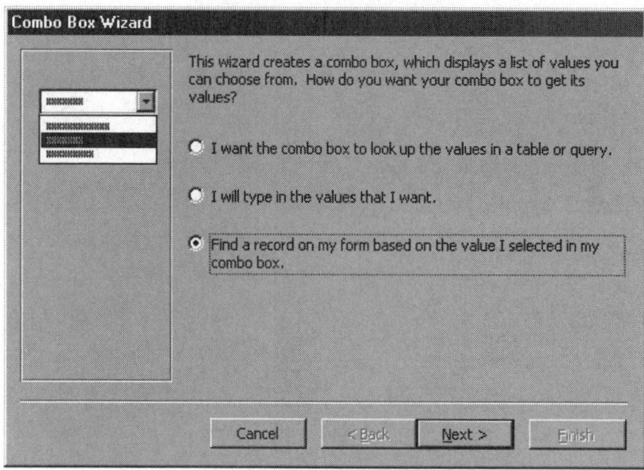

Figure 19-5
The Combo Box Wizard offers to find a matching record.

Double-click the new combo box control in the header to view the Combo Box Properties window. The wizard assigned a default name to the control—probably something like Combo3. Don't change the name yet; it is linked to an event handler.

The Combo Box Wizard created the combo box to locate a single record, but you want to be able to locate a group of records, so you will need to make some modifications to the combo box's properties. On the Data tab of the Combo Box Properties window, the Control Source property is blank. This combo box control is not linked to a field, and that prevents the combo box from changing the value of an existing record. The Row Source property contains an SQL statement generated by the wizard. This SQL statement determines the rows that will fill the box. Click in the Row Source property box, and then click the ellipsis button on the right side of the text box to display the Query Builder window shown in Figure 19-6. The Query Builder is a miniature Query Design view window; it edits SQL statements that are not actual Query objects.

This query retrieves the ProductID and CategoryName for each product in the table. You want only a unique list of Category names. Click the ProductID column header above the field list box in the query grid and press Delete to remove it. Double-click the query background on the top of the grid to display the Query Properties window, change the Unique Values property to Yes, and then close the Query Properties window. Change the Sort property of the CategoryName field to Ascending by clicking in the Sort property drop-down list in the design grid and choosing Ascending from the list.

To save your changes, do not click the Save button. Doing so will only save the SQL statement as a stand-alone Query object. Instead, close the Query Builder window, and click Yes when the Query Builder asks if you want to save the changes back to the control's Row Source property.

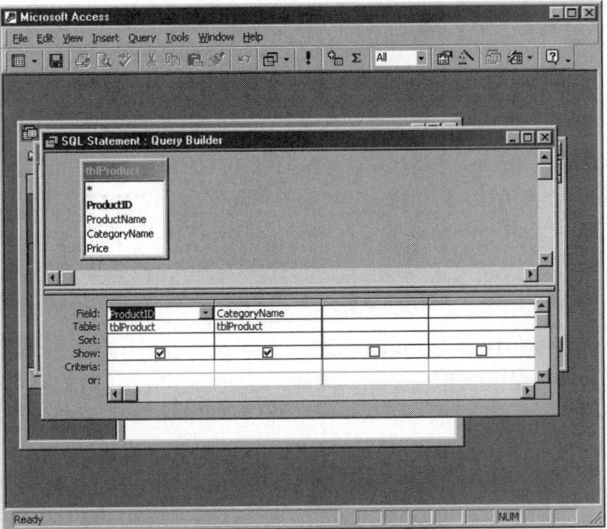

Figure 19-6
The Query Builder edits an SQL statement.

The combo box is still prepared to handle two columns. Switch to the Format tab of the Combo Box Properties window, change the Column Count property to *1* and clear the contents of the Column Widths property box. Then close the Properties window. Save the form and display it in Form view.

Making a Combo Box Filter Records on a Form

Your form now contains a new combo box. The combo box is empty, but if you click the arrow on the right side of the control, the three category names will appear in the drop-down list. Selecting one of the category names will result in a Type Mismatch error. The Combo Box Wizard added an event handler to select a single product from the drop-down list. For some reason, the event handler can't find the ProductID field. Click Debug in the error message box to switch to the Visual Basic Editor and see the event handler displayed in Figure 19-7.

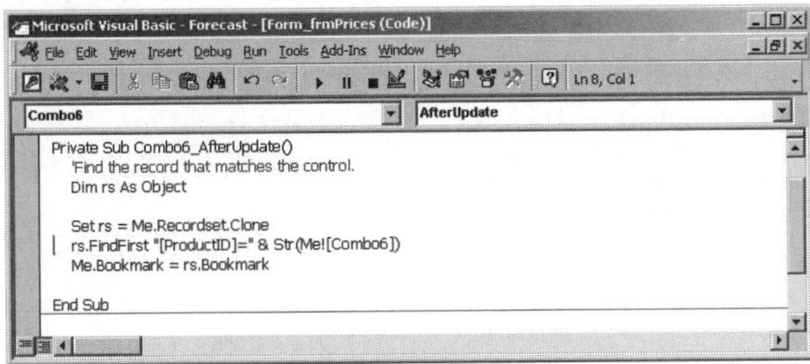

Figure 19-7
The Combo Box Wizard created an event handler.

The event handler created by the Combo Box Wizard is completely inappropriate for filtering records based on a category, but at least it shows which event to use—the AfterUpdate event of the combo box. Click the Reset toolbar button in the Visual Basic Editor to stop the procedure. The event handler created by the wizard uses a Recordset object and is a little complicated. ("Extracting Values From a Form's Recordset," later in this chapter, shows how to use a Recordset object when populating a chart.)

As with all event handlers, the name of the control with which the event is associated is the name of the event handler. This would be a good time to rename the combo box. Delete the procedure generated by the wizard, switch to Access, and change to Design view. On the Other tab of the Combo Box Properties window, change the name of the control to *lstCategory*. Click the Events tab. The After Update text box includes an entry labeled [Event Procedure], reflecting the fact that the Combo Box Wizard created an event handler for this event. Click the ellipses button next to that entry to create a new event procedure.

Assuming that you would only select an existing category name from the combo box drop-down list, the following *lstCategory* event handler will be sufficient to filter the list:

```
Private Sub lstCategory_AfterUpdate()
    Filter = "CategoryName = '" & lstCategory.Value & "'"
    FilterOn = True
End Sub
```

Assuming that you select Meats from the list, the procedure creates the string *CategoryName = 'Meats'* and assigns it to the form's Filter property. The single apostrophes around the name of the filter item are essential; the filter is equivalent to a WHERE clause of an SQL statement (omitting the WHERE keyword). Assigning a value to the Filter property is equivalent to using the context menu to set a filter and then clicking the Remove Filter button: the filter is there, but it is inactive. Assigning *True* to the FilterOn property is equivalent to clicking the Apply Filter toolbar button.

A combo box allows you to type a new value into the field (unless you specifically tell it not to by setting its Limit To List property to Yes). You can take advantage of that ability: set the event handler to turn off the filter if you type anything other than an existing category name. Here is the expanded event handler:

```
Private Sub lstCategory_AfterUpdate()
    If lstCategory.ListIndex = -1 Then
        lstCategory.Value = ""
        FilterOn = False
    Else
        Filter = "CategoryName = '" & lstCategory.Value & "'"
        FilterOn = True
    End If
End Sub
```

The ListIndex property of a list or combo box gives the sequential number (counting from zero) of the selected item. The value *–1* indicates that no item from the list is selected. Switch back to Access, save the form, display it in Form view, and then test the Category combo box.

Note If you do create a combo box that is limited to the values in a list, you might want to initialize the combo box to the first item in the list when the form opens. To do that, create a *Form_Load* event handler that includes the following statement:

```
lstCategory.ListIndex = 0.
```

Chapter 19

Preventing Changes to a Field

You are creating a form specifically to change the prices of existing products. You don't want to be able to change the product name or the category name. You can prevent changes to the CategoryName field by removing its text box from the Detail section of the form. To prevent changes to the ProductName field, you can set its control properties.

Switch to Design view, delete the CategoryName text box and label, and reposition the remaining fields on the form. Double-click the ProductName text box. On the Data tab of the Text Box Properties window, there are two interrelated properties: Enabled and Locked. The default value for Enabled is Yes, and the default value for Locked is No. If you change the Enabled property of a control to No, Access prevents you from selecting the control, and it also grays it out. If you change the Locked property of a control to Yes, the control remains highlighted, and Access displays an error message if you try to change it. If you change both controls to the opposite of their default values—that is, change the Enabled property to No and the Locked property to Yes—Access understands that you are trying to make it a read-only control. In that case, you can't select the control (which prevents changes), but it is not grayed out.

You do not want to use this form to add new products, partially because you deleted the CategoryName text box and, as a result, have no way to specify the CategoryName for a new product. You can easily prevent the addition or deletion of products using the form. Double-click the Form Selector box, click the Data tab in the Properties window, and assign the value *No* to the Allow Deletions and Allow Additions properties. Then save and close the form.

Creating a Form with a Linked Subform

Suppose you want to create a form that allows you to add new Product records—again, with the products grouped by category. Filtering records on a form does not automatically enter the value of the filter into new records. If you have a Category table that contains a single record for each category, you can create a master form that displays one category at a time, and you can then include a subform that displays all the products for that category.

Creating a Subform

To create the master form, click New in the Forms object group of the Database window. Select AutoForm: Columnar, select the tlkCategory table, and then click OK. The form shows records from the Category table, one record at a time. Switch to Design view and enlarge the window. Since header and footer sections are only useful on a Continuous Form report, remove them by clicking Form Header/Footer on the View menu. Change the form's caption property to Edit Products and save the form with the name frmEditProducts.

You can now add a linked subform to this form based on the Product table. In the Toolbox window (click the Toolbox button on the toolbar if the Toolbox is not open), click the Subform/Subreport button, and click below the form box in the detail section of the window. Access will automatically enlarge the form to include the new subform.

Note The Subform Wizard is not installed as part of a typical Office 2000 installation. You will need to have your installatio media handy the first time you use this feature.

When the Subform Wizard begins, select Use Existing Tables And Queries, ignore the list of form names at the bottom, and click the Next button. In the second step of the Subform Wizard, select the Product table, add all the fields except the ProductID to the Selected Fields box, and then click the Next button. The third step of the wizard displays a list of field names that match between the main form and the subform, as shown in Figure 19-8. Accept the proposed matching names and click the Next button.

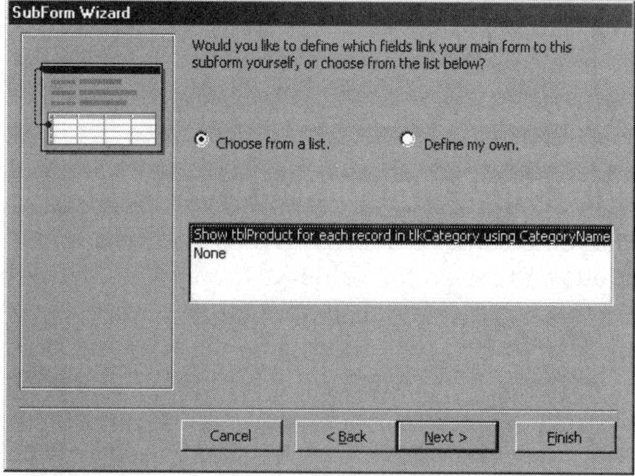

Figure 19-8
Access suggests matching field names for linking the forms.

The fourth step of the Subform Wizard asks for a name for the subform. Type *frmEditProducts(List)* and click the Finish button. The first portion of the name matches the name of the main form, which causes the forms to appear next to one another in the report list. The suffix *(List)* in parentheses identifies this form as a subform. Once the wizard finishes creating the subform, delete the label it adds above the subform control, and change the size of the subform control to about 1.5 inches tall.

Note To select the container of the subform, you must first select a control on the main form, and then click once anywhere within the subform. When you click a second time on a subform, you select an object within the subform. To get back to the container (so that you can move it, resize it, or change its properties), you must click a control on the main form and then click once on the subform again, or click the border of the subform.

Using a Subform Report

Click the View button to switch to Form view. In the subform, only the records matching the category on the main form will appear. Each form has a set of record navigation controls. As you use the lower navigation controls to move through the category products, the subform changes which records it displays, as shown in Figure 19-9.

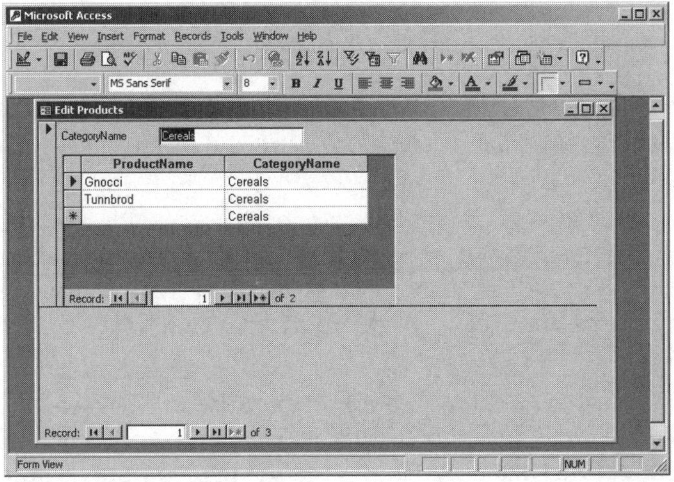

Figure 19-9
A subform displays only records where the linked fields match.

You can see in the new record of the subform that the appropriate category name has already been entered. When you use a subform with linked fields, Access simplifies adding new records.

If the field that links the Category and Product tables is defined as having a *Cascading Update relationship* (see "Modifying Table Relationships" in Chapter 17), changing the category name in the Category Name box on the main form then changes the corresponding name in all the records of the subform. Figure 19-10 shows the effect of changing the name of the Cereals category to Grains.

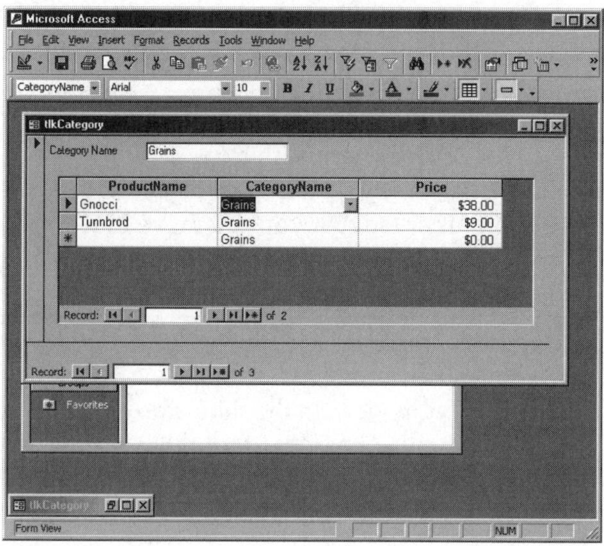

Figure 19-10
Changing the category name can change all related records.

If you change the name of a category in a record in the subform, the record will then be associated with a different category. The record does not disappear from the subform until you select a new category record, or until you press F9 to refresh the form.

If you don't want to be able to change the category of an existing product, you can either remove the field from the subform (since it is not needed for adding a category to a new record), or you can change the Enabled and Locked properties as explained in "Preventing Changes to a Field," earlier in this chapter.

If the subform displays only a few records at a time, you might want to remove its record navigation controls to reduce the confusion between two sets of controls. To do that, in Design view, double-click the Form Selector box of the subform. On the Format tab of the Properties window, change the Navigation Buttons property to No.

If you want to be able to use a drop-down list to select a category for the main form, create an unbound combo box control that applies a filter to the main form, as described in "Making a Combo Box Filter Records On a Form," earlier in this chapter.

Creating Dynamic Reports

Access reports are powerful and flexible. They also can be difficult to create. A particularly tedious type of report to create—but one that is very commonly needed—is one that contains multiple columns. One example of this type of report is a summary report based on a Crosstab query.

Creating Reports with Headings and Totals

The basics of defining a multi-column Access report are logical. You add label controls and bound text boxes to lay out the report. The problem is that you must create and position each control individually. You must line up field labels, detail text boxes, and summary boxes. The process can be tedious and maddening. The Report Wizard is a truly invaluable tool for simplifying the process. Even if you make dramatic changes to a report after creating it with the Report Wizard, you can usually make the changes across a large section of the report at once. You also might delete items added by the Report Wizard, and it is often much easier to delete items than to add new ones.

Preparing a Crosstab Query for the Report

Before using the Report Wizard, you must already have a table or query ready to use. The qxtData query contains a crosstab view of the data in the qryData query. Figure 19-11 shows the definition of the query. (See “Creating a Crosstab Query,” later in this chapter, for more details about creating a Crosstab query.)

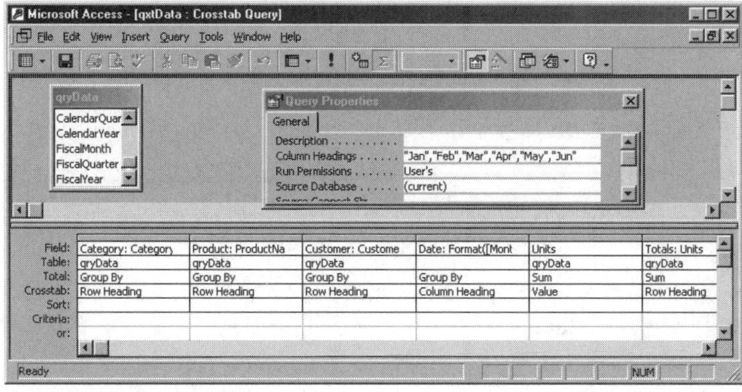

Figure 19-11
Start with an existing query definition.

In addition to the cross-tabulated data fields, the query also calculates the total for the six-month time period as a separate Row Heading field.

Note The query has three-character abbreviations for month names as the Column Headings. It also has Column Headings defined in the Query properties to keep the month names in the correct order. Without the Column Headings, Access would sort the month labels alphabetically.

Using the Report Wizard to Create a Summary Report

In the Database window, activate the Queries object group, select the qxtData query, click the arrow next to the New Object button on the toolbar, and click Report. The two AutoReport options are extremely basic. In most cases, you would probably simply print the query datasheet rather than use one of those reports. Select the Report Wizard option, and click OK.

In the first step of the wizard, add all the fields from the query into the Selected Fields list and click the Next button. The second step of the wizard, shown in Figure 19-12, allows you to specify grouping levels.

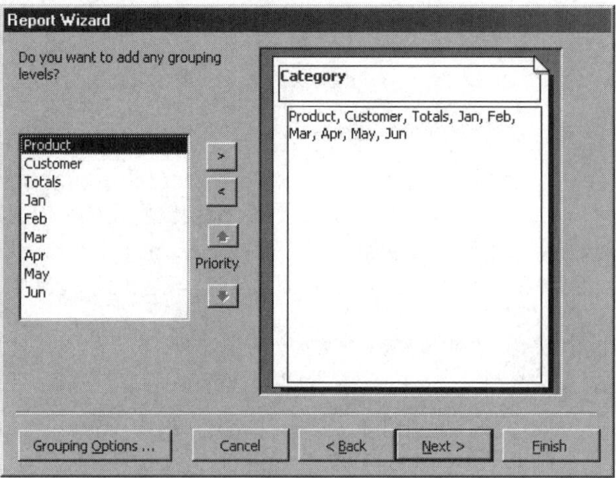

Figure 19-12
Summarize levels using the Report Wizard.

One of the most useful features of the Report Wizard is that it can add summation text boxes at the bottom of each grouping level. These summation boxes are tedious to create by hand, but they are easy to delete. It is even relatively easy to rearrange the order of the grouping levels. Unless you have a report design clearly in mind, you might want to always leave only one row heading ungrouped. In this report, select Category and Product as grouping levels, and then click the Next button.

The third step of the Report Wizard allows you to determine the sort order of the detail rows. The sort order is very easy to change if you change your mind later. Do not overlook the Summary Options button at the bottom of this step, however. This is the most important part of the entire wizard, and it is very easy to miss. Clicking the Summary Options button displays the dialog box shown in Figure 19-13.

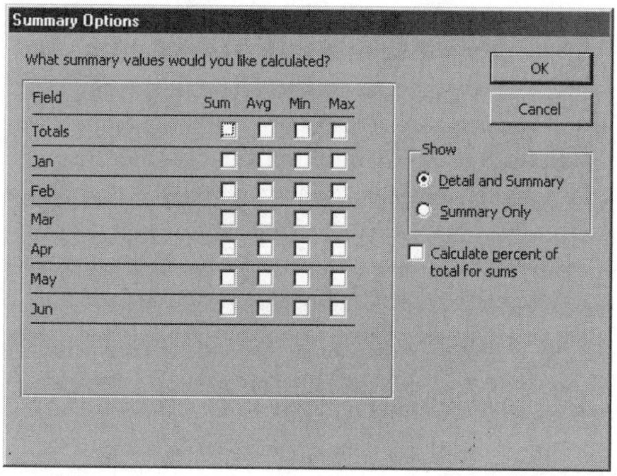

Figure 19-13
Creating summary values is the most valuable part of the Report Wizard.

For a Crosstab report, you will certainly want to add a Sum total for each numeric field. It is annoying to have to select the check box for each field individually—particularly since you can't even use the Down arrow key to move directly from the Sum box of one field to the same box in the next field—but selecting check boxes is much easier than manually creating Sum total boxes. The choice between showing Detail And Summary or Summary Only appears important, but it really is not. It simply controls a single, easily modified property of the Detail section of the report. In this report, after selecting the Sum check box for each field, click OK and then click the Next button. The next step, shown in Figure 19-14, allows you to select layout options.

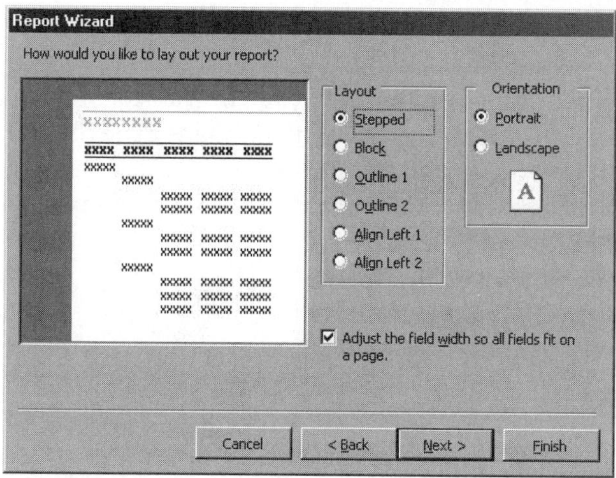

Figure 19-14
Selecting an appropriate layout is important.

The Block option is identical to the Stepped option, except that with the Block option, the heading labels are lined up with the first detail row in each section, creating a more compact report. Even after creating the report, it is easy to convert between the Stepped and Block layouts. The other options overlap the heading fields at different levels and are harder to change. For this report, select the Stepped layout and click the Next button.

The next step of the Report Wizard, shown in Figure 19-15, allows you to choose one of six styles for the report. After the report is created, you can change the style, so this is not an important decision.

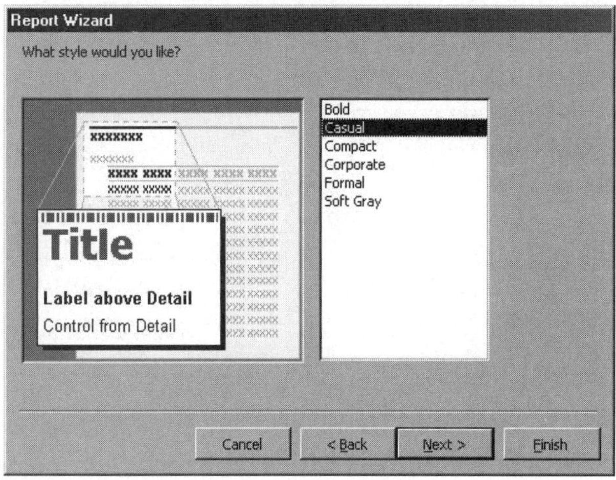

Figure 19-15
You can easily change the style after the report is created.

For this report, select the Casual style, and click the Next button.

The final step of the wizard allows you to specify the title for the report. The default title is the name of the query the report is based on. Change the title for this report to Customer Order Forecasts and click the Finish button. Click Save As on the File menu, and give the report the name rptData. Figure 19-16 shows a portion of the generated report.

Modifying an Existing Report

The Report Wizard creates a good, basic report, but you often need to make modifications to it. Some customizations are trivial. Others require more work.

Customizing Report Formatting

To start customizing the report, switch to Design view. You probably don't want a description of the number of records in each section, so the first task is to delete the boxes that display the number of records in both the Product and the Category

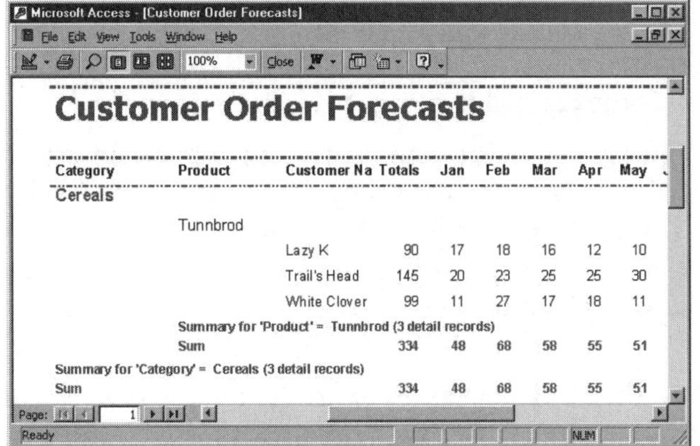

Figure 19-16
The automatically generated report is close to perfect.

groups. Select the box in the Product footer (with the text that begins "Summary for" and press the Delete key. Do the same in the Category footer section. After doing that, click in the ruler at the left of the form window to select all the controls in a section, and drag them all up close to the top of the section. Then drag the following section's border up to remove the extra space.

Suppose that once you have created the report, you decide you don't like the style that you chose. You can change the style by using the AutoFormat toolbar button. For example, to change the entire report to use the Corporate style, click the Report Selector box at the intersection of the rulers, click the AutoFormat toolbar button, select Corporate and click OK. You can use the AutoFormat button to change the style of individual sections of the report—or even individual controls—but mixing styles on a report might create a strange effect. If you click the Options button in the AutoFormat dialog box, you can select whether to apply Fonts, Colors, or Borders from the style. To completely fine-tune the formatting, you can copy formatting from one control to another. To do that, select the source control, click the Format Painter toolbar button, and then click the target control.

Customizing Report Layout

Suppose that once you have created the report, you decide you don't like the layout that you chose. Perhaps, rather than the Stepped layout, you want that you had chosen the Block layout—or even a hybrid of the Block and Stepped layouts. Specifically, rather than having each new Product name take up an entire row, you would like it to appear to the left of the detail row.

To convert a stepped heading into a block heading, drag the text box control for the Product header down to the Detail section. Then, with the heading control still selected, open the Text Box Properties window, and on the Format tab, change the Hide Duplicates property to *Yes*. You can change the value of the Hide Duplicates property for any control on the report, but it is ignored unless the control is in the Detail section. When Hide Duplicates is set to *Yes*, if the value of the control matches the value in the preceding record, the control becomes invisible.

After moving the Product name to the detail row, you might want to add the Product name to the Sum label in the Product group footer. To do that, select the Product text box—the one you just moved into the Detail section—and click Duplicate on the Edit menu. This creates a copy of the control. Drag the copy of the control to just after the Sum label in the Product Footer section. Use the Format Painter to copy the format of the Sum label to the new Product text box.

You might want to link the Sum label and the Product text box so that if you move one, the other will move with it. This is the way that Access creates labels and text boxes when you add a new field to a form or report. To link an existing label to an existing text box, select the label and cut it to the clipboard. Then select the text box, and paste the label. The label is now linked to the text box. To reposition one linked control without moving the other, drag the dark box in the upper left corner of the field (when the mouse pointer is a dark, upward-pointing finger).

Changing Sorting and Grouping Properties

To remove the newly emptied header section for the Product header section, click the Sorting And Grouping toolbar button. On top of the Sorting And Grouping window, select the Product field. In the Group Properties section on the lower half of the dialog box, change the Group Header property to No, as shown in Figure 19-17. (Access will warn you if the section contains controls that would be deleted by removing the section.)

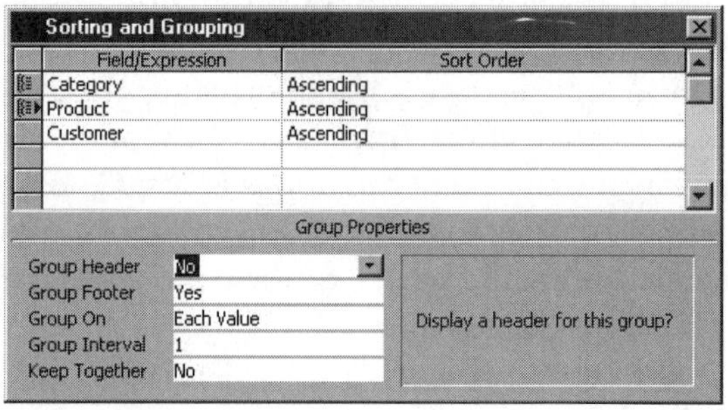

Figure 19-17
You can remove an unused group header.

If you change your mind about the order in which the fields would be grouped, simply drag the Field Group box (to the left of the Field name in the Sorting And Grouping window) up or down to a new position. Any header or footer sections for the affected fields will swap places.

Another important feature of the Sorting And Grouping window is the Keep Together property for a group. Setting this property for a group keeps Access from moving some of the records to a new page. If not all the records will fit on the current page, the entire group moves to the new page. Obviously, you should use that property with caution. Unfortunately, there are no widow and orphan properties that prevent a group from having a single member at the top or bottom of a page.

Creating a Summary Report

You might want to have the report display only the summary sections, hiding the records in the Detail section. (This was an option in the Report Wizard.) To hide the detail rows, select the Detail section, and on the Format tab of the Section properties window, change the Visible property to No. This is an easy change to make, but suppose that you want two versions of the report, one with the detail rows visible, and another with them hidden. As soon as you create two copies of an identical report, you create a maintenance nightmare. Any time you make a change to one of the reports, you must remember to make the identical change to the other report.

Using an Event Handler to Create a Summary Report

Rather than create two reports and assign different property values to each report, you can make a report smart enough to know whether it should display the detail rows or not. You can add an event handler to the report that decides whether to print the detail rows based on the name of the report. If the last seven characters of the report name equal *Summary*, don't print the Detail section. You still have two named copies of the report, but aside from the name, they are exact duplicates of one another. If you make changes to one of the reports, you simply delete the other report, make a copy of the revised report, and rename the copy to the name of the deleted report.

To add the following *Detail_Format* event handler, select the Detail section. On the Event tab of the Form Properties window, click in the On Format drop-down list. Then, click the ellipsis button next to the box, select Code Builder, and click OK. The shell of the event handler appears. Type the following procedure into the Code window:

```
Private Sub Detail_Format(Cancel As Integer, FormatCount As Integer)
        If Right(Name, 7) = "Summary" Then
            Cancel = True
        End If
End Sub
```

One of the arguments for the *Detail_Format* event is *Cancel*. If the procedure assigns *False* to that argument, the section is not formatted. (Technically, the name of the event should be BeforeFormat, because events that typically have a Cancel argument begin with the prefix *Before*.) The rest of the procedure should be self-explanatory. After adding the event handler to the report, make sure that the Detail section of the rptData event report is visible, save the report, make a copy of the report named rptDataSummary, and then preview the two reports.

Data Access Pages

Data access pages are a new feature in Microsoft Office 2000. A data access page is a hybrid of a Web page and an Access form or report. You create a data access page in Access, and then view the page using either Access or Internet Explorer (version 5.0). A data access page uses an .html file extension and theoretically can be opened in any browser on any computer. In actuality, for a data access page to operate properly, it must be opened on computer with a Windows operating system running Internet Explorer 5.0 or later, have Access 2000 installed on the computer, and have a file-sharing connection to the data source.

A computer that meets those requirements could simply open the Access database and use native forms and reports. For a power user who develops database applications for personal or departmental use, forms and reports are most likely a more efficient solution than data access pages.

Adding Dynamic Charts to Forms and Reports

Charting originated with Microsoft Excel. To add charts to other Office applications, the Excel group created an almost exact clone of Excel charting called Microsoft Graph.

Note Microsoft Graph is not installed by default when you install Office 2000. You will need to have your Office 2000 media handy when you begin this exercise so that the installer can add it for you.

The major difference between an Excel chart and a Graph chart is the way in which they each link to data values. An Excel chart is specifically designed to retrieve values from a worksheet. A Graph chart is designed to link to other data sources. In Access specifically, a Graph chart can work much like a subform, extracting values from an SQL statement while linking to a field on the main form. Managing data links on an Access form is easier with a Graph chart than with an Excel chart, but there might be times when you want to integrate an Excel chart with a form.

Note Even though this section describes adding a chart to a form, the process is essentially identical when adding a chart to a report.

Adding a Simple Chart to a Form

For this example, you want to create a form that charts forecasted orders by customer and month for a product. The form will display a new chart each time you move to a new product.

Creating a Simple Chart on a Form

Since each record in the frmEditProducts form corresponds to a product, create a main form based on the product table. In the Forms object group of the Database window, click New, select Form Wizard, select the Product table (tblProduct), and click OK. In the next step, add only the ProductName field to the Selected Fields list, and click the Finish button. Switch to Design view, enlarge the window, and click Form Header/Footer on the View menu to remove the unnecessary sections of the form. Save the form, giving it the name frmGraph.

There is no Chart icon in the Toolbox window. To add a chart, click Chart on the Insert menu, and then click below the form. You will base the query for the chart on the qryData query described in "Creating a Combination Query" in Chapter 18. In the first step of the wizard, select the Queries option, select the qryData query, and click the Next button. In the second step, add the CustomerName, Month, and Units fields to the Fields For Chart list and click the Next button. In the third step, select the Area Chart option (you can refine or change the chart type after creating it), and then click the Next button. In the fourth step, drag the Month field box to the Category area below the sample chart, and the CustomerName field box to the Series area to the right of the sample chart, as shown in Figure 19-18. (The Units field should have already been placed in the Data box by default.)

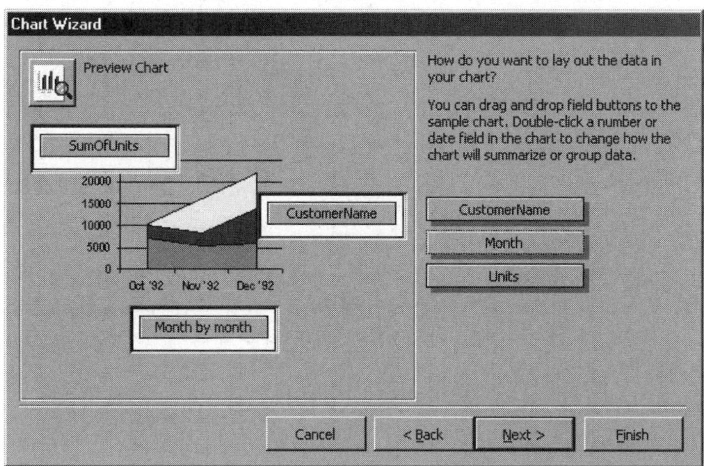

Figure 19-18
Drag fields to the appropriate location on the chart.

This is an important step, because it determines how the wizard will construct the Crosstab query for the chart. The next step of the wizard suggests that you link the ProductID fields between the chart query and the main form. Click the Next button to accept the suggestion. The final step of the Wizard asks for a name for the embedded chart. This is actually the title for the chart. Change the title to Customers by Month, and click the Finish button. Double-click the Chart to active it. The result should look like Figure 19-19.

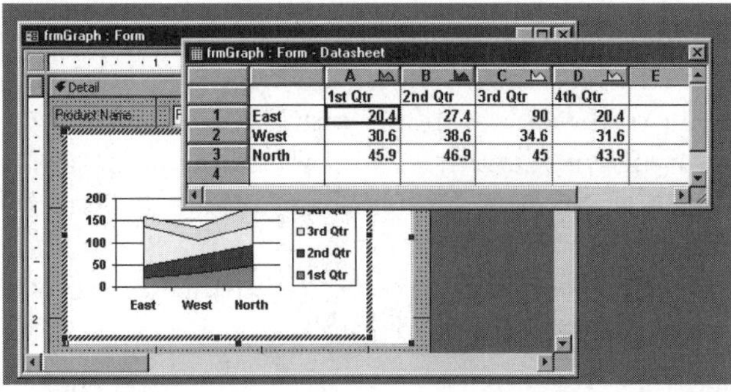

Figure 19-19
Editing a chart adds a datasheet and a Chart menu.

You can close the datasheet window after saving your form. The datasheet is useful if you create a chart that is not linked to a query, but in a chart linked to a Row Source, the values from the datasheet will be replaced as you display the form. The Chart menu is similar to the Chart menu in Excel. The Source Data and Location commands are missing, for obvious reasons. You can use the Chart Type command to choose any chart type available in Excel charts, even those not displayed in the wizard. In the sample chart, you can see gaps at the sides of the chart. To make the charted fill the horizontal axis, double-click the category axis labels, activate the Scale tab, and clear the Value (Y) Axis Crosses Between Categories check box. Once you have finished modifying the appearance of the chart, click anywhere on the form outside the chart.

Modifying the Query for a Simple Chart

If you need to modify the query for the chart—for example, to restrict the chart to show only values for the Corporate scenario—select the chart container box and open the Chart Properties window. On the Data tab, select the Row Source property box and click its ellipsis button. The query is a Crosstab query, with the Row Heading field as the Category axis labels, and the Column Heading field for the Series axis labels. If you want to switch the orientation of the chart, swap the Row Heading and Column Heading assignments.

Add the ScenarioName field to the field grid, type *Corporate* in the Criteria row, and change the Total property for the field to *Where,* to indicate that the field will not appear in the chart, but is used only as a criterion field.

Because the query contains a date field, the Chart Wizard created a calculated field as the Row Heading field. The formula is *Expr1: (Format([Month],"mmm"" '""yy")).* This expression creates a text version of the date, displaying the month and a two-digit year. There is also a Group By field that does not appear on the chart. (Its Crosstab value is blank.) The formula for the calculated field is *(Year([Month])*12+Month([Month])-1).* This formula calculates a numeric value that combines the year and month in an order that sorts the months in calendar order, unlike the text dates. Without this calculated field, the month labels would appear sorted in alphabetical order. Close the Query Builder window, accepting the offer to save changes.

Save the form and switch to Form view to see the chart change as you move from product to product. Figure 19-20 shows the chart for one product.

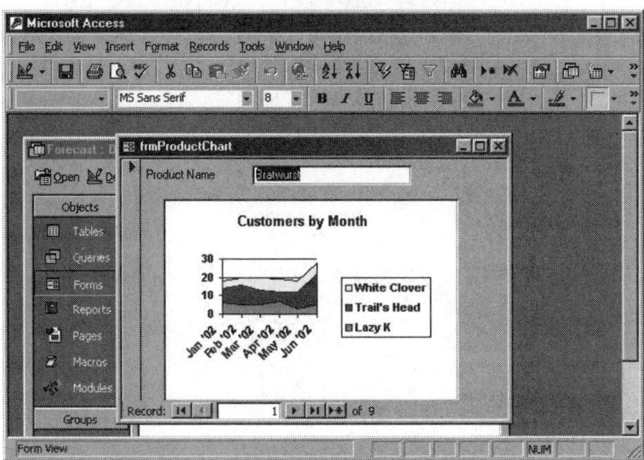

Figure 19-20
The chart values change for each product.

Adding an Excel Chart to a Form

Both Graph charts and Excel charts have object models, and both support Automation. The object models for the two tools are very similar, but not identical. If you will need to use Visual Basic for Applications (VBA) to modify a chart in Access, you might prefer to simply use an Excel chart. According to the Help file, you can add an Excel chart to a form, but it will be static, not changing as you switch from record to record. You can create an Excel chart that changes data when you switch records, but you must add the data into the chart yourself. This involves two processes: extracting data from Access, and adding data to an Excel chart without using a worksheet. Even if you never add an Excel chart to a form or report, you might need to use one of these processes in another context.

Adding a Subform to Create a Usable Recordset

Before adding data to an Excel chart, you must extract the data from Access. A collection of records in Access—whether the records are in a form, a query, or bound to a report—is called a *Recordset*. As you will learn in the next section, the easiest way to retrieve a recordset is to borrow the recordset belonging to a form. Thus, the easiest way to create a chart that changes from record to record is to create a subform that displays the desired values as they change from record to record.

Switch to the Database window. In the Forms object group, click New, select Design View, and click OK. Click the Form Selector box. On the Data tab of the Form Properties window, select the RecordSource box and click the ellipses button to define a data source.

In the Show Tables dialog box that appears, add the qryData query, and then close the dialog box. Add the ProductID, CustomerName, Month, Units, and ScenarioName fields to the field grid. Type *Corporate* as the criterion for the ScenarioName field, and clear that field's Show box. Select Ascending in the Customer Name field sort box and in the Month field Sort box. Figure 19-21 shows the final data source definition. Click the View button if you want to see the result of the query. After defining the data source, close the window, saving the changes back to the form.

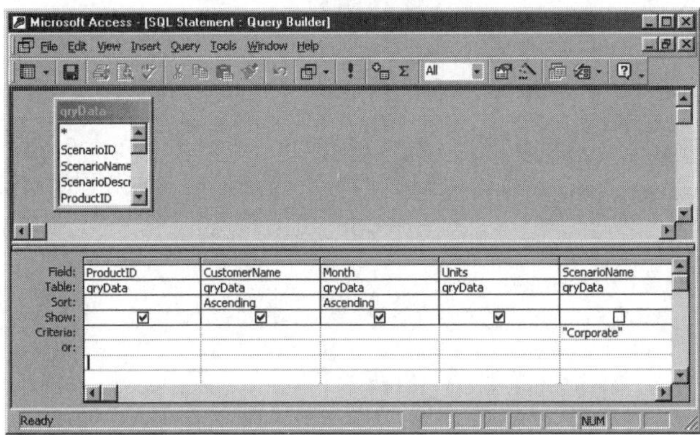

Figure 19-21
A subform requires fixed Column Headings for a Crosstab query.

Back in the subform definition, you can add the fields to the form. You will eventually hide the subform, so it doesn't need to be pretty. As you develop the form, however, it might be useful to see the values change. To add the fields, click the Field List button on the toolbar, and then double-click the Field List title bar to add all the selected fields to the form. Change the Default View property for the form to Datasheet view, save the form with the name *frmExcel(Data)*, and close the form.

Create a copy of the frmGraph form and give it the name *frmExcel*. Open the new form in Design view, and then select and delete the chart object. Then click the Subform/SubReport button in the Toolbox window and click the background of the form. In the first step of the Subform Wizard, select frmExcel(Data) from the list of forms, and then click the Next button. In the next step of the wizard, accept the defaults and click the Next button. In the final step, give the subform control the name *frmData*, and then click the Finish button to create the subform. Click the View button to switch to Form view and browse the product records to see the subform values change. For each product, the query returns a list with CustomerNames, Months, and Units, as shown in Figure 19-22. The sort order of the records will be very important. The customer names are all grouped together, and the months for each customer are in an appropriately ascending order.

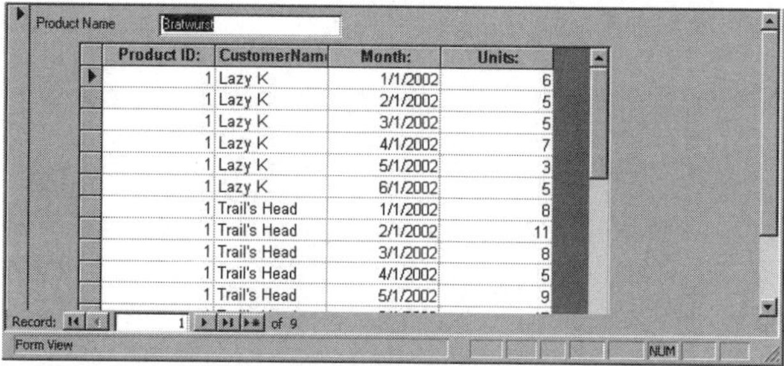

Product ID:	CustomerName	Month:	Units:
1	Lazy K	1/1/2002	6
1	Lazy K	2/1/2002	5
1	Lazy K	3/1/2002	5
1	Lazy K	4/1/2002	7
1	Lazy K	5/1/2002	3
1	Lazy K	6/1/2002	5
1	Trail's Head	1/1/2002	8
1	Trail's Head	2/1/2002	11
1	Trail's Head	3/1/2002	8
1	Trail's Head	4/1/2002	5
1	Trail's Head	5/1/2002	9

Figure 19-22
The subform returns a list you can access from a VBA procedure.

Extracting Values From a Form's Recordset

Once the subform exists and properly retrieves data linked to the main form, you can create an event handler that extracts the values from each field into an array in preparation for adding the values to an Excel chart. Select the Form Selector box of the main form in Design view. On the Event tab of the Properties window, select the On Current event, click the ellipsis next to the box, and select Code Builder to create a VBA event handler.

Caution Before creating a procedure that uses a Recordset object from a form, you must make a change to the libraries in the Access VBA References dialog box. There are actually two different object libraries that have Recordset objects: Data Access Objects (DAO)—which have been used in the past few versions of Access and Visual Basic, and the ActiveX Data Objects (ADO)—which have recently been introduced. The Recordset linked to a form is a DAO recordset, but Access VBA defaults to include a reference to the ADO library, not to the DAO library.

To change to the DAO library, click References on the Tools menu, and then clear the check box next to the Microsoft ActiveX Data Objects 2.1 Library entry. Then select the check box next to the Microsoft DAO 3.6 Object Library entry and click OK. If you do not make this change, when the procedure attempts to assign the Recordset from a form to a variable declared as a Recordset, you will get a Type Mismatch error.

The following *Form_Current* event handler reads each record in the Recordset once for each field that will appear on the report. Each iteration through the Recordset, the procedure stores the values into an array. Later, you will add code to the event handler to move the values into an Excel chart each iteration through the array.

```
Option Compare Database
Option Base 1
Option Explicit

Private Sub Form_Current()
    Dim rs As Recordset
    Dim myName As String
    Dim x(), y() As Variant
    Dim i, j As Long

    Set rs = frmData.Form.RecordsetClone

    rs.MoveFirst
    i = 0
    Do Until rs.EOF
        i = i + 1

        Erase x
        Erase y

        myName = rs.Fields(1)
        j = 0
        Do While rs.Fields(1) = myName
            j = j + 1

            ReDim Preserve x(j)
            ReDim Preserve y(j)
            x(j) = rs.Fields(2)
            y(j) = rs.Fields(3)

            rs.MoveNext
            If rs.EOF Then Exit Do
        Loop
    Loop
End Sub
```

Three option statements are listed at the top of the module. The *Option Explicit* statement is there if you require variable declaration as recommended in "Creating Variables" in Chapter 4. Access adds the statement *Option Compare Database* to the top of each module to facilitate localization of comparisons. You must add the statement Option Base 1 yourself. Normally, arrays in Visual Basic begin with zero as the first element in the array. Because this procedure contains so many collections and counters—most of which begin with 1 as the first element—the code is simpler if the arrays begin with 1, as well.

To refer to a subform, a procedure must first refer to the container object in the main form. This object name is based on the name of the form, so the term *frmData* refers to the container of the subform. The expression *TypeName(frmData)* identifies the data type as a subform. To access the form inside the container, you must use the container object's Form property. The form inside the subform has a recordset bound to it.

A form that is bound to a data source has a Recordset property. The Recordset object always retrieves field values from the current record in the Recordset. To change the current record, you use MoveFirst, MoveNext, and similar methods, which correspond to clicking the navigation buttons at the bottom of a form. Changing the current record of a recordset bound to a form changes the current record in the form, which is not always desirable. Because of that, a form has a separate RecordsetClone property, which refers to the same set of records as the Recordset property, except that it maintains a separate pointer to the current record. You can move through the Recordset object returned by the RecordsetClone property without affecting the form.

The EOF property identifies when the current record has moved past the end of the recordset. The procedure can loop until the EOF property is *True*, as long as the loop contains a MoveNext method to move through the loop. The procedure contains nested *Do* loops. The inner loop process once for each record in the recordset—with each record corresponding to a new data point on the chart. The outer loop processes once, each time the customer name changes. The procedure uses *i* as a counter to keep track of the separate customers, and *j* as a counter to keep track of individual data points for each series. X values—the dates from the Month field—will be stored in the X array. Y values—the values from the Units field—will be stored in the Y array. Before accumulating new values for a Series, the procedure erases both arrays. The procedure retains the customer name from the first record in a group as a way to identify when the customer name changes.

For each new point within a series, the procedure increases the size of the array by one element, while maintaining the existing values. The procedure has no way of knowing how many points there might be for a given series. The subsequent statements in the inner loop simply assign the values from the current record to the newest element of each array. After retrieving a new record, the inner loop must determine if the end of the recordset has been reached. Otherwise, the *Do* statement for the inner loop—the one that checks for a new name—will display an error message at the end of the recordset because there will be no value in *rs.Fields(1)* to compare with.

To test the procedure, set a breakpoint on the second *Loop* statement and run the procedure. When the procedure reaches the breakpoint, type the command *For Each z in x:?z:Next* into the Immediate window and press Enter. This single-line loop will display all the values stored in the X array. Then do the same for the Y array. Press F5 to cycle through the next customer and test the arrays again. Each time through the outer loop, the arrays will contain new values.

Adding an Excel Chart to the Form

To add an Excel chart to a form, click Object on the Insert menu with the frmExcel form in Design mode, select Microsoft Excel Chart from the list box in the Insert Object window, and then click OK. The chart will appear, opened and ready for customizing, as shown in Figure 19-23.

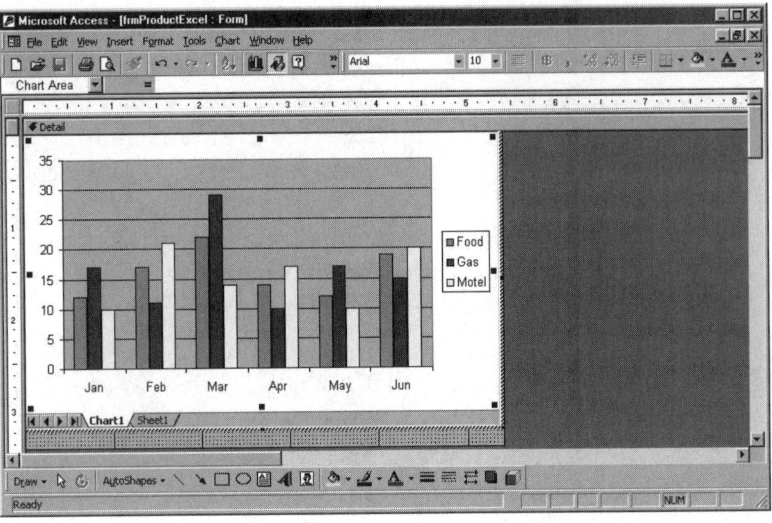

Figure 19-23
Adding an Excel chart adds an entire workbook.

The chart is accompanied by the Sheet1 worksheet. When you embed an Excel chart, you create an entire workbook. You can actually add additional worksheets to this embedded workbook if you like. Any changes you make to the workbook while the form is open in Design mode will remain while you run the form. Change the Chart type from the Chart menu. In the Chart Type window, select Area from the Chart Type list box, and then select Stacked ARea from the Chart Sub-Type list. Then click OK. Click Chart Type on the Chart menu, convert the chart to a stacked Area chart, and click OK. As with the Graph chart, don't worry about the sample data; the event handler will replace the data values with new ones anyway.

When you are through customizing the chart, press the Escape key to deactivate the Chart object. (Depending on what is selected on the chart, you might need to press the Escape key more than once.) At this point, the subform will appear on top of the Chart object. If you don't want the subform in the way in Design view, make the chart smaller and drag it off to a corner. If you don't want to see the subform in Form view, change the Visible property of the container object to *No*.

Move or resize the chart's container object as needed to see the ProductName text box. You will refer to the chart's container object from the event handler, so give it a better name than the default (OLEUnbound, plus a suffix number). To rename the chart's container object, right-click in the container and select Properties. On the Other tab of the Unbound Object Frame Properties window, type *xlChart* as the Name property, and then press Enter. Close the Properties window.

Using VBA to Add Data to a Chart

There are several ways to add data values into an Excel chart. One option is to enter the values into the Sheet1 worksheet that accompanies the chart, and then adjust the chart data source to match the new data range.

As a second option, if you don't want to enter the data values into a worksheet, you can assign values directly to the Values property and the XValues property of a series. You can assign the values either as a comma-delimited string or as an array. The problem with assigning values this way is that they go directly into the SERIES formula of the chart as constants, and you quickly encounter the maximum length of that formula, depending on the length of the data items. With single-digit values, the limit is approximately 20 data items.

There is a third option which, like the first option, allows hundreds of data points per series. Also, like the second option, the method does not require entering values into the worksheet cells. This option utilizes the fact that an Excel Chart series can reference a defined name for the values. "Charting an Algebraic Function" in Chapter 13 explains how to enter a mathematical function into an Excel-defined name. You also can enter an array constant into a defined name. An array constant in a defined name can be much larger than a constant entered into the SERIES formula of a chart.

Chapter 19

Note Before referencing an Excel chart in a VBA procedure, you must add a reference to the Excel object library. To do that, activate the Visual Basic Editor, click References on the Tools menu, select the check box next to the Microsoft Excel 9.0 Object Library entry, and click OK. (See "Using Objects from Other Office Applications" in Chapter 5 for details about adding references between Office applications.)

Here is the revised *Form_Current* event handler procedure. The new portions are bracketed by lines of asterisks. This procedure creates a new Excel defined name at the end of pass through the form's recordset object.

```
Private Sub Form_Current()
    '**********************************
    Dim myWorkbook As Workbook
    Dim myWorksheet As Worksheet
    Dim myChart As Chart
    Dim mySeries As Series
    Dim myFormula As String
    '**********************************
    Dim rs As Recordset
    Dim myName As String
    Dim x(), y() As Variant
    Dim i, j As Long
```

```
    '**********************************
    Set myWorkbook = xlChart.Object

    Set myChart = myWorkbook.Charts(1)
    Do While myChart.SeriesCollection.Count > 0
        myChart.SeriesCollection(1).Delete
    Loop

    Set myWorksheet = myWorkbook.Worksheets(1)
    myWorksheet.Cells.Clear
    '**********************************

    Set rs = frmData.Form.RecordsetClone

    rs.MoveFirst
    i = 0
    Do Until rs.EOF
        i = i + 1

        Erase x
        Erase y

        myName = rs.Fields(1)
        j = 0
        Do While rs.Fields(1) = myName
            j = j + 1

            ReDim Preserve x(j)
            ReDim Preserve y(j)
            x(j) = rs.Fields(2)
            y(j) = rs.Fields(3)

            rs.MoveNext
            If rs.EOF Then Exit Do
        Loop
    '**********************************
        myWorkbook.Names.Add Name:="Sheet1!PlotX" & i, RefersToR1C1:=x
        myWorkbook.Names.Add Name:="Sheet1!PlotY" & i, RefersToR1C1:=y
        myChart.SeriesCollection.Add myWorksheet.Cells(1), , False, False
        Set mySeries = myChart.SeriesCollection(i)

        myFormula = ",Sheet1!PlotX" & i
        myFormula = myFormula & ",Sheet1!PlotY" & i
        myFormula = myFormula & "," & i
        myFormula = "=SERIES(" & myFormula & ")"
        mySeries.Formula = myFormula
        mySeries.Name = myName
    '**********************************
    Loop
End Sub
```

In the first block of the added executable statements, the first statement retrieves a reference to the Excel chart. An embedded chart has a container object on the form. This is the object that you named earlier. The expression *TypeName(xlChart)* returns the type name ObjectFrame. The ObjectFrame's object property returns a reference to the Automation object it contains. In this case, the ObjectFrame's object property does not really return a Chart object; rather, it returns an entire Excel workbook object, which the procedure assigns to a variable.

The chart exists on a Chart sheet in the workbook. Because there is only one Chart sheet in the workbook, it can be referenced by retrieving the first element from the Charts collection. After setting a reference to the chart, the loop deletes each data series currently in the chart. As the main form moves through different products, some might have more customers than others. Clearing all the series keeps the chart from displaying too many series.

Retrieving a reference to the Worksheet object is analogous to retrieving a reference to the Chart object. Just for good measure, the procedure clears the entire Worksheet containing the sample data.

The final block of added executable statements occurs after accumulating all the points for a single series. The procedure adds two new Excel names for each series: one for X values and one for Y values. (For most chart types, only the X values from the first series are actually used, but the procedure is capable of generating the data for an XY chart, where each series uses its own X values.) For the X values, the procedure uses the name Sheet1!PlotX, suffixed with the series number. This is a sheet-local name on the Sheet1 worksheet. ("Managing Local and Global Names" in Chapter 13 for details about sheet local names.) The reason for using a sheet-local name is that a SERIES formula uses external references to the workbook. A workbook-level name requires the workbook name as part of the reference and, as you will see when you watch the procedure run, Excel creates a new temporary workbook with a new temporary name each time you load the form. You can reference a sheet-local name by using the worksheet name, however, which never changes.

After adding the array values to defined names, the procedure adds a new series. It defines the series with a single-cell data source, with no row or column headings. According to the Help topic for the SeriesCollection.Add method, you should be able to create a new series by specifying an array of values as the source. Unfortunately, it doesn't work this way. There is no way to create a new series on a chart in a VBA procedure without specifying a worksheet range somewhere as its source. The procedure then retrieves a reference to the new series.

The final task is to construct a SERIES formula that uses the newly defined range names for the *Category* and *Value* arguments. A VBA procedure can assign an array or a comma-delimited string of values directly to the Values or the XValues properties of a collection, but a procedure cannot use an object property to assign a defined name. The only way to assign a defined name to a chart series is to replace the

Formula property with an old-fashioned SERIES formula. The procedure first creates the SERIES formula in a string variable so it's easy to inspect the formula while stepping through the procedure.

After assigning the SERIES formula to the series, the final statement in the loop assigns the name of the current customer as the name of the series. The name could have been included as the first argument of the SERIES formula, but that would have required constructing a string that contains nested quotation marks, which is very difficult to do correctly. Because a series does have a Name property, the procedure takes advantage of that property.

Caution When using a VBA procedure to define a name, be careful not to use a name that could be a cell address in either A1 notation or in R1C1 notation. For example, don't use a name like Y1 or C. Excel will allow the procedure to create the name, but when you attempt to reference the name, it will become confused and could crash.

Testing an Access Procedure that Modifies an Excel Chart

Before testing the procedure, be sure to save all your work. The interaction between Access and Excel is such that a seemingly minor error in your code can cause your computer to hang.

Note The interaction between Access and Excel does not appear to be any more or less robust than the interaction between Access and Graph. Whether you create an Excel chart or a Graph chart, Access must launch a separate application and manage the information transfer between them. In fact, if you already have Excel running on the computer, the chart does not need to load an additional application like it does when using Graph to create a chart.

Set a breakpoint at the beginning of the event handler procedure. In Access, switch the form to Form view display, and then begin stepping through the procedure. If Excel is not already running, the statement that retrieves a reference to the Workbook object launches a hidden copy. Launching Excel might take a few seconds. Once the Workbook reference has been assigned, you can use it to make Excel visible. Type the statement *myWorkbook.Application.Visible = True* in the Immediate window and press Enter. The workbook window is also hidden within Excel. To make it visible, type the statement *myWorkbook.Windows(1).Visible = True* and press Enter. If you activate Excel after performing these steps, you will see the chart and worksheet with the sample data that was visible in Design mode. As you step through the procedure, you can watch the statements that clear the existing series.

Once the procedure starts the loop, set a breakpoint on the statement that assigns a SERIES formula to the series. Press F5 to run to that point, and then step through the code and press F8 as needed to watch the values that appear on the chart, as shown in Figure 19-24. Press F5 again to loop through the values for the next series.

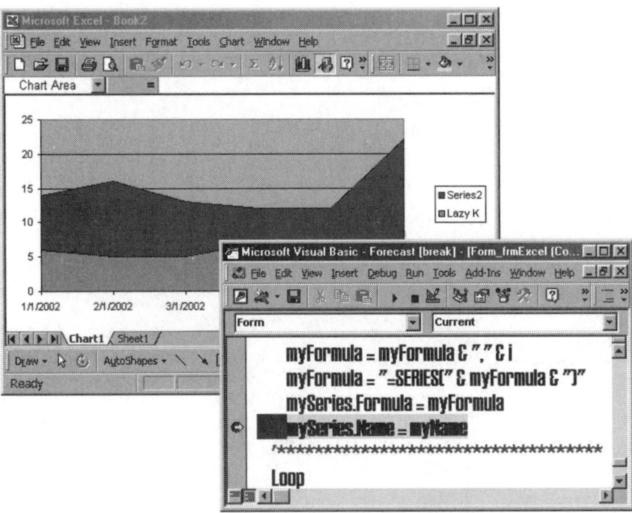

Figure 19-24
You can watch as an Access procedure modifies an Excel chart.

Once the chart for a product has finished, switch to Access and navigate to the next record to repeat the process. Clear the breakpoints to watch the uninterrupted creation of the chart. Even though it might seem that a lot of code is executed for each product, the charts appear very quickly. The speed is much the same even for a chart that contains hundreds of data points per series.

Part 6

Other Office Tools

Chapter 20

Organize Your Life with Outlook

by Alan Neibauer

In This Chapter

Microsoft Outlook 2000 is a full-fledged personal information manager (PIM) and communications program. As a PIM, it helps you organize and manage your time. As a communication program, it lets you send and receive e-mail over the Internet and your local area network.

The main problem with all PIM programs, however, it getting organized. As the amount of information stored in the program increases, so does the complexity of putting it in the correct order so you can easily access it. In this chapter, you'll learn how to organize your information to get the most use out of it.

Appointments, Meetings, and Events

Before looking into the specifics of Outlook, you should understand how Outlook categorizes information. All Outlook data is stored in folders, each containing certain types of information. The Calendar folder stores information about appointments, meetings, and events, and you should understand the differences between them:

- **An Appointment** is a time period you set aside on your calendar, and for which you are not using Outlook to invite others. It might or might not be an actual appointment with another person. You can, for example, create an appointment to reserve time to work on a project, or to make a phone call. As you will learn, you can associate an appointment with a person in your contact list so their name is recorded as part of the item.
- **A Meeting** is an appointment to which you invite other users. As part of the process of creating a meeting, Outlook actually mails out invitations—either over your computer network or the Internet. In Outlook terms, if you invite others to an appointment, it then becomes a meeting. Likewise, if you cancel all the invitations to a meeting, it then becomes an appointment.
- **An Event** is something that lasts an entire day. It could be a day-long conference, an anniversary, or a birthday. You also can create an Invited Event with which you use Outlook to invite others to participate via e-mail. If you choose to make the event less than an entire day, Outlook changes it to an appointment or a meeting, depending on whether you have invited others.

Associating Information with Contacts

When you create an item in Outlook, you can associate it with one or more contacts in your Contacts folder. This way, you can quickly list all your Outlook activities that relate to the contact by opening the Activities page of the contact's listing. For example, suppose you create several tasks and then schedule a meeting relating to a project you are working on for a client. You can associate those items with the client so you can review all related activities in one location. Before calling the client to review your invoice, you open the client's Activities page to use as a reference.

To associate an Outlook item with a contact, open the item and click the Contacts button. (With e-mail messages, click Options on the message window toolbar, and then click the Contacts button.) In the Select Contacts dialog box, which is shown in Figure 20-1, click the contact's name and then click OK or Apply. To associate multiple contacts at one time, hold down the Ctrl key as you click each contact's name.

Associating a meeting or an appointment with a contact does not add the contact to the attendees list. If you want to invite a contact to a meeting or assign them a task, do so from the meeting or task window as you normally would. This also inserts an item for the meeting or task in the contact's Activities page so you do not have to also associate

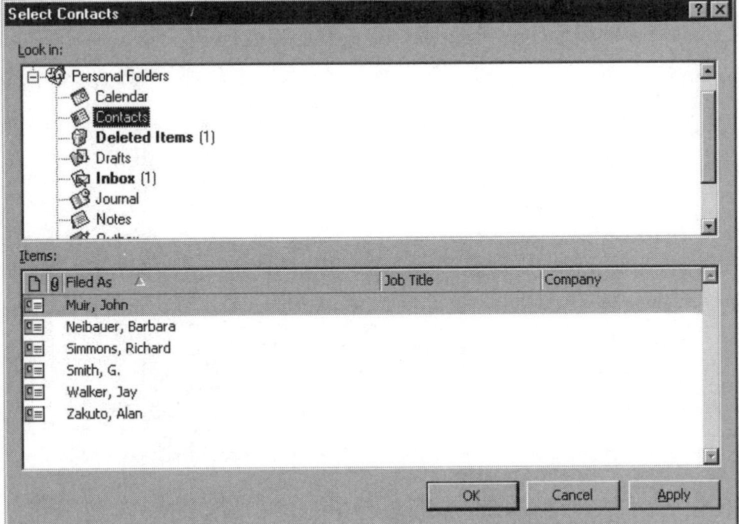

Figure 20-1
The Select Contacts dialog box.

the contact with the item. The only time you might want to invite and associate a contact is when you'll want to sort or filter calendar items by their contacts.

Linking Documents to Contacts

You also can associate any document on your disk—or an existing Outlook item—with a contact without opening the document. This is especially useful when you want to associate an e-mail message with a contact who was not the sender or a recipient of the message.

To associate a document with a contact, select and then open the contact's listing, choose Link from the Actions menu, and then click File. In the Choose A File dialog box, select the document and then click Insert. When the Journal Entry dialog box appears, more information can be added if you want. Then click Save And Close to close the contact item.

To associate an existing Outlook item with a contact, select and then open the contact's listing, choose Link from the Actions menu, and click Items to open the Link Items To Contact dialog box shown in Figure 20-2. Choose the Outlook folder containing the item, select the item itself, and then click OK.

A listing for each linked item appears on the contact's Activities page. Double-click the listing to open the selected document or Outlook item.

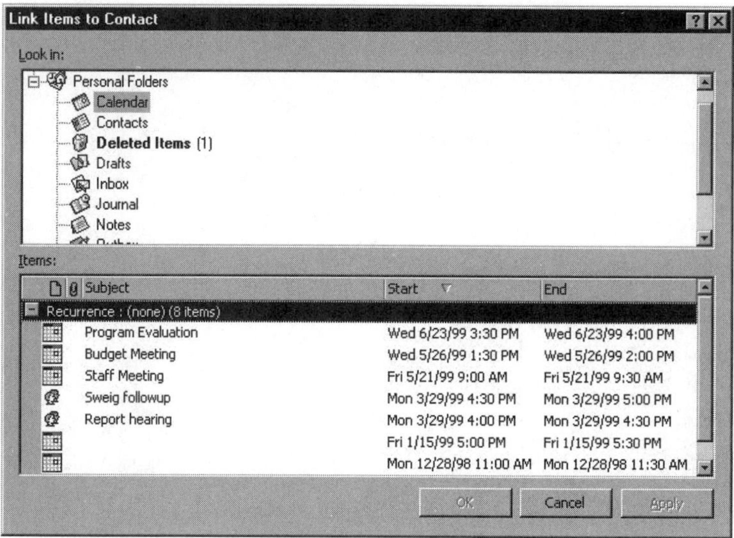

Figure 20-2
The Link Items To Contact dialog box.

Opening the Contact Activities Tab

When you want to see all Outlook items associated with a contact, open the contact's item in the Contacts folder and click the Activities tab. When you click the Activities tab, Outlook takes a moment to scan all its folders looking for items linked to that contact, and then lists them as illustrated in Figure 20-3. You'll see, for example, all e-mail messages you sent to or received from this contact—even messages still in your Outbox and messages you have deleted that are still in the Deleted Items folder. You'll also see all meetings to which the contact was invited and all tasks assigned to the contact. You can double-click an item in the list to open it.

Click the Show list to choose which items are displayed. Your choices are All Items, Contacts, E-Mail, Journal, Notes, and Upcoming Tasks/Appointments. Select the types of activities you want to see.

Mail Merging to Contacts

While we're on the subject of contacts, Outlook 2000 lets you use your Contacts folder to create a merge document in Microsoft Word. You use Word to write and format the letter (or an envelope or mailing label), and then merge it with the address or other information in the Contacts folder. You can even choose which contacts to use for the merge. When you want to send a personalized message to a number of contacts, follow these steps.

1. Open the Contacts folder.
2. To send a message to a group of contacts, select the contacts in the folder.

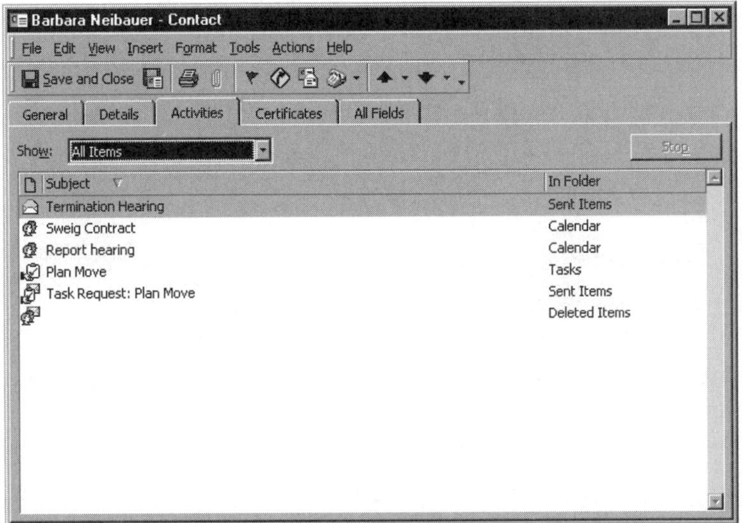

Figure 20-3
The Contact Activities page.

3. Choose Mail Merge from the Tools menu to display the Mail Merge Contacts dialog box shown in Figure 20-4.

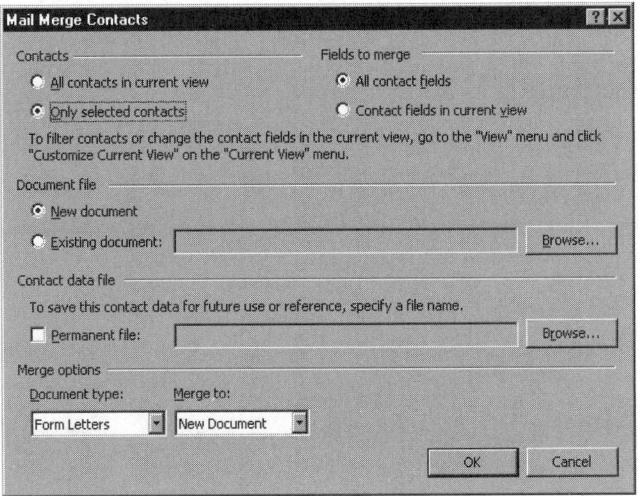

Figure 20-4
The Mail Merge Contacts dialog box.

4. Select an option that determines which contacts to use for the merge. You can choose to use all contacts in the current view, or just the selected contacts.
5. Choose which fields to use—all fields in the Contacts folder, or just the fields in the current view.

6. Next choose to either create a new Word merge document, or to use an existing merge document. If you select the Existing Document option, click Browse and choose the document in the Open dialog box.
7. Choose if you want to save the resulting data in a separate file. If you do, click the Permanent File check box and enter the name of the file in the text box to its right.
8. Choose the document type for the merge: Form Letter, Mailing Labels, Envelopes, or Catalog.
9. Choose the destination for the merge document. Your options are to save the merge document to a new document for use in Word, to have Word merge the individual documents directly to the printer, or to send the documents by e-mail.
10. Click OK. Outlook opens Microsoft Word and creates a mail merge document.
11. Finish preparing the document in Word, using the Insert Merge Field button on the Merge Toolbar to insert codes where you want contact information to appear. A typical merge document might look like the one shown in Figure 20-5.

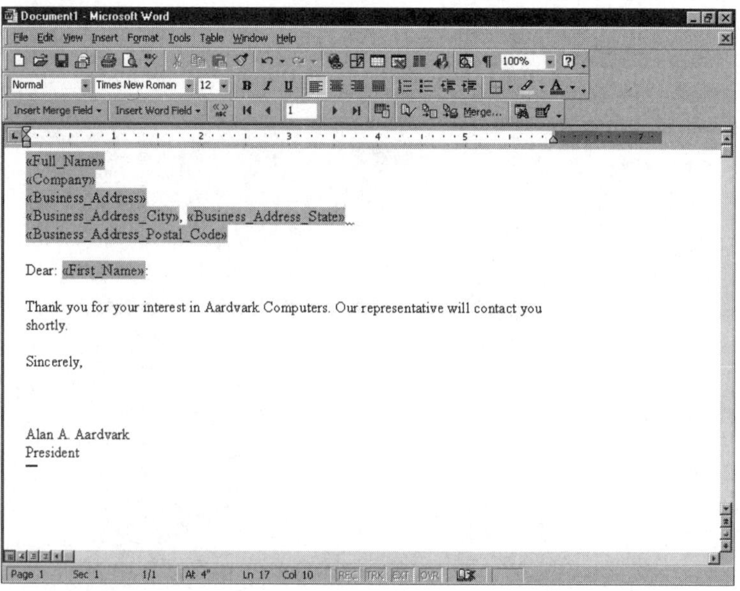

Figure 20-5
A typical merge document in Word.

When you have completed the document, click the Mail Merge button on the Merge toolbar and then click Merge in the Mail Merge Helper dialog box.

Working with Categories

Associating an Outlook item with a contact is just one way to organize information for easy recall. You also can associate items with one or more categories. Outlook provides a number of built-in categories, and you also can add your own categories. For example, you can create a category for each project you are working on, so that you can then easily list all your activities that relate to that project for reviewing your progress or reporting to clients. You also can use categories to associate items with people who are not in your Contacts folder. Categories are ideal for organizing information.

You can assign an item to one or more categories as you create it. Here is how to use categories when you are creating an item:

- For a calendar item or task, click the Categories button in the lower-left corner of the item's Task page.
- For an e-mail message, click Options on the message window toolbar and then click the Categories button in the Message Options dialog box.
- For notes, click the icon in the upper-left corner of the note window and choose Categories from the menu.
- If you have already created the item, you can right-click it and choose Categories from the shortcut menu.

Outlook opens the Categories dialog box shown in Figure 20.6.

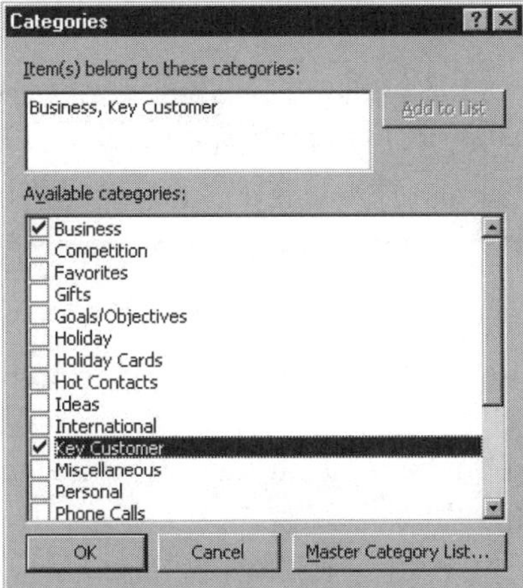

Figure 20-6
The Categories dialog box.

Select the check boxes for as many categories as you want to assign to the item, and then click OK. Clear the check box if you want to remove an item from a category.

You also can use the Organize feature to assign categories in the Calendar, Contacts, Tasks, or Journal folders. Click the Organize button on the Standard toolbar, and then select the items you want to assign to a category. With a calendar option open, for example, click Using Categories in the Organize pane to see these options:

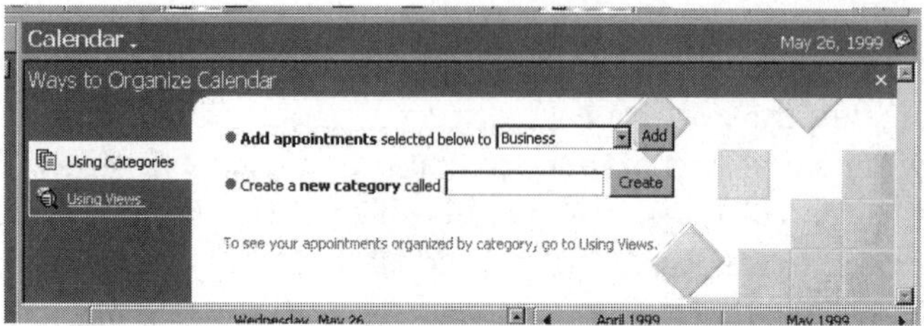

Choose an existing category from the list and click Add, or type in a new category in the Create A New Category Called text box and click Create. Specify as many categories as you want, and then click the Organize button again to close the Organize pane.

Adding Your Own Categories

The categories provided by Outlook might not satisfy all your requirements. You might want to group items, for example, by a specific project or client. To get the most from this Outlook feature, create your own categories to add to the list using the following steps:

1. Open a folder and select an item that you'd like to assign to a new category.
2. Right-click the item and choose Categories from the Shortcut menu to open the Categories dialog box.
3. Type the new category name in the Item(s) Belong To These Categories text box. If you are adding more than one category, separate the names with a comma.
4. Click Add To List. Outlook adds the new category to the list so that you can easily assign other items to this new category later.
5. Click OK.

If you are synchronizing items with a laptop or hand-held device, the added category will appear with the items assigned to it, even though the category has not been added to the other device's category list. You have to manually add the new category to the list if you want to select it for other items.

Managing the Master Category List

You add and remove categories—or reset the category list to Outlook's default categories—using the Master Category List box. From the Categories dialog box, click the Master Category List button to see the dialog box shown in Figure 20-7. Type the name of a new category and click Add to create a new category; use the Delete button to remove a category; or use the Reset button to restore all the original categories.

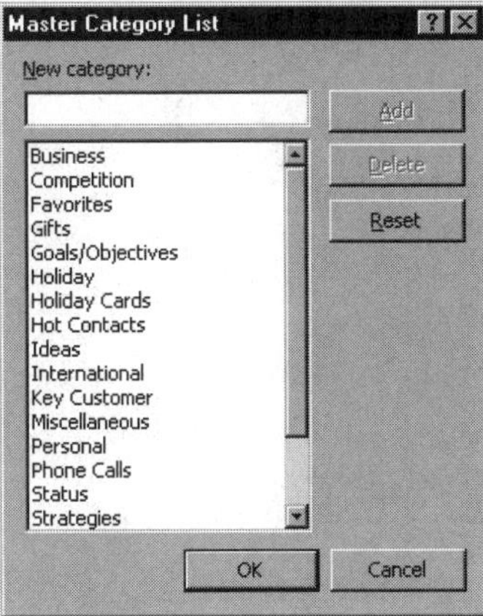

Figure 20-7
The Master Category List dialog box.

Deleting a category from the Master Category List dialog box doesn't remove the category from any items that have already been assigned to it. You will still be able to sort, group, and filter items by the deleted category.

Grouping Views

The standard way to change views is to select Current View on the View menu, and then to select one of the options on the View submenu. Grouping views By Category, By Company, or By Location will group items under those headings that correspond to the various entries in the Category, Company, or Location fields. For example, choose By Person Responsible to group tasks by the name of the person responsible for the task. Grouping is a way to organize folder items to more easily find and examine related items.

If there is no built-in view that groups items the way you want, you can create a custom view either visually from within the folder window, or by selecting up to four fields in a dialog box. The dialog box method has the added advantage of letting you group an item that is not displayed in the current window.

Visually Grouping Items

The quickest way to group items is to right-click a column heading and choose Group By This Field from the shortcut menu. Outlook organizes the items on the selected field and then displays the field name in the Group By box above the column headings, as shown in Figure 20-8. Notice that the field no longer appears in the column headings.

You can then add one or more subgroups to further organize the items. To add a subgroup, use either of the following two methods.

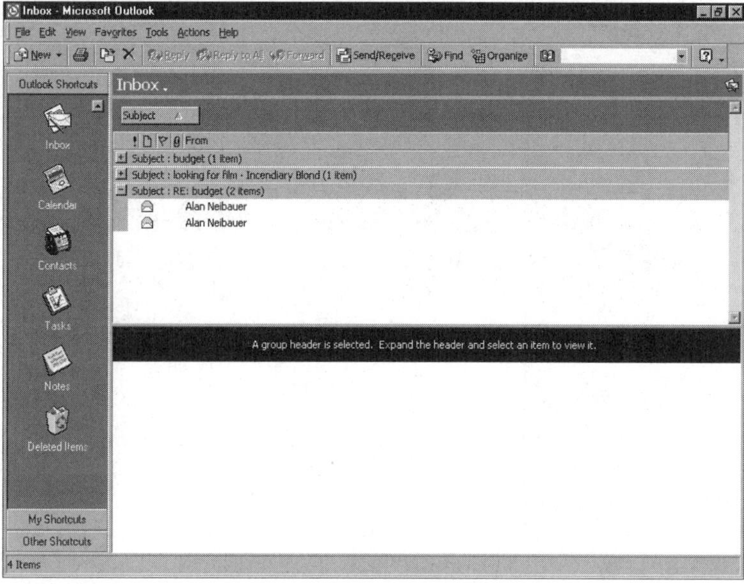

Figure 20-8
Grouping items using the Group By box.

- Right-click the field and choose Group By This Field from the shortcut menu.
- Drag the field heading to the Group By box.

When you use multiple levels of grouping, Outlook first groups the items by the first field you specified for the group. Then, within each one of those groups, Outlook creates subgroups based on the second field chosen, and so on. The fields will be indented in the Group By box to visually illustrate this grouping order, as shown earlier in Figure 20-8. If an item contains no information in the specified field, it is listed first and labeled (None).

To change the order in which the fields are used for grouping, rearrange the fields within the Group By box. For example, to change a subgroup into the primary grouping field, drag it to the left of any other groups in the Group By box and then release the mouse.

When you no longer want to group by a field, drag it from the Group By box back to the column heading, or right-click the field name in the Group By box and choose Don't Group By This Field from the shortcut menu.

If you no longer want to display the Group By box, right-click a column heading and choose the Group By box from the shortcut menu. (You also can use that option to open the Group By box at any time.)

Using the Group By Dialog Box

As an alternative to dragging fields into the Group By box, you can group items using a dialog box. The Group By dialog box lets you group items based on up to four fields, select fields that aren't visible, select the order of the fields, and choose how you want the groups expanded or collapsed.

First, you should understand how Outlook organizes fields. A field is nothing more than a column heading—a category of information stored in a folder. Outlook's fields are organized into groups called *field sets*. In many cases, when you want to select a field for some purpose, you first have to select the set that contains the type of field you want to group by. You can then choose the specific field from the field set. To change the way items are grouped in an open folder, follow these steps:

1. Choose Current View on the View menu, and then choose Customize Current View from the Viewmenu.
2. Click Group By in the View Summary dialog box to display the Group By dialog box shown in Figure 20-9.

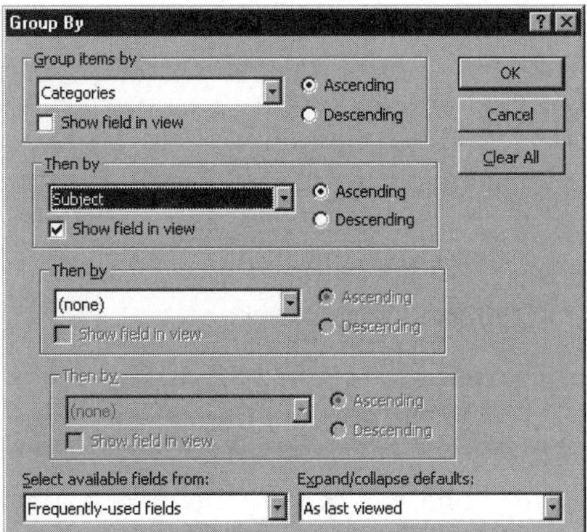

Figure 20-9
Grouping items using the Group By dialog box.

3. In the Select Available Fields From drop-down list, select the field set containing the fields you want to use for grouping.
4. Start with the Group Items By list box and select the primary field to group by.
5. Select the Show Field In View check box if you want to display the field in the column heading, as well as in the Group By box.
6. Choose Ascending or Descending order in the Group Items By dialog box for sorting the field items. The default order is Ascending.

7. Repeat steps 3 to 6 to group by as many as three additional fields. Note that you can change the field set in step 3 for any of the additional levels of grouping.
8. Select how you want the items displayed. Your options are As Last Viewed, All Expanded, or All Collapsed.
9. Click OK.

To remove all groupings from a folder view, open the Group By dialog box and click the Clear All button.

Sorting Views

Sometimes the easiest and quickest way to organize information is just by sorting. You can then scan down the list looking for items of interest and make some quick decisions, such as which contacts are taking up most of your time.

Outlook gives you two ways to sort folder items: using the mouse and using the Sort dialog box. You can sort by as many as four fields. Sorting can display items in the same order as grouping them, but sorting does not add group headings or labels to the list.

Sorting with the Mouse

Sorting with the mouse is quick and convenient, but you can use this method only in a view that has columns. You can sort items in either ascending or descending order.

- To sort items in ascending order, click the heading of the column you want to use to sort the items so it shows an upward-pointing triangle.
- To sort items in descending order, click the column heading again so it shows a downward-pointing triangle.
- To sort items by more than one sorting field, click the column headings in reverse order. Begin by clicking the heading of the last column you want to sort by, and end by clicking the heading of the first column you want to sort by. For example, if you want to sort tasks first by subject, then by priority, and then by the due date, click the Due Date heading, the Priority heading, and then the Subject heading.

Sorting with the Sort Dialog Box

The Sort dialog box provides more sorting options than you have available using the mouse, such as sorting on a field that is not visible in the current view of the folder. You also can use the Sort dialog box to sort in card and icon views, in addition to table views. To sort folder items using the Sort dialog box, follow these steps.

1. Open a folder and select table, card, or icon view.
2. Choose Current View on the View menu, and then choose Customize Current View from the View menu to display the View Summary dialog box.
3. Click the Sort button to display the Sort dialog box.

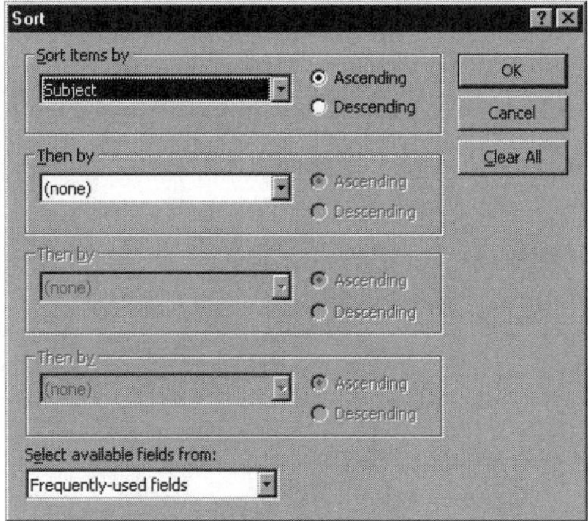

4. In the Select Available Fields From drop-down list at the bottom of the dialog box, select the field set containing the fields you want to use for sorting. If you sort by more than one field, you can select the fields from more than one field set.
5. Select the first sorting fields in the Sort Items By list, and choose either Ascending or Descending order.
6. Use the Then By list boxes to select a second, third, and fourth sort level and their sort order.
7. Click OK.

If you select a field for sorting that isn't displayed in the current folder view, Outlook asks whether you want to display that field. Click Yes to display the field for each item in the view. (If you are using a table view, for instance, this can be a handy way of adding a column to the view.) Click No to keep the current folder view, without displaying the additional field. Whichever choice you make, Outlook can sort items by the fields you choose, even if the fields are not visible.

If you select (None) as a sorting key in any box in the Sort dialog box, all the boxes below it automatically revert to (None), just as if you click the Clear All button in the Sort dialog box. The sort order will remain in the order you last set.

Filtering Items in Folders

If you have a great many items in a folder, sorting and grouping can help you organize them, but you still have to scroll down the list to locate items of interest. As an alternative, you can create a filter. A filter temporarily hides items you are not interested in seeing, making it easier to analyze information without interference from irrelevant items. When you remove the filter, you can see all the items again.

To set up and apply a filter for the current view, display the Filter dialog box using the following steps:

1. Open the folder.
2. Choose Current View on the View menu, and then choose Customize Current View from the View menu to display the View Summary dialog box shown in Figure 20-10.
3. Click the Filter button.

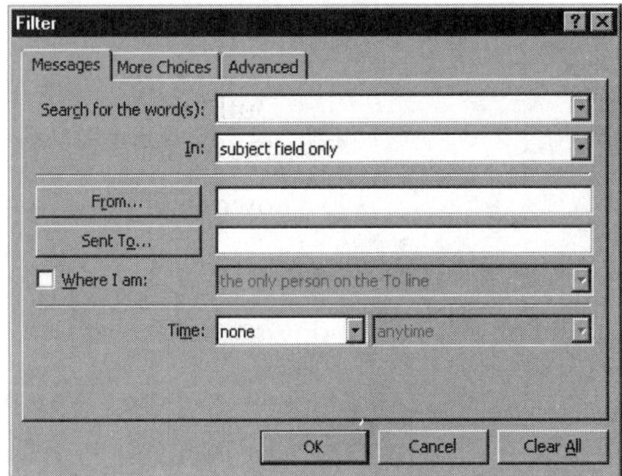

Figure 20-10
The Filter dialog box for the Inbox folder shows the Messages tab.

You can use all three of the tabs in this dialog box to set up criteria for a filter. For example, you could use the Filter dialog box to display only Inbox messages sent by Billy Joe pertaining to an excavation project using the following steps:

1. Open your Inbox folder.
2. Open the Filter dialog box.
3. On the Messages tab of the Filter dialog box, type the word *excavation* in the Search For The Word(s) text box.
4. Select Subject Field And Message Body from the In drop-down list.
5. In the From text box, type *Billy Joe*. You can select addresses from the Address Book by clicking either the From or the Sent To buttons.
6. Click OK to close the Filter dialog box.
7. Click OK again to close the View Summary dialog box and apply the filter.

Your Inbox folder now displays only messages sent by Billy Joe that contain the word *excavation* in either the subject line or in the body of the message. Notice that Outlook adds the words Filter Applied to the status bar (in the lower left corner of the folder window) and to the right of the folder window's title bar.

If you want to narrow your filter even further, you can set additional filter criteria on the Messages tab—specifying messages sent during a certain time range, for example—or on either the More Choices or Advanced tabs in the Filter dialog box. A folder item must meet all criteria specified on all tabs to appear in the filtered view of the folder.

Setting Other Filter Options

The first of the three tabs in the Filter dialog box varies according to the type of folder that is currently open. For instance, you'll see the Messages tab shown earlier in Figure 20-10 if you are setting up a filter for a folder that contains message items. If you open a different type of folder to set up a filter, Outlook changes not only the name of the first tab in the Filter dialog box, but also the options it contains.

The More Choices tab of the Filter dialog box, shown in Figure 20-11, is the same for most types of folders.

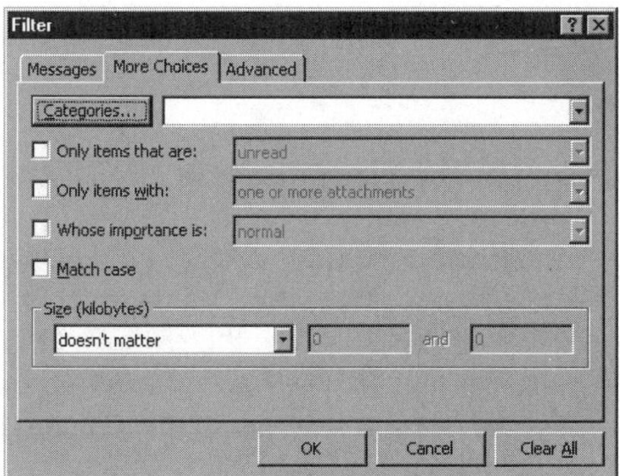

Figure 20-11
The More Choices tab of the Filter dialog box.

When you use categories as filter criteria, Outlook displays folder items that have been assigned to the categories you list. Type the category names, separated by a comma, or click the Categories button to select category names in the Categories dialog box. (If you want to specify categories you used in a previous filter, select them from the list where Outlook stores them.) Use the other options in the tab to:

- Select *Only Items That Are* Read or Unread.
- Select *Only Items With* One Or More Attachments or No Attachments.
- Select items *Whose Importance Is* High, Normal, or Low.

- Choose to *Match Case* of the characters you type in the Search For The Word(s) box on the first tab.
- Limit the *Size* to items size, in kilobytes, matches a specified size range.

If you need to refine the filter even further, use the Advanced tab, shown in Figure 20-12, to select a field and specify a condition and a value for the field.

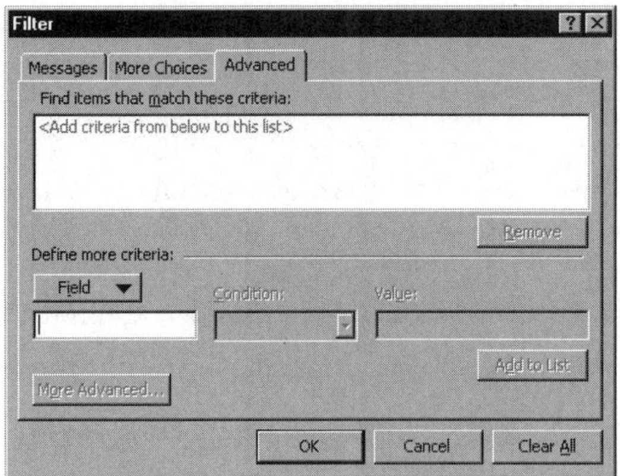

Figure 20-12
The Advanced tab of the Filter dialog box.

You can enter multiple values in the Value box. For text fields, use the word And or a blank space to filter items whose field contents match both values. For instance, to display messages that you've assigned to both the categories Key Customer and International, type *Key Customer and International* in the Value text box. To display messages that you've assigned to either category, use the word Or, a comma, or a semicolon instead of the word And. For date fields—used most often with the conditions On, On Or After, and On Or Before—you can use AutoDate to describe the value. For example, you can assign Birthday for the Field contents, On Or Before as the Condition, and you can type *two days* for the value. The Filter will show only those Contacts whose birthday is on or before today's date.

Turning Filters Off

To turn off a filter, take these steps:

1. Open the folder.
2. Choose Current View on the View menu, and then choose Customize Current View from the View menu to display the View Summary box.
3. Click the Filter button.
4. In the Filter dialog box, click the Clear All button.
5. Click OK in both dialog boxes to return to the unfiltered folder.

Setting Up Columns

Another way to organize information is to control what columns appear in table views. You can add or remove columns, and you can rearrange the order of the columns to suit your needs. You also can adjust the width of the columns to show more or less information or to display more columns without needing to scroll the window.

Adding Columns from the Field Chooser

The Field Chooser is a window, grouped by field sets, listing the fields you can add to a table view, as shown in Figure 20-13. When you use the Field Chooser, you first select the field set that contains the type of field you want to add, and then you drag the specific field to the table to the position where you want the column to appear. You can add fields from more than one set. After adding fields from one set, for example, just choose another field set and drag any fields from it to the table.

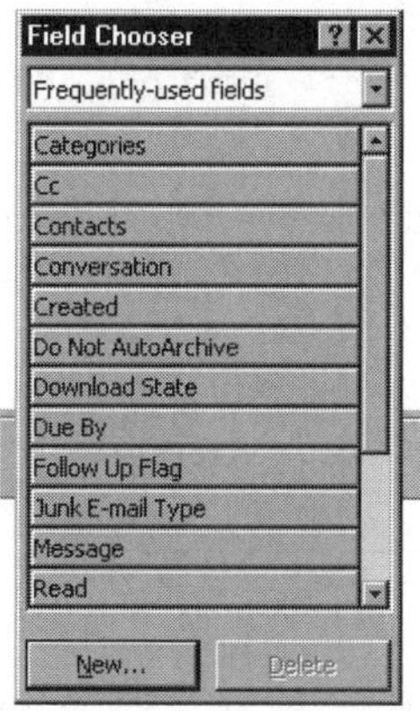

Figure 20-13
The Field Chooser window.

To add columns to a folder view using the Field Chooser, follow these steps:

1. Open a folder and select a view that has columns.
2. Right-click the column headings and choose Field Chooser from the shortcut menu.
3. Click the down arrow at the top of the Field Chooser window to see a list of field sets.
4. Select the field set containing the field you want to add. When you select a field set, Outlook displays the fields contained in the set in the lower portion of the window.
5. Drag the field name from the Field Chooser into the folder window and position it at the location in the column headings where you want it to appear.

(Outlook displays two red arrows to show you where the column will be inserted.) When you release the mouse button, Outlook adds the column to the folder view, with the field name as the new column heading. Outlook also removes the field name from the Field Chooser.

6. When you've added as many columns as you want, click the Close button in the upper-right corner of the Field Chooser window.

Removing Columns

If you no longer want a column to appear in a folder view, you can easily remove it from the screen without actually deleting the information contained in the column. You can later reinsert the column from the Field Chooser to display the information again. To delete a column, use either of the following two techniques:

- Drag the field name away from the column heading until you see a large black X appear over the field, and then release the mouse button.
- Right-click the column heading you want to remove, and then choose Remove This Column from the shortcut menu.

Note When you want to quickly move a column to a new position, just drag its column heading to the new location and release the mouse button. As you move the column heading between existing columns, you'll see two red arrows pointing to where the column will be inserted when you release the mouse button.

Using the Show Fields Dialog Box

The general way to add, remove, and rearrange a column is by using the Show Fields dialog box. Begin by opening a folder and selecting a view that has columns, and then follow these steps:

1. Choose Current View on the View menu, and then choose Customize Current View from the View menu to open the dialog box shown in Figure 20-14. You also can right-click the column heading and choose Customize Current View from the shortcut menu.
2. Click the Fields button to display the Show Fields dialog box shown in Figure 20-15.
3. To add a field, select the field set, choose the field in the Available Fields drop-down list, and click the Add button.
4. To remove a field, select it in the Show These Fields In This Order drop-down list, and then click Remove.

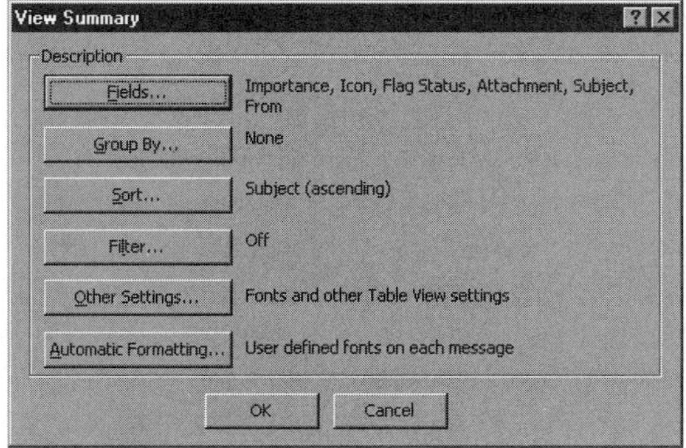

Figure 20-14
The View Summary dialog box.

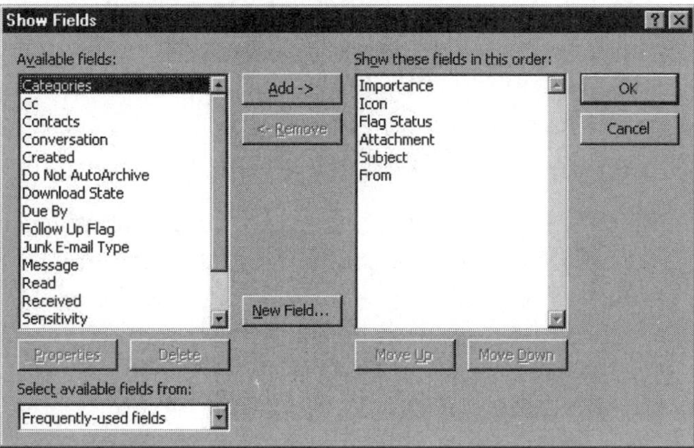

Figure 20-15
The Show Fields dialog box.

5. To change the position of a field, select it and then click the Move Up button to move the field to the left, or click the Move Down button to move the field to the right.

Working with Custom Fields

Outlook lets you create your own fields when you cannot find a built-in field that serves your needs. Use the field to display information, to perform calculations, or to group items in the folder.

Note You cannot create custom fields for timeline, day/week/month, note, or icon views.

When you create a custom field, it is only available to the folder in which you created it. The custom field name appears in the User-Defined Fields In Folder list in the Sort, Filter (Advanced Fields), and Group By dialog boxes. You can create three kinds of custom fields: simple, combination, and formula.

- Add a basic piece of information to folder items, such as a column in a table view or a row on a card view, using a simple field.
- Combine the values in existing fields so the information contained in the fields appears in a single column or a single row in a folder using a combination field.
- Perform calculations that involve information contained in other fields using a formula field.

Each new custom field must be based on a specific data type—that is, the field must be able to contain the appropriate kind of data: text, numbers, dates, or other data. The basic steps for creating all three types of custom fields are the same, although combination and formula fields involve a few additional steps.

Creating a Simple Custom Field

A simple custom field lets you insert one piece of information. For example, you might add a field called Evaluation Date in your Tasks folder, into which you can record the date you wrote and submit an evaluation of the completed project. You could then add this field to the Completed Tasks view. To create a simple custom field for a folder, use this procedure:

1. Open the folder for which you want to create a custom field.
2. Select a table view or a card view.
3. Choose Current View on the View menu, and then choose Customize Current View on the View menu to display the View Summary dialog box.
4. Click the Fields button.
5. In the Show Fields dialog box, click the New Field button to see this dialog box:

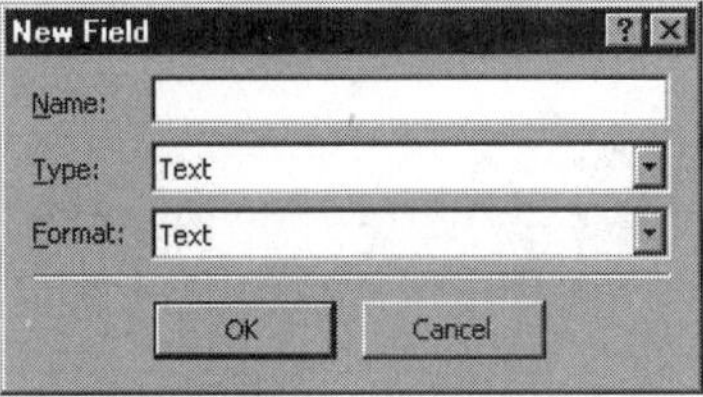

6. Type a name for the field.
7. Select the data type.
8. Select the format. (The options depend on the data type.)

9. Click OK.
10. In the Show Fields dialog box, you can click the Move Up button to change the position of the field.
11. Click OK in the Show Fields dialog box, and then click OK in the View Summary dialog box.

Tip In the Contacts folder, create a new field by opening the item, clicking the All Fields tab in the item's window, and then clicking the New button.

When you create a custom field, you select a data type in the Type box of the New Field dialog box. The data type determines the kind of information you'll be storing in the field. Your options are:

- Text
- Number
- Percent
- Currency
- Yes/No
- Date/Time
- Duration
- Keywords
- Combination
- Formula
- Integer

Chapter 20

For each data type except combination and formula, you also can choose a format in which the information will appear.

Creating a Combination Field

You might have a number of fields that you'd like to combine and display in one column or row. For example, you might create a column that combines the City, State, and Zip fields in an address list to save space. To create a combination field, follow these steps:

1. Open the New Field dialog box and enter a new field name.
2. Select Combination in the Type drop-down list.
3. Click Edit to see the dialog box shown in Figure 20-16.
4. Choose to join the fields together, or to show only the first field that has data and to ignore subsequent fields.
5. Click the Field button, and then choose the field set and field for the first field you want. Repeat for each field you want to combine.
6. In the Formula text box, you can add any additional text—such as a comma and a space between the City and State fields.

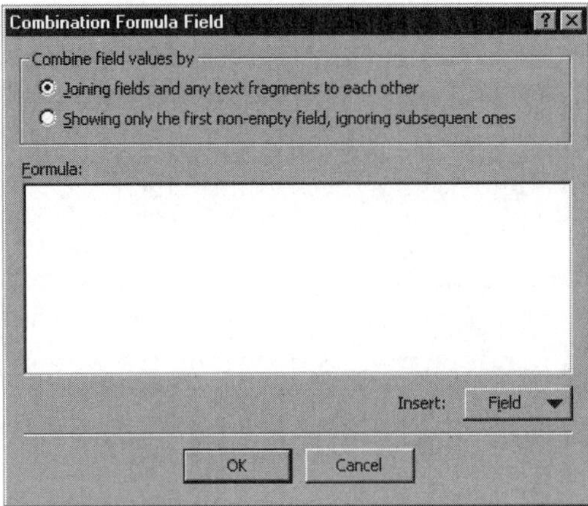

Figure 20-16
Creating a combination field.

7. Click OK in the Combination Formula Field dialog box and again in the New Field dialog box.
8. In the Show Fields dialog box, you can click Move Up to move your new field up the list if you want to adjust the position in which the field will be displayed in the folder window.
9. Click OK in the Show Fields dialog box.

To add or change the information in a combination field, you must add or change the information in the simple fields that make up the combination field. For example, if you create a combination field consisting of city and state names, you need to add or change the city name in the simple City field and the state name in the simple State field. You can't directly edit the information in a combination field.

Creating a Formula Field

You use a formula field to perform calculations that involve information from other fields. A formula field, for example, might show the number of days since each message was received. To create a formula field, follow these steps:

1. Open the New Field dialog box and type a new name.
2. Select Formula in the Type drop-down list.
3. Click Edit to open the Formula Field box shown in Figure 20-17. In this formula box, you insert the fields, functions, and operators needed to create the calculation.
4. To insert a function, choose a category in the Function drop-down list and then click the function. The function appears in the Formula box with the names of any arguments it requires.

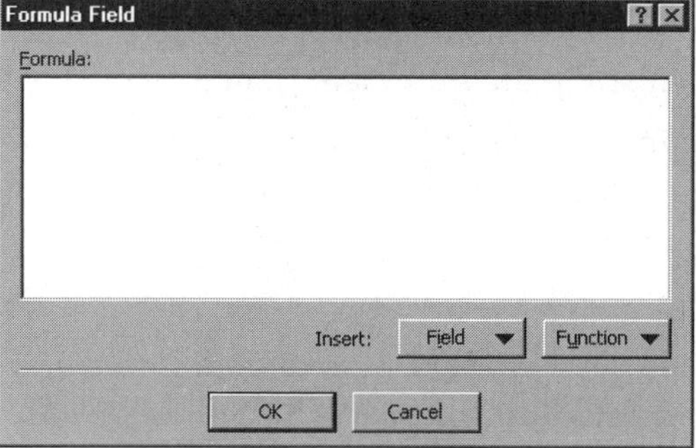

Figure 20-17
The Formula Field dialog box.

5. To insert a field, choose the field set and then click the field. To insert a field inside a function argument, select the function argument in the Formula box and then choose the field.
6. Type any operators or literal information—such as text and numbers—that are needed to complete the calculation.
7. Click OK in the Formula Field dialog box, and then click OK in the New Field dialog box.
8. In the Show Fields dialog box, click the Move Up button if you want to adjust the position of the field in the list.
9. Click OK in the Show Fields dialog box.

Chapter 20

Note You cannot sort, group, or filter the contents of a formula field.

If you need to add or change the information contained in a formula field, you must add or change the information in the simple fields that make up the formula; you can't directly edit the information in a formula field.

Changing a Custom Field

You can change a custom field only by changing the format or the formula. You can't change the field name or the data type. To change the format or formula for a custom field, use this procedure:

1. Choose Current View on the View menu, and then choose Customize Current View from the View menu to display the View Summary dialog box.
2. Click the Fields button.
3. If you're using the custom field, move it from the Show These Fields In This Order drop-down list to the Available Fields drop-down list. (Either double-click the field name, or select it and then click the Remove button.)

4. Select the field name in the Available Fields drop-down list, and then click the Properties button to display the Edit Field dialog box.
5. For a formula field, type a new formula in the Formula box. (You also can click the Edit button, change the formula in the Formula Field dialog box, and then click OK.)
6. Click OK.
7. If you want to use this newly edited custom field in the folder, add it back to the Show These Fields In This Order list. (Either double-click the field name, or select it and then click the Add button.)
8. Click OK in the Show Fields dialog box.

Creating and Changing Views

Now that you know ways to organize information, consider techniques for changing and creating views. You can create custom views to display information any way you like. When you create a new view, you give the view a name and you determine the fields, the sorting, the grouping, and the filtering you want to use. To create your own view, follow these steps:

1. Open the folder in which you want to define a new view.
2. Choose Current View on the View menu, and then choose Define Views on the View menu to open the Define Views For dialog box.
3. Click New to open the Create A New View dialog box shown here.

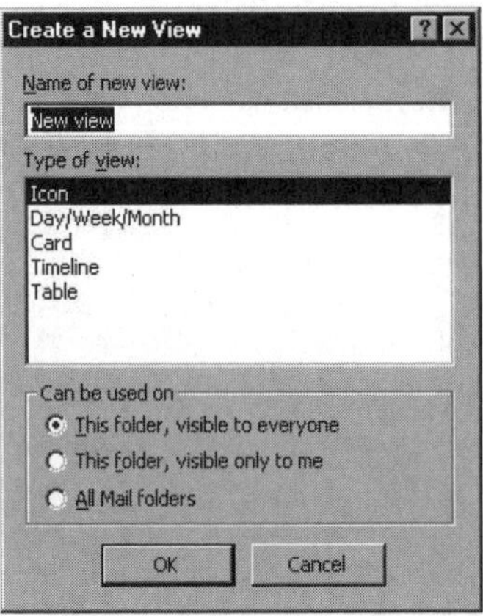

4. Type a name for the new view and then choose its type.
5. Choose an option in the Can Be Used On section to specify where the view can be used and who can use it.

- To make the view available only in the folder in which you created it, choose This Folder, Visible To Everyone. Anyone with permission to open the folder can choose to display the view from the Current View menu.
- To make the view available only in the folder in which you created it, choose This Folder, Visible Only To Me. This does not allow other people to use the view.
- To make the view available to all folders that are the same type as the folder in which you created the view, choose All [Folder Type] Folders. Anyone with permission to open a folder of this type can use this view to organize items in a similar folder.

6. Click OK. Depending on the type of view you've chosen, Outlook displays the View Settings dialog box or the View Summary dialog box, shown in Figure 20-18, which provides a complete description of the view as it currently exists.

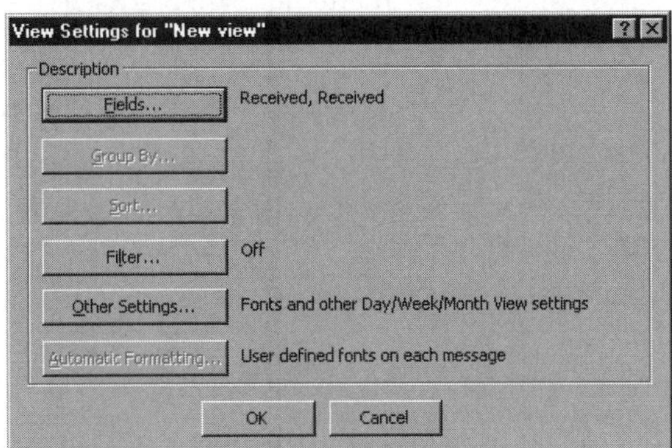

Figure 20-18
The View Summary dialog box.

7. Use the buttons in this dialog box to set up the elements of the new view. Some buttons might be unavailable, depending on the type of view you're defining.
8. When you've finished setting up the elements of the view and have closed the relevant dialog boxes, click OK in the View Summary dialog box to close it and return to the Define Views For dialog box.
9. If you want to apply the new view to the folder that is currently open, select the view from the list, and then click the Apply View button; otherwise, click the Close button.

Copying a View

Outlook also provides a shorter method for creating a new view. Instead of starting from scratch and defining every part of a new view, you can base a new view on the current arrangement of fields, filters, groups, and sort order. Open the folder in which you want to define a new view, choose Current View on the View menu, and then choose Define Views from the menu to open the Define Views For dialog box.

Select the view that you want to use as the basis for the new one, and then click Copy to display the Copy View dialog box. Type a name for the new view, choose a Can Be Used On option, and click OK. In the View Summary dialog box, use the available buttons to change any of the view settings as desired, and then click OK.

Modifying a View

If a view isn't quite right, you can modify it so that it better suits your needs. To modify either a view you created or one of Outlook's built-in views, follow these steps:

1. Open the folder that contains the view you want to change.
2. Choose Current View on the View menu, and then choose Define Views from the menu to open the Define Views For dialog box.
3. Select the name of the view you want to change.
4. Click the Modify button to open the View Summary dialog box.
5. In the View Summary dialog box, use the available buttons to modify the view as needed.
6. When you've finished modifying the view and have closed the relevant dialog boxes, click OK in the View Summary dialog box to close it and return to the Define Views For dialog box.
7. If you want to apply the modified view to the folder that is currently open, click the Apply View button in the Define Views For dialog box; otherwise, click the Close button.

Formatting Automatically

In addition to changing what appears in a view, you can change how the information is displayed. To customize the font, color, and lines in a view, for example, click the Other Settings button in the View Summary dialog box to see the available options for the view you're customizing.

In some folders, not every item is displayed the same way in the item list. In e-mail folders, for example, unread messages are shown in bold, expired messages are shown in strikeout, and scheduled mail is shown in italic. In the Tasks folder, overdue tasks are displayed in red and completed tasks are displayed in strikeout. Formatting items based on their condition or status is called *automatic formatting*, and it helps you visually distinguish items on the list.

You can modify the formats that Outlook applies to folder items, and you can create your own rules for identifying and formatting items. For example, you might want to display messages from a certain individual or regarding a specific topic in color to call your attention to them. To modify the way Outlook formats items, follow these steps:

1. Display the view that contains the type of items you want to automatically format.
2. Choose Current View on the View menu, and then choose Customize Current View from the View menu to open the View Summary dialog box.
3. Click the Automatic Formatting button to display the Automatic Formatting dialog box shown in Figure 20-19.

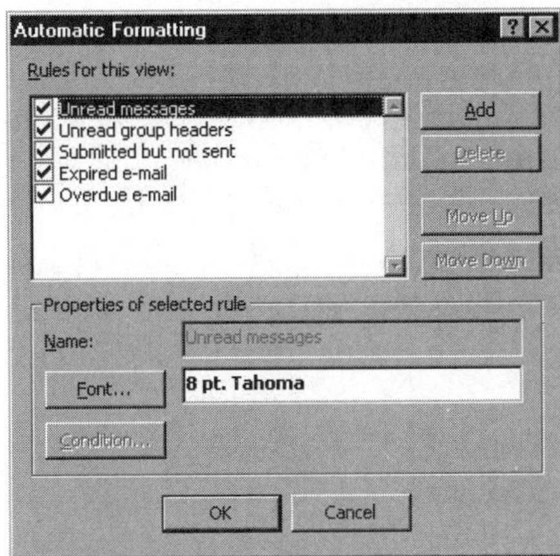

Figure 20-19
The Automatic Formatting dialog box.

4. Select the rule whose formatting you want to modify.
5. Click Font on the Font dialog box, choose the formats to apply to the item type, and then click OK twice.

To create your own rules for identifying and formatting an item, you have to establish the conditions that identify the item type. For example, a condition might be the name of the sender for an e-mail item or the subject of a task. You can then apply formats to items that meet those conditions. To create a new rule in the Automatic Formatting dialog box, use this procedure:

1. Click Add to create a new rule. Outlook activates the Name text box.
2. In the Name text box, enter an identifying name for the rule.
3. Click Font, choose the formats to apply to the items that meet the rule, and then click OK.
4. Click Condition to display the Filter dialog box, specify the conditions for the item, and then click OK to close all the open dialog boxes.

Keeping a Journal

Outlook's Journal folder is often overlooked, especially because it is located in the My Shortcuts group in Outlook 2000. That's a pity, because the Journal is a great help in keeping track of your activities and the documents you work on. Once you prepare the Journal by selecting the functions you want it to perform, the Journal can keep a record of all your Microsoft Office activities—e-mail messages, task and meeting requests and responses, and interactions with contacts. The Journal identifies each action and records the date and time you performed it. You also can set Outlook to record a journal entry each time you create, open, close, or save a file in an Office application.

Outlook can automatically record activities in the Journal, and you can manually add Journal entries yourself. Add your own entries, for example, for activities that you've already performed and for activities that Outlook cannot automatically record. You can even add entries that act as shortcuts to files on your hard disk or to files on another computer on your network so that you can open those files from your Journal folder.

The Journal folder displays a timeline showing each document you worked on and each call, meeting, or other Outlook activity for which you created a Journal entry, as shown in Figure 20-20.

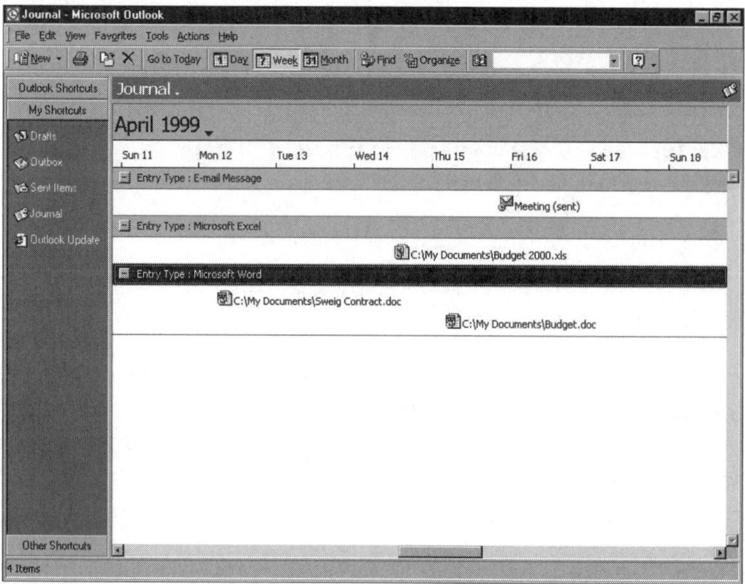

Figure 20-20
The Journal folder.

Preparing the Journal

Before using the Journal folder, you should do the following:

- Choose which Outlook activities are recorded.
- Choose the contacts for whom Outlook activities are recorded.
- Choose the Microsoft Office programs for which activities are recorded.

Here are the steps to prepare the Journal to automatically record your activities:

1. Choose Options on the Outlook Tools menu, click the Preferences tab, and then click Journal Options to open the dialog box shown in Figure 20-21.

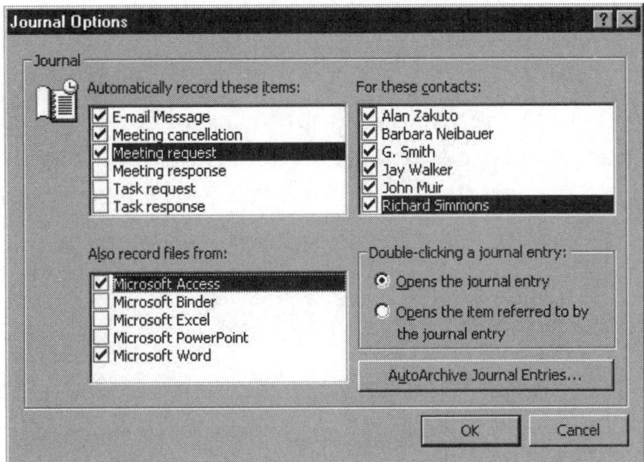

Figure 20-21
The Journal Options dialog box.

2. In the Automatically Record These Items list, select the check boxes for the Outlook activities you want to record.
3. In the For These Contacts list, select the check boxes for the contacts for which you want Outlook to record activities.
4. In the Also Record Files From list, clear the check boxes for the applications whose file activities you do not want Outlook to record.
5. In the Double-Clicking A Journal Entry section, select what should happen when you double-click a Journal entry.
6. Click OK.

Adding Entries to Your Journal

The Journal Options dialog box lets you record entries for Office and other application activities, e-mail messages, and task and meeting requests, and responses. To record Journal entries for other Outlook activities (such as appointments, notes, and phone calls), for Office files and documents that you haven't opened, or for files and documents you create with applications that are not a part of Office, you have to manually add the Journal entries. You also have to manually create Journal entries for contacts whose check boxes you did not select in the Journal Options dialog box.

To manually add a new Journal entry, you need to open the Journal folder and then open a new Journal entry window, like the one shown in Figure 20-22, using one of these techniques:

1. Choose New Journal Entry from the Actions menu.
2. Choose New on the File menu, and then choose Journal Entry from the menu.
3. Click the New Journal button on the Standard toolbar.
4. Press Ctrl+N.

If you want to include the time you are about to spend creating this entry as part of the time spent on the activity, click the Start Timer button. Complete the other information in the window and then click the Save And Close button.

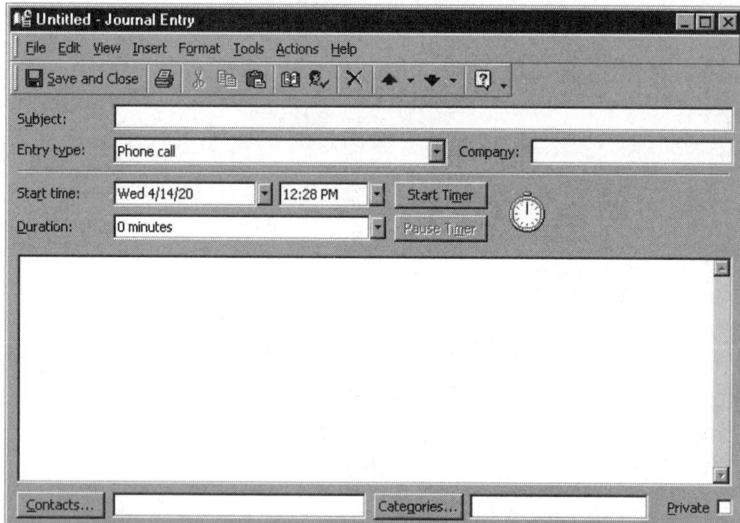

Figure 20-22
The Journal Entry window.

Using the Timer

A Journal entry's timer gives you a record of how much time you spend on activities such as completing a task, making a phone call, or meeting with a contact. To use the timer, simply open the Journal entry window and click the Start Timer button. As you work, leave the Journal entry window open. (Minimize the window if you need to see more of the screen.) You can pause the timer if a phone call or a visit that isn't related to the matter at hand interrupts you. When you finish the activity, click the Save And Close button in the Journal entry window. Outlook stops the timer for you.

Adding Existing Outlook Items to Your Journal

When you've worked on a task, held a meeting, or e-mailed a contact, for example, and you haven't recorded a Journal entry for the activity, you might want to add an entry afterward. Here's how to add a journal entry for an existing Outlook item:

1. Open the Outlook folder containing the item for which you want to add a Journal entry and select the item.
2. Drag the selected item and drop it onto the Journal folder icon on the Outlook Bar.
3. Outlook opens a Journal entry window for the item. You can add or change information for the entry as needed. Outlook sets the entry type based on the type of item you add. For example, if you add a contact to your Journal, Outlook sets the entry type to Phone Call. If necessary, you can select a more accurate description from the Entry Type list.
4. When you've made your adjustments to the Journal entry, click the Save And Close button.

Adding Existing Documents to Your Journal

You've probably already created documents and files in other applications that you might want to add to your Journal folder. Adding existing files and documents to your Journal allows you to organize a list of entries that all relate to a single project or task. Also, a Journal entry makes it possible for you to open the file or document from Outlook rather than searching with other tools—such as Windows Explorer or My Computer.

To create a Journal entry for an existing file or document created in another application, take these steps:

1. Click Other Shortcuts in the Outlook Bar.
2. Click My Computer in the Other Shortcuts group.
3. Open the folder containing the file or document you want to add as a Journal entry and select the file or document.
4. Click Outlook Shortcuts in the Outlook bar.
5. Drag the selected item and drop it onto the Journal folder icon on the Outlook Bar.
5. Outlook now opens a Journal entry window for the file or document. A shortcut icon for the file or document appears in the message area of the window,

and the name of the file or document appears in the Subject box. You can change the entry name or the entry type and add other information that you want to record with the Journal entry.

6. Click the Save And Close button.

Opening and Changing Journal Entries

To open a Journal entry to view or edit its details, perform one of the following actions in the Journal folder:

1. Right-click the entry, and then select Open from the shortcut menu.
2. Double-click the entry.
3. Select the entry and choose Open from the File menu.
4. Select the entry, and then press Ctrl+O.

You can review, add, or change information in the Journal entry. If you make additions or changes, be sure to click the Save And Close button when you want to close the window.

Creating Reports

Printing a copy of an item from a Microsoft Outlook folder is a simple matter. In fact, Outlook comes with a default print style for each Outlook folder and for each view of that folder. To print folder items using the standard print style, select the items that you want to print, and then click the Print button on the Standard toolbar.

If you're not pleased with the default print settings and style, however, you can change the settings to generate all types of reports.

Changing Printing Settings

To set basic print options, open the Print dialog box, shown in Figure 20-23, rather than printing the item immediately. To open the dialog box, use any of these techniques:

- Choose Print from the File menu.
- Choose Page Setup on the File menu, and then choose a style (or define a new style and then choose it). Then click the Print button in the Page Setup dialog box.
- Choose Print Preview from the File menu, and then click the Print button on the Print Preview toolbar.

Use this dialog box to set the following print options:

- **Printer Name** Select a different printer, if necessary.

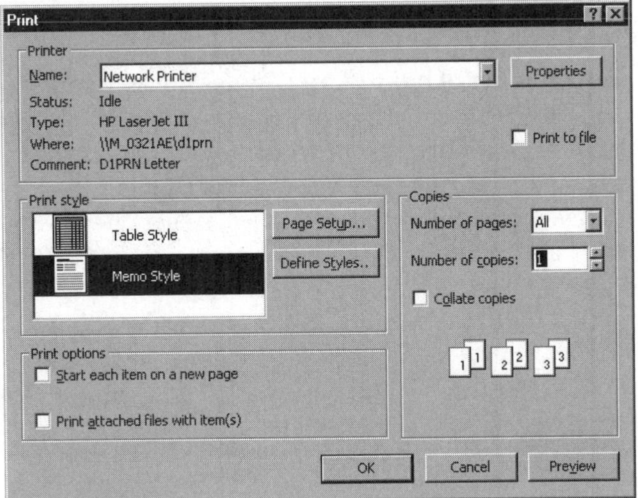

Figure 20-23
The Print dialog box.

- **Properties** Click this button to adjust the global settings for the selected printer driver for this and all other Windows-based applications, if necessary.
- **Print To File** Select this check box to send the job to a file instead of the printer. If you don't have the selected printer connected to your system, you can take the file to another computer and copy the file to the printer.
- **Print Style** Select one of the available print styles, or click Define Styles to create your own print style.
- **Number of Pages** Select which pages to print (All, Even, or Odd).
- **Number of Copies** Set the number of copies you want to print.
- **Collate Copies** Select this check box to print complete sets of the job if you are printing multiple copies of more than one page. If you clear this check box, printing might be faster, but all page 1's will print first, then your page 2's, and so forth. You will have to manually collate them into sets.
- **Print Options; Print Range** This section's name and contents vary with the type of items selected, such as whether to start each item on a new page, whether to print attachments, which items or rows to print, and which dates to include from the Calendar.
- **Preview** Click this button to see a preview of the printed page on your screen.

Choosing an Alternate Print Style

Outlook includes a number of built-in print styles for each folder. The styles determine what information prints and how it appears on the printed page. To select an alternate print style for a report, first open the folder that contains the folder items you want to print and choose the view by selecting Current View on the View menu and selecting the view from the submenu. Next, select one or more items that you want to print, and select Print from the File menu to open the Print dialog box. Select the print style you want to use and click OK.

Note As an alternative, you also can choose Page Setup on the File menu, choose the style from the submenu that appears, and then click Print in the Page Setup dialog box.

- The **Memo** style prints one or more selected folder items in a standard memo format. It is also the only built-in print style for individual items you open. For instance, a printout of an appointment on your calendar might look like this:

Subject:	Lunch with Mark
Start:	Thursday 3/18/99 12:30 PM
End:	Thursday 3/18/99 2:00 PM
Recurrence:	(none)

- The **Table** style prints either selected folder items or all items in the current view. The information appears in a table arrangement, with the items in rows with the same column headings that are shown in the current view.
- **Daily**, **Weekly**, and **Monthly** styles print a day, week, or month of calendar entries on one page.
- The **Tri-fold** style prints your daily calendar, weekly calendar, and TaskPad in three equal sections, using landscape orientation.
- The **Card** style prints either selected contact cards or all cards in the current view of your Contacts folder. Contact cards appear in alphabetical order, marked by letter tabs, from top to bottom on the page in two columns. Outlook prints two blank cards at the end.
- The **Small Booklet** and **Medium Booklet** styles are designed for contact cards in the Contacts folder. Small Booklet prints on both sides of a sheet of paper, with eight pages per sheet. Medium Booklet prints on both sides of a sheet of paper, with four pages per sheet.
- The **Phone Directory** style prints names and telephone numbers for all your contacts or for selected contacts. The list is in alphabetical order, marked by letter tabs. Other contact information is omitted.

- The **Calendar Details** style each day prints on a page, with all the information on each calendar item.

Setting the Print Range or Options

The settings below the Print Style section of the Print dialog box are labeled either Print Options or Print Range, based on the selected style. Table 20-1 lists the print styles and the options available for each style. When you print your calendar in the Daily, Weekly, Monthly, Tri-fold, or Calendar Details print styles, you also can choose not to print the details of private appointments.

Print Style	Print Range Options	Description
Memo	Start Each Item On A New Page	Select this check box to print each folder item on a separate page.
	Print Attached Files With Item(s)	Select this check box to print the contents of attachments with the text of each folder item.
Table	All Rows	Select this check box to print all items in a folder view.
	Only Selected Rows	Select this check box to print only the folder items you selected before opening the Print dialog box.
Daily, Weekly, Monthly, Tri-fold, Calendar Details	Start	Select or type the earliest date of the items you want to print.
	End	Select or type the latest date of the items you want to print.
	Hide Details Of Private Appointments	Select this check box if you don't want to print the details of any appointments marked as Private.
Phone Directory, Card, Small Booklet, Medium Booklet	All Items	Select this check box to print all items in a folder view.
	Only Selected Items	Select this check box to print only the folder items you selected before opening the Print dialog box.

Table 20-1
Print Range Options Available for Each Print Style.

Chapter 20

Printing and Assembling a Booklet

The booklet print styles are designed so that you can print pages on both sides of a sheet of paper and then cut and staple the pages to create a booklet. (In Outlook, paper refers to a physical sheet of paper. Page refers to the area of the paper that is actually printed.) The layout and page numbering for the booklet are arranged automatically by Outlook.

You can print a booklet on either a duplex printer (a printer that can print on both sides of the paper) or on a printer that prints on only one side of the paper at a time. When using a duplex printer, be sure it is set up for duplex printing. Click the Properties button in the Print dialog box to open the Properties dialog box for your duplex printer. Select the Flip option you prefer. (Note that None is the default and is for one-sided printing only.) If you are using a printer that prints on only one side of the paper at a time, print even-numbered pages first (by selecting Even in the Number Of Pages drop-down list in the Print dialog box). Then load the printed pages into the printer again so that their blank sides will be printed on, starting with the lowest-numbered page first (usually Page 2), and then select Odd to print the odd-numbered pages. Make sure you have additional blank sheets in the printer, in case there is an extra odd-numbered page at the end.

Before you start printing, click the Page Setup button, and then click the Paper tab when the Page Setup dialog box opens. Set Paper Type to the size of the paper in your printer, and then select the Page Size to the right. Page Size lets you print one page on each sheet of paper or two, four, or eight pages per sheet of paper if you select 1/2 Sheet Booklet, 1/4 Sheet Booklet, or 1/8 Sheet Booklet. You also can select the orientation of the pages. Click Print Preview to check your settings, and then click OK to start printing.

After the booklet's pages are printed, cut the paper into the number of sections you specified. For example, if you specified a 1/8 Sheet Booklet, cut the paper into four sections. Each section will show two pages (the odd-numbered page on the left or right side and the even-numbered page on the opposite side). Stack the sheets of paper in the order of the page numbering, and fold along a ruler or straight edge. You can then staple the sheets of paper together into a booklet.

Previewing Printing

Before you print an item or a view, you can preview it to see what it will look like on paper. Print Preview uses the settings for the currently selected print style in the Print and Page Setup dialog boxes.

To preview a selected item or a view before printing, take one of the following actions:

- Choose Print Preview from the File menu.
- Choose Page Setup on the File menu, choose the print style you want to preview, and then click the Preview button in the Page Setup dialog box.
- Choose Print from the File menu, and then click the Preview button in the Print dialog box.

Figure 20-24 shows a preview of a calendar printout.

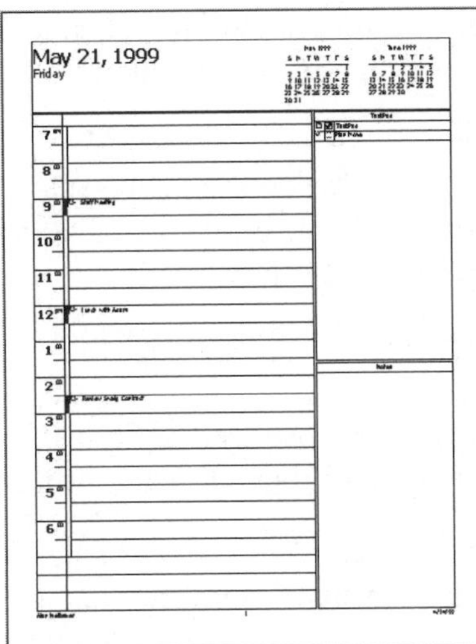

Figure 20-24
The Print Preview of a Calendar page.

Print Preview displays a full-page layout of the items to be printed, reducing the size of the folder item text to display an entire page, one screen at one time. It's an extremely useful feature when you want to check how the various print styles look on the page, how columns line up, whether the print style needs adjustment, and so on.

If you don't like what you see in Print Preview, you can click the Page Setup button on the Print Preview toolbar to open the Page Setup dialog box. You can then adjust the current print style as explained in "Modifying a Print Style" later in this chapter, returning to Print Preview whenever you want to check the results of your changes. Or, if you decide to try a different print style, you can click the Print button either on the Print Preview toolbar or in the Page Setup dialog box to open the Print dialog box and select a new style.

If you need to see the text in its actual size while you are in Print Preview, click anywhere on the page (the pointer will show a magnifying glass with a plus sign (+)). To switch the view back to full page, click again inside the page area (now the pointer shows a minus sign (-)). To see multiple pages, move the pointer outside the page area (another minus sign (-) appears), and click again. You also can switch between viewing sizes by using the Actual Size, One Page, and Multiple Pages toolbar buttons.

When you're ready to print, click the Print button on the Print Preview toolbar, and then click OK in the Print dialog box.

Modifying a Print Style

You can make a number of changes to a print style—including changes to its format, to its standard paper settings, and to the information included in headers or footers. To change the print style, you have to open the Page Setup dialog box. You can do this using any of the following techniques:

- Choose Page Setup on the File menu, and choose the print style you want to use from the menu. (The menu lists the available built-in styles, as well as any print styles you have created that apply to the view.)
- Choose Print on the File menu, choose the print style you want to change, and then click the Page Setup button.
- Choose Page Setup on the File menu, and choose Define Styles. In the dialog box, choose the style you want to change and then click the Edit button.

Now you can review and change any of the settings shown in the Page Setup dialog box (described in more detail in the next three sections) to customize the print style.

You also can use the Print Preview feature in this process. As you make your changes in the Page Setup dialog box, you can click the Print Preview button at any time to see how your adjustments affect the printed page. If you're dissatisfied with the results, click the Page Setup button on the Print Preview toolbar to return to the Page Setup dialog box so that you can continue refining the print style.

When you're satisfied with what you see in Print Preview (and if you don't want to change another print style), click the Close button on the Print Preview toolbar to return to Outlook, or click the Print button on the same toolbar to open the Print dialog box, where you can begin printing as soon as you click OK.

Changing Format Tab Settings

The Format tab on the Page Setup dialog box always provides a small preview picture of the print style. For all print styles, you can change the fonts used in headings and in the body of the folder items, and you have the option of printing with or without gray shading. Figure 20-25 shows the Format tab for the Table print style; the tab for the Memo style is very similar.

Formatting Tab Settings for Printing Calendars

The Format tab for the Calendar Details print style is similar to the tab shown in Figure 20-25, except it also contains these options:

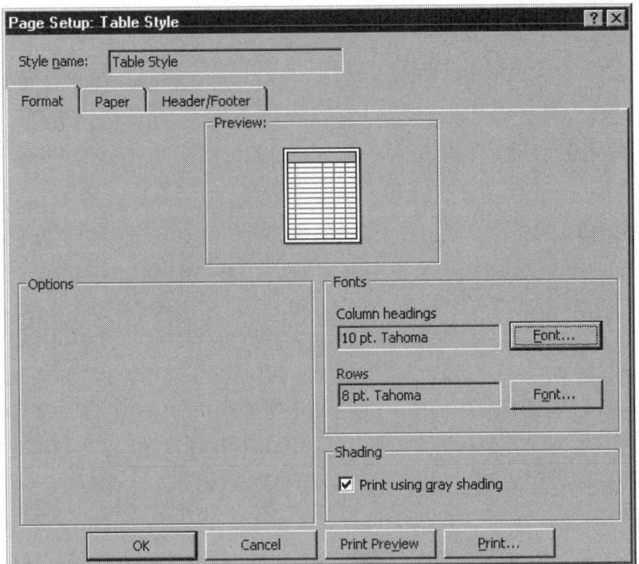

Figure 20-25
The Format tab for the Table print style.

- **Start A New Page Each** This option lets you choose to start a new page for each day, week, or month.
- **Print Attachments** This option lets you choose whether or not to print attachments with the calendar item.

You also can change the format of the Daily, Weekly, Monthly, and Tri-fold print styles that are used to print calendar items. Again, you can use different fonts for date headings and for appointments, and you can print with or without gray shading. The Options area gives you some additional layout choices, as shown here for the Daily print style:

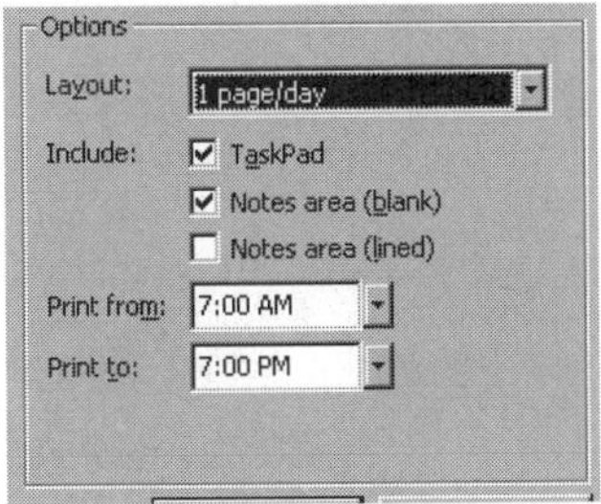

In the Layout box for the Daily print style, you can tell Outlook to print the day's calendar on two pages rather than one, giving you more room to write in information about your appointments and meetings. You can choose to include or omit the TaskPad (which is lined) and the Notes section (which is lined or unlined), and you can specify the range of time to be printed for the day (in the Print From and Print To boxes).

The Format tabs for the Weekly and Monthly print styles are similar to the Daily print style, with the following variations:

- The Format tab for the Weekly print style offers the same options you find for the Daily print style. (In this case, of course, you choose whether to use one or two pages to print a week rather than a day.) In addition, this tab contains two Arrange options: click Top To Bottom to have Outlook arrange the seven days down two columns on the page (omitting hour markers), or click Left To Right to have Outlook set up seven columns across the page, one for each day, including hour markers. (If you choose Top To Bottom, Outlook turns off the Print From and Print To boxes—there's no need to specify a range of hours when the hour markers are omitted.)
- The Format tab for the Monthly print style provides the Layout option, which prints a month on one page or two, and the Include options to print the TaskPad and the Notes section, but it omits the Arrange options and the Print From and Print To boxes. You also can choose not to print weekends and to print exactly one month on each page.

The Format tab for the Tri-fold print style is a little different. It contains only three options: Left Section, Middle Section, and Right Section. For each section (fold) of a tri-fold printing, you can specify one of the following items to print in that section:

- Daily calendar
- Weekly calendar
- Monthly calendar
- TaskPad
- Notes (blank)
- Notes (lined)

Formatting Tab Settings for Printing Contacts

The Format tabs for the Card, Small Booklet, and Medium Booklet print styles, used for printing contact items, are identical, and the Options area contains these choices:

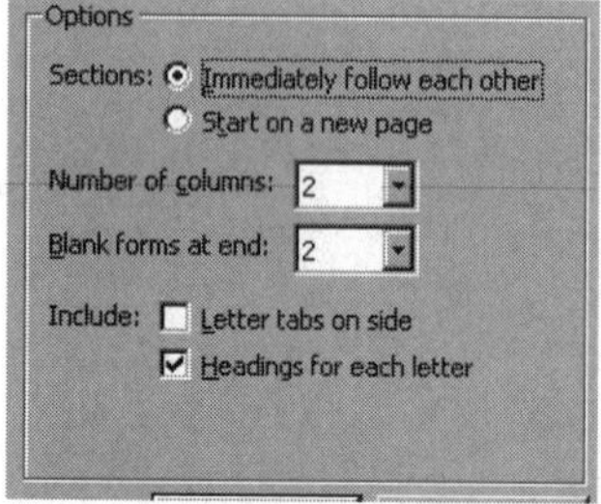

Sections refers to the alphabetical sections of your contact list. You can print alphabetical sections one after another in continuous columns, or you can begin the entries for each letter of the alphabet on a new page. You also can specify the number of columns per page, and you can tell Outlook to include blank contact cards (forms) at the end of the printing—these are useful when you're out of the office and need to hand-write contact information to be entered later into your contact list in Outlook. In addition, you can include or omit headings for each alphabetical section as well as letter tabs on the side of the page. When you include letter tabs, they appear on the right side of the page in a shaded column, as shown in Figure 20-26. Notice how the color of the tabs indicates which contacts are on each page so that you can use the tabs to quickly find the information you need.

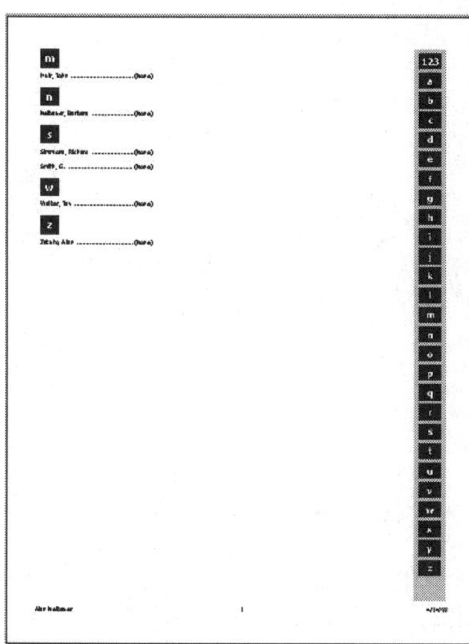

Figure 20-26
A page of contact information, previewed using the Card print style with letter tabs on the side.

Finally, the Format tab for the Phone Directory print style is fairly simple. You can specify the number of columns to print, and you can include or omit headings for each alphabetical section and letter tabs on the side of the page.

Changing Paper Tab Settings

The various print styles have their own paper settings—paper size (or type), page size, orientation, paper source (the tray or trays in your printer), and margins. You can adjust these settings on the Paper tab of the Page Setup dialog box, as shown in Figure 20-27.

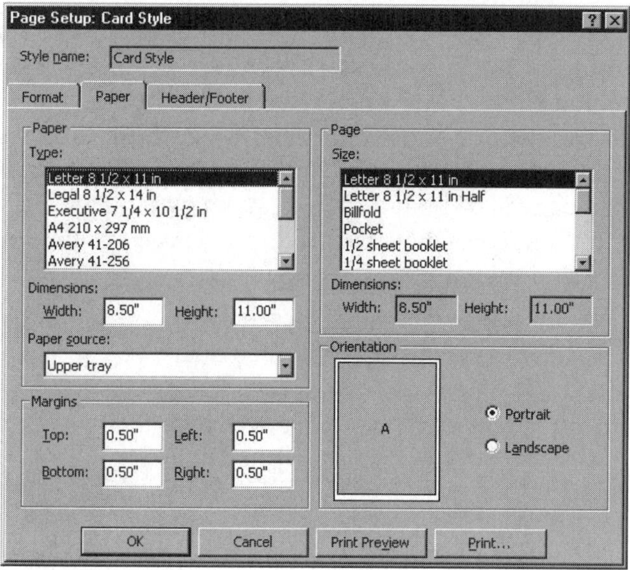

Figure 20-27
The Paper tab for the Memo print style.

Setting Paper Type and Page Size

The Paper tab displays the same information for all print styles. You can select a paper size or enter dimensions for a custom page, choose the appropriate paper feed, and set the page margins and the orientation. In the Size box of the Page section, you set the area each formatted Outlook page occupies on each sheet of paper. For example, you can choose to print your calendar on standard letter-sized paper but only in half-sheet booklet size.

When printing Outlook items and views, it's important to understand how Outlook distinguishes between paper and page. In Outlook, paper and paper type refer to the physical sheet of paper you put in the printer. Page refers to the area of that sheet of paper that each formatted Outlook page will be printed on. You can print several of these pages on a single sheet of paper. For example, in the Small Booklet print style, you can select 1/8 Sheet Booklet and print eight pages of a booklet on a single sheet of paper.

Each print style starts with a default paper type and page size, which you can modify. When you select a paper type, the list of page sizes available for use with that paper type is displayed in the Page Size list. Settings for paper type and page size in the Page Setup dialog box take precedence over any paper settings you select in the Properties dialog box for your printer (which you open by clicking the Properties button in the Print dialog box). Settings you make in the Orientation area of the Paper tab apply to pages, not to paper type.

Let's say you want to use the Daily print style to print four days worth of calendar items. By default, Outlook prints the items for each day on a separate sheet of 8½-x-11 inch paper. If you want to have all four days appear on one sheet of paper, select Pocket from the Size list on the Paper tab, or select the Half setting to print two pages on one sheet of paper.

Setting a Custom Paper Size

You can set up any custom paper size you want. To specify a custom paper size, simply select Custom in the Paper Type drop-down list, and then set the width and height of the paper in the Dimensions boxes in the Paper Type section.

Note If you change the width or height of a listed paper type in the Dimensions boxes, Outlook automatically selects Custom in the Paper Type list.

When you set up a custom paper size, the Page Size list includes the appropriate page size choices for that paper size. Outlook also adds Custom and Custom Half as the first two items in the Page Size list.

Setting Margins

When you change the margin settings, you're changing the width and height of the blank space at the borders of the page. Keep margins small unless you like lots of blank space around the printed information. The larger the margins, the more cramped the information appears because it must fit into a smaller space. You'll often need to print on more sheets of paper if you use large margins.

Outlook's default margins are .50 inch for the top, bottom, left, and right borders of the page. You can click the Print Preview button in the Page Setup dialog box to see the effect of changes you make to the margins.

Changing Header/Footer Settings

The process of setting up headers and footers is the same for all print styles. The Header/Footer tab of the Page Setup dialog box provides six boxes in which you can insert the text and fields that you want Outlook to print in headers and footers, as shown in Figure 20-28. For some print styles, Outlook presets parts of the header or footer, but you can change any section of the header or footer, as you like. The toolbar below the footer area lets you insert the page number, total number of pages, the date printed, the time printed, and the user name.

You can use text only, fields only, or a combination of text and fields in your headers and footers. Placing information in the left, center, and right boxes of the Header and Footer sections controls how the information is displayed on the printed page—if you enter text only in the center header box, for instance, Outlook prints a centered

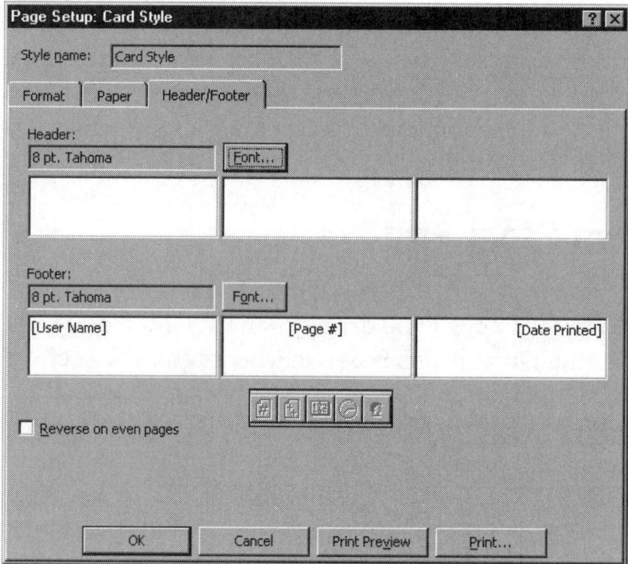

Figure 20-28
The Header/Footer tab of the Page Setup dialog box.

header on each page. Text entered in the left boxes is aligned on the left margin of each page, and text in the right boxes is aligned on the right margin. For the footer setup in Figure 20-28, Outlook will print the user's name on the left, the page number in the center, and the date of printing on the right.

Note The term *field* refers to a location that shows data or to an empty box that you (or Outlook) can fill in with information.

To insert a field into a header or footer, click in the boxes where you want to insert a field, and then click one of the field buttons on the Header/Footer tab.

Outlook displays an inserted field as words inside square brackets: [Page #], for example. (You can type the field in the header or footer box instead of clicking a button if you type it in this format.) During printing, Outlook replaces the field with the proper information—the page number, the date of printing, and so on.

You can type any text in any of the header and footer areas. The text might be some special information about the printed items, such as the date range of appointments, meetings, or tasks. You might want to type the word *Page* before the Page Number field. Or you might type the word *of* between a Page Number field and a Total Pages field and then type the word *pages* after the Total Pages field—this way, on each page Outlook prints a header or footer such as five of 10 pages.

If you want the same headers and footers to print on every page, leave the Reverse On Even Pages check box cleared. But if you're printing on both sides of the paper or if you're going to photocopy single-sided printed pages back-to-back to assemble a booklet, you might have Outlook always print the text in the leftmost box of the header or footer on the inside edge of all pages, and the text in the right box on the outside edge of all pages. This would, for instance, allow page numbers in the right box to appear on the outside edge of each of two facing pages (both odd and even pages), as you might see in a book. To do this, select the Reverse On Even Pages check box.

Resetting a Print Style

After you make changes to a built-in print style, you might want to restore the original settings. To reset a built-in print style, take these steps:

1. Choose Page Setup on the File menu, and choose Define Print Styles from the menu to open the dialog box shown in Figure 20-29.

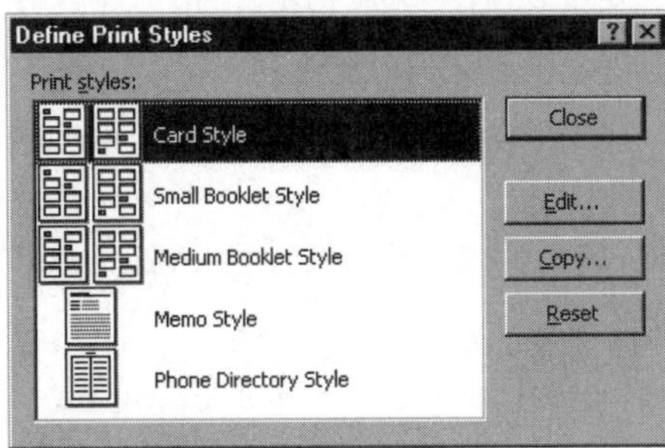

Figure 20-29
The Define Print Styles dialog box.

2. Select the print style you want to reset.
3. Click Reset.
4. When Outlook asks you to confirm resetting the print style, click OK.
5. Repeat steps 2 through 4 for each built-in style you want to reset.
6. When you've finished, click the Close button in the Define Print Styles dialog box.

Note You can't reset a print style that you have created. You can only modify it or delete it.

Creating a Print Style

What if you want to modify a print style but only want it to apply to certain print jobs? Rather than changing a built-in print style, which will affect the printing of all folder items for which you use the style, you can create a print style of your own.

Start by first making a copy of a built-in print style (or a copy of a print style you've already created). This method gives you several advantages. First, you start from an existing batch of settings, which means that you need to modify only the specific settings that you want to change, rather than having to set all the options yourself. Second, in any instance in which the print style you copied applies, your custom style also appears on the Page Setup menu (after you exit and restart Outlook) and in the Print dialog box for easy selection. You don't have to recreate your special print style for every view or folder.

Here's how to create a print style:

1. Choose Page Setup on the File menu, and choose Define Print Styles from the menu to see the Define Print Styles dialog box. As an alternative, you can choose Print from the File menu, select the print style in the Print Style list, and then click the Define Styles button.
2. In the Define Print Styles dialog box, select the print style you want to copy.
3. Click Copy to see the Page Setup dialog box.
4. In the Style Name text box, type a name for your custom style to replace the Copy Of text.
5. Change any settings on the three tabs in the Page Setup dialog box.
6. Click OK in the Page Setup dialog box.
7. Click the Close button in the Define Print Styles dialog box.

Tip

You also can use the Print Preview feature in this process. As you make your changes (step 5), you can click the Print Preview button at any time to see how your style will appear on the printed page. If you're dissatisfied with the results, click the Page Setup button on the Print Preview toolbar to return to the Page Setup dialog box and continue creating the print style.

Deleting a Print Style

If you no longer want or need a print style that you created, you can delete it. To do so, take these steps:

1. Choose Page Setup on the File menu, and choose Define Print Styles from the menu. As an alternative, you can choose Print from the File menu, select the print style in the Print Style list, and then click the Define Styles button.
2. In the Define Print Styles dialog box, select the print style you want to delete, and then click the Delete button.

3. When Outlook asks you to confirm that you want to delete the print style, click OK. Repeat steps 2 and 3 for each custom style that you want to delete.
4. When you have finished, click the Close button in the Define Print Styles dialog box.

By taking advantage of Outlook's extensive printing features, you can format and organize the information you usually access on screen to produce an attractive printed form suitable for traveling, sharing, or producing reports. Your printouts also can serve as a backup reference in case you delete an item by mistake. For even better insurance against losing important information, however, you can archive Outlook data for safekeeping, as you will learn how to do in the next chapter.

Chapter 21

Communicate Smoothly with E-Mail

by Alan Neibauer

In This Chapter

Microsoft Outlook is all about communicating with other people through e-mail and fax, and about keeping you and others informed about appointments, meetings, and tasks. E-mail and fax are quickly becoming the methods of choice for many individuals and businesses because of their convenience and speed. E-mail is immediate—for example, popping up in the recipient's inbox—without the delay of sealing, stamping, and mailing. In this chapter, you'll learn how to deal with some of the more sophisticated issues of communicating with Outlook via e-mail and fax. You'll also learn how to back up your Outlook information, to keep your e-mail and addresses safe and sound.

Selecting the E-Mail Service Option

Outlook can be used as an e-mail client with Microsoft Windows 2000/Windows NT and Microsoft Exchange Server, on a peer-to-peer network using Microsoft Windows 95/98, and with Internet E-mail through a dial-up account or a network connection. The first time you start Outlook after you install it, you will have the chance to select the type of service. Here are some available options.

- Corporate/Workgroup
- Internet Only
- No E-Mail

Generally, it is best to select the Corporate/Workgroup option if you intend to connect to a network—any type of network—at any time, even if you use a laptop computer and only occasionally connect to the office network. The Corporate/Workgroup version allows you to send and receive e-mail through your network, as well as through the Internet, so you won't be missing anything. Choose the Internet Only option if you will never be connecting to a network.

If you choose the Corporate/Workgroup option, you'll then be taken through the Inbox Setup Wizard where you specify the services you'll be using. You will learn how to set up services in a personalized profile later in this chapter.

Don't worry if you make the wrong choice of services; you can always change your e-mail service option at any time. Just have your Microsoft Office 2000 or Microsoft Outlook 2000 CD-ROM handy, and follow these steps:

1. Start Outlook.
2. Select Options from the Tools menu, and click the Mail Services tab.
3. Click the Reconfigure Mail Support button, choose the support option, and click OK.
4. If a message appears with information about the change, read it and then click Yes.
5. Insert your Outlook 2000 or Office 2000 CD-ROM in your computer to complete your changes, and then exit and restart Outlook.

Note Every person who uses Outlook on your machine must use the same service option, even if each has an individual user profile established.

Outlook will retrieve the necessary files from your hard disk or CD-ROM to change the service options. Changing service options does more than switch the way e-mail is sent, so you should be aware of the consequences. For example, Outlook supports two fax types—Microsoft Fax using the Corporate/Workgroup setup and Symantec Fax Starter Edition for the Internet Only setup. When you switch options, the previously installed fax service is disabled as an Outlook service, although its drivers remain on your system.

The most significant effects of changing services, however, involve your Outlook folders, such as the Inbox containing mail you have received, along with your calendar of meetings and appointments. If you switch from Corporate/Workgroup mode to Internet Only mode, any Internet e-mail accounts that were set up in your profile will be transferred to your Internet Only setup automatically, along with your personal address book and personal folders. If your messages are stored on an Exchange Server network, they will no longer be available when you switch to Internet Only mode. To access your network files, you must use Offline folders that you can access when you are not connected to the network, and then synchronize the files before switching to Internet Only mode. When you switch back to Corporate/Workgroup later, the Exchange Server service will no longer be in the default profile; you'll have to add the service to the profile again and restart Outlook.

Setting Dialing Options

Before you dial up any Internet service provider (ISP) or fax number using your computer, you should make sure your telephony options are set correctly. You will also have to select the location when creating a dialup networking account.

To access these settings, double-click the Telephony icon in the Windows Control Panel to see the Dialing Properties dialog box shown in Figure 21-1. The figure shows the dialog box for Windows 98 (the box in Windows 95 is slightly different, but with the same basic options). The dialog box lets you set up the locations from which you make calls for either e-mail or faxes.

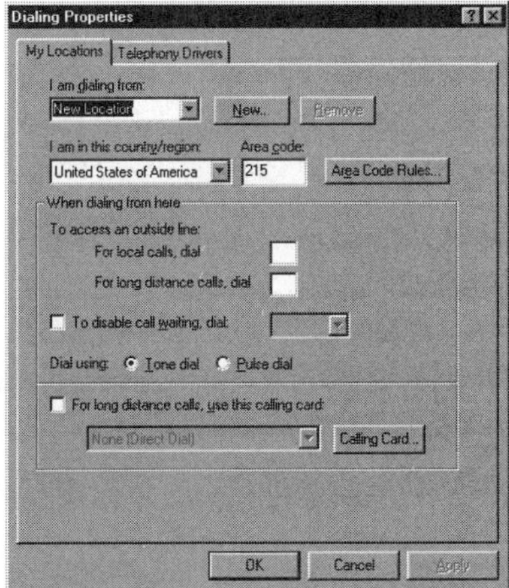

Figure 21-1
Setting telephone options.

If you are using a desktop computer, you'll be dialing from only one location. However, if you are using a laptop computer, you may be dialing from multiple locations. Location specifies the area code and country for the dialing location, accessing an outside line, the type of dialing, and calling card information. You can then quickly change locations when you move your laptop.

To create a new location, click the New button and then click OK to the message that appears. The notation New Location appears in the I Am Dialing From drop-down list. Select and edit the name to reflect your location, such as From Home or At The Field Office.

For each location, indicate the area code and country, along with the numbers to dial to access an outside or long distance line. If the location has call waiting, enable the To Disable Call Waiting check box, and then type the numbers to dial in the text box or select from frequently used choices.

In some locations, there are local numbers for which you still have to dial the prefix 1, or 1 plus the area code. If you are calling any such numbers—or you want to turn on 10-digit dialing for all your calls—click the Area Code Rules button to open the dialog box shown here:

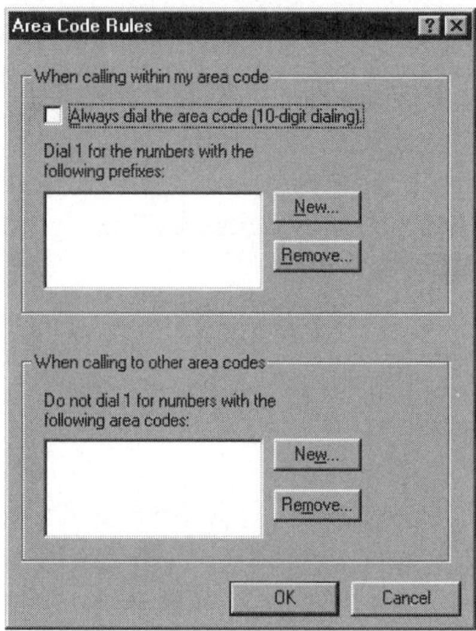

If you must use all ten digits for calls in your local area, enable the check box labeled Always Dial The Area Code (10-Digit Dialing).

You also can indicate which telephone number prefixes in your area code require you to dial 1 before the number. Click the New button in the top of the dialog box, type the prefix in the box that appears, and then click OK. Use the lower section of the dialog box to indicate any area codes for which you do not have to dial 1.

Setting Up Calling Card Dialing

If you use a calling card for long distance numbers, you should specify the card type for each location. In the Dialing Properties dialog box, enable the check box labeled For Long Distance Calls, Use This Calling Card, and then select your card type from the list. You need to indicate the access number to dial to use the card next, if any, along with your PIN number. Click the Calling Card button to open the Calling Card dialog box shown in Figure 21-2.

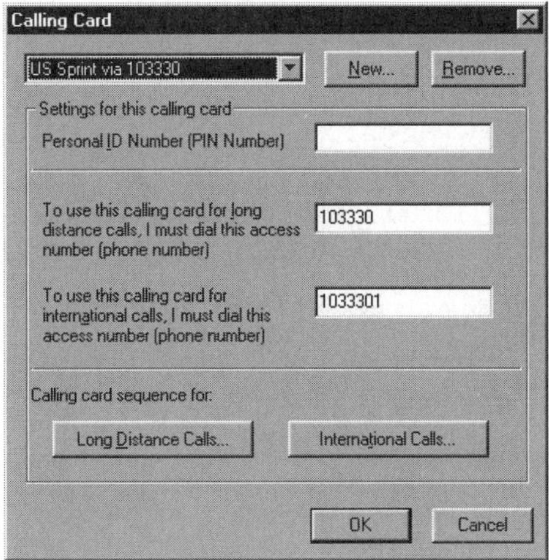

Figure 21-2
Setting up a calling card.

Click the arrow on the drop-down list at the top and select your card. If it is not listed, click New, type the card name, and click OK. Next, type your PIN number in the Personal ID Number text box, and type the proper access numbers for long distance and international calls, if they are not already shown.

Some calling cards require a special series of steps to make a connection. After dialing the calling card number, for example, you might have to wait until a tone sounds or until a certain number of seconds pass to dial the destination number or PIN number. These steps should already be defined for your card, but you can check them by clicking the Long Distance Calls and International Calls buttons. The Calling Card Sequence dialog box that appears for Long Distance Calls, for example, is shown in Figure 21-3. If you have to change the settings, choose an option from the list box, and then pull down the Then Wait For list and choose either the tone or the number of seconds you want to wait before the next step is executed.

When you have finished setting up your calling card and the dialing properties, click OK to close each of the open dialog boxes.

E-Mail for Corporate/Workgroup Users

Before you can use Outlook to send and receive e-mail or faxes, you have to set it up for your mail service. If you are using Outlook on a network, you create a *profile*—a collection of settings that tell how you want to use Outlook to communicate. If you are not on a network, and you are using the Internet Only installation, you have to set up one or more Internet e-mail accounts—you don't have to worry about profiles.

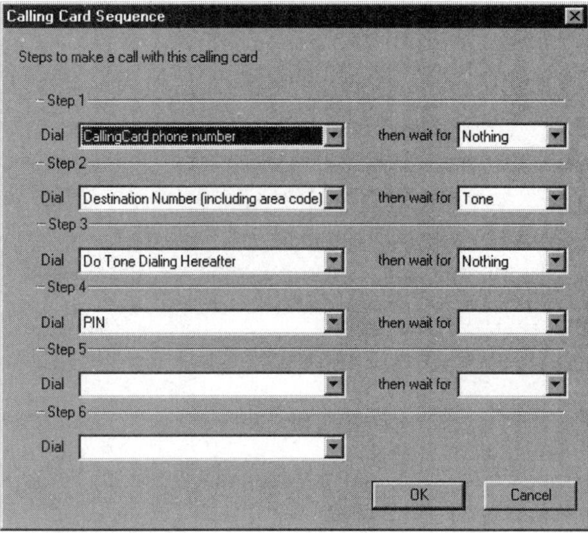

Figure 21-3
Defining Dialing Rules.

Establishing Your Profile

You can use a single profile to send and receive mail through your Exchange Server network, through a Windows-based peer-to-peer network, and through your Internet service provider. You also can establish multiple profiles, such as one to use when you are connected to the network and one to use when you're on the road with your laptop.

If you are connected to a network and are having any problems starting Outlook or sending and receiving mail, there is probably something wrong with your profile. To take a look at your profile and troubleshoot any problems you may be having, start with these steps:

1. Click Start on the Windows taskbar, point to Settings, and click Control Panel.
2. Open the Mail icon in the Control Panel. The Microsoft Outlook Internet Settings Properties dialog box appears, listing the services in the default profile, as shown in the following illustration.
3. Follow the instructions to set up and check your profile.

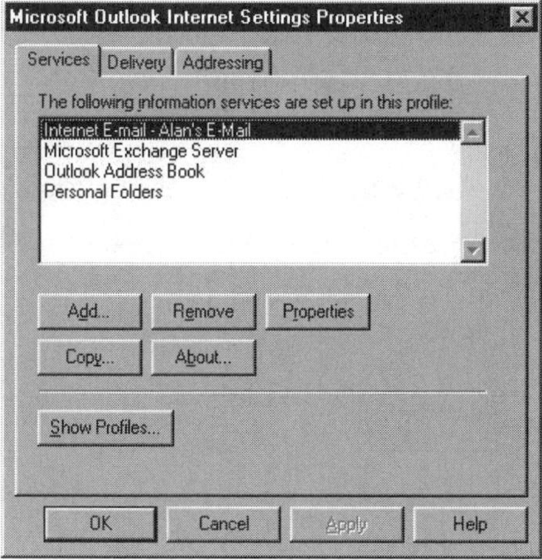

Setting Up for Microsoft Exchange Server

If you connect to a Windows NT server, your profile has probably been set up for you to communicate through Microsoft Exchange Server. Select Microsoft Exchange Server from the list, and click the Properties button to see the Microsoft Exchange Server dialog box shown in Figure 21-4. Click the Check Name button if you want Windows to confirm you've used the correct mailbox name. You also can choose to connect to the Exchange Server automatically or when prompted, and you can define the number of seconds to wait for connection.

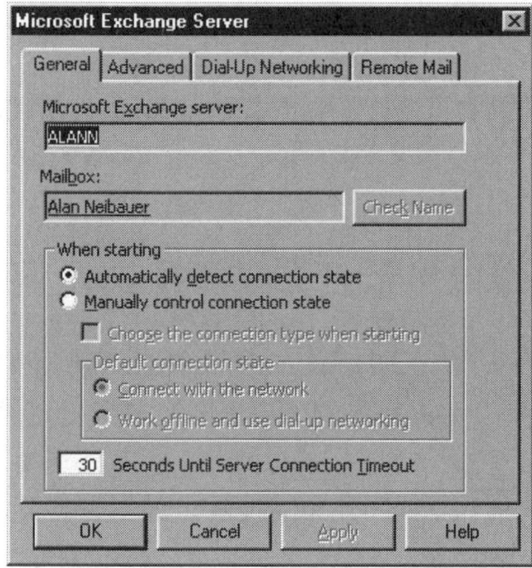

Figure 21-4
The Exchange Server properties dialog box.

If Exchange Server is not listed in the Microsoft Outlook Internet Settings Properties box, then you need to set it up before you can connect to and communicate over the network.

1. Click the Add button to open the Add Service To Profile dialog box.
2. Click Microsoft Exchange Server, and then click OK to open the Microsoft Exchange Server dialog box.
3. Enter the name of your server. If the mailbox name is not correct, change it.
4. Click the Check Name button to confirm the mailbox.
5. Click OK.

Setting Up Personal Folders

When you are using Microsoft Exchange Server, you can choose to have your files stored on the server or on your own disk. This is called the *delivery point.* To store your Outlook data on your own disk, however, you need to have Personal Folders as part of your profile and select them as the delivery point.

First, check to see if the Personal Folders service already exists. Open the Properties box for the profile and see if Personal Folders is included in the list of services. If not, follow these steps to create personal folders.

1. On the Services tab of the Properties dialog box for the profile, click the Add button to display the Add Service To Profile dialog box.
2. Select Personal Folders and click OK.
3. In the dialog box that appears, select the location for the new folder. If you already have personal folders on your disk and want to use them for this profile, enter the path and name, or select it using the Browse button.
4. In the File Name box, type the name for the new folder, or select an existing file.
5. Click the Open button to display the Create Microsoft Personal Folders dialog box shown in Figure 21-5.
6. Type a name for your personal folders in the Name text box as you want it to appear in Outlook.
7. Choose an encryption setting. Encryption and a password are only needed if you share your computer with others, or if you want to ensure that no other network users can access your files.
8. Type an optional password. Type the same password again for verification.
9. Enable the Save This Password In Your Password List check box if you don't want to be prompted for the password when you use the folder, and click OK.

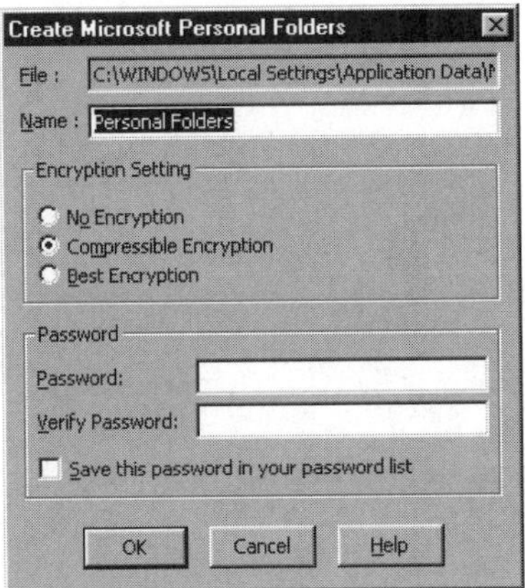

Figure 21-5
The Create Microsoft Personal Folders dialog box.

Setting the Delivery Point

You now have to choose where you want your messages and other Outlook data to be stored—in your network mailbox or in your personal folders.

Some network gurus suggest always using your network mailbox. They feel this provides some degree of security and that the server should have enough storage to handle even the largest inbox. If you are usually connected to the network, then using your server mailbox is not a bad idea. You should also create a set of offline folders so you can still access your Outlook data when the network is down. We'll cover offline folders later.

If you are mobile user with a laptop computer, if your server is frequently down, or if you connect to both an Exchange Server and a peer-to-peer network at different times, you should use Personal Folders as the delivery point. This ensures that you always have the most current data available when you start Outlook.

1. To set the delivery point, click the Delivery tab on the Microsoft Outlook Internet Settings Properties dialog box for your profile, as shown in Figure 21-6.
2. Choose a delivery point from the Deliver New Mail To The Following Location drop-down list:
   - Select the item labeled Mailbox followed by your mailbox name if you want all your incoming mail and other Outlook information to be stored in folders on the server.
   - Choose Personal Folders from the Deliver New Mail To The Following Location list if you want to store your Outlook data on your own disk.
3. Click OK.
4. If Outlook is running, exit and restart the program.

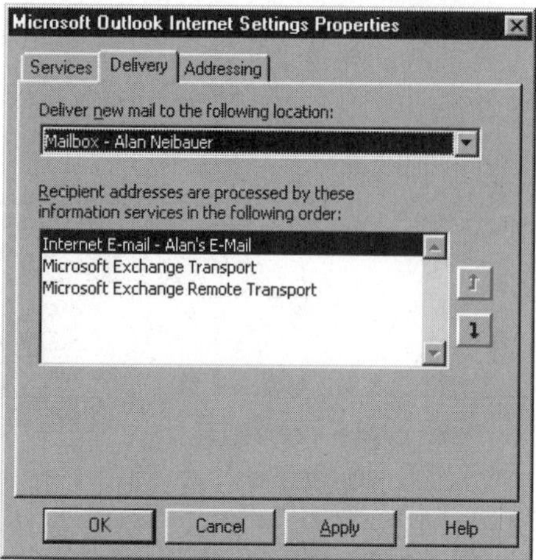

Figure 21-6
Setting the delivery point.

Note

If you want to share personal folders on more than one machine, see "Sharing Personal Folders," later in this chapter.

Changing Delivery Points

Setting up a delivery point does not mean that you are locked into it forever. You can always change delivery points if you want, but it should be done with caution. First, let's recap how to change delivery points from within Outlook.

1. Choose Services from the Tools menu from within Outlook, or double-click the Mail icon in Windows Control Panel.
2. Click the Delivery tab on the Properties dialog box.
3. Select the Deliver New Mail To The Following Location drop-down list, and choose the delivery point from the list.
4. Click OK.

The next time you start Outlook, you'll get a message reporting that your delivery point has changed. Click OK to accept the change and start Outlook.

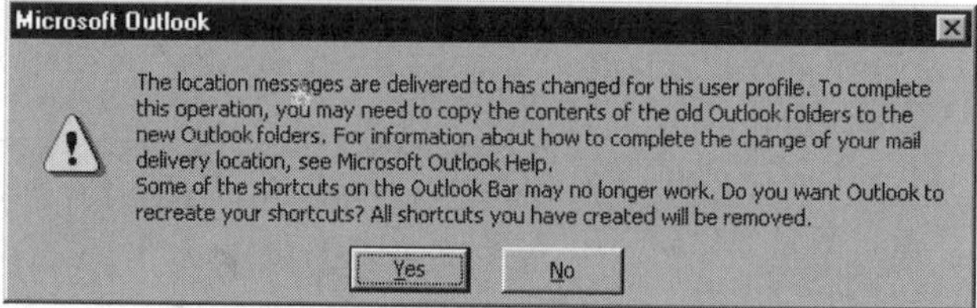

Now let's assume your delivery point was originally set to Personal Folders. This means that any messages that were received when you were connected to the network were placed in the *.pst* file on your local disk. If you now change the delivery point to the network mailbox, none of those messages will appear in the Inbox of the mailbox folder because they are not on the server. You'll have to change to Personal Folders in the folder list to access them. Any new messages you receive will be stored on your server mailbox and will be accessible only when you are connected to the network or when you are using updated offline folders.

Now let's assume that your delivery point originally was your server mailbox. The messages are listed in the Inbox when you start Outlook and have connected to the network. If you change the delivery point to your personal folders and connect to the network, all your mail on the network server—no matter how old—is now transferred to your personal folders and deleted from the mailbox. If you later restore the delivery point to your mailbox, those messages will no longer appear in your inbox. You'd have to display your personal folders in the folder list to access them. To return them to the server for storage, you'd have to drag them from the personal folder to the mailbox folder.

Sharing Personal Folders

If you are using Microsoft Exchange Server, you can work with a copy of your server files remotely using offline folders. You can then synchronize the offline folders when you are connected to the server later to make sure your desktop and laptop files contain the same information. This means that any changes to Outlook information you make on the laptop while not connected to the server will automatically be updated to the network when you go online, and vice versa.

You cannot automatically synchronize Outlook folders on your desktop and laptop using a peer-to-peer network or with no network selected. What you can do, however, is use a *Briefcase* to keep two sets of your Outlook folders synchronized. A Briefcase is a special file that lets you share information—and keep it up-to-date—between computers.

In this discussion, we'll assume that you want to share your Outlook folders between a laptop and a desktop computer, and that the folder you want to share is originally located on the desktop. You also can use the same techniques to share a folder with two computers on a network.

1. Connect your laptop to the network.
2. On the laptop, open the folder in which you want to store the Briefcase. You also can store the Briefcase directly on the desktop for convenience.
3. Right-click the folder on the desktop, point to New, and click Briefcase. If Briefcase is not an option, you have to install it. Change the name of the Briefcase so you can identify it easily.
4. Copy your personal folder file (with the .pst extension) from the desktop computer into the Briefcase. You can do this by opening the Briefcase on the laptop

and the folder on the desktop computer in which the .pst file is stored, and then dragging the .pst file into the Briefcase.

Now that your desktop's folders are on the laptop, you have to access them. For the most efficient use, set the folder in the Briefcase as Outlook's default Personal Folders folder and make it the delivery point. This way, Outlook automatically starts using the information in the Briefcase. Here's how:

1. Select Services from the Tools menu and click the Add button.
2. Choose Personal Folders from the Available Information Services list and click OK.
3. The Create/Open Personal Folders File dialog box appears. Navigate to the Briefcase, open it, and double-click the .pst file.
4. Click OK on the Delivery tab.
5. Choose Personal Folders from the drop-down list at the top of the dialog box and click OK.

Updating the Briefcase

You now have a copy of your .pst file on your laptop. Let's assume that you travel with your laptop and make some changes to your Outlook folders. Before using Outlook on your desktop again, you have to update the .pst file on the desktop with any changes you made on the laptop. Connect the laptop to the desktop, open the Briefcase on the laptop, and then look at the Status column. If it says Needs Updating, you have to update the files on one of the computers.

Click the Update All button on the Briefcase toolbar, or choose Update All from the Briefcase menu. If you see an arrow pointing to the right with the word Replace beneath it, as shown in Figure 21-7, the file in the Briefcase is newer than the corresponding .pst file on the desktop. Click the Update button.

When you are finished working with Outlook on the desktop, repeat the same process to update the Briefcase. In this case, the arrow should be pointing to the left. Click the Update button, so that the new information is then transferred to the Briefcase on the laptop.

During this process, keep in mind that the folders are not being synchronized in the same sense as they are with Exchange Server. Updating the Briefcase simply copies the most recent version of the folders from one system to the other. For example, consider this series of events:

- You update the Briefcase.
- While working on the laptop, you send an e-mail message. A copy of the message goes into the Sent Items folder of the .pst file in the Briefcase.
- Without updating the Briefcase to the desktop, you run Outlook from the desktop and send an e-mail message.

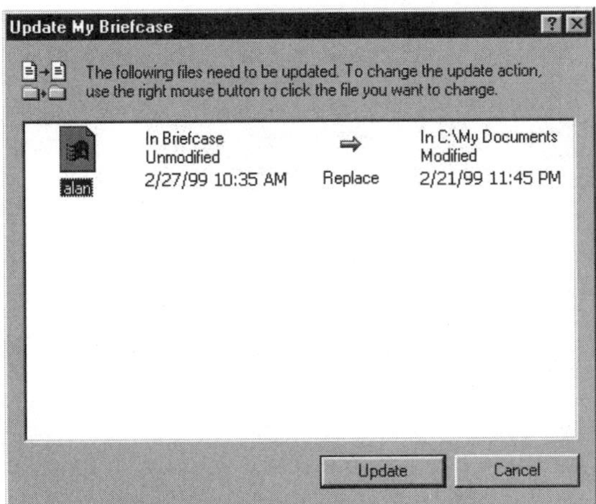

Figure 21-7
Updating the Briefcase file.

There are now changes to both .pst files, so updating one to the other will lose at least one message.

Using Offline Folders

So far, it seems simple. You use personal folders to store information on your computer, and you use your mailbox folder to store information on the server. If you want to get the best of both worlds, however, use offline folders.

Offline folders are copies of your server folders, which you synchronize when you are online so that both contain the most up-to-date information. When you are connected to the network, you can send and receive mail, and work with other Outlook information, directly in your server mailbox. However, if your server goes down or you're working with your laptop computer away from the network, you have all the most current information from the server to work with. You can even create new mail, and then send it once you are back online.

Setting Up Offline Folders

The first task you need to perform is to create a set of offline folders. These will be stored on your hard disk in a file with the *.ost* extension. Before starting, however, connect to the network and make sure your mailbox is set as the delivery point.

Next, start Outlook, choose Services from the Tools menu, select Microsoft Exchange Server in the list of services, and then click Properties. In the Microsoft Exchange Server dialog box, click the Offline Folder File Settings button on the Advanced tab to see the Offline Folder File Settings dialog box shown in Figure 21-8.

Outlook suggests a name for the offline folder file. If you already have offline folders set up from another installation, click Browse to find the file. Otherwise, click OK

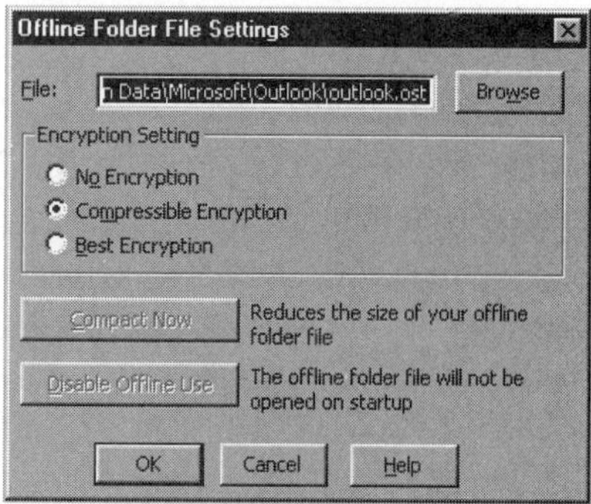

Figure 21-8
Creating offline folders.

to accept the default name and close the dialog box. Select the check box labeled Enable Offline Use and then close all the open dialog boxes.

Icons appear beside each of Outlook's folders in the Outlook Bar and on the Folder List, if it is displayed, indicating that they are available for offline use:

Now when you work offline, you can see all the information that was in your mailbox on the server. Of course, any actions you take, such as composing new messages or deleting or moving messages, won't be reflected in your mailbox until you go online and synchronize the folders. *Synchronizing* means updating the contents of your offline and server mailbox folders so that they both contain identical sets of the most up-to-date information.

Note If you plan to stop working offline, clear the Enable Offline Use check box.

Getting Your Offline Address Book

If you want to address e-mail to persons on your network while you are offline, you have to create an offline address book of network users. This is a copy of the server's address book on your own computer.

To create an offline address book, connect to your network, choose Synchronize on the Tools menu, and click Download Address Book to open the Download Offline Address Book dialog box shown in Figure 21-9.

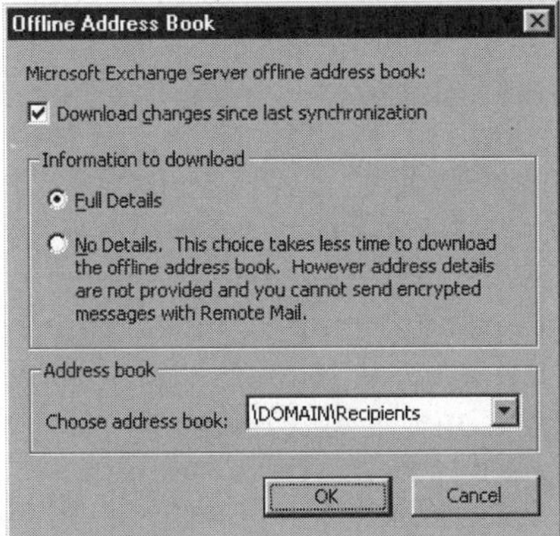

Figure 21-9
The Download Offline Address Book dialog box.

Select the level of detail you want for the offline address book. The Full Details option downloads the entire address book. The No Details option downloads only the essentials. This second option is faster, but you won't be able to send encrypted mail remotely. Click OK to download the address book.

You should periodically update your offline address book to reflect changes on your network. Update the book by downloading it again, but first select the check box labeled Download Changes Since Last Synchronization.

Synchronizing Folders

You need to periodically synchronize the offline folders with their corresponding folders on the server. During synchronization, any new items in your offline folders are uploaded to your server mailbox, and any new items in your server mailbox are downloaded to your offline folders.

Outlook automatically synchronizes offline folders when you connect to Microsoft Exchange Server. You should also synchronize offline folders before closing Outlook. You can synchronize folders manually, or set up Outlook to do it automatically. To synchronize all your offline folders at one time, point to Synchronize on the Tools menu, and then choose All Folders from the submenu. To synchronize a specific folder, open the folder, point to Synchronize on the Tools menu, and choose This Folder.

Synchronizing Offline Folders Automatically

Rather than try to remember to synchronize folders yourself, however, you can have Outlook automatically synchronize offline folders when you exit Outlook, or at periodic intervals.

When you are working online, choose Options from the Tools menu, and then click the Mail Services tab. Enable the When Online, Synchronize All Folders Upon Exiting check box, and then click OK. This guarantees that your offline folders will be up-to-date when you start to work offline. On the Mail Services tab, you also can select to automatically synchronize folders at periodic intervals—such as every 60 minutes—when you are online or when you connect remotely offline.

Setting Up for Internet E-Mail

If you have problems sending and receiving Internet mail when using the Corporate/Workgroup setup, your profile or account setup is not configured properly. First, check to see if Internet E-Mail is already installed in your profile. Open the Properties box for your profile and see if Internet E-Mail is included in the list of services. If it is, check to make sure it is set up correctly. Click Internet E-Mail and then click Properties to see the E-Mail Properties dialog box shown in Figure 21-10. On the General tab, make sure your own e-mail address is correct. On the Servers tab, check these settings:

- The name of the outgoing mail server, sometimes referred to as the SMTP (Simple Mail Transfer Protocol) Server.
- The name of the incoming mail server, sometimes called the POP (Post Office Protocol) Server.
- Your mail server logon name, which is usually the first part of your e-mail address.
- Your mail server password, which may be different from your ISP logon password.

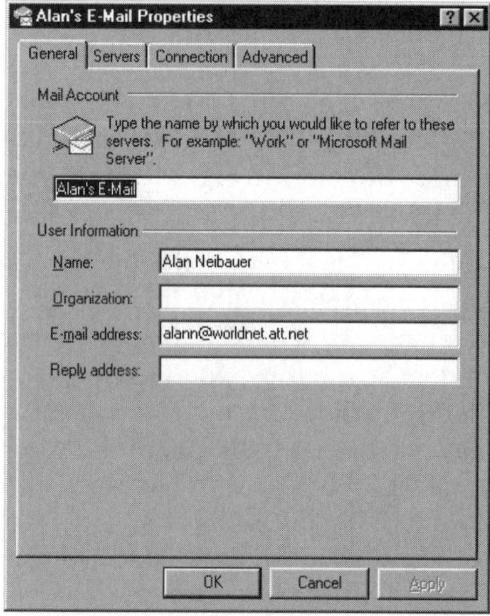

Figure 21-10
The Internet e-mail properties dialog box.

On the Connection tab of the E-Mail Properties dialog box, shown in Figure 21-11, you specify how you want Outlook to connect to the Internet.

- Choose Connect Using My Local Area Network (LAN) if you connect to the Internet though your network.
- Choose Connect Using My Phone Line if you have a dial-up account and use the modem connected to your computer. If you choose this option, select your network connection in the Use The Following Dial-Up Networking Connection drop-down list.
- Choose I Establish My Internet Connection Manually if you connect to the Internet yourself before using Outlook to send and receive mail.

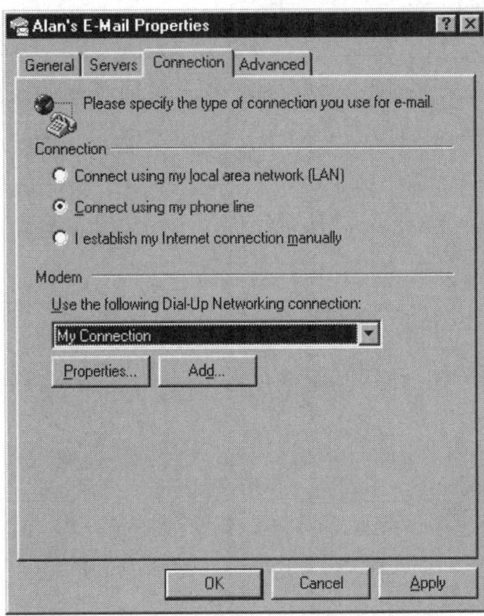

Figure 21-11
Setting the connection.

If you do not have an Internet e-mail service setup, you need to add one to your profile.

1. On the Services tab of the Properties dialog box for the profile, click Add to display the Add Service To Profile dialog box.
2. Select Internet E-Mail and click OK to open the Mail Account Properties dialog box.
3. Specify the settings on the tab of the dialog box and then click OK.

Sending Mail with Multiple Accounts

You can send and receive e-mail over the Internet using multiple accounts. You also can share a single mail account—perhaps with members of your family—so mail goes out under the name of the person who wrote it. How you do so depends on whether you've installed Outlook using the Corporate/Workgroup option or the Internet Only option.

If you have more than one ISP and are using the Corporate/Workgroup option, create an Internet E-Mail service in your profile for each account. When you are ready to send mail, choose Send And Receive from the Tools menu, and then click the account you want to use from the submenu that appears. To share an account with another member of the family, use these steps:

1. Create an address book listing in the Address Book for each family sharing your e-mail address. Use their name but your e-mail address.
2. In the message window, choose From Field on the View menu to insert the From box above the To box.
3. Click From and select the name of the family member sending the message.
4. Complete the message as usual, and click Send.
5. Click the Send/Receive button on the toolbar.

When the message arrives, the name you selected for the From field will be shown as the sender.

Selecting a Startup Profile

If you have more than one profile set up, you can select which profile to use as the default in the Mail application from the Control Panel. Click Show Profiles to see a list of the profiles you've created, click the When Starting Microsoft Outlook Use This Profile drop-down arrow, and choose the profile to use by default from the list.

You can select a default profile, or you can choose to select one each time you start Outlook. When Outlook is running, choose Options from the Tools menu and click the Mail Services tab.

- Choose Prompt For A Profile To Be Used if you want to select a profile each time Outlook starts.
- Choose Always Use This Profile and select the profile name from the list next to the option to always use the same profile.

Using Internet Only Mode

If you are using the Internet Only mode of Outlook, you set up one or more mail accounts, either from within Outlook or from the Mail icon in the Windows Control

Panel. You can use more than one account if you have multiple ISPs, or you can share a single account with several people. If you have already set up such an account in Microsoft Internet Explorer or Microsoft Outlook Express, Outlook automatically uses that account for its e-mail service. If not, you must set up the account before you can send and receive e-mail. Follow these steps to check which e-mail accounts you already have and to set up additional accounts:

1. Select Accounts from the Tools menu, or open Mail from the Windows Control Panel, to open the Internet Accounts dialog box, as shown in Figure 21-12.

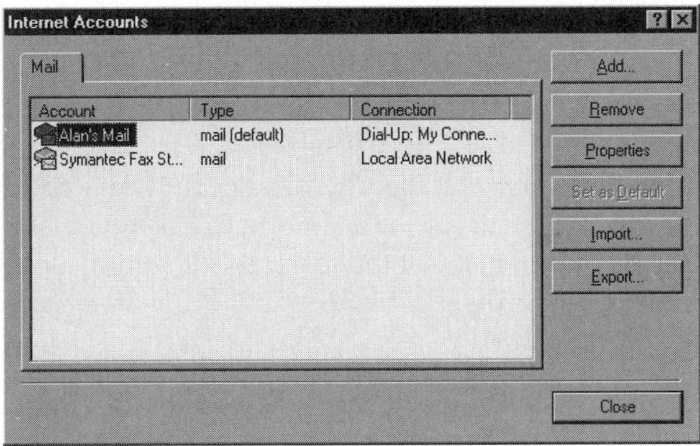

Figure 21-12
Creating Internet mail accounts.

2. If there is no e-mail account already shown, or if you want to set up an additional e-mail account, click Add. Then click Mail in the menu that appears to start the Internet Connection Wizard.

   If you already have at least one e-mail account and don't want to set up any more accounts, you can skip the rest of this procedure.

3. On the first page of the Internet Connection Wizard, enter the name you want to appear in the From field of your messages and click the Next button.
4. Type your e-mail address and click the Next button.
5. Click in the My Incoming Mail Server drop-down list and choose either POP3 or IMAP. POP3 is the most common type of mail server used by dial-up Internet service providers. If you are not sure, check with your ISP.
6. Enter the name of your incoming mail server and your outgoing mail server and click the Next button.
7. Type your mail account name. This is usually the first part of your e-mail address—the information to the left of the @ symbol.
8. Type your e-mail password, which is often different from your ISP logon password.

9. Enable the check box labeled Remember Password if you do not want to enter your password each time you check your mail.
10. Unless your ISP has told you otherwise, do not enable the Log On Using Secure Password Authentication (SPA) check box. This is a special password required to access some Internet servers through a firewall. Click the Next button.
11. Choose a connection type and click the Next button.

If you didn't choose Connect Using My Phone Line, click Finish to complete your account setup. If you did select to use your telephone line to connect, choose an existing account in the Dial-Up Connection dialog box that appears, or choose to create a new one and complete the Internet Connection Wizard. When you're finished, click Finish to complete your account setup.

The new account will be shown in the Internet Accounts dialog box. If the account is listed under its mail server name in the Internet Accounts dialog box, you might want to change the displayed name of the server to something more meaningful, like Alan's E-Mail. To change the display name or make any other necessary changes to an account, follow these steps:

1. Choose Accounts from the Tools menu to display the Internet Accounts dialog box, if it's not already open.
2. Select the Mail tab of the dialog box, and then select the account you want to change from the list.
3. Click the Properties button to display the account's Properties dialog box, shown here.

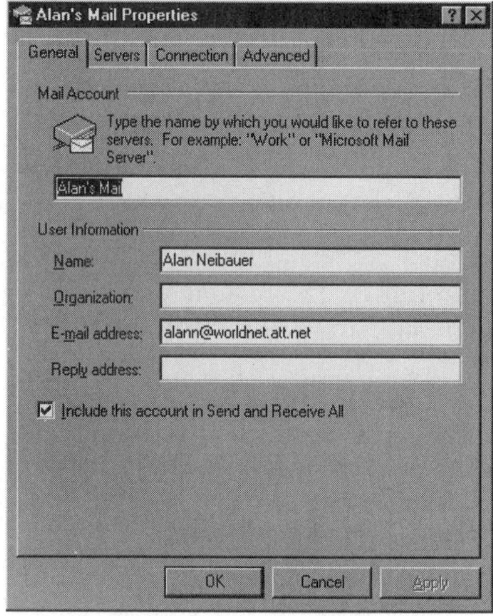

Change the desired settings in the Properties dialog box using the appropriate tabs. Here are a few possibilities:

- Change the display name of your mail server account, your user information, or your e-mail address on the General tab.
- Change the name of the incoming or outgoing mail servers, as well as your logon name and password, on the Servers tab.
- Change your dial-up connection method on the Connection tab.
- Set security for your account on the Security tab.
- Set server port numbers, timeouts, and delivery rules (for advanced users only) on the Advanced tab.

Fin y, you must set your mail account (or one of your accounts if you have more than one) as the default. This is especially important if the Symantec Fax service is set as the default. Here's how:

1. Click the name of your only mail account or your primary mail account in the Internet Accounts dialog box. (Choose Accounts from the Tools menu if the dialog box is not open.)
2. Click the Set As Default button.
3. Click OK to close the dialog box.

The mail account will now be shown as the default:

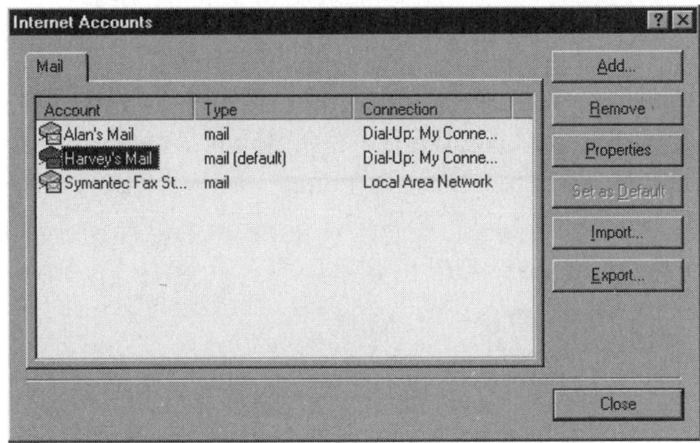

Sending Mail with Multiple Accounts

If you have more than one ISP, you must set up a mail service for each. When you create a message, you select the ISP through which to send it. You can check all your ISPs for mail at the same time.

When you share an account, multiple people use the same ISP account, but mail is sent and received under each individual's name. You can even configure Outlook so that each person has a separate set of mail folders.

With the Internet Only installation of Outlook, you can have more than one e-mail account set up and switch between them. You can check for mail on more than one service, select which e-mail account to use for outgoing mail, and change your selections as often as you want. You can add additional e-mail accounts at any time by following the steps you learned in the previous section.

If you want to choose another account for sending a specific message, compose the message as you would normally. In the New Message window, however, do not click Send. Instead, click the small down arrow next to the Send button and then click the account name you want to use. You also can select Send Using on the File menu and then choose the account:

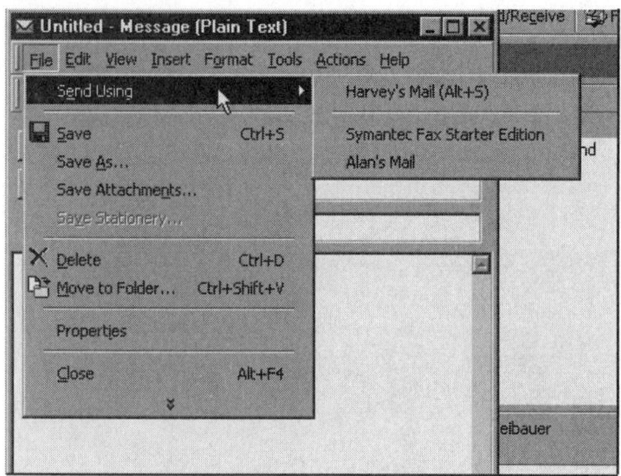

If Outlook is not set up to send mail immediately, mail from all the accounts is stored in the Outbox. To send mail later, click the Send/Receive button on the toolbar. Outlook will send all messages in the Outbox and receive mail for all accounts. If you've set up each account to dial its own ISP, Outlook will automatically dial each account for you and process the mail for each one.

To send and receive mail from a specific account, point to Send/Receive on the Tools menu and choose the account you want to use.

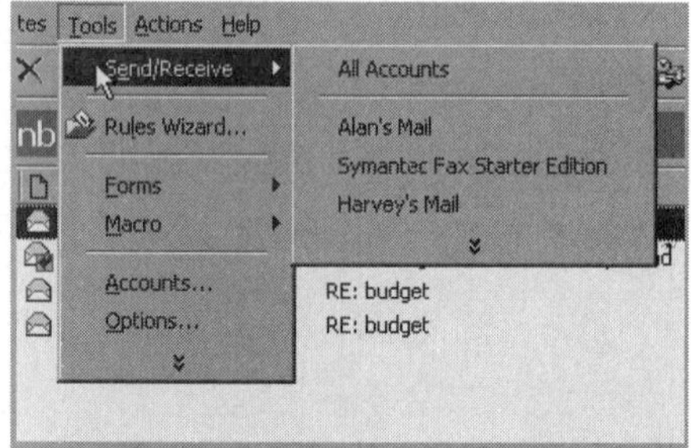

If you have many accounts set up, you may want only some accounts to be included when you click the Send/Receive button. This way, for example, you can send and receive from several accounts at one time, while excluding others.

To exclude an account from the Send/Receive function, choose Accounts from the Tools menu, select the account you want to exclude, and click the Properties button. On the General tab of the Properties dialog box, clear the check box labeled Include This Account In Send And Receive All. When you do want to send or receive via this account, point to Send/Receive on the Tools menu and choose the account.

Backing Up Outlook

No doubt you make regular back ups of all your important files at regular intervals. Just in case you don't, or you don't make them often enough, you should regularly make backup copies of your Outlook data. How regularly? Ask yourself how many days of messages, new appointments and meetings, and other Outlook information you'd mind losing. You've answered the question yourself.

It is easy to back up your Outlook data. You can back up most of your Outlook data from within Outlook. If you are using personal or offline folders, you also can back up your information using basic Windows techniques. The first task is to locate the files that you'll need to back up.

Locating Files for Windows Backup

The information that you can back up from Outlook includes:

- Personal folders
- Offline folders
- Personal Address book
- Outlook Bar settings
- Signature and virtual Business Card files
- Rules Wizard rules
- Nicknames
- Global views and menu customizations

If you are not in Outlook, locate the files using the Find command on the Start menu.

1. Click the Start button on the Taskbar, point to Find, and click Files Or Folders.
2. In the Named box, type **.pst* and press Enter to locate the personal folder files. If only one is listed, make a note of its location, or drag the file onto the backup disk.
3. In the same way, use the following extensions to locate files:
    - **.OFT* to locate offline folders
    - **.PAB* to locate personal address books
    - **.FAV* to locate Outlook Bar settings

- **.NICK* to locate nickname files
- **.RWZ* to locate Rules Wizard files
- **.VCF* to locate Virtual Business Card files
- *OUTCMD.DAT* to locate the file with global views and menu customizations

Note Custom folder views are stored in the same folder as your Outlook folders.

AutoSignatures are stored in three files with these extensions:

- *.rtf for rich text formatted messages
- *.htm for HTML formatted messages
- *.txt for plain text messages

They are all stored in the folder C:\Windows\Application Data\Microsoft\Signatures, so you may want to back up the entire folder.

The .fav, .nick, and .rwz files are stored in the folder C:\Windows\Application Data\Microsoft\Outlook. You can back up the entire contents of that folder, if you like. Each of these files is preceded by the name of your profile, such as Microsoft Exchange.fav. If you want, you can back up just the files for your profile. That folder also contains the Outcmd.dat file that you should also back up.

Custom forms can be found in one of two locations. If you are not using Windows user profiles, the forms are located in the following folder:

C:\Windows\Local Settings\Application Data\Microsoft\Outlook\Forms

If you are using profiles, the forms are in the following folder:

C:\Windows\Profiles\{User Name}\Local Settings\Application Data\Microsoft\Outlook\Forms

In some cases, you may have more than one file with the same extension. To make sure you are backing up the correct file, locate its path from within Outlook. Here's how:

1. Start Outlook using the profile that contains the personal and offline folders you want to back up.
2. Choose Services from the Tools menu to open the Services dialog box. Click Personal Address Book, and then click Properties. Make a note of the path and name of the address book file in the Path text box of the dialog box that opens. It will have the .pab file extension. Click Cancel.
3. Click Personal Folders, and then click Properties.
4. Make a note of the path and name of your personal folders file in the Path text box of the dialog box that opens. It will have the .pst file extension. Click Cancel.

5. Click Microsoft Exchange Server, and then click Properties.
6. In the Microsoft Exchange Server dialog box, click the Advanced tab, and then click the Offline Folder File Settings button.
7. Make a note of the path and name of your office folders file in the File text box of the dialog box that opens. It will have the .ost file extension. Click Cancel and then close the Services dialog box.

Now that you know where your files are located, use standard Windows techniques to make copies of the .pab, .pst, and .ost files. If you have to restore your .pab and .ost files, copy the backup files to their original locations. You'll lose any changes you've made since your last backup, but you'll at least get the bulk of your Outlook data.

Backing Up Server Information

Rather than depend on your network administrator to maintain backup copies of your Microsoft Exchange or post office mailbox, you can maintain your own backup copies using the Export feature. You also can use Export to back up personal folders from within Outlook and to make incremental copies as you add and delete information. The first time you perform the operation, it creates an entire copy of your folders. Then each subsequent time you export the folders, it simply adds any new information that was not previously recorded.

1. Select Import And Export from the File menu to open the Import And Export Wizard.
2. Choose Export To A File in the Import And Export Wizard and then click the Next button to see the dialog box shown here.

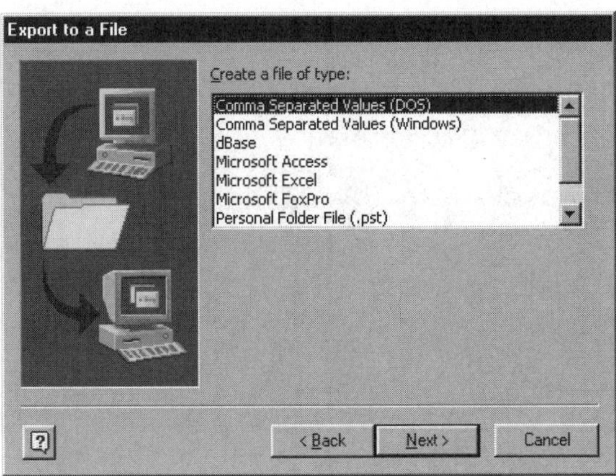

3. Select the Personal Folder (.pst) file type and then click the Next button. You'll see a dialog box listing your Outlook folders. One or more folders may be expanded, showing all the individual folders contained within it.

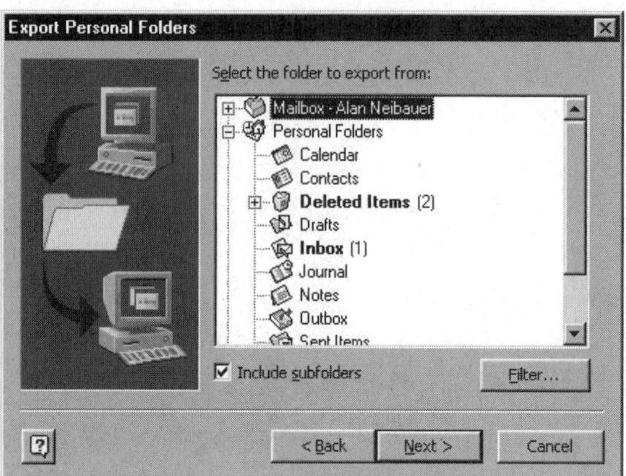

4. Select the item starting with Mailbox to back up your server folders. Select Personal Folders to back up your personal folders file.
5. Enable the check box labeled Include Subfolders to export all the mailbox folders.
6. Click the Filter button if you want to filter the messages and other items that are exported. In the dialog box that appears, you can choose to filter messages based on their content, sender, recipient, or other items. Do not filter if you want a total backup.
7. Click the Next button to see the dialog box shown in Figure 21-13. There will already be a suggested default path and name for the file, Backup.pst. Change the path and name, if desired.

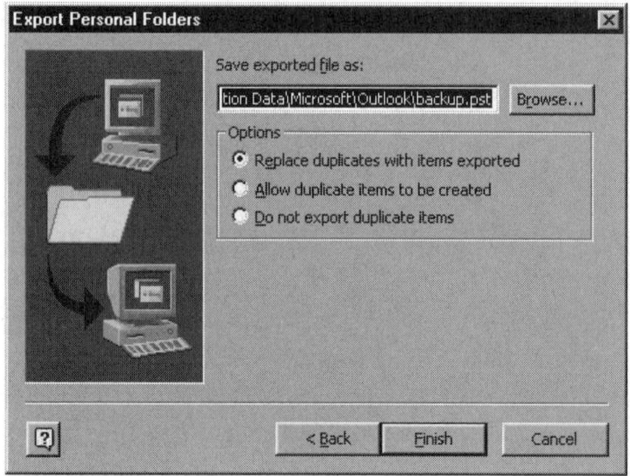

Figure 21-13
Backing up server files.

Select how you want to handle duplicate items. To perform an incremental backup, choose either Replace Duplicates With Items Exported or Do Not Export Duplicate Items. Choose the default Replace option to make sure that any changes you made to Outlook items will be recorded in the backup file. Click the Finish button.

If the backup file does not yet exist, you'll see the Create Microsoft Personal Folders dialog box. You cannot change the path and file name in this box, but you can set the name the folder will have if you open it in Outlook. The default name is Personal Folders—change this to something like MyBackup to differentiate it from your default personal folders. If you want, enter a password that will be required to open the file, and click OK.

If you ever need to open the backup file, choose Open from the File menu and click Personal Folders File (.pst). Locate the folder and file and click OK.

Other Export Options

You also can use the Export feature to save copies of specific folders rather than the entire mailbox. In addition, you can use it to save Outlook information in a format usable by other applications, such as Microsoft Excel and Access. For example, you could export your Contacts folder to an Access database to prepare mailing labels or print invoices. The Formats you can export to include:

- Microsoft Exchange Personal Address Book
- Comma-separated text file
- Tab-separated text file
- Microsoft Access
- Microsoft Excel
- Microsoft FoxPro
- dBASE

If the program you want to export the information to is not listed, check for a format the program can use. For example, you can use information in Lotus 1-2-3 by saving the information as a comma-separated file and then importing it into Lotus 1-2-3.

Select Export To A File in the Import And Export Wizard and then click the Next button. Select the format and then click the Next button. You'll see a dialog box listing your Outlook folders. Select the folder whose contents you want to export and then click the Next button. Type the path and name for the file, and click the Next button to see the dialog box shown at the top of page 842.

Confirm that the description of the action is accurate. If it is not what you want to perform, click the Back button and make any changes in the wizard dialog boxes. You also can use the Map Custom Fields button to change the order in which the

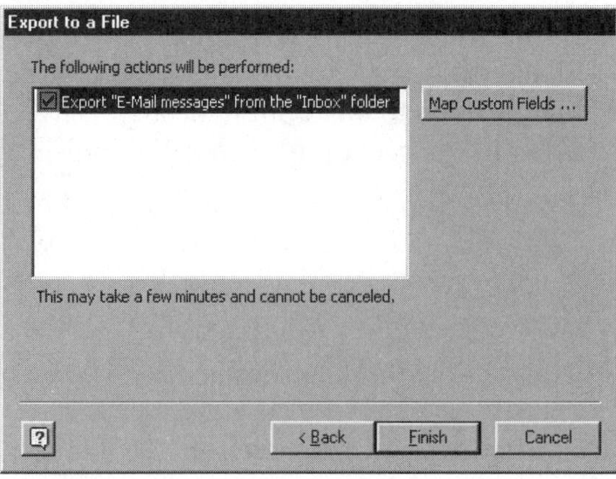

information is stored or to remove fields that you do not want to export. Click the Finish button when you are done.

Mapping Fields

Mapping fields means that you can change the order of the fields in the resulting file or remove fields. For example, in the Inbox, messages are stored starting with the fields Subject, Body, and From (Name). When you export the file, the information also is in that order. You may want to change the order of the fields so you can merge the resulting file with another document that is already in another order, such as storing the senders name first, and then the subject.

When you click Map Custom Fields, Outlook opens the Map Custom Fields dialog box shown in Figure 21-14.

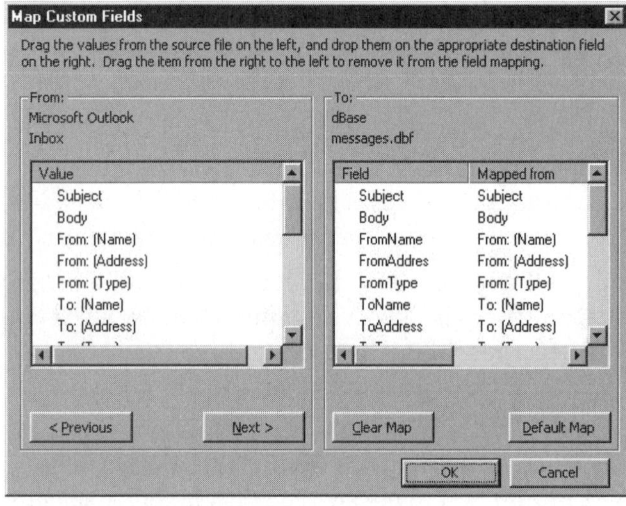

Figure 21-14
The Mapping Custom Fields dialog box.

To remove a field so that it is not exported, drag it from the list on the right to the list on the left. Click the Clear Map button to remove all the fields from the list on the right. You can then drag the fields that you want to export from the list on the left to the right side. Click the Default Map button to undo all your changes.

To change the order of a field, drag it from the list on the left to the position you want it on the right.

You may find it easier to adjust the order of fields if you're looking at the actual information rather than just the field names. Click the Next and Previous buttons to scroll through the folder, displaying the contents of each item in place of the field names.

Importing Data to Outlook

If you backed up information by exporting to another format, you have to import the information to later restore it into Outlook folders. To begin the process, select Import And Export from the File menu to open the Import And Export Wizard, select the import option for the type of file to import, and then click the Next button. The Wizard boxes that appear will depend on the file type you are importing. Work your way through the wizard and then click Finish.

You also can use the Import command to use address or mail files that you created with another e-mail program. This is useful if you are switching to Outlook for the first time. Here's a review of the types of files you can import:

- **Internet Mail Account Settings** adds to your profile the mail server, e-mail address, and logon details you've already entered in programs such as Eudora, Netscape Mail and Messenger, Microsoft Mail and News, or Outlook Express.
- **Internet Mail and Addresses** lets you import your address book and message folders from Eudora, Netscape Mail and Messenger, Microsoft Mail and News, or Outlook Express.
- **VCARD File (.vcf)** imports into your Contacts folder the name and address information that you stored as a VCARD using an e-mail program or address books.
- **ICalendar Or VCalendar File (.vcs)** imports into your Outlook calendar appointment and meeting information that you may have created with another program or received over the Internet.
- **Another Program File** lets you import information created with many popular applications, such as Excel and Access, or stored in a text file—you choose the Outlook folder in which to place the imported information.

Sending and Receiving Faxes

Even with the growing popularity of e-mail, faxes are still an important means of communicating. Faxing offers the opportunity to send a hard copy of documents that you create or scan into your computer. Faxes are also useful for communicating with persons who do not have e-mail.

There are two ways to fax: you can use a stand-alone fax machine, or you can send an electronic fax from your computer, if you have a fax-capable modem. An electronic fax can be a document you type in Microsoft Word or some other Microsoft Windows application or a message that you want to send in Outlook. The person receiving the fax can do so either with a stand-alone fax machine or with a fax modem.

To determine if your computer is already set up for faxing, click Start, Settings, and choose Printers. If you see an item with the word Fax, it is already installed. If you use Windows 95, faxing capabilities are automatically installed with Microsoft Messaging or Microsoft Exchange. If you use the Internet Only setup of Outlook, its own faxing program is also installed on your computer.

Corporate/Workgroup Faxing

If you choose the Corporate/Workgroup Outlook installation, you should use Microsoft Fax as your faxing program because it is free and well integrated into Outlook.

With Windows 95, faxing capabilities are automatically installed with Microsoft Messaging or Microsoft Exchange. If it is not installed on your computer, you have to install Microsoft Fax from the Microsoft Windows CD-ROM. Use the Add/Remove Programs icon in Windows Control Panel. Select the Windows Setup tab in the Add/Remove Programs dialog box, and select the Microsoft Fax component.

Windows 98 does not install fax service by default, and it does not offer it as a regular setup option. To install fax capability, you have to run a program called Awfax.exe in the \Tools\Oldwin95\Message\Us (or \Intl directory for international users) of the Microsoft Windows 98 CD-ROM.

Because Microsoft Fax was designed before Outlook 2000, however, it may replace some files that Outlook needs to operate. Therefore, if you do install Microsoft Fax after you install Outlook or Office 2000, you have to replace some of the newer files. If you installed Outlook as a separate program and not as part of Office 2000, simply reinstall Outlook after you install Microsoft Fax. If you installed Outlook as part of Office 2000, use the Repair Office function to restore the necessary files.

Setting Up a Fax Profile

If you had fax service installed before you installed Outlook, you might have already added it to your profile using the Inbox Setup Wizard. If not, you need to add fax service to your Outlook profile before you can send or receive faxes.

The process is similar to adding Internet e-mail to a profile, but with additional options for dialing and preparing faxes. You can install it from within Outlook using the Services command on the Tools menu, or you can install it from the Mail icon in Windows Control Panel. We'll outline the procedure for using Control Panel.

1. Double-click the Mail icon in the Control Panel. If the profile you want to add fax service to is not displayed, click Show Profiles, select the profile you want to change, and then click the Properties button.
2. Click the Add button to open the Add Service To Profile dialog box. Select Microsoft Fax in the list of services and then click OK. A message asks whether you are ready to supply your name and fax number.
3. Click Yes to open the Microsoft Fax Properties dialog box shown in Figure 21-15.

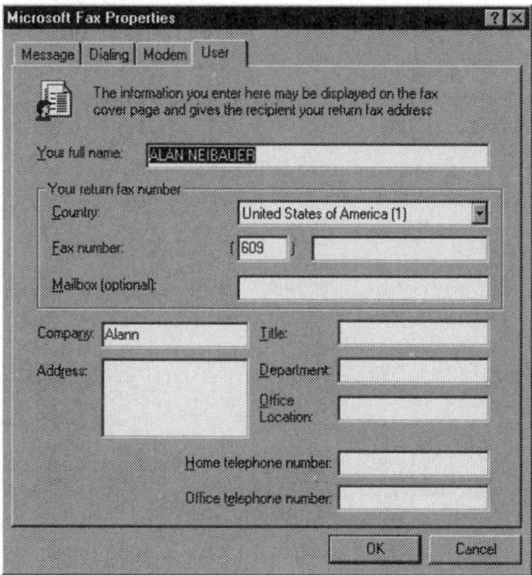

Figure 21-15
The Fax Properties dialog box.

4. On the User tab, type your fax number and any other information you want to insert.
5. Click the Modem tab and make sure it is set for the modem you are using. If you have more than one modem, choose the one you'll be using, and then click the Set As Active Fax Modem button. Complete the other tabs of the dialog box as explained in the following section.
6. Click OK in each of the open dialog boxes.

Note You can set and change Fax options by choosing Microsoft Fax Tools on the Tools menu and clicking Options from the submenu.

Setting Message Options

You use the Message tab of the Microsoft Fax Properties dialog box, shown in Figure 21-16, to choose a standard message format, set up a default cover page, and select the time when you want Outlook to send your faxes.

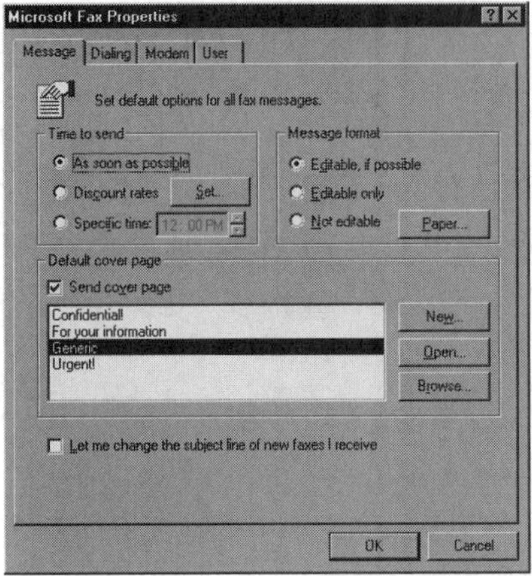

Figure 21-16
The Message tab of the Microsoft Fax Properties dialog box.

Setting Dialing Options

The options on the Dialing tab of the Microsoft Fax Properties dialog box, shown in Figure 21-17, let you set up the locations from which you send faxes, create a list of telephone numbers with toll prefixes, and specify how many times Outlook will retry to send a fax if it doesn't go through on the first attempt.

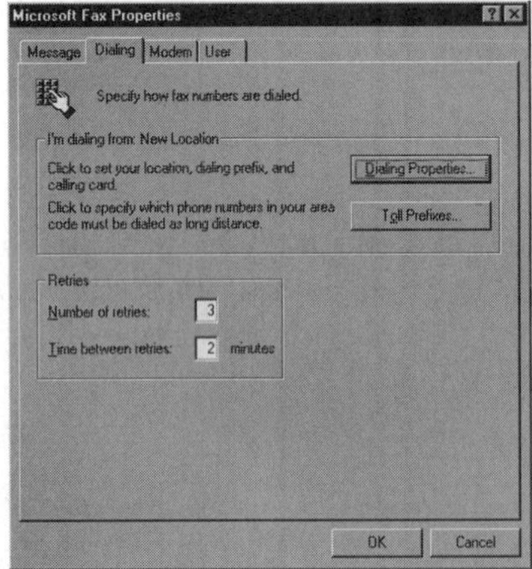

Figure 21-17
Define dialing options for sending faxes.

The Retries section of the dialog box allows you set the number of retries and to set how long you want Outlook to wait between retries

Setting Modem Options

The Modem tab of the Microsoft Fax Properties dialog box lets you select the modem that Outlook will use for faxes, and to set the options for that modem. If the modem you want to use is not listed, you can add it. You can add either a local modem (a modem in your computer or attached to it) or a network modem.

You also can set up your modem to answer incoming calls, adjust the modem speaker volume, and set your call preferences. To set modem properties, select your fax modem from the Available Fax Modems list, and then click the Properties button to display the Fax Modem Properties box shown in Figure 21-18.

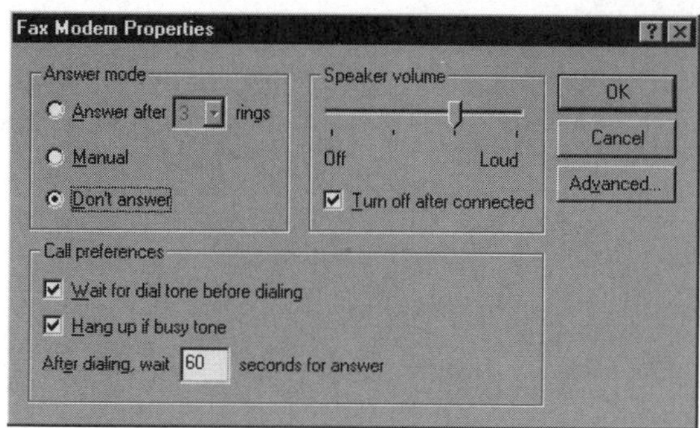

Figure 21-18
The Fax Modem Properties dialog box.

Sharing a Modem

Not everyone on your network may have a fax modem installed in his or her computer. If this is the case, you can share a fax modem with other users as long as you enable sharing and establish permissions for the device.

To share your modem with other users on the network, enable the check box labeled Let Other People On The Network Use My Modem To Send Faxes on the Modem tab of the Microsoft Fax Properties dialog box. If the Select Drive dialog box appears, select the drive on your local machine that you want the network fax service to use, and then click OK.

Next, click the Properties button to open the NetFax dialog box shown in Figure 21-19. You use this dialog box to enter the share name and to designate network users who have permission to share your modem.

Make sure the Shared As option button is selected, and then select Full in the Access Type section. You may choose Depends On Password if you want to require users to have a password to send and receive faxes. If you want to restrict access to

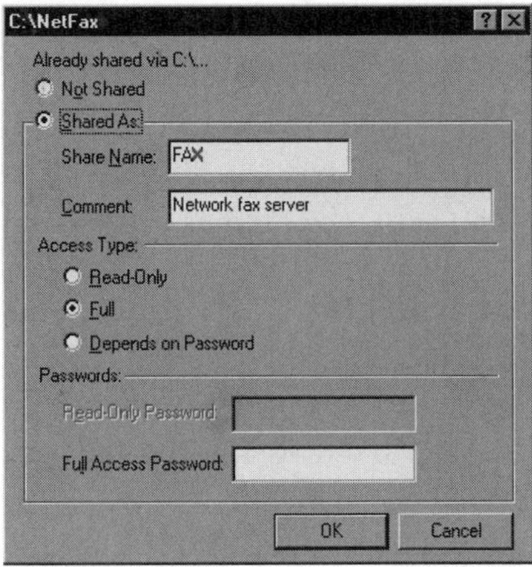

Figure 21-19
The NetFax dialog box.

those with a password, enter the password in the Full Access Password text box. Click OK.

Receiving a Fax

How you receive faxes depends on the Answer Mode option you've chosen:

- If you selected the Answer After option, simply let Outlook answer the call and receive the fax.
- If you selected the Manual option, when a call comes in and you pick up your phone and hear the fax warble, click the Answer Now button in the Microsoft Fax Status window and hang up the phone after Outlook has answered the call. If the Microsoft Fax Status window does not appear when the telephone rings, click the Fax icon in the System tray (at the right edge of the Windows taskbar).

Received faxes appear in your Inbox, just as e-mail messages do. You can then treat the faxes just as you treat any folder item in Outlook.

Retrieving a Fax from a Service

A *fax service* is a company that stores faxes on their computer so you can pick them up when it is convenient. When you are ready to retrieve your faxes, point to Microsoft Fax Tools on the Tools menu, and then choose Request A Fax from the submenu. You'll see the first panel of the Request A Fax Wizard, shown in Figure 21-20.

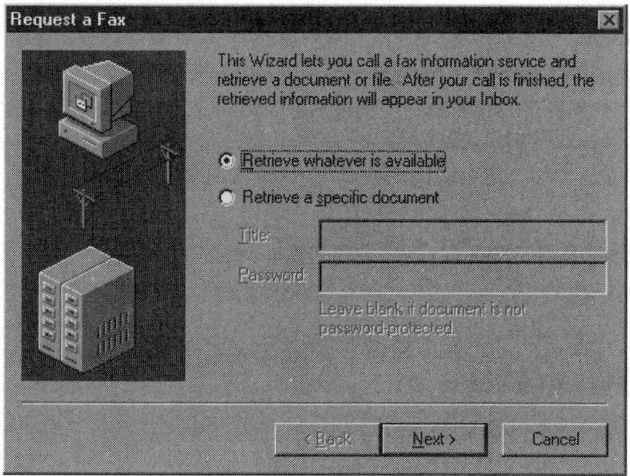

Figure 21-20
The Request A Fax Wizard dialog box.

Select to receive whatever faxes are available or just a specific fax. If you choose to receive a specific fax, enter its name and your password, if applicable. In a series of dialog boxes, you perform these tasks:

- Enter the name of the fax service in the To box, and select the appropriate country from the drop-down list.
- Protect the fax with a password or encrypt the fax.
- Type the fax service's fax number, and select the Dial Area Code check box if needed.
- Select the time you want Outlook to send the request—as soon as possible, when telephone rates are discounted, or a specific time.

Sending and Receiving Secure Faxes

If you are sending a fax to a recipient's fax modem, you can add a password to the fax or encrypt the fax to protect it from unauthorized persons. A password ensures that only recipients to whom you give the password can receive the fax. Encryption scrambles the fax so that it is unreadable except to those recipients who have your key.

Adding a Password to a Fax

You can add a password to a fax, whether you create it using the New Fax Wizard or as an Outlook message.

- If you use the New Fax Wizard, click the Options button in the third Wizard dialog box.
- If you are creating a fax as an Outlook message, select Send Options from the File menu when you create the message, then click the Fax tab.

In both cases, click the Security button in the dialog box that appears to open the Message Security Options dialog box shown in Figure 21-21. Select the Password Protected option button and then click OK. In the dialog box that appears, enter and then re-enter the password and click OK. Continue using the New Fax Wizard, or complete and send the message.

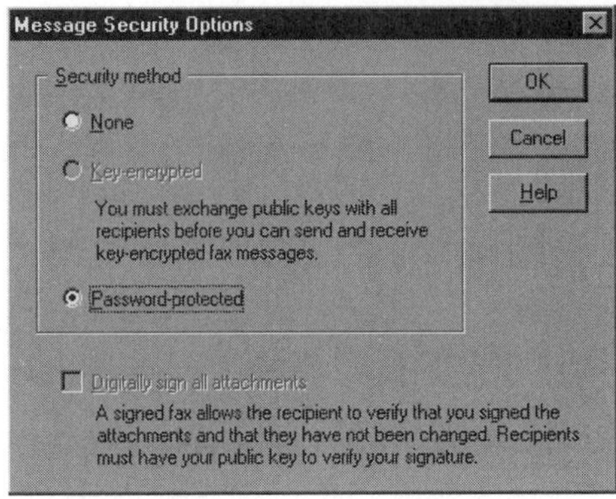

Figure 21-21
The Message Security Options dialog box.

Protecting Faxes with Encryption

When you encrypt a fax, the recipient needs to have two special passwords, called *keys*, to make the fax readable. One is the public key of the person receiving the fax. The other is the sender's own private key, created with a combination of a special password and the sender's user information. The keys are stored together in a *key set.*

You can only send an encrypted fax to recipients who have previously sent you their public key. Likewise, a person can only send you an encrypted fax if you have sent them your public key.

To create your key set so that you can send and receive encrypted faxes, choose Microsoft Fax Tools from the Tools menu, and select Advanced Security to open the Advanced Fax Security dialog box. Click the New Key Set button to display the dialog box shown here.

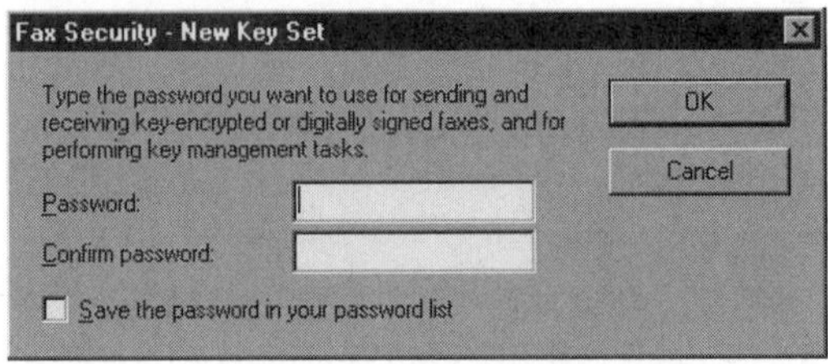

Type a password in the Password text box, and enter it again in the Confirm Password box. Because asterisks appear, rather than the characters you type, be careful as you make your entries. Click OK and then close the dialog box.

Sending Your Public Key to Fax Recipients

You now have to send your public key to anyone who you want to send you encrypted faxes. Follow these steps:

1. Open the Advanced Fax Security dialog box and click the Public Keys button. If the Fax Security-Key Set Password dialog box appears, type your password and click OK. The Fax Security-Managing Public Keys dialog box appears.
2. Click the Save button to open the Fax Security-Save Public Keys dialog box.
3. Select your name and the names of others whose public keys you want to share, click the To button, and then click OK.
4. In the Fax Security-Save Public Keys dialog box, navigate to the location and folder where you want to save your public key file. Type a filename, and then click the Save button.
5. Click the Close button in the Fax Security-Managing Public Keys dialog box, and then click Close in the Advanced Fax Security dialog box.
6. Send the public key file as an attachment in an e-mail message.

Internet Only Fax Service

If you installed Outlook using the Internet Only setup option, Outlook provides its own fax service automatically, which is called the Symantec WinFax Starter Edition. In fact, the first time you run Outlook—or after you select to send or receive a fax for the first time—the Symantec WinFax Starter Edition Setup Wizard will appear. In a series of dialog boxes, you'll be asked to specify your fax information:

- Type your name, company, fax number, voice number, and station identifier (typically, your fax number or name).
- Type your address and click the Next button.
- If you want Outlook to automatically answer the telephone and receive a fax, specify the number of rings when receiving and the number of retries when sending.
- Add your modem settings.
- Specify a default cover page style.

Sending Faxes

To send a fax, choose New Fax Message from the Actions menu to open a mail window. To address a fax to a person in the Contacts folder who has a fax number, enter the name of a recipient. You also can send a fax by typing a fax number in the To box using the form FAX@555-5555. If you need to dial a number to reach an outside line, use the syntax FAX@9w555-5555. In this case, nine is the number to reach an outside line, and the letter "w" tells Outlook to wait for a dial tone before dialing. Complete the message as you would any other, and then click Send.

If you started the message using the New button on the toolbar, do not click Send. Instead, click the drop-down arrow next to the Send button and choose Symantec Fax Starter Edition from the list. You also can click the Options button, open the Send Message Using list, and then choose Symantec Fax Starter Edition. Then close the Message Options dialog box, and then click Send.

Receiving Faxes

If you set up Symantec WinFax to automatically receive faxes, Outlook will answer the telephone and start receiving incoming faxes. If you share one telephone line for your voice and fax service, however, you probably should not set Outlook to automatically answer.

If you get a telephone call and hear a fax tone, manually start Symantec WinFax by choosing Receive Fax from the Tools menu.

Getting Read and Delivery Receipts If you send e-mail to an invalid address, you'll get a return message reporting that it could not be delivered. Just because a message is not returned, however, doesn't mean that it has been delivered and opened by the recipient.

If you want to know when a message is delivered, you can request a delivery receipt. A delivery receipt indicates that the recipient's server has received the message, not necessarily that it has been transmitted from the server to the recipient's personal folder.

You also can request a read receipt. A read receipt indicates that the recipient has opened the message, but there is no way of knowing if they have actually read the message! With Outlook, you can request receipts for individual messages or for all new messages.

As you create a message, request a receipt by clicking the Options button in the message window toolbar. In the dialog box that appears, select either or both of these options:

- Request A Delivery Receipt For This Message.
- Request A Read Receipt For This Message.
- Click OK to close the Options dialog box and then complete and send the message.

If you want to request receipts for all messages, use these steps:

1. Select Options from the Tools menu.
2. Click the Preferences tab.
3. Click the E-Mail Options button.

4. Click the Tracking Options button to see the Tracking Options dialog box, shown in Figure 21-22.
5. Select one or both of the options:
   - Request A Read Receipt For All Messages I Send.
   - Request A Delivery Receipt For All Messages I Send.

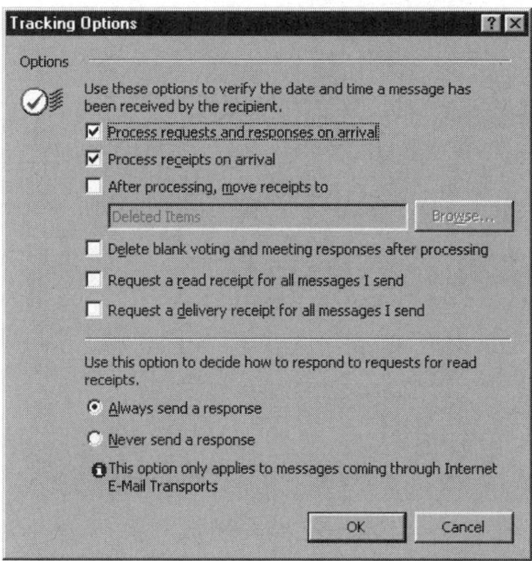

Figure 21-22
The Tracking Options dialog box.

Voting Options Delivery and read receipts are just one type of feedback you can get from Outlook e-mail. Sometimes, you send an e-mail that requires a Yes or No response, such as "Do you favor the contract?" To make it easy for recipients to respond to such questions, and to automatically tabulate the results, you can use voting buttons. Voting buttons appear on the e-mail message like this:

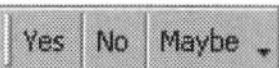

When you create the message, click the Options button on the message toolbar and enable the Use Voting Buttons check box. The associated drop-down list contains three choices—Approve;Reject, Yes;No, and Yes;No;Maybe. Choose the set of buttons you want to include in your message, or create your own set of voting buttons. To create your own set of buttons, type your choices in the text box, separating them with semicolons, as in *OneStar;TwoStars;ThreeStars.* Then complete and send the message. When Outlook delivers the message, the recipients will see the buttons in the message window, along with the instruction "Please Respond Using The Buttons Above."

You will not see the buttons on your screen when you are composing the message, but they will appear on the message in your Sent Items folder.

When the recipient clicks one of the buttons, you'll receive an e-mail informing you of their selection. Read the e-mail to see the response and any additional comments. The original message in your Sent Items folder is now marked with a special icon indicating that responses have been received. When you open the message, it will contain a Tracking tab that lists all recipients and the status and date of their replies, as well as any delivery and read receipts, as shown in Figure 21-23.

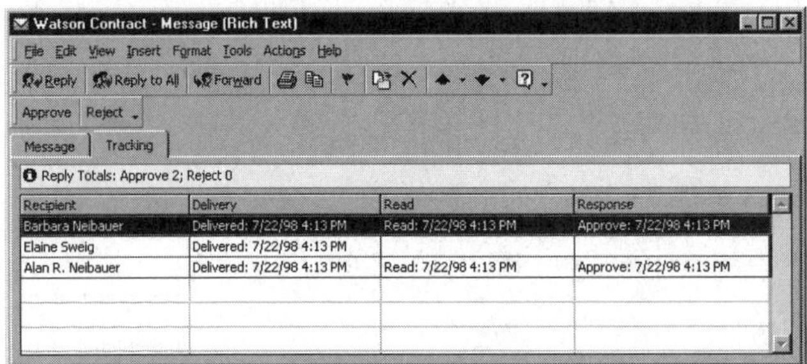

Figure 21-23
The Tracking tab lets you keep track of votes, message delivery, and read receipts.

Recalling and Resending a Message Mail you send through your Microsoft Exchange Server network is stored in the recipient's mailbox. Until a recipient moves the message to their inbox or their personal folder, you can take either of these actions:

- You can recall the message you've already sent, removing it from the recipient's inbox.
- You can resend the same message after correcting or updating it.

First find the message you've already sent by opening the My Shortcuts group on the Outlook Bar, opening the Sent Items folder, and double-clicking the sent message to open it.

To recall or replace the message, follow these steps:

1. Open the message and choose Recall This Message from the Actions menu on the message window.
2. In the Recall This Message dialog box, do one of the following:
    - To receive a notification about the success or failure of recalling or replacing the message for each recipient, select the Tell Me If Recall Succeeds Or Fails For Each Recipient check box.
    - To recall the message, select the Delete Unread Copies Of This Message option button, and then click OK.

- To replace the message with another, select the Delete Unread Copies And Replace With A New Message option button, and then click OK. In the new message window that appears, type the new message, and then click the Send button.

To simply resend the message (rather than recall or replace the message), follow these steps:

1. Open the message and choose Resend This Message from the Actions menu of the message window.
2. In the message window that appears, make any necessary changes, and then click the Send button.

Sending and Receiving Secure Messages

Long ago, when you wanted to send a secure message, you melted a little wax and stamped a seal onto the flap of an envelope. If you received the message with the seal broken, you knew it had been intercepted en route.

E-mail messages travel through your network or over the Internet where they also can be intercepted. Anyone can configure a mail program to send messages that appear as if the messages were sent by someone else.

When you want to be certain your messages are safe from tampering, you can include a *digital signature* that verifies that you are the actual person who sent the message, and you can encrypt the message to ensure that only authorized persons can read the message.

To set up Outlook for secure messages, you use the Security tab on the Options dialog box, as shown in Figure 21-24.

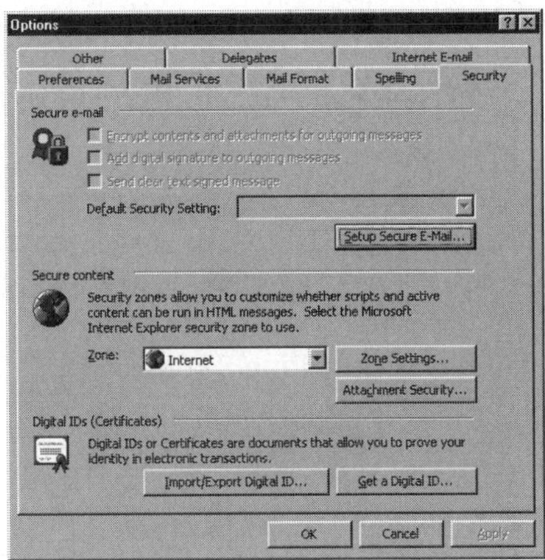

Figure 21-24
The Security tab of the Options dialog box.

Getting a Digital Certificate

To take full advantage of these security features, you must have a security certificate that verifies who you are to others. There are two types of certificates available in Outlook: an Exchange certificate to use over an Exchange Server network and a Secure/Multipurpose Internet Mail Extensions (S/MIME) certificate that you obtain and then use over the Internet. Exchange certificates are free, and S/MIME certificates are available for a small annual fee—usually less than $10, depending on the type of service and the level of security desired. Before applying for an Exchange Server certificate, ask your network administrator for a special password called a *token*. If you are on a network that is connected to the Internet, you can use both types of security certificates. When you are ready to apply for the certificate, follow these steps:

1. Choose Options from the Tools menu, and click the Security tab.
2. Click Get A Digital ID.
3. If you're not connected to a security-enabled Exchange Server network, Outlook launches your Web browser and connects you to a site that provides information on security certificates.
4. If the Get A Digital ID dialog box appears, choose either Get A S/MIME Certificate From An External Certifying Authority or Set Up Security For Me On The Exchange Server, depending on the type of security you want to use.

If you choose to obtain an S/MIME certificate, follow the instructions on the screen to apply for a digital certificate. In most cases, after you apply, you'll be notified by e-mail that your certificate is ready. You'll then need to connect to the vendor's Web site to accept it. When the site verifies your certificate, it will download and install it on your system.

If you choose to obtain an Exchange Server certificate, a dialog box will appear into which you enter the token given to you by the network administrator. The box also shows a key set name that identifies you. When you click OK to close the dialog box, you will see a message reporting that your request for a certificate has been sent to the network. Click OK to close all open messages and dialog boxes.

Once the server processes your request, it sends an e-mail informing you that your security has been enabled. When you open the message, a dialog box appears reporting that Outlook is writing the Exchange signing key to your system. Click OK to display a message box reporting that Outlook is writing the encryption key to your system, and click OK again. A message appears reporting that you are now security-enabled.

Securing Contents

E-mail messages using HTML formatting also can contain active content—elements that have the potential to run programs and perform operations on your computer.

While it is unlikely that you will receive such a message, it pays to be careful. The Zone setting in the Secure Content area of the Security tab lets you control how active content is handled in both e-mail messages and attachments.

In the Zone list, you can select from two zones: Internet Zone and Restricted Sites Zone. The Internet Zone offers a medium level of security that will warn you before active content is accepted and run. The Restricted Sites Zone offers a high level of security that simply excludes any active content. To change the degree of security in a zone, click the Zone Settings button to see the dialog box shown below, and then follow these steps:

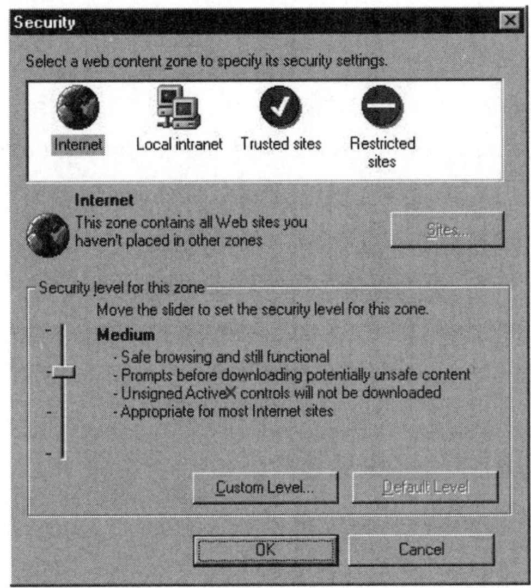

1. Choose the zone you want to change.

   If you choose Restricted Sites, click Sites to enter specific Web sites to restrict.
2. Select the level of security for the zone you selected.
3. Click OK.

You also can click Custom Level to enable, disable, or warn for each of a list of specific types of content.

Active content also can be found in message attachments. Again, it is highly unlikely that you will receive an attachment with dangerous content but, by default, you will be warned of the potential problem when you save or open some attachments. If you do not want to receive this warning, click the Attachment Security button, choose None in the dialog box that appears, and then click OK.

Using Message Security

To use security with all messages, select the encryption and digital signature check boxes on the Security tab of the Options dialog box.

- Select the Encrypt Contents And Attachments For Outgoing Messages check box to encrypt your messages.
- Select the Add Digital Signature To Outgoing Messages check box to add a digital signature to each message you send so your recipient can be sure that the message originated from you.
- Select the Send Clear Text Signed Message check box if you want recipients who cannot read S/MIME signatures to be permitted to read your message.

You can, of course, clear the encryption and digital signature check boxes on the Security tab, as explained earlier. If you do, you can encrypt a single message or add your digital signature to a single message by clicking the Options button on the Standard toolbar when composing a message, and then selecting the Encrypt Contents And Attachments check box or the Add Digital Signature To Outgoing Message check box. You also can clear these check boxes to turn off security for an individual message.

When you are sending an encrypted message over the Internet, you must have the recipient's public key stored with their address in your address book. If you are using Exchange security, one of three things will happen:

- If your security level is set to the default Medium level, a message appears reporting the level of security. Click OK to send the message.
- If your security level is set to Low, the message is sent immediately.
- If your security level is set to High, you must supply a password to send the message. Type your password and then click OK.

If you do not have the recipient's key, or if an Exchange recipient doesn't have security set up, you'll see a message box telling you so. You then have two choices for delivering the message:

- Click the Don't Encrypt Message button to send the message anyway. When encryption is turned on, this is the only way to send a message to a recipient who doesn't have advanced security.
- Click the Cancel Send button if you decide not to send the message to someone who doesn't have advanced security.

Swapping Security Certificates

To send encrypted mail over the Internet, you need the security certificate of the recipient. Before the recipient can send an encrypted message to you, he or she must first send you a message that is digitally signed so you can add their certificate to your address book. If you want to receive an encrypted message from a person, you have to send them your certificate.

1. Choose Options from the Tools menu and select the Security tab.
2. Click the Change Settings button.
3. In the Security Settings Name list, make sure you select the setting for S/MIME Internet security.
4. Select the Send These Certificates With Signed Messages check box.
5. Click OK in each of the remaining dialog boxes.
6. Send the person a message that is digitally signed.

When your message arrives, the recipient must perform these steps:

1. Double-click the message to open it.
2. Right-click your name.
3. Choose Add To Contacts from the shortcut menu to create an address listing for you that also contains your public key.
4. When the Contacts form opens displaying the sender's address book information, click the Save And Close button on the form's Standard toolbar.

Now the sender's public key is included in your Contacts folder with all your other information about that person, and the key will be available for decrypting secure messages from the sender in the future. Certificates do not need to be exchanged for secure traffic across a Microsoft Exchange Server network. The network administrator sets up certificates that reside on the server, and they don't need to be distributed locally to the individuals on the network.

Getting Rid of Spam

Spam is junk mail—those advertisements and come-ons that clog your inbox and that seem to multiply exponentially each day. You can sometimes prevent further e-mail from specific senders by responding with the word REMOVE in the subject line. More often than not, though, it is easier to avoid paying taxes than it is to get off a spammer's mailing list.

Fortunately, Outlook helps you avoid reading spam by automatically moving it to your Deleted Items folder or marking it in a different color so it is easily identified in your Inbox. Outlook has two categories for such mail—Junk and Adult Content. *Junk mail* is mail that is received from persons whom you identify as junk mail senders, or who are listed in the Rules Wizard as known junk-mailers. *Adult Content mail* is similar, but can be classified either by the sender or by the content of the subject line and message text.

The easiest way to handle spam is to use the Organize button on the toolbar. Click Organize and then click the Junk E-Mail tab in the Organize pane to see the options shown in Figure 21-25.

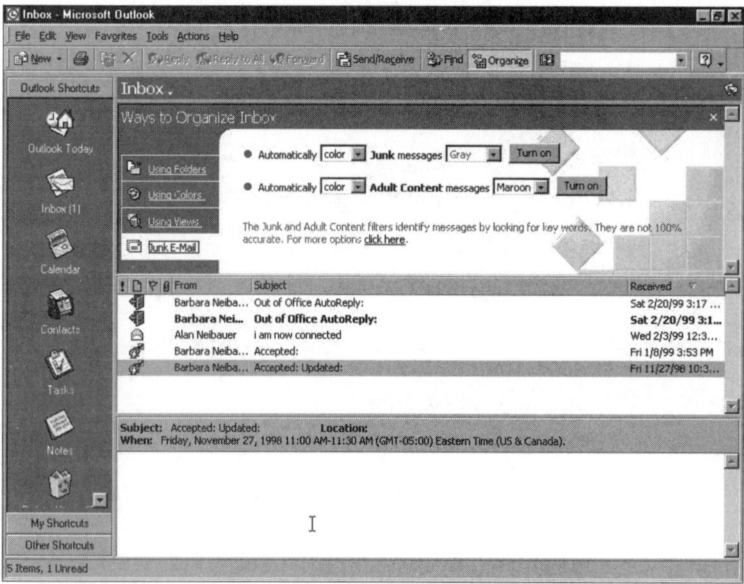

Figure 21-25
Working with junk mail.

To move mail to another folder, choose Move from the first box in either the Junk Mail or Adult Content sections. Then, click the drop-down arrow above the Organizer and select Junk E-mail, Deleted Items, or Other Folder from the drop-down list. To change the color of the mail, choose Color from the first box and select a specific color from the list. Finally, click Turn On to activate the feature. If you do not yet have a Junk E-Mail folder, Outlook will ask if you want to create it. Select Yes to create the folder. The Junk E-Mail folder is not automatically added to the Outlook Bar, but it will be included in the Folder list.

Now that you have specified how you want spam to be handled, you can add the e-mail addresses of spam senders to the junk mail list easily. Simply right-click a message in the inbox from a spammer, and choose either Add To Junk Senders List or Add To Adult Content Senders List from the shortcut menu.

Organizing Messages

When you set up Outlook to handle junk mail, you are actually creating one or more *rules* that determine how incoming mail is handled. You are saying, for example, "If any mail comes from a specific sender, move it to the deleted items folder." You can create other types of rules to move and respond to mail of all sorts.

Using the Rules Wizard, you can configure Outlook to automatically sort, forward, or reply to messages. If you are on an Exchange Server network, you also can use the Out Of Office Assistant to tell people who send you messages that you are away, when you'll be back, and who to contact or what to do during your absence. The Out

Of Office Assistant also can automatically sort, move, forward, and delete messages while you are away.

Using the Rules Wizard

When you want to specify how an incoming message is handled, use the Rules Wizard. Start by choosing Rules Wizard from the Tools menu to display the dialog box shown in Figure 21-26. If you are using Outlook with Microsoft Exchange Server, you must be online to use the Rules Wizard.

Figure 21-26
The Rules Wizard dialog box.

To create a new rule, click the New button to open the Rules Wizard dialog box shown in Figure 21-27.

On this page, you use the Which Type Of Rule Do You Want To Create? list to choose the general type of rule you want to create. For example, select Check Messages When They Arrive if you want to perform some action as soon as a message is received, such as sending a reply or forwarding the message to another recipient. Select Move Messages Based On Content if you want to move messages relating to a specific subject matter—such as a budget or personnel—to a selected folder

As you select options in the Rules Wizard, the logic of the rule appears in the Rule Description list box. In some cases, the description will contain hyperlinks which appear as underlined text. This means that you must click the hyperlink to further refine the rule. If you select the Move New Messages From Someone link, for example, you'll see the description shown here:

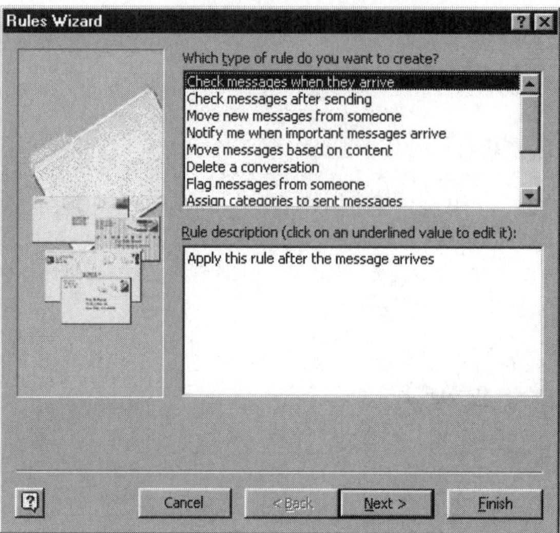

Figure 21-27
Use this page of the Rules Wizard to create a new rule.

```
Apply this rule after the message arrives
from people or distribution list
move it to the specified folder
```

This means you have to click the People Or Distribution List hyperlink to select the sender you want to check for, and then click the Specified hyperlink to choose the folder in which to place the message.

After you've chosen the type of rule, click the Next button to display the On Which Condition(s) Do You Want To Check? page. For example, you could create a rule that checks messages to determine if they are from a specific sender, if they have to do with budgets, or if they contain attachments. The availability of options depends on the type of rule you are creating.

After you select the conditions, click the Next button to open the What Do You Want To Do With The Message? page. On this page, you specify the actions that will be applied to messages that meet the conditions of your rule. For example, if you want to send an automatic reply to a message, select Reply Using A Specific Template. A few of the other actions you might choose include deleting the message, forwarding it to a list of recipients, playing a sound, or moving to a folder you specify. Click the Next button after making your choices.

Your rules will be applied in the order in which they are listed in the Rules Wizard list box. Once a rule is found that fits a message, no other rules are applied to it. You may have a message that fits two rules, for example, but only the first rule in the list will be used because the first rule's condition has been met.

You can change the order of rules to customize the way they are applied. Select the rule whose position you want to change and then click the Move Up or Move Down buttons to change the order or the application of the rules.

You also can use the Rules Wizard dialog box to copy, modify, rename, or delete rules. For additional control over how rules are applied, click the Options button to display the Rules Wizard Options dialog box, as shown in Figure 21-28.

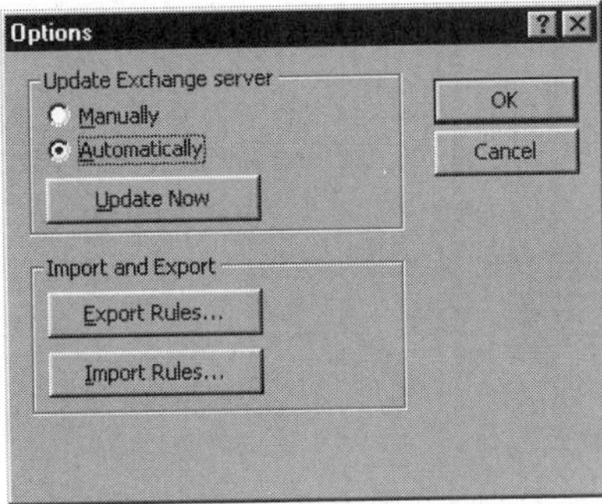

Figure 21-28
The Rules Wizard Options dialog box.

Normally, the rules you create are applied only to new messages as they are received or sent. To apply the rules to existing messages, click Run Now in the Rules Wizard dialog box to see the options shown in Figure 21-29.

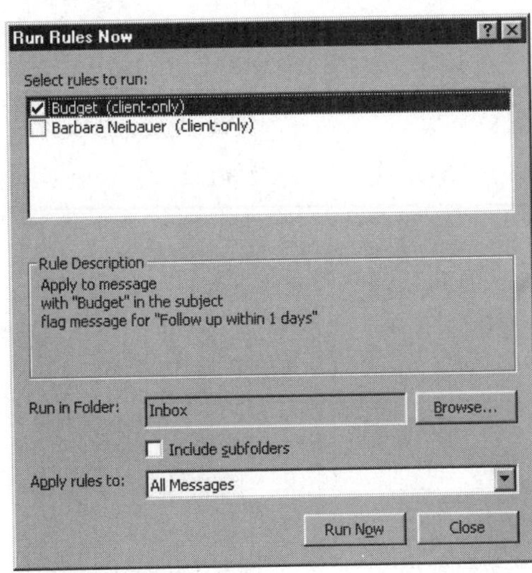

Figure 21-29
The Run Rules Now dialog box.

Select the check boxes for the rules you want to apply, and then choose the folder you want to apply the rules to. You can select only one folder at a time, but if you select a higher level folder, you can choose to apply the rules to messages in subfolders as well. You also can choose to apply the rules to all messages, only to messages that have been read, or to unread messages only in the selected folder(s). Click Run Now to apply the rules.

Create Rules with Other Methods

In addition to using the Rules Wizard to define each part of the rule, you can speed up the process in two ways.

If you already received a message from a sender or about a subject for which you want to create a rule, open the message and choose Create Rule from the Actions menu. The Rules Wizard opens with the message's sender, recipient, and subject already listed as conditions. Now complete the rule by choosing the conditions and actions you wish to apply.

You also can create a rule that moves a message from a specific sender or to a specific recipient using the Organize pane. Click Organize and then click the Using Folders tab. Select From or Sent To, and then enter the name of the sender or recipient, if necessary. Select the destination folder and then click Create Rule. The rule will be inserted into the Rules Wizard list and activated.

Using the Out Of Office Assistant

When you're away from your office—on vacation, for example—and you want people who write you to know that you're not available for a while, use the Out Of Office Assistant to automatically reply to each message you receive. You can use the Out Of Office Assistant only if you are using Outlook with Microsoft Exchange Server.

To set up the Out Of Office Assistant, take these steps:

1. Select Out Of Office Assistant from the Tools menu to open the dialog box shown in Figure 21-30.
2. Enable the option button labeled I Am Currently Out Of The Office to turn on the Out Of Office Assistant. When you later return to the office and can answer your mail, enable the button labeled I Am Currently In The Office.
3. In the AutoReply text box, type the reply you want the Assistant to send when a message is received.
4. Click OK.

When someone on your Exchange Server network sends you a message, whether or not you have Outlook running or not, your reply text is automatically sent to the sender, with the text Out Of Office Reply added to the subject line.

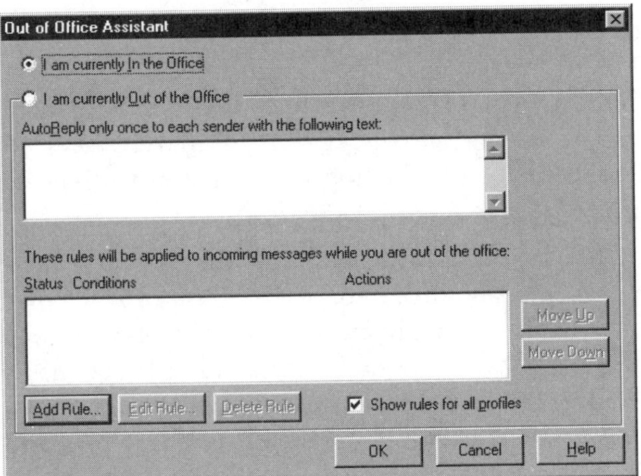

Figure 21-30
The Out Of Office Assistant dialog box.

The next time you start Outlook, you'll see a message reporting that the Out Of Office Assistant is currently activated and asking if you want to turn it off. Select Yes if you want to be considered in, or No if you are still out.

Until you turn the Out Of Office Assistant off and then on again, only one reply is returned to each sender. If a person sends you a second message while you are out, a reply is not sent automatically.

In addition to sending a simple reply, you also can use the Out Of Office Assistant to create and apply additional rules. In the Out Of Office Assistant dialog box, click the Add Rule button to open the Edit Rule dialog box, as shown in Figure 21-31.

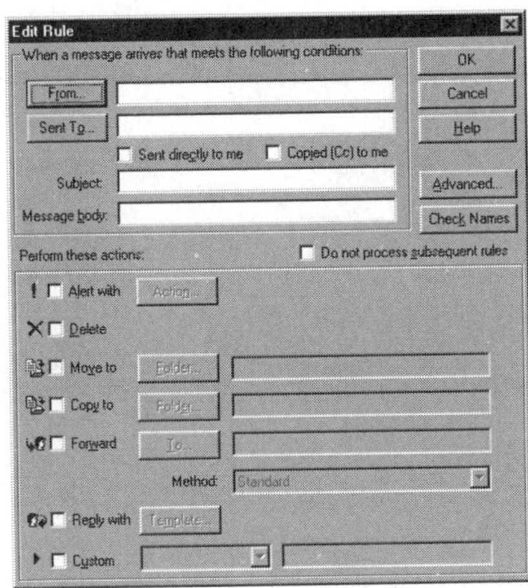

Figure 21-31
The Edit Rule dialog box.

For example, you can create a rule that sends a reply when a message is from a specific sender or contains specific text in the subject or body. To designate more detailed criteria for the message, click the Advanced button. In the dialog box that appears, you can specify criteria for the message size, the date it was sent or received, the attachments it might contain, and the Importance and Sensitivity designations.

Click the Check Names button to check names you've entered in the From and Sent To boxes against the entries in your address book. If Outlook finds a matching name, it underlines the name and turns it into a hyperlink to the address book entry. If you typed a partial name, such as just a first name, Outlook completes the name with the full listing from the address book. If Outlook locates multiple matches, such as several persons with the same first name, it asks you to select the correct name from a list. If Outlook does not find a match, it asks if you want to create a new address listing.

Next, designate the actions to take in the lower half of the Rules dialog box. You can choose to have Outlook do the following things:

- Alert you that the message has arrived by displaying the New Items Of Interest Box with the sender's name, subject, and message date, optionally playing a sound. If Outlook is not running, the alert will appear the next time you start it.
- Delete the message.
- Move the message to a folder.
- Copy the message to a folder.
- Forward the message to another person.
- Reply to the message with a template.
- Perform a custom action, if any have been provided.

When you close the Edit Rule dialog box, all your rules will be listed in the Out Of Assistant box, as shown here:

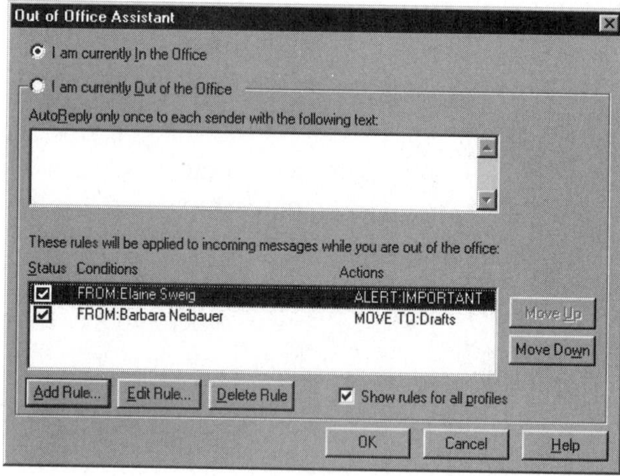

You can turn individual rules off or on by checking or clearing their check boxes, and you can change the order in which they are applied.

Turning off the Out Of Office Assistant does not delete the rules. You can set up the Out Of Office Assistant in advance and then turn it on and off as needed. You also can leave intact the rules you create so that you have to set them up only once.

Office 2000 and E-Mail

So far, we've been addressing sending e-mail through Outlook. Office 2000 also includes Outlook Express, a powerful program used for sending and receiving e-mail over the Internet and working with news groups.

E-mail, in fact, is built right in to the Office 2000 interface, so you do not have to launch Outlook or Outlook Express to send mail. From within the major Office 2000 applications, for example, click the E-Mail button on the Standard toolbar or choose Send To from the File menu and select either Mail Recipient or Mail Recipient (As Attachment).

Note Just type an Internet e-mail address—in the format name@xxxx.xxx—to create a mail hyperlink, and click the hyperlink to send mail to the recipient.

- In Microsoft Word, clicking the E-Mail button opens an e-mail window within Word showing the current document as the text of the message. Just type the recipient's address and a subject, and then click Send on the message window toolbar.
- In Microsoft Excel, clicking the E-Mail button lets you choose either the Send The Entire Workbook As An Attachment option or the Send The Current Sheet As The Message Body option.
- In Microsoft PowerPoint, clicking the E-Mail button gives you the option to send the entire presentation as an attachment or to send the current slide as the message body.
- The Send To command on the File menu might also include the options Fax Recipient and Routing Recipient. Choose Fax Recipient when you want to fax the current document using your fax modem.

Routing a document lets you e-mail the document to more than one person as an attachment. You can choose to send the document to recipients either all at one time or in sequence. You create a routing slip similar to the one shown in Figure 21-32 that specifies how you want to send the document and keep track of its progress.

The Return When Done option sends the document back to you as e-mail once everyone on the list has reviewed it. The Track Status option sends you e-mail as each recipient forwards it to the next.

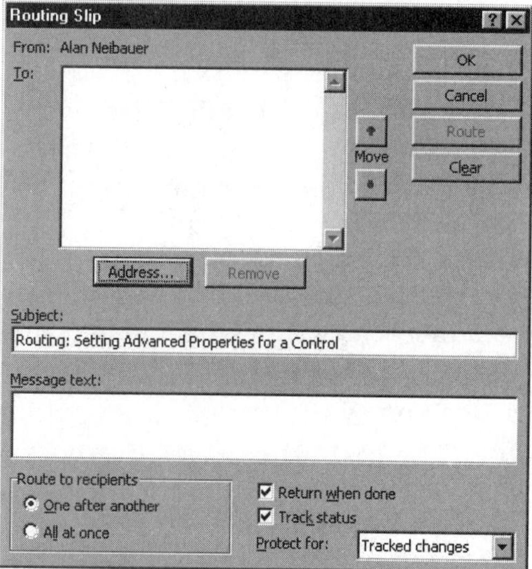

Figure 21-32
The Routing Slip dialog box.

Use the Protect For list to control the type of changes that recipients can make to the document. You can choose from the following options:

- **None** allows recipients to make changes to the document without tracking the changes.
- **Tracked Changes** allows recipients to change the document but turns on revision marking.
- **Comments** allows recipients to insert, but not to change, the contents.
- **Forms** prevents recipients from changing the structure of a routed form.

When you are finished selecting options, click Route to send the e-mail, or click Add Slip (which replaces the OK button) if you want to send the document later. If you choose Add Slip, send the document by selecting Send To from the File menu and choosing one of the following options:

- Next Routing Recipient lets you route the document or simply send it without the routing slip.
- Other Routing Recipient opens the routing slip so you can choose the recipient.

The recipient receives e-mail with the document attached, which they can then open and read or edit. The recipient can then choose the Next Routing Recipient or Other Routing Recipient option from the Send To menu to continue the routing process.

Chapter 22

Manage Web Sites with FrontPage

by Jim Buyens

In This Chapter

Anyone who is familiar with Microsoft Office applications and who has been on the Internet for more than a few minutes would never confuse an Internet Web site with a Microsoft Word document or a Microsoft Excel spreadsheet. Compared to other types of Office documents, Web pages are small in size, long on interactivity, complex in organization, and high in impact.

Web pages can be internally complex, as well. What might be a single document in Word or PowerPoint could be dozens of independent documents, or pages, on the Internet, and each of those pages might include a dozen or more pictures, plug-ins, ActiveX Controls, Java applets, and other component files. Rather than a single Word or PowerPoint file, the Web requires that you keep hundreds of individual files properly linked and organized. Fortunately, Microsoft FrontPage can help.

At first, many fledgling Web designers approach FrontPage as nothing more than a What You See Is What You Get (WYSIWYG) Web page editor. Using FrontPage editor, designers with little or no HTML knowledge can create interesting pages in a very short period of time. At the same time, FrontPage handles all the integration needs for the many files that make up each page.

The next step, of course, is for FrontPage to remember the component and hyperlink relationships within and among all the pages on a Web site, and to use this information for automatically updating those pages as things change. This second step is the topic of this chapter.

In the context of FrontPage, the word *user* is a very confusing term. Is the user the person who creates pages in FrontPage, or is the user the person intended to view those pages? To avoid ambiguity, we'll call those who create pages Web designers, and we'll call those who view those pages Web visitors.

Automating Web Site Organization

A FrontPage Web is a collection of Web pages, picture files, and other components that FrontPage manages as a unit. A FrontPage Web begins in a folder, and includes all the files and folders within it. There are two kinds of FrontPage Webs:

- A **Disk-Based Web** resides in an ordinary folder on your hard disk or file server. This is the simplest type of FrontPage Web to understand and create. The FrontPage desktop software updates this type of Web directly.
- A **Server-Based Web** resides in a folder on a Web server. The FrontPage desktop software updates this kind of Web indirectly, by communicating with special software installed on the Web server. This makes server-based Webs more complex to manage and use.

In terms of Web page creation and Web site management, both types of Webs offer equal features. The difference comes into play when you go beyond delivering static Web pages and start running programs on the Web server when a visitor requests a certain page. These types of programs can run only on Web servers, and testing them (or sometimes even developing them) requires a server-based Web.

One FrontPage Web can reside within another; such Webs are called nested Webs. The inner Web is called a child Web or a subweb, and the Web that contains it is called a parent Web. Content within a subweb doesn't appear as content within its parent Web, however. No file or folder can belong to two Webs at once.

FrontPage maintains various cross-references and indexes for each FrontPage Web. This is where FrontPage records all its information about the files contained in the Web—title, date and time the file was saved, the person who last maintained it, comments, and so forth. This information can become outdated if you create a FrontPage Web and then change it through means other than using FrontPage. The consequences are incomplete or incorrect results. The best approach, therefore, is to always modify FrontPage Webs using FrontPage, the Web Folders icon in My Computer, or the Web Folders icon on the Office 2000 Save As dialog box. If that isn't possible, you should periodically run the FrontPage Recalculate Hyperlinks command to rebuild all the indexes from scratch.

Initializing a FrontPage Web

A FrontPage Web is much more than a collection of content files. It also contains system files and programs put into place and maintained by the FrontPage software. The phrase *creating a FrontPage Web* doesn't necessarily mean creating a set of content files; it means initializing the special folders and files FrontPage will use to manage that content. FrontPage can include an existing body of content when it creates a new Web, or even populate a new Web with prototype content. Nevertheless, creating a new Web means preparing a folder tree for management by FrontPage. Populating the FrontPage Web with Web pages and related content files is really a separate operation.

You can create FrontPage Webs in a variety of ways, but they all require that you use the FrontPage desktop software or the FrontPage Server Extensions. You can't, for example, create a FrontPage Web from the Web Folders icon in My Computer or the Web Folders icon in the Office 2000 Save As dialog box.

Initializing a Disk-Based FrontPage Web

The simplest way to create a FrontPage Web is to start using FrontPage to save Web pages into a specific folder, and then wait for FrontPage to display the web conversion dialog box shown in Figure 22-1. This occurs the first time you use a FrontPage feature requiring the use of a FrontPage Web. Click Yes to convert the current folder into a FrontPage Web.

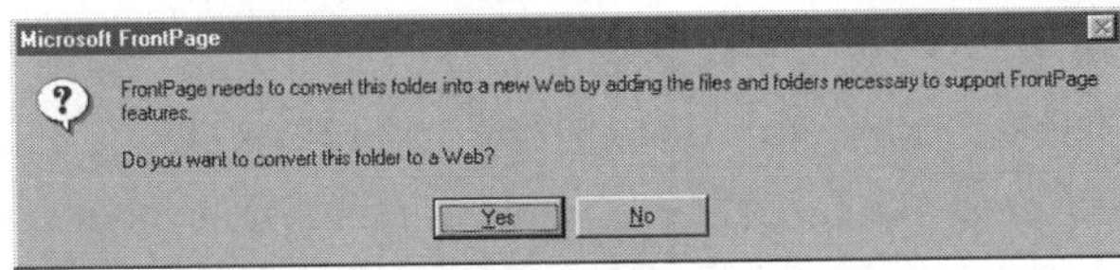

Figure 22-1
The FrontPage Web conversion dialog box.

You also can create a FrontPage Web explicitly using the following procedure:

1. Start the FrontPage desktop software.
2. Choose New from the File menu, and then choose Web.

3. When the New dialog box shown in Figure 22-2 appears, choose a Web type from the Web Sites dialog box.
4. Enter or select a location for the Web type in the Specify the Location of the New Web drop-down list on the right. Entering a disk location creates a disk-based Web, while entering a location beginning with http://<server name> creates a server-based Web.
5. Click OK.

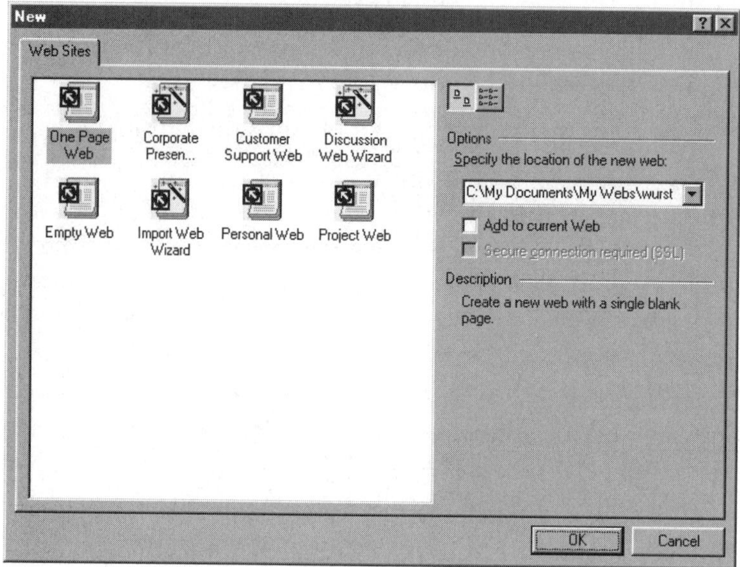

Figure 22-2
Select a FrontPage Web type in the Web Sites dialog box.

The icons in the Web Sites dialog box shown in Figure 22-2 control the Web's initial content.

- **Empty Web** creates a Web, but adds no content.
- **One Page Web** creates a new Web with an empty home page.
- **Import Web Wizard** displays several dialog boxes that prompt you for a source location and related settings, and then creates a new Web with content from that location. You can specify either a disk folder or an http:// URL as the source location.
- **Discussion Web Wizard** creates a Web that functions as a threaded discussion group. Web visitors can post new messages, browse and search existing messages, and respond to messages. Because discussion Webs involve server-side programs to create and index any new messages a Web visitor might submit, they require a server-based Web for testing and deployment.

Initializing a Server-Based FrontPage Web

For most users just starting out with FrontPage, a disk-based Web provides maximum simplicity and adequate capability. However, for advanced users requiring maximum capability, nothing but a server-based Web may suffice. Creating a server-based Web requires five distinct steps.

- First, an administrator must install Web server software on the computer that will host the FrontPage Web. This will create one logical Web server, often called the default server.

  If you're installing a personal Web server on your own computer, then the administrator will probably be you.

- Second, if the computer will support more than one virtual Web server, an administrator must define and configure each one. Each additional Web server is called a virtual Web server, which responds to a different IP address. This is how one physical computer can support multiple sites such as www.artichokes.com, www.attitudes.com, and www.mensa.org.

  The Microsoft Personal Web Servers for Windows 95/98 and Windows NT Workstation support only a single, default server. That is, they don't support virtual servers.

- Third, a system administrator working at the Web server's console must install the FrontPage Server Extensions. Significantly, this step doesn't activate the server extensions for any Web servers that may exist on the server itself.

  Performing this step generally involves running a setup program supplied with the version of the FrontPage Server Extensions designed for the installed Web server.

- Fourth, the system administrator must activate the FrontPage Server Extensions on each desired virtual Web server. This step converts that Web server's existing content into a single FrontPage Web called the root Web.

  Installing the FrontPage Server Extensions on a server normally completes step one for the whole server, and step two for the first (that is, the default) Web server. However, the administrator must initiate step two manually for any Web servers other than the first. When installing the FrontPage Server Extensions on a Personal Web Server that doesn't support virtual servers, steps three and four are always combined.

  The software for performing this step varies according to the type of Web server. The possibilities include Microsoft Management Console and a collection of command-line utilities, and a collection of HTML forms provided with the FrontPage Server Extensions.

  After installing the extensions on a virtual server, the system administrator usually delegates administration of the root Web to the client.

- Fifth, the administrator of any FrontPage Web—including the root Web—can optionally create new subwebs and designate other users as administrators of those subwebs. Splitting a large site into several Web sites improves performance, localizes related content, and provides different security for different parts of the site.

Microsoft provides the following Web servers for the various Windows operating systems. To install any of these servers on your own computer—either for production or for testing—obtain and install the Windows NT Server 4.0 Option Pack from Microsoft's Web site at the following URL:

```
http://www.microsoft.com/NTServer/all/downloads.asp
```

This will install one of the following Web servers on your computer, depending on your operating system:

- Microsoft Personal Web Server for Windows 95 and Windows 98
- Microsoft Personal Web Server for Windows NT Workstation
- Microsoft Internet Information Server for Windows NT Server

Unless Microsoft updates the Option pack, do not install the included version of the FrontPage Server Extensions. Instead, install the FrontPage Server Extensions Resource Kit from Office 2000 or FrontPage setup or, if you prefer, the Office Server Extensions from the \OSE folder on one of the Office 2000 distribution discs.

Examining a FrontPage Web

Figure 22-3 shows FrontPage 2000 displaying a new disk-based Web. Beneath the title bar, menu bar, and toolbars are a Views bar at the left, a Folder List in the center, and an editing window at the right.

The six options in the Views bar provide the following functions:

- **Page View** provides the WYSIWYG editing window. To edit a Web page, double-click it in the Folder list or choose Open from the File menu.
- **Folders View** replaces the WYSIWYG editing window with a list of files contained in the current Web, organized by folder. Although the Folder List still appears in the center window, the Folder view on the right provides more detail.
- **Reports View** displays a summary report showing statistics about the current Web, along with 12 detailed reports you can optionally view and sort.
- **Navigation View** contains a hierarchical view of the Web reflecting its menu structure. As we'll learn in the next section, this is something you supply manually, not something that FrontPage gleans from hyperlink analysis.
- **Hyperlinks View** displays a structural diagram of the FrontPage Web based on hyperlink analysis.

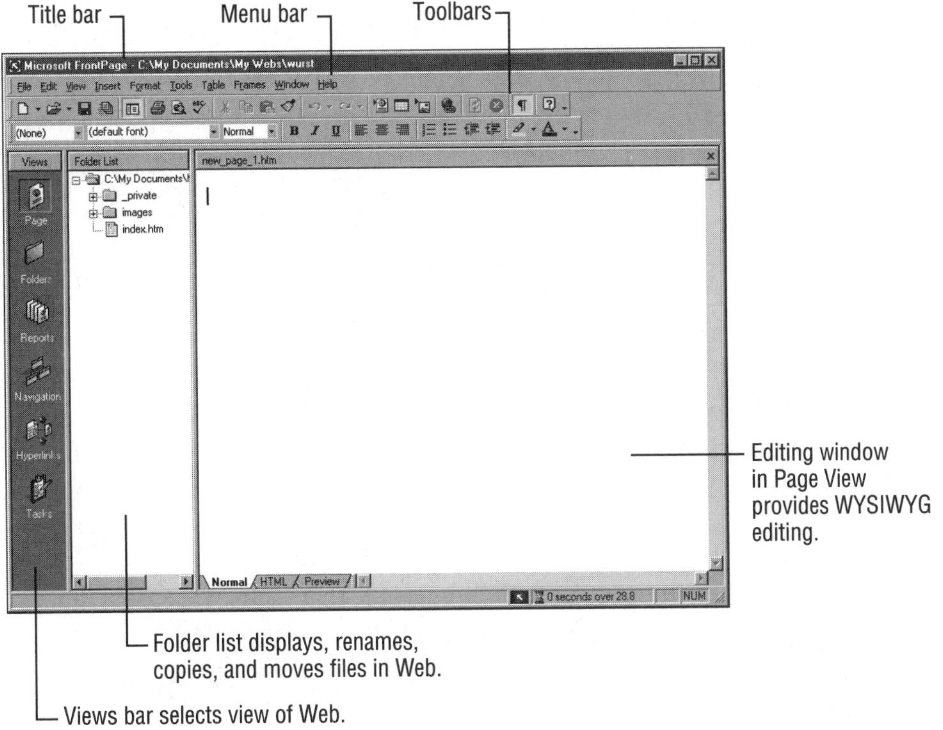

Figure 22-3
This is how FrontPage displays a new one-page Web.

- **Tasks View** provides a mechanical to-do list for your Web. You can add, update, and delete tasks manually, and FrontPage can automatically create tasks while initializing new pages, scanning for spelling errors, or looking for broken hyperlinks.

Note Office Server Extensions are available only for Windows NT Server. They include the FrontPage Server Extensions, plus additional features that work with Office 2000 applications.

Once your Front Page Web exists, you can create new pages by choosing New from the File menu, by clicking the New Page toolbar button, by right-clicking a folder in the Folder List and choosing New Page, by copying and pasting files in the Folder List, and through various other commands conveniently located in nooks and crannies throughout the application.

There are many ways to create hyperlinks, as well. Dragging a page from the Folder list into the WYSIWYG editing window, for example, creates a link from the edited page to the page you dragged. The dragged page's Title text—as entered under Page

Properties—will become the hyperlink text. In the Page view editor, you can perform the following actions:

1. Select any text or picture.
2. Click the Hyperlink toolbar button, choose Hyperlink from the Insert menu, or right-click the selected area and then choose Hyperlink from the context menu.
3. Use the resulting dialog box to enter or locate the desired hyperlink location.
4. Click OK.

Organizing Your Site Using Navigation View

Building hyperlinks is one way to organize your site's structure, but this is laborious up front and difficult to maintain over time. That's why FrontPage provides Navigation view, described in this section. Figure 22-4 illustrates FrontPage displaying nine Web pages in Navigation view.

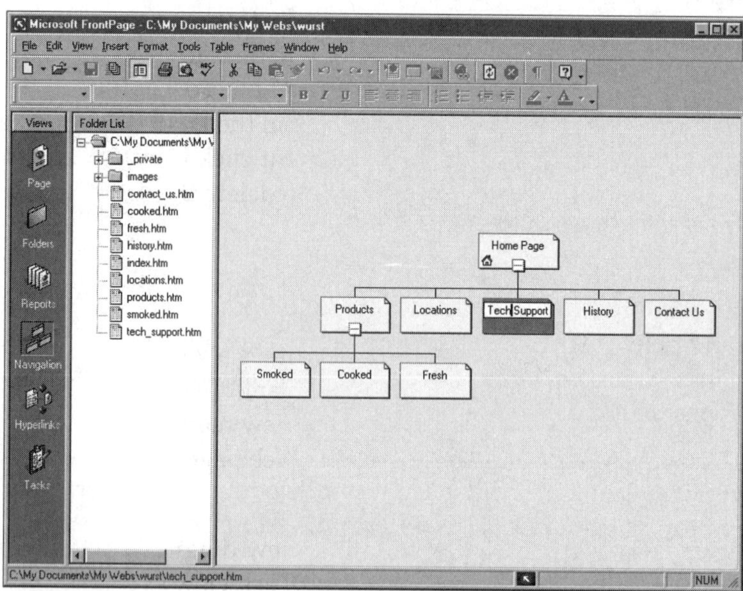

Figure 22-4
Navigation view records and displays the structure of the Web pages in a FrontPage Web.

To duplicate this structure, take the following steps:

1. Create a new one-page Web. For this example, we'll use the disk-based Web shown earlier in Figure 22-2.
2. Click the Navigation icon in the FrontPage Views bar.

3. Select the Home Page. Initially, this will be the only page in the Web, and also the one diagrammed in the Navigation view window.
4. Click the New Page toolbar icon to add a new page hierarchically beneath the currently selected page, just under the Home Page.
5. The new page's title will say New Page *n*, where *n* is a sequential number. Give the page a better title by clicking it, pressing F2, and typing in a new name. To recreate Figure 22-4, title this page "Products."
6. Repeat steps 3 through 5 to create the Locations, Tech Support, History, and Contact Us pages. Enter these page titles in step 5.
7. Select the Products page, and then repeat steps 4 and 5 to create the Smoked page.
8. Repeat step 7 to create the Cooked and Fresh pages.

At this point, the Navigation view structure will exist, but the associated Web pages will not. Switching out of Navigation view will save blank Web pages, with default names for each node that don't already have a physical page.

To update the Navigation view, simply drag pages from one part of the diagram to another. FrontPage will draw temporary structure lines to show what a page's parent would be if you dropped it at its current location. To add a page that exists in your Web but not in Navigation view, drag it from the Folder list window into the Navigation view diagram. To remove a page, right-click it and choose Delete from the context menu. FrontPage will ask whether to delete the page entirely from the Web, or just from Navigation view.

Using the Page Banner Component

Creating a nice-looking Navigation view structure is a wonderful exercise, but the resulting Web pages have a big problem: they're blank! To correct this, one of the first things you need is a way to use the Navigation view name of each Web page as its heading. The following procedure will update a Web page so its heading matches its Navigation view name:

1. Double-click the page in the Navigation view diagram in the Folder List or anywhere else you see it displayed (except Task view). For this example, we'll double-click the Home page index.htm.
2. FrontPage will switch to Page view and open the blank page for editing.
3. Make sure the insertion point is flashing within the blank page, and then choose Page Banner from the Insert menu. This will display the Page Banner dialog box shown in Figure 22-5.

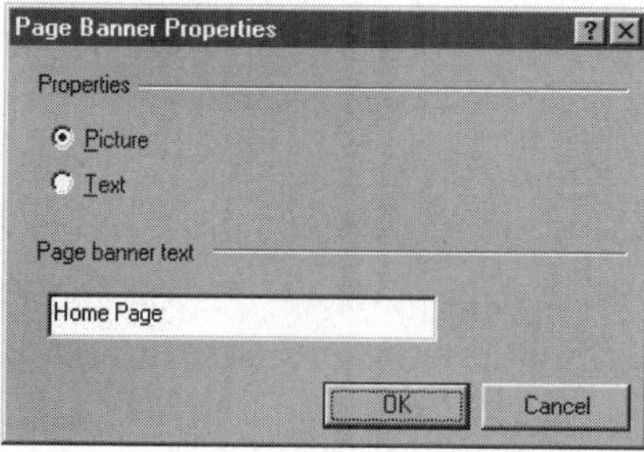

Figure 22-5
This dialog box inserts a Web page's Navigation view name as text.

4. Verify that the Picture option is chosen under Properties, and that the Page Banner Text is correct. Updating the Page Banner Text field actually updates the Navigation view name.
5. Click OK.

After you complete step 5, the page's Navigation view name should appear as text within the Web page. You can format this text in any of the usual ways. For example, you could select it and center it on the page using the Center toolbar button, or you could change its text style or font using the formatting toolbar or the Format menu. But for this example, we'll disregard these possibilities and worry about inserting a Navigation bar instead.

There are three equivalent ways to reconfigure an existing Page banner:

- Double-click it, or
- Right-click it and choose Properties from the context menu, or
- Select it and then either choose Properties from the Format menu or press Ctrl+Enter.

Using the Navigation Bar Component

The next embellishment to our home page will be a menu bar that points to each of the pages we created just beneath it. The FrontPage Navigation Bar component can create such menu bars automatically. Here are the necessary steps:

1. Pick the position where you want the menu bar to appear. For this example, click the right edge of the Page Banner component we inserted in the previous section, and then press Enter to start a new paragraph.
2. Choose Navigation Bar from the Insert menu.
3. When the Navigation Bar Properties dialog box shown in Figure 22-6 appears:
   - Under the heading Hyperlinks To Add to Page, choose Child Level Under Home.

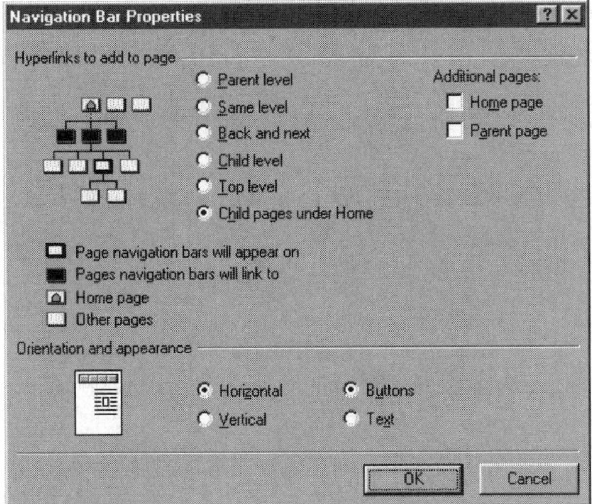

Figure 22-6
The Navigation Bar Properties dialog box controls which hyperlinks appear in a given Navigation bar.

- Under Orientation And Appearance, choose Horizontal and Buttons.

4. Click OK.

Figure 22-7 shows how the Web page should now appear. Notice the hyperlinks to the five pages. The Navigation bar component displays hyperlinks to the five pages we positioned beneath the Home page in Navigation view, in the order we arranged them. This is no accident; in fact, switching back to Navigation view and changing the diagram would automatically change the Navigation bar, even if none of the affected pages were open in Page view. This is where the power of Navigation view really starts showing. Change your Web's structure once in Navigation view, and all the links connecting all the diagrammed pages automatically change.

Using the Page Banner and Navigation bar components means that the same page will be identified by the same text everywhere in your Web.

Standardizing Your Web with Shared Borders

Manually inserting Page Banners and Navigation bars into each page in a Web isn't terribly difficult, but it isn't terribly interesting or glamorous, either. Fortunately, FrontPage provides a way to insert such components throughout your site, and to keep them up-to-date as well. The method to this madness is the FrontPage Shared Border component.

Once you apply Shared Borders to a Web, FrontPage adds borders along the top, bottom, left, and right edges—in whatever combination you wish—for each page in the Web. FrontPage then ensures that those borders contain exactly the same content for every page in your Web.

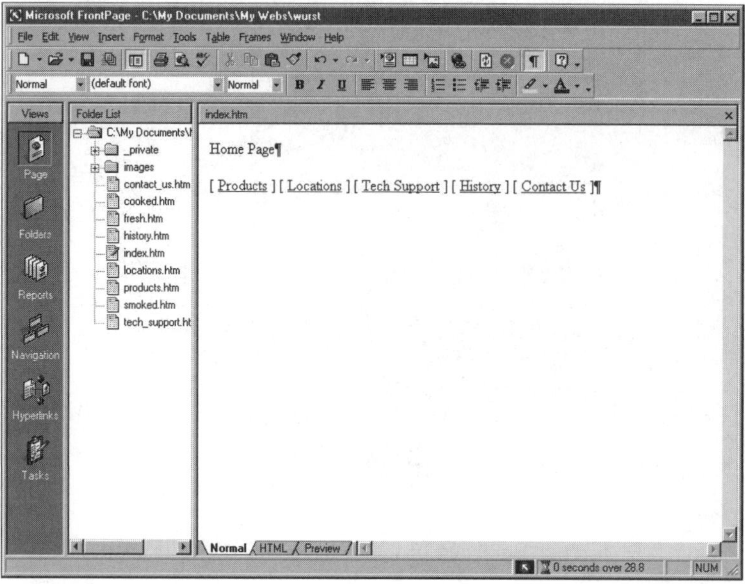

Figure 22-7
The second line on this Web page is a FrontPage Navigation bar component that derives all its text and links from the Web's Navigation view structure.

Adding the same top border to every page in a Web might seem a bit silly; after all, you want every page to have a different heading. But if you place a Page Banner component in the top Shared Border, the Page Banner component will display the Navigation View name of each page where it appears. The same is true for Navigation bars; a Navigation bar in a Shared Border customizes itself for each page where it appears.

Figure 22-8 shows the dialog box you use to add Shared Borders to a Web page. To display it, choose Shared Borders from the Format menu. The following fields apply.

- **Apply To** chooses a set of pages that will receive the Shared Borders. In this example, we'll choose All Pages, which will apply Shared Borders to every page in the FrontPage Web. Choosing Selected Page(s) applies Shared Borders only to the currently selected pages in the active FrontPage window.

If you apply Shared Borders to All Pages and also to Selected Pages, the settings for the selected pages will override the settings for the entire Web.

- **Top, Left, Right,** and **Bottom** toggle Shared Borders on and off for the corresponding edges. In this example, we'll choose Top and Bottom only.
- **Include Navigation Buttons** controls whether a Navigation bar will be present in the associated border (top or left), which is the option we'll use for the top Shared Border.

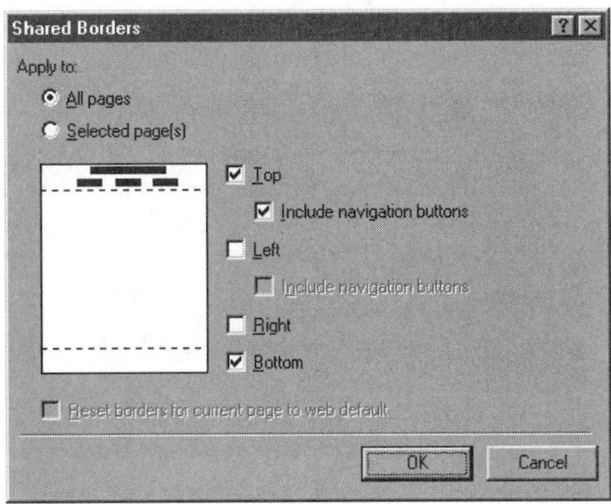

Figure 22-8
Shared borders replicate identical content and components to every page in a Web.

- **Border For Current Page To Web Default** reverses the effect of applying Shared Borders for a selected page. After turning this box on, clicking OK causes the current Web page to revert to the default Shared Border settings in effect for the FrontPage Web as a whole.

The best way to edit Shared Borders is simply to edit any Web page that contains them. Remember, though, that changing the content of a Shared Border in one Web page changes the contents of the same border in every other page in the same Web. Never place content appropriate to just one or two pages within a Shared Border.

Figure 22-9 shows the example site's Home page after applying Shared Borders to the entire Web, and after a bit of additional editing. The top Shared Border appears above the upper dotted line, and the bottom Shared Border appears below the lower dotted line.

The top Shared Border contains the Page Banner component we configured previously, plus the Navigation bar that came from selecting Include Navigation Buttons when we created the Shared Borders. It also contains a Comment component, which displays text while you're editing the page in FrontPage, but suppresses it when Web visitors see the page. FrontPage generated the comments that appear in Figure 22-9, but you can add your own comments anywhere in a Web page by setting the insertion point and then choosing Comment from the Insert menu.

The bottom Shared Border begins with a standard HTML horizontal line. To insert a horizontal line, set the insertion point, and then choose Horizontal Line from the Insert menu.

Below the horizontal line is some ordinary text, "Last changed by," followed by a FrontPage Substitution component. This component displays named values defined elsewhere in the Web. Here are the steps for using the Substitution component:

1. Set the insertion point where the Substitution component should appear. For this example, we'll place it within the bottom Shared Border.

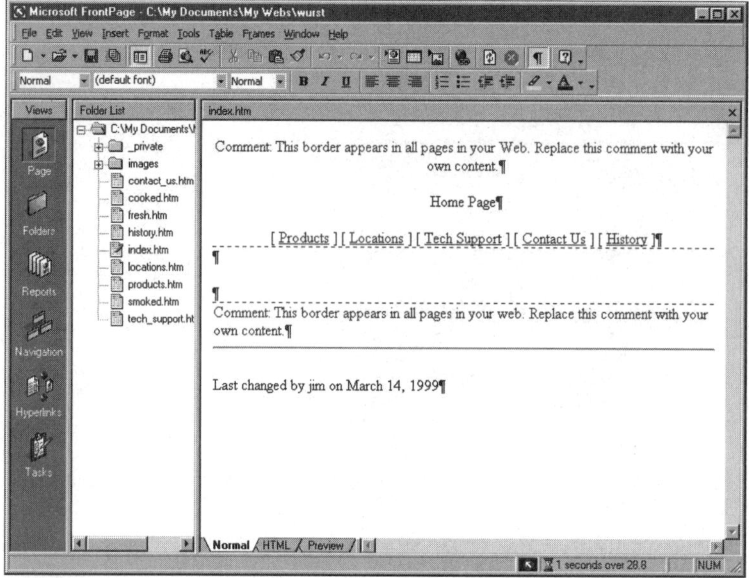

Figure 22-9
Shared borders replicate the same content to selected edges of every page in a Web.

2. Choose Component from the Insert menu, and then choose Substitution.
3. In the Substitution Properties dialog box displayed in the graphic below, choose Modified By in the drop-down list.
4. Click OK.

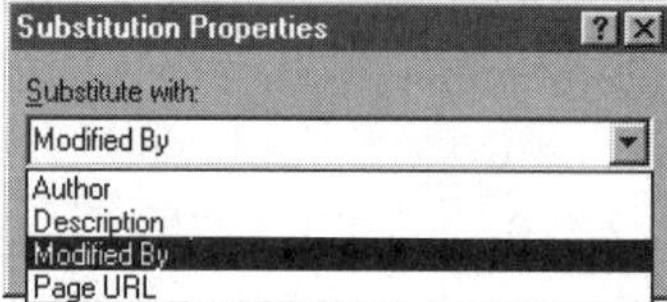

The four choices shown in the illustration are built-in variables representing the following four values:

- **Author** indicates the name of the person who originally created the Web page. FrontPage automatically collects and records this information.
- **Description** contains a comment string you can modify by right-clicking the Web page in the Folder List, choosing Properties from the pop-up menu, and filling in the Comments box on the Summary tab.
- **Modified By** indicates the name of the person who last changed the Web page. FrontPage automatically collects and records this information.

- **Page URL** displays the Web location of the current page. FrontPage automatically obtains this information.

You can define additional variables by choosing Web Settings from the Tools menu, and then choosing the Parameters tab. When you have a string of text that will appear on multiple Web pages, and that string of text occasionally changes, you should consider defining it as a Web Parameter and use the Substitution component to display it. That way, when the value changes, you only have to update it in one place.

Referring again to Figure 22-9, the word "on" is ordinary text, but the date "March 14, 1999" is a FrontPage Date and Time component. The Date and Time component is another object that displays information automatically recorded by FrontPage. Here's the procedure to add the Date and Time component to your page:

1. Set the insertion point where you want the Date and Time component to appear. In this example, we'll place it within the bottom Shared Border.
2. Choose Date and Time from the Insert menu.
3. In the Date and Time Properties dialog box shown below, choose Date This Page Was Last Edited, the date format you prefer, and a time format of (none), and then click OK.

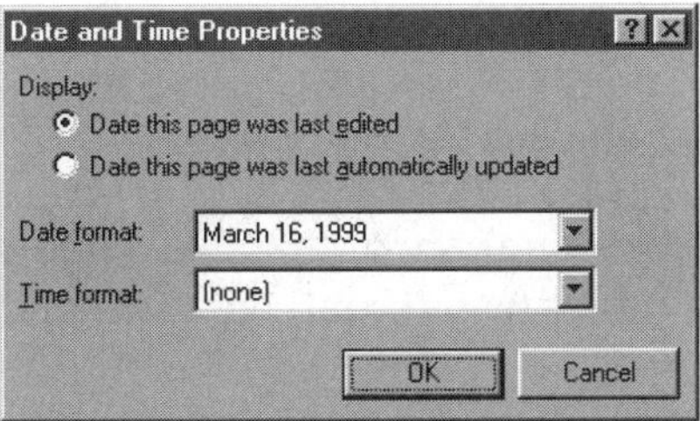

When displaying dates on the Web, it's always best to use spelled-out months and four-digit years. A date like 01/02/03 could mean February 3, 2001, January 2, 2003, or February 1, 2003 to people from different parts of the world.

Figure 22-10 shows three pages in our Web. The index.htm file is the one we've been working on, but all the content in the other pages came directly from FrontPage. The top border area in each page is the same, in one sense; for each page. it contains a Page Banner component and a Navigation Bar component. Although identically configured, these components display different information depending on the page that contains them. The result is a set of Web pages properly linked, uniformly named, and ready for individual content, all done automatically and correctly—and with very little work on your part.

The real payback comes when it is time to add, remove, or reposition pages in your site. If you make such changes in Navigation view, FrontPage will update all the site Navigation bars automatically.

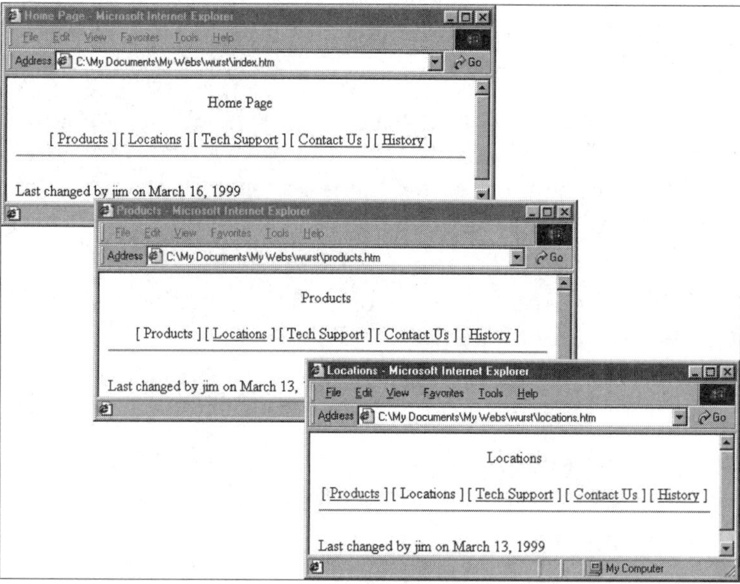

Figure 22-10
The Navigation bars on each of these pages are configured identically, and each bar reflects the Navigation view position of its host Web page.

Creating a Table of Contents for Your Web

In this section, we'll look at one more component that organizes content. Then, in the next section, we'll learn how to use a major FrontPage feature that controls Web site appearance.

The Table of Contents component creates a map of your Web's structure and displays it in a Web page. This helps your Web visitors quickly find the page they need. Here's the procedure for adding a Table Of Contents page to the sample site:

1. Click the Navigation icon in the Views bar.
2. Highlight the home page, and then click the New Page toolbar button.
3. Using the mouse, drag the new page to the left of the home page, and then drop it. As shown in Figure 22-11, there should be no connector lines to other pages in the Web.
4. Name the new page Site Map.
5. Double-click the Site Map page to open it in Page view.
6. Set the insertion point in the body of the Web page—that is, between the top and bottom Shared Borders.
7. Choose Component from the Insert menu, and then choose Table of Contents.

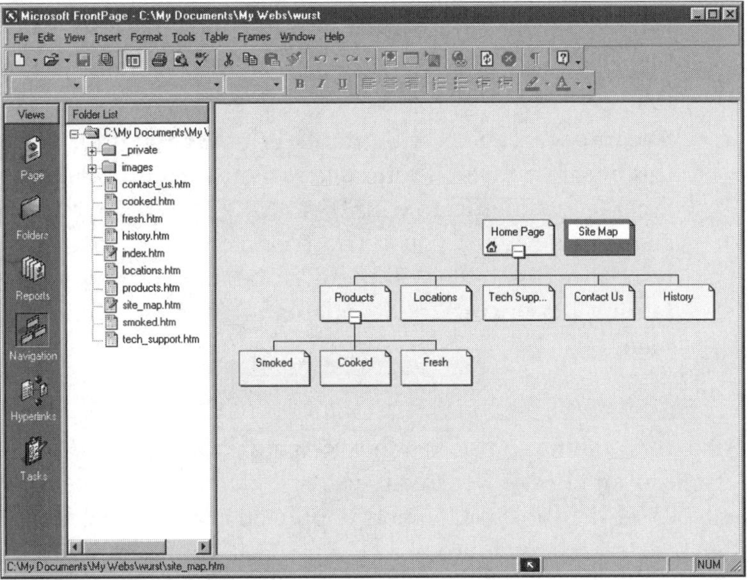

Figure 22-11
Pages positioned to the left or right of the Home page aren't part of a Web's hierarchy.

8. When the dialog box shown in Figure 22-12 appears, specify these values:
   - **Page URL for Starting Point Of Table** Enter the URL that should appear at the top of the Table of Contents. In our example, we want to map the entire FrontPage Web, so we specify the URL of the home page: index.htm.
   - **Heading Font Size** Select the font size FrontPage should use for the page at the top of the Table of Contents. A value of 1 means Heading 1 (H1) style; a value of 2 means Heading 2 (H2) style, and so forth. Choose 3.
   - **Show Each Page Only Once** Select this box if, when a Web page appears more than once in the structure, you want only the first occurrence displayed. This makes no difference in our example, but we'll check it anyway.

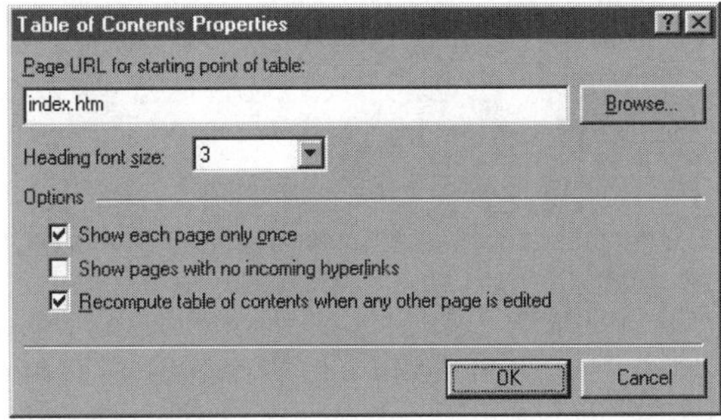

Figure 22-12
The Table of Contents Properties dialog box configures the starting point and other settings for a table of contents based on hyperlink analysis.

- **Show Pages With No Incoming Hyperlinks** Select this box if you want the Table of Contents to include any Web pages not specified in any hyperlink on your Web.
- **Recompute Table Of Contents When Any Other Page Is Edited** Select this box if you want FrontPage to recreate the Table of Contents each time you make a change to your Web. Note that this operation takes extra processing time when you save a Web page. If you leave the box unchecked, refreshing the table will require opening and saving the Web page containing it or using the Recalculate Hyperlinks command on the Tools menu.

9. Click OK.

The Table of Contents component has two quirks you should be aware of. First, the table itself doesn't display correctly in Page view; all you see is a dummy Table of Contents. To see the Table of Contents populated in all its glorious detail, save the page and then preview it in your browser. Figure 22-13 shows both FrontPage and Internet Explorer displaying a Web page that contains a Table of Contents component.

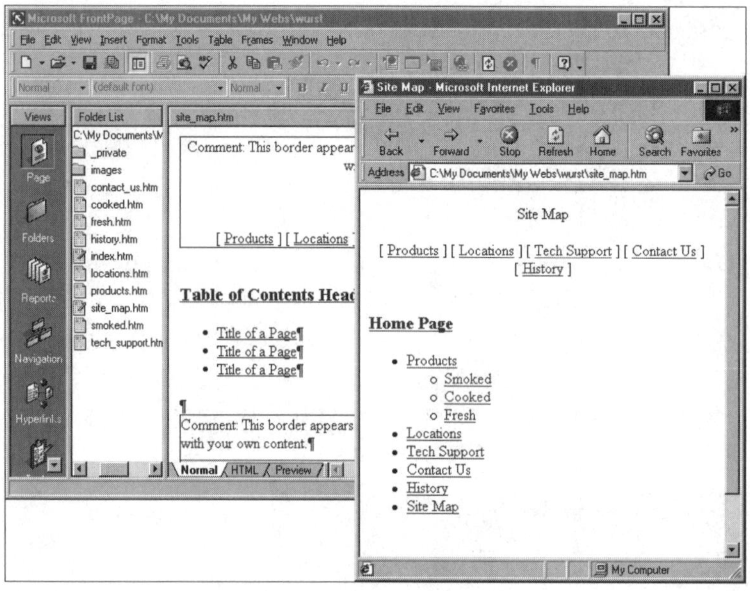

Figure 22-13
FrontPage displays Table of Contents components with placeholder contents only.

The second quirk is that the Table of Contents component isn't based on the current Web's Navigation view structure. Instead, the table is based on hyperlink analysis. FrontPage scans the starting page for hyperlinks within the current Web and constructs Level 1 headings accordingly. Then, it scans each Level 1 page for additional hyperlinks to get that page's Level 2 headings. This process continues until there are no more hyperlinks to list.

In the sample site, we let Navigation bars build all our hyperlinks for us, based on Navigation view. Therefore, hyperlink analysis produces the original Navigation view structure. This generally wouldn't be true if we built any or all of the hyperlinks by hand.

Note When you construct a Table of Contents, FrontPage always ignores pages that are parents of the current page. In the Wurst Web example used earlier in this chapter, for example, the Home page links to the Products page, and the Products page also links to the home page. To avoid an infinite loop, FrontPage ignores any link from a child page (like Products) to its parent (the Home Page, in this case).

Using FrontPage Themes

FrontPage has a rich collection of formatting commands that can improve the appearance of Web pages like those in the previous section. However, applying these commands individually to every page in your Web site is generally tedious and inconsistent. What's needed is a way to summarily impart the same appearance to every page in a Web site, and this is exactly what FrontPage Themes provide.

Using Existing Themes

The process of choosing and applying a FrontPage Theme is simple. To begin, open the Web site in FrontPage and then choose Theme from the Format menu. This will display the Themes dialog box shown in Figure 22-14. As you select each theme listed in the scroll box at the left, FrontPage previews that theme in the Sample of Theme window at the right. When you click the OK button, one of two things will happen, depending on the Apply Theme To setting in the upper left corner of the dialog box:

- **All Pages** applies the selected theme to every page in the current Web site except for any pages that have individual overrides. In other words, the selected theme becomes the default theme for the Web site.
- **Selected Pages** overrides the default theme for any pages currently selected in the Folder list, selected in Folder view, or open for editing in Page view. The choice goes to whichever of these you last clicked.

Notice the two special options at the top of the themes list in Figure 22-14. The entry beginning (Default) tells FrontPage that the currently selected pages should always use the default theme for the Web site. Note the difference between choosing (Default) Bubbles and choosing Bubbles. If you choose (Default) Bubbles and later change the default theme for this Web site, the pages you selected here will inherit the new theme.

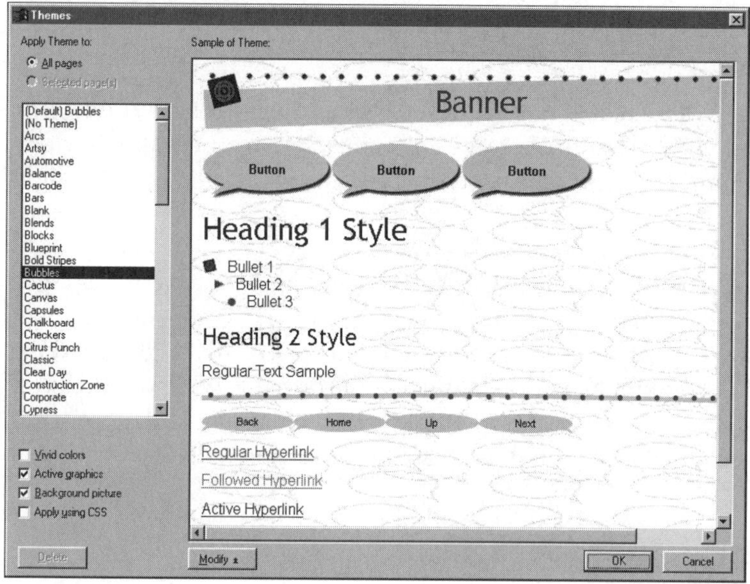

Figure 22-14.
With a single choice, the Themes dialog box configures a myriad of visual settings.

If you choose Bubbles for a group of pages, those pages will always use the Bubbles theme, even if you later change the default theme from Bubbles to something else.

Note Applying a theme replaces existing colors, text styles, and other formatting in the affected pages, with no possibility of undo. Applying a theme and then backing off to (No Theme) resets formatting to the defaults of HTML, not to their original appearance.

The (No Theme) entry tells FrontPage not to apply any theme to the currently selected pages or Web.

There are four options at the lower left of the dialog box that provide variations on a theme.

- **Vivid Colors** Selects a richer, more brilliant set of colors. However, if the theme only provides one set of colors, this setting has no effect.
- **Active Graphics** Specifies that button images should change appearance when the mouse pointer passes over them.
- **Background Picture** Specifies that the background of each page should consist of a repeating pattern.
- **Apply Using CSS** Tells FrontPage to use Cascading Style Sheets (CSS) to apply the characteristics of the theme. With the box unchecked, FrontPage will

use ordinary HTML commands. (CSS is generally more accurate and more efficient than ordinary HTML commands, but not all browsers support it.)

For the example Web, we'll choose the Bubbles Theme and choose Apply Theme To All Pages. In the lower left corner, we'll choose Active Graphics and Background Picture, but not Vivid Colors or Apply Using CSS. This produces the results illustrated in Figure 22-15.

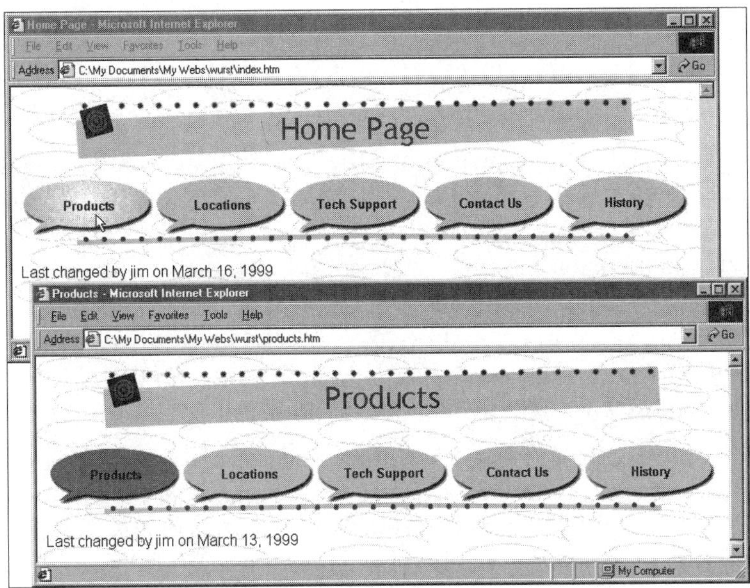

Figure 22-15
Using Themes, a single command can impart a uniform appearance to every page in your Web.

When applying themes to existing Web pages, the effects are often less dramatic than you might expect. There are two reasons for this:

- The dramatic banner graphic applies only to Page Banner components. The only way to specify the heading text that appears in a Page Banner component is to diagram and name the page in Navigation view.
- The dramatic button graphics apply only to Navigation bar components. The only way to specify the hyperlinks that appear in Navigation bar components is to diagram and name the relevant pages in Navigation view.

Note The FrontPage Hover Button component provides a way to construct your own graphic buttons that change appearance as a mouse pointer passes over them. To create a hover button, choose Component from the Insert button, and then choose Hover Button.

Creating Custom Themes

FrontPage comes with an assortment of interesting themes, and third-party sources offer more. Even so, it is inevitable that sooner or later you'll want to modify an existing theme or create a completely new one. This capability is now built into FrontPage. The following procedure describes how to modify an existing theme:

1. Display the Themes dialog box, as shown earlier in Figure 22-14, by choosing Themes from the Format menu.
2. Select the theme that is closest to the style and color you want to use.
3. Click the Modify button at the bottom of the dialog box.
4. Five new buttons will appear above the Modify button and below the Sample Of Theme window. Use these buttons to change the following selected theme options:
   - **Colors** displays a window that modifies the colors for the current theme. You can choose colors using any one of three methods: from a list of professionally chosen combinations, by picking a key color and letting FrontPage calculate the rest mathematically, and by individually choosing colors for each element in the theme.
   - **Graphics** displays a window that specifies pictures in the current theme. First, you select how the graphic will be used—Background Picture, Banner, Bullet List, and so forth—and then you type the filename you want to use, or locate the picture you want to use. FrontPage will overlay pictures with text.
   - **Text** displays a window that specifies the font for each type of text element controlled by a theme. First, select the type of text element, and then select the font. Finally, click More Font Styles to control size, color, and additional properties.
   - **Save** updates the current theme with any new values you've entered. However, this option is dimmed for any theme supplied with FrontPage.
   - **Save As** creates a new theme that includes all attributes of the original theme, plus any changes you've made.

Strictly speaking, you can't create a new theme from scratch. However, there's nothing preventing you from opening an existing theme, modifying it beyond recognition, and saving it with a completely different name.

To delete a theme, select it in the main Themes dialog box, and then click the Delete button in the lower left corner.

Note FrontPage has a feature called Text On GIF that makes it relatively easy to superimpose formatted text on any picture. To use this feature, display the Picture toolbar, select the graphic, click the Picture toolbar's Text icon (a capital A), size the text area, and then type.

Distributing Themes

Themes you save in FrontPage reside in a folder which is accessible to other Office 2000 applications, as well. Not all Office 2000 applications use such themes, but those that do—including Word 2000—have access to them immediately.

There are two ways to distribute Themes from one computer to another: by direct file copy and by Web.

Distributing a Theme by Direct File Copy

To distribute a theme to computers other than your own requires copying one folder that contains two or three files. By default, themes supplied with FrontPage reside in the following folder:

C:\Windows\Application Data\Microsoft\Themes

Theme files you create yourself reside in the following folder:

C:\Program Files\Common Files\Microsoft Shared\Themes

The folder, the files within it, and the theme will generally have similar names. For example, the New Bubbles theme resides in the New bubbles folder, and the included files are named New bubbles, plus a file extension.

To copy a theme from one computer to another, copy its folder to an intermediate location—such as a diskette, a file server, or an FTP location—and then copy it from that location to the Themes folder on the other computer.

Figure 22-16 shows the Themes folder, the New bubbles folder, and the included files on a typical Windows 98 installation.

Distributing a Theme by Web

When you apply a theme to a page in a FrontPage Web, FrontPage copies the theme files into that Web. Then, when another FrontPage user opens the same Web, their Themes list contains two types of entries:

- Themes residing on their local system
- Themes residing in the current FrontPage Web

If the second FrontPage user applies a theme that resides only on the FrontPage Web, FrontPage will offer to download the theme and install it locally. This provides an efficient means to propagate themes.

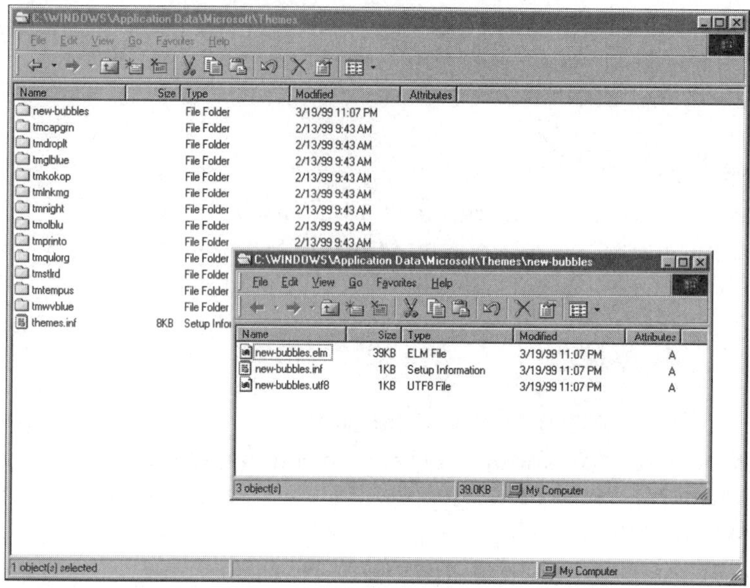

Figure 22-16
Themes reside in a common files area accessible to other Office 2000 applications.

Editing Web Pages as Code

FrontPage can edit and debug source code—Visual Basic and JavaScript—designed for the following three environments:

- On the Web visitor's browser
- On the Web server that delivers the page
- Within the FrontPage authoring environment

By coincidence, FrontPage also provides three ways to edit code. However, the three kinds of code and the three ways to edit them aren't related in any one-to-one relationship. Table 19-1 illustrates each editor's capabilities. Later sections will discuss each editor in more detail.

Code Type	Function	HTML View	Microsoft Script Editor	Visual Basic Editor
HTML	Edit	●	●	○
Browser Scripts	Edit	●	●	○
	Debug	○	●	○

Table 19-1
Functions of Built-In FrontPage Code Editors.

(continued)

Table 19-1 *(continued)*

Code Type	Function	HTML View	Microsoft Script Editor	Visual Basic Editor
Server-Side Scripts	Edit	●	●	○
	Debug	○	●	○
FrontPage Macros	Edit	○	○	●
	Debug	○	○	●

Legend: ●=Available ○=Unavailable

Using FrontPage HTML View

Opening a Web page in Page view doesn't lock you into WYSIWYG editing mode. To look at and work with the underlying HTML code, simply click the HTML tab at the bottom of the editing window. The resulting view displays and edits HTML, CSS, script code, and whatever else you manage to throw in. All this code is color-coded as to code type, and you can even control the color coding by choosing Page Options from the Tools menu and then clicking the Color Coding tab. By default, normal code is black, HTML tags are blue, CSS code is gray, and script code is red.

Figure 22-17 shows FrontPage displaying a Web page in HTML view. Even though the Web page appears as code, many of the normal FrontPage menu commands still work. For example, you can find and replace text, modify file properties, and use formatting commands on the tag that includes the insertion point.

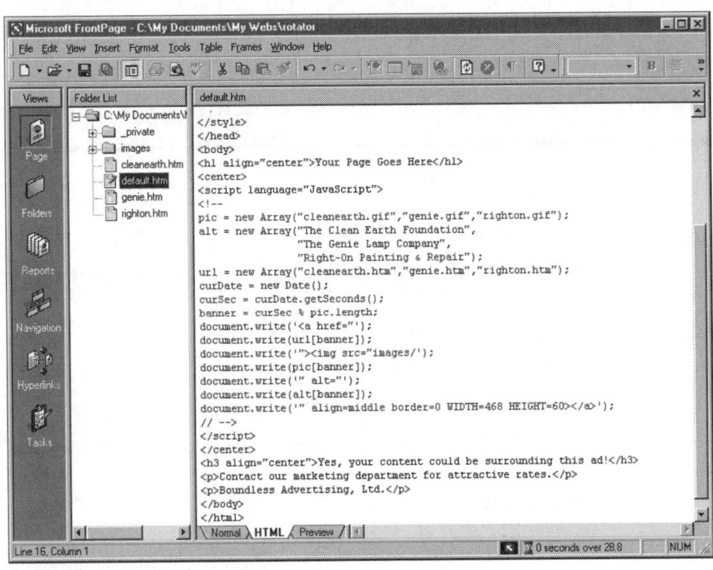

Figure 22-17
FrontPage can display and edit Web page as code. The script shown here displays one of three advertising images at random.

Take the following steps to enter a block of browser-side script code anywhere in the current Web page:

1. If the script will produce displayed output, set the insertion point where the output should appear.
2. Click the HTML tab at the bottom of the editing window.
3. Verify that the insertion point is set correctly within the HTML code.
4. Enter the four lines of code shown below:

```
<script language="JavaScript">
<!--

// -->
</script>
```

5. Enter your script code between the second and third lines above.

The first and fifth lines in step 4 begin and end a block of script code. The second and fourth lines begin and end a block of comments. The comment tags mark your code as comments for browsers that don't support scripting and thus ignore the <script> and </script> tags.

The code shown in Figure 22-17 implements an Advertisement Rotator that randomly displays advertising pictures for three different clients, and which jumps to a different URL for each client. The first three statements each define an array: a *pic* array that contains the filenames of three advertising pictures, an *alt* array that contains the corresponding alternate text, and a *URL* array that contains the three hyperlink locations.

To randomly select one of the three advertising pictures, the following code first creates a new object—named *curDate*—that contains the current date and time:

```
curDate = new Date();
```

The next line of code obtains the seconds portion of the date and time, placing it in *curSec*. The seconds portion of the current time is a fairly random number.

```
curSec = curDate.getSeconds();
```

The third line of code divides *curSec* by the number of entries in the *pic* array and places the remainder in a variable called *banner*. The remainder gives us the random number between 0 and 2, inclusive, that we need to choose which banner to display.

```
banner = curSec % pic.length;
```

The seven document.write statements remaining in Figure 22-17 then write an <IMG> tag surrounded by <A> and </A> tags. The <IMG> tag uses the picture filename from the *pic* array and the alternate text from the *alt* array. The <A> tag uses the URL from the *URL* array.

Figure 22-18 shows the result in both FrontPage WYSIWYG view and in Internet Explorer. The script doesn't execute in the FrontPage environment, so it appears with a "J" icon to indicate JavaScript.

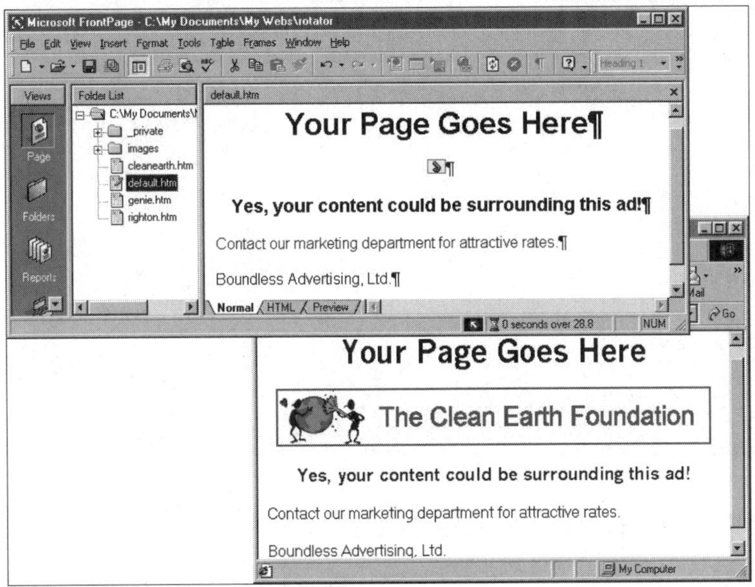

Figure 22-18
Script code doesn't execute in FrontPage, but merely shows up as a small icon.

Note If you decide to use this script in your own Web page, be sure the number of entries in the *pic*, *alt*, and *URL* arrays are always equal. Also, when you make up entries for the *URL* array, you'll need to use fully qualified http:// addresses for any locations not on the local server.

Using the Microsoft Script Editor

Figure 22-19 shows the second editor capable of working with HTML, script, and CSS code. FrontPage calls this environment the Microsoft Script Editor, even though the environment calls itself the Microsoft Development Environment. To edit the current Web page using this editor, choose Macros from the Tools menu and then choose Microsoft Script Editor. If you prefer invoking the editor from the keyboard, press Shift+Alt+F11.

The large central window contains the code for the current Web page. As in HTML view, you can work on the code directly or through commands on the menu bar, toolbar, or context menus. If this working environment seems familiar, you've probably used Visual InterDev, of which Microsoft Script Editor is a subset.

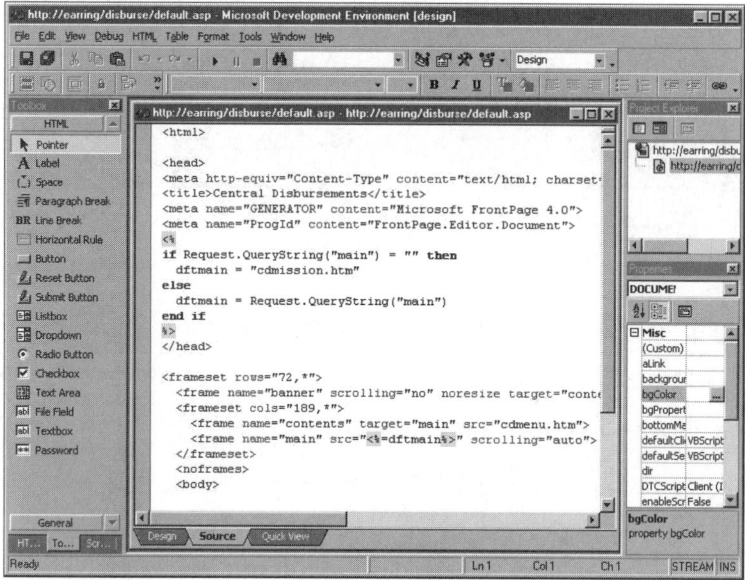

Figure 22-19
Microsoft Script Editor provides another way to edit Web pages as code.

Compared to FrontPage, Microsoft Script Editor has the disadvantage of being a new and different program to learn. However, it offers the major advantage of including a Script Debugger. The Script Debugger traces execution of your script one line at a time, always highlighting the current statement, or it runs the script at full speed until it completes or crashes. If it crashes, the Script Debugger highlights the statement that was executing at the time of the crash. This works for both browser-side and server-side scripts, although in the case of server-side scripts, the Web server and Microsoft Script Editor need to be running on the same machine. The Script Debugger also can set breakpoints and can display run-time values while the script is running.

The Web page illustrated in Figure 22-19 is a frameset named default.asp. The filename extension ASP stands for Active Server Page, and it flags the Web page for execution on the Web server. When a Web visitor requests an ASP page, any script code enclosed by <% and %> tags executes on the Web server as the server delivers the page to the visitor. If the script generates any HTML code, it appears intermixed with ordinary HTML in the same page.

Figure 22-20 shows the default.asp page as it normally appears in a browser. Obviously, the frame sources aren't fully developed Web pages, but they're sufficient to illustrate the example. The large frame touching the lower right corner is titled Main, and its default frame source—which appears in the figure—is a Web page named cdmission.htm.

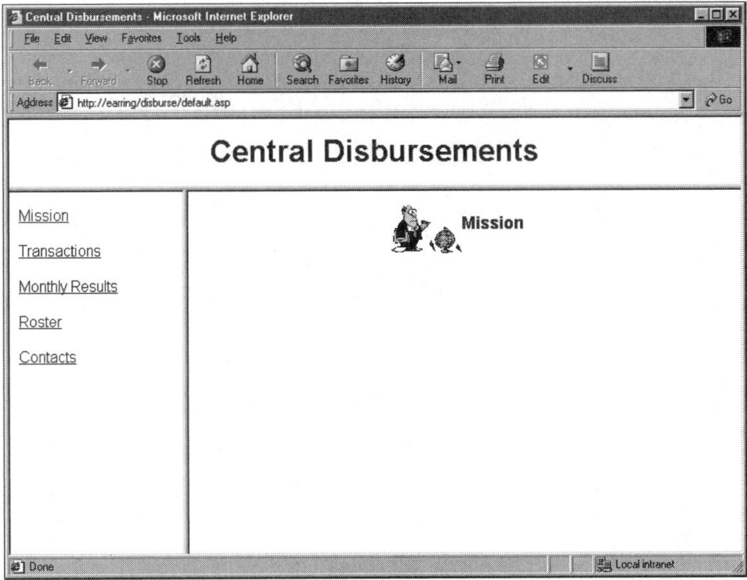

Figure 22-20
The home page in the Wurst Web is a typical frameset.

The server-side scripting in default.asp provides an unusual, but highly useful, feature. Specifically, hyperlinks from other pages can display the frameset with any page they wish in the main window. For example, to load the frameset with cdtrans.htm as the target of the main frame, the URL would be:

```
http://earring/disburse/default.asp?main=cdtrans.htm
```

The string *?main=cdtrans.htm* appended to a URL is a query string. The browser transmits this string to the Web server along with the normal HTTP request. The Web server places each *name=value* pair thus received in a collection called *Request.QueryString.* If the query string appended to the URL were *?first=one&second=two,* then *Request.QueryString("first")* would contain *one* and *Request.QueryString("second")* would contain *two.*

The first block of script code shown in Figure 22-19 tests the value of *Request.QueryString("main").* If the string is blank, the script sets the variable *dftmain* to *cdmission.htm.* If *Request.QueryString("main")* contains a value, the script sets *dftmain* to that value.

The second block of script code is very short; it consists entirely of the following characters:

```
<% =dftmain %>
```

An equal sign (=) at the beginning of a line of ASP code works the same as *document.write*; that is, it evaluates the subsequent expression and then merges the result into the outgoing HTML. Thus, specifying *src="<% =dftmain %>"* within a

<FRAME> tag sets the frame's default source to the Web page named as the value of the script variable *dftmain*.

Active Server Pages are only supported on Microsoft Web servers, and the Web server must be configured to consider the folder where the ASP file resides as executable. If your Web server doesn't support Active Server Pages or the folder isn't configured as executable, the ASP file will probably download as data rather than execute as described above.

Although it's beyond the scope of this book, Active Server Pages also can access files, databases, and other resources located on the Web server.

Using Visual Basic for Applications in FrontPage

The third type of scripting FrontPage supports is Visual Basic for Applications (VBA). This type of scripting is completely unavailable to your Web visitors; instead, it benefits Web designers by automating the FrontPage environment.

Because controlling FrontPage with VBA is quite a different application from controlling a browser or Web server with JavaScript or VBScript, creating and testing VBA code requires a different editor: the Visual Basic Editor. To invoke the Visual Basic Editor, choose Macros from the Tools menu, and then choose Visual Basic Editor. Alternatively, you can press Alt+F11. Figure 22-21 shows the Visual Basic Editor development environment.

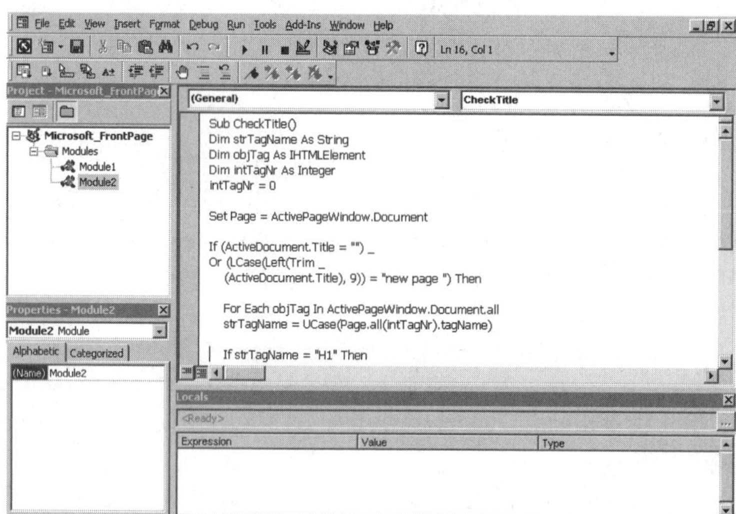

Figure 22-21
The Visual Basic Editor integrates Visual Basic for Applications with FrontPage.

Complete descriptions of the Visual Basic Editor and the Visual Basic for Applications language are lengthy topics, quite deserving of books in their own right. Briefly, however, all VBA code is contained in procedures, forms, modules, or Class modules. You can create any of these objects by using the Insert menu, and you can import and export these objects from the File menu. Exporting and importing provides a means for developing macros on one machine and installing them on another.

The macro shown in Figure 22-21 consists of a single subroutine named *CheckTitle*. This macro checks the title of the current Web page (normally configured under Page Properties, General) to see if it's blank or begins with the string *new page*. If so, it searches the Web page for a paragraph formatted with the Heading 1 style. When it finds such a paragraph, the macro copies its text into the title field.

```
Sub CheckTitle()
Dim strTagName As String
Dim objTag As IHTMLElement
Dim intTagNr As Integer
```

In order, these four lines of code initialize and name the subroutine, and then define three variables. Note that the *objTag* variable has the type *IHTMLElement*, which means it has the properties of an object on a Web page. *IHTMLElement* is a type that's specific to FrontPage.

```
intTagNr = 0
Set Page = ActivePageWindow.Document
```

These two statements initialize the *intTagNr* variable to *0* and establish an object called Page that points to the document that is open in the current FrontPage editing window.

```
If (ActiveDocument.title = "") _
Or (LCase(Left(Trim _
    (ActiveDocument.title), 9)) = "new page ") Then
```

These three lines actually comprise one statement; the underscore character at the end of the first and second lines is a continuation character. The first code line tests for an empty title value. The second and third lines use the *Trim* function to remove any leading or trailing spaces from the title, the Left function to get the first nine characters of that result, and then the Lcase function to convert those nine characters to lowercase characters. The last line then compares the overall result to the string *new page*. (When FrontPage creates a new page, it creates titles like New page 1, New Page 2, and so forth.)

```
    For Each objTag In ActivePageWindow.Document.all
```

If either comparison is *True*, the above statement sets up a loop that scans each HTML tag in the document. The *objTag* variable points to the HTML tag selected during each iteration of the loop.

```
    strTagName = UCase(Page.all(intTagNr).tagName)
```

This statement obtains the tagName property of the *Nth* tag on the page, where *N* is the counter *intTagNr*. The tagName property is the tag's identifier: P stands for paragraph, IMG stands for image, A stands for anchor, and so forth. Recall that we previously set up the *Page* variable so it points to *ActivePageWindow.Document.* The Ucase function converts the tag name to uppercase characters.

```
    If strTagName = "H1" Then
        ActiveDocument.title = Page.all(intTagNr).innertext
        MsgBox "Page title set to:" & vbCrLf & vbCrLf & _
            ActiveDocument.title, vbInformation
        Exit Sub
    End If
```

In the above listing, the first line of code determines if the tag name of the current tag is H1. If so, the second line of code sets the active document's title to the H1 tag's innertext property. This property contains everything that appears between the <H1> and </H1> tags, but excludes any other tags such as <B>, <BR>, and <IMG>. The macro then displays an informational message and exits the subroutine.

```
        intTagNr = intTagNr + 1
    Next
End If
```

If the macro hasn't found an H1 tag (and therefore hasn't exited the subroutine), the first statement above increments the tag number by one in preparation for the next iteration through the loop. VBA collections are zero-based, so the counter needs to be zero the first time through the loop, one for the second loop, and so forth. The *Next* statement terminates the range of the *For Each* loop, and the *End If* statement terminates the range of the check for a blank or new page title.

```
MsgBox "Page Title remains:" & vbCrLf & vbCrLf & _
    ActiveDocument.title, vbInformation
End Sub
```

The *Msgbox* statement notifies the page designer that the macro has made no changes, and the *End Sub* statement marks the end of the subroutine.

Aside from the tasks of learning the Visual Basic language and the Visual Basic Editor, discovering the expression that names a required FrontPage object, property, or method can be daunting. FrontPage exposes virtually every aspect of its operation, every object in a FrontPage Web, and every object and property in an open Web page to VBA, if only you can ascertain the object's nomenclature. And therein lies the rub.

The Visual Basic Editor provides some help through its Object Browser and AutoList features. To search for the object that contains the tagName property, for example, take the following steps:

1. Display the Object Browser by choosing Object Browser from the View menu, or by pressing F2.
2. Use the Object Browser's top, leftmost drop-down list to choose the project or library to search.
3. Type or select a text string in the box just below the Project/Library box.
4. Click the Search button (the binoculars icon).
5. Search the result for the object you want to work with. Figure 22-22 shows a typical search result.

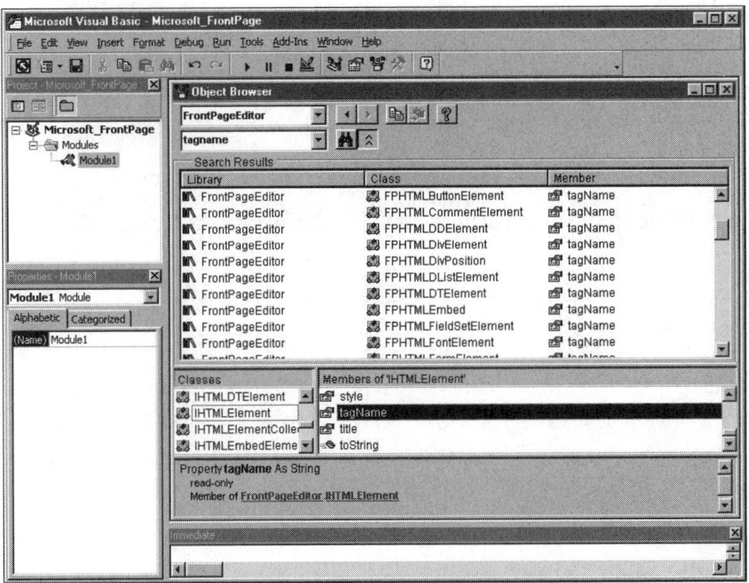

Figure 22-22
VBAs object browser is useful for locating objects and properties not indexed any other way.

The AutoList feature shown in Figure 22-23 works automatically whenever you type the name of a valid object and then a period. Typing the period cues the Visual Basic Editor to display a scrollable list of the object's subordinate objects, properties, and methods. To continue, make a selection from the list and then press the Tab key.

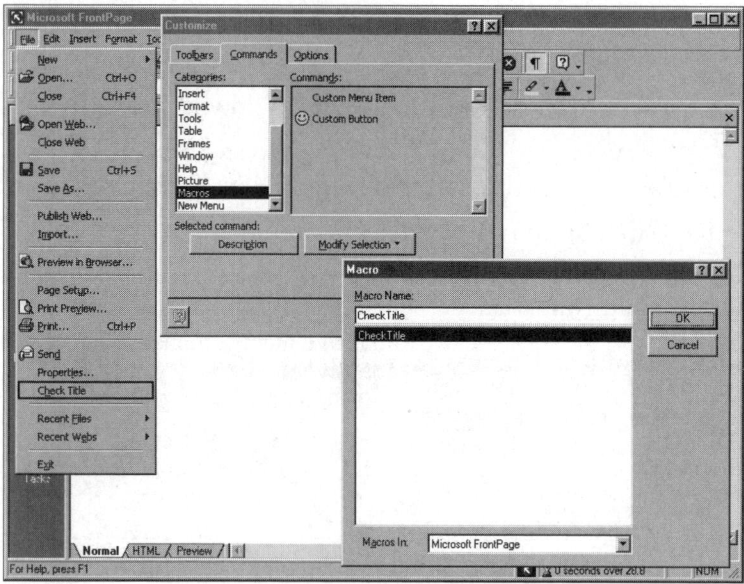

Figure 22-23
The AutoList feature in the VBA editor presents a drop-down list of properties and methods whenever you type a valid object name and a period.

Despite these facilities, discovering the names and organizational structure of FrontPage objects remains somewhat of a black art. Watch for additional documentation—possibly on Microsoft's Web site—and for sample code posted around the Internet.

Index

Numbers and Symbols

A

B

C

D

E

F

G

H

I

J

K

L

M

N

O

P

Q

R

S

T

U

V

W

X

Y

Reed Jacobson provides creative training, consulting, and custom development services for Microsoft Office and Visual Basic for Applications. Reed received a B.A. in Japanese and Linguistics and an M.B.A. from Brigham Young University, and a graduate fellowship in Linguistics from Cornell University. In addition to running his own consulting firm, he worked as a Software Application Specialist for Hewlett-Packard for 10 years, has been a Vice President for LEX Software Systems, and teaches courses in multi-dimensional database management for OLAP Train, Inc.

Reed is the author of *Excel Trade Secrets for Windows*, *Microsoft® Excel 97 Step by Step*, *Microsoft® Excel 97 Step by Step, Advanced Topics*, and *Microsoft® Excel 2000/Visual Basic® for Applications Fundamentals*. He has given presentations on Excel at Tech•Ed and other Microsoft conferences and seminars; he has created CD-ROM training materials for Microsoft Excel, Microsoft Access, Visual Basic; and has contributed articles to *Inside Visual Basic*.

Reed Jacobson
P. O. Box 3632
Arlington, WA 98223
reed@expertcompanion.com

The manuscript for this book was prepared and galleyed using Microsoft Word 97. Pages were composed by Black Hole Publishing Services using Adobe PageMaker 6.52 for Windows, with text in Palatino and display type in Helvetica Condensed. Composed pages were delivered to the printer as electronic prepress files.

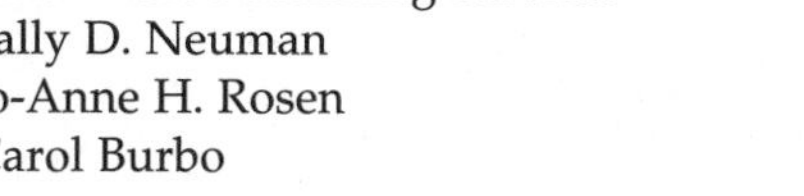

Cover Designer:	Tom Draper Design
Interior Graphic Designer:	James D. Kramer; Phyllis Beaty (Magnolia Studio)
Editorial and Production:	Black Hole Publishing Services
Technical Editor:	Sally D. Neuman
Principal Compositor:	Jo-Anne H. Rosen
Indexer:	Carol Burbo

Optimize Microsoft Office 2000 with multimedia training!

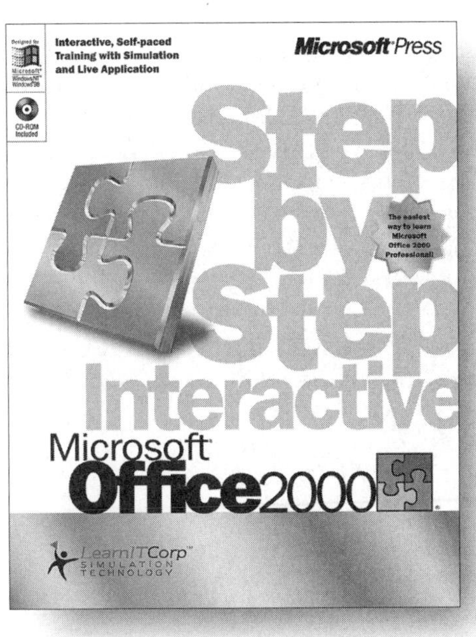

U.S.A. **$29.99**
U.K. $27.99 [V.A.T. included]
Canada $44.99
ISBN 0-7356-0506-8

MICROSOFT® OFFICE 2000 STEP BY STEP INTERACTIVE is a multimedia learning system (in both audio and text versions) that shows you, through 20 to 30 hours of simulated live-in-the application training, how to maximize the productivity potential of the Office 2000 programs: Microsoft Excel 2000, Word 2000, Access 2000, PowerPoint® 2000, Outlook® 2000, Publisher 2000, and Small Business Tools. If you already use Microsoft Office 97, this learning solution will help you make the transition to Office 2000 quickly and easily, and reach an even greater level of productivity.

Microsoft Press® products are available worldwide wherever quality computer books are sold. For more information, contact your book or computer retailer, software reseller, or local Microsoft Sales Office, or visit our Web site at mspress.microsoft.com. To locate your nearest source for Microsoft Press products, or to order directly, call 1-800-MSPRESS in the U.S. (in Canada, call 1-800-268-2222).

Prices and availability dates are subject to change.

mspress.microsoft.com

MICROSOFT LICENSE AGREEMENT

Book Companion CD

IMPORTANT—READ CAREFULLY: This Microsoft End-User License Agreement ("EULA") is a legal agreement between you (either an individual or an entity) and Microsoft Corporation for the Microsoft product identified above, which includes computer software and may include associated media, printed materials, and "online" or electronic documentation ("SOFTWARE PRODUCT"). Any component included within the SOFTWARE PRODUCT that is accompanied by a separate End-User License Agreement shall be governed by such agreement and not the terms set forth below. By installing, copying, or otherwise using the SOFTWARE PRODUCT, you agree to be bound by the terms of this EULA. If you do not agree to the terms of this EULA, you are not authorized to install, copy, or otherwise use the SOFTWARE PRODUCT; you may, however, return the SOFTWARE PRODUCT, along with all printed materials and other items that form a part of the Microsoft product that includes the SOFTWARE PRODUCT, to the place you obtained them for a full refund.

SOFTWARE PRODUCT LICENSE

The SOFTWARE PRODUCT is protected by United States copyright laws and international copyright treaties, as well as other intellectual property laws and treaties. The SOFTWARE PRODUCT is licensed, not sold.

1. **GRANT OF LICENSE.** This EULA grants you the following rights:

   a. **Software Product.** You may install and use one copy of the SOFTWARE PRODUCT on a single computer. The primary user of the computer on which the SOFTWARE PRODUCT is installed may make a second copy for his or her exclusive use on a portable computer.

   b. **Storage/Network Use.** You may also store or install a copy of the SOFTWARE PRODUCT on a storage device, such as a network server, used only to install or run the SOFTWARE PRODUCT on your other computers over an internal network; however, you must acquire and dedicate a license for each separate computer on which the SOFTWARE PRODUCT is installed or run from the storage device. A license for the SOFTWARE PRODUCT may not be shared or used concurrently on different computers.

   c. **License Pak.** If you have acquired this EULA in a Microsoft License Pak, you may make the number of additional copies of the computer software portion of the SOFTWARE PRODUCT authorized on the printed copy of this EULA, and you may use each copy in the manner specified above. You are also entitled to make a corresponding number of secondary copies for portable computer use as specified above.

   d. **Sample Code.** Solely with respect to portions, if any, of the SOFTWARE PRODUCT that are identified within the SOFTWARE PRODUCT as sample code (the "SAMPLE CODE"):

      i. **Use and Modification.** Microsoft grants you the right to use and modify the source code version of the SAMPLE CODE, *provided* you comply with subsection (d)(iii) below. You may not distribute the SAMPLE CODE, or any modified version of the SAMPLE CODE, in source code form.

      ii. **Redistributable Files.** Provided you comply with subsection (d)(iii) below, Microsoft grants you a nonexclusive, royalty-free right to reproduce and distribute the object code version of the SAMPLE CODE and of any modified SAMPLE CODE, other than SAMPLE CODE, or any modified version thereof, designated as not redistributable in the Readme file that forms a part of the SOFTWARE PRODUCT (the "Non-Redistributable Sample Code"). All SAMPLE CODE other than the Non-Redistributable Sample Code is collectively referred to as the "REDISTRIBUTABLES."

      iii. **Redistribution Requirements.** If you redistribute the REDISTRIBUTABLES, you agree to: (i) distribute the REDISTRIBUTABLES in object code form only in conjunction with and as a part of your software application product; (ii) not use Microsoft's name, logo, or trademarks to market your software application product; (iii) include a valid copyright notice on your software application product; (iv) indemnify, hold harmless, and defend Microsoft from and against any claims or lawsuits, including attorney's fees, that arise or result from the use or distribution of your software application product; and (v) not permit further distribution of the REDISTRIBUTABLES by your end user. Contact Microsoft for the applicable royalties due and other licensing terms for all other uses and/or distribution of the REDISTRIBUTABLES.

2. **DESCRIPTION OF OTHER RIGHTS AND LIMITATIONS.**

   - **Limitations on Reverse Engineering, Decompilation, and Disassembly.** You may not reverse engineer, decompile, or disassemble the SOFTWARE PRODUCT, except and only to the extent that such activity is expressly permitted by applicable law notwithstanding this limitation.
   - **Separation of Components.** The SOFTWARE PRODUCT is licensed as a single product. Its component parts may not be separated for use on more than one computer.
   - **Rental.** You may not rent, lease, or lend the SOFTWARE PRODUCT.
   - **Support Services.** Microsoft may, but is not obligated to, provide you with support services related to the SOFTWARE PRODUCT ("Support Services"). Use of Support Services is governed by the Microsoft policies and programs described in the

user manual, in "online" documentation, and/or in other Microsoft-provided materials. Any supplemental software code provided to you as part of the Support Services shall be considered part of the SOFTWARE PRODUCT and subject to the terms and conditions of this EULA. With respect to technical information you provide to Microsoft as part of the Support Services, Microsoft may use such information for its business purposes, including for product support and development. Microsoft will not utilize such technical information in a form that personally identifies you.

- **Software Transfer.** You may permanently transfer all of your rights under this EULA, provided you retain no copies, you transfer all of the SOFTWARE PRODUCT (including all component parts, the media and printed materials, any upgrades, this EULA, and, if applicable, the Certificate of Authenticity), **and** the recipient agrees to the terms of this EULA.
- **Termination.** Without prejudice to any other rights, Microsoft may terminate this EULA if you fail to comply with the terms and conditions of this EULA. In such event, you must destroy all copies of the SOFTWARE PRODUCT and all of its component parts.

3. **COPYRIGHT.** All title and copyrights in and to the SOFTWARE PRODUCT (including but not limited to any images, photographs, animations, video, audio, music, text, SAMPLE CODE, REDISTRIBUTABLES, and "applets" incorporated into the SOFTWARE PRODUCT) and any copies of the SOFTWARE PRODUCT are owned by Microsoft or its suppliers. The SOFTWARE PRODUCT is protected by copyright laws and international treaty provisions. Therefore, you must treat the SOFTWARE PRODUCT like any other copyrighted material **except** that you may install the SOFTWARE PRODUCT on a single computer provided you keep the original solely for backup or archival purposes. You may not copy the printed materials accompanying the SOFTWARE PRODUCT.

4. **U.S. GOVERNMENT RESTRICTED RIGHTS.** The SOFTWARE PRODUCT and documentation are provided with RESTRICTED RIGHTS. Use, duplication, or disclosure by the Government is subject to restrictions as set forth in subparagraph (c)(1)(ii) of the Rights in Technical Data and Computer Software clause at DFARS 252.227-7013 or subparagraphs (c)(1) and (2) of the Commercial Computer Software—Restricted Rights at 48 CFR 52.227-19, as applicable. Manufacturer is Microsoft Corporation/One Microsoft Way/Redmond, WA 98052-6399.

5. **EXPORT RESTRICTIONS.** You agree that you will not export or re-export the SOFTWARE PRODUCT, any part thereof, or any process or service that is the direct product of the SOFTWARE PRODUCT (the foregoing collectively referred to as the "Restricted Components"), to any country, person, entity, or end user subject to U.S. export restrictions. You specifically agree not to export or re-export any of the Restricted Components (i) to any country to which the U.S. has embargoed or restricted the export of goods or services, which currently include, but are not necessarily limited to, Cuba, Iran, Iraq, Libya, North Korea, Sudan, and Syria, or to any national of any such country, wherever located, who intends to transmit or transport the Restricted Components back to such country; (ii) to any end user who you know or have reason to know will utilize the Restricted Components in the design, development, or production of nuclear, chemical, or biological weapons; or (iii) to any end user who has been prohibited from participating in U.S. export transactions by any federal agency of the U.S. government. You warrant and represent that neither the BXA nor any other U.S. federal agency has suspended, revoked, or denied your export privileges.

DISCLAIMER OF WARRANTY

NO WARRANTIES OR CONDITIONS. MICROSOFT EXPRESSLY DISCLAIMS ANY WARRANTY OR CONDITION FOR THE SOFTWARE PRODUCT. THE SOFTWARE PRODUCT AND ANY RELATED DOCUMENTATION ARE PROVIDED "AS IS" WITHOUT WARRANTY OR CONDITION OF ANY KIND, EITHER EXPRESS OR IMPLIED, INCLUDING, WITHOUT LIMITATION, THE IMPLIED WARRANTIES OF MERCHANTABILITY, FITNESS FOR A PARTICULAR PURPOSE, OR NONINFRINGEMENT. THE ENTIRE RISK ARISING OUT OF USE OR PERFORMANCE OF THE SOFTWARE PRODUCT REMAINS WITH YOU.

LIMITATION OF LIABILITY. TO THE MAXIMUM EXTENT PERMITTED BY APPLICABLE LAW, IN NO EVENT SHALL MICROSOFT OR ITS SUPPLIERS BE LIABLE FOR ANY SPECIAL, INCIDENTAL, INDIRECT, OR CONSEQUENTIAL DAMAGES WHATSOEVER (INCLUDING, WITHOUT LIMITATION, DAMAGES FOR LOSS OF BUSINESS PROFITS, BUSINESS INTERRUPTION, LOSS OF BUSINESS INFORMATION, OR ANY OTHER PECUNIARY LOSS) ARISING OUT OF THE USE OF OR INABILITY TO USE THE SOFTWARE PRODUCT OR THE PROVISION OF OR FAILURE TO PROVIDE SUPPORT SERVICES, EVEN IF MICROSOFT HAS BEEN ADVISED OF THE POSSIBILITY OF SUCH DAMAGES. IN ANY CASE, MICROSOFT'S ENTIRE LIABILITY UNDER ANY PROVISION OF THIS EULA SHALL BE LIMITED TO THE GREATER OF THE AMOUNT ACTUALLY PAID BY YOU FOR THE SOFTWARE PRODUCT OR US$5.00; PROVIDED, HOWEVER, IF YOU HAVE ENTERED INTO A MICROSOFT SUPPORT SERVICES AGREEMENT, MICROSOFT'S ENTIRE LIABILITY REGARDING SUPPORT SERVICES SHALL BE GOVERNED BY THE TERMS OF THAT AGREEMENT. BECAUSE SOME STATES AND JURISDICTIONS DO NOT ALLOW THE EXCLUSION OR LIMITATION OF LIABILITY, THE ABOVE LIMITATION MAY NOT APPLY TO YOU.

MISCELLANEOUS

This EULA is governed by the laws of the State of Washington USA, except and only to the extent that applicable law mandates governing law of a different jurisdiction.

Should you have any questions concerning this EULA, or if you desire to contact Microsoft for any reason, please contact the Microsoft subsidiary serving your country, or write: Microsoft Sales Information Center/One Microsoft Way/Redmond, WA 98052-6399.

PN 097-0002296